Short Story Criticism

Guide to Gale Literary Criticism Series

When you need to review criticism of literary works, these are the Gale series to use:

If the author's death date is:	You should turn to:
After Dec. 31, 1959 (or author is still living)	***CONTEMPORARY LITERARY CRITICISM*** for example: Jorge Luis Borges, Anthony Burgess, William Faulkner, Mary Gordon, Ernest Hemingway, Iris Murdoch
1900 through 1959	***TWENTIETH-CENTURY LITERARY CRITICISM*** for example: Willa Cather, F. Scott Fitzgerald, Henry James, Mark Twain, Virginia Woolf
1800 through 1899	***NINETEENTH-CENTURY LITERATURE CRITICISM*** for example: Fyodor Dostoevski, Nathaniel Hawthorne, George Sand, William Wordsworth
1400 through 1799	***LITERATURE CRITICISM FROM 1400 TO 1800 (excluding Shakespeare)*** for example: Anne Bradstreet, Daniel Defoe, Alexander Pope, François Rabelais, Jonathan Swift, Phillis Wheatley
	SHAKESPEAREAN CRITICISM Shakespeare's plays and poetry
Antiquity through 1399	***CLASSICAL AND MEDIEVAL LITERATURE CRITICISM*** for example: Dante, Homer, Plato, Sophocles, Vergil, the Beowulf Poet

---

Gale also publishes related criticism series:

CHILDREN'S LITERATURE REVIEW
This series covers authors of all eras who have written for the preschool through high school audience.

SHORT STORY CRITICISM
This series covers the major short fiction writers of all nationalities and periods of literary history.

POETRY CRITICISM
This series covers poets of all nationalities and periods of literary history.

DRAMA CRITICISM
This series covers dramatists of all nationalities and periods of literary history.

ISSN 0895-9439

Volume 9

Short Story Criticism

Excerpts from Criticism of the Works of Short Fiction Writers

Thomas Votteler
Editor

Laurie DiMauro
Cathy Falk
David Kmenta
Marie Lazzari
Thomas Ligotti
David Segal
Bridget Travers
Associate Editors

STAFF

Thomas Votteler, *Editor*

Laurie DiMauro, Cathy Falk, Tina Grant, David Kmenta, Marie Lazzari, Thomas Ligotti, David Segal, Bridget Travers, *Associate Editors*

Jennifer Brostrom, Rogene M. Fisher, Judy Galens, Ian A. Goodhall, Kyung-Sun Lim, Susan Peters, Johannah Rodgers, Bruce Walker, *Assistant Editors*

Jeanne A. Gough, *Permissions & Production Manager*
Linda M. Pugliese, *Production Supervisor*
Paul Lewon, Maureen Puhl, Camille Robinson, Jennifer VanSickle, *Editorial Associates*
Donna Craft, Brandy C. Johnson, Sheila Walencewicz, *Editorial Assistants*

Maureen Richards, *Research Supervisor*
Mary Beth McElmeel, Tamara C. Nott, *Editorial Associates*
Kathleen Jozwiak, Amy Kaechele, Julie K. Karmazin, Julie A. Synkonis, *Editorial Assistants*

Sandra C. Davis, *Permissions Supervisor (Text)*
Maria L. Franklin, Josephine M. Keene, Denise M. Singleton, Kimberly F. Smilay, *Permissions Associates*
Michele M. Lonoconus, Shelly Rakoczy, Shalice Shah, *Permissions Assistants*

Margaret A. Chamberlain, *Permissions Supervisor (Pictures)*
Pamela A. Hayes, *Permissions Associate*
Amy Lynn Emrich, Karla Kulkis, Nancy Rattenbury, Keith Reed, *Permissions Assistants*

Mary Beth Trimper, *Production Manager*
Mary Winterhalter, *Production Assistant*

Arthur Chartow, *Art Director*
C. J. Jonik, *Keyliner*

The paper used in this publication meets the minimum requirements of American National Standard for Information Sciences—Permanence Paper for Printed Library Materials, ANSI Z39.48-1984 ™

Library of Congress Catalog Card Number 88-641014
ISBN 0-8103-2558-6
ISSN 0895-9439

Printed in the United States of America

Published simultaneously in the United Kingdom

by Gale Research International Limited
(An affiliated company of Gale Research Inc.)

Contents

Preface

Short Story Criticism (SSC) presents significant passages from criticism of the world's greatest short story writers and provides supplementary biographical and bibliographical materials to guide the interested reader to a greater understanding of the authors of short fiction. This series was developed in response to suggestions from librarians serving high school, college, and public library patrons, who had noted a considerable number of requests for critical material on short story writers. Although major short story writers are covered in such Gale series as *Contemporary Literary Criticism (CLC), Twentieth-Century Literary Criticism (TCLC), Nineteenth-Century Literature Criticism (NCLC),* and *Literature Criticism from 1400 to 1800 (LC),* librarians perceived the need for a series devoted solely to writers of the short story genre.

Scope of the Work

SSC is designed to serve as an introduction to major short story writers of all eras and nationalities. Since these authors have inspired a great deal of relevant critical material, *SSC* is necessarily selective, and the editors have chosen the most important published criticism to aid readers and students in their research.

Approximately ten to fifteen authors are included in each volume, and each entry presents a historical survey of the critical response to that author's work. The length of an entry is intended to reflect the amount of critical attention the author has received from critics writing in English and from foreign critics in translation. Every attempt has been made to identify and include excerpts from the most significant essays on each author's work. In order to provide these important critical pieces, the editors will sometimes reprint essays that have appeared in previous volumes of Gale's Literary Criticism Series. Such duplication, however, never exceeds twenty percent of an *SSC* volume.

Organization of the Book

An *SSC* author entry consists of the following elements:

- The **author heading** cites the name under which the author most commonly wrote, followed by birth and death dates. If the author wrote consistently under a pseudonym, the pseudonym will be listed in the author heading and the author's actual name given in parentheses on the first line of the biographical and critical introduction.

- The **biographical and critical introduction** contains background information designed to introduce a reader to the author and the critical debates surrounding his or her work. Parenthetical material following the introduction provides references to other biographical and critical series published by Gale, including *CLC, TCLC, NCLC, Contemporary Authors,* and *Dictionary of Literary Biography.*

- A **portrait of the author** is included when available. Many entries also contain illustrations of materials pertinent to an author's career, including holographs of manuscript pages, title pages, dust jackets, letters, or representations of important people, places, and events in the author's life.

- The list of **principal works** is chronological by date of first publication and lists the most important works by the author. The first section comprises short story collections, novellas, and novella collections. The second section gives information on other major works by the author. For foreign authors, the editors have provided original foreign-language publication information and have selected what are considered the best and most complete English-language editions of their works.

- **Criticism** is arranged chronologically in each author entry to provide a useful perspective on changes in critical evaluation over the years. All short story, novella, and collection titles by the author featured in the entry are printed in boldface type to enable a reader to ascertain without difficulty the works discussed. Also for purposes of easier identification, the critic's name and the publication date of the essay are given at the beginning of each piece of criticism. Unsigned criticism is preceded by the title of the journal in which it appeared.

- Critical essays are prefaced with **explanatory notes** as an additional aid to students and readers using *SSC.* The explanatory notes provide several types of useful information, including: the reputation of a critic, the importance of a work of criticism, and the specific type of criticism (biographical, psychoanalytic, structuralist, etc.).

- A complete **bibliographical citation,** designed to help the interested reader locate the original essay or book, follows each piece of criticism.

- The **further reading list** appearing at the end of each author entry suggests additional materials on the author. In some cases it includes essays for which the editors could not obtain reprint rights.

Beginning with volume six, *SSC* contains two additional features designed to enhance the reader's understanding of short fiction writers and their works:

- Each *SSC* entry now includes, when available, **comments by the author** that illuminate his or her own works or the short story genre in general. These statements are set within boxes or bold rules to distinguish them from the criticism.

- A **select bibliography of general sources on short fiction** is included as an appendix. Updated and amended with each new *SSC* volume, this listing of materials for further research provides readers with a selection of the best available general studies of the short story genre.

Other Features

A **cumulative author index** lists all the authors who have appeared in *SSC, CLC, TCLC, NCLC, LC,* and *Classical and Medieval Literature Criticism (CMLC),* as well as cross-references to other Gale series. Users will welcome this cumulated index as a useful tool for locating an author within the Literary Criticism Series.

A **cumulative nationality index** lists all authors featured in *SSC* by nationality, followed by the number of the *SSC* volume in which their entry appears.

A **cumulative title index** lists in alphabetical order all short story, novella, and collection titles contained in the *SSC* series. Titles of short story collections, separately published novellas, and novella collections are printed in italics, while titles of individual short stories are printed in roman type with quotation marks. Each title is followed by the author's name and the corresponding volume and page numbers where commentary on the work may be located. English-language translations of original foreign-language titles are cross-referenced to the foreign titles so that all references to discussion of a work are combined in one listing.

A Note to the Reader

When writing papers, students who quote directly from any volume in the Literary Criticism Series may use the following general forms to footnote reprinted criticism. The first example pertains to material drawn from periodicals, the second to material reprinted from books:

[1] Henry James, Jr., "Honoré de Balzac," *The Galaxy* 20 (December 1875), 814-36; excerpted and reprinted in *Short Story Criticism,* Vol. 5, ed. Thomas Votteler (Detroit: Gale Research, 1990), pp. 8-11.

[2] F. R. Leavis, *D. H. Lawrence: Novelist* (Alfred A. Knopf, 1956); excerpted and reprinted in *Short Story Criticism,* Vol. 4, ed. Thomas Votteler (Detroit: Gale Research, 1990), pp. 202-06.

Suggestions Are Welcome

Readers who wish to suggest authors to appear in future volumes, or who have other suggestions, are invited to contact the editors by writing to Gale Research, Inc., Literary Criticism Division, 835 Penobscot Building, Detroit, MI., 48226-4094.

ACKNOWLEDGMENTS

The editors wish to thank the copyright holders of the excerpted criticism included in this volume, the permissions managers of many book and magazine publishing companies for assisting us in securing reprint rights, and Anthony Bogucki for assistance with copyright research. We are also grateful to the staffs of the Detroit Public Library, the Library of Congress, the University of Detroit Library, Wayne State University Purdy/Kresge Library Complex, and the University of Michigan Libraries for making their resources available to us. Following is a list of the copyright holders who have granted us permission to reprint material in this volume of *SSC*. Every effort has been made to trace copyright, but if omissions have been made, please let us know.

COPYRIGHT EXCERPTS IN *SSC*, VOLUME 9, WERE REPRINTED FROM THE FOLLOWING PERIODICALS:

American Imago, v. 20, Winter, 1963 for "Aiken's 'Mr. Arcularis': Psychic Regression and the Death Instinct" by James W. Tuttleton. Copyright 1963 by The Association for Applied Psychoanalysis, Inc. Reprinted by permission of the publisher and the author.—***American Literary Realism 1870-1910,*** v. 10, Spring, 1977. Copyright © 1977 by the Department of English, The University of Texas at Arlington. Reprinted by permission of the publisher.—***The Antioch Review,*** v. 32, 1973. Copyright © 1973 by the Antioch Review Inc. Reprinted by permission of the Editors.—***Conradiana,*** v. 12, 1980 for "Conrad's 'The Secret Sharer': Complexities of the Doubling Relationship" by Joan E. Steiner; v. 14, 1982 for "The Issue of Racism in 'Heart of Darkness' " by Hunt Hawkins. Both reprinted with permission of Texas Tech University Press.—***Criticism,*** v. XXVII, Fall, 1985 for " 'Heart of Darkness': Anti-Imperialism, Racism, or Impressionism?" by Patrick Brantlinger. Copyright, 1985, Wayne State University Press. Reprinted by permission of the publisher and the author.—***English Journal,*** v. 60, December, 1971 for "Jackson's 'The Witch': A Satanic Gem" by Robert L. Kelly. Copyright © 1971 by the National Council of Teachers of English. Reprinted by permission of the publisher and the author.—***ESQ: A Journal of the American Renaissance,*** v. 18, 2nd quarter, 1972. Reprinted by permission of the publisher.—***Essays in Literature,*** v. XV, Fall, 1988. Copyright 1988 by Western Illinois University. Reprinted by permission of the publisher.—***The Georgia Review,*** v. XXVII, Fall, 1973 for "Carson McCullers' Literary Ballad" by Joseph R. Millichap. Copyright, 1973, by the University of Georgia. Reprinted by permission of the publisher and the author.—***Hartford Studies in Literature,*** v. VI, 1974. Copyright © 1974 by the University of Hartford. Reprinted by permission of the publisher.—***Indian Literature,*** v. II, 1968 for "An Analysis of Indic Tradition in Hermann Hesse's 'Siddhartha' " by Bhabagrahi Misra. Reprinted by permission of the author.—***The Journal of Narrative Technique,*** v. 18, Spring, 1988. Copyright © 1988 by *The Journal of Narrative Technique.* Reprinted by permission of the publisher.—***The Literary Criterion,*** v. XXII, 1987. Reprinted by permission of the publisher.—***The Massachusetts Review,*** v. XVIII, Winter, 1977. © 1977. Reprinted from *The Massachusetts Review,* The Massachusetts Review, Inc. by permission.—***The Midwest Quarterly,*** v. IV, January, 1964. Copyright, 1964, by *The Midwest Quarterly,* Pittsburg State University. Reprinted by permission of the publisher.—***Monatshefte,*** v. 63, Summer, 1971. Copyright © 1971 by the Board of Regents of the University of Wisconsin System. Reprinted by permission of The University of Wisconsin Press.—***Mosaic: A Journal of the Comparative Study of Literature and Ideas,*** v. 3, Spring, 1972. © Mosaic 1972. Acknowledgment of previous publication is herewith made.—***New Orleans Review,*** v. 12, Spring, 1985. © 1985 by Loyola University, New Orleans. Reprinted by permission of the publisher.—***The New Republic,*** v. 143, November 28, 1960. © 1960, renewed 1988 The New Republic, Inc. Reprinted by permission of *The New Republic.*—***The New York Times,*** March 10, 1958. Copyright © 1958, renewed 1986 by The New York Times Company. Reprinted by permission of the publisher.—***The New York Times Book Review,*** September 15, 1968; February 11, 1973. Copyright © 1968, 1973 by The New York Times Company. Both reprinted by permission of the publisher./ May 10, 1925; April 17, 1949. Copyright 1925, renewed 1953; copyright 1949, renewed 1977 by The New York Times Company. Both reprinted by permission of the publisher.—***The New Yorker,*** v. X, March 31, 1934 for "Worlds, Public and Private" by Clifton Fadiman. Copyright 1934, renewed © 1958 by The New Yorker Magazine, Inc. Reprinted by permission of the author.—***Novel: A Forum on Fiction,*** v. 8, Winter, 1975. Copyright © 1975 Novel Corp., 1975. Reprinted by permission of the publisher.—***Pembroke Magazine,*** n. 20, 1988 for "Carson McCullers' Anti-Fairy Tale: 'The Ballad of the Sad Cafe' " by Margaret Walsh. Copyright © 1988 the author. Reprinted by permission of the publisher.—***Revue des langues vivantes,*** v. 42, 1976 for " 'The Morgaged Heart': The Workshop of Carson McCullers" by Melvin J. Friedman. Reprinted by permission of the author.—***Saturday Review,*** v. XLIX, September 17, 1966. © 1966 *Saturday Review* magazine.—***Slavic and East-European Journal,*** v. VII, 1963. © 1963 by AATSEEL of the U.S., Inc. Reprinted by permission of the publisher.—***The Southern Literary Journal,*** v. XXII, Fall, 1989. Copyright 1989 by the Department of English, University of North Carolina at Chapel Hill. Reprinted by permission of the publisher.—***The Southern Quarterly,*** v. XXI, Fall, 1982; v. XXVI, Spring, 1988. Copyright © 1982, 1988 by the University of Southern Mississippi. Both reprinted by permission of the publisher.—***Southwest Review,*** v. 63, Winter, 1978 for " 'Freaking Out': The Short Stories of Carson McCullers" by Robert Phillips. © 1978 Southern Methodist University. Reprinted by permission of the author.—***Studies in American Fiction,*** v. 18, Spring, 1990. Copyright © 1990 Northeastern University. Reprinted by permission of the publisher.—***Studies in the Literary Imagination,*** v. I, October, 1968. Copyright 1968, Department of English, Georgia State University. Reprinted by permission of the publisher.—***Studies in Short Fiction,*** v. I, Fall, 1963; v. I, Winter, 1964; v. IX, Winter, 1972; v. X, Fall, 1973; v. XI, Fall, 1974; v. XII, Fall, 1975; v. 15, Winter, 1978; v. 15, Summer, 1978; v. 16, Winter, 1979; v. 19, Spring, 1982; v. 19, Summer, 1982. Copyright 1963, 1964, 1972, 1973, 1974, 1975, 1978, 1979, 1982 by Newberry College. All reprinted by permission of the publisher.—***Studies in Weird Fiction,*** n. 6, Fall, 1989. Copyright © 1989 by Necronomicon Press. Reprinted by permission of the publisher.—***Texas Studies in Literature and Language,*** v. V, Autumn, 1963 for " 'La Femme Adultère': Camus's Ironic Vision of the Absurd" by Anthony Zahareas; v. X, 1969 for " 'The Secret Sharer': Conrad's Psychological Study," by Gloria R. Dussinger. Copyright © 1963, 1969 by the University of Texas Press. Both reprinted by permission of the publisher and the respective authors./ v. IV, Winter, 1963. Copyright © 1963 by the University of Texas Press. Reprinted by permission of the publisher.—***The Times Literary Supplement,*** n. 3631, October 1, 1971. © The Times Supplement Limited 1971. Reproduced from *The Times Literary Supplement* by permission.—***Twentieth Century Literature,*** v. 20, January, 1974. Copyright 1974, Hofstra University Press. Reprinted by permission of the publisher.—***Western Humanities Review,*** v. XXXI, Winter, 1977. Copyright, 1977, University of Utah. Reprinted by permission of the publisher.

COPYRIGHTED EXCERPTS, IN *SSC,* VOLUME 9, WERE REPRINTED FROM THE FOLLOWING BOOKS:

Aiken, Conrad. From ***Selected Letters of Conrad Aiken.*** Edited by Joseph Killorin. Yale University Press, 1978. Copyright © 1978 by Mary Hoover Aiken and Joseph I. Killorin. All rights reserved. Reprinted by permission of Brandt & Brandt Literary Agents, Inc. and the editor.—Boddy, Gillian. From ***Katherine Mansfield: The Woman and the Writer.*** Penguin Books, 1988. Copyright © Gillian Boddy, 1988. All rights reserved. Reprinted by permission of Penguin Books Australia Limited.—Bowen, Elizabeth. From an introduction to ***Stories.*** By Katherine Mansfield, edited by Elizabeth Bowen. Vintage Books, 1956. © copyright, 1956, renewed 1984, by Alfred A. Knopf, Inc. All rights reserved. Reprinted by permission of Curtis Brown Ltd., London.—Braun, Lev. From ***Witness of Decline: Albert Camus, Moralist of the Absurd.*** Farleigh Dickinson University Press, 1974. © 1974 by Associated University Presses, Inc. Reprinted by permission of the publisher.—Brooks, Cleanth. From an interpretation of "The Lottery," in ***Understanding Fiction.*** Edited by Cleanth Brooks and Robert Penn Warren. Second edition. Appleton-Century-Crofts, 1959. Copyright © 1959, renewed 1987, by Appleton-Century-Crofts, Inc. All rights reserved. Reprinted by permission of Prentice-Hall/A Division of Simon & Schuster, Englewood Cliffs, NJ.—Carr, Virginia Spencer. From ***Understanding Carson McCullers.*** University of South Carolina Press, 1990. Copyright © University of South Carolina 1990. Reprinted by permission of the publisher.—Chekhov, A. P. From a letter in ***Tolstoy: The Critical Heritage.*** Edited by A. V. Knowles. Routledge & Kegan Paul, 1978. © A. V. Knowles 1978. Reprinted by permission of the publisher.—Christian, R. F. From ***Tolstoy: A Critical Introduction.*** Cambridge at the University Press, 1969. © Cambridge University Press 1969. Reprinted with the permission of the publisher and the author.—Cryle, P. M. From ***The Thematics of Commitment: The Tower & the Plain.*** Princeton University Press, 1985. Copyright © 1985 by Princeton University Press. All rights reserved. Reprinted by permission of the publisher.—Davidson, Cathy N. From ***The Experimental Fictions of Ambrose Bierce: Structuring the Ineffable.*** University of Nebraska Press, 1984. Copyright 1984 by the University of Nebraska Press. All rights reserved. Reprinted by permission of the publisher.—Eisinger, Chester E. From ***Fiction of the Forties.*** The University of Chicago Press, 1963. © 1963 by Chester E. Eisinger. Reprinted by permission of The University of Chicago Press and the author.—Ellison, David R. From ***Understanding Albert Camus.*** University of South Carolina Press, 1990. Copyright © University of South Carolina 1990. Reprinted by permission of the publisher.—Erskine, Thomas L. From "The Two Worlds of 'Silent Snow, Secret Snow'," in ***From Fiction to Film: Conrad Aiken's "Silent Snow, Secret Snow."*** Edited by Gerald R. Barrett and Thomas L. Erskine. Dickenson Publishing, 1972. Copyright © 1972 by Dickenson Publishing Company, Inc. All rights reserved. Reprinted by permission of the publisher.—Forster, E. M. From ***Two Cheers for Democracy.*** Harcourt Brace Jovanovich, 1951, Edward Arnold, 1951. Copyright 1939, renewed 1967 by E. M. Forster. Reprinted by permission of Harcourt Brace Jovanovich, Inc. In Canada by Edward Arnold (Publishers) Ltd.—Fullbrook, Kate. From ***Katherine Mansfield.*** Indiana University Press, 1986. © Kate Fullbrook, 1986. All rights reserved. Reprinted by permission of the publisher.—Gordon, Ian A. From an introduction to ***Undiscovered Country: The New Zealand Stories of Katherine Mansfield.*** Edited by Ian A. Gordon. Longman, 1974. © Introduction: Longman Group Limited 1974. All rights reserved. Reprinted by permission of the publisher.—Gossett, Louise Y. From ***Violence in Recent Southern Fiction.*** Duke University Press, 1965. Copyright © 1965 by Duke University Press, Durham, NC. Reprinted by permission of the publisher.—Guerard, Albert J. From ***Conrad the Novelist.*** Cambridge, Mass.: Harvard University Press, 1958. Copyright © 1958 by the President and Fellows of Harvard College. Renewed 1986 by Albert Joseph Guerard. Reprinted by permission of the author.—Gurr, Andrew and Clare Hanson. From ***Katherine Mansfield.*** St. Martin's Press, 1981, Macmillan, London, 1983. © Clare Hanson and Andrew Gurr 1981. All rights reserved. Used with permission of St. Martin's Press, Inc. In Canada by Macmillan, London and Basingstoke.—Hankin, C. A. From ***Katherine Mansfield and Her Confessional Stories.*** St. Martin's Press, 1983, Macmillan, London, 1983. © C. A. Hankin 1983. All rights reserved. Used with permission of St. Martin's Press, Inc. In Canada by Macmillan, London and Basingstoke.—Hanson, Clare. From ***Short Stories and Short Fictions, 1880-1980.*** St. Martin's Press, 1985. © Clare Hanson 1985. All rights reserved. Used by permission of the publisher.—Hassan, Ihab. From ***Radical Innocence: Studies in the Contemporary American Novel.*** Princeton University Press, 1961. Copyright © 1961, renewed 1989 by Ihab Hassan. All rights reserved. Reprinted by permission of the author.—Jackson, Shirley. From "Biography of a Story," in ***Come Along with Me.*** Edited by Stanley Edgar Hyman. Viking Press, 1968. Copyright 1948, 1952, © 1960 by Shirley Jackson. Used by permission of Viking Penguin, a division of Penguin Books USA, Inc.—Kaplan, Sydney Janet. From ***Katherine Mansfield and the Origins of Modernist Fiction.*** Cornell University Press, 1991. Copyright © 1991 by Cornell University. Used by permission of the publisher, Cornell University Press.—Kazin, Alfred. From "On Ambrose Bierce and 'Parker Adderson, Philosopher'," in ***The American Short Story.*** Edited by Calvin Skaggs. Dell Book, 1977. Copyright © 1977 Alfred Kazin. All rights reserved. Reprinted by permission of the author.—Kittredge, Mary. From "The Other Side of Magic: A Few Remarks About Shirley Jackson," in ***Discovering Modern Horror Fiction.*** Edited by Darrell Schweitzer. Starmont House, 1985. Copyright © 1985 by Starmont House, Inc. All rights reserved. Reprinted by permission of the publisher.—Lazere, Donald. From ***The Unique Creation of Albert Camus.*** Yale University Press, 1973. Copyright © 1973 by Yale University. All rights reserved. Reprinted by permission of the author.—Mileck, Joseph. From ***Hermann Hesse: Life and Art.*** University of California Press, 1978. Copyright © 1978 by The Regents of the University of California. Reprinted by permission of the publisher.—Moller, Peter Ulf. From ***Postlude to the Kreutzer Sonata: Tolstoj and the Debate on Sexual Morality in Russian Literature in the 1890s.*** Translated by John Kendal. Brill, 1988. © copyright 1988 by E. J. Brill. All rights reserved. Reprinted by permission of the publisher.—Nathan, Rhoda B. From ***Katherine Mansfield.*** Continuum, 1988. Copyright © 1988 by Rhoda B. Nathan. All rights reserved. Reprinted by permission of the publisher.—Noyer-Weidner, Alfred. From "Albert Camus in his Short Story Phase," translated by Ernest Allen, in ***Essays in Camus's "Exile and the Kingdom."*** Edited by Judith D. Suther. Romance Monographs, 1980. Copyright © 1981 by Romance Monographs, Inc. Reprinted by permission of the publisher.—Pelz, Manfred. From "The Function of Interior Monologue in 'The Renegade'," translated by Stephen K. Wright, in ***Essays on Camus's "Exile and the Kingdom."*** Edited by Judith D. Suther. Romance Monographs, 1980. Copyright © 1981 by Romance Monographs, Inc. Reprinted by permission of the publisher.—Picon, Gaëtan. From " 'Exile and the Kingdom'," in ***Camus: A Collection of Critical Essays.*** Edited by Germaine Brée. Prentice-Hall, 1962. © 1962 by Prentice-Hall, Inc. Renewed 1990 by Germaine Brée. All rights reserved. Reprinted by permission of Mercure de France S. A. and the editor.—Reilly, Joseph J. From ***Of Books and Men.*** Julian Messner, 1942. Copyright 1942, renewed 1970, by Joseph J. Reilly. Reprinted by permission of Julian Messner, Inc., a division of Simon & Schuster, Inc.—Rose, Ernst. From ***Faith from the Abyss: Hermann Hesse's Way from Romanticism to Modernity.*** New York University Press, 1965. © 1965 by New York University. Reprinted by permission of the publisher.—Rosenthal, Raymond. From a foreword to ***Fables and Fairy Tales.*** By Leo Tolstoy, translated by Ann Dunnigan. New American Library, 1962. Translation copyright © 1962, renewed 1990 by Ann Dunnigan. Foreword copyright © 1962 by New American Library of World Literature, Inc. All rights reserved. Used by permission of New American Library, a Division of Penguin Books USA Inc., New York, NY.—Schorer, Mark. From a preface to ***The Collected Short Stories of Conrad Aiken.*** The World Publishing Company, 1960. Copyright © 1960 by Conrad Aiken. Renewed 1988 by Ruth P. Schorer. All rights reserved. Reprinted by permission of Harpercollins Publishers, Inc.—Showalter, English, Jr. From ***Exiles and Strangers: A Reading of Camus's 'Exile and the Kingdom.'*** Ohio State University Press, 1984. © 1984 by the Ohio State University Press. All rights reserved. Reprinted by permission of the publisher.—Simmons, Ernest J. From ***Introduction to Tolstoy's Writings.*** The University of Chicago Press, 1968. © 1968 by The University of Chicago. All rights reserved. Reprinted by permission of the publisher.—Tarrow, Susan. From ***Exile from the Kingdom: A Political Rereading of Albert Camus.*** University of Alabama Press, 1985. Copyright © 1985 by The University of Alabama Press. All rights reserved. Reprinted by permission of the publisher.—Warren, Robert Penn. From an introduction to ***The Collected Short Stories of Conrad Aiken.*** Schocken Books, 1982. Introduction copyright © 1982 by Robert Penn Warren. Reprinted by permission of the William Morris Agency, Inc., on behalf of the Estate of the author.—Wasiolek, Edward. From ***Tolstoy's Major Fiction.*** The University of Chicago Press, 1978. © 1978 by The University of Chicago. All rights reserved. Reprinted by permission of the publisher and the author.—Weiand, Hermann. From "Typhoon," in ***Insight II: Analyses of Modern British Literature.*** Edited by John V. Hagopian and Martin Dolch. Hirschgraben-Verlag, 1965. Reprinted by permission of the publisher.—Weimer, David R. From "Ambrose Bierce and the Art of War," in ***Essays in Literary History Presented to J. Milton French.*** Edited by Rudolf Kirk and C. F. Main. Rutgers University Press, 1960. Copyright © 1960 by Rutgers, The State University. Renewed 1988 by Rudolf Kirk. Reprinted with permission of the publisher.—Woodruff, Stuart C. From ***The Short Stories of Ambrose Bierce: A Study in Polarity.*** University of Pittsburgh Press, 1965. Copyright © 1964, University of Pittsburgh Press. Reprinted by permission of the publisher.—Ziolkowski, Theodore. From "Siddhartha: The Landscape of the Soul," in ***The Novels of Hermann Hesse: A Study in Theme and Structure.*** Princeton University Press, 1965. Copyright © 1965 by Princeton University Press. Reprinted by permission of the publisher.—Ziolkowski, Theodore. From an introduction to ***Pictor's Metamorphoses and Other Fantasies.*** By Hermann Hesse, translated by Rika Lesser. Farrar, Straus and Giroux, 1982. Introduction and translation copyright © 1981, 1982 by Farrar, Straus and Giroux, Inc. Reprinted by permission of Farrar, Straus and Giroux, Inc.—Ziolkowski, Theodore. From an introduction to ***Stories of Five Decades.*** By Hermann Hesse, translated by Ralph Manheim and Denver Lindley. Farrar, Straus and Giroux, 1972. Translation copyright © 1954, 1972 by Farrar, Straus and Giroux, Inc. Reprinted by permission of Farrar, Straus and Giroux, Inc.

PHOTOGRAPHS AND ILLUSTRATIONS APPEARING IN *SSC*, VOLUME 9, WERE RECEIVED FROM THE FOLLOWING SOURCES:

© Rollie McKenna: **p. 1;** Courtesy of Clarissa Lorenz Aiken: **p. 21;** Courtesy of Mary Hoover Aiken: **p. 38;** Culver Pictures, New York: **p. 48;** The Bettmann Archive: **pp. 77, 362;** Courtesy of Jean Camus: **p. 102;** Collection of Mme. Catherine Camus: **p. 109;** Photograph by T. R. Annan & Sons: **p. 139;** Courtesy of Thames and Hudson Ltd.: **p. 170;** Photograph by Grete Widmann: **p. 209;** Schiller-Nationalmuseum, Marbach am Neckar: **p. 233;** Courtesy of Laurence Hyman: **p. 248;** Courtesy of Barry Jackson: **p. 255;** Courtesy of Sarah H. Stewart: **p. 257;** Courtesy of Arthur and Bunny Hyman: **p. 263;** Courtesy of the Brockways: **p. 271;** Photograph by Louise Dahl Wolfe: **p. 321.**

Conrad Aiken

1889-1973

(Full name Conrad Potter Aiken; also wrote under the pseudonym Samuel Jeake, Jr.) American poet, novelist, short story writer, critic, essayist, and journalist.

INTRODUCTION

An influential and highly regarded poet and critic, Aiken is also known for such often-anthologized stories as "Silent Snow, Secret Snow" and "Mr. Arcularis." In these and many other fictional and poetic works Aiken blended psychological and philosophical elements to explore facets of modern existence and the nature of human consciousness. Aiken's short stories have been praised in particular for their compelling portrayal of the tension between the internal realities of his protagonists and the external, social reality of the worlds they inhabit.

Aiken's short stories generally focus on character rather than plot, emphasizing the emotional state of his protagonists over their actions or intellectual development. Commentators have suggested that many of the stories are highly autobiographical, and the experiences of several of Aiken's protagonists have been related to traumatic events in his own life, most notably the murder of his mother by his father and his father's subsequent suicide. Aiken himself discouraged emphasis on the autobiographical aspects of his works, claiming that such a view would accord him "no credit as an artist" for his conscious shaping of material. The influence of the psychoanalytic theories of Sigmund Freud is frequently noted in Aiken's works, and his short fiction is often discussed from a psychoanalytic viewpoint.

With his first collection, *Bring! Bring!,* which was published in 1925, Aiken garnered praise for his lyrical prose style, unobtrusive narrative technique, and avoidance of formulaic plots and stock characterizations. In addition, the mood of several stories in *Bring! Bring!* is considered reminiscent of the predilection for the surreal and macabre familiar in his poetry of the era. For example, "Strange Moonlight" portrays a young boy's attempt to comprehend the death of a playmate, and contains numerous allusions to the works of Edgar Allan Poe. The stories in Aiken's second collection, *Costumes by Eros,* were written during a long period of intense personal suffering for Aiken that included a divorce from his first wife and his suicide attempt in 1932. Many of these stories focus on relationships between women and men. In "Your Obituary, Well Written," the narrator reminisces about his brief friendship with a female writer modeled on Katherine Mansfield, with whose works Aiken's short stories are frequently compared, while "I Love You Very Dearly" focuses on the relationship between a father, who has gone abroad after a family argument, and his married daughter, who is engaged in an adulterous affair.

Aiken's third collection, *Among the Lost People,* which contains his best-known works of short fiction, "Silent Snow, Secret Snow" and "Mr. Arcularis," focuses on individuals whose experiences isolate them from society and everyday reality. In "Mr. Arcularis" an elderly man recuperating from an operation undertakes a sea voyage during which he experiences a series of disturbing dreams, awakening each time to discover that he has been sleepwalking in search of a coffin stored on the ship. At the end of the story, it is revealed that he died during the operation, a disclosure that has led some critics to view Mr. Arcularis's "voyage" as a symbolic confrontation with the philosophical and psychological problems of his own death. In "Silent Snow, Secret Snow," which is often discussed as a case history of schizophrenia, twelve-year-old Paul Hasleman wakes one morning with a vision of "a secret screen of new snow between himself and the world." Realizing that the essence of his vision cannot be communicated, Paul tells no one what he perceives, determined that "at whatever pain to others . . . one must persevere in severance, since the incommunicability of the experience demanded it." The family doctor is unable to find any physical ailment, yet Paul becomes increasingly alienated, ultimately withdrawing into his private world. Paul's estrangement is commonly explained as the onset of mental illness, but others have also found his experience symbolic of the alienation of the artist from society.

While some reviewers frequently found Aiken's short stories inexplicable or merely morbid, others perceived a symbolic significance in the pathological states Aiken presented and expressed admiration for his narrative technique. Discussing the detailed descriptive style Aiken employed, Robert Morss Lovett noted that Aiken "is disarmingly casual in his presentation of the external world of associations and contacts, but behind this affectation of indifference there is always matter of intense significance to the individual soul. Indeed Mr. Aiken's pervasive theme may be said to be this contact between the uncomprehending world and the mind intensely concerned with its own life, and tragically lonely in its pursuit." Recent critics have also praised the craftsmanship of Aiken's short stories, noting their complex symbolic structures and literary allusions, as well as their importance in the development of his literary career.

PRINCIPAL WORKS

SHORT FICTION

Bring! Bring! 1925; also published as *Bring! Bring! and Other Stories,* 1925
Costumes by Eros 1928
Among the Lost People 1934
The Short Stories of Conrad Aiken 1950
The Collected Short Stories of Conrad Aiken 1960

OTHER MAJOR WORKS

Earth Triumphant, and Other Tales in Verse (poetry) 1914
The Jig of Forslin: A Symphony (poetry) 1916
Turns and Movies, and Other Tales in Verse (poetry) 1916
Nocturne of Remembered Spring, and Other Poems (poetry) 1917
The Charnel Rose, Senlin: A Biography, and Other Poems (poetry) 1918
Scepticisms: Notes on Contemporary Poetry (criticism) 1919
The House of Dust: A Symphony (poetry) 1920
Punch: The Immortal Liar, Documents in His History (poetry) 1921
Priapus and the Pool (poetry) 1922; also published as *Priapus and the Pool, and Other Poems* [enlarged edition], 1925
The Pilgrimage of Festus (poetry) 1923
Blue Voyage (novel) 1927
Selected Poems (poetry) 1929
John Deth: A Metaphysical Legend, and Other Poems (poetry) 1930
The Coming Forth by Day of Osiris Jones (poetry) 1931
Preludes for Memnon; or, Preludes to Attitude (poetry) 1931
Great Circle (novel) 1933
Landscape West of Eden (poetry) 1934
King Coffin (novel) 1935
Time in the Rock: Preludes to Definition (poetry) 1936
A Heart for the Gods of Mexico (novel) 1939
And in the Human Heart (poetry) 1940
Conversation; or, Pilgrims' Progress (novel) 1940
Brownstone Eclogues, and Other Poems (poetry) 1942
The Soldier: A Poem (poetry) 1944
The Kid (poetry) 1947
**The Divine Pilgrim* (poetry) 1949
Skylight One: Fifteen Poems (poetry) 1949
Ushant: An Essay (autobiography) 1952
Collected Poems (poetry) 1953; also published as *Collected Poems, 1916-1970* [enlarged edition], 1970
A Letter from Li Po, and Other Poems (poetry) 1955
Mr. Arcularis [adaptor; from the short story "Mr. Arcularis" by Conrad Aiken] (drama) [first publication] 1957
A Reviewer's ABC: Collected Criticism (criticism) 1958; also published as *Collected Criticism,* 1968
Sheepfold Hill: Fifteen Poems (poetry) 1958
The Morning Song of Lord Zero: Poems Old and New (poetry) 1963
The Collected Novels of Conrad Aiken (novels) 1964
Thee: A Poem (poetry) 1967
The Clerk's Journal: Being the Diary of a Queer Man (poetry) 1971
Selected Letters of Conrad Aiken (letters) 1978

*This work contains revised versions of "The Charnel Rose," "The Jig of Forslin," "The House of Dust," and "Senlin: A Biography," as well as "The Pilgrimage of Festus" and "Changing Mind."

Malcolm Cowley (essay date 1925)

[*A prominent American critic, Cowley made several valuable contributions to contemporary letters, including his editions of the works of important American authors, his writings for the* New Republic, *and above all, his chronicles and criticism of modern American literature. Cowley's literary criticism does not attempt a systematic philosophical view of life and art, nor is it representative of a neatly defined school of critical thought. Rather, Cowley focused on works that he considered worthy of public appreciation and that he believed personal experience had qualified him to explicate, such as the works of the "lost generation" writers whom he knew. The critical approach Cowley followed is undogmatic and is characterized by a willingness to view a work from whatever perspective—social, historical, aesthetic—that the work itself seemed to demand for illumination. In the following essay, Cowley reviews* Bring! Bring!, *focusing on "The Orange Moth."*]

Ideally considered, the short story is a plot which contains four elements. There is a situation (or event); an emotion which the event calls forth; an idea crystallized from the emotion; finally an action. Most stories follow this outline with surprising fidelity; it is even the standard of the popular magazines, although they have a tendency to emphasize the fourth element at the expense of the other three. In ***Bring! Bring!*** the action is almost negligible. A boy comes to realize, slowly, the fact of his playmate's death. A man receives a letter from a stranger, who is dying. Or a drunken woman goes wandering through the rain, crawls into a taxi-cab, and falls asleep. There is no climax, no real conclusion; a chain of obscure causes leads to an emotion which is almost disembodied.

In still another story, Marie Schley visits her dying grandmother and there, at the bedside, remembers her own childhood. She steals away to meet her lover. That evening, in the electric dusk of a theatre, listening to a singer with gold teeth and a cork-blackened face, she feels the ecstasy of abstract surrender. "A delicious feeling of weakness, of dissolution, came over her. Life seemed to her extraordinarily complex, beautiful and miserable."

Imagine the same story as written by another author. Marie, at her grandmother's death-bed, would be overcome with pity, remorse, a sudden respect for the family gods. These emotions would crystallize into the idea of giving up her lover; she would act on the idea. The story would end perhaps in a grim parting, perhaps in a reconciliation with her husband. In Mr Aiken's handling, the idea (third element in the ideal plot) is omitted like the action. Marie is left with a purposeless emotion, unexpressed, drowned in her mind as in a pool of standing water. It is perhaps not difficult to understand why most of Mr Aiken's characters are tormented by the sense of futility and defeat.

They are people who live in boarding-houses and speak in the terms of a rag melody. They have an income, but forget their antecedents. Their life is one of pure physical sensation. At times they refer to Fichte or Spinoza; they make elegant allusions to Venus "rising out of Duxbury Bay on a good-sized clam shell," but these are only the tarnished last-souvenirs of their classical education. They study and think no longer. Instead they feel, dream, passively accept.

This dangerous passivity, the neglect of logical thought, the distaste for action (growing into a contempt for action): all these are symptoms of the malady which afflicts the more intelligent writers of our time. Their books are concerned with people who drift, accept, surrender to their passions. A strain of inherited agnosticism, applied first to God, then to society, has finally centred in the self. They are palsied with doubt; afflicted, characters and authors, with an atrophy of the will.

And correspondingly the emotions are exalted. Every other element in Mr Aiken's stories becomes subordinate. The first of the elements, even—the situation or event—is altered into something less definite. It becomes a background for emotion: a park where robins sing louder and larger than life, where ducks stand on their heads and trees are green as verdigris. Or observe the city of maggots: "their heads are small and wedge-shaped, and glow with a faint bluish light." Every detail is magnified, distorted by feeling. The story itself becomes a lyric poem, a brief threnody of suffering and delight, almost a chemically pure emotion.

These are a poet's stories. In a world of neat plots, made by experienced mechanics, they have an unprofessional air which does not detract from their effect. They are better, indeed, than Mr Aiken's poems. It has always seemed to me that heretofore his published work has been something less than a measure of the man. The writing was distinguished, the emotions profound, but there was a gap between the two, perhaps a mechanical failure, a failure in the mechanics of expression rather than in those of verse. I can't point to line and stanza, but I might quote from Conrad Aiken's own caricature of a poet who suffered from the same disability in a far more exaggerated manner.

Young Cooke, the hero of **"The Orange Moth,"** was always trying to write like Pater or De Quincey; to stimulate his talents with yellow or blue paper, with pads and blank books of many shapes, with red or violet inks. A ridiculous figure; still, his emotions were delicate, his vision clear. He liked to ride on the Elevated and stare through the open tenement windows, where he could see "people moving there, inside, folding newspapers, taking pots from stoves, turning back bed covers, reaching up arms to light the gas. He liked the heavy Jewesses leaning out into the evening, apathetic, their massive breasts spread out on the cool stone, their faces like the faces of oxen. . . . There it was, so close to him, so immediate, yet he could do nothing with it. Some poison in his brain turned it all to dullness, to mud—no, worse than that, to a kind of lifeless simulacrum, a mechanical formula—as soon as he tried to touch it. Oh, God, if he could only get hold of beauty."

He decided, one glutinous summer night, that he was a failure. De Quincey couldn't help him; neither could Pater. He crawled into bed, pulled the sheet over him, and dreamed. "An orange-coloured moth flew heavily in through the window, and settled with wide velvet wings on the opened pages of the blank book. The orange wings covered the two pages completely. He sprang up, shut the book, and the beautiful thing was caught. When he opened the book, he found that the pages were soft orange moth wings; and incredibly fine, indecipherable, in purple, a poem of extraordinary beauty was written there."

Of course the humour of the story is that anybody should try to set a trap for beauty, in blank books of any special shape. Impossible, ridiculous, and yet—would it be too much to say that in this volume, with its atmosphere of drowned emotions, "complex, beautiful and miserable," Conrad Aiken has captured the orange moth? (pp. 507-09)

Malcolm Cowley, "The Orange Moth," in The Dial, *Chicago, Vol. 79, December, 1925, pp. 507-09.*

The New York Times Book Review (essay date 1925)

[*In the following review of* Bring! Bring!, *the critic discusses Aiken's strengths as a prose stylist while expressing dissatisfaction with the collection as a whole.*]

[In ***Bring! Bring!***] Conrad Aiken, hitherto generally known as poet and critic, . . . brings together thirteen short stories which combine poetry of feeling with criticism of life in prose narrative. Whether they are veritable short stories according to academic canons is somewhat problematical; they seem to belong, for the greater part, to the school of which Katherine Mansfield was perhaps the most successful exponent.

Not that Mr. Aiken is imitative; he is much too fine and individual an artist to tag with such a phrase. But these tales, like so many of the Mansfield narratives, merely exploit the dramatics of a situation or a mood, or explore the subtleties of a character rather than attempt a short story proper in any commonly accepted sense of the term.

The title story, for example, deals with a household in which a man and three women are curiously related. The husband, according to his wife, is an arrant philanderer. She is either in reality or imagination a semi-invalid. Her nurse, from whose point of view the story progresses, is apparently jealous of the wife's sister, who is housekeeper and who also bears a somewhat shadowy and problematical relationship to her brother-in-law. This neuropathological household is pictured intimately and the nurse's mind turned inside out with deftness and diabolical insight. And yet the story disappoints, perhaps because of a lingering impression that the whole situation is thought out from the angle of psychoanalytic theory rather than merely allowed to live itself out.

As in his poetry, Mr. Aiken shows his penchant for the subterranean, the shadowy, the sometime morbid and demoniacal. He has certain affinities with Poe, and **"Smith and Jones"** is in this vein or in that of Stevenson's "Markheim." He is rather fascinated by the obscure, the dark, the morbid, the bizarre. And yet he can turn out **"Hey! Taxi!"** in which a homeless street girl is driven to take refuge from the rain in the car of a sleepy and unwilling chauffeur. There is something sardonic, almost mordant even, in his humor.

"Strange Moonlight," a wistfully beautiful study of a child's mind in its attempt to grasp the tragedy of existence, is a most appealing thing. The sense of tears in mortal things and of death touching the mind is ever present in Mr. Aiken's work, and even in his poetry it has hardly been brought out with more terrible beauty than in this sketch of the childish effort to understand the loss of his first love. **"The Orange Moth"** seems more nearly poetry than prose in conception, and possesses something of the evanescence of music in its appeal; it is like some brief overtoned nocturne.

In **"The Disciple"** Mr. Aiken perhaps comes nearest hitting his mark fairly and by that same token most disappoints. That immortal figure the Wandering Jew, now a shopkeeper, recognizes Judas in a customer; an unconscious Judas whose memory is difficult to touch. Something of the grotesque, the macabre, is achieved, and then the end flats woefully.

Mr. Aiken's endowment is so exceptional and his accomplishment so fine, that one feels a more than ordinary sense of disappointment in his unfulfilled promises. In almost every story in the present collection that promise is very high. His insight into character, his feeling for the truly dramatic and intensely poetic, are so sure, that, liking these stories as one assuredly must, they nevertheless leave behind them an irritation almost inevitable and a well warranted regret.

"Mr. Aiken's Stories," in The New York Times Book Review, *May 10, 1925, p. 8.*

R. N. Linscott (essay date 1928)

[*In the following review, Linscott discusses style and theme in* Costumes by Eros.]

Picking up Mr. Aiken's new book [***Costumes by Eros***], letting one's thoughts drift down through the pages of its fourteen predecessors, one speculates upon the mind of their creator. It is, one feels, amazingly perceptive, "all tremulous awareness," as he himself says of one of his characters, a speculative mind preoccupied with the problems of consciousness; a susceptible and dissatisfied mind continually shifting its point of attack, forever adapting novel forms in its search for a style appropriate to each new theme.

Meditating upon this susceptibility, one opens Mr. Aiken's new book with a question. Has he succumbed to the clipped and stripped style of the younger story-tellers? And sure enough, one finds half way through the volume a perfect example of the new method. **"Farewell! Farewell! Farewell!"** is the story of an Irish servant girl who falls in love on a transatlantic liner. It is competently done, and completely in character. It is solid, simple, sharply objective; everything, in short, that a story of this kind should be. In a way one welcomes it as evidence that the author, if he chooses, can pass beyond the orbit of his own consciousness and fully explore an alien mind. And yet, at the same time, one feels certain that Mr. Aiken has taken the wrong path, that he has turned his back upon the enchanted forest where he is at home. For he is still a poet, and most happy in those themes that allow for the free play of the imagination and that are better expressed by lingering and involute cadences than by the abrupt rhythms of the new prose.

In **"Your Obituary, Well Written,"** he has found such a theme and has made from it a story of poignant and delicate beauty. Its "plot" is of the slightest. Starting from the thesis that the most illuminating record of a life would be the relation of one single central episode "in whose small prism all the colors and lights of one's soul might be seen," the narrator looks back over his own life and selects as such an episode his meeting with a woman novelist whom he enormously admired. The novelist is young, beautiful, unhappily married and condemned by a fragile heart to imminent death. Their meeting is brief, they have little to say; yet in those few words the author somehow breaks through the boundaries of the solid world and gives one a fourth-dimensional glimpse of the human soul.

> It was strange, at that moment, how everything seemed to be conspiring to make this mutual recognition complete: the long room lined with book cases; the high mantel of cream-colored wood and the pale Dutch tiles which surrounded the fireplace; the worn Khelim rug which stretched between us, and the open window,

> which it seemed not improbable that the thorn-tree itself had opened, in order that its fragrance and the London spring might come in to us—all these details were vividly and conspiratorially present to me, as if they were indeed a part of the exquisite mingling of our personalities at that poised instant of time. . . . Destiny was in this; æons of patient evolution and change, wars and disasters and ages of darkness, the sandlike siftings of laws and stars, had all worked for the fulfilment of this intimate minute, this perfect flowering of two meeting minds.

It is this capture of the "ultimate minute" so perfectly achieved in **"Your Obituary, Well Written"** that furnishes the touchstone with which to measure the success of Mr. Aiken's other stories. In **"Spider, Spider,"** he describes a woman's attempt to seduce a man who loves another, reaching a perfection almost as complete, but on a lower level, for the theme does not permit the same magic sense of ecstasy. **"State of Mind," "The Moment,"** and **"Field of Flowers"** are slighter, but equally flawless exercises in virtuosity. Two of the stories—**"The Necktie"** and **"The Woman-Hater"**—are comparative failures, the first because it is an expanded anecdote, the second because the device of an overheard conversation cramps the development of the theme.

Throughout the book, as might be inferred from the title, love is the dominant theme. Each story presents a different aspect of the relation of the sexes and taken together, they make a formidable case against the blind god. As in his novel, *Blue Voyage,* Mr. Aiken has depended largely upon the stream of consciousness method and has scrupulously avoided the use of plot, relying for interest upon the skill with which he lays bare the subtlest emotions, the most delicate nuances of feeling.

As a whole the new volume is more competent in treatment than ***Bring! Bring!*** (Mr. Aiken's previous collection), but slightly less exciting in content. One feels that the author is gradually deserting fantasy for realism; moving down on the scale from Dostoievsky toward Chekov. It is this unquenched zest for experiment that makes Mr. Aiken one of the major figures in the literary scene; this together with a comprehension of the finer shades of character worthy of Henry James; an ability to communicate emotion, particularly the keen and narrow emotion of spiritual ecstasy and pain, comparable with that of Katherine Mansfield, and a style that is a perfect instrument both of beauty and of precision, and a perpetual reminder that Mr. Aiken is first of all a poet.

R. N. Linscott, "Conrad in Quest of Reality," in The Saturday Review of Literature, *Vol. V, No. 12, October 13, 1928, p. 212.*

Clifton Fadiman (essay date 1934)

[*Fadiman became one of the most prominent American literary critics during the 1930s with his insightful and often caustic book reviews for the* Nation *and the* New Yorker *magazines. In the following excerpt, Fadiman offers a favorable assessment of* Among the Lost People, *particularly praising "Silent Snow, Secret Snow."*]

I don't want to be quoted on this, but in a way, it seems to me, perhaps the only "pure individuals" are babies and lunatics. The baby (at least during the first half-hour or so of its career) flaunts a complete and somewhat cynical detachment from its environment. It refuses to play the social game on any terms. The lunatic, unable to fit into a public world, does the next best thing. He constructs his own personal one. He is a kind of capitalist of the emotions, retaining the principle of private ownership of the psychoses. As a matter of fact, he is the only genuinely rugged individualist.

Most novelists, these days, observe man as a social animal, but a few still work with the ego as it approaches a state of isolation. They are interested in human beings as islands rather than isthmuses. Newborn babies just don't lend themselves to the novel; consequently, writers like Faulkner and Conrad Aiken tend to deal with people who are either quite mad or definitely on the way.

I prefer Mr. Aiken. He seems less Gothic and his stories are always quite clear, no matter how murky may be the states of mind they describe. In him three talents converge: that of a crafty story-teller, that of a brilliant stylist, that of a trained psychoanalyst. He is an Edgar Allan Poe who has been to Vienna—and, by the way, he affords a pretty convincing refutation of the prevalent gossip that Freud is played out as a source of literary material.

His new collection of short stories is called ***Among the Lost People,*** and the title gives you the idea. Most of the tales are very fine, a few not so good. All are highly readable and, with the exception of **"Mr. Arcularis,"** you can't really call them morbid. Mr. Aiken finds a certain beauty in his mental cancers and communicates his weird delight to all except those who do deep-breathing exercises before open windows.

The book offers a memorable cruise among human islands. Meet Mr. and Mrs. Lynton, who live desperately in an eggshell world of whimsy; Mr. Arcularis (Lord, what a story!), who literally dreams himself to death; the two Willard women, whose revenge mania is set off by the chance phrase of an itinerant evangelist; Michael Lowes, the unconscious kleptomaniac; twelve-year-old Paul Hasleman, gently, pleasantly, inexorably retreating into his fantasy universe, where all things are shrouded in falling snow. Tossing all restraint to the winds, I hereby nominate this last tale, **"Silent Snow, Secret Snow,"** as the finest short story written in America since Mr. Hemingway knocked us over with "The Killers."

Most of Mr. Aiken's narratives are laid in the world of childhood, or play back and forth between the adult present and the vaguely remembered childhood past. In psychoanalytic fiction, we get an intensified sense of a new time dimension. The Now is relatively unimportant. Just as the revolutionary novel gives the effect of being written partially in the future tense, so the Aiken-Faulkner novel works patiently, subtly in the past tense. Each form is freighted with its own unique richness and "thickness."

Clifton Fadiman, "Worlds, Public and Private," in The New Yorker, *Vol. X, No. 7, March 31, 1934, pp. 56, 58.*

Robert Morss Lovett (essay date 1934)

[*An American literary critic, educator, and statesman, Lovett served on the editorial staff of the* New Republic *during the 1920s and 1930s. The book reviews that he contributed to that periodical as well as his editorial policy reflected Lovett's leftist social and political thought. An advocate of numerous liberal causes, Lovett was president of the League for Industrial Democracy, president of the Sacco-Vanzetti National League, and on the executive committee of the American Civil Liberties Union. In the following excerpt from a review of* Among the Lost People, *Lovett praises narrative style in the collection and discusses the psychological focus of the stories.*]

In his fiction as in his poetry no one can doubt Conrad Aiken's originality. If in [***Among the Lost People***] as in its predecessors, he reminds one of James Joyce or Katherine Mansfield, of Sherwood Anderson or Ernest Hemingway, it is because of their participation in a common spirit of modernity, not because of any direct influence. That Mr. Aiken should suggest so many other writers is a mark of his virtuosity; that amid variety he is extremely like himself is a sign of his originality. As in his first volume of short stories, ***Bring! Bring!*** he writes sometimes in recollected narrative of low key and extreme simplicity; sometimes in the present stream of consciousness, gropingly gathering about matters of fact. He is disarmingly casual in his presentation of the external world of associations and contacts, but behind this affectation of indifference there is always matter of intense significance to the individual soul. Indeed Mr. Aiken's pervasive theme may be said to be this contact between the uncomprehending world and the mind intensely concerned with its own life, and tragically lonely in its pursuit. Unquestionably this preoccupation reflects Mr. Aiken's own pessimism, his sense of a civilization past the age of belief or hope. The half-sane madness of his early poetry, and his recent *Preludes to Memnon* with their recurrent lament from "chaos to chaos," are the cry of a poet whose eyes are turned inward and who hears reflected in his own mind this noise of a world riding to ruin. The fantastic score of his novel *Blue Voyage* likewise reflects what Mr. Peterson calls, in his valuable interpretation of the book, *The Melody of Chaos.*

The stories in [***Among the Lost People*** as in Aiken's earlier volumes of short fiction] have a psychological rather than a social focus; their psychology is of the type known in more innocent days as abnormal, and their characters tend to become studies in incongruity. **"O How She Laughed"** is the story of a woman who paints badly, who knows that she paints badly, but who shows the usual failure of the neurotic to face reality. **"Impulse"** is the experience of a man, a failure in life, who tries to rehabilitate himself in his own eyes by stealing a safety razor in a drug store. **"The Bachelor's Supper"** is that of a sentimental, sensitive bridegroom exposed to masculine prenuptial obscenities. **"Pure as the Driven Snow"** is that of a sensual Puritan using his scruples to evade the obvious requirements of a night with a chorus girl. **"No, No, Go Not to Lethe"** is the downfall of an egoist who aspired to personal imperialism by penetrating and controlling the little lives about him without giving anything of himself. The most touching and beautifully written story in the collection is **"Silent Snow, Secret Snow,"** in which a young boy uses a casual hallucination as a defense mechanism against an encroaching world.

A neurologist tells us that, given the present rate of increase in nervous diseases, the civilized world will be insane in a couple of centuries. Mr. Aiken's work is a prophecy of that grim future. His detachment, his underemphasis, his humor, are in a way deceptive, and conceal from us the fact that many of his characters, even those who are so like ourselves that we exclaim, "There but for the grace of God go I," are on, or beyond, the verge. There is no heaviness or melodrama in their tragedy; they may even amuse us. But they are lost people in a sense more real than figurative, lost to the world, sometimes even lost to themselves. (pp. 80-1)

Robert Morss Lovett, "The Melody of Chaos," in The New Republic, *Vol. LXXIX, No. 1017, May 30, 1934, pp. 80-1.*

Horace Gregory (essay date 1950)

[*Gregory was a noted American poet, critic, and translator of classical Latin verse. In the following review of* The Short Stories of Conrad Aiken, *he considers Aiken's accomplishments as a short story writer.*]

No academic reader of the short story in America is likely to overlook the prose writings of Conrad Aiken. Mr. Aiken is widely known as a poet of exceptional gifts and when one looks for examples of poetic sensibility in prose, it is natural enough to seek them out in his short stories and novels. His work belongs to a generation that made a trans-Atlantic, or rather, a Boston-Common-to-Russell-Square, discovery of Symbolism. Impressionism and twentieth century psychology, and in Mr. Aiken's case that discovery was attended by a strong attraction to the invested moralities of gas-lit diabolism, that strange light that glimmered from the pages of *The Yellow Book.* And in these excursions, through fair weather and foul, Mr. Aiken has been rescued by a gift for writing lyrical poetry and prose.

[***The Short Stories of Conrad Aiken***] is an anthology of the best of his short fiction, and it brings back into print the familiar titles, **"Bring, Bring," "Mr. Arcularis"** and **"Silent Snow, Secret Snow."** The book represents the work of the last twenty-eight years that Mr. Aiken has devoted to the short story and the volume seems to have been thoughtfully edited and presented. Of the twenty-nine stories in the book two are of unquestionable merit; they are **"Mr. Arcularis"** and **"Silent Snow, Secret Snow"**: Mr. Arcularis, spinning in cold through polar and starry distances toward death is a memorable figure, and so is the boy who finds that the vision of snow is the singular expression of his being. It is important, I think, that both stories contain the images of deathly cold and that both man and boy are inclosed within a world of self-obsession: and the internal meaning of these stories also contains an echo of the phrase, "in the midst of life we are in death."

To the serious reader of Mr. Aiken's prose the other stories in the book are far less fortunate and far less profound;

and many are overshadowed by the presence of a middle-aged Bostonian who is too consciously aware of diabolic impulses and the need to exhibit a neatly burnished cloven hoof. He is too often the central figure in the story, and though he is deliberately candid and unashamed, he is less wicked than he hopes to be; his encounters with faithless girls and women recall adventures that were the details of gossip thirty years ago; it soon becomes clear, which is depressing and tinged with sentimental sadness, that he has fallen out of fashion. Sex is, of course, one of the timeless subjects of literature, but fashionable ways of viewing its distresses and disillusionments change with the times and Mr. Aiken's middle-aged Bostonian seems unaware of Wordsworth's warning.

> the Gods approve
> The depth, and not the tumult, of the soul.

Whenever Mr. Aiken's Bostonian does not lean too bleakly upon the reader's shoulder (I have never read of any one who is more sentimental about sin than he is), the pages of the book are illuminated by descriptive passages of lyrical brilliance; in **"Bow Down, Isaac,"** there are fine and highly sensitive sketches of a New England countryside and in **"A Pair of Vikings"** the reader's eye is charmed by a summer carnival in an English country town; this is the kind of writing in which Mr. Aiken's sensibility is manifest, and one is under no obligation to think or feel too deeply; the people in the two stories do not greatly matter for they are observed with less penetration than the scenes around them.

The last story in Mr. Aiken's book, **"Your Obituary, Well Written,"** also has its moments of persuasive charm: the scene is London and its central figure is a woman novelist and short-story writer who died in 1923. (I shall leave to the readers of Mr. Aiken's book the pleasure of rediscovering her familiar features, the familiar cut of her straight, dark bobbed hair, and then naming her.) In the story the famous lady speaks of Henry James . . . "her small pointed chin resting upon her clasped hands. . . . 'No one else—*no* one—has made such beauty, and such *intricate* beauty, out of the iridescence of moral decay!' " This remark, which has all the charms of archful youth and naughtiness, shows more of Mr. Aiken's fondness for the cloven hoof than a perception of the serious aspects of Henry James's art. Or was it an intention to make the lady seem a shallow reader of the writer she so knowingly admired?

After reading this, one returns to the more brilliant and, I think, more enduring story of how Mr. Arcularis dies, for in that story there is a parallel to the best of Mr. Aiken's poetry. One should remember that Mr. Aiken is a poet and that most of his writing is on the side of the all too obviously lost and fallen angels.

Horace Gregory, "A Poet-Story Teller on the Side of the Fallen Angels," in New York Herald Tribune Book Review, *October 22, 1950, p. 7.*

Seymour L. Gross (essay date 1957)

[In the following excerpt, Gross discusses allusions to the works of Edgar Allan Poe in "Strange Moonlight."]

Most of Conrad Aiken's short stories are hauntingly elusive, full of provocatively mysterious effects and connotations. An Aiken story, as Mark Schorer remarked [in his 1952 essay in *Wake*] after quoting a portion of **"Strange Moonlight,"** is "a horror all wrapped up in an actuality, a fantasy all rooted and real." In such a texture it is unfortunately easy for explication to lose its way.

The textural landscape of **"Strange Moonlight"** is no less crowded with the dense foliage of Aiken's imagination than, say, **"Silent Snow, Secret Snow,"** but in the former there is a track which, when followed, can lead us to the meaning of the story. This "track" is Aiken's deliberate use of Poe's "Annabel Lee" for the purpose of thematic contrast so that in its final effect the story is an ironic commentary on the poem.

No one can fail to be struck by the frequency with which Poe is directly or indirectly evoked in the story. That these allusions are not merely the half-conscious echoings of a literate and literary mind, such as are found in many modern fictions, can be assumed from the introduction of Poe into the very first paragraph of the story. The young boy has filched a volume of Poe from his mother's bookcase, and, as a consequence, has dreamed himself into a "delirious night in inferno." In his nightmare he is accompanied by what would seem to be a dream-distortion of a raven: "Down, down he had gone with heavy clangs about him . . . and a strange companion of protean shape and size, walking and talking beside him. For the most part, this companion seemed to be nothing but a voice and a wing—an enormous jagged black wing, soft and drooping like a bat's." And further on in the story the boy does not take a book of Poe with him to the beach only because he knows his parents would not approve.

Other more indirect "reflections" of Poe weave in and out of the story. The description of Caroline Lee (whose name, in view of the context, can hardly be accidental) is highly suggestive of Poe's descriptions of such women as Ligeia, Berenice and Morella. Like these figures, Caroline Lee has an "extraordinarily strange" beauty, with "dark hair and large pale eyes, and . . . forehead and hands curiously transparent." Caroline Lee's house, "dim and exciting" and "mysterious and rich," full of rich tapestries, clocks, trophies, statues and winding staircases, conjures up (because of the context) images of the houses in which various of Poe's characters work out their strange destinies. Moreover the boy's obsessive preoccupation with various objects—a bird, a medal, a goldpiece—reminds one of the neurotic concentration on sensory phenomena of several of Poe's characters. But most important, the central situation in both story and poem is precisely the same: a young girl dies, leaving the boy who loves her to come to terms with the loss.

Even though Poe's poem is quite well known, it is necessary to pause for a moment on the implications of the final stanza. After recounting the nature and history of his love for the dead girl in the first four stanzas, the poet asserts that he cannot, or at any rate will not, accept the distinction between memory and perception, between life and death: in the night he "dreams" himself across the barrier of death and lies down with his darling "In her sepulchre there by the sea." His solution to the anguish of loss is, in effect, to wipe out its reality. That this solution is ultimately destructive to the moral and esthetic resources of life is the main burden of **"Strange Moonlight."**

The boy in Aiken's story must also reconcile himself to the death of a loved one. At first, the death of Caroline Lee leaves the boy "stifled" and "frightened," but above all "incredulous": "How was it possible for anyone, whom one actually knew, to *die*? Particularly anyone so vividly and beautifully remembered. . . . *Had* she actually died?" And before the pressures of an insistent reality force him to withdraw from it, the boy's solution is Poe's: Caroline Lee hadn't really "died"; there is no death unless you believe in it. Accordingly, he projects a wish-fulfillment fantasy much like the final stanza of Poe's poem. "What does it feel like to die—were you sorry?" he asks the dead child. Caroline Lee assures him that it is not at all what he thinks, that when the funeral is over "you just get up and walk away. You climb out of the earth just as easily as you'd climb out of bed." And most comforting for the boy, she tells him that at night, if he brings a lantern, he can come and see her.

The death of Caroline Lee, however, is the crisis not the inception of the boy's struggle to break through the limitations of his adolescent mind. The death of the child and the other incidents in the "tremendous week" "all seemed to unite, as if they were merely aspects of the same thing." The boy's bewildered anguish at the death of Caroline Lee, as Aiken indicates, is but the logical culmination of the boy's inability to distinguish between the various levels of experience: everything strikes his delicately receptive sensibilities with hard but essentially undifferentiated impact. This confusion is first shown in a passage which is a symbolic prefiguration of the crisis. After having received a medal at school, the boy runs to a nearby park which had once been a graveyard and opens the box. "He was dazzled. The medal was of gold, and rested on a tiny blue satin cushion. His name was engraved on it—yes, actually cut into the gold; he felt the incisions with his fingernail. It was an experience not wholly to be comprehended. He put the box down in the grass and detached himself from it . . . and stared first at the tombstone and then at the small gold object, as if to discover the relationship between them. . . . Amazing." To the mind unable to grasp the qualitative differences in experience, the medal given to the living and the monument erected to the dead—each hard, emblematic, incised—run together. Here, as in the instance of Caroline Lee, the outlines of life and death are blurred.

This distortion shows up in still another passage. While playing with his sister and brother, the boy sees a goldfinch fly into the room, dart to and fro, and then flash out over the trees. "This was beautiful," he thinks, "it was like the vision in the infernal city, like the medal in the grass." But the distorting equation of shadow and substance vaguely disturbs him; suddenly sensing a crucial moment in what he dimly knows as an "inevitable approach toward a vast and beautiful or terrible conclusion," he begins to ponder the death of Caroline Lee (who had died a few days earlier) and arrives, as we have seen, at the "beautiful" not the "terrible" conclusion—that there is no death.

The insubstantiality of this conclusion, however, is first symbolized at the beach where his family has gone on a picnic, and in which the "chief event of the afternoon was the burial of his father, who had his bathing suit on." The very grammar of the sentence with its startling final qualifying clause hints at the resolution. As the boy watches his father in the "grave" of sand, he thinks that "It was singularly as Caroline had described it, for there he was all alive in it, and talking, and able to get up whenever he liked." But the disturbing impact of the details of his father's body as he runs down to the sea—the brown upturned soles, the mouth blowing water, the strong white arms flashing in the sunlight—prefigures the boy's final understanding of death.

On the way home from the beach the boy senses that "everything was changed." The nature of this change is brilliantly dramatized in the final paragraph, in which the polarities which have bewildered the boy are subtly organized.

> And their house, when at last they stopped before it, how strange it was! The moonlight, falling through the two tall swaying oaks, cast a moving pattern of shadow and light all over its face. Slow swirls and spirals of black and silver, dizzy gallops, quiet pools of light abruptly shattered, all silently followed the swishing of leaves against the moon. It was like a vine of moonlight, which suddenly grew all over the house. . . . He stared up at this while his father fitted the key into the lock, feeling the ghostly vine grow strangely over his face and hands. Was it in this, at last, that he would find the explanation of all that bewildered him? Caroline, no doubt, would understand it; she was a sort of moonlight herself. He went slowly up the stairs. But as he took the medal and a small pink shell out of his pocket, and put them on the desk, he realized at last that Caroline was dead.

Here the death of Caroline Lee and the boy's lingering awareness of her presence are brought into perspective. Caroline Lee still "is," but only like moonlight ("She was a sort of moonlight"), which depends upon being reflected from a solid substance for its existence. (Earlier, the boy thinks that the "mystery" of Caroline Lee's death is "like the moonlight on the white wall. Surely beneath it there was something solid and simple.") Like "the vine of moonlight" on the boy's face and hands, Caroline Lee exists only as a poignant shadow, a "ghostly" memory, a ray of moonlight. The gold medal and pink shell, however, are something "solid and simple," palpable objects of the world of substance, no longer "like" the vision in his dream or the haunting presence of the dead girl. But the "terrible" conclusion—what Poe cannot accept—is really the "beautiful" one, for now the boy can feel the beauty of *life as life,* the intensity of which, tragically enough, depends upon the full awareness of death. Perhaps the final irony is that the moon, which in Poe's poem is the magical prerequisite for experiential distortion ("For the moon never beams without bringing me dreams / Of the beautiful Annabel Lee") is here the mechanism for the boy's clarification of the terms of human life, and the consequent extension of its moral and esthetic resources. (pp. 185-89)

Seymour L. Gross, "The Reflection of Poe in Conrad Aiken's 'Strange Moonlight'," in Modern Language Notes, *Vol. LXXII, No. 3, March, 1957, pp. 185-89.*

Mark Schorer (essay date 1960)

[*Schorer was an American critic and biographer who wrote the definitive life of Sinclair Lewis. In his often anthologized essay "Technique as Discovery" (1948), Schorer argued that fiction deserves the same close attention to diction and metaphor that the New Critics had been applying to poetry. He determined that fiction viewed only with respect to content was not art at all, but experience. For Schorer, only when individuals examine "achieved content," or form do they speak of art, and consequently, speak as critics. Schorer also maintained that the difference between content and art is "technique," and that the study of technique demonstrates how fictional form discovers and evaluates meaning, meaning that is often not intended by the author. In the following essay, Schorer defines prominent characteristics and identifies thematic concerns of Aiken's short stories.*]

Recently a letter appeared in one of the literary reviews that reminded its editors that we have in the United States at least one writer who may still appropriately be called a man of letters, and the name was Conrad Aiken. It is curious how, year after year for more than four decades now, general readers and editors alike have *had* to be reminded of that name, which does indeed support an achievement that, in its brilliant distinction and, more than that, in its scope, makes Conrad Aiken so much more than a writer alone. He has the range of the literary master: the beautiful bulk of his poetry in all its formal splendor and variety; literary essays of pioneering quality; one of the most extraordinary autobiographies in the language; four novels, at least two of which—*Great Circle* and *King Coffin*—must endure; a play; more than forty short stories.

If the entire work of Conrad Aiken demonstrates this mastery of a range possessed by few modern writers, the forty-one short stories [in ***The Collected Short Stories of Conrad Aiken***] demonstrate a range of mood and method, within the scope of the single form, that is almost as surprising; yet all of them, like the whole body of his work, are stamped with the mark of his imagination, and could have been written by Conrad Aiken alone.

In that complex imagination, there is a prominent strain of rather bemused irony that, when he gives it free rein, produces stories that are essentially comic, even rather light-hearted, with a satiric edge that cuts into a human foible or a paradox of personality or a turn of fate's screw, cuts deftly, delicately, without either the ritual air of major surgery or the thrust of passionate involvement. Such stories are **"No, No, Go Not to Lethe," "The Necktie," "West End," "O How She Laughed!"** and a good many others. They seem to say, with an air of the literary shrug, "Well, there it is. What do you think? Odd, isn't it?" Or, "Queer, isn't it, although surely he had it coming?" Or, "Amusing?" Yet even in these stories there is usually another strain, a note struck off from the taut strings of the stretched nerves, something sharp, shrill or somber, sinister, or mockingly morbid, an echo out of psychic chaos. Think only, for example, of that quite alarming hero of **"No, No, Go Not to Lethe,"** whose ambition it is to enfold and paralyze others in the coils of his observation of them without ever himself becoming in the least involved. It is a comic story, but the laughter seems to come eerily up from the bottom of a very deep and a very old well.

This is, of course, the note that characterizes the most splendid and the best known of Conrad Aiken's short stories, those stories in which he moves from the mundane into the mysterious, into hysteria, horror, hallucination, phobia, compulsion, dream, death, and, more often than not, back again into the mundane. The sudden penetration into the shadows of consciousness, a veil surprisingly pulled back and dropped again, something beyond our perception perceived in it, a mythical beast suddenly gazing curiously up at us from the shrubbery at the end of our own well-kept garden: these are the gestures that are made by stories like **"Silent Snow, Secret Snow"** and **"Mr. Arcularis"** and many another. But let us consider one of the stories that is less well known.

"Life Isn't a Short Story" ought to be among the first documents in the demonstration materials of all people who profess to "teach" the writing of fiction, and among the instructional materials of all people who wish to learn to do it. It is about a story writer who "had run out of ideas; he had used them all; he was feeling as empty as a bath-tub and as blue as an oyster." This drudge of the imagination is having his breakfast—sitting in the window of a white-tiled restaurant, staring rather vacantly out into a busy city street, suddenly catching sight of a woman who might, if she were plumper, serve as the physical model for the woman in a story he is thinking about: for he isn't, after all, it seems, quite empty.

The story. The seed of the story had been planted in his mind as, passing through the lounge of a theater, he overheard phrases of a greeting—*"as I live and breathe!"* and *"in the flesh!" I am alive* and *you are alive;* these phrases translated themselves in his mind, and that, alive and not alive, was, he saw, the difference between life and a short story, even as he thought of his character, Gladys, a plump, commonplace creature who cannot tolerate such clichés, so plump and commonplace, any more readily than she can tolerate her simple and unrefined husband. So, sitting in the restaurant window, he imagines the proper town for Gladys to live in (Fitchburg, Massachusetts, seems right), imagines her apartment, imagines her story, which is the story of her intolerable marriage. Meanwhile, a horse-drawn laundry wagon has pulled up in front of the window, and the story writer's eye rests on the dejected horse, beaten by rain, while the story, through all its grimy fatalities, grows in his presumably disengaged, vacantly staring mind. When it reaches its climax, we know not only that the whole, dreary life of the street outside, bleary and rain-soaked, has been assimilated into the atmosphere of the life of Gladys and her husband, but we know also, as the writer does *not* know, any more than Gladys knows, that her poor old drone of a husband is the horse that pulls the laundry wagon. With their identification, the story is finished. Then we follow the horse up the street. "What did he think about, as he plodded from one dirty restaurant to another, one hotel to another, carrying towels? Probably nothing at all; certainly no such sentimental thing as a green meadow, nor anything so ridiculous as a story about living and breathing. It was enough, even if one was a slave, to live and breathe. For life, after all, isn't a short story."

Life isn't a short story because life, that spavined hack, keeps going on its rounds and never meets a climax; but a short story is life because, no matter where it may go all through its middle, it begins in life and it ends there, and if we look twice, we will see that, through that extraordinary process of imaginative osmosis whereby the details of life are lifted up into the patterns of art, its middle, too, is in large part the street outside the real window. A story by Conrad Aiken, in the characteristically fine middle, seems to rear up on its hind legs and throw its head into white clouds and among patterned stars, or it seems to race down into abysses of peculiar horror and shrill alarm, but all the time, poor creature (and the poor creatures that make it up), it is out there in the street, stodgy in the rain.

> At the same time, there was the awful commonplaceness of the two phrases, the cheapness of them, the vulgarity—they were as old as the hills, and as worn; æons of weather and æons of handshake lay upon them; one witnessed, in the mere hearing of them, innumerable surprised greetings, innumerable mutual congratulations on the mere fact of being still alive. The human race seemed to extend itself backwards through them, in time, as along a road—if one pursued the thought one came eventually to a vision of two small apes peering at each other round the cheeks of a cocoanut and making a startled noise that sounded like "*yoicks!*" Or else, one simply saw, in the void, one star passing another, with no vocal interchange at all, nothing but a mutual exacerbation of heat. . . . It was very puzzling.

Puzzling, indeed, since it all starts in the lounge of the Orpheum, with a couple of portly blondes, and then at once loops out into space and history and mystery and the perfect terror of human experience as it plods through its generic hysteria, most of the time not knowing where it is, whether in the rainy street or in the stifled scream, when it is always in fact in both.

This is a story by Conrad Aiken: a horror all wrapped in an actuality, a fantasy all rooted and real, all rooted in a real detail. "For the most part, this companion seemed to be nothing but a voice and a wing—an enormous jagged black wing, soft and drooping like a bat's; he had noticed veins in it." *He had noticed veins in it.* If one could define the rhetorical mystery of this sentence, of this justaposition of the mad anatomy and the graphic physiology, one would probably have defined the effect of Mr. Aiken's fiction.

Just as the structure of these stories characteristically develops in the effort of the material to assert a reality beyond or below its mundane shape, so their drama characteristically arises within an individual mind as it struggles to break over the edge of its own limitations. This whole considerable body of fiction, long and short, has, for this reason, a central core of formal as well as psychological concern, an implicit, primary unity that marks it over and over as the product of this imagination and no other, as the work of this author. In one story, at least, the implicit becomes the explicit. **"Gehenna"** has as its protagonist an urban Everyman ("Smith, or Jones, or Robinson, or whatever his name happened to be") who reflects at the outset, "How easily . . . our little world can go to pieces! And incidentally, of course, the great world . . . " and then contemplates the imminence in the materials of consciousness of that disorganization of reality that is madness. But is that disorganization any less real than the organization which it has dispelled?

> In an instant it will be as if I had stepped through this bright cobweb of appearance on which I walk with such apparent security, and plunged into a chaos of my own; for that chaos will be as intimately and recognizably my own, with its Smith-like disorder, as the present world is my own, with its Smith-like order. Here will be all the appurtenances of my life, every like and dislike, every longing or revulsion, from the smallest to the greatest; all the umbrellas—so to speak—of my life, all the canceled postage stamps and burnt matches, the clipped fingernails, love letters, calendars, and sunrises; but all of them interchanged and become (by change) endowed with demonic power. At a step, I shall have fallen into a profound and perhaps termless Gehenna which will be everywhere nothing but Smith. Only to the name of Smith will the umbrella-winged demons of this chaos answer.

This possibility of the altered kaleidoscope of being and the further possibility of altering that kaleidoscope by an act of will fascinates Smith—or Jones or Robinson. "Perhaps I could achieve this gradually," he thinks, "and step by step, just as I pace to and fro across the four rugs from Persia which cover the floor; item by item I would tear down the majestic fiction which is at present myself and the world, and item by item build up another. Exactly as one can stare at a word until it become meaningless, I can begin to stare at the world." In his bathroom, he stares at a door-knob, and through a kind of self-hypnosis, he allows the process to get under way, only, at the last moment, through another effort of will, to rip himself out of this new prison that his consciousness is already building. He goes to bed and dreams of "a small glass aquarium, square, of the sort in which goldfish are kept."

> I observe without surprise that there is water in one half of it but not in the other. And in spite of the fact that there is no partition, this water holds itself upright in its own half of the tank,

Scene from Gene R. Kearney's film adaptation of "Silent Snow, Secret Snow."

> leaving the other half empty. More curious than this, however, is the marine organism which lies at the bottom of the water. It looks, at first glance, like a loaf of bread. But when I lean down to examine it closely, I see that it is alive, that it is sentient, and that it is trying to move. One end of it lies very close to that point at which the water ends and the air begins; and now I realize that the poor thing is trying, and trying desperately, to get into the air. Moreover, I see that this advancing surface is as if sliced off and raw; it is horribly sensitive; and suddenly, appalled, I realize that the whole thing is simply—consciousness. It is trying to escape from the medium out of which it was created. If only it could manage this—! But I know that it never will; it has already reached, with its agonized sentience, as far as it can; it stretches itself forward, with minute and pathetic convulsions, but in vain; and suddenly I am so horrified at the notion of a consciousness which is pure suffering, that I wake up. . . . The clocks are striking two.

It is at this margin, at this edge, where, without barrier, the water of daily human experience stands against the wall of air that is outside it—it is at this margin that Conrad Aiken's fiction is written. (His extraordinary novels develop and amazingly sustain the central concern of the stories.) And thus his fiction asks its great questions: "Was the North Star hung at the world's masthead only in order that on a certain day in a certain year an ugly wallpaper should be glued to the walls of this room?" Human tragedy exists because of the suffering that must inhere in a consciousness that can ask the question at all. It persists, with life itself, because the clocks in the city do strike, and with their reverberations, draw the invisible circles around that consciousness, saving it for its order, yes, but in the very act of saving it, re-committing it to an area within which questions must go on being asked.

We have, I think, no other body of fiction like this—so centrally coherent, its very coherence derived from a contemplation of the intransigence of that incoherence that lies scattered on all sides of us, and above and below, and, worst of all, within. But also best of all. For rationality would be a poor and shriveled thing if it did not have all that other to nourish no less than to alarm it. As life would be if it did not have the basic resources that can make it into art. (pp. vii-xiv)

Mark Schorer, in a preface to The Collected

Short Stories of Conrad Aiken, The World Publishing Company, 1960, pp. vii-xiv.

John Updike (essay date 1960)

[*Considered a perceptive observer of the human condition and an extraordinary stylist, Updike is one of America's most distinguished writers. Best known for such novels as* Rabbit Run *(1960),* Rabbit Redux *(1971), and* Rabbit Is Rich *(1981), he is a chronicler of life in Protestant, middle-class America. Against this setting and in concurrence with his interpretation of the thought of Søren Kierkegaard and of Karl Barth, Updike presents people searching for meaning in their lives while facing the painful awareness of their mortality and basic powerlessness. A contributor of literary reviews to various periodicals, he has frequently written the "Books" column in the* New Yorker *since 1955. In the following essay, Updike discusses presentations of love and death in Aiken's short stories.*]

When I had finished reading this big book [***The Collected Short Stories of Conrad Aiken***], I closed it, and looked at the back, and my tired eyes, without my willing it, went out of focus, placing, to the right of Aiken's face and slightly lower, a dimmer duplicate. Eerily, this secondary image, though less sharp, seemed more *real* than the image it echoed. The shadows around the mouth called into relief muscles potentially expressive of humor and wrath; the cheekbones and eyelids seemed curved and tactile; the hornrim spectacles perched forward dimensionally on the stout, white, pugnacious nose. The photograph was just a photograph, but the photograph's ghost was a man—a man who, when I tried to study him closely, of course vanished. And I wondered if these 41 stories might best have been viewed, by some hypnotic relaxation of the cerebrum, in the same way; for their truth, seems to exist, invisibly, to one side of their vivid surfaces.

Love and death, those two organic imperatives, are Aiken's all but exclusive subjects. The stories about death—conceived as an ethereal incoherence bombarding our humanity from all sides—are the more strikingly original, and account for his reputation as a teller of sophisticated shudder stories. But he is poles removed from a spook-monger like H. P. Lovecraft; the horror of Aiken's fiction lies not in the possibility that other worlds exist but in the certainty that they do not. The cosmic vacuity, the central *nihil* haunts him; "the great white light of annihilation" illuminates his scenes and to an extent bleaches them. In retrospect many of his stories seem black-and-white film clips from the twenties and thirties. His characters wake from comic dreams and, singing empty little snatches of song to themselves, move through a world crowded with ticking clocks and seething snow and visual details ("dead matches, a rusty horse-chestnut burr, a small concentration of eggshell, a streak of yellow sawdust which had been wet and now was dry and congealed, a brown pebble, and a broken feather") observed with an intensity befitting an insane universe. Aiken's world is so morally insubstantial that hallucinations effortlessly permeate it. In his famous **"Silent Snow, Secret Snow,"** thickening snow becomes the sensible manifestation of an uncaused apathy which closes over a young boy and lures him to death. In **"Mr. Arcularis"**—a superb fantasy that must be read to be believed—a shipboard romance, rumbling engines, the threat of icebergs, fog, a coffin in the hold, and a sleepwalking exploration of the frozen stars give body and form to a man's progress toward death on an operating table.

"The fair page of the world, thus reset, becomes a brilliant but meaningless jumble of typographical errors"—this from **"Gehenna,"** Aiken's most concentrated and dense explication of a "world of which the only tenable principle is horror." The horror is not Hitlerian but Einsteinian; crime seldom and war never intrude in these stories, but the interstellar gulfs, the chasms in subjectivity, and the atomic near-void are translated into sensual acrophobia. His compulsion to give shapelessness shape does generate, by backwards thrust, a kind of supernaturalism. **"The Disciple,"** more than any other American story I have read, breathes life into Christianity in its guise as local European folklore; Judas and the Eternal Jew meet and talk in an atmosphere supercharged *à la* Isak Dinesen and Dostoevsky. But in the end, Aiken himself backs away, leaving the reader suspended between realities and doubtful of the author's good faith. Metaphysical fantasy, lacking the conviction of delirium, subsides into allegorical gossip; **"Smith and Jones,"** for instance, reminded me too much of those dental pamphlets in which Irving Incisor and Max Molar debate fluoridation. Perhaps, indeed, Death (as opposed to dying, which is a species of living) is a better subject for meditation than for fiction, since it is, however conceived, unknowable, and emotional effects aimed from one conception of it can too easily, by a slight shift of philosophy, be evaded.

I found myself more affected, on the whole, by Aiken's stories of love. He moves with ease in the swimming minds of women willing to fall in love (**"Bring, Bring," "All, All Wasted"**); he tastes the uncanny innocence of promiscuity (**"Thistledown," "West End"**); he conveys, in the tiny interval before the spangled curtain of good taste descends, a strong sexual flavor—"Tom took her gloved hand, inserted his finger in the opening, and stroked her palm. A delicious feeling of weakness, dissolution, came over her." Not that, under the skies of heavenly apathy, seduction is either very difficult or very rewarding. "We came together as naturally as leaf touches leaf or the grass bends to the wind," one adulterer says. In **"Hey, Taxi,"** a cabdriver and a girlish tramp drift into each other's arms like two snowflakes in the universal descent of fatigue. Such energy as is needed, the women provide; their aggression can be monstrous (**"Spider, Spider"**). But men are feeble beasts, preoccupied with themselves and their wives, and they send their mistresses alone into howling trolley cars (**"The Night before Prohibition"**), betray them to satyrs (**"Thistledown"**), and begrudge them even the present of a dollar print (**"Field of Flowers"**). Small wonder, since boredom and abuse invariably follow the scattering of the pollen, that the most moving and ecstatic of these love-stories are those in which nothing—physically speaking—happens. The flower opens, the bee hovers, and that is all. In **"Farewell! Farewell! Farewell!"** an Irish maid and a young architect exchange one kiss. In **"Your Obituary, Well Writ-**

ten," nothing is exchanged but some childhood memories about the rain. It *is* well-written; the poet trembles up out of the prose and the page is solid with sensation. Aiken is impressive when he snows, but delicious when he rains; I wish that somehow the climate had permitted him to rain more.

So as not to end on a damp note: in addition to stories already mentioned I especially admired **"State of Mind,"** an Occidental *koan;* **"I Love You Very Dearly,"** a letter of fatherly advice from an expatriate roué; **"The Dark City,"** which makes happy domestic life seem rich and terrible with mystery; **"Strange Moonlight,"** which does the same for childhood; the Gogolian humor of **"The Necktie"**; the Mack Sennett humor of **"The Moment"**; **"Fly Away Ladybird,"** swift and clean as an arrow; and **"Life Isn't a Short Story"** and **"The Orange Moth,"** which deal with that most unpromising of subjects, trying to write. (pp. 26-7)

John Updike, "Snow from a Dead Sky," in The New Republic, *Vol. 143, No. 23, November 28, 1960, pp. 26-7.*

Conrad Aiken (letter date 1961)

[*In the following letter to Jay Martin, Aiken comments on a draft of Martin's critical study* Conrad Aiken: A Life of His Art *(1962) and discusses the degree of invention and autobiographical detail in his short stories.*]

Dear Jay: Thanks for letters and the rewrite. Alas, me no likee AT-all, as you'll see by some pretty pungent marginal comments! Forgive the slang-shots, please, but I do think once again you're way up the wrong tree, and again being positively *perverse* in this obsession of yours about all the fiction being autobiographical! To begin with, you're misusing the word autobiographical *passim.* Autobiography implies self-revelation, self-disclosure, the analysis of oneself and one's history: to claim this for Arcularis or practically all the others is absurd. The use of a fragment of personal experience, or encounter, or something told one, or a remembered person, as a jumping-off place for an invented piece of poiesis does not make that poiesis autobiographical. In this sense, this whole section on the fiction is mistaken and, for your readers, misleading: the net result is that I will be given no credit whatever for being an artist, for using materials of ANY sort and making artifacts of them, and what's more, of great variety. This vitally important fact you suppress or misconstrue in the interests of proving your initial *assumption*—which I do not grant anyway—that the fiction played a special role. You tend to take this assumption as proved, and then argue from it. Moreover, as this whole section seems to me trivial, of really no interest to anyone *per se, not* very well stated, and really on the order of W Winchell gossip, I hope you will take my advice and drop it out entirely. Instead, put in a page or two on the subject, but in general terms, NOT taking up the stories item by item, a dull business, but *relating* them to the poetry—particularly to the early narrative poems—*T and Movies,* "Youth," *Forslin, H of D, Punch,* etc.—maybe "Tetélestai" too—and also to the later narrative poems, "Deth," "Osiris," "Landscape," "Ruby," "Kid" and "Soldier." And two important middle-period poems, "Psychomachia" and "Electra," written at the same time as Chap. 1 of *Blue Voyage* and **"Bring Bring."** This would make much better reading, and if you can bring out the similaritites of artification in the prose and verse it would be extremely useful. You see, the current you are interested in, as I have insisted before, was working, or running, *all* the time in both mediums, from the very beginning. Remember that the "Deceitful Portrait" was written in 1917, "Tetélestai" either that year or the next: in these you have the germ of everything that follows. What was being enriched, in both forms from now on, was the *articulation.* And *most* of the fodder of "experience" had already been laid in. . . . as ev Conrad

(The following are [Aiken's] comments on the degree of autobiography and invention in each of his stories, which he enclosed with this letter.)

"Bring! Bring!" Actual experience of Eunice, but of course greatly altered and amplified, and given a Duxbury setting.

"The Last Visit" Completely autobiographical.

"Mr. Arcularis" Based on a combination of a dream on shipboard and the simultaneous encounter with the real Mr. A. Fundamentally an invention of the imagination.

"The Bachelor Supper" An invention suggested by going to a bachelor supper in Boston at T Wharf.

"Bow Down, Isaac" Complete invention—can't remember ANY sources.

"A Pair of Vikings" Actually happened—I knew them in Rye. Story not changed at all.

"Hey, Taxi!" Complete invention, suggested by a taxi driver telling me of a freak trip from Boston to Hanover, Mass.

"Field of Flowers" Autobiographical. In another country. And besides, the wench dying.

"Gehenna" Invention.

"The Disciple" Invention. Got stuck in it too, had to put it aside for a year before I cd find a way to finish it.

"Impulse" Invention. In toto.

"The Anniversary" Invention, but with Uncle A[lfred] as hero, with Aunt E[dith] his wife: story invented, the portrait true.

"Hello, Tib" Actual occurrence, the cat's death; the setting or preceding situation invented to fit it.

"Smith and Jones" Completest invention!

"By My Troth, Nerissa!" Invention, out of chronic acedia.

"Silent Snow, Secret Snow" . . . [Invention] imagination going far afield from a small premise.

"Round by Round" Invention plus biographical, based on a newspaperman-friend-of-mine's experience, plus my own reporting of an actual fight—middleweight championship, Vince Dundee and someone whose name began with a B.

"Thistledown" True portrait of a gal I knew well, and who's alive, so nameless.

"State of Mind" Invention coming to the rescue of personal tension.

"Strange Moonlight" Invention and synthesis coming to the rescue of disorder and early sorrow.

"The Fish Supper" True story, happened to a friend of mine.

"I Love You Very Dearly" Found a similar letter in a book I was looking at in someone's library—built it up from there.

"The Dark City" Invention, but using the house and family of a friend of mine—story invented, the portraits true.

"Life Isn't a Short Story" Complete invention, based on a casual greeting between two strangers in a theatre lobby.

"The Night before Prohibition" Autobiographical.

"Spider, Spider" Autobiographical. Names cyant be mentioned.

"A Man Alone at Lunch" Autobiographical. As above.

"Farewell! Farewell! Farewell!" Autobiographical. Verbatim. It's her own name.

"Your Obituary, Well Written" Autobiographical, and suggested by the ad in the Times, with embellishments.

"A Conversation" Autobiographical.

"No, No, Go Not to Lethe" Complete invention—know no sources.

"Pure as the Driven Snow" True story, happened to a friend of mine.

"All, All Wasted" True story, observed from back window of my house in Rye.

"The Moment" True story, combination of TWO friends of mine.

"The Woman-Hater" True story, another friend of mine, with a famous musical comedy star, name forgotten.

"The Professor's Escape" True story, happened to the friend of mine who figures in Dark City.

"The Orange Moth" Autobiographical—with Van Wyck Brooks, papa Yeats et al. thrown in, and the dream was actual.

"The Necktie" True Story, the uncle, but nameless.

"O How She Laughed!" True story, I was there.

"West End" True story, told to me by a woman in London, but with many embellishments.

"Fly Away Ladybird" Based on the situation of two people I knew, but with my own ending supplied. It turned out to be prophetic. (pp. 311-14)

Conrad Aiken, in a letter to Jay Martin on November 12, 1961, in his Selected Letters of Conrad Aiken, *edited by Joseph Killorin, Yale University Press, 1978, pp. 310-14.*

James W. Tuttleton (essay date 1963)

[In the following excerpt, Tuttleton examines the revelation of the subconscious and the death instinct in "Mr. Arcularis."]

Once asked about his credo, Conrad Aiken replied: "How extraordinarily little I know about myself." His answer implies curiosity not only about the complexities of his own being but also about the mystery of life as a whole. This curiosity is responsible for Aiken's extraordinary interest in Freudian psychology as an instrument capable of revealing the deeply hidden, mysterious, secret self. "Almost alone in his generation," the psychiatrist Henry A. Murray has written [in his 1952 essay in *Wake*], "Aiken proved equal to the peril. He allowed the Freudian dragon to swallow him, and then, after a sufficient sojourn in its maw, cut his way out to a new freedom. When he emerged he was stocked with the lore of psychoanalysis but neither subjugated nor impeded by it. Aiken and Freud were, in a profound sense, fellow-spirits. . . . "

One of Freud's principal theories—that the creation of a work of art is a revelation of the artist's hidden self, a day-dream release of hidden desires and repressed erotic complexes—has had its obvious effect on Aiken's poetry and prose. Aiken has also extrapolated from the work of Freud a theory of literary criticism. Because historical, biographical, and aesthetic criticism cannot explain the *cause* of art, the critic may need to employ the techniques of the psychologist, the anthropologist, or the biologist. Of the origins of art Aiken has said:

> It has been urged that in the day-dream, or art, we do not really seek to escape from ourselves, but, precisely, to find ourselves. But what part of ourselves is it that we find? Is it not exactly that part of us which has been wounded and would be made whole: that part of us which desires wings and has none, longs for immortality and knows that it must die, craves unlimited power and has instead "common sense" and the small bitter "actual"; that part of us, in short, which is imprisoned and would escape? . . . There can be little question about it, and it is precisely of the associations connected with these major psychic frustrations that we have evolved the universal language of healing which we call art. Let us not hastily condemn this view simply because it savors of the often-flouted "new" psychology. Freud is not, by two thousand two hundred years, the first to see art as primarily a process of wish-fulfillment. Let us recall Aristotle's theory of catharsis, and rub our eyes. The difference between catharsis and wish-fulfillment is slight to the point of disappearance. [*A Reviewer's ABC*]

If for Aiken art is then the therapy by which the psychic wound is healed, it is not surprising that a theme of greatest frequency in his fiction is the inward-turning eye, the deep descent into the mysteries of one's own psyche, toward that "frontier within man's consciousness where the individual, like a diver, plunges into his own depths to sound them, and in so doing believes himself effectually to have sounded the world" [Aiken's description of the Spiritual history of Ralph Waldo Emerson]. Aiken's **"Mr. Arcularis"** is one such exploration of the frontier of consciousness-nonconsciousness. To understand it properly the literary critic must think in the categories of the psychologist.

This short story is a narrative of an ether-dream experienced by Mr. Arcularis as he lies upon the operating table in a hospital. Under the anesthetic, Mr. Arcularis dreams that the operation, which he is undergoing, was a success, that he left the hospital and took passage aboard ship for a long voyage of convalescence. Aboard ship he meets Clarice Dean, a younger woman, is mysteriously drawn to her, but suffers a feeling of doom surrounding the voyage. With unaccountable anxiety, Mr. Arcularis discovers that there is a corpse aboard—in the hold. On the first and second nights of the voyage, Mr. Arcularis dreams that he soars up through space, at incredible speed, each time a little farther from the ship, traversing an orbit that circumnavigates the moon, the North Star, Polaris, Betelgeuse—towards Arcturus, the last signpost of finity. When he awakes from these two dreams he finds himself near the hold of the ship, having walked in his sleep in search of the coffin, which he fears will be empty. On the third night he again has the nightmare, and awakes, presumably to find the coffin empty and ready for his occupancy.

The story has its origin in a generalization of Aiken's personal credo—that we know extraordinarily little about ourselves. In the story Mr. Arcularis' recurrent sleep-walking nightmare leads him to remark "how extraordinarily little we know about the workings of our own minds and souls" and to ask, "After all, what *do* we know?" To this Miss Dean responds: "Nothing—nothing—nothing—nothing." And Mr. Arcularis emphasizes: "*Absolutely* nothing."

"Mr. Arcularis" thus takes us inside the mind of a man on the operating table at the point of death, anesthetized by ether, in order to show us the workings of our own minds and souls: to show us how latent thoughts in the subconscious mind, counterpointed by preoperative anxieties of death, are distorted in the manifest dream-content by the activities of the dream work—condensation, displacement, visual representations in plastic images, secondary elaboration, and dream symbolism. To understand the meaning of Mr. Arcularis' subconscious thought, the literary critic must, like the psychoanalyst, demolish the manifest content of the dream and pierce through to what lies beneath. The mode of representing this process is the stream-of-unconsciousness—a beautiful and rare example of the unity of subject matter (the activity of the subconscious mind) and narrative point of view; only in the final three paragraphs of the story is Aiken obliged to move outside the subconscious mind of Mr. Arcularis to verify our growing awareness that Mr. Arcularis is dying upon the operating table. The drama enacted upon that table, in the mind and soul of Mr. Arcularis, is a struggle between life and death, between Eros—the life instincts, and Thanatos—the death instinct.

Aiken's interest in the distortions within the subconscious mind produced by ether-dreams is recorded in an essay ["Gigantic Dreams"] about three of his own dreams while he lay etherized upon the table. His description of the characteristics and content of these ether-dreams, in view of the light they shed on the meaning of **"Mr. Arcularis,"** is worth our closest attention:

> It [the ether-dream] is, to the ordinary dream, what the epic is to the short story. It is gigantic; it is grandiose; it transcends the limits of time and space; it is cosmic; and when it is at its best, it gives the dreamer an annihilating sense of understanding, a divine comprehensiveness of foreknowledge and memory. There is always one moment, in the ether-dream, when everything, the whole universe, becomes blindingly clear and simple. The sensation is, perhaps, a sensation of light—which makes one wonder whether the dream occurs usually as one is first returning to consciousness, first relaxing one's eyelids. And there is usually, also, a rather terrifying use of repetition. The pattern of the dream unfolds, and then returns upon itself and unfolds again. The movement, the drama, of the dream is as likely as not cyclic, and one draws from it an apalling sense of the everlasting determinism of things.

In the first of his ether-dreams Aiken saw the world as a chessboard in which the moves were "as pre-ordained as the moves of knights and bishops." (Thus aboard ship the chess game indicates to Mr. Arcularis the rigorous determinism of life.) In the second ether-dream Aiken witnessed himself on an endless voyage with Columbus. In mid-Atlantic he fell overboard, settled in spirals to the bottom and was transmogrified into an oyster shell. Looking up he saw three keels and said to himself, " 'Good Lord, I won't be there when they discover America!' For I knew vaguely," Aiken continued, "that America had been already discovered four hundred years ago; but I also knew that it was not *yet* discovered. I had stepped clear out of time and space; my consciousness was both before and after the event; I had become God. I felt a kind of pity and contempt for poor Columbus, who knew so little; and for myself also I felt pity, because I knew so much." Thus the Kantian postulate of time as a necessary mode of thought is short-circuited in the dream. This effect in dreams was brilliantly discussed by Freud in *Beyond the Pleasure Principle,* where he contended that "unconscious mental processes are in themselves 'timeless.' That is to say to begin with: they are not arranged chronologically, time alters nothing in them, nor can the idea of time be applied to them." This work, as we shall later see, has a most significant bearing on the meaning of **"Mr. Arcularis."**

In the third dream Aiken saw himself witnessing the creation of the world. At first he dreamed of Chaos. Gradually he perceived the emergence of order, of the evolution of the solar-system and of life. As he witnessed the evolution of Man's consciousness, he was aware that

> Phases of consciousness succeeded each other like so many flashes. I was aware, somehow, that we had reached the fifth or sixth century B.C. And at this point the dream hit upon a device for the demarcation of one phase of sophistication from another, the progress from consciousness to consciousness of consciousness, and so on, which showed an extraordinary ingenuity. To begin with, some perfectly simple remark was made: I forget what it was, but it was something as obvious as 'Here we are, then.' An age then passing in a flash, and a second stage of sophistication being reached, the remark was repeated, but this time with a double quotation: ' "Here we are, then." '

This statement, according to Aiken, was made several times, producing a "visual image of quotation marks, quotation marks at either end of a simple statement, building themselves out at either end of the statement into infinity. The simple statement became, with each addition, more appallingly and unfathomably complicated: it had become, in fact, the world itself: it had become *everything that was knowable.*" Then, unaccountably, Aiken continues, the full burden of consciousness narrowed in and focused on Aiken himself as he lay on the operating table—it reached its *reductio ad absurdum* in himself. Then the process began again: "the dream became cyclic, and I beheld, innumerable times, the evolution of the world to its final flowering—magnificent egotism, profound solipsism!—in my own consciousness. Everything had become intelligible: the world no longer had any secrets from me. I now knew the world for what it was—a mere senseless nightmare of fatalistic and orderly but meaningless change; a mechanical ring from which no one was ever destined to escape."

The description of what happened in Aiken's three ether-dreams provides an enlightening corollary to the ether-dream of Mr. Arcularis, who transcends both space in a fixed, recurrent, and repetitive cosmic orbit, and time as he regresses, psychotemporally, into his childhood and beyond, as he lies dying upon the table. He perceives with clarity life's meaning and is annihilated at last in the full comprehension of the burden of his own consciousness. The principles by which the distortion of the latent dream-thought of Mr. Arcularis' ether-dream may be explained are those discussed by Freud as mechanisms of the dream-work: the dream-censor distorts the latent dream-thoughts by *displacement,* the process by which latent dream-elements are replaced with something remote from them, something in the nature of an allusion, or by which the psychic accent is transferred from an important element to an unimportant element in the dream; by *condensation,* in which elements in the latent dream-thoughts are omitted from the manifest dream-content, appear in it only in fragments, or are blended in it into a single whole; by the transformation of latent thoughts into *visual images* or *plastic word-representations;* and by *secondary elaboration,* the mechanism by which incoherence and chaos in the latent-dream elements are reduced to a coherent unity. Together with these mechanisms, which disguise and distort the real meaning of the latent dream thoughts of the subconscious, there must also be added the mechanism of *dream symbolism,* the constant relationship between a dream-element and its translation. How these principles operate in the story deserve our closest scrutiny.

One of the most important dream symbols in the story is the symbolic voyage of Mr. Arcularis. Clearly it is the voyage to death he must make. Freud is explicit in stating that "departing on a journey is one of the commonest and best authenticated symbols of death." Long before the final three paragraphs in which we discover that he has died upon the operating table Aiken provides indications that Mr. Arcularis is dying. As Harry drives him past the Harvard Club bar, on their way to the ship, Mr. Arcularis quotes a fragment of "Crossing the Bar"—Tennyson's representation of his own death as a voyage out to sea. When Harry asks where the line comes from, Mr. Arcularis identifies it as from the *Odyssey*—the Homeric epic of the wandering voyage of Ulysses. Harry's comment " 'We're here because we're here because we're here,' " to which Mr. Arcularis responds, " 'Because we're here' " is a hitherto unnoticed allusion to an anonymous World War I song entitled "Here We Are," to be sung, I have been told, to the tune of "Auld Lang Syne":

> We're here because we're here,
> Because we're here, because we're here;
> Oh, here we are, and here we are,
> And here we are again.

This apparently aimless allusion, however, is in reality an echo of the "simple statement" of Aiken's third ether-dream—"Here we are, then"—a statement which in *that* dream became the world and all knowable reality. In this context the allusion suggests a displacement of the rational and fatalistic determinism from which Mr. Arcularis wishes to but cannot escape—all that can be known about reality.

Moreover, the ship on which he sails out on the voyage to death is a dream symbol of Mr. Arcularis' body. The pulsations of the motors of the ship are geared to the pulsations of his own physical pain, so that at times Mr. Arcularis cannot tell whether he feels the vibrations of the engines or of his own heart. Later, as he approaches death, on the operating table, the ship is barely moving, and the rhythm of the engines is "slower, more subdued and remote." The fog and mist which obscure his sight are suggestive of waves of "nonconsciousness" as, approaching annihilation, his life wavers on the table. Another clear indication that Mr. Arcularis is dying is that he is always cold—the warmth of vitality is slowly fading from him. This coldness is explained to him, however, as the result of the ship's proximity to icebergs. Mr. Arcularis—his subconscious objectifying his body as the ship—muses upon all the ships which have sunk after collisions with icebergs. He is prepared for an imminent catastrophe, such as his own shipwreck, for the coffin in the hold inauspiciously augurs bad weather on the voyage. The sense of doom surrounding the voyage reflects his pre-operative anxiety that he would not survive the operation. He remembers the *Titanic* and the *Empress of Ireland,* shipwrecks that foreshadow his own imminent death. The finale of the *Cavalleria Rusticana,* which he had heard from the streets just before leaving the hospital and which the ship's band plays, is displaced in his subconcious by "Nearer My God to Thee," which, ironically, was played by the orchestra of the *Titanic* as it foundered upon the ice.

His dream censor exploiting the mechanisms of displacement and dream symbolism, Mr. Arcularis moves through four stages of psychotemporal regression (comparable at many points to, and clearly based upon, Aiken's three ether-dreams). These stages of psychotemporal regression mark out the phases of the struggle between Eros—the Principle of Life, and Thanatos—the Principle of Death. The first stage of regression takes Mr. Arcularis back to his childhood; the second withdraws him further to the mother's womb; the third takes him further back to a prehistoric stage of phylogenetic evolutionary development; and the fourth takes him back to the genesis of all things, the moment of creation—and beyond it to Chaos, to the swirling bright and white light of nothingness, annihilation. Each of these stages helps us to understand how Aiken employed his own experience under ether and his knowledge of Freud's commentary on dreams and the death instinct to enrich and deepen the significance of the voyage to death of Mr. Arcularis and of the workings of the mind and soul.

1. *The Return to Childhood:* The most bewildering problem for Mr. Arcularis is the identity of Miss Clarice Dean, who accompanies him on the mysterious voyage. Throughout the early part of the story he tries vainly to recollect where he has seen her before, who she is. It grows upon him that she reminds him of the freckle-faced young girl at the hospital, an assistant at the operation who had been especially kind during his stay there. But this association is not totally satisfactory to Mr. Arcularis. The freckle-faced girl, in turn, reminds him of something else long ago. "The little freckle-faced girl at the hospital was merely, as it were, the stepping-stone, the sign-post, or, as in algebra, the 'equals' sign. But what was it they both 'equalled'?" Mr. Arcularis associates them both with jackstones and his Aunt Julia's rose-garden at sunset, yet he perceives an inherent ridiculousness in this identification. "It couldn't be simply that they reminded him of his childhood! And yet why not?" This is the first stage in the psychotemporal regression of Mr. Arcularis: Clarice Dean, the hospital assistant, and his Aunt Julia are blended together, by the mechanism of condensation, into a composite figure suggesting some repressed memory of his early childhood—undoubtedly a memory of his mother.

The imminence of death reveals to Mr. Arcularis the beauty of life as only a child perceives it. He sees with joy the June spring in Boston—the streetcars, the green leaves, the drops of sparkling rainwater. Moreover, his father appears in the condensed figure of the doctor at the hospital, who reappears to him in his ether-dream as the doctor aboard ship who prescribes a simple bromide as a remedy for the horrible sleepwalking dream. Of the doctor Mr. Arcularis says to himself, " 'But why was it that doctors were all alike? and all, for that matter, like his father, or that fellow at the hospital?' " In such a way do people from his childhood appear in composite forms in his ether-dream.

In his attempt to recollect what these childhood memories "equalled," the sense of time becomes distorted in the mind of Mr. Arcularis. Once he thinks that time has ceased. Later his sense of time vanishes completely and he thinks that he has perhaps been on the ship for aeons. This confusion of the sense of time implies not only the irrelevance of time in dreams but also the timelessness of death, Eternity as the timeless Absolute. In addition, it also suggests that Mr. Arcularis has nearly completed the great circle of life and, at the point of death, is psychotemporally regressing by degrees to his childhood and birth. His feeling on leaving the hospital is, " 'Why should he feel sad about it and want to cry like a baby' " when " 'new life would be opening before him' "? He associates his experiences with events of his childhood, but he cannot rationally define the relationship between these associations. The return to his childhood, however, is only one arc in the regressive orbit of Mr. Arcularis.

2. *The Return to the Womb:* Gradually it grows upon Mr. Arcularis that his obsession with his childhood has significance. Miss Dean tells him not to worry about the nightmare search for the coffin because, as she says, " 'We aren't children any longer!' " and he replies " 'Aren't we? I wonder!' " When he has the nightmare on the second night he is horrified to wake up at the bottom of the stairway, as *he* emphasizes it, " *'crawling on my hands and knees.'* " On the third night Miss Dean says, " 'Be a good boy and take your bromide,' " and he replies, " 'Yes, mother, I'll take my medicine.' " These facts suggest that Mr. Arcularis' voyage to death is, like Aiken's third ether-dream, psychotemporally regressive; it is an example, as Aiken put it in his novel *Great Circle,* of "the end that is still conscious of its beginnings. Birth that remembers death." The great circle, the naked orbit, fixed and determined in its terrifying logical curve, is then a return not only to childhood but also to his genesis, to the mother's womb. In this respect one is reminded of Dylan Thomas "I dreamed my genesis in a sweat of sleep."

This suggestion of the return to the womb is supported by Mr. Arcularis' conversation with Clarice Dean about the ship stewards who are "dead souls." He asks, " 'How could they be stewards otherwise? And they think they've seen and known everything. They suffer terribly from the *déjà vu.*' " the sense of having already been at some strange place, seen or experienced something before in the unremembered past. Mr. Arcularis' certainty about them (" 'I'm sure of it. I'm enough of a dead soul myself to know the signs!' ") is not merely a subtle hint that he is dying, but also an indication that his voyage is wombward as well. Freud's comment [in *The Interpretation of Dreams*] on this psychological phenomenon of the *déjà vu* supports this interpretation: "But *'Déjà vu'* has a special significance in dreams. In this case the locality is always the genitals of the mother; of no other place can it be asserted with such certainty that one has been here before." That Mr. Arcularis' dream search for the coffin implies his subconscious search for the mother's womb is also suggested by his free association at the point of death with the word "coffer." The word "coffer" suggests not only coffin but also "box," which in German (*"Büchse"*) and in English is a slang term for the female genitals. Although this word association may seem arbitrary and therefore suspect, no less an authority than Freud himself may again be cited in its support. His analysis in *The Interpretation of Dreams* of the association of these words with the female genitals is carefully defined and expanded there to include even *Schachtel, Loge, and Kasten.* Moreover, other obvious word plays and associations appear in **"Mr. Arcularis,"** for example, the pun on Absolute/Obsolete=Absolete/Obsolute. Both Frederick J. Hoffman [in *Conrad Aiken*] and Jay Martin [in *Conrad Aiken: A Life of His Art*], moreover, have shown that Aiken had read Freud's *The Interpretation of Dreams* in 1915 and was thoroughly familiar with the work of Freud and his colleagues. It is not too much to say, then, that Mr. Arcularis' free association at the point of death is suggestive of his psychotemporal return to the womb.

But the identification of Miss Dean and the freckle-faced girl with Mr. Arcularis' mother and the suggestion, therefore, of his regression to the womb is, as such, too narrow to explain several indications in the story that she is in some sense also a projection of his own alienated psyche. In one passage he wonders: " 'I wish I could remember who you are." And she replies, " 'And you—who are you?' "—to which he answers, " 'Myself.' " Thereupon she says, " 'Then perhaps *I* am yourself.' " Taken aback, he responds, " 'Don't be metaphysical!' " And she concludes, " 'But I *am* metaphysical.' " Later this hint is developed further in Mr. Arcularis' meditation about Clarice Dean: "He broke off his sentence and looked hard at her—how lovely she was, and how desirable! No such woman had ever before come into his life; there had been no one with whom he had at once felt so profound a sympathy and understanding. It was a miracle, simply—a miracle. . . . He had only to look at her, and to feel, gazing into those extraordinary eyes, that she knew him, had always known him. It was as if, indeed, she might be his own soul." Only with her can he share the horror of his recurrent nightmares; only she communes with him. Only she expresses the wish that she could go with him. Only she expresses the wish that she could go with him on his dream orbits around the stars toward infinity. On the last night, just before Mr. Arcularis retires for the night, and for the third and last sleep-walking search which will lead him to the coffin in the hold, and for the third and last dream-within-a-dream which will take him out beyond the stars on the voyage to infinity, Mr. Arcularis and Clarice (whose names rhyme with each other and with "Polaris") embrace. In some sense or other they experience an infinite union, are in fact each other. "It was then that they first embraced—then, at the edge of the infinite, at the last signpost of the finite. They clung together desperately, forlornly, weeping as they kissed each other, staring hard one moment and closing their eyes the next. Passionately, passionately, she kissed him, as if she were indeed trying to give him her warmth, her life." The absolution expressed in this passage, the healing of what Aiken has called "the deep psychic wound," can be explained, I believe, by examination of a literary allusion to Plato dropped earlier in the story. It clarifies Clarice Dean's role in the story and perhaps suggests something about the nature of Mr. Arcularis' wound which would be made whole.

As he passed the Harvard Club on his trip to the ship, Mr. Arcularis thought, "There it was, with the great flag blowing in the wind, the Harvard seal now concealed by the swift folds and now revealed, and there were the windows in the library, where he had spent so many delightful hours reading—Plato, and Kipling, and the Lord knows what . . . ". F. L. Gwynn [in his 1956 essay in *Twentieth-Century Literature*] is right, I believe, in citing Kipling's interest in dreams and in the transmigration of souls in "The Bridge-Builders," "The Brushwood Boy," "Wireless," and "The Finest Story in the World." But his explanation of why Mr. Arcularis thinks of Plato (that Plato is distant in time and substance from Kipling, is concerned with the soul in *Phaedo* and the *Republic,* and is the originator of the motif of the Absolute and the Infinite) is not altogether satisfactory. One possible suggestion may come from a dialogue Gwynn overlooks—Plato's *Symposium.* This dialogue deals principally with the praise of love. Yet it is Plato's analysis of the origins of the sexes, put into the mouth of Aristophanes, that accounts for Mr. Arcularis' memory of Plato and for Clarice Dean's multiple role in the story.

As Aristophanes presents it, the sexes were originally three in number: man, woman, and the union of the two—called "androgynes." Because the powerful androgynes assaulted the gods, Zeus humbled them by dividing them in two. As a result, man separated spent his lifetime searching for his "other half," possessed by the ancient implanted desire to reunite "our original nature, making one of two, and healing the state of man. Each of us when separated, having one side only, like a flat fish, is but the indenture of a man, and he is always looking for his other half." When one meets his other half, "the actual half of himself," "the pair are lost in an amazement of love and friendship and intimacy,"—their desire not "the desire of lovers' intercourse, but of something else which the soul of either evidently desires and cannot tell, and of which she has only a dark and doubtful presentiment."

The union with Clarice Dean, it seems to me, symbolizes not only a return to childhood and beyond to his mother's womb but also a reunification with a part of himself. Their ecstatic union, or re-union, in the final passages of the story indicates that at long last Mr. Arcularis is coming to perfect union with himself, in other words, that he has, for the first time, possessed his own soul ("It was as if, indeed, she might be his own soul"). But unconscious repressions displace the recollection of his own birth and interfere with his instinctive yearning for fulfillment and completeness, of which he has only "a dark and doubtful presentiment." This interpretation of the story is thus consistent with Freud's contention that the dream is on the whole "an act of regression to the earliest relationships of the dreamer, a resuscitation of his childhood, of the impulses which were then dominant and the modes of expression which were then available."

This repression of the trauma of birth is illuminated in a second allusion, from *Macbeth,* which deepens and intensifies the significance of an unaccountable feeling of guilt which seems to oppress Mr. Arcularis. As Mr. Arcularis stands with Clarice, "They leaned, shoulders touching, on the deck-rail, and looked at the sea, which was multitudinously incarnadined." This line seems clearly to me an allusion to *Macbeth* (II, ii, 60-63), where Macbeth agonizes because he cannot wash away the blood of murdered Duncan:

> Will all great Neptune's ocean wash the blood
> Clean from my hand? No, this my hand will rather
> The multitudinous seas incarnadine,
> Making the green one red.

If the allusion suggests that Mr. Arcularis is torn by guilt, the origin of his guilt is obscure unless we assume a general Oedipal connection. Clearly enough, the inability of Mr. Arcularis to identify Miss Dean until the point of death is the effect of the repression of an infantile psychological trauma. The parson aboard ship senses that Mr. Arcularis' sleep-walking nightmare arises from a sense of guilt: " 'You feel guilty about something. I won't be so rude as to inquire what it is. But if you could rid yourself of the sense of guilt—' ". Aiken's *play version* of the story, published in 1957 (twenty-six years later than the publication of the story), defines explicitly the origin of Mr. Arcularis' guilt: as a child he had witnessed his mother's illicit love affair with her husband's brother. But the source of guilt explicit in the play, however, cannot help us to interpret the story. In the first place, there is no direct evidence in the story that Mr. Arcularis witnessed the infidelity of his mother. Aiken invented the play's mother-uncle motif to repair the damage done to the story by Diana Hamilton, whose previous play version included an invented wife for Mr. Arcularis. This interpolation was so obviously unsatisfactory that Aiken repaired it by borrowing a mother-uncle motif from the middle section of his novel *Great Circle.* Thus the play version is so different from the story and so late an invention that only a rash critic would attempt to gloss it from the play. The conclusions of the two versions, story and play, are, as Rufus Blanshard suggests [in his 1957 essay in the *Sewanee Review*], "*separately* right as resolutions," but they are not, as he claims, "so akin as to gloss one another." Perhaps an interpretation more consistent with the psychological context out of which this story issues is that Mr. Arcularis is repressing the trauma of birth; the red ocean might therefore suggest not guilt but the breaking of waters, or the escape of the amniotic fluid at birth. Birth and the sea are identified so commonly in the literature of psychology that perhaps we need not press the issue further. Mr. Arcularis' psychotemporal return to the womb, the second stage of his regression toward death, is in itself merely an attempt to return to a condition of security prior to the birth trauma, a motive determined by the pleasure principle. But this regressive voyage reaches back beyond the recollection of ejection from his prenatal home.

3. *The Return Through the Phylogenetic Development:* In his discussion of regression in dreams to the state of childhood, Freud continued: "Behind this childhood of the individual we are then promised an insight into the phylogenetic childhood, into the evolution of the human race, of which the development of the individual is only an abridged repetition influenced by the fortuitous circumstances of life." Aiken has shown us this phylogenetic development in the rehearsal of his own ether-dream; it is also present in **"Mr. Arcularis."** This devolutionary return to the past is indicated in Mr. Arcularis' reference to the prehistoric time when his operation might have been performed: " 'Centuries ago. When I was a tadpole and you were a fish.' " This comment alludes to a poem by Langdon Smith—"Evolution" (1895), of which these lines are pertinent:

> When you were a tadpole and I was a fish,
> In the Paleozoic time,
> And side by side on the ebbing tide,
> We sprawled through the ooze and slime, . . .
> My heart was rife with the joy of life,
> For I loved you even then.

This evolutionary period before human life is the third stage in Mr. Arcularis' psychotemporal regression to death. That the history of the human race is contained in the development of the embryo ("ontogeny recapitulates phylogeny") is a theory perhaps no longer seriously believed by biologists. Nevertheless, the process of Mr. Arcularis' regression toward annihilation is based upon this concept and upon, I believe, Freud's discussion of it.

4. *The Return to the Creation of the Universe:* The fourth stage in Mr. Arcularis' voyage to infinity takes him beyond childhood, beyond the womb, even beyond the prehistoric evolutionary development of the race. It takes him back to the moment of the creation of the universe, to the frontier of Time and Eternity, Creation and Chaos, Being and Nothingness or Annihilation. Just as Aiken witnessed in his third ether-dream the creation of the universe, order evolving from chaos, so Mr. Arcularis' subconscious mind regresses psychotemporally toward the moment of Creation and, when he arrives at it, he is annihilated. The coincidence of Mr. Arcularis' death at the moment when he had crossed beyond finity into infinity is not accidental; figured lineally it is the "great circle," "the end that is still conscious of its beginnings," "birth that remembers death."

Why, after all, it may be asked, should Aiken have isolated these four stages in Mr. Arcularis' passage to death, his annihilation? The question itself, or one similar to it, was also asked by Aiken in his interesting little piece **"State of Mind."** There a man who wished to annihilate himself asked: "How could one project, in satisfactory form, this desire for annihilation? Not in suicide, but in imagination?" **"Mr. Arcularis"** is, in fact, an imaginative projection of the desire of a man for annihilation. The desire is, however, an instinct for annihilation. In *Beyond the Pleasure Principle* Freud proposed a theory of instinct beyond the pleasure principle which would account for the regressive phenomenon of the death instinct. He argued that "in the traumatic neuroses the dream life has this peculiarity: it continually takes the patient back to the situation of his disaster, from which he awakens in renewed terror." Mr. Arcularis' search for the coffin, or the prenatal security of the womb, is thus an expression of what Freud called the compulsion "to *repeat* as a current experience what is repressed, instead of, as the physician would prefer to see him do, *recollecting* it as a fragment of the past." It is this "repetition-compulsion" which defines the "regressive character of instinct." Beyond the pleasure principle is "*a tendency innate in living organic matter impelling it toward the reinstatement of an earlier condition. . . .* " Mr. Arcularis' attempt to return to the prenatal unity and security of the womb is thus a manifestation of the pleasure principle. Beyond it is the inward struggle of Eros and Thanatos, the sexual instincts of life combatting the death instinct. The identity of Clarice Dean becomes clearer: symbolically a part of himself, she personifies Eros (the life or sexual instincts which minister to and preserve the existence of the organism). She yearns to stay with him, to give him her warmth and vitality. But beyond Eros, beyond the sexual instincts, is Thanatos, an instinct more primitive and powerful, which inevitably leads to death. Freuds' proposition was that " *'The goal of all life is death,'* and casting back. *'The inanimate was there before the animate,'* " It is worth pointing out that Aristophanes' speech in the *Symposium* about the quest of the androgynes for reunion exactly fulfills one condition of Freud's theory of the death-instinct: it derives an instinct "from the *necessity for the reinstatement of an earlier situation.*" Though admittedly Plato's account is a myth, Freud argued that "Plato would not have adopted any such story . . . had he not himself felt the truth contained in it to be illuminating."

Mr. Arcularis' search for the coffin reflects the organism's compulsion to return to an earlier inanimate state—"a state never hitherto reached," yet the "final goal of all organic striving," the "ancient starting point, which the living being left long ago, and to which it harks back again by all the circuitous paths of development." Mr. Arcularis reaches that goal at precisely the moment when he finds the coffin, when he passes the frontier of Time and Eternity, when he passes the last signpost heading toward Infinity. At that point he is immersed in the bright white swirling light of annihilation. (pp. 295-312)

James W. Tuttleton, "Aiken's 'Mr. Arcularis': Psychic Regression and the Death Instinct," in American Imago, *Vol. 20, No. 4, Winter, 1963, pp. 295-314.*

Ann Gossman (essay date 1964)

[In the following essay, Gossman considers the symbolic significance of Paul Hasleman's psychological withdrawal in "Silent Snow, Secret Snow."]

William M. Jones has [in *Explicator,* March 1960] analyzed Conrad Aiken's **"Silent Snow, Secret Snow"** as a study, done imaginatively and sympathetically, but almost clinically, of schizophrenia. He interprets the isolation of the hero as a schizophrenic repudiation of reality that culminates in a catatonic trance. Such an explication, such an analysis of Paul Hasleman's case, reflects the laboratory wisdom—the laboratory knowledge, rather—of this world. Very probably, the doctor called in to examine the boy might have offered just such a diagnosis to the Haslemans if he had been privileged to read Paul's thoughts.

That such an intention was Aiken's, however, is considerably less demonstrable. It is the purpose of this paper to suggest another interpretation which also fits the facts that Aiken has given but which deals with a symbolic, not a clinical, reading of these facts.

Since the story is told from the point of view of Paul himself, without any explicit commentary from Aiken in the person of storyteller, Paul's vision must contain almost all the clues that Aiken intended to give us, with one exception to be mentioned later, and this technique compels us to create our own commentary upon the available clues. My thesis is that Paul's withdrawal is not psychopathic, but rather the alienation of the artist from society, and that the price of this creative *apartheid* is death. Such a theme stems, of course, from the romantic movement and appears in much of the literature of the twentieth-century, *e.g.,* in Willa Cather's "Paul's Case," in much of Kafka and Joyce and Yeats, and in Mann's *Tonio Kröger;* and it has been traced back to the theme of the artist's melancholia in Burton and in Dürer, through Coleridge, Baudelaire, and the French Symbolists. As Frank Kermode points out in *The Romantic Image,* to experience that " 'epiphany' which is the Joycean equivalent of Pater's vision," the artist has to suffer profoundly, risk his very soul, and be alone, "not only to be separate from all others, but to have not even one friend." Such a price in isolation is the inevitable concomitant of the artist's perception of what Kermode calls "the Image as a radiant truth out of space and time."

Aiken applies the term "counterpoint" to Paul's two kinds of vision: his strange perception of the snow and his recognition of a pattern of visible details of the world of phenomena. Jones says of even the quaint observation of Dierdre's freckles, which formed the pattern of the Big Dipper, that it is a manifestation of abnormal psychology; and he cites Carl Jung's account of "fascination" [in *The Psychology of Dementia Praecox*] as a "distraction to the environment in order to conceal the vacuum of inner associations or the *complex* producing the vacuum." Aside from the fact that Paul has a vision, not a vacuum, to depart from and that he does not welcome any departure, it would seem a highly dangerous reading of far too much into an innocent observation. Any poet who "numbers the streaks of the tulip," it seems, would be in danger of the same kind of analysis. One is reminded of the late Professor Irwin Edman's anecdote of the psychiatrist who offered to *cure* him of his philosophy. Even if Paul were a schizophrenic (a point of view which I palpably do not accept), he would still be a valid symbol of the alienated artist, and the diagnosis of madness would leave unanswered the larger question of an ethically mad or spiritually blind society, guilty of the organized, bizarre sanity that can be cured only through such humane figures as Giraudoux's Madwoman.

What Aiken does with the details of Paul's awareness, though, seems less a study of psychological "fascination" than an application of Conrad's precept that the artist should make us *see* the visible universe, as well as share the artist's private, inner vision of what is enduring.

The entire story is, to use Aiken's term, a delicate counterpointing of two ways of considering reality: one, under the aspect of eternity, and the other, simply as phenomena are perceived, or as they might be perceived, by either a poet or a sharp-eyed, spontaneous child. The conflict in Paul between these two levels of vision, which finally become irreconcilable, culminates in a choice which he must make, and ultimately it results in his death.

The vision which manifests itself through the symbolism of the snow is at first undemanding; it comes unsought as a precious mystery, conveying "a beautiful sense of possession." It carries with it a simple delight. Just so, the artist is always entranced initially with the beauty and charm of what Robert Graves calls the White Goddess; only later is he painfully enchanted, left alone and palely loitering. The snow is "just an idea," that is, a country of the mind which Paul may inhabit at the same time that he is counting Deirdre's freckles or contemplating the green and yellow continents of his geography class. Paul is abstracting "one degree from actuality" and naturally turns to images to express his miraculous vision, which is superior to "mere actuality."

Almost at once Paul's vision becomes a screen that covers with beauty the ugliness of the world of particulars, such as the little "deltas of filth" in the gutter. Aiken is by no means the first artist of our century to perceive the aesthetic discontinuity experienced by any serious lover of beauty in a world of "ambition, distraction, uglification, and derision." And as Paul's vision becomes more demanding, it imposes itself between the merely actual world and Paul. Hence he must lead a double life. His artistic integrity makes demands: he must be true to his vision "at whatever pain." His reward is that he may inhabit his unusual country of the mind. The proof of his controlling intellect is that he may inhabit his usual world as well whenever he needs to do so. The beauty is "beyond anything," pure, remote, and peaceful; but Paul is still sane and no fool as the world judges, even as the shrewd Miss Buell judges. When she suspects him of the usual childish day-dreaming or failure to pay attention in class and challenges him, "I'm sure Paul will come out of his day-dream long enough to be able to tell us. Won't you, Paul?" he finds it amusing to make the required effort of attention immediately and answer her question about the Hudson River, however trivial it strikes him.

Aiken in his middle thirties.

As the vision narrows and sharpens, "how sharply [is] increased the amount of illusion that [has] to be carried into the ordinary business of daily life," for the ideal is a cold transforming light upon the so-called real. Aiken here applies to the artist's vision terms that suggest a Platonic dichotomy between the absolute ideal forms and the multiple, various realm of "becoming."

Part of the pain which Paul must suffer results from the demand of secrecy that the vision imposes. Aiken's treatment of this portion of the story is meaningful in terms of the artist's conflict of loyalties and his need for creative solitude. It is also (like Forster's "The Celestial Omnibus") an indictment of the hampering adults who would limit the sensitive child and deprive him of his right of privacy. The increased demand for secrecy is surely justified: "Was it wrong to want a secret place?" The vision becomes inexorable as Paul crosses the river homeward, and it ascends from mere things to images or thoughts of them and thence to eternity. Such an account accords well with the phenomenological progression with its "eidetic reduction," and it is also a kind of ascent up the Platonic ladder of beauty. Mortal limitations make the terrifying process partly incomprehensible to Paul.

For instance, Paul is not aware of the full implications of the developing crisis of family loyalties, though he has sensed that "at whatever pain" can mean pain to others as well as to himself. Nor does he think of the snow as akin to death, but merely akin to sleep. For the reader, though, who watches Paul pass almost insensibly through the degrees toward eternity, it is evident that Paul must reach this eternity ultimately only through dying. There is a kind of dramatic irony in Paul's failure to perceive that the steps have finally reached his house. He does begin to wonder whether this means that he will never hear the postman again. Jones takes this figure merely to be "news from the outside world," but that is a confusion of the two levels of reality, which have already been defined.

In the third division of the story, the world exacts its price from Paul. If the spiral of snow is inexorable, it is overbalanced by the cruel inquisition which is held. The parents, frightened by the calm and courteous quality of Paul's separateness as much as by, one suspects, the separation itself, call in a doctor. Paul can answer the doctor's questions, of course, and he also understands perfectly well what the doctor is assuming. Mrs. Hasleman is sympathetic, but Paul recognizes very soon his father's "punishment voice," which is inexorable and cruel. Paul himself sees that the ordeal reduces him to the status of a performing dog (surely an indictment of the psychologists) and feels cruelly spotlighted as well. Aiken is not just giving us Paul's bias; he plainly offers objective facts and the emotionally charged glare of the investigation the way Paul experiences them; they ought to speak for themselves. It is damning evidence against a society of philistines that they would choose this method of limiting the artist, destroying him, or—worst of all—curing him.

If the inquisition does not plainly offer the clues for its own interpretation, there is yet another profoundly beautiful and ironic commentary upon Paul's ordeal: the passage which he reads aloud for the benefit of the Haslemans and the doctor. Its ostensible use is to test Paul's ability to hold a book correctly and read accurately the words on a printed page, and to everyone but Paul it is merely that. What it is to him—that is, what the passage means to him—he does not say, but it is his own choice: the choral ode at the heart of *Oedipus at Colonus,* the section praising the Grove of Athens, haunt sacred to love and the hospitable gods and the Muses—Athens, honored by the gods with the gifts of ships and horses that men might tame. The choral poem is the lyrical and symbolic statement of the meaning of the last play that Sophocles wrote, in which the reviled and banished Oedipus is at last granted a fair dismissal: first to be received magnanimously and compassionately by Theseus, then to find, though in darkness, a way into the mystic grove and a death that is rather an apotheosis. A reference to this choral poem, then, is a highly allusive way for the author to suggest an interpretation of all the facts of the story: a hero tragically isolated and wrongly condemned by society, the images of artistic control and understanding, and finally a vision of death and the transcendence of pain.

Aiken allows this Sophoclean passage to be read, but unsullied by any possible misunderstanding on the part of the parents or the doctor. They, instead, proceed to force Paul to some admission about his private vision. Under the pressure of these inquisitors Paul does reveal that his secret is "just thinking," and he comes as close as he dares to his image of the snow. He must not interpret it. It is possible that he could not have done so satisfactorily, for he is a child of twelve. What is more important, it is characteristic of the romantic image that it is "an aesthetic monad," original and rich in suggestion, but superior in its organic aliveness to any sort of limiting "discursive truth" about it. To paraphrase, to translate, to explain the image is to debase and destroy the ineffable vision which cannot be communicated save through symbolic language.

It is probable that if Paul had tried to tell his parents and the doctor about the snow, they would have pronounced him mad, and Paul and his vision would thus have been sacrificed in vain. Therefore Paul willingly elects the sacrifice of himself alone by keeping his silence. He chooses the "timeless, shapeless, world-wide ideas." At once the reward of his ethical commitment is vouchsafed, a new and even more beautiful revelation. Ironically, just as the crisis seems to be over, this new revelation is interrupted by the harsh, mundane light; and it is Paul's mother, not his father, against whom he must cry out his rejection of even the well-meaning sensible world when it would seek to cut off his vision and deprive him of his truth. When the flower becomes seed in Paul's new revelation, Jones interprets the image as evidence of the "maturity process arrested, even diminishing. . . ." Jones is right, in one sense. Paul himself is the flower that becomes seed: he has flourished as an artist, and he must die rather than "mature" into perhaps another Mr. Hasleman. But the seed is a rich image that suggests also that Paul holds Infinity in the palm of his hand. When eternity becomes accommodated to its containing artistic symbol, the artist achieves his ultimate cold peace. (pp. 123-28)

Ann Gossman, " 'Silent Snow, Secret Snow': The Child as Artist," in Studies in Short Fiction, *Vol. I, No. 2, Winter, 1964, pp. 123-28.*

Thomas L. Erskine (essay date 1972)

[In the following excerpt, Erskine discusses the "two different worlds" motif in "Silent Snow, Secret Snow."]

Conrad Aiken, an early convert to the teachings of Freud, effectively portrays in **"Silent Snow, Secret Snow"** a young boy's psychological affliction. In criticism of the story one inevitably finds reference to "neurosis," "psychosis," "Oedipal complex," "schizophrenia," terms which critics use to describe the content, or subject, of the story. That the short story is more than a clinician's case study of a patient is obvious if one contrasts it to Hall's fictitious language-of-science version of the story [Lawrence Hall, in *How Thinking Is Written*]. As Clifton Fadiman points out [in his *Reading I've Liked,* 1941], although the story could not have been written before the advent of psychiatry, Aiken treats his subject in an "unclinical" manner. Arguing for an interpretation of Paul as artist, Ann Landman states [in an essay originally published in *Studies in Short Fiction* under the name Ann Gossman] that the psychological criticism of the story merely reflects the "laboratory knowledge" of the world, and then she offers a "symbolic" reading of the "facts" of the story. While I have reservations about Mrs. Landman's reading of the story, I do share her belief that the symbolism in the story is literary as well as psychological. It is this "blend of the symbolic and the psychological," as Reuel Denny calls it [in *Conrad Aiken*], which removes the story from the case history genre and qualifies it as an excellent short story.

An example of the symbolic and psychological simultaneously at work is Aiken's use of the "two different worlds" motif, which most critics mention only in passing. The motif is explicit: "But how then, between the two worlds, of which he was thus constantly aware, was he to keep a balance?" "Balance" is important psychologically because the term describes Paul's precarious hold on reality, but the nature of the two worlds and Paul's attitude toward them are conveyed symbolically in the story by the geography and explorer imagery. Like Keats' "On First Looking into Chapman's Homer," the short story concerns discovery.

In the first paragraph of his story Aiken juxtaposes the two worlds, portrays them, and suggests the image of Paul as explorer. For Paul, the snow world is a "delicious" secret, which he savors because it gives him a sense of both possession and protection: "It was as if, in some delightful way, his secret gave him a fortress, a wall behind which he could retreat into heavenly seclusion." The reference to "fortress," "wall," and "retreat" suggest the need to flee from the real world and also anticipate the hostility Paul sees during the "inquisition" (he refers to his parents and the doctor as "hostile presences"). The snow world is compared to a series of objects, which possess individuality, uniqueness, and almost, because of their protective function, a magical quality. On the other hand, the real world of the school is stylistically depicted as humdrum and dull by Aiken's prose: "The green and yellow continents passed and repassed, questions were asked and answered. . . ."

In the first paragraph Paul moves from his snow world to the real world, but he does so through the use of Deirdre as reference point. Like a navigator at sea, Paul charts his course by the stars: "Deirdre, who had a funny little constellation of freckles on the back of her neck, exactly like the Big Dipper. . . ." At the end of Part I Paul is again returned to reality through the bell *and* Deirdre: "He saw Deirdre rise, and had himself risen almost as soon—but not quite as soon—as she."

The geography lesson, which occupies the bulk of Part I, serves to sharpen the contrast between the two worlds and to develop Paul's role as explorer. The boundary lines between the two worlds are established by Miss Buell, who stresses the "imaginary" quality of the line about the middle of the earth. During the remainder of the lesson Miss Buell deals with geographical facts; Paul deals with his ideas about those facts. Paul's attention focuses on the white regions, the Arctic and Antarctic; but Miss Buell begins in the tropics, which are in green and which reflect life, even fertility (the animals and birds are like *"living"* jewels). As Paul thinks about the postman, the harbinger of the snow world, and of the peace, remoteness, cold, and sleep the snow world offers, Miss Buell moves north from the tropics to the "vast wheat-growing areas in North America and Siberia." When she reaches the Arctic region, she describes it as the "land of perpetual snow," a land which lacks fertility and life. How inadequately her brief one-liner describes Paul's land of enchantment!

In the course of Part I Paul finds it increasingly difficult to maintain the balance between his two worlds. In fact, he ironically must use "illusion" to remain in the real world:

> Each day it was more difficult to go through the perfunctory motions of greeting Mother and Father at breakfast, to reply to their questions, to put his books together and go to school. And at school, how extraordinarily hard to conduct with success simultaneously the public life and the life that was secret.

As Paul puts it, "It was as if he were trying to lead a double life." He prefers the snow world:

> He had to explore this new world which had been opened to him. Nor could there be the slightest doubt—not the slightest—that the new world was the profounder and more wonderful of the two. It was irresistible. It was miraculous. Its beauty was simply beyond anything—beyond speech as beyond thought—utterly incommunicable.

The decision to "explore" the new world significantly occurs just after Miss Buell tells the class about Hendrick Hudson's search for the Northwest Passage and after a discussion with his mother about geography (history, the recording of the past, is "dull"), the North Pole, and explorers like Peary, Scott, and Shackleton. The allusions are instructive: Scott reached the South Pole, but he perished on the return trip; Hudson searched for a passage to the Orient, a region seen as exotic and beautiful, but, as Paul answers, Hudson was "disappointed." By mentioning Scott and Hudson, Aiken suggests that explorations like Paul's sometimes involve failure and death.

In Part II Aiken again implicitly compares Paul with an explorer, this time Columbus, who likewise sought a new route to the Orient, but found something else. On an odyssey of his own, Paul walks homeward (and Aiken's question "Homeward?" suggests Paul's "home" may not be with his parents) and sees a gateway, which itself is symbolic of passage from one world to another:

> Then came the gateway with two posts surmounted by egg-shaped stones which had been cunningly balanced on their ends as if by Columbus, and mortared in the very act of balance: a source of perpetual wonder. On the brick wall just beyond, the letter H had been stencilled, presumably for some purpose. H? H.

The details, presumably there for Aiken's purpose, suggest the identification of Paul Hasleman with Columbus, the precarious nature of the balance, the juxtaposition of two worlds, and the association of the egg-shaped stones with birth and, paradoxically, death.

The epiphany is particularly appropriate, because it is as a result of his journey homeward that he becomes increasingly interested in "miracles" rather than in the ugly details of daily life. In a richly evocative passage, the "items of mere externality" assume symbolic roles:

> Dirty sparrows huddled in the bushes, as dull in color as dead fruit left in leafless trees. A single starling creaked on a weather vane. In the gutter, beside a drain, was a scrap of torn and dirty newspaper, caught in a little delta of filth: the word ECZEMA appeared in large capitals, and below it was a letter from Mrs. Amelia D. Cravath, 2100 Pine Street, Fort Worth, Texas, to the effect that after being a sufferer for years she had been cured by Caley's Ointment. In the little delta, beside the fan-shaped and deeply runneled continent of brown mud, were lost twigs, descended from their parent trees, dead matches, a rusty horse-chestnut burr, a small concentration of sparkling gravel on the lip of the sewer, a fragment of eggshell, a streak of yellow sawdust which had been wet and now was dry and congealed, a brown pebble, and a broken feather.

The images suggest dirt and filth (the sparrows, newspaper, delta), isolation ("a single starling" who "creaks," not sings), death ("dead matches"), and sterility (the "rusty horse-chestnut burr," the "fragment of eggshell" [particularly effective when contrasted with the balanced "egg-shaped stones"]). Some of the items also seem to demand a symbolic interpretation. Paul is like a "lost twig" descended from parent trees, and in his crippled emotional state ("broken feather") he is on the brink of losing his balance (like the "sparkling gravel on the lip of the sewer"). All the details, including the ECZEMA advertisement with its adult hypocrisy and false promise of "cures," serve as a microcosm of the real world that Paul would leave. After all, the tiny patch of mud becomes a "delta" and even a "continent," implying its universal application.

The real world accordingly turns Paul away, and while his snow world becomes more extensive, the real world contracts. On the walk home, for example, he sees the real world, but "something," the snow world, "teases" at the corner of his eyes and mind. The process of shutting out the real world progresses rapidly in Part II, and the "audible compass of the world" narrows until in Part III the snow world eventually rules him.

From Paul's eyes the eye examination is an "inquisition," but Aiken chooses to present extensive dialogue without editorial comment, without criticism. From a reading of the dialogue we view the eye examination objectively: two concerned parents with a doctor's help attempt, somewhat foolishly but not maliciously, to find out what is "wrong" with their son. Yet Paul, who now sees everything with snow-affected eyes, terms the examination a "cross-examination," as well as an "inquisition." From his point of view, the real world is phony, prosaic ("gross intelligences," "humdrum minds"), but also threatening (his father's "punishment" voice). In his paranoid condition the real is false, the illusion real. He even believes that there is "proof" of his world, while the material "proof" seen by the impartial observer testifies against Paul.

Except for his mother's brief appearance, Paul spends most of Part IV in the snow world. The "audible compass of the world" shuts out everything: we don't hear any noises from the real world. On the other hand, the hiss of the snow breaks into a roar. So complete is his citizenship in the snow world that he regards his mother's entrance as "something alien," something "hostile" from another world, which he can hardly understand. It is significant that he does remember the "exorcising words" which sever the cord between mother and son.

In these last moments, however, Aiken's imagery reflects his earlier use of the explorer motif. Paul as navigator is in his room, where "the bare black floor was like a little raft tossed in waves of snow." The "enormous whispering sea-waves" seem to swallow up the raft. In this final scene Aiken evokes an image of a young boy who seeks to discover a new world, although he is out of his depth, without a guide, with only a fragile, precarious craft. He finds peace, remoteness, cold, sleep, but he may also have found, by our reckoning, insanity or death. (pp. 86-91)

Thomas L. Erskine, "The Two Worlds of 'Silent Snow, Secret Snow'," in From Fiction to Film: Conrad Aiken's "Silent Snow, Secret Snow," *edited by Gerald R. Barrett and Thomas L. Erskine, Dickenson Publishing Company, Inc., 1972, pp. 86-91.*

Carolyn Handa (essay date 1975)

[In the following excerpt, Handa examines the structure and imagery of "Impulse," focusing on the psychological state of the protagonist. For an opposing view, see the essay by Bernard Winehouse dated 1978.]

Conrad Aiken remains firmly established in his exalted position as one of America's most neglected contemporary writers. One can only hope, however, that critics of American literature will begin examining the mammoth canon of his work in an attempt at a serious evaluation of his artistic abilities. Too much of the small amount of Aiken criticism has been spent arguing over the merits of his poetry, as opposed to his novels, or his short stories, and is primarily a defense rather than an exploration of Aiken's accomplishments in one of the three genres. Malcolm Lowry was especially upset by a *Time* review of ***The Short Stories of Conrad Aiken*** for stating that "though his reputation has been largely based on his poetry, Aiken may well be remembered most for his short stories." Indeed, Lowry's perturbation with this remark may have been justified, since Aiken's poetry might very well deserve as much notice as his fiction, but the glaring critical shortcoming, obvious now, twenty-five years after the *Time* reviewer's comment, is that today even his short stories are forgotten. *Neither* these stories *nor* his poetry are receiving anything approximating the adequate amount of attention needed for a proper assessment of his achievements.

At this point in his studies, Aiken's accomplishments in both fiction and poetry are quite important to remember. When approaching his work, critics aware of these two facets of Aiken's artistic temperament will then immediately understand that each genre, rather than taking precedence over another, helps instead, to illuminate the others. In [*Conrad Aiken: A Life of His Art,* 1962] Jay Martin points out that "Since the appearance of Aiken's autobiographical 'essay,' *Ushant,* it has been clear that Aiken himself understands his literary career in terms of the experience he has been able to express in his fiction. With the sole exception of *The Kid,* he mentions his poems in only a cursory fashion in *Ushant,* while he discusses his fiction at length. Although Aiken does this ironically, he also intends thereby to emphasize his fiction. For the critic of Aiken, then, the novels assume critical importance aside from their individual merits, since an understanding of his fiction helps toward an elucidation of his poetry." Although Martin considers only the novels in his brief discussion of Aiken's fiction, his comment is worth noting because it suggests that type of stylistic and thematic genre interchange which I have just mentioned. Aiken, in fact, uses poetic methods in his fiction; more specifically, he utilizes near-poetic form and symbolism in his stories and novels. In point of fact, I hope to show that such extremely careful, semi-poetic techniques structure one of his lesser-criticized but widely-anthologized stories, **"Impulse."** If Aiken's short stories in any way indicate the wealth of artistry critics might uncover by examining his fiction closely, an alert reading of this story will yield a veritable gold mine of clues to Aiken's intricate fictional and poetic styles.

Artistically, **"Impulse"** is finely-constructed, so carefully molded that its structure and imagery adhere tenaciously to its theme, lending this theme an appropriate form and serving as more than adequate vehicles of expression. Aiken constantly welds images and overall design to reinforce his point of view: that "civilization is only skin-deep"; once shaved of that paper-thin skin of civility, mankind shows itself to be "criminal, ex-post facto." The imagery, consequently, relates to shaving and the breaking of bonds, and the form the story takes—that of the " 'V' turned upside down" mentioned in its first paragraph—assumes significance for this tale of a man defeated by exposing his inherently criminal nature.

Before going into detail about the inverted-V structure of the story, however, perhaps I should further explain the theme of the story, a theme that emerges during the early conversation at the bridge game. One of the men admits that conceding to impulses would simply be human: " 'What would be more human? We all want things. Why not take them? Why not do them? And *civilization is only skin-deep*' " (italics mine). Giving form to this story is Aiken's idea that civilized nature is only a thin veneer beneath which every human feels similar impulses, and which, when punctured, releases man's anti-social tendencies. Once aware of the theme, we immediately begin to see juxtaposed the "civilized" and "uncivilized" actions in the story. The idea that civilization is only skin-deep provides the chief thrust for the story's main action. In addition, Aiken heaps level upon level of irony since we realize that except for civilization, the men would not be contemplating impulse in such a cerebral manner, Michael would not feel tempted to test an impulse within this civilization's constructs, and of course, the instrument which Michael steals would probably not exist. According to Frederick Hoffman [in *Conrad Aiken*], Aiken often experiments with themes, exploring the consequences of civilized versus uncivilized actions: "In general, the struggles of Aiken's heroes to establish an emotional middle ground—between an extreme hatred of the flesh, of the corruptibility of the human species, and an emotional void—seem to be . . . efforts to recover a lost balance and stability from the past. Many of the short stories are centrally concerned with this kind of tension: the illusion of a gracious and sophisticated society, and the insistent threat posed by a naturalistic reduction (or annihilation) of its pretenses."

In the face of this type of theme, the V-structure of the story is quite interesting. Aiken's opening line introduces us to Michael Lowes, whose surname appropriately suggests his present situation in life; just having argued with his wife about his unpaid bills, he is at a low point. Although he hums, he is not optimistic, for he thinks "there would be more of them [the unpaid bills], probably, beside his plate. The rent. The coal. The doctor who had attended to the children. Jeez, what a life." However, this life apparently begins looking up for Michael Lowes as he contemplates his "bi-weekly day of escape, when he would stay out for the evening and play bridge with Hurwitz, Bryant, and Smith," and he senses the rising movement continue through breakfast: Dora does not mention their financial discussion and he manages to slip quietly out of the house. I consider the progression of the story here as a motion upward since these incidents seem to help Michael overcome what he considers petty cares. Although he appears irresponsible to others, he himself feels each successive and successful move restoring a solipsistic peace of mind. This ascending side of the inverted-V shows Michael continually inflating his escapist illusions.

Dinner with the three other men, the bridge game, and the conversation during the game further remove Michael from his past life and bring him to a higher realm of delusion. The discussion of impulses amazes, yet comforts Michael, because he finds that he shares such feelings with all the men in the room: "Michael was astonished at this turn of the talk. He had often felt both these [erotic and selfish] impulses. To know that this was a kind of universal human inclination came over him with something like relief."

Having left the bridge game, Michael still pursues his deluded incline while he walks through the drug store after he has decided to give in to his impulses. He is thoroughly pleased, yet: "Oddly enough, . . . not in the least excited. . . . On the contrary, he was intensely amused; not to say delighted. He was smiling as he walked slowly along the right-hand side of the store toward the back."

However, Michael does not long continue in this movement because the theft of the shaver both catapults him to the peak of the structure of the story and marks the beginning of his downward plunge. Michael acts in an attempt to prove to himself his oneness with the rest of civilization—his connection to all those who act impulsively. But because his acceptance of society's pretentious veneer has so thoroughly hindered any direct sensitivity to his inherent nature, ironically only the failure of his roundabout attempt at establishing a connection finally reveals his consanguinity with a humanity which is guilt ex-post facto.

Each successive incident after the theft, accordingly, draws Michael down to a lower level. Under the circumstances, his friends desert him one by one; first Smith cannot be located and then the others deny knowing him well enough to account for his erratic behavior. Even his superficial marital bond with Dora dissolves completely. As she says in her final note to him: " 'Michael, . . . I'm sorry, but I can't bring up the children with a criminal for a father, so I'm taking proceedings for a divorce. This is the last straw.' "

Aiken's structure consists of an upward movement towards a peak situation, followed by an immediate reversal of the previous action. Michael begins at a low point made comfortable by illusions, rises in his comfort due to an increase of illusions, then performs his impulsive, catalytic act which triggers a series of confrontations that bring him back to a most painful reality. The second half of the structure thus complements the first through its reversed movement (we see the coming down of what went up), and reversed perceptions (reality follows illusions; what was flatly literal assumes a deeper figurative cast).

As we might expect, Aiken's imagery follows and accentuates the structure of the story while reinforcing the "civilization is only skin-deep" theme. One of the primary sets of images centers around the "civilized" ritual of shaving. Aiken emphasizes this action subtly and first depicts Michael shaving—literally: "Michael Lowes hummed as he shaved, amused by the face he saw." Structurally, we can place Aiken's first reference to shaving at the foot of one side of the inverted-V shape of the story. The next reference to shaving occurs in the scene at the apex of the inverted-V where Michael acts to bring about his downfall. Here Michael receives his fatal impulse to steal the very instrument used in the act of shaving: "a *de-luxe* safety-razor set, of heavy gold,"—in other words, a *shaver*. Aiken includes no final direct reference to shaving, but does infer, indirectly, to the state of a "shaved" man in the last scene. We see Michael Lowes sitting on the edge of his bed in his cell, thinking of his past life—his childhood, his college years, his days as a husband and a father. By the final line of the story, Michael realizes: "It [that whole life] had all come foolishly to an end." He is now figuratively a shaved man. His theft has erased his entire previous life and leads him back down, in the structure of the story, to the second low point of the inverted-V. Just as Michael's movement from the peak of illusion to harsh reality places him in a more painful situation than his first low illusory state, this shaving is more drastic than Michael's first ritual action, because it exposes that lower side of his human nature which lies beneath civilization's thin skin. Finally perceiving his degradation mirrored in Dora's last glance, Michael guesses she is probably "wondering what sort of people criminals might be. Human? Sub-human?" And through that one short reference to sub-humanness, we can sense Aiken wondering how far mankind has indeed developed since its cave man days.

The less obvious imagery of the card game is also noteworthy. The four men are playing bridge, and, more specifically, contract bridge. Aside from their use as card game titles, both "bridge" and "contract" suggest attempts to overcome some type of abyss separating human beings, and Aiken plays with these definitions through his tale. The noun and verb forms of "bridge" denote times, places, means of, or attempts at connection or transition. In the first half of the story, Michael feels that he has achieved reasonable connections in many of his relationships; but this first half, we remember, shows Michael's growing illusions about himself, and we can see that he is just as deluded in his belief that he has established any true relationships with others. His only thoughts before breakfast with Dora concern ways to avoid her possible questions about his irresponsible ways. For this reason, he cannot confront her with the fact that he will not be home after work: "He would wait till late in the afternoon, and then telephone to Dora as if it had all come up suddenly. Hello, Dora—is that you, old girl? Yes, this is Michael—Smith has asked me to drop in for a hand of bridge—you know—so I'll just have a little snack in town. Home by the last car as usual." Because Michael takes Dora for granted, his attitude cannot help to establish a strong relationship between them. In addition, Michael's three friends, if friends they can be called, are hardly closer to him than his wife. Too distant from these men to call any of them by their first names, Michael refers to them simply as "Hurwitz, Bryant, and Smith." And the only kind word Michael has to say about Hurwitz is that he "always provided good alcohol." Actually, his first thoughts about the three men are extremely condescending: "Not that he liked Hurwitz or Bryant or Smith—cheap fellows, really—mere pick-up acquaintances. . . . They were all right enough. Good enough for a little escape, a little party." His feeble attempts to bridge the chasm separating all individuals are superficial and ritualized, and require only as much thought and effort as his morning shave. Rather than being solid networks of communication and understanding, Michael's bridges are as insubstantial as if they had been built with shaving lather.

The second half of the story exposes Michael's "insubstantial bridgework" for all its flimsiness, and follows the V-structure of the story, just as the shaving imagery did. Both images are pictured as literal actions in the first half of the story; the second half, however, reveals them in a reversed, figurative, and more disastrous light. Thus Michael begins with the act of shaving, but ends figuratively shaved; he also begins playing a game of bridge, but by playing the wrong cards in life, ends up destroying all his bridges to the present point.

Here we might examine one final use of the term "bridge." Anyone acquainted with the rudiments of contract bridge knows that players must remain alert and account for the cards which have been played. Yet Michael is not at all engrossed in the game after the discussion about impulse. At one point after "the game was resumed," we find him dreamily contemplating various impulses—both his own and those of other people. Then Aiken tells us: "the game interrupted his recollections." If Michael has been able to entertain all these thoughts before the game interrupts him, he has either been playing a very bad hand, or has been sitting idly by with reason—the reason being that he has been the "dummy" for this hand.

Indeed, considering the four men in the room, we see that only Michael is fool enough to bid for and contract the undertaking of such an impulse without realizing its entire implication. And to continue with the bridge game terminology, we might say that because of his lack of insight regarding the repercussions a failure might bring, he is a real dummy. Having failed to take the decisive trick, Michael finally loses the game of life he has thus far bridged.

Aiken leaves us with no doubts about Michael's downfall in this story. The author's imagery shows his character shaved and isolated, and his structure brings the man to a lower point than ever before. Once Michael had seen the inverted-V in the mirror, he should have known that the hand his human nature had been dealt contained sufficient points only for defeat—not victory. (pp. 375-80)

Carolyn Handa, "'Impulse': Calculated Artistry in Conrad Aiken," in Studies in Short Fiction, *Vol. XII, No. 4, Fall, 1975, pp. 375-80.*

Bernard Winehouse (essay date 1978)

[*In the following essay, Winehouse disputes Carolyn Handa's interpretation of "Impulse," basing his argument on an examination of point of view, characterization, and biblical allusions in the story. For Handa's commentary, see the essay dated 1975.*]

This article was prompted by the reading of Carolyn Handa's analysis of Conrad Aiken's **"Impulse"** in *Studies in Short Fiction.* As I see it, Miss Handa interprets this story in a manner diametrically opposed to the spirit and the form of its conception. She describes **"Impulse"** as a "tale of a man defeated by exposing his inherently criminal nature"; civilized and uncivilized elements in the story are juxtaposed and Michael Lowes, the protagonist is criminally arraigned as uncivilized. Michael's act of stealing is, according to Miss Handa, illustrative of "man's anti-social tendencies" and that it is Aiken's purpose in this story to show mankind as "criminal ex-post facto". The structure is described in terms of an inverted "V" in which Michael, after a faint upward swing of illusion, falls to ignominy and defeat. I find that Miss Handa's discussion of rather peripheral symbolism such as the inverted "V", the bridge game and the act of shaving lead us into an analysis which moves away from the central concerns of the story; these concerns in fact call upon the reader to make an almost total identification with Michael Lowes, a character whom Miss Handa would make the villain of the piece. I will illustrate Aiken's "calculated artistry" in terms of point of view, characterization and biblical allusion, all of which serve in **"Impulse"** to exonerate rather than condemn the protagonist.

The point of view in **"Impulse"** makes a very clear call for sympathy with Michael Lowes. The technique of third person limited omniscience allows the events of the story to be seen almost entirely through the prism of Michael's thought—with surprisingly little ironic intrusion, explicit or implied, on the part of the omniscient narrator. No moral condemnation of any kind is made by the narrator. The reader's insight into Michael's mind reveals a bored little man in a lonely and hideously alien world who seeks cheap palliatives for his condition. Michael himself is seen to evince a considerable degree of self-knowledge as to the realities of his situation. He speaks of his bi-weekly "day of escape" from his miseries; his card-partners are "cheap fellows" and he sees no harm in his unashamed deceptions of his wife, Dora. Michael soberly acknowledges that his outing is merely "a little night off" and no more than "a little diversion." He inhabits a world in which he finds that the only solace from the day's dumb round is "a little escape," "a little party" or in the exercise of impulse in the search for "real satisfaction" in life. Likewise, Michael is well aware of the "real reason" for entering the shop from which he will steal. His repeated choice here of words like "little" and "real" suggests that he understands his motives quite clearly. In fine, point of view, whether in the reporting of thought process or in the exercise of the narrator's privilege of comment, consistently refuses to apportion any criticism to Michael's behaviour.

A vital complement to the psychological realism embodied in the third person (central) limited omniscient point of view is the use of peripheral characterization to underscore questions of theme. Such characterization in **"Impulse"** delineates a world in which self-knowing neer-do-wells such as Michael Lowes are decidedly preferable to any of the time-serving or establishment figures who betray and outlaw him. Without exception, there is no character in the story who is in any sense "reliable," who would suggest in terms of the fictional world created, a valid criticism of Michael. Dora is a fair-weather wife who kicks her husband when he is down. The coldness and cliché style of her significantly brief letter indicate the narrator's distaste for her. Michael's friends deny him even the minimum of help in his trouble and the repulsive detective who arrests him is portrayed with brief venom. Finally, the judge and his verdict are presented in satirical terms: "He [Michael] was a college man of exceptional education and origin, and ought to have known better. His general character might be good enough, but as against all this, here was a perfectly clear case of theft, and a perfectly clear motive." The judge, like the world at large, has no doubts as to questions of guilt, so Michael is sentenced, in the pomposity-larded words of the judge, "to three months in the house of correction." All is betrayal: "There but for the grace of God go I" becomes a mirror in which no character can see himself.

But the most persuasive signposting of all, though, as we have seen, point of view and characterization have been powerful in their impact, is found in the central, expanding allusion in the story to the myth of Eden. Surprisingly, Miss Handa makes no reference at all to this very rich element in the story. This pattern of allusion is first made evident in the course of the card game which precedes the theft. The conversation during the game and Michael's thoughts are punctuated throughout with a connotatively precise group of words: "impulse," "temptation," "stealing," "caught, by God," "opening . . . eyes wide," "Christ," "hell," "yield," "fascinating," "thrills." Likewise there are four references in the conversation of the card players to woman's temptation of man. Michael's theft of a "snakeskin box," "a delicious object" which contains a "gold razor" is a clear reference to the theft of Eve, and his attempts to escape from the detective recall those of Adam and Eve as they hid amongst the trees of Eden. The pre-lapsarian world of Michael appears to have the beauty and the blessing of God: "The lights on the snow were very beautiful. The Park Street Church was ringing, with its queer, soft quarter-bells, the half-hour." His exit in the custody of the detective, after the theft, is described in very different terms. What we have here is a parody of the exit from Eden: " . . . he was firmly conducted through a back door into a dark alley at the rear of the store. It had stopped snowing. A cold wind was blowing. But the world which looked so beautiful fifteen minutes before, had now lost its charm. They walked together down the alley in six inches of powdery snow, the detective holding Michael's arm with affectionate firmness." Michael's direct appeals to God and the God-like lieutenant at the police station "writing slowly in a book" serve to expand the allusion further. Finally, Michael's despairing reaction to his wife's betrayal of their marriage suggests a vision of Adam seeing his Eve naked for the first time:

> He gazed at this queer cold little female with intense curiosity. It was simply extraordinary—simply astonishing. Here she was, seven years his wife, he thought he knew her inside and out, every quirk of her handwriting, inflection of voice; her passion for strawberries, her ridiculous way of singing; the brown moles on her shoulder, the extreme smallness of her feet and toes, her dislike of silk underwear. Her special voice at the telephone, too—that rather chilly abruptness, which had always surprised him, as if she might be a much harder woman than he thought her to be. . . . He knew all these things, which nobody else knew, and nevertheless, now, they amounted to nothing.

The quiet close of this story of maturation takes the form of an epiphany in which Michael Lowes realizes clearly that his past life, which had been composed of "trivial and infinitely charming little episodes," had come to an end. Michael will or will not change but he is now a wiser man. But the central theme of this story is concerned with the frightening tedium of the human condition which can be relieved only by an occasional act of "impulse" made for "kicks"—as that Americanism puts it. Often the richness of allusion allows a literary work to make a comment on the source of the borrowing. Aiken says, perhaps, that God overacted in dooming the inhabitants of Eden to expulsion, just as society overacts in this story by betraying Lowes for a very ordinary piece of human behaviour. Aiken implies that the reader should not commit the same act of betrayal for Lowes is a mirror of our own being. "What would be more human," asks Michael as he begins to see himself as a "Columbus of the moral world." Impulse is a momentary circumvention of the stabilizing Ego, a hubristic refusal to accept the dictates of "a cockeyed world" of boredom and routine, the disciplines of life's Eden. Lowes "remembers his mother always saying, 'Michael, you *must* learn to be orderly.' " The First Sin was and still is the Sin of all mankind; the extended biblical allusion of this story and the clear functional thrust of point of view and characterization persuade us that indeed "impulse" is a "universal human inclination." No, this is not "the tale of a man defeated by exposing his inherently criminal nature," as Miss Handa would persuade us. (pp. 107-10)

Bernard Winehouse, " 'Impulse': Calculated Artisty in Conrad Aiken," in Studies in Short Fiction, *Vol. 15, No. 1, Winter, 1978, pp. 107-10.*

Arthur Waterman (essay date 1979)

[In the following essay, Waterman provides an overview of Aiken's short stories.]

In 1921, Conrad Aiken [in an essay collected in his *A Reviewer's ABC*] called Chekov "possibly the greatest writer of the short story who has ever lived." Aiken supported this claim by praising Chekov's colloquial tone, which gave his stories a "quality of natural, seemingly artless, actuality—casual and random in appearance," and by saying that Chekov's genius lay in his evocation of mood, his "range of states of consciousness." Aiken called Chekov a poet, in the sense that he was the kind of writer who improvised without adopting the careful selectivity of incidents that James did and without following the well-made frame of Maupassant. Chekov was an author who emphasized mood by conveying an impression of life, creating, thereby, a lyric mood missing in more conscious writers. Next, Aiken praised Katherine Mansfield as a short story writer of "unique sensibility," who followed Chekov in preferring mood over form, but who lacked the tremendous range of the Russian master. A few years later, when Aiken published his first volume of short stories, ***Bring! Bring!*** (1925), he revealed that he, too, was a disciple of Chekov, and Andreyev; for he wrote his stories in a direct, almost artless, tone, emphasized the quality of an experience more than character delineation or plot development, and created a variety of incidents and voices that surpassed Miss Mansfield's limited range. Although the eclectic nature of ***Bring! Bring!*** was somewhat narrowed by an emphasis on love in ***Costumes by Eros*** (1928) and by a focus on the failure of consciousness in ***Among the Lost People*** (1934), the thirty-nine stories that make up these three volumes prove that, with the exception of less than a dozen tales, Aiken was following Chekov, not James. These stories stress experience rather than technique, life not art, the immediate impression instead of the deliberate artifact. So, when Aiken collected twenty-nine of his stories for the ***Short Stories of Conrad Aiken*** (1950), he placed them in random order, with no perceivable chronological, thematic, or technical progression. They were being presented, that is, as unselected impressions, as haphazard and spontaneous as the reality they mirrored, yet broad enough in range and varied enough in mood to be true to the living world from which they came.

Their range is astonishing. We meet professors, prostitutes, farmers, businessmen, journalists, writers, nurses, taxidrivers, tourists, carnival performers, children, and that ubiquitous everyman "Smith, or Jones, or Robinson, or whatever his name happened to be." And the moods they express are equally varied: humorous, sad, ironic, satiric, macabre, cruel, insane, sentimental, erotic, and melancholy. For all their infinite variety, however, these stories are clearly the work of one writer, "stamped," according to Mark Schorer [in his preface to ***The Collected Short Stories of Conrad Aiken,*** 1960], "with the mark of his imagination . . . written by Conrad Aiken alone." Since they carry the clear imprint of Aiken's imagination, they are much more than an up-to-date echo of Chekov. They continue the emphasis found in all Aiken's writings, one that places him at the center of twentieth-century literature, namely his consistent use of psychology as the basis for his art.

He once said [in the *Paris Review,* 1968], "Freud was in everything I did," which meant that in Freudian psychology Aiken discovered both an explanation for the cultural and personal chaos he saw as a condition of modern life, and also as a possible resolution to that chaos. In the five novels he published alternately with his volumes of short stories, Aiken explored man's capacity to grow in self-knowledge through an "evolution of consciousness." His fictional heroes are so driven by their subconscious repressions that they cry out their inner pain, expose their anguish, and then, through a confession, begin to free themselves from those inner frustrations so they can turn away from them to the living world outside. They make a journey of the mind, even in one case directed by a psychiatrist, which is told in a modified stream-of-consciousness style, using the dream-confession as the means for self-knowledge. The short stories, however, are far more restricted in the extent of the psychological evolution they can develop, so Aiken usually limits the hero's discovery to a single, compelling moment in his life, an insight not revealed through the complex symbolism of the dream, but related by means of a letter or reminiscence. The emphasis in both the novels and the tales is the same—the growth in consciousness through self-knowledge—but the development is different. In the stories we take a step along the journey the novels complete. Jay Martin [in his *Conrad Aiken: A Life of His Art*] identifies the focus in the short stories as "confessional" fiction, where "the writer conceals his art because he is primarily interested in elucidating the experience itself. He will ferret out the crucial moments of life when the individual—arriving at what Carl Jaspers calls 'frontier situations'—is able to understand momentarily the basic things of the soul. Life as he sees it, is not a problem to be solved, but a reality to be experienced."

Because the stories do not trace the intricate psychological growth of the novels, they substitute impressions of reality. The tales are often fragments taken from someone's life, with little shape, direction, or completeness, almost devoid of plot or character. In following Chekov, Aiken risks slicing his life a little too thin and sometimes offers his readers incidents that border on the trivial. An example is the story **"I Love You Very Dearly,"** where a perturbed father writes a letter to his married daughter after a quarrel between them has caused him to go abroad. He confesses his responsibility for the quarrel and hints that he would like to return and live with her, but he goes on to chastize her for having an affair. In an outpouring of jealousy and concern, he uses his own life as an example of the cruelty possible in human relationships, admitting his errors in the past in the hope that she will profit from them. We feel the poignancy of his appeal and recognize the unconscious irony in his confession, but the story ends before we discover whether or not his letter has succeeded, either in persuading her to invite him back or in convincing her to drop her affair, and whether his confession has taught him anything about himself. What saves many of Aiken's stories from the ephemeral quality of a piece like **"I Love You Very Dearly"** is his tough honesty, a trait he admired in Chekov. Aiken sees life as it is and knows how limited we are in coping with its complexities. He likes to begin a story with a description of the "living world," as he once called it [in his preface to *Three Novels,* 1965]: "the taste, touch, sight, smell, immediacy and rankness, and sheer appallingness, of the living world itself, in its inevitable and daily appearance: the brutal and beautiful here-and-now of it, its absurdity, the inexhaustible comicality of it, its cruelty, even its lunacy."

Many of Aiken's characters evade or deny the demands of the real world, answering instead to the call of self, insisting that the "here-and-now" is what they neither deserve nor desire. In love, or facing death, however, they encounter two significant moments that test their consciousness, "frontier situations" that force them to balance the imperatives of self with the harsh cries of reality. Love is the key which unlocks the prison of self, for it requires that we reach out and risk involvement, hazard the pain of denying the ego to gain the reward of loving another person. Death is the ultimate moment when we face the burden of our lives and have to account for our destiny. As he lies dying on a hospital operating table Mr. Arcularis imagines that he is on a sea voyage. He makes an unconscious confession that reveals to the reader, and perhaps to himself, that his life has been as empty and cold as are the images that convey his death. The distant stars, the inescapable cold, the fog and mist, the lost opportunity for affection with Miss Dean, the voyage itself—all manifest his unconscious realization that he is dying, and they also serve to symbolize the terms of his lonely and pathetic life. James W. Tuttleton [in his 1963 essay in *American Imago*] has convincingly shown that Mr. Arcularis undergoes a kind of Jungian atavism as the tale develops: "The first stage of regression takes Mr. Arcularis back to his childhood; the second withdraws him further to the mother's womb; the third takes him further back to a prehistoric stage of phylogenetic evolutionary development; and the fourth takes him back to the genesis of all things, the moment of creation." Thus Mr. Arcularis traces a universal and frightening journey, in which he both dreams his own death and repeats the regressive history of man. Indeed, it seems probable that as he reviews his lost life in the deepest recesses of his mind, Mr. Arcularis wills his death, transmuting the emblems of that wasted life into the "great white light of annihilation." Death, Aiken says, is the test of life, the moment when the burden of the history of man as a single self and as everyman, comes full circle. This moment reveals to Mr. Arcularis his failure to live, to love, and consequently causes him to accept death willingly.

"The Last Visit" juxtaposes love and death to show how a woman in love cannot possibly comprehend the anguish of another woman who is dying. Marie Schley visits her dying grandmother as an excuse so she can also spend the day with her lover. Her visit evokes from her remembrances of her childhood, when she lived with the older woman, causes her to wonder what the dying woman wants from her, and leads her to anticipate her afternoon's dalliance with her lover. Her grandmother cries out to her, "I can't die! I can't die! . . . I want to die and I can't!" and Marie is struck by the differences between the old woman's fear and loneliness and her own passion and vitality: "Life suddenly seemed to her extraordinarily complex, beautiful, and miserable." But when she tries to articulate her mixed feelings to her lover, he says simply, "It's the way things are." To show the way things are is the purpose of the story, which depicts a woman dying alone, afraid and upset, another moved by her lover's touch to a "delicious feeling of weakness." Encompassing them both is reality, symbolized by the figure of a vaudeville singer, who is coarse, colorful, amoral, and vital: "A blackface singer, on the stage, was singing coarsely. The blinding disc of spotlight, with its chromatic red edge, illuminating his bluish makeup, made his tongue an unnatural pink, sparkled the gold fillings in his wide teeth. *'[H]ot lips,'* he intoned grinning, *'that are pips . . . and no more conscience than a snake has hips'* . . .".

Another story, **"Your Obituary, Well Written,"** combines love and death to question whether the physical side of love can hamper its more spiritual side. In trying to determine what his obituary might say, the narrator decides that "the best, and perhaps the only, way of leaving behind a record of one's life . . . was that of relating some single episode of one's history; some single, and if possible central, episode in whose small prism all the colors and lights of one's soul might be seen." The narrator, who could be Aiken himself, tells of a brief, platonic relationship he had with a writer, Reine Wilson, who is modeled on Katherine Mansfield, with whom the narrator found an immediate and mutual rapport. She is dying, which gives a peculiar poignancy and delicacy to their meetings and draws the narrator's attention to her special sensitivity: "Her burning intensity of spirit, the sheer naked honesty with which she felt things, and the wonderful and terrible way in which she could appear so vividly and joyfully, and yet so precariously, alive. . . . It was, for me, terribly disturbing. I was going to fall in love with her—and I was going to fall hard and deep." Like Marie Schley, he is moved by the wonder and terror of life, so much so that he is afraid to alter the sensitive nature of their relationship by some overt act of passion, afraid that "some unguarded shaking of the tree [might] destroy the whole rare miracle." When, later, he hears of her death, he wanders in the Borghese Gardens, dazed by his loss, regretful that he never physically had loved her, yet grateful that she showed him the way to live by how she faced death; and Aiken brings out all these complex emotions in a brilliant passage summarizing his imaginary obituary by saluting the richness of life. In this closing paragraph, Aiken catches, not the strident coarseness of reality he depicted in **"The Last Visit,"** but the pain, beauty, and tender fragility of both love and death:

> Without knowing how I got there, I found myself presently in the Borghese Gardens. There was a little pond, in which a great number of ducks were sailing to and fro, gabbling and quacking, and children were throwing bread into the water. I sat down on a bench under a Judas-tree—it was in blossom, and the path under it was littered with purple. An Italian mother slapped the hand of her small boy who was crying, and said harshly, 'Piangi! . . . Piangi! . . .' Cry! Cry! . . . And I too felt like weeping, but I shed no tears. Reine Wilson the novelist was still alive; but Reine Wilson the dark-haired little girl with whom I had fallen in love was dead, and it seemed to me that I too was dead.

"Thistledown" contrasts with Aiken's tender tribute to Katherine Mansfield in **"Your Obituary, Well Written"** by presenting an ambiguous study of a nymphomaniac. The most Jamesian story Aiken ever wrote, **"Thistledown"** might be called an inverse *Daisy Miller.* Unlike James's narrator, Winterbourne, Aiken's narrator, Philip, does sexually possess his Coralyn, but like Winterbourne, he fails to understand and save the girl he might have loved. No Daisy, Coralyn is compared to a dandelion seed, beautiful, delicate, above all, fickle. In a sentence that expresses the ease and amorality of that moment, Philip recalls the day they became lovers: "We came together as naturally as leaf touches leaf or the grass bends to the wind." True to her vagrant nature, Coralyn soon leaves to live in New York. When Philip visits her and stays the night with her, she confesses to having had six affairs since their last meeting, and insists that her promiscuity is part of her naturalness. Yet she also admits, "I'm afraid, Philip! I'm afraid. I really am." Shocked, Philip offers advice instead of comfort, admonitions rather than security. With Philip as the central narrator, we trace in a series of dramatic scenes Coralyn's decline over a number of years: more affairs, a bad marriage, an inevitable hardening of her fragile nature. "I'm hard-boiled now," she warns him. Motivated by his conscious moral disapproval and subconscious sexual jealousy, Philip betrays her by betting a friend, notorious for his sexual escapades, that he cannot seduce Coralyn. Eventually the friend admits failure because Coralyn would sleep with him only on the condition that he pay her one-thousand dollars, and he tells Philip, "You know, I think she's in some sort of trouble." But it's too late for Philip to rescue Coralyn. She disappears and he ends the story expressing the hope that "for her sake, she is dead." Philip's point of view and involvement with Coralyn blur the readers' understanding of her; for, as in James, our reactions are ambiguous. Like Philip, we are charmed by her naturalness, offended by her actions, and confused by her appeals. But we are never sure how much of her irresponsible behavior derives from her desperate need for security and permanence. Obviously her tragedy is partly a result of her nature, but it is also a result of Philip's unwillingness to respond to her needs and give her the assurances she craved. I think Aiken wants us to view Philip as we do Winterbourne, that is as one who failed the test of love because he was selfish, who judged when he should have loved. He knew Coralyn too well, perhaps, and condemned her too quickly. He is the opposite of the narrator of **"Your Obituary, Well Written,"** because his sexual knowledge of Coralyn blinds him to her other qualities.

Some of Aiken's most terrifying tales are concerned with a different kind of failure than the failure to love or to understand the shock of death. These stories deal with the failure to face and accept "the sheer appallingness of the living world itself." Aiken calls his characters who refuse to accept reality "lost people," condemned to a hell of their own solipsism. Paul Hasleman, the autistic boy in **"Silent Snow, Secret Snow,"** who prefers his imaginative inner world of whiteness to the real world outside, is the most famous of these lost people. The power of **"Silent Snow, Secret Snow"** lies in its credibility, in Aiken's success in convincing us that Paul's vision is possible, even preferable, to the mailman, the school teacher, and his own parents. These outsiders intrude noisily into his secret peace and demand that he answer their letters, questions, and concerns. At first Paul is aware of and responds to these outer claims. He hears his teacher's voice and notices the freckled hand of the girl sitting in front of him, is pleased by the familiar and drab details of his walk home from school. But he is also inexorably attracted to the other world of falling snow, a new world that "was the profounder and more wonderful of the two. It was irresistible. It was miraculous. Its beauty was simply beyond anything." Only twelve years old, Paul cannot explain his double life, but he is sensitive and precocious enough to know that he must somehow balance the two worlds: "One must get up, one must go to breakfast, one must talk with Mother, go to school, do one's lessons—and, in all this, try not to appear too much of a fool. But if all the while one was also trying to extract the full deliciousness of another and quite separate existence, one which could not easily (if at all) be spoken of—how was one to manage?" His dilemma culminates when he realizes that he must choose either to return to the living world where the mailman's steps can be heard on the cobblestones, or to descend into his private world where nothing, not even the mailman, can enter. The busy, querulous inquisition of his parents and the doctor makes his choice easy and his schizophrenia turns into an autistic vision, closing inward upon itself to cold, silent death. Aiken's mastery in creating psychological studies, almost case-histories, is wonderfully exhibited by **"Silent Snow, Secret Snow."** As in his novel *King Coffin,* Aiken centers the narrative inside the mind of a disturbed person, a stylistic achievement in its psychological accuracy and believability. Surrounded by fragments of the rough real world, torn newspapers, dirty sparrows, discarded letters, Paul prefers "a ghost of snow falling in the bright sunlight, softly and steadily floating and turning and pausing, soundlessly meeting the snow that covered, as with a transparent mirage, the bare, bright cobbles." Not surprisingly, we willingly choose with Paul to reject the dirty, noisy world for his secret, silent whiteness, for we have been hypnotized by Aiken's superb rendition of his mad but credible vision.

Paul's case is extreme, perhaps, but not unique. In **"Gehenna,"** for example, the narrator muses on the possibility that anyone's "world can go to pieces," if he allows his mind to loose itself from reality and drift into "the glorious Gehenna which we are." Like Paul, he wills his mind to concentrate on a doorknob to the exclusion of everything else, collapsing to the point where he is alone in a self-made world "of which the only tenable principle is horror." Here, he faces the ultimate question of self-existence: "Is my name Smith? But how preposterous. What on earth is a Smith? Would the Pole Star know me? Would the Pleiades take off their hats to me, or a jury of molecules pronounce me a unit? In short, would the universe admit that it had produced me, or assume the slightest responsibility for me?" His questions are answered by a dream he has, where his mind is completely detached from reality, adrift in a solipsistic nightmare. What he sees in his dream is an aquarium in which some kind of creature on one side is trying to crawl to the other side, from water into air, and he realizes that this is consciousness "trying to escape from the medium out of which it was created . . . and suddenly I am so horrified at the notion of a consciousness which is pure suffering, that I wake up." He wakes to the sound of a clock striking the hour, sounds of order which negate the implications of the dream. Although **"Gehenna"** is a little too absurd to be acceptable, even a bit sophomoric in its metaphysical doubts, it does establish the two worlds of much of Aiken's fiction, and their precarious relationship to each other.

In **"Gehenna,"** the two worlds exist side by side, with the image of consciousness unable to reach across from its water world of self to the air world of externality, suggesting that man lives in a universe in which he is an alien. What might be even more interesting is the possibility that the two worlds in fact depend upon and emerge from each other, that the nightmare and the stars share a common source. Such a possibility ought to alleviate the dread which permeates **"Gehenna,"** but in **"The Dark City"** this possibility leads to harrowing conclusions. The story is a parable of a sinister Eden. A man returns from his busy business life in the city to his suburban paradise, where he is happily enslaved by a wife, three children, and a garden. Hoeing his peas he imagines he is pleasing mother earth by scratching her back; transplanting strawberries he pretends he is in "the best of all possible worlds" where, God-like, he bestows life. The first two sections of the story are brimming with delight and harmony: family, nature, self—all in apparent Edenic rapture. Then, after supper, he looks out over the shadowed land "to see once more the dim phantasmal outlines of the dark city, the city submerged under the infinite sea, the city not inhabited by mortals. Immense, sinister, and black, old and cold as the moon . . . it faded, a profound and vast secret, an inscrutable mystery." He explains to his wife that the city is inhabited by "maggots of perhaps the size of human children . . . it is the universe that they devour; and they build above it, as they devour it, their dark city like a hollow tomb. . . . Extraordinary that this city, which seen from here at dusk has so supernatural a beauty, should hide at the core so vile a secret . . ." Although a first reading might suggest that the bright bucolic outer reality is at odds with the disturbed inner vision of the dark city, we should realize that the garden and the city actually mirror each other. The maggots who inhabit the city are human size, like the narrator's own children, who quarrel among themselves and complain while they eat supper and even urge their father to squash and kill caterpillars. His wife cannot stay awake for their evening chess game and dreams that her husband is Bluebeard. He identifies with his primitive, ape-like ancestors as he works his garden. The point is that he has repressed these imperfections beneath a cloak of ironic chatter and deliberate foolishness. But the more he deceives himself in order to maintain the purity of his paradise, the more vile and grotesque will be his subconscious vision, for to deny the chaotic nature of reality is to foster irrational terrors within the mind. Eden is a lie, because the garden and the city are one.

The secret snow, the terrifying dream, the dark city—these are manifestations of the failure of consciousness. For Aiken, modern man is not "lost" in the traditional sense of being removed from God, but in the psychological sense of denying the truth about life, whose nature is suggested by the approaching mailman, the striking clock, and the imperfect garden. Many of Aiken's characters are lost in this psychological, secular sense. In **"Anniversary,"** a man drunkenly fantasizes killing his wife so that he can be free to enjoy what he imagines to be the carefree life of a bachelor friend, who is in fact an overworked doctor, with no time for chorus girls and the like. In **"Impulse,"** a man thinks shoplifting will be a thrilling experience; but when he steals, he is caught, tried, convicted, and jailed. Over and over Aiken records the tragedies of losers, people who neither know themselves nor understand the nature of reality. Yet a few of Aiken's people overcome the failure of consciousness by growing away from the confines of self and through love and self-knowledge learn to accept, even welcome, the "beautiful and brutal here-and-now of it." A line in one of Aiken's poems goes, "Walk with me world, upon my right hand walk," and these people are saved by walking with the world. If our Gehenna is secular, so must be our salvation.

The secular emphasis in Aiken's stories is nowhere better seen than in **"Life Isn't a Short Story."** Here, the tough honesty Aiken so admired in Chekov, which is the hallmark of his own criticism and autobiography *Ushant,* establishes a realistic commentary on life and art. Caught by two phrases he has overheard, "as I live and breathe!" and "in the flesh!", a writer begins to imagine a story about Gladys, whose absurd pretensions of culture cause her to separate from her ordinary husband, Sidney. To Gladys, Sidney is as cheap and as vulgar as is his favorite saying, "As I live and breathe"; to the writer, Gladys is equally silly and vulgar. He believes she is destroying both her own and Sidney's lives by her false illusions and her refusal to accept life "in the flesh." But Aiken provides a third perspective, one which neither Gladys nor the writer has realized: what about Sidney? While the writer has been constructing his tale, he casually watches a deliveryman's horse quietly, patiently making his rounds through "thick and thin." Sidney and the horse represent the ordinary business of living, of getting through the day, with neither the falseness of Gladys nor the fantasies of the writer. In his closing paragraph, constituting his own imaginative rendition of the commonplace, Aiken superbly renders the living world in the flesh:

> The towel-supply man came running back with a basket, flung it into the wagon, banged the dripping doors shut, and then jumped nimbly up to his seat, unhooking the reins. Automatically, but as if still deep in thought, the horse leaned slowly forward, lowered his head a little, and began to move. A long day was still ahead of him, a day of crowded and noisy streets, streets full of surprises and terrors and rain, muddy uneven cobbles and greasy smooth asphalt. The wagon and the man would be always there behind him; an incalculable sequence of accidents and adventures was before him. What did he think about, as he plodded from one dirty restaurant to another; one hotel to another, carrying towels? Probably nothing at all; certainly no such sentimental thing as a green meadow, nor anything so ridiculous as a story about living and breathing. It was enough, even if one was a slave, to live and breathe. For life, after all, isn't a short story.

"Strange Moonlight" turns what might have been a Poe-like horror tale into an initiation story, where a child discovers the meaning of life. A boy wins a gold medal at school, but instead of happily showing it off to his parents, he hides his award to keep himself from any involvement in outward achievement. In place of his own lively family, he prefers to visit the Lees, who live in a dim, mysterious house, strangely silent and dark. He is especially drawn to Caroline Lee because she is "strange and beautiful," quite different from his bothersome brother and sister and quarrelsome parents. Obviously, he is on his way into the same kind of withdrawal Paul makes in **"Silent Snow, Secret Snow,"** and when Caroline dies he begins to imagine conversations with her in which he asks the dead girl what death is like: "But after they've shut you up in a coffin and sung songs over you and carried you to Bonaventure and buried you in the ground, and you're down there in the dark with all that earth above you—isn't that horrible?" He imagines her answering, "You climb out of the earth just as easily as you'd climb out of bed." In his innocence, the child can only equate the mystery of death to what he knows of life: the grave is a bed where one sleeps. Death, therefore, is like the living world, only better. But, one day, the boy and his family travel to the beach where the children bury their father in the sand. To the boy his father appears to be in a grave, and like Caroline, "alive in it, and talking, and able to get up whenever he liked." But, suddenly, his father "leapt out of his tomb, terrifying them, scattered his grave clothes in every direction, and galloped gloriously down the beach into the sea." The transformation of the entombed father into the living man helps the boy realize the difference between Caroline's strange and secret death and the terror and glory of life. When the family returns home that evening, the moonlight completes his initiation by allowing him, as Hoffman says [in *Conrad Aiken*], "to translate from the imaginary to the real, even though both have aspects that are strangely alike." The moonlight reminds him of death because it is so strange, "like a deep river," touching and smothering everything with its silent, silver presence. Its very strangeness, that is, emphasizes its difference from the real and normal, so when the child goes to his room to tell Caroline about the moonlight, "he realized at last that Caroline is dead." Her death at first accelerated his tendency to withdraw from life, but in the end her death saves him by making him recognize that death is strangely different from life.

The delicious, difficult, reluctant, pleasures and pains of love are caught in **"Spider, Spider."** As he is explaining to Gertrude why he wants to marry May, Harry lets himself be persuaded to forget his love for the absent May and take, instead, the willing Gertrude who stands before him. The delightful humor in the story comes from a juxtaposition of Harry's inner thoughts and Gertrude's aggressive acts. He watches himself, in bemused fascination, become her partially willing victim, letting her mock his affection for May, resisting her not too subtle appeals, consciously analyzing her actions, while, at the same time, he is being drawn closer to her web. "She had the restlessness of a caged animal," he thinks to himself, "feline, and voluptuous, and merciless. She wanted to protect him, did she, from that 'designing' May? But she also, patently, wanted to devour him." For a moment at the end of the story, Aiken touches on the dangers and fears of giving oneself to another stronger, more determined self: "Good God—

how horrible! He closed his eyes to the chaos and terror of the future; to the spiritual deaths of himself and May; the betrayal and the agony. . . ." But Aiken saves Harry and the story by continuing, "And then he felt himself beginning to smile; while with his finger and thumb, he gently tweaked a tiny golden watch-spring of hair which curled against the nape of the white neck." Quite possibly the victim has skillfully arranged his capture and the seduced is really the seducer. Emily Dickinson once wrote, "Love is its own rescue"; and with exactly the right tone and in scenes of sharply realized detail, Aiken shows us love's rescue; its demands, complications, difficulties, along with its playfulness, eroticism, and joy. We recall lines from the last Prelude in *Time in the Rock,* which put into a lyric cry what **"Spider, Spider"** is about:

> Simple one, simpleton,
> when will you learn the flower's simplicity—
> lie open to all comers, permit yourself
> to be rifled—fruitfully too—by other selves?
> Self, and other self—permit them, permit them—

I quote from the poetry to remind us, quite frankly, that Aiken is a greater poet than he is a writer of short stories. His forty-three tales reflect the psychological basis found in all his art, and they would be the foundation of a literary reputation for some authors. But in Aiken's case they are the lesser part of a larger canon. Taken together the stories do not make a larger whole, do not develop toward a divine pilgrimage as does the poetry. Their limitations, however, bring out an aspect of Aiken's writing frequently overlooked when we discuss the novels or the poetry. Unlike the extended psychological journey to consciousness traced in the novels, or unlike the growth, in symphonic structure, toward spiritual regeneration found in the poetry, Aiken's short stories are confined to secular concerns. At their worst they are limited by their Chekovian impressionism to become no more than fragments of experience, insubstantial, even trivial. They succeed in what is essentially an achievement of style, or styles, that record how man encounters reality. As we have seen, the tales often treat "lost" people who are cut off from the harsh world around them and who have retreated into an inner vision. Aiken masterfully creates that other world, the secret, inner world of the nightmare, where a man dreams his death, a child wills himself into a white sleep, a garden cloaks a horrifying vision, and love can be twisted into jealousy and betrayal. His stylistic "rightness," at once psychologically accurate and emotionally credible, easily carries the reader into that "lost" world:

> And the mist of snow, as he had foreseen, was still on it—a ghost of snow falling in the bright sunlight, softly and steadily floating and turning and pausing, soundlessly meeting the snow that covered, as with a transparent mirage, the bare, bright cobbles. He loved it—he stood still and loved it. Its beauty was paralyzing—beyond all words, all experience, all dream. No fairy story he had ever read could be compared with it—none had ever given him this extraordinary combination of ethereal loveliness with a something else, unnameable, which was just faintly and deliciously terrifying.

On the other hand, some of the most memorable scenes from the stories are those that depict the acute realness of things as they are: a man recalling a lost love while surrounded by crying children (Piangi! . . . Piangi!), ducks gabbling, and purple flowers; a boy frightened by the apparition of his father rising from his grave of sand; a horse standing patiently while rain pours off his back; a man happily succumbing to the wiles of the seductress before him. These two worlds—things as they are and our imaginative version of them—shape Aiken's short stories and affirm their secular nature. We can say of these tales what Aiken says about Chekov: in them we are made aware of "the sound of life," and we discover "beings through whose rich consciousness, intense and palpable, we are enabled to live, backward and forward, in time, lives as appallingly genuine as our own." (pp. 19-31)

Arthur Waterman, "The Short Stories of Conrad Aiken," in Studies in Short Fiction, *Vol. 16, No. 1, Winter, 1979, pp. 19-31.*

Edward Butscher (essay date 1982)

[An American critic and educator, Butscher is the author of Conrad Aiken: Poet of White Horse Vale *(1988), a critical biography of Aiken. In the following essay, Butscher discusses "Silent Snow, Secret Snow," "Mr. Arcularis," and "Strange Moonlight," focusing on the biographical, literary, and psychological influences on Aiken's short fiction.]*

Frederick J. Hoffman, whose [*Conrad Aiken*] is punctuated by numerous shrewd insights, has declared that at his best "Aiken is a superb storyteller. He succeeds much more often in the short form than in the novel." The validity of his judgement is, I believe, beyond question, since none of Aiken's five novels ever achieves the organic power necessary to guarantee whatever passes for immortality in literature, despite the professional flow of their narratives and the presence of individual sections of great beauty and acumen. Even in the impressive short stories, which number over fifty, excluding the handful written and published at Harvard during Aiken's undergraduate years, rarely does the most sympathetic critic come across that essential melding of method and complex means required for a literary transcendence of time, place, and self. Probably only three stories—**"Silent Snow, Secret Snow," "Mr. Arcularis,"** and **"Strange Moonlight"**—are destined to remain a permanent part of our cultural heritage.

The reasons for this are many and varied, at least on the surface, but the fundamental cause of Aiken's lack of ultimate success with fiction can be traced back to the basic quality of his imagination, which was that of a lyric poet, almost autistic in its concentration upon self, incapable of 'inventing' other characters and their realities because never sufficiently aware of other people's existence. Sympathy and craft are possible to such an ego, but the broad empathy necessary to recreate the interior dimensions of exterior beings never is. Without it, fiction becomes, inevitably, the poet's story, the story of the vulnerable self that can but fragment experience into component egos (Eliot's "broken bundle of mirrors") rather than into legitimate human alternatives, contrary personalities. Its energy is the energy of lyric mourning over its own wounds and lost past, and its most natural form of expression is the stream-of-consciousness technique that emerged in full bloom with the publication of the initial volume of *À la recherche du temps perdu* in 1913.

It should be remembered that fiction for Aiken began as a way of making money, a very inadequate way as it turned out, and his first short stories, again excepting the Harvard pieces, started to appear in the early twenties after he had already written some six or seven collections of poetry, poetry marked by a variety of derivative styles, large thematic debts to Nietzsche, Freud, and T. S. Eliot, and a facile taste for meditative narratives. This was the period when Katherine Mansfield, who died in 1923, was regarded in both England and America as one of the leading short story writers, despite the fact that her tales retained an anecdotal frame and an old-fashioned concept of mental processes strikingly at odds with the sophisticated stream-of-consciousness approach being practiced by Dorothy Richardson and James Joyce and handled with growing mastery by Virginia Woolf. Indeed, her style, a darkish compound of Chekhovian terseness and occasional O. Henry twists, seems far more at home with the nineteenth than the twentieth century, which might help explain why so few of her own works have endured.

And yet, it was the example of Mansfield, whom he had met and admired—she is "Reine Wilson" in his **"Your Obituary, Well Written"**—that had the most profound impact upon Aiken's short fiction. But Aiken, ever the astute critic, was never blind to either the precise nature of her achievement or its intrinsic limitations. In his 1921 review of *Bliss and Other Stories* for the *Freeman,* he isolated the undeniable Chekhovian influence but insisted upon elucidating its specific effect:

> What provokes one to say "Chekhov" is the fact that almost alone among writers of fiction in England and America Miss Mansfield has followed Chekhov in choosing to regard . . . the short story "form" not as the means to the telling of a tale, and not always or wholly as the means for the "lighting" of a single human character, but rather as the means for the presentation of a "quintessence," a summation of a human life or group of lives in the single significant "scene" or situation or episode; and, by implication, the illumination . . . of life itself. This, one observes, is the method of poetry.

After conceding Mansfield's narrowness of range in contrast to her Russian mentor, Aiken celebrated her "genius for a kind of short narrative poem in prose, a narrative lyric."

A year later, while reviewing *The Garden Party* for the same magazine, he reiterated his primary interpretation of the Mansfield logos, "the fact that Miss Mansfield goes to the short story as the lyric poet goes to poetry," locating her in the configuration of the "subjective" artist and stressing that her sensibilities, though original, were "remarkably limited." The crucial portion of the review dealt with characterization or, more appropriately, the lack of genuine characterization in the Mansfield sphere, where the people "are all Miss Mansfield, all speak with her voice, think as she thinks, are rapidly ecstatically aware, as she is aware; share her gestures and her genius; and represent, in short, not so many people or lives, but so many projections of Miss Mansfield's mind and personality into other people's bodies and houses." And in a final review four years after her death—this time of *The Journal of Katherine Mansfield* for *The Bookman*—he compared her to a Keats writing stories, praised her intensity, and continued to decry her lack of range, concluding that "in the finest sense, she *was* a poet: her nature was essentially a poetic one. Her stories were poems; they were as characteristically the products of the unconscious as any poems ever written."

The final note, so typically Freudian, suggests that Aiken grasped the foundational difference between poetry and fiction, at least between lyric poetry and standard fiction, though it can and should also be argued that the strongest fiction vents as much of the unconscious as the strongest poetry. Significantly, he realized that Mansfield's special talent lay not in the consciousness of alien consciousness, which tends to govern the fiction of, say, a Tolstoy or a Dickens, but in the ability of her finest stories, i.e., "The Garden-Party" and "Bliss," to convey the intensity of her unique perceptions through a persona that embodied a component ego. She was, then, like Dostoievsky, Proust, and her modernist contemporaries, a subjective writer, a poet's prose writer, who succeeded best when working close to the bone of emotion most directly affecting her own sensitive psyche, its particular obsessions.

Leaving aside considerations of the treacherous terrain sketched in by terms such as "subjective" and "objective," which was perhaps epitomized during Aiken's heyday as a critic by *The Sun Also Rises* and *The Great Gatsby,* what makes his acute reaction to Mansfield's art paramount, of course, is that it can be applied with equal force and weight to his own short fiction. It is easy to see that the three stories of his most deserving of permanence are precisely those in deepest contact with the psyche of their creator, if not always with his external biography. Two of these, **"Silent Snow, Secret Snow"** and **"Mr. Arcularis,"** have already attained consensus status as masterpieces of the genre, as frequent anthology appearances attest, and it is possible to pursue the knobbed trunk of their stubborn power back to fertile roots in Aiken's lifelong obsession with and fear of death and insanity.

In *Ushant,* which must be read with caution as the progress of a secular saint, a dazzling *tour de force* of autobiographical fiction superior to its main model, George Moore's *Confessions of a Young Man,* and comparable to Whitman's last revisions of *Leaves of Grass,* Aiken reveals the extent of death's grip upon his unconscious, manifesting itself in an endless chain of nightmares: "it was even arguable that in this sense what had happened was predestined, and inevitable, and that the act [a 1932 suicide attempt], in the end, and as it had so fortunately worked out, provided its own cure. Weren't his dreams, his whole lifetime of dreams, that unparalleled parade of monstrous fantasies and malformations, convincing enough evidence of this? The obsession with death, with abnormal sensibility and death, informed them everywhere: the reek of decay and dissolution and corruption arose from them every morning of his life."

Further on in the same passage, he alludes to a recurrent dream in which he perceives himself drawing "cartoons or portraits" of himself ("D.") that became "the real thing; a series of portraits or cartoons, of D.—D. in the process of dying; D., hurrying towards his death, into death; in each new panel the figure becoming more gaunt and skeletalized, the eyes further sunken into the hollow eye-sockets, the ribs more nakedly prominent, as it ran, stumbled, and fell, towards the sea—desperately trying to get to the sea, with some obscure notion of then swimming out into the sunset, into the light: until, in the final panel of all, the skeleton, at last bare, now lay prone, with empty and out-stretched hands, on the beach at the water's edge; disclosing, within the rib-case, where the heart should have been, but itself rotten and falling apart, and with crumbling amulets among the perishing pages, a copy of *The Book of the Dead.*"

Without essaying any glib analysis of the obvious return-to-the-womb *leit motif* laid bare here, it is evident that the terror of death pervaded Aiken's unconscious mind with vivid tenacity, a terror which relates to the murder-suicide of his parents when he was eleven years old. The death of a parent is devastating at any age, shifting an offspring's demise that much nearer, but the abrupt loss of both parents in adolescence has to entail awesome psychological ramifications. Added to and complicating this fear of death was a concomitant apprehension of madness, of going insane, the "*petit mal*" mentioned often in *Ushant,* which stemmed from the memory of the paranoia that had driven his once-adored father to shoot his wife and then himself in a fit of jealousy and despair. In spite of his subsequent commitment to the major tenets of Freudian theory emphasizing environmental factors over heredity, Aiken was convinced that the cause of his father's instability could be found in his marriage to a relative, a second cousin, that the *petit mal* ran in the family. When his sister Elizabeth had to be institutionalized in her thirties, he naturally regarded it as proof of the family's strain of madness, a conviction shared by his brother Kempton, a doctor, who refused to have children of his own because of it.

Aiken's oldest daughter, novelist Jane Aiken Hodge, when queried about her father's dread of insanity, replied, "I think all his life, yes, he felt himself a risk. . . . I certainly remember his saying to me that one of the reasons why he married my mother was because, as he put it, she was peasant stock." . . . Doubtless, the fear played a major role in his own nervous breakdown during the late 1920s and early 1930s, culminating in the suicide attempt described in *Ushant* and the evolution of his greatest poetic accomplishment, the two *Preludes* sequences. It is certainly no accident, further, that **"Silent Snow, Secret Snow"** and **"Mr. Arcularis"** date from the same fecund period.

Thanks to the efforts of Jay Martin, who Aiken accused of "being positively *perverse* in this obsession of yours about all the fiction being autobiographical," Aiken's comments on the supposed sources of almost all of his tales are available. For **"Silent Snow, Secret Snow,"** he drew upon "invention, imagination going far afield from a small premise," and the memory preserved in *Ushant,*" of a postman's footsteps in Rye "once muffled by a mirage of snow." Of **"Mr. Arcularis"** he was no less definite: "Based on a combination of a dream on shipboard and the simultaneous encounter with the real Mr. A. Fundamentally an invention of the imagination." In both instances Aiken is careful to give "invention" and "imagination" the bulk of the credit, downplaying whatever autobiographical elements were present. There is no reason to question the veracity of his statements regarding the stories' genesis, but his own background, his dedicated study of the convoluted psychological machinery motoring the creative impulse, which infused his critical method as a reviewer, must have made him aware of the inadequacy of his responses, that is, of their refusal to expand upon key obsessional connections between the minimal biographical data proffered and the trigger function it served.

It seems advisable to scrutinize the fictions themselves, if solely to reconfirm their "poetic" structure and the underlying drives behind their realization. In **"Silent Snow, Secret Snow,"** as in **"Strange Moonlight,"** the third-person narrative voice belongs to a child, Paul Hasleman, age twelve, a child articulated by another party, another self, which has the technical advantage of permitting insights to quicken in the cosmopolitan syntax and lexicon of an adult perspective. The opening two sentences deftly establish the tone of the story and the dominant conflict between Paul's inner vision and the factual authority of his parents, without yet specifying the nature of the boy's delusion: "Just why it should have happened, or why it should have happened just when it did, he could not, of course, possibly have said; nor perhaps would it even have occurred to him to ask. The thing was above all a secret, something to be preciously concealed from Mother and Father; and to that very fact it owed an enormous part of its deliciousness." The enigmatic start does its job well, impaling the reader on his curiosity, and the physical scene is soon blocked in with skillful economy, a classroom lesson in geography, little Deirdre sitting in front of Paul, nape freckles like the Big Dipper, Mrs. Buell, "old and grayish and kindly" of face lecturing about the tropics, while Paul in dramatic contrast muses on the globe's white "Artic and Antarctic regions."

Before discussing internal mechanisms, one should say that Aiken's architecture is, as usual, sturdily constructed along traditional lines, the thrust of a narrative hook, constant alterations of inner and outer realities, and a gradual, insistent movement towards the cleverly foreshadowed climax, a climax of horror for the reader and ambiguous delight for the protagonist, which provides the kind of supratextual echoes serious literature demands. He had learned well from Mansfield and, more importantly, from his and her master, Chekhov—"He's been my ghostly godfather all my life"—and even from the lesser art of O. Henry, who presides over the 'trick' conclusion of **"Mr. Arcularis."** Jane Aiken Hodge has pointed out her father's odd loyalty to the latter, noting that he kept "a complete set" of O. Henry's stories in the Rye house. But it is Poe who stands foresquare at the heart of **"Secret Snow, Silent Snow,"** at its adolescent heart, the gothic Poe whom Aiken had treasured since the age of nine in Savannah, associating him with Colonial Park across the street from his house, an old graveyard where he played among decrepit tombstones. Poe is always present in spirit, the touchstone sensibility, and insofar as the tale is a horror tale about a child on the verge of madness and manhood, he is present in the surface texture of its terrifying unraveling as well.

Poe, indeed, binds together the two levels of the story's remorseless development, the aesthetic engine and its catalytic fear of death and insanity, although it is Freud—the psychoanalytic schema of the "family romance" and his philosophic *Beyond the Pleasure Principle*—who figures most heavily in transforming **"Silent Snow, Secret Snow"** into the marvel that it is. Paul's steady retreat from the real world into the fantasy calm offered by the increasing snowfall in his mind, which is marked by increasing hostility towards adults, his parents and a doctor ostensibly concerned about his health, acquires a new measure of potency when considered within a Freudian framework. However entranced by his own story, Aiken was too conscious a craftsman not to feel the need to supply a firm psychological context for his alter ego's drift into madness. Consequently, the poetic refrain, that litany of cold, peace, remoteness, and sleep tendered by the snow, advances down a path of artfully defined signposts—"H" on the wall *versus* "Homeward," the magic numbers seven and thirteen, etc.—that activate a universe of symbolic proportions, of screen memories and Freudian fairy tales, where every gesture, word, and human mass connotes the subconscious dilemmas of the teller's (and audience's) psychosexual history.

Never individualized, the father assumes a threatening Oedipal tone towards his son, the deceptive voice of regal authority, speaking "softly and coldly" in "a silken warning" (unspecified) to him, his voice later depicted as "resonant and cruel," so that the pleasure Paul experiences from the rapid encroachment of the snowfall is partially explained as a defense against this threat, a means of escape from male pressure. But in the climactic moment, when the dual pattern of the narrative is fusing into a single strand, fantasy's total triumph, the "exorcising" words, "I hate you," are flung at the mother, not the father, which would appear to confound any strict Oedipal interpretation. And yet, the turn is in keeping with the vague guilt attached to Paul's delusion from the beginning, a mystery's anticipated surprise sprung at last, and it does maintain the magical properties of the tale-within-a-tale markers inserted along the way. To admit, in other words, to a hatred for the mother, for Eros, for the queen, for the womb that is death's eternal antithesis, energizing the core of Paul's superficially inexplicable detachment from phenomena—a psyche's swoon into oblivion, after all—is to concede the snowfall's insidious opposition to love, the life principle.

Hoffman has characterized the snow as "death, or the means to death, a confrontation of infinity or of natural immensities," and Martin opines that "we never, in the story, transcend the snow itself, whose meanings remain secret." Both views are correct without touching upon the interior constructs of **"Silent Snow, Secret Snow,"** where the twin obsessions of Aiken's entire life, the fear of death and madness, are relieved, fulfilled, though not resolved, by their melding into Freud's notion of the death instinct, life's perpetual desire for rest. In a 1923 article on *Beyond the Pleasure Principle* for *The Dial,* which Aiken must have read, George Santayana treats Freud's tome with surprising warmth as "an admirable counterblast to prevalent follies" because its satisfying admixture of biology and myth produces a bedrock verity: "The transitoriness of things is essential to their physical being, and not at all sad in itself; it becomes sad by virtue of a sentimental illusion, which makes us imagine that they wish to endure, and that their end is always untimely, but in a healthy nature it is not so."

Aiken's protagonist, whose mental demise *is* untimely, has reversed the illusion, seeking salvation in death, but the poet's story is neither noetic system nor random existence. Freud's conviction, gleaned from Schopenhauer, that the "goal of all life is death" can only prevail upon its mechanical procedures, the organism's entropic drift into inertia (peace, coldness, remoteness, sleep) as the victory of the pleasure principle, childhood's appetite, over the reality principle, while the story's creative tension, its struggle between generations in Paul's psychodrama and between the riven halves of a divided self, can never abate. The horror remains in the snowfall's relentless progress, Poe's whiteness from *Eureka,* the absence of all values, not merely the black threat of antagonistic poles—even Paul refers at one point to the event of the animistic snow as a "menace." And Aiken has the genius, conscious or otherwise, to perceive in Freud's account of the instinctual "tendency in living organic matter impelling it towards reinstatement of an earlier condition" the lineaments of a potent return-to-the-womb fiction that could merge mother and her antithesis into a fatal entity.

In **"Mr. Arcularis,"** which does not quite possess the hypnotic power of **"Silent Snow, Secret Snow,"** perhaps because of the absence of the insanity obsession, morbid personal anxiety is translated into grandiose cosmic terms, a frequent childhood impulse. Aiken is again deeply engaged in the story, despite the presumed distance between him and his middle-aged main character, nailed there by the actual dream of himself in a coffin at the bottom of a ship and the absolute self-absorption that gives the death obsession its enormous force. Old age, scary in itself as a carnal deterioration of youthful faculties, is the last step before extinction, the child's projected terror centered upon that easily imagined terminal plateau in his own life. Thus, **"Mr. Arcularis"** is not only another poet's story; it is **"Silent Snow, Secret Snow"** *redux,* the same inner journey in a different format, more complexly plotted.

Like Paul, like Paul grown old—Arcularis's friend Harry tells him, "You're tottering like an octogenarian!" when assisting him out of the hospital—the protagonist is confronting annihilation, physical death plus the death instinct, which guarantees his tale its fierce emotive ambivalence, shared by the reader, who is ensnared in the archetypal design of its subtext. Also like Paul's case, the internal drama depends upon the resolution, temporary and treacherous, of a family romance crisis, though now shaped more blatantly around psychoanalytic symbols and cosmic imagery. Poe's influence is much stronger throughout, the adolescent Poe who could contemplate reality as "a dream within a dream" and the Poe of "Manuscript in a Bottle," where a horrified passenger is taken to his death at the South Pole by a ghost ship and its crew of corpses, who welcome the destruction. (In the pentultimate prelude of the contemporaneous *Preludes to Memnon,* Aiken's poetic quest for a godhead in expanding human consciousness, the last lines are: "Come dance around the compass/ pointing north/ Before, face downward, frozen,/ we go forth.") Although the praxis of **"Mr. Arcularis"** exhibits expected evidence of debts to Mansfield and O. Henry, flags are again and again erected to map out an interior voyage uncharted by their modest talents, flags that also affirm the closeness of the author to his hero, who assumes his past and his reading habits, his sensibility and, of course, his compulsive fascination with death.

Arcularis jokingly refers to the bored stewards as "dead souls" suffering from *déjà vu* (his own ironic condition), and earlier he has alluded to *The Odyssey* of Homer, which is followed by a simile coupling the porthole in his stateroom, "his forlorn and white little room," to "the eye of a cyclops." From the start the literal voyage is paralleled by an interior one, the dual construct of **"Silent Snow, Secret Snow"** reasserted and elaborated, and the story itself, as the surprise coda will demonstrate, is a nightmare *after* death. Fictional margins, like the swamp boundaries between autobiography and literature, are thereby rendered unreliable, which is what myth and Freudian dream analysis elicit in the end, the downward search for unconscious truth that Aiken is transmuting into an upward, nothern flight.

Early in **"Mr. Arcularis,"** the inner journey is repeatedly drawn to the past, particularly childhood; from the hospital window, the streetcars look to Arcularis "as they used to look when he was a child," and he later asks himself, "Had he become a child again?" More relevant, when he meets Clarice Dean on board ship—Aiken was married to Clarissa Lorenz at the time, his second wife, who, like his other two wives, bore a resemblance to his mother—she reminds him first of the freckled-faced girl he had met at the hospital, reminding us of little Deirdre in **"Silent Snow, Secret Snow,"** and then of "Someone far back in his life: remote, beautiful, lovely." This identification tends to confirm the paradoxical tropes of inner and outer voyages, as Arcularis commences to have his dreams about flying (sexual) to the North Star, after finding himself in "a wide plain covered with snow," lost and cold until he stumbled on an iced signpost with the word "Polaris" on it, which engendered an "awful feeling of despair." While narrating the initial dream to Clarice, including the frightening aftermath of waking up outside his stateroom door, she again reminds him of the hospital girl, but this time he realizes that both girls are mere stepping stones, "the signpost" to "Long ago and far away," to, at last: "It couldn't be simply that they reminded him of his childhood! And yet why not?"

In the background, always, is the ship's engines, which "followed one like the Hound of Heaven," [The critic adds in a footnote: "Francis Thompson was one of Aiken's beloved authors, and the reference here to that poet's strongest work reiterates the way in which the protagonist's personality has been filled by Aiken himself."] and they, their sound and pulse, help propell him in his dream "out into space, making the round trip by way of Betelgeuse and Polaris, sparkled with frost," icicles on his fingers and toes, "on the verge of the Unknown." Antinomies and implacable repetitions typify dream and reality, and the exhilaration of his nocturnal soarings is stained by fear, "the feeling as of everything coiling inward to a center of misery," though he senses that "he was almost home—almost home. . . . would be. Safe and sound. Safe in his father's house." The course is the "Great Circle," taking him back to his youth, directly to his father, who is surely Aiken's flesh father also: "But why was it that doctors were all alike? And all, for that matter, like his father."

The fact that the ship doctor writes poetry forms part of the cyclical mosaic—Aiken's father tried his hand at creative writing, writings which his son saved—and limns an image of Aiken on the same ship, crouched "in there, in his cabin, night after night, writing . . . all about the stars and flowers and love and death; ice and the sea and the infinite; time and tide." Narrative lines have crossed and recrossed, like a painting of a painter painting himself painting, a spiral into a refracted self, Poe's whirlpool, an old man returning to the primal scene, his childhood, where he has already faced his father as a doctor and as an allegorical home—Paul's doctor had a "false" smile—but finding something missing, someone. If the internal trek is a simultaneous drift into death, desire for inertia and terror of oblivion, and a return to the family romance and its trauma, then the next revolution must encompass Clarice, the surrogate mother, who is his last chance for salvation from doom.

Inescapably, as Arcularis trembles on the brink of his zenith dream, having awakened in the previous one at the bottom of the stairway leading to the hold, where the coffin is located, *"crawling on my hands and knees!"* like an infant, she expresses a desire to accompany him, a desire he fervently wishes could be satisfied, noticing that in her loveliness and allure it "was as if, indeed, she might be his own soul," his anima. They passionately kiss and embrace, the ship (again like Poe's ghost vessel) "seemed scarcely to be moving—it was as if anchored among walls of ice and rime," while she kisses him "as if she were indeed trying to give him her warmth, her life." At the acme of bliss and fear, mother has become lover, the child's dearest hidden wish fullfilled, which explains the "guilt" the parson had told Arcularis he was nursing unknowingly. Since Clarice is mother and other self in their union, this means that both voyages can now reach a climax. "Be a good boy and take your bromide!" are her parting words to him, and his playful retort fuses life and death, past and present, into the horror of womb as tomb and *vice versa:* "Yes, mother, I'll take my medicine!"

The final trip into the "Unknown," final in the temporal margins of the text, is a replay of Paul's schizophrenic passage into the snow, into "light, delight, supreme white and brightness, whirling lightness above all—and freezing—freezing—freezing." Reinforcing Freud's observation that we never really forget or lose anything, the shock at story's end, the discovery that Arcularis had not recovered from his operation—the doctor, the father, had failed to save him, to deliver the baby from his side—returns us to the beginning, denying death, completing the circle without, naturally, resolving the perpetual conflict between reality and pleasure principles. As in **"Silent Snow, Secret Snow,"** the puissance of the tale stems from a matrix of personal obsession and deliberate manipulation of Freudian metaphors, from its transfigured self-absorption, not an empathetic recreation of alien fields of vision. The unseen event behind the story, the father's paranoia turning him against son and wife at a crucial phase in Aiken's youth when the Oedipal situation had not yet been transcended, might grease the wheels of the plot too, but knowledge of absent biographical information is unnecessary to comprehend or experience the anguished impact of the two stories, which is why they are such efficient objectifications of private but universal predicaments.

In comparison, **"Strange Moonlight,"** which predates both and is far more autobiographical in details, is somewhat less compelling, more muted. Of it, Aiken admits that "imagination takes a hand, to be sure, and transmutes it, but the material is deeply and closely personal, and is allowed to remain so," later summarizing: "Invention and synthesis coming to the rescue of disorder and early sorrow." Two intelligent critics, Seymour Gross [in his 1957 essay in *Modern Language Notes*] and Mary M. Rountree, have offered sensitive readings of the story, identifying several pertinent literary influences and techniques at work, but neither manages to penetrate to the radium hub of its psychological dynamo. Gross perceptively isolates the way in which Aiken manipulates Poe, his "Annabel Lee" poem, to create a thematic contrast between the story and the poem, but this leads him to mistakenly conclude that the protagonist's solution to the problem of how to deal with death, with the first death, is, like Poe's, "to wipe out its reality. That this solution is ultimately destructive to the moral and aesthetic resources of life is the main burden of **'Strange Moonlight.'** "

Aided by Aiken's own statement—"The story is a sonata, or quarter, the motif is *gold:* goldfish, medal, goldpiece, and, in a sense, Caroline Lee, with moonlight as the counterpoint"—Rountree emphasizes the music analogy with impressive precision, "the symbolic counterpoint" evolved between "sunlight and moonlight, gold and silver, life and death," and links the boy's dream at the tale's thematic center, which "involves a journey of discovery," with the pivotal battle between highly charged tropes of animate and inanimate worlds, relating the whole business back to the Poe-drenched tales written at Harvard. Her last paragraph deserves to be quoted: "Like the sonata, Aiken's four-part composition resolves its conflict with a poise and balance that points up the resonant complexity of its theme. As both his apprentice stories at Harvard and his note on the structure of **"Strange Moonlight"** make clear, Aiken learned that he could, through the discipline of his art, reach a state of poise and balance by turning his personal pain into tender and compassionate renderings of universal human experience."

Portrait of Aiken by his third wife, Mary Hoover Aiken.

Such critics have managed to illuminate important technical aspects of the story without ever drilling beneath its proficient surface to mine the vein of psychological correspondences that grant it distinction, timeless emotive drive. Therefore, they are unable to appreciate **"Strange Moonlight"** as the first of the poet stories, the seedling precursor of **"Silent Snow, Secret Snow"** and **"Mr. Arcularis,"** where Aiken is wrestling almost nakedly with the traumatic material that had aided his metamorphosis into the artist, the creature who stands outside his own existence, forever divided from self and life. It is a direct assault upon the origins of the two obsessions that would impel and shape his career, a career that mandates a permanent and tragic existential distance from all other human beings, the egocentric gestation of the Great Circle.

In the first section of **"Strange Moonlight,"** Poe's gothic imagination is immediately linked with the adolescent consciousness narrating the tale (another adult-masked voice) by a family romance tie, a book of his short stories stolen from "mother's bookcase." During the nightmare that ensues, the husband appears also, a huge bat-like wing and a disembodied voice, "placid and reasonable, exactly in fact, like his father's explaining a problem in mathematics." Father seems to be Dante's Lucifer and Virgil abstracted and combined to suit the dream work. As in the two later poet stories, there are a mystery and a voyage towards it, a mystery "vast and beautiful" in the black-walled "infernal city," which has Hades, the descent into unconscious realms, for its domain, though paradise nestles it, pleasure and terror merging. The enigma persists into daylight consciousness, a nagging sense that its solution is imminent, but Prize Day at school intervenes to endow the boy with a medal, which he unboxes in Colonial Park amid the ancient tombstones, his name engraved in gold as if in a gravestone: "It was an experience not wholly to be comprehended." Inexplicably, like Paul's snowfall, it is also an experience "to be carefully concealed from mother and father," though the latter discovers the honor and rewards him with glory.

The medal, the tombstones, and the dream mystery are intimated to possess a subtle relationship, a relationship that has the medal for its focus, which summons up inappropriate emotions, severe mental pain and shame when discovered by the father, its presence in his pocket burning "him unceasingly," the price of sin. Section two supplies a time frame of a week, but the story doubles back upon itself—everywhere "lurked that extraordinary hint of the enigma and its shining solution." While he and his siblings, John and Mary, play with toy soldiers, emulating the Battle of Gettysburg, a goldfinch suddenly flies into the room and blunders about frantically before making its escape, gold again connecting the diverse elements in Aiken's musical schema, but its secret song is a dirge, depending upon the old superstition that a bird indoors portends a death. Accordingly, the boy goes off by himself to lie down and recall Caroline Lee, a girl dead of scarlet fever—Aiken's brother Robert (Taylor) was actually the one who contracted the disease in their youth—whom he had visited once at her brother's invitation. Her house is the familiar Freudian symbol of the womb and its vagina, perhaps too blatantly so, "dim and strange," the wallpaper beside the staircase leading up to her "rough and hairy," and she herself a nubile Poe heroine *par excellence,* "extraordinarily strange and beautiful . . . thin, smaller than himself, with dark hair and large pale eyes, and her forehead and hands looked curiously transparent."

From here to death is not far, from innocence through Poe to the depths of the hell (sexual identity) that death impresses upon prepubescent minds. The other symbols Aiken feels compelled to interject, Caroline's goldpiece, pink shell, and Egyptian necklace (*Book of the Dead* talisman) are the plot tokens of the musical analogy that tends to disguise rather than uncover the subterranean corridors where dwell their real significance, the source of their electricity and meaning. They contribute, these surface images, to the boy's idealization of "a vision that was not to be repeated, an incursion in a world that was so beautiful and strange that one was permitted of it only the briefest of glimpses," but her literal, unwitnessed death three days after he learned of her illness—the magic number endemic to the grim fairy tales of Poe *and* Freud—brings home (apt word) the narrative's molten core: "The indignity, the horror, of death obsessed him." The red quarantine sign on her door is, portentously, replaced by a white notice of death, and as he watches her silent house, knowing her corpse is lying inside, he thinks of the goldpiece he had almost stolen from her, as he will "filch" Poe from his mother, and intuits that the mystery "was once more about him." Clearly, Caroline Lee and his mother are mated in the house, sexual treasures frightening and desirable, ripe with death and perilous to his identity, burdened by anchorless guilt, as was (or will be) Paul and Arcularis.

It is proper, then, that section three commences with him in bed, watching the moonlight on the "white outhouse door" and deciding to arise to secure a better view of its enchanting effect upon two trees. Instead, he is treated to the unsettling knowledge that his parents are sexual beings, one of childhood's inevitable traumas, as he peers down the stairs, adolescent observer frozen in time and sorrow, and sees his mother and father together: "His mother had just called his father 'Boy'! Amazing!" Worse yet, his father laughs in a "peculiar angry way," threatening his wife with another child if her behavior does not improve, and what the boy observes "filled him with horror. His mother was sitting on his father's knee, with her arms about his neck. She was kissing him. How awful!" The scene, akin to the embraces exchanged by Arcularis and Clarice, is "offensive" to him, his parents not behaving like parents at all but like "children."

What is happening here is crucial, and it certainly conforms to the riddle-like death images, the punishing medal and the irrational shame and attendant terror and curiosity, but its ramifications are even more profound than perhaps Aiken was willing to concede at this juncture in his aesthetic growth, despite his sympathetic perusal of Freud and Freudian disciples like Jung and Rank. The piece of the puzzle that does not fit is the position of the parents, her on his knee, which is natural enough but seems at odds with the Oedipal tensions implicit in the boy's excessive reaction, a boy on the threshold of sexual desire (Caroline's home) but too young to have yet resolved the Oedipus Complex Freud posited as an essential step in the ego's psychosexual maturation. *Ushant* renders the scene differently as "the house at Savannah, and the gay card-parties . . . and the extraordinary quarrels—as in that mysterious episode which he had introduced into an early story, when he had looked down over the banisters to see his father sitting on his mother's knee, with his arm around her."

This account squares more readily with the idea that part of the child's reaction, its unspoken rage and envy, resides in his comprehension of the father replacing him in the mother's arms, the father who is (in all three poet tales) ambivalently perceived as god and rival, potential savior and destroyer. And his shame, remorseless, wells from the guilt, the guilt that also haunts **"Silent Snow, Secret Snow"** and **"Mr. Arcularis,"** that he experiences below consciousness for desiring his mother and, probably, wishing his father dead. In the story as it is, the general disgust over parental sexuality is made to carry the entire thematic load, to integrate it with the enigma orbiting around

Caroline's innocent death and the coin he wanted to take from her. Death itself, the death-obsession, is in its nascent stage, its symbolic displacements, inversions, condensations, and the like not yet capable of a rational fusion. But the narrative maintains a dual approach, and the boy's flight from the disturbing scene between his parents to the dead Caroline, whom he imagines holding a conversation with him, swings nearer to one, when she tells him—she is buried in "Bonaventure" cemetery, where Aiken's parents were interred—"it's nicer than being alive," that death is not complete: "You climb out of the earth just as easily as you'd climb out of bed." Death and sex are thus entwined, hopefully obviated, and what is next must be a return to the family romance.

This comes at Typee Beach, when the boy continues to puzzle over the mystery and its array of gold symbols, grasping a web-frail bridge between the medal burning and buzzing in his pocket and a dream of thrusting his hand deep into a sea-chest of goldpieces. It is the medal in the sand, where he has now lain it, that causes him to wish Caroline was alive, and was with him, her house their house, "their house would be perfect," a union of self and death. The father certifies that resurrection is plausible, his wife acting playful, "as if she was a girl," when he leaps "out of his tomb, terrifying them, scattered his grave clothes in every direction" and races into the water, a deifical figure who can inflict fear from beyond the grave, father rival and conqueror of death. Yet the ambiguous crux remains, though it glides closer to some elemental meaning when the family rides the streetcar home. The ride is metamorphosized by the moonlight, light of the boy's unquiet mind and its unconscious associative process, into Arcularis's voyage towards a death that could be cosmic: "Where was it they were going—was it anything so simple as home . . . or . . . like a fiery comet towards the world's edge, to plunge out into the unknown and fall down and down forever?"

Their house is now drowned in the moonlight, transformed into something "ghostly" and "strange" (compulsive, inadequate adjective), and the horror is pure Poe, the strip of light the jolt delivered by the climaxes of his generic tales of terror: "It was like a vine of moonlight, which suddenly grew all over the house, smothering everything with its multitudinous swift leaves and tendrils of pale silver, and then as suddenly faded out." It is while the father is slipping the key into the lock, opening the door to a solution and violating the house, their shared home, the mother, that the boy falls prey to the moonlight, the "ghostly vine grow strangely over his face and hands." This eventuates in the insight that Caroline, Poe heroine and incestuously loved alter-ego, is "a sort of moonlight," poisonous and beautiful, remote as death, yet strangling him as he climbs the Freudian staircase, enters self-knowledge.

The end of the story, overt climax to the enigma's musical structure, depends upon his palming the medal and the pink shell, which lifts him into a new consciousness, a new level of consciousness, his felt awareness "at last that Caroline was dead." The manifest mystery is solved, or at least sufficiently patterned to permit some release from the intensities projected, but the story itself is the maze for the maze of the mystery's latent tell-tale heart. To reduce, as Gross does, the finale to a didactic warning against Poe's solipstic romanticism is to foresake the larger maze's telic design and quest, to miss the nearness of the invention to Aiken's psyche. Rountree hovers closer, detecting the artist's self-scrutiny, but she too veers off before discerning the obsessive dynamic behind the poise and balance achieved by the sonata's reassuring reciprocities. Remember: the Oedipal conflict fueling the plot is directed towards death, and implicit in the story's every action is the loss of ambivalently conceived parents that looms ahead, and its subsequent trail of guilt.

The major discovery is that the death of Caroline, which represents the parental deaths to come off-stage, has ushered the protagonist out of normal reality forever, centered him absolutely on the self, trapped in the phase of infantile neurosis Freud and Aiken would agree simulates the artist's lot. Art as cathartic wish-fulfillment, another view they held in common, amplifies the two resurrections. The boy's realization that Caroline is indeed gone, his first death, should be considered in conjunction with a relevant passage from *Ushant:* "To be able to *separate* oneself from one's background, one's environment—wasn't this the most thrilling discovery of which consciousness was capable? and no doubt for the very reason that as it is a discovery of one's limits, it is therefore by implication the first and sharpest discovery of death." A bit beyond, Aiken speaks of "the terror that was light's invariable accompaniment" and of the self-absorption that must result as "one was consciously a tropism of exquisite response in the very center of one's own world."

It is also in *Ushant* that the author of **"Strange Moonlight"** brings the story's internal voyage into dock, conceding that "voracious egotism" was one of his parents' gifts to him, a gift of art: "And, granted that the egotism, as in his own deplorable case, was a nuisance and a menace, wasn't it also the very material for the all-transforming smithy of artifaction?" Furthermore, the narrative's interior rubric of an unresolved, reenacted Oedipus Complex and consequent egocentricity has the additional emotional factor of the death-obsession in embryonic formulation, the convergence of obsession and art that is generating the sad tale of imagination's birth under the prod of extinction, sentenced to an existence detached from life yet wracked by fears of its finite nature.

If not equal to **"Silent Snow, Secret Snow"** and **"Mr. Arcularis"** in literary courage, its dangerous content too intent upon abstract distances, **"Strange Moonlight"** is like them in being able to exert a breathless hold on the reader's emotions and unconscious energies. Like them, and unlike other exceptional Aiken stories, such as **"Bring! Bring!," "Round by Round,"** and **"Life Isn't a Short Story,"** where expert craftsmanship avoids tapping obsession's mother lode, it never resolves the human mystery, merely revitalizes and expands its moving nodes of expression, proceeds beyond the page, like the serial stories Aiken used to invent each night for his children, "neverending—and never-ended." (pp. 99-117)

Edward Butscher, "Conrad Aiken's Short Fic-

tion: 'The Poet's Story'," in The Southern Quarterly, *Vol. XXI, No. 1, Fall, 1982, pp. 99-118.*

Robert Penn Warren (essay date 1982)

[An American poet and critic, Warren was named poet laureate of the United States in 1985. Consistently in the vanguard of American scholarship, he began his career as a member of the Fugitive group of Southern poets during the 1920s. The intent of the Fugitives was to create a literature utilizing the best qualities of modern and traditional art. After 1928, Warren and several other Fugitives joined with other writers to form the Agrarians, a group dedicated to preserving the Southern way of life and traditional Southern values. Warren, John Crowe Ransom, and Allen Tate eventually left Agrarianism and went on to become prominent founders of New Criticism, one of the most influential critical movements of the mid-twentieth century. Although the various New Critics did not subscribe to a single set of principles, all believed that a work of literature had to be examined as an object in itself through a process of close analysis of symbol, image, and metaphor. For the New Critics, a literary work was not a manifestation of ethics, sociology, or psychology, and could not be evaluated in the general terms of any nonliterary discipline. In the following excerpt from his introduction to The Collected Short Stories of Conrad Aiken, *Warren discusses the unifying subjects and themes that characterize Aiken's short fiction and praises Aiken's achievement as a short story writer.]*

A short story here and there may give a momentary enlightenment, but if we are to realize the deep inner meaning of a writer we must read many of his stories. With certain obvious exceptions (often forced by economic necessity) the different pieces by a really good short story writer all belong to the same family. They bloom from the same trunk. They deal with aspects of the same deep issues. (p. viii)

When I was invited to do an introduction to [***The Collected Short Stories of Conrad Aiken***], I was hesitant, and the hesitancy persisted until I discovered that, after some fifty years, story after story of Aiken, even with the proper title, popped clearly and significantly back into my head, and beyond that the unique atmosphere of the stories in general also returned. I suddenly knew that I must read the stories again. I wanted to verify the fact that he had "created" his world. Now I have done that.

I have said, or implied, that all or most of the stories (or novels or poems) of a good writer are hewn out of the same block. That big block is, of course, the writer's self—but the self that neither he nor his friends may know much about. (In fact, the real self may be what is created by the hewing.) And in a way that is one of the germinal things Aiken writes about. In one of his most famous and most memorable stories (**"Mr. Arcularis,"** one of the first that came into my mind when the project was suggested), we have a passage that might be taken as a Golden Text of Aiken's work. The main event may be assumed to be actually occurring on a liner on a real sea voyage, when an aging man recovering from an operation is on deck talking with a charming and mysterious young girl, or we may take it all as the illusion of a dying man. (The story ends with the death of the patient on the operating table, long before he could go on any sea voyage.)

> [Mr. Arcularis is speaking.] ". . . how extraordinarily little we know about the workings of our own minds or souls. After all, what do we know?"
>
> "Nothing—nothing—nothing—nothing," said Miss Dean slowly.
>
> "*Absolutely* nothing."
>
> Their voices had dropped and again they were silent; and again they looked at each other gently and sympathetically, as if for the exchange of something unspoken and perhaps unspeakable. Time ceased.

However we take the event, it still holds good as a Golden Text. The stories, by and large, are about the moment when some piece of the ambiguous "workings of our own minds or souls" is made manifest in the story (if not necessarily to a character therein).

We need not depend, however, on a Golden Text. There are many examples—in action stated or suggested or aborted. For instance, poor Hamerton of **"The Moment"** has a theory that "one's life consisted of at most half a dozen moments of supreme experience, or perhaps not even as many as that." The discovery of, or failure to discover, such a moment is a "story." A revelation may be seized or pass unrecognized, but in either instance, a crisis of awareness has come into being. Such a crisis may have its ironical turn, as in **"No, No, Go Not to Lethe."** This is the tale of a man who prides himself on being the totally detached observer of others, drawing a sense of total power from a creation of their lives and committing himself to nothing. He is an "intellectual" who finds that a young lady daily "observed" in his boarding house has fallen in love with him. When he had defined her to herself and extracted an avowal of love, he retreats into his self-sufficiency and pride—only to find too late that she has fled and is indispensable. He has become the "observed." But thus he finds that he has never "observed" his real self. He has never even faced the question of what a self is.

Stated so flatly, as in the Golden Text, the work of Aiken sounds as though it were cut to a pattern, poured into a mold, mixed to a formula. In one sense, it is. It is so in the way that the work of every good writer is. In many writers who are famously good, we seem to see first a random variety—for without the variety there is the death of serious achievement, a danger in, say, even the greatness of a Beckett.

In this connection, let us think for a moment of the infinite variety of characters and scenes in Shakespeare. But if we shift our angle of vision, all is different. We see that the characters of Shakespeare belong to a relatively small family after all. Isabella in *Measure for Measure* is a sister of Cordelia in *Lear* or, in a strange way, of Malvolio in *Twelfth Night.* Cordelia is truly noble, is disgusted by pretense, and loathes a lie, especially the lie for gain: and horror follows horror in the irony of virtue. In other words, abstract virtue leads to disaster, in a grisly paradox. Isabella sees the virtue of female chastity as an abstraction—as an absolute definition of virtue in whatever context—and is sorely disappointed when her brother Claudio does not rejoice at the prospect of being beheaded to save her maidenhead. This play is not a tragedy, and so by a cynical trick both head and maidenhead remain intact. But the two ladies are female twins. And Brutus is, shall we say, an elder brother. He will sacrifice his dear friend to save a republic that any fool could see is no longer a republic. It is a mob. But Brutus, like the ladies, lives by abstraction.

It is easy to see that Toby Belch and Falstaff are kin, but a little analysis will show that Antony and Cleopatra are related to them, only in a different tonality. And let us see, in passing, the kinship of Augustus and Bolingbroke, those cold-blooded artists of power.

What I am getting at here is that though we may seem to find a mechanical and limited statement as a definition of an Aiken story, there is still a very great variety—if somewhat less than in Shakespeare, Balzac, Dickens, Faulkner, or Dreiser, each of whom had his own "thing," which he kept turning in varying lights and shadows.

Let us return to examine some of the varying lights and shadows that give Aiken's Golden Text its variety. The story entitled **"The Dark City"** is, in a sense, very explicit and abstract, but one may try to observe even here how Aiken has sought to flesh out, to harmonize, the subject. Andrew, the hero, is a very prosperous businessman in the "Dark City," bored with his job, who comes home by the same train every afternoon to a charming house and happy family and putters delightedly in his garden, thinking comically to himself: "Ridiculous! that this solemn singular biped, whom other bipeds for convenience call Andrew, should stand here with a stick and scratch the skin of this aged planet." In such a vein he muses on and on, goes in to a good meal and jolly little children, but taking time beforehand to watch dusk descend over the city he loathes. Then he plays chess with his delightful wife. Accustomed to his habits and his hatred of the "Dark City," she asks has he watched it tonight, as usual, at dusk. In his air of comedy, he replies: "A city of the dead . . . the people are maggots—maggots of perhaps the size of human children; their heads are small and wedge-shaped and glow with a faint bluish light. . . . What horrible feast is it that nightly they celebrate there in silence? . . . Extraordinary that this city, which seen from here at dusk has so supernatural a beauty, should hide at the core so vile a secret."

His wife stares at him, then says: "Really, Andrew, I think you are going mad."

And he replies, in his comic vein: "Going? I'm gone! My brain is maggoty."

At this they laugh and put the chessmen away.

We ask ourselves how much madness is in Andrew's comedy. And if he is going mad are we all held off from that fate by the skin of our teeth? As we regard the momentary beauty of the Dark City? But Aiken does not ask such a question. He tells us only of the chessmen being put away, and that the wife is beautiful in her drowsiness. Perhaps the story is totally ambiguous, a comedy of ambiguity, which for some people may be neither ambiguous nor comic.

But we do not always have such ambiguity. In **"Spider, Spider"** we see a gentleman, who has fallen desperately in love with an unsophisticated "shy arbutus" of a young woman, now calling on the beautiful widow of a friend. And we see the widow, bit by bit, as the gentleman makes his confession, turn his romance into a silly farce for him, until the moment comes when he leans forward to touch a "tiny golden watch-spring of hair which curled against the nape of the white neck" of the woman of the world. The gentleman had failed, alas, to know himself, even though he knew before the event that there would be spiritual death.

In this collection of forty-one stories there are some that fail, for all their skill (for instance, **"Bow Down, Isaac!"** or the near novelette **"Thistledown"**), and these are those that fail to find contact with Conrad's deepest impulse. But the very best here are superb and have the atmosphere of permanence, the good are very good indeed. After not having read a story by Conrad Aiken for years, I was vividly and happily surprised to find how many I remembered in such detail and with such pleasure. And with the pleasure of remembering came, too, the pleasure of discovery, for the stories remain freshly a testament of a complex, learned, and witty mind staring at the world and asking itself a question—question presented as a possibility:

> I am myself only a momentary sparkle on the swift surface of this preposterous stream. My awareness is only an accident and moreover my awareness is less truly myself than this stream which supports me, and out of which my sparkle of consciousness has for a moment been cast up.

I cannot end this piece without two parting remarks. First, these stories, I emphasize, are not merely a collection. They constitute a unity, a significant and haunting unity. Second, if a few of these stories should please a reader, he must lay hand as soon as possible on the poems of Conrad Aiken, many of which are permanent signposts of the last age, and a signpost for this. (pp. viii-xiii)

Robert Penn Warren, in an introduction to The Collected Short Stories of Conrad Aiken, *Schocken Books, 1982, pp. vii-xiii.*

Jesse G. Swan (essay date 1989)

[In the following essay, Swan argues for a positive interpretation of "Silent Snow, Secret Snow" based on an examination of the concept of silence in Aiken's poem "Senlin: A Biography."]

In "Senlin: A Biography" and **"Silent Snow, Secret Snow,"** Conrad Aiken explores the psyches of two people, one an old man, the other a child, who seem to be confronting something much larger than they are. In both pieces, the central figures experience something to which no one else seems to be sensitive. As this experience is uncommon, the depiction of it demands uncommon material. Aiken succeeds in presenting these nebulous experiences by carefully casting silences in his work. Aiken's silences surround man, embody man, and are embodied by man. They also resemble the Christian God in their ubiquity as well as their comprehensiveness. In both pieces, Aiken tries to communicate the import of these silences, and he does this by stretching our consciousness to include the edges of our minds. Although "Senlin" is an early poem of Aiken's and **"Silent Snow, Secret Snow"** is a later short story, both rely on silence to convey their intendment. Realizing that Aiken employs silence in "Senlin" and develops that employment in **"Silent Snow, Secret Snow,"** we not only develop a greater understanding of Aiken's *Weltanschauung,* we also perceive new possibilities for reading Paul Hasleman's confrontation with the silent snow.

Aiken conceives of silence and silent entities as the neglected component of human reality. In "Senlin: A Biography," for example, Aiken shows us an Everyman character, Senlin "the generic 'I' " as Aiken calls him, struggling in the zone of truth where silence dominates. Aiken tries to explain Senlin's character in his 1949 preface to the poem [in the collection *The Divine Pilgrim*] by writing that Senlin grapples with "the basic and possibly unanswerable question, *who and what am I.* . . . Unanswerable except in a kind of serial dishevelment of answers, or partial answers. . . . Is the answer really nothing but a kind of shimmering series?" "Senlin" shows that the answer is indeed a shimmering series, vacillating between sound and silence. Similarly in his short story **"Silent Snow, Secret Snow,"** Aiken shows us a person trying to work out the tension between the regular, pedestrian, mundane world of civilization and the more beautiful and rich world of silence. The obvious difference is that whereas Senlin is "the 'little old man' that each of us must become," Paul Hasleman is the twelve year old boy that each of us once was. At the edges of life, it appears, humanity confronts the edges of accepted reality as articulated in language and custom. In both works, the protagonists "breathe in silence / And strive to say the things flesh cannot say."

The confrontation with silence involves more than simply experiencing the vague border between silence and sound. It demands a choice. The tension generated by such key points as this, where man is forced to accept or reject a usually vague, if not invisible, part of his being and world, is a favorite of Aiken's. "Senlin" makes this clear. As in Flannery O'Connor where, she claims, "There is a moment in every great story in which the presence of grace can be felt as it waits to be accepted or rejected, even though the reader may not recognize this moment," Aiken's best work deals with such moments. For O'Connor they are moments of grace, but for Aiken they are more ambiguous. In "Senlin," for example, we have "a silent shore," a silent garden, a silent mountain as well as a "sunlit silence," "the heart of silence," and a "cloud of silence." The ambiguity begins to clear if we realize that "silence" is the core, it is the default state of man and the world. Silence is at once a quality as well as an independent entity and Senlin"—"the generic 'I' "—both embodies silence and is embodied by silence.

These two concepts of "silence," as a quality and an autonomous entity, inform the whole poem. The first part of the poem emphasizes the silent nature of various beings and objects. The first item related to silence is, significantly, " . . . Our shadows." This is the omnipotent narrator speaking and the shadows are ours. They do not belong to some group in the poem, they belong to the readers. This early connection between the poem and the readers pulls us into the poem and encourages us to experience what Senlin experiences directly. "Our shadows revolve in silence / Under the soulless brilliance of blue sky" much as Senlin, in the end of the poem, lets us know that "Alone, in silence, / I ascend my stairs once more." Our shadows and Senlin are both doing something silently as well as doing that something—revolving and ascending—"in silence." Silence is both a characteristic of action as well as the piece of action.

This silent characteristic is not merely an absence of sound as it possesses an uncommon form of eloquence and meaning which somehow provides answers. Senlin, speaking to us directly, points to a tree and reveals the fact that it

> Utters profound things in this garden;
> And in its silence speaks to me.
> I have sensations, when I stand beneath it,
> As if its leaves looked at me, and could see;
> And these thin leaves, even in windless air,
> Seem to be whispering me a choral music,
> Insubstantial but debonair.

The tree contains some truth, and it explains that truth in silence which is, presumably, lost on most people. But not Senlin since he is sensitive to silence and can understand the tree. In fact, he understands the tree so well that "Sometimes, indeed, it appears to me / That I myself am such a tree." Senlin is such a tree inasmuch that he has a silent component, like the tree, which encompasses universal truth. This silent "component" is really the basis for other components in the poem, such as sound.

That this silence is generally positive seems to be made clear when Senlin associates silence with God. Senlin wonders if in the morning he should "not pause in the light to remember god?" He decides that he should and that he "will dedicate this moment before my mirror / To him alone, for him I will comb my hair. / Accept these humble offerings, cloud of silence!" But this god is not an external entity, though he surrounds Senlin, as he becomes an image of Senlin. Senlin rises from "a bed of silence" to "stand before [his] mirror / Unconcerned, [to] tie [his] tie." Senlin then wonders, later in his day: "But is god, perhaps, a giant who ties his tie / Grimacing before a colossal glass of sky?" Is Senlin god, god Senlin? Yes. At the end of the poem, when the narrator returns to lull us into a Senlinic silent state, the narrator describes the events or sensations of Senlin's room which we are to feel. "We plunge in a chaos of dunes, white waves before us / Crash on kelp tumultuously . . . The sun is swallowed . . . Has Senlin become a shore? / Is Senlin a grain of sand beneath our footsteps." The answer is yes though "we would say, this is no shore at all, / But a small bright room with lamplight on the wall; / And the familiar chair / Where Senlin sat, with lamplight on his hair." Senlin is both man and shore, man and god, alive and dead, articulate and silent.

Senlin's ability to be these impossible combinations comes from his recognition and acceptance of the silence that surrounds him. Senlin leaves us trying to communicate the silent secret of life. He cries:

> Listen! . . . and you will learn a secret—
> Though it is not the secret you desired.
> I have not found a meaning that will praise you!
> Out of the heart of silence comes this music,
> Quietly speaks and dies.

Presumably we want a secret that will praise us by telling us that we will live forever or that we will be happy or the like. But this secret, the universal secret and truth, says nothing and only Senlin has the ability to perceive it. We can perceive it too if we stretch our minds and examine the edge of language where silence is magnified. If we let go and "listen!" to the fringe of the poem, we will understand what Senlin does. But we do not let go, choosing instead to concentrate exclusively on words and actions. The narrator knows that this is what we do as he tells us that Senlin—"the generic 'I' "—spoke, but found you could not understand him— / You were alone, and he was alone." Here is the message again. Exclusive focus on speaking and what is spoken does not advance knowledge of our human situation. We need to listen to "the heart of silence," which is punctuated with speech, to understand Senlin.

To an even greater extent, silence motivates the events of Aiken's greatest work, his short story, **"Silent Snow, Secret Snow."** Like "Senlin," **"Silent Snow, Secret Snow"** is an investigation of a psyche that involves much more than only the psyche. Indeed in an even more developed fashion, **"Silent Snow, Secret Snow"** reveals a struggle that, it appears, Aiken believes we all experience. Some dismiss the confrontation with silence in the story as puberty or madness. However, since the silence in the story develops the silence of "Senlin," it appears that this story, like the poem, depicts a serious confrontation with eternity, with truth, with silence.

A common temptation is to view the silent snow negatively. Paul, we may be tempted to say, is going mad. This conclusion, however, is one that Mr. and Mrs. Hasleman would form. Paul knows that he cannot tell his parents about his silent snow, "No—" he thinks, "it was only too plain that if anything were said about it, the merest hint given, they would be incredulous—they would laugh—they would say 'Absurd!'—think things about him which weren't true. . . . " And clearly the parents would think him insane, but we are not to do so. The parents are "gross intelligences . . . humdrum minds so bound to the usual, the ordinary" that they cannot experience something "irrational." This description from Paul's point of view, if not wholly accurate because of its extremity, does represent the parents' general character. Perhaps it is inappropriate to be so harsh on the parents for being "normal," but they clearly are normal. The parents notice a change in their son's usual, acceptable character and think that something must be wrong with him. If they knew that he was listening to silent snow, they *would* think him mad. They do not see it, so, for them, it is not there. Like any good parent, they decide to call in an authority—the family physician.

The physician epitomizes the typical adult. We believe that there must be a "rational" explanation for everything and that the world is a rationally understandable environment. Anything supernatural cannot be accounted for and is therefore relegated to the realm of "irrationality," "madness," and the like. The parents believe this as does the physician. The physician asks Paul, "Now, young man, tell me,—do you feel all right?" When Paul tells him that he feels fine—indeed Paul feels exceptionally well because of his silent, secret snow—the doctor performs a physical survey of Paul which includes Paul's reading from a passage of a book. When this reveals nothing out of the ordinary, "silence thronged the room," and the doctor asks Paul, moving to a psychological survey assuming that if nothing is physically wrong, something psychologically *must* be wrong with Paul, whether there is "anything that worries you?" Since Paul's answer remains "No," the doctor becomes exasperated and exclaims: "Well, Paul! . . . I'm afraid you don't take this quite seriously enough." The doctor has given Paul numerous chances to declare himself mad, but since he does not, the doctor concludes that Paul is not only mentally troubled but unacceptably obstinate. Thinking about the doctor's and the parents' actions and portraits, it seems that Paul is not so unreasonable. Concluding that the story is about a boy "whose mind finally breaks down" [Edward Stone in his *Voices of Despair: Four Motifs in American Literature*] ignores the possibility, if not fact, that the parents and physician are blind, insensitive and thereby negative agents in the story and that the silent snow and Paul's embrace of it are the positive agents. Such a narrow reading reveals that the readers, like the parents, are "so bound to the usual, the ordinary . . . [that it is] impossible to tell them about" the positive beauty and peacefulness of the silent snow. These readers, like the parents and the doctor, have pushed away the silence which surrounds them and have chosen to embrace the rational, language centered world. Paul, many try to conclude, is mad, and the parents and doctor, they silently assume, are the standard by which to judge sanity and madness.

That the silent snow is positive not only provides additional support for reading the story as a representation of one of Aiken's favorite points in human development, it also seems rather obvious to the unprejudiced reader. From the very beginning the silent snow is a pleasant experience. In the opening scene where Paul is in class, we find out that

> he was already, with a pleasant sense of half-effort, putting his secret between himself and the [Miss Buell's] words. Was it really an effort at all? For effort implied something voluntary, and perhaps even something one did not especially want; whereas this was distinctly pleasant, and came almost of its own accord.

Although this can be read negatively, as a sign of Paul's ensuing madness, a more positive reading suggests itself as well. The silent secret comes on to Paul, perhaps as "madness" does "a schizoid personality" [William M. Jones in his 1960 *Explicator* note], but also as nature's breezes and soothing sounds do. A breeze is not an effort, but we often feel a half-effort to experience it fully. Like the silent secret, a breeze is not voluntary and it is often pleasant. Hence, the silent secret snow is not ipso facto madness and therefore negative. In fact, it seems really quite a positive experience for Paul, much like a mystical experience must be for a devout Christian or a cognitive insight for a critical theorist.

The development of the silent, secret snow seems to provide further evidence that the snow is a positive force. As in "Senlin," the silence is first a quality that characterizes as well as surrounds, and second it is an entity itself. The silence in the story characterizes the snow which comes to surround Paul's world and then becomes "the most beautiful and secret story" in the end. In class, Paul contemplates the fact that

> All he now knew was, that at some point or other—perhaps the second day, perhaps the sixth—he had noticed that the presence of the snow was a little more insistent. . . . There, outside, were the bare cobbles; and here, inside, was the snow. Snow growing heavier each day, muffling the world, hiding the ugly, and deadening increasingly—above all—the steps of the postman.

The snow is "hiding the ugly" of the world much like Percy Bysshe Shelley claims poetry does in his *A Defence of Poetry.* Shelley claims that "Poetry turns all things to loveliness; it exalts the beauty of that which is most beautiful, and it adds beauty to that which is most deformed. . . . It subdues to union under its light yoke, all irreconcilable things. It transmutes all that it touches. . . . " The snow, then, may resemble poetry. If the snow resembles poetry, is Paul a poet? Perhaps, but since Aiken concerns himself with Everyman and not just artists, it seems more likely that Paul is an Everyman. The snow may be poetic without Paul being a poet if the silent snow is universal truth that poets, children, and old people are sensitive to.

If the snow is universal truth that includes both the rational and the irrational, as it is in "Senlin," the significance of its "deadening increasingly—above all—the steps of the postman" may be ambiguous. The postman has been seen as representing death as well as, more modestly, "the plain ordinary world in which small boys have to get up, eat breakfast, go to school, listen attentively, and do all the other things expected of small boys" [Ballew Graham, *English Journal,* 1968]. The more modest view seems more appropriate especially if we see the silent snow as positive. If the snow hides what is ugly, as poetry does, it would muffle the sound of the postman since the postman is "the bringer of information from the outside world." The postman, with the parents and the doctor, becomes associated with the adult and loud world that has chosen to ignore the silent truth Paul decides to embrace. By incessantly assaulting the beauty of Paul's newly discovered world with news from the adult's mundane world, the postman must be silenced by the purifying silent snow.

The silent snow, after imposing itself on the world, reveals the essential silent entity that embodies everything. Toward the end of the story, when Paul is being interviewed by the physician, the silent snow becomes an entity that "Even here, even amongst these hostile presences, and in this arranged light, he could see the snow, he could hear it—it was in the corners of the room, where the shadow was deepest." The snow occupies the corners—the fringes—of the room much like silence encompasses the edges of sound. Moreover, this silent snow tells Paul to resist his parents and the doctor so that it can provide him with "something new! Something white! something cold! something sleepy! something of cease, and peace, and the long bright curve of space!" This is a rather tempting promise to make, especially when contrasted with what the parents and the world they represent offers him.

The end of the story presents Paul's realization of the silent secret of the universe. The silent snow exclaims:

> Listen! . . . We'll tell you the last, the most beautiful and secret story—shut your eyes—it is a very small story—a story that gets smaller and smaller—it comes inward instead of opening like a flower—it is a flower becoming a seed—a little cold seed—do you hear? We are leaning closer to you.

This statement, compounded by the closing line that describes the snow becoming a fierce "moving screen of snow—but even now it said peace, it said remoteness, it said cold, it said sleep," leads many readers to conclude that Paul dies, that his death wish is fulfilled. But the scene has other possibilities, as Jay Martin notes that "we seem always about to break through to the truths contained in the 'secret' snow. But we never, in the story, transcend the snow itself, whose meanings remain secret." Secret they remain to those who, as "reasonable" adults, embrace only what can be understood with mere human language. The snow's depiction of the secret as a flower growing inward back to the beginning of life seems more positive than what is normal—i.e., a flower growing outward and dying! If the secret grows inward it can grow outward again, and repeat this cycle infinitely. The secret that grows inward is related to the silence that developed before Paul dashed up to bed. That "silence seemed to deepen, to spread out . . . to become timeless and shapeless, and to center inevitably . . . on the beginning of a new sound." Hence, we have the most beautiful and secret story; namely, we have the story of the dynamics of eternal life. Life grows out to grow in, indefinitely.

There is certainly more to it than this. However, as the meaning is obviously ultimately silent, all that any of us can do is approximate the truth. Approaching the truth is what Aiken does best. He takes us to the edge of our minds momentarily innumerable times in his poetry and fiction. Senlin has been recognized as a character who probes the problem of understanding who we are. However, Paul, because he is a child, has received incomplete recognition. Like Senlin, Paul is encountering silent truth. Like Senlin, Paul embraces this beauty which "was simply beyond anything—beyond speech as beyond thought—utterly incommunicable." But unlike Senlin, Paul is twelve years old and the "reasonable" modern adult reader naturally seems to recoil from accepting Paul's choice as courageous and insightful. Perhaps the modern reader recognizes the situation and resents Paul for having the courage that only old men, such as Senlin, usually have. In both cases, Aiken clearly presents a person at a critical point in a human's life—that is, at the edge of sound and silence—and both choose the one which encompasses the other. (pp. 41-8)

Jesse G. Swan, "At the Edge of Sound and Silence: Conrad Aiken's 'Senlin: A Biography' and 'Silent Snow, Secret Snow'," in The Southern Literary Journal, *Vol. XXII, No. 1, Fall, 1989, pp. 41-9.*

FURTHER READING

Bibliography

Bonnell, F. W., and Bonnell, F. C. *Conrad Aiken: A Bibliography (1902-1978).* San Marino, Calif.: Huntington Library, 1982, 291 p.

Bibliography of Aiken's books and pamphlets, his contributions to books and periodicals, translations of his works, and miscellaneous publications and adaptations of his works.

Biography

Butscher, Edward. *Conrad Aiken: Poet of White Horse Vale.* Athens: University of Georgia Press, 1988, 518 p.

First volume of a projected two-volume critical biography, covering Aiken's life through 1925.

Lorenz, Clarissa M. *Lorelei Two: My Life with Conrad Aiken.* Athens: University of Georgia Press, 1983, 231 p.

Autobiography of Aiken's second wife that focuses primarily on the years between their meeting in 1926 and divorce in 1938. Lorenz includes a brief biographical sketch of Aiken and numerous comments about his short stories and other works.

Criticism

Aiken, Conrad. Introduction to *Mr. Arcularis,* by Conrad Aiken, pp. v-ix. Cambridge: Harvard University Press, 1957.

Discusses Aiken's theatrical adaptation of his short story "Mr. Arcularis."

Albrecht, W. P. "Aiken's 'Mr. Arcularis.' " *The Explicator* VI, No. 6 (April 1948): Item 40.

Discusses the constellations in "Mr. Arcularis."

Barrett, Gerald, and Erskine, Thomas L., eds. *From Fiction to Film: Conrad Aiken's "Silent Snow, Secret Snow."* The Dickenson Literature and Film Series. Encino, Calif.: Dickenson Publishing Co., 1972, 193 p.

Collects primary and secondary sources for study of Aiken's "Silent Snow, Secret Snow." The volume includes "Silent Snow, Secret Snow," reprints of critical essays by various authors focusing on Aiken's short story, a scene-by-scene analysis of Gene R. Kearney's film adaptation, and critical essays discussing the film.

Bryant, J. A., Jr. "Recent Short Fiction." *The Sewanee Review* LXXI, No. 1 (Winter 1963): 115-16.

Favorable review of *The Collected Short Stories of Conrad Aiken.* Bryant comments: "[Aiken's] admirable qualities are reflected in the publisher's claim that 'he writes in the tradition of Henry James, Walter de la Mare, Katherine Mansfield, and Guy de Maupassant,' which is not so far-fetched as it may sound. If anything, the list should probably be expanded, for Aiken is fundamentally a clever and tasteful craftsman who can and does manipulate a variety of techniques at will."

Cowley, Malcolm. "The Dark City." *The Saturday Review of Literature* 1, No. 47 (27 June 1925): 851.

Discusses settings and characterization in the short stories collected in *Bring! Bring! and Other Stories* and praises Aiken's prose style.

Denney, Reuel. *Conrad Aiken.* University of Minnesota Pamphlets on American Writers, no. 38. Minneapolis: University of Minnesota Press, 1964, 48 p.

Includes a brief discussion of "Silent Snow, Secret Snow."

Fadiman, Clifton. "Conrad Aiken: Commentary." In his *Reading I've Liked,* pp. 734-35. New York: Simon and Schuster, 1941.

Introduction to "Silent Snow, Secret Snow" in which Fadiman comments that: "What makes 'Silent Snow, Secret Snow' a masterly piece of writing is not that it is a successful study of the mechanism by which a mind fatally splits itself. The value of the tale lies in its human sympathy."

Fytton, Francis. Review of *The Collected Short Stories of Conrad Aiken,* by Conrad Aiken. *The London Magazine* 6, No. 5 (August 1966): 115-18.

Favorable review of Aiken's short stories. Fytton comments: "The publication of [Aiken's] *Collected Stories* is a sharp reminder of just how neglected these works have been."

Gwynn, Frederick L. "The Functional Allusions in Conrad Aiken's 'Mr. Arcularis.' " *Twentieth-Century Literature* 2, No. 1 (April 1956): 21-5.

Examines allusions to literature, art, and music in "Mr. Arcularis."

Hamalian, Leo. "Aiken's 'Silent Snow, Secret Snow.' " *The Explicator* 7, No. 2 (November 1948): Item 17.

Psychoanalytic discussion of the protagonist of "Silent Snow, Secret Snow."

Hoffman, Frederick J. *Conrad Aiken.* New York: Twayne, 1962, 172 p.

Critical and biographical study with a chapter devoted to Aiken's fiction.

Jones, William M. "Aiken's 'Silent Snow, Secret Snow'." *The Explicator* XVIII, No. 6 (March 1960): Item 34.

Interprets the protagonist's break with reality as a manifestation of his mental illness.

Martin, Jay. *Conrad Aiken: A Life of His Art.* Princeton, N.J.: Princeton University Press, 1962, 280 p.

Critical study of Aiken's poetry that includes a section discussing the relationship between his prose fiction and poetic works.

Paterson, Isabel. "Poetic but Ectoplasmic." *New York Herald Tribune Review of Books* 10, No. 30 (1 April 1934): 4.

Faults the characterization in the stories collected in *Among the Lost People.*

Perkins, George. "Aiken's 'Silent Snow, Secret Snow.' " *The Explicator* XXI, No. 3 (November 1962): Item 26.

Notes allusions to Gaelic legend in "Silent Snow, Secret Snow."

Rascoe, Burton. "Contemporary Reminiscences: The Hard Brilliance of Ernest Hemingway; Sherwood Anderson's New Phase; and Other Literary Matters." *Arts & Decoration* XXIV, No. 1 (November 1925): 57, 79, 82.

Brief, unfavorable review of *Bring! Bring!* Rascoe concludes: "The disillusions of life, the impermanence of passion, the remembrance of youth, the carnal base of the most spiritual love—these are forever good themes for the poet, especially the poet who has Aiken's skill at verbal harmonics, his delicacy of rhythm. But Aiken has not a like skill for making these themes interesting in prose."

Rountree, Mary Martin. "Conrad Aiken's Fiction: 'An Inordinate and Copious Lyric'." *The Southern Quarterly* 21, No. 1 (Fall 1982): 9-27.

Discusses Aiken's prose fiction, focusing primarily on his novels. Rountree briefly discusses "Silent Snow, Secret Snow," praising it as "one of Aiken's most brilliant achievements."

Slap, Laura A. "Conrad Aiken's 'Silent Snow, Secret Snow': Defenses against the Primal Scene." *American Imago* 37, No. 1 (Spring 1980): 1-11.

Examines Paul Hasleman's breakdown from a psychoanalytic perspective, maintaining that the protagonist's illness "is a reaction to his realization of his parent's sexual activity."

Strauss, Harold. "Mr. Aiken's Stories." *The New York Times Book Review* (8 April 1934): 6-7.

Praises the psychological insight of the stories collected in *Among the Lost People.*

Tabachnick, Stephen E. "The Great Circle Voyage of Conrad Aiken's *Mr. Arcularis.*" *American Literature* XLV, No. 4 (January 1974): 590-607.

Examines the theme of the "great circle" voyage in several of Aiken's poetic and fictional works, including the short story "Mr. Arcularis" and Aiken's theatrical adaptation of this work.

Tebeaux, Elizabeth. " 'Silent Snow, Secret Snow': Style as Art." *Studies in Short Fiction* 20, Nos. 2-3 (Spring-Summer 1983): 105-14.

Stylistic analysis of "Silent Snow, Secret Snow." Tebeaux argues: "Close analysis of the story reveals that Aiken carefully implements a number of poetic devices that mesh sound and sense and content to convey the stages, development, and intensity of Paul's experience."

"Faintly Bitter." *Time* LVI, No. 14 (2 October 1950): 80.

Reviews *The Short Stories of Conrad Aiken,* asserting that "[though] his reputation has been largely based on his poetry, Aiken may well be remembered most for his short stories."

Wake, Special Conrad Aiken Issue, No. 11 (1952): 3-128.

Includes an essay by Jean Garrigue on the play *Mr. Arcularis,* which Aiken adapted from the short story.

Wright, Russell. "Juxtaposition." *The New York Herald Tribune Books,* No. 37 (31 May 1925): 11.

Favorable review of *Bring! Bring! and Other Stories.*

Additional coverage of Aiken's life and career is contained in the following sources published by Gale Research: *Concise Dictionary of American Literary Biography, 1929-1941; Contemporary Authors,* Vols 5-8, rev. ed., Vols. 45-48 [obituary]; *Contemporary Authors New Revision Series,* Vol. 4; *Contemporary Literary Criticism,* Vols. 1, 3, 5, 10, 52; *Dictionary of Literary Biography,* Vols. 9, 45; and *Something about the Author,* Vols. 3, 30.

Ambrose Bierce

1842-1914?

(Full name Ambrose Gwinnett Bierce; also wrote under the pseudonyms Dod Grile and William Herman) American short story writer, journalist, poet, essayist, and critic.

INTRODUCTION

Bierce's literary reputation is based primarily on his short stories of the Civil War and of the supernatural, most prominently "An Occurrence at Owl Creek Bridge," "Chickamauga," and "The Death of Halpin Frayser." Often compared to the tales of Edgar Allan Poe, Bierce's stories share a similar attraction to death in its more bizarre forms: they feature uncanny manifestations and depictions of mental deterioration, and express the horror of existence in a meaningless universe. Like Poe, Bierce was concerned with the pure artistry of his work; at the same time he was intent on conveying his personal attitudes of misanthropy and pessimism.

Bierce was born in Meigs County, Ohio. His parents were farmers, and he was the tenth of thirteen children, all of whom were given names beginning with "A." In 1846 the family moved to Indiana, where Bierce attended primary and secondary school. He entered the Kentucky Military Institute in 1859, and at the outbreak of the Civil War enlisted in the Union army, serving in such units as the Ninth Indiana Infantry Regiment and Buell's Army of the Ohio. Bierce fought bravely and extensively in numerous military engagements, including the battles of Shiloh and Chickamauga and in Sherman's March to the Sea. After the war Bierce traveled with a military expedition to San Francisco, where he left the army in 1867.

Bierce's early poetry and prose appeared in the *Californian* magazine. In 1868 he was hired as the editor of the *News Letter,* for which he wrote his famous "Town Crier" column. Bierce became a noted figure in California literary society, establishing friendships with Mark Twain, Bret Harte, and Joaquin Miller. In 1872 Bierce moved to England, where during a three-year stay he wrote for *Fun* and *Figaro* magazines and acquired the nickname "Bitter Bierce." His first three books of sketches, *The Fiend's Delight, Nuggets and Dust Panned Out in California,* and *Cobwebs from an Empty Skull,* were published during this period. He returned to San Francisco and worked in a government mint office for one year before becoming associate editor of the *Argonaut* in 1877. Bierce worked for a mining company in South Dakota for two years, but he returned in 1881 to become editor of the weekly *Wasp.* In 1887 Bierce began writing for William Randolph Hearst's *San Francisco Examiner,* continuing the "Prattler" column he had done for the *Argonaut* and the *Wasp.* This provided him with a regular outlet for his essays, epigrams, and many of the short stories subsequently collected in *Tales of Soldiers and Civilians* in 1891 and *Can Such Things Be?* in 1893. A committed opponent of hypocrisy, prejudice, and corruption, Bierce acquired fame as a journalist, becoming an admired but often hated public figure, a man of contradiction and mystery. In 1914 he informed some of his correspondents that he intended to travel to Mexico and join Pancho Villa's forces as an observer during that country's civil war. He was never heard from again, and the circumstances of his death are uncertain.

Bierce's major fiction was collected in *Can Such Things Be?* and *Tales of Soldiers and Civilians.* Many of his stories draw on his experiences in the Civil War, earning him a reputation as a realistic author of war fiction. However, Bierce was not striving for documentary realism, as critics have pointed out and as he himself admitted, for his narratives often fail to supply sufficient verisimilitude. Rather, Bierce focused on the adept manipulation of the reader's viewpoint: a bloody battlefield seen through the eyes of a deaf child in "Chickamauga," the deceptive escape dreamed by a man about to be hanged in "An Occurrence at Owl Creek Bridge," and the shifting perspectives of "The Death of Halpin Frayser." The structure of Bierce's tales commonly hinges on an ironic, surprise conclusion;

as Alfred Kazin has noted, "There is invariably a sudden reversal, usually in a few lines near the end, that takes the story away from the reader, as it were, that overthrows his confidence in the nature of what he has been reading, that indeed overthrows his confidence." Similarly Bierce's tales of the supernatural often feature unexpected conclusions that allow the events of the narrative to be interpreted as both the effect of a supernatural agency and the result of hallucination or other psychological phenomena. In *The Devil's Dictionary,* a lexicon of its author's witticisms, Bierce defines *Ghost* as "the outward and visible sign of an inward fear"—clarifying his fundamentally psychological approach to the supernatural. For instance, the eponymous protagonist of "The Death of Halpin Frayser" dies on his mother's grave either by the hand of her widowed husband or in a symbolic, mysterious struggle with the ghost of his mother. Critics have maintained that "An Occurrence at Owl Creek Bridge" plumbs the depths of a condemned man's psyche during execution; though ostensibly a war story, it is sometimes included in supernatural anthologies for its depiction of abnormal phenomena and has been cited as an early and significant exploration of psychology in fiction.

Bierce's narrative methods have sometimes caused critics to view his works as little more than technical exercises. "Too many of his stories," David Weimer has stated, "lean heavily on crafty mechanics, on a kind of literary gadgeteering." Yet, according to H. E. Bates, the structure of Bierce's stories is significant because "Bierce began to shorten the short story; he began to bring to it a sharper, more compressed method: the touch of impressionism." In addition, Bierce's stories typically display a marked use of black humor, particularly in the ironic deaths the characters often suffer. For example, several stories center on a protagonist who, through a confusion of identities or circumstances, is responsible for the murder of a beloved family member. While critics have both condemned and praised Bierce's imagination as among the most vicious and morbid in American literature, his works are counted among the most memorable depictions of human existence as a precarious, ironic, and often futile condition.

PRINCIPAL WORKS

SHORT FICTION

Tales of Soldiers and Civilians 1891; published in England as *In the Midst of Life,* 1892
Can Such Things Be? 1893

OTHER MAJOR WORKS

Nuggets and Dust Panned out in California [as Dod Grile] (sketches) 1872
The Fiend's Delight [as Dod Grile] (sketches) 1873
Cobwebs from an Empty Skull [as Dod Grile] (sketches) 1874
The Dance of Death [with Thomas A. Harcourt under the pseudonym of William Herman] (satire) 1877
Black Beetles in Amber (poetry) 1892
The Monk and the Hangman's Daughter [translator; with Gustav Adolph Danzinger] (novel) 1892
Fantastic Fables (satire) 1899
Shapes of Clay (poetry) 1903
The Cynic's Word Book (satire) 1906; also published as *The Devil's Dictionary,* 1911
The Shadow on the Dial, and Other Essays (essays) 1909
Write It Right (essay) 1909
The Collected Works of Ambrose Bierce. 12 vols. (short stories, sketches, poetry, essays, and satire) 1912

The Critic (essay date 1892)

[*In the following essay, the critic reviews* Tales of Soldiers and Civilians, *finding some stories in the collection to be theatrical and repetitive in their employment of the surprise—and often improbable—ending.*]

Tales of Soldiers and Civilians by Ambrose Bierce, is a book that comes from the Pacific coast with a distinct challenge as to its merits. A little notice on a front page states that, 'denied existence by the chief publishing-houses of the country, this book owes itself to Mr. E. L. G. Steele'; also that, 'in attesting Mr. Steele's faith in his judgment and his friend, it will serve its author's main and best ambition.' Who that loves a contest can refuse to accept the challenge? *We* cannot; and therefore we reluctantly acknowledge ourselves on the side of power and tyranny—to wit, the publishers. Mr. Bierce has a charmingly lucid style, a delicate fancy, an instinct for the insignificantly salient and a pleasing faculty of making it significant—in other words, he has caught the modern knack of telling a story about nothing and telling it well. But this is not all: he sometimes commits the fault of telling about something, and not telling it well but theatrically. The stories also lack variety, in fact are tiresomely alike. The nymphs attendant upon Makart's Diana are not more surely done after a single model than are these tales. Read one and the construction of all is known to you; the only variation is in their point—a point often delayed down to the last word of the last line. Mr. Bierce's tales present to us the incongruous mental picture of a story like a top standing on its end—and we are so occupied in seeing how small a thing can evenly sustain such an elaborate superstructure that we are apt to underestimate its other qualities.

There are many masters of this art of balancing a story on a single point, not the least of whom is Mr. Aldrich, who in his 'Olympe Zabriskie' has done in an altogether different style what Mr. Bierce has so nearly succeeded in doing. Three of his stories—**'At Owl Creek Bridge,' 'The Affaire at Coulter's Notch'** and **'Haïta, the Shepherd'**—are delicate and poignant bits of writing that will remain long in the memory. It is in such tales as **'A Watcher by the Dead'** and a **'Tough Tussle'** that he becomes overstrained and theatrical.

A review of "Tales of Soldiers and Civilians," in The Critic, *New York, Vol. 17, No. 3, March 19, 1892, p. 167.*

The Bookman **(essay date 1898)**

[*In the following essay, the critic praises* In the Midst of Life *as a collection of short stories that are equal to those of Edgar Allan Poe, Rudyard Kipling, and Guy de Maupassant.*]

Under this new title [***In the Midst of Life***] appears a volume containing those stories by Mr. Bierce formerly published as ***Tales of Soldiers and Civilians,*** with the addition of several more. Mr. Bierce's reputation is so well established with lovers of good literature, that we can do little more than note the fact of this book's appearance. We think it very safe to say that with the single exception of Poe, no American writer has ever written any short stories that can compare with these. Intensely dramatic, condensed in such a way as to make their very brevity heighten the effect which they produce, the construction and development of each of these tales is a model of literary art. They are as striking as Kipling's, they are as powerfully unpleasant as some of the best of Maupassant's. We like most the stories whose scene is laid on or near the battlefield, and the more so as they are not purely and simply "war stories," but bring into the web of the plot those threads of love and hate, of ambition and intrigue and disgrace that display the intensely human man under the soldier's garb. Nowhere can the art of how and when to end a story be more perfectly exemplified than in some of these remarkable tales.

A review of "In the Midst of Life," in The Bookman, *New York, Vol. VII, No. 3, May, 1898, p. 257.*

H. E. Bates (essay date 1941)

[*Bates was one of the masters of the twentieth-century English short story and the author of* The Modern Short Story *(1941), an excellent introduction to the form. He was also a respected novelist and contributor of book reviews to the* Morning Post *and* The Spectator. *In the following excerpt, Bates identifies elements in Bierce's oeuvre that anticipated the modern short story.*]

Of far greater significance than Bret Harte, a better writer, speaking from an intensely personal attitude, offering moreover a picture and some comment on the shattering history of his time, is the mysterious Ambrose Bierce. Bierce served as an officer in the Civil War. A whole literature, dressed up, fattened out, romanticized, has now sprung up about that war in very much the same way as a whole literature sprang up in the nineteenth century about the Napoleonic Wars. It is comparatively easy now to sit back and, getting the perspective right, produce a *Gone with the Wind.* It is a very different matter to record the battle before the smoke has died away. In some dozens of forceful unromanticized war-sketches Bierce did that, and more. Bierce introduced the psychological study: perhaps more truthfully the pathological study. That he failed to raise it to the level where the pathological interest ceased to be obtrusive, to be sufficiently absorbed, does not really matter. Bierce is important as a sign of the days to come: the days when the short story was to interpret character not through a series of bold and attractive actions but through casual and apparently irrelevant incidents. As a man of action who in the stink of battle could retain a detached viewpoint Bierce was remarkable enough, and the famous "**The Horseman in the Sky**" alone would put him into the front rank of all commentators on the futility of war; but as a man of action who was interested in the psychological value of the apparently insignificant moment or event Bierce was some years ahead of his time. It is interesting that he showed an inclination to keep the stories of action and the stories of interpretation separate, as if his two methods were imperfectly correlated. In Bierce, as in all writers of more than topical importance, and certainly not as in Bret Harte, two forces were in incessant conflict: spirit against flesh, normal against abnormal. This clash, vibrating in his work from beginning to end, keeping the slightest story nervous, restless, inquisitive, put Bierce into the company of writers who are never, up to the last breath, satisfied, who are never tired of evolving and solving some new equation of human values, who are driven and even tortured by their own inability to reach a conclusion about life and thereafter remain serene.

But Bierce, who as a writer tirelessly impinging a highly complex personality on every page will always remain interesting, is significant in another respect. Bierce began to shorten the short story; he began to bring to it a sharper, more compressed method: the touch of impressionism.

> The snow had piled itself, in the open spaces along the bottom of the gulch, into long ridges that seemed to heave, and into hills that appeared to toss and scatter spray. The spray was sunlight, twice reflected; dashed once from the moon, twice from the snow.

The language has a sure, terse, bright finality. In its direct focusing of the objects, its absence of wooliness and laboured preliminaries, it is a language much nearer to the prose of our own day than that of Bierce's day.

Again the same "modern" quality is found:

> A man stood upon a railroad bridge in northern Alabama, looking down into the swift water twenty feet below. The man's hands were behind his back, his wrists bound with a cord. A rope closely encircled his neck.

Note that this is the beginning of a story, the famous **"An Occurrence at Owl Creek Bridge."** Note that there is no leading-up, no preliminary preparation of the ground. In less than forty words, before the mind has had time to check its position, we are in the middle of an incredible and arresting situation. Writers throughout the ages have worked with various methods to get the reader into a tractable and sympathetic state of mind, using everything from the bribery of romanticism and fantasy to the short bludgeon blow of stark reality. But Bierce succeeds by a process of absurd simplicity: by placing the most natural words in the most natural order, and there leaving them. Such brief and admirable lucidity, expressed in simple yet not at all superficial terms, was bound to shorten the short story and to charge it in turn with a new vigour and reality. Not that Bierce always uses these same simple and forceful methods. Sometimes the prose lapses into the heavier explanatory periods of the time, and unlike the passages quoted, is at once dated; but again and again Bierce can be found using that simple, direct, factual method of description, the natural recording of events, objects, and scenes, that we in our day were to know as reportage.

Born too early, working outside the contemporary bounds, Bierce was rejected by his time. A writer who wants to be popular in his time must make concessions. Bierce made none. With a touch of the sensuous, of the best sort of sentimentalism, of poetic craftiness, Bierce might have been the American Maupassant. He fails to be that, and yet remains in the first half-dozen writers of the short story in his own country. Isolated, too bitterly uncompromising to be popular, too mercurial to be measured and ticketed, Bierce is the connecting link between Poe and the American short story of to-day. (pp. 52-6)

H. E. Bates, "American Writers after Poe," in his The Modern Short Story: A Critical Survey, *1941. Reprint by The Writer, Inc., 1956, pp. 46-71.*

M. E. Grenander (essay date 1957)

[*Grenander is an American critic and educator. In the following essay, she disputes the claim that Bierce is a literary scion of Edgar Allan Poe, and asserts instead that Bierce wrote unique tales of terror that achieve their effect through irony.*]

Sponge-like, the glamorous life and elusive personality of Ambrose Bierce have absorbed the attention of scholars, who have studied the author instead of his literary output. Accordingly, such off-hand critical judgments as the numerous writers on Bierce have offered are usually either wrong, or right for the wrong reasons. For example, in the Autumn, 1954, issue of the *Hudson Review,* Marcus Klein pauses in the midst of an article discussing the hatefulness of Ambrose Bierce to break a parenthetical lance on the collective heads of those who dismiss Bierce's stories as mere imitations of Poe's. For the Bierce stories are, according to Mr. Klein, "unlike the satin horrors of Poe" because "they did a job. They drew an indictment. They served."

Mr. Klein's conclusion immediately sets him up in opposition to a long line of critics and literary historians, of varying degrees of scholarship, who have either tried to establish, or subscribed blindly to, the thesis that Bierce was a follower of Poe. The attempt began in Bierce's own lifetime, and never failed to arouse his articulate wrath and his stout disclaimers that his tales had really been sired by Poe. On September 6, 1909, he wrote Silas Orrin Howes with wry irony: "If I had left the tragic and the supernatural out of my stories I would still have been an 'imitator of Poe,' for they would still have been stories; so what's the use?"

Bierce's repeated denials of Poe's influence on his tales did not, however, prevent a succession of reviewers and critics from continuing to trace this same illegitimate genealogy. The effort reached its solemn apotheosis in Arthur Miller's scholarly attempt to establish the bar sinister in the ancestry of Bierce's stories. In an article in *American Literature* (May, 1932) entitled "The Influence of Edgar Allan Poe on Ambrose Bierce," Mr. Miller marshalled an imposing array of similarities between the work of the two men, but offered no proof that Bierce "borrowed" from Poe. And the recent *Times Literary Supplement* issue on American literature (September 17, 1954) was only following conventional procedure in treating the two authors together as part of our national tradition of dark horror.

Hence Mr. Klein's heresy is a welcome corrective to an uncritical bromide which has been accepted more or less on faith by generations of readers. But the grounds on which Mr. Klein bases his conclusion are disturbing in their implications. For few writers have been more insistent than Bierce that it was *not* the function of literature to do a job, draw an indictment, or serve. These chores he relegated to journalism, for which, despite the very good living it paid him ($100 a week from William Randolph Hearst), he had only contempt. But literature was something else again. "The Muse will not meet you if you have any work for her to do" is a characteristic statement of Bierce's views on the subject.

Nevertheless, despite what I consider his false premises, I believe Mr. Klein to have arrived at a sound conclusion, for I think it is demonstrable that Bierce's stories are completely "unlike the satin horrors of Poe," though for aesthetic rather than didactic reasons. In the first place, besides his tales of horror Bierce wrote many other types: comic stories, tales of pathos, stories of tragic pity, etc. In the second place, when we do concentrate on his horror tales we find that they differ specifically from Poe's in a way that has not yet been analyzed and that constitutes them as a distinct form, an examination of which yields illuminating differentiae. I therefore propose, in this essay, to scrutinize some of Bierce's tales of terror and to show in what way their form differs from that of Poe's.

Briefly, I believe that Bierce's unique contribution to the development of the short story is the particular way in which he combined irony with terror. In any terror tale, the emotional effect is basically an intense degree of fear. Poe uses all the devices at his command to enhance and increase it to a climactic crescendo, relying heavily, for example, on bizarre settings: a lonely decayed old house on the brink of a miasmal tarn, a torture chamber of the Spanish Inquisition, a subterranean tomb in the vaults of an ancient family castle.

Bierce's method, however, was quite different. He added an ironic twist, which rests primarily on a certain kind of relationship between plot and character, so that we feel an intense fear coupled with a bitter realization that the emotion is cruelly inappropriate. What emerges is really a new form. Poe's tales of terror are nearly all simple in plot and cumulative in their emotional impact; Bierce's best ones are complex in plot and involve an element of irony in their emotional effect.

Bierce's handling of irony was, moreover, highly individual. Most authors who have cultivated it—O. Henry comes instantly to mind—have done so by manipulating the manner of representation. In other words, the narrator self-consciously conceals or holds back vital bits of information until he can spring them on the unsuspecting reader—often with little regard for the demands of probability in either plot or character—at a point in the representation where he thinks they will achieve their maximum effect of surprise. (The revelation is frequently so unexpected, and rests on so slight a foundation of probability, that not uncommonly the effect can, indeed, be more accurately described as stupefaction.) When this technique is applied to the terror story, we get what might be termed "the ironical tale of terror."

Bierce was not above using this artificial device. But in his best stories, the irony lies not in a self-conscious coyness on the part of the narrator, but in a certain relationship between a given character and the incidents of the plot. Hence I have chosen to call these stories, not ironical tales of terror, but tales of ironical terror, since the irony is not a factitious thing tacked on by the narrator, but an integral part of the action itself.

How is this effect of ironical terror achieved? Fundamentally, it depends on a firm psychological grasp of the connection between intellectual, emotional, and sensory factors in the human personality. In Bierce's tales of ironical terror, a character's reaction to given circumstances involves all three of these factors. First, he has an intellectual awareness of a dangerous situation—typically one which he believes threatens his life or his honor. Second, this knowledge arouses in him an emotion of fear, deepening to terror, and frequently thence to madness. Third, this emotional involvement results in a particular kind of physical reaction—usually a tremendous heightening and acceleration of sensory perceptions, the latter often indicated by a slowing-up of subjective time.

Obviously the base of this psychology is the intellectual awareness of danger. Just as obviously this psychology could be used in a good nonironical horror story showing the steadily increasing effects of terror on the protagonist. (As a matter of fact, this is the kind of story Poe writes.) Bierce, however, makes the intellectual awareness on which the whole psychology of his protagonist's terror rests a wrong one; hence all the emotional and sensory reactions which follow are erroneous, and the reader's perception of this gruesome inappropriateness to the facts of the real situation is what gives their peculiar distillation of horror to the Bierce tales.

Let us say that a character sees a deadly snake in his bedroom. He "knows" that the snake's bite will be fatal. This intellectual perception results in an emotional reaction of fear. Or suppose that a man, after a long absence, returns home and sees his cherished wife running to meet him. He "knows" that they will soon be reunited; consequently he "feels" joy. In either of these cases, the intellectual perception is accurate and the emotional reaction proper and appropriate. But suppose that in the second example, the man sees a woman running to meet him who he thinks is his wife; she is in fact, however, a neighbor who is hurrying to tell him of his wife's death. His emotional reaction in this case will be the same as in the former—*i.e.,* joy; but the effect of the story will be ironical, since his intellectual perception is inaccurate and his emotional reaction therefore painfully inappropriate.

That this relationship between thought and emotion was an integral part of Bierce's interpretation of human psychology and not a factitious schema superimposed on his stories by the present writer is indicated by comments he made in two letters. Writing to his protégé, George Sterling, on January 29, 1910, he said: "You know it has always been my belief that one cannot be trusted to feel until one has learned to think." And to Percival Pollard he wrote, on July 29, 1911: "To feel rightly one must think and know rightly."

The story **"One Kind of Officer"** probably isolates more clearly than any other the importance of the intellectual perception of danger to Bierce's psychology. Although I conceive this tale to be one of retributive tragedy rather than one of terror, I introduce it at this point because it shows the tremendous importance Bierce puts on a character's "knowledge" of a situation. In this story even the army, for example, has a subconscious kind of knowledge: "Beneath the individual thoughts and emotions of its component parts it thinks and feels as a unit. And in this large, inclusive sense of things lies a wiser wisdom than the mere sum of all that it knows." Hence the men "had a dumb consciousness that all was not well" and "felt insecure," while the officers "spoke more learnedly of what they apprehended with no greater clearness."

But Captain Ransome, who is in "conditions favorable to thought," understands the situation with greater precision. General Cameron, however, has told him: "It is not permitted to you to know *anything*"—an order which Ransome takes quite literally and repeats to Lieutenant Price. Cameron, we discover, has been tragically mistaken in thinking Ransome "too fond of his opinion," for the captain commits the fatal error of acting contrary to knowledge he himself possesses. With the "mechanical fidelity" which all the army is showing that day, Ransome does no more than his duty, callously following orders and consciously slaughtering his own men. And he must pay the price for his lethal actions: when General Masterson asks him if he does not know what he had been doing, he admits his knowledge. Masterson, shocked, says: "You know it—you know that, and you sit here smoking?"

Ransome tries to excuse himself on the grounds of following orders, even though they ran counter to his knowledge, but when he turns to Lieutenant Price (General Cameron has been killed) with the query, "Do you know anything of the orders under which I was acting?" Price, who has also been told it was not permitted him to know *anything,* says: "I know nothing." And Ransome is doomed by the same kind of officer he himself is: one who obeys orders mechanically, knowing they are wrong, and sends men to their death in the process.

"One Kind of Officer" is unique among Bierce's stories, not for its irony—that is typical—but because the protagonist does not act on his knowledge. For typically in a Bierce story the character acts, or reacts, all too thoroughly on the basis of the best knowledge that he has, irony arising because his knowledge is fatally wrong.

The situation in terror stories must be one that will arouse fear; hence it must either be dangerous or be thought dangerous. Bierce's best tales of ironical terror can be divided into two groups: those in which the actual situation is harmful, with the protagonist conceiving it to be harmless and reacting accordingly; and those in which the actual situation is harmless, with the protagonist conceiving it to be harmful and reacting accordingly. In either of these groups, the reader may share the protagonist's misconception of the situation, not realizing the truth until the end of the story; or he may realize all along that the protagonist is wrong. What the reader's grasp of events will be is controlled by the method of narration.

In the first category come such stories as **"An Occurrence at Owl Creek Bridge"** and **"Chickamauga."** In both, the protagonist thinks himself safe in what is really a harmful situation. Peyton Farquhar's sensations in **"Owl Creek Bridge"** are at first "unaccompanied by thought. The intellectual part of his nature was already effaced; he had power only to feel." Suddenly, however, "the power of thought was restored; he knew that the rope had broken and he had fallen into the stream . . . . His brain was as energetic as his arms and legs; he thought with the rapidity of lightning." He thinks (wrongly) that he has made a miraculous last-minute escape from being hanged.

The child in **"Chickamauga"** believes that the group of maimed and bleeding soldiers he comes upon is "a merry spectacle," which reminds him "of the painted clown whom he had seen last summer in the circus." He fails to recognize his home when he sees its blazing ruins, and thinks them a pleasing sight.

Accompanying these intellectual misunderstandings are emotional reactions which are gruesomely inappropriate. Farquhar eagerly makes his way homeward (he thinks), joyfully anticipating a reunion with his wife. The boy in **"Chickamauga"** has a gay time playing with the pitiful specimens he comes upon, "heedless . . . of the dramatic contrast between his laughter and their own ghastly gravity." He even tries to ride pig-a-back on one of the crawling and broken soldiers, and he dances with glee about the flaming embers of his home.

In both stories the protagonist also has unusual physical reactions. Farquhar's senses are preternaturally acute: "Something in the awful disturbance of his organic system had so exalted and refined them that they made record of things never before perceived." He feels each ripple of water on his face; he sees the veining of individual leaves in the forest on the bank of the river, the insects on them, and the prismatic colors of the dew in the grass. He even sees through the rifle sights the eye of the man on the bridge who is firing at him. And he hears "the humming of the gnats . . . ; the beating of the dragon-flies' wings, the strokes of the water-spiders' legs," the rush of a fish's body. Accompanying all this is the slowing up of time; the interval between his falling and suffocating is "ages," and the ticking of his watch is so strong and sharp it "hurt[s] his ear like the thrust of a knife."

The "Chickamauga" boy, on the other hand, has senses which are subnormally dull. He is a deaf-mute, a fact which accounts for his sleeping through the battle: "all unheard by him were the roar of the musketry, the shock of the cannon." When he recognizes the torn and mangled body of his dead mother, and a belated understanding bursts upon him, he can express himself only by "a series of inarticulate and indescribable cries—something between the chattering of an ape and the gobbling of a turkey—a startling, soulless, unholy sound, the language of a devil."

In **"An Occurrence at Owl Creek Bridge,"** the reader does not realize the true state of affairs until the end of the story. In **"Chickamauga,"** he is constantly aware of the true situation and the irony of the boy's reaction to it; the narrator tells us immediately: "Not all of this did the child note; it is what would have been noted by an elder observer." For this reason, in **"Chickamauga"** the horrific effect is stronger, and the ironic element in it is maintained more consistently from beginning to end. We are not conscious, as we are in **"Owl Creek Bridge"** of the narrator's manipulation of point of view. We lose the element of surprise at the end; we gain a more powerful and more constant emotional effect.

In the second group of stories—represented by **"One of the Missing," "One Officer, One Man,"** and **"The Man and the Snake"**—the technique of ironic terror is reversed. A basically harmless (or at least, not very harmful) situation is misinterpreted as an extremely perilous one; the protagonist has all the emotional reactions which would be appropriate to a situation of terrible danger, and the story concludes with his death.

Jerome Searing in **"One of the Missing"** is convinced that a loaded rifle, set on a hair-trigger and pointed directly at his forehead, will go off if he makes the slightest move. In **"One Officer, One Man"** Captain Graffenreid not only misinterprets his situation, he misinterprets his own character. Thinking himself a courageous man, "his spirit was buoyant, his faculties were riotous. He was in a state of mental exaltation." But after the shooting starts, "his conception of war" undergoes "a profound change. . . . The fire of battle was not now burning very brightly in this warrior's soul. From inaction had come introspection. He sought rather to analyze his feelings than distinguish himself by courage and devotion. The result was profoundly disappointing." In his change from ignorance to knowledge of his own character, he realizes his cowardice, but he still thinks he is engaged in a dangerous battle.

In **"The Man and the Snake"** Harker Brayton thinks the reptile under his bed a real one which is trying to hypnotize him with its malevolent glare. At first he is "more keenly conscious of the incongruous nature of the situation than affected by its perils; it was revolting, but absurd." He thinks of calling the servant, but it occurs to him "that the act might subject him to the suspicion of fear, which he certainly did not feel." Then he considers the offensive qualities of the snake: "These thoughts shaped themselves with greater or less definition in Brayton's mind and begot action. The process is what we call consideration and decision. It is thus that we are wise and unwise." But he overestimates his own powers of emotional resistance, and makes a fatal mistake: " 'I am not so great a coward as to fear to seem to myself afraid.' "

In all these cases, the protagonist reacts emotionally to what he thinks is a situation of extreme jeopardy. Jerome Searing is a brave man, and as he creeps forward on his scouting expedition, his pulse is "as regular, his nerves . . . as steady as if he were trying to trap a sparrow." When he sees the rifle pointed at his head and remembers he has left it cocked, he is "affected with a feeling of uneasiness. But that was as far as possible from fear." Gradually, however, he becomes conscious of a dull ache in his forehead; when he opens his eyes it goes away; when he closes them it comes back. He grows more and more terrified. As he stares at the gun barrel, the pain in his forehead deepens; he lapses into unconsciousness and delirium.

> Jerome Searing, the man of courage, the formidable enemy, the strong, resolute warrior, was as pale as a ghost. His jaw was fallen; his eyes protruded; he trembled in every fibre; a cold sweat bathed his entire body; he screamed with fear. He was not insane—he was terrified.

Captain Graffenreid, as he hears his men laughing at his cowardice, burns with "a fever of shame," and "the whole range of his sensibilities" is affected. "The strain upon his nervous organization was insupportable." Agitation also grips Brayton, though he is a reasonable man. The snake's horrible power over his imagination increases his fear, and finally he, too, screams with terror.

In these stories, as in those of the first group, the protagonists react with unusual physical sensations. Searing "had not before observed how light and feathery" the tops of the distant trees were, "nor how darkly blue the sky was, even among their branches, where they somewhat paled it with their green. . . . He heard the singing of birds, the strange metallic note of the meadow lark." Time slows up, space contracts, and he becomes nothing but a bundle of sensations:

> No thoughts of home, of wife and children, of country, of glory. The whole record of memory was effaced. The world had passed away—not a vestige remained. Here in this confusion of timbers and boards is the sole universe. Here is immortality in time—each pain an everlasting life. The throbs tick off eternities.

Captain Graffenreid, in his state of terror, grows "hot and cold by turns," pants like a dog, and forgets to breathe "until reminded by vertigo." Harker Brayton is also affected physically. When he means to retreat, he finds that he is unaccountably walking slowly forward. "The secret of human action is an open one: something contracts our muscles. Does it matter if we give to the preparatory molecular changes the name of will?" His face takes on "an ashy pallor," he drops his chair and groans.

> He heard, somewhere, the continuous throbbing of a great drum, with desultory burst of far music, inconceivably sweet, like the tones of an aeolian harp. . . . The music ceased, rather, it became by insensible degrees the distant roll of a retreating thunder-storm. A landscape, glittering with sun and rain, stretched before him, arched with a vivid rainbow framing in its giant curve a hundred visible cities.

The landscape seems to rise up and vanish; he has fallen on the floor. His face white and bloody, his eyes strained wide, his mouth dripping with flakes of froth, he wriggles toward the snake in convulsive movements.

All three men die of their fright: Brayton and Searing from sheer panics Graffenreid a suicide because he can no longer tolerate the disorganization of his nervous system. But all their terror and pain was needless—Searing's rifle had already been discharged; Graffenreid's battle was a minor skirmish; Brayton's snake was only a stuffed one with shoe-button eyes. In these stories, as in **"Chickamauga"** and **"An Occurrence at Owl Creek Bridge,"** Bierce has given the terror tale an ironic turn of the screw. (pp. 257-64)

M. E. Grenander, "Bierce's Turn of the Screw: Tales of Ironical Terror," in Western Humanities Review, *Vol. XI, No. 1, Winter, 1957, pp. 257-64.*

David R. Weimer (essay date 1960)

[In the following essay, Weimer provides an overview of Bierce's war stories.]

As American commentators on Ambrose Bierce have universally remembered and then forgotten, there is something to be gained from sitting down with his stories and reading them—as stories. History in the twentieth century has, to be sure, furnished causes for our having spent less time with what Bierce wrote than with what he stood for. At the same time that two world wars have stimulated an interest in his fiction, particularly in the war stories, they have made still more intriguing to postwar sensibilities the remote, lonely figure Bierce was. The faintly sensational nature of his public life has served, also, to divert attention from his writings.

This biographical questing seems to me regrettable, but not entirely so. A momentary loss in literary appreciation may, after all, be a gain elsewhere; and so it has proved with Bierce. In undervaluing him as a writer, we have elevated him as a symbol—with results suggestive of fundamental ideas shared by American intellectuals and perhaps the public generally. It tells us something valuable about ourselves, I believe, to learn that in the 1920's Americans conceived of Bierce as a Rebel, an Alienated Artist, an Iconoclast—all fundamentally social ideas implying the possibility of the individual's reconciliation with society—whereas our own postwar era has seen him as a Nihilist or Stoic, that is, in terms of isolated moral positions, as either denying all values or preserving one's own. It is worth a small literary sacrifice to know that.

But the same argument does not apply to the long run. Like Juvenal, his spiritual brother-in-arms, Ambrose Bierce will eventually be known only by his few scribblings. It is time that we become better acquainted with some of them.

Because the most thoughtful and eloquent appraisals of Bierce's work have appeared in the wake of World Wars I and II, it is worthwhile to discover what he was about in his battle fiction, a literary type of predictable appeal to postwar generations. Bierce wrote twenty such short pieces, all told, fifteen of them brought together (with eleven tales of unmilitary terror) in 1891 as ***Tales of Soldiers and Civilians.*** The best known of these Civil War episodes is **"An Occurrence at Owl Creek Bridge,"** but equally typical of the subject matter and approach of the whole collection are **"A Horseman in the Sky," "Chickamauga," "A Son of the Gods," "One of the Missing," "The Coup de Grâce"** and **"One Officer, One Man."** Since these seven are, I think, also the best of his war stories, we may appropriately look at them more closely than at the others.

What are their characteristic features? They usually have one main character and are simply plotted. As a rule, they begin *in medias res,* follow a B-A-B structure (with a chronological reversion or flash back in the middle section), and end ironically. Frequently they depend on extreme devices to shock the reader, as when (in **"The Coup de Grâce"**) a soldier discovers that swine have ripped open the abdomen of a wounded friend of his, still alive on the ground, and have been feeding on his entrails. (How cautious we should be in dismissing such incidents in the tales as *mere* contrivances is nicely illustrated by the fact that in the Cheat Mountains of western Virginia in 1861 Bierce had actually seen corpses whose faces had been eaten away by wild swine.) Furthermore, like Poe, to whom he owed a great literary debt, Bierce was strongly concerned with creating an effect. He also had a flair for building and sustaining mood, for developing motivation realistically and selecting the most cogent detail.

Now these observations are all pretty fragmentary, and I offer them here partly as evidence of the sort of criticism Bierce's war stories have commonly received to date. From H. L. Mencken, who argued in 1929 that Bierce's tales "are probably read today, not as literature, but as shockers," to Harry T. Levin twenty years after, who perceived in the war tales chiefly the thematic contrast "between the civilian's preconceptions of military glory and the soldier's experience of ugliness and brutality," critics of the war stories have viewed them from one angle or another, but never in the round. Even Carey McWilliams, who offered the fullest and in many respects the most sensible literary account of the short stories in his biography of some thirty years ago, played them down as coherent artistic achievements.

While I am as susceptible as anyone to quarreling with readers who see a short story only as bits and pieces, I find a certain justice in the piecemeal comments on Bierce's work. Too many of his stories lean heavily on crafty mechanics, on a kind of literary gadgeteering. Small wonder that critics have given tit for tat.

But despite all this, each of Bierce's best war tales does have an artistic center. Many have sensed it, if no one has yet squarely confronted and described it. **"A Horseman in the Sky"** is the clearest example. Almost the entire action of this twelve-page story occurs near the top of a steep cliff in the mountains of Virginia. A Union soldier, Carter Druse, awakes as if intuitively from a forbidden sleep at his sentinel post:

> He quietly raised his forehead from his arm and looked between the masking stems of the laurels, instinctively closing his right hand about the stock of his rifle.
>
> His first feeling was a keen artistic delight. On a colossal pedestal, the cliff,—motionless at the extreme edge of the capping rock and sharply outlined against the sky,—was an equestrian statue of impressive dignity. The figure of the man sat the figure of the horse, straight and soldierly, but with the repose of a Grecian god carved in the marble. . . . The gray costume harmonized with its aerial background; the metal of accoutrement and caparison was softened and subdued by the shadow; the animal's skin had no points of high light. A carbine strikingly foreshortened lay across the pommel of the saddle, kept in place by the right hand grasping it at the "grip"; the left hand, holding the bridle rein, was invisible. In silhouette against the sky the profile of the horse was cut with the sharpness of a cameo; it looked across the heights of air to the confronting cliffs beyond. The face of the rider, turned slightly away, showed only an outline of temple and beard; he was looking downward to the bottom of the valley. Magnified by its lift against the sky and by the soldier's testifying sense of the formidableness of a near enemy the group appeared of heroic, almost colossal, size.

Private Druse raises his rifle, pauses, recognizes the rider, then fires at the horse. Abruptly the point of view shifts to that of an officer in the Union army. Climbing from below the mountain on which Druse reposes, the officer hesitates:

> Lifting his eyes to the dizzy altitude of its summit the officer saw an astonishing sight—a man on horseback riding down into the valley through the air!
>
> Straight upright sat the rider, in military fashion, with a firm seat in the saddle, a strong clutch upon the rein to hold his charger from too impetuous a plunge. From his bare head his long hair streamed upward, waving like a plume. His hands were concealed in the cloud of the horse's lifted mane. The animal's body was as level as if every hoof-stroke encountered the resistant earth. Its motions were those of a wild gallop, but even as the officer looked they ceased, with all the legs thrown sharply forward as in the act of alighting from a leap. But this was a flight!

As we suspected, the man whom the dying horse carries to his death is Private Druse's father. That is the trick of the thing. But one is likely to remember from the story, I believe, not so much the trick as the sharply sketched images of the motionless rider astride the horse. These images give us the most intense, most expressive part of the narrative, even as they interrupt it momentarily. They provide the emotional center of the story, the point which should—and I think for the most part in Bierce's battle tales does—coincide with the center of the author's implicit values.

Bierce's values will be clearer if we examine another passage from the tales. In **"Chickamauga,"** a six-year-old boy, a deaf-mute, wanders from home, plays soldier in the woods and becomes lost. Suddenly he sees strange creatures moving with a terrific slowness on the ground among the trees. They are men, hundreds of them, wounded in battle, now crawling away from it. To the child, observing this dreadful scene,

> it was a merry spectacle. He had seen his father's negroes creep upon their hands and knees for his amusement—had ridden them so, "making believe" they were his horses. He now approached one of these crawling figures from behind and with an agile movement mounted it astride. The man sank upon his breast, recovered, flung the small boy fiercely to the ground as an unbroken colt might have done, then turned upon him a face that lacked a lower jaw—from the upper teeth to the throat was a great red gap fringed with hanging shreds of flesh and splinters of bone. The unnatural prominence of nose, the absence of chin, the fierce eyes, gave this man the appearance of a great bird of prey crimsoned in throat and breast by the blood of its quarry. The man rose to his knees, the child to his feet. The man shook his fist at the child; the child, terrified at last, ran to a tree near by, got upon the farther side of it and took a more serious view of the situation. And so the clumsy multitude dragged itself slowly and painfully along in hideous pantomime—moved forward down the slope like a swarm of great black beetles, with never a sound of going—in silence profound, absolute.

Here, as in **"A Horseman in the Sky,"** the image is set amidst utter silence, but against an implied background of shattering sound—of the rifle shot or the battle just past, the crash of the horse and rider or the shrieks of the wounded about to come.

Both images are of motion, too, yet of no motion at all. In the first story the man and horse are initially "motionless," form "an equestrian statue"; plunging from the cliff, the man still does not change position, while the horse only seems to gallop on the earth. Similarly, in **"Chickamauga"** the great black beetles move so slowly as to make their motion appear as illusory as the rest of their "hideous pantomime." Equestrian statuary, cameos, pantomimes, beetles—Bierce's metaphors are drawn from different spheres of art and nature, but they all imply the ideas of arrested motion, of suspended sound.

We would seem to be in the presence of a writer whose treatment of his materials, indeed whose conception of external reality, is highly pictorial; and so we are. If Bierce is a slighter artist than Henry James or Faulkner, as he unquestionably is, the way he visualizes experience nonetheless has a great deal in common with that of the creator of the famous scene in *The Ambassadors* in which Lambert Strether, coming unexpectedly upon Mme. de Vionnet and Chad Newsome together in a boat, is forced to take a new view of the pair ("It was suddenly as if these figures, or something like them, had been wanted in the picture . . . and had now drifted into sight, with the slow current, on purpose to fill up the measure"); or with the creator of that natural world where the moment of a ten-year-old boy's first confronting an enormous bear takes on mythic proportions ("It did not emerge, appear: it was just there, immobile, fixed in the green and windless noon's hot dappling, not as big as he had dreamed it but as big as he had expected, bigger, dimensionless against the dappled obscurity, looking at him").

Still other features of the war stories become artistically significant when we place them in the light of Bierce's graphic intentions. As in his handling of sound and motion, Bierce interrupts, restrains, telescopes time. His most signal use of this device is in **"An Occurrence at Owl Creek Bridge,"** a tour de force in which elaborate memories and fantasies flood through a hanged man's mind in the few seconds between his drop from the gallows (the bridge) and his losing consciousness. But Bierce manipulates time frequently in the stories, nearly always in constructing the type of scene already described.

He likewise exhibits a marked interest in light, shadow, and color and in exact, sparing description. He favors dramatic presentation over narrative, a restricted point of view (with only occasional shifts to the omniscient author), and the use of his main character in the role of spectator—all elements that work directly toward the creation of a single, vivid, static scene. This pictorial focus has been felt, rather than articulated, by American critics. They have shown an awareness of it chiefly in their metaphors, as when Bertha Clark Pope observed, in the course of introducing an edition of the *Letters* (1922), that "above all writers Bierce can present—brilliantly present—startling fragments of life, carved out from attendant circumstance . . . sharply bitten etchings of individual men under momentary stresses and in bizarre situations." In his *Portrait of the Artist as American* (1930), Matthew Josephson came closest of all the critics to touching the mainspring of the war stories, commenting on the equestrian scene in **"A Horseman in the Sky"** as "almost sculptural" in quality, on "the picture of the lost child" in **"Chickamauga"** and also on Bierce's "love for the purely kaleidoscopic, through his perception of form and mysterious beauty in each accidental effect of light."

Though Pope and Josephson stopped this side of developing their insights, both sensed that the painter's eye was not peripheral to the method of the war stories but somehow right in the middle of it. Roaming around a bit more among the better stories, they might have noted the central, organizing image in each. In **"A Son of the Gods,"** a young officer braves enemy fire to reconnoiter the opposing troop positions and (after a few suspenseful minutes of astonishing bravery) is killed. In **"One of the Missing,"** a courageous private scouts Confederate gun emplacements only to be trapped by a freak accident in a wooden shed where (after a brief, disciplined attempt to free himself from the wreckage) he dies of terror. In **"The Coup de Grâce,"** an officer (glancing in a second from a herd of swine to his wounded friend upon the ground) realizes that he must kill the man to spare him further agony. In

Bierce during his military service with the Ninth Indiana Infantry.

"One Officer, One Man," a well-intentioned army captain (during the first, shocking barrage of enemy gunfire) abruptly commits suicide.

While the arrested moment in these stories sometimes brings self-discovery to one of the characters, that is not really Bierce's main point. What the characters undergo—and what matters to Bierce—is an instant, always brightly attractive in its brief duration, of intensely felt or intensely perceived experience.

It is not in every case a moment of heroism, though often it is. Acute and pleasurable intensity—that is the distinguishing characteristic. And there is another: transience. The horse and rider will surely, swiftly fall, the groans of the dying soldiers resound, the courage go for naught. This is almost certainly what Josephson meant in referring to the war stories as creating "moments of instability—as in a dance—of ingenious, dire paradox on the part of the universe." The grotesquely unstable, fragile, precarious nature of the individual's rare and therefore valuable experience is precisely Bierce's theme.

A recognition of this theme makes it possible to understand both the incompleteness and the force of Carey McWilliams's statement that the war fiction conveys "the sense of an indescribable malevolence . . . mixed up in a strangely inseparable manner with the good and beautiful." And it makes possible, too, the proper evaluation of other critical judgments, such as Mencken's assertion (in his *Prejudices,* 1927) that Bierce's "war stories, even when they deal with the heroic, do not depict soldiers as heroes; they depict them as bewildered fools, doing things without sense, submitting to torture and outrage without resistance, dying at last like hogs in Chicago. . . . " Mencken had a surer grasp of Bierce's over-all place in American letters (minor but important) than of the literary subleties.

We can judge, furthermore, what is sound and what is not in Ludwig Lewisohn's condemnation of all Bierce's tales as "morally and therefore in the last analysis creatively sterile, because Bierce showed himself conscious of no implication and disengaged no idea. The naked horror sufficed him." The remark is, within limits, perspicacious. Bierce was assuredly not conscious *enough* of the implications of his imagined world, not conscious enough to be thought of as a first-rate literary mind. But the naked horror did not suffice him. If less deeply, less complexly than his literary superiors of a later day, Bierce saw very far into the ambiguities of the war experience. (pp. 229-38)

David R. Weimer, "Ambrose Bierce and the Art of War," in Essays in Literary History Presented to J. Milton French, *edited by Rudolf Kirk and C. F. Main, Rutgers University Press, 1960, pp. 229-38.*

Eugene E. Reed (essay date 1962)

[*In the following excerpt, Reed examines how in* "Chickamauga" *Bierce contrasts the perspective of the central character with that of the reader to convey the horror of war.*]

"Chickamauga" gives instant notice that Bierce does not intend a horror story in the tradition of the tales which make up the bulk of the collection, ***In the Midst of Life.*** The child who on the warm fall afternoon strays from home to enter a wood unobserved is seen initially as a symbol of the historical context as it has been formed over the centuries. It is this child's spirit which "in bodies of its ancestors, [has] for thousands of years been trained to . . . feats of discovery and conquest—victories in battles whose critical moments were centuries, whose victors' camps were cities of hewn stone". Thus juxtaposed immediately in the selection are the eternal and the immediate, the universal and the particular; evoked, too, is a contrast made the more poignant by the author's choice of symbol, the child general with the wooden sword, the militant descendant of warrior generations who falls "upon the rearguard of his imaginary foe, putting all to the sword" only then to be vanquished by a rabbit from which he flees "calling with inarticulate cries for his mother, weeping, stumbling . . . his little heart beating hard with terror". He falls asleep to awaken to a scene of idyllic tranquility which is not only opposed to his erstwhile panic, but, in the light of that which follows, serves to emphasize the indifference of a nature "unconscious of . . . pity".

As the child stands alone in the descending twilight, the

mist rising from the brook nearby, he sees some distance before him "a strange moving object which he [takes] to be some large animal—[perhaps] a dog, a pig". The child is unafraid, for to him the approaching shape lacks the menace of the rabbit. The shape is joined by others; "to right and to left [are] many more; the whole open space . . . alive with them—all moving toward the brook . . . [creeping] upon their hands and knees . . . [using] their hands only, dragging their legs . . . [using] their knees only, their arms hanging idle at their sides". These are not dogs or pigs, an allusion which now seems to border upon the obscene, but men. "Not all of this did the child note . . . he saw little but that these were men, yet crept like babes". The child's view is thus an outside view; it is oblivious of its own innocence, which is in turn in counterpoint to the evil which it surveys—unconscious of horror, it serves to instil that consciousness, that horror, in us; there is no intermediation which might reduce the impact which the bizarre contrast must have upon the reader. "[The child moves among the men] freely, going from one to another . . . peering into their faces with childish curiosity. All their faces were singularly white and many were streaked and gouted with red. Something in this—something, too, perhaps, in their grotesque attitudes and movements—[recalls] the painted clown whom he had seen last summer in the circus, and he [laughs] as he [watches] them. But on and on they [creep], these maimed and bleeding men, as heedless as he of the dramatic contrast between his laughter and their own ghastly gravity". Again obscenity is skirted in the evocation of contrast—the contrast between the horrid facts of death and mutilation, the intent gravity of suffering, and the merriment of the child to whom these relics of recent history are but clowns. Heedless of the drama of this contrast as are both child and torn men, the reader is not; the antipodal stresses of the scene effect his disorientation, and it is the dissonance of the child's outside view which generates the requisite impact. A grotesque crescendo is reached as the gleeful boy mounts one of the ruined men as he might a pony. The man falls, recovers, flings the child to earth to turn upon him "a face that [lacks] a lower jaw . . . The unnatural prominence of nose, the absence of chin, the fierce eyes, [giving] this man the appearance of a great bird of prey crimsoned in throat and breast by the blood of its quarry". Three unconventional contrasts are simultaneously present: the contrast between the nature of the action and the context in which it occurs; the contrast between the act itself and the character of its object; the contrast between that which the man's appearance suggests, the "bird of prey", and that which he is—once predator, now quarry. Note again, too, the omnipresent contrast initially created through the evocation of the historical context, for in counterpoint to that race of conquerors the descendant of which is the child is this race of victims—this "clumsy multitude [dragging] itself slowly and painfully along in hideous pantomime . . . forward down the slope like a swarm of great black beetles, with never a sound of going—in silence profound, absolute"—a paradoxical silence which shrieks aloud to the reader and of which only he is conscious.

"Through the belt of trees beyond the brook [shines] a strange red light", and the child, whose anticipation of pleasure has become an index of the reader's apprehension, moves toward that light with his grotesque companions "his wooden sword still in hand . . . solemnly [directing] the march, conforming his pace to theirs . . . Surely such a leader never before had such a following". Indeed not. A scene of infernal desolation now confronts the reader, and, quite as before, his horror is heightened by the dancing glee of the child who runs about collecting fuel, ultimately ending his military career with the sacrifice of his sword to the flames in "surrender to the superior forces of nature". At this climactic moment the emotions of reader and child briefly converge as both discover that it is the child's home which burns and his mother who lies twisted in death upon the ground. But even this is not enough—deftly, the greater burden of agony is shifted to the reader: "The child [moves] his little hands, making wild, uncertain gestures. He [utters] a series of inarticulate and indescribable cries—something between the chattering of an ape and the gobbling of a turkey—a startling, soulless, unholy sound, the language of a devil. The child [is] a deaf mute". Thus, through the reduction of the reflex of grief to the uncouth and animal—to terms which the reader cannot accept as adequate to contain grief's need for communication, for expression—the reader himself is compelled to articulate inwardly this reflex, to supply grief a voice, to bear additionally the weight of pity paradoxically tempered by an inevitable revulsion that the answer to idiot tragedy is an idiot cry.

How different, how much more forceful all this as compared with the many more conventional fictional and historical records of human conflict! Whence the force? Are we not accustomed to say that war is horrible, implying that an identity, war, exists *and,* among other things, is horrible? The very nature of the language of prose, which is perhaps closest to the language in which we think, seems to compel a separation of identity and attribute—a separation which cannot be without its effect upon the creative process as it operates in the prose medium. No experience can be perceived as an existential entity, communicated as an entity, perceived again at tertiary remove as an entity as long as perception and communication are, as processes, subject to the divisive dictates of descriptive language. What then of the predicament of the writer to whom it is not sufficient to say that war is horrible—who will rather state that the particular identity, war, is never without its attribute, horror—that war *is* horror? Generally speaking, his problem is to translate that which he has accidentally perceived as an existential whole, the experience of war, into terms that will permit that experience to be perceived entire by the reader. Descriptive language tends to preclude this exercise, for at the writer's disposal is only that frightening tool which prescribes, as a first step in knowing, a reduction of the whole to its parts and, in communication, has the further tendency to enforce separate consideration of these with the result that true consciousness of the identity of the object is impossible. By the same token, since we think in language, we, as readers, have come in our vicarious experience of war to divorce that identity from its attribute, horror, which we consider in semi-isolation, denatured through removal. Bierce's problem, as I have tried to show, is thus one of restoration of identity—this managed within the confines of language through the skillful use of the device of the outside view. Horror is awakened; subjective attribute is welded to objective experience; a terrible identity is felt in all its horrific intensity of presence. (pp. 50-3)

Eugene E. Reed, "Ambrose Bierce's 'Chickamauga': An Identity Restored," in Revue des langues vivantes, *Vol. 28, No. 1, 1962, pp. 49-53.*

Eric Solomon (essay date 1964)

[In the following essay, Solomon provides an overview of Bierce's war fiction and asserts that the power expressed by these tales is unsurpassed within the tradition of war literature.]

In his brilliant study, *The Art of Satire* (1940), David Worcester defines cosmic irony as the satire of frustration which has a particular relevance for post-Copernican man, who is no longer the center of his universe. Ambrose Bierce's short stories of war, ***Tales of Soldiers*** (1891), are vignettes of cosmic irony wherein man is brought to realize his insignificance in the face of the all-encompassing universe of war as well as the futility of all "normal" acts and aspirations. Only Stephen Crane has written as powerfully as Bierce about the shock of recognition brought on by the Civil War.

The keynote of Bierce's war fiction is frustration. His soldiers are chagrined by their limits of knowledge and their lack of control. As Bierce states in his military memoirs, "Bits of Autobiography," "It is seldom indeed that a subordinate officer knows anything about the disposition of the enemy's forces . . . or precisely whom he is fighting. As for the rank and file, they can know nothing more of the matter than the arms they carry." Man in war, afflicted by the failure of reason and the impact of collective suffering, is also unable to live up to his preconceived ideals. Again in the memoirs, we find Bierce telling us of a gallant charge that has been beaten back by a heavy fire: "Lead had scored its old time victory over steel; the heroic had broken its great heart against the commonplace. There are those who say that it is sometimes otherwise." These two concepts, unreason and failure, provide the basis for the bitter irony of Bierce's brief, rapid anecdotes, which silhouette the blackest side of war.

The fifteen extremely short "Tales of Soldiers" included in the collection, ***In the Midst of Life,*** strike a mean between violently contrived naturalism—replete with disgusting ugliness and shocking coincidence—and the accumulation of exact, realistic, and factual observations of combat life. There can be no doubt that the author loads the dice in each of his tales. The theme of every story is the death of the good, the honest, and the brave. A Northern soldier kills his rebel father; a young enlisted man on guard duty discovers his brother's corpse; a gunner destroys his own house, murdering his wife and children. All the gestures of heroism turn out to be empty. Certainly the coincidences are over-emphasized for added ironic effect in these war stories as in all of Bierce's work. The mordant cynicism of *The Devil's Dictionary* and ***Fantastic Fables,*** the misanthropic savagery of Bierce's treatment of insanity and the supernatural in ***Can Such Things Be?*** do not lead to an objective point of view. Life is terrible, and war is the epitome of its misery.

War fits Bierce's philosophy perfectly. The very nature of combat that involves a heightening, a tension, an absurdity of situation, an incongruity that calls for satire, suits his dark approach. In Bierce's "Tales of Civilians" which make up the second half of ***In the Midst of Life,*** his stories seem labored and contrived. The writer must spend much more time to build up the situation than in the war stories, where the background may be taken for granted simply because war is war. The later stories become discursive—an almost fatal flaw for an epigrammatic method—since Bierce must describe the mining camps or the San Francisco social hierarchy; within the war context everything is understood at once. The military situation, by its nature rapid and simple, supplies its own foreshortening. Wilson Follett, perhaps Bierce's most acute critic, points out that the chief artistic weakness in his fiction comes from the substitution of an external irony for the irony inherent in the nature of things. War, with its own frame of irony, is the finest subject for "Bitter Bierce's" corruscating, witty excursions into fiction.

Bierce had ample opportunity to learn about war firsthand. He enlisted in the Ohio Volunteers at the age of nineteen, young enough for the ironies of war to become an integral part of his education. Bierce later spoke of his six years of soldiering as spent under a magic spell, "something new under a new sun." He was a success as a soldier. He rose through the ranks to become a sergeant, then a lieutenant, and finally, as a topographical engineer, he became a member of the staff of General W. B. Hazen. Bierce sums up his war experiences with an old soldier's quiet modesty: " . . . although hardly more than a boy in years, I had served at the front from the beginning of the trouble, and had seen enough of war to give me a fair understanding of it."

He was at Shiloh, Stone's River (Murfreesboro), Chickamauga, Kenesaw Mountain, and Franklin, among other engagements. Like almost every veteran who lives long enough, Bierce is able in his memoirs to cast a gloss of sentiment over army life, but he is realistic enough to comprehend that this warm sentiment is not called for. "Is it not strange" he reminisced, "that the phantoms of a blood-stained period have so airy a grace and look with so tender eyes?—that I recall with difficulty the dangers and death and horrors of the time, and without effort all that was gracious and picturesque?" We must not be misled by his fine war record and vintage memories. Bierce's war recollections are also sprinkled with the materials that go into his stories—the irony of a man named Abbot being killed by a shell with the foundry mark "Abbot" on it, or the ghastly sight of his dead comrades after they had been trampled by a herd of swine. While Bierce enjoyed the test of combat, the companionship and the excitement of war, he was revolted, intellectually, by the harsh brutalities of a repellent, paradoxical world.

Moving from memoir to fiction, Bierce found the short, almost elliptical story to be his ideal form. As critics have been quick to point out, Bierce learned a great deal from

Edgar Allan Poe's theories of fiction. Like Poe, Bierce is highly selective, fixing upon the decisive, revealing moment. For example, he catches the instant of an execution in his famous **"An Occurrence at Owl Creek Bridge,"** the intense immediacy of the discovery of cowardice and courage in the two protagonists of **"Parker Adderson, Philosopher,"** or the momentary stasis in **"A Horseman in the Sky,"** where a boy quietly presses the trigger and his father's body slowly falls into space.

Unquestionably, Bierce's plots are forced. Consider the manipulation for effect in **"An Affair of Outposts."** Here a young man, Armisted, informs the governor of his state that he wants a commission in the army in order to die in battle because his wife has taken up with some unknown person. Much later, the governor visits the battlefield, wanders too far, is endangered by an enemy attack, and saved by Armisted, who dies in the attempt—but not until both men realize that they share the knowledge that the governor is the villain of the piece. The bare plot outline, as always, hardly does justice to the story, which gains its effect from the conjunction of the civilian and military frames of reference and the bitingly sarcastic tone of the narrative. Yet this example shows how Bierce uses a highly unusual military situation that focuses the whole history of his characters onto one remarkable event. Since war is full of startling chances, the author's controlling hand is less obtrusive than it might be.

Although Bierce's figures are flat (to use E. M. Forster's term), each story expresses a deep psychological trauma, one that ends in madness or loss. Again, war is the proper setting for the intensified emotion Bierce presents. In war character becomes automatized, part of the military machine. Relying on this firm military context, Bierce easily sketches as much or as little of his heroes' past lives as he desires. The immediate impression is important in the war construct. So the hero of **"An Occurrence at Owl Creek Bridge"** is a spy who is about to be hanged—that much is germane to the story. We take for granted the reason for his being in this situation and what his beliefs are.

Bierce provides the barest minimum of character description:

> Peyton Farquhar was a well-to-do planter of an old and highly respected Alabama family. Being a slave owner and like other slave owners a politician, he was naturally an original secessionist and ardently devoted to the Southern cause. Circumstances of an imperious nature, which it is unnecessary to relate here, had prevented him from taking service with the gallant army . . .

Who he is makes little difference. How he reacts to war is important. Bierce's attitude towards plot and character may be cursory, but his fictional treatment of war is, with the exception of the work of Crane (and possibly Rudyard Kipling), the most extensive in nineteenth century English and American fiction. Bierce's subject is man in war. He does not heighten his fiction with the details of war in the manner of John W. De Forest or John Esten Cooke; rather he steeps his stories in the aura, the meaning of battle. Bierce captures the principle that lies behind the facts. He catches war at its sources, and he makes it an intensification of personal experience.

A remarkable aspect of Bierce's very short war stories is that in each one he manages to evoke the feeling of reality, the sense of fact and place that makes war not an abstract moral condition but a concrete physical actuality. Even in an allegory such as **"A Son of the Gods,"** Bierce shows the solid circumstances of war, "the occasional rattle of wheels as a battery of artillery goes into position to cover the advance; the hum and murmur of the soldiers talking; a sound of innumerable feet in the dry leaves that strew the interspaces among the trees; hoarse commands of officers." He reproduces the serious minutiae of battle, the sound and impact of shells, the ugliness of death (his corpses, festering, with entrails spread on the ground, are as brutally portrayed as anything in the pages of Erich Remarque or Henri Barbusse), the boredom and the sweat, the mass movements and the isolation of the individual who "was alone . . . His world was a few square yards of wet and trampled earth about the feet of his horse." The war stories include all types of soldier: the gay, devil-may-care spy who cracks under pressure at the last moment; the serious young officer who obeys orders even when he knows he is killing his own men; the sensitive, poetic private who deserts when he finds his brother's dead body; the blindly courageous officer who is constantly attempting to prove his courage and repress his fear.

It is a dark world, but there is a feeling of movement and excitement. "Color-bearers unfurled the flags, buglers blew the 'assembly,' hospital attendants appeared with stretchers. Field officers mounted and sent their impedimenta to the rear in care of Negro servants."

Bierce assumes that once the unique war world is created, his readers will themselves set the characters in their proper military context, as captain or private, cavalryman or infantryman. Bierce analyzes the matter of the uniqueness of the war situation brilliantly in his story **"An Affair of Outposts."** We have already mentioned the rather melodramatic plot of this tale. The particular quality of the story derives from the superb contrasting of the two worlds—the easy, ordered life of the governor, that enables him to carry a traditionally romantic conception of war in his mind, and the harsh, incongruous position of the soldier, that enforces a sardonic, anti-heroic outlook.

The governor and his staff, well-mounted and impeccably tailored, visit the fairly quiet combat area. "Things of charm they were, rich in suggestions of peaceful lands beyond a sea of strife. The bedraggled soldier looked up from his trench as they passed, leaned upon his spade, and audibly damned them to signify his sense of their ornamental irrelevance to the austerities of his trade." This coda of the story sets up the basic conflict. The author takes the position of a veteran dweller in the war world into which these others came as strange interlopers (such contempt for civilians becomes a familiar pattern in the angry war novels of the twentieth century, from John Dos Passos to John Horne Burns). The governor wanders too near the front and has to rush away—but he cannot escape the sight of the actualities of combat, the wounded struggling back, feebly dragging themselves to the cover of their comrades' fire. Now writing from the governor's angle of vision, Bierce sets forth his artistic credo as far as war is concerned:

> In all this there was none of the pomp of war—no hint of glory. Even in his distress and peril the helpless civilian could not forbear to contrast it with the gorgeous parades and reviews held in honor of himself—with the brilliant uniforms, the music, the banners, and the marching. It was an ugly and sickening business . . . revolting, brutal, in bad taste. . . . "Where is the charm of it all? Where are the elevated sentiments, the devotion, the heroism, the—?"

The author takes over at this point in the narrative and supplies the answer to the governor's question. The heroism is in the clear, deliberate voice of the captain, the austere devotion to duty that brings about a bayonet charge, savage hand-to-hand fighting, cutting, bludgeoning—and the death of the captain. The story ends with an added Biercean ironic twist: the cynical civilian is careless of all this dutiful military courage that saves his life. Yet this plot device also underlines the disparity between the honor of the battlefield and the deceit of the marketplace.

Bierce's fiction is tempered by his anti-romanticism, an attitude drawn from experience. The essay, **"On a Mountain,"** compares the natural beauties of the Virginia landscape with the shocking sight of decaying corpses. Romance must give way to realism in the war setting:

> How romantic it all was; the sunset valleys full of visible sleep; the glades suffused and interpenetrated with moonlight . . . Then there was the "spice of danger" . . . As we trudged on we passed something—some things—lying by the wayside . . . How repulsive they looked with their blood smears, their blank, staring eyes, their teeth uncovered by contraction of the lips!

This conscious rejection of the glorious view of war that characterized nearly all war fiction before the shock novels of World War I is carried over into Bierce's stories. Although Bierce the essayist occasionally lets a nostalgic note creep into his work, in the fashion of Kipling or De Forest, Bierce the creator of fiction refuses to conceive any sentimental picture of war's glories. His heroes are not heroic; his cowards are not castigated.

In **"One Kind of Officer,"** a condemnation of the entire military structure, Bierce merges plot and setting to show the irrationality of war. The general orders a captain of artillery to hold his position at all costs and to ask no questions. Obeying his orders to the letter, the captain fires on his own men. But the general is killed in the action, and the captain must be shot for carrying out his orders, since there is no one to defend him. This mordant story is at an incredible distance from previous war fiction. Not even Emile Zola rigs his war plots in quite so nihilistic a manner. And Bierce's setting is equally anti-heroic. Rain, mud, rubber ponchos, dripping corpses—how different from the glittering pomp of Charles Lever's battle scenes! Bierce refuses to accept even a hint of the heroic. "Very repulsive these wrecks looked—not at all heroic, and nobody was accessible to the infection of their patriotic example. Dead upon the field of honor, yes; but the field of honor was so very wet! It makes a difference." It does indeed make a difference. The cosmic irony of a world out of joint leads to the use of certain special fictional techniques.

Bierce might be called the first really modern war writer working in the English language. With the exceptions of Tolstoy and Stendhal, nobody writing fiction in the nineteenth century sustained an ironic approach to war so consistently as Bierce did. There are five fictional methods in which he anticipates the writers of the next century: the treatment of time, the process of animism, the approach to nature, the use of religious symbolism, and, finally, the employment of the theme that was to be raised to its finest schematization by Stephen Crane, the development from innocence, through war, to experience.

It is to be expected that such tightly condensed tales as those of Bierce should demand a certain element of foreshortening. Characters are mere shadows; one action is usually the basis for the tale, and dialogue is held to a bare minimum. Bierce recognizes a basic fact of combat: that in an intense situation the time scheme is often upset; an event that seems to take an eternity may in reality happen in a matter of minutes, and the converse is equally possible.

An outstanding example of this first type of time-manipulation appears in Bierce's most frequently anthologized war story, **"An Occurrence at Owl Creek Bridge."** Like much of his writing, it is in essence a tour-de-force. The hero, Peyton Farquhar, is about to be hanged from a railroad bridge. Bierce supplies a mournfully slow, cadenced description of the bridge, the soldiers guarding it, the officer in charge, and the preparations for the hanging. Farquhar becomes conscious of the labored, measured passage of time when he hears a steady stroke sounding for all the world like a death knell; the noise comes from his watch. The trap is sprung, and first the author provides a flashback to Farquhar's previous life, then an increasingly tense narration of his escape from the noose, his rapid flight down the turbulent river, through the bullets of the sentinels and the grape-shot of the artillery. He makes good his escape, returns to his wife—and the last, shocking line utterly destroys the carefully wrought illusion. "Peyton Farquhar was dead; his body, with a broken neck, swung gently from side to side beneath the timbers of the Owl Creek Bridge."

The ordering of time, extending the felt experience far beyond the actual number of minutes involved, has become a commonplace in modern fiction. It is important in the context of the war genre because the extension of time to include the past histories and the future hopes of the participants in a military action has been an extremely effective technique for writers who must keep their focus on the battle circumstances in order to sustain the suspense, and yet move away in time and space from the physical restrictions of the battlefield to vary the effects.

The same device is used with even greater success in **"One of the Missing,"** where a scout is crushed by a timber in a recently shelled barn. The narrator works from the scout's point of view, slowly drawing out the reveries, the mental agony, and the final, abortive suicide attempt, before the soldier dies from the strain of his long isolation. For the ironic twist in the O. Henry manner that Bierce greatly enjoys, the narrative shifts to the victim's brother who looks at his watch the instant the barn is hit by the shell and automatically checks the timepiece again when he comes across the unrecognizable body of his brother. Bierce accomplishes a double irony; the scout appears to have been dead a week, so great was the degenerative process of his fear; the watch indicates that only twelve minutes have passed. Again, sense of time supplies the macabre point to the story. Quite obviously, the shock effect is the product of Bierce's rather special sensibility. Still, the facts of war, where time is of transcendent importance, yet normally confused, where action may occur incredibly swiftly, or life may consist of tedious waiting—where, in short, time cannot be controlled by the individual—fits Bierce's treatment.

If **"One of the Missing"** would seem overly contrived in most settings, it does not seem out of place in war. We have but to compare Poe's "The Pit and the Pendulum" which is based on a similar stratagem. For all its horror and steady increase of suspense, Poe's tale has no connection with a realistic world. The Gothic terror of Poe, Le Fanu, and Blackwood is, by definition, abnormal, and it calls for a suspension of disbelief. War is normally abnormal, so that the terror of Bierce's story receives the reinforcement of a thoroughly possible contemporary setting. Bierce can play with time in his war fiction and not destroy the illusion of reality.

In calling the Civil War the first modern war, military historians mean to draw attention to both the scale of manpower involved and the increased mechanization of weapons—the use of ironclad ships or railroad guns, for example. Throughout the fiction of the nineteenth century, from Fenimore Cooper and Sir Walter Scott to De Forest and Kipling, there has been a movement away from the positive view of war as an affair of glory to a consideration of it as an unpleasant necessity. The imagery of Ambrose Bierce and, to a far greater extent, Stephen Crane, supports the naturalistic conception of war.

There is a dual process observable in the war fiction of these two authors. First, they both lean heavily on the pathetic fallacy, the personification of inanimate objects. This animation is not new. As far back as Achilles' shield or Arthur's sword, Excalibur—or Natty Bumppo's rifle, "Kill-Deer"—weapons were given names and almost personal qualities. Animism is not a new technique, but Bierce and Crane anticipate its widespread use by modern war writers.

Language is further disrupted. Man is dehumanized, referred to either in terms of animals or machines. The modern war chronicler is attracted to violent imagery for the same reasons that motivated the metaphysical poets to seek out shocking and incongruous images to express their emotional disturbance over the changing world of the Renaissance. Bierce is equally disturbed by the absurdity of war which, after all, reverses the natural processes. It is against natural law to die young, and Bierce registers his complaint by reversing his imagery, turning men into beasts (as war does) and endowing the instruments of death with human attributes.

Any sensitive observer of army life immediately notices the fundamental irony of man's loss of individuality as he becomes part of the military machine. The most disturbing event in a young soldier's life is the realization that he is only the agent of another's volition. The machine is not only the metaphor of mass warfare, it is also the basis for the severest trauma of the civilian-soldier. In brief, the face of war changes in the nineteenth century, and the writers substitute a sardonically naturalistic picture for the shining armor and glowing hopes portrayed in earlier battle fiction. The hero is no longer the splendid chevalier who guides his horse over the highest barriers. He becomes, if the expression is permissible, the dogface who burrows deep in his fox-hole.

Bierce provides the first really extensive examples of this type of imagery in war fiction. He sets forth the rationale for animism in his memoirs. "There is something that inspires confidence in the way a gun dashes up to the front, shoving fifty or a hundred men to one side as if it said, 'Permit *me*!' Then it squares its shoulders, calmly dislocates a joint in its back, sends away its twenty-four legs and settles down. . . . " The fiction extends these images, often giving the impression that the guns are more important than the men in the war world. In a sentimental story by Thomas Nelson Page, for example, the survivors of a Confederate force at the war's end sadly bid farewell to their cannon which, under the names of Matthew, Mark, Luke, John, The Eagle, and The Cat, have become real personalities in the men's eyes. A cannon to Bierce is "something horrible and unnatural: the gun was bleeding at the mouth," or "The army's weapons seemed to share its military delinquency. The rattle of rifles sounded flat and contemptible."

To a similar extent, men in war are turned into beasts. A man with his jaw shot away has "the appearance of a great bird of prey crimsoned in throat and breast by the blood of its quarry." Bierce's wounded are always inarticulate; they crawl away like "a swarm of great black beetles." Equipment is their spoor; a trapped soldier is "conscious of his own rathood." Bierce chooses these images to convey his disgust with the whole process of war. He is particularly disturbed by the mutilated victims of the malignant weapons. The author expresses genuine compassion for "a writhing fragment of humanity, this type an example of crude sensation." In order to sustain the distance from his characters necessary for the ironic detachment he seeks, Bierce employs an imagery that shows contempt for men and admiration for guns—the reverse of his actual feeling.

What of nature itself in these passages? Bierce does not have the poet's eye for detail displayed by Crane. Instead, Bierce, the former topographical engineer, sets each story in an exactly planned and restricted composition. Relying on what von Clausewitz calls *Ortisinn*—sense of locality—Bierce puts his vignettes of war in a frame that includes a hill on which the observer is usually stationed (it is called an "acclivity," apparently Bierce's favorite word), and from which a long view stretches out over a field. A farmhouse is located on one side of the field, and a body of woods is behind the hill. There are variations, naturally, but Bierce is ordinarily satisfied with some such clearly defined stage for his military operations. His idea of nature is inconsistent. At times the landscape is indifferent. He shows the sheer beauty of the sight of a horseman poised on a cliff, outlined against the blue sky, looking down on a stream that runs through the valley below. Immediately after this vision, the horse and rider are plunged to their deaths. Or the natural setting is deliberately contrasted to the ugliness of the events it shelters: "He could imagine nothing more peaceful than the appearance of that pleasant landscape with its long stretches of brown fields over which the atmosphere was beginning to quiver in the heat of the morning sun." And in a moment, the observer of all this beauty will kill himself in a paroxysm of fear in order to escape an enemy attack!

As the attitude towards war grows more serious in nineteenth century fiction, a religious note creeps into the writing. Again, this is hardly a new departure, but rather a return to a much older tradition. The gods took part in the Homeric struggles; the Old Testament is packed with battles. As far back as the Old English *Dream of the Rood,* Christ has been portrayed as an heroic warrior. If the earlier historical novelists did not consider the spiritual side of war, Zola and Tolstoy constantly remind the reader that combat has its religious overtones.

Ambrose Bierce brings forth the religious motif in one of his finest, and least known, stories. **"A Son of the Gods"** is perhaps his most perfectly constructed war tale. It is a thinly disguised allegory. The story is told from the point of view of an anonymous soldier and is subtitled "A Study in the Present Tense." The atmosphere is heavy with the sense of mystery and silence that exists when the position of the enemy is unknown. The army is almost paralyzed, in a fog of hesitation and doubt, in awe of the incomprehensible.

The observer, a veteran staff-officer, is talking about the realities of war, and he employs the plainest terms, speaking of "an old saddle, a splintered wheel, a forgotten canteen." Suddenly, in sharp contrast, the narrator raises his eyes to see an anomolous entrant upon the subdued scene:

> . . . a young officer on a snow-white horse. His saddle blanket is scarlet. What a fool! No one who has ever been in action but remembers how naturally every rifle turns toward the man on a white horse . . . He is all agleam with bullion—a blue-and-gold edition of the poetry of war.

The old soldier's immediate reaction is one of mockery, he finds himself emotionally attracted to the figure. "But how handsome he is!—with what careless grace he sits his horse!"

Bierce combines the mystical religious connotations of this knight with the basic realities of the military problem. There is a hedge-lined wall on the top of a hill behind which the enemy may be stationed in force. The normal procedure would be to send out a body of skirmishers to prove the enemy's presence by drawing fire, but in this position it would mean annihilation for those troops. So the young horseman, ten thousand eyes focused on him and the sun shining its benediction on his shoulder-straps, offers to sacrifice himself in place of the skirmishers. His act draws forth a spirit of ecstasy from the troops. The religious emotion inherent in Bierce's prose here recalls the intensity of Gerard Manley Hopkins' lyrics. As the officer rides on, "He is not alone—he draws all souls after him. But we remember that we laughed . . . Not a look backward. O, if he would but turn—if he could but see the love, the adoration, the atonement!"

The narrator pictures the burly commander-in-chief and the hardened killers who are accustomed to death in its ugliest forms—they are men who can play cards among the corpses of their comrades—and they are all equally involved with the fate of the young hero. The author does not attempt to conceal the young officers' symbolic configuration. " 'Let me pay all,' says this gallant man—this military Christ!"

The tone of pure enchantment is sustained perfectly up to this point. Having established the beauty and heroism of the act, the narration changes from the enchanted mood to one of direct suspense as the hero rides before the enemy guns and momentarily manages to escape their withering fire. Finally, after his horse has been shot down, the officer, still miraculously alive, signals with his sword to the watching troops that he has given his life for them. "His face is toward us. Now he lowers his hand to a level with his face and moves it downward, the blade of his sabre describing a downward curve. It is a sign to us, to the world, to posterity. It is a hero's salute to death and history."

If Bierce had ended his story here, it would exist as a remarkably sensitive and lyrical evocation of the spirit of sacrifice in war, a tale of sympathetic, elegiac loveliness—that would make war appear a thing of beauty. Bierce's philosophical approach to the realities of a war that is cruel and illogical will not allow such treatment of the religious theme to stand. Like much of later war fiction, **"A Son of the Gods"** must pervert the religious elements in order to remain true to the author's dark vision of war. We have qualified Bierce's philosophy as one of cosmic irony. One of the concomitants of this discipline is the certainty that God is an enemy, not a friend, of man. He is a careless God. Following such an ideology, Bierce needs to end his war story on a savagely ironic note.

The onlooking troops are brought to a state of religious frenzy by the hero's last sign to them. They break the rules of their world of war—since the knight is the symbol of another, supposedly higher world—and disobey their orders, charging in the direction of the dead body. The enemy opens fire, and by the time the preternaturally calm commander has the bugler sound the retreat, a mass of dead and wounded are left on the field. Taking the commander as an image of the father-God, and the officer the son-Christ, we see that the traditional sacrifice has been twisted out of shape. The Christ figure, whose action was planned to save even the skirmishers, has excited the army to such an extent that not only the skirmishers but also many other soldiers are killed *because* of the intended sacrifice. The most biting aspect of the irony is that the information was gained, and the officer's mission might have been a success. In war, however, not even religion obeys any rules—everything is perverted. The despondent voice of Bierce breaks through the narrator's sad cry of agony and anger that ends the story:

> Ah, those many, many needless dead! That great soul whose beautiful body is lying over yonder, so conspicuous against the sere hillside—could it not have been spared the bitter consciousness of a vain devotion? Would one exception have marred too much the pitiless perfection of the divine, eternal plan?

Throughout his war fiction, Bierce remains within the ethical system he has constructed. **"A Son of the Gods"** indicates that unless a writer has some sort of optimistic attitude towards war, the religious theme must show the horrible unreasonableness of a world whose real god is not Christ but Mars. Another piece, **"The Story of a Conscience,"** emphasizes this point. Bierce follows the same routine, preparing the reader, through the tale of a spy who had once gratuitously saved his captor's life, for a moment of positive humanity. But the war ethic prevails; the spy who had once shown "a divine compassion" is shot, and his captor commits suicide. There can be no compromise with the illogic of war.

The archetypal character of modern war fiction is the innocent youth who gains an understanding of life through his war service. Many of Bierce's stories—**"One Officer, One Man,"** or **"The Mocking Bird,"** for example—examine the psychological problem of the extraordinary pressures brought about by the first introduction to war.

To express the innocence-to-experience theme, Bierce turns to the same mixture of realism and allegory used in **"A Son of the Gods." "Chickamauga"** carries the figure of the innocent back to its proper source, a six-year-old child. The story follows the adventures of a little boy who wanders away from home one sunny afternoon in wartime. It becomes immediately clear that the child, clutching a wooden sword and endowed with an inherited love of military books and pictures, represents the idea of romantic war, since, " . . . this child's spirit, in bodies of its ancestors had for thousands of years been trained to memorable feats of discovery and conquest." One aspect of the story is sheer parody. The little boy is a dreamer who savagely destroys his enemies, slashing to the right and to the left with his sword, until he is suddenly terrified—by a rabbit. Thus reality—and a reversed reality at that for the rabbit is the least frightening of beasts—ruins his game for a time, and he goes to sleep amid a strange, muffled sound of thunder.

He awakes to see a procession of revoltingly wounded men staggering bloodily through the woods. This, too, is reality, but the innocent who only comprehends the romance of war finds these victims of combat less terrible than the rabbit. He laughs with glee at the clownish antics of these agonized creatures, and even mounts one, a man whose jaw has been shot away. The little boy goes to the head of the column of dying and mutilated men and leads them forward to the gestures of his wooden sword. "Surely such a leader never before had such a following."

Bierce continues the dreadful parody of reality almost to the breaking point. The child's lack of experience is emphasized; he does not recognize drowned men for what they are, nor notice the signs of a great retreat. The innocent must learn the truth, however, and Bierce destroys the maddening illusion in two swift strokes. The boy, a knight on a quest, leads his troops towards the red glow of a fire. Eager to add fuel to the flames, he searches for wood, but everything he finds is too heavy. "In despair he flung in his sword—a surrender to the superior forces of nature. His military career was at an end." His first understanding of reality comes from the comprehension of his own inferiority in the face of nature's indifference, and he gives up his romantic dreams of military conquest.

Bierce has an additional irony in reserve, moreover. The child discovers that the burning dwelling is his own home. He comes upon the Goya-like scene of his mother's disgusting and dismembered corpse. The romantic vision of war died when the sword went into the fire. Now the sickening reality of everything he has been experiencing is brought home to the boy. Bierce compounds the irony with a third note of horror by making the child a deaf-mute. The shock of the story is overwhelming, but the author's meaning is clear. War is not what it seems to be in books and pictures. Only experience, personal experience, can wipe out the false impression and teach the essentials of war. Like all those caught up in war, the child learns the tremendous disparity between the vision and the actuality.

Ambrose Bierce never loses sight of the incongruous and the shocking aspect of war. The illusion-reality theme runs throughout his war stories. His grim portrait of combat anticipates the modern attitude towards war, but the compressed force of his war stories has never been equalled. (pp. 147-65)

Eric Solomon, "The Bitterness of Battle: Ambrose Bierce's War Fiction," in The Midwest Quarterly, *Vol. IV, No. 2, January, 1964, pp. 147-65.*

Stuart C. Woodruff (essay date 1965)

[In the following excerpt, Woodruff discusses Bierce's war stories as expressions of a pessimistic worldview.]

In his journalism and satiric verse, and especially in *The Devil's Dictionary,* Bierce is primarily concerned with castigating a flawed humanity, "a world of fools and rogues, blind with superstition, tormented with envy, consumed with vanity, selfish, false, cruel, cursed with illusions—frothing mad!" In his short stories, on the other hand, Bierce's characteristic theme is the inscrutable universe itself, whose mechanisms checkmate man's every attempt to assert his will or live his dreams. If the universe is not actively hostile or malevolent, as in many of his tales of the supernatural, it is at best always indifferent to human need. From birth, that "first and direst of all disasters," to death, life is but the "spiritual pickle preserving the body from decay." This dismal concept of the human situation is Bierce's central imaginative impulse in his short stories, the idea that gives shape to his fictional world. Repeatedly, his protagonists become enmeshed in some fatal trap or are destroyed by uncontrollable fears. They move in ignorance toward their destiny, ground into oblivion by some spectacular ordering of events, or else unhinged by their encounter with the supernatural. To Bierce the picture was "infinitely pathetic and picturesque." (p. 19)

Perhaps Bierce's most violent diatribe against the inhospitable universe and the clearest expression of his attitude occurs in an essay sarcastically entitled "Natura Benigna." Despite the mannered and rhetorical flourishes, the violence of Bierce's assault suggests something of his own frustration and rage over a world in which "Howe'er your choice may chance to fall, / You'll have no hand in it at all." Because Bierce always insisted, as did Poe, that a storyteller must remain detached and impersonal in his narrations, such personal concern is usually disguised in his fiction. Its deliberate concealment or distortion in the direction of macabre humor has caused several of Bierce's critics to call him "inhuman" or "without pity." As the following quotation from "Natura Benigna" indicates, however, Bierce's frequent claim that "nothing matters" requires careful qualification:

> In all the world there is no city of refuge—no temple in which to take sanctuary, clinging to the horns of the altar—no "place apart" where, like hunted deer, we can hope to elude the baying pack of Nature's malevolences. . . . Dodge, turn and double how we can, there's no eluding them; soon or late some of them have him by the throat and his spirit returns to the God who gave it—and gave them.

Particularly evident in this essay is Bierce's compulsive desire to assault what disturbs him most profoundly. The thought of that "pack of Nature's malevolences" triggers a kind of frenzied despair:

> What a fine world it is, to be sure—a darling little world, "so suited to the needs of man." A globe of liquid fire, straining within a shell relatively no thicker than that of an egg—a shell constantly cracking and in momentary danger of going all to pieces! Three-fourths of this delectable field of human activity are covered with an element in which we cannot breathe, and which swallows us by myriads. . . . Of the other one-fourth more than one-half is uninhabitable by reason of climate. On the remaining one-eighth we pass a comfortless and precarious existence in disputed occupancy with countless ministers of death and pain—pass it in fighting for it, tooth and nail, a hopeless battle in which we are foredoomed to defeat. Everywhere death, terror, lamentation and the laughter that is more terrible than tears—the fury and despair of a race hanging on to life by the tips of its fingers! And the prize for which we strive, "to have and to hold"—what is it? A thing that is neither enjoyed while had, nor missed when lost. So worthless it is, so unsatisfying, so inadequate to purpose, so false to hope and at its best so brief, that for consolation and compensation we set up fantastic faiths of an aftertime in a better world from which no confirming whisper has ever reached us across the void. Heaven is a prophecy uttered by the lips of despair, but Hell is an inference from analogy.

Such a chilling vision, nourished by Bierce's own experiences in the Civil War, his incisive knowledge of "how it was," provides the main creative impulse for many of his stories, especially those contained in ***Tales of Soldiers and Civilians.*** The war became for Bierce a controlling metaphor of the world and its ways. Always irrationally destructive, war reduced life to its lowest common denominators; the war-world he depicted made a unifying dramatic action of the hopeless struggle for existence. Its elements of surprise, confusion, and the predatory instinct constituted that blind causality which struck with devastating and unpredictable finality. The common soldier, an expendable pawn ignorant of the larger strategies and issues, was shifted about at random, fighting his enemies in treacherous forest depths or dense fog. Shells leapt out at him from nowhere, stupid or depraved officers gave disastrous orders, irrational terror overwhelmed him. Under such pressures individual will or desire became not only impossible but irrelevant, or was converted into an obsessive longing to rush wildly into certain annihilation.

The story that most clearly embodies Bierce's concept of the destructive universe is **"One of the Missing."** Its protagonist, Jerome Searing, is a scout sent by division headquarters to reconnoiter enemy positions. "An incomparable marksman, young, hardy, intelligent and insensible to fear," Searing is presented as the ideal professional soldier. Leaving his companions behind he creeps forward stealthily and is soon "lost to view in a dense thicket of underbrush." Upon reaching the Confederate trenches he finds them empty, but moves further ahead "to assure himself beyond a doubt before going back to report upon so important a matter." He takes cover in a dilapidated plantation building which commands an excellent view of the enemy, a "half-mile away," executing an orderly withdrawal. At this point, Searing has "learned all that he could hope to know," but instead of starting back immediately for his own lines, he makes an offhand decision to send an "ounce and a quarter of lead hissing" into the midst of the retiring troops. It is a seemingly trivial act of will, unpremeditated and unmotivated.

> But it was decreed from the beginning of time that Private Searing was not to murder anybody that bright summer morning, nor was the Confederate retreat to be announced by him. For countless ages events had been so matching themselves together in that wonderful mosaic to some parts of which, dimly discernible, we give the name of history, that the acts which he had in will would have marred the harmony of the pattern.

Searing's unwitting Atropos is a Confederate artillery officer "some two miles" away from where the scout stands cocking his rifle. "Some twenty-five years previously the Power charged with the execution of the work according to the design" had caused

> the birth of a certain male child in a little village at the foot of the Carpathian Mountains, had carefully reared it, supervised its education, directed its desires into a military channel, and in due time made it an officer of artillery. By the concurrence of an infinite number of favoring influences

the officer comes to America, joins the Confederate army, and is placed in command of a battery near Searing's observation post. "Nothing had been neglected—at every step in the progress of both these men's lives, and in the lives of their contemporaries and ancestors . . . the right thing had been done to bring about the desired result." The artillery officer makes an idle decision as seemingly inconsequential as Searing's: "Having nothing better to do while awaiting his turn to pull out and be off, [he] amused himself by sighting a field-piece obliquely to his right at what he mistook for some Federal officers on the crest of a hill, and discharged it. The shot flew high of its mark."

With the jerk of the lanyard, Searing becomes the victim of the mindless and ineluctable configurations of human destiny. With a "horrible roar," the shell "sprang at him out of the sky," smashing his hideout into "matchwood" and pinning the scout helplessly under a pile of "débris which towered above his narrow horizon." " 'Jerome Searing,' " he tells himself with unnecessary emphasis, " 'you are caught like a rat in a trap—in a trap, trap, trap.' " What Bierce has done in tracing the infinitely slow, infinitely complex "mosaic" of events leading up to Searing's predicament is to emphasize that the trap has existed from the beginning of time, as certain as it is inscrutable. The screaming shell and collapsed building are but the end result of that mysterious "work according to the design." Searing, "perfectly conscious of his rathood, and well assured of the trap that he was in, remembering all and nowise alarmed, again opened his eyes to reconnoitre, to note the strength of his enemy, to plan his defense."

At this point the story undergoes a significant shift in emphasis as Bierce pursues a theme closely allied to that of the destructive universe. Because of his "narrow horizon," Searing does not understand that there is no defense against the "enemy" that faces him now—his own capacity for terror. If the external ordering of events trapped the "brave" scout, it is his uncontrollable fear that finally destroys him. Like many of Bierce's stories, **"One of the Missing"** becomes the study of a mind coming unhinged, annihilated by its inability to cope with primitive emotions. At first Searing is relatively calm, even when he discovers that his rifle—which he mistakenly believes still cocked—points directly at his head, and that some loose boards touch the trigger. As the tension mounts the scout lapses into periods of unconsciousness and delirium. His world narrows to the "confusion of timbers and boards":

> No thoughts of home, of wife and children, of country, of glory. The whole record of memory was effaced. The world has passed away—not a vestige remained. . . . Here is immortality in time—each pain an everlasting life. The throbs tick off eternities.

Unable to place a board so as to deflect the bullet should his rifle discharge, Searing's "terror returned, augmented tenfold." Suddenly he gives up all effort to escape the trap: "a new design had shaped itself in his mind—another plan of battle." Seizing a strip of board and "closing his eyes," Searing "thrust it against the trigger with all his strength! There was no explosion; the rifle had been discharged as it dropped from his hand when the building fell. But it did its work." Later, Searing's brother, a Federal lieutenant, passes by the ruined building and notices "a dead body half buried in boards and timbers." Only twenty-two minutes have elapsed between the explosion of the artillery shell and the discovery of the body, yet Lieutenant Adrian Searing is unable to recognize the terror-twisted features of his brother: " 'Dead a week,' said the officer curtly, moving on and absently pulling out his watch as if to verify his estimate of time."

In the actions and images of **"One of the Missing"** we have an instructive paradigm of Bierce's fictional world of gratuitous horror and purposeless destruction. Private Searing himself is the prototype of the Biercean hero, his skill and apparent fearlessness subjected to an impossible test, his death utterly without dignity or significance, except to reveal the flawless efficiency of "the design." His lonely journey into the forest and his poignant ordeal—a frequent pattern in Bierce's war stories—constitute a kind of truncated myth in which the hero invariably fails to solve the riddle or return with the saving boon. Under the baleful gaze of an indifferent cosmos, he can only submit to his fate. The sky above Searing "appeared almost black," and even the "singing of birds, the strange metallic note of the meadow lark" makes an ominous sound "suggesting the clash of vibrant blades." In his delirium Searing falls into "pleasant memories of childhood" and dreams of the time he "entered the sombre forest . . . and with timid steps followed the faint path to Ghost Rock, standing at last with audible heart-throbs before the Dead Man's Cave and seeking to penetrate its awful mystery." His reverie is a compressed symbol of the whole pattern of his life and of man's inability to "penetrate its awful mystery." All his life Searing has been on "the faint path" that leads to "Dead Man's Cave," for the cave merges symbolically into the tiny ring of steel pointing at his head. This is what circumscribes his life and simultaneously defines man's perilous existence "in disputed occupancy with countless ministers of death and pain." As Bierce once wrote in his essay "The Ancestral Bond," "man travels, not the mental road that he would, but the one that he must—is pushed this way and that by the resultant of all the forces behind him."

Bierce's fatalism is very similar to Thomas Hardy's, and both writers must necessarily rely on coincidence to enforce their particular vision. **"One of the Missing,"** for example, is reminiscent of Hardy's poem "The Convergence of the Twain" in which the ship *Titanic* and the gigantic iceberg move relentlessly toward a collision that "jars two hemispheres." Both story and poem, moreover, point up the futility of any assertion of human will. But in a way "coincidence" is a misleading term, for Hardy and Bierce are careful to show at work an intricate pattern of causal connection, unseen by those involved but all too discernible to the detached gaze of an omniscient author. As Edmund Wilson once said of Dickens's novels, the mysterious connection events have with each other becomes the moral of the tale. And in Bierce, the plot becomes the trap that snaps shut on the helpless protagonist. Virtually all of Bierce's stories, in fact, have what has been called a "snap ending"; while the term is sometimes justly used in a pejorative sense, it is important to see how Bierce's conclusions derive from his ironic point of view.

In **"The Mocking-Bird,"** a tale whose central features resemble those of **"One of the Missing,"** Private Grayrock of the Federal army fires a random shot at night while on picket duty and kills his beloved brother, a Confederate soldier. The theme of divided kinsmen was a common one in stories about the Civil War, but Bierce uses it as another example of that "wondrous mosaic" destructive to the young and the brave. Grayrock's hopeless ignorance of the forces conspiring against him is symbolized by his lonely vigil in the forest: "A landscape that is all trees and undergrowth . . . lacks definition, is confused and without accentuated points upon which attention can gain a foothold." As the minutes of his watch drag by, Private Grayrock loses his sense of direction: "Lost at his post—unable to say in which direction to look for an enemy's approach . . . Private Grayrock was profoundly disquieted." When he hears "a stir of leaves and a snap of fallen

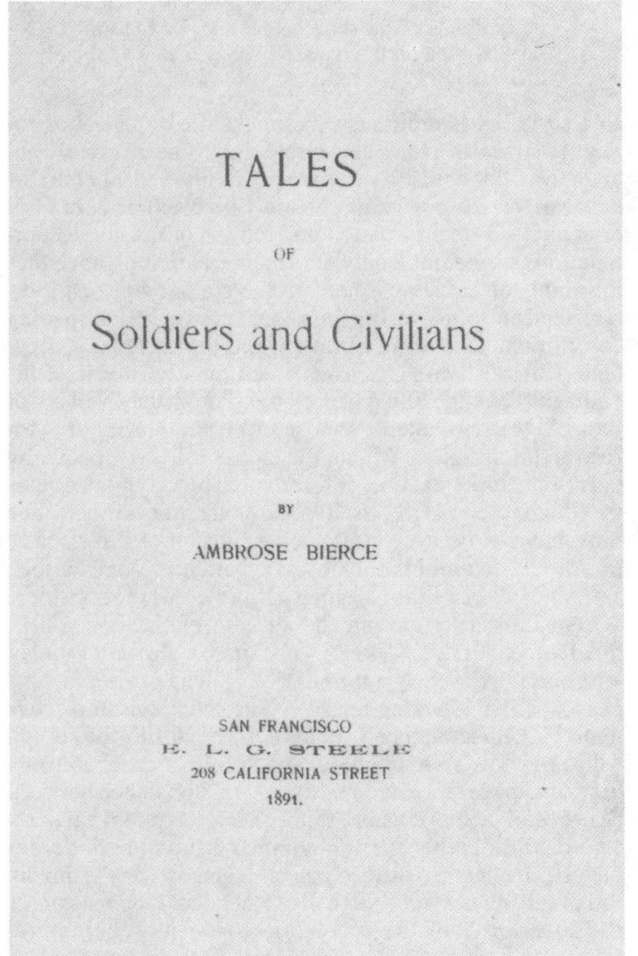
TALES
OF
Soldiers and Civilians
BY
AMBROSE BIERCE
SAN FRANCISCO
E. L. G. STEELE
208 CALIFORNIA STREET
1891.

Title page for the American edition of one of Bierce's short story collections.

twigs" he fires blindly into the dark. The next day he returns to his post to search for the man he thinks he must have killed. Like Searing, he lapses into a reverie of his happy boyhood with his brother John when they "walked in paths of light through valleys of peace, seeing new things under a new sun. And through all the golden days floated one unceasing sound—the rich, thrilling melody of a mockingbird in a cage by the cottage door." Significantly, such light-drenched scenes are now only dreams, and when Private Grayrock awakes the rays of the setting sun "projected from the trunk of each giant pine a wall of shadow traversing the golden haze to eastward until light and shade were blended in indistinguishable blue." In the "heart of the little thicket" he finds "the body of John Grayrock, dead of a gunshot wound, and still warm!" Bierce calls the strange discovery a "masterwork of civil war," brought to completion when William Grayrock kills himself out of grief and remorse.

Suicide, in fact, is committed with significant regularity in Bierce's stories, and its occurrence illuminates the very heart of his "vision of the human race, trapped and betrayed in the wilderness of the world" [Leroy J. Nations, "Ambrose Bierce: The Gray Wolf of American Letters," *South Atlantic Quarterly,* 1926]. In the war tales alone, in addition to **"The Mocking-bird"** and the abortive suicide of **"One of the Missing,"** it occurs in **"Killed at Resaca," "One Officer, One Man," "The Story of a Conscience," "George Thurston,"** and **"A Tough Tussle."** Bierce vigorously defended the right of "taking oneself off" if circumstances made life unbearable. Among those qualifying for suicide he included people who were "threatened with permanent insanity," burdened with "disease," "addicted" to some "destructive or offensive habit," "without friends, property, employment or hope," or who had somehow "disgraced" themselves. "The time to quit," Bierce argued [in **"Taking Oneself Off"**], "is when you have lost a big stake, your foolish hope of eventual success, your fortitude and your love of the game." Since Bierce's pathetic protagonists are always losing "a big stake" or their "fortitude" to the "keeper of the table," the suicide rate in the tales is understandably high. With the paradoxical irony some modern existentialists are so fond of, Bierce regarded self-destruction as a kind of creative act, a weird moral achievement in a universe virtually drained of moral purpose and meaning. It was as if the individual could only assert his will by relinquishing it altogether in a final destructive act. Suicide became a last salute to all those dark forces conspiring against man, a Pyrrhic victory that ushered in the "good, good darkness."

In **"The Mocking-bird,"** as we have seen, suicide is prompted by grief and remorse; in **"One of the Missing"** Searing tries to end his suffering because of terror and overwhelming hopelessness. **"The Story of a Conscience"** presents still another motive: guilt, coupled with an unbearable sense of disgrace. Captain Hartroy, a Federal officer, captures a Confederate spy who turns out to be one Dramer Brune, a former Union soldier who has deserted on principle to the Confederate cause. Assigned to guard Brune years before, Hartroy had fallen asleep at his post, but had been humanely wakened by Brune himself before his crime could be detected:

> "Ah, Brune, Brune, that was well done—that was great—that—"
>
> The captain's voice failed him; the tears were running down his face and sparkled upon his beard and his breast. Resuming his seat at the table, he buried his face in his arms and sobbed. All else was silence.

Here again, as in so many of his stories, Bierce enforces the ironic and tragic conjunction of events destructive of human life. The irony is not lost on Captain Hartroy. He realizes only too well that he might have saved Brune years before by reporting his prisoner's magnanimous act, but that he failed to for fear of his own court-martial. Trapped between his obligation to have Brune shot as spy and deserter and a terrible longing to repay Brune's former generosity, Hartroy turns over his command to a fellow officer who gives the order to the firing squad. Seconds later a "single pistol shot" reveals that Captain Hartroy has "renounced the life which in conscience he could no longer keep."

By far the most important motive for Bierce's fictional suicides, however, is the inability to cope with the enemy within: one's fatal susceptibility to uncontrollable fear. To Bierce, no one was immune to its devastating effects, not even that brave and resourceful soldier, Jerome Searing. With the unpredictable suddenness of the shell that "sprang at him out of the sky," fear could reduce a man to helpless imbecility (as in many of Bierce's ghost stories), or else goad him into some spectacular act of compensatory bravery that would result in death. An inherited tendency, part of the instinctive life of the race, it was perhaps even more bitterly ironic in its lethal possibilities—and more convincing—than a whimsical ordering of external circumstance. The story **"Parker Adderson, Philosopher,"** for example, reveals the painful inadequacy of man's rational faculties when pitted against his primitive heritage. Parker Adderson, confessed spy, is seated with his captor, General Clavering, in the latter's tent. Assuming he is to be shot according to custom the following morning, Adderson dumbfounds the general by his composed attitude toward his impending death. To Clavering "Death is horrible!"; to Adderson, on the other hand, it is but "a loss of which we shall never be conscious," one that "can be borne with composure and therefore expected without apprehension." The would-be philosopher tries to explain the fear of death as an inheritance from "our savage ancestors":

> To us it is horrible because we have inherited the tendency to think it so, accounting for the notion by wild and fanciful theories of another world—as names of places give rise to legends explaining them and reasonless conduct to philosophies in justification.

At this point in Adderson's lecture, the provost marshal enters the tent and is instructed to take the spy out and shoot him immediately. Hearing that he is to die right away, Adderson suddenly goes berserk and pulls the tent down on the three of them. In the wild melee that follows, the provost marshal is stabbed to death; Clavering is mortally wounded. When order is restored we find Parker Adderson, philosopher, "cowered upon the ground" uttering "unintelligible remonstrances." As he is led away "begging incoherently for his life," General Clavering, the man who had thought death "horrible," dies serenely, "with a smile of ineffable sweetness" upon his face.

The instinctive hereditary fear that unravels Parker Adderson as a rational human being leads directly to the protagonist's suicide in **"One Officer, One Man,"** and in **"George Thurston,"** In the former tale we find Captain Graffenreid facing his first experience under fire after an irksome tour of duty at his state capitol. Aware that his battle-hardened companions assume he has been "forced unwillingly into the field," Graffenreid looks forward buoyantly to proving himself in combat:

> He was in a state of mental exaltation and scarcely could endure the enemy's tardiness in advancing to the attack. . . . How his heart leaped in his breast as the bugle sounded the stirring notes of "assembly"! With what a light tread, scarcely conscious of the earth beneath his feet, he strode forward at the head of his company, and how exultingly he noted the tactical dispositions which placed his regiment in the front line! And if perchance some memory came to him of a pair of dark eyes that might take on a tenderer light in reading the account of that day's doings, who shall blame him for the unmartial thought or count it a debasement of soldierly ardor?

In a style that simultaneously mocks the language of romantic adventure tales and Graffenreid's naïve concept of his heroic possibilities, Bierce sets up his central contrast between, on the one hand, the individual's illusion of freedom and self-determination and, on the other, some combination of inherent frailty and external circumstance that inevitably defeats the protagonist. A similar contrast is established in **"One of the Missing,"** through the opening descriptions of Searing's bravery and professional competence, or in Private Grayrock's sentimental reverie of his youthful days in "the paths of light" and the "valleys of peace." Many of Bierce's most successful stories are stories of initiation in which the opportunity to profit by hard-won understanding is terminated by violent death, or in which the insight itself makes life unbearable. The movement is typically from some illusion of life's sunny promise to an annihilating forest experience. For example, several of Bierce's tales begin with a reference to sunshine: "One sunny afternoon in the autumn of the year 1861" **("A Horseman in the Sky")**; "The time, a pleasant Sunday afternoon in the early autumn of 1861. The place a forest's heart" **("The Mocking-bird")**; "One sunny autumn afternoon" **("Chickamauga")**. In all of these stories the setting belies the true state of affairs and sets up a cruel contrast between appearance and reality, a fatal imbalance between desire and achievement. While Bierce's plots have received considerable attention, largely from the standpoint of their artificiality or mechanical ingenuity, his symbolic use of setting has gone virtually unnoticed. One reason for the superiority of the war stories over his supernatural tales, however, is that in the former Bierce's settings and dramatic actions often function as integrated metaphors for the process of psychological collapse.

Graffenreid's initiation into the harsh realities of life begins when the enemy fires an artillery barrage "from the forest a half-mile in front." Cowering from a shell which explodes harmlessly to his left, he hears "a low, mocking laugh" from his first lieutenant.

> He had not known that the flight of a projectile was a phenomenon of so appalling character. His conception of war had already undergone a profound change, and he was conscious that his new feeling was manifesting itself in visible perturbation.

Forced to take cover beside a dead soldier, Graffenreid gets an instructive worm's-eye view of the face of death: "It looked yellow already, and was repulsive. Nothing suggested the glory of a soldier's death nor mitigated the loathsomeness of the incident." During a momentary lull in the action "had come introspection. He sought rather to analyze his feelings than distinguish himself by courage and devotion. The result was profoundly disappointing. He covered his face with his hands and groaned aloud." When the order is given to attack, Graffenreid is paralyzed with fear. He stares transfixed at "the sinister silence of the forest in front." Seconds later a sergeant behind the terrified officer sees a strange sight: "a sudden reaching forward of the hands and their energetic withdrawal, throwing the elbows out, as in pulling an oar." From between the officer's shoulders springs "a bright point of metal which prolonged itself outward, nearly a half-arm's length—a blade!"

The protagonist in **"George Thurston,"** instead of becoming suddenly aware of his cowardice, knows it all along and tries to subdue it by recklessly exposing himself to danger. As the stammering quartermaster explains the matter at mess one day, "It's h-is w-ay of m-m-mastering a c-c-consti-t-tu-tional t-tendency to r-un aw-ay." Inflexible and aloof, Thurston fights his private war by walking into the hottest battles with arms folded and head erect. Although he is wounded, he leads an apparently charmed life. Back in camp one day, he joins a group of men amusing themselves on a swing some fifty feet high. Pumping himself to dizzying heights, heedless of the warnings from below, Thurston soon drives his swing past the level of its anchorage. Suddenly the rope goes slack and Thurston, catapulted out beyond its arc, lands with a sickening impact. When they reach his mangled body they find the arms "folded tightly across the breast." Of death itself the shaken narrator remarks: "We did not know that he had so ghastly resources, possibilities of terror so dismal." George Thurston, the "man in the sky," a speck "sharply outlined against the blue," becomes a symbol of man's pitiful existence in an alien world.

The fate that overtakes such characters as Jerome Searing, William Grayrock, and George Thurston, originates in what Bierce conceived of as the "pitiless perfection of the divine, eternal plan." Whether this fate manifests itself as some arbitrary pattern of external circumstance or as an inner "constitutional tendency" makes no difference. The result is the same: the annihilation of the protagonist or of his private dream. Sometimes death is preceded by a stupefying sense of disillusionment or horror; sometimes it comes so swiftly there is no time for reflection. In many of the war stories, Bierce creates a bitter contrast between the main character's hopes or youthful dreams and the harsh reality that reduces him to a meaningless cipher. Focusing on single moments of intense crisis and awareness, Bierce shows his characters being hounded into a corner where their affliction becomes "an acclimatizing process preparing the soul for another and bitter world." Their brief life in present time is "a little plot of light" where "we enter, clasp a hand or two, and go our several ways back into the darkness." Death ends their dreams of that "imaginary period known as the Future," the "realm of song" where "Hope flies with a free wing, beckoning to temples of success and bowers of ease." To Bierce, the ultimate horror of the "eternal plan" was that man could learn nothing from his ordeal except the lesson of his own futility and purposelessness. Perhaps this was the "awful mystery" that Jerome Searing, in his delirium, tried to "penetrate" as he stood before "Dead Man's Cave." Like Searing, Bierce found existence to be "A transient, horrible, fantastic dream, / Wherein is nothing yet all things do seem." (pp. 21-38)

The congealing sense of doom that permeates Bierce's war stories suggests a Calvinism from which all sense of grace or benevolent purpose has been removed. As one critic has put it:

> Bierce had rejected the God of his New England ancestors and his Puritan upbringing, but the code that he retained implied a metaphysic almost identical to the Calvinism that he denied. A harshly personal God was replaced by a harshly impersonal Fate. Every man's slightest action was preordained, and his duty was to submit to the mysterious workings of the supernatural. ["New Letters of Ambrose Bierce," *Opinion,* 1930]

One important effect of this rigid fatalism is to minimize or ignore the question of man as moral agent in favor of portraying the effects of a deterministic universe. This is not to say that Bierce was indifferent to moral values—the whole body of his journalism and satire shows how accountable he held man. But in the short stories his characters have no inner moral life in any decisive sense. What they do have is a kind of rudimentary psychology which reacts according to the stimulus they receive and their "constitutional tendency." Bierce's characters are really human types—types of susceptibility—rather than fully drawn individuals. They may have a history, but they lack an identity apart from the circumstances they are exposed to.

Since these circumstances are invariably destructive in one way or another, the story ends when the maximum pressure has been brought to bear on the protagonist. If he does not actually die, at the very least his private world collapses and death would even seem preferable. . . . If the protagonist commits suicide, it is either because he realizes he is inextricably caught or because, like George Thurston, he has long recognized his fate as some inherent compulsion which makes life unbearable. In any event Bierce's characters are never responsible for what happens to them. Often, like . . . Jerome Searing, they are good, brave men or, like the child in **"Chickamauga,"** merely ignorant and naïve. Essentially passive, sometimes literally immobilized like Prometheus in his chains, they have an interior life of acute sensation. Because we can know them only through their feelings, which are usually very unpleasant or painful, we can only respond to them with pity. We do not really know *them;* we know their suffering.

Because it was the reality of their suffering and frustration that Bierce responded to, his war figures make a serious claim upon our attention. Only in the war stories does Bierce achieve the sense of genuine concern for human frailty endlessly cheated and baffled by life. His characters are credible even when their dilemmas are not, because he believed in the agony of their ordeal, even if he believed in little else. (pp. 52-3)

Stuart C. Woodruff, in his The Short Stories of Ambrose Bierce: A Study in Polarity, *University of Pittsburgh Press, 1965, 193 p.*

William Bysshe Stein (essay date 1972)

[*Stein is an American critic and educator. In the following essay, he describes Bierce's use of Gothic elements to depict the limits of human consciousness in* "The Death of Halpin Frayser."]

> Mind, n. A mysterious form of matter secreted by the brain. Its chief activity consists in the endeavor to ascertain its own nature, the futility of the attempt being due to the fact that it has nothing but itself to know itself with.
>
> *The Devil's Dictionary*

Whatever its European origins and whatever its reflections of the unresolved dualisms of the Protestant sensibility, the Gothicism of American fiction remains an artistic phenomenon. Almost as if by dynastic succession, Brown, Poe, Hawthorne, James, and Bierce labor to bring larger stretches of the chartless domain of human consciousness under control of the word. The exorcizing of the demons and ghosts of dream, reverie, fantasy, nightmare, and compulsion is for each of them an irresistible challenge to invent a narrative method that will magically effect a conjunction of the subjective and objective worlds. But unlike literary critics, not one of these writers presumes to call the one illusory and the other real. With the exception of Brown who learned the same lesson from, I think, Sterne, they learn from one another that the practice of fiction is an art of illusion far more reliable than the artifact of history in revealing the essentially ahistorical activity of the mind. Accordingly, they undertake to create discrete worlds of rhetoric that incarnate the meaning of experience in their reconstruction of the processes of consciousness. Beginning with Brown and continuing through Bierce (or even Faulkner), they manipulate the language of prose as if composing poetry, intent upon allowing the mind to speak in the multiple idioms in which it thinks or thinks it thinks. For them the perception of anything has little to do, ultimately, with the faculty of reason which, as scientists are beginning to realize, is simply a pragmatic instrument—a convenient and useful mental habit for condensing a combination of noted, half-noted, and unnoted observations into an expedient crutch for carrying on the clumsy business of life. Or, put in another perspective, these practitioners of Gothicism, each in his own way, attempt to capture all the associations and dissociations of thought that merge into a single perception of what is called reality. In spite of his swaggering penchant for sensationalism, Bierce is a virtuoso in the handling of this "poetics" of consciousness—and no more so than in **"The Death of Halpin Frayser"** with its baffling rhetorical orchestration.

. . . . .

In the first three chapters the use of the "poetics" of consciousness is conspicuous yet baffling, and in the fourth and last chapter, except for a teasing flourish of poetic fancy in the first paragraph, inconspicuous yet revealing. This masking reflects a carefully planned strategy for the resolution of the action. The story is finally filtered through the minds of conventional stereotypes of rationality—the sheriff Holker (a pun on "holk," to dig or turn things up), who manipulates clues with the empty zeal of a checker player, and the detective Jaralson (perhaps a pun on "son of jarl," suggesting an "eagle-eye"), who is a kind of caricature of Sherlock Holmes in his dogmatic omniscience on irrelevant matters. They reduce the process of reason to a pattern of absurd cause and effect far more terrifying in its implications than Halpin Frayser's dream that he is murdered by the vengeful ghost of his jealous mother.

To achieve this astonishing reversal, Bierce, a connoisseur of red herrings with the odor of mockery, dangles an epigraph, attributed to Hali, under the nose of the typical reader of ghost and horror tales. It sets up the motif of the soulless creature that will appear to strangle the hero, albeit in a dream. Then with a backward glance at Shakespeare and the enduring wisdom of his remark that "The lunatic, the lover, and the poet / Are of imagination all compact," Bierce establishes the seasonal setting of the action on a "dark night in midsummer." Here it must be remembered that in his dream Halpin Frayser becomes a poet—what kind probably has to be determined by the derivation of Halpin from "elfin." Nor is this sleight-of-hand nonsense on his part (or mine). It simply follows the logic of a definition in *The Devil's Dictionary,* a parody of Descartes' *cogito ergo sum* that converts the faculty of thought into a wayward mischief-maker: "I think that I think, therefore I think that I am." Or put another way, consciousness is an "elfin phraser"; whatever its mode of expression, it makes fools of us all. The etymological pun, however, is no doubt a verbal ploy that Bierce employs to alert the curiosity of anyone who, after a few readings of the story, begins to realize that Bierce's rhetorical hocuspocus disguises an obsession with the uncharted avenues of perception.

Indeed, even for the reader who comes to this horror tale willing to suspend disbelief in the marvels of the supernatural, the substance of the next paragraph of narration may well serve to deflect the inclination:

> He [Halpin Frayser] lived in St. Helena, but where he lives now is uncertain, for he is dead.

> One who practices living in the woods with nothing under him but the dry leaves and the damp earth, and nothing over him but the branches from which the leaves have fallen and the sky from which the earth has fallen, cannot hope for great longevity, and Frayser had already attained the age of thirty-two. There are persons in this world . . ., and far away the best persons, who regard that as a very advanced age. They are the children.

As the lore of spiritualism and theosophy ("but where he lives . . .") collides with mythic cosmogony ("the sky from which . . .") and then dissolves into the enchanted world of the *puer aeternus* ("They are the children"), Bierce deliberately short-circuits any attempt on the part of the reader to set up a consistent train of associations. Seen in the perspective of the entire story, this tactic undermines the plausibility of the three solutions to Halpin Frayser's murder that the narrator presents: the hero as a victim of the soulless ghost, of the second husband of his mother, or of his own misguided mind. The cryptic references invalidate the authority of the motif of incest jealousy, the psychological extension of the content of the epigraph. They also controvert the sheriff's logical reconstruction of the crime and the parody of Descartes' radical separation of mind and body. However, the disconcerting, if not confusing, exposition at issue rings with a solemnity that precludes an outright dismissal of its importance, particularly when contrasted with the narrator's later whimsical and sardonic intrusions. As subsequent analysis will show, it functions to reveal Bierce's vision of the individual as a fragment of cosmic consciousness. To the extent the act of creation is an embodiment of divine thought as capricious as the rhetoric suggests, then the dead Halpin Frayser lives on as an orphaned mind. Nor is it difficult to understand why the children of the world take for granted this inescapable fate. They play out the fiction that existence is real while knowing full well that consciousness in its human expression is no more than a dream in the endless cycle of reciprocal becoming and passing away because for them death and life are ultimately the same. Of course, this explanation directly reflects the epigraph to this essay; that is, how can the isolated thought ever apprehend the process that produced the thought in the infinite regression of cause and effect underlying the endless manifestations of cosmic consciousness.

The hugger-mugger of Bierce's preceding commentary leads directly into the apparently prosaic circumstances of Halpin Frayser's nightmare. Lost in the hills and barred from any descent by impenetrable "thickets of manzanita" (apple trees), he at last falls asleep "near the root of a large madrono" (mother tree). Here surrogates of the tree of knowledge and tree of life are polarized in order to externalize the way ego consciousness sinks into the womb of unconsciousness and seeks an escape from the vexations of insecurity. For next the narrator proceeds to describe the expulsion from the paradise of infantile bliss—the awakening to the uncertainties of existence:

> It was hours later, in the very middle of the night, that one of God's mysterious messengers, gliding ahead of the incalculable host of his companions sweeping westward with the dawn line, pronounced the awakening word in the ear of the sleeper, who sat upright and spoke, he knew not why, a name, he knew not whose.

The trite, gushing rhetoric reduces the diurnal paradigm of creation to a parody of the providential "let there be light" of Genesis, for the inscrutable name, "Catherine Larue" hints at the virtual impossibility of ever arriving at a comprehension of the divine mind. The subversion of the sacred also echoes in the casual reference to the witching hour ("in the very middle of the night"), especially in connection with the semantics of rue (the herb of grace used to exorcise demons and also used by witches for the opposite reason, in the latter instance as implied in Halpin Frayser's poem). As a mock epiphany, the passage debases the validity of mystical perception, relating all such insights to cultivated modes of consciousness. This explication finds corroboration in Halpin Frayser's reaction to the strange event: "Halpin Frayser was not much of a philosopher, nor a scientist. The circumstance that, waking from a deep sleep at night in the midst of a forest, he had spoken a name aloud did not arouse an enlightened curiosity to investigate the phenomenon. He thought it odd. . . ." The careful differentiation between Halpin Frayser's discrimination and the hypothetical discernment of a philosopher or a scientist clearly indicates that Bierce categorizes the mental responses of individuals in accordance with conditioned outlooks on so-called reality. In effect, he argues that what we take for the mind is for the most part a culturally inherited mind—an externally imposed method of thinking.

The description of the outset of Halpin Frayser's dream confirms this assumption, as again an incongruous rhetorical intrusion alerts the reader to heed the character of thought: "in the land Beyond the Bed surprises cease from troubling and the judgment is at rest." What this implies is that during sleep the silenced voices of other levels of consciousness assert their right to speak. And it is this psychoscape that the hero now trods: "a road less traveled, having the appearance, indeed, of having been long abandoned, because, he thought, it led to something evil, yet he turned into it without hesitation, impelled by some imperious necessity." What he thinks at this point expresses less the actuality of circumstances than the fear of an encounter with an unknown aspect of his being. Thus the threat to the security of an accepted order of self-knowledge evolves into a premonition of evil. As Bierce later indicates, Halpin Frayser has been trained to be a lawyer, and as a consequence in this particular situation of the dream he resorts to the simplistic cause-and-effect logic that explains everything but resolves nothing. Even granting that the sudden manifestation of the destroying mother seems to support the assumption of impending malevolence, the vision also belongs to an established outlook on things that is not necessarily connected with any Oedipal complex.

The unreliability of Halpin Frayser's responses emerges in his interpretation of the voices heard along the unused road:

> As he pressed forward he became conscious that his way was haunted by invisible existences

> whom he could not definitely figure to his mind. From among the trees on either side he caught broken and incoherent whispers in a strange tongue which yet he partly understood. They seemed to him fragmentary utterances of a monstrous conspiracy against his body and soul.

The qualifications about the identity of the unseen creatures and about their intentions hardly lend credence to his impressions. He sees in his imagination the auditory apparitions of the received cultural formula of good and evil, of God withstanding the devil. Yet there is an incongruity in this association, the linking of "body and soul," that bespeaks the presence of a voice long repressed by tyrannical routines. As this subsequent envisagement of the struggle with the ghost suggests, it is the voice of body whose language takes the form of physical activity. When the dominance of pragmatic consciousness relaxes in a crisis of existence, it achieves freedom of expression:

> [H]is mind was still spellbound, but his powerful body and agile limbs, endowed with a blind, insensate life of their own resisted stoutly and well. For an instant he seemed to see this unnatural contest between a dead intelligence and a breathing mechanism only as a spectator . . . then he regained his identity almost as if by a leap forward into his body, and the straining automaton had a directing will. . . .

The casual "seemed" (Bierce's controlling word in modulating the hero's impressions of the dream) clearly casts doubt on Halpin Frayser's interpretation of the experience. On the other hand, his envisagement of the restoration of his identity isolates the uncensored reaction to the struggle, dramatizing the inseparable union of the mind and the body. As the description of the momentary alienation indicates, the ego consciousness derives its identity from its physical vessel, the sanctuary so desperately reclaimed. Despite adding an abstract purpose to the energetic motions of the body, the ego still serves the primary instinctual impulse of the body to survive. Thus the so-called automaton automates thought, not vice versa. The machine which thinks in **"Moxon's Master"** is the correlative of this line of action; and probably to a greater degree than any other Gothic specialist in mental terror, Bierce intuitively perceives the cybernetic mechanisms of human biology.

The redefinition of the monitoring power of intelligence is clearly foreshadowed in Bierce's ironical account of Halpin Frayser's attempts to translate the language of the flesh and blood (the chemistry of dread) into a usable illusion of logic. Falling back upon the retributive fiction of conventional Christian morality, he proceeds to create another fiction upon its foundation: "All this . . . *seemed* not incompatible with the fulfillment of a natural expectation. It *seemed* to him that it was all in expiation of some crime which, though conscious of his guilt, he could not rightly remember. To the menaces and horrors of his surroundings the consciousness was an added horror" (italics mine). Of course, here Bierce teasingly invites an association with Halpin Frayser's alleged Oedipal complex and its burden of inward anxiety and guilt. But as the gist of the quotation suggests, it is the bent of his individualized consciousness that induces the estrangement within his dream. He restricts his vision of life to what he has been taught to think it is, not to what it is—a reciprocal interplay of a mind lodged in the body and of a body interwined in the convolutions of the brain. His refusal to come to terms with the incarnate thought of body (and the machine of the cyberneticists) explains why he becomes a poet; he seeks to remake himself in the making of a poem: " 'I will not submit unheard. There may be powers that are not malignant traveling this accursed road. I shall leave them a record and an appeal. I shall relate my wrongs, the persecutions that I endure—I, a helpless mortal, a penitent, an unoffending poet!' Halpin Frayser was a poet only as he was a penitent: in his dream." But Halpin Frayser is not even a poet in his dream: he is a lawyer. The fragment of consciousness that he takes for his mind is the product of the roboting memory of his education. It is he who curses the road of his traveling mind. It is he who is his own murderer. The gruesomely Gothic Gongorism of his poem adds the final touch of grotesque comedy to his ordained fate:

> Conspiring spirits whispered in the gloom,
> Half-heard, the stilly secrets of the tomb.
> With blood the trees were adrip; the leaves
> Shone in the witchlight with a ruddy bloom.
>
> I cried aloud!—the spell, unbroken still,
> Rested upon my spirit and my will.
> Unsouled, unhearted, hopeless and forlorn,
> I strove with monstrous presages of ill!

He is what he makes himself—an echo of borrowed consciousness.

. . . . .

Commonly Bierce launches the action of his Gothic exercises *in medias res,* and then at the point of climax (in this case the manifestation of the supposed ghost of the mother) disrupts the continuity of the horror sequence with a retrospect. Devisedly (and often flippantly) clumsy and mechanical, this formula of suspense calls attention to itself but for an ulterior purpose. It usually is the vehicle of a revelation crucial to the understanding of the previously delineated states of consciousness, and is thus a test of a reader's perception. As in the case of this story, what is treated dismissively or ironically is far more important than what invites careful scrutiny, to wit, "the sexual element" in the relations between Halpin Frayser and his mother. The exposition so depressed involves a summary of the hero's social background and heredity, both a target of implicit ridicule:

> The Fraysers were well-to-do. . . . Their children had the social and educational opportunities of their *time and place,* and had responded to good associations and instruction with agreeable manners and cultivated minds. Halpin . . . was perhaps a trifle spoiled. He had the double disadvantage of a mother's assiduity and a father's neglect. Frayser *père* was what no Southern man of means is not—a politician. His country . . . made demands upon his time . . . so exacting that to those of his family he was compelled to turn an ear, partly deafened by the

> thunder of the political captains and the shouting, his own included. (first italics mine)

Obviously, Halpin Frayser's sensibility is a product of his conditioning, even like his father's. He inherits a pattern of stock responses, intellectual and emotional, that reflect the ethos of the time and the place. "Dreamy, indolent, and rather romantic," he is further taught to believe "that in him the character of the late Myron Bayne, a maternal great-grandfather, had revisited the glimpses of the moon—by which orb Bayne had in his lifetime been sufficiently affected to be a poet of no small Colonial distinction." In effect, Bierce dictates the scenario of the dream in the context of these quotations. Along with his training in law, environment and heredity (or their spurious influences) shape the protagonist's male ego and, by extension, the romantic attachment to his mother who "was herself a devout disciple of the late and great Myron Bayne." Surely, the pun on the name of the grandfather presages a curse on Halpin Frayser—a "myronic" fatality, bitter as myrrh, despite the fact that "myron" is a chrism. Just as in the play on the hero's name, the cynical frivolity of the planted association with Byron traces poetic inspiration to a quirk of consciousness, to a search for a disinherited sense of being.

Significantly, Myron Bayne figures importantly in the situation that Bierce contrives to titillate the sensibilities of Freudian critics—the Oedipus complex. This involves a Gothic subterfuge on the part of the mother to keep her son from going to California on legal business. What it suggests is that Halpin Frayser is the surrogate of the grandfather, a displacement for his mother's romantic attachment to a figure warmer in emotions than her husband:

> Grandfather Bayne had come to me in a dream, and standing by his portrait . . . pointed to yours on the wall [.] And when I looked it seemed I could not see the features; you had been painted with a face cloth, such as we put upon the dead. Your father has laughed at me, but you and I, dear, know that such things are not for nothing. And I saw below the edge of the cloth the marks of hands on your throat. Perhaps you have another interpretation. Perhaps it does not mean you will go to California. Or maybe you will take me with you.

But for all the blatant foreshadowing of the implacable succubus of the dream, this dialogue is a red herring. It betrays the mother's feeling for the son, not his for her. Indeed, Halpin Frayser without being a politician is not unlike his father in adapting to the "odd notions of duty" decreed by his professional persona. Furthermore, as Bierce points out in Halpin Frayser's reaction to the sinister portent of his departure, the latter is totally unaware of his mother's perverted love: "[T]his ingenious interpretation of the dream *in the light of newly discovered evidence* [of his legal case] did not wholly commend itself to the son's more logical mind . . . it foreshadowed a more simple and immediate, if less tragic, disaster than a visit to the Pacific coast. It was Halpin Frayser's impression that he was to be *garroted on his native heath*" (italics mine). Apparently some oversight in his handling of a case has left him open to the threat of revenge. Which is to say that the figure of his dream is his client in the dissociated form of the mother. So much then for the incest guilt so easily misread into the equivocal account of his nightmare.

But if that crux is resolvable in a distortion of memory, such is not the case with the action of the fourth chapter, which centers on the putative unraveling of the murders of Halpin Frayser and his mother. Indeed, at the outset Bierce's omniscient narrator plays around with a description that comments equally on weather and whether:

> A warm, clear night had been followed by a morning of drenching fog. At about the middle of the afternoon of the preceding day a little whiff of light vapor—a mere thickening of the atmosphere, *the ghost of a cloud*—had been observed clinging to the western side of Mount St. Helena, away up along the barren altitudes near the summit. It was so thin, so diaphanous, so *like a fancy made visible,* that one would have said: "Look quickly! in a moment it will be gone." (italics mine)

The deliberate reversal of the continuity of time, the inversion of the usual connotations of night and day, the implicit pun on vapor, the dream ghost lurking in the ghost of a cloud, and the notion of a materialized fancy (an optical illusion in tether to a fiction of the imagination): these observations all mock the self-reliance of rational thought and sensory perception. Moreover, the lyrical ecstasy of the breathless moment so readily shared with the reader collapses into a nonsensical joke. A dense fog immediately forms as the wisp of a cloud joins "small patches of mist that appeared to come out of the mountain side on exactly the same level, with an intelligent design to be absorbed."

Properly, Bierce brings a pair of manhunters into the narrative on the morning after this weather develops, as they set out on a journey to lift the fog of mystery surrounding the murder of a woman (Mrs. Frayser) by her second husband (Branscom). And once more the narrator enjoins the reader to share a moment of pointless mutual superiority in awareness: "They [Holker the sheriff and Jaralson the detective] carried guns on their shoulders, yet no one having knowledge of such matters could have mistaken them for hunters of bird or beast." As the plot thickens in the unthickening fog, white turns black in the movement of the two men towards their destination, though in a kind of educative jest:

> "The White Church? Only a half mile farther," the other [Jaralson] answered. "By the way," he added, "It is neither white nor a church; it is an abandoned schoolhouse, gray with age and neglect. Religious services were once held in it—when it was white, and there is a graveyard that would delight a poet."

Counterpointing the narrator's subversion of the tone of the story (though not Bierce's cynical disdain for the power of thought), Jaralson's reversals of anticipation signal a total *reductio ad absurdum* of a commonsensical resolution of the mystery of Halpin Frayser's murder. Like the principals of the main plot, the detective also suffers from a perceptual quirk. The manipulated conjunction of methodical literality and romantic sentiment projects the peculiar balance of reason and emotion that enters into his judgments of factual reality. As the one faculty colors the functions of the other, he exercises as little control over his associations as Halpin Frayser.

In effect, both find themselves dominated by equivalent patternings of consciousness. One a lawyer and the other a detective, they build their outlook on the dislocations of life from similar points of view, and in a grimly hilarious coincidence Myron Bayne's Gothic poetry feeds the yearnings of their imagination. This strategy of identity is contrived to cast as much doubt upon Jaralson's objectivity in criminal investigation as Halpin Frayser's subjectivity in nightmare characterization. Ordinary thought, at least from Bierce's standpoint, differs not a whit from the dream fantasy. Although Jaralson's purpose in coming to White Church is to find the grave of Mrs. Frayser who has been murdered by her second husband, it is hardly a wonder that he discovers the dead body of the son sprawled by the headboard. Nor, by the same token, is it unpredictable that Holker stumbles upon the manuscript of Halpin Frayser's poem. This convergence of plot and subplot rehearses the usual scenario of the horror tale on the verge of resolution, but that convention does not actually apply in this story.

For when the narrator describes the strangled body of the protagonist, the unsaid and the unanswered beg for scrutiny, especially since the two manhunters immediately jump to the conclusion that he has been murdered by Branscom: "The body lay upon its back, the legs wide apart. One arm was thrust upward, the other outward; but the latter was bent acutely, and the hand was near the throat. Both hands were tightly clenched. The whole attitude was that of a desperate but ineffectual resistence to—what?" Yet these and other gruesome details are taken in "almost at a glance" by the two men. They fail to heed the message of the clenched, confessional hands—the answer to the unanswered questions of the story and a cross-reference to the dream in which the body, responding to the promptings of its own irrepressible language, usurps the authority of the mind. This parallel finds support in the terror, similar to Halpin Frayser's, that begins to overwhelm Jaralson. Like Frayser, he also feels haunted by a phantom murderer, the figure of the Branscom conjured up in his imagination. Bierce insistently draws attention to this condition in the description of his physical movements: "making a vigilant circumspection of the forest, his shotgun held in both hands and at full cock." "The work of a maniac, he said, without withdrawing his eyes from the enclosing wood." "[He] continued scanning the dim gray confines of their narrow world and hearing matter of apprehension in the drip of water from every burdened branch." Thus Bierce urges the reader to note the correspondence in the state of consciousness of the awake Jaralson and the dreaming Halpin Frayser.

The purpose behind this rhetorical strategy emerges when Holker reads aloud from the latter's poem; for Jaralson's dogmatic identity of its author establishes the voice of the verse as a flow of consciousness that transcends person, time, and place: " 'Myron Bayne, a chap who flourished in the early years of the nation—more than a century ago. Wrote mighty dismal stuff; I have his collected works. The poem is not among them, but it must have been omitted by mistake.' " Here Bierce's use of the casual "dismal" (etymologically, to cause dread or consternation) associates the voice with an impulse of life hostile to the norms of ordinary awareness. As such, it speaks for the body, for all the desires of liberation from cultural automatism that receive expression in the rebellious language of poetry, fantasy, murder, and dream. Thus the gathering at White Church, the dead and the living, marks the convergence in and out of time of all the characters in the story who have been lured into traveling the forbidden road of consciousness so dramatically evoked in the recorded dream and poem.

Accordingly, Bierce next deftly concretizes the specious factuality of historical identity in the dialogue that follows the discovery of Mrs. Frayser's grave marker, " 'Larue, Larue!' exclaimed Holker, with sudden animation. 'Why, that is the real name of Branscom—not Pardee. And—bless my soul! how it all comes to me—the murdered woman's name had been Frayser.' " Constantly delineated as incurious and unimaginative, Holker personifies the limitations of empirical reason. For all his piecing together of evidence, nothing has been solved. The still uncaptured Branscom or Larue (surrogate of the Oedipal son) is no more or less a murderer than Mrs. Frayser in her son's dream or Myron Bayne in the ecstasies of morbid inspiration or Jaralson in arresting an assassin. If there is a criminal at large, he is for Bierce the creator of the mind of man: the trickster God (Descartes' *Dieu trompeur*) who delights in betraying every aspiration for truth or certitude that the creatures of His creation harbor in their thoughtless thought. For it is the sound of that thought, echoing out of the spaceless and timeless distances of consciousness, that Holker and Jaralson hear or think they hear emanating out of the forest. The sound actually originates at the source of all consciousness and records the pitiless indifference of the creator of all things for the fragments of His consciousness. This horrifying cry, always keyed to the bitter frustrations of human thought, is the signature of American Gothicism—the subjective condition of the ingrained Puritan sensibility of the American even when he is in the grip of the consoling illusion of self-reliance. And this is the nightmarish voice that haunts the fiction of Brown, Poe, Hawthorne, James, and Bierce. Listen attentively: it sounds loudest in the silences of the sun under the supreme manifestation of the illusion-making Word. (pp. 115-22)

William Bysshe Stein, "Bierce's 'The Death of Halpin Frayser': The Poetics of Gothic Consciousness," in ESQ, *Vol. 18, No. 2, 2nd quarter, 1972, pp. 115-22.*

B. S. Field (essay date 1977)

[*In the following essay, Field asserts that critics tend to dismiss Bierce because they fail to recognize the significance of his tales within the tradition of American comic writing.*]

Ambrose Bierce is a comic writer and ought to be judged as one. Once that observation is acknowledged, his position among the traditions of American literature takes on a new perspective. Sometimes minor writers are made to seem inappropriately insignificant in the histories of the literatures to which they belong, because critics compare them with "major" writers, rather than with other writers within their own tradition. Such has been the fate of the work of Ambrose Bierce.

Bierce's popularity with the common reader has never abated, but his work has not been given the treatment it deserves by critics of American literature. Critics commit this disservice because they let themselves be tempted by the grim tone of some of his stories, and by their own tendency to place any grim fiction in the category of the "serious," the "philosophic." That has led to a further temptation to regard Bierce as a philosophic writer who strives to make his audiences aware of the absurdist-tragic quality of their lives. To succumb to that temptation is to misvalue Bierce's work in two ways: first, to force upon it comparison with genuinely philosophic work, by which comparison it clearly suffers and is made to look weaker than it really is; and second, to fail to measure it against the other work in the tradition of American comic writing where it belongs, and where it stands up very well indeed.

To value Bierce's work correctly we need to understand that all of it, however solemnly philosophic it may be made to seem, has a comic aim. It has always been obvious that the element of the grotesque joke is important in part of Bierce's fiction. Richard O'Connor, Bierce's biographer, comments [in *Ambrose Bierce*] that if Bierce is ever "rediscovered," it would be as a black humorist. Edmund Wilson in his *Patriotic Gore* speaks consistently of Bierce's characters in his tales as "the helpless butts of sadistic practical jokes."

So the idea of Bierce as a joker is not a new one. Nor is the idea of Bierce as practitioner of black comedy new. His biographers all repeat that Bierce, in one way or another, was a misanthropist, indeed a pessimist. Representative of this point of view is Clifton Fadiman, who, in the introduction to a volume of Bierce's *Collected Writings* published in 1946, speaks of Bierce as "a pessimism machine. He is Swift minus true intellectual power, Rochefoucauld with a bludgeon, Voltaire with stomach ulcers." Fadiman, entering the Age of the Bomb, takes Bierce's misanthropy as the stalking horse for his own Atomic Angst. Fadiman also comments that if Bierce really did die in Mexico in 1914, "it seems rather a pity. The current scene would have filled him with so pure a pleasure."

In 1963 a volume of Jacques Papy's translations of Bierce's tales was published in Paris by Julliard under the title *Au Coeur de la Vie.* It was designed, I suspect, to coincide with the premiere of a French movie based on some of the stories in the volume. This collection also contained an explanatory introduction by Jacques Sternberg, and in this essay, Sternberg divided Bierce's important work into two groups—the seriously misanthropic and the less seriously so. He termed the latter group *humour noir.* Under this latter heading he includes such things as the four tales from "The Parenticide Club," the ***Fantastic Fables,*** and *The Devil's Dictionary.* Among the seriously misanthropic, he cites, among those that appeared in ***Tales of Soldiers and Civilians,*** **"Killed at Resaca," "Occurrence at Owl Creek Bridge," "Chickamauga,"** and **"Coup de Grâce."**

Sternberg takes some trouble to demonstrate for his French readers that Bierce's misanthropy was not a pose; it was to be taken seriously. But the evidence that he cites in order to prove his point comes from the works that he has listed under the heading of *humor noir.* By the same logic, why may not one treat the stories that Sternberg calls seriously misanthropic as *humour noir* as well? Where, indeed, is the point to any of them if there is no ironic comedy in them?

A comparison of the techniques of tales which are patently comic in intention, such as those in "The Parenticide Club," with the technique of some of the tales that Sternberg takes as seriously misanthropic will demonstrate that the technique in both groups is roughly the same. **"Oil of Dog"** from "The Parenticide Club" is overtly comic. Its style, its choice of vocabulary tells us so. It starts:

> My name is Boffer Bing. I was born of honest parents in one of the humbler walks of life, my father being a manufacturer of dog-oil and my mother having a small studio in the shadow of the village church, where she disposed of unwelcome babes.

The choice of the word "studio," as Fadiman remarks, is a happy thought. Bierce closes his story with a similar device. After the action of the tale reaches its climax as Boffer Bing's parents murder each other—the father stabbed, dragging the mother with him into a boiling vat of dog-oil—the narrator concludes:

> Convinced that these unhappy events closed to me every avenue to an honorable profession in that town, I removed to the famous city of Otumwee, where these memoirs are written with a heart full of remorse for a heedless act entailing so dismal a commercial disaster.

And of course the choice word here is "commercial." All the tales from the "Parenticide Club" function in similar forms. Another tale from the same group, **"An Imperfect Conflagration,"** opens:

> Early one June morning in 1872, I murdered my father—an act which made a deep impression on me at the time.

Still another, **"The Hypnotist,"** has no opening joke, but it does have a delicious closing sentence. The first matter in the tale is a long disquisition on the new science or art of mesmerism, followed by a description of a series of the narrator's experiments with it. The last of these revolves around the narrator's discovery of his parents out on a picnic. He convinces them that they are both wild stallions and deadly enemies. They promptly kick each other to death. The narrator concludes:

> Such are a few of my principal experiments in the mysterious force or agency known as hypnotic suggestion. Whether or not it could be employed by a bad man for an unworthy purpose I am unable to say.

A representative selection from another group, "Negligible Tales," is the brief **"Curried Cow."** The narrator's Aunt Patience owned a cow which was fond of kicking to death anyone who approached. Her husband tried to cure the cow of this habit by setting up a cast iron figure of himself in the cow's stall. The cow wore itself out kicking the figure and seemed to have a chastened temper. The tale concludes:

> Her entire character appeared to be radically altered—so altered that one day my Aunt Patience, who, fondly as she loved her, had never before so much as ventured to touch the hem of her garment, as it were, went confidently up to her to soothe her with a pan of turnips. Gad! how thinly she spread that good old lady upon the face of an adjacent stone wall! You could not have done it so evenly with a trowel.

All these tales, as appears in the passages quoted above, are couched in the genteel style of Bierce's day, a device that encourages the genteel reader to expect that complacent genteel cliché, this multiplying the force of the dénouement which overturns these complacent expectations.

We can find that same genteel style in more "serious" groups of Bierce's stories, and used for the same ends as those we have just cited. **"Killed at Resaca"** provides a simple model. The tale begins by telling of a Lieutenant Herman Brayle's foolish bravery. But occasionally a sharp word or phrase, reminiscent of the "choice" words in the comic tales, can be detected as satire or irony:

> He would stand like a rock in the open when officers and men alike had taken cover; while men older in service and years, higher in rank and of unquestionable intrepidity, were loyally preserving behind the crest of a hill lives infinitely more precious to their country, this fellow would stand, facing in the direction of the sharpest fire.

The word "loyally" in that passage and such phrases as the cliché, "infinitely more precious," the derogatory connotation of "fellow," all suggest an ironic view of the men behind the crest of the hill.

There are other devices besides the genteel style with which to arouse and abuse expectations. Brayle is eventually killed, his belongings are divided among the survivors, and his wallet falls to the narrator. The narrator, on his way to California after the war, looks through the wallet a second time and comes across a letter he had previously missed, to Brayle from a girl in San Francisco. Part of it reads:

> Mr. Winters, whom I shall always hate for it, has been telling that at some battle in Virginia, where he got his hurt, you were seen crouching behind a tree. I think he wants to injure you in my regard, which he knows this story would do if I believed it. I could bear to hear of my soldier lover's death, but not of his cowardice.

The narrator calls on the girl in San Francisco and delivers the letter in a room where a fire is burning.

> She mechanically took the letter, glanced through it with deepening color, and then looking at me with a smile, said:
>
> "It is very good of you, though I am sure it was hardly worth while." She started suddenly and changed color.
>
> "This stain," she said, "it, it—surely it is not—"
>
> "Madam," I said, "pardon me, but that is the blood of the truest and bravest heart that ever beat."
>
> She hastily slung the letter on the blazing coals. "Uh! I cannot bear the sight of blood!" she said. "How did he die?"

The narrator considers the girl and the burning paper for a moment and then replies:

> "He was bitten by a snake."

Clearly the effect at the end of this story is that of a joke, of the arousing and then the betrayal of expectations.

Let us examine the converse of the proposition: when Bierce's tales are not effective, they are not so because they are not good jokes. **"One of the Missing"** is about a Federal scout, a man of unexampled bravery, who leaves camp in order to have a look around the Confederate lines. As he stands in a partially wrecked building he sees the Confederate elements pulling back. He cocks his rifle to shoot and then thinks better of it. At this moment a chance Confederate shell knocks the building down on top of him, trapping him in the rubbish. When he regains consciousness, he sees his rifle aimed straight at his eye. He is afraid that if he moves, his rifle with its especially devised hair-trigger will go off. He dies of fright, and then we learn that the rifle has already been discharged when the building fell. Bierce has now made his point, that is, if the story is merely a horror tale. But Bierce goes on. Twenty-four minutes later the body is discovered by the scout's own brother, who looks at the contorted face without recognition, judges him "dead a week," and moves on. The story is weak because neither the dead brother nor the live one comes to any consciousness of the state of things. Neither has any expectations to be betrayed. The story fails as a joke fails.

On the other hand, the close of the tale **"Coup de Grâce"** is a real moment of truth. The story of Captain Downing Madwell, his best friend, Sergeant Caffal Halcrow, and his worst enemy, the brother of the sergeant, Major Creede Halcrow, opens as Madwell searches a battlefield, and finds in the wilderness the sergeant mortally wounded and in intense, inarticulate pain. After pages of indecision, Madwell finally gives the sergeant what he obviously wants, a *coup de grâce.* As he tries to withdraw his sword from the sergeant's body,

> . . . three men stepped silently forward from behind a clump of trees which had concealed their approach. Two were hospital attendants and carried a stretcher.
>
> The third was Major Creede Halcrow.

A similar effect is attempted in **"George Thurston."** We learn that the title character is depressed. In a rest camp, the men have hung a swing from a high branch. Thurston's turn on this toy is remarkable for the great length of the arcs he swings, and he attracts a crowd, among them the narrator. Then Thurston flies off the rope.

> Thurston and the swing had parted—that is all that can be known; both hands at once had released the rope. The impetus of the light swing exhausted, it was falling back; the man's momentum was carrying him, almost erect, upward and forward, no longer in his arc, but with an outward curve. It could have been but an instant, yet it seemed an age. I cried out, or thought I cried out: "My God, will he never stop going up?" . . . At this distance of many years I can distinctly recall that image of a man in the sky, its head erect, its feet close together, its hands—I do not see its hands. All at once, with an astonishing suddenness and rapidity, it turns over and pitches downward. There is another cry from the crowd, which has instinctively rushed forward. The man had become merely a whirling object, mostly legs. . . .

The description of his descent, of the noise he makes when he lands, and of the position of the body continues for six or seven more lines of text, and then on through still another paragraph before we reach the last and enlightening touch:

> The arms were folded tightly across the breast.

This tale is not as weak as **"One of the Missing,"** for at least the narrator is capable of seeing the state of affairs, but it does not impress as such a story might. The butt is missing. Not even the narrator clearly suffers any shock or surprise.

The effects of **"One of the Missing"** and of **"George Thurston"** miss the same targets that stories like **"Killed at Resaca"** or **"Coup de Grâce"** hit. This kind of joke needs a butt. A butt is a person capable of comprehending the situation and of suffering because of it, that is, of seeing his expectations betrayed. There is no butt in **"One of the Missing."** Only the narrator in **"George Thurston"** is available for the function of the butt, and little is made of what he suffered. But for Lieutenant Brayle's girl friend or for Captain Madwell, the possibilities for suffering are various, very various.

There are further variations possible. Critics monotonously repeat that **"Occurrence at Owl Creek Bridge"** is a study of an abnormal psychological state. Perhaps it is. Edmund Wilson tells us that the central character is the butt of a practical joke. But the central character is not the only available butt. To be presented with the tale of a man who apparently escapes death by hanging because the rope breaks in the process, to follow his fall into the river, his swim to shore, his run cross-country to his home, only to learn, just as the man is about to clasp his wife in his arms, that all these events are imaginary ones that have passed through his mind between the springing of the trap and the snapping tight of the noose, is to be the butt of a practical joke. **"Chickamauga,"** we are assured, is a study in point of view. It may be so. But by the time the narrator has described, through the eyes of a child, the wounded and dying men, has described the child's playing "horsey" with them as they crawl toward water, has described their drowning in the creek because they are too weak to lift their faces out after drinking, and has described the mangled body of the child's mother in the ruins of their home, the information that the child is deaf and dumb cannot affect us with horror, even though it explains the child's insensitivity to the battle around him, nor with disgust either, for it is too tasteless. In other words, it, too, is a joke. Not funny, but the butt of a joke seldom finds his own plight comic.

Ambrose Bierce.

It has been a critical commonplace among critics of American literature that somehow the reputation of Ambrose Bierce ought to be a little higher on the literary stock market than it is. Apparently Bierce's reputation has always been on the verge of rehabilitation, without ever achieving it. O'Connor points out that as early as 1893 Bierce was tired of hearing that he was about to be discovered. O'Connor also cites a passage, from the *London News Age* of 1909, in which Arnold Bennett named Bierce as an example of an "underground reputation." And underground that reputation has remained. Ten or a dozen of his stories have been reprinted over and over in various periodicals in the last sixty years. At least one among this group of stories is always being included in the latest anthology of short fiction. But most attempts to discuss Bierce and his writing, like Woodruff's book, study him in the wrong context.

To study Bierce in the same category with Twain or Crane is to show only how he fails to measure up to such writers without giving him credit for having written in another tradition entirely. All of the work of Bierce, not just some of it, regardless of how fascinating or repulsive one may find his so-called misanthropy, ought to be judged as the work of a joker and a practitioner of *humor noir,* in the not inconsiderable American tradition of writers like O. Henry, H. L. Mencken, and Don Marquis. There he occupies a respectable if extreme position in the spectrum of American writers of comic fiction. (pp. 173-80)

B. S. Field, Jr., "Ambrose Bierce as a Comic," in Western Humanities Review, *Vol. XXXI, No. 1, Winter, 1977, pp. 173-80.*

F. J. Logan (essay date 1977)

[In the following essay, Logan contends that "An Occurrence at Owl Creek Bridge" *has been the object of numerous critical misreadings and is far superior as a work of literature than its reputation as an anthology-piece would suggest.*]

Ambrose Bierce's **"An Occurrence at Owl Creek Bridge"** has a history of both popularity and critical inattention. The result is misreading. The story has languished in anthologies, chiefly those used in secondary schools, perhaps because it has been so frequently offered as an action tale of extreme power written by an otherwise unfamiliar Civil War writer.

It is fitting that, if Bierce's slender popular reputation must rest on any one story, it should rest on this one since it is among his best; it is unfortunate that the story should be generally valued for its accidents and not its essence—that the fine Biercean imagination, grisly wit, and poignant irony should be slighted or overlooked entirely—and that it should be most often read, as Cleanth Brooks and Robert Penn Warren read it [in *Understanding Fiction*], as a war yarn with a gimmicky ending, a reverse O. Henry twist.

Because **"Owl Creek Bridge"** is still misunderstood, a correction is in order. Recent evidence of this general misunderstanding is a puzzling article by Fred. H. Marcus, titled "Film and Fiction: 'An Occurrence at Owl Creek Bridge' " [California English Journal, 1971]. Professor Marcus sees the story as a "narrowly homogenized Gothic tale of horror," "spiced by authorial intrusions of sardonic observation." He has noticed two of Bierce's more important sentences ("What he heard was the ticking of his watch." "He was a Federal scout."), and contends that here "the horror reaches its apogee in the terse closing phrase which flares like luminous evil over the preceding lines"; and that "the eerie light illuminates section I and maintains the chill mood of Bierce's horror tale." The persona's observation that Farquhar was evidently "no vulgar assassin" reflects Bierce's "social consciousness of caste," according to Marcus (this is one of the story's three themes, as Marcus reads it); and Farquhar's post-imaginary-plunge hypersensitivity reveals "man's usual insensitivity to the vibrant, throbbing life pulsating about him." Marcus reviews a cinematic adaptation of the story following this observation, and closes his article with the reflection that, since the filmmaker used a number of details which trivialize death," and since this "trivializing of death suggests contemporary events only too clearly," *therefore,* "the late nineteenth-century story becomes highly relevant to our time and place."

This most shopworn and factitious of all conclusions puts a period to ten pages of what Bierce and every good Biercean reader would surely brand as "bosh." In those places where Marcus is neither obvious, nor silly, nor trite, he is dead wrong. He is wrong about the protagonist, the story, and the intended effect of the story on the reader; and he is therefore wrong about Bierce. In those places where his meaning is accessible he seems to be arguing that **"Owl Creek Bridge"** is a sensational thriller à la Poe (probably the most widely held interpretation of the story). I will show that it is not.

The story is, incidentally, an action tale; *essentially,* its concern is with what may be loosely called philosophical questions: it is a speculation on the nature of time and on the nature of abnormal psychology, particularly on processes of abnormal perception and cognition. The story also explores or exploits epistemological issues and the logic upon which this epistemology rests. So the story is philosophy, but it is satire as well—two kinds: first, it is a burlesque of the orthodox war yarn in which the hero's death or survival is noble and significant; and second, it is thus in effect a lampoon-in-progress against those who, expecting the usual war yarn, mistake **"Owl Creek Bridge"** for their standard fare and overlook its central concerns. And its ending is thus a sharp rap across the sensibilities for "that cave-bat, 'the general reader,' " dealt in punishment for woolgathering.

For the reader, to the extent that he likes and is like Farquhar, to the extent that he ignores reason and irony, to the extent, that is, that he does not really *read,* the end of the story is a sad shock. Would Bierce purposely lampoon the inattentive? Yes. He detested "bad readers—readers who, lacking the habit of analysis, lack also the faculty of discrimination, and take whatever is put before them, with the broad, blind catholicity of a slop-fed conscience or a parlor pig."

Bierce, by the way, was himself a *close* reader. For example, in an essay written in 1903 titled "The Moon in Letters," he takes a number of authors to task for their "private systems of astronomy," for "their ignorance of what is before their eyes all their blessed lives." After listing several celestial impossibilities in a novel by H. Rider Haggard, he says,

> A writer who believes that the new moon can rise in the east soon after sunset and the full moon at ten o'clock; who thinks the second of these remarkable phenomena can occur twenty-four hours after the first, and itself be followed some fourteen hours later by an eclipse of the

> sun—such a man may be a gifted writer, but I am not a gifted reader.

The novelist William Black has been even less attentive than Haggard:

> In dismissing Black I cannot forbear to add that even if the moon could rise in the south; even if rising into the dome when it should be setting . . . [etc.] . . . I have found similar blunders in the poems of Wordsworth, Coleridge, Schiller, Moore, Shelley, Tennyson and Bayard Taylor. Of course a poet is entitled to any kind of universe that may best suit his purpose, and if he could give us better poetry by making the moon rise "full-orbed" in the northwest and set like a "tin sickle" in the zenith I should go in for letting him have his fling. But I do not discern any gain in "sweetness and light" from these despotic readjustments of the relations among sun, earth and moon, and must set it all down to the account of ignorance, which, in any degree and however excusable, is not a thing to be admired.

Similarly, here is Bierce once more on the primacy of precision: "We think in words; we cannot think without them. Shallowness or obscurity of speech means shallowness or obscurity of thought." And this is an application of that dictum:

> The other day, in fulfillment of a promise, I took a random page of [Howells'] work and in twenty minutes had marked forty solecisms—instances of the use of words without a sense of their importance or a knowledge of their meaning—the substitution of a word that he did not want for a word that he did not think of. Confusion of thought leads to obscurity of expression. . . . Words are the mechanism of thought. The master knows his machine, and precision is nine parts of style. This fellow Howells thinks into the hopper and the mangled thought comes out all over his cranky apparatus in gobs and splashes of expression."

The point to this digression is to establish at the outset the certainty that Bierce as reader demanded accuracy, and therefore the high probability that Bierce as writer provided it. . . . I am contending that **"Owl Creek Bridge"** is not, *pace* Marcus and nearly all other critics good and bad and indifferent, some sort of hysterical gothic horripilator; it is, on the contrary, as tightly controlled and meticulously organized as any story is likely to be. Bierce knew what he was doing—among other things, here, dispensing fine satiric comment, and seeing to it that the story's protagonist gets his fair share.

. . . . .

Poor Peyton Farquhar—"such an attractive figure: brave, sensitive, highly intelligent. . . . It is," Stuart Woodruff mourns [in his *The Short Stories of Ambrose Bierce*], "the tragic waste of such a man which engages our sympathies." Woodruff is mistaken: Farquhar is not brave, he is foolhardy; he is not sensitive, he is callous ("a civilian who was at heart a soldier, and who in good faith and without too much qualification assented to at least a part of the frankly villainous dictum that all is fair in love and war"); and he is not highly intelligent. He is, as we shall see, rather stupid.

Farquhar, poised on the bridge, "looked a moment at his 'unsteadfast footing.' " If recognized as an allusion, this must have seemed a mere gratuitous one to readers for the last eighty years, because no one, so far as I know, has bothered to follow up this little tag. It is worth following up. Here is the allusion in the context (Worcester trying to placate Harry) of *Henry IV,* Part I:

> Peace cousin, say no more.
> And now I will unclasp a secret book,
> And to your quick-conceiving discontents
> I'll read you matter deep and dangerous,
> As full of peril and adventurous spirit
> As to o'er-walk a current roaring loud
> On the unsteadfast footing of a spear.

Harry is interested:

> If he fall in, good night. Or sink, or swim!
> Send danger from the east unto the west,
> So honor cross it from the north to south,
> And let them grapple! O the blood more stirs
> To rouse a lion than to start a hare.
>
> NORTHUMBERLAND.
>
> Imagination of some great exploit
> Drives him beyond the bounds of patience.
>
> HOTSPUR.
>
> By heaven methinks it were an easy leap
> To pluck bright honor from the pale-fac'd moon,
> Or dive into the bottom of the deep,
> Where fadom-line could never touch the ground,
> And pluck up drowned honor by the locks. . . .

So by means of his short allusion Bierce has strongly suggested Farquhar's pedigree: he is a sort of latter-day Warmspur, not as splendid and formidable as Harry, but just as restive and foolhardy. What other evidence have we that this is so, that Farquhar is a satiric object?

We have the burlesques. Here, for example, is the beginning of the story's second section:

> Peyton Farquhar was a well-to-do planter, of an old and highly respected Alabama family. Being a slave owner and like other slave owners a politician he was naturally an original secessionist and ardently devoted to the Southern cause. Circumstances of an imperious nature . . . had prevented him from taking service with the gallant army that had fought the disastrous campaigns ending with the fall of Corinth, and he chafed under the inglorious restraint, longing for the release of his energies, the larger life of the soldier, the opportunity for distinction. That opportunity, he felt, would come, as it comes to all in war time. Meanwhile he did what he could. No service was too humble for him to perform in aid of the South, no adventure too perilous for him to undertake.

Now I read this as a thumbnail burlesque of martial rhetoric: words like "gallant," "inglorious," "opportunity," "distinction," and "adventure" begin cropping up immediately. They are symptoms of Farquhar's terminal "Walter Scott disease," as Mark Twain called it. Bierce's inclusion in this *mimesis* of alliteration ("longing . . . release . . . larger . . . life") helps the burlesque along by inflating these words and phrases, rendering them emptier than they inherently are, giving them—to borrow Bierce's own metaphor from a different context—"the martial strut of a boned turkey." This calls attention to them and thus to the irony lurking within them (Hemingway fans will note resemblances here). Bierce emphasizes his burlesque with the figure *isocolon,* here, that hoariest of encomia for the stay-at-home ("No service . . . too humble, no adventure too perilous"), and follows this with a sentence epitomizing chivalric fatuity: the Federal scout asks for a drink of water, and "Mrs. Farquhar was only too happy to serve him with her own white hands."

[In his essay "Crossing the Bar Twice: Post-Mortem Consciousness in Bierce, Hemingway, and Golding," *Studies in Short Fiction,* 1969] John Kenney Crane has mistaken satire for mawkishness. He assures us that "it is, of course, the blatant sentimentality that mars the story," and it is presumably such passages as these which lie at the root of his objection. Crane assumes that the vocabulary is Bierce's, but there is no reason why he should. To assume that stupid words necessarily signify authorial obtuseness is to ignore the author's option of addressing his readers indirectly; such words may well be a sign of authorial astuteness, as they are here in section two of **"Owl Creek Bridge."**

Let me emphasize this point. No one, for example, has objected to James Joyce's occasionally sounding like his characters: "But wasn't Maria glad when the women had finished their tea and the cook and the dummy had begun to clear away the tea-things!" When reading sentences like this, nobody accuses Joyce of being himself a dummy; everybody assumes that this is masterly first person narrative couched in the third person; nobody doubts his genius, much less his competence.

If Joyce, why not Bierce? Why assume that what strikes us as Victorian gingerbread would not have struck Bierce as contemporary treacle? Why not give him the benefit of the doubt? As it turns out, however, there is no need to do so; nearly everything about the sickly Victorian novel, including the hackneyed "white hands" convention, did strike Bierce as being tiresome frippery. In **"The Captain of 'The Camel,' "** for example, starving mariners are reduced to eating volumes of current genteel fiction, with the result that

> Our diction consisted, in about equal parts, of classical allusion, quotation from the stable, simper from the scullery, cant from the clubs, and the technical slang of heraldry. We boasted much of ancestry, and admired the whiteness of our hands whenever the skin was visible through a fault in the grease and tar.

The irony, then, is Bierce's; the timidity, triteness, and inanity are Farquhar's. The words are not the author's but the character's, and they establish him as part villain manqué, part fool. The flaws Crane finds in the story are flaws in Farquhar's character, and Gordon W. Cunliffe, in writing that "the sympathy evoked by the description of the main figure is here [in section two] confirmed," would have been correct had he written not "confirmed," but "cancelled."

"I will ease my heart / Albeit I make a hazard of my head" (*Henry IV,* Part I.) These are Hotspur's words, but they could serve, with the simple substitution of "neck" for "head," as Farquhar's motto. Obsessed with honor, he neglected the "dusty horseman," neglected to ask him about his regiment, and so forth—to see if this man were what he seemed. "Gray-clad" is good enough for Farquhar. And when the horseman tells him that the piled driftwood "is now dry and would burn like tow," Farquhar's reaction (inferred from his subsequent predicament) is like Harry's: "Why, it cannot choose but be a noble plot!" As an unreflecting and ingenuous glory hunter, who reveals his tragicomic flaw in his lexicon, who wears his soldierly heart on his sleeve, and who seems never to have heard (though "all is fair," though he is himself an agent) that there exists such folk as spies, Farquhar gets what is coming to him:

> His neck was in pain and lifting his hand to it he found it horribly swollen. He knew that it had a circle of black where the rope had bruised it. His eyes felt congested; he could not close them. His tongue was swollen with thirst; he relieved its fever by thrusting it forward from between his teeth into the cold air. How softly the turf had carpeted the untraveled avenue—he could no longer feel the roadway beneath his feet!

Here Bierce's own tongue is thrust firmly in his cheek, and we can catch a clear echo, particularly in the last sentence here, of his charnel wit. This almost jovial description of the hanged man, plus the burlesque, plus the allusion to Farquhar's literary lineage, make it obvious that for Bierce he is negligible and expendable, and fair satiric game.

But Farquhar is, like Henry Fleming, Gulliver, Hotspur, Huck, a satiric vehicle as well as a satiric object. If Farquhar is all too human, as the euphemism has it, then his executioners, the Union company, are all too inhuman. This is how Bierce presents them. This is how, in so doing, he maintains the necessary semblance of neutrality toward his characters, but also, having discouraged sympathy for Farquhar, retains the reader's interest in him. Farquhar, however much a figure of fun he may be, is definitely a human character. We know something about him, as a man; but of the Union soldiers, as men, we know nothing.

Biercean *metonymy* is at work here. It is distinct and distinctive enough in his war writing, that [in his *The Beginnings of Naturalism in American Fiction*] Lars Ahnebrink has called it a "process of animism." Bierce invented this technique (just as he invented the drastic fictional distortion of time). This value of this "process of animism"—which might better be called a "process of deanimism"—is this: by confounding men with things, Bierce, and later Stephen Crane, were able to convey in a subtle but telling manner man's insignificance and subhumanity in his own horrendous conflicts. The latter-day Union soldiers are introduced in terms of the arms they bear, as extensions of their weapons. Just as Farquhar's vice and folly make him liable to lampooning, so the soldiers' apparent lack of any feeling or thought makes them liable to the same. And that is what they get. The sentinels at either end of the bridge and facing outward stand in the "support" position with their rifles. They are not spectators but merely blockades; they "might have been statues to adorn the bridge." The main body of the company stands "staring stonily, motionless," with their rifles at "parade rest," lined up like the tree trunks of the stockade. A lieutenant stands with his hands folded over the hilt of his sword. The captain stands silently.

This tableau is the machine of death in repose. In action it is hardly less regular, suggesting as it does the automata that emerge from the works of Swiss town hall clocks to elaborately chime the hours (an apposite suggestion, since Bierce's main theme is the concept of time, and since his protagonist becomes a "pendulum.") A robot-like series of movements transposes the sergeant and the captain; a nod from the captain removes the sergeant from the plank and precipitates Farquhar. This is the rhetorical trope *hypotyposis,* mimicry of acts, another Biercean favorite.

And these robot-like actions are conveyed by and reflected in a pattern of robot-like sentences and phrases ("The preparations . . . the two . . . The sergeant . . . These movements . . . the end . . . This plant . . . the arrangement"). Such a flatfooted series—article/subject, article/subject—reads like an army training manual on the field-stripping of rifles. Here is more jargon. Bierce has allowed his military persona (for that is the speaker as the story opens) to drift into a burlesque of military diction. The denatured and clumsy language both describes the graceless maneuvers and blurs their significance. This is *mimesis,* again, and it functions with the *metonymy* and the *hypotyposis* to make Bierce's point, unobtrusively but effectively, about the soldiers. Furthermore, this burlesque complements Farquhar's jingoism, already noted, which comes a page later. The jargons interact, military litotes with military hyperbole, revealing the weaknesses of each. The language is objective but the anti-war message is subjective indeed, and the passages together constitute another example of dry and rarefied Biercean wit. "Humor is a sweet wine," he tells us elsewhere, "wit a dry; we know which is preferred by the connoisseur." **"Owl Creek Bridge"** contains vintage wit, is vintage satire. But it is more than satire; it is philosophy.

. . . . .

"A man stood upon a railroad bridge in northern Alabama, looking down into the swift water twenty feet below." This is the first sentence. A few lines later, the "man," Farquhar, is again gazing at the water which we already know is "swift," and he watches it "swirling" and "racing madly" below. Then:

> A piece of dancing driftwood caught his attention and his eyes followed it down the current. How slowly it appeared to move! What a sluggish stream!

The "swift" stream has suddenly turned "sluggish." Bierce is tampering with time in these latter three sentences, for each reflects a different point of view.

The water is swift. What thoughts this current calls up for the doomed man are at first open to conjecture since we are still observing Farquhar and his surroundings, not yet observing through him. The point of view is limited, the narrator acutely perceptive but disinterested. We are met with a series of uncertainties which communicate the narrator's limitations. Things beyond the moment and the field of vision are not definitely known, and the narrator is careful to separate, precisely, surmise from certainty: the captain is definitely a captain because he is in the uniform "of his rank," but the sergeant "*may*" (my emphasis) in civil life have been a deputy sheriff—and then again he may not have been; there is no way to be sure. Also, because the railroad was "lost to view" in the forest after a hundred yards, the narrator can only infer from military usage that "doubtless there was an outpost farther along." Similarly, Farquhar was "apparently" thirty-five years old, "evidently" no vulgar assassin, and a civilian and planter "if one might judge from his habit."

Bierce's handling of this persona—a man who knows what he knows and what he does not—is as deft as it is unobtrusive. But despite this persona's seeming objectivity and anonymity, we can still know a bit about him because his language gives him away. For example, he is (the irony indicates) slightly amused: "The liberal military code makes provision for hanging many kinds of persons, and gentlemen are not excluded." And this raises another point: this persona seems to know a great deal about the military. In the first part of section one we are treated to explanations of martial code, etiquette, usage, terms, and postures. In brief, the story's title and its first section smack of the general officer's memoirs—perhaps those of an old soldier who is at heart a *litterateur.*

This military observer (to refer again to the three sentences quoted above) notices the object catching Farquhar's attention and Farquhar's eyes following that object; this limited observer becomes an omniscient one in the next sentence, and is thus able to relate how this object appears to Farquhar; and in the third sentence the observer again becomes limited, but it is now a different observer, Farquhar himself. The reversal is complete. (And this is only the first of what becomes a pattern of such reversals, ranging from minute [the three sentence about-face], through extensive [the intrusion of the omniscient narrator—and reality—into fancy, at the close of each section], to all-inclusive [the last such intrusion, the whiplash ending].) This momentary but significant glance through Farquhar's eyes sets a precedent; the character has become, briefly, a second persona, and may do so again.

These three sentences merit a bit more attention. Bierce signals this reversal, accompanies and helps accomplish it, by supplanting prose with near-verse for as long as the reversal takes. Sentence one begins with four iambs ("A piece of dancing driftwood caught"); sentence two consists of the same ("How slowly it appeared to move!"); and sentence three begins with two trochees ("What a sluggish stream!"). That is the meter. The first sentence's *d*-alliteration gives way to the *s*-alliteration of sentences two and three. Bierce varies this alliteration in the last two words, slowing them, by juxtaposing *s-* and *sh-*sibilants, thus joining sound to sense; it is impossible to articulate, quickly, "sluggish stream."

We are now and momentarily inside the protagonist's brain, and that brain is definitely malfunctioning. In the next paragraph, the first full one on page thirty, the ticking of Farquhar's watch becomes to his ears thunderous, and more and more infrequent. ("No reader," Professor Marcus assures us, "could possibly fail to be reminded of Poe's story of 'The Tell-Tale Heart' "; Marcus does not, however, say why an essentially unlike and woefully inferior story should so inevitably come to mind, and one must therefore assume that he is simply resorting to the easy and stereotypic but wrong preconceptions that preclude an adequate reading of Bierce—in this instance, the persistent misconception that Bierce aped Poe.) Again we are perceiving through Farquhar. The sound "seemed" both distant and close, but then the interposed consciousness of the omniscient narrator again disappears; the intervals of silence did not "seem to grow," they *"grew"* and the sound *"increased"* (my emphases). It is, must be, his own brain, with thoughts being "flashed" upon it, that misinterprets this subdued and regular sound, and thus flaws the narrative. (Professor Marcus, however, does not think this is a disguised first person intrusion because he has discovered that the whole story is told by—and this would have pleased Bierce—an "omniscient author." One might point out to him, though—without quibbling over the distinction between "author" and "narrator"—that his "omniscient author" is at times strangely ignorant: "What he heard was the ticking of his watch." "What a sluggish stream!"). As Farquhar's mind works at ever higher speed everything else correspondingly slows, and we should be prepared for, not an escape, but a hallucination.

And this is what fascinated Bierce: the grim possibility that there is no death which is mercifully instantaneous since ordinary time may not apply. Mary Grenander, in her Twayne book on Bierce, first found this intriguing and revealing passage in his essay on the then new electric chair:

> The physicians know nothing about it; for anything they know to the contrary, death by electricity may be the most frightful torment that it is possible for any of nature's forces or processes to produce. The agony may be not only inconceivably great, but to the sufferer it may seem to endure for a period inconceivably long. That many of the familiar physical indications of suffering are absent (though "long, shuddering sighs" and "straining at the straps" are not certainly symptoms of joy) is very little to the purpose when we know that electricity paralyzes the muscles by whose action pain is familiarly manifested. We know that it paralyzes all the seats of sensation, for that matter, and puts an end to possibilities of pain. That is only to say that it kills. But by what secret and infernal pang may not all this be accompanied or accomplished? Through what unnatural exaltation of the senses may not the moment of its accomplishing be commuted into unthinkable cycles of time?

Hence Farquhar, his senses "exalted and refined," in his "unthinkable arcs of oscillation."

Later in this essay Bierce comes to the point: "Theories of the painlessness of sudden death appear to be based mostly upon the fact that those who undergo it make no entries of their sensations in their diaries." The third section of **"Owl Creek Bridge Bridge"** is a fictional attempt at just such a diary.

And logic is our guide through its mad pages. How do we know what we know? Bierce raises the epistemological question subtly but persistently. Indeed the whole story is "a lesson in perspective," as Stuart Woodruff so aptly titled his consideration of it. Or, what comes to the same thing, it is an exercise in "the faculty of discrimination," a faculty dormant or absent in both Farquhar and "bad readers."

There is an initial, strange uncertainty: could a man—however "exalted and refined" his "organic system"—see a million distinct blades of grass, and the dewdrops on each blade, and the prism in each drop, and the colors in each prism? Not likely. Thomas Erskine is probably right in saying that most readers accept this "outrageous hyperbole." But there is no excuse for such readers—Marcus among them—to do so, because Farquhar's perceptions are, in the strict sense of the word, preposterous.

And Bierce even points this out, as directly as he is able; Farquhar's senses are making "record of things never before perceived." This is the rhetorical trope *adianoeta,* deliberate ambiguousness, a Biercean favorite. Here it enables Bierce to ask his reader, indirectly but pointedly, perceived by whom? If by Farquhar only, then to make this explicit, "they had" should appear between "things" and "never." But the wording as it is leaves the question barely open: it may be only Farquhar who has never sensed such things; it may well be that no human being has ever sensed them; probably no percipient creature has ever done so. The conclusion following the latter two interpretations is obvious, and these two are supported by the record of Farquhar's astonishing sensations.

Could he (to take another example) hear a water spider's legs moving on the same flood in which he is now ostensibly immersed? Could he hear this above the rush of the torrent and the rasp of his own half-strangled breathing? Perhaps; very probably not—despite Professor Marcus's conviction that, were it not for our "usual insensitivity," we could, just as Farquhar did, thrill to this "vibrant, throbbing, pulsating," albeit infinitesimal, "life." "A fish slid along beneath his *eyes* and he *heard* the rush of its body parting the water" (my emphases). Bierce's phrasing suggests that Farquhar comes close to a synaesthetic experience here, that not only does he hear the inaudible but he does so with his eyes, and this at a time when he is supposedly bending every effort to stay alive. Again, however, this may not be absolutely impossible.

But when we are told that as he surfaced he could see the bridge and the fort (that is, he was far enough downstream for such a comprehensive view), but that the figures on the bridge were at this distance gigantic; and when we are told that at this distance he could see the eye and the color of the eye of the soldier who is shooting at him (which feat is in itself extremely improbable), although this man is to Farquhar a *silhouette*—by definition a dark featureless form in outline—then we must conclude that the gray eye is Farquhar's own, that it is turned inward, and that the "visible world" of which he is the "pivotal point" is also all his own. We *know* that Farquhar could not have seen these last two sights for the same reason we know that God can make neither a colossal midget nor a square circle.

No critic, so far as I know, has caught these two clear logical contradictions. And Woodruff, moving from a consideration of things he thinks *could* not have happened—seeing the dewdrops, etc.—to a consideration of things that did not happen, even quotes part of the passage in question: "Excited soldiers, silhouetted 'against the blue sky,' shout and gesticulate, Farquhar is spun and buffeted by the current, shots spatter all around him and he dives 'as deeply as he could.' " Woodruff comments: "It is this kind of specific detail [presumably including the eye in the silhouette and the gigantic soldiers in the distance] that keeps persuading the reader that perhaps the impossible has happened, that the rope did break and that soon Farquhar will be safe in the forest."

Not so. Farquhar is hallucinating and we know it. But, one may object, he is doing so too quickly: he is compressing an imaginary twenty-four hours into a fraction of a second.

Yet this is of course just Bierce's point. He makes it in his electric chair essay; he makes it implicitly throughout the story, beginning with the preposition *at* in the title; he makes it explicitly in the story's last sentence, ruling out any possibility of the comparatively slow death by strangulation: Farquhar had a "broken neck" and his dreaming was therefore done in an instant. Bierce, with his passion for precision and concision, would hardly have included such a detail inadvertently. No. Farquhar's death sentence was (and note the typically Biercean irony in this word's connotation) *"commuted"* only in the sense that death by electrocution may be "commuted"—that is, subjectively. "Swift" Owl Creek and the perceived behavior of the watch tell us that Farquhar's mind was accelerating (geometrically, in the manner of the falling body that he is) in proportion to the world's apparent deceleration; as real time left to him dwindles to nothing, subjective time expands this remnant, maintaining the balance. This is the hypothesis for the "careful and analytic record of" Farquhar's "sensations at every stage of his mischance"; this is the logical foundation for Bierce's **"A Diary of Sudden Death; By a Public-Spirited Observer on the Inside."** Farquhar is the guinea pig; Bierce is the real "student of hanging."

The theoretical arrow of Zeno is a good analogy here since the story's premise can be understood as a corollary of this ancient conundrum. Zeno's arrow never reached its target because, before it could do so, it had first to traverse half the distance, then half the remaining distance, etc., with eighths, sixteenths, thirty-seconds, sixty-fourths, and so on, endlessly interposing themselves. The arrow can get very close, but since a mathematical line has only location and direction, and not area, one can always be squeezed in half way between approaching point and static plane. For the archer this would be sufficiently discouraging. But when he reflects that his arrow can never get more than half-way anywhere, then he will realize that the shaft can never even leave the bow and that motion is impossible; and he will trudge sadly home. Zeno's assumption is that space is infinitely divisible; Bierce's, that time is infinitely divisible. It follows that if the human brain could perform that function and thus generate its own reprieve-in-progress, then death would be impossible, and Farquhar, thinking "with the rapidity of lightning," would be forever *in extremis*—immortal in some private fifth dimension.

Woodruff writes, toward the close of his discussion of the story, that "somehow the reader is made to participate in the split between imagination and reason, to *feel* the escape is real while he *knows* it is not." Woodruff is right, but his "somehow" could be improved upon. My suggestion is that the story gets much of its power from the opposition of two logics, that this is the submerged origin of Woodruff's "split." Bierce pairs unanswerable philosophical logic with the implacable logic of natural law. To Farquhar, death cannot be real so the escape must be; to the Biercean reader, the reader who keeps his eyes open and his sympathies in check, who therefore sees the series of gross improbabilities, contradictions, and shifts in point of view, to such a reader it is just the other way around—because the human brain, even a first-rate one, cannot perform the function of dividing time infinitely. The shaft hits home and the man's neck breaks.

To sum up: Bierce knew what he was doing, and we can know what he did. He did not write a Radcliffean cliff-hanger, nor a soap operetta, nor a slam-bang action yarn. All the evidence, both inside and outside the story, points the other way. The logic lets us know that we are participating in a hallucination, and that whatever else the reality behind the hallucination may be, it is not tragedy. This is simply the record of an "occurrence"—a rehearsal of the way things are. But it is also a broad hint at the warless way life should be, as well as an imaginative guess at the way death may be.

And it is superb art. Brooks and Warren ask, expecting the answer *no,* "is the surprise ending justified; is it validated by the body of the story; is it, in other words, a mere trick, or is it expressive and functional?" We do not drink fine wine to quench thirst; we do not read Bierce to kill time. Brooks and Warren expected mediocrity, read the story accordingly, and misunderstood this masterpiece of fiction—complaining, as they do, about the sad lack of "meaningful irony" and so forth. One might as reasonably dismiss a lofty vintage, gulped from the bottle, for the bitterness of its lees. The correct answer to Brooks and Warren's question is a resounding *yes. Yes,* the ending is justified, validated, expressive, and functional because the story's satiric content requires it, because the story's premise demands it, and because, realizing these necessities, Bierce took care that the ending should be in the beginning and throughout. Stephen Crane, as good a reader and critic as he was a writer, did *not* misunderstand **"Owl**

Creek Bridge": "That story has everything," he wrote. "Nothing better exists." (pp. 101-11)

F. J. Logan, "The Wry Seriousness of 'Owl Creek Bridge'," in American Literary Realism 1870-1910, *Vol. 10, No. 2, Spring, 1977, pp. 101-13.*

Alfred Kazin (essay date 1977)

[*A highly respected American literary critic, Kazin is best known for his essay collections* The Inmost Leaf *(1955),* Contemporaries *(1962), and* On Native Grounds *(1942). In the following essay, he examines Bierce's technique as a short story writer as it relates to his pessimistic philosophy.*]

Ambrose Bierce was only seventeen years old when he entered the Union Army during the Civil War. The war was the great experience of his life, and everything he was to write would be colored by this experience.

Bierce's writing is thus distinguished by a particular point of view, a slant, an angle of vision, that is somehow more original and more compelling than his narrative art itself. Unlike his contemporary, Henry James, who virtually created the modern realistic, psychological novel in America, Bierce was not a great craftsman in fiction and invented nothing that was to have a technical influence on the development of modern fiction. As will be seen, even so acute a story as **"Parker Adderson, Philosopher"** depends on Bierce's favorite device, a sudden reversal of character, rather than on a deeply worked out plot.

But Bierce's "point of view," his particular slant on life, was his ace in the hole. This was something new in American history and American literature. It was a form of war-hardened cynicism, as we so lightly say; it was the profoundest kind of disbelief, as we should say, a disbelief that overturned the usual balance of things as the American mind considered it. Bierce delighted in bringing into his *dénouement,* in story after story, not a *deus ex machina,* but the crunch of a devil out of the machine—a devil not so much in man as a steady accuser of man, a perpetual adversary of our poor human nature that delighted in showing up man as a hypocrite, self-deluder, sentimentalist, fool.

The secret of the world, Emerson once wrote with the typical confidence of his "spiritual" generation before the Civil War, is the tie between person and event. Character is fate, said Heraclitus. These are moral statements that suggest that the reason why human beings fail, why they fail themselves, is that they are not "good" enough. This was certainly the belief of American writers before the Civil War. Emerson, the prince of them all, thought that a man properly in touch with the gods—a man, that is, in touch with his supposedly "immortal" nature—could accomplish everything he meant to.

Bierce, like so many writers in his later generation, believed that we are ruled by circumstances. But this subservience to circumstances is not due to a lack of morality or higher purpose, as Emerson and other sages before the Civil War would have said. To Bierce the law of things (and there is an unyielding design that makes us do not what we want but what circumstances beyond our control invariably compel) is to trip man up, to show him up. The law of life is what the literary naturalists, the imitators of science in literature, liked to call determinism. We are determined by the formula inherent in things, by forces that operate on us as if we were inorganic particles—in short, by circumstances. Even when these circumstances are in ourselves, and display themselves as some corrupting, shameful, above all unexpected and contradictory weakness, this weakness is rooted in our psyches and hereditary nature, so that it works on us as if it were outside.

No one can really say why Ambrose Bierce of Ohio, who grew up on the old frontier and served in the Civil War, became a professional newspaperman mocker and iconoclast, became "Bitter Bierce," as a biographer in the twentieth century was to call him. No one can really say why Bierce made a point of parodying and inverting the status quo in his many columns, sketches, and stories for San Francisco papers, or why he made a point of scaring his Victorian audience, invariably showing human nature at its worst. He had been wounded in the head during the Civil War, and it would be tempting to say of him, as of twentieth-century war writers like Hemingway and Céline, who never recovered from the wounds they suffered in the First World War, that he was a permanent victim of war. But it might be truer to say that Bierce was somehow not altogether sorry to suffer terrible wounds in war because of the literary capital he could wrest out of his disillusionment.

The central fact about Bierce, as about Hemingway after him, is that he very early found his one distinctive note—skepticism about the prevailing ethos of American life—that he pursued this, with unequal success, through one story after another, for the pleasure of accomplishing a particular emotional and pictorial effect.

Bierce specialized in the "piece," the column, the squib, the satire, the story that was often a very short story indeed. He was never a novelist, but rather a natural writer of newspaper articles, stories, and satire. He was a man with a specific design on the reader, as all journalists must be. This explains Bierce's startling, provocative effect on readers. It does not explain the peculiarly obsessive, almost fanatically unyielding quality of his work.

Bierce wanted to create specific effects, and he did. He wanted in some way to unsettle the reader, to transmit his own taste of bitterness. The effect of a Bierce story can be described as the surprise ending made into a moral quality, a principle of life according to Ambrose Bierce. There is invariably a sudden reversal, usually in a few lines near the end, that takes the story away from the reader, as it were, that overthrows his confidence in the nature of what he has been reading, that indeed overthrows his confidence. Bierce intends to leave the reader with a dizzying feeling that life is a trick, and that the only sure element in it is a totally mischievous, insidious kind of surprise.

But we must grant Bierce a higher degree of artistry, above all of intellectual purpose, than is suggested by the words "trick," or "surprise ending." For Bierce spoke for a whole generation of writers after the Civil War when, in his repeated use of this trick ending, he made clear his absolute belief that life itself at the end of the nineteenth century had become, for a nation of proverbial innocents and believers, a game that human beings are not allowed to win. In one important respect, however, Bierce differs from other realists of his generation who shared something of Bierce's general view of life, though in a considerably subtler form. Bierce has a kind of strictness, or monomania, about what he believes, that is unlike relatively more genial writers like Henry James and Mark Twain, for whom the contest between the individual and his fate demands the expansive working out that is a novel.

Bierce is not a great writer, for he described life as an ordeal without dealing with the individual nature of each ordeal. He does not deal with character in depth; indeed, he never explores character for its own sake. His interest is all too much in shocking the reader. By writing straight at the reader, by working on his feelings, Bierce himself becomes the trickster rather than the uncoverer of life as a trick.

But in Bierce's **"Parker Adderson, Philosopher"** we see brought to its highest level of ironic concentration Bierce's mischievous design, his scornful kind of narrative economy. **"Parker Adderson"** is one of Bierce's best stories. The trick or surprise *dénouement* at the end is original. The captured Federal spy is philosophic and even condescending to the Confederate general because he knows that spies are shot at sunrise. He goes to pieces as soon as he discovers that he is to be shot right away. Falling upon his captors, he manages to kill the general's aide and to wound mortally the general himself. The general becomes the real "philosopher" of the story, but this—surprise again!—only because of his weary, unconscious death wish.

"Parker Adderson" succeeds without question (as too many of Bierce's stories do not) because both the captured spy and the general have their characters defined with some care. And of course Bierce's most brilliant thrust is to show that while Parker Adderson is not superior to his own death, the general, brought down from his lofty detachment about other men's deaths, somehow welcomes the death that he must share with Parker Adderson himself. The point made is again the old Greek adage that "character is fate." In some way that is closer to Freud than the Greeks, the general in **"Parker Adderson"** has unconsciously wished for death. In this brilliant, tough little story, Bierce makes once again the point American writers in the generation that followed his were to swear by, that although life is full of accidents and reversals, nothing that happens is simply arbitrary. It is we, sooner or later, who somehow help to dislodge the rock that falls on us. There is a merciless pattern of cause and effect to human life. We are in the hands of forces beyond ourselves—though it is we, every time, who somehow (surprise!) set these forces in motion. (pp. 31-4)

Alfred Kazin, "On Ambrose Bierce and 'Parker Adderson, Philosopher'," in The American Short Story, *edited by Calvin Skaggs, Dell Book, 1977, pp. 31-5.*

James G. Powers (essay date 1982)

[*In the following essay, Powers argues that "An Occurrence at Owl Creek Bridge" anticipates the psychological principles outlined in the writings of Sigmund Freud.*]

Much has been written of Ambrose Bierce's predilection for bizarre topics—his penchant [according to Stuart C. Woodruff in *The Short Stories of Ambrose Bierce: A Study in Polarity*] for "gratuitous horror and meaningless annihilation," his cynicism rooted in an idealism which collided with the "crudities of the Gilded Age" at the turn of the century; his love-hate relationship to war; finally, his pioneer treatment of the "clock of consciousness" in a relentless time world. In this last respect, John Crane observes [in "Crossing the Bar Twice: Post-Mortem Consciousness in Bierce, Hemingway, and Golding," *Studies in Short Fiction* 4 (Summer 1969], alluding to **"An Occurrence at Owl Creek Bridge,"** that the hero, Peyton Farquhar, "has imposed a *temporary reality,* the desires of the heart, upon the true reality within the swollen moments of his post-mortem consciousness."

It is these "desires of the heart," welling up in the unconscious of Peyton Farquhar, at the moment of his departure from the observable fixities of this world, that this [essay] addresses. Little has been said of Bierce's psychological treatment of fiction, except a terse reference in Robert A. Wiggin's short reflection, *Ambrose Bierce,* wherein he mentions that "Bierce was precocious in his rebellion against the oppressive intellectual atmosphere of the community." He adds, "Biographers with a Freudian bias might speculate upon the extent to which boyhood hostilities were acted out in the writer's numerous stories involving patricide and matricide." The author notes, however, that "such speculation is fruitless; we do not have enough evidence to support a detailed psychological portrait." Despite this advice later in the same work. Wiggins does not hesitate to assert, analyzing Bierce's **"The Death of Halpin Frayser,"** that ". . . apart from the evident skill and effectiveness in its telling, it is an interesting pre-Freudian study in an Oedipal theme."

I submit, especially in **"An Occurrence at Owl Creek Bridge,"** that there exist significant pre-Freudian allusions to open for us a valid, fuller interpretation of this provocative short story. If the *owl* remains a symbol of mysterious knowledge, perhaps it is a happy coincidence that the hero of this story reveals a hidden aspect to his personality against the backdrop of a bridge named after this inscrutable creature.

It seems clear that the "Occurrence" suggests more than a physical experience; it represents a psychological one as well. It is not accidental that Bierce describes Farquhar's plunge from the Bridge not in the passive voice, which a reader might expect in a description of a hanging victim, but *active voice.* Farquhar takes the initiative in this journey: "Farquhar dived—dived as deeply as he could." The author proceeds to expand on the scene by associating it with a *Voice:* "The water roared in his ears like a voice of Niagara. . . ." Who was this Peyton Farquhar to whom this "Voice" directs its words? Early, we are told that he was "A well-to-do planter, of an old and highly respected

Alabama family." Obviously, he was from a structured background, born into an ordered world where formalities counted much among the gentry. After all, the narrator informs us that the hero was unable to participate as a soldier in the Southern cause because "circumstances of an imperious nature" forbade it. Because of this, Peyton "chafed under inglorious restraint." Truly, Farquhar found himself inhibited by social and historical strictures, and so, "longed for the release of his energies," dominated by the *ego's* mandates.

In other words, beneath this reserve, this decorum which governed his life, surged another Peyton Farquhar for whom "no adventure was too perilous for him to undertake." The hero, in fact, was, we are told, a proponent of the "villainous dictum that all is fair in love and war." Furthermore, Peyton characterizes himself as a "Student of Hanging." Is it excessive to suggest that this stable paragon of southern aristocracy also wrestled with expression of a pleasure principle, analogous to Freud's *libido*? Is it any wonder in Farquhar's downward plunge into a dream world, suggestive of the *Id,* encompassed by a "luminous cloud," that the thrilling experience was grasped as nonrational in nature, composed rather of "sensations unaccompanied by thought"? Clearly, the hero, at this point, who has "power only to feel," contends with the ungovernable, that force, which, like the unconscious, is "distant and how inaccessible."

It cannot be ignored, in this struggle for emancipation and emotional fulfillment, while immersed in the depths, that Peyton gropes and claws at the hangman's rope, which, interestingly, is said to resemble a "water-snake"—a symbol rich in archetypal implications. In ripping it free, Farquhar hears the command: "Put it back, put it back!" He ignores the order—possibly because he only "thought he shouted these words to his hands. . . ." Once he makes the choice to override this moral imperative, Peyton, the narrator alerts us, was "blinded by sunlight" and engulfed by a great draught of air, "which he expelled in a shriek." We now witness an exquisitely sensuous and liberating moment which Farquhar's untrammeled soul luxuriously responds to with all the emotional and physical resources at its command.

Once on shore, the first reaction of Peyton was to dig his fingers into the sand (even though it had already cut him) and weep with delight. Here, everything appears magnified, enchanting, deliciously beautiful. In tossing sand over his body, "It looked like gold, like diamonds, rubies, emeralds; he could think of nothing beautiful it did not resemble." Farquhar, like Odysseus among the Lotus Eaters, debates about remaining in this paradise with its provocative "roseat light," but shortly springs to his feet and, casting aside all reserve, penetrates a forest, wild and untamed, unchartered and void of paths. This traveller, formerly so circumspect, confesses that "He had not known that he lived in so wild a region." The reader too, with the surprised hero, has been introduced to that hidden domain of Farquhar's personality, passionate in nature—his unconscious world, alien to anything rational and clamoring for spontaneous expression. No wonder that the hero recognizes the entire episode as "uncanny" and thrills to it. Finally, at the climax of this delirious odyssey, Farquhar is rewarded by a vision of unsurpassed beauty, represented by a "flutter of female garments." Though the narrator interjects that this is "his wife, looking fresh and cool and sweet," we have every reason to believe that Peyton thrills to something more than this, namely, the apotheosis of feminine loveliness and gratification standing before him. This may be inferred because no earlier description of a tantalizing, entrancing wife has been created. Instead, we know her only as "Mrs. Farquhar" with "white hands," who "fetches water" and appears domestic enough to sit with her husband on a "rustic bench" and to welcome a stranger and serve him dutifully. But Farquhar's vision radiates much more: a "smile of ineffable joy" and "matchless grace and dignity." It is at this Beauty Peyton literally springs, attempting to "clasp her." However, the spell is broken; darkness descends and we return to the world of reality and observable consciousness, namely, the Owl Creek Bridge, where swings a "dead" Peyton Farquhar, whose lively sally into the dream world, albeit brief, permitted him to taste emotions long subliminated, but undeniably vibrant and powerful, once they surfaced and allured him to shore.

Carey Williams's *Ambrose Bierce: A Biography,* insists that the author "was much more interesting as a personality than important as a writer." Obviously, in one sense, this stands true; however, it seems equally clear that through fiction like **"An Occurrence at Owl Creek Bridge"** with its early exploration into psychology, Bierce's contribution as a writer deserves further attention and reflection. (pp. 278-81)

James G. Powers, "Freud and Farquhar: An Occurrence at Owl Creek Bridge?" in Studies in Short Fiction, *Vol. 19, No. 3, Summer, 1982, pp. 278-81.*

Cathy N. Davidson (essay date 1984)

[An American critic and educator, Davidson has written and edited several works on Bierce. In the following excerpt, she asserts that Bierce anticipated modern fiction through his experimentation with narrative form and his depiction of reality as indeterminate.]

Bierce's definitions of *realism* as "the art of depicting nature as it is seen by toads" and *reality* as "the nucleus of a vacuum" attest that he had little in common with what he referred to as the "Reporter school" of late-nineteenth-century American literature. His vision of life, of language, and of fiction, evidenced especially in stories such as **"The Death of Halpin Frayser,"** is worlds away from a literature that details the everyday actions of ordinary human beings. That he particularly despised writers who reduced the complexities of life and fiction to simple fictional structures and metaphysical teleologies is also demonstrated in his essay "The Short Story." Here he explicitly discredits the idea that literature should be grounded in the mundane and the explicable:

> Probability? Nothing is so improbable as what is true. It is the unexpected that occurs; but that is not saying enough; it is also the unlikely—one

> might almost say the impossible. . . . Considered from a viewpoint a little anterior in time, it was most unlikely that any event which has occurred would occur—any event worth telling in a story. Everything being so unearthly improbable, I wonder that novelists of the Howells school have the audacity to relate anything at all.

Bierce set himself several different tasks completely at odds with the established literary orthodoxies of his day. He sought to make the impossible reality of reality (whatever that might be) fictionally convincing:

> Fiction has nothing to say to probability; the capable writer gives it not a moment's attention, except to make what is related *seem* probable in the reading—*seem* true.

Thus we note the careful arranging of telling details, the deployment of surprisingly relevant disgressions, and the penchant for hidden clues that will direct the reader along a course parallel to but not synonymous with the one taken by an obtuse protagonist. At the same time, Bierce is a "higher realist" (to use Howard Bahr's term ["Ambrose Bierce and Realism," *Southern Quarterly,* 1963]) who explores the way constructs of reality are formulated. How do humans come to see as they do? Even more important is the question of why they do not see better than they do. . . . [Almost] all of the stories show how fallacious the protagonists' preconceptions usually are. That latter demonstration, incidentally, does not require that Bierce, as the author, be clearly aware of the truth that the characters in his fiction fail to discern. One does not have to see the bird the hunter did not hit to know he missed when he sends the bullet through his toe. Often, indeed, the clearest view of the intended target is the vision that sees it is not there and wisely holds its fire.

This brings us to Bierce's final purpose and an objective that subsumes the others just described. Again and again Bierce insists that common vision and common sense mostly confirm common errors. It is for this reason that so many stories examine the perceptual process, that so many of these same stories demonstrate the disastrous consequences that befall characters who conventionally read the texts that life sets for them. This concern extends from the isolated individual to the whole society. In stories such as **"One of the Missing"** or **"The Eyes of the Panther"** we trace out the genesis of individual disasters or family tragedies. In **"Chickamauga"** we see the necessary consequences of a whole society's subscribing to the heroic view of war that is also disastrously embraced by the deaf-mute child in that story. (pp. 115-17)

Bierce's coherence is a coherence of vision, not a rigidity of technique. . . . Paradoxically, Bierce fosters this end by demonstrating, in the individual stories, how limited human vision is. . . . We see the dangers of being positively wrong along with the difficulty of changing a made-up mind, the impossibility of effective communication when dialogue is mostly the clashing of contradictory misperceptions, the relativity of all perspectives and the consequent tentativeness of any attempts at truth. This tenuous division better reflects the totality of Bierce's fictional work than does the traditional dichotomy of the war stories versus the ghost stories (with, sometimes, the tall tales recognized as a third class).

Just as there is one overriding element in Bierce's different intentions as a writer, so too is there one basic element in his different strategies. They are all ways of calling perspectives into question. . . . Consider, for example, **"Haïta the Shepherd,"** Bierce's one attempt at pastoral fable. To start with, the pastoral setting is incongruously beset with howling wolves, troops of bears, and disastrous floods. The world of nature in which Haïta at first finds the promise of the presence of "friendly . . . shy immortals" can just as easily speak—as nature, for Haïta, soon does—in the "whispers of malign deities whose existence he now first observed." It all depends on what one is listening for. Yet, strangely, it does not at all depend on what one is looking for. The "beautiful maiden," who three times appears to Haïta and promises to "abide" with him, disappears each time he seeks to assure himself that she will permanently remain. The ostensible point of the fable is that happiness comes only when unsought. As the maiden emphasizes just before her third and final disappearance, if Haïta had "learned wisdom," he would take her as she was and not "care to know" how long she planned to stay. When Haïta, in the final episode of the story, seeks wisdom from the wise old hermit, he admits that by questioning the beautiful presence he three times "drove her away in a moment." " 'Unfortunate youth!' said the holy hermit, 'but for thine indiscretion thou mightst have had her for two.' " This concluding counsel promises little to the wise and is itself undercut by the fable's beginning: "In the heart of Haïta," we are told in the first sentence, "the illusions of youth had not been supplanted by those of age and experience." Furthermore, Haïta was happy before the maiden appeared. He was unhappy before he knew he had lost her. A better allegorical meaning of this seemingly simple fable might be that happiness, like the tale in which it is examined, will not sustain critical analysis.

Other seemingly atypical stories differently illustrate Bierce's pervasive questioning of conventional points of view. Often this objective is partly achieved even on the level of diction itself, as in **"A Baby Tramp."** There is a late-Victorian self-indulgent sentimentality inherent in such a title and such a protagonist. But Bierce, from the very beginning, subverts the maudlin by overstating it—a *baby* tramp, a vagrant toddler? In the story too a mordant wit both emphasizes sentimentality and undermines it. When we are told that "at the age of one whole year Joseph set up as an orphan," the incongruous "set up as" serves to emphasize that being "an orphan" is indeed young Joseph's profession. He must sell his suffering to the sentimental, a transaction that they would prefer to indulge in on their own terms by never noticing how cheaply their charity supports their self-complacency. In a difficult buyer's market, "Jo was indeed . . . wonderfully besmirched, as by the hand of an artist." But that capable display of his wares goes unrewarded, and he dies—most sentimentally, most unsentimentally—of exposure.

A few stories do not quite fit into the individual categories that I have employed. A few others, such as **"The Famous**

Gilson Bequest," combine them all. In this tale we see . . . how perception evolves rapidly to death. Henry Brentshaw, who has just vindicated through "five long years" of litigation an executed criminal's reputation, thinks he encounters the criminal's ghost at ghostly pilfering. Brentshaw was the prime mover in effecting the original sentence and the subsequent execution and then long argued that the verdict was unjust. The shock of seeing how greatly he has been duped kills him. Furthermore, we have extensive dialectics of misperception in the prehanging and posthanging debates regarding Gilson's honesty. The story, finally, juxtaposes countering perspectives to call much of its subject matter—and certainly the formal workings of law and the propriety of those who pretend that they live by law—into question.

Those countering perspectives begin, again, even on the level of diction. Since "it was impossible to repress the abounding energies of such a nature as his," Gilson bounces merrily from one illegality to another. But this "enterprising" character comes to grief when one of his "modest essays in horseherding" is interrupted by Brentshaw, the man most convinced that Gilson is a criminal. The apprehended horse rustler is soon tried, sentenced, executed:

> So Mr. Gilson was—I was about to say "swung off," but I fear there has been already something too much of slang in this straightforward statement of facts; besides, the manner in which the law took its course is more accurately described in the terms employed by the judge in passing sentence: Mr. Gilson was "strung up."

By thus emphasizing the incongruities between the terms employed and the deeds thereby described, Bierce humorously manages to call both the portrayed deed and the portraying word into question.

The protagonist achieves in his way what the author imitates in his. Gilson bequeaths all of his property to Brentshaw as his "lawfle execeter"—unless it can be proven any time during the next five years that, as public opinion long alleged, Gilson was a thief, in which case the estate is to be divided equally among any and all that were robbed by the deceased. When a subsequent cursory search of Gilson's personal effects proves that the supposed ne'er-do-well was actually incredibly rich, the gold rush is on: "The country rose as one man." For five years the territorial courts are tied up with Gilson suits and countersuits. Brentshaw buys off judges right and left and counters "mendacious witnesses" by hiring "witnesses of superior mendacity." In short, the criminal justly hung for dishonesty engineers a postmortem joke whereby he demonstrates that justice and honesty are both shams. He also takes his revenge on the man who apprehended him. The whole fortune goes to defend the fortune. Brentshaw is not only penniless at the end of the five years, he is also mentally broken by the expedients that did not save his treasure. He is left clinging to the solace of "an unshaken belief in the entire blamelessness of the dead Gilson." But even that faith is shattered when Brentshaw visits the cemetery to commune with the spirit of the honest dead but sees the ghostly Gilson still about his business. The tale concludes with the consequence of that vision:

> Perhaps it was a phantasm of a disordered mind in a fevered body. Perhaps it was a solemn farce enacted by pranking existences that throng the shadows lying along the border of another world. God knows; to us is permitted only the knowledge that when the sun of another day touched with a grace of gold the ruined cemetery of Mammon Hill his kindliest beam fell upon the white, still face of Henry Brentshaw, dead among the dead.

The unomniscient narrator presents two conflicting explanations for Brentwood's sudden demise. But both hypotheses are at once undermined as theories ("to us is permitted only the knowledge . . .") and then further undermined by the mawkish sentimentality of what is known (that the golden dawn illuminated the cemetery, that the sun shone kindliest upon dead Brentshaw). The story, conjoining . . . such diverse fictional forms as a tall tale, a Bret Harte western, a courtroom drama, a satire on law, to revenge tragedy, *and* a ghost story, remains indeterminate to the end.

"The Famous Gilson Bequest" is all of a contradictory piece, and so is the corpus of Bierce's fiction. Of course, we do not know whether Brentshaw died of natural or supernatural causes. Bierce delights in these similarities and oppositions. Through such fictional equations, the logician's *either/or* becomes the writer's *both/and,* an open-ended refusal to dichotomize which means, Bierce would also insist, that the writer, and not the logician or the philosopher, must work out the workings of the human mind. The logician merely indicates how men think they should think. *Logic,* it will be remembered, is no more than "the art of thinking and reasoning in strict accordance with the limitations . . . of the human misunderstanding." *Philosophy,* introducing the additional problem of what humans think they should think most seriously about, is even more diffuse. It is "a route of many roads leading from nowhere to nothing." In the nineteenth century, psychology was, of course, a branch of philosophy and would be, for Bierce (faculty psychology then and clinical psychology now) another artful science that confused the issue.

If internal cogitations did not illuminate the interior psychic world, neither did objective observation and the experimental method fully uncover the external physical world. As his treatment of scientists in such stories as **"The Man and the Snake"** and **"Moxon's Master"** indicates, Bierce was most skeptical about the objectivity of observation and the validity of ostensibly disinterested deduction. He also suspected that a good deal of science was based upon self-affirming propositions or the circular rephrasing of the problem and the facts. His definition of *gravitation* in *The Devil's Dictionary* perfectly illustrates his reaction to the discoveries of such science:

> **Gravitation,** n. The tendency of all bodies to approach one another with a strength proportioned to the quantity of matter they contain—the quantity of matter they contain being ascertained by the strength of their tendency to approach one another. This is a lovely and edifying illustration of how science, having made A the proof of B, makes B the proof of A.

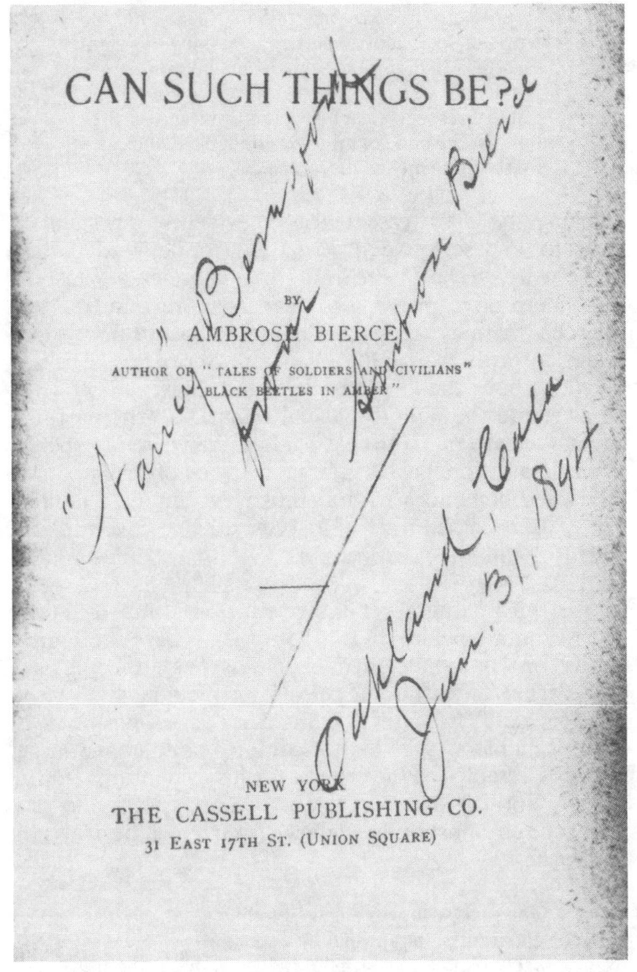

CAN SUCH THINGS BE?

BY

AMBROSE BIERCE

AUTHOR OF "TALES OF SOLDIERS AND CIVILIANS"
"BLACK BEETLES IN AMBER"

NEW YORK
THE CASSELL PUBLISHING CO.
31 EAST 17TH ST. (UNION SQUARE)

Inscribed title page for Bierce's 1893 collection of short stories.

For Bierce the universe was not made sensible by the certainties of much late-nineteenth-century science. His view . . . resembles [Charles S.] Peirce's, particularly Peirce's concept of "scientific fallibilism" and his early work in relativity. Bierce would also have appreciated more modern scientific notions such as the Heisenberg dictum that elevates "uncertainty" to a principle, and would insist that the Heisenberg principle applies to much more than subatomic particles.

The uncertainties that most concern Bierce are, finally, the unresolvable problems of mind. Other questions, of course, arise. But such matters as the possible existence of the ghost beyond the ken of some observer or the present whereabouts of Charles Ashmore strangely vanished still bring us back to the real focus in all of Bierce's fiction—the perceiver, what he (very rarely, she) thinks he perceives, how he puts nebulous thought into nebulous words and then reacts to what he thinks he thinks. All of which, contradictory and confused, can be shown only in words. But can language explore the limitations of language? Can story (defined in the late-nineteenth-century primarily as "plot") transcend the "plottedness" of story? It is Bierce's answers, unprecedented in his time, to these difficult questions (questions for the writer and the reader) that distinguish him as an author.

Anticipating more modern fictions, Bierce's experimental stories confuse and confound such fundamental Western dichotomies as reason and superstition, reality and art, even reader and writer. Mimesis, the foundation for late-nineteenth-century realism, is turned inside out. Bierce's texts hold up a mirror, but it is not a mirror held up to nature. It is a mirror held up to consciousness—with all its conscious, subconscious, and unconscious tricks and turnings. When the stories work, the reader necessarily participates in the creation of the fiction. But as [can be] seen in stories such as **"An Occurrence at Owl Creek Bridge,"** the reader's participation (being duly "tricked" by the ending) is intended at least partly to make the reader aware of his or her own limitations and, by extension, the limitations of human understanding. In short, Bierce more than any other nineteenth-century American writer anticipates the revolutions in ideas of art and life that characterize the innovative and experimental fictions of the present era. (pp. 117-23)

Cathy N. Davidson, in her The Experimental Fictions of Ambrose Bierce: Structuring the Ineffable, *University of Nebraska Press, 1984, 166 p.*

Harriet Kramer Linkin (essay date 1988)

[In the following essay, Linkin analyzes narrative technique in "An Occurrence at Owl Creek Bridge."]

In **"An Occurrence at Owl Creek Bridge"** Ambrose Bierce's linguistic strategies deliberately dislocate his readers to effect a mimetic correspondence between the audience's perception of the text and Peyton Farquhar's sensory understanding of his world. Bierce reproduces the condemned man's psychological disorientation among the members of his audience through temporal displacements and shifting points of view, conditioning the reader's temporary acceptance of what cannot possibly occur during **"An Occurrence at Owl Creek Bridge."** Using innovative narrative techniques, Bierce plays a cat and mouse game with his readers in the tale; the first section not only reveals Peyton's distended sense of time quite directly, but also foregrounds the perceptual distance between Peyton's consciousness and the narrator's when the narrator self-reflexively declares "these thoughts, which have here to be set down in words, were flashed into the doomed man's brain rather than evolved from it." Though that first section contains all the hints we require to read accurately, we steadfastly ignore them when Bierce drops a series of false interpretive clues in the second section—where Peyton himself falls victim to the duplicitous words of the Yankee scout. As the third section begins, we suspend disbelief, and marvel at Peyton's escape; as the section proceeds, we start to lose confidence in our understanding of what really occurs at the Owl Creek bridge. Only when we reach the final paragraph does Bierce abruptly tug us back to the narrator's supposed "objective" time just as the noose breaks Peyton Farquhar's neck. By shifting back and forth between at least two different kinds of narrative consciousnesses—Peyton Farquhar's and the narrator's—Ambrose Bierce effects the ironic temporal trick that concludes the tale.

Bierce begins under the deceptively straightforward guise of a conventional third-person narrator whose physical perspective establishes a panoramic view of the scene before him: initially focused on the condemned man, the narrator's vision pans out to encompass a much larger tableau. Sharing the distanced perspective of this first narrator beguiles readerly self-assuredness, given the inventory he provides. The only information lacking involves the identity and physical location of the narrator himself, whose competent observation may or may not indicate participation. Readers easily recognize the generally military thrust of his rhetoric, however. Wasting little descriptive space on nonmilitary concerns, he concentrates on the rank and function of those before him, even describing nature in a military context:

> The other bank of the stream was open ground—a gentle acclivity topped with a stockade of vertical tree trunks, loopholed for rifles, with a single embrasure through which protruded the muzzle of a brass cannon commanding the bridge.

His few personal interjections carefully hedge any hypotheses unvalidated by direct sensory evidence, as if he fears some backlash from fellow soldiers: he theorizes that the sergeant "*may* have been a deputy sheriff" in civil life, that "It *did not appear to be* the duty of these two men to know what was occurring at the center of the bridge," and "*Doubtless* there was an outpost farther along" (emphasis mine). At the same time he demonstrates a nice awareness of the civilian constituency of his audience by defining military terms such as "support" and "parade rest" (which he considerately places in quotes in the text). Those definitions reveal his military values; in explaining "support" as positioning a rifle "vertical in front of the left shoulder, the hammer resting on the forearm thrown straight across the chest" he admits it to be "a formal and unnatural position" (as a civilian might comment), but proudly goes on to say it enforces "an erect carriage of the body." The definitions also establish the nonmilitary reader's distance from the narrator; such a reader probably fails to share the narrator's expressed values (and is more susceptible to identifying with the man about to be hanged when learning of his civilian status).

The narrator voices his proud acceptance of military values more emphatically towards the end of the second paragraph, where he moves from natural observation to an almost poetic rendition of the soldiers' silent stand as "statues to adorn the bridge" (which contrasts interestingly with his nonpoetic description of nature). That movement towards a military poetics culminates in a philosophical rumination which asserts the narrator's firm belief in the military code:

> Excepting the group of four at the center of the bridge, not a man moved. The company faced the bridge, staring stonily, motionless. The sentinels, facing the banks of the stream, might have been statues to adorn the bridge. The captain stood with folded arms, silent, observing the work of his subordinates, but making no sign. Death is a dignitary who when he comes announced is to be received with formal manifestations of respect, even by those most familiar with him. In the code of military etiquette silence and fixity are forms of deference.

Because the last two sentences so evidently interrupt the narrator's descriptive observations, some readers take these words to be Bierce's authorial commentary inscribing interpretive principles. Readers more familiar with Bierce's writings recognize the gap between Bierce's attitudes towards war and the narrator's expressed beliefs. Even without the larger background, however, we learn to attribute these philosophical remarks to the narrator, given the pattern of the next paragraph: when it too begins with description, passes into poetic or emotional observations and concludes with a similar evocation of military code, we become aware of a stylistic habit governing the narrator's mode of expression.

In the third paragraph military ethics continue to inform the narrator's perspective as he turns his gaze more insistently on the condemned man. Although the narrator once again bases his judgments on seemingly objective sensory data, he carefully modifies his suppositions by using qualifiers (such as "apparently" or "if one might judge"), establishes the criteria for his evaluations (for instance clothing as an indicator of profession), and provides the circumstantial evidence from which he draws his inferences:

> The man who was engaged in being hanged was apparently about thirty-five years of age. He was a civilian, if one might judge from his habit, which was that of a planter. His features were good—a straight nose, firm mouth, broad forehead, from which his long, dark hair was combed straight back, falling behind his ears to the collar of his well-fitting frock coat.

Because "good" is relative, the narrator wisely identifies how the condemned man's features might be defined as good. Only when he looks directly into the condemned man's eyes does the narrator's strong military description begin to waver. Instead of hedging his evaluations, the narrator states "his eyes were large and dark gray, and had a kindly expression which one would hardly have expected in one whose neck was in the hemp." Using "one" to describe both the observor and the observed, the narrator collapses distinctions between the condemned man and himself (and the audience) even as those distinctions are made. As we will momentarily see, Bierce effects the same collapsing of distinctions through personal pronouns in the next paragraph. Here the narrator's linguistic identification with the condemned man is complemented by a new mode of analysis; he not only concludes that the condemned man's eyes appear kindly (without offering a rationale, as he does in identifying the condemned man's profession and looks) but he also assumes one would not expect a kindly expression in the eyes of a condemned man. These newly personal judgments begin to close the gap between readers and the military narrator, and more importantly, stir sympathies for the attractive, kindly condemned man.

The narrator follows his idiosyncratic comment by returning to more circumstantial judgment: "Evidently this was no vulgar assassin". Such a statement fits more readily with the narrator's previous rhetorical habits as it uses another qualifier ("evidently") and bases its conclusion on observable information (physical description, although the narrator's moment of subjectivity makes the validity of such description problematic). As if the narrator recognizes he has gone too far in assessing the kindly expression in the condemned man's eyes, he reins himself in by brusquely citing military code again (and reopens the gap between his and his readers' values): "The liberal military code makes provision for hanging many kinds of persons; and gentlemen are not excluded." Repeating the pattern of the second paragraph, the narrator follows a shift into poetic or emotional expression by asserting military rules. These discursive shifts differ in their revelation of identity, however: the first instance glorifies the military by attributing poetic beauty to the soldiers; the second instance endangers the narrator's military integrity by sympathizing with the enemy. Significantly, the military narrator's breakdown occurs when he looks into the condemned man's eyes—the very eyes that establish perspective—for we are about to move from the military narrator's presumably "reliable" eyes to the "unreliable" eyes of the condemned man himself.

The narrative transfer that occurs in the fourth paragraph constitutes the first trick in Bierce's text: just as we begin to see how the narrator is more than a camera carefully recording data, just as we begin to surmise something of his values, just as we begin, even, to detect a pattern in his speech, Bierce jumps from the military narrator into the consciousness of the condemned man himself. Because the linguistic structure of the paragraph at first seems to conform to the military narrator's idiolect, it takes us some time before we understand our new location. Bierce deliberately obscures the shift through the use of the imprecise personal pronouns and intentionally confusing referents. For a moment we too stand upon the wooden plank, uncomfortably suspended in an unidentified point of view, waiting to find out what will happen next:

> These movements left the condemned man and the sergeant standing on the two ends of the same plank. . . . This plank had been held in place by the weight of the captain, it was now held by that of the sergeant. At a signal from the former the latter would step aside, the plank would tilt and the condemned man go down between two ties. The arrangement commended itself to *his* judgment as simple and effective. *His* face had not been covered nor *his* eyes bandaged. *He* looked a moment at *his* "unsteadfast footing," then let *his* gaze wander to the swirling water of the stream racing madly beneath *his* feet. A piece of dancing driftwood caught *his* attention and *his* eyes followed it down the stream. How slowly it appeared to move! What a sluggish stream! (emphasis mine)

Storytelling consciousness shifts just as the soldiers change position on the bridge, accompanied by language that begins to unravel. In retrospect we easily pinpoint exactly where the shift in consciousness occurs, but as we read we seem to ease imperceptibly into the consciousness of the condemned man.

In the excerpt cited above, the sergeant and captain not only replace each other but in turn are replaced by the impersonal adjectives "former" and "latter"; when the text begins substituting the possessive pronoun "his" for the figures on the bridge we experience no small degree of difficulty locating its referent. Grammatically, "his" should (and does) refer to "the condemned man" since that noun occurs last in the sequence; nevertheless we hesitate to attribute "The arrangement commended itself to his judgment as simple and effective" to the condemned man given the difficulty of believing he would approve the manner of his execution. Instead, we look to the military judgment of either the sergeant or the captain as a potential source (and wonder if it is the former or the latter). The next "his" clearly indicates the condemned man, but might be observed by either of the soldiers: "His face had not been covered nor his eyes bandaged." In the sentence that follows, Bierce throws us completely off balance by the multitude of pronouns allowing a variety of identifications, as well as the presence of an expression in quotes: "unsteadfast footing." Some readers recognize the hand of the original military narrator here, who so thoughtfully identified "support" and "parade rest" earlier. Since that same narrator noted the "swift water" in the opening sentence of the tale he might again observe the "swirling water of the stream racing madly" at this point. Surely that observation cannot come from the mind of the condemned man, who reflects "What a sluggish stream!" By the time we hear the actual thoughts of the condemned man at the end of the paragraph, we share his disordered sensory awareness through Bierce's narrative manipulations; only when we reach the end of the paragraph do we possess the evidence enabling our retrospective assigning of identity.

Although Bierce deliberately tricks us in shifting from the military narrator's consciousness to that of the condemned man's, he seems to right matters at the beginning of the next paragraph by providing clear narrative location; once again eyes symbolize perspective when the condemned man "closed his eyes in order to fix his last thoughts upon his wife and children," thereby shutting off the view of external reality so carefully established by the military narrator. That we are in the condemned man's consciousness is clear from a variety of signs, not least of which is the new poetic sensibility of nature as "water, touched to gold by the early sun, the brooding mists under the banks at some distance down the stream." Now, instead of focusing on the purportedly objective description of the military narrator, we glimpse the condemned man's subjective internal reality quite clearly; for the man about to be hanged, time slows down, his senses are disoriented and he experiences hypersensitive perception:

> Striking through the thought of his dear ones was a sound which he could neither ignore nor understand, a sharp, distinct, metallic percussion like the stroke of a blacksmith's hammer upon the anvil; it had the same ringing quali-

> ty. . . . The intervals of silence grew progressively longer; the delays became maddening. With their greater infrequency the sounds increased in strength and sharpness. They hurt his ear like the thrust of a knife; he feared he would shriek.

Our view of the disarranged senses of the condemned man concludes with a sentence that brings us back to seeming objectivity: "What he heard was the ticking of his watch." If we believe that the condemned man himself understands the sounds as the ticking of his watch, we also believe he resumes normal perspective and sensory awareness. The narrative consciousness in this final sentence, however, might not be the condemned man's but the narrator's. Once again personal pronouns make interpretation confusing. Because Bierce never returns to a direct evocation of the condemned man's perceptions in the first section—as he might if he had characterized how the condemned man views the water below him when he opens his eyes—we have no way of ascertaining the final state of the condemned man's sensory awareness. Perhaps his senses are still disarranged; perhaps not. Bierce's authorial silence in the face of the reader's need for commentary leaves open the possibility of escape later.

When the condemned man opens his eyes he seems to return to "objective" external reality: "He unclosed his eyes and saw again the water below him." Certainly the reader experiences normalcy because we return to the military narrator's perspective, a report of the condemned man's thoughts more conventionally as dialogue (versus the free indirect discourse of the preceding paragraphs): " 'If I could free my hands,' he thought, 'I might throw off the noose and spring into the stream. By diving I could evade the bullets and, swimming vigorously, reach the bank, take to the woods and get away home.' " Perhaps more wishful thinking than viable plan, at least these thoughts approach a degree of rationality, particularly when compared to the reader's last foray into the condemned man's hypersensitive consciousness. Bierce's decision to report these thoughts as dialogue fosters a level of ambiguity that becomes a critical crux once the third section begins. Later we may view these thoughts as a plan which seems to come true and thereby lends validity to the "escape" (occurring before the sergeant steps aside and the condemned man drops); at the end of the story we may understand these thoughts are retold from the condemned man's hypersensitive perspective in the third section (occurring *as* the sergeant steps aside and the condemned man drops). For now, Bierce enjoys the irony of unclosing his character's eyes while he blindfolds the reader with easily misinterpreted information.

Although the penultimate paragraph in the first section artfully sets us up, the final paragraph "corrects" any misimpressions by providing all the information we honestly need to understand the third section. Either the military narrator or the implied author (here the distance narrows to a fraction) clearly identifies the condemned man as "doomed." Nevertheless, readers are free to construe such identity as a writerly synonym for condemned." More telling, he carefully explains how the condemned man's "thoughts, which have here to be set down in words, were flashed into the doomed man's brain rather than evolved from it." With retrospective vision we recognize the hint that warns us of the still existing difference between the condemned man's sense of time and ours: what appears to develop gradually as a scheme of escape actually occupies an instant of objective time. Because of the self-reflexive insert, however, Bierce allows us to hypothesize a comparison between the diachronic nature of writing versus the sometimes synchronic nature of thought. Winking at us all the way through, Bierce tells us just enough to maintain the careful dualism necessary for the story to work. Then, as we reach the end of the paragraph, anticipating the culmination of the activities on the bridge, Bierce once again leaves us hanging. We read "The sergeant stepped aside" and expect to drop into the swift waters of Owl Creek with the condemned man; instead we plunge into the flashback that constitutes the second section of the tale.

Before we quite recognize the second section as a flashback, we experience frustration through Bierce's modal shift from dynamic plot to static exposition in the first paragraph, Bierce compounds our sense of dislocation in two important ways. First, we meet a seemingly new character named Peyton Farquhar. Although it quickly becomes clear that Peyton Farquhar is the condemned man of the first section, Bierce teases us by witholding his identity for a brief period, adopting a technique mimetically appropriate to the section's general focus on identity. Second, while the paragraph opens under the guise of a strong third-person narrator (perhaps, even, the military narrator of the first section), by the third sentence we seem to have slipped inside Farquhar's consciousness. The narrator's language moves from clear reportage to the glittering generalities that constitute Farquhar's own rhetorical code:

> Peyton Farquhar was a well-to-do planter, of an old and highly respected Alabama family. Being a slave owner and like other slave owners a politician he was naturally an original secessionist and ardently devoted to the Southern cause. Circumstances of an imperious nature, which it is unnecessary to relate here, had prevented him from taking service with the gallant army that had fought the disastrous campaigns ending with the fall of Corinth, and he chafed under the inglorious restraint, longing for the release of his energies, the larger life of the soldier.

As in the first section's slippery use of personal pronouns, we might argue about where to pinpoint the shift in consciousness; such arguments demonstrate Bierce's narrative skill in deceiving the reader. Again, retroactive vision enables us to see where we first entered into Farquhar's mind. For the second time in **"An Occurrence at Owl Creek Bridge"** we unknowingly share Farquhar's perspective. We will share it yet a third time, to devastating effect.

The second paragraph returns us rather squarely to the hands of a conventional narrator who announces his story with a variant of the standard "once upon a time": "One evening while Farquhar and his wife were setting on a rustic bench. . . ." Like the military narrator of the first section, Bierce imbues this narrator with personal characteristics. The narrator seems to share some of Peyton Farquhar's Confederate values—or at least the chivalric code of the South—in describing how "Mrs. Farquhar was only too happy to serve [the gray-clad soldier] with her own white hands," in calling her a "lady," and mentioning that the soldier "thanked her ceremoniously." Instead of the careful attention to visual images exhibited by the first section's military narrator, however, this section's narrator focuses on sound. Recording the dialogue Farquhar shared with a gray-clad soldier, he not only reveals why Farquhar is about to be hanged but also the deliberately duplicitous origins of his situation. Guilty of the desire to further the Confederate cause, Farquhar is first tempted and then tricked by a Federal scout into believing he has the opportunity and means to serve the Confederacy. The soldier reports a supposed order issued by the Yankee commandant that speaks directly to Farquhar's civilian dreams of grandeur: "any civilian caught interfering with the railroad, its bridges, tunnels or trains will be summarily hanged." Earlier Farquhar declares "no adventure too perilous for him to undertake if consistent with the character of a civilian who was at heart a soldier"; the threat of hanging like a soldier increases the appeal of sabotaging the bridge. When Farquhar accepts the bait by asking " 'Suppose a man—a civilian and student of hanging—should elude the picket post and perhaps get the better of the sentinel . . . what could he accomplish?'," the soldier reels in the line: "I observed that the flood of last winter had lodged a great quantity of driftwood against the wooden pier at this end of the bridge. It is now dry and would burn like tow." Hooked by false possibilities, Farquhar dooms himself.

Just at the Yankee scout sets a trap for Farquhar, Bierce conveys information that later snares us into believing Farquhar possesses the means and opportunity to escape when Farquhar curiously identifies himself as a "student of hanging." Might the "plan" of the first section contain merit? Does Farquhar know any tricks himself? Do we have reason to hope for Farquhar's escape? Bierce's false clue fosters the level of correspondence between his character's situation and his reader's; while the soldier's deceiving words (and the larger deceptions fostered by the rhetoric of the Confederacy) victimize Farquhar, Bierce's linguistic strategies disarm us. Narrative displacements in the first two sections effectively close the gap between Peyton Farquhar and the reader; we share his consciousness twice unknowingly and sympathize with his plight (as even the disciplined military narrator of the first section threatens to do before he corrects himself). When the third and final section opens, we remain susceptible to belief.

Bierce's strategic jump into the past furthers the reader's vulnerability to deception by dislocating our sense of time (and increasing our likeness to the condemned man). Busy absorbing new expositional material, we experience a moment of disjunction as Bierce begins the third section by picking up on the plot events of the first section exactly where he left off. Narrative voice further complicates our re-entry when the section almost immediately shifts from an unidentified third-person narrator to the free indirect discourse of Farquhar himself:

> As Peyton Farquhar fell straight downward through the bridge he lost consciousness and was as one already dead. From this state he was awakened—ages later, it seemed to him—by the pain of a sharp pressure upon his throat, followed by a sense of suffocation.

Because Bierce offsets Farquhar's consciousness with two different third-person narrators in the other two sections, he might use either of them, or even a third omniscient narrator to relate the final section. Knowing who speaks matters if we hope to determine what actually happens and where Farquhar's consciousness takes over. Bierce shuts down all narrative cues after the first few words, leaving us in a state of suspension. Without the careful tableau of the first section's narrator, or the straightforward reported dialogue of the second section's narrator, the reader possesses no standard against which to measure Farquhar's distended sensations. Critics who insist only careless readers fail to recognize the third section as hallucination ignore how brilliantly Bierce tricks the reader through silence. In the first section we understand Farquhar's hallucinatory sensations as a distortion of natural phenomena, not a creation of reality. The military narrator's careful observations enable comparison. Because the third section never displays the qualifying vision of an alternate narrator we lack evidence to believe Farquhar fantasizes a new reality; instead we accept the lessons of the first section. Careful readers suffer most when they learn how Farquhar "swung through unthinkable arcs of oscillation, like a vast pendulum"; knowing that hanging victims generally die of broken necks, they possess reason to believe the unbelievable—that the condemned man might escape—with no objective markers' to clarify vision.

Given Bierce's authorial silence, we interpret the events described in the third section through the screen of Farquhar's distorted senses. Just as Peyton reads his world incorrectly, we pursue a false reading of the story, trying to figure out what causes the condemned man's responses. The process acquires credibility through careful details: Farquhar momentarily loses consciousness, awakens to feelings of pain about his neck and congestion in his head, and loses the ability to think as he becomes a creature of sensation alone. When the plunge into Owl Creek restores the power of thought (formally indicated by the introduction of quotes around some of those labelled thoughts), Farquhar himself provides the detached observation we miss from an external narrator, expressing surprise at the turn of events:

> To die of hanging at the bottom of a river!—the idea seemed to him ludicrous. . . . "To be hanged and drowned," he thought, "that is not so bad; but I do not wish to be shot. No; I will not be shot; that is not fair."
>
> He was not conscious of an effort, but a sharp pain in his wrist appraised him that he was trying to free his hands. He gave the struggle his attention, as an idler might observe the feat of a juggler, without interest in the outcome. What splendid effort!—what magnificent, what superhuman strength! Ah, that was a fine endeavor! Bravo!

His frequent interjections make the escape more plausible; at the same time they indicate a new level of identity that noticeably increases our sense of Farquhar's vitality. As several critics remark, the condemned man's passive acceptance of his fate in the first section and the rhetoric of the Confederacy in the second changes to a bold assertiveness in the third section. Now Farquhar revises his unqualified assent to the dictim "all is fair in love and war" by declaring what is "not fair." Earlier he "feared he would shriek" at the sound of the ticking watch; as his hands tear away the noose, he thinks he shouts " 'Put it back, put it back!' " When he finally reaches the water's surface "his lungs engulfed a great draught of air, which instantly he expelled in a shriek!" Less inhibited by former codes of behavior, Farquhar strikes out in a new direction that ironically makes him seem most alive.

The hypersensitive senses Farquhar acquires as he surfaces surprise him as well as the reader; Farquhar conveniently provides an explanation:

> He was now in full possession of his physical senses. They were, indeed, preternaturally keen and alert. Something in the awful disturbance of his organic system had so exalted and refined them that they made record of things never before perceived. He felt the ripples upon his face and heard their separate sounds as they struck. He looked at the forest on the bank of the stream, saw the individual trees, the leaves and the veining of each leaf.

In the first section nature serves to contrast the military narrator's point of view with the condemned man's more poetic sensibility. Farquhar's microscopic awareness of nature in the third section potentially demonstrates how yet another rhetorical system overwhelms his reemergence: the ecstatic language of a doomed man reborn to a world made precious through near loss. Although critics reasonably insist we must recognize Farquhar's hallucination at this point, his mode of perception curiously augments that of the first section. Without other access to the actual scene before him, we accept Farquhar's reading as a distortion of natural stimuli rather than a hallucination. While his observations seem fantastic, the rhetorical system that governs the third section allows for such perceptions.

If Bierce finally provides an authorial hint to rectify our blind belief in Farquhar's escape, such a hint surfaces once again through the larger symbol of eyes that determine perspective; after Farquhar surfaces, observing how "the visible world seemed to wheel slowly round, himself the pivotal point," he notices the soldiers first pointing and then shooting at him:

> He heard a second report, and saw one of the sentinels with his rifle at his shoulder, a light cloud of blue smoke rising from the muzzle. The man in the water saw the eye of the man on the bridge gazing into his own through the sights of the rifle. He observed that it was a gray eye and remembered having read that gray eyes were keenest, and that all famous marksmen had them. Nevertheless, this one had missed.

Because the military narrator of the first section calls attention to the condemned man's gray eyes, Bierce hints that Farquhar still stands on the bridge, seeing his own eye reflected in the sights of the rifle. Interpretation remains open in part through the deliberate use of definite articles that keep identity indefinite ("The man in the water saw the eye of the man on the bridge" rather than explicit reference to "the sentinel" or even "he"). Once again retrospective vision enables our recognition that Farquhar's gray eyes miss being keenest, given his distorted senses. During a first reading, however, the subtlety of Bierce's hint generally evades the reader's understanding.

Instead we marvel at Farquhar's effectiveness in implementing part of the planned escape he conceived in the first section; although he lands in the stream by accident (versus his hope of freeing his hands, throwing off the noose, and springing into the stream), once there he takes the next step, diving deeply into the water to evade the soldiers' bullets. Since the soldiers fire simultaneously, his chances of avoiding their bullets improve. Farquhar's reported thoughts on strategy lend greater credibility: " 'The officer,' he reasoned, 'will not make that martinet's error a second time. It is as easy to dodge a volley as a single shot. He has probably given the command to fire at will.' " Instead, the soldiers fire the cannon; again, Farquhar's reasoning fosters belief: " 'They will not do that again,' he thought; 'the next time they will use a charge of grape.' " Luck saves him from a second firing when a vortex sweeps him to safety.

When the vortex appears, the underlying rhetoric of the third section shifts in degree toward the jubilant tones of high Romanticism. Farquhar not only whirls about in a Blakean vortex that cleanses perception, but is also flung out upon sand that looks "like diamonds, rubies, emeralds; he could think of nothing beautiful which it did not resemble." After he blesses the jewel-like sands he becomes aware of how the wind makes "the music of aeolian harps" in the trees' branches. Nature reveals paradisaical qualities that foster revelations of higher order or divine presence for Farquhar:

> The trees upon the bank were giant garden plants; he noted a definite order in their arrangement, inhaled the fragrance of their blooms. A strange, roseate light shone through the spaces among their trunks. . . . He had no wish to perfect his escape—was content to remain in that enchanting spot until retaken.

Though we recognize not only the language of Romanticism at work but also Farquhar's newly religious overtones, that "strange, roseate light" might awaken suspicions among readers who recall the first section's careful pinpointing of the "early sun." Most of Farquhar's hypersensitive responses connect with reasonable stimuli (or so Bierce wants us to believe); the roseate light, difficult to associate with a natural phenomenon, becomes a worrisome detail hinting at a different level of religious enlightenment. Has Farquhar ascended to paradise? Did a bullet hit him unawares? Any growing doubts readers entertain on the nature of Farquhar's escape momentarily cease, however, when a final cannon shot interrupts Farquhar's joyous idyll.

Those doubts quickly return when Farquhar undergoes strange difficulties finding his way home again. Beyond his own surprise "that he lived in so wild a region" comes a comment uttered ostensibly in Farquhar's consciousness but quite possibly shared by Bierce himself: "There was something uncanny in the revelation." The unsettling remark points towards, indeed initiates, the story's uncanny resolution. When the homewards-bent Farquhar finally happens upon a curiously untraveled road he knows "to be the right direction," we wonder where the road truly leads. Because "no fields bordered it, no dwelling anywhere. Not so much as the barking of a dog suggested human habitation" some readers suddenly anticipate the worst: Farquhar approaches an unearthly, hellish abode. As Farquhar himself loses the ability to understand the signs projected by his immediate environment, we experience a corresponding loss of faith in our own reading of the story, so dependent on Farquhar's interpretations of reality:

> The black bodies of the trees formed a straight wall on both sides, terminating on the horizon in a point, like a diagram in a lesson in perspective. Overhead, as he looked up through this rift in the wood, shone great golden stars looking unfamiliar and grouped in strange constellations. He was sure they were arranged in some order which had a secret and malign significance. The wood on either side was full of singular noises, among which—once, twice, and again—he distinctly heard whispers in an unknown tongue.

Farquhar clearly passes into the dark side of the rhetorical or metaphorical system that governs the language of the third section, hypothesizing malign significance in the stars instead of the former grace he perceived in the arrangement of the trees.

Farquhar's fading interpretive skills here signal the larger blindness he exhibits throughout the third section, as Bierce hints in having Farquhar resee the arranged trees as "a diagram in a lesson in perspective." A companion remark to the self-reflexive comment that occurs near the end of the first section ("these thoughts, which have here to be set down in words, were flashed into the doomed man's brain rather than evolved from it"), Bierce warns us how Farquhar's tunnel vision provides a dangerously limited field of interpretation for the reader. When Farquhar's description of pain repeats the pattern that began the third section—losing the power to think, turning into a creature of sensation—we know, finally, he is dying or dead:

> His neck was in pain and lifting his hand to it he found it horribly swollen. . . . His tongue was swollen with thirst; he relieved its fever by thrusting it forward from beneath his teeth into the cold air. How softly the turf had carpeted the untraveled avenue—he could no longer feel the roadway beneath his feet!"

Half-suspecting as much for the past few paragraphs, we now realize Farquhar's efforts to escape his fate meet with failure. Though we share Farquhar's perceptions through most of the third section, we finally regain some measure of control as our interpretations begin to diverge.

The markedly changed perspective in the penultimate paragraph seems to confirm the reader's hypothesis by making Farquhar appear ghostlike as the narrational mode shifts from past tense to present tense. Such tense disjunction signals the return of an external narrator, who slips inside Farquhar's consciousness to share narrational duties:

> now he sees another scene—perhaps he has merely recovered from a delirium. He stands at the gate of his own home. All is as he left it. . . . he sees a flutter of female garments; his wife, looking fresh and cool and sweet, steps down from the veranda to meet him. At the bottom of the steps she stands waiting, with a smile of ineffable joy, an attitude of matchless grace and dignity.

Positive Farquhar never approaches his home—for surely his wife would run to meet him—we easily dismiss this episode as a deathbed fantasy experienced on the road (or perhaps a Biercean version of the afterlife). Finally we step outside Farquhar's limited vision through our own interpretive skills. What surprise, then, to learn how death claims Farquhar: "he feels a stunning blow upon the back of the neck; a blinding white light blazes all about him with a sound like the shock of a cannon—then all is darkness and silence!" Why a blow on the back of the neck? Why a sound like the shock of a cannon? The paragraph's strategic emphasis on time should condition us for Bierce's last trick: "Peyton Farquhar was dead; his body, with a broken neck, swung gently from side to side beneath the timbers of the Owl Creek bridge." Like the noose that breaks Farquhar's neck, the return of a third person narrator jolts us back to real time with an abruptness that matches the narrator's impersonal tone.

Bierce manipulates the reader throughout **"An Occurrence at Owl Creek Bridge"** but never lies outright. Although he shifts narrational and temporal modes several times to keep us off-balance—or within the displaced sensibility of Farquhar himself—the clues exceptional readers require to share Bierce's perspective are always available. Three of the most important sentences in the text deliberately begin with the time-indicative conjunction "as": the ending of the first section ("As these thoughts, which have here to be set down in words, were flashed into the doomed man's brain rather than evolved from it the captain nodded to the sergeant. The sergeant stepped aside."), the beginning of the third section ("As Peyton Farquhar fell straight downward through the bridge he lost consciousness and was as one already dead"), and the next to last sentence of the third section ("As he is about to clasp her he feels a stunning blow upon the back of the neck; a blinding white light blazes all around him with a sound like the shock of a cannon—then all is darkness and silence"). Bierce simply makes it easier to miss these clues and accept what appears as true. Sharing more than Peyton Farquhar's time frame, we learn of our own susceptibility to rhetoric; just as Farquhar succumbs to the tempting glory offered by the Confederacy and a falsely clothed spy, readers of Bierce's tale fall victim to easy belief in narrative consciousnesses possessing partial truths. Like Peyton Farquhar we become students of hanging, but we escape with our lives. (pp. 137-50)

Harriet Kramer Linkin, "Narrative Technique in 'An Occurrence at Owl Creek Bridge'," in The Journal of Narrative Technique, *Vol. 18, No. 2, Spring, 1988, pp. 137-52.*

G. Thomas Couser (essay date 1990)

[Couser is an American critic and educator. In the essay below, he examines "Jupiter Doke, Brigadier-General."]

Among Ambrose Bierce's stories of the Civil War, **"Jupiter Doke, Brigadier-General"** is exceptional in its satiric intent, humorous tone, and epistolary format. Economical in its method, shrewd in its implied commentary on the administration of the war, the tale is an isolated but impressive experiment. Dense and subtle in its historical allusions, it incorporates a sly but trenchant burlesque of some identifiable Civil War luminaries, most notably Ulysses S. Grant. Its most significant achievement is that it cleverly and unsparingly lampoons the process by which war is written, both as and after it is waged. A minor comic masterpiece, the tale manages to satirize at once the fighting and the writing of the Civil War, its "conduct" and its textual reconstruction.

Unlike most of Bierce's war stories, which take the form of retrospective monologues, this one consists of eighteen "documents" that chronicle the career of the incompetent Jupiter Doke from his initial (political) appointment as a brigadier-general of Illinois volunteers in November of 1861 through numerous military blunders that result, ironically, in his promotion to the rank of major general in February of 1862. The author of several of the longer documents, Doke is a caricature of the self-seeking, politically ambitious general; through his interaction with other military and political figures, the story broadly but efficiently satirizes a whole range of targets: military bungling, cowardice, and incompetence; wartime profiteering, corruption, and nepotism; official deception, manipulation of subordinates, and verbal face-saving.

In this polyphonic tale, Bierce lets the participants condemn themselves by their own written testimony. The documents, which include official military correspondence (such as orders and battle reports), Doke's diary entries, a newspaper editorial, and a congressional resolution, are carefully devised so that, taken singly, each text displays its author's hypocrisy and, taken together, the documents expose one another's distortions and evasions. Throughout the fiction, Bierce manipulates the forms of official discourse in such a way as to disclose a kind of hidden civil war, the battle among fellow officers for advancement, profit, power, and fame.

The satire functions simultaneously on another, more fundamental, level that has not hitherto been fully appreciated: the incidents of the story, though exaggerated to the point of absurdity for comic effect, are loosely based on actual events. Paradoxically, the most incredible of the tale's incidents is the only one for which an historical source has been noticed. The rather intricate plot climaxes in the abrupt and entirely accidental reversal of a night attack by Confederate troops on Doke's headquarters. When an alert black servant, alarmed by the sound of Southern voices, awakens Doke, the general's panicked flight in his shirttail triggers a massive mule stampede that utterly destroys the attacking army. In his 1967 biography of Bierce, Richard O'Connor noted: "Undoubtedly the story was based on a similar victory of the vainglorious General Hooker's in which a stampede also scattered the enemy, during the Chattanooga campaign, in which Bierce participated."

O'Connor has the right episode, but his association of the story exclusively with Hooker is misleading for two reasons. First, Doke is ultimately a composite of several high-ranking Union officers, a kind of generic general to whom Bierce attributes the worst traits of a number of individuals. Second, if any officer is to be singled out as his model, it is not Joseph Hooker but Ulysses S. Grant. The primary clue that Doke is a caricature of Grant lies not in biographical similarity but in a nominal one: the resemblance of their names, both of which combine ambitiously allusive, trisyllabic given names with prosaic, monosyllabic family names. Both names start out soaring, then plunge to earth. To an ear like Bierce's, easily offended by euphemism and grandiloquence, the name "Ulysses Grant" might have had an oxymoronic ring; the elevation of "Ulysses" to "Jupiter" and the reduction of "Grant" to "Doke" amplifies the clash between the first and last names. That Grant is the primary model for Doke is implicit in Doke's first name, for just as Jupiter was the supreme Roman god, Ulysses Grant was the highest-ranking Union general (and later commander in chief and president of the entire reconstructed nation).

Bierce's low regard for Grant's generalship is easily documented. Indeed, he singled him out for explicit criticism in his war writing, both fictional and nonfictional. For example, in the story **"An Affair of Outposts,"** the narrator refers offhandedly to Grant's "manifest incompetence" at Pittsburg Landing. The narrator of **"The Mocking-Bird"** comments acerbically on the same battle: "On the morning of the memorable 6th of April at Shiloh, many of Grant's men when spitted on Confederate bayonets were as naked as civilians; but it should be allowed that this was not because of any defect in their picket line. Their error was of another sort: they had no pickets."

In **"Jupiter Doke,"** Bierce's attack is oblique, but his quarry and his animosity are finally unmistakable. Of the numerous correspondences between the plot and characters on the one hand and historical events and personages on the other, most point to General Grant as the chief butt of Bierce's satire. Broad parallels between the careers of Doke and Grant reinforce the resonation of their names. When first commissioned as Civil War officers, both are residents of Illinois, and Doke's address, Hardpan Crossing, echoes the name of Grant's failed Missouri farm, Hardscrabble. Doke's career takes off after military success in Kentucky, like Grant's after his campaign in Tennessee. Thus, after the "battle" at Jayhawk, Doke is given the rank of major general, the rank to which Grant was promoted after the taking of Fort Donelson, "the first important Union victory in the Civil War," according to William S. McFeely. And just as Doke is considered a potential presidential candidate after his "victory," Grant was first mentioned as a candidate in the aftermath of Chattanooga (when he was also promoted to lieutenant general, a rank no one had held since George Washington).

Doke's brief military career in Kentucky also evokes that of Grant in Tennessee by conflating two of Grant's important victories, for the tale telescopes into a few months battles that transpired over the course of a couple of years. First, as O'Connor points out, the story alludes to an incident from the Chattanooga campaign of the autumn of 1863, when Union troops broke out of the besieged city and pushed the Confederates deeper into the South. Grant's rather low-key description of the episode in his account of Chattanooga for the *Century Magazine* explained that

> on the night of the 28th-29th [of October] an attack was made on Geary, at Wauhatchie, by Longstreet's corps. When the battle commenced, Hooker ordered Howard up from Brown's Ferry. . . . Before he got up, Geary had been engaged for about three hours against a vastly superior force. The night was so dark that the men could not distinguish one another except by the light of the flashes of their muskets. In the darkness and uproar Hooker's teamsters became frightened, and deserted their teams. The mules also became frightened, and, breaking loose from their fastenings, stampeded directly toward the enemy. The latter no doubt took this for a charge, and stampeded in turn. By 4 o'clock in the morning the battle had entirely ceased, and our "cracker line" was never afterward disturbed.

This event is, in a sense, the historical kernel of the story. Although the stampeding mules may have been Hooker's, the campaign was under Grant's direction, and Grant took credit for it.

In any case, the mule stampede is merely the tip of the iceberg of the historicity of the story. While the stampede alludes to one of Grant's crucial victories, other details point to an earlier triumph in Grant's Tennessee campaign: the taking, in quick succession, of Fort Henry and Fort Donelson on the Tennessee and Cumberland rivers, respectively. The dates of the story's "battle" at Jayhawk (February 2-3, 1862) correspond almost exactly to those of the Henry-Donelson campaign (February 3-16, 1862). Just as Doke arrives safely at Distilleryville after the way had been cleared for him, Grant and his troops arrived at Fort Henry after it had already surrendered to Union gunboats. (Indeed, the storms that facilitate Doke's arrival by steamboat have their parallel in the rains that eased the taking of Fort Henry by submerging several of the cannon facing the river.)

Even the improbable casualty figures, virtually 100% on the Confederate side, virtually nil on the Union side, have their historical equivalent in the extremely lopsided losses of the two sides at Forts Henry and Donelson: only one Union soldier was killed in taking Fort Henry, and at Fort Donelson the Union troops suffered about 3,000 casualties while taking some 12,000 Confederate troops prisoner. Finally, the names of the Confederate generals whose troops are demolised by Doke's mules at Jayhawk (Gibeon J. Buxter, Simmons B. Flood, and Dolliver Billow) are scrambled versions of the names of three of the generals Grant defeated at Fort Donelson (Simon Bolivar Buckner, John Floyd, and Gideon Pillow). So while the stampede derives from the Chattanooga campaign, the names of the defeated generals allude unmistakably to another Grant victory and another Confederate fiasco.

Though the careers of Doke and Grant are parallel, their *characters* are dissimilar. By most accounts, as a general, Grant lacked Doke's most obvious characteristics: his venality, his political ambition, and his cowardice. Whereas Grant was known for his dislike of profiteers, Doke is portrayed as seeking every opportunity for nepotism and personal profit. But while the venality attributed to Doke had no parallel in Grant's *military* career, it did have its analogue in Grant's administration, if not in his personal conduct as president. Grant's biographer, William S. McFeely, offers ample evidence of unethical, if not illegal, behavior on the part of Grant's appointees, associates, and relatives during (and after) his presidency. Thus, just as the tale condenses two Grant victories into one of Doke's, it may also conflate Grant's several careers (military, political, and business) into Doke's brief military one. The name of the town to which Doke is first ordered (Distilleryville, Kentucky) may be a sly reference to Grant's reputation as a hard-drinking officer, to the Whiskey Ring scandal of his presidency, or to both.

Whereas Grant had no discernible political ambition before the war, Doke is a politician first and foremost. Indeed, one of the narrative's running jokes, conveyed through his style, is that Doke sees everything in political terms. He characteristically calls the enemy soldiers "Democrats" rather than Confederates; he even refers to his own children as "the vital issues." In response to a terse letter of appointment from the secretary of war, which requires only a yes-or-no answer, he sends a fulsome letter with overblown language that exposes him as a self-promoting politician. His pastiche of patriotic clichés cannot conceal his ulterior concerns:

> The patronage of my office shall be bestowed with an eye single to securing the greatest good to the greatest number, the stability of republican institutions and the triumph of the party in all elections; and to this I pledge my life, my fortune and my sacred honor.

Doke's obvious political ambitions satirize a notable syndrome of nineteenth-century American politics, in which wartime generalships were frequently parlayed into political careers, if not always, as in Grant's case, successful presidential candidacies.

Grant was the proximate target of Bierce's satire not because he was particularly venal or politically ambitious but because of costly military lapses that Bierce had witnessed first hand and because, of all the Union generals, he was the first and most obvious political beneficiary of victory. But given the timing of Bierce's war fiction, most of which was apparently written in the late 1880s and early 1890s, it would appear that his chronic criticism of Grant was impelled not only by a lingering sense of outrage at Grant's wartime bungling and by indignation at the laxness, to put it generously, of his administration of the executive branch but also by dissatisfaction with, and resentment of, Grant's literary reconstruction of his military career. By parlaying his military career into a literary as well as a political one, Grant was of course venturing onto Bierce's turf, an incursion with commercial and critical success that may have intensified Bierce's ire. Ultimately, however, the satire of **"Jupiter Doke"** has a larger target than Grant. It is best understood as part of Bierce's complex response to the chronicles of the war that appeared in the 1880s; collectively, these recreated the war in a heroic mold that Bierce found both unrecognizable and intolerable.

Books about the Civil War began to pour from the presses in the 1880s. In addition to the *Official Records of the Union and the Confederate Armies,* which the Government Printing Office began to publish in 1880, numerous memoirs were issued independently by officers on both sides. In particular, the enormously popular series of accounts published in the *Century Magazine* between November of 1884 and November of 1887, and collected in the four-volume *Battles and Leaders of the Civil War* (1887-88), epitomizes the authorized discourse of the war. Inevitably, Ulysses Grant figured prominently in the writing of the war; the editors deemed his participation in the *Century* project essential to its success, and his *Century Magazine* accounts of Shiloh, Vicksburg, Chattanooga, and the Wilderness formed the basis of his two-volume *Personal Memoirs.*

Focusing on major battles and campaigns, the official war narratives were written by, and from the point of view of, commanding officers. Stressing strategies and outcomes, they inevitably minimized the chaos and casualties of war and neglected the experience of the ordinary combatants. Thus, as history (in two senses), the war belonged to its high-ranking officers, who were twice commissioned: once to fight, and once to write, the war. Indeed, officers controlled its campaigns much more authoritatively as writers in the 1880s than they had as participants in the 1860s: errors made in the field could be minimized or rationalized in retrospect.

Bierce responded to this official discourse in various ways. One was to challenge accounts of the war directly in his own war memoirs. As Napier Wilt has argued [in "Ambrose Bierce and the Civil War," *American Literature,* 1929], Bierce reconstructed his own war history by inserting himself into gaps in official narratives, rather than by relying solely on his own memory. His desire to supplement and correct the official accounts of the war and to salvage the soldier's war is manifest in the opening of **"The Crime at Pickett's Mill":**

> There is a class of events which by their very nature, and despite any intrinsic interest that they may possess, are foredoomed to oblivion. They are merged in the general story of those greater events of which they were a part, as the thunder of a billow breaking on a distant beach is unnoted in the continuous roar. To how many having knowledge of the battles of our Civil War does the name Pickett's Mill suggest acts of heroism and devotion performed in scenes of awful carnage to accomplish the impossible? Buried in the official reports of the victors there are indeed imperfect accounts of the engagement: the vanquished have not thought it expedient to relate it. It is ignored by General Sherman in his memoirs, yet Sherman ordered it. General Howard wrote an account of the campaign of which it was an incident, and dismissed it in a single sentence; yet General Howard planned it, and it was fought as an isolated and independent action under his eyes. Whether it was so trifling an affair as to justify this inattention let the reader judge.

Here Bierce not only puts Pickett's Mill on the map of Civil War battles but also, as his polemical title suggests, indicts those in charge. Similarly, in **"What I Saw of Shiloh,"** he explicitly disputed Grant's leadership at a more familiar battle.

One of Bierce's responses to the sanctioned, but distorted, accounts of the war was to "right" them by supplying his own conflicting accounts. Such a response, however, was of limited effectiveness. Bierce's accounts were unlikely to convey the authority, or to reach the audience, of official accounts; moreover, because of their deliberate incompleteness and limited perspective, they would not satisfy the desire for comprehensive, definitive accounts of the war. In any case, to answer memoirs with counter-memoirs was to allow others to establish the conventions of the discourse and to define its agenda. It was to fight on the enemy's field by the enemy's rules.

Bierce came to realize that the official discourse misled not only by means of its selective contents but also by means of its distanced retrospective narrative, the Olympian perspective of which effaced the chaos, confusion, and carnage of war. Thus, after setting the scene at Pickett's Mill, he interrupts his own narrative to comment on its inadequacy:

> The civilian reader must not suppose when he reads accounts of military operations in which relative positions of the forces are defined, as in the foregoing passages, that these were matters of general knowledge to those engaged. Such statements are commonly made, even by those high in command, in the light of later disclosures, such as the enemy's official reports. It is seldom, indeed, that a subordinate officer knows anything about the disposition of the enemy's forces—except that it is unamiable—or precisely whom he is fighting. As to the rank and file, they can know nothing more of the matter than the arms they carry. . . . It may be said, generally, that a soldier's knowledge of what is going on about him is coterminous with his official relation to it and his personal connection with it; what is going on in front of him he does not know at all until he learns it afterward.

In addition to disputing and emending the official records, Bierce sought to write a different kind of "record" of the war, one that would render its disorderly quality, as experienced on the battleground, rather than represent it in a seamless teleological narrative, recollected in tranquillity and safety.

Bierce distinguished his accounts of the war by emphasizing their subjective and fragmentary nature: hence titles like **"What I Saw of Shiloh"** and **"A Little of Chickamauga."** Also, rather than writing a single sequential narrative of his war-time experience, on the model of an officer's memoirs, Bierce confined himself to short, unconnected narratives ("Bits of Autobiography") in which his own role was not dominant. For Bierce, war could be properly narrated only in short takes, if at all. His ambition was to simulate, as nearly as possible, the less privileged point of view of the subordinate officer and even to communicate a sense of what war was like to the ignored "rank and file." The mannered quality of most of Bierce's narratives, however, suggests what Bierce may have suspected: that his attempts to escape literary mediation in his nonfiction narratives of war could never entirely succeed.

Another strategy for writing the war was to exploit, rather than to disdain, literary license, to turn from the relatively direct but constrained forms of historical and autobiographical narrative to the oblique but presumably freer forms of fiction. The plots of Bierce's Civil War stories contrast sharply with the comforting teleology of official narrative; his emphasis on his protagonists' generally disastrous fates runs counter to the tendency of summary accounts to overlook individual fatalities. But, although some of Bierce's Civil War stories are powerfully gruesome, they rely compulsively on ironic coincidences. When his stories are read in sequence, the cruel coincidences become predictable; the effect is not so much to shock as to draw attention to their own artifice. Their ultimate effect is to present war as a series of tidy, isolated dramas overseen and arranged by a perverse intelligence. Perhaps, as many believe, Bierce's work, fictional and nonfictional, contains some of the finest writing about the Civil War. The trouble is that too often his rendering of the war is "fine writing," the very refinement of which weakens its impact. Bierce's supreme command of language, manifest in his intricate plots, elevated diction, and elaborate syntax, had the effect of depicting the war as *too* "civil."

There was, however, another approach to the problem of writing war. Instead of trying to correct the errors of official discourse, or to sidestep literary mediation entirely, or to simulate the experience of war in fiction, one might lampoon the process by which war gets written. This is the strategy, uniquely, of **"Jupiter Doke, Brigadier-General."** Significantly, the basic format, which mixes various kinds of documents, mimics that of *The Official Records.* Bierce's use of an epistolary format amounts to a kind of tactical retreat; he relinquishes his own narrative voice and point of view in order to subvert those of the authorized writers of war. Thus, while the military action climaxes in an absurd victory brought about by a mule stampede, its "speech action" culminates in a series of mutually inconsistent reports of the "battle" by three of the routed generals and one bystander. Though the Confederate generals presumably know, more or less, what hit them, they cannot admit it; nor, scattered in defeat, can they collude in accounting for the fiasco. Indeed, they variously ascribe their inexplicable loss to "one of the terrible tornadoes for which this region is famous," "fifty thousand cavalry," and "somdings . . . I know nod vot it vos."

The face-saving tendency of officers' retrospective accounts of battle is particularly transparent, but it had its precedent in the sort of documents that Bierce read. Indeed, Bierce's inspiration for these rationalizations by the vanquished may have come from a footnote to Grant's account of Chattanooga in *Battles and Leaders,* in which a Southern officer, Major J. L. Coker, disputed Grant's version of the battle at Wauhatchie. Coker begins by minimizing the importance of the episode ("The engagement of Wauhatchie, or Lookout Valley, was of minor importance; but it is well to have errors corrected"), then goes on to say that Geary was attacked not by Longstreet's *corps* but by Colonel John Bratton's *brigade* (the clear implication being that Geary was not so much outnumbered as surprised). He concludes by rebutting the "mule charge": "The battle lasted about one hour and a half, and was brought to a close on account of General Howard's advance threatening Bratton's rear, and not by a Confederate stampede caused by a *'mule-charge'* in the dark. When the order to retire was received, the brigade was withdrawn in good order." Although Bierce's Confederates' accounts are written quite soon after the battle, they display tendencies evident in subtler form in accounts composed some twenty years after the war.

Bierce's objection to the monopolization of the writing of the war by interested parties is evident earlier in the story as well, in the editorial that accompanied Doke's "thrilling account, in another column, of the Battle of Distilleryville." The "Battle of Distilleryville" hardly merits mention in Doke's diary; after being mistakenly fired upon by reinforcements whom they have left their camp to greet, his troops return to their base to find "that a deputation of the enemy had crossed the river in our absence and made a division of the loaves and fishes." The editor goes on to note, with unconscious irony,

> verily, truth is stranger than fiction and the pen is mightier than the sword. When by the graphic power of the art preservative of all arts we are brought face to face with such glorious events as these, the *Maverick's* enterprise in securing for its thousands of readers the services of so distinguished a contributor as the Great Captain who made the history as well as wrote it seems a matter of almost secondary importance.

Bierce's point is that in this case, at least, "making" history and writing it were the same thing. The identity of the author of the account is of primary, not secondary, importance.

While **"Jupiter Doke"** makes no attempt to render the war realistically, it does go part way toward returning authority to the literarily as well as politically disenfranchised by leaving the last words to Doke's black servant:

> Dat was a almighty dark night, sho', and dese

> yere ole eyes aint wuf shuks, but I's got a year like a sque'l, an' w'en I cotch de mummer o' v'ices I knowed dat gang b'long on de far side o' de ribber. So I jes' runs in de house an' wakes Marse Doke an' tells him: "Skin outer dis fo' yo' life!" An' de Lo'd bress my soul! ef dat man didn' go right fru de winder in his shir'tail an' break for to cross de mule patch! An' dem twenty-free hunerd mules dey jes' t'nk it is de debble hese'f wid de brandin' iron, an' dey bu'st outen dat patch like a yarthquake, an' pile inter de upper ford road, an' flash down it five deep, an' it full o' Confed'rates from en' to en'! . . .

There is obvious irony in the fact that the only reliable witness to events is an aged, nearly blind servant; there is irony, too, in the fact that the truth emerges not from any military document but from the oral testimony of an illiterate civilian. There is further irony in this character's name, Hannibal Alcazar Peyton. His first name, Hannibal, associates him with the Carthaginian military genius of ancient history, and his middle name, Alcazar (which refers to a Moorish fortress), reinforces his association with African conquest of European territory.

The resolution of the story is particularly noteworthy because it seems to violate one of Bierce's explicit aesthetic principles, avoidance of dialect in fiction:

> To take for a hero or heroine a person unable to speak the language of the tale, whose conversations are turbid swirls in the clear stream of the narrative is an affront justifiable only by a moral purpose presumably in equal need of justification.

Bierce evidently found his moral purpose, for although Peyton is not the story's protagonist, he is its covert hero in two senses. First, he is Doke's savior; by alerting him, he triggers the chain of events that converts impending disaster into triumph and Doke's deserved shame into undue fame and glory. Second, he provides the only authoritative account of the episode at Jayhawk. The use of his dialect to end the narrative exposes the pretense and pretension of the official prose that precedes it. (Though Peyton's phonetically rendered dialect may resist quick apprehension, it is Doke's prose that could be described as "turbid swirls" by comparison.)

Yet the status of his account in the collage of documents is somewhat ambiguous. Because there is no indication of the time, place, or manner of the deposition of his account (it is headed simply "Statement of Mr. Hannibal Alcazar Peyton, of Jayhawk, Kentucky"), it is not clear what sort of authority Peyton's testimony has within the world of the narrative. The lack of authenticating details suggests that this information is not available to the other characters, and that, if it were, it would be dismissed out of hand as the figment of a superstitious imagination. But it persuades the *reader;* though no more *plausible* than the competing accounts, it is the only *credible* one precisely because, alone among those who narrate the incident, Peyton has no apparent stake in the matter. The inclusion of Peyton's definitive account of the "battle" of Jayhawk by the invisible hand of the "editor" admits, and implicitly authorizes, a point of view and a language generally excluded from official records.

It may be worth noting that the actual mule stampede to which the tale alludes gave rise to some unofficial or "folk" responses, traces of which may be found in some accounts of the war. For example, according to Horace Porter's *Campaigning With Grant,* after the rout at Wauhatchie, General Howard's quartermaster requested that the mules be promoted to the rank of horses. The success of the mule stampede inspired an anonymous ballad, "Charge of the Mule Brigade." Bierce goes a good deal further outside of the mainstream to recuperate a suppressed form of discourse, one he himself tended to discredit. Bierce resented the domination of the history of the war by those who first "ordered" it. In ending his story with an unofficial yet trustworthy statement in black dialect, Bierce affords the reader a sense of what history might look like if it were written from the bottom up, rather than from the top down.

Unlike Bierce's more typical, and more critically esteemed, war stories, which have little dialogue and which are generally narrated from an omniscient point of view, this one is entirely dialogical. It involves not only a variety of speakers but a range of styles and languages, from the terse utilitarian prose of the secretary of war, through Doke's bombast, to Peyton's dialect. It is a discursive Civil War, presented entirely in the words of the characters, most of whom ruthlessly manipulate others by means of verbal ruses. The story culminates in a narrative contest for *mastery* of history in which three generals compete, in writing, to determine the official record of a battle they lost only to be trumped by the oral account of an illiterate member of a race whose oppression they fought to perpetuate.

"Jupiter Doke" represents a logomachy, a war of words, in the sense that it stages a verbal power struggle for the control of war. In the context of Bierce's war writing as a whole, it can be seen as enacting a war *on* words as well in that it suggests the extremes to which Bierce was driven in his attempt to find linguistic and narrative modes adequate to his experience of war. Finding other strategies (correction of official accounts, direct transcription, and imaginative reconstruction of combat) inadequate to the task of writing the war, in this instance Bierce ingeniously reproduces, in satiric miniaturization, the complex process by which war is verbally administered and reconstructed. The inconsistency of the various documents and the narrative's lack of complete closure require readers to fill in gaps in the narrative and to correct defective accounts; the epistolary form arms them with skepticism. Failing to write his own war, perhaps, Bierce undertook here to rewrite, and unwrite, that of others. (pp. 87-97)

G. Thomas Couser, "Writing the Civil War: Ambrose Bierce's 'Jupiter Doke, Brigadier-General'," in Studies in American Fiction, *Vol. 18, No. 1, Spring, 1990, pp. 87-98.*

FURTHER READING

Bibliography

Gaer, Joseph, ed. *Ambrose Gwinett Bierce: Bibliography and Biographical Data.* 1935. Reprint. New York: Burt Frank, 1968, 102 p.

Primary and secondary bibliography that includes a biographical sketch and several brief critical assessments.

Biography

Fatout, Paul. *Ambrose Bierce: The Devil's Lexicographer.* Norman: University of Oklahoma Press, 1951, 349 p.

Comprehensive biography.

McWilliams, Carey. *Ambrose Bierce: A Biography.* New York: Albert & Charles Boni, 1929, 358 p.

Early biography with a chapter devoted to criticism of the short stories.

Criticism

Ames, Clifford R. "Do I Wake or Sleep? Technique as Content in Ambrose Bierce's Short Story, 'An Occurrence at Owl Creek Bridge.'" *American Literary Realism 1870-1910* 19, No. 3 (Spring 1987): 52-67.

Examines how Bierce's concealed manipulation of narrative reliability in "An Occurrence at Owl Creek Bridge" conduces to a formal ambiguity that parallels the story's thematic focus upon the confusion between subjective perception and objective events.

Cooper, Frederick Taber. "Ambrose Bierce." In his *Some American Story Tellers,* pp. 331-53. New York: Henry Holt and Co., 1911.

Praises Bierce's technique in the short stories while deprecating his choice of subject as having "too much the flavor of the hospital and the morgue."

Fabó, Kinga. "Ambrose Bierce: An Occurrence at Owl Creek Bridge." *Acta litteraria academiae scientiarum Hungaricae* XIV, Nos. 1-2 (1982): 225-32.

Identifies the formal devices Bierce uses to characterize Peyton Farquhar's mental state immediately preceding his death in "An Occurrence at Owl Creek Bridge."

Grenander, M. E. *Ambrose Bierce.* New York: Twayne, 1971, 193 p.

Analysis of Bierce's fiction aimed at an "understanding of a limited number of works, rather than a superficial coverage of everything he wrote."

Roth, Russell. "Ambrose Bierce's 'Detestable Creature'." *Western American Literature* 9, No. 3 (November 1974): 169-76.

Biographical reading of "Killed at Resaca."

Stark, Cruce. "The Color of 'The Damned Thing': The Occult as the Suprasensational." In *The Haunted Dusk: American Supernatural Fiction, 1820-1920,* edited by Howard Kerr, John W. Crowley, and Charles L. Crow, pp. 211-25. Athens: University of Georgia Press, 1983.

Cites Bierce's supernatural and psychological horror stories as a response to scientific theories and discoveries that challenged spiritual beliefs in the nineteenth century.

Ward, Alfred C. "Ambrose Bierce: *In the Midst of Life.*" In his *Aspects of the Modern Short Story, English and American,* pp. 60-72. London: University of London Press, 1924.

Defends the sincerity of Bierce's war tales and discusses "A Horseman in the Sky" as the most technically successful work in *In the Midst of Life.*

Additional coverage of Bierce's life and career is contained in the following sources published by Gale Research: *Contemporary Authors,* Vol. 104; *Dictionary of Literary Biography,* Vols. 11, 12, 23, 71, 74; and *Twentieth-Century Literary Criticism,* Vols. 1, 7, 44.

Albert Camus

1913-1960

Algerian-born French novelist, essayist, dramatist, journalist, short story writer, and critic.

INTRODUCTION

One of the most important literary figures of the twentieth century, Camus is best known for such works as the novel *L'étranger (The Stranger)* and the essay *Le mythe de Sisyphe (The Myth of Sisyphus).* In these and other writings, Camus examined themes relating to alienation, meaninglessness, absurdity, and revolt. In his only short story collection, *L'exil et le royaume (Exile and the Kingdom),* Camus employed a variety of narrative techniques to explore subjects similar to those of his novels and essays.

The six stories in *Exile and the Kingdom,* which were published late in Camus's career, portray conflicts and interdependencies between individuals while reflecting his interests in colonialism and politics. Although the stories recall themes that are familiar from his earlier novels and essays, they are considered generally less allegorical and more lyrical than the novels and intensify the sense of ambiguity that Camus instilled in all his writings. Each story presents an uneasy conclusion that leaves the reader to reflect on the unresolved moral conflict that has been described. Mirroring the paradoxical title of the volume, the stories unfold in a landscape that is simultaneously foreign and familiar. The best-known story in the collection, "L'hôte" ("The Guest"), concerns Daru, an Algerian-born French schoolteacher assigned to a remote post in Algeria. When asked by a French police officer to assume responsibility for an Arab prisoner being delivered to officials in another town during a political uprising, the pacifistic Daru at first refuses, preferring to remain aloof from the ongoing political conflict between France and Algeria. Eventually he agrees to guard the prisoner but unbinds him and treats him as a guest as soon as the officer has left. Daru subsequently allows the prisoner to choose between captivity and freedom when he leaves him on a forked road that leads in one direction to the police headquarters and in the other out of the district. When the schoolmaster last glimpses the prisoner, he sees him walking toward the police station, and Daru, on returning to his classroom, finds a threatening message written on the blackboard: "You handed over our brother. You will pay for this." This abrupt and enigmatic conclusion underscores the paradoxical nature of the situation: in refusing to ally himself with either the French or the Arabs, Daru discovers that he is unable to escape the conflict. The title of the story in French, "L'hôte," means both guest and host, signalling the ambiguous configuration of power in the guest-host relationship and in the colonial situation.

In "Le femme adultère" ("The Adulterous Woman"), Camus documents the conflict between Arabs and French colonialists through the story of Janine, a middle-aged French woman who is travelling with her husband through North Africa. Using reminiscence and current observation, the narrative relates Janine's momentary escape from the confinement of her marriage and her preconceived notions of herself as a European in Algeria. "La pierre qui pousse" ("The Growing Stone"), set in Brazil, also treats the issue of colonialism. In this story, a French engineer tours the countryside as an ambassador of technical knowledge while wishing to be accepted by the native population. "Le renégat" ("The Renegade") takes place in North Africa and ostensibly relates a missionary's crisis of faith and his adverse experiences in a pagan community. Thematically, the story examines the duality of good and evil and is, stylistically, Camus's most innovative. Narrated from the perspective of the missionary, the story utilizes interior monologue, characterized by violent language and abrupt shifts in tone, to effectively represent his confused mind. "Les muets" ("The Silent Men") focuses on a coopers' strike to portray the fate of the working class in the industrial age, while "Jonas ou l'artiste au travail" ("The Artist at Work") features a painter whose experiences mirror Camus's own difficulties in reconciling his public and private identities as a writer. "The Artist at Work" delineates what is essentially the organizing motif of *Exile and the Kingdom*—the relationship between self and others—by ending with a description of a canvas on which Jonas has painted a word that can be read as both *solitaire* (solitude) and *solidaire* (solidarity).

Commentators have been restrained in assessing Camus's ability as a writer of short fiction. Many critics have identified autobiographical elements in *Exile and the Kingdom* and interpret the stories as reflecting Camus's own quandaries concerning the issue of colonialism. Others have drawn parallels between these stories and Camus's earlier works, noting, for instance, similarities between the arid, harsh landscape of "The Renegade" and the descriptions of Algiers in *The Stranger.* While many critics concede that Camus's stories are occasionally clumsy and implausible, they have been praised for their psychologically complex characterizations and have been ultimately evaluated as an indication of Camus's versatility as a writer.

PRINCIPAL WORKS

SHORT FICTION

L'exil et le royaume 1957
[*Exile and the Kingdom,* 1957]

OTHER MAJOR WORKS

L'envers et l'endroit 1937 (essays)
["The Wrong Side and the Right Side" published in *Lyrical and Critical Essays,* 1968]
Noces 1939 (essays)
["Nuptials" published in *Lyrical and Critical,* 1967]
L'étranger 1942 (novel)
[*The Stranger,* 1946; also published as *The Outsider,* 1946]
Le mythe de Sisyphe 1942 (essay)
[*The Myth of Sisyphus,* 1955]
**Caligula* 1944 (drama)
**Le malentendu* 1944 (drama)
La peste 1947 (novel)
[*The Plague,* 1948]
Les justes 1949 (drama)
[*The Just Assasins,* 1958]
L'homme revolté 1951 (essay)
[*The Rebel,* 1954]
La chute 1956 (novel)
[*The Fall,* 1956]
***Requiem pour une nonne* 1956 (drama)

*These works were translated and published together as *Caligula and Cross Purpose,* 1947.

**This work was adapted from William Faulkner's novel *Requiem for a Nun.*

Gaëtan Picon (essay date 1957)

[*In the following essay, originally published in the* Mercure de France, *Picon discusses the naturalistic qualities that distinguish the stories in* Exile and the Kingdom *from such allegorical works as* The Stranger *and* The Plague.]

I do not think that any of the six tales contained in ***Exile and the Kingdom*** can be ranked with Albert Camus's most accomplished writings; but no other book by Camus has made me more keenly aware of the profound nature and actual status of his work. The quest, the intensity, the distribution of this work; what it has attempted and still is attempting to do; what new horizons open up before it: all seem to me to be more clearly visible here than anywhere else.

None of these tales are able to strike us, to hold our attention, to inscribe themselves in our memory with the force of *The Stranger, The Plague,* or even *The Fall.* The reason for this is evident. All of Camus's previous books carry through to conclusion a particular line of thought, which finds its form in the simplification and enlargement of a mythical image. These extremes of perspective, the massive writing have an imperious eloquence. Here we are brought back to a state of in-betweens, of confusion, to the careful fusing of the characteristics of everyday existence. Even when it is dramatic, this existence is composed of humble, day-to-day details. **"The Silent Men," "The Guest," "The Adulterous Woman"** are presented as realistic accounts: that is the way things actually happened, and there is always some detail, attesting to the brutish thoughtlessness of reality, which prevents the narrative from disappearing into the pure and inflexible line of myth. There is always some detail which describes an existing situation without any mental reservation. **"The Artist at Work"** and **"The Growing Stone,"** on the other hand, have somewhat the appearance of fables. In **"The Artist at Work"** the irony of the narrator is directed visibly toward the narrative, dispelling the dust of insignificant facts. In **"The Growing Stone"** the tone is that of legend, but there is also amusement in this irony: the pleasure of recounting in a legendary tone. At any rate, it seems to me that these tales are the first in which Camus takes into consideration the actual subject matter of his narrative and dwells upon the details. Whereas previously he had sought the most exact and most simplified coincidence between a thought impulse and a dramatic action, here he is observing, imagining—caught in the web of reality.

It is possible that these tales will disappoint the admirers of Camus. As for myself, whom he has never quite satisfied, I feel that they announce a very salutary reappraisal. The author's impress is not as visible as usual: we no longer entirely recognize his austerity, his haughty abstraction, his willful reduction to bare essentials. The discordancy of tone may be perplexing because legend succeeds parody, interior monologue succeeds behaviorist narrative. Even the value accorded to geographical location is such as to surprise us. The Algeria of *The Stranger* and of *The Plague* was scarcely less allegorical than the Holland of *The Fall.* Here the setting is more than a conventional situation, or an allegorical agreement between space and mind: the Brazilian forest of **"The Growing Stone,"** the North Africa of the other narratives—it is a fact, a reality which attracts to itself a large portion of that attention which had previously been fixed upon the moral and the symbol.

Each tale has a presence, a sort of material weightiness which, one might fear, could entail a weakening in meaning. But it suffices to go from one to the other to perceive that the collection of tales is animated by a significance which is scattered, flowing, diffuse, hence all the more active. Certainly Camus did not write the book for the purpose of amusement—or as an exercise in narration and observation after so many moral treatises. He has dispersed his secrets; he has simply set them down and let them live instead of giving them the too-evident appearance of allegory. Until this work, Camus had clung to an attitude which, although temporary, had been pushed to its extreme limit, thus imparting to each book a character both excessive and incomplete. Now, at last, he abandons himself to the fluctuations of life. In the place of abstractions we have here the agitation of waters at their dividing line. His preceding work was indeed in search of something, but, in regard to this quest, it only blocked out certain main perspectives. *The Stranger* and *The Fall* immobilize the quest at its limit in the trajectory, which goes beyond the existentialist surface of the story. *The Plague* fixes the quest in a circular kind of composition and compromise. For the first time, in ***Exile and the Kingdom,*** one feels a certain movement—a movement which allows the author to say everything without betraying anything.

Camus's problem is to relate the unity of artistic expression with a vibrant inner experience, torn apart so that it may live. How can one gather into unity of expression that which escapes all unity? Sometimes in his linear narrative the unity of myth achieves artistic efficacy only by belying the truth of the experience: the *roman-hypothèse* achieves unity solely because it is false; it has the air of a dangerous abstraction. Sometimes, notably in *The Plague,* Camus tried to integrate his inner diversity with the unity of a form by composing, in mid-stream, a somewhat disappointing fusion. To go in one direction only, but to its extreme limit—or to bring into balance opposing tendencies: Camus hesitates between Descartes and Gide, between utmost rigor and infinite comprehension. But the true path lies beyond this hesitation. The present work, rather than being entrapped by the author's fame is still in the process of defining itself, of seeking out its rightful place. I have always thought this, and I find a moving and comforting confirmation of this idea in these lines which Camus wrote for an edition of *L'Envers et l'endroit* (Betwixt and Between): "The day when a balance shall be struck between what I am and what I do; on that day perhaps, I scarcely dare write it, I shall be able to give substance to the work of which I have always dreamed."

The work he dreamed of is not ***Exile and the Kingdom,*** but this collection of stories allows him to envision it somewhat better. ***Exile and the Kingdom*** and, as I can imagine solely from the nature of the title, *L'Envers et l'endroit* are faithful to the author's concept of truth because they are based on a constant coming and going, on a particular tempo. *The Stranger, The Plague, The Fall* all contain effective myths, rigorous thoughts, but because of that unity which is reflected by the single word in their titles, they destroy the rhythmical truth of a life seeking to know itself. It is the image of tension which, one should recall, charged the concluding pages of *The Rebel* with the violence of experience, thus coloring the drabness of conciliatory dialectic:

> In this hour when each one of us must arch his bow in readiness to prove himself, to conquer within the bounds of history—and in spite of it—those things which he already possesses: the meager harvest of his fields, the fleeting love of the land; at the moment when, at last, we are born into manhood, we must leave behind us the frenzied agitation of adolescence. The bow strains, the wood screeches. At the utmost peak of tension an arrow flies out, straight and true, the result of the firmest and freest of shots.

Only strict adherence to this experience will reconcile Camus's writings with his personal being.

The drama—the theater—with its bold, conflicting characters would have been ideal for expressing "this dialogue which we are." Camus has a passion for the theater; but he does not seem to have the necessary genius. He wrote one theatrical masterpiece: *Requiem for a Nun,* but only by drawing upon Faulkner. His plays grow weaker as their structure becomes more dramatic. The finest one, *Caligula,* is simply a monologue. The best of Camus's writings up to the present have not touched upon this element of dialogue which is inherent in Camus. To be more precise, they suppressed or mitigated it; but here, in the succession of stories in ***Exile and the Kingdom,*** the tempo which myth destroyed, and which the theater reflected but feebly, imposes its rhythmical beat.

Only this tempo can simultaneously express and overcome the inner fluctuation. Only this tempo can retrieve what is destroyed by the various alternatives of thought. The preceding books show us first the right then the wrong side of the cloth: this one begins by placing the fabric in our hands. We must not separate the absurd from the joy of living, revolt from love, inner nobility from the militant refutation of evil. Each of Camus's books conformed to the other because each one brought forth only one word in its title instead of emitting the rhythm of an entire phrase. Thus *The Fall* corresponded to *The Plague* as *The Plague* corresponded to *The Stranger.* ***Exile and the Kingdom*** does not in the least correspond to *The Fall;* it does not add another segment in the formation of a line; but in contrast to the successes of abstraction, it poses an attempt at completeness.

The Fall was to have been included in this collection; but the author took it out because of its unforeseen bulk. It is important to note that the two books are not alike. *The Fall* fully explores one path, leaving us suspended on the verge of an answer which it cannot possibly give, because to do so it would have to return to the point of departure. Like all the preceding books, *The Fall* corresponds to a point in progression (which could, as is the case in this instance, assume a regressive pace), while ***Exile and the Kingdom*** contains a definite movement. In *The Fall* there is only an exile without a kingdom. There is no answer to the discovery made by Clamence (good itself is evil)—at least no answer which does not oblige us to start afresh from nothing. Here the answer is always given with the question, the right with the wrong side, the kingdom with the exile.

This book is not based upon a contradiction, and herein lies its success. The exile and the kingdom are not two continents separated by an ocean: they are two aspects of the same breath and heartbeat. The kingdom is in the exile, the exile is a path toward the kingdom—in fact, exile could actually be the kingdom. **"The Artist at Work,"** with swift, ironical verve, evokes the life of an artist separated from his work by his family and friends. He finally isolates himself in his workshop by constructing a sort of cage—in which he dies. One word, in very small characters, is written in the center of the white canvas he leaves behind him. We do not know whether the word is *solitary* or *solidarity.* These two words are enough alike so that we need not oppose them too brutally. Without a doubt, Jonas dwelt in exile among his own circle of family and friends. He found his true home in the solitude of his work, but his circle remains the same. The cage wherein he dies is a mock kingdom. For the workers who are on strike in **"The Silent Men,"** exile is the hostility of society—the kingdom is their silent revolt. They experience a feeling of fraternity which they could not have known without undergoing exile. In **"The Adulterous Woman"** the opposing elements seem particularly clear: exiled both in her marital life and in her daily work, Janine has but to cast a glance upon the desert to discover the free, untrammeled existence of the kingdom:

> From the dawn of time, upon the dry, barren soil of this immeasurable land, a small band of men had trod relentlessly, owning nothing, serving no one; the wretched but free lords of a strange kingdom. Janine did not know why this idea filled her with a sadness so sweet and so vast that it obliged her to close her eyes. She knew only that this eternal kingdom had been promised her, and that, except for this fleeting moment, it would never again be hers. . . .

Drab as it may be, does it not yield possibilities of tenderness, of depth? In the very last lines she joins her sleeping husband and whispers, "my darling."

In **"The Guest,"** which is perhaps the most effective story in the collection, we see clearly that the conflict is not between solitude and fellowship, or liberty and submission. The hero does not oscillate between two forms of solitude: one, the cruelest of exiles, is a solitude in which the gestures of fraternity turn against us—the solitude of incomprehension; the other, which constitutes the sole portrayal of the kingdom, is the solitude in which we are aware of what we have done, and realize that it was necessary to do what we did. Is this the opposing of two attitudes: building up a good point and tracking down a bad one? Not at all. The book invites us to probe the very pulse of existence—which unfolds, then shuts up tight; reveals itself in a flash of light, then veils itself in obscurity; waxes and then wanes. The moralist who isolates and dissects is succeeded by the poet who puts together and restores the one complex throb of life. (pp. 152-56)

Gaëtan Picon, " 'Exile and the Kingdom'," in Camus: A Collection of Critical Essays, *edited by Germaine Brée, Prentice-Hall, Inc., 1962, pp. 152-56.*

Orville Prescott (essay date 1958)

[Prescott is an American critic. In the following excerpt, he faults the stories in Exile and the Kingdom *for their lack of artistry, cryptic themes, and enigmatic conclusions.]*

It is M. Camus' failure as an artist in fiction that he ignores "the greatest number of men" and writes ambiguous and symbolical parables. In his first two novels, *The Stranger* and *The Plague,* the symbolism was reasonably clear and simple. But in his last novel, *The Fall,* it was darkly obscure and in his new book, ***Exile and the Kingdom,*** a collection of six short stories, the symbolical fog is as damp and thick as ever.

Most short stories are either stories in the old-fashioned sense or they are studies of character, emotion and the meaning of particular behavior or circumstances. Both kinds require a minimum of lucidity in communication. But M. Camus' short stories are beautifully written and highly suggestive puzzles. Any reader can interpret them to suit himself. The professor's answer is no more likely to be correct than the freshman student's. This kind of short fiction, no matter how morally earnest—and M. Camus' stories are written with deadly earnestness—can only be a sort of fashionable, intellectual game to be enjoyed by a small coterie. When cryptic hints and solemn posturing become the substance of fiction, life itself is drained from it.

The six stories in ***Exile and the Kingdom*** are all riddles in the reader's path. M. Camus has hinted at their meaning by his title. His people, who are never fully characterized, are exiles, lonely, unhappy and frightened exiles from some desirable kingdom. Perhaps the land of heart's desire? Maybe even the kingdom of God? At any rate, they are enduring what M. Camus calls "the long anguish of living and dying" with no pleasure, little courage and little competence.

Three stories seem to me more peculiar and more exasperating than the other three and at the same time more representative of M. Camus' method. The first is about a woman traveling by bus in the African desert with her husband, who is selling dry goods to Arab merchants in the oasis cities. The woman is irritable, bored, stupid. Scornful of her husband, frightened of life, she responds to some mysterious compulsion and leaves their hotel bedroom to spend a few minutes on the city wall in a vaguely rapturous communion with the desert night. The story is called **"The Adulterous Woman."**

Riddle: In what symbolical fashion was the woman adulterous? Since she was physically faithful, since she was not even unfaithful in her imagination, answers are not easy. I can think of several; but thinking of them is a dull way of wasting time and a story like this seems to me a sterile and tiresome performance.

The second story consists of the stream of consciousness, or the interior monologue, of a Roman Catholic missionary who has been driven mad by torture. In a city of salt somewhere in the Sahara the crazed man cowers before the tribal fetish of his captors and masters. His tongue has been cut out and he now despises his former faith and worships the fetish of his masters and glories in their cruelty and evil. **"The Renegade"** is a gruesome nightmare.

Riddle: Is the madman "converted" by pain a symbol of the peoples who are subject to totalitarian tyranny; or is he a sardonic comment on fear as the original source of religion? or what?

In the third story, **"The Growing Stone,"** a French engineer watches the bizarre religious rituals of an isolated Brazilian village. At first repelled by their primitive and savage character, he eventually succumbs to the general infection and participates.

Riddle: Is the need to belong greater than educated intelligence? Are exiles from the kingdom so desperate they will compromise on a miserable counterfeit of it?

Orville Prescott, in a review of "Exile and the Kingdom," in The New York Times, *March 10, 1958, p. 21.*

Victor Brombert (essay date 1960)

[Brombert is an American educator and critic who has written extensively on modern French literature, including a major study of the works of Gustave Flaubert. In the following essay, he analyzes the narrative technique that Camus utilized in "The Renegade" and portrays the title character's conversion to absolute evil.]

Is **"The Renegade"** merely a poetic exercise in violence? Future generations may well admire, above all the rest of Camus' work, the nightmarish perfection of this parable, with its incantatory rhythms and blinding images of pain. It is, however, a disturbing text. Brutality assumes hysterical proportions. Feverish, convulsive images build up to an apocalypse of cruelty.

"Quelle bouillie, quelle bouillie"! The opening words refer to the pulp-like state of the narrator's mind. But it is his body which was first literally beaten to a pulp. In an unlivable, "maddening" landscape, under the rays of a savage sun, the human flesh is exposed to the worst indignities. In the white heat of an African summer, the victim is whipped and salt is lavishly sprinkled on his wounds. Beaten about the head with wet ropes until his ears bleed, he is left moaning under the eyes of a blood-thirsty Fetish. Sadistic women assist his torturers, while he in turn is forced to witness the torture and rape of others. Inhuman cries, bestial matings, orgiastic rituals culminate in scenes of mutilation. His tongue is cut out, his mouth filled with salt. But nothing seems to satisfy this lust for pain. The victim himself—willing collaborator of his tormentors—yearns for more punishment.

Punctuated by onomatopoeic effects (the submissive interjection *ô*, the guttural *râ, râ*, the haunting rattle of thirst, hate and death), this frenzied tale offers no respite. But what is all this violence about? Why does the narrator accept it with gratitude, even with relish? On the surface, the story appears simple enough. A student in a theological seminary is consumed with the desire to convert heathens, to force upon others the truth of his faith. He decides to set out as a missionary to the African "city of salt," Taghâza—a "closed city" which few have entered, and from which even fewer have returned. Having heard of the spectacular cruelty of its inhabitants, he feels attracted by the glorious possibility of converting them to the God of Love. Although warned by his superiors that he is not ready, not "ripe," he dreams of penetrating into the very sanctuary of the Fetish, of subjugating the savages through the sheer power of the Word.

Events, however, take an unexpected turn. He discovers that Evil is stronger than he thought, and soon accepts this strength as the only Truth. The tortured missionary is thus, ironically, converted by the very Fetish he set out to destroy. He discovers the joy and the power of hatred. His new masters teach him how to despise love. He adores, as he has never adored before, the ax-like face of the Fetish who "possesses" him. At the end of the story, as though to outdo his new masters and to avenge himself on his old ones, he savagely kills the new missionary, while calling for the eternal Reign of Hatred.

The virtuosity of these pages is remarkable. Nowhere else has Camus revealed himself so accomplished a master of images, sounds and rhythms. The fulgurating whiteness of the landscape, the piercing sunfire of this white hell, the liquefaction of time under the burning refraction of a thousand mirrors—all this is suggested in the hallucinating interior monologue which presses forward as though indeed the only speech left the tongueless narrator were the metaphorical "tongue" of his feverish brain. In this "cold torrid city" of Taghâza, with its iron name and the steel-like ridges of its landscape, a defiant race has built a surrealistic city of salt.

The salt and the sun—these are indeed the basic images in **"The Renegade."** The word sun, in itself symbol of absolute violence, appears up to four times in the same paragraph. "Savage" and "irresistible," it is the sun of death and of flies. It "beats," it "pierces," making holes in the overheated metal of the sky. Visual images, as well as images of sound and touch, are relentless reminders of the theme of hardness. The narrator hears in his own mouth the sound of rough pebbles. He fondles the barrel of his gun, while the stones and rocks all around him crackle from the heat. There is hardly a transition between the icy coldness of the night and the crystal-like dazzlement of the day. But it is the very rhythm of the speech—panting, harsh, elliptical yet smooth—which marks the greatest achievement of this text. Audacious, yet pure in a Racinian manner, the language and the syntax swiftly glide from affirmation to negation.

Virtuosity is, however, not Camus' purpose. Even when originally inspired by vivid personal impulses and sensations (surrender to air, sun, water; love of nature; pagan sensuality), most of Camus' writing seems irresistibly drawn toward an allegorical meaning. The very titles of his work which so often suggest a loss, a fall, an exile or a spiritual disease, point to a parabolic tendency and at times even seem to come close to Christian theological concerns. He may be, like Jean-Baptiste Clamens in *The Fall,* an *ailing* prophet, sick with the very illusions and weakness he feels compelled to denounce. But this solidarity with illness only makes the diagnosis more urgent.

The missionary in **"The Renegade,"** who discovers that only guns have souls, is very sick indeed. His sickness, a particularly dangerous one: the obsessive quest for the absolute. His superiors at the seminary are perfectly right: he does not know "who he is." This ignorance of his true self sets the stage for the most shocking discoveries. But, on the symbolic level, it also points to the transcendental urges which bring about self-negation and self-destruction.

Who, indeed, is the narrator? Who is this missionary-renegade with his desire for "order" and his dream of absolute power? "Dirty slave," he calls himself with characteristic self-hatred. Intelligent, but hard-headed ("mulet," "tête de vache"), he is from his youth on attracted to cruelty, finding the very idea of Barbarians exciting. A hunter of pain, he imagines that the very girls in the street will strike at him and spit in his face. He dreams of teeth that tear, and enjoys the voluptuous image of his imagined pain.

This masochistic eroticism which instinctively leads him to Taghâza is clearly of a symbolic nature. The rape by the Evil Fetish is perpetrated not so much on his body as on his mind. The missionary surrenders to the Fetish in a quasi-sexual ecstasy of pain. But this surrender is of an intellectual nature: the allegory deals with the drama of the mind. In a climate whose extreme heat precludes contact between human beings, his new masters, these "lords" of the salt mines, succeed in brainwashing the absolutist, or rather in converting him. *Absolute* dedication to good is transmuted into *absolute* dedication to evil.

The allegorical identity of the Renegade thus emerges. He is the modern intellectual, heir to a Humanist culture, but now impatient with the "seminary" coziness of his tradition and with its shams, and who, in search of systems and abstract ideologies, espouses totalitarian values that have long declared war (and he knows it!) on the thinker and his thought. Thus amorous hate and amorous surrender are the logical consequence of a denial of life in favor of meaning. The missionary-intellectual believes he is out to convert the barbarians; in fact he seeks tyranny in order to submit to it. Brutalized, tortured, humiliated in his flesh and in his spirit, he adores his enemy and proclaims the omnipotence of the sadistic Fetish.

The symbolism of his quest and of his punishment—his tongue is cut out, his mouth filled with salt—are quite transparent. But it is interesting to note that he feels betrayed by his own culture ("my masters have deceived me"), that even in his original desire to convert others there was the yearning for "absolute power," that in fact he adores the Fetish long before he sets out on his journey. The sense of this betrayal remains ambivalent. On the one hand, it shows up the poison of ideological absolutes; on the other, it reveals the deep-rooted suicidal impulses of the intelligentsia. The missionary-renegade, bitter against his former teachers and ashamed of his cultural heritage, seeks not only the destruction of what he is, but of what he represents. He has "an account to settle" with his entire culture. That is, one must assume, the meaning of his murdering the new missionary. By killing him, he attempts to kill what he himself stands for, as well as the spiritual guild to which he belongs. The betrayal is a vengeance, but this is also self-punishment!

The terror of the absolute, so powerfully conveyed by this story, is one of Camus' permanent themes. The missionary who reneges on his mission does so because his thirst for a despotic ideal can only find satisfaction in evil. For evil, unlike good, can be absolute in human terms. The Renegade, seeing that good is a constantly postponed and tiring project, refuses to pursue any further an ever receding boundary. He knows that the Reign of Goodness is impossible. So he turns to the Reign of Evil as to the only abstraction that can be translated into a flawless truth. For only the "square" truth, the "heavy" and "dense" truth, can be acceptable to the seeker of the absolute. "Only evil can go to its own limit and reign absolutely." The conversion, to be sure, leads to a denial of all values. "Down with Europe, down with reason, honor and the cross." But this is the price to pay: the militant need for absolute affirmation implies absolute negation. Ideology replaces life. The missionary-intellectual becomes a grave-digger who prepares his own burial.

No problem of our time has preoccupied Camus more than this disastrous temptation of the absolute and the death-wish of the modern intellectual. Eloquent spokesman for a new Humanism, he has steadily rejected all transcendent "Kingdoms," whether religious or political, and sung instead with pagan accents the "implacable grandeur" of a life in which all the idols have feet of clay. He is, as Germaine Brée reminds us, suspicious of all absolutes. His books, whose very titles point to the themes of exile and nostalgia, assert the need to rediscover a lost birthright and cling desperately to man's most precious virtue: the "generous exigence of happiness." Happiness and love are indeed key words in his vocabulary. But above all, he has reaffirmed in lyric fashion the need to return to the modest "mortal" condition. Like Odysseus, he rejects Calypso's deceptive offer of immortality. For his intellectual pilgrimage is also a return from the world of gods and monsters back to the world of men. (pp. 81-4)

Victor Brombert, " 'The Renegade' or the Terror of the Absolute," in Yale French Studies, *Vol. 25, Spring, 1960, pp. 81-4.*

Alfred Noyer-Weidner (essay date 1960)

[*In the following excerpt from an essay originally published in the journal* Zeitschrift für französische Sprache und Literatur, *Noyer-Weidner offers general guidelines for interpreting the stories in* Exile and the Kingdom *and discusses Camus's understanding of the short story genre.*]

The older [French] narrative tradition of the nineteenth century, which has not yet been entirely discarded, gradually brought up the object of the narration and calmly advanced to the central story from a relatively detailed exposition. In contrast to this, Camus tends more toward the technique of what is understood by the English type of "short story" as used in its narrow, technical sense. This technique transfers the reader into the middle of the events and later adds the facts which are necessary for comprehension. Although this approximation of the novella to the "short story" can be found before Camus, the uniqueness of his stories consists in their immediate and recurrent descriptive imagery. . . . [The] technique of presenting events from the point of view of his characters illustrates the fact that Camus's short stories frequently begin with a rather long, drawn-out observation which reflects upon the events taking place. One must add that these stories also advance in a series of stages of development, each stage of which is a complete description in itself. The descriptions, especially during the river crossing, the reception by the city dignitaries, the dance orgy of the natives, and the beginning of the procession, clearly dominate the large phases of the development of **"The Growing Stone"**; even the conversations, in part those between D'Arrast and the "cook," have more of a descriptive than a plot-advancing function. Even toward the end of the story where the action becomes concentrated, it can hardly be said that this action attains the autonomy of a continuous forward drive. Every forward step of the plot is interrupted by the narrator's use of a kind of *tableau vivant.* So it is when the natives come to the hut where D'Arrast has thrown down the stone:

> They found D'Arrast standing with his shoulders against the back wall and eyes closed. In the center of the room, in the place of the hearth, the stone was half buried in ashes and earth. They stood in the doorway without advancing and looked at D'Arrast in silence as if questioning him. But he didn't speak.

Scarcely have they entered and sat down when the narrator's gaze is already moving around again: "They were squatting in a silent circle around the stone. No sound but the murmur of the river reached them through the heavy air. Standing in the darkness, D'Arrast listened without seeing anything. . . . " Although such analytical character scenes are found elsewhere in ***Exile and the Kingdom,*** their frequency and descriptive detail is especially striking in **"The Silent Men."** At each new stage of development the behavior of each individual is closely examined. Here, to be sure, this method is especially substantiated by the author's ultimate objective, as will be shown later on.

This recurrent lingering reveals what Camus's attempts to mislead the reader and to heighten his suspense can only partly conceal: namely, how thinly-plotted his short stories basically are. Furthermore, the characters' past histories bring no plastic description of events into the stories. The concrete events of the past become blurred and vague; and in **"The Growing Stone"** they are even more concealed than in the other stories. For example, what kind of experience had almost driven D'Arrast himself to make a vow? Thus the heroes' past lives are essentially reduced to descriptive contrasts of their past and present, such as the beginning and the later form of Janine's married life with Marcel, the account of Daru's difficulties in adapting to an isolated elementary schoolhouse which cuts him off from the rest of the world, and his final assimilation to the solitude of the desert: "It was this silence that had seemed painful to him during the first days. . . . And yet, outside this desert neither of them [neither he nor the Arab prisoner], Daru knew, could have really lived." We see similar examples of descriptive contrasts when Janine, skipping over in her memory a period of twenty-five years, sees her present life projected against the background of her youth, and when Yvars looks from the perspective of a man of forty back to the time when he was twenty. Also characteristic of the parallel between the two stories is the indefinite time formula: "The years had passed" in **"The Adulterous Woman"** and "Then the years had passed" in **"The Silent Men,"** which effectively omits what lies between and thus guarantees a pure impression of contrast. When it is absolutely necessary to relate at least the most important part of the intervening events in Yvars' life, then this information is conveyed as a series of isolated states as opposed to an epic experience: "*there had been* Fernande, the birth of the boy." **"The Silent Men"** uses this method of presentation even more extensively than **"The Adulterous Woman."** Although ***Exile and the Kingdom*** contains little continuous dynamic narration in the form of hurrying from event to event, this "there had been" still has a special significance in the framework of this particular story. It is the only time that Camus uses the words "there is" or "there are" (with appropriate verbal constructions) in his stories in the same manner as in *The Stranger;* its function there has been analyzed by Sartre [in *Situations* I, 1974]. What had already been expressed at the beginning of the story through the alternation between the author's commentary and the characters' points of view becomes more evident here in the image of the principal character's passivity.

Another aspect of the narrative technique of *The Stranger* in ***Exile and the Kingdom*** will be taken up in a later passage. On the whole, however, the specific method of presentation of Camus's earlier narrative works rarely becomes evident in the stylistic form of this volume of stories. For example, the particular style features of *The Plague* reappear only sporadically, such as when people are depicted in the image of animals, the colonial soldier in **"The Adulterous Woman"** as a jackal and the mayor in **"The Growing Stone"** as a weasel. This weasel reminds one strikingly of the owl of *The Plague.* The animal metamorphosis is presented here, as in the other work, as an ironic device. Irony is also evident in **"The Growing Stone"** where it permeates the trite rhetorical expressions of the judge and gives a special flavor to D'Arrast's reception. One cannot assert that Camus did not make any extensive use of irony before *The Rebel.* However, he has never made such skillful use of irony or pushed it to the point of sarcasm and cynicism as in his last phase of development, notably in *The Fall* and **"The Artist at Work."** Naturally the content of the stories is correspondingly stamped with irony, but first of all this phenomenon is symptomatic of the "stylistic law" which dominates the entire volume of stories, in which *The Fall* was also originally supposed to appear. Camus was seeking the most forceful impression by presenting spectacularly heightened characterizations. The intensification of irony in *The Fall* serves the same purpose as the confused, blurred style, the stream-of-consciousness technique of **"The Renegade."** These stories are primarily artistic experiments in presenting more precise characterizations; they do not signify unconditionally an intensification of the character traits themselves. Perhaps one can already conclude from this experimental approach the later position of ***Exile and the Kingdom*** in the complete works of Camus. As [André] Gide found his way from the smaller experiment to the form of the larger work, from *Isabelle* to *Lafcadio's Adventures,* so also may *The Fall* and ***Exile and the Kingdom*** be viewed as a preparation for the novel on which Camus is now working.

In whatever direction the artistic experiment of ***Exile and the Kingdom*** may move, its common denominator remains the attempt to increase the impact of the writing. This aspiration is also detectable in those stories which are written in a less eccentric form than **"The Renegade"** and **"The Artist at Work."** It is also evident in Camus's continuous preference for statuesque grandeur, for impressive images in general. There are the large landscapes of Africa and South America, the Algerian desert in **"The Adulterous Woman"** and **"The Guest,"** the fantastically exaggerated description of the city of salt, the "cold torrid city" of **"The Renegade,"** and the Brazilian jungle river of **"The Growing Stone."** The "sea of vegetation" of the latter, "vast and savage like the continent of trees stretching beyond it for thousands of kilometers," is put into just as affective vibration as the "vast horizon" of the "realm of stones" with its "thousands of miles" in **"The Adulterous Woman."** Of course this lyrical expansion never slips away from the author's intellectual awareness, not even in **"The Renegade."** In this respect Camus does not abandon his favorite notion of "Mediterranean lucidity." His clearly ordered train of thought is just as visible in the sharply defined individual phases of the river experience as in the way he methodically builds the description of the desert panorama which unfolds before Janine and Marcel during the climb to the tower. There is first of all the widening of the horizon during the climb itself which is enclosed in a chiastic framework: "As they climbed . . . an even broader light . . . a vibration increasing in length as they advanced. . . . " This passage is followed by an initial great synthetic impression, inserted between the "vast horizon" and the "limitless expanse," and then finally by the contemplation of the individual parts in a scholarly analytic continuation: "From east to west, in fact, her gaze swept slowly . . . Beneath her . . . Farther off . . . Still farther off . . . At some distance from the oasis . . . Above the desert. . . . "

In such a framework, the pathos of the nature image is heightened at the lyrical climaxes to a monumental human vitality, whether it be to the "motionless progress" of the sky at the end of **"The Adulterous Woman,"** or to the "wild river," which "strained under the craft," at the beginning of **"The Growing Stone."** On the other hand, the monumentality of nature also encompasses the people, insofar as the particular story content permits. The key words of the nature vision, "motionless" and "silent," with their synonyms and variants signify, in addition, the

Francine and Albert Camus in Stockholm, at the time he was awarded the Nobel Prize.

manner in which the author describes his characters from the first story to the last. Janine is accompanied in the bus by a "mute escort" of Arabs whose "silence" and "impassivity" is repeated outside the bus in a group of "forms . . . standing still . . ." which suddenly emerges, "Mute, . . . [having] come from nowhere." In a short passage the words "motionless" and "silent" return several times during the description of the river crossing beginning with "the silence and immobility of this broad clearing in the virgin forest" up to the "each remained in his place, motionless and quiet." The end of the collection of stories reinforces their general tendency toward monumentality as D'Arrast stands unmoving and silent after his deed.

After his deed—we must come back to it once more—D'Arrast raises himself up, "suddenly enormous," and therein is included a further key word of Camus's short story style, a detail which confirms what has been said up to now. With an almost excessive use of expressions of suddenness, of "soudain" and "subit" ("sudden"), "soudainement" and "subitement" ("suddenly"), and "[tout] d'un coup" ("all of a sudden"), Camus attempts to give to the events, to the experiences of the characters, a more than normal significance. It is his goal to transpose the minimum of events which are presented in the stories into a maximum of visible plasticity.

Camus has not always avoided the danger of his descriptive talents, for the descriptions sometimes become an end in themselves. However, they do not threaten the total effect of the story as long as he explicitly removes them from the narrative, as, for example, the fly, which he uses as a point of departure in the first story. Nevertheless he accomplishes this explicit removal with an accuracy of description which is rather disturbing in view of the insignificance of the incident: "The fly shook a chilled wing, flexed its legs, and took flight." The total effect is threatened, however, when he creates, through forceful imagery, a crucial point of a story which does not at the same time represent a crucial point of the actual plot. The lyrical heightening of the nature experience in **"The Adulterous Woman"** has its justification in the climax of the plot. Its counterpart, the same strong emphasis on nature in **"The Growing Stone,"** produces a false accent, an incongruity of form and content. The main event of the story, which occurs later, is not equal to the stirring, energetic nature prelude and has no direct causal connection with it. Even D'Arrast's statuesque size does not bridge the gap. Thus **"The Growing Stone"** does not go beyond a masterful reporting of a loosely connected series of events. It never attains the compactness of a true short story, which can be accomplished only by means of "productive omission."

In general, through careful planning, the language and imagery remain related to the concealed objective of the story and thus correspond to Camus's frequently stated intention of using a conscious working style "when imagination and intelligence are fused" [*Lyrical and Critical Essays*]. This is true of the foreword to the new edition of *The Wrong Side and the Right Side,* which was written at approximately the same time as ***Exile and the Kingdom.*** The outward appearance of the characters is a figure for their inner nature, and even the simplest statements frequently and surprisingly reveal a deeper symbolic meaning. Occasionally this interrelation penetrates to the level of language, as seen in the case of D'Arrast's "big, hearty laugh that resembled him," and also when it is said of Yvars: "This morning he was pedaling along with his head down, feeling even *heavier* than usual; his heart too was *heavy.*" If one consistently pursues these opening statements, one sees how little Camus leaves to the free play of the imagination. The appearance and gestures of his characters reflect a deeper, symbolic significance.

If we wish to understand the behavior of the Arab in **"The Guest,"** we can already find a point of reference in the conspicuous feature of his physical appearance: "At first Daru noticed only his huge lips." Conspicuously the story insists upon this physical peculiarity, up to a last pointing up of the observation regarding this "animal mouth." This reference, in fact, directly precedes the first failure of the Arab to grasp a question of a higher moral order: "Obviously he did not understand." His animal-like physiognomy turns out to be the consciously stylized exterior manifestation of an inner primitiveness, of a passivity devoid of understanding, which is subsequently brought more and more clearly into relief: "The Arab watched him without seeming to understand," "was looking at him blankly," "as if he didn't know what to do with what was being given him." Upon closer examination, even such an apparently insignificant scene as this acquires deeper meaning: " 'Go ahead,' [said Daru]. The fellow didn't budge. 'I'm coming,' said Daru. The Arab went out." For here is anticipated *in nuce* the behavior of the Arab in the decision at the crossroads, where suddenly "a sort of panic" appears on his face, where he stands for a long time hesitating and looks at Daru, thus again hoping for instructions from him. When the Arab is finally shown "on the road to prison," this occurs without any commentary. "The prison" has, of course, in addition to its literal meaning, an allegorical contrast relationship to the "kingdom" of the collective title. Another important clue to the meaning of the passage lies in the fact that the Arab appears predestined to failure after the description of his outward appearance, or, more specifically, from our first physical impression of him. The solution of Camus's stories lies, to formulate it paradoxically, not just in their endings but already at their beginnings; it is, in its essence, already given in the description of the first appearance of the characters.

In this characteristic practice of the "coded technique" of the collection is reflected the polarity between the "exile" and the "kingdom." In a different way from the Arab's, but no less clearly, the characters of Yvars and Marcel are also predetermined by a negative sign from the very beginning; this is the point of convergence of the details already presented to the reader from the first pages of **"The Silent Men,"** and this is the reason for the stylistic emphasis of the portrait of Marcel: "With wisps of graying hair growing low on a narrow forehead, a broad nose, a flabby mouth, Marcel looked like a pouting faun." Does not the Arab's mouth also give him a "pouting look"? In Marcel's portrait, as part of his equipment as a merchant, is a sample case about which he is constantly concerned. When finally the object takes the place of the man, then his unconscious self-abasement and the meaningless, monotonous routine of Janine's life with him is illustrated in a manner as simple as it is glaringly obvious: "Janine *followed the trunk,* which made a way for her through the crowd." Marcel's sample case, which at first seems so natural and so harmless, turns out in the long run to be the symbol of the "unexamined life" which is constantly ridiculed by Camus.

If, however, we establish as fact such interrelationships from the beginning in regard to the characters who turn out badly, then we must also assume that it is not merely a coincidence that similar interrelationships exist when we examine those characters who turn out well. At some points the analogy of their outward appearance is made even more strikingly obvious, with the presentation of Daru as "a husky fellow," with the introduction of Janine as "tall and sturdy," and of D'Arrast with "his huge broad frame," whose body in the spotlight appears "taller and more massive each time he came back to life." Should not these powerful figures, just as in the case of the Arab whose outward appearance seemed to be planned for his future failure, also be considered a stylization, only exactly in the opposite direction, predestining them for a positive final impression? Would it not otherwise be curious that the concrete events in Janine's past are so vague and blurred, whereas her former sports ability is intentionally stressed? The positive valuation of an athletic physique, which is well-known as a constant factor in Camus's works, makes an important contribution to the final objective of the story. Obviously, therefore, the details in these stories and, to a special degree, the physical, external characterization of the stories' heroes are formulated with a view to the total effect.

We are now in the domain of Poe's "pre-established design" which has already influenced the literature of the nineteenth century and which, certainly by no coincidence, authors of modern novellas and short stories are now adopting. Anyone who does not grasp this principle of presentation, which is followed throughout the stories, easily falls into a false critical perspective. Thus Theis took the physical appearance of D'Arrast in an absolute manner and suspected Camus of turning toward race ideology. This inference is, in the case of the resistance-moralist of *Letters to a German Friend,* absurd in itself, but where is it actually stated in the text, which he claims to have examined closely, that D'Arrast is more than a powerful man, that he is a "blond, Nordic giant," "a concession to the vulgar taste?" [Raymond Theis, "Camus's Return to Sisyphus," *Essays on Camus's "Exile and the Kingdom,"* 1980].

It is neither possible nor necessary here to go into further details on the mutual dependence of exterior and interior elements in ***Exile and the Kingdom.*** Additional references will appear in the content of the stories. This analysis, however, rests on the certainty that the obscurity of meaning in the stories can be adequately explained by the clarity of contour of the description, and that the unstated can be explained by the stated. The fact that this unity of foreground or external description and underlying meaning is particularly evident in the area of human relationships is an indication of the center of gravity of the entire volume of stories. (pp. 56-65)

Alfred Noyer-Weidner, "Albert Camus in his Short Story Phase," translated by Ernest Allen, in Essays on Camus's "Exile and the Kingdom," *edited by Judith D. Suther, Romance Monographs, Inc., 1980, pp. 45-87.*

Laurence Perrine (essay date 1963)

[Perrine is a Canadian educator and critic. In the following excerpt, he examines the moral complexity of "The Guest."]

The protagonist of **"The Guest"** is Daru, a French Algerian who teaches a one-room school for Arab children in the middle of the bleak Algerian plateau where he was born and which he loves. Into his solitude during a spell of bad weather comes the gendarme Balducci, leading an Arab who has killed his cousin in a dispute over some grain. Balducci insists on handing the prisoner over to Daru for delivery to police headquarters at a village some four hours distant. Daru protests that this is not his job; but Balducci, citing police shorthandedness in the face of an incipient Arab revolt, makes Daru sign for receipt of the prisoner, and departs.

A sensitive, humane, and compassionate man, Daru treats his hostage as a human being rather than as a member of a subject race, as a guest rather than as a prisoner. He unties the Arab's wrists so that he can drink his hot tea; he refuses to put the rope back on him afterwards; he eats his supper beside the Arab, much to the latter's surprise, for the Arab is not used to being treated as an equal by a Frenchman; he neglects to keep a pistol near his bed that night, though he has given the Arab a cot in the same room. Even though he is a French civil servant, he rebels against the notion of handing the Arab over to French authorities for trial.

The story centers around Daru's dilemma. Should he do what Balducci would consider his duty, obey orders, and deliver the prisoner? Or should he follow his own human impulse and give the Arab his freedom? On the one hand, Daru is responsible for the prisoner; he has been given an order; he has signed a receipt. In addition, he is a Frenchman; he will fight against the Arabs if war is declared; for him, as for Balducci, the French are "us" and the Arabs are "they." Moreover, the Arab is a murderer; and Daru, a peaceable man, cannot repress his wrath against all men who wantonly kill, motivated by hate, spite, or blood lust. But then, on the other hand, the Arab is a human being, and it offends Daru's "honor" to treat him, however guilty, with anything less than human dignity. Such treatment demands that the Arab should be judged by his own people, not by alien French masters. It also demands that the Arab shall be treated as a "guest" while under Daru's roof. But this very treatment introduces an additional complication into Daru's dilemma, and one that is morally irrelevant. The stranger's presence in his room that night

> imposed on him a sort of brotherhood he refused to accept in the present circumstances; yet he was familiar with it. Men who share the same rooms, soldiers or prisoners, develop a strange alliance as if, having cast off their armor with their clothing, they fraternized every evening, over and above their differences, in the ancient community of dream and fatigue.

A guest, even an unwanted guest, exercises a rationally unjustifiable claim on one's loyalties.

The necessity of moral choice can be an almost intolerable burden, and Daru several times wishes he were free of it. In the afternoon, when he awakes from his nap, Daru is "amazed at the unmixed joy he derived from the mere thought the Arab might have fled and that he would be alone with no decision to make." During the night, when the Arab gets up to urinate, Daru at first thinks, "He is running away. Good riddance!" In the morning the Arab's continued presence irks him. "He simultaneously cursed his own people who had sent him this Arab and the Arab who had dared to kill and not managed to get away." But the decision must be made.

Daru solves his dilemma by taking the Arab a two hours' journey across the plateau to where two ways divide. Giving him a thousand francs and enough food to last for two days, he first points out the way to prison, a two-hour walk, and then the way to freedom, a day's journey to the pasturelands where the nomads will take him in and shelter him according to their law. When Daru looks back, later, he sees "with heavy heart" the Arab walking slowly on the road to prison. Still later, back in the classroom, he finds "clumsily chalked up" on the blackboard the words, "You have handed over our brother. You will pay for this."

Camus' story is about the difficulty, the agony, the complexity, the necessity, the worth, and the thanklessness of moral choice. It tells us that moral choice may be difficult and complex, with no clear distinction between good and evil, and with both rational and irrational, selfish and unselfish claims justifying each course of conduct. It tells us that moral choice is a burden which man would willingly avoid if he could, but also that it is part of the human condition which man cannot evade and remain man. It shows us that man defines himself by moral choice, for Daru makes the choice which the reader wants him to make, and establishes his moral worth thereby. But the story also shows that moral decision has no ulterior meaning, for the universe does not reward it. Not only does the Arab fail to take the freedom offered him, but ironically the Arab's tribesmen misinterpret Daru's action and threaten revenge.

In large terms, Daru is representative of moral man, and his desert is representative of the world. Daru is essentially alone in this world, which is "cruel to live in," and life in it has no overarching or transcendental meaning.

> This is the way it was: bare rock covered three quarters of the region. Towns sprang up, flourished, then disappeared; men came by, loved one another or fought bitterly, then died. No one in this desert, neither he nor his guest, mattered.

In Camus' world man lives alone, makes his moral decisions alone, suffers alone, and dies alone. At the end of the story, in consequence of the very action by which Daru has affirmed his selfhood, he has cut himself off from those he had tried to aid. "In this vast landscape he had loved so much, he was alone." His aloneness is both literal and symbolical.

This account is doubtless incomplete, but it provides a context for discussing the major misinterpretations to which the story seems peculiarly subject. These are as follows:

1. *The main conflict is between conscience and society.* Daru must choose between doing what he himself believes right and what is expected of him. He must decide between his own standards and society's.

This interpretation is not so much wrong as it is an oversimplification. It is true that Balducci, the gendarme, is the voice of society, and that by Balducci's standards Daru's duty is clear and unequivocal. It is true also that Daru's immediate human impulse, his individual inner direction, is opposed to Balducci's concept. But the story is not a fictional counterpart of Emerson's *Self-Reliance* or Thoreau's *Civil Disobedience,* with individual right opposed to social wrong. Actually Daru's conscience is divided: it is on both sides of this conflict, and so are his loyalties. He does consider it contrary to honor and humanity to hand the prisoner over; but he is also revolted by the Arab's "stupid crime," which deserves trial and punishment. He does feel loyalty to the Arab as a member of the human race, but he also feels loyalty to his countrymen, with whom he will fight if war breaks out. What is required of Daru is not simply the courage to resist the pressures of society and do what is right, it is the courage to make a moral decision between alternatives neither of which is right. Balducci is not the representative of shallow social convention, nor is his request unreasonable: it makes sense in terms of ordinary "justice" and in terms of the national danger. Balducci, it must be noticed, is not portrayed unsympathetically. Though not so quickly sensitive as Daru, he is a fundamentally decent and kindly man, careful not to ride too fast and hurt the Arab, quick to approve of removing the bonds from the Arab's wrists, still ashamed, when he thinks of it, of putting a rope on another man. Fond of Daru as he is of his own son, he will not denounce Daru and he trusts Daru to tell the truth. He is representative, moreover, as is Daru, of a government which has tried to educate the Arabs and which provides wheat in times of drought. Daru is reluctant to hurt such a man, and feels remorse when he has done so. Conscience, that is, is on Balducci's side as well as on the Arab's.

2. *The story concerns the impossibility of isolating oneself from society and from human responsibility.* Though a man cannot accept the world, he is inevitably a part of the world. However hard he tries to escape it, the world will break in upon him and compel him to acknowledge its claims. (pp. 52-5)

Again, this statement of theme is not so much wrong as it is an oversimplification. The story does show the impossibility of escaping human involvement. But Daru has fled neither responsibility nor mankind. He is an employee of the French government. He is engaged in the responsible task of education. In times of drought he distributes wheat, and deals not only with his pupils but with their fathers. If war comes, he will be a soldier, as he has been before, not a deserter. He has chosen this isolated region to live in because he loves it, not because he hates mankind. "Daru had been born here. Everywhere else, he felt exiled." This is the place where he is rooted, not one that he has fled to. If his schoolhouse is remote from human habitation, it is probably so in order to serve all the neighboring villages equally. Moreover, he "had requested a post in the little town at the base of the foothills"; it was not his own choice that had assigned him to this more isolated spot, where at first he had found "the solitude and the silence" hard to bear.

3. *Daru evades making a decision.* Taking the easy way out, he shifts the entire responsibility for decision to the Arab. By thus refusing to become involved in the affairs of men, he rejects their brotherhood, and the consequences of his failure to act are worse than either of the alternative choices would have been.

It is true that Daru several times wishes he might be relieved of the necessity of choice. It is true also, as one perceptive student wrote, that Daru in pointing out the two ways to the Arab, "was trying to transfer some of the weight of decision from himself to the Arab." *Some* of the weight—precisely. For Daru is not paralyzed by inaction. He does not simply wait in indecision till the authorities or the Arabs crash in on him. By putting the Arab two hours on his way, by giving him a thousand francs and enough food to last two days, Daru takes positive action. The decision to let the Arab make his own decision is itself a decision. In effect, moreover, Daru is presenting the Arab with his freedom, if he will only take it. That the Arab does not take it leaves Daru with a "heavy heart," and is an ironical reward for all his trouble and agitation. He needn't have troubled himself. Except that, by troubling himself, he defines himself as a man, however little the action means to the total cosmos. He has not, like Pilate, washed his hands of evil; rather, in allowing the Arab to make his own choice, he has given the Arab the ultimate freedom—the only real freedom, Camus might say, that men have.

4. *The Arab chooses the road to prison* because *of Daru's kindness.* Responding to Daru's humane treatment, he feels that it would be dishonorable to violate Daru's trust. Like Daru he has a moral decision to make for right or wrong, and, like Daru, he chooses right. This decision is a point of honor to him.

If this interpretation is correct, then Daru's decision has indeed made some impact on the outer world, has meaning, however ironical, beyond a meaning for Daru himself. For this reason the reader who is repulsed by Camus' bleak portrayal of life is tempted to accept it. But it rests on too little evidence. From the beginning the Arab is pictured as passive, uncomprehending, a little stupid. Though his face has "a restless and rebellious look," he at no point makes any motion toward attempting to escape. When Daru asks Balducci, "Is he against us?" Balducci replies, "I don't think so." A prior attempt to escape, or an act of rebellion, would be necessary to establish a change of attitude on the Arab's part after Daru's decision. Instead, his passivity is stressed from the beginning of the story. He first appears, following Balducci, hands bound and head lowered, and the point is made that he not once raises his head. In the schoolroom he squats "motionless in the same spot" and "without stirring." During the night he makes no attempt to get away or to seize Daru's pistol, though he might easily have done so. His incomprehension also is emphasized. When Daru asks him why he killed the cousin, he gives an almost inconsequential answer. When Daru asks, "Are you sorry?" the Arab stares at him openmouthed. "Obviously he did not understand." He sleeps with "his mouth open"; the next morning his expression is "vacant and listless"; when Daru returns, after the journey has begun, to investigate a noise, the Arab watches "without seeming to understand"; when Daru gives him the food and money, he acts "as if he didn't know what to do with what was being given him." The Arab *is,* of course, anxious about his fate at the same time that he seems resigned to it. He wants to know whether Daru is the judge, and whether the gendarme is coming back the next day. He is also warmed by Daru's humanity; but his response is that he wants Daru to accompany him and Balducci to the police headquarters. Exactly what he is trying to communicate to Daru when Daru finally leaves him is of course a matter of speculation.

> The Arab had now turned toward Daru, and a sort of panic was visible in his expression. "Listen," he said.

But a good guess is that he is trying to repeat his earlier request, "Come with us." He doesn't want to be left alone in a hostile world. He wants the man to come with him who has treated him as a human being.

Camus' **"The Guest"** is a subtle and complex story. At one level it tells us about the French situation in Algeria between World War II and the Algerian War, a situation as difficult as Daru's, where also no choices were right ones. But primarily it is less about a political situation than about the human situation. It is about the difficulty, the complexity, the futility, and the glory of human choice. (pp. 56-8)

Laurence Perrine, "Camus' 'The Guest': A Subtle and Difficult Story," in Studies in Short Fiction, *Vol. I, No. 1, Fall, 1963, pp. 52-8.*

Camus on his art:

I cannot live as a person without my art. And yet I have never set that art above everything else. It is essential to me, on the contrary, because it excludes no one and allows me to live, just as I am, on a footing with all. To me art is not a solitary delight. It is a means of stirring the greatest number of men by providing them with a privileged image of our common joys and woes. Hence it forces the artist not to isolate himself; it subjects him to the humblest and most universal truth. And the man who, as often happens, chose the path of art because he was aware of his difference soon learns that he can nourish his art, and his difference, solely by admitting his resemblance to all. The artist fashions himself in that ceaseless oscillation from himself to others, midway between the beauty he cannot do without and the community from which he cannot tear himself. This is why true artists scorn nothing. They force themselves to understand instead of judging. And if they are to take sides in this world, they can do so only with a society in which, according to Nietzsche's profound words, the judge will yield to the creator, whether he be a worker or an intellectual.

From his Nobel Prize acceptance speech (1957)

Anthony Zahareas (essay date 1963)

[In the following excerpt, Zahareas analyzes the characterization of Janine and the themes of alienation and absurdity in "The Adulterous Woman."]

An oscillation between the conviction that man's existence has no meaning and a positive attitude that another road may yet be open to man, is implicit in almost all of Camus's writings. It is the degree of stress upon the one or the other view that generally determines the particular tone of a given work. Since the development of Camus's ideas is often hesitant, tentative, and at many points exploratory, this oscillation results in many contradictions which are not always resolved. This coexistence of two seemingly opposing views springs from his acknowledgment of a paradox: human solidarity in the face of and, in a sense, because of absurdity.

No single piece of Camus's fiction illustrates this paradox more consistently than **"La femme adultère" ["The Adulterous Woman"]**, the two ideas of which—"l'absurd" and "la révolte"—constitute the basic philosophical concepts of all of Camus's work. On the symbolic level, the story is an examination of the meaning of life; its main character, typically, stakes her life on the chances of this earth, and against immortality. Moreover, it contains often-used symbols: water, dryness, night, stars. In short, this carefully planned novelette appears to be just another parable about the absurd isolation of man in a senseless universe. But there yet remains, I think, a deeper level of significance which is communicated by the structure and imagery. **"La femme adultère"** contains the culminating expression of Camus's view of the tragic irony in man's fate. The awareness of life's meaninglessness creates a feeling of absurdity and revolt; such a feeling may intensify man's immediate sense of truth but it can also, if carried too far, deprive him of an awareness of the fellowship between human beings, a fellowship without which life is unbearable; a need for human solidarity, however, can lead man to overcome, temporarily at least, the nihilistic tendencies of the absurd. The real mystery lies, therefore, not in the incomprehensibility of the universe but in the ironic fact that in a world obviously deprived of any meaning, human beings manage somehow to live and act together.

. . . . .

"La femme adultère" is set in the Algerian desert. What there is of plot can be summed up briefly:

Janine, a married woman for some twenty years, accompanies her husband on business. They travel by bus on a cold, windy, winter morning. During the slow, tedious journey Janine recalls her youth and contemplates the fact that she is childless. They arrive in town at noon, eat rapidly, and visit a few Arab stores where her husband sells his products. Around five o'clock they visit a fort, which offers a good view of the desert's vastness; Janine is especially impressed by the black tents of the Nomads in the distance. Back in their room, she is restless, cannot sleep, and is unable to remove the desert from her mind. As if compelled, she gets out of bed, dresses quietly, and leaves the room with all the precautions of a thief. She arrives at the fort alone and in the cold night is momentarily exalted by the starry sky and the mute desert. She finally returns to her room and accidentally awakes her husband. When he notices that she is crying, she tells him that "it is nothing."

The implications of Janine's action, i.e., her "adultery," are developed in four dramatic moments of the narrative: while on the bus, Janine feels a gap between herself and her husband and is filled with revolt against a married life which has lost its original meaning; she sees the Nomads and the absurdity of her particular existence is intensified; she abandons her husband, begins to live out her revolt, and, alone at the fort, experiences momentarily in herself the void of the desert and the universe; finally, she chooses to return to her husband whom she needs but does not love. A closer examination of each of these moments will clarify the novelette's central philosophical lines.

First moment: Janine attempts to pick up a suitcase, but has difficulty bending down. She instantly recalls her youth and specifically her erect but flexible body doing gymnastics and swimming. She is anguished by the relentless passage of time which has made her old and which will lead to death. For twenty years she has been embedded in the habitual, deadening routine of married life. Her past hopes, dreams, and desires are set off by opposition to the limitations of her immediate present:

"Non, rien ne se passait comme elle l'avait cru." "L'été, les plages, les promenades, le ciel même étaient loin." She is suddenly face to face with a life which is senseless. Her absurd condition is symbolized by aridity and barrenness: she did not bear a child and because of her husband's concern with business and future security, she has had a monotonous life.

Second moment: Janine next takes a closer look at the impenetrable, purposeless universe around her. She cannot take her eyes away from the Nomads who in their tents, "sans maisons, coupés du monde, ils étaient une poignée à errer sur le vaste territoire qu'elle découvrait du regard." They are a fitting symbol of the absurd life: tied to the desert and stripped of a purposeful life, they reach an accord with the emptiness of the desert. . . . In their futile traveling, in accepting a life which lacks a definite direction, they become equal to their destiny—like Sisyphus to his rock. The Nomads thus help Janine to grasp consciousness of her own identity with the world and this sets the stage for her nightly escape. "Elle savait seulement que ce royaume, de tout temps, lui avait été promis."

Third moment: Abandoning the warmth of her husband's bed to answer the mute call of the desert, turning her eyes on the expanse of the night, revolving with the stars which "la réunissait peu à peu a son être le plus profond," Janine opens to the emptiness of the desert, becomes aware of the final equality of things, and feels a primitive and serene indifference to everything and even to herself: "Elle respirait, elle oubliait le froid, le poids des êtres, la vie démente ou figée, la longue angoisse de vivre et de mourir." This is the moment of existential fatigue, the moment when man dwells at the threshold of a forbidden kingdom, in anguish and peace, fully aware and as if outside himself. Like Meursault in his prison cell, Janine communicates with the indifference of the world in a moment of detachment.

Fourth moment: Janine finally returns to her husband. This is a puzzling act, a little unexpected, because it has no parallel in Camus's fiction (with the possible exception of the swimming scene in *La Peste*). Yet it has been subtly prepared, and, although a little paradoxical, is never inconsistent. It is central in Camus's ironic vision of the absurd and revolt. Before her escape, Janine reflected upon her husband: "Depuis plus de vingt ans, chaque nuit ainsi, dans sa chaleur, eux deux toujours, même malades, même en voyage comme à present." Now, after her so-called adulterous act, she is not prepared to put an awareness of absurdity above what she and her husband are actually experiencing in their everyday life. Their marriage is characterized by physical love and mutual dependence: "Ils s'aimaient dans la nuit, sans se voir, à tâtons." The expression most often used in the relations between Janine and her husband, that is, the *leit-motif* of their human intercourse, is need (*bésoin*). . . . It is the need not to be alone physically, which links her directly to her husband and establishes a bond between them in the face of the absurd. Need, expressed as physical, immediate dependence becomes a symbol of human solidarity and along with the anguish of the absurd forms an element of common human nature. This need, as opposed to the abstract conception of "love," is a concrete truth in Janine's consciousness; it is neither Christian nor Romantic nor Sentimental: it is viewed as a need of man for man, an experience of love—"by feel" (*à tâtons*)—which remains beyond the reach of rational categories.

The title of the story now becomes clearer: Janine is not adulterous in the literal sense, since she never entertains physical unfaithfulness. Her transgression is directly related to her independence, that is, her momentary rejection of dependence upon her husband. Yet she does not give up for long human dependence in the here and now. "Elle s'accrochait à cette épaule avec une avidité inconsciente, comme à son port le plus sûr." She accepts her limitations, faces an existence without lasting values and certainly without hopes, but not alone. Thus Janine's return is a reaction, paradoxically, against the very forces of the absurd and revolt that lead her to adultery. Her revolt is not nihilistic; the offshoot of nihilism in such a situation would probably be, ironically, real adultery. Her tears in the end, rationally inexplicable, affirm a kind of joint human interest. To paraphrase the last line of *The Myth of Sisyphus:* despite her absurd marriage, one must not imagine Janine totally unhappy.

Camus is very skillful in giving us this transition from "l'absurd" to "le bésoin." He overcomes the difficulties of an abrupt shift by carefully alternating throughout the narrative that feeling of the absurd which leads to the adultery and that anxiety for security which leads to Janine's return. The oscillation during the trip moves from an anguish due to solitude and the passing of time to the consideration that maybe her husband loved her: "elle aimait être aimée . . . elle n'était pas seule"; from feeling tired, useless, and desperate, to the realization that she may not love her husband but that she needs him: she feels his shoulder "avec une avidité inconsciente"; finally, from an urge to leave her husband and run to the fort to a suggestion that her husband's warmth has not been negated: "L'instant d'après, la chaleur du lit la quittait, le froid la saisit."

Two things are important in the above oscillation: first, the expressions of need are only hints, and subtly form a secondary theme under the predominating thematic force of absurdity and revolt; second, the alternation leads to two climaxes: Janine's feeling of independence at the fort and her return to the hotel room to join her husband. Although our last impression is that of her return, this is no indication of an end of the absurd; rather, it is a counteraffirmation of the latent theme of human need. Her return exemplifies both the void felt by someone who experiences the absurd and the emergence of human solidarity.

Up to the end, the predominant theme of absurdity is balanced by the suggestions of the secondary theme of need. Despite the transition from one to the other the thematic balance is maintained in the end: Janine's revolt is not cancelled, but collapses gracefully in the background during her brief but effectively described return. Without the impression of a sudden shift, the action is given over to the secondary theme of need and acceptance of human limitations. Janine's return is personal; it never becomes a proposed solution but rather a clarification of man's position. Immediate need is as much a truth for man as is absurdity or nihilism. In Janine's case, it does not eliminate anguish, but tempers it, at least temporarily. (pp. 319-23)

The coexistence of nihilism and life, of hopelessness and aliveness, of end and continuity breeds a tension of irreconcilable entities in Camus's thought. In **"La femme adultère"** this coexistence is given such an ironic twist that it helps to clarify further Camus's views on the absurd. The one idea around which is spun the novelette's theme is established by Janine's reflection that "nothing turned out as she had expected." The ironic twist—which resembles somewhat the Greek tragedies—is that despite the overpowering truth of this awareness not all was lost, and not all was so terrible. In both outcomes—before and after awareness—what is mocked is first the sentimental and then the rational "fitness" of things. First, things should have turned out: Janine's health should have produced a child, and her sensuality an enjoyable life. The opposite happened. Next, things should not have turned out: Janine finds Marcel unattractive, their marriage purposeless, and their love nonexistent. The opposite again happens because through need and dependence some things do turn out. Marcel's observation on the day's trip, the slowness and discomfort of which becomes symbolic of man's life, is very telling: " . . . le voyage ne serait pas inutile." (p. 327)

Anthony Zahareas, " 'La Femme Adultère': Camus's Ironic Vision of the Absurd," in Texas Studies in Literature and Language, *Vol. V, No. 3, Autumn, 1963, pp. 319-28.*

Manfred Pelz (essay date 1970)

[In the following excerpt from an essay originally published in the journal Die neueren Sprachen, *Pelz discusses the structure and function of the interior monologue in "The Renegade."]*

The English edition of *The Fall* takes a quotation from the Russian novelist [Mikhail Yuryevich] Lermontov as its epigraph: "*A Hero of Our Time,* gentlemen, is in fact a portrait, but not of an individual; it is the aggregate of the vices of our whole generation in their fullest expression." This observation holds true to an even greater extent for

Camus's short story **"The Renegade."** Like Clamence, the renegade missionary is an abstraction; like the former, he embodies an attitude that, together with all its consequences, is examined and illuminated by a penetrating mind. Nevertheless, both works can only be understood as parables. The actual theme consists not of a definite, verifiable subject matter, but rather of the experience of Being that is concealed behind the word in the foreground. The ethical nihilism in the case of Clamence has its equivalent in **"The Renegade"** in a metaphysical nihilism: a diametrical inversion of good and evil. Both heroes are borderline cases; their situation is the *Grenzsituation,* the existential borderline situation. Having experienced the absurdity of the world, they have lost every shred of belief even in the dignity and worth of man. They react to this situation with a cry of despair which only the interior monologue seemed able to capture.

On the whole, interior monologue as the general structural principle of a short story is nonsense. Even in its modern form, the short story requires considerable emphasis on the narrative content as such. (pp. 189-90)

Yet Camus transformed the interior monologue so as to serve the short-story genre as well as his own purposes. Camus refuses to represent his characters' streams of consciousness as "the murmuring of existence that barely escape the inarticulate" [Julius Rütsch, "Situation des französischen Romans," *Trivium:*]. and thereby reduce meaning to external form alone. Interior monologue as it is used [in *The Fall*] is kept under very close control. Clamence had someone to talk to, someone to whom he could pour out his flood of words. His vision was directed outwards: realistic details glimpsed at random were drawn into the monologue situation. A certain continuity could be traced running through his statements. Shifts in setting, albeit within a limited framework, performed specific functions leading up to a carefully prepared effect at the end of the novel. The same characteristics, with some qualifications, are found in **"The Renegade,"** with one clear exception: as in true interior monologue, the missionary has no interlocutor. The words addressed to the Sorcerer at the end of the story ("is it you, Sorcerer . . .") remain totally integrated in the flow of speech and have no bearing either on the narrative content or on the structure of the monologue. Lacking an intermediary to talk to, the narrator addresses the reader directly. It seems that he can only communicate through a self-destructive sadism, a sadism that is even more intense here than in *The Fall.*

But like Clamence, the renegade is able to see. The external world can be an integral part of his thought processes without losing any of its clarity. Corresponding to the constant interplay between past and present is the shift from one to another of three carefully described settings from which two of his memories spring: cool, rainy central France and Taghâsa, the blazing city of salt in the desert. The missionary assumes a symbolic position between them: he sits in the shade beneath a boulder outside the city. At regular intervals his consciousness returns from its memories to this place, only to set out again for one of the two opposite points on the periphery. Evocative power is a function of the temporal and spatial distances involved. The insistent lyrical intensity with which Taghâsa is described stands in sharp contrast to the sober stylization of the French landscape. Three words suffice to characterize the missionary's distant homeland: rain, snow, mountains. In his mouth they betray his dislike of France and the lack of any emotional attachment to it. As in [Camus's] play *Cross-Purpose (The Misunderstanding),* the landscape becomes the vehicle of a thematic statement, and an individual's attitude to it is a symbolic reference to his human condition: "Oh, I wanted to get away, leave them all at once and begin to live at last, in the sunlight, with fresh water." Walled in as if in a prison, one tries to break out and go to a land "over which summer breaks in flame . . . and where . . . things are what they are."

In Taghâsa things are what they are. They have subjugated man and made him part of themselves. The land has usurped man's active role. As if on its own authority, the city has chiseled itself out of the salt: "the white terraces . . . had all together tackled a mountain of salt. . . . " Its inhabitants are pillars of salt rising up out of the seething substratum of boiling crystal. Here, too, a thematic statement is woven into the description of a landscape: nature no longer confronts man with a benign indifference, but rather is made so intense that it becomes a power destroying everything human. Being is experienced as a chaos into whose whirlpool all living things plunge as soon as they reach a high enough level of consciousness. The recurring symbols for this experience are sun and salt.

This clarifies the distinction between the monologue as Camus uses it and true interior monologue. The latter "does not see; it directly gives voice to the incalculable slimy debris of the existing consciousness" [Rütsch, 1955]. The missionary's speech, on the other hand, is a mixture of perception and proper motion. In addition to the impersonal "murmuring of existence" there is a narrative component, the description that originates in memory. In this way the "narrative," which interior monologue has gradually driven out of fiction, again increases in constitutive significance. The amorphous monologue becomes a goal-oriented report. As such, it can portray events and the places connected with them.

More strikingly than in the other stories in the book, the first paragraph of **"The Renegade"** immediately introduces us to the situation of importance for the narrator. The curious ambivalence of perspective is already unmistakable in **"The Silent Men."** Yvars is surrounded by sparkling sunlight, but he seems not to notice it. His situation is the inability to see: Yvars is cut off from all communication. The same is true of Janine: the image of the fly at the beginning of **"The Adulterous Woman"** suggests a situation from which there is no exit. In both stories the events that follow confirm the impression given in the opening sentences.

The missionary's situation consists of an inner compulsion to speak. He is the "garrulous slave" An irrepressible torrent of words forces its way out of his mouth in a "jumble." They seem to come from an unknown depth for which this particular person is a mere mouthpiece. But the narrator himself is aware of this fact; he is not a "confused mind" in an absolute sense. He tries to put his thoughts in order. In the French edition, the word *ordre* appears four times on the first page alone. As a result of his efforts, statements about the narrative content become more lucid toward the end of the introductory paragraph. The reader learns that the narrator's tongue has been cut out; this comment elevates the whole monologue to an almost ironically distanced and irreal plane. An exact time and place is specified: "Here I am on the trail, an hour away from Taghâsa. . . . Day is breaking over the desert." In the cold desert morning someone from whom we have heard only empty phrases is waiting for someone else; a missionary who is supposed to pass by this spot sometime during the day. The narrator's attention is totally fixed on that event, so that the monologue situation is augmented by a suspense-building sense of anticipation that is sustained until the story's end.

The first paragraph, then, has two functions to perform:

1. It introduces the interior monologue of a narrator who is completely unknown to the reader. A momentary glance back at the past ("I always longed for order") must be left for the time being before it can offer any approach to a deeper understanding of the story. The nature of the speech itself together with a statement about the content ("I've been here I don't know how many years") create an atmosphere of formless and timeless flowing to which the narrator seems to have been helplessly abandoned.

2. It orients the monologue situation to a real event. The physical mutilation of the narrator, the details of time and place, and the reference to the missionary all call for an explanation. Questions come to mind: Who is delivering this monologue? What was his past like? What does he plan to do? Only the unfolding of the story that follows will give the answers.

Both of these functions, each in its own way, are at work throughout the entire monologue: the first as a sense of entrapment or of being enclosed that results from the very act of delivering a monologue, the second as a development and clarification of the narrator's situation which is left vague at the story's outset. It seems to be the main concern of the story to present these two functions as concretely as possible. (pp. 191-95)

The missionary's interior monologue takes place within a fixed temporal framework such as has become characteristic of all Camus's work. The monologue situation spans a full day, beginning in the early morning hours of an arbitrary day and lasting until well after nightfall. The function of the narrative forms used varies during this time: the monologue report that recalls the earliest facts of a distant past changes, more pronouncedly as it nears the present, and finally takes the form of narration. At the same time, the object of our anticipation becomes more and more clear. Retrospection turns into expectation as the narrator looks forward to a definite event in the near future. When this event finally takes place, the interior monologue merges with the present.

Statements about the narrative content are related to the time of day and the changing intensity of the sunlight. Memories of Europe, the rain and snow in the mountains, and the misty horizons correspond to the cold of the desert morning. The narrator's attitude to this part of his past is one of rejection. As the sun climbs higher in the sky, the tone grows calmer. It reaches its lowest pitch at noon in the account of the missionary's arrival in Taghâsa. This second narrative segment stands at the exact center of the interior monologue. It tells of the most important fact in the renegade's life: his encounter with evil and his capitulation. Everything that has gone before has led up to this moment; everything that follows takes its departure from it. There is good reason to regard this point as the axis of the story's structure and meaning. For a moment the flow of narration slows to a standstill. It is as if the narrator could only put himself in touch with the past intuitively. The accounts of both of the other episodes come in the afternoon. They are shorter and no longer have the autonomy of the central event. In comparison with them, the description of the narrator's inner development increases in significance. He undergoes a catharsis for the sake of evil. The interior monologue, now the vehicle of the missionary's settling of accounts with Christianity, swells to a hymn of hatred that celebrates evil as the central principle of Being. The speech becomes even more intense as evening approaches. A sense of inevitability, already suggested by the monologue situation itself, is the result. The development leads with logical necessity to a climax that is reached as night falls. As at the story's beginning, the cold of the time of day corresponds to a hatred that nearly overwhelms the narrator. Here, as at the beginning, sadism takes the form of self-destructive masochism, with the difference that at the outset of the interior monologue it was grounded in memory alone ("I wanted to be offended") while now it is expressed as an agony experienced in reality and relished with enthusiasm: "Ah! the pain, the pain they cause me, their rage is good and on this cross-shaped war-saddle where they are now quartering me, pity! I'm laughing, I love the blow that nails me down crucified."

There are no more climaxes in the rest of the interior monologue. The reader participates in the inner growth of a new decision: the reconversion of the renegade missionary. The consciousness of the defeat he has suffered is compounded by the consciousness of possible guilt: "Ah! supposing I were wrong again!" Both statements continue to be of fundamental significance throughout the rest of the story. They generate a dialectical tension that brings the interior monologue close to analytical reflection—but it is a reasoning process for which there seems to be no rationally tenable conclusion. With the return to the world of love and kindness a new narrative phase sets in, one which directly reproduces the momentary fluctuations of mental processes and which grows imperceptibly out of the first part of the interior monologue. At this point Camus interrupts the flow of the monologue. The last sentence is written from the author's point of view: "A handful of salt fills the mouth of the garrulous slave." The shift of perspective, a common structural principle found in most stories, is used only at this salient point in **"The Renegade,"** and so offers the most important approach to an interpretation of the story.

. . .The style of **"The Renegade"** is marked by a single characteristic: the monologue situation. Consequently, it is a "spoken style" in the truest sense. As such, it is the direct expression of the narrator and his situation, a situation that can be characterized as one of entrapment or of being enclosed. The narrator is helplessly abandoned to his situation: he must speak, virtually in spite of himself. The stream of words and sentences flows out of his mouth incessantly without first being ordered and clarified by an overseeing intellect. Punctuation is used only rarely and irregularly. What seems to be of importance is not unity of syntax, but rather the more significant unity of meaning, which at the lyrical climaxes of the narrative flow coincides with the limits of the respective passages.

The most emphatic intensity of speech is found at the beginning and end of the story, as well as at those points where the narrator considers his current situation. Here the monologue becomes a direct comment on the present and seems to be functionally dependent on extrahuman phenomena. The concentrated use of light and heat metaphors, the expressions of the strong, the enormous, and the mineral, and the evocative power of the description all point to a power beyond conscious thought and action for which the narrator is only an intermediary and a mouthpiece.

In the middle of the story the tone grows calmer without letting this impression fade. Clearly outlined events from the immediate past emerge from the flowing stream of consciousness, but they seem to lack concreteness. The narrator sees the past only at an irreal distance. *He* does not speak about it, but rather *it* seems to speak out of him. The heavy use of perfective tenses, especially the present perfect (*passé composé*), marks everything the narrator says and does as something that has always been. The "I" of the present moment is totally different from the "I" of yesterday. As in *The Stranger,* it looks at itself: it is a stranger to itself.

What should this style be called? Behind it one detects an elemental inability to act otherwise, an enormous "must," the depths of a mind from which the boundaries have been removed. The flow of the monologue has no end, not even when a real event takes place within it. In the end, it is mere formalism, an indulgence in "intoxicating quantitative conceptions" [Karl Jaspers, *The Perennial Scope of Philosophy*], in power without positive thematic content—a style, therefore, of absolute entrapment in a situation. Camus recognizes this as a symptom of our time and counters it with the sharpest criticism: by virtue of his authorship he uses the final sentence to interrupt the interior monologue with an abrupt, almost cynical stroke. In this way the renegade's fall maintains its homogeneous character to the end and is once again glaringly illuminated with biting irony by this closing gesture. In this harsh light the possible reconversion of the missionary finds no justification—it is at best a stylistic device to provide contrast. (pp. 199-202)

Manfred Pelz, "The Function of Interior Monologue in 'The Renegade'," translated by Stephen K. Wright, in Essays on Camus's "Exile and the Kingdom," *edited by Judith D. Suther, Romance Monographs, Inc., 1980, pp. 189-202.*

Donald Lazere (essay date 1973)

[*Lazere is an American educator and critic. In the following excerpt, he disparages the style and polemical tone of the "The Growing Stone" and suggests that the story's weaknesses are evidence of Camus's difficulties with the short story genre.*]

"The Growing Stone" presents the most optimistic version of [***Exile and the Kingdom***'s] recurrent themes, which is undoubtedly one reason Camus placed it last. It also has the most involved plot: D'Arrast, the engineer exiled for reasons we never learn from his native France, comes to Iguape, Brazil, to build a dike protecting the poor section of the town from a flooding river. There he is annoyed by the superstitious local Catholicism and by the white bureaucracy—the mayor, the chief of police who drunkenly harasses him, the inevitable judge, predictably grandiloquent and self-righteous, who insists against D'Arrast's will that the police chief be punished for his indiscretion. He feels more companionship toward the poverty-stricken black natives, but they resent his presence. He finally befriends a mulatto ship's cook with whom he attends a night of Dionysian native dancing, but as the dancing nears orgiastic pitch, the cook approaches D'Arrast: "Coldly, as if speaking to a stranger, he said: 'It's late, Captain. They are going to dance all night long, but they don't want you to stay now.' " Afterward D'Arrast reflects morosely: "Yonder, in Europe, there was shame and wrath. Here, exile or solitude, among these listless and convulsive madmen who danced to die."

The cook, recently saved from a shipwreck, has vowed in gratitude to Jesus to carry a hundred-pound stone on his head to the church in the procession at the Festival of the Good Jesus, so named for a statue of Christ placed in a grotto where another stone miraculously grows and replaces the bits chipped off by pilgrims. But, too weak willed to refrain from dancing until dawn the night before the procession, the exhausted cook hasn't the strength to reach the church with his penitential burden. D'Arrast picks up the fallen stone for his friend, carrying it on his own head but continuing with it past the church, against the cries of the townspeople, to the cook's miserable hut, where his family, previously hostile to D'Arrast, now ask him to sit down among them.

This ending is obviously laden with symbolism. D'Arrast is rejecting official social institutions—government, church, civic endeavors (the dike he is to build)—in favor of a personal bond between men. Camus may be expressing in parable form his pessimism over all social organization, partially offset by his faith in individual relationships, particularly those between well-meaning whites and colonized natives; certainly the latter relationship ends more promisingly here than in **"The Guest."** By carrying the rock to the cook's hut instead of to the church, the agnostic D'Arrast affirms secular love for men over sacred love for Jesus; he feels more brotherhood with the cook for his fleshly frailty of will than for his religious resolution. In Camus's familiar technique of reversing Christian symbolism, the rock D'Arrast carries away from the church suggests the rock of Peter, on which a secular church will be built, or the cross carried by a Christ in opposition to the mystical Christianity that distracts the poor natives from their human condition. In place of the supernatural growing stone in the grotto of the Good Jesus, D'Arrast's stone grows from one man's burden into a symbol of shared, earthly responsibility. Camus must also have chosen this symbol of solidarity as a counterpart to *The Myth of Sisyphus,* where Sisyphus's rock was his solitary burden.

"The Growing Stone" is one of Camus's weaker pieces of writing. The Crucifixion symbolism of the ending, which he has used so many times previously, has become tiresomely predictable and is exposed heavy-handedly, with too abrupt a shifting of gears from the previous realistic mode. In realistic terms it is implausible, if not downright silly; the last thing a destitute native family needs is a hundred-pound rock in the middle of their living room. The story reveals no lucid political consciousness of the colonial situation; its tone, on the contrary, is patronizing toward the noble savages. D'Arrast's background in insufficiently developed. What has his life been previously? Why has he left Europe? What is the promise he has failed to keep? Up to the night of dancing, the story is too long, with tedious, superfluous stretches of local color that Camus took from the notebooks of his 1949 trip to Brazil for realistic authenticity. (He is a rather pedestrian writer when he attempts passages of straight realism; he is at his best when he blends realistic with symbolic or lyrical elements.) Several strands of plot and symbolism are also incompletely developed—for instance, the dike, which seems to be forgotten halfway through the story, or D'Arrast's attraction to the "black Diana," presumably the cook's sister or niece. She is among the family who welcomes D'Arrast at the end, but we get no hint of where their potentially provocative relationship might lead. Imagery of water is prominent throughout the story, but its significance is vague. There is a suggestion, as in **"The Adulterous Woman,"** that it is associated with sexual potency, particularly near the end, when "the sound of the waters filled him with a tumultuous happiness. With eyes closed, he joyfully acclaimed his own strength; he acclaimed, once again, a fresh beginning in life. At that moment, a firecracker went off that seemed very close." But this theme too is inadequately developed.

"The Growing Stone" is the most obvious instance of the impression the whole book gives that Camus had not fully mastered the short-story form. **"The Guest"** is the only story that ranks with the three novels in successful cohesion of theme, structure, expository technique, characterization, and realistic and symbolic elements. **"The Renegade"** is perhaps equally well written but is emotionally unmoving, perhaps because its narrator is the only one of Camus's central characters who is totally unsympathetic. **"The Adulterous Woman"** is too obviously written around the tour de force ending; like **"The Growing Stone,"** the realistic scene setting of its first half is somewhat listless and unnecessarily long. **"The Artist at Work,"** on the other hand, is a moderately effective study in satirical realism up to the ending where, as in **"The Growing Stone,"** the sudden shift to highly contrived symbolism disrupts the previous development and tone. **"The Silent Men"** is successful as far as it attempts to go but is too short for us to become fully absorbed in its characters or situation. It and **"The Growing Stone"** might have served better as points of departure for longer fictional works; in fact, **"The Silent Men"** may provide us with a hint of the direction Camus would have taken in the work based on his youth in Algiers that he projected in the 1958 preface to *L'Envers et l'endroit.* But the subjects of these and several of the other stories are also precisely those he had had the least success dealing with in depth: realistically portrayed working-class and colonial situations, marital relationships, the feminine viewpoint. Perhaps his very choice of the short-story medium, which is a constricted one to begin with and which by the 1950s was becoming even more obsolescent than the novel, was a tacit admission of his inability to treat these subjects with the fullness they require. (pp. 207-10)

Donald Lazere, in his The Unique Creation of Albert Camus, *Yale University Press, 1973, 271 p.*

Lev Braun (essay 1974)

[Lev Braun is a Czechoslovakian-born American educator and critic. In the following excerpt, he interprets "The Silent Men" as an expression of Camus's political beliefs and his understanding of the problems facing the working class in the industrial age.]

"I did not learn rebellion in Marx, I learnt it in misery," wrote Camus when lectured by Sartre about working-class solidarity. The fact is that, in contrast to many French radical intellectuals of bourgeois background, Camus related to the proletariat without effort and had no feeling of hereditary sin concerning his origins. Accordingly, there is nothing compulsive in Camus's attitude with regard to social problems, and he is not obsessed with revolutionary romanticism. In fact—leaving out *State of Siege,* in which the Plague symbolizes the totalitarian system, not capitalism—Camus's writings are inspired only twice with a revolutionary mood: during the Spanish war, with *Revolt in Asturia,* and, for a brief period, after the liberation of Paris. Otherwise, Camus was a radical reformist convinced that social justice could and should be enforced by democratic means. This, however, did not exclude conflict; indeed, it presupposed unrelenting pressure, and nothing could be further removed from Camus's outlook than a naïve belief in plain good will. A convinced trade-unionist, he believed that nothing could be gained without strikes and the threat of social disorder. What worried him was the increasing control of the French trade unions by the Communist Party, and the dehumanization of the class struggle in the age of large industry, materialism, and the masses. (pp. 229-30)

[In 1955, Camus] published a short story conceived a few years earlier, about a strike in a small cooper shop in Algiers. . . . The short story, **"The Silent Men,"** which describes the coopers' feelings, was called half jokingly by Camus "an exercise in socialist realism." The coopers had always been silent, and in exploring their inner lives Camus goes back to the figures of his childhood: his silent mother and the uncomplicated men and women of Belcourt. The "Mediterranean man," as described in Camus's earlier short stories, had a brief youth, centered on bodily pleasures, then an endless middle-age, the boredom of which was relieved by work, the reading of sports papers, and an occasional drink of anisette. Such was his fate, for "there was no other form of happiness in this country" than physical life "and that happiness disappeared with youth." The picture is familiar to every reader of Camus's books. Yet, as we know, the "Mediterranean man" does not become positively unhappy, for he has a sense of the beauty of the world and lives attuned to nature. Thus feels Yvars, watching the night fall on the terrace at the moment his neighbors "would suddenly lower their voices": "At least he felt in harmony at such moments; he had nothing to do but wait quietly, without quite knowing for what." Such was his basic understanding of the world. His wife and child were so much a part of the substance of his existence that he was hardly conscious of their presences, yet they added warmth and security to his life. Yvars would call himself "happy," meaning that he was, on the whole, content.

For such a man, work in a small cooper's shop had nothing in common with the industrial inferno Camus later discovered in Paris. The work required skill and care, and Yvars was proud of his proficiency. The love of work well done as an essential part of a worker's life is never mentioned in the story, but it is suggested as closely as possible as the reader follows Yvars's thoughts: "The good cooper, the one who fits his curved staves and tightens them in the fire with an iron hoop almost hermetically, without rafia or oakum. . . . " The concrete terminology drives the point home. Camus's uncle had worked in such a small cooper's shop; such talk must have been familiar to him as a boy.

The kind of life described here is that of artisans. It is a hard life, but lived at a human level. The work itself, far from being a curse, could give meaning to one's life if only the pay were a little better, so that there would be no need to work overtime on Saturdays and even on Sundays to bring one's child up decently. The other men were old acquaintances; comradeship in work *almost* blotted out national and racial difficulties, although the Arab mentioned here is only a helper. As for the boss, "he was not a bad sort." He still remembered that his father had been an apprentice; he lived in a modest middle-class house almost enclosed in the shop, in which his whole life was encompassed. Hardly more sophisticated than his workers, he remained chummy, although he had become Monsieur Lasalle; moreover, his whole life, his very presence, was a reminder that every good worker could become a boss in due course. This had happened to Camus's own uncle and would have been the luck of his father, too, had he not been killed at Verdun.

This was a human world, or rather had been a human world, for it was dying out. Camus is acutely conscious of this: "What can coopers do when the cooper-age disappears?" The pathos of this deceptively simple story is derived from the subtle interplay of human emotions and inhuman economic laws which drive men against each other and reject them out of humanity.

What can coopers do in the age of the large container factory? "One does not change trades at forty." This is not due to dumbness, but to something else: "You don't change trades when you have gone to the trouble of learning one. . . . Changing trades is nothing, but to give up what you know, your master craftsmanship, is not easy." Your trade is part of your being. But all trades are disappearing, together with the cooper-age, and craftsmen become gradually hollowed out. One day, they will go and work in a container factory, submit to clock work and the assembly line, and forego their pride of craftsmanship. This is the tragedy of the men whose human dignity is threatened because their talents are no longer wanted and they themselves are destined to a kind of work in which the difference between good workers and bad workers is blurred; all are interchangeable, and none of them will ever be able to build a shop of his own.

What can cooper bosses do if the situation pits them against one another as competitors and against their employees for the sharing of diminished profits? Then the worst features in human nature come out. Until then, patriarchal conditions had prevailed. Camus does not idealize them, knowing the kind of conflicts and unavoidable resignation they entailed. But he clearly prefers them to the industrial world. In the cooper-age, the system was hierarchical, yet it did not exclude human equality, born of daily contacts and mutual esteem; and it was alleviated both by the hope of a better lot for oneself or one's children, and by the existence of trade unions, whose equalizing role was the main source of the workers' dignity. Small enterprise and trade unions made working conditions bearable. However, conditions were changing and Camus's prevalent mood was pessimistic at the time he wrote the story; his compulsion to go back to the world of his childhood at that time was probably due to his nostalgia for a dying world that was hard materially, but in which the absurdity of life was compensated by human values and natural beauty. To Camus, the new world seemed not only hard materially, but without beauty or values. This new world is not shown in the story, since the protagonists are not aware of its looming. They just feel that times are getting difficult, and they react by hardening their relations to one another: The boss refuses a raise, although he knows that the cost of living is going up. He acts selfishly, in order to preserve his profits. How else should it be? Can one expect the boss to be a saint? Moreover, he has to act as other bosses do, or face ruin. He is partly selfish and partly caught. The workers understand that. They need a raise. So, they resort to their old weapon: the strike. A half-hearted strike, half-heartedly backed by the union, which has other business to take care of than looking after a handful of outmoded artisans. The strike fails, of course, and the class conflict between boss and workers hardens into irreparable hostility which nobody really wanted.

Once again, as in **"The Guest,"** the tragedy is one of lost brotherhood and mutual incomprehension. The initial guilt rested with the boss. He not only refused the raise, but did it in an offensive way—probably to overcome his bad conscience and his suspicion that his own trade was becoming unwanted. His take-it-or-leave-it attitude infuriated the workers, who embarked on a punitive strike. Here was a subtle paradox: embittered class conflict prevailed

Camus (kneeling at front, in black apron) at his uncle's cooperage, 1920.

where all were unconscious victims of a developing new order of things. The boss stood by his bosshood, the workers by their rights, although it was really a matter of coopers surviving the end of the cooper-age and, in fact, of independent work.

After the failure of the strike, the defeated workers devised another punishment for the boss: silence. Perhaps devised is the wrong word, for nothing was agreed among them and none of them decided it. It was less a decision than a natural outcome of an inextricable situation. On the day work resumed, Yvars's wife was worried: "What will you men say to him?"—"Nothing." Indeed, there was nothing to say. And a wave of silence fell upon the workshop. The boss had intended to show his masterhand once more by letting the men wait in front of closed doors in the morning, and then return to joviality; but his high spirits collapsed before the sullen silence of the men. In an interview with the oldest worker, he said what he should have said before the strike: that "when business picks up," he would give them the raise without even being asked. His proposal failed to dispel the gloom. Why? Were they so hurt by his earlier high-handedness, or did they all know that business would never pick up, that it was all "wind"? Sullenness set in, as in **"The Guest."** Nobody wanted it, but it happened. Perhaps they were taking out on each other their anguish at being survivors of the cooper-age? All that is obscure. Only, "anger and helplessness sometimes hurts so much that you can't even cry out." Here, as in **"The Guest,"** it is insinuated that at one point men lose their grip on the situation and inhuman laws start grinding. In **"The Guest,"** the fleeting moment when brotherhood and generosity could prevail was hardly perceptible, and the blind determinism of race hatred was unmistakably symbolized by the writing on the wall: "You handed over our brother, you will pay for this." In **"The Silent Men,"** the opposite occurs: the fleeting moment becomes a clear opportunity to make peace—when the boss's child is taken dangerously ill and all the men are genuinely anxious. However, the men remain silent. Not that they want to, but they cannot help it. They were silent by nature, shy in expressing their emotions; then they become deliberately silent. Now, they are numb. Although the boss has again become a man to them, they still find nothing to say to him: "When it occurred to Yvars that someone ought to call him, the door had already closed." Later on, when talking about it to his wife, he concluded: "It is his own fault!" Here the words on the wall are written almost imperceptibly. But they are written.

In this story of refusal, a minute symbolic incident is inserted. It is as ambiguous as in **"The Guest."** The workers' hostility to the boss brought them nearer to each other. In this new atmosphere of warmth, during the lunch break, Yvars suddenly noticed Saïd, the Arab helper, lying in a pile of shavings. Perhaps he dimly sensed that they had been behaving to Saïd as the boss to them. In the new mood of class brotherhood, he approached him, somewhat hesitantly, and asked him if he had already finished. Saïd said he had eaten his figs. Yvars stopped eating. The uneasy feeling that hadn't left him since the interview with Lassalle suddenly disappeared to make room for a pleasant warmth. He broke his bread in two as he got up and, faced with Saïd's refusal, said that everything would be better next week. "Then it'll be your turn to treat," he said. Saïd smiled. Now he bit into the piece of Yvars's sandwich, but in a gingerly way, like a man who isn't hungry.

"The Silent Men" inevitably brings to mind some pieces of pre-war French social literature, such as Jean Guéhenno's *Journal d'un homme de quarante ans* and, Louis Guilloux's *La Maison du Peuple,* to which Camus wrote a preface in 1953 for a new edition. Guilloux's short masterpiece is in many ways in keeping with Camus's own feeling of life among the poor, as expressed in **"The Silent Men"** and *The Right and the Wrong Side of Things.* This similarity is due to complex factors. First and foremost is the fact that both writers were born among the poor and could speak from firsthand experience. As Camus observes ironically in his preface to *La Maison du Peuple,* "Almost all the French writers who set themselves forth as speaking for the people today were born of rich or well-to-do families. . . . One can try to explain this paradox by asserting—like a wise friend of mine—that by speaking of what you don't know you eventually learn it." What Camus resents in those self-appointed spokesmen is what he regards as their false tone: either a glorification of "the proletariat" or "the masses," born of the bourgeois intellectual's own guilt feeling or revolutionary busybodiness (it is easy to guess whom Camus has in mind); or the high-handed sociological approach of the "experts in progress" who study the proletariat as "a tribe with peculiar customs." It is hard to say what is more insulting—the "disgusting sycophancy" of the former or the "candid contempt" of the latter. Those who have experienced poverty, Camus observes, tend to be impatient with those who speak about it without firsthand knowledge.

Besides their proletarian origins, Camus and the social writers he mentions have something else in common: they speak of a world that is no longer theirs, since they have become intellectuals and comparatively well off. Moreover, they speak of the world of their youth that was already anachronistic at the time they lived in it. Their warmheartedness is mingled with a double nostalgia—for their youth, and for the by-gone age of artisans, when work still had a soul.

Today's proletariat has little in common with old-time artisans. It looms on the horizon as an unknown factor in history and has indeed acquired the quality of "a tribe with strange customs"; *the masses* is a hideous phrase, suggesting some human raw material, explosive and undifferentiated, that aimlessly proliferates where there used to be men and women of the people. Although Camus does not care to admit it, the new proletariat is as strange to him as to "bourgeois intellectuals" or "experts in progress." Camus's notes and letters show that the discovery of large-scale industry was a kind of nightmare to him. The industrial inferno he discovered in Paris and Saint Etienne on his arrival in Metropolitan France found no place in Camus's artistic work. Perhaps the experience was too overwhelming. It just influenced—negatively—the nostalgic remembrance of *The Stranger* and ***Exile and the Kingdom.*** (pp. 230-36)

Lev Braun, in his Witness of Decline: Albert Camus, Moralist of the Absurd, *Farleigh Dickinson University Press, 1974, 283 p.*

English Showalter, Jr. (essay date 1984)

[Showalter is an American educator and critic. In the following excerpt, he examines "The Guest" as an expression of the existential conflict between meaning and nothingness and criticizes the emphasis that other commentators have placed on the issue of French colonialism in Algeria in their interpretations of the story.]

One character aids or shelters another who would normally be the former's enemy. This literary topos, which lies at the heart of Camus's **"The Guest,"** can be found in many versions, from folklore and legend to modern popular culture. It was especially popular with the romantics, in works like *Hernani* and *The Lady of the Lake,* and with other writers preoccupied with heroism, like Corneille and Saint-Exupéry. In these heroic versions, the guest's identity is often revealed late, and the host is presumed to be strongly motivated to harm the guest, even as he protects him in accordance with the laws of hospitality. Typically, the guest responds to this honorable behavior by promising to return for a second encounter between equals.

Camus gives us a distinctly modern variant, which could be outlined—still very abstractly—as follows. A schoolteacher in an isolated area is ordered by a policeman to keep a prisoner overnight and conduct him to jail. The teacher treats the prisoner kindly, offers him several opportunities to escape, and in the end gives him food and money and shows him the road to freedom. The prisoner, however, takes the road toward the jail.

Not only are schools, police, and prisons institutions of the modern state, but also the teacher's attitude reflects a very contemporary alienation. Policeman and teacher, agents of the same social order—indeed, both civil servants in this story—share no common sense of law. The conflict that was internal in the heroic versions has given way to a division of labor and the alienation that it entails. Yet the policeman and the teacher of the story are not enemies, either; they share a racial, cultural, and class background in contrast to the prisoner; and before the incident of the story, they had been friends.

With so bare an outline, one could imagine several reasons for the teacher's attitude: approval of the prisoner's crime, or belief that the prisoner had not committed any crime, or doubt that the prisoner would be treated fairly, or fear, or inability to carry out the orders. None of these, however, is the reason given by the story. The teacher, Daru, expresses no sympathy for the prisoner's act or any mistrust of the judicial system, and Camus has taken some pains to establish Daru's ability to do the job. He simply does not want to because he does not want to accept that responsibility. If he suffers from any inner conflict, it is of a sort quite different from the dilemmas of the romantic heroes, for he feels no desire at all to harm his guest. Despite the fact that the man has committed murder, Daru feels no obligation to participate in the process by which society attempts to deter such crimes.

The prisoner's last gesture, then, is highly ironic, a black parody of Hernani's vow to reconstitute himself prisoner of Don Ruy. It remains, moreover, unexplainable. As we shall see, many suggestions have been advanced to justify the prisoner's decision; but with the story narrated rigorously from Daru's perspective, there can be no fully persuasive explanation. In the earlier versions, the comparable twist in plot transformed this topos from mere episode to plot element by installing some weight from the past within the hero. Camus ends the encounter at this parting, but Daru's concern about the prisoner's decision reveals an involvement in it that contradicts his previous professions of indifference. Like it or no, he too has been weighted with the responsibility of the prisoner.

Camus, of course, added a final, uniquely modern touch of irony. When he returns to his school, Daru finds a threat written on the blackboard: "You handed over our brother. You will pay for this." This message contains still more mystery than the prisoner's actions. We never know the identity of its authors or their actual relationship to the prisoner; for "brother" can be taken literally, as blood kin, or more loosely, as an active member of some organization (a political party, for example), or more loosely still, as a passive member of some group (fellow countryman, for example). Why they prefer making the threat to freeing the so-called brother, an easy task under the circumstances, is not explained. And, of course, we never learn what happens afterward.

I have deliberately generalized this story before mentioning its most important particulars. Set in Algeria in the mid-1950s, it is the only story that alludes to the political crisis of the time. The prisoner is an Arab; Daru and the gendarme, Balducci, are both "pieds-noirs," Algerian-born of European descent. Balducci refers vaguely to the rebellious violence that led ultimately to the end of French rule in Algeria, and both he and Daru wonder whether the Arab might be a revolutionary terrorist, although they think not. Now, a quarter of a century later, Algeria has long since won its independence from France; but the real problem touched on has by no means disappeared. Given Camus's personal involvement in the early stages of debate, critics have quite naturally looked for political interpretations. In my view, this is a mistake. In revising, Camus consistently softened the possible contacts between fiction and reality. As the real conflict worsened, Camus made the story less and less precise. One could easily transpose the story into dozens of other settings without significantly altering its meaning.

To be sure, many elements drawn from reality support the basic story line. It is useful that racial, religious, linguistic, cultural, and class differences parallel the radical difference between an accused prisoner and everyone else—useful, but not necessary. Equally useful, at least for the moment, is the well-known existence of a liberation movement in Algeria; one accepts without question the rumors of a forthcoming revolt, knowing that in fact it came. But in how many places, in how many causes, have similar resistances occurred by now? A fictional underground would serve as well. We are accustomed by the events of our age to credit such things, including their most important trait, a certain irrational violence, born of weakness and anger. This trait, in the end, was as much a mark of the reactionary "Algérie française" movement, the clandestine secret army organization (O.A.S.) and terrorists of the right, as of nationalist or leftist guerrillas at the start. **"The Guest"** has nothing to teach about the Algerian conflict, except insofar as its problems were those of all conflicts, in all ages and in all places, between all sorts of people and for all sorts of reasons.

The question that inevitably preoccupies readers of this story is why the Arab takes the road east toward Tinguit, where the jail is, instead of the path south toward the plateau, where the nomads will provide protection. . . . Roughly speaking, we can judge the Arab along four scales. First, and most basic I think, a passive/active scale: is he docile and dependent, or is he deliberate and autonomous? Second, a social/asocial scale: is he allied with an Algerian nationalist movement, or is he a loner, acting for personal reasons? The first two scales deal with questions of fact, although that does not imply that we can give a clear yes or no answer. The third scale concerns his placement in a social category: is he to be regarded primarily as a criminal, or as a victim of circumstances beyond his control? Within this scale would fall the matter of his guilt or innocence in the murder for which he was arrested, with all the extenuating circumstances that the judicial system recognizes; but also, more broadly, the possibility that French justice has intruded into a foreign domain, so that the Arab, having acted under one set of principles, is now to be tried under a different set that he may not even comprehend. Finally, the fourth scale of interpretation is really literary: is the Arab a hero—one who incarnates the author's conception of good or right behavior in some fashion—or is he a villain—one who denies the author's message or remains unaware of it and obstructs its accomplishment?

Each of the four scales can be applied independently of the others, so that there are sixteen possible characterizations, with of course a considerable range of shadings within many of them. Roughly, they can be arranged as follows:

The Arab as hero. In general, such interpretations look on the Arab's decision to go to jail as an effort to help Daru in one way or another. If the Arab is taken to be more intelligent and purposeful than he seems, then his choice is an existentialist's act of assuming responsibility. Whether he is a rebel or a loner, whether he is a common criminal or the hapless victim of an unjust colonial regime, he is sufficiently affected by Daru's fraternal attitude to be converted. His choice may represent an effort to please Daru, to honor Daru's system of justice, to dignify Daru's inevitable and unjust punishment. If, on the other hand, the Arab is taken to be ignorant, passive, and helpless, his final act is hardly a choice at all but a pathetic mistake. He may be trying to please Daru, or he may be so conditioned to dependence that he is afraid of freedom, or he simply may not understand and be taking the more familiar route. In any case, he means Daru no harm. If he has been a rebel, he must be trying to please an unexpectedly kind man. If the other was an existentialist reading, this one is liberal or humanist. Both Daru and the Arab (and even Balducci) are men of good will, trying to do the right thing, yet bringing misfortune on each other. The Arab's character, his passivity and ignorance, his possible rebelliousness and criminality, are creations of the government Daru represents.

The Arab as villain. The most extreme interpretation would make the Arab a conscious terrorist, who goes in the direction of Tinguit to deny Daru any sense of brotherhood; we do not know, after all, that he goes as far as the jail. One critic has suggested even that he turns himself in to provoke increasing violence, sacrificing himself as a sort of martyr for the revolution. It is perhaps more plausible to suppose that his "brothers" had planned an ambush along the road to Tinguit, and that he expects to rejoin them. If we consider the Arab as a loner, his motive must be simply an insurmountable hatred of Europeans. In any case, such readings can be characterized as extremist; they divide the characters into good and bad, and that division matches the division between European and Arab, between master and servant, between comfortable and impoverished, between policeman and prisoner, and so forth. From the bourgeois European perspective of the usual reader the following summary would be accurate: "to a Frenchman who gives him a great proof of humanity, an Algerian responds only with hate" [Franz Ranhut, "Du nihilisme à la 'mésure' et à l'amour des *hommes,*" *Configuration critique d'Albert Camus,* Richard Thieberger, ed.]. It should be noted, however, that an Algerian could equally well turn the extremist reading inside out; the prisoner's intransigent hostility would then be a heroic virtue. It seems highly unlikely to me that Camus meant the characters to be separable into good and bad.

A more subtle version of the Arab as villain arises when he is regarded as a passive figure. Obviously, he cannot be held morally responsible in quite the same way. As a brutelike creature, killing a fellow Arab on blind impulse, seeking the easy way by instinct, he brings violence and hate in his wake. If we assume that he has become a political terrorist, we must suppose that it was because of his preference for easy answers. He goes toward Tinguit at the end, perhaps to rejoin his "brothers" along the way, perhaps to have a secure bed and three meals a day during hard times, but in any case untouched either by Daru's concern for his motives or by Daru's kindness. Daru, a kind of Camusian saint, has met his opposite and failed to awaken him to freedom. These readings are fundamentally pessimistic and tragic. The saints are few, the brutes many; and if the stupidity of the latter brings ruin to the former, there seems little hope that dreams of brotherhood could ever be realized.

Although the advocates of one or another interpretation will disagree, I do not find any explanation of the Arab's character and behavior satisfactory. Some are more plausible than others; but none is entirely without flaws, and none can be demonstrated false. Camus surely intended it that way. Daru does not understand, and we are to share his confusion, not view the events with an omniscient superiority. The presentation of the Arab in the story, scrutinized closely, confirms this ambiguity as intended. The Arab speaks only twelve utterances, totaling fewer than fifty words. Six are questions, three are imperatives, two are the single word "yes," leaving only the reply, "He ran away. I ran after him" to Daru's question "Why did you kill him?" as a direct statement of the Arab's view of anything. The rest is all our inference, much of it influenced by Daru's own inferences. The Arab's eyes are "full of fever," his forehead "obstinate," his look "restless and rebellious." He watches Balducci "with a sort of anxiety," looks at Daru with eyes "full of a sort of woeful interrogation." In the darkness, the Arab turns toward Daru "as if he were listening attentively"; and at their parting, the Arab takes the package "as if he didn't know what to do with what was being given him." Daru thinks he hears the Arab moan and thinks that he is escaping." The Arab's expression the next day is "frightened," then "vacant and listless"; twice he seems not to understand; and in our final close view of him, "a sort of panic was visible in his expression." In short, Camus has been very careful to give us no authorial insights into the Arab, but to link every judgment of Daru's to a precise physical source. Daru is sometimes wrong, however, as when he thinks that the Arab is escaping.

The ending of the story appears to mean that, in some significant way, Daru has misapprehended the situation. Analyses that attempt to explain the Arab simultaneously attempt to explain the story by revealing the nature of Daru's error, and certainly a valid reading must focus on that error. Yet, as I have just shown, we cannot hope to solve the problem through understanding the Arab because Camus does not tell us enough about him.

The policeman Balducci is the only other character actually present in **"The Guest."** Since he departs early, it would be structurally odd for him to represent the central focus. Nonetheless, he offers Daru a possible fraternal relationship, which does in fact go awry, at least temporarily. His role is worth considering, if only to see how it compares to the more important relationship between Daru and the Arab.

Balducci, of course, shares with Daru all those traits that separate the two of them from the Arab; no circumstantial barrier exists between them. Their past friendship has been close, almost familial. Despite being a policeman, Balducci expresses some misgivings about his role, and his attitude toward the Arabs is not unlike Daru's. He can speak some Arabic, he willingly agrees to untying the prisoner, he sympathizes with Daru's reluctance to hold the Arab: "I don't like it either. You don't get used to putting a rope on a man even after years of it, and you're even ashamed—yes, ashamed." Certainly he is not presented as a man who has forfeited his claim to fraternal solidarity with other men.

Before the Arab, Balducci represents responsibility to

Daru. He brings orders from their common master, the French government. Even though he is unhappy about it, Daru readily accepts this responsibility by signing the paper. The understanding between the two men on this point is perfect. Balducci knows that Daru will tell the truth in any case, Daru accepts the fact that the rules require a signature. By signing, Daru releases Balducci and takes on the responsibility himself. At the same time, Daru refuses to follow the orders. He reaches that decision promptly and tells Balducci bluntly: "But I won't hand him over." Moreover, he repeats his decision twice. Balducci disapproves, but his own sense of obligation stops short of denouncing Daru. Their disagreement on the ethical question weakens the ties of friendship between them, but no misunderstanding occurs.

As Balducci leaves, Daru offers a ritual gesture of friendship: "I'll see you off," which the gendarme declines, saying, "There's no use being polite. You insulted me." Daru's refusal amounts to a criticism of Balducci's conduct. Their disagreement remains open and frank, however; canceling politeness keeps the superficial forms of their contact in harmony with its underlying truth. Between these two there are none of the false starts, words left unsaid, or half-gestures that characterize the relations between Lassalle and his workers in **"The Silent Men,"** for example. Balducci even softens his rejection somewhat, by saying, "Good-bye son," as he goes out. One feels that their long-standing camaraderie will not be permanently destroyed by the momentary conflict. Daru, it should be observed, neither contradicts Balducci nor apologizes for the insult. As with the responsibility for the prisoner, Daru acknowledges the disagreement readily if not gladly.

In short, Daru's relationship with Balducci comes near to being an ideal fraternal bond, capable even of surviving the inevitable troubled moments and crises that less-than-ideal reality produces. Critics who have blamed Daru for hesitation and indecision should reread the opening more carefully; Daru decides almost instantly to take responsibility for the prisoner but not to hand him over, and nothing in the story suggests that he is ever tempted to change his mind. The prisoner himself is too mysterious a figure for us to know with certainty how Daru ought to have acted, assuming that he ought to have done something different. A last critical resort has been to accuse Daru of some general complicity in his fellow Frenchmen's presumed guilt toward the Arabs. Daru, so the reasoning goes, represents an imperialist culture. He is master of his school, he feels like a lord by contrast to the poverty-stricken people around him. He is paternalistic, doling out the food and supplies, along with the civilization, shipped in from France. He is elitist, equating knowledge with the French school curriculum and imposing it on his pupils. Perhaps the best symbol of his clash with his surroundings is the map of French rivers chalked in four colors on his blackboard—the ruling country imposed on its subject, rivers in a desert, colors in a landscape turned black, white, and gray by the snow. It is the fitting spot for the threat to be written at the end.

Yet, though there is a certain symbolic justice in the desecration of the map, and a certain truth in regarding Daru as superior (in a pejorative sense), in human terms we must recognize that he has done about all anyone could to overcome his Otherness among these people. His feeling of lordship stems not from wealth but only from his acceptance of what little he has as enough. Undeniably he has had privileges of training and of comfort, but he is trying to share what he has and to give these poor people some of his privileges. Perhaps it is misguided to teach them the geography of France, although I see nothing to suggest that Daru does it with any spirit of condescension or of domination; I think that one must be frighteningly sure of one's own opinion to condemn him just for not knowing the best way to accomplish a worthy goal. Daru's treatment of the prisoner recapitulates his general attitude toward the Arabs. He insists on the prisoner's humanness, on his freedom, and on his equality with himself. They eat together and sleep in the same room, two rituals of fraternal bonding. Daru supplies the Arab with shelter, food, even money, and makes a small effort to educate him, not only about the route to freedom, but also, in asking about the murder, about moral responsibility. It seems from the changes in the Arab's expression and behavior that Daru wins his trust. Whether his gifts, his instruction, his kindness, his example of humanity succeed in making a lasting impression on the prisoner remains forever unknown.

In the end, there is nowhere to fix the blame and no place to locate Daru's misapprehension, unless it be that he misunderstands reality. He is a humanist in an inhuman or dehumanized world. He genuinely sees a brother in the Arab, but Balducci and the Arab's "brothers" can see only a criminal or a victim, a pretext for vengeance or a problem, an object within a system of objectified relationships. Daru is further more a respecter of ambiguity, who lives appropriately on the plateau between the desert and civilization, who wants to be a middleman between knowledge and ignorance, between plenty and poverty. But his world is growing increasingly polarized; one must be for or "against us," as Daru puts it, an act must be right or wrong, a person must be guilty or innocent. Daru is in many respects the most tragic, or at least the most moving, of Camus's heroes in ***Exile and the Kingdom. . . .*** (pp. 73-82)

[However,] it is, in the final analysis, a silly romantic daydream to think that Daru could have done any more for the prisoner than he did. Can anyone seriously believe that Daru could have joined the Algerian nationalists who were fighting a guerrilla war against the French? Or ought he then to have accompanied the prisoner to the nomad tribes? It would have made no difference in the outcome. The threat was coming to Daru, regardless of what he did, and regardless of what the prisoner did. If there is any immediate connection between the prisoner and the "brothers," between the fate of the prisoner and the acts of the "brothers," that connection defies analysis, given the paucity of information available to Daru and to us. Daru's choice is between turning the prisoner in and setting him free. That is a moral choice for Daru, and he makes what is probably the right decision (although how many of us, given the chance, would free a presumed murderer?). The bitter irony of **"The Guest,"** which makes it the most bleakly pessimistic of Camus's stories, is that right moral choices do not change the world.

If there is a villain in **"The Guest,"** it is the same one as in the other stories, not a person or a society, but the universe itself. That is the truly silent, completely passive and indifferent element in every story. In many regards, the Arab is explicitly identified with this impersonal natural reality. His skin is "weathered" and "discolored by the cold," like the landscape. Balducci refers to him as a "zèbre" and compares the murder to the slaughter of sheep. All this recalls Daru's opening meditation on the region and the climate, ending: "The sheep had died then by thousands, and even a few men, here and there, sometimes without anyone's knowing." Later, he thinks again about the same general themes, and sums up the passage of history in the region: "Towns sprang up, flourished, then disappeared; men came by, loved one another or fought bitterly, then died. No one in this desert, neither he nor his guest, mattered." The Arab belongs to that eternal cycle, like the stones cracking in the sun, the stinging wind, the tireless waves, the wheeling stars, motifs that recur in almost every story. The Arab is just someone who passes by. His actions—the murder, his words to Daru, his staying at the school, his taking the road to Tinguit—signify no more than do the changes in the weather. If a mind and soul inhabit that body, they stay as unrecognizable as the mind and soul of the material universe.

Daru's error, then, is this: he had believed that his monastic life, his solitude, his love for others and his acceptance of his place, had created a harmony between him and his universe. The story ends on the line, "In this vast landscape he had loved so much, he was alone." He loved a landscape and nourished a delusion that it loved him, that in it he was not alone. He is, and always has been, alone in his moral existence. The honor he chooses to obey is his, not Balducci's or the Arab's, and certainly not the world's. (pp. 84-5)

The Arab is not a puzzle we are meant to solve but rather a blank, eternally, irrevocably meaningless. It is pathetic that Daru becomes interested in him, and actually cares what road he takes, after Daru has any chance left to be involved. It is pathetic in the same way that Daru cares enough about honor to offend Balducci by refusing to go along with orders. Daru is a quixotic figure—Don Quixote too freed prisoners out of honor, and suffered for it later. But Camus's vision of the universe is a blacker one than Cervantes'. This confrontation between Daru and the universe is the very locus of the absurd. Daru lives through a pointless, meaningless, and unresolved incident, yet he invests it with a conclusion, fits it into a signifying system, and projects a resolution. Since we see it all through his eyes, we share his desperate yearning to make sense of it. Even though this longing may be an error, pathetic, quixotic, self-deluding, foredoomed, the human refusal to subside into purely passive insignificance is our glory, our one possibility of revolt against the absurd. (pp. 85-6)

English Showalter, Jr., in his Exiles and Strangers: A Reading of Camus's "Exile and the Kingdom", *Ohio State University Press, 1984, pp. 73-87.*

Susan Tarrow (essay date 1985)

[*In the following excerpt, Tarrow discusses the character Marcel in "The Adulterous Woman" in relation to the themes of colonization and alienation.*]

All the stories in ***Exile and the Kingdom,*** published in 1957, deal with people who do not belong in the world in which they find themselves. In 1947 Camus had declared Algeria "my true homeland" [*Lyrical and Critical Essays*]. But by 1950 he would write in his notebook: "Yes, I have a native land: the French language" [*Notebooks II*]. There was no longer a land to which he belonged, but merely a form of expression; he became increasingly aware of his francophone core, an "Algerian Frenchman," while his sympathy for France and its values declined. And his recurrent episodes of artistic sterility were exacerbated by the fact that the French language was his medium; his inability to use it fruitfully underlined his feelings of exile.

Algeria was a paramount factor in political debate in France during the 1950s. The tug-of-war between East and West in Europe seemed to have ended in a stalemate, at least for the time being, and events in France's colonies were giving cause for alarm. The conflict in Indo-China was decided in 1954 with the fall of Dien Bien Phu to the Vietminh. Once Mendès-France had negotiated a settlement in 1955, he had to turn his attention to North Africa. Tunisia and Morocco were already suffering terrorist attacks by rebels and European right-wing extremists; the situation in Algeria had not yet deteriorated to the same degree, but the likelihood of violence was imminent, particularly since the problems of poverty and overpopulation were even more acute there than in the two neighboring countries. Decolonization dominated French political life in the fifties and sharply divided the country.

Camus returned briefly to journalism in 1955; he contributed articles to *L'Express* to support Mendès-France's candidacy for the premiership and to express his views on the Algerian situation. After an unsuccessful appeal for a civilian truce in Algiers in 1956, he withdrew from regular journalism, and limited his activities to behind-the-scenes interventions on behalf of imprisoned activists. The publication in 1958 of *Actuelles III: Chroniques algériennes,* elicited scant reaction at a moment when violence was at its height, and de Gaulle had once more been called in to save France. Camus's call for a confederation seemed irrelevant, when the ultimate choice now lay between massive repression and the granting of independence.

The short stories of ***Exile and the Kingdom*** return to Camus's early themes of estrangement and misunderstanding. Many of the characters are misfits in their environment, even when they feel they belong there. (pp. 172-73)

In his preface to the first edition of **"The Adulterous Woman,"** published by Schumann in Algeria in November 1954, Camus acknowledged the autobiographical element in the story: "In Laghouat I met the characters of this story. I am not certain, of course, that their day ended as I have told it. Doubtless they did not go forth to the desert. But *I* went, some hours after that, and during all that time their image pursued me and challenged what I saw."

This impression of opposition, of conflict, is apparent in the portrayal of Janine and her husband Marcel as they travel in unknown territory in the Algerian interior. On the most obvious level, Janine finds the desert the opposite of what she had expected: instead of warm sand and palm trees, there is a bitterly cold wind blowing over a landscape of stone. Physical discomfort is a dominant feature of the couple's experience.

Marcel is a stereotype of the petty-bourgeois *pied-noir* whom Camus ridiculed in his notebooks, who believes that Arabs are uncivilized and whose aim is a house full of furniture from the Galeries Barbès. Marcel's attitude is that of the fault-finding tourist, who complains of anything that is different. Even in the final version of the story, Marcel's comments are full of racial slurs; it is significant that in earlier versions his comments are even stronger. The typical racist epithets—lazy, dishonest, incompetent—are applied to various Arabs. Marcel expresses a commonly held attitude towards emancipation: "They're supposed to be making progress, said Marcel. To make progress, you have to work. And for them, work is like pork, forbidden."

Camus may, in Quilliot's view, have diluted Marcel's racism because of the worsening situation in Algeria between 1952, when the story was first drafted, and 1954, when it was published in Algiers. It seems more likely, however, that Camus wanted to make his character more sympathetic by emphasizing his limitations and the narrowness of his outlook in general, rather than presenting him as a hardened racist. Marcel is just another frightened human being, who works hard and takes no risks in order to assure both economic and emotional security. It is the exposure to a strange land with undefined parameters that elicits his hostile criticism. On a realistic level, his racist attitude arises from fear of two well-documented threats: economic and sexual competition. The economic crisis that followed World War II had forced Marcel to dispense with intermediaries, and to try and sell his fabrics directly to the Arabs. For the first time, he must deal with Arabs in the small towns of the interior, and to be successful he must deal with them as equals. Also for the first time, perhaps, he must speak Arabic. In the city, where French is the language of the dominant class, he can assert that dominance with his perfect mastery of that language. Now he finds the roles reversed, and the Arab has the upper hand because of his linguistic fluency. Marcel resents the Arabs' haughtiness, and his own position of suppliant: "He became irritable, raised his voice, laughed awkwardly, he seemed like a woman who is trying to be attractive and is unsure of herself." His manhood is put in doubt, and his response is to make scornful comments to Janine about Arab conceit. The final insult is administered by the magnificent Arab who crosses the town square and almost walks over Marcel's case of samples. "They think they can get away with anything nowadays," remarks Marcel. Even Arab cooking is inferior: "*We* know how to cook"; the French rendering of the emphatic "we" *(nous autres)* underlines the otherness Marcel feels in a predominantly Arab town.

Marcel does not actually voice his fears for Janine's security, yet her reaction to the strange environment is physical. "Adulterous" may seem an extreme epithet in view of the reality of Janine's experience, but she is disloyal to the structure of the little world she lives in with her husband, to their marriage. She feels drawn toward the autonomy of these people of the interior, who seem not to depend on material comforts or possessions for their well-being. Janine is encumbered by overweight, luggage, a complaining husband, a heavy meal, the years of conjugality: in the oasis town, people display a freedom and independence such as she enjoyed in her youth. The Arabs do not even seem to notice her existence: "She found that even when they were dressed in rags, they had a proud demeanor, which was not the case with the Arabs in their home town." The Arabs in the coastal towns depend on the Europeans for a living, and therefore adopt a more servile attitude, but here in the interior the French presence is minimal—pork served in the hotel restaurant, and a military decoration on the chest of the old Arab waiter. Out in the desert, the nomads are sovereign.

Hostility or serene indifference greet the French couple, both inside and outside the town. The local people and their landscape are at one in their autonomy vis-à-vis the strangers. All is cold and hard; even Janine's experience of physical union with the world is like a cold flood rather than a warm glow, as she leans against the stone parapet of the fortress. But Janine's fear is stronger than her yearning for freedom, and she returns to the warmth of her husband "as her safest haven."

The impression of physical weight that Camus evokes in his portrayal of these characters makes them real and tangible people, what E. M. Forster would call "round" characters rather than the somewhat abstract characters of *The Plague.* Marcel and Janine are among Camus's most successful fictional creations: they are creations of flesh and blood rather than the stereotypical image of the *pied-noir.* Marcel may represent the reactionary racist European in Algeria, yet at the same time he is just a man, beset by the fear of death, loneliness and poverty like any other. Camus's old Algiers friend, Charles Poncet, suggested that, living in Paris as he did, "Camus may have felt more of a duty to defend the interests of the *pied-noir* against the unanimous hostility of the French left" [Herbert Lottman, *Albert Camus: A Biography*]. Camus certainly wanted to dissipate the "image d'Epinal" disseminated by some of the French press, which portrayed Algeria as a colony "inhabited by a million *colons* with whips and cigars, riding around in Cadillacs."

"The Adulterous Woman" does not defend the interests of the *pied-noir,* but rather reveals the extent to which fear inspires scorn and hostility. Marcel and Janine are quite literally out of their element in central Algeria: they need the definition of a coastline to feel secure, for the desert is as limitless as the ocean; the prevailing imagery of the descriptive passages is drawn from the open sea. Even in their home town, the couple no longer goes to the beach, but exists in an ever more restricted area: "The years had passed in the shadowy light they maintained with the shutters half-closed." It is only a half-life, and what characterizes both the conjugal relationship and Janine's experience in the desert is sterility. The story suggests that the couple has no future, only a precarious present. Janine's encounter with the desert makes her newly aware of the vastness of space and time, into which the Arabs seem to fit while she remains excluded, unable to read "the obscure signs of a strange writing whose meaning had to be deciphered."

Camus's attitude to the Algerian situation at this point is revealed as more humanistic than political. Marcel's opinions are obviously distasteful, yet Camus mitigated them in order to make the character more universal. The two sides are not black and white, and a solution does not lie in the eviction or enslavement of one party in the dispute. And yet in this story as in **"The Guest,"** the characters are not really at home in the country they regard as their own.

In **"The Adulterous Woman"** a hostile natural environment is handled with equanimity by the Arabs, while the Europeans are acutely uncomfortable. A sandstorm is blowing, a "mineral mist" surrounds the bus on which Janine and her husband are traveling. A few palm trees seem to be "cut out of metal," and Janine's dream of a desert of soft sand is disappointed: "The desert was not like that, but was only stone, stone everywhere, in the sky that was still overcast with the dust of the stone, cold and rasping." In the jolting bus, the Arabs "looked as though they were asleep, wrapped up in their burnoose. Some had tucked up their feet on the seat and swayed more than the others with the movement of the vehicle. . . . The passengers . . . had sailed in silence through a kind of pale night." Janine notices that "despite their voluminous garments, they seemed to have plenty of room on the seats which were only just wide enough for her and her husband." She and Marcel are impeded by their clothes and their baggage, but "all these people from the South apparently traveled empty-handed."

Only when Janine stops all movement can she begin to understand the desert and its people. "For a long time, a few men had been traveling without respite over the dry earth, scraped to the bone, of this unbounded land, men who had no possessions but were no man's slave, wretched but free lords of a strange kingdom." The scene recalls the end of *Crime and Punishment,* where Raskolnikov sees the nomads across the river from his prison. For a moment Janine shares this accord, but she is brought back to reality by her husband. "She felt too tall, too solid, and too white for this world she had just entered." She is a misfit in the landscape. (pp. 174-78)

Susan Tarrow, in her Exile from the Kingdom: A Political Rereading of Albert Camus, *The University of Alabama Press, 1985, 221 p.*

P. M. Cryle (essay date 1985)

[*In the following excerpt, Cryle utilizes the philosophical discussion of self-consciousness in Camus's early absurdist treatise* The Myth of Sisyphus *to explicate the themes found in "The Artist at Work" and "The Growing Stone."*]

It happens frequently that when reading Camus' work, we find ourselves attending to the experience of being already in the world—of being caught up, indeed, in the tedious rhythms of routine. One may think at first that the sense of freedom, the possibility of a new beginning, are not to be found: there is a kind of inertia that tends to exclude commitment as choice. Thus the old woman of *Le Malentendu,* in whom the source of all new emotion seems to have dried up, goes on with the *habit* of killing: It all happened years and years ago. So many years ago that I don't remember how it began, and I've forgotten what I was then.

She could be described in terms of our thematics—if one were not too fearful of the ridicule that can attach to such analogies—as a tragic militant.

On a less dramatic and more general level, we find that everyday routine seems often to continue of its own accord: the passages of *Le Mythe de Sisyphe* describing the succession of work-travel-sleep are some of those most frequently quoted from Camus' work. Yet *Le Mythe de Sisyphe* draws our attention to this experience precisely in order to emphasize the decisive, if temporary, *interruption* of these stultifying rhythms. The possibility of choice appears, often quite suddenly, at a certain point in time:

> But one day the "why" arises and everything begins in that weariness tinged with amazement. "Begins"—this is important. Weariness comes at the end of the acts of a mechanical life, but at the same time it inaugurates the impulse of consciousness. It awakens consciousness and provokes what follows. What follows is the unthinking return into the chain/production line, or it is the definitive awakening. At the end of the awakening comes, in time, the consequence: suicide or recovery.

So it happens that there *is* a beginning at the end of, in the midst of, continuity. The space of freedom opens up, allowing one to choose, in the broadest and most radical terms, between suicide and going on. There is patently no question of another life or another world. The "definitive" awakening of consciousness does not constitute an escape into the air, a glorious—or even involuntary—flight: it simply emerges as the understanding, the analysis, of habit. Freedom can be used to stop, or to begin *again.*

This is the lesson to be learned from Sisyphus as mythical hero. His fate—his behavior, so to speak, within his fate—is exemplary insofar as it develops a rhythm of consciousness, associated with spatial displacement, while following the constraints of an eternal routine. We should consider Sisyphus most closely at the point where he turns around, at the top of the slope:

> It is during that return, that pause, that Sisyphus interests me. A face that toils so close to stones is already stone itself! I see that man going back down with a heavy yet measured step toward the torment of which he will never know the end. That hour like a breathing-space which returns as surely as his suffering, that is the hour of consciousness.

Being invited to "imagine Sisyphus as a happy man," we should bring the effort of our imagination to bear on the space-time of freedom, the moment at which Sisyphus decides to turn, or turns to decide. The rock turns over quite simply because of the force of gravity, but the human gravity of Sisyphus is not of the same order: it is not a mechanical necessity. "Volt of the rock and revolt of Sisyphus," says Blanchot [in "Le Détour vers la simplicité," *N.R.F.,*] with admirable conciseness.

For freedom to be discerned thus in the midst of habit requires a narrow spatio-temporal focus. Sisyphus must not be thought of merely as a laborer or even as a mountaineer. The imagination of climbing leads us to the material understanding of muscular effort, as Bachelard has pointed out [in *La terree et les rêveries de la volonté,* 1948]; but this is precisely what renders it inappropriate here. Descent, on the other hand, requires little exertion and thus permits more general kinds of awareness. It is a phase of reflection that prolongs the pause at the top: the athletic heroism of the climber consists only in feeling the rock hard against his face, whereas the man, the moral creature who walks down, knows his life and his fate because he sees the rock before him. For Camus, the story of Sisyphus is not an ascension myth: its most vital, or most instructive, phase is that of re-descent. Sisyphus's climb can thus be understood as entailing not so much the *risk* of falling—so often the mark of heroism—as the *certainty* that his rock will soon be coming down again. He knows himself to be caught up in a cycle, so his upward effort can never amount to a movement out of the world or out of time. There is no state of detachment because there is no achievement of height for its own sake. There is no edifice, then, on top of the hill, no tower or church in which he might stand. Is there even a hill whose shape can be discerned? Sisyphus belongs on a slope.

It happens thus that a certain spatial and moral superiority occurs without in fact having been sought: "At each of those moments when he leaves the heights and gradually moves down toward the lairs of the gods, he is superior to his fate. He is stronger than his rock." Superiority is experienced and enjoyed as a moment, not one gloriously dilated, eternal moment but a series of instants occurring in his routine. The time of beginning again is distinctive because it is reliably associated with the space of contemplation and lucidity. This is when Sisyphus goes down to commitment, separated from his rock by the space of knowledge, and seeing his fate as the continuing entailment of his present action:

> At that subtle moment when man glances backward over his life, Sisyphus, as he turns back to his rock, contemplates that series of unrelated actions which becomes his fate, created by him, combined under his memory's eye and soon sealed by his death.

We see here, undoubtedly, the most modest, the most literally pedestrian, form of commitment we have yet encountered, not only because of its spatial reduction—the more noble symbols of dominant verticality have given way to the humble slope—but also because it is reduced and situated in time, occurring regularly within the space of an instant. The "exercise in detachment and passion" described in *Le Mythe de Sisyphe* as that which consummates "the splendour and futility of a man's life" is here organized rhythmically. Passion occurs during the climb, when he is totally involved in his labor, and detachment—the detachment that belongs at the heart of commitment—occurs during the descent. He never looks upward, one supposes—why would he look at the sky?—but he does have time to look at or toward the plain:

> At the very end of his long effort measured by *skyless space* and time without depth, the purpose is achieved. Then Sisyphus watches the stone rush down in a few moments toward that lower world whence he will have to push it up again toward the summit. He goes back down into the plain. (my italics)

There is nothing miraculously privileged here about the experience of vertical contemplation: it involves no angelic lightness, no complicity with the gods. Being above is not the beginning of the story: it occurs at the end of a period of passionate effort. Yet the pause at the top of the slope, the moment of conscious elevation is also the time when one recognizes that there is no end, no end other than death. Freedom is not a durable state but an attitude that allows the measurement of bondage, that very measurement being a (fleeting) triumph of intelligence. There is more in Camus' work than drudgery and militancy, as we can see, but we are likely to find often that freedom emerges within the framework of a certain fatality, whether that fatality be understood as divine punishment—traditionally the case with Sisyphus—or whether it be thought of as social or historical necessity. (pp. 242-46)

[A] positive commitment, one that might be read as continuing the tradition of Sisyphus . . . can be found in **"Jonas ou l'artiste au travail."** Jonas the painter lives in a world that has well-defined limits. Essentially, he belongs in his apartment—any attempt to live outside it being characterized as escape—and the problems of his existence are proper to this space. The particular constraints of this apartment are such as to distinguish it immediately from the *malconfort* of *La Chute:* its horizontal exiguity actually requires those who live in it to assume a vertical position:

> the kitchen was next to the water closet and a nook graced with the name of shower room. Indeed, it might have been a shower if only the fixture had been installed vertically, and one were willing to stand utterly motionless under the kindly spray.
>
> They could also at a pinch eat in the kitchen, provided that Jonas or Louise was willing to remain standing.

The apartment presents us with what might be called, in the context of commitment, a spatial paradox. Normally, the domestic interior is likely to appear as the place of comfortable ignorance, an uncoordinated womb-like space, a nest or cocoon, in which certain vital problems, especially general ones, are never posed. Here, however, we find that the vertical axis is inscribed *within* the apartment and that it resists a certain facile domestication. It cannot, for instance, be simply divided and partitioned by the owners, as the horizontal plane has been, to double the number of apartments. . . . [We] find here a certain resolution of horizontal and vertical, and the possibility that specific problems posed by the apartment as living space will reflect those of the world at large.

Now Jonas's art—his vocation as an artist—is associated, by a piece of humdrum symbolism, with his star. The star shines above him, in the sky, in the place of disembodied entities, in the place of those eternal values so scorned by Sartre. Yet it so happens that there may be room for this romantic oddity *within* the apartment. The ceiling is so high that it cannot be lit by normal, domestic means, in any case: "Jonas had been particularly entranced by the largest room, the ceiling of which was so high that there could be no question of installing a lighting system." In this place, there could be room for starlight, for the artist's lofty vocation, for that relative transcendence that takes one, not into Clamence's heavenly abyss, nor even to Drieu's mountainous roof of the world, but just as far as a high ceiling. Why should we not take the relationship between floor and ceiling here as homologous to that between earth and sky? The world of "Jonas" may be teaching us, not to rail against the sky, nor indeed to claim it as a simple possession, but to understand it in modestly human terms.

Jonas is characterized by a "simplicité d'artiste" that leads us to suppose that he belongs in the purity of the air, or on the singular vertical axis. His simplicity can be opposed, as we might expect, to the diverse preoccupations of those around him. There is an industrious "ant," his wife, who, like his friend Rateau, bears a name (Poulin) that has animal connotations. Both she and Rateau are small, energetic, and practical, whereas Jonas is tall and absent-minded. The horizontal plane, the floor of the apartment, then tends to become the domain of multiplicity—"For his part, Rateau had produced a multiplicity of ingenious inventions."—being crowded with children, paintings, and especially visitors. This is where Louise works out *her* vocation: "Louisa's vocation was activity." It is likely to be the place of her active, plural intellectuality:

> She read everything without order, and in a few weeks became capable of talking about everything.
>
> She dedicated herself at once to the visual arts, visited museums and exhibitions, dragged Jonas to them although he didn't quite understand what his contemporaries were painting and felt bothered in his artistic simplicity.

Now this arrangement, in all its whimsical facility, is not allowed simply to endure; it comes under pressure because of the spatial constraints of the apartment: "The birth of the children, Jonas's new occupation, their restricted quarters [etc.] left only *limited room* for the *double activity* of Louise and Jonas." (my italics) Will there be room in the same living space for the star and the children? Or, if we continue to take the apartment as a representation of the world, will there be room in a crowded and busy community for such diverse vocations? "each of us has his workbench," says Louise, but where can the workbenches be built? "The problem of living space was, however, by far the greatest of their problems, for time and space shrank simultaneously around them." It hardly suffices to know that art is an "elevated" preoccupation and shopping, for instance, a "lowly" if respectable one: some specific *modus vivendi* needs to be worked out, and the function of the apartment is to make this problem progressively more acute. Despite the vagueness of his dreams and his futile attempts to escape, Jonas comes to see more and more clearly that "It was hard to paint the world and men and, at the same time, to live with them."

The problems of living space exist, in fact—such is the microcosmic completeness of this place—on both axes. Not only is there clutter on the horizontal plane, there is uncomfortable and insecure vertical movement:

> The really extraordinary height of the ceilings and the narrowness of the rooms made of the apartment an odd assortment of parallelepipeds almost entirely glassed in, all doors and windows, with *no place to stand the furniture,* and with the human beings *floating about like bottle imps in a vertical aquarium.* (my italics)

(pp. 268-71)

To the double problem of crowding and floating, Jonas finds a precisely adequate solution. He finds the only possible standpoint, the only conceivable working- and resting-place that could reconcile the conflicting exigencies of his situation. With an admirably geometrical logic that responds to the terms of the problem—"cubage," "volume," "surface," "parallel-pipeds," "the square of sky outlined by the court"—he builds a loft half-way up, half-way between the floor and the ceiling, the earth and sky. He is now exactly half-way between the demands of commitment and detachment. It is indeed, as he says with resolute, if rather tired, optimism: "a very good solution." The loft is not flooded by light or noise: it has the "shade" and the "half-silence" of a desert or a tomb (my italics). He has an experience of distance without absence, of (partial) detachment without abstraction:

> The only direct sounds he heard came from the kitchen or the lavatory. The other noises seemed distant, and the visits, the ringing of the doorbell and the telephone, the comings and goings, the conversations, reached him *half-muffled,* as if they came from out on the street or from the farther court. (my italics)

It is hard for us, of course, to accept this absurdly simple, fifty-fifty "solution" to the problems of commitment. It seems rather to be their *reductio ad absurdum,* the ultimately sophisticated, humorous comment on the thematics of verticality and horizontality. Yet we would do well to note that Jonas's geometry does have some ironic force as an answer to the more spectacular or lyrical forms of commitment found, for instance, in Drieu and Barrès and parodied in Sartre. Instead of polemical caricature—discernible not only in "Erostrate" but in **"Le Renégat"** and *La Chute*—we find here a kind of resolute mediocrity, a grimly optimistic determination to mark the place of art in relation to other human activity. While excluding the metaphysical verticality of heaven and hell, of the *axis mundi,* **"Jonas"** affirms the desire to achieve more—a little more—than routine horizontality. Not for him the totalist, and usually totalitarian, drama that consumes a whole succession of Camusian characters: Caligula, Nada (*L'Etat de siège*), the renegade, Clamence. Like Sisyphus, and like most of the characters in *La Peste,* he addresses himself to the most pressingly concrete problems.

The loft built by Jonas is neither an eagle's nest nor a *mal-confort:* it is simply a slightly elevated living space with its own internal dimensions, one that continues to include, despite its strictly punctual situation in space, some kind of verticality. It is "narrow, but high and deep." Jonas is thus able to stay in it for a time, having at last achieved immobility and darkness. "he remained motionless in darkness all day long." Early in the story, he would say naively of his good fortune, "It's the same old [continuing] luck," as if it had never had a beginning. Now, he knows that he has to stop in order to begin again more deliberately: "He had a great work, really new, to create; everything was going to begin all over again. As he was talking to her, he felt that he was telling the truth and that his star was there. All he needed was a well-organized system." The relative discretion, the intermittent presence, of the star is such that it is there *to be found,* unlike the inhumanly powerful sun of **"Le Renégat"** whose presence or absence seems brutally decisive for all forms of awareness. To see his star again, to have it emerge from the shadows, Jonas has to develop a clear understanding of the significance of his activity: "He still had to discover what he had not yet clearly understood, although he had always known it and had always painted as if he knew it." By giving him the time and space in which to do this, the loft represents for Jonas the possibility of genuine commitment.

At the end of this period of withdrawal and reflection, we see Jonas fall. . . . His fall is only a form of punctuation: it does not mark the drastic end of a previous existence. We are told, in fact, that the world is "still there, young and lovable" and that he will get better. He says, it is true, that he will never work again, but we ought no doubt to read this as a sign of catharsis, the measure of his satisfaction. Has he not managed, after all, to see his star once again in the darkness? Has he not, by virtue of this inspiration, produced a (verbal) painting that is one of the more succinct examples of the "literature of commitment"?

> Rateau was looking at the canvas, completely blank, in the center of which Jonas had merely written in very small letters a word that could be made out, but without any certainty as to whether it should be read *solitary* or *solidary.*

His new work is . . . a more complex and ambiguous solution than the construction of the loft, but it continues to relate the *solitaire* of detachment to the *solidaire* of commitment, not allowing us to choose one at the expense of the other. And space is not forgotten: each of these inseparable—but nonetheless resolved—terms contains the spatial elements *sol* [ground] and *air* [air] in which the drama of commitment has been traditionally played out. The fatality of the human situation "frames" this understanding, just as the apartment frames Jonas's whole existence; yet within the experience of exiguity, there is a limited but nonetheless decisively different range of options. Between the floor and the ceiling lies the margin of freedom, and Jonas the artist uses his freedom to stand half-way, affirming the need for both.

Following **"Jonas,"** and completing the collection ***L'Exil et le royaume,*** **"La Pierre qui pousse" ["The Growing Stone"]** continues to elaborate, although in a rather different way, the positive imagination of commitment. By its geographical setting, it may seem to be closer to **"Le Renégat"** and *La Chute* than to **"Jonas."** Indeed, we find here not only a kind of exoticism that might readily be associated with escape from routine constraints but also some of the marks of traditional privilege, of the freedom to approach and enter the world of others from a superior position. Yet d'Arrast's travel is unmistakably a (hesitant and uncertain) search for integration and his privilege a mere remnant of the kind of initial superiority found, for instance, in the work of Drieu. He has the name of an aristocrat, it is true, but this is a virtually empty inheritance, as we see in his conversation with the cook:

> "But you're a noble. Socrates told me." "Not I. But my grandfather was. His father too and all those before his father. Now there is no more nobility in our country." "Ah!" the black said, laughing. "I understand; everybody is a noble." "No, that's not it. *There are neither noblemen nor common people.*" (my italics)

The society from which he comes is in fact an undifferentiated world governed by police and merchants.

Now we can relate the social perspective to the geographical here in a way that is strangely reminiscent, at first glance, of *L'Homme à cheval.* South America—Camus' Brazil or Drieu's Bolivia—contrasts with Europe by its marked differentiation of upper and lower classes. Between the aristocracy and the people, as here between d'Arrast and the cook, there can be a kind of non-bourgeois or antibourgeois complicity: "Buying and selling, eh! What filth!" The vital difference between the two stories is that whereas *L'Homme à cheval* maintains and glorifies a vast social gap as the space to be played on by the artists of commitment, **"La Pierre qui pousse"** focuses on the relatively narrow but nonetheless quite precise margin that separates a tawdry group of "notables" from the desperate horizontality of the poorest people. Instead of the palatial cliff-top salon, we find a "club" that is "a sort of small bar on the first floor furnished with a bamboo counter and iron café tables"; the balcony of privileged observation is found, not above an abyss, but on the first floor of a judge's or a mayor's residence.

Faced with this difference, d'Arrast the vestigial aristocrat is not content to settle comfortably in the lowly heights, enjoying the unimpressive superiority of the "notables." He is less interested in the club than in the situation of the poor people, those who live, both socially and spatially, at the lowest level. When he asks to visit one of their huts, he sees, not the "very interesting things" promised absurdly by the "commandant" who is escorting him, but precisely a certain *absence* that is a sign of the fundamental. There are no picturesque objects, only the bare earth and minimal furniture:

> In the hut, D'Arrast saw nothing at first but a dying fire built right on the ground in the exact

> center of the room. Then in a back corner he made out a brass bed with a bare, broken mattress, a table in the other corner covered with earthenware dishes, and, between the two, a sort of stand supporting a color print representing St. George. Nothing else but a pile of rags to the right of the entrance and, hanging from the ceiling, a few loincloths of various colors drying over the fire. Standing still, D'Arrast breathed in the smell of smoke and poverty that rose from the ground and took hold of him.

Visibly, this is the place of "the poorest," of those who live right at the surface of the earth. To enter fully into their world seems very difficult indeed, not because the initial situation of the *notable* or the aristocrat is one of lofty superiority, but because this horizontality is so pure and so radical. To reach this level, one would need to attain the absolutely rudimentary, the very perfection of simplicity.

So it is that, in keeping with **"Jonas,"** the vertical axis is dramatically important—it is the space to be crossed by an act of commitment—while being in fact of quite unspectacular proportions. Limited verticality is once again a given of the situation, being "given" in fact not by any particular political or economic force identified in the text, but by material, atmospheric conditions: the oppressive, all-enveloping humidity of the place is such that the sky, the stars, the buildings, the birds—all the symbols of elevation—seem to suffer from an insurmountable fatigue:

> In the black sky stars flickered/trembled.
>
> . . . without really seeing them, he was looking at the faint/exhausted stars still swimming in the damp sky.
>
> . . . a tired flight of ragged urubus.
>
> Above the forest the few stars in the austral sky, blurred by an invisible haze, were glowing dimly. The humid air was heavy.

The stars that might have been a guide for the traveler or a call to higher things are simply extinguished and washed out of the sky:

> The pale-black sky still seemed liquid. In its transparent dark water, stars began to light up, low on the horizon. Almost at once they flickered out, falling one by one into the river as if the last lights were trickling from the sky.

The buildings and the central square itself—"the bumpy [half-subsided] square, which looked even larger because of the low structures surrounding it"—seem to slump beneath this weight. In such conditions, the flight of a bird can have no romantic force; it is merely a comically measurable fiasco:

> a humid heat weighed upon the town and the still forest. . . . The almost clear blue sky *weighed down on top of the first dull roofs.* Yellowish urubus, transfixed by the heat, were sleeping on the house across from the hospital. One of them suddenly fluttered, opened his beak, ostensibly got ready to fly away, flapped his dusty wings twice against his body, *rose a few centimeters* above the roof, fell back, and went to sleep almost at once. (my italics)

"A few centimeters": such is the extent of lyrical verticality in the world of **"La Pierre qui pousse."**

With respect to this atmospheric oppression, it might seem that the poorest people, by the very horizontality of their existence, occupy a position of stability, if not exactly of strength. They too, however, are threatened, threatened by water in its more visibly aggressive, its more muscular, form. The huts are built just above the level of the river and are in constant danger of being flooded or even washed away: "they had to be strengthened at the base with heavy stones." This is of course the official reason for d'Arrast's visit and for his preoccupation with the poor people: he is to build a dam that will protect their homes from the river.

It could be said, then, that the story of **"La Pierre qui pousse"** defines two tasks: from the point of view of commitment, there is a space of action—a vertical social distance—to be crossed, and from the more narrowly professional standpoint, the people of Iguape require specific material help. There is every indication, furthermore, that d'Arrast is well qualified to complete the two at the same time. His aristocratic name may itself be read as a noble version of that which is most humble, *à ras d(e) t(erre),* and his sheer size and physical strength seem particularly appropriate. He is, we are told, a "colosse," already "solidly planted on the ground." . . . (pp. 272-80)

It seems, indeed, that he may be about to experience a kind of ritual integration into this earthy society through his attendance at the dance: "Then he noticed that he himself, though without moving his feet, had for some little time been dancing with his whole weight." But he does not go through with this; he has an experience of weakness, a kind of fall that merely brings him to an uncomfortable and irresolute crouching position: "D'Arrast let himself slide down the wall and squatted, holding back his nausea." His nausea is in fact a symptom of nonbelonging; to be a part of this horizontal life is virtually impossible:

> This land was too vast, blood and seasons mingled here, and time liquefied. *Life here was flush with the soil, and, to become part of it, one had to lie down* and sleep for years on the muddy or dried-up ground itself. (my italics)

At this point in our story there is a rather surprising hiatus. We are obliged to recognize, in fact, that this is *not* a classical narrative of commitment, at least insofar as the perspective of future integration—which emerged so clearly when we considered its spatial organization—tends at certain moments to disappear. Spatial position—in particular, d'Arrast's natural, or cultural, superiority—does not seem to correspond, in the (phenomenological) way we might expect, to a specific form of consciousness. Instead of serene prospection and the clear measurement of future possibilities, we find in d'Arrast an element of doubt and relative passivity: he is waiting but does not know what he is waiting for. His nausea and his continuing uncertainty serve thus to mark the limits of his freedom. He may be an aristocrat and a wanderer, he may be endowed with the earthy qualities of strength and solidity, but he cannot simply "go to the people" as and when he chooses. In this sense integration, if it occurs, will be found in time and rather against the odds: "commitment" is framed and limited by chance.

When d'Arrast is above, looking down from the "town hall balcony," he does not have a clear spectacle before his eyes but rather a certain emptiness that provokes nausea and anguish: "The empty street with its deserted houses *attracted and repelled him at one and the same time.* Once again he wanted to get away from this country; at the same time he thought of that huge stone; he would have liked that trial to be over." (my italics). His attitude has none of the simplicity of benevolence (or of scorn): how could such ambivalence be a clear preparation for the action of commitment? Yet when he sees that the cook is not in his place in the procession, he acts suddenly and impulsively, bringing to an end his long period of alienation and inactivity: "In a single bound, without excusing himself, he left the balcony and the room, dashed down the staircase, and stood in the street under the deafening sound of the bells and the firecrackers." It is not the case that integration, in its perfection, is achieved by this one downward movement. Rather, we see the hero move quickly from one hiatus to another, by a series of impulsive gestures that lead him to walk beside the cook "without knowing why," to grab hold suddenly of the piece of cork that is used to support the stone, to change direction "abruptly" when he seems to be taking the stone to the church, to open the door of the hut and throw the stone onto the fire "brusquely." Little wonder that he should be filled with "an obscure joy that he was powerless to name." It is only at this point, as he pauses, as he stands in solitude after completing an act of solidarity, that he is able to ratify what he has done. Retrospective understanding is accompanied by the passionate enjoyment of his own strength: "he joyfully acclaimed his own strength."

It is here that we, too, can see the point of d'Arrast's strength. It is not something to be contemplated in itself, like the body of the fascist leader—the colossus stands illuminated on a "hill" at the beginning of the story, but no crowd gathers around him. Rather, it is a quality that enables him to accomplish a particular task or set of tasks. It is not simply the strength of Sisyphus that allows one to cope (successively) with the weight of the rock and with the absurdity of one's fate. D'Arrast must also deal with the crowd, carrying his stone through it, struggling against the inertia of the tide:

> There he had to struggle against the crowds of merrymakers, the taperbearers, the shocked penitents. But, irresistibly, bucking the human tide with all his weight, he cut a path in such an impetuous way that he staggered and almost fell when he was eventually free, beyond the crowd, at the end of the street.

More generally, and in much the same way, he must deal with the water that threatens to dissolve or drown the whole place, and stone—so often the symbol of concentrated strength—is the substance that can resist this process. Indeed, there has already been once before a mythical triumph of stone over water in Iguape, when a statue of Jesus came out of the sea. This elemental victory, however, did not last: the stone is now kept in a damp grotto, where people go to break off pieces of wet schist. It might be a miraculous growing stone, but it does not act as a dam: it has become absorbed into the general process of dissolution and liquefaction, broken up by the drizzling rain of "grace."

With more immediate purpose than Sisyphus had, and with concomitantly more material opposition, d'Arrast accomplishes a particular, decisive act, carrying his stone down the slope—"the slope was slippery"—to the "poor areas" where it is needed. He throws it, finally, into the fire that burns in the center of this world of poverty. Dried and hardened in this way, it will presumably be better able to resist the infiltration of humidity and the invasion of the flood:

> "In the center of the room, in the place of the hearth, the stone was half-buried in ashes and earth."

The story ends, as did **"Jonas,"** with a moment of resolution: stone and water are clearly opposed, as were *solitaire* and *solidaire.* Yet this is also, as in Jonas's painting, a synthesis of opposites. Michael Issacharoff says:

> we can see taking place here, in a protagonist who was previously quite unyielding, a harmonious metaphorical fusion (still on the spatial level): now that he has accomplished his act of solidarity with the blacks by carrying the stone, he *accepts* water, the element which had been disturbing him and which he had been rejecting all through the story: "the sound of the waters filled him with a tumultuous happiness." [*L'Espace et la nouvelle,* 1967]

There is no scorn here, of course, no rejection of the horizontal, nor is there simple capitulation: d'Arrast does not finally have to lie down in the mud in order to be absorbed into this place. He is invited to sit (or crouch) as part of the family group: "They were squatting in a silent circle around the stone. . . . The brother moved a little away from the cook and, half turning towards D'Arrast but without looking at him, pointed to the empty place and said: 'Sit down with us.' "

In a sense, **"La Pierre qui pousse"** goes beyond the myth of Sisyphus without being essentially unfaithful to it. D'Arrast's act is no doubt more dramatic and more decisive than that of his heroic predecessor: he has achieved a more perfect stability, having actually found a point at which the stone can stop. Here, it is half-buried in the earth, in the exact center of this limited, human world: it can be both a foundation and a new, pagan miracle, a second growing stone, partaking thus, in true mythical fashion, of the cultural and the natural. Moreover, the stone is now the object of collective contemplation, just as the carrying of it involved more than one person. It is not d'Arrast, with his strength, nor for that matter the cook, with his weakness, who stands in the middle. There is no admiration of d'Arrast as leader—the cook's brother does not even look at him when inviting him to sit down—merely the visible hardness, the durable significance, of the completed act. Strength is what is required—and represented—by the rock: it is not opposed to the weakness or dependence of the other. There is no intersubjective conflict, no mastery or slavery, no judgment or penitence. . . . All that is left is for this group of human beings to pause together after a period of strenuous effort before continuing their existence at earth level.

Both **"Jonas"** and **"La Pierre qui pousse,"** the former in its literal-minded geometry, the latter in its radical diminution of the vertical axis, may be read as sophisticated and no doubt, by virtue of such modification, ironic reprises of the classical imagination of commitment. But it would be rash, as we have suggested, to associate this irony too closely with that of Sartre. Whereas Sartre ridicules elevation, denouncing and paradoxically despising it from below, working to achieve—or to consecrate—his own fall and the fall of the other, Camus seems determined to maintain height in some vestigial form. This can been seen in his discursive writings, which—although they seem to be concerned, almost as much as Sartre's, with a spatial projection of the role of the intellectual, with the definition of his *place*—develop quite a different emphasis. (pp. 280-86)

P. M. Cryle, "Routine Elevation: 'Le Mythe de Sisyphe', 'La Peste', 'L'Exil et le royaume', 'La Chute'," in his The Thematics of Commitment: The Tower & the Plain, *Princeton University Press, 1985, pp. 242-94.*

Camus on leaving Algeria:

Once more I left Tipasa, returning to Europe and its struggles. But the memory of that day sustains me still and helps me meet both joy and sorrow with equanimity. In the difficult times we face, what more can I hope for than the power to exclude nothing and to learn to weave from strands of black and white one rope tautened to the breaking point? In everything I've done or said so far, I seem to recognize these two forces, even when they contradict each other. I have not been able to deny the light into which I was born and yet I have not wished to reject the responsibilities of our time. It would be too easy to set against the gentle name Tipasa other names more sonorous and more cruel: there is, for man today, an inner path that I know well from having traveled both ways upon it, which leads from the summits of the mind to the capitals of crime. And, doubtless, one can always rest, sleep on the hillside or settle into crime. But if we give up a part of what exists, we must ourselves give up being; we must then give up living or loving except by proxy.

From "Return to Tipasa" (1954)

David R. Ellison (essay date 1990)

[In the following excerpt, Ellison examines Camus's interpretation of the biblical Jonah in "The Artist at Work" and stresses the relevance of Camus's own experiences as an artist to the themes of the story.]

The Old Testament of the Bible tells the story of a man named Jonah whom God asks to go to Nineveh in order to denounce the wickedness of its citizens. Wishing to escape his duty to the Lord, Jonah embarks upon a boat instead, but soon he and the members of the crew are tossed by a terrible tempest. Realizing that he is the cause of this life-threatening storm, Jonah volunteers to be thrown overboard; when he is in the sea, the tempest suddenly stops. Camus chooses to place before the beginning of his own story the passage from the book of Jonah in which the reluctant prophet says to his companions on ship: "Take me up and cast me forth into the sea . . . for I know that for my sake this great tempest is upon you" (Jonah 1:12). The cautionary tale of Jonah is most famous, of course, for what follows this initial episode: when he finds himself in the sea, Jonah soon is swallowed by a whale, in whose belly he lives for three days and three nights. It is not this part of the story in isolation that interests Camus most, however. Rather, the modern writer concentrates his attention on two aspects of the beginning of the Biblical narrative: 1. Jonah's efforts to flee his duty (which in this case is the prophetic denouncing of a city and its sins); 2. the necessity of his punishment and suffering so that his fellow humans can live in tranquillity.

The protagonist of [**"Jonas ou l'artiste au travail ("The Artist at Work")**], a painter who not only achieves success in artistic circles, but also a degree of public notoriety, is called Gilbert Jonas. Camus's tale is about the frustrations of the artist in the modern world, about the demands placed upon him by his family, friends, colleagues, rivals, and business associates. In framing his allegory with the Biblical quotation and in naming his hero Jonas, Camus establishes what might be called a one-to-one correspondence between his own story and that of the Bible. Just as the Old Testament Jonah attempted to flee the Lord, in the same way Jonas attempts to escape his artistic duty in various ways; just as it was necessary for the ancient Jonah to suffer so that his fellows might have peace, in the same way, Camus suggests that the artist must live through a certain kind of punishment and pain so that his public can pursue its everyday life in security and without anguish.

"The Artist at Work" is, for Camus and for ***Exile and the Kingdom,*** a curious, somewhat anomalous creation. It is the only one of the six stories that takes place in Europe (various signs in the tale point unambiguously to Paris); it is autobiographical in an unusually transparent way; and its style can only be described as a pastiche of Voltaire. **"The Artist at Work"** is a humorous but also bittersweet rewriting of *Candide,* in which the leitmotiv of the Voltairian hero, "tout est pour le mieux dans le meilleur des mondes" ("all is for the best in the best of worlds") is replaced by Jonas's equally naive belief in his "star" (that is: the infallibility of his success, the inevitability of his secure happiness). Like Voltaire, Camus views his protagonist from a distinctly ironical distance, but this distance and this irony are the more remarkable because Jonas, in a crucial sense, *is* Albert Camus. Whereas Voltaire delighted in crushing Candide with exaggerated misfortune as a means of dismantling the tenets of Leibnizian optimism (for which, of course, he had no philosophical admiration), Camus, in loading his hero with the burdens of our hectic modern-day world, was tracing his own self-portrait and was detailing the confrontation between his own naive optimism and the calamities that beset the thinking person in the twentieth century.

The story of Jonas is quite simple and linear in its development. It begins when Jonas is thirty-five years old and his works have attracted the attention of several influential critics. We follow Jonas's career from this early modest success to the apex of his renown in the public eye, then through the eclipse of his name to final obscurity. As the years pass and his artistic work moves through its phases, he marries, has several children, is surrounded then abandoned by numerous hypocritical admirers and false friends, then retreats into ultimate solitude. Beyond the love of his wife and children, there are two constants in his life: the ever-faithful friendship of a man named Rateau, who visits him almost daily, and the regularity of his artistic production, on which he can count until the final stages of his evolution toward silence.

The exceedingly simple narrative framework of the story allows Camus the freedom to express some of his deep convictions on the mission of the artist in the modern world in an apparently off-hand and humorous way. The surface wit of the comments does not remove the sting of the author's observations, however. What Camus has to say about the phenomenon of artistic discipleship, for example, is both funny and sad: funny for the reader to contemplate from the outside, sad (and aggravating) for the artist, who must endure such stupid and non-disinterested "admiration." In the following passage, one hears Camus's own voice:

> Jonas now had disciples. At first he had been surprised, not understanding what could be learned from someone who himself had everything to discover. The artist, in him, walked in darkness; how could he have taught the true paths? But he understood rather quickly that a disciple was not necessarily someone who aspires to learn something. More often, on the contrary, one became a disciple for the disinterested pleasure of teaching one's master. . . . The disciples of Jonas explained in detail what he had painted and why. Thus Jonas discovered in his work many hidden intentions that surprised him a bit, and many things that he had not intended.

In this and other similar passages, Camus makes clear that the essential work of the artist takes place in "darkness" and solitude. Whereas the disciples want Jonas to remain faithful to one coherent set of aesthetic principles, the protagonist knows intuitively that the best art does not proceed dogmatically from neat and codifiable theories. As the false admirers progressively invade his life (and his territory: in a literal and physical sense, soon Jonas has no more space in his apartment in which to paint), the conflicts between the artist's natural inclination toward sociability and the demands of his work grow ever greater: "It was difficult to paint the world and men while simultaneously living with them."

As the story moves toward its conclusion, Jonas becomes increasingly incapable of painting. This creative sterility, which resembles Camus's own "writer's block" after *The Rebel,* is coupled with a sentiment that might properly be called existential anguish: that is, the less he is capable of work, the more Jonas reflects on the meaning of his existence. When, at the conclusion of the tale, he isolates himself from friends and family in a small loft he has constructed above the rest of the apartment, when he does not lift his brush but merely listens to "the silence within himself," he has attained a state of absolute emptiness in which life seems to have become a desert without points of reference, without significance. Only after he has reached bottom does he finally trace one small word on his canvas—a word that can be deciphered either as *solitaire* (solitary) or *solidaire* (solidary).

With conscious intent, Camus has left the ending of his story open. Just as it is impossible for Rateau to determine whether the central letter of the painted word is a "t" or a "d," in the same way it is impossible for the author to know whether he can choose between the privilege of artistic solitude on the one hand and the duty of solidarity with his fellow humans on the other. It is probable that the choice cannot be made, that the position of the artist is always an uncomfortable one—that his career is necessarily an alternation between solitude and solidarity, in which neither side ever permanently attains dominance. In **"The Artist at Work"** Camus has returned to the same fundamental problem that he developed in **"The Guest,"** where Daru was forced to choose between his preferred solitary life and an act of solidarity—either toward Balducci or toward the Arab prisoner. The difference between the stories is one of emphasis and tone, but in both cases Camus refuses to grant his protagonists—or himself—the luxury of an easy self-involved isolation beyond the cares and conflicts of the brutal, disorderly world in which we all live. (pp. 199-204)

David R. Ellison, in his Understanding Albert Camus, *University of South Carolina Press, 1990, 232 p.*

FURTHER READING

Biography

Lottman, Herbert R. *Albert Camus: A Biography.* Garden City, N.Y.: Doubleday and Co., 1979, 753 p.

Traces Camus's life and intellectual development. Also includes a critical history of his works.

McCarthy, Patrick. *Camus: A Critical Study of His Life and Work.* London: Hamish Hamilton, 1982, 359 p.

Biographical study that reevaluates the life and work of Camus after his death and seeks to answer the question "what remains of Camus and how do we look back on him?"

Criticism

Amoia, Alba della Fazia. "*Exile and the Kingdom:* A Diorama." In her *Albert Camus,* pp. 125-34. New York: Continuum, 1989.

Compares the characters in Camus's short stories, which illustrate "the muted struggle of oppressed figures in everyday life," with the more mythical figures that populate Camus's dramas and essays.

Barbeito, Patricia. "Perception and Ideology: Camus as 'Colonizer' in 'The Adulterous Woman'." *Revue Celfan/Celfan Review* 7, No. 3 (May 1988): 34-8.
Examines the characterization of Arabs and descriptions of the female body in "The Adulterous Woman."

Black, Moishe. "Camus's 'L'hôte' as a Ritual of Hospitality." *Nottingham French Studies* 28, No. 1 (Spring 1989): 39-52.
Presents "The Guest" as a "ritualized drama of hospitality" that is directed by ancient rituals of Bedouin hospitality and rules of the guest-host relationship in classical antiquity.

Blythe, Hal and Sweet, Charlie. "Speaking in 'Tongues': Psychoses in 'The Renegade'." *Studies in Short Fiction* 25, No. 2 (Spring 1988): 129-34.
Argues that the narrative inconsistencies in "The Renegade" are not signs of artistic laxity but Camus's attempt to realistically render the missionary's schizophrenic speech.

Cervo, Nathan. "Camus's 'L'hôte'." *The Explicator* 48, No. 3 (Spring 1990): 222-24.
Discusses the symbolism in the names of characters and locations and examines the significance of Daru's political beliefs in "The Guest."

Claire, Thomas. "Landscape and Religious Imagery in Camus' 'La Pierre qui pousse'." *Studies in Short Fiction* 13, No. 3 (Summer 1976): 321-29.
Analyzes "The Growing Stone" by exploring "the fashion in which d'Arrast's development is delineated, with particular emphasis upon the landscape and religious imagery that reflects his development."

Crant, Phillip. "Conflict and Confrontation: An Essay on Camus's 'L'hôte'." *The University of Southern Florida Language Quarterly* XII, Nos. 1-2 (Fall-Winter 1973): 43-6.
Discusses how the conflict between Daru and the Arab in "The Guest" is reflected and supplemented by other oppositions presented in the story, including man versus man, man versus nature, and nature versus nature.

Curtis, Jerry L. "Alienation and the Foreigner in Camus's *L'exil et le royaume.*" *French Literature Series* II, (1975): 127-38.
Reviews the stories included in *Exile and the Kingdom,* highlighting the theme of alienation and the role of the foreigner.

———. "Structure and Space in Camus's 'Jonas'." *Modern Fiction Studies* 22, No. 4 (Winter 1976-77): 571-76.
Examines the character of Gilbert Jonas and the relationship between solidarity and solitude in "The Artist at Work."

Davis, Robert Gorham. "Faith for an Age without Faith." *The New York Times Book Review* (9 March 1958): 1, 26.
Praises the short stories in *Exile and the Kingdom* for their artistry and philosophical rigor.

Day, Loraine. "The Theme of Death in Camus's 'La femme adultère' and 'Retour à Tipasa'." *Essays in French Literature* No. 20 (November 1983): 67-94.
Discusses similarities between "The Adulterous Woman" and Camus's "Retour à Tipasa," a journal kept by him during his visit to Laghouat, Algiers.

Festa-McCormick, Diana. "Existential Exile and a Glimpse of the Kingdom." In *Critical Essays on Albert Camus,* edited by Bettina L. Knapp, pp. 107-16. Boston: G. K. Hall, 1988.
Examines the importance of community throughout *Exile and the Kingdom.*

Fischler, Alexander. "Camus's 'La Pierre qui pousse': Saint George and the Protean Dragon." *Symposium* XXIV, No. 3 (Fall 1970): 206-17.
Focuses on Camus's allusions to classical myth and the Bible in "The Growing Stone."

Fitch, Brian T. *The Narcissistic Text: A Reading of Camus's Fiction.* Toronto: University of Toronto Press, 1982, 128 p.
A semiotic reading of "The Guest" and "The Artist at Work."

Goodhand, Robert H. "The Omphalos and the Phoenix: Symbolism of the Center in Camus' 'La Pierre qui pousse'." *Studies in Short Fiction* 21, No. 2 (Spring 1984): 117-26.
Examines the symbolism in "The Growing Stone."

Grobe, Edwin P. "The Psychological Structure of Camus's 'L'hote'." *The French Review* 40, No. 3 (December 1966): 357-67.
Analyzes the meeting between Daru and his Arab guest, the psychology of both characters, and the cultural influences that condition the responses of guest to host.

Haig, Stirling. "The Epilogue of *Crime and Punishment* and Camus' 'La femme adultere'." *Comparative Literature Studies* 3, No. 4 (1966): 445-49.
Compares similarities in the language and themes of Camus's "The Adulterous Woman" and the epilogue to Dostoevsky's *Crime and Punishment.*

Howe, Irving. "Between Fact and Fable." *The New Republic* 138, No. 13 (31 March 1958): 17-18.
Characterizes the major themes in Camus's fiction and reviews the stories that make up *Exile and the Kingdom.*

Johnson, Patricia J. "An Impossible Search for Identity: Theme and Imagery in Camus' 'Le renégat'." *Research Studies* 37, No. 1 (March 1969): 171-82.
Examines the disparate experiences that contribute to the identity of the missionary in "The Renegade."

Joiner, Lawrence D. "Reverie and Silence in 'Le renegat'." *Romance Notes* XVI, No. 2 (Winter 1975): 262-67.
Analyzes the significance of delusion and speechlessness in explicating the character of the missionary.

———. "Camus' 'Le Renégat': Identity Denied." *Studies in Short Fiction* 13, No. 1 (Winter 1976): 37-41.
Analyzes the character of the missionary and how his identity contributes to the themes of "The Renegade."

———. "Camus's 'The Renegade': A Quest for Sexual Identity." *Research Studies: Washington State University* 45, No. 3 (September 1977): 171-76.
A psychoanalytic interpretation of "The Renegade" that discusses the childhood experiences of the missionary and compares the characteristics exhibited by him to the symptoms that Freud outlines in his "Character and Anal Eroticism."

Jones, Rosemarie. "Camus and the Aphorism: *L'Exil et le royaume.*" *The Modern Language Review* 78, No. 2 (April 1983): 308-18.

Notes the abundance of binary oppositions in *The Exile and the Kingdom* and the impossibility of assigning a single interpretation to each story as being evidence that the collection shares certain traits with the aphoristic form.

Keefe, Terry. " 'Heroes of Our Time' in Three of the Stories of Camus and Simone de Beauvoir." *Forum for Modern Language Studies* XVII, No. 1 (January 1981): 39-54.

Contends that the similarities between Camus's "The Artist at Work" and de Beauvoir's *Les mandarins* illustrate the sympathy that existed between the existentialism of Sartre and de Beauvoir and the moralist philosophy of Camus.

King, Adèle. "Jonas ou l'artiste au travail." *French Studies* XX, No. 3 (July 1966): 267-80.

Cites allusions to the biblical Jonah in "The Artist at Work" and compares the story to Henry Miller's "Un etre étolique" and George Orwell's "Inside the Whale."

LaVallee-Williams, Marthe. "Arabs in 'La femme adultere': From Faceless Other to Agent." *Revue Celfan/Celfan Review* IV, No. 3 (May 1985): 6-10.

Examines the role of the Arab in "La femme adultère" and considers Camus's characterization of Arabs in several other works.

Miles, O. Thomas. "Three Authors in Search of a Character." *The Personalist* XLVI, No. 1 (Winter 1965): 65-72.

Compares Camus's *Exile and the Kingdom* to Arthur Miller's *Death of a Salesman* and Aldous Huxley's *Brave New World.*

Minor, Anne. "The Short Stories of Albert Camus." *Yale French Studies* 25 (Spring 1960): 75-80.

One of the earliest critical studies of *Exile and the Kingdom* in English that reviews the plot, themes, and structure of each story.

Pasco, Allan H. " 'And Seated Ye Shall Fall': Some Lexical Markers in Camus's 'Jonas'." *Modern Fiction Studies* 28, No. 2 (Summer 1982): 240-42.

Examines the solitary/solidarity duality in "The Artist at Work" and draws parallels between the character Jonas and the life of Camus.

Petry, Sandy. "Speech, Society and Nature in Camus's 'Les muets'." *Romance Notes* 22, No. 2 (Winter 1981): 161-66.

Discusses the major themes in "The Silent Men" and explains the importance of class identity in the story.

Quillot, Roger. "An Ambiguous World." In *Camus: A Collection of Critical Essays,* edited by Germaine Brée, pp. 157-69. Englewood Cliffs, N.J.: Prentice-Hall, 1962.

Discusses the stories in *Exile and the Kingdom* in relation to Camus's other works and with respect to the difficulties that Camus experienced in his later career.

Rhein, Phillip H. "The Kingdom of Man." In his *Albert Camus,* pp. 116-30. New York: Twayne, 1969.

Examines the themes, style, and plots of the stories in *Exile and the Kingdom.*

Rooke, Constance. "Camus' 'The Guest': The Message on the Blackboard." *Studies in Short Fiction* 14, No. 1 (Winter 1977): 78-81.

Considers the possibility that Daru wrote the accusatory message on the blackboard himself and discusses the intent and meaning of the story as if it is based on guilt rather than cultural misunderstanding.

Simon, John K. "Camus' Kingdom: The Native Host and Unwanted Guest." *Studies in Short Fiction* 1, No. 4 (Summer 1964): 289-91.

Analyzes the characterization of Daru in "The Guest" and defends the common assertion that Daru's refusal to dictate the fate of the Arab is a "type of decision."

Sterling, Elwyn. "A Story of Cain: Another Look at 'L'hôte'." *The French Review* 54, No. 4 (March 1981): 324-29.

Discusses the many allusions to the Bible in "The Guest" with particular attention to Cain, the prelapsarian landscape, and the fall.

———. "Albert Camus's Adulterous Woman: A Consent to Dissolution." *Romance Quarterly* 34, No. 2 (May 1987): 155-63.

Addresses the issue of what constitutes Janine's adulterous act in "The Adulterous Woman" by referring to the opinions of other critics and analyzing the events in the story.

Storey, Michael L. "The Guests of Frank O'Connor and Albert Camus." *Comparative Literature Studies* 23, No. 3 (Fall 1986): 250-62.

Examines similarities in plot, characterization, setting, and themes of Frank O'Connor's short story "Guests of the Nation" and Camus's "The Guest."

Suther, Judith, ed. *Essays on Camus's* Exile and the Kingdom. University, Miss.: Romance Monographs, 1980, 329 p.

A collection of essays that address thematic and stylistic concerns in the stories and provides a number of previously untranslated essays in English.

———. "The Concept of 'Kingdom' in Camus' 'La femme adultere' and Colette's *La vagabonde.*" In *Selected Proceedings 32nd Mountain Interstate Foreign Language Conference,* edited by Gregorio C. Marté, pp. 367-71. Winston-Salem, N.C.: Wake Forest University, 1984.

Compares the ambiguity of the word *royaume* (kingdom) in Camus's "La femme adultère" to the relative clarity of the term in Colette's novel *La Vagabonde.*

Thody, Philip. "Exile, Humanism and a Conclusion." In his *Albert Camus,* pp. 95-112. London: Macmillan, 1989.

Discusses the stories in *Exile and the Kingdom* with reference to the theme of spiritual exile.

Womack, William R., and Heck, Francis S. "A Note on Camus's 'The Guest'." *The International Fiction Review* 2, No. 2 (July 1975): 163-65.

Praises "The Guest" as a "nearly perfect short story" and offers an interpretation of the enigmatic conclusion.

Additional coverage of Camus's life and career is contained in the following sources published by Gale Research: *Contemporary Authors,* Vols. 89-92; *Contemporary Literary Criticism,* Vols. 1, 2, 4, 9, 11, 14, 32, 63; and *Dictionary of Literary Biography,* Vol. 72.

Joseph Conrad

1857-1924

(Born Jozef Teodor Konrad Nalecz Korzeniowski) Polish-born English novelist, short story writer, essayist, and autobiographer.

INTRODUCTION

Considered one of the greatest novelists of the twentieth century, Conrad is also esteemed as a preeminent writer of short fiction. Two stories in particular, *Heart of Darkness* and "The Secret Sharer," have been proclaimed as the works of a consummate literary artist and an entertaining storyteller. In these and other stories Conrad employed an introspective narrator to focus attention on the teller as well as the tale. Like many of his novels, Conrad's short fiction deals with several recurring themes: the ambiguity of good and evil, the corruption of moral ideals, and the human propensity for self-deception.

Critics generally divide Conrad's literary career into two periods: works written before or during 1912 and those written after 1912. Works of the first period include Conrad's widely acclaimed stories of the sea, most prominently "Youth," "Typhoon," "The End of the Tether," "The Secret Sharer," as well as the novella *Heart of Darkness.* Stories of the second period are less highly regarded and are typified by such romantic melodramas as "Because of the Dollars," "The Planter of Malata," "The Tale," and "The Warrior's Soul." Typical of the early works, *Heart of Darkness* is based in part on personal experiences. In 1890, after more than a decade as a seaman, Conrad requested the command of a Belgian steamer sailing for Africa. A diary kept by Conrad during the subsequent voyage up the Congo River documents the nightmarish aspects of his experience and provides evidence that many of the characters, incidents, and impressions recalled in *Heart of Darkness* have factual bases. In his preface to *Youth: A Narrative, and Two Other Stories,* in which *Heart of Darkness* appeared, Conrad stated that the story is "experience pushed a little (and only very little) beyond the actual facts of the case." Despite this contention, critics have found that Conrad's grim depiction of the African environment and his emphasis on greed, savagery, and psychological regression in the novella are the products of Conrad's pessimistic view of human nature, specifically his belief that individuals cannot live up to their fundamental moral codes and ideals. *Heart of Darkness* tells the story of Marlow—who also appears in *Lord Jim* and "Youth"—and his journey up the Congo River to relieve Kurtz, the most successful trader in ivory working for the Belgian government. Prior to meeting Kurtz, Marlow admires the trader and is excited at the prospect of their encounter. When Marlow finally meets him, he is repulsed by Kurtz's barbarism, subjugation of African peoples, and thirst for power. Upon Kurtz's death, Marlow realizes that the heart of darkness—the human potential for evil and savagery—lies within him as well.

Whereas in *Heart of Darkness* Conrad focused on Marlow's intensified awareness of evil in human nature through his identification with Kurtz, Conrad used the idea of a "double" in "The Secret Sharer" to portray the protagonist's growth toward self-knowledge. "The Secret Sharer" is the account of a young captain who harbors a criminal on his ship while at sea. The captain aids in the escape of Leggatt, a man wanted for murder, because he believes him to be his ideal self, his "secret sharer of life." Some critics have contended, however, that Leggatt is far from any human ideal. Instead, they argue, he displays cowardice, murderous instincts, and irrationality and represents the evil in the captain and in humankind. Conrad's ambiguous portrayal of characters has inspired extensive critical debate and stems from his goal as a writer to present the complexities of events and individuals without pretense of explanation. As Conrad stated in the preface to *The Nigger of the "Narcissus"*: "My task which I am trying to achieve is, by the power of the written word, to make you feel—it is, before all, to make you *see.* That—and no more, and it is everything."

Critics note that Conrad was less successful in making his readers "see" in his later works. While popular with readers of the time, Conrad's works written after 1912—including the novels *Chance, Victory, The Shadow-Line,* and the short story collections *Tales of Hearsay* and *The Sisters*—are considered inferior to his earlier writings. In such stories as "Because of the Dollars," "The Planter of Malata," and "The Warrior's Soul," Conrad abandoned complex narratives and characterizations and focused instead on romance, violence, and sentiment. "The Planter of Malata," for example, tells the story of Geoffrey Renouard, a young man in love with Felicia Moorsam, who is engaged to another man. Wanting to keep Felicia close to him, Geoffrey deceives her into sailing away to the remote island of Malata. When Felicia learns of Geoffrey's duplicity, she scorns him, and a brokenhearted Geoffrey kills himself. Disappointed by what they consider romantic melodrama, scholars generally dismiss Conrad's later short fiction.

Most critics affirm that the superiority of Conrad's earlier stories can be attributed to their basis in his own life, particularly his experiences at sea and his private struggle with questions of morality, loyalty, and human fallibility. Some have commented that toward the end of his career, Conrad was more concerned with selling books than in creating works of literature. Nonetheless, even in his weakest stories, as Lawrence Graver has observed, Conrad was "preeminently concerned with man's response to the hazards of circumstances or to the unexplored vulnerability of his own nature."

PRINCIPAL WORKS

SHORT FICTION

Tales of Unrest 1898
Typhoon 1902
**Youth: A Narrative, and Two Other Stories* 1902
Typhoon, and Other Stories 1903
A Set of Six 1908
†*'Twixt Land and Sea* 1912
Within the Tides 1915
Tales of Hearsay 1925
The Sisters 1928
The Complete Short Stories of Joseph Conrad 1933

OTHER MAJOR WORKS

Almayer's Folly (novel) 1895
An Outcast of the Islands (novel) 1896
The Children of the Sea (novel) 1897; also published as *The Nigger of the "Narcissus"*, 1898
Lord Jim (novel) 1900
The Inheritors [with Ford Madox Ford] (novel) 1901
Romance [with Ford Madox Ford] (novel) 1903
Nostromo (novel) 1904
One Day More (drama) 1904
The Mirror of the Sea (autobiography) 1906
The Secret Agent (novel) 1907
Some Reminiscences (autobiography) 1908; also published as *A Personal Record,* 1912
Under Western Eyes (novel) 1911
Chance (novel) 1913
Victory (novel) 1915
The Arrow of Gold (novel) 1917
The Shadow-Line (novel) 1917
The Rescue (novel) 1920
Notes on Life and Letters (essays) 1921
Notes on My Books (essays) 1921
The Rover (novel) 1923
The Nature of a Crime [with Ford Madox Ford] (novel) 1924
Suspense (novel) 1925
Last Essays (essays) 1926
Conrad to a Friend: 150 Selected Letters from Joseph Conrad to Richard Curle (letters) 1928; also published as *Joseph Conrad to Richard Curle,* 1928
The Collected Edition of the Works of Joseph Conrad. 21 vols. (novels, short stories, essays, and memoirs) 1946-55
Congo Diary, and Other Uncollected Pieces (diary and short stories) 1978

*This work contains the novella *Heart of Darkness,* which was published separately in 1942.

†This work contains "The Secret Sharer."

Edward Garnett (essay date 1902)

[*Garnett was a prominent editor for several London publishing houses and introduced the works of Conrad, John Galsworthy, and D. H. Lawrence to the reading public. In the following excerpt from a review originally published in* Academy and Literature *in 1902, he favorably appraises "Youth," "The End of the Tether," and* Heart of Darkness. *Responding to Garnett's review, Conrad wrote: "My dearest fellow you quite overcome me. And your brave attempt to grapple with the foggishness of* H. of D., *to explain what I myself tried to shape blindfold, as it were, touched me profoundly."*]

The publication in volume form of Mr. Conrad's three stories, **'Youth,'** ***Heart of Darkness,*** **'The End of the Tether,'** is one of the events of the literary year. These stories are an achievement in art which will materially advance his growing reputation. Of the stories, **'Youth'** may be styled a modern English epic of the Sea; **'The End of the Tether'** is a study of an old sea captain who, at the end of forty years' trade exploration of the Southern seas, finding himself dispossessed by the perfected routine of the British empire overseas he has helped to build, falls on evil times, and faces ruin calmly, fighting to the last. These two will be more popular than the third, ***Heart of Darkness,*** a study of 'the white man in Africa' which is most amazing, a consummate piece of artistic *diablerie.* On reading ***Heart of Darkness*** on its appearance in *Blackwood's Magazine* our first impression was that Mr. Conrad had, here and there, lost his way. Now that the story can be read, not in parts, but from the first page to the last at a sitting, we retract this opinion and hold ***Heart of Darkness*** to be the high-water mark of the author's talent. It may be well to analyse this story a little so that the intelligent reader, reading it very deliberately, may see better for himself why Mr. Conrad's book enriches English literature.

Heart of Darkness, to present its theme bluntly, is an impression, taken from life, of the conquest by the European whites of a certain portion of Africa, an impression in particular of the civilising methods of a certain great European Trading Company face to face with the 'nigger.' We say this much because the English reader likes to know where he is going before he takes art seriously, and we add that he will find the human life, black and white, in ***Heart of Darkness*** an uncommonly and uncannily serious affair. If the ordinary reader, however, insists on taking the subject of a tale very seriously, the artist takes his method of presentation more seriously still, and rightly so. For the art of ***Heart of Darkness***—as in every psychological masterpiece—lies in the relation of the things of the spirit to the things of the flesh, of the invisible life to the visible, of the sub-conscious life within us, our obscure motives and instincts, to our conscious actions, feelings and outlook. Just as landscape art implies the artist catching the exact relation of a tree to the earth from which it springs, and of the earth to the sky, so the art of ***Heart of Darkness*** implies the catching of infinite shades of the white man's uneasy, disconcerted, and fantastic relations with the exploited barbarism of Africa; it implies the acutest analysis of the deterioration of the white man's *morale,* when he is let loose from European restraint, and planted down in the tropics as an 'emissary of light' armed to the teeth, to make trade profits out of the 'subject races.' The weirdness, the brilliance, the psychological truth of this masterly analysis of two Continents in conflict, of the abysmal gulf between the white man's system and the black man's comprehension of its results, is conveyed in a rapidly rushing narrative which calls for close attention on the reader's part. But the attention once surrendered, the pages of the narrative are as enthralling as the pages of Dostoevsky's *Crime and Punishment.* The stillness of the sombre African forests, the glare of sunshine, the feeling of dawn, of noon, of night on the tropical rivers, the isolation of the unnerved, degenerating whites staring all day and every day at the Heart of Darkness which is alike meaningless and threatening to their own creed and conceptions of life, the helpless bewilderment of the unhappy savages in the grasp of their flabby and rapacious conquerors—all this is a page torn from the life of the Dark Continent—a page which has been hitherto carefully blurred and kept away from European eyes. There is no 'intention' in the story, no *parti pris,* no prejudice one way or the other; it is simply a piece of art, fascinating and remorseless, and the artist is but intent on presenting his sensations in that sequence and arrangement whereby the meaning or the meaninglessness of the white man in uncivilised Africa can be felt in its really significant aspects. If the story is too strong meat for the ordinary reader, let him turn to **'Youth,'** wherein the song of every man's youth is indeed sung.

The third story, **'The End of the Tether,'** is not, we think, so remarkable an artistic conception as are the other two; but in the close study of the old English captain, a seaman of the old school, Mr. Conrad has given us the best piece of character painting he has yet achieved. (pp. 131-33)

As a picture of sea life the story is absolutely convincing; it is only in the total effect on the reader's nerves that **'The End of the Tether'** strikes us as being less subtle in arrangement, less inevitable in its climax than is ***Heart of Darkness.*** If we are to judge the story, however, as a series of continuous and interdependent pictures of life, cunning mirages of actual scenes, exquisitely balanced and proportioned, delicate mirages evoked as by an enchanter's wand, then indeed Mr. Conrad is easily among the first writers of to-day. His special individual gift, as an artist, is of so placing a whole scene before the reader that the air, the landscape, the moving people, the houses on the quays, the ships in the harbour, the sounds, the scents, the voices in the air, all fuse in the perfect and dream-like illusion of an unforgettable reality. **'The End of the Tether'** is a triumph of the writer's art of description, but we must repeat that ***Heart of Darkness*** in the subtlety of its criticism of life is the high-water mark of the author's talent. (p. 133)

Edward Garnett, in an excerpt from Conrad: The Critical Heritage, *edited by Norman Sherry, Routledge & Kegan Paul, 1973, pp. 131-33.*

Robert Lynd (essay date 1912)

[*Lynd, an Irish journalist and author, served as literary editor of the* London News Chronicle *and contributed regularly to the* New Statesman and Nation. *His literary criticism has been described by J. B. Priestley as "acute, witty, yet tolerant." In the following excerpt from a review originally published in the* Daily News *in 1912, he lauds* 'Twixt Land and Sea, *declaring "The Secret Sharer" a masterpiece.*]

If anyone has any doubts of Mr. Conrad's genius he will do well to read **'The Secret Sharer,'** the second story in [***'Twixt Land and Sea***]. I confess repentantly that I once had such doubts. But I had not read **'Typhoon'** then. None of the three stories in ***'Twixt Land and Sea*** possesses the cosmic or rather the infernal, energy of **'Typhoon.'** In reading **'Typhoon'** one has constantly, as it were, to catch hold of something solid in order to keep oneself from being swept off one's feet by the fury of the author's sensitive and truthful genius. **'The Secret Sharer'** is work of a quieter mood. It is as different from **'Typhoon'** as still water is from a storm. But it is to an equal extent a mastering vision of a world which Mr. Conrad knows and nobody else knows—a world of artistically uncharted seas—a world the seas of which have at once the reality of the seas we know, and something of the still intenser reality of the phantom seas of 'The Ancient Mariner.'

Everyone who has read Mr. Conrad's stories knows how sensitively and how surely he can create a living atmosphere as he adds nervous sentence to nervous sentence. Every sentence has a nerve; that is one of the distinguishing features of his writing. It is not clever writing—at least, not deliberately so. If his genius fails him, he has none of those glittering reserves of cleverness to fall back upon, such as enable Mr. Kipling always to achieve vividness even when he does not achieve life. But in what has been called the sense of life, Mr. Conrad is, within his limits, far richer than Mr. Kipling.

It is true that he expresses his sense of life rather through his winds and seas and ships than through his human beings. His human beings are, on the whole, small and eccentric creatures compared to those elements which spring upon them and lie in wait for them like the messengers of gods and devils. His characters, in other words, do not belong to that aristocracy of passion of which [Walter] Pater wrote. Even though they perform miracles of endurance in their warfare against wind and wave, it is the latter who are the mighty characters of his books. Compared with them, the captains and the sailors seem at times to be just a sort of odd playthings.

Thus his characters have frequently something of the quality of victims. One is very conscious of this as one reads **'Freya of the Seven Isles,'** in the present book. This is a wonderful pitiless story of revenge in the Dutch East Indies. It tells how a Dutch naval lieutenant, an ugly, surly, thick-bodied man, was enabled to get his rival, a young English trading captain, into his clutches in a manner that cost a charming and generous young man his reason, and a charming and high-hearted girl her life. The especial pitilessness of the story arises from the fact that the Dutchman's bitterness would hardly have been able to plan the destruction of his rival unaided. It was fate that struck the young man down—struck him down, too, not through his vices, but his virtues. For a man to whom he had done a service stole, in a moment of drunken weakness, the firearms belonging to his ship, and sold them to the natives on one of the Dutch islands, with the result that the young trader was delivered into the lieutenant's power. No one but Mr. Conrad could have described with such intense imaginative excitement—excitement free from every trace of melodrama and rhetoric—that calculated devilish tragedy when the lieutenant manœvred Jasper Allen's beautiful white ship to its doom upon the reef where it would lie long afterwards, a grey ghost, haunting the insane eyes of its owner as he watched it, the ghost of a man, from the shore.

In his description of human beings subjected to some terrible fascination Mr. Conrad excels. 'Studies in fascination' would be a not inapt description of the three stories in this book. The first of the three, **'A Smile of Fortune,'** which also has its scene among tropical seas, is a study of the spell cast on the captain of a ship by a mysterious outcast, shy, untamed, animal of a woman. It is good, but not supremely good. **'The Secret Sharer,'** on the other hand, which tells of the spell cast upon another captain by a mate charged with murder, who has taken refuge in his ship, is surely a masterpiece. Here Mr. Conrad himself casts a spell.

Ever from that midnight moment, when the captain, lonelily pacing the deck of his anchored ship in islanded eastern seas, looks over the side and beholds the apparently headless body of a man in the phosphorescent water at the foot of the ladder, the story grips one in its quiet, inevitable sentences. There is marvellous psychological insight shown in the way in which the captain, having clothed the man in his clothes and hidden him in his room and heard his strange story, like a secret, in intimate whispers, gradually comes to associate his own identity with the identity of the fugitive. It is the captain and not the fugitive who jumps at sudden sounds and at chances of discovery. The great elation of the story, however, does not arise from its study of the psychology of fascination or curious sense of identity or alarm. All this is necessary to produce it, but all this alone would not produce it. In his eagerness for the escape of his double, who insists upon dropping over the ship's side at night and swimming to one of the islands where he can live as one dead, a marooned and forgotten man, the captain compels his crew, almost still with horror, to bring the ship right up under the shadow of the land on a pretence of looking for land winds. That scene gives us one of the great thrills of modern literature.

> Such a hush had fallen on the ship that she might have been a bark of the dead floating in slowly under the very gate of Erebus.
>
> 'My God! Where are we?'
>
> It was the mate moaning at my elbow.

As the helmsman gives his answers to the captain's orders 'in a frightened, thin, childish voice' we, too, are still and tense like the horror-stricken crew. Then comes the fugitive's escape in the dark water. After that, the escape of that fine ship herself from the shadow, as it were, of the everlasting night—an escape that is one of the wonderful things of the literature of the sea. The elation that we get from this story is the elation which all great literature, even tragic literature, ought to give. Let all the bells of praise ring for so fine a piece of work. (pp. 251-53)

Robert Lynd, in an excerpt from Conrad: The Critical Heritage, *edited by Norman Sherry, Routledge & Kegan Paul, 1973, pp. 251-53.*

"I daresay **'Freya'** is pretty rotten. On the other hand the **'Secret Sharer,'** between you and me, is *it.* Eh? No damned tricks with girls there. Eh? Every word fits and there's not a single uncertain note. Luck my boy. Pure luck."

—Joseph Conrad in a letter to Edward Garnett, 1912

Joseph J. Reilly (essay date 1942)

[Reilly was an American educator, author, and critic. In the following essay, he examines the "moral test" facing each protagonist in Conrad's short fiction.]

The phrase "shorter stories," in Conrad's case, requires a word of explanation for, apart from full length novels, it means for the purposes of this essay stories as short as **"The Lagoon"** (4,000 words) and as lengthy as **"The End of the Tether"** (60,000 words). Conrad's finest stories of less than novel length do not fall within the typical short story bounds. What are his finest shorter stories? I think they are, in addition to the two named above, **"Youth,"** ***Heart of Darkness,*** **"Falk," "Secret Sharer," "Typhoon," "Smile of Fortune," "Freya of the Seven Isles,"** and **"Amy Foster,"** with **"Karain," "Tomorrow,"** and **"Outpost of Progress"** as additional possibilities.

The problems which concern Conrad's chief characters are not even in **"Typhoon"** primarily physical but moral and ethical. They have little to do with strength of muscle, everything to do with those inner qualities, that spiritual energy, that loyalty (often unconscious) to standards of conduct, which we imply in the phrase "strength of character." The hostile force against which strength of character must be shown may be the fury of fire or storm or, more subtly, temptations presented in guises uniquely seductive, or the threatened loss of a beloved woman, or ignorance coupled with fear, or human cunning and rapacity, or dangers growing out of the defiance (however benevolently intended) of established law.

The persons with whom Conrad's characters are chiefly concerned are not weaklings. If they triumph they deserve to and the reader applauds. If they fail it is because they have been subjected to tests which no man could promise himself to endure. Most of them are in a real sense tragic figures, at bottom good, wishing the right, struggling to maintain it but finally overcome. Kurtz, Captain Whalley, Yanko, Jasper Allen, Arsat—"There but for the grace of God go I."

Conrad once protested against the popular notion that he wrote "sea stories." What he meant was that the challenges his chief characters face have nothing essentially to do with the sea, but in one form or another confront men at all times and in every corner of the world. Conrad wrote about the men he knew best, who "go down to the sea in ships, who do business in great waters," of whom he was one from his sixteenth till his thirty-seventh year. Captain Whalley in **"The End of the Tether"** might have been a railroad engineer; Marlow, the hero of **"Youth,"** a flier with his first plane; the Captain in **"A Smile of Fortune,"** almost any young man who toyed to his hurt with half evil, half tender sensations. Significantly, Kurtz, the chief character in ***Heart of Darkness,*** the most powerful of all Conrad's shorter stories, is not a seaman at all and the sea plays no direct part in the tale.

Let us see to what moral test (what test of character if you prefer) the leading figures of his shorter stories are subjected.

In his first short story **"The Lagoon,"** Arsat the Malayan, in his flight with the wife of his chief, is aided by his brother. When the three are cornered by their pursuers, Arsat, compelled to make a choice, sacrifices his brother and saves the woman.

In **"Karain,"** written a few months later and thrice as long, the problem is similar: faced with the choice between the beloved woman and his dearest friend, Karain kills him to save her. In each case the decision must be on the instant, and however made is bound to bring remorse in its wake. Life, Conrad intimates, never tires of posing moral challenges. What complexities usually surround them, what undreamed of consequences are in their train!

The centaur-like hero of **"Falk"** has his own problem. Loving life with the deep-rooted instinct of an animal, he feels a comparable passion for an Olympian girl so generously alive that "she could have stood for an allegoric statue of the Earth." His conscience bids him confess to her a secret known to himself alone: once on a derelict ship he saved his life by murder and maintained it by cannibalism. To make this confession is almost certainly to horrify the girl and alienate her forever. But for Falk, with whom conscience and the hunger for life are equally exigent, there is no other way.

If we penetrate beneath the surface of **"The Secret Sharer"** we discover two ethical problems implied but never brought into the light. The youthful captain who knowingly harbors a murderer aboard his ship acts contrary to law (becoming an accessory after the fact), and in providing him an opportunity to escape imperils the safety of ship and crew entrusted to his care. In following this course the captain yields to the claims of compassion rather than to the claims of responsibility and law; he acts as a private individual rather than as the chief officer of a ship and a good British subject. What he faces, Conrad implies, is a conflict between duties defined by law and universally observed and the generous instincts of his youth, which appear heroic when we realize that in yielding to them he runs the risk of disgrace and ruin.

In **"The End of the Tether"** Captain Whalley, retired, who "never lost a ship nor consented to a shady transaction," returns to the sea to earn money for his impoverished daughter. When his sight begins to fail he keeps the fact secret, continuing in service and risking the safety of his ship. His conscience bids him resign his post but his daughter's need cries out against it. Love and duty clash but duty is not the victor.

The test which in **"Amy Foster"** confronts Yanko, the Polish castaway on English soil, is, unlike Captain Whalley's, not an ethical one. He survives homesickness and unreasoning suspicions; but when the dull unimaginative peasant girl who has married him out of pity runs from him in terror, taking their child with her, he can endure no more.

In **"Freya of the Seven Isles,"** Jasper Allen has so long associated his girl and his brig together in his thoughts that they become merged in a single all-absorbing passion, beyond which he has no desire, no future, no life. Thus when his rival, Heemskirk, deliberately wrecks the *Bonito* he wrecks the lives of the lovers as well, for Jasper does not seek out Freya and win fresh hope and courage from her who is so rich in both, or attempt to conquer some brave new world with her at his side, but broods over his loss till he goes insane and leaves to the heart-broken girl no release but death. Allen's weakness, cautiously revealed in the course of the story, is a lack of maturity, a certain want of self-discipline, a fatal flaw in an otherwise attractive character.

In **"Youth"** Jim Marlow at twenty-one as mate of the *Judea* does not escape his test. Conrad does not picture him tormented by fears, but he does not on that account mean to imply that fears—breath-taking fears—would not be justified. Were it otherwise this story could not have been written. It is not that Jim is unaware of their presence or lacks nerves and imagination but that he is so intoxicated by youth, so uplifted by its unreflecting gusto, that peril is a joy and tragedy but an aspect of a thrilling adventure. Thus, says Conrad, men act in the divine hour of youth; later they may also prevail but then they act stolidly or stoically or cynically or by force of habit or from shame or by an effort of will.

In **"Typhoon"** a similar test confronts the crew of the *Nan-Shan,* attacked not by fire but by the confederate violence of sea and sky, and attention is focussed no longer on one man getting his first initiation in responsibility but on four men, the Captain and his seasoned chief officers. What effects does this "act of God," this most prodigious storm in the whole of literature, have on each of these men and how, besides, do they react to the problem of justice and compassion involved in the presence of a supercargo locked in the hold and maddened by terror?

"An Outpost of Progress" (ironic title) recalls two similar stories of men isolated from civilization, "The Seventh Man" by Quiller-Couch and "In a Far Country" by Jack London. The scene of Conrad's tale is equatorial heat; the scene of the other two, arctic cold. Solitude and frayed nerves play a part in all three but the significant difference is that Conrad's story deals with moral degeneration. The tragedy which overtakes Carlier and Kayerts is traceable beyond a mental upset to a sly and enormous greed which condones and profits by murder.

In a story of much ampler scope, subtlety, and power, ***Heart of Darkness,*** Conrad returns to a similar theme. Kurtz is gifted, magnetic, and idealistic as Carlier and Kayerts never are, and the temptations which assail and finally destroy him are more insidious in their workings and more completely ruinous in their results than the vulgar ones to which they yield. Their spiritual potentialities are meagre, his enormous; at best they might have been commonplace executives in minor positions but Kurtz has it in him to become a world figure, an immortal in the history of social regeneration. The test comes when he discovers that the way to an independent fortune is heart-breakingly slow, and yet without it the door is closed against both his marriage and his vast ambitions for the altruistic development of central Africa. He finds means to quicken it but his course involves him in hateful alliances and tribal feuds, in sinister practices and monstrous relationships culminating in terrorism, lust, and murder.

While writing his first short story, **"The Lagoon,"** Conrad informed a friend that it was "a tricky thing with the usual forests, rivers, stars, wind, sunrise and so on." By this he meant, I think, that it is in miniature a typically Conradean story in the sense that it provides a vital test of the chief personage's character, and it tries to present that character in different situations, in revealing moments, and in actions whose consequences are more widespread and more tragic than one has foreseen. Finally, it provides a setting wherein the power and opulence of Nature are revealed in their fulness, and the sense of fear and solitude, beauty, wonder, and mystery is deepened, till her domain and that of human creatures who in the midst of life walk in the shadow of death, seem to mingle in a cosmic pattern more vast and awesome than they can comprehend.

Conrad at age seventeen.

"The romantic feeling of reality," said Conrad, "was in me an inborn faculty." This sense of reality explains why at the core of his stories is an incident of which he had either personal experience as in **"Youth"** or direct knowledge as in ***Heart of Darkness;*** or an episode currently known like Heemskirk's villainy in **"Freya"** or like the murder at sea in **"The Secret Sharer."** Conrad's romantic feeling explains why his best tales are not merely sailors' yarns but great stories that have been lifted into literature through the power of his emotion and imagination. Thus, to take **"The Secret Sharer"** again, he broods on what seems to be a vulgar homicide committed by a nameless sailor, until the wrong-doer is transformed from less than a shadow into a living man who, instead of being sent to England, to trial and imprisonment (as in the original episode), falls into the hands of a person responsive to the claims of compassion and poetic justice.

Once the murderer and his deed become actual to Conrad he faces what he called "the problem." "The problem," he wrote, "was to make unfamiliar things credible. To do that I had to create for them, to reproduce for them, to envelop them in, their proper atmosphere of actuality," so that the reader may see what Conrad has come to see and every aspect of the setting: not only, for example, the storm which assails the *Nan-Shan* and makes every sailor's nerves tense, not only the other ship (in **"Secret Sharer"**) on which the murderer Leggatt seeks refuge, but the friendly young captain's compassion, his curious notion that Leggatt is a kind of *alter ego,* the suspicions of the crew that the captain is getting "queer," and finally the scene at night when the captain (to the consternation of the crew) orders his ship to stand in close to shore to give his dangerous guest a chance to escape: "The black southern hill of Koh-ring seemed to hang right over the ship like a towering fragment of the everlasting night. . . . Then stillness again with the great shadow gliding closer, towering higher, without light, without sound. Such a hush had fallen on the ship that she might have been a bark of the dead floating in slowly under the very gate of Erebus." The fugitive noiselessly lowers himself into the sea and as the ship edges away strikes out for the shore and the chance—shrouded in similar darkness and mystery—of a new life.

The facts of this story, as of all Conrad's best tales, might be told in a few words but then it would not be his; the distinguishing features would be gone. The readers must share the captain's sympathy for the murderer; therefore they must know something about him: his background, his upbringing, his courage, his inherent decency; about the murdered sailor: his meanness, insolence, and cowardice; about the captain, who is going to be so impressed by the mitigating circumstances surrounding the crime and to feel such compassion for the murderer, that he will harbor him in defiance of law and risk everything to give him a chance to escape. The incredible must be made credible, and to solve that "problem" by the only medium open to him, words, "the old, old words," as he called them despairingly, "worn thin, defaced by ages of careless usage," Conrad toiled in a very agony of resolve, sometimes in tears. It is the proof of his genius that his successes were striking, his failures few.

To Conrad a character in his stories is immeasurably more than a person to whom something happens. He is a creature of immense importance partly because he is a human soul endowed with fears, longings, hopes, the capacity to foster illusions and to die of heartbreak, and partly because he possesses a conscience which, no matter what name he gives it, plays an inescapable role in his life. As an entity in that human creation which is the sum and crown of things, he commands attention not only for what he does and for what happens to him but for what he thinks and feels, since his thoughts and emotions help to explain the course he pursues and his reactions to the consequences. He is a complex being whose name is mystery, and Conrad, understanding this, leaves to the reader the sense of a secret truth, of a hidden reality in his full length characters that lie beyond the reach of any probe. It is with reverence no less than with despair that he notes "how incomprehensible, wavering, and misty are the beings that share with us the sight of the stars and the warmth of the sun." It is typical of Conrad that he succeeds in probing so deep, revealing so much, and conceding with fine but gratuitous humility his limitations of vision.

In order to make unfamiliar things credible—scenes, events, people—to make us, as he once put it, "hear, feel, before all, *see*" with his own sense of reality, Conrad has recourse to certain devices. Like More in *Utopia* (to take one instance out of many) he employs in all his finest shorter stories, except **"Typhoon"** and **"The End of the Tether,"** a narrator who is alleged to speak with first hand knowledge. Conrad does not handle this device with unfailing skill and in spite of his best efforts he sometimes wearies or exasperates. Many a reader would gladly proclaim the willing suspension of his unbelief if on such terms this supernumerary might be banished! As another expedient, Conrad adduces reinforcing testimony as to facts and goes to almost grotesque lengths to establish the moral and personal antecedents of his characters and to reveal the varied estimations in which they are held. The three officers of the *Nan-Shan* are one regarding the fury of the typhoon but not regarding Captain MacWhirr's idiosyncrasies; Captain Whalley discloses to the friendly VanWyk the story of his pride and his humiliation and we are permitted to see him through the eyes of VanWyk, Massy, and Sterne. So also with Kurtz: to Europe he is a great name, associated rather vaguely with a kind of humanitarian crusade; to the Company officials, an amazingly successful producer of ivory, a result made possible, it would seem, by some curious influence he wields over the natives; the natives themselves think him a kind of God whose ways are strangely wrought of good and bad; in Marlow's eyes he is evil, in those of the sweetheart who awaits his return to Paris and who cherishes beautiful memories, another Bayard without fear and without reproach.

How are so many points of view possible? How does it come about that Kurtz is known to two continents and why are judgments so divergent? Conrad cannot answer these questions lightly. Being Conrad, having a passion for establishing the reality of his stories, he must answer carefully, meticulously, even at the risk of wearying his readers. We must be informed that it is Marlow who tells this story, that as he does so he is on board a cruising yawl. What is her name? The *Nellie.* Where is she? Anchored in the Thames. What time of day is it? As dusk is falling on the river and London is becoming "a lurid glare under the stars." To whom does Marlow tell the tale? To the Director of Companies and three other men. Who are they? Who is Marlow? How did he happen to go to Africa and specifically up the Congo river? All these questions are answered and countless more as the story slowly gathers itself together and begins to move. As it moves it gains not speed but weight, the weight of endless detail added bit by bit with infinite patience; nothing is overlooked, from the two women "knitting black wool as for a warm pall" in the waiting-room of the Company, to the black helper in the wheelhouse who, spitted through the heart by a spear, "looked at me over his shoulder in an extraordinary, profound, familiar manner, and fell upon my feet." Conrad is in no hurry. If a story seems to him worth telling he insists on telling it in his own way, that is, in the only way which will make you see it—people, setting, and events—full of light and darkness and mysterious emanations, as he sees it himself. A lover of Conrad unendowed with patience and imagination is a contradiction in terms.

The strange seas and remote shores, the lonely rivers whose virgin waters have never been ploughed by a white man's craft, the alluring islands that "lie upon the level of a polished sea, like a handful of emeralds on a buckler of steel," are as unknown to Conrad's readers as the Aegean and the adjacent lands were to Byron's and they are invested with a similar lure. Says Marlow in **"Youth"**: "The mysterious East faced me, perfumed like a flower, silent like death, dark like a grave."

Therein lies a phase of Conrad's problem, of his task of making the incredible credible. He must present this mysterious East to his readers as it appears to him, to Marlow, his other self, for it does things to men, especially to sensitive and imaginative men, the kind whose stories he likes best to tell and the kind through whose eyes he watches those stories unfold. This explains why his descriptions of nature are so interpenetrated, so curiously colored, by human fancies and moods that it becomes impossible to say how much of the scene the senses perceive and how much they create. Instances are countless: "The contorted mangroves seemed to writhe at us in the extremity of an impotent despair." "The woods were unmoved, like a mask—heavy, like the closed door of a prison—they looked with their air of hidden knowledge, of patient expectation, of unapproachable silence." The fury of sky and tropical sea in **"Youth"** is released upon Marlow's ship: "Whenever the old dismantled craft pitched heavily with her counter high in the air, she seemed to throw up, like an appeal, like a defiance, like a cry to the clouds without mercy, the words written on her stern: *Judea,* London. Do or die." Who can remain unaware of these seemingly insentient forces that work their mysterious and evil will on everything that dares approach them? We read of the tall, emaciated Kurtz: "The wilderness . . . had caressed him, and—lo!—he had withered; it had taken him, loved him, embraced him, got into his veins, consumed his flesh, and sealed his soul to its own by the inconceivable ceremonies of some devilish initiation."

Read again the description of the *Judea* burning in the night and you cannot fail to notice the transforming power of certain words. A good journalist, a writer devoted to reality stripped of romantic feeling, could write, "At daylight she was only a charred shell, floating still under a cloud of smoke and bearing a glowing mass of coal within." But only Conrad, to whom "the romantic feeling of reality," to repeat, "was an inborn faculty," would write of "the blood-red play of gleams," of "a disc of water glittering and sinister," of "an immense and lonely flame," or speak of the burning craft as "mournful and imposing like a funeral pile" and of her "magnificent death" which came "like a grace, like a gift, like a reward" at "the end of her laborious days. The surrender of her weary ghost to the keeping of stars and sea was stirring like the sight of a glorious triumph."

It is easy to point out in such passages as these the similes, the analogies, the metaphors, the instances of the pathetic fallacy, the "fresh choice and allocation of words and phrases, somewhat in the Gallic order" (to quote Dean Cross), but the important thing is that magic, mystery, and beauty rise from these pages like exhalations, beguiling the fancy till it roam whither "no eye can follow, no hand can grasp," conveying to us some realization of the restless and invincible illusions through which, each in his own degree, his men and women wander.

The word illusion, like the words mystery, fear, evil, and loneliness, are common in Conrad. He uses it to express those conceptions known to most men which approximate reality but are too painful or too joyful, too gloomy or too bright, too full of hope or of despair, to conform with it exactly. Few of us have such complete command of our fears and hopes that we can confront for what it is a world whose naked facts seem so brutal. Some illusions pass only to be replaced by others; some suffer a disenchantment from which there is no recovery; but almost universally illusions of one kind or another remain for they are "invincible." Generally Conrad uses the word to imply a conception that gives more joy, hope, serenity or courage than reality warrants; but he tells us that illusions may imply the opposite as was the case with Falk who was tortured by the illusion that his guilty tale of murder and cannibalism would stir his Juno to revulsion but found with joy that she was moved to pity instead.

Virtually all Conrad's chief characters have their own peculiar illusions: Jasper Allen that he is beyond the reach of Heemskirk's vengeance; old Nelson that Freya does not love Allen and so will stay on to comfort his own old age; Yanko that marriage to an Englishwoman will win him peace of mind and the security of his own hearth; the youthful Marlow that life will always remain thrilling and wonderful; Captain Whalley that his physical powers will never flag; Kurtz that his idealism will survive the forces of evil which lie in wait for him in the tropics, far from the steadying influence of Europe, and so on to the end of the long Conradean gallery. When the cold touch of reality destroys a bright illusion the victim occasionally finds refuge in another, as Kurtz does for a time when he tells himself that he can play with the fires of lust and murder and remain unscathed; or he re-creates it by an effort of memory and for an hour tastes the heady joy of it again, like the middle-aged Marlow when he recounts his early experiences in **"Youth."** Kurtz, from the very fact that he is intellectual, imaginative, and idealistic, manages to create a succession of fresh illusions as his earlier ones fall from him, but in the end on his way back to the coast, broken in health and will, death overtakes him; in that dark presence, earth's last reality, his final illusion dissolves, and with a cry, "The Horror," he sees himself as the thing he is. Jasper Allen swings from one illusion to its opposite, from the extreme of confidence to the extreme of despair, for after tasting Heemskirk's vengeance he falls victim, not to the reality, harrowing though it is, but to the hope-destroying illusion that the wreck of the *Bonito* is the wreck of his world.

Whether or not Conrad studied the *Apologia* it is hard to say, but he is as sensitively aware as Newman of the isolation of every individual soul. In the hour of crisis each of us must make his own decisions, play his own part, fight his own battle, morally as remote from his fellows as Crusoe on his island. Conrad's Slavic temperament, reinforced by his years at sea, helps to explain his consciousness of this truth, as when he speaks of "the tremendous fact of our isolation, of the loneliness, impenetrable and transparent, elusive and everlasting." By no other writer of English fiction is this note made so pervasive, so insistent; in no other English work but *Everyman* and *The Dream of Gerontius* is it so pronounced. You find it everywhere in Conrad's tales; Kurtz, Leggatt, Il Conde and Gaspar Ruiz (***A Set of Six***), Yanko, Arsat, Jasper Allen, Renouard (**"The Planter of Malata"**), each is alone in his fateful hour, alone with fear, with despair, with the passion for life, with the mystery of death. So it is with Captain Whalley upon the deck of the sinking *Sofola,* as the shouts of his crew and the sound of their hurrying feet die away; so with Karain, tortured not only by the memory of the friend he has killed but by the desolation that loss has brought him.

The most gripping pages of the **"Typhoon"** are, as Conrad intended, those which describe Captain MacWhirr on the bridge of the *Nan-Shan,* clawed at by wind and tumultuous waters and in the sudden darkness "feeling stricken by a blind man's helplessness." In the duel between the elements and this man he can expect neither a helping hand nor an encouraging voice; he is alone with his iron courage, alone with his responsibility for the safety of his ship and of every soul aboard. Jukes, the mate, stumbles through storm and darkness to join him, not helping but adding to his burdens. "Our boats are going now, sir." Then "with a penetrating effect of quietness in the enormous discord of noises, as if sent out from some remote spot of peace beyond the black wastes of the gale" he hears the Captain's voice—"the frail and indomitable sound that can be made to carry an infinity of thought, resolution and purpose, that shall be pronouncing confident words on the last day, when heavens fall, and justice is done—again he heard it, and it was crying to him, as from very, very far—'All right.' "

Almost all Conrad's finest shorter stories belong to tragedy or tragi-comedy. Even **"Youth,"** that paean of joy in remembered gusto, has as its refrain regret over precious, irrecoverable things, while **"Falk"** and **"The Secret Sharer"** though ending "happily" grow out of tragic episodes.

Why should this be so? Why did tragedy capture Conrad's attention and commend itself to him under a variety of guises, as the stuff from which he could—and did—shape his finest stories? The answer, I think, is to be found in several things: in his childhood, darkened by the savage repression which followed the insurrection of 1863; memories of an exiled mother treated with ruthless severity and of a cultured and talented father recalled from exile only to follow her to the grave; in a racial strain in which melancholy has always been deeply marked; in an imagination shadowed by apprehensions and fears; in his twenty years of struggle as a writer in the face of poverty and popular indifference; in, finally, a supersensitive nature which Conrad's wife tells us was not a happy one.

Life, Horace Walpole once observed, is a tragedy to him who feels, and Conrad no less than Thomas Hardy is a notable instance. Hardy's rebellion against what he deemed the pitiless injustice of the ultimate force (Chance, Destiny, God, "It," President of the Immortals,) made him so complete a pessimist that he sometimes creates the impression of trying to justify his attitude by loading the dice against his chief characters. It is significant that Conrad entered a spirited denial of the charge that he was either a pessimist or a cynic. It is true that there are passages in his tales which the casual reader may cite in support of one or both charges. But if Conrad said that the history of men might be written in the phrase: "They were born, they suffered, and they died," he was prompt to confess that it was as difficult to be wholly sad as wholly joyous on this earth. If he was acutely aware of the isolation of the individual soul, he cherished nevertheless an invincible belief in the spiritual and emotional solidarity of all human kind, in a communion uniting "the dead to the living and the living to the unborn." If he bears testimony to a universe full of haunting terror, pain, sorrow, toil, uncertainty, and disillusionment, he bears equal testimony to "its wonder and beauty, its infinite passion, its illimitable serenity." He never lets us forget that if men hate, they love; if they despair, they hope; if they are deadened by the ugly and the commonplace, they are uplifted by the sublime.

All writers, he says, give themselves (and their morality) away "in about every third sentence" and he himself is no exception. Let us see. All lands and they that dwell therein "lie under the inscrutable eyes of the Most High" and must run their course and meet the challenges of good and ill. Man, the universe, the ways of God, are full of mystery; nevertheless there is a supreme law which He established and through which He operates, and the individual conscience to which He speaks. Each of us has an appointed task on this earth; we must endure the vicissitudes of life with a "steeled heart" and see in death the very condition of immortality. Add courage, compassion, love capable of faith and abnegation, a stern sense of duty, the wisdom of discipline, and you have a glimpse of the "morality" (or if you prefer, the philosophy of life) in which Conrad believed and which he reveals "in about every third sentence." In moods when the burthen of the mystery chilled his heart he spoke of life as "a futile tale," but in a loftier and truer mood he could look upon the face of a man dead and say: "His soul, delivered from the trammels of his earthly folly, stood now in the presence of Infinite Wisdom."

These things explain why Conrad denied that he was either cynic or pessimist and why he declared, "I have never sinned against the basic feelings and elementary convictions which make life possible to the mass of mankind." (pp. 79-92)

Joseph J. Reilly, "The Shorter Stories of Joseph Conrad," in his Of Books and Men, *Julian Messner, Inc., 1942, pp. 79-92.*

Douglas Hewitt (essay date 1952)

[*In the following excerpt from a study originally pub-*

lished in 1952, Hewitt discusses "The Secret Sharer," contending that the story marks the end of a phase in Conrad's writing career and that Conrad's later writings deal less with the theme of "secret doubles" and more with the virtues of honesty, courage, and fidelity.]

Though it was not published until 1912 in the volume ***'Twixt Land and Sea*****, "The Secret Sharer"** was written in November, 1909. Conrad had taken up and set aside *Chance,* finished *The Secret Agent,* just completed *A Personal Record,* and was engaged in writing *Under Western Eyes,* which he finished two months later.

It is a remarkable story and its extraordinary virtues have attracted surprisingly little attention. It belongs very obviously, in the nature of the interests displayed and in some similarities of treatment, to the same phase of his writing as ***Heart of Darkness,*** *Lord Jim* and *Nostromo.* But it marks the end of this period. The previous works show the central character confronted by some realization of the nature of his beliefs or by some "deadly incubus"—the knowledge of the link with Mr. Kurtz or Gentleman Brown, the disturbing awareness of "the foundation of all the emotions" or of the disastrous results of Don Carlos Gould's idealism. From this knowledge or from these relationships there is no escape; in the nature of the case no solution of the problems is possible. The narrator of **"The Secret Sharer"** is similarly faced by the realization of a bond between him and Leggatt, but he finds a solution; at the end of the story he frees himself from the haunting presence of his "other self".

The setting of the story is typical of Conrad's work in its emphasis on the isolation of the little self-contained world of the ship and on the supremely important position of the narrator-captain. So far as outward power is concerned, he reflects: "I could do what I liked, with no one to say nay to me within the whole circle of the horizon". At the end, when he is giving Leggatt, the secret sharer of his cabin, an opportunity to escape, although he seems to his officers and men to be wantonly running the ship aground yet he is still obeyed. The crew know that their safety is in his hands, yet he is still the captain and they leave their fate to him.

The intruder on this isolation is Leggatt, the fugitive who swims out to the ship, and it is made abundantly clear that he is only able to come on board because of the state of mind of the captain, a state in which he feels "somewhat of a stranger" to himself. He decides to set no anchor-watch and to stay on deck alone and explains that:

> My strangeness, which had made me sleepless, had prompted that unconventional arrangement, as if I had expected in those solitary hours of the night to get on terms with the ship of which I knew nothing, manned by men of whom I knew very little more.

It seems at first as though he will achieve his purpose. In a passage whose irony very soon becomes apparent, he says:

> . . . as I passed the door of the forecastle I heard a deep, quiet, trustful sigh of some sleeper inside. And suddenly I rejoiced in the great security of the sea as compared with the unrest of the land, in my choice of that untempted life presenting problems, invested with an elementary moral beauty by the absolute straight-forwardness of its appeal and by the singleness of its purpose. The riding-light in the fore-rigging burned with a clear, untroubled, as if symbolic flame, confident and bright in the mysterious shades of the night.

Immediately after this he notices that the rope-ladder has not been hauled in as it should, but checks his annoyance with the reflection that his own action is responsible for this. The ladder is there because he has decided to dismiss all hands and keep watch himself in the endeavour to overcome his feeling of "strangeness". When he tries to pull the ladder aboard, he finds the man hanging on the bottom of it. Leggatt asserts later, when he is the "secret sharer" of the narrator's thoughts, that it was the ladder alone which saved him.

> I wasn't capable of swimming round as far as your rudder-chains [he says] And, lo and behold! there was a ladder to get hold of.

The captain does not consciously decide to conceal the fugitive, any more than Marlow consciously decides to accept the "unforseen partnership" with Kurtz. As soon as he sees him, he reflects later: "A mysterious communication was established already between us two—in the face of that silent, darkened tropical sea." Leggatt speaks of him as talking to him quietly—"as if you had expected me". The closeness of this mysterious communication is emphasized from the very start of their relationship, first because of the accident of a similarity of clothes:

> In a moment [the captain says] he had concealed his damp body in a sleeping-suit of the same grey-stripe pattern as the one I was wearing and followed me like my double on the poop.

As Leggatt tells his story it is as though the captain were seeing his own reflection "in the depths of a sombre and immense mirror", so that he can say: "I saw it all going on as though I were myself inside that other sleeping-suit". There is a phrase which is strongly reminiscent of those which tell of the link between Lord Jim and Gentleman Brown: "He appealed to me as if our experiences had been as identical as our clothes". This is, above all, what is stressed—the bond between the captain and the intruder with his burden of guilt. The bond is the closest possible; Leggatt is described as his "double" or his "other self" more than twenty times in the course of the story. When the captain of the *Sephora* comes in search of Leggatt and says that he "wasn't exactly the sort for the chief mate of a ship like the *Sephora,*" the captain reflects:

> I had become so connected in thoughts and impressions with the secret sharer of my cabin that I felt as if I, personally, were being given to understand that I, too, was not the sort that would have done for the chief mate of a ship like the *Sephora.*

He feels "utterly incapable of playing the part of ignorance properly", so that, as he says;

> I could not, I think, have met him by a direct lie,

> also for psychological (nor moral) reasons. If he had only known how afraid I was of his putting my feeling of identity with the other to the test! But, strangely enough—(I thought of it only afterward)—I believe that he was not a little disconcerted by the reverse side of that weird situation, by something in me that reminded him of the man he was seeking—suggested a mysterious similitude to the young fellow he had distrusted and disliked from the first.

The link is not, as in ***Heart of Darkness*** or *Lord Jim,* with someone obviously wicked. The crime of Leggatt is a very modified one in the eyes of the narrator and we remember that when a reviewer described him as a "murderous ruffian" Conrad said that he was "simply knocked over" by such a misunderstanding. But there is, in Leggatt, a feeling of guilt, the knowledge that he has, like Lord Jim, transgressed against the code of society. He can speak of the man he has killed as one of the "miserable devils that have no business to live at all", but he is prepared to accept "the 'brand of Cain' business". "I was ready enough", he says, "to go off wandering on the face of the earth".

We are not, moreover, concerned with the precise nature of Leggatt's offence, for there is no indication that the captain feels any shadow of guilt specifically because the man he is hiding is a murderer. Leggatt is an embodiment of his original feeling of being "a stranger" to himself, of that fear that there are parts of himself which he has not yet brought into the light of day and that these aspects of his personality may interfere with "that ideal conception of one's own personality every man sets up for himself secretly". What disturbs him is that there is a secret sharer at all, for he brings to light his own suspected insecurity.

The captain leads a life of whispers and sudden concealments and, inevitably, his nerves begin to go to pieces. He shouts at men or whispers suddenly, stops men from entering his state-room, feeling all the time that "it would take very little to make me a suspect person in the eyes of the ship's company". They begin to assume that he is either mad or drinking, and his mental state expresses itself for him, too, in the knowledge that it impairs his ability to command.

> This [he says] is not the place to enlarge upon the sensations of a man who feels for the first time a ship move under his feet to his own independent word. In my case they were not unalloyed. I was not wholly alone with my command; for there was that stranger in my cabin. Or rather, I was not completely and wholly with her. Part of me was absent. That mental feeling of being in two places at once affected me physically as if the mood of secrecy had penetrated my very soul.

As a result the orders which should spring to his lips without thinking or reflection do not come; "all unconscious alertness" deserts him; it requires an effort of will to call his mind back from his "secret double" to the "conditions of the moment".

Every detail of the story is perfectly concrete, perfectly naturalistic, yet this is far more a nightmare story than any other—far more than such obviously "painful" stories as **"Freya of the Seven Isles",** which appeared in the same volume. The feeling of "duality" is pushed to the point at which the captain fears for his sanity, because this "confused sensation of being in two places at once" is set against his endeavour to retain his grasp on normality—embodied here as the ability to command his ship and deal with his crew. During breakfast, on the morning after Leggatt has come aboard, he says:

> . . . all the time the dual working of my mind distracted me almost to the point of insanity. I was constantly watching myself, my secret self, as dependent on my actions as my own personality, sleeping on that bed, behind that door which faced me as I sat at the head of the table. It was very much like being mad, only it was worse because one was aware of it.

On the fourth day of "miserable juggling with the unavoidable" he reaches the climax of this torment of trying to reconcile the knowledge of the secret sharer with his duty as shipmaster. The steward goes to hang up the captain's coat, opens the door of the bathroom, where Leggatt is concealed, and does not see him hiding in the bath. The captain waits for the inevitable discovery, and, when it does not come, his bewilderment and his mixture of feelings about Leggatt come out in his first reflection:

> "Saved", I thought. "But no! Lost! Gone! He was gone!"

At this stage in his experience he actually fears that he may already be insane.

> . . . an irresistible doubt of his bodily existence flitted through my mind [he says]. Can it be, I asked myself, that he is not visible to other eyes than mine? It was like being haunted . . . I think I had come creeping quietly as near insanity as any man who has not actually gone over the border.

But from this position escape is possible, as it is not possible for the central characters of the earlier stories. This is because the situation of the narrator in **"The Secret Sharer"** is a stage nearer the purely symbolic than that dealt with in the other works. As I have shown, the presence of Leggatt is so nightmarish, not because he makes the captain aware of any inadequacy or wrongness in his ideas and beliefs, but rather because the relationship between them is itself an objective correlative of such knowledge. After the death of Kurtz, Marlow is left with his mind uneasy and with the feeling that the last words of the dying man were "a moral victory", but in **"The Secret Sharer"** the whole of the narrator's "strangeness" has been so completely embodied in the person of Leggatt that seemingly it can be got rid of.

Leggatt can, in fact, be marooned on one of the islands that fringe the Gulf of Siam. But the captain feels that he cannot do this easily. Although he knows that he may be endangering his ship by taking such a risk, he feels that, as he says, "It was now a matter of conscience to shave the land as close as possible". Clearly it is not physical considerations alone which determine this need: Leggatt can swim too well for that. It seems, rather, that the captain feels that to exorcise his "other self" he must run as close to disaster as possible, knowing all the time, as he says, that

> all my future, the only future for which I was fit, would perhaps go irretrievably to pieces in any mishap to my first command.

Thus, finally, the narrator and Leggatt are separated; even that hat which the captain thrusts on the fugitive's head falls off in the water and acts as a mark by which he can gauge the progress of the ship.

> Now I had what I wanted [the captain says]—the saving mark for my eyes. But I hardly thought of my other self, now gone from the ship, to be hidden forever from all friendly faces . . . I watched the hat—the expression of my sudden pity for his mere flesh. It had been meant to save his homeless head from the dangers of the sun. And now—behold—it was saving the ship, by serving me for a mark to help out the ignorance of my strangeness.

Now at last the captain can feel certain of his ability to command, as he could not when he gave his first order and knew that he was not "wholly alone" with his command. Now he can say:

> Already the ship was drawing ahead. And I was alone with her. Nothing! no one in the world should stand now between us, throwing a shadow on the way of silent knowledge and mute affection, the perfect communion of a seaman with his first command.

"Strangeness"—the knowledge of the "secret double"—has been exorcised and normality restored.

This story, as I have pointed out, marks the end of one phase of Conrad's work; the preoccupations are fundamentally the same as in the earlier books but the situation is so presented that a solution can be offered. It is noticeable that after this a change comes over his writing, and when we consider the form which it takes we are struck at once by a parallel between it and **"The Secret Sharer"**. The story might almost be an allegory of Conrad's future development.

The Conrad of the group of stories and novels which we have been considering is as obsessed by the consciousness of the "other self" as the narrator of **"The Secret Sharer"**. There is a potentially evil or discreditable side to the natures of all his central characters, a seed of corruption in all their idealisms, a suspicion that all our most elevated feelings derive at bottom from the same root as the hunger of Falk which had to be satisfied by cannibalism.

There can be little of quietness or optimism or security in such a view of human life, and the works are indeed disturbing and, like Marlow's reminiscences, "inconclusive". The price of peace of mind for Conrad seems to be much the same as it is for the narrator of this story. He turns away from these preoccupations. In the later works, as we shall see, there is no longer this emphasis on the sense of guilt and this indefinable compact with the "secret double". The simple virtues of honesty, courage and fidelity to one's comrades, whose insufficiency has been one of the main themes of works like ***Heart of Darkness*** and *Nostromo,* are in the later books sufficient guides. It would, of course, be too much to say that no doubts of them are ever expressed, but such expressions are rarely more than perfunctory and they never carry the same weight of feeling and criticism as in the early books. One consequence of this removal of tension from the experience of his central figures is that his characters tend more and more to fall into two groups—the good and the bad.

The contrast in outlook is very clearly seen if we compare the significance of the description in this story of the

> great security of the sea . . . that untempted life presenting no disquieting problems, invested with an elementary moral beauty by the absolute straightforwardness of its appeal and by the singleness of its purpose

with similar passages in *Chance,* or with an extract from a letter to Mrs. Sanderson which he wrote in 1917:

> The naval training has a peculiar quality, and forms a very fine type. For one thing it is strictly methodized to a very definite end which is noble in itself and of a very high idealistic nature, while on its technical side it deals with a body of systematized facts which cannot be questioned as to their value. . . .

In **"The Secret Sharer"** the reflection is profoundly ironic, coming as it does immediately before the appearance of Leggatt, who presents the most "disquieting problems" it is possible to imagine. For the Conrad of the early works the "strictly methodized" and "highly idealistic" sea life is no defence against the recognition of the presence of the secret sharer. The virtues which it fosters are unable to deal with Mr. Kurtz or with the dilemma of Captain Whalley. But there is no irony in such references in *Chance* or the later letters. It is in this context that we must think of Conrad's idealization of naval life after he had become a public figure. It is not enough to see it merely as an ageing man's nostalgia for the life he had led as a young man nor as a romanticization for the newspaper public. Rather is it an inevitable result of this turning away from the preoccupations of the works before **"The Secret Sharer"**.

I prefer to restrict speculation on the significance of this story's coming soon after he had finished the plunge into his own Polish past which took shape—carefully edited, as all Conrad's reminiscences are—in *A Personal Record,* and while he was writing *Under Western Eyes,* in which his feelings about his early life under the Tsarist tyranny are clearly involved. It is possible that by such speculation we could construct plausible and even correct theories about his feelings concerning his childhood and adolescence, but it would help us little in the task of evaluating his work. What we are concerned with is the presence of a crisis within the works, and of the existence of this there can be little doubt.

There seems to have been within him a continual war between the recognition of the "heart of darkness" and the desire to rest securely on unquestioned values. His letters tend to show that the desire for security was the more conscious, but in the best of the early works the "other self" cannot be denied. We have seen something of the struggle emerging in the flaws and insufficiencies of parts of *Lord Jim.* With **"The Secret Sharer"** Conrad seems to resolve this conflict for his peace of mind. . . . (pp. 289-95)

Douglas Hewitt, "The Secret Sharer," in The Art of Joseph Conrad: A Critical Symposium, *edited by R. W. Stallman, Michigan State University Press, 1960, pp. 289-95.*

Tom Hopkinson (essay date 1957)

[*Hopkinson was an English novelist, editor, and critic who specialized in the study of Africa. In the following excerpt, he presents an overview of Conrad's short stories.*]

Joseph Conrad wrote half-a-dozen magnificent short stories, two or three times as many moderately good ones, and one or two so bad that they read like parodies of himself.

The best have certain things in common. They are all enormously long—up to 200 pages, short novels rather than short stories. They were written, on the whole, early in his writing career. With one exception, they are all either stories of the sea or of remote parts of the world—and even in these last a sea-substitute, such as a river with river-steamers, plays an important part.

The half-dozen which seem to me outstanding are **'The Return'** from ***Tales of Unrest*** (1898); ***Heart of Darkness*** from ***Youth*** (1902); **'Typhoon'** and **'Falk'** from ***Typhoon*** (1903). In addition to these are the two referred to by Conrad as his 'Calm-pieces'—**'The Secret Sharer'**, first published in *Harper's Magazine* in 1911, and **'The Shadow Line'** which was written about 1916. This last might almost be described as an inverted **'Typhoon'**—a sailing-ship becalmed, as against a steamer in a storm.

All of these stories have a force, solidity and grandeur which is Conrad's own, and despite the occasional lavishness of description they give the effect of a tight rein and strong control. The writer could go further and deeper if he wanted. For anyone unfamiliar with—or forgetful of—Conrad's quality when in his stride, a few sentences from **'Typhoon'** may serve as sample.

> At its setting the sun had a diminished diameter and an expiring brown, rayless glow, as if millions of centuries elapsing since the morning had brought it near its end. A dense bank of cloud became visible to the northward; it had a sinister dark olive tint, and lay low and motionless upon the sea, resembling a solid obstacle in the path of the ship. She went floundering towards it like an exhausted creature driven to its death.

Compared with the great masters of the form, Tchehov, Turgeniev, Maupassant, Conrad approaches the short story from an entirely different point of view. For them, and particularly for the greatest of all, Tchehov, the essence of every story is the behaviour of human beings, which we are invited to watch as if personally present. The character of a man or woman is not given to us in long description, but revealed in action.

'It was said that a new person had appeared on the sea-front: a lady with a little dog. Dmitri Dmitrich Gurov, who had by then been a fortnight at Yalta, and so was fairly at home there, had begun to take an interest in new arrivals. . . . ' So begins one of the most famous and beautiful of Tchehov's stories.

Conrad begins **'Typhoon'**: 'Captain MacWhirr, of the steamer *Nan-Shan,* had a physiognomy that, in the order of material appearances, was the exact counterpart of his mind: it presented no marked characteristics of firmness or stupidity; it had no pronounced characteristics whatever; it was simply ordinary, irresponsive, and unruffled.'

He goes on to a four-page description of MacWhirr, his childhood, character and background. Tchehov reveals: Conrad describes—and this difference in technique derives from a totally different attitude towards the physical world. To Tchehov, to Maupassant, and in a lesser degree to Turgeniev, the world is simply a place where human beings live and act. Its interest at any given moment derives from what is being done or said.

Like a producer who cannot be bothered with complicated sets and stuffy draperies, Tchehov shows only what is vital to his story, to establish a place as real and to disclose the state of a character's mind through what he does or does not take in of his surroundings. In the story whose opening words I quoted, 'The Lady with the Dog,' when Gurov finally goes to visit Anna in her own town, all we are given of the town is the broken inkstand in his hotel room and the fence opposite Anna's house where he walks up and down hoping to see her.

To Conrad, by contrast, the world appears as a succession of tremendous backcloths, deserving—demanding—to be set before the reader in their fullest detail. Backcloths not required by the story may be brought in for sheer display. In ***Heart of Darkness,*** one of the finest stories, we get not only long and detailed descriptions of the African river and the trading-post upon which the action centres, but we begin with an impressive word-picture of the Thames and Sea-Reach at sunset—with glimpses of the same scene in Roman times—before going on to the Continent to visit the headquarters of the Company which manages the main depot, upriver from which lies the trading-post . . . and so on.

In contrast to the Tchehovian technique of plunging straight to the heart of the story—'The Lady with the Dog' is only twenty-five pages, and one has the feeling of having lived through an additional lifetime—Conrad works backwards away from the action. He does this partly by concentrating on the settings, partly by his, to my mind most wearisome, device of having many of his stories told by people, who are themselves frequently repeating the accounts of events seen, or heard about, by others.

In **'Il Conde'** for instance, the final story in ***A Set of Six,*** two layers of story-teller are interposed between the reader and the unconvincing melodrama. Similarly, in **'Gaspar Ruiz'**, from the same volume, a General Santierra is described for us at length, in order that he instead of Conrad may tell Ruiz's tale. Marlow is, of course, Conrad's favourite interpositary device, an *alter ego* whose interest for the reader he greatly overestimated, and of whom he wrote: 'I don't think that either of us would much care to survive the other.'

In **'Youth,'** Marlow's recurring outbursts—'Oh, the glamour of youth! Oh, the fire of it . . . '—provide a note of false romanticism which goes far to spoil the story. In ***Heart of Darkness,*** the constant interruptions in the narrative due to Conrad's need to get back to his story-teller, Marlow, are simply exasperating.

At a crucial moment, following the attack by savages on the river-steamer, we get: ' . . . Why do you sigh in this beastly way, somebody? Absurd? Well, absurd. Good Lord! mustn't a man ever—Here, give me some tobacco. . . . ' His match has to go out, and a lot of back-chat has to be addressed to Marlow's nameless—and indeed meaningless—companions before we can return to the savages.

One word comes before long to haunt the mind of any persistent reader of Conrad's stories—the word 'melodrama'. Why does he do it? What has he got against ordinary human life? What is the purpose of all these feuds, assassinations, revolutionary plottings, these fearful disasters and betrayals—against which, it seems, only the stolid application to duty of the totally unimaginative can hope to hold its ground?

In Conrad's first collection, ***Tales of Unrest*** published in 1898, there are five stories in all. One is of a Malayan princeling haunted by the brother he betrayed; a second is of parents who can only beget idiots, and the mother—after stabbing the father—throws herself to destruction; in the third, two stupid white men, left in charge of a trading-post, quarrel and both die; **'The Return'** is a gloomy and powerful account of a final breach between husband and wife; with the last, **'The Lagoon',** we are back where we began with the betrayal of brother by brother for the sake of a woman.

Already the pattern has taken shape which later stories on the whole bear out, often with less regard for probability and correspondingly less success. The world is a series of stupendous settings. Only plots or stories which are fantastic, bloody or disastrous provide action to suit the sombre magnificence of what Conrad refers to at times explicitly as 'the stage'.

'It was the stage where, dressed splendidly for his part, he strutted, incomparably dignified . . . ', and again, a few lines further on: 'In many successive visits we came to know his stage well . . . .'

In these dramas staged by the author, the actors are men and ships—the ships for the most part maintaining the appearance of man's instruments, but occasionally, as in **'The Brute,'** actually taking charge and acting on their own. The rôle of women in Conrad's stories is as secondary beings. Either—as with Mrs MacWhirr in **'Typhoon'** or Mrs Davidson in **'Because of the Dollars'**—they are utterly unaware of what their husbands undergo, pointing the contrast to the man's sufferings by their own triviality and folly; or else their rôle is to act as stimulants upon the men, to ends which are usually either ruinous or evil. Occasionally, as with Hermann's niece in **'Falk'** or Kurtz's 'Intended' in ***Heart of Darkness,*** they are passive influences for good—but it is the idea of them in the minds of their men that has importance not themselves. It is significant how many of them are almost, or totally, silent.

The equation can be simplified even a stage further. Conrad's short stories tend to centre upon a single theme—the loyalty of man to man, a high proportion of them dealing with betrayal. The natural world, particularly the brilliant and vivid landscape of the Far East, is the setting for each crucial test. The fellowship of the sea supplies, frequently, the bond which men either keep or break. Woman is the temptation to betrayal, or occasionally the inspiration to hold on.

It is this over-simple pattern, disguised though it is with philosophical musings and moral reflections, which gives to so much of Conrad's work a sense of schoolboy limitations, of being written within a series of conventions by which in fact human beings do not live. Even the betrayals tend to be breaches of a code or the result of artificial dilemmas of 'honour', rather than acts of villainy or baseness.

Just as to Thomas Hobbes the civil contract is the one thing which prevents man sliding into anarchy, so to Conrad—it seems—the accepted codes and standards of behaviour are man's sole protection against bloody ruin and abandonment. Rarely indeed do we get even a glimpse, as in **'The Return,'** of a man trying to live by a gleam of inner truth rather than by accepted standards.

An over-simplification of man's problems in the world; an over-complication of technique; a tendency to false dramatization and philosophizing; these are basic faults in Conrad as a story-writer. His qualities are an unsurpassed power of description of natural forces, scenery and setting; a tremendous sense of man's conflict with his environment, and of the need for every man to discover and prove himself in struggle; with, finally, a bitter sardonic humour.

This last has received less than its due. We English talk with pride of Conrad's admiration for our race, but I know of no harsher, more incisive description of the well-brought-up, well-to-do Englishman than that of Alvan Hervey in **'The Return,'** beginning: 'He was tall, well set up, good-looking and healthy; and his clear pale face had under its commonplace refinement that slight tinge of overbearing brutality which is given by the possession of only partly difficult accomplishments; by excelling in games, or in the art of making money; by the easy mastery over animals and over needy men . . . ' on to 'They moved in their enlarged world amongst perfectly delightful men and women who feared emotion, enthusiasm, or failure, more than fire, war, or mortal disease; who tolerated only the commonest formulas of commonest thoughts, and recognized only profitable facts. It was an extremely charming sphere, the abode of all the virtues, where nothing is realized and where all joys and sorrows are cautiously toned down into pleasures and annoyances.'

Like Dickens, Conrad uses his sardonic humour to express an angry pity: this comes out strongly in ***Heart of Darkness,*** in describing the horrible treatment of the native helpers at the Company's African base. A page or two later comes an echo. . . .

> Once a white man in an unbuttoned uniform, camping on the path with an armed escort of lank Zanzibaris, very hospitable and festive—not to say drunk. Was looking after the upkeep of the road, he declared. Can't say I saw any road or any upkeep, unless the body of a middle-aged negro, with a bullet-hole in the forehead, upon which I absolutely stumbled three miles farther on, may be considered as a permanent improvement.

Many people, I know, detest any attempt to evaluate writers: to me it seems an inevitable part of critical activity. Because of his consciously developed powers, working on a kind of experience which can never be repeated, the best of Conrad will always be unique: because of his limitations, a diet of Conrad quickly becomes wearisome. As a writer of so-called 'short' stories, he belongs to my mind not with the few supreme masters—who threw them off, it seems, almost at will—but with the larger number of those—such as Poe, Tolstoy, Lawrence, Hardy, Herman Melville, Joyce—who have written a small number of stories which can truly be called great. (pp. 36-41)

Tom Hopkinson, "The Short Stories," in London Magazine, *Vol. 4, No. 11, November, 1957, pp. 36-41.*

Albert J. Guerard (essay date 1958)

[*Guerard, an American novelist and critic, has written extensively on Conrad. His* Conrad the Novelist *is considered the standard critical interpretation of several of Conrad's works, including* Heart of Darkness. *In the following excerpt from that study, he examines Marlow's growth toward self-awareness and a knowledge of evil in* Heart of Darkness.]

Joseph Conrad was one of the most subjective and most personal of English novelists. And his best work makes its calculated appeal to the living sensibilities and commitments of readers; it is a deliberate invasion of our lives, and deliberately manipulates our responses. (p. 1)

[We] cannot ignore the personality and temperament that pervade the best writings (and some of the worst) and largely determine their form. For we are concerned with a style that is unmistakably a speaking voice; with a certain way of constructing novels that may derive from temperamental evasiveness; above all with an intense conflict of novelistic judgment and sympathy presumably reflecting divisions in Conrad himself. (pp. 1-2)

Heart of Darkness is the most famous of [Conrad's] personal short novels: a *Pilgrim's Progress* for our pessimistic and psychologizing age. . . . The living nightmare of 1890 seems to have affected Conrad quite as importantly as did Gide's Congo experience thirty-six years later. The autobiographical basis of the narrative is well known, and its introspective bias obvious; this is Conrad's longest journey into self. But it is well to remember that ***Heart of Darkness*** is also other if more superficial things: a sensitive and vivid travelogue, and a comment on "the vilest scramble for loot that ever disfigured the history of human conscience and geographical exploration." (pp. 33-4)

Heart of Darkness thus has its important public side, as an angry document on absurd and brutal exploitation. Marlow is treated to the spectacle of a French man-of-war shelling an unseen "enemy" village in the bush, and presently he will wander into the grove at the first company station where the starving and sick Negroes withdraw to die. It is one of the greatest of Conrad's many moments of compassionate rendering. The compassion extends even to the cannibal crew of the *Roi des Belges.* Deprived of the rotten hippo meat they had brought along for food, and paid three nine-inch pieces of brass wire a week, they appear to subsist on "lumps of some stuff like half-cooked dough, of a dirty lavender color" which they keep wrapped in leaves. Conrad here operates through ambiguous suggestion (are the lumps human flesh?) but elsewhere he wants, like Gide after him, to make his complacent European reader *see:* see, for instance, the drunken unkempt official met on the road and three miles farther on the body of the Negro with a bullet hole in his forehead. ***Heart of Darkness*** is a record of things seen and done. But also Conrad was reacting to the humanitarian pretenses of some of the looters precisely as the novelist today reacts to the moralisms of cold-war propaganda. Then it was ivory that poured from the heart of darkness; now it is uranium. Conrad shrewdly recognized—an intuition amply developed in *Nostromo*—that deception is most sinister when it becomes self-deception, and the propagandist takes seriously his own fictions. Kurtz "could get himself to believe anything—anything." The benevolent rhetoric of his seventeen-page report for the International Society for the Suppression of Savage Customs was meant sincerely enough. But a deeper sincerity spoke through his scrawled postscript: "Exterminate all the brutes!" The conservative Conrad . . . speaks through the journalist who says that "Kurtz's proper sphere ought to have been politics 'on the popular side.' "

Conrad, again like many novelists today, was both drawn to idealism and repelled by its hypocritical abuse. "The conquest of the earth, which mostly means the taking it away from those who have a different complexion or slightly flatter noses than ourselves, is not a pretty thing when you look into it too much. What redeems it is the idea only. An idea at the back of it; not a sentimental pretence but an idea; and an unselfish belief in the idea . . . " Marlow commits himself to the yet unseen agent partly because Kurtz "had come out equipped with moral ideas of some sort." Anything would seem preferable to the demoralized greed and total cynicism of the others, "the flabby devil" of the Central Station. Later, when he discovers what has happened to Kurtz's moral ideas, he remains faithful to the "nightmare of my choice." . . . The Kurtz who had made himself literally one of the devils of the land, and who in solitude had kicked himself loose of the earth, burns while the others rot. Through violent not flabby evil he exists in the moral universe even before pronouncing judgment on himself with his dying breath. A little too much has been made, I think, of the redemptive value of those two words—"The horror!" But none of the company "pilgrims" could have uttered them.

The redemptive view is Catholic, of course, though no priest was in attendance; Kurtz can repent as the gunman of *The Power and the Glory* cannot. ***Heart of Darkness*** (still at this public and wholly conscious level) combines a Victorian ethic and late Victorian fear of the white man's deterioration with a distinctly Catholic psychology. We are protected from ourselves by society with its laws and its watchful neighbors, Marlow observes. And we are protected by work. But when the external restraints of society and work are removed, we must meet the challenge and temptation of savage reversion with our "own inborn strength. Principles won't do." This inborn strength appears to include restraint—the restraint that Kurtz lacked and the cannibal crew of the *Roi des Belges* surprisingly possessed. The hollow man, whose evil is the evil of *vacancy,* succumbs. And in their different degrees the pilgrims and Kurtz share this hollowness. (pp. 34-6)

As for Kurtz, the wilderness "echoed loudly within him because he was hollow at the core." Perhaps the chief contradiction of ***Heart of Darkness*** is that it suggests and dramatizes evil as an active energy (Kurtz and his unspeakable lusts) but defines evil as vacancy. The primitive (and here the contradiction is only verbal) is compact of passion and apathy. "I was struck by the fire of his eyes and the composed languor of his expression . . . This shadow looked satiated and calm, as though for the moment it had had its fill of all the emotions." Of the two menaces—the unspeakable desires and the apathy—apathy surely seemed the greater to Conrad. Hence we cannot quite believe the response of Marlow's heart to the beating of the tom-toms. This is, I think, the story's minor but central flaw, and the source of an unfruitful ambiguity: that it slightly overdoes the kinship with the "passionate uproar," slightly undervalues the temptation of inertia.

In any event, it is time to recognize that the story is not primarily about Kurtz or about the brutality of Belgian officials but about Marlow its narrator. (p. 37)

Substantially and in its central emphasis ***Heart of Darkness*** concerns Marlow (projection to whatever great or small degree of a more irrecoverable Conrad) and his journey toward and through certain facets or potentialities of self. F. R. Leavis [in *Scrutiny,* 1941] seems to regard him as a narrator only, providing a "specific and concretely realized point of view." But Marlow reiterates often enough that he is recounting a spiritual voyage of self-discovery. He remarks casually but crucially that he did not know himself before setting out, and that he likes work for the chance it provides to "find yourself . . . what no other man can ever know." The Inner Station "was the farthest point of navigation and the culminating point of my experience." At a material and rather superficial level, the journey is through the temptation of atavism. It is a record of "remote kinship" with the "wild and passionate uproar," of a "trace of a response" to it, of a final rejection of the "fascination of the abomination." And why should there not be the trace of a response? "The mind of man is capable of anything—because everything is in it, all the past as well as all the future." Marlow's temptation is made concrete through his exposure to Kurtz, a white man and sometime idealist who had fully responded to the wilderness: a potential and fallen self. (p. 38)

On this literal plane, and when the events are so abstracted from the dream-sensation conveying them, it is hard to take Marlow's plight very seriously. Will he, the busy captain and moralizing narrator, also revert to savagery, go ashore for a howl and a dance, indulge unspeakable lusts? The late Victorian reader (and possibly Conrad himself) could take this more seriously than we; could literally believe not merely in a Kurtz's deterioration through months of solitude but also in the sudden reversions to the "beast" of naturalistic fiction. Insofar as Conrad does want us to take it seriously and literally, we must admit the nominal triumph of a currently accepted but false psychology over his own truer intuitions. But the triumph is only nominal. For the personal narrative is unmistakably authentic, which means that it explores something truer, more fundamental, and distinctly less material: the night journey into the unconscious, and confrontation of an entity within the self. . . . It little matters what, in terms of psychological symbolism, we call this double or say he represents: whether the Freudian id or the Jungian shadow or more vaguely the outlaw. And I am afraid it is impossible to say where Conrad's conscious understanding of his story began and ended. The important thing is that the introspective plunge and powerful dream seem true; and are therefore inevitably moving.

Certain circumstances of Marlow's voyage, looked at in these terms, take on a new importance. The true night journey can occur (except during analysis) only in sleep or in the waking dream of a profoundly intuitive mind. Marlow insists more than is necessary on the dreamlike quality of his narrative. . . . Even before leaving Brussels Marlow felt as though he "were about to set off for the center of the earth," not the center of a continent. The introspective voyager leaves his familiar rational world, is "cut off from the comprehension" of his surroundings; his steamer toils "along slowly on the edge of a black and incomprehensible frenzy." As the crisis approaches, the dreamer and his ship move through a silence that "seemed unnatural, like a state of trance"; then enter (a few miles below the Inner Station) a deep fog. "The approach to this Kurtz grubbing for ivory in the wretched bush was beset by as many dangers as though he had been an enchanted princess sleeping in a fabulous castle." Later, Marlow's task is to try "to break the spell" of the wilderness that holds Kurtz entranced.

The approach to the unconscious and primitive may be aided by a savage or half-savage guide, and may require the token removal of civilized trappings or aids. . . . In ***Heart of Darkness*** the token "relinquishment" and the death of the half-savage guide are connected. The helmsman falling at Marlow's feet casts blood on his shoes, which he is "morbidly anxious" to change and in fact throws overboard. . . . Here we have presumably entered an area of unconscious creation; the dream is true but the teller may have no idea why it is. So too, possibly, a psychic need as well as literary tact compelled Conrad to defer the meeting between Marlow and Kurtz for some three thousand words after announcing that it took place.

We think we are about to meet Kurtz at last. But instead Marlow leaps ahead to his meeting with the "Intended." . . . This is the "evasive" Conrad in full play, deferring what we most want to know and see; perhaps compelled to defer climax in this way. The tactic is dramatically effective, though possibly carried to excess: we are told on the authority of completed knowledge certain things we would have found hard to believe had they been presented through a slow consecutive realistic discovery. But also it can be argued that it was psychologically impossible for Marlow to go at once to Kurtz's house with the others. The double must be brought on board the ship, and the first confrontation must occur there. (pp. 39-41)

Hence the shock Marlow experiences when he discovers that Kurtz's cabin is empty and his secret sharer gone; a part of himself has vanished. . . . And now he must risk the ultimate confrontation in a true solitude and must do so on shore. "I was anxious to deal with this shadow by myself alone—and to this day I don't know why I was so jealous of sharing with anyone the peculiar blackness of that experience." . . . We are told very little of what Kurtz said in the moments that follow; and little of his incoherent discourses after he is brought back to the ship. "His was an impenetrable darkness. I looked at him as you peer down at a man who is lying at the bottom of a precipice where the sun never shines"—a comment less vague and rhetorical, in terms of psychic geography, than it may seem at a first reading. And then Kurtz is dead, taken off the ship, his body buried in a "muddy hole." With the confrontation over, Marlow must still emerge from environing darkness, and does so through that other deep fog of sickness. The identification is not yet completely broken. "And it is not my own extremity I remember best—a vision of grayness without form filled with physical pain, and a careless contempt for the evanescence of all things—even of this pain itself. No! It is his extremity that I seem to have lived through." Only in the atonement of his lie to Kurtz's "Intended," back in the sepulchral city, does the experience come truly to an end. "I laid the ghost of his gifts at last with a lie . . . "

Such seems to be the content of the dream. If my summary has even a partial validity it should explain and to an extent justify some of the "adjectival and worse than supererogatory insistence" to which F. R. Leavis (who sees only the travelogue and the portrait of Kurtz) objects. I am willing to grant that the unspeakable rites and unspeakable secrets become wearisome, but the fact—at once literary and psychological—is that they must remain *unspoken.* A confrontation with such a double and facet of the unconscious cannot be reported through realistic dialogue; the conversations must remain as shadowy as the narrator's conversations with Leggatt. So too when Marlow finds it hard to define the moral shock he received on seeing the empty cabin, or when he says he doesn't know why he was jealous of sharing his experience, I think we can take him literally . . . and in a sense even be thankful for his uncertainty. . . . [It] may be the groping, fumbling ***Heart of Darkness*** takes us into a deeper region of the mind. If the story is not about this deeper region, and not about Marlow himself, its length is quite indefensible. But even if one were to allow that the final section is about Kurtz (which I think simply absurd), a vivid pictorial record of his unspeakable lusts and gratifications would surely have been ludicrous. I share Mr. Leavis' admiration for the heads on the stakes. But not even Kurtz could have supported many such particulars.

"I listened on the watch for the sentence, for the word, that would give me the clue to the faint uneasiness inspired by this narrative that seemed to shape itself without human lips in the heavy night air of the river." Thus one of Marlow's listeners, the original "I" who frames the story, comments on its initial effect. He has discovered how alert one must be to the ebb and flow of Marlow's narrative, and here warns the reader. But there is no single word; not even the word *trance* will do. For the shifting play of thought and feeling and image and event is very intricate. It is not vivid detail alone, the heads on stakes or the bloody shoes; nor only the dark mass of moralizing abstraction; nor the dramatized psychological intuitions apart from their context that give ***Heart of Darkness*** its brooding weight. The impressionist method—one cannot leave this story without subscribing to the obvious—finds here one of its great triumphs of tone. The random movement of the nightmare is also the controlled movement of a poem, in which a quality of feeling may be stated or suggested and only much later justified. But it is justified at last. (pp. 41-4)

[The] narrative advances and withdraws as in a succession of long dark waves borne by an incoming tide. The waves encroach fairly evenly on the shore, and presently a few more feet of sand have been won. But an occasional wave thrusts up unexpectedly, much farther than the others: even as far, say, as Kurtz and his Inner Station. Or, to take the other figure: the flashlight is held firmly; there are no whimsical jerkings from side to side. But now and then it is raised higher, and for a brief moment in a sudden clear light we discern enigmatic matters to be explored much later. Thus the movement of the story is sinuously progressive, with much incremental repetition. The intent is not to subject the reader to multiple strains and ambiguities, but rather to throw over him a brooding gloom, such a warm pall as those two Fates in the home office might knit, back in the sepulchral city.

Yet no figure can convey ***Heart of Darkness*** in all its resonance and tenebrous atmosphere. The movement is not one of penetration and withdrawal only; it is also the tracing of a large grand circle of awareness. It begins with the friends on the yacht under the dark above Gravesend and at last returns to them, to the tranquil waterway that "leading to the uttermost ends of the earth flowed sombre under an overcast sky—seemed to lead into the heart of an immense darkness." (pp. 44-5)

The travelogue as travelogue is not to be ignored. . . . Presently Marlow will discover a scar in the hillside into which drainage pipes for the settlement had been tumbled; then will walk into the grove where the Negroes are free to die in a "greenish gloom." The sharply visualized particulars suddenly intrude on the somber intellectual flow of Marlow's meditation: magnified, arresting. The boilermaker who "had to crawl in the mud under the bottom of the steamboat . . . would tie up that beard of his in a kind of white serviette he brought for the purpose. It had loops to go over his ears." The papier-maché Mephistopheles is as vivid, with his delicate hooked nose and glittering mica eyes. So too is Kurtz's harlequin companion and admirer, humbly dissociating himself from the master's lusts and gratifications. . . . And even Kurtz, shadow and symbol though he be, the man of eloquence who in this story is almost voiceless, and necessarily so—even Kurtz is sharply visualized, an "animated image of death," a skull and body emerging as from a winding sheet, "the cage of his ribs all astir, the bones of his arm waving."

This is Africa and its flabby inhabitants; Conrad did indeed have a "feel for the country." Yet the dark tonalities and final brooding impression derive as much from rhythm and rhetoric as from such visual details: derive from the high aloof ironies and from a prose that itself advances and recedes in waves. (pp. 45-6)

The insistence on darkness, finally, and quite apart from ethical or mythical overtone, seems a right one for this extremely personal statement. There is a darkness of passivity, paralysis, immobilization; it is from the state of entranced languor rather than from the monstrous desires that the double Kurtz, this shadow, must be saved. In Freudian theory, we are told, such preoccupation may indicate fear of the feminine and passive. But may it not also be connected, through one of the spirit's multiple disguises, with a radical fear of death, that other darkness? . . .

It would be folly to try to limit the menace of vegetation in the restless life of Conradian image and symbol. But [it] . . . reminds us again of the story's reflexive references, and its images of deathly immobilization in grass. Most striking are the black shadows dying in the greenish gloom of the grove at the first station. But grass sprouts between the stones of the European city, a "whited sepulcher," and on the same page Marlow anticipates coming upon the remains of his predecessor: "the grass growing through his ribs was tall enough to hide his bones." The critical meeting with Kurtz occurs on a trail through the grass. Is there not perhaps an intense horror behind the casualness with which Marlow reports his discoveries, say of the Negro with the bullet in his forehead? (p. 47)

Heart of Darkness . . . remains one of the great dark meditations in literature, and one of the purest expressions of a melancholy temperament. (p. 48)

Albert J. Guerard, in his Conrad the Novelist, *Cambridge, Mass.: Harvard University Press, 1958, 322 p.*

John Howard Wills (essay date 1961)

[In the following essay, Wills examines setting, characterization, plot, and theme in "The Secret Sharer."]

In a particularly frank moment Conrad wrote to Edward Garnett, " **'The Secret Sharer',** between you and me, is *it.* Eh? No damned tricks with girls there. Eh? Every word fits and there's not a single uncertain note." Few recent critics have quarreled with Conrad's estimate. There seems among recent critics, in fact, as much unreserved admiration for this story as for almost any in the language. Yet, in spite of such general acclaim, the work has not received its critical due.

For one thing, it has not been openly recognized for the exciting adventure story it is. In its first few pages, our apprehension is aroused, and from the seventh page to the last, we remain in the story's grip. Its narrative excitement recalls other nineteenth century English masters of suspense—Scott, Dickens, Collins, Thomas Hardy. It is particularly reminiscent of the "police tale," so beloved by Dickens and his Russian admirer, Dostoievski.

The major difficulty has been in correctly interpreting the story. The majority of Conrad's critics find the fugitive, Leggatt, for all his aid to the narrator and his single-handed rescue of the *Sephora,* to be guilty of murder. Miss Bradbrook, Thomas Moser, and Albert Guerard frankly pronounce him guilty, while Douglas Hewitt and Walter Wright feel he has somehow erred. Are not these critics, by condemning Leggatt, bringing to their own judgments the very standards Conrad sought to ridicule? The standards of Archbold (the captain of the *Sephora*), the crews of the two ships, the "old fellow in a wig and the twelve respectable tradesmen"? Are they not missing a major aspect of the story's theme? The ironic comment upon the injustice of civil justice? Certainly the narrator does not believe Leggatt has erred, for he speaks of him admiringly throughout the story, sees in a moment that he is no "homicidal ruffian," fiercely protects him from the moment he comes on board, and, finally, risks his life and his future in order to set a deserving man free. And there is strong reason to believe that Conrad himself regarded Leggatt as his narrator did. (Isn't the narrator, after all, as in all the other sea stories, a projection of Conrad's self?) Conrad was in fact completely flabbergasted when a reviewer described Leggatt as a "murderous ruffian." No, I agree with Carl Benson that "it is the stupidly conscientious captain of the *Sephora* and not the narrator (or Conrad) who regards the accidental killing of a mutinous sailor as murder" [*PMLA,* 1954].

It seems to me that the major reason Conrad's critics have misinterpreted this story is that they have failed to examine it in anything like its entirety. I don't mean only its symbolism, shadow imagery, point of view, tone, and style (although they have in these areas been neglectful also). I mean they have neglected to examine even the subject matter of the story with any degree of thoroughness. I do not believe the theme of the story will really come clear to us unless we consider the several backdrops, objects, characters, and actions in relation to one another. We must, in our search for theme, examine both the spatial and temporal aspects of subject matter—both the world (setting and static characterization) of the story and the life (character in action) moving through that world. Let us begin with the story world.

The world of **"The Secret Sharer"** is a world of huge distances and staggering heights. Around the narrator's ship there is "no sign of human habitation as far as the eye . . . [can] reach." On one side are the sea and a "few barren islets"; on the other, "the straight line of the flat shore joined to the stable sea, edge to edge"—all this under "the enormous dome of sky." It is a world so large that any one piece of it—whether island, river, jungle, ship, or man—appears insignificant in relation to the whole. It is a world, in brief, in which man must constantly struggle to complete the "long and arduous enterprise" of his life. He must struggle because he can never expect aid from a benevolent god sitting above, performing miracles in his behalf. Above and around him sky and sea, when they are not actually threatening his existence, act only as "spectators and judges." At such times the world is "an immense stillness"—a kind of huge vacuum—in which man must make his own breaks, find land breezes to blow him homeward when there is no sea breeze, set a reefed foresail to save his ship when no one else will set it, escape imprisonment to save his own life when no one will let or help him escape.

Quite often, however, man's free will is severely limited. The world, as Leggatt's gruelling experience demonstrates to the narrator, contains plenty of "special surprises for . . . [man's] discomfiture." Furious storms come, men half-crazed with fear commit mutinous acts, while other men crazed with the same fear do nothing to prevent either those acts or the acts of mutinous winds and seas.

Conrad's view of society (that is, society without Leggatt or the revitalized captain) in this story is heavily satirical, almost scornful. It is true that he only scantily delineates that society, but his strokes are swift and telling. The chief trouble is that few men understand the world in which they live. They view the mysterious water about them as so much H_2O. A criminal is a criminal as far as they can make out. The best sort of fellows, in their view, are fellows one can account for. They themselves are, admittedly, plain men. Constantly we see them slavishly adhering to man-made laws and traditions which are outworn or otherwise inexpedient. They will not, like Frost's neighbor in "Mending Wall," go behind their father's saying; and, when anyone else does—even though he is in the right—they either stand open-mouthed (How many open mouths there are, literally, in this story!) or—when they feel the heresy to be dangerous—attempt to crucify the culprit. When they are successful in their attempts to rid society of him (and they are successful in this story by driving Leggatt off), they deprive society of his potential, extremely necessary leadership—to say nothing of the injustice they do him. I say "necessary leadership" because these men give repeated indications of being unable to act responsibly and courageously themselves in time of crisis. A Leggattless society in **"The Secret Sharer"** is a society completely ill-equipped to meet the problems of existence.

Conrad's mistrust of the bourgeois is especially evident in the works of his middle period—in *Nostromo, The Secret Agent,* **"Gaspar Ruiz," "An Anarchist," "The Informer,"** and *Under Western Eyes.* These works of course almost wholly concentrate upon "shore people," men who, in Thomas Moser's words, appear to be secure only because they have never been tested" [*Joseph Conrad: Achievement and Decline*]. Whenever shore people are tested, they fail miserably. Captain Mitchell of *Nostromo* (he is, after all, a shorebound sailor) for all his courage and fidelity, becomes, in Moser's words, "the unwitting dupe of the 'material interests' that are destroying Costaguana"; Winnie Verloc of *The Secret Agent,* for all her kind and loving nature, becomes the unwitting dupe of her husband's nefarious activities—and must thereby be held partly responsible for her brother's death; the titular hero of **"Gaspar Ruiz,"** for all his strength and good intentions, becomes the unwitting dupe of his wife's heartless, tyrannical schemes.

"The Secret Sharer" is the first story in which Conrad savagely attacks the bourgeois upon ship deck. The dupe and bungler frequently appear in *The Nigger of the "Narcissus,"* **"Youth,"** and ***Typhoon,*** but in those works Conrad is so concerned with establishing the superiority of sea life over shore life that he remains at most amused over the stolidity of his Bakers, Beards and MacWhirrs. That he is far less amused by the ships' officers of **"The Secret Sharer"** possibly results from his increasing impatience with human stupidity in the intervening years. For one thing, his letters during the period 1902-1909 reveal his increasing annoyance with most of the critics of his work. He more than ever found himself being considered a spinner of sea yarns, an exotic romancer, and a Kipling of the Malay Archipelago. For another thing, during the writing of *Nostromo, The Secret Agent,* and most of the stories in ***A Set of Six,*** Conrad apparently came to understand that unthinking man can help only to destroy society, never to deliver it. However it came about, **"The Secret Sharer"** is the most pessimistic sea story Conrad ever wrote. With the exception of Leggatt and the narrator, there is not one sympathetic seaman in all of the story's pages. Like James's stories of misunderstood artists and Faulkner's novels of fallen patricians, **"The Secret Sharer"** is militantly pro-intellectual.

Let us observe the bourgeoisie more closely. The first thing we notice about them is that they are caricatures rather than characterizations. Again, as in ***Typhoon,*** the influence of Dickens is strongly in evidence. In delineating each of these characters, Conrad sacrifices the fullblown figure for the detail. The narrator repeatedly refers to his first mate's whiskers, frequently neglecting to mention the man behind them at all. In like manner, he several times refers to the trembling lip of his young second mate, the wide eyes of his steward, and the mumbling delivery of the *Sephora* skipper. Even Leggatt refers to the old judge on shore in terms of his wig. Further, the narrator puts tag lines into the mouths of both the first mate and steward—"Bless my soul, sir, you don't say so" and "Beg pardon, sir."

In themselves, these caricatures are inferior to most of Dickens' caricatures. None of Conrad's bourgeoisie are nearly as humorously or as vitally conceived as Dickens' Gradgrind, Turveydrop, Jefferson Brick, Captain Cuttle, or Veneering. (Of course, none can approach MacWhirr either.) Conrad's caricatures are, however, more thematically significant than Dickens' caricatures. They are, in fact, doubly significant. The trembling whiskers and lips, the saucer-like eyes, and the mumbling delivery of Conrad's bourgeois seamen—these images in themselves suggest cowardice and ignorance: moral and intellectual fragmentariness. Also suggesting fragmentariness is the fragmentary nature of the images. As mere pieces of men the bourgeois seamen are presented in pieces.

The key images of the bourgeois conspiracy are wide-eyed, quivering faces and huddled, nodding heads. Constantly we see the stolid officers and men of the narrator's ship falling back in amazement before one or another of their young captain's heresies. Repeatedly, the chief mate's eyes grow round, his whiskers tremble, and he stammers breathlessly, "Bless my soul, sir! You don't say so!" The lower lip of the second mate visibly quivers almost every time the narrator addresses him. The eyes of the crew, like the eyes of the helmsman, exhibit an "unusual roundness" whenever the narrator appears before them. And the "pale-faced steward," who frequently has business in the narrator's cabin, several times leaps backwards before his frightening captain—eyes wide, mouth agape. The seaman aboard the *Sephora* react in like manner to the heresies of Leggatt. At the sight of the man Leggatt has killed they and their captain run "screaming" about the deck "like a lot of lunatics." The captain trembles "like a leaf" when he converses with Leggatt. And both captain and men constantly wear sick expressions when they confront their "criminal" shipmate. "To see some of their faces you'd have thought they were afraid I'd go about at night strangling people."

After recoiling in surprise, the startled men of the narrator's ship generally gather in groups to discuss the latest heresy of their captain. The following is typical:

> Directly I put my head out of the companion I saw the group of my two officers, the second mate barefooted, the chief mate in long india-rubber boots, near the break of the poop, and the steward halfway down the poop ladder talking to them eagerly. He happened to catch sight of me and dived, the second ran down on the main deck shouting some order or other, and the chief mate came to meet me, touching his cap.

We can well imagine what kind of huddled, nodding conspiracies took place outside the locked doors of the cabin in which Leggatt was confined after the killing. Considering the malicious natures of the old second mate and steward—the "two chaps . . . [who] ran the ship"—the schoolteacherish wife of the captain (with her "brand of Cain" ideas about Leggatt), the captain himself, and his men, these conspiratorial huddles were probably both numerous and keenly engaged in.

The aristocrats in the world of **"The Secret Sharer"** are much more attractive than the bourgeoisie. Leggatt, the fugitive, is one of the most heroic characters in Conrad; and that circumstance is of course hugely ironic in that Leggatt, acording to civil law, is a criminal, "with the mark of Cain on his brow." Like Dostoievski's Myshkin he is an immensely paradoxical figure—the only bright man in a world of idiocy—or, better, the only just man in a world of injustice. In the world of **"The Secret Sharer"** Leggatt is the natural aristocrat—the one man who not only understands the perils surrounding his fellow men, but who actively protects his fellow men from those perils. By setting the reefed foresail of the *Sephora* during a tremendous gale when his captain was too paralyzed by fear to give the order, Leggatt reveals himself as a born leader of men—responsible and actively courageous.

It might of course be argued, in the spirit of the cynical older speaker in *What Is Man?* by Mark Twain, that Leggatt—even though preserving society momentarily from the encroachments of chaos—was motivated like all heroes by selfishness rather than selflessness. And to a certain extent this is true. Throughout his works, Conrad seems to hold in suspect any fine or noble action. At least he leaves us in question as to the purity of his heroes' motives. Thus Marlow constantly questions the sincerity of Jim, the western teacher of languages the sincerity of Razumov, and an omniscient Conrad the sincerity of Heyst and several other pseudo-chivalric heroes of the late novels and stories. Leggatt, it might reasonably be argued, acted as any animal would act: set the foresail only to save himself from drowning and swam to the narrator's ship only to save himself from hanging.

The entire truth is a little more complex. Leggatt is as conscientious and responsible as man can be in Conrad. Having, like young Jim, been brought up in two institutions—the parsonage and the maritime training school for officers—which teach, among other things, man's responsibility to man, Leggatt is considerably bothered by the fact that he has killed a man. So much so, that he is constantly talking about the "ugly business" to the narrator—not because Leggatt (like Jim in his talks with Marlow) is seeking justification (he is convinced of the justice of his act), but because he feels bad about having taken the life of a human being, whatever sort of ruffian the fellow was. He tells the captain that while a cabin prisoner aboard the *Sephora,* he refused to smash the door of his cabin to save himself, because he feared that if he did he might have to kill someone else—and he did "not want any of that."

Another mark of Leggatt's humanity is his immense loneliness. He is a man who longs for friendship and understanding. Aboard the *Sephora* he was friendless, even before the killing. Everyone aboard was, like Archbold, a "plain man." When Leggatt tells of finding the narrator's ship's ladder after spending hours in the sea, we almost feel he has swum all that way merely to talk to another human being:

> When I saw a man's head looking over I thought I would swim away presently and leave him shouting—in whatever language it was. I didn't mind being looked at. I—I liked it. And then you speaking to me so quietly—as if you had expected me—made me hold on a little longer. It had been a confounded lonely time—I don't mean while swimming. I was glad to talk a little to somebody that didn't belong to the *Sephora* . . . I don't know—I wanted to be seen, to talk with somebody, before I went on. I don't know what I would have said . . . "Fine night, isn't it" or something of the sort.

Though Leggatt does not seek justification for his deed, he does require understanding. Thus, when he realizes the narrator does understand him "thoroughly," their relationship appears to Leggatt "very wonderful." It seems so wonderful, in fact, that he does not wish to profane it by accepting, before his departure, the money his friend offers him. It is difficult to believe that any "homicidal ruffian" could feel about another as Leggatt feels about the narrator. Consider the narrator's account of their last moments together: "Our eyes met; several seconds elapsed, till, our glances still mingled, I extended my hand and turned the lamp out." And a few moments later: "Our hands met gropingly, lingered united in a steady, motionless clasp for a second . . . No word was breathed by either of us when they separated."

These passages reveal the narrator's admiration for Leggatt every bit as much as they reveal Leggatt's admiration for the narrator. If we read carefully, we realize that, almost from the moment of their meeting, the narrator has admired the fugitive. The narrator constantly describes Leggatt in admiring terms. Leggatt has a "strong soul," "rather regular features," a "smooth square forehead," "a good mouth" with "white, even teeth." His expression is "concentrated, meditative." He is, all in all, a "well-knit young fellow." And notice the flattering manner in which the narrator refers to him, after letting him off at Koh-ring, in the concluding sentence of the story:

> Walking to the taffrail . . . I was in time to catch an evanescent glimpse of my white hat left behind to mark the spot where the secret sharer of my cabin and of my thoughts, as though he were my second self, had lowered himself into the water to take his punishment [the only just punishment for an innocent man being freedom]: a free man, a proud swimmer striking out for a new destiny.

Such is the world of **"The Secret Sharer"**—a menaced community without a leader. Precisely how it acquires its leader and thus its hope of temporary salvation is recounted in the narrator's story. Having considered setting and characterization, let us now consider plot, and then attempt to formulate a statement of theme.

At the outset of the story, the narrator—"appointed to the command only a fortnight before" and "untried as yet by a position of the fullest responsibility"—is still "a stranger to himself." "I was willing to take the adequacy of the others for granted. They simply had to be equal to their tasks; but I wondered how far I should turn out faithful to that ideal conception of one's own personality every man sets up for himself secretly." His lack of confidence is most clearly revealed in his relationships with his fellow officers. He constantly fears their criticism, several times regretting even giving them certain orders:

> I felt painfully that I—a stranger—was doing something unusual when I directed him [the first mate] to let all hands turn in without setting an anchor watch . . .
>
> I asked myself whether it was wise ever to interfere with the established routine of duties even from the kindest of motives. My action might have made me appear eccentric.

Precisely how does this shy and diffident young captain gain the confidence required for his "long and arduous enterprise"? The answer is obvious. He comes to know Leggatt and to learn from him that to be a responsible commander he must, like Leggatt, become a man willing to act according to his convictions.

It is not difficult for him to become like Leggatt (that is, once he has "understood" the fugitive's story "from first to last"), for his "secret self" and Leggatt are identical. In the words of R. W. Stallman, Leggatt is "the embodiment of the Captain's moral consciousness. His appearance answers the Captain's question—'I wondered how far I should turn out faithful to that ideal conception of one's own personality every man sets up for himself secretly' " [*The Art of Modern Fiction*].

The narrator becomes aware of Leggatt's strong resemblance to himself from almost the moment of their meeting. At first he notices only material resemblances: their looking somewhat alike, their standing in identical attitudes, their wearing identical clothing, their having been graduated from the same training school for maritime officers. He soon recognizes, however, that the resemblance is more profound. In spite of the fact that Leggatt was only first mate of the *Sephora,* the narrator gradually discovers that Leggatt was regarded by his shipmates in much the same way the narrator is regarded by his shipmates—as something of an eccentric intellectual not to be trusted.

Quite naturally, he listens with a sympathetic ear to Leggatt's "sufficiently fierce story," and the story adds tinder to the "secret partnership" which is beginning to blaze between the two officers. Leggatt does not have to finish justifying his "criminal" deed. "I needed no more," the narrator claims. "I saw it all going on as though I were myself inside that other sleeping-suit." He recognizes immediately that his "double there was no homicidal ruffian," and rather more gradually that Leggatt's "crime" was no crime at all. As he is able to phrase it later on, the "same strung-up force which had given twenty-four men a chance, at least, for their lives, had, in a sort of recoil, crushed an unworthy mutinous existence."

The narrator thereby makes a strong effort to protect Leggatt. When Archbold, the elderly commander of the *Sephora,* comes aboard looking for his homicidal mate, the narrator employs every means short of a lie—he could not lie, he asserts, "for psychological (not moral) reasons"—to protect his "secret sharer." Also, he repeatedly risks what little reputation he has left on board his ship to keep Leggatt from the prying eyes of his officers and men.

This loyalty to Leggatt drives the narrator to the brink of insanity; for a long time he feels trapped between conflicting loyalties of love and duty, of personal and social justice—his dilemma being cleverly symbolized by his being forced to divide his time between cabin and deck, and while on deck by his feeling of being "in two places at once." Finally, however, his officers and Archbold so offend him with their aggressive snooping that he takes up the cudgel in behalf of his "secret self." He comes up on deck, gives orders, and sees that those orders are carried out. Certain at last that he is more capable to command the ship than his officers are, he realizes he must gain their complete respect and obedience if all aboard are going successfully to complete their "long and arduous enterprise." Thus when putting Leggatt ashore on Koh-ring, he takes his ship in dangerously close to the rocks chiefly to convince his officers and men—"a matter of conscience," he calls it—that he is going to be boss from that day forward.

Then comes the action which reveals precisely how much like Leggatt the narrator has become. When the bewhiskered first mate mutinously protests the narrator's daring act, the narrator grabs and shakes the blubbering creature. And here the narrator's action is reminiscent of Leggatt's during his time of crisis. By now Leggatt and the narrator are essentially the same man. Both have taken the advice Stein offers Marlow in *Lord Jim:* "A man that is born falls into a dream like a man who falls into the sea. If he tries to climb out into the air as inexperienced people endeavor to do, he drowns—*nicht wahr?* . . . No! I tell you! The way is to the destructive element submit yourself, and with exertions of your hands and feet in the water make the deep, deep sea keep you up."

The narrator realizes his salvation has been achieved shortly after Leggatt leaves the ship and the hat—a symbol of his and Leggatt's "secret partnership"—appears upon the surface of the water, "serving me [as Leggatt so well had served him] for a mark to help out the ignorance of my strangeness." Out from under the shadow of Erebus, and for the first time in open water, he voices his newly found confidence: "Already the ship was drawing ahead. And I was alone with her. Nothing! No one in the world should stand now between us, throwing a shadow on the way of silent knowledge and mute affection, the perfect union of a seaman with his first command."

Considering the evidence of setting, characterization, and plot, the theme of **"The Secret Sharer"** might be stated as follows: Because of the dangerous and chaotic world in which mankind lives, it is imperative that men of wisdom control and protect the lives of their fellows.

The light and shadow imagery of the story also suggests such a reading. There is little sunlight in the world of **"The Secret Sharer."** The sea and sky are almost always etched in grays and blacks. Yet within this huge globe of darkness, the tiny riding light in the forerigging of the narrator's ship burns "with a clear, untroubled, as if symbolic, flame, confident and bright in the mysterious shades of the night." The captain of the ship, however, does not burn with such a flame until he meets a lighted man: "a faint flash of phosphorescent light, which seemed to issue suddenly from the naked body of a man, flickered in the sleeping water with the elusive, silent play of summer lightning in a night sky." After meeting this man, who sits "glimmering white in the darkness" of the deck, the narrator also, if slowly, becomes "confident and bright." Befriending the lighted man literally saves the narrator from the darkness of chaos, for his own floppy hat—a symbol of that befriending—"white on the black water," saves him and his crew from being dashed to pieces against the black rocks of Koh-ring.

The theme of the story is also dissolved in other story elements—in point of view, tone, and symbolism. Let us examine these in our concluding pages.

It is interesting to note that **"The Secret Sharer"** is unique among Conrad's artistic successes for exhibiting a minimal degree of distances between narrator and narrative. His best works usually exhibit, like ***Typhoon*** and *The Secret Agent,* distance imposed by an ironically omniscient author or, like ***Heart of Darkness*** and *The Nigger of the "Narcissus,"* distance imposed by a first person narrator looking back upon one of his early experiences, or, like **"Il Conde"** and *Under Western Eyes,* distance imposed by a detached (or relatively detached) observer. If we consider each of these points of view in relation to **"The Secret Sharer,"** we shall understand the wisdom of Conrad's choice. Had he chosen any one of those methods he would probably have undermined our sympathies with the "secret partnership" and established bonds with the bourgeois officers and men. Seen from a distance, the narrator would certainly have appeared more ludicrous than heroic—dodging in and out of his cabin and wandering up and down the decks in his sleeping suit. Leggatt, likewise, hiding in the narrator's cabin and bathroom, would probably have appeared more cowardly than courageous. By allowing the young captain to tell his own story, and, particularly, by allowing him to become deeply involved in his own story, Conrad precluded almost any possibility of our losing sympathy with the "secret partnership."

Only once during the entire story do we become aware of any appreciable distance between the time of narration and action. During the recounting of Archbold's visit to his ship, the narrator brings up the question of the latter's name, and then remarks parenthetically, "it was something like Archbold—but at this distance of years I hardly am sure." This token appeal to our credulity more nearly shocks than convinces us, for almost from the outset of the story until that moment the action appears to have occurred only moments before the telling. We have, in fact, been so caught up in the Dostoievski-like intensity of the narrative as actually to be unaware of the question of narrative distance at all.

Tone of course inevitably derives from point of view, and is thus appropriate in this story. Whereas in **"Youth"** the narrator is sufficiently removed from his youthful exploits to see the comedy in them and thus comes to regard them from time to time with strong tinges of irony, the narrator of **"The Secret Sharer"** is too close to his story to be other than as serious, anxious, and excited as his younger self was. In short, since his values are apparently the same as those of his younger self, his attitudes are also.

The structure and style of the story are unobstrusive, but admirably support its theme. The structure is extremely compact and highly selective, thus helping to intensify our response. Also, Conrad seems to have known where to begin and conclude the narrator's story. Given the story's theme, material from an earlier or later stage in the narrator's history would have been irrelevant. The style, likewise, is admirably economical and convincing. It is rarely onomatopoeic (except for the *s's* of whispering men) or pictorially brilliant, but then if the style of such a dark and silent story were, its fabric would be irremediably damaged. The style does perform major organic functions: through its choice of recurring words ("ghost," "phantom," "dream," "sleep," "double," etc.) it helps to establish the nightmarish atmosphere of the story, and, at the same time, helps to erect the story's symbolistic overtones. Let us examine those overtones in some detail.

Until now we have been considering **"The Secret Sharer"** as a realistic story—that is, as a story which does no violation to the laws of nature as we know them. And we have been right in doing so, for the major portion of the story operates on a realistic level. If we concluded our examination at this point, however, we would be missing certain important things the story has to offer: in brief, its symbolic overtones. These overtones not only help to erect and sustain the story's theme, but also complicate and enrich it.

In spite of the intelligent things Jocelyn Baines has to say about **"The Secret Sharer,"** his interpretation is severely limited by his inability to recognize Conrad's symbolic intentions. "I do not believe," he writes [in *Joseph Conrad: A Critical Biography*], "that Conrad intended **'The Secret Sharer'** to be interpreted symbolically." Further: "There is no suggestion of a transcendental relationship between Leggatt and the captain or of the 'double' being a psychological manifestation of an aspect of the original as there is in Poe's vulgar, trashy 'Richard Wilson' [surely, 'William Wilson'] or Dostoevsky's obscure nightmare, 'The Double.' " After reading these statements, one wonders whether Baines could have read the story very closely. One also wonders whether he has carefully considered the "Preface" to *The Nigger of the "Narcissus"* or Conrad's letter to Barrett H. Clark in May of 1918.

If **"The Secret Sharer"** has any noticeable failing, in fact, it is that some of its symbolic overtones are *too* obvious. There are, in brief, too many signposts. I grow a little weary of constantly hearing about "my double," "my other self," "my secret sharer," "my secret self," "my second self," and "my very own self." I am sure all of us understand Conrad's point about the third time we hear such sentiments.

Except for this single kind of obviousness, the overtones are subtle and inevitable. Leggatt is the "ideal conception of . . . [the narrator's] personality . . . [the narrator] sets up for himself secretly." Thus he is also the stalking id of the narrator's dreams, the ghost (or dead spirit) of the narrator, and the mirrored, or true, image of the narrator.

Let us examine these patterns one at a time. In the first pattern, Leggatt appears to the narrator at night when the narrator is attired in his sleeping suit. The fugitive (naked, like the id) rises from the "sleeping water" and comes aboard the narrator's ship (as a thought often bursts the surface of consciousness). The narrator first clothes the fugitive in a sleeping suit like his own, then beds him down in the captain's bunk, and feeds him the captain's breakfast coffee all the while the ship is becalmed in "the sleepy gulf" of Siam. Finally, when the narrator has no longer any reason to be troubled by a repressed id, Leggatt disappears as a "faint, phosphorescent flash" into the "sleeping water."

In the second pattern, Leggatt appears in the water as a "greenish cadaverous glow"—"ghostly, silvery, fish-like." And he comes on board to haunt the narrator's troubled mind. His movements are "as noiseless as a ghost." Some of his remarks resemble "something that a ghost might have said." He is, the narrator ultimately recognizes, "my own grey ghost." "Can it be," he finally asks himself, "that he is not visible to other eyes than mine?" And he concludes, "it was like being haunted." At last, when the narrator's spirit is no longer dead, the ghost dissolves within the "phantom sea."

In the third pattern Leggatt initially appears as a headless body in the "darkling glassy shimmer" of the sea (as if the narrator's head, exactly above, belongs on Leggatt's body); a few seconds later the fugitive's face is "upturned exactly under" the narrator's. Then, after Leggatt has come upon deck and has begun to tell his story, the narrator feels "as though I had been faced by my own reflection in the depths of a sombre and immense mirror." At other times he notices the fugitive's facing him in identical attitudes:

> He rested a hand on the end of the skylight to steady himself with, and all that time did not stir a limb, so far as I could see . . .
>
> One of my hands, too, rested on the end of the skylight; neither did I stir a limb, so far as I knew. We stood less than a foot from each other.

And again:

> He had turned about meantime; and we, the two strangers in the ship, faced each other in identical attitudes.

These symbolic overtones add richness to the story. Not only do they offer us alternate readings and help subject us to the narrator's nightmare, they enable us better to understand that nightmare. The nightmare is guilt in the form of hallucination. When the guilt leaves, the *doppelgänger* leaves. (pp. 115-26)

John Howard Wills, "Conrad's 'The Secret Sharer'," in The University of Kansas City Review, *Vol. XXVIII, No. 1, October, 1961, pp. 115-26.*

John Howard Wills (essay date 1963)

[*In the following essay, Wills lauds "Youth" as a neglected masterpiece, praising the work's characterization, tone, style, and symbolism.*]

Of all Conrad's short works of fiction, **"Youth"** is the most seriously underestimated. Most critics admire it for its pictorial loveliness, its verve, and its authenticity, but finding it lacking in multiple symbolic levels and in dark journeys within tormented heroes, ultimately dismiss it as minor. [In his *Conrad the Novelist,* Albert J.] Guerard speaks for the majority when he asserts that "the story requires no interpreting. It seems more than any other of Conrad's to invite a simple enjoyment of its surface charm." Among Conrad's major critics only Thomas Moser seems fully to recognize Conrad's "very sophisticated use of the personal narrator" and skillful employment of symbolism [*Joseph Conrad: Achievement and Decline*]. "Although **'Youth'** lacks the explicit seriousness of some of the early works,"

Moser writes, "much serious meaning does come through implication. The prose reveals the important qualities of the early style: vigor, irony, symbolic imagination, emotional richness."

The story is not perfect. But it has only one fault worth talking about—a certain nineteenth-century obviousness. At the outset Marlow makes sure his cronies cannot misinterpret him: "You fellows know there are those voyages that seem ordered for the illustration of life, that might stand for a symbol of existence." And, "to me she [the *Judea*] was not an old rattletrap carting about the world a lot of coal for freight—to me she was the endeavour, the test, the trial of life." And, "She was tired—that old ship. Her youth was where mine is—where yours is—you fellows who listen to this yarn." Also, he several times interrupts his story to deliver eulogies to his heroic British merchantmen.

But such explicitness is not what comes to mind when we remember **"Youth."** What comes to mind is the nostalgia, the irony, the seascapes and landscapes, the controlled ambiguity and, above all, the organic artistry.

The surface triumphs have been acknowledged by virtually all readers and critics during the past several generations. What has not been acknowledged is the story's deeper triumph—in the language of the Preface to *The Nigger of the "Narcissus,"* its "perfect blending of form and substance." In **"Youth,"** as in so many of Conrad's novels and stories, theme is dissolved in plot, character, setting, structure, symbolism, point of view, tone, and style.

In order to experience the brief happiness life has to offer, man must, while young, entertain the illusion that he is strong and important; for he will, when older, be unable to entertain such an illusion. This is the theme of **"Youth."** It is also, with a slightly more serious accent, the theme of *Victory:* "Ah, Davison, woe to the man whose heart has not learned while young to hope, to love—and to put its trust in life!"

Let us discern the dissolution of this theme in the fictional fabric of **"Youth"**—first in plot, character, and setting, and then in structure, point of view, tone, style, and symbolism.

A middle-aged former merchantman named Marlow, apparently grown tired of "success" and "love" on shore, sits drinking in an English pub with four other ex-merchantmen. Partially because he senses "the strong bond of the sea" between him and his audience, and partially because he is in need of catharsis, Marlow tells his companions the story of his first voyage to the East, twenty-one years earlier. He warns them that the story is to be construed as an "illustration of life," a "symbol of existence." "You fight, work, sweat, nearly kill yourself, sometimes do kill yourself, trying to accomplish something—and you can't. Not from any fault of yours. You simply can do nothing, neither great nor little—not a thing in the world—not even marry an old maid, or get a wretched 600-ton cargo of coal to its port of destination." The story Marlow tells bears him out. It is a lengthy and impressive record of nature's physical overthrow of man, and of man's concerted, but unsuccessful effort to prevail. Several times the *Judea* barely gets started towards Bangkok when an accident overtakes her: twice she runs into gales; once she is rammed by another ship; another time she begins to come apart at the seams. And always she is hauled back to the nearest port for repairs—the last time for longer than three months. Finally, she does get under way; but, once she has entered Eastern waters, her cargo catches fire. The heroic efforts of her men do not avail her. An explosion soon occurs below deck, causing the fire, until that time only smouldering, to leap out onto the deck and gradually to consume the old ship until she eventually goes down. Her officers' plans to reach Bangkok are thereby frustrated; for now they can only row for the nearest island, with the sole hope that, once there, an English ship might give them "a passage somewhere."

This is not the entire story Marlow tells. If it were, he would not be allegorizing the theme of **"Youth."** And he does allegorize the theme—especially when focussing upon his younger self. Young Marlow regards the various accidents which befall the *Judea* as exciting fun. During the gale which batters the ship shortly after she leaves the Tyne, he says to himself, "By Jove! This is the deuce of an adventure—something you read about; and it is my first voyage as second mate—and I am only twenty—and here I am lasting it out as well as any of these men." Even when the *Judea* sinks, he is overjoyed at the prospect of seeing "the East first as a commander of a small boat." It doesn't particularly bother him that he will not reach Bangkok. The island he is rowing for will do. He proves that by ignoring potential rescue ships and by excitedly regarding the island and her people. And while he thrills to the splendors of the East, his older fellow seamen, having lost their illusions, sleep in the stranded longboats.

Frequently during Marlow's recitation, he sighs, laments the cruelty of Time, and drinks from the bottle. Thematically, he is as important as an actor as he is as a narrator. Important also as actors are the members of his audience. Like the old men of the *Judea*—Beard, Mahon, and all the "battered and bandaged scarecrows" who make up the crew—Marlow and his drinking companions (and perhaps his readers also) are significantly contrasted with the youthful hero. Contrasted also, as in all Conrad's sea stories, are sea and shore, the places respectively of spiritual life and of death. Both sets of contrasted elements are strongly emphasized in the novel's conclusion. Marlow is speaking:

> "You here—you all had something out of life: money, love—whatever one gets on shore—and, tell me, wasn't that the best time, that time when we were young at sea; young and had nothing, on the sea that gives nothing, except hard knocks—and sometimes a chance to feel your strength—that only—what you all regret?"
>
> And we all nodded at him: the man of finance, the man of accounts, the man of law, we all nodded at him over the polished table, that like a still sheet of brown water reflected our faces, lined, wrinkled; our faces marked by toil, by deceptions, by success, by love; our weary eyes looking still, looking always, looking anxiously

> for something out of life, that while it is expected is already gone—has passed unseen, in a sigh, in a flash—together with the youth, with the strength, with the romance of illusions.

In terms of point of view, **"Youth"** represents a big advance over *The Nigger of the "Narcissus."* By employing a frame—Marlow as a narrator within a narrator—Conrad was able to give the novel additional authenticity and power. When we see Marlow (in his cups) through the eyes of a member of his audience, he appears more real than ever. He is then the same old sentimental escapist the rest of us are. And at the conclusion of the novel we are strongly affected by Marlow's sentimentality, partially because our narrator is affected by it: "And we all nodded at him: the man of finance, the man of accounts, the man of law, we all nodded at him." At this point, as Wilson Follett once observed [in *Joseph Conrad: A Short Study*], Marlow's audience have "quite literally and physically" been drawn "in one by one, until they are indistinguishably lost, and the reader with them, in a single tense personality."

But excluding the frame, the most fruitful result of the point of view is the convincing double perspective it opens upon the action. Throughout Marlow's narrative we often see the same events from the vantage point of both youth and age, illusion and reality, hope and fatality. **"Youth"** is, as Marlow says, a "romance of illusions," but it is a comedy of illusions as well. In its exoticism and nostalgia it looks back to the Malayan works and *The Nigger;* in its irony, forward to **"Typhoon"** and *The Secret Agent.* Perhaps only in the early comedies of Shakespeare—*Love's Labour's Lost, As You Like It, Much Ado About Nothing, A Midsummer Night's Dream,* and *Twelfth Night*—does romantic-comic ambiguity achieve as large a measure of success. One of the fine things about **"Youth"** is that, given the *Judea* world and Marlow's being twenty years removed from that world, both his ironic and romantic attitudes clearly reveal theme. **"Youth"** is a masterpiece of tonal art.

"Comedy," Conrad once wrote, "is but a matter of the visual angle," thus providing us with the key to the comedy of **"Youth,"** as well as to the comedies of **"An Outpost of Progress," "The Duel,"** and *The Secret Agent.* In a world inexorably governed by chaos and death, man's optimism appears necessarily comic when seen from the vantage point of omniscience. From such a vantage point, Marlow regards a large portion of his youthful voyage. It amuses him that everyone sees the world as it is not. And when he several times lets us glimpse the darkness hovering about the horizon's rim, we are also amused. All human endeavor then seems laughable. Mrs. Beard's last-minute reminder to young Marlow, for example: "You are a good young man. If you see John—Captain Beard—without his muffler at night, just remind him from me to keep his throat well wrapped up." And the men's trimming of the yards, about which Marlow wryly says: "Do you see the lot of us there, putting a neat furl on the sails of that ship doomed to arrive nowhere?" The men's heroics seem especially ludicrous whenever Marlow reminds us of the commercial squabbles going on back in London among "the owner, the underwriters, and the charterers" of the *Judea.* The two principal comedians of the voyage are Captain Beard and young Marlow. They are completely different types. Both see the world as it is not, but for different reasons: Beard because he is excessively preoccupied with details, young Marlow because he is excessively preoccupied with abstractions.

Marlow turns his arrows upon Beard immediately after the explosion, when the good Captain rushes onto the main-deck and—without responding to the devastation about him—angrily demands to know the whereabouts of the cabin-table. He is here like MacWhirr in the middle of the typhoon worrying about the whereabouts of his matchbox. Marlow does not allow Beard to get off easily:

> "Do you know what he wanted next? Well, he wanted to trim the yards. Very placidly, and as if lost in thought, he insisted on having the foreyard squared. 'I don't know if there's anybody alive,' said Mahon, almost tearfully. 'Surely,' he said gently, 'there will be enough left to square the foreyard.'
>
> "The old chap, it seems, was in his own berth winding up the chronometers, when the shock sent him spinning. Immediately it occurred to him—as he said afterwards—that the ship had struck something, and he ran out into the cabin. There, he saw, the cabin-table had vanished somewhere. The deck being blown up, it had fallen down into the lazarette of course. Where we had our breakfast that morning he saw only a great hole in the floor. This appeared to him so awfully mysterious, and impressed him so immensely, that what he saw and heard after he got on deck were mere trifles in comparison."

Young Marlow is the chief comedian of the voyage. Whenever the aging Marlow remembers his youthful naïveté, his tone becomes ironic. From the outset of the voyage, the youthful Marlow, like the uninitiated Jukes and Lord Jim, believes the world to be ruled by a benevolent deity, whose only purpose is to cater to the needs of young men like himself. He pictures Bangkok as a Utopia which will magically satisfy his every need; the "rattletrap" *Judea* as a stately galleon; and his body as something which will "last forever, outlast the sea, the earth, and all men." He is not at all dismayed by the gales which several times threaten the *Judea;* he thinks of them only as providing "the deuce of an adventure." Nor is he dismayed by the cynical prophesies of the Falmouth citizenry who, constantly pointing out to visitors the ill-starred *Judea* and her crew, sneer, "She will never get to Bankok [*sic*]." "That's all you know about it," the young mate replies scornfully. During the "attempt to dig down to the fire," confident of a benevolent providence, he leaps "down to show how easily it . . . [can] be done," and has to be fished out "with a chainhook tied to a broomhandle." Then comes the episode during and immediately following the explosion. As young Marlow is standing upon "the main-deck for a moment," he suddenly becomes "aware of a queer sensation, of an absurd delusion"; he seems "somehow to be in the air." Stunned after finding himself again on deck, with everywhere about him "a wilderness of smashed timber," he looks imploringly out to the world beyond—expecting to find it "convulsed with horror"; but the elements wear no expression of commiseration. Old Marlow asserts that, to the youth, "the peace of the sky and the serenity of the sea were distinctly surprising." Young Marlow then looks to his captain for sympathy, but Beard affords him "a frightful shock" by merely asking about the location of the cabin-table. As a last resort, the young man pins his hopes for sympathy upon a Malay boatman coming alongside the stricken *Judea,* but even he does "not deign to lift his head for a glance." Astounded, the young man laments: "I thought people who had been blown up deserved more attention."

The early portions of Marlow's narrative are more comic than romantic. The romantic flavor does not predominate until the full outbreak of the fire. From that point on Marlow becomes so involved in his youthful adventure that he loses his ironic perspective. He forgets to ask for the bottle any more (at the conclusion of his narrative, however, when the vision begins to fade, he remembers his forlorn existence and twice drinks deeply) and several times even lapses into the present tense.

There are three kinds of romance in **"Youth."** First, there is the romance of adventure. Again and again Marlow shows that men's illusions are responsible for their heroism as much as for their buffoonery: that when men think their cause worthwhile, the world harmless, or themselves powerful, they engage in all sorts of daring ventures. He remembers the spiritual victories the men of the *Judea* attained over the elements and over themselves—the victories of age as well as youth: Beard "saving heroically in his arms that old woman—the woman of his life"; Mahon digging down to the fire and fainting there; all the "battered and bandaged scarecrows" braving the smoke to put "a neat furl on the sails of that ship." He remembers that both officers and men had "something in them, something inborn and subtle and everlasting . . . something solid like a principle, and masterful like an instinct . . . of that hidden something . . . that shapes the fate of nations." And he remembers the *Judea* herself. She was heroic because her men were heroic. When the "old dismantled craft" threw "up like an appeal, like a defiance, like a cry to the clouds without mercy, the words written on her stern: '*Judea,* London. Do or Die'," she was reflecting the spirit of her crew.

He remembers also that his youthful self was heroic; that in the myriad material defeats of the voyage, he too had achieved his spiritual triumphs. He remembers, during the furious gales which attacked the *Judea,* fighting the elements for long, miserable hours. And he remembers pulling into the island, his arms aching from the days of rowing, his throat "dry as a cinder," with about him the "drawn faces" of dejected men, and feeling only "the first sign of the East on . . . [his] face . . . like a whispered promise of mysterious delight."

At this point **"Youth"** becomes a romance of wonder. When Marlow recalls pulling into the island, he becomes lost in his vision—so lost, in fact, that he lapses into the present tense:

> "I have the feel of the oar in my hand, the vision of a scorching blue sea in my eyes. And I see a bay, a wide bay, smooth as glass and polished like ice, shimmering in the dark. A red light burns far off upon the gloom of the land, and the night is soft and warm. We drag at the oars with aching arms, and suddenly a puff of wind, a puff faint and tepid and laden with strange odours of blossoms, of aromatic wood, comes out of the still night."

And he can still see how marvelous the East looked to him when he opened his "young eyes on it" the following morning:

> "I see it now—the wide sweep of the bay, the glittering sands, the wealth of green infinite and varied, the sea blue like the sea of a dream, the crowd of attentive faces, the blaze of vivid colour—the water reflecting it all, the curve of the shore, the jetty, the high-sterned outlandish craft floating still, and the three boats with the tired men from the West sleeping, unconscious of the land and of the people and of the violence of sunshine."

The first glimpse of the island was beautiful enough, but the remembrance of that glimpse is even more beautiful. Old Marlow is shore-bound. Confronted by "a still sheet of brown water" on a table top in a public house, he yearns for "the sea blue like the sea of a dream." The tone of **"Youth"** is predominantly elegiac. Conrad rightly spoke of the story's "mood of wistful regret, of reminiscent tenderness." And Wilson Follett appropriately labelled it "the threnody of a past that was beautiful and is vanished." **"Youth"** is an ironic comedy, a romance of adventure, and a romance of wonder; but it is these only fitfully and fragmentarily. Essentially, like *Huckleberry Finn* and *A Sportsman's Notebook,* it is a romance of nostalgia—a hymn to the vanished past. Nostalgia intensifies the blueness of the seascape set inside the dingy frame. Time after time Marlow loses himself in his memories, but each time is jolted back to reality. "Youth! All Youth! The silly, charming, beautiful youth," he exclaims. His memories of the East he saw for the first time from the jetty of an Eastern island especially move him. As he recalls he sighs, and as he sighs he drinks.

> "I have known its fascination since; I have seen the mysterious shores, the still water, the lands of brown nations, where a stealthy Nemesis lies in wait, pursues, overtakes so many of the conquering race, who are proud of their wisdom, of their knowledge, of their strength. But for me all the East is contained in that vision of my youth. It is all in that moment when I opened my young eyes on it. I came upon it from a tussle with the sea—and I was young—and I saw it looking at me. And this is all that is left of it! Only a moment; a moment of strength, of romance, of glamour—of youth! . . . A flick of sunshine upon a strange shore, the time to remember, the time for a sigh, and—good-bye—Night—good-bye . . . !"
>
> He drank.
>
> "Ah! The good old time—the good old time. Youth and the sea. Glamour and the sea! The good, strong sea, the salt, bitter sea, that could

> whisper to you and roar at you and knock your breath out of you."
>
> He drank again.

The language of **"Youth"** has several times been attacked for being florid and overwrought. So imposing a critic as [F. R.] Leavis has spoken of its "cheap insistence on glamour" [in *The Great Tradition*] and so discerning a critic as [Morton Dauwen] Zabel has mentioned its "cloying lyric verbalism" [Introduction to *The Portable Conrad.*] I cannot believe that either critic has seriously considered the organic character of the novel, or he would have noticed that the language is only insistent on glamor and cloyingly verbal where it should be—toward the conclusion of the narrative, when Marlow is hopelessly involved in his vision.

It should be observed that Marlow's recollection begins in tranquility—in language almost as colorless as the grey Western ocean he is engaged in describing—and that he does not become rhapsodic until (in Wordsworth's language) "an emotion kindred to that which was before the subject of contemplation, is gradually produced, and does itself actually exist in the mind." Such an emotion overwhelms him during the concluding moments of his tale: the sinking of the *Judea,* his entering the bay as captain of a small-boat, his first view of the East and her people. Until those closing moments his language is quite different. It is, in fact, casual and chatty. His account of joining the *Judea* is typical: "It was twenty-two years ago; and I was just twenty. How time passes! It was one of the happiest days of my life. Fancy! Second mate for the first time—a really responsible officer! . . . The ship also was old. Her name was the *Judea.* Queer name, isn't it? She belonged to a man Wilmer, Wilcox—some name like that." Even during the more exciting early portions of his narrative, Marlow's language rarely becomes glamorous or lyrical. He frequently asks questions of his cronies, calls for the bottle, comments ironically upon his youthful folly, and in various other ways reveals that he is highly conscious of being twenty-two years removed from the voyage. Were he to remain at twenty-two years removed during the conclusion of his narrative, the fabric of the story would be fatally damaged. As we have seen, he does not. He relives his experience.

And the language is organic in yet another way: sense is frequently suggested by sound. Guerard's example of the story's onomatopoeic effects can hardly be improved upon:

> Suddenly there was a frightful racket, rattle, clanking of chain, hiss of water, and millions of sparks flew up into the shivering column of smoke that stood leaning slightly above the ship. The catheads had burned away, and the two red-hot anchors had gone to the bottom, tearing out after them two hundred fathoms of red-hot chain. The ship trembled, the mass of flame swayed as if ready to collapse, and the fore-topgallant mast fell. It darted down like an arrow of fire, shot under and instantly leaping up within an oar's length of the boats, floated quietly, very black on the luminous sea.

The last sentence is particularly admirable, in that sense—as so often in Conrad—is suggested by rhythm and pace as well as by consonants and vowels.

It remains for us to examine the symbolistic overtones of **"Youth"** to see in what way they enrich the literary organism. (Oddly enough, these overtones have received little, if any, notice from several generations of critics.) Several times Marlow suggests that the voyage of the *Judea* is symbolic not only of the life of modern man, but of ancient man—particularly of the Hebrew. As he considers his first voyage to the East, he thinks "of men of old who, centuries ago, went that road in ships that sailed no better, to the land of palms, and spices, and yellow sands, and of brown nations ruled by kings more cruel than Nero the Roman, and more splendid than Solomon the Jew." Toward the conclusion of his tale, when recalling his first view of the island and her people, Marlow reflects that "this was the East of the ancient navigators, so old, so mysterious, resplendent and sombre, living and unchanged, full of danger and promise. And these were the men." The ship is appropriately named the *Judea.* She is captained by the very, very old Beard. Her first mate's name is "pronounced Mann," and he is also "a very, very old chap." Her steward is the ancient Abraham. Also, young Marlow feels as though he has "lived in her for ages." There is just enough to suggest an alternate allegory.

But, other than to suggest the timeless significance of young Marlow's voyage, what is the function of this allegory? Is it merely to glorify human endurance? Isn't it, rather, thematically to reveal the hopelessness of that endurance. We must not ignore "the *Celestial* from Singapore on her return trip," that ship which young Marlow hails in the name of his captain in order to secure "a passage somewhere." That she is commanded by a cursing skipper; that she carries "no light" to combat the darkness everywhere around her; and that a place in her hold is the ultimate "reward" of the men of the *Judea*—all these facts suggest that Conrad meant her name to be ironic; that he was, through her, revealing the true nature of the heavenly city, which Western men, from biblical times onward, have desperately struggled to attain. Human happiness must derive from illusion, not reality, from youth, not age. And, considering the sinking of the *Judea,* the spiritual death of her aged officers and crew, and the character of the *Celestial,* is it not possible that Conrad was suggesting, more specifically, the waning influence of Christianity upon his own generation?

"Youth" is more than a great tale of the sea, more even than an organic work of fiction; it is an abiding vision of modern man. (pp. 591-601)

John Howard Wills, "A Neglected Masterpiece: Conrad's 'Youth'," in Texas Studies in Literature and Language, *Vol. IV, No. 4, Winter, 1963, pp. 591-601.*

Hermann Weiand (essay date 1965)

[*Weiand is an American educator and critic. In the following essay, he analyzes the character of Captain MacWhirr in "Typhoon."*]

[**"Typhoon"**] was written when Conrad was at the height of his writing power (1901) and is one of his great sea-stories (beside *The Nigger of the Narcissus* and **"Youth"**, written before, **"The Secret Sharer"** and *The Shadow Line,* written much later). It is pervaded with the spirit of the "deep conviction" with which Conrad "approached the subject of the story. This conviction, presented through the typhoon and Captain MacWhirr, . . . is the product of 20 years of life. My own life." (Author's Note)

Conrad tells his story as an objective narrator and views MacWhirr with a mixture of admiration and contempt, with affection and scorn. MacWhirr's simple mind being too dull a mirror to reflect events or to provide insight, by far the greater part of the story is seen through the eyes of young Jukes. Although he is at times treated with mild paternal irony, his evaluation of events would therefore seem to come closest to the author's, who, in real life, also served as chief mate under a Captain MacWhirr.

The ponderous centre of the story is nevertheless MacWhirr. Even if he is not seen, his presence is intensely felt, and all episodes are related to him. Just as a number of cameras can be aimed at the same object from different angles and distances, providing pictures from various aspects and stressing outstanding traits, so we get a variety of information about MacWhirr from secondary characters. They qualify MacWhirr and are evaluated by him and through their attitude to him in turn, just as a picture tells us something about the quality of camera and photographer alike when compared with the real object. The reader of course knows much more about MacWhirr than any of the single characters, as their accumulated knowledge is made available for him. Jukes' mind, being the exact opposite of that of MacWhirr, is used as a contrast throughout the story, often with a comic effect.

First we have the author's picture of MacWhirr. He is thick-set and sturdy of limb. In appearance he is plain and crude to the point of cutting a comic figure. In conversation he conveys an impression of timidity and bashfulness. When in command, he creates an atmosphere of harmony and peace. In the very first sentence of the story we are informed that "Captain MacWhirr . . . had a physiognomy that . . . was the exact counterpart of his mind: it had no pronounced characteristics whatever; it was simply ordinary, irresponsive, and unruffled." Later we learn that his "mind" was "much too simple to be perplexed by anything in the world except men's idle talk for which it was not adapted". He had "just enough imagination to carry him through each successive day, and no more, [and therefore] he was tranquilly sure of himself; and . . . not in the least conceited . . . It was, in truth, as impossible for him to take a flight of fancy as it would be for a watchmaker to put together a chronometer with nothing except a two-pound hammer and a whip-saw in the way of tools." He is "entirely given to the actuality of bare existence". "Faithful to facts, which alone his consciousness reflected", MacWhirr perceives but their surface, and acts accordingly. It never occurs to him that they may mean more than what can actually be seen or heard of them. When he notices the fall of the barometer that "was of a nature ominously prophetic", his face betrays "no sort of inward disturbance". The worst he had known till then were "gales in the nature of dirty weather", and he cannot conceive anything beyond that, never having come across it; "omens were nothing to him, and he was unable to discover the message of a prophecy till the fulfilment had brought it home to his very door". There is a lot of trash in books—people talking about things they have never known themselves; how can a captain say e.g. he has dodged a typhoon when he never met it, swerving, presumably, from its path. The "past to his mind is done with, and the future not there yet". He is "neither loquacious nor taciturn . . . There were matters of duty of course", but "the more general actualities of the day required no comment, because facts can speak for themselves with overwhelming precision." His utter lack of imagination is further elucidated by the example of the Siamese flag-elephant, or by his utter amazement at a two hours' conversation between Jukes and an engineer, or by his bewildered consternation at Jukes' "wild" figurative language. It is summed up in Jukes' statement: "He's so jolly innocent that if you were to put your thumb to your nose and wave your fingers at him he would only wonder gravely to himself what got into you", not noticing that he was being jeered at. Given entirely to the facts of bare existence, living merely to exist and help others to exist, MacWhirr is entirely incapable of becoming perplexed by the enigmas and contradictions of human life.

But along with this simplicity and innocence go other qualities which make MacWhirr admirable—which people with complex and subtle minds lack: singleness of purpose, devotion to duty, skill, reliability, an unwavering sense of responsibility and unflinching courage,—altogether incorruptible strength.

This then is the objective narrator's picture of MacWhirr: a blend of admiration and scorn. It is enhanced throughout the story by the reaction of the secondary characters to MacWhirr's naïveté. It is also conveyed through the letters written by MacWhirr himself, by Jukes and the first engineer, old "Solomon" Rout. In the first chapter MacWhirr himself writes to his parents, and his father, who had a "gift for sly chaffing, which to the end of his life he exercised in his intercourses with his son, a little pityingly, as if upon a half-witted person", comments on him: "Tom's an ass." Old Solomon talks of a "dull ass" and a "fool". Jukes writes that he cannot get over how "dense, dull, innocent, exasperating" his skipper is and displays a pose of tolerant and generous mental superiority.

In the last chapter we have again a group of letters, which now express admiration for MacWhirr's achievement. "That captain of the ship . . . a rather simple man . . . has done something rather clever", Solomon says; "wonders will never cease". Jukes thinks "that he got out of it very well for such a stupid man". MacWhirr's letters are left lying open for the steward to read and let the reader know their contents. MacWhirr's wife, for whom her husband is but a necessary commodity, glances wearily through his letters because they are "so prosy, so completely uninteresting". Having seen better days, she thinks herself "quite superior" to him and is resigned to the necessity of her mésalliance as long as her husband is far away. She is utterly incapable of understanding the implications of her husband's "prosy" statements about the typhoon.

There is a whole range of secondary characters omitted in the school editions: the Scottish shipbuilders, who know MacWhirr's value very well, the Siamese shipowner, old Mr. Sigg, who at once recognizes the sterling quality of this taciturn man, the second mate, who "loses his nerve" at the climax of the typhoon and is fisticuffed by MacWhirr, the "profane" second engineer, the third engineer Beale, the helmsman Hackett.

MacWhirr's peculiarities are strongly thrown into relief by contrast to young Jukes, the first mate, who has a blossoming gift of imagination, a quick wit, intelligence and a rare gift of expression. He is typical of all Conrad's young heroes with artists' minds who because of these same qualities are excessively endangered and mostly perish. With their "quick, forestalling vision" (*Lord Jim*) they are open to fear, anguish, doubt and temptation. Conrad seems to be taking revenge on the young romantic heroes of light literature who seduced him when he was a boy.

Although dull MacWhirr is no match for Jukes' quick intelligence, the latter would have been lost in the fury of the typhoon had he not caught hold of his sturdy captain, when his feet were blown from under him. Unlike the other young heroes he has, in a literal sense, a good example in his hour of greatest need, when he is ready "to let everything go". Backed by his captain, he passes his "supreme test", which most of the others like him, lacking a MacWhirr, fail. He is now armed to meet the worst for the rest of his life.

> [In the centre of the typhoon] Jukes experienced an access of confidence, a sensation that came from outside like a warm breath, and made him feel equal to every demand. The distant muttering of the darkness stole into his ears. He noted it unmoved, out of that sudden belief in himself, as a man safe in a shirt of mail would watch a point.

In structure, movement and mood the story is of one cast. Its end is definite and conclusive in form and contents. There is a unity of place, action and time. The scene is the ship, the action the struggle against the typhoon, the time a chronological, definite number of hours on one trip. Circumstances of action, place and time are rendered with great factual precision, visually and audibly. The author, after a general exposition of people and ship in the first chapter, gives us the initial time and the fact of the ominous fall of the barometer, and then sets the clock and the changes in men and nature going—launching the story at a good pace and keeping it up right through.

The story proper starts off one morning, and we learn that the sun is out, what the sky is like, the swell of the sea, the wind and its direction and strength, the temperature, the general state of the atmosphere, the course of the ship and the temper of the individual members of the crew. Throughout the story Conrad keeps registering the changes in all components of the scene, showing the gradual development of the typhoon and the different phases of the struggle against it in a precise rendering of visual and audible detail.

In the unleashed fury of waters and winds, in the impenetrable, almost solid darkness the assuring light of the instruments in the wheel-house seems a last hold: symbol of the ingenuity of the human mind, of man's intrepid spirit set against the chaotic forces of the elements. The helmsman, meeting the assaults from the dark with swift turns of the wheel, is assisted by the men in the heart of the ship. The speaking tube connects the chaotic upper world with the engine-room, a dome of light with a steely, metallic core, submerged in the destructive element. Jukes gets a glimpse of it in the decisive stage of the struggle: of the powerful motions of the shiny metallic limbs of the engine, controlled by the signals of the telegraph with its meaningful inscriptions and its restless hand, of the controlling function of steam-gauge and water-gauge, of the hectic efforts of the engineers to keep all this smooth functioning intact, of the frantic labours of the demon-like stokers in front of the fiery glow of the boilers.

What is the "significance" of this story then, as dramatized mainly in the person of MacWhirr and in his opponent, the typhoon? First of all, there is constant insistence on the notion of order. MacWhirr clings so abjectly to it that he sends Jukes down to re-establish order in the 'tween-deck at the height of the typhoon, when the latter is very badly needed on the bridge. The typhoon abates as soon as order is restored. MacWhirr lives in a rigidly ordered little world, where next to nothing is left to chance, in which everything has its appointed place down to the smallest objects (e.g. the place for MacWhirr's towel or the box of matches in his cabin; the repeated reference to it as a "symbol", an example for the usefulness of a painstaking habit upheld for years, which previously may have seemed utterly pedantic and useless).

The ship can be seen as a symbol for individual man as well as for a community. As soon as one part refuses to function, the whole is endangered. As seen from the canon of Conrad's whole work, we can say that the chaotic disorder in the 'tween-deck at a moment of greatest danger represents one of the sorriest aspects of society, of the "land": a reckless and unscrupulous greed for money. The coolies are "chasing the dollars"—a phrase repeatedly used in Conrad's early work for the evil greed of the white man. Their fighting amongst each other alongside the gallant effort of the crew, who risk their lives to ward off the terrific blows of the common enemy, is "odious" to MacWhirr and seems mad to the sailors. They "rig up lif-lines" to give the coolies a hold. After their initial hesitation, caused by the stunning first blow of their foe, they readily submit to the rule of conduct imperative in their calling and put up a brave fight. In all of Conrad's sea-stories disorder on the ship provokes the destructive forces of nature, and these can only be held at bay if order is restored. As long as discipline and self-control, submission to the requirements of the common need are intact, ship and crew are not only able to withstand the worst that the typhoon can do, but they even defy it. The ship is "breathing into the still core of the hurricane the excess of her strength", and the "small" human voice is repeatedly heard above the typhoon—an unfailing source of strength and consolation. When Jukes is listening through the speaking tube, MacWhirr's "small voice shoved aside the shouting hurricane quietly".

The first part of Conrad's conviction then is that for man to survive and exist order must be indefatigably maintained. MacWhirr's scrupulous orderliness is the outcome of a "humane intention" and "a vague sense of the fitness of things". Only when every individual fulfils his duty in his allotted place can the whole survive, and he draws personal value from the quality of his service (MacWhirr's tacit appreciation of the perseverance of the helmsman). Neglect of duty means destruction (the second mate "loses his nerve" and "is lost").

The second part is that in order to fulfil one's duty properly it is indispensable to be efficient in one's craft. An efficient sailor or engineer is, for MacWhirr, "a good man". Only reliable men can produce the reliable instruments necessary for survival. The *Nan-Shan* is a "good ship" and survives. When MacWhirr sets his foot on board for the very first time, he at once perceives a "rubbishy lock". "Rubbishy locks" prove a great nuisance in the typhoon, and what first seemed petty pedantry to one of the shipbuilders now turns out to have been precious foresight.

The third part is that, apart from his technical skill, man must ever be ready to meet the unexpected, as "Mr. Rout—good man—was ready". He must never tire of standing up against his foe, never lose his courage and his confidence in himself and the ship. "Keep her facing it . . . Facing it—always facing it—that's the way to get through. You are a young sailor. Face it. That's enough for any man. Keep a cool head." That is MacWhirr's crucial advice, which makes Jukes' heart flutter in a sudden access of confidence in the middle of the typhoon and makes him "feel equal to every demand".

There is, however, another ironic side to this story. Life is such a complex thing that man does not generally know what to do at any given moment, in the same way as a sailor knows this because of his training and tradition within the limited circle of his ship and his duties. Although the *Nan-Shan* had been "sighting, verily, even the coast of the Great Beyond", Conrad deliberately turns his back on ultimate issues of human existence. To raise them would have been incompatible with MacWhirr's cast of mind; there are merely occasional hints. The question which imposes itself most strongly is, however, why MacWhirr, despite his limitations, is so eminently fit for his business!

The answer is, that he is so efficient because of his very limitations. He stands in and for a tradition and has adopted its rules wholeheartedly. There is repeated stress laid on his unquestioning acceptance of facts. Just because he is uncritical, unquestioning and unimaginative he is a perfectly efficient sailor. When he tries "to do what's fair", he applies the rules of his inherited tradition. "His only need is to exist", like that of the invulnerable young Russian in Conrad's ***Heart of Darkness,*** and to provide means of existence for some people ashore. Because he has no imagination and little intelligence, he has no needs beyond the mere necessities of existence, and he cannot be tempted or led astray by aspirations and dreams. He is nothing but a sailor. His extraordinary, almost heroic strength results from his extraordinary limitation, his eminence is paid for by shortcomings which make him ridiculous in the eyes of his fellowmen—and of the author. On the other hand—as both parties grudgingly admit—he is one "of that good stupid kind we like to feel marching right and left of us in life . . . not disturbed by the vagaries of intelligence and the perversions of—of nerves, let us say" (*Lord Jim*), one of those men and women "whose very existence is based upon honest faith, and upon an instinct of courage . . . a power of resistance . . . an unthinking and blessed stiffness before the outward and inward terrors, before the might of nature and the corruption of men . . . "

It is Conrad's conviction that men like MacWhirr, although they may be dull, boring and uninspiring, are the backbone of our kind. With equal composure, they plod through their daily task or perform heroic feats, without expecting praise or reward beyond their daily bread. Beside the almost neurotic young heroes with their romantic dreams they seem incredibly sane and efficient, and absurd at the same time. In Conrad's world, however, it is the romantic young hero who fails, and it is the simple, prosaic, down-to-earth fellow who survives.

Whether his achievements are real victories however, whether reaching another port is just a respite granted to him before he is turned back into an even more violent sea till final disaster comes—that is a question not touched upon in Conrad's sea-stories, but forming the core of his more important work. (pp. 49-55)

Hermann Weiand, "Typhoon," in Insight II: Analyses of Modern British Literature, *edited by John V. Hagopian and Martin Dolch, Hirschgraben-Verlag, 1965, pp. 49-58.*

James C. Dahl (essay date 1968)

[*In the following excerpt, Dahl discusses the depiction of the dark side of human nature in* Heart of Darkness.]

The awakening to the darkness of the human heart and the consequences of this act are the subjects of this paper on Joseph Conrad's novel ***Heart of Darkness.*** This kind of introspective journey into the dark side of human personality is the subject of much of the best of modern literature and modern psychology and is generally considered to be necessary for human happiness and mental balance. Yet it is probably the most frightening and disruptive moral act human beings are called to undertake, and as Conrad's novel indicates, some do not survive the journey. What ***Heart of Darkness*** reveals of the inner journey is of great importance to our present age, especially since the Biblical promises of forgiveness and internal change are now so little understood, trusted, and acted upon.

In the novel, Mr. Kurtz, the gifted artist, intellectual, and idealist, is the most obvious case of degeneration. His motive for taking a position with the Belgian trading company in the Congo is that of bringing the fruits of civilized life to the natives of the upper reaches of the Congo River.

In fact, Kurtz has been commissioned by the Society for the Suppression of Savage Customs to write a report on conditions among the natives and, presumably, to offer advice on how to change life in that region. Kurtz writes seventeen pages of the report, emphasizing the potential for good the white man enjoys in the Congo because of the almost supernatural reverence in which he is held by the natives. Later, we learn through Marlow that Kurtz's idealism changes to savagery. The postscript to Kurtz's report is the infamous command "Exterminate all the brutes!" In action, Kurtz becomes more savage and ruthless than any native in the novel, and his final summing up of himself and his achievements in the Congo is "The horror! The horror!"

What reasons for Kurtz's degeneration does the novel offer? First of all, the story makes it very clear that Kurtz had no idea of his potential for savagery before his experiences in Africa. Kurtz is presented as one of the most brilliant products of nineteenth-century European civilization, and in the story Marlow tells specifically what Kurtz's background is: "The original Kurtz had been educated partly in England, and—as he was good enough to say himself—his sympathies were in the right place. His mother was half-English, his father was half-French. All Europe contributed to the making of Kurtz." Idealistic, progressive, optimistic—these are the qualities of nineteenth-century intellectual opinion which Kurtz is the product of. The suggestion here is clearly that Kurtz is more than a mere case study in abnormal psychology; rather he is representative of the shallowness of philosophical thought of his era. In Kurtz all of intellectual Europe is mirrored, and his fate seems to be the almost inevitable result of a philosophy of optimism about human nature, with its complete ignorance of the human capacity of savagery. With only the conviction of moral superiority to the natives and the idealistic mission to civilize them, Kurtz is helpless against the temptations of the abominable which he encounters in his isolation at the inner station. This inadequate appraisal of his character, his ignorance of his potential for evil, is what Marlow means when he says Kurtz is hollow at the core. In a civilized setting, Kurtz is protected from himself by the pressure of public opinion and the law, and therefore, while in Europe, Kurtz's idealistic oratory causes him to be regarded as a genius and a promising liberal politician. Away from the restraints of civilization, Kurtz is unprotected and helpless against his inclination toward the abominable. As Marlow says of Kurtz in Africa: "But the wilderness had found him out early, and had taken on him a terrible vengeance for the fantastic invasion. I think it had whispered to him things about himself which he did not know, things of which he had no conception till he took counsel with this great solitude—and the whisper had proved irresistibly fascinating. It echoed loudly within him because he was hollow at the core." Kurtz, like another of the gifted intellectuals of modern literature, Mann's Gustave von Aschenbach of *Death in Venice,* has all the positive characteristics of mind except those which can protect him from himself, and both men undergo a degeneration of like degree. Kurtz becomes a ruthless egomaniac who has himself worshipped by the natives; Aschenbach passes from a highly respected intellectual historian to a childish pervert, hopelessly in love with a fourteen-year-old Polish boy.

Marlow's discovery of his dark side is as dramatic as Kurtz's, and most thoughtful readers of the story see Marlow's self-discovery as the principal theme of the story. In temperament and intellect, however, Marlow and Kurtz are certainly far from alike, and their reasons for the African venture are also very dissimilar. Marlow is not an intellectual, and prior to his knowing the Belgians of the Central Station and Kurtz, Marlow is not an idealist either. Adventure and the desire to fulfill a childhood dream are his motives for going to Africa. Only the amorality of the Belgians and their admiration, though insincere, of the idealism of Kurtz bring to consciousness Marlow's idealism. The company men are avaricious and sadistic as well as stupid, and even before leaving the Central Station, Marlow declares his interest solely in Kurtz and Kurtz's ideals: " . . . I was curious to see whether this man, who had come out equipped with moral ideas of some sort, would climb to the top after all, and how he would set about his work when there."

Africa and Kurtz provide the opportunities for self-discovery for Marlow. His murderous reaction to the demand by his fellow European on the journey from the coast to the Central Station (the fat French companion of Marlow wants him to kill a bearer for leaving his duties) is the first jolt to Marlow's naive self-esteem. It is now that he first recognizes his potential for murder. Later, Marlow hears and sees the natives singing and dancing, and he confesses to an inner reaction not previously known: " . . . the thought of their humanity—like yours—the thought of your remote kinship with this wild and passionate uproar. Ugly. Yes, it was ugly enough, but if you were man enough you would admit to yourself that there was in you just the faintest test of a response to the terrible frankness of that noise, a dim suspicion of their being a meaning in it which you—you so remote from the night of first ages—could comprehend."

On learning of the reversion of Kurtz, Marlow is faced with a serious crisis of loyalty. The Manager speaks of Kurtz's murders and marauding for ivory in wholly amoral terms; Kurtz's "method is unsound." Marlow's reaction to this judgment—"It seemed to me I had never breathed an atmosphere so vile, and I turned mentally to Kurtz for relief—positively for relief—" is that of a young man forced by circumstances into thoughtfulness about life. However, why Marlow continues to be faithful to Kurtz, even after his complete megalomania is obvious to Marlow, is a question as perplexing as it is significant. One would expect that Marlow would view Kurtz's action as viler than the Manager's since the latter has never entertained a moral viewpoint. Kurtz, on the other hand, came to Africa for the expressed purpose of furthering morality and the rule of law, the gifts of civilization, and in the course of his career at the inner station has become the monster he came to suppress. Why, then, does Marlow remain loyal to Kurtz?

I believe the answer to this question is that Marlow, who labels Kurtz as hollow at the core, is himself fearful of hollowness. For Marlow, the triumph of Kurtz is that in spite of his savage acts and ideas, he has pronounced a judgment on himself and on life itself. This is Marlow's reaction at the time of Kurtz's summing up: "Anything approaching the change that came over his features I have never seen before, and hope never to see again. Oh, I wasn't touched. I was fascinated. It was as though a veil had been rent. I saw on that ivory face the expression of sombre pride, or ruthless power, of craven terror—of an intense and hopeless despair. Did he live again in every detail of desire, temptation, and surrender during that supreme moment of complete knowledge? He cried in a whisper at some image, at some vision—he cried out twice, a cry that was no more than a breath: 'The horror! The horror!' "

Immediately after Kurtz's final words, Marlow speaks of his own nearness to death, for he, like Kurtz, is suffering from jungle fever. Marlow's thoughts now are of his own summing up, and his fear is this: "I was within a hair's breadth of the last opportunity for pronouncement, and I found with humiliation that probably I would have nothing to say. This is the reason why I affirm Kurtz was a remarkable man. He had something to say. He said it. . . . I like to think my summing-up would not have been a word of careless contempt. Better his cry—much better. It was an affirmation, a moral victory paid for my innumerable defeats, by abominable terrors, by abominable satisfactions. But it was a victory! That is why I have remained loyal to Kurtz to the last. . . . " Marlow has seen himself mirrored in the amorality and shallowness of the Company men, and his fear of nihilism leads him to affirm the man whose soul he acknowledges as mad.

The Roi des Belges, *the ship Conrad commanded on his journey to the Congo.*

What keeps Marlow from the Kurtzian is then not superior moral fibre or greater internal restraint; rather, the story indicates that only the gospel of work and the dissimilar circumstances of Marlow protect him from the temptations to which Kurtz succumbs. Again and again, Marlow stresses the importance of work activity as protection from one's dark side. The savagery of the native dance appeals to Marlow, but it is his duties as captain of the river steamer, not moral restraint, which keep him going ashore. Marlow also lays great stress on the fact that his circumstances are never those of Kurtz. Kurtz is isolated in the jungle, albeit by his own choice (the Company had sent him an assistant but Kurtz had ordered that man back to the Central Station), while Marlow is among Europeans during his entire stay in Africa.

At the point in the story where Kurtz attempts to escape from his rescuers back to the camp of the natives, Marlow comes closest to being in Kurtz's circumstances. As he stalks Kurtz in the middle of the jungle night, Marlow is beseiged by the irrational and savage in his own subconscious: "I had some imbecile thoughts. The knitting old woman with the cat obtruded herself upon my memory as a most improper person to be sitting at the other end of such an affair. I saw a row of pilgrims squirting lead in the air out of Winchesters held to the hip. I thought I would never get back to the steamer, and imagined myself living alone and unarmed in the woods to an advanced age. Such silly things—you know. And I remember I confounded the beat of the drum with the beating of my heart, and was pleased at its calm regularity." Here Marlow is most nearly in a situation like that of Kurtz at the inner station, and his fantasy includes the thought of living alone in the jungle and the oneness of his heartbeat with the beat of the jungle drums. These are dangerous thoughts for one to entertain whose own opinion of his moral armor is that only work and circumstance differentiate him from a man who has become a monster. This passage binds Marlow and Kurtz more closely than any other in the novel. But Marlow's fear of his own hollowness, that is of having nothing to say of his experiences or of life itself, keeps him loyal to Kurtz, madman though Marlow knows Kurtz to be.

If what Marlow learns of his dark side during the African journey is that no fundamental difference exists between Kurtz and himself, then Marlow's neurotic actions and thoughts back in Brussels are not unexpected. He returns to that city sick in body and soul, deeply shaken by his newfound awareness of his shadow side. As Marlow says, "It was not my strength that wanted nursing, it was my imagination that wanted soothing." Marlow despises the citizens of Brussels for their superficiality and ignorance of life, characteristics of Marlow himself before Africa.

By the time of his telling the story to his friends on board the *Nellie,* Marlow has obviously recovered his emotional stability, but his extremely pessimistic comments on life clearly echo the shattering and humiliating self-discoveries of Africa and Kurtz. In fact, Marlow states that, though not wholly clear, the African venture has thrown a kind of light on his experiences. Marlow's thoughts on human life are of central importance to an understanding of the theme of the story—self-discovery and its consequences—and these observations have been little noted by critics of the novel.

For instance, of the possibility of real communication between men and hence of real affection between them, Marlow's summing up is this: "No, it is impossible; it is impossible to convey the life-sensation of any given epoch of one's existence—that which makes its truth, its meaning—its subtle and penetrating essence. It is impossible. We live, as we dream—alone."

Of the failure of idealism in difficult circumstances, we have the example of Kurtz himself. One cannot fail to note that though Marlow alludes to the necessity of faithfulness to an idea (in the story the faithfulness is to the idea of civilization) as the means to overcome the temptation of reversion to the savage, Kurtz succumbs, in spite of the fact that he is the strongest possible advocate of the benefits of civilized life. The most outspoken and convincing idealist falls prey to "the fascination of the abomination." Marlow surely cannot fail to see that, under similar circumstances, his faithfulness to the idea of civilization would likely not protect him from the temptation of the savage.

Of the nature of human life itself, Marlow emerges from the African venture with this conclusion: "Droll thing life is—that mysterious arrangement of merciless logic for a futile purpose. The most you can hope from it is some knowledge of yourself—that comes too late—a crop of inextinguishable regrets." One is reminded here of the disillusionment of Marlow in Conrad's story **"Youth,"** written immediately before ***Heart of Darkness.*** The theme of that story is that youthful idealism is impossible to maintain in the face of life's inevitable disappointments, but the tragedy is that without idealism, the human heart ". . . grows dim, grows cold, grows small, and expires—and expires too soon, too soon—before life itself."

Finally, what do we know of Joseph Conrad himself and his reactions to what he learned of himself during the actual months of his African venture in 1890? First, like Marlow, whose motive for the journey is adventure, Conrad reportedly described himself as shallow and naive before Africa. To his friend Edward Garnett, Conrad reportedly said, "Before the Congo, I was just a mere animal." To what degree the story mirrors actual people, events, and insights no one can say for certain, though it is generally held that Marlow is the spokesman for Conrad. Of the consequences of Conrad's journey into self we have the pessimistic statements of Marlow in the story and a very important letter about her husband's African experience written by Jessie Conrad in 1930, six years after Conrad's death. Mrs. Conrad wrote, "I know that he returned a disillusioned and broken man and the consequences of that ill-advised visit to the Congo coloured all the rest of his life."

We also know that Conrad lost his religious faith early in life, a fact of major significance, I believe, in the matter of self-discovery. Of Christianity, Conrad wrote, "I am not blind to its services but this absurd oriental fable from which it springs irritates me. Great, improving, softening, compassionate it may be, but it has lent itself with amazing facility to cruel distortions, and is the only religion which, with its impossible standards, has brought an infinity of anguish to innumerable souls—on this earth." Thus, having dismissed Christianity with its acknowledgment of the human tendency to evil but its assurance of forgiveness of sin and spiritual rebirth from natural depravity, is it surprising that Conrad emerged from Africa extremely pessimistic about human life and its potential for meaning and happiness? For the unbeliever, the descent into self is indeed a reckless one, and it is not surprising that for many the insight into the human heart of darkness is so shattering. Kurtz, unaware of his potential for savagery, becomes the very thing he came to Africa to change. Marlow and Conrad emerge from Africa only as wiser but sadder men.

To Swiss psychologist Carl Jung, the recognition of the shadow side of human personality is of the utmost importance to wholeness and balance. If unrecognized or repressed, the danger is a fate like Kurtz's—the uncontrollable emergence of the savage side of man. Jung is also strongly convinced of the importance of religious belief to human happiness, especially with regard to this descent into self, for the major religions of the world all promise spiritual rebirth. For us in the third quarter of the twentieth century, the decline, if not near absence, of deep religious convictions is a matter of grave consequence with regard to the dangers of reversion to savagery. As Jung writes in the chapter "Approaching the Unconscious" in *Man and His Symbols,* "Our times have demonstrated what it means for the gates of the underworld to be opened. Things whose enormity nobody could have imagined in the idyllic harmlessness of the first decade of our century have happened and have turned our world upside down. Ever since, the world has remained in a state of schizophrenia. Not only has civilized Germany disgorged its terrible primitivity, but Russia is also ruled by it, and Africa has been set on fire. No wonder that the Western world feels uneasy." (pp. 33-40)

James C. Dahl, "Kurtz, Marlow, Conrad and the Human Heart of Darkness," in Studies in the Literary Imagination, *Vol. I, No. 2, October, 1968, pp. 33-40.*

Gloria R. Dussinger (essay date 1969)

[*In the following essay, Dussinger argues that "The Secret Sharer" is successful as a work of fiction only if read as a psychological study.*]

"The Secret Sharer" is a criticism-riddled story. Appreciating its importance in the Conrad canon, critics have attempted repeatedly to give this story its due. So much stirring of the waters has, alas, only muddied them; pronouncements have been made that Leggatt is and is not the captain's ideal self, that his presence aids and hinders the captain in fulfilling his duties, and that the captain carries Conrad's approval and opprobrium. Consequently, the student turns from **"The Secret Sharer"** convinced that the tale is meaningful but bewildered as to the meaning.

There remains one way of reading **"The Secret Sharer"** which forestalls plaguing contradictions: the action must be seen to occur in a social vacuum. It can be soundly demonstrated that social morality is irrelevant to **"The Secret Sharer."** Indeed, as soon as ethical judgments are brought to bear, the story breaks in two, contradictory readings appear plausible, conclusions antithetical to Conrad's other writings are made possible, and Conrad's artistry comes under suspicion. **"The Secret Sharer"** becomes coherent, unified, and thoroughly Conradian only when read as a psychological study, an investigation of identity as the basic existential fact. The author has deliberately filtered out social considerations in order to observe without distraction the process of self-discovery.

Conrad's asocial focus in **"The Secret Sharer"** is admittedly bold, and misinterpretation of the story is the price he paid for his experiment. By creating a laboratory environment for the captain's confrontation of himself, Conrad achieved a concentrated and powerful expression of his truth, but he sacrificed verisimilitude. It is the reader's prior knowledge of the relationship of each man to all men that causes misunderstanding of **"The Secret Sharer,"** for the reader invariably measures Conrad's captain by social standards. He confronts the fact that Leggatt is a murderer and that the captain in sheltering him defies the law on which his role aboard ship depends. No matter how skillfully the critic justifies the harboring of a criminal by juggling internal and external laws, he cannot absolve the captain of a still greater crime: the risk of his crew and his ship in an act of needless bravado. The reader is faced with two choices: he can apply social criteria to the captain's behavior and find him guilty, thereby converting the story's triumphant conclusion into irony, or he can close his mind temporarily to the judgments of custom and accept only the values of Conrad's artistic world.

If the reader stays within the limits of the little world created by Conrad, experiences only what Conrad offers, he will avoid confusion. Through imagery, characterization, setting, mood, and direct statement, Conrad has drawn our attention to the psychological drama and left the rest of the playhouse—man's relationship to his fellows—in the dark. The imagery of depth psychology figures so largely in **"The Secret Sharer"** that Conrad has been charged by [Marvin] Mudrick with a lack of indirectness:

> And who could possibly miss, on the most inattentive first reading, Conrad's oversimplified, imposed mythical structure, symbol to character in the crudest one-to-one relationship, nailed into the flesh of the narrative in almost every sentence? [*Hudson Review,* 1954]

Scholars persist in looking beyond the psychological images in spite of the fact that Conrad has included them in greater profusion and concreteness than his art allows him elsewhere. Is it naïve to conclude that he did so purposely to prevent misinterpretation, even at the cost of an uncharacteristic obviousness?

Leggatt's coming naked from the sea (the primal element) at night (the time of dreams), his wearing of a sleeping suit (the garment of the unconscious), his concealment, and his customary position near the bedplace all reinforce the psychological import of the story. Also suggestive of the unconscious life are the rope ladder and the rope's end by means of which Leggatt gets into and out of the ship: they represent the umbilical cord. During the time Leggatt is hidden in the captain's room, he sits "on the low stool, his bare feet close together, his arms folded, his head hanging on his breast—and perfectly still" in what is obviously the fetal position. When the captain and his double slip "through a tiny dark passage . . . a sliding door" into the cramped sail locker, they are, imagistically, in the womb. Here, as identical twins, they experience the closest sympathy. The captain, who has always maintained enough objectivity to call Leggatt "the secret sharer," now completely merges identities with the fugitive: "I saw myself wandering barefooted, bareheaded, the sun beating on my dark poll." It is apparent that Leggatt has no conscious identity aboard the captain's ship; his psychological status equals that of the unborn. Conrad tells us this by never allowing the captain to use Leggatt's name, for the individual name is the sign of personality. The man who was Leggatt elsewhere becomes aboard ship merely an element of the captain's psyche.

As imagery focuses on the psychological, so does characterization of the narrator, to the exclusion of moral overtones. The fact is that the captain not once considers Leggatt's moral standing; never does he weigh the rightness or wrongness of sheltering an outlaw. On the contrary, the story emphasizes repeatedly the instantaneous and complete sympathy between the two men: "He appealed to me as if our experiences had been as identical as our clothes," and "I quite understand," to quote only two statements. Both the captain's comments on the murder are lacking in any hint of condemnation: " 'Fit of temper,' I suggested, confidently," and "It was all very simple. The same strung-up force which had given twenty-four men a chance, at least, for their lives, had, in a sort of recoil, crushed an unworthy mutinous existence." To introduce a dual set of laws—internal and external—as though the captain were choosing, is specious. The captain's relation to Leggatt is a psychological one which Conrad has deliberately kept clear of moral judgments. To argue from omission that something is wrong with the captain because he ignores social morality is to step outside the limits of Conrad's story into the void of the uncreated artistic world. That chaos affords no critical footing.

Still, readers may be tempted to invert the captain's statements and attitudes because they suspect him of egotism. In distrust they may read him ironically, as one is forced to do frequently with Henry James's narrators. Conrad, however, has forestalled such an interpretation through his setting and over-all mood, which support rather than contradict a straightforward acceptance of the narrator. At the outset Conrad carefully constructs a scene of unmitigated isolation: "for there was no sign of human habitation as far as the eye could reach." In order to focus his spotlight *only* upon the captain and the ship, Conrad underscores the lack of human company: "And then I was left alone with my ship. . . . There was not a sound in her—and around us nothing moved, nothing lived, not a canoe on the water, not a bird in the air, not a cloud in the sky." The crew and the social mores they illustrate are not to be considered. At the climax of the narrator's story, as the ship bears down upon the islands, society is once again excluded: "But all that forenoon . . . I saw no sign of man or canoe in the field of the telescope I kept on pointing at the scattered group." The author has attempted to make his setting suggest a social vacuum, thereby allowing the psychological to be displayed in its purest state.

In addition to setting, Conrad offers a general mood that agrees with the captain's direct statements and assures us of their reliability. Readers are aware of Conrad's consummate ability to evoke a feeling of the uncanny, the unreal, as he does in the nightmare ***Heart of Darkness.*** In **"The Secret Sharer"** this power has not been called into use. Far from surrounding the captain's experience of Leggatt with a mood of doubt or incredulity, Conrad consistently marks it with calm acceptance. There can be no conflict in the captain's breast between the law of the individual and the law of society when the psychic atmosphere is one of welcome and instant sympathy. Conrad's mood urges us to share the narrator's internal experience; it nowhere invites the application of societal judgments.

To bolster the imagery, characterization, setting, and mood of **"The Secret Sharer,"** all of which function on the psychological level, Conrad includes a number of statements that make a strictly psychological reading of the story imperative. For example, our attention is early restricted, in the second paragraph, to the captain and the ship: "the appointed task of both our existences to be carried out, far from all human eyes, with only sky and sea for spectators and for judges." Society, of which the crew forms a part, becomes inessential to the plot; the captain rules out any effect of his ordeal upon the crew: " . . . I was willing to take the adequacy of the others for granted. They had simply to be equal to their tasks . . . ." When the moment of severe testing arrives—the steering of the ship under the shadow of Koh-ring—the captain expresses his fear: "and I realized suddenly that all my future, the only future for which I was fit, would perhaps go irretrievably to pieces in any mishap to my first command." That his fear is personal and shows no concern for the safety of the seamen does not prove the captain's egotism; it simply proves that this is a story about the relation of a captain to his ship and not about the relation of a captain to his crew. Conrad would have eliminated the crew entirely were it not for the demands of realism. Instead he shoved them out of sight by means of these statements.

While these quotations limit our scrutiny to the captain aboard his ship, a few others clarify the narrator's relation to the law represented by the captain of the *Sephora.* Observing the visiting captain's distress, the narrator reflects, "perhaps I should have sympathized with him if I had been able to detach my mental vision from the unsuspected sharer of my cabin as though he were my second self." The narrator's psychological involvement with his double prohibits any moral judgment. When debating how he should have acted toward the *Sephora*'s captain, the narrator says, "And yet how else could I have received him? Not heartily! That was impossible for psychological reasons, which I need not state here." The young captain's identification with Leggatt causes him to respond as Leggatt would respond. Moreover, the captain of the *Sephora* had already made clear that the narrator would not do for chief mate aboard his ship. Heartiness would have been the falsest of affectations under these circumstances. At the climax of the interview, the narrator fears a direct question about Leggatt: "I could not, I think, have met him by a direct lie, also for psychological (not moral) reasons." To say that Leggatt was not present would represent an immense psychological lie, for he was present in the identity of the captain. These three statements expressly hold the story to the psychological at the very point closest to social involvement.

Thus through imagery, characterization, setting, mood, and direct statement, Conrad has made clear that **"The Secret Sharer"** records a psychological and only a psychological experience. It is the story of a young captain coming to know himself and thereby becoming adequate to the command of his ship. The critic may quarrel with Conrad's having set up a situation whose social simplicity belies reality. Moral ramifications are strictly controlled in **"The Secret Sharer,"** and the story is therefore false to the randomness of life. But if readers are willing to grant the author his *donnée,* they will see in this tale Conrad's most compressed and most dramatic insight into the human personality.

What is the truth Conrad has artfully contrived **"The Secret Sharer"** to reveal? A youthful captain is about to be tested by his first command. He feels unsure of his ability to meet the responsibility because his strangeness to the ship and to himself prevents him from recognizing his resources. Whatever degree of courage he may possess is useless to him until he can know of it. The story traces the captain's self-confrontation, his unflinching recognition of total identity, including those raw, impulsive forces that men keep hidden in the unconscious under firm control of the ego ideal. As a result of self-knowledge the captain becomes a free man, able to commune with his ship because he dares commune with himself. He has stripped reality to the existential truth of selfhood and, standing firmly on this ground, can face whatever a chance-ridden universe can bring.

At the beginning the captain shares with Conrad's other uninitiated young men a belief in the orderliness of the universe:

> And suddenly I rejoiced in the great security of the sea as compared with the unrest of the land, in my choice of that untempted life presenting no disquieting problems, invested with an elementary moral beauty by the absolute straightforwardness of its appeal and by the singleness of its purpose.

These words fairly shriek from the page for refutation, and the student of Conrad knows that they will be scathingly dealt with. A second sign of the captain's immaturity is his belief in an ideal self: " . . . I wondered how far I should turn out faithful to that ideal conception of one's own personality every man sets up for himself secretly." Conrad had already provided his audience with a masterful statement on such idealism in *Lord Jim.* The ideal toward which Jim strove was shown to be unreal and false, both by the exaggerated actions which it inspired and by its source: Jim garnered his ideal of courageous behavior from "light holiday literature," we are told in Chapter One of that novel.

An echo of this basing one's view of human nature on shallow "romantic" literature can be heard in **"The Secret Sharer,"** where Conrad fittingly condemns it. When Leggatt proposes that he be put ashore among the islands, the captain protests, " 'Maroon you! We are not living in a boy's adventure tale!' " Leggatt scornfully replies, " 'We aren't indeed! There's nothing of a boy's tale in this'." The story concerns a frightening confrontation of the realness of identity; there is no room here for ideal heroes who contain no taint of the uncontrolled libido.

The captain's ego ideal, about which he is fearful at the opening of the episode, is not meant to be measured up to; it is meant to be expanded because it is inadequate. Quite obviously, the young lack the experiental wherewithal to form an adequate notion of what it takes to be a man. The critics who regard Leggatt as the embodiment of the ideal and who argue that the captain in protecting the fugitive gains those "qualities of decisiveness, ability, and courage he himself seems to lack" [Leo Gurko, *Joseph Conrad: Giant in Exile*] appear in error on two counts. First, they disregard Conrad's suspicion of the "ideal conception of one's own personality" throughout his works. Second, they miss the many demonstrations of the captain's decisiveness, ability, and courage in **"The Secret Sharer."** The captain does not lack these qualities; he is only a stranger to himself, which means that he is unaware of his potential. From the beginning he exhibits those traits that will make him successful as a captain: he accepts Leggatt with a matter-of-fact assurance, almost as if he were expecting him; there is none of Jim's childish refusal to see himself for what he is. He gives orders firmly, subdues the sneering second mate, and asserts his command arbitrarily. His first order—that the men sleep rather than maintain an anchor watch—reveals a decisiveness that outfaces custom. Even the fear of being thought eccentric does not paralyze him as it would a less self-confident master of men.

Although the untried young captain at first has no inkling of the amoral force within himself (a condition of ignorance in which the "ideal" flourishes), he identifies unhesitatingly with the "man from the sea" as soon as that figure emerges. The naturalness of his acceptance of Leggatt testifies to the potential of his personality. In Leggatt he recognizes the concealed part of his personality, the instinctual energy that is vital and lawless. As long as Leggatt remains hidden below, however, the captain suffers from a loss of instinctiveness: "But all unconscious alertness had abandoned me. I had to make an effort of will to recall myself back (from the cabin) to the conditions of the moment." A feeling of duality has caused this loss; instinctiveness cannot be recovered until the captain sees Leggatt not as an other self but as himself. That is, the captain must go beyond his unconscious reception of vital impulse to a conscious acknowledgment. When, in the sail locker, the captain is struck by a sudden thought—"I saw myself wandering"—his ego has accepted Leggatt fully. The transference of the hat which is the Jungian symbol of personality marks this complete identification.

And it is the hat, sign of the captain's unreserved acceptance of the libido, that saves the narrator and opens the future for him. Had he been unwilling to admit his potential for murder, he would have stifled his potential for saving the ship. Leggatt represents both. The innate force that allows man to work good or evil is suggested in **"The Secret Sharer"** by the contrasting words, "saved" and "lost." Trying to justify Leggatt to his captain, the narrator states, " 'That reefed foresail saved you'." When the steward comes out of the cabin without showing signs of having seen Leggatt, the captain gasps, " 'Saved,' I thought. 'But, no! Lost! Gone! He was gone!' " The mate's anguished answer to his own cry " 'My God! Where are we?' " is the single word " 'Lost!' " Lastly, the captain sees his hat become "the saving mark for my eyes." Conrad has shown in the opposition of "saved" and "lost" the ambivalence of instinctive force: it can save man by giving him full selfhood; it can destroy him unless harnessed by the ego (witness Kurtz!). Without it man cannot act at all and thus cannot exist.

Paralleling the irrational—Leggatt's element—in microcosmic man is the factor of chance in the macrocosm. Those who have faith in the ideality of personality share their trust with those who conceive of an orderly universe governed by moral laws constituted in nature. In **"The Secret Sharer"** Conrad asserts the need to recognize libidinal power as the fountainhead of identity, but he points out that such force is morally undifferentiated. Irrationality or psychic chaos is the price one pays for this power. On the cosmic level, disorder manifests itself in chance or accident. Good and evil are irrelevant to chance, which merely effects the dynamism of the universe.

The chief mate with his terrible whiskers represents belief in an orderly world: "He was of a painstaking turn of mind. As he used to say, he 'liked to account to himself' for practically everything that came in his way . . . ." Through the exercise of reason, the chief mate attempts to fit all experience into a tidy pattern. The incident of the scorpion that inexplicably drowns in the inkwell, contrary to all "natural laws" governing scorpion behavior, presages both Leggatt's impulsiveness and the element of chance. When the captain has difficulty pulling in the side ladder, he tries the mate's method to "account" for the unexpected. This failing, he ceases to reason and begins to act: "In the end, of course, I put my head over the rail." His willingness to move into the unknown signifies his coming enlightenment.

Recognizing in Leggatt his own instinctive nature, the captain learns to accept the philosophic corollary of his psychological awareness. He sorrowfully acknowledges that Leggatt's standing is incompatible with a belief in an ordered universe: "The very trust in Providence was, I suppose, denied to his guilt. Shall I confess that this thought cast me down very much?" Identifying with Leggatt demands the sacrifice of the captain's security in a divinely ordained world. He, too, is denied a trust in Providence.

That the narrator alters his world view from one of benign order to one of indifferent randomness is shown in his decision to steer toward the islands. The rationalistic mate looks aghast at the captain's plan: " 'Do you mean, sir, in the dark amongst the lot of all them islands and reefs and shoals?' " But the captain has come to understand that traveling in the dark among reefs and shoals is the necessary condition of man's life. The perilous journey to Koh-ring manifests his acceptance of the terms of existence. (pp. 599-608)

Gloria R. Dussinger, " 'The Secret Sharer': Conrad's Psychological Study," in Texas Studies in Literature and Language, *Vol. X, 1969, pp. 599-608.*

John Howard Weston (essay date 1974)

[In the following excerpt, Weston discusses "Youth" as both a stepping-stone to later works and an artistic achievement in its own right.]

Because critical examinations of Conrad's **"Youth"** tend almost universally to fall into one or another critical perspective—the story is typically of interest either as an isolated work of art or as Conrad's stepping-stone from *The Nigger of the 'Narcissus'* to ***Heart of Darkness*** and *Lord Jim*—a more balanced look at the story is in order. Those who see the story in isolation seem always to claim too much: while **"Youth"** is the "existential comedy" [J. Oates Smith, *Renascence,* 1963] and "masterpiece" [J. H. Wills, *Texas Studies in Language and Literature,* 1963] they show it to be, they never show it to be more than a comedy of severely limited implications and a masterpiece of small compass. On the other hand, those who see the story as revealing "in modest and undeveloped form many of [Conrad's] characteristic devices and themes" [Murray Krieger, *College English,* 1959] never show it to be even a minor masterpiece. The shortcoming of the first approach is that the critic does not use his privileged hindsight, does not read **"Youth"** as a possible analogue to ***Heart of Darkness*** in order to enlarge his awareness of the possible thematic content of **"Youth."** The shortcoming of the second is that in showing how the story is a crucial step on Conrad's path to ***'Heart of Darkness,'*** the critic concerns himself largely with Conrad's narrative technique and neglects to use his hindsight to discover, to the story's advantage, how much of the "darkness" is inchoate in **"Youth."**

In both cases, the stumbling-block seems to be Conrad's relation to Marlow: either the critic does not deal with the ironic relation between Conrad and his narrator in ***Heart of Darkness,*** and thus does not import his knowledge of that relation into his examination of **"Youth,"** or he simply sees the ironic relation in the later novel as a sophisticated technique that has as its antecedent Conrad's naive use of Marlow in the earlier story. The only study I know of that attempts to treat **"Youth"** fully both on the terms of the story and in its place in the Conrad canon is Lawrence Graver's *Conrad's Short Fiction,* but even Graver does not escape the second weakness: while he sees that **"Youth"** is unique among Conrad's stories because "it is the only extended study of the natural egoist," he also writes that "**'Youth'** is an attractive work with which to begin a discussion of Conrad's major period, for it allows an easy entrance into the complex world of ***Heart of Darkness.***" I would argue, however, that "Youth" is in itself a complex work, in which Conrad plumbs depths which, epistemologically if not morally, are as deep as those of ***Heart of Darkness.***

Critics generally agree that **"Youth"** represents a significant technical advance over *The Nigger of the 'Narcissus.'* For example, William York Tindall argues [in *From Jane Austen to Joseph Conrad*] that "the idea of Marlow can be traced back to the inner demands of Conrad's work . . . The story of . . . the ship *Narcissus* is told by someone who . . . is nameless and apparently disembodied. . . . [H]e seems not altogether there. . . . Marlow, developing from this voice, improves it. Equipped with personality, character, limits, attitude, and tone—in a word, with body—Charlie Marlow and his conspiring voice become authentic." The authenticity of Marlow's voice should lead us further. Like the tone of *The Nigger,* the tone of Marlow's narration in **"Youth"** is elegiac; in each work, Conrad's narrator presents us with an heroic past from which the present is sadly fallen away. But while, in *The Nigger,* the narrator sees in modern "sympathy" the source of all modern weakness, he is himself highly sympathetic: in his bodilessness, he is able, for instance, to drift into James Wait's consciousness, an exercise in sympathy *par excellence.* And further, by presenting the travail of the *Narcissus* crew with the very sympathy he deplores, the narrator muddies forever the crucial distinction upon which the novel is founded, the distinction between sympathy and, as Conrad put it in the preface, "solidarity." In this contradiction between narrative form and thematic content, there is a high potential for irony, but because that potential is not realized by Conrad, the authenticity of the narrator's voice is dubious indeed.

In ***Heart of Darkness,*** however, the ironic relation between Conrad and Marlow is actualized to the full. When, for instance, Marlow proposes that "What redeems [the 'conquest of the earth'] is the idea only . . . and an unselfish belief in the idea—something you can set up, and bow down before, and offer a sacrifice to . . . ", we must see what Marlow does not see: that he is presenting us with an image of Kurtz. The authenticity of Marlow's voice derives itself, that is, from the authenticity of Marlow as a limited human being with a human being's limited perception, and only through Conrad's irony is the limitation in Marlow's perception established.

What I have called, from one point of view, Marlow's "limited perception" may be seen, from another, as his "imagination." Playing a central role in all of Conrad's works, imagination always has a dual quality: "illusion"-generating as it is—**"Youth"** ends with Marlow's audience yearning after "the romance of illusions"—imagination may also envision a world in which the affirmation of "solidarity" is a real possibility. In ***Heart of Darkness,*** Marlow attempts to maintain his image of a world in which his belief in the "saving illusion" of work has a place, but ironic conjunctions of language such as the one noted above continually remind us, if not Marlow himself, of the futility of such illusions. If Marlow's stance—what he has learned and his attitude toward it—is by the end of ***Heart of Darkness*** still indeterminable, in **"Youth"** it is not; as far as Marlow is concerned, he is a disillusioned, wiser, and weaker man, regretting his bygone "chance to feel [his] strength." But to take Marlow's word for his final condition in the story is to ignore what we have learned from ***Heart of Darkness***; a close look at **"Youth"** will reveal the operation of a similar ironic relation between Conrad and his narrator, and reveal, too, that Marlow remains incorrigibly imaginative.

The narrative dimension of **"Youth: A Narrative,"** as the full title of the story indicates, is basic to the tale; more than any other of Conrad's works, time is the stuff out of which the story is made. Time is, first, structurally important, and units of time are given apparently disproportionate attention. The *Judea* takes sixteen days to sail from London to the Tyne, spends a month there, because she arrived late, waiting to load, and is then hit in the dock and forced to lie up for three weeks' of repairs. At this point, Marlow, arithmetically incompetent and, perhaps, enlarging the magnitude of his past ordeal, says: "When we made that start for Bankok we had been already three months out of London. We had expected to be a fortnight or so—at the outside." Soon after departing from the Tyne, the *Judea* runs into a gale and springs a leak: "We pumped watch and watch, for dear life; and it seemed to last for months, for years, for all eternity, as though we had been dead and gone to a hell for sailors. We forgot the day of the week, the name of the month, what year it was, and whether we had ever been ashore." After a limping return, complete with more headwinds, the *Judea* lies up in Falmouth for more repairs for at least six months: "Morally it was worse than pumping for life. It seemed as though we had been forgotten by the world, belonged to nobody, would get nowhere; it seemed that, as if bewitched, we would have to live for ever and ever in that inner harbour . . . ." Eventually, after "lumber[ing] on through an interminable procession of days," the *Judea* enters the Indian Ocean, and the fire begins. Although the units in which time is expressed now diminish from eternities to hours, the quality of eternity remains. The sixteen hours from the explosion to the lifeboats' departure—the length of time is stated after the occurrence—comprise in their effect the longest period of time in the story: together they consume twelve pages, or almost one-third. And finally, the witchery of time makes itself felt in Marlow's simultaneously temporal and eternal ordering of his experience in the open boat: "I remember nights and days of calm, when we pulled, we pulled, and the boat seemed to stand still, as if bewitched within the circle of the sea horizon . . . and I remember sixteen hours on end with a mouth dry as a cinder . . . ." The final "spell" lasts eleven hours. For these darkly magical shiftings in duration, for the progressive eternalization of time and temporalization of eternity, there are very good artistic and thematic reasons.

"Youth" turns on the difference between the ways in which Marlow the forty-year-old narrator and Marlow the twenty-year-old participant see the voyage of the *Judea.* To the older Marlow, "there are those voyages that seem ordered for the illustration of life, that might stand for a symbol of existence. You fight, work, sweat, nearly kill yourself, sometimes do kill yourself, trying to accomplish something—and you can't. Not from any fault of yours. You simply can do nothing, neither great nor little—not a thing in the world . . . ." But to the younger Marlow the *Judea* "was not an old rattletrap carting about the world a lot of coal for a freight—to me she was the endeavour, the test, the trial of life." When the ship is about to be abandoned, young Marlow thinks: "I wasn't going to sail in a squadron if there were a chance for independent cruising." Unlike the captain, he is not at all downhearted by the sinking of the *Judea,* for he has been cruising independently all along.

Marlow gives himself and his younger self away in speculating on "what made [the crew] obey me when I, thinking consciously how fine it was, made them drop the bunt of the foresail twice and try to do it better": "They had no professional reputation—no examples, no praise. It wasn't a sense of duty . . . They didn't think their pay half good enough. No; it was something in them, something inborn and subtle and everlasting. I don't say positively that the crew of a French or German merchantman wouldn't have done it, but I doubt whether it would have been done in the same way. There was a completeness in it, something solid like a principle, and masterful like an instinct—a disclosure of something secret—of that hidden something, that gift of good or evil that makes racial difference, that shapes the fate of nations." It may seem here that Conrad is "straining to find something public to praise," but it is Marlow, not Conrad, who does the praising. Just as the history of the criticism of ***Heart of Darkness*** shows a marked turning away from [F. R.] Leavis' attack on Conrad's "adjectival and worse than supererogatory insistence on 'unspeakable rites,' 'unspeakable secrets,' 'monstrous passions,' 'inconceivable mystery,' and so on" [The *Great Tradition*], so should critics of **"Youth"** turn away from regarding any purely verbal section of the story as Conrad's intrusion. For Marlow deceives himself here; what sustains the crew is not of national origin, but rather what supports young Marlow: the conscious thought of "how fine it was." Marlow and the crew are working in eternity rather than in time, disregarding their temporally limited knowledge that the masts are almost sure to fall, and living in the eternal knowledge that they are in the process of discovering themselves. For the man who, like young Marlow, imagines himself to be tested, both the world and time exist to serve him because he turns them into images of himself: the mere fact that the masts might fall is inconsequential, for experience is "the endeavour, the test, the trial of life." Objective reality—the physical world and chronological time—ceases to exist and becomes pure subjective experience for the youthful, imaginative magician.

Less evident, perhaps, is the older Marlow's inverse legerdemain. Time is for him certainly not eternity, but neither is it chronological succession; rather, it is brutal succession: "Oh, the glamour of youth! Oh, the fire of it, more dazzling than the flames of the burning ship, throwing a magic light on the wide earth, leaping audaciously to the sky, presently to be quenched by time, more cruel, more pitiless, more bitter than the sea—and like the flames of the burning ship surrounded by an impenetrable night." Similarly, the reality of the physical world is neither benevolent nor objectively indifferent, but purposeful and cruel: "It blew day after day: it blew with spite, without interval, without mercy, without rest. The world was nothing but an immensity of great foaming waves rushing at us, under a sky low enough to touch with the hand and dirty like a smoked ceiling." The older Marlow has not been so much disillusioned as re-illusioned; for him, time and physical reality are as hostile as they are encouraging to his younger self. Both Marlows are wizards and symbol-makers, and the symbols they create are simply projections upon the outer world of their own inner lives.

Conrad's East, in his early works a symbol of dissolution, in **"Youth"** comprises both aspects of existence, physical reality and time. Having looked forward to the mysteries of the exotic East, young Marlow arrives in Java to hear it speak "in a Western voice. A torrent of words was poured into the enigmatical, the fateful silence; outlandish, angry words, mixed with words and even whole sentences of good English, less strange but even more surprising. The voice swore and cursed violently; it riddled the solemn peace of the bay by a volley of abuse." In spite of the ugly, potentially illusion-shattering force of this diatribe, Marlow is strong in his vision of reality, rendering the curses powerless by creating his own romantic symbol, a unity of eternity and physical stasis, in which they can have no place: "the men of the East . . . stared down at the boats, at the sleeping men who at night had come to them from the sea. Nothing moved. The fronds of palms stood still against the sky. Not a branch stirred along the shore, and the brown roofs of hidden houses peeped through the green foliage, through the big leaves that hung shining and still like leaves forged of heavy metal. This was the East of the ancient navigators, so old, so mysterious, resplendent and sombre, living and unchanged, full of danger and promise." But the older Marlow is equally sure in his vision; concentrating on what had so appealed to his younger self 's early-Yeatsian feeling for shimmering motionlessness, he finds what is, for him, the East's animating demon: " . . . I have seen the mysterious shores, the still water, the lands of brown nations, where a stealthy Nemesis lies in wait, pursues, overtakes so many of the conquering race, who are proud of their wisdom, of their knowledge, of their strength." Then, bringing to a head the conflict between youthful romance and middle-aged skepticism, he continues: "But for me all the East is contained in that vision of my youth. It is all in that moment when I opened my young eyes on it. I came upon it from a tussle with the sea—and I was young—and I saw it looking at me. And this is all that is left of it! Only a moment; a moment of strength, of romance, of glamour—of youth! . . . A flick of sunshine upon a strange shore, the time to remember, the time for a sigh, and—good-bye!—Night—Good-bye . . . !" Characteristically, old Marlow minimizes the moment, but to young Marlow, the moment is all-important.

As Marlow's response to his memory of his Eastern experience shows, skepticism is as much an image—as much an "illusion"—as is romantic idealism. Each mode of vision is a projection of the inner life, especially onto time; the romantic sees eternity in every moment, the skeptic sees every moment evanescing before the brutal, onrushing flow of succession. Neither skepticism nor romantic idealism sees "facts," for each outlook is the magical transmutation of existence by a particular and distorting view of time.

But if existence is protean for his character, it is not, though it may be unknowable, for Conrad, and in his works, any epistemology always has its moral ramifications. Conrad could never rest satisfied as a relativist, and his strong moral and pragmatic bias does not allow the images projected by skepticism and romantic idealism to rest in their differences. He must test out the two images against each other, searching for the nature of the inner life each projects, the survival value each affords, and the power for the affirmation of solidarity each fosters.

The medium of comparison is, of course, the story itself: not Marlow's story of his younger self, but the story of Marlow's change from youth to middle-age. Young Marlow, naive as he is, is an appealing figure, and his appeal resides in his almost infinite capacity for action, his romantic readiness to do whatever must be done to get to Bankok. The older Marlow, on the other hand, is suspended and withdrawn throughout; as much as he excites himself over his previous exploits, he treats his earlier self with a bemused patronization. He tells the story, it seems, to confront and justify his and his friends' aging paralysis, and his minimal effort is to shape existence in such a way that suspension and withdrawal are the only appropriate response. His frequent resorts to nostalgic apostrophes and claret only show how far he has come from his long-lost immediate engagement with life.

Both Marlows see existence as something to define themselves against, either as "test" or as brutality, but young Marlow's vision seems to offer greater survival value because it affords the chance of success: a test can—in **"Youth,"** at least—be passed. Yet neither image—and here we are back to Conrad's basic preoccupation—affords the possibility of the affirmation of human solidarity. As soon as the boats are launched from the burning ship, young Marlow's desire is to "part company," and when he later sights a ship, he is relieved to find that his crew does not see it. His goal has never been to get the *Judea* to Bangkok safely, but to get to Bangkok. Always the romantic egoist, he risks his and his crew's lives, all for "independent cruising." Similarly, the older Marlow is cut off from affirmative action by the way in which he shapes his tale and, essentially, his world; in the face of the innate cruelty of existence, nothing is possible. Yet the older Marlow's image of existence is clearly more enduring than that of his younger self, and from a careful look at the structure of the tale, we can see why.

With **"Youth"** Conrad does indeed have his first masterpiece, in which a complex and significant structure comments on and complements the language of time. The several frames of the central, static "picture," the burning of the *Judea,* are shot through with a dynamic movement that progresses from West to East, from youth to age, and from dynamism to stasis. Framing the almost still-life picture of the burning ship, itself an explicit symbol of youth succumbing to time, are young Marlow the participant, then old Marlow the narrator, then his immediate audience, then the reporter of the story, and finally us. The language, too, has a framing effect: Marlow asks for the bottle five times before the ship burns, and does not drink again until the last page; and references to concrete units of time are common near the beginning and end of the story, while eternities are at its center. The effect of these various frames is to subject young Marlow's experience to old Marlow's interpretation of it, while at the same time to suggest that old Marlow cannot cope with the eternal moment that, he tries so hard to capture in the web of time. But through this eternal still-life with its multiple shimmering frames runs time, brutal in its merciless succession, on the move from one place to another, from the naivete of a "crack Australian clipper" to a "stealthy Nemesis [that] lies in wait," from innocence to experience, from a West believing in affirmation and progress to an East of contemplation and stasis. The vision of Marlow the narrator dominates because **"Youth"** is his story; to paraphrase Faulkner's Darl, the older Marlow is *is,* the younger Marlow is *was.*

But just as the older Marlow wins an incomplete victory—his younger self and the burning *Judea* tend to break out of their restraining meshes—the victory he does win is Pyrrhic and, finally, tragic: " . . . I remember my youth and the feeling that will never come back any more—the feeling that I could last for ever, outlast the sea, the earth, and all men; the deceitful feeling that lures us on to joys, to perils, to love, to vain effort—to death; the triumphant conviction of strength, the heat of life in handful of dust, the glow in the heart that with every year grows dim, grows cold, grows small, and expires—and expires, too soon, too soon—before life itself." Marlow has exchanged one image for another, one of great beauty for one of less; and never seeing the "facts" of existence in themselves, he sees them only, whether he is old or young, in relation to himself.

Yet it cannot be denied that, at this point in Conrad's life, the vision of the older Marlow was, at times, Conrad's own. Shortly after finishing **"Youth"** (in late May or early June, 1898), he wrote to his close friend, the socialist reformer R. B. Cunninghame Graham (I have reproduced exactly Conrad's somewhat imperfect French):

"Il n y a pas des convertis aux idées de l'honneur, de la justice, de la pitié, de la liberté. Il n y a que des gens qui sans savoir, sans comprendre, sans sentir s'extasient sur les mots, les repétent, les crient, s'imagiment y croire—sans croire a autre chose qu'au gain, a l'avantage personel, a la vanité satisfaite. Et les mots s'envolent; et il ne reste rien, entendez vous? Absolument rien, oh homme de foi! Rien. Un moment, un clin d'oeil et il ne reste rien—qu'une goutte de boue, de boue froide, de boue morte lancée dans l'espace noir, tournoyant autour d'un soleil éteint. Rien. Ni pensée, ni son, ni âme. Rien." Conrad's vision of cold mud, black space, an extinguished sun, and "nothing" is certainly close in tone, if not entirely in substance, to Marlow's. Yet this partial conjunction of the older Marlow with Conrad should not, in spite of their ironic relation in **"Youth,"** surprise us, nor should it lead us to forget the conjunction—again partial—between young Marlow and Conrad. Conrad's letters to Cunninghame-Graham are like his letters to no one else: seeing in Graham the politically and existentially romantic and idealistic side of his own nature, he wrote with as much political and existential skepticism as he could muster. In **"Youth,"** however, Conrad projects his romantic hopes onto young Marlow, and his profound skeptical misgivings onto his narrator. And he denies final validity to both images of existence because he sees in both their essential quality of egoistic self-projection. What we see in **"Youth"** are the first full fruits of Conrad's effort to transcend himself by seeing himself in perspective: not only his "past," romantic self, but his "present," skeptical self. Only through such efforts could he attain the vision of these middle years that no view of life is final because any view is the projected image of a particular self. In this vision is the origin of ***Heart of Darkness*** and *Lord Jim*—and of **"Youth."** (pp. 399-407)

John Howard Weston, " 'Youth': Conrad's Irony and Time's Darkness," in Studies in Short Fiction, *Vol. 11, No. 4, Fall, 1974, pp. 399-407.*

Addison C. Bross (essay date 1975)

[In the following essay, Bross discusses the nature of individual and societal beliefs in A Set of Six, *focusing on the stories "Gaspar Ruiz," "The Informer," "An Anarchist," and "Il Conde."]*

In Conrad's fiction men create the conditions of their corporate and individual lives and determine the qualities of their existence through a process known as belief. Their own beliefs or those of their respective societies decide men's actions and define their destinies by imposing meaning upon the motives and consequences of their deeds. It may be claimed that Conrad's single great theme is this act of belief in its fullest variety, with its crucial propensity to control men's perceptions of the exterior world as meaningful symbol or meaningless void, to determine a man's evaluation of himself and his fellows, to establish the conventional notions of a society, which often frustrate an individual in his search for identity. The questions raised in Conrad's greatest works always concern the nature of belief—whether Decoud's withdrawing skepticism is more honorable than Don Carlos Gould's fidelity to a corrupted idealism, whether the heat of Kurtz's original idealism contributed to his corruption and whether his ability to perceive or believe in his own vileness really does constitute a moral victory, whether one's achievements must be won "in the ranks"—within the limited moral vision of Western society—as Marlow's "privileged friend" in *Lord Jim* insists, or whether Jim's final rehabilitation, based neither on Patusan's nor on the West's standard of success, but only on Jim's private sense of duty, is valid.

This theme, pervasive in the major novels, appears also in the shorter fiction and quite saliently in the short stories in ***A Set of Six,*** which critics have only recently begun to appreciate as substantial works. Many of these brief and relatively simple pieces treat the theme of belief with a pungent directness unattainable in the longer works. They were written after the gargantuan creative effort of *Nostromo,* and either before or just after *The Secret Agent* definitely indicated the turn of Conrad's interest to the political scene. One or perhaps two of them justifies Conrad's typically self-deprecatory comment that he had tried in this volume to be "simply entertaining." Nevertheless, both in their own right and as illuminating companions to the accepted masterpieces, most of them reward close reading.

One of the tales in this volume concerns the phenomenon of human belief as it affects man's perception of the non-human world. Conrad showed an interest in this subject early in his career. In **"The Idiots,"** his first short story (excluding **"The Black Mate"**), a Breton peasant is driven to distraction by the nagging suspicion that some obscure, hostile, semi-personal force is immanent in his paternal plot of farmland, continually resisting his attempts to manage its chaotic fertility, and that this same force is responsible for his consistently begetting none but retarded offspring. The spectacle of nature seems to waver between blank and impersonal phenomena and an antagonistic will. Conrad's aesthetic manifesto, the "Preface" to *The Nigger of the "Narcissus,"* acknowledges the uncertain nature of the exterior world and the pathetic instability of man's interpretation of it. The "visible universe" to which art attempts to render "the highest kind of justice" is an "enigmatical spectacle." The meaning of the exterior world is imposed upon it, he claims, by the activity of the human temperament, and does not reside in phenomena: fiction must appeal to the "innumerable temperaments whose subtle and resistless power endows passing events with their true meaning, and creates the moral, the emotional atmosphere of the place and time."

In ***A Set of Six,*** **"The Brute,"** a slight tale hardly more than "entertaining," nevertheless bears witness to the truth that the meaning of the phenomenal world is elusive. The physical universe is epitomized here by a ship which, with tantalizing regularity and through no discernible structural imperfection, kills one person per voyage by means of freakish "accidents." Its regularity tempts one to see in the ship an inimical will, despite the slim possibility that the "killings" are chance occurrences.

The captain's wife, the pretentious and formal Mrs. Colchester, gruffly disparages all allusions to the ship's purposeful evil as "Stuff and Nonsense!" She alone likes the ship because it affords her a luxurious home—its builders gave it a decidedly domestic character and proportions of Victorian sumptuousness. She herself attains something of the ship's obscurely malevolent nature, for she continually defends its reputation under a guise of scoffing at superstition, all the while, perhaps, secretly condoning the murders she knows of for the sake of her comfort. She is also linked with the ship in appearance: she struts about the deck with a heavy gold cord flopping about on her bosom as a ship's cable hangs from its prow.

On one voyage the chief mate, determined for once to cheat the ship of its murder, manages to outwit the vessel on the open sea. But on the Thames, within sight of the dock, things go oddly amiss. His *fiancée* disregards his advice to go below during docking operations. The ship seems to put an unaccountably great weight on the towing tug, and its cable breaks. In the ensuing tangle of ropes the anchor "accidentally" jerks itself overboard, carrying its seemingly intended victim: "Its great, rough iron arm caught Maggie round the waist, seemed to clasp her close with a dreadful hug, and flung itself with her over and down in a terrific clang of iron." Maggie is drowned and the ship takes its prey.

The story's major flaw lies in its failure to establish genuine ambiguity in the phenomenal world, which here is too definitely possessed of malevolence, to suggest the ambivalence usually inherent in the act of belief as it figures in Conrad's fiction.

It is interesting that women characters are associated throughout the story with the ambiguously evil vessel and with the vaguely antagonistic force in the physical world which the ship represents. I have mentioned the identification between the furtively hostile ship and the ostentatiously domestic Mrs. Colchester, who condones its killings. Another woman in the tale pretends to moral probity but on the sly is less than upright. She holds the obviously domestic position of governess to children of a quite proper family, but her seductive antics by night cause the second mate to run the ship aground. Furthermore, the ship is mistakenly identified as a woman by Conrad's first narrator when he enters the pub where the second narrator is spinning the yarn and hears of "*her* going about the world murdering people." The barmaid too links innocent domesticity with obscure malevolence as do the ship, Mrs. Colchester, and the governess. The narrator repeatedly notes her exaggerated propriety and is thus shocked by her bland expression as she overhears the sailor's tale of violence. Significantly, the barmaid's name is Miss Blank, suggesting the inscrutability of refined and dangerous women and of the enigmatical inanimate world with which they are linked in this story.

The most substantial stories in ***A Set of Six*** are **"Gaspar Ruiz," "The Informer,"** and **"Il Conde."** Taken together they show Conrad's concern with the phenomenon of belief in its several forms—idealism, egoism, hypocrisy, naiveté, gullibility, cynicism, fanaticism. Each of these stories presents a nightmare world created through the process of belief.

"Gaspar Ruiz" raises the doubtful question whether a cynical and audacious egoism or a spurious idealism, corrupted by the passionate determination of its adherents, is the more honorable. The story is linked with **"An Anarchist"** as the pathetic tale of a man caught between the forces of two implacable ideologies which he does not understand. It is set in nineteenth-century revolutionary Chile in a war in which both groups of believers sacrifice honor for the achievement of their ideals. Amid this conflict a humble, apolitical peasant of superhuman strength, Gaspar Ruiz, is abducted into the Army of Independence, then captured by Royalists and forced to advance in their front rank. Next he is recaptured by the Republicans and sentenced to be shot as a deserter. But the firing squad only wounds him. Left for dead, he crawls to the house of the family of destitute Royalists. Their beautiful, haughty daughter nurses him back to health and wins his love. Later she uses his great strength and military acumen to take vengeance on the Republicans for reducing her proud family to life of poverty. Directed by her cunning, Gaspar Ruiz gets himself reinstated in the Republican army and becomes a captain, but he soon quarrels with a Republican civil official and murders him. He goes into the hills with his followers and becomes a partisan leader for the Royalist cause and a genuine threat to the safety of the new Republic. The Republicans through treachery capture Doña Erminia, his aristocratic wife. Gaspar Ruiz beseiges the fort where she is imprisoned but is frustrated by the lack of a gun-carriage on which to mount his cannon. He attempts to serve as a human gun-carriage on his hands and knees, but expires from the strain after the successful shot. Doña Erminia assures him of her love just before he dies. While being taken to the capital under custody of Republican troops, Doña Erminia leaps from the narrow mountain road to her death.

The story is presented in part by an omniscient narrator and partly, in retrospect, by the aged Republican General Santierra. Though his usefulness as narrator had been questioned, Santierra's attitude toward the events is crucial to the story's representation of a noble but futile idealism. The validity of all idealism is called in question when Santierra reluctantly but repeatedly acknowledges that his ideal of human liberty has been betrayed by the passionate vindictiveness of those who fought for it, and even by his own deep feelings. Santierra is not a grossly gullible fanatic. He does not whitewash the Republicans who shot down a lone messenger from Gaspar Ruiz or the Republican officer who laughed at his compassion for the unjustly condemned peasant. It is the man's basic fairness and objectivity which make his occasional self-delusion seem all the more damning. During his account he slips now and then into a deluded, propagandistic phrase. The omniscient narrator has sardonically described the Royalists' confiscation of Gaspar Ruiz' parents' possessions, leaving the old people "sitting under a bush in the enjoyment of the inestimable boon of life." This sardonic tone makes the General's self-delusion all the more palpable when he later explains ingenuously that Doña Erminia's father was left "wandering ruined and houseless, and burdened with nothing but his life, which was left to him by the clemency of the Provisional Government." The two opposing armies are equally cruel, but Santierra's self-deluding reverence for his ideal of liberty causes him to present the Republicans' brutality as clemency. At times it is difficult not to mistake the old man's fervent self-delusion for cynicism. He declares that all men are brothers, for, he says, only brothers could fight so fiercely against each other. Only his earnest manner convinces his listeners that this remark is sincere, not cynical.

Santierra's reverence for his corrupted ideal becomes even more strained. It is clear that certain of his deeply rooted sentiments run counter to his professed convictions. Despite his egalitarianism, he cannot bear to think that Doña Erminia, "only a short time before, the admired of all the balls in the Viceroy's palace, should take by the hand a guasso, a common peasant." He finds it repulsive that her seduction of Gaspar Ruiz was occurring almost under his nose: "I rode past the house every day almost . . . and this was what was going on within. But how it was going on no mind of man can conceive. Her desperation must have been extreme."

The anguished believer, General Santierra, is one of Conrad's most appealing representations of man's tenacious reverence for a flawed ideal. Doña Erminia as a believer presents a more difficult moral anomaly. Her hatred has led her into a glaring inconsistency. To avenge her aristocratic pride, she has debased herself and wooed a common peasant. (Her name refers ironically to the legend that the ermine may be caught by surrounding its lair with filth, for it will be captured or die rather than stain its coat.)

Yet in a sense the inconsistency in her act is extremely short-lived. In the heat of her vengefulness, her class feeling has long ago disappeared. Republicans are not her political adversary but merely her hated enemy. In its awesome intensity, her extreme egoism makes her inconsistency seem insignificant. She considers the total ruin of the new Republic as not too much to assuage her sense of outraged honor, nor does she find marriage to a peasant too great a price to pay for revenge. The dying Gaspar Ruiz asks if it is true that she has loved no one else in all the world. In her final words to him, the Olympian assurance of her pride is rather striking. That she has loved none but him is "As true as that there is no mercy and justice in this world." True to her unwavering egoism, this speech affirms the validity of her private emotion in the very moment that it denies the validity of the human community's standard of justice. Like Kurtz, she has "kicked herself free of the earth."

Throughout the tale this intensity of private, subjective belief, void as it is of an exterior sanction, dismays the shame-faced idealist Santierra. When she hands over her child to him and leaps into a mountain chasm rather than submit to the Republicans' power, he is shaken to the roots of his being. He later explains his hysteria with a phrase which suggests that what truly appalls him in Doña Erminia is her rejection of the community's moral standard, her complete moral autonomy, which shocks his own need for a communally shared ideal verified and supported by something more than one's own lonely belief. She arouses his fear of ideological emptiness: "I cannot describe to you the sudden and abject fear that came over me at that dreadful sight. It was a dread of the *abyss*" (italics added). The story exposes Santierra's pathetic fidelity to a sullied cause and his reluctance to accept in real life the logical consequences of the egalitarian ideal he espouses. It also suggests that though Doña Erminia's egoism is fanatically antisocial, and though it brings her to compromise the aristocratic pride which she seeks to avenge, her fierce hatred constitutes a diabolical integrity that may be preferable to Santierra's inconstant self-delusions.

Like Gaspar Ruiz, the central character of **"An Anarchist"** is forced into a role foreign to his own nature by the adherents of two opposing fanaticisms equally lacking in integrity. As such these two stories are forerunners of Conrad's longer study of the same situation in *Under Western Eyes.*

Paul, a simple young French mechanic, gets drunk on his name-day and becomes enraged when a pair of anarchists tell him that the rich live off the blood of exploited workers. He shouts subversive slogans, breaks things, and is thrown into jail. His ardent anarchist lawyer presents him as a martyr to the cause and gets him sent to prison. He is denied employment on release and hounded by his anarchist "friends," who refuse to let so pliable a comrade escape their nurturing. They get him involved in a bank robbery and sent to an island penal colony. He escapes, only to be enslaved by the petty agent of a meat-extract concern on a neighboring island.

Paul has clearly been victimized by a certain type of spurious, gratuitous belief—the anarchists and their enemy, conventional society, ironically similar in their obsessive, fanatical thinking, have denied him his simple, unsensational identity and forced upon him the label of "anarchist." Here the moral choice between two opposing camps of belief is still more hopeless than in **"Gaspar Ruiz,"** for they are more precisely matched in hypocrisy, word-mongering, and blind self-delusion. Many of the actions of the anarchists are ironic parodies of their own theory. When the prisoners in the penal colony rebel, their revolt becomes a microcosmic representation of the anarchist movement: the oppressed prisoners rise up and overcome the guards, who represent society's laws and institutions; yet the second phase—the immediate, spontaneous establishment of a Utopian brotherhood—somehow does not follow. What does follow is chaos, in which men treat each other like animals; the convicts pursue the surviving wardens into the brush on a "warden-hunt"; troops arrive from a nearby military base and begin a "convict-hunt." Paul overhears a mob of desperate prisoners taking counsel—a frightening epitome of mankind without order: "The fierce whispering of that dark mass of men was very horrible."

The failure of anarchism to serve as a worthy idealism is also epitomized in personal relationships. To escape the thickest of the melée, Paul takes a boat and rows around the island. When he comes ashore he is met by Simon and Mafile, his anarchist mentors since his unfortunate name-day party. They "prove" that his boat is really theirs, since they outnumber him two to one, and the anarchist brotherhood becomes a relationship between oppressor and oppressed, as in conventional capitalist society. They grudgingly allow Paul to escape with them, since he knows navigation. Paul suddenly reverses their relationship and becomes himself the oppressor. He draws a revolver from his blouse and forces them to row long past the point of exhaustion far out into the ocean. The three men in the open boat, totally isolated from civilized society, constitute a micro-society, a bitter parody of the anarchists' classless brotherhood. In this test situation the anarchists betray their favorite theory. Mafile invokes the classical anarchist notion that the oppressed worker has nothing to lose but his chains and should unite with his fellows in open assault upon the oppressor. He urges Simon to join him in a rush on Paul. But his more basic fears and desires run counter to this theory. "While he spoke he pulled; and Simon kept on pulling too. It made me smile. Ah! They loved their life, these two, in this evil world of theirs, just as I used to love my life, too, before they spoiled it for with with their phrases." When they sight a ship Simon and Mafile, self-styled rebels against oppression, praise Paul for his use of oppression, for, as they say, they never could have rowed out so far into the ship routes had Paul not held them at gun point. While acknowledging this they continue to address each other as "comrade." "Ah, what a good word! And they, such men as these two, had made it accursed."

Paul murders the two men and is picked up by the ship, then left on another island, the principal grazing land for the huge meat-extract corporation. Here Paul, having just escaped from the imprisoning force of the anarchists' fanaticism, is subjected to similar treatment at the hands of a flunky of capitalism. Harry Gee, the pompous overseer for the pasture land of the B.O.S. Co. Ltd., is the perfect representation of the hypocritical, self-deluding conventional society, and, ironically, the precise counterpart of the anarchists Simon and Mafile. Like them he is hypocritically companionable. The narrator is repelled by his hollow garrulousness and his facile branding of people with nicknames which he thinks clever. Like the anarchists, he exercises power over the simple Paul by foisting upon him the label of "anarchist"—he knows there are anarchists among the other island's prisoners, and though he does not really think Paul is one, he sees the possibility of monetary gain in calling him one. When he learns Paul is a mechanic, he keeps him on the island to tend his steam launch and spreads gossip in the town among the simple population that Paul is an anarchist. This gratuitous calumny, by which he blackmails Paul, allows him to have the services of a mechanic without having to pay one's salary.

Harry Gee's company also uses words dishonestly but on a larger scale. Their slick circulars purvey sentimental slogans, and their gaudy trademark pictures a bull trampling upon a snake, which "symbolizes disease, weakness—perhaps mere hunger, which last is the chronic disease of the majority of mankind." Like the anarchists, the meat-producers claim to feel a profound compassion for the world's hunger and to make every sacrifice to minister to it. One of their products offers nourishment "not only highly concentrated, but already half digested. Such apparently is the love that Limited Company bears to its fellowmen—even as the love of the father and mother penguin for their hungry fledglings." It is quite apt that Paul's final service to conventional society is performed for cattle, which symbolize the docile, unthinking "herd" of society—though Harry Gee warns him that (like the society they symbolize) they are senselessly vicious and would have trampled him immediately had Harry not "rescued" him upon finding him on the shore.

Harry, the epitome of a hypocritical society, unwittingly exposes the shallowness of his and his society's pretentious belief when he comments on the anarchist movement: "That subversive sanguinary rot of doing away with all law and order in the world makes my blood boil. It's simply cutting the ground from under the feet of every decent, respectable, hard-working person. I tell you that the consciences of people who have them, like you or I, must be protected in some way; or else the first low scoundrel that came along would in every respect be just as good as myself. Wouldn't he, now? And that's absurd!" In admitting that a low scoundrel might possibly be as good as a decent hard-working person, Harry shows that he and his society are moral skeptics masquerading as sincere believers. For moral lowness is as good as decency only if man's conduct has no inherent significance whatever, and the value or rightness of man's actions is entirely dependent on the arbitrary, ephemeral beliefs of his group—only, that is, if moral standards have no real, objective existence.

What proves to Harry the wrongness of the anarchists is not that they contradict a set of ideals which are self-evident. He does not find it absurd that his ideals (decency and hard work) may be set at naught, but his naive egoism finds it absurd to imagine himself the mere equal of a "low scoundrel." Harry's and his society's hypocrisy consists in their clothing such naive egoism in the guise of a true idealism, a true sense of value. They uphold ideals with only a cloudy understanding of them, and for merely selfish reasons.

Imprisoned by the society which Harry serves, Paul loses all hope of escaping the web woven by its false beliefs about him, and his standard reply to all accusations is "I deny nothing." Even when the narrator, a wandering butterfly collector, offers to help him escape, Paul is too broken in spirit to make the attempt.

In **"The Informer,"** another tale of anarchists, Mr. X, an extremely refined radical, quite knowledgeable in the arts, tells a story to a sheltered, overcivilized member of the *haut monde,* a connoisseur of Chinese bronzes to whom he has been introduced by a mutual acquaintance, a "collector" of intriguing personalities. While the two men are dining, X remarks casually, "There's no amendment to be got out of mankind except by terror and violence." His pedantic companion is extremely shocked. X illuminates his remark with a story which, like **"An Anarchist,"** shows that human beings are quite incapable of being influenced by the ideals they profess—that though a few retreat into an inhuman skepticism, most people live by means of gestures with no genuine belief in the meaningfulness of their actions. Complacent people delight in reading X's radical pamphlets, and the majority of the upper class is so incapable of serious conviction, or indeed of any serious thought, that some of its members, seeking diversion from their boring lives, have actively patronized anarchist agitators.

In X's tale a young woman of emanicipated sensibility, a would-be individualist, daughter of a wealthy public official, donates a building she has inherited to a group of anarchists for the publication of a radical journal. She works with delighted, naive enthusiasm, reading proof and writing fierce, iconoclastic articles. She does not know that on the third floor *coups* are being plotted and bombs prepared. She completes her self-delusion with the notion that she is in love with Sevrin, one of the members of the group, who, unknown to her and to the serious anarchists, is an accomplished spy and is informing the police of all their plots. Having become an anarchist from a vague humanitarian impulse, he has since suffered a depletion in the optimism necessary for a true radical and become just as fanatical in betraying the cause he once served. But he is in love with the young amateur anarchist in earnest. X becomes suspicious of an evident security leak among this group and stages a mock raid upon the house with anarchists impersonating policemen, hoping that the informer will expose himself, but Sevrin, along with the others, seems to react as a surprised anarchist should, for he must preserve his pose even before men he takes to be policemen if he is to retain his effectiveness as a spy. Then the young lady enters the room. Her amateur anarchism seems to have led her into a difficult situation, and she appeals to Sevrin, not as a young enthusiast in the movement to her radical hero, but as an aristocratic young lady to her escort, whose duty is to protect her. Sevrin urges the leading "policeman" to get her out of the house and hands over his credentials as a police spy to authorize his demand. He tries to leave the building with her, but is thrown backward on the floor and realizes the true nature of the situation. The young lady is bewildered, not knowing whether to be relieved at the disappearance of the imminent threat of scandal, or to feel shocked on learning her lover's true character, but Sevrin, fearful of losing her esteem, assures her that he has dedicated himself to anti-anarchism "from conviction." He half-kneels before her and seems about to touch the hem of her dress. Her bewilderment disappears when she is presented with this opportunity for a perfect theatrical gesture. She quickly jerks her skirt away from his touch and averts her face from him. He swallows some poison kept ready for such a disaster and X leads the lady away. After this roiling of her shallow soul, she goes into retirement, then enters a convent. "I can't tell where she will go next. What does it matter? Gestures! Gestures! Mere gestures of her class."

This story presents a tangled web of compounded hypocrisy which challenges the imagination to unravel. The lady is a false anarchist and quite falsely in love, though she imagines herself in earnest on both counts. The object of her false love is himself a false anarchist but genuinely in love with her. Unlike her, he is aware of his masquerade as an anarchist, but he is not aware of his own self-delusion. He thinks he has escaped from a hollow fanaticism in his apostasy from anarchism, but he is really just as rabid in his present obsession. He has not turned to some more substantial doctrine but has simply compounded anarchism's basic error, its belief in the efficacy of destruction. As once he believed it good to destroy society, now he thinks it good to destroy anarchism.

Sevrin's shift from one belief to its opposite extreme recalls the apostasy of such other Conradian figures as Kurtz and shows the pervasiveness of Conrad's interest in such leaps of faith. The plot of the story and the different statuses of the characters as believers recalls *Under Western Eyes,* wherein a young, idealistic Russian woman feels a rather uncertain affinity with the cause of revolution but is not nearly so culpably naive or hypocritical as the girl in **"The Informer."** Nathalie Haldin is at first proud of her brother, who has assassinated a Czarist minister and been executed. But, being separated from the actual scene of revolutionary activity, she does not know its full horror and its insidious egoism. She later comes to have strong reservations about her brother's deed and about violence, terrorism and radicalism generally. The young man in the novel who corresponds with Sevrin, becomes a police spy not through a sort of reversed fanaticism, but rather by being forced by pressure from both Czarists and revolutionists, in much the same way that Paul the mechanic has a false identity thrust upon him by two fiercely opposing factions. A comparison of the short story and the novel shows Conrad's amazing ambivalence and flexibility of judgment. He treats Nathalie's inadequately scrutinized commitment with genuine compassion while he scorns the shallowness of the girl in **"The Informer"** though between the two moral conditions, the two phases of belief, there is "not the thickness of a piece of paper."

As in **"An Anarchist"** so in this tale, the reader turns from one set of characters to another, continually disappointed of relief from a pervasive hypocrisy. The "true believers," the anarchists, in the very heat of their passionate convictions, have long since lost a vision of their goal. When X tries to warn one of them that his group is infiltrated with spies, the old firebrand answers "with irrelevant exaltation: 'I have something in hand that shall strike terror into the heart of these gorged brutes.' " Another, the explosives expert, is quite as indifferent to this practical concern: "He shrugged his shoulders disdainfully and turned away to his balances and test-tubes." Ardent belief seems hardly more effective than empty posturing.

If the girl's life is merely a matter of gestures, so is the connoisseur's. His idea of morality is so pedantically refined as to be irrelevant to real human life. It concerns merely "a suave and delicate discrimination of social and artistic values." He does not believe in the existence of evil and violence. To him these are "as unreal as the giants, ogres, and seven-headed hydras whose activities affect, fantastically, the course of legends and fairy-tales!" The sterility of his existence is amply indicated by the decor of the room in which he and X admire his Chinese bronzes—quite a cold room, for he does not allow fires to be lit there, containing, as its only furniture, the glass cases which house the bronzes. So empty is his character that between him and Mr. X, the cynical proponent of violence, the reader is faced with another Conradian "choice of nightmares."

The connoisseur's friend, who sent X to him, is still worse. He has allowed the collector's vice of soulless triviality to stultify his human relationships; to him his fellow men seem to exist merely to gratify his idle curiosity. "He observes them, listens to them, penetrates them, measures them, and puts the memory away in the galleries of his mind." Ironically he himself verifies X's opinion about the necessity of terror and violence, for when he and the connoisseur meet again, the friend remarks that X "likes to have his little joke sometimes," indicating that he has failed to take seriously the dangerous realities clearly presented in X's words and in his character.

Even the excellent Mr. X fails to provide the various hypocrites and fanatical believers with a humanly practicable corrective. The connoisseur, for all his fastidiousness, raises a valid objection to X's way of life. He wonders how X or any other serious anarchist performs the simple and ordinary acts of which life is made—how he sleeps, eats, and appreciates bronzes while expecting and planning a holocaust. One may wonder how X can maintain his faith that terror and violence improve mankind, aware as he is of the several anarchists' failings. Furthermore, his mixture of anarchism with a profound appreciation of art, a product of civilization, seems a gross inconsistency.

The story remains a frightening if exaggerated compendium of culpable manifestations of the phenomenon of belief: fanaticism, hypocrisy, self-delusion, cynicism. It is full of witty absurdity—X the anarchist has a *bombe glacée* for dessert; the radicals ship their explosives from the laboratory in tins containing the innocuous Stone's Dried Soup; the amateur anarchist's brother, a young man in knickerbockers with a vacuous stare and arched eyebrows, entertains the joyless proletariat with comic songs—but the dominant tone is that of an extremely bitter farce.

"The Duel" rivals **"The Brute"** in being little more than "simply entertaining," largely because the separate dueling incidents which make up the plot, though they are exciting, do not work together to complicate and develop the psychological and moral conflict beyond its very simple dimensions at the beginning of the tale. There is latent in the story the situation of the innocent man forced into an inappropriate role by the gratuitous, simplistic beliefs of his fellows, but this remains a forgotten potential.

The tale takes place during the Napoleonic wars. The quarrel between Lieutenants D'Hubert and Feraud begins when their respective cavalry regiments are quartered for a short period of peace in a small German town. D'Hubert is sent by the commanding general to find Feraud and order him to confine himself to quarters for fighting a duel that morning. The hot-headed Feraud resents the punishment and challenges D'Hubert to immediate combat. D'Hubert knows the idea is senseless, that Feraud has no just reason to take offense, and that he himself is therefore not bound by objective standards of honor to fight him; but he also knows Feraud *thinks* quite the opposite and will be able to make him the object of disgust among the regiments. He agrees to fight and wounds Feraud. In this way Feraud's gratuitous, obsessive belief in an imaginary offense begins to dominate both his and D'Hubert's lives and their military careers, causing a series of duels between them which continues throughout Napoleon's wars and beyond. D'Hubert for most of this time would like to see the senseless affair forgotten, but Feraud is obstinate in his delusion. Even his suspicions that he may be wrong goad him into imagining more and more subtle offenses from D'Hubert. Later, in a black mood after Napoleon's demise, Feraud convinces himself that D'Hubert "never loved the Emperor." After the Restoration this opinion, now become a rumor, affords D'Hubert favor with the new regime and gets him an enviable post in the royal army. Feraud, sulking in a provincial town on half pay, hears of this and imagines it is D'Hubert's crowning atrocity, committed simply to infuriate him. He breaks parole and goes with seconds to find D'Hubert at his sister's estate. They arrange a stalking duel with pistols in a nearby wood. The cool D'Hubert, knowing Feraud is the better shot, succeeds in drawing his fire so that Feraud has shot both his bullets before D'Hubert has fired once. D'Hubert decides to grant him his life on the condition that on D'Hubert's command he will shoot himself.

D'Hubert has told only his fiancée's uncle of his plan to meet Feraud. The young lady learns about the duel early on the very morning of the encounter and comes running alone distraught, her hair down, to the estate. D'Hubert has been afraid he would fail to win her genuine personal affection, for he is much older than she, and his sister and her mother have arranged the match. After her open show of concern, their relationship is immediately freed from the strained formality which D'Hubert had assumed in his fear of finding her love merely dutiful. He feels that the recalcitrant Feraud is responsible for his happiness. After the birth of their son, he writes Feraud to offer reconciliation, but the hot-headed Gascon rejects his suit because D'Hubert has not named his son after Napoleon, proving beyond doubt that he "never loved the Emperor."

D'Hubert's destiny has been manipulated by the wilful obsession of Feraud. Also the credulity, the speculation, and the reasoned opinion of the entire cavalry division, which both men have respected, have prolonged the quarrel and occasionally distorted its meaning. D'Hubert's plight is thus basically similar to that of Gaspar Ruiz and Paul the mechanic, whose feelings, lives, and even identities are determined by the gratuitous beliefs of the people who surround them. The theme gets a new twist here, for though Feraud's delusion continually endangers D'Hubert's life and forces him to accept an antagonism he does not really reciprocate, at the end it is the means by which he comes to know his true self—to feel confident of his fiancée's affection.

"Il Conde," one of the best stories in this collection, examines again the psychic phenomena of over-refined idealism and insidious egoism and reveals how a man may live and die entirely by the occult force of his imagination. This is the fate of the Count, a kindly and aristocratic sojourner in Naples, whom the first-person narrator meets while admiring Pompeiian bronzes in a museum. The opening scene recalls X's inspection of the connoisseur's bronzes in **"The Informer."** The Count is of the same type as the connoisseur, though more truly genteel and treated more sympathetically. The story hinges on the ambiguous moral status of his extremely high standard of refinement and his lofty sense of self-esteem and honor.

Like the connoisseur, the Count is unaware or skeptical of the existence of violence and is repelled by the slightest hint of it. He turns with mild aversion from the museum's busts of Roman emperors—"Their faces were too vigorous, too pronounced for him." Again and again comes the hint that his refinement implies a separation from reality, from a truly substantial existence. His fortune was not of his own making, for "his nature was too kindly for strife." His delicate constitution verifies the suggestion of unworldliness. He is staying in Naples because only that city's climate mitigates his "rheumatic affections." "His white hair brushed upwards off a lofty forehead gave him the air of an idealist, of an imaginative man."

His insulation from the reality of violence ends one evening when a sullen young South Italian of aristocratic appearance prods him with a long knife and demands his money and valuables, a short distance from where a strolling crowd is listening to a band concert. The Count is profoundly disturbed by the robber's wanton ferocity and scathing contempt, which increases when he finds that the old man has only a few lire and a cheap watch—he has left most of his money at the hotel desk, and his regular watch is in a repair shop. When the man demands his rings, the Count refuses and closes his eyes. The villain takes his money and leaves, only to reappear in a cafe where the Count, having discovered a gold piece in an odd pocket, has stopped to calm himself and have a risotto. The robber curses him bitterly for withholding some of his cash, threatens that he is not yet done with him, and departs. The Count learns from an old cigar vendor that his adversary is a student from a fine family from Bari and the chief of a very powerful Camorra respected by even the University professors. The narrator hears the Count's story but is unable to soothe his shocked feelings. The old man is intent on leaving Naples, though he is certain that he will die outside its protective climate. The narrator sees him off at the station with the feeling of paying his last respects to his funeral cortege.

Like other protagonists in this volume, the Count is the victim of what other men believe he is, or of what he thinks they believe of him. His tranquil and lofty self-esteem, hitherto supported by others' deference, is outraged by the robber's contempt. "He was disgusted with himself. . . . He was shocked at being the selected victim, not of robbery so much as of contempt. . . . His life-long, kindly nicety of outlook had been defaced."

The Count, in his lofty conception of his dignity, exaggerates this offense. He generalizes it as the hostility not of one man only, but of a whole society. Like St. Anthony in the paintings of his temptation, he has become, in his imagination, the center of the world of grimacing, threatening faces. Just before and after the robbery he has seen scores of young men in the streets with the identical physiognomy and expression of the Camorra chief; and it is the same look of "cruel discontent" which he had observed on the busts of the Roman emperors. Furthermore, the young man from Bari has the respect of the University, and his sulky demands make the Neapolitan waiters, who are usually slow, rush to him and fawn upon him. The world seems to be with the sullen young student and against the Count. It is no small matter to be the object of a whole society's arbitrary contempt. "A man's real life is that accorded to him in the thoughts of other men," as Conrad's narrator holds in *Under Western Eyes.*

The Count's exaggerated refinement and self-esteem are morally suspect as manifestations of the phenomenon of belief, despite his charm. The narrator suggests that there is something alien, exotic, or occult in his sense of refinement by comparing it to the Oriental tradition of hara-kiri, which is unfathomable to the Western mind. It isolates him from all normal and commendable human feeling; the narrator is restrained from expressing his commiseration, for he knows that the Count finds all manifestations of emotion repugnant.

Most damaging to the moral assessment of his character is the unacknowledged egoism inherent in his sense of refinement. If he were not egocentric he would not believe that he was personally singled out as the victim of contempt. The egoism appears subtly here and there in his conversations with the narrator; and it is always genuine and deeply ingrained, quite free from pretension. His unconscious, natural identification with the ancient Roman aristocracy is charming: "He thought it extremely probable that the Romans of the higher classes were specially predisposed to painful rheumatic affections. . . . He argued from personal experience. He had suffered himself from a painful and dangerous rheumatic affection till he found relief in this particular spot of Southern Europe."

His egoism and his indolence, though mitigated by his urbane kindliness, link him, ironically, with his adversary. He is dismayed when all the waiters fawn upon the young man, because he is accustomed to similar if less extreme deference from hotel acquaintances and from all the menials of the street. Though his expression is not sulky like that of the young man, the Count too expects the world to please him—thus he goes out on the night of the robbery to look at the crowd, with quite a patronizing air, as if it were an entertaining spectacle arranged for him. The relationship between Count and Camorra chief is actually a conflict between a mild-mannered egoist and a violent one. Beneath the grossest violence and the most exquisite refinement lies the same egoism.

There is also a suggestion that the Count finds his ultimate fulfillment as a man of refinement in this loathsome incident. Paradoxically, his extreme fastidiousness and his scrupulous self-esteem are nowhere more emphatically revealed than in the disgust with which he reacts to this experience. The high value which he places upon the perfect, even tenor of his life is defined by the incident, for he believes that merely being robbed is quite enough to desecrate its pristine purity. The act of hara-kiri is mentioned twice in descriptions of the Count's reaction to the robbery. Hara-kiri is at once both a reaction to the loss of honor and a means of restoring it; the act most of all indicates the height of one's self-esteem. During the robbery, the young man places the point of his knife at the precise spot "where a Japanese gentleman begins the operation of the Hara-kiri." The young man not only affords the Count the occasion to show his exaggerated sense of honor, but he also seems to assist the Count in the act of hara-kiri, which is the means of restoring that honor.

Refinement consists in a high standard of propriety or an ability to appreciate the best, but it can also be defined as a high sensitivity to outrage. The Count's exaggerated sense of honor has achieved perfect expression through being outraged by the young man's violent contempt. It has also been secured thereby, for the Count's imminent death will preclude any possible defilement, just as, in the story's opening paragraph, the delicate perfection of the Pompeiian bronzes "has been preserved for us by the catastrophic fury of a volcano." The final sentence alludes to this passage and connects the Count with the bronzes by describing him as if he were a glass-cased museum piece, quite as delicate and out of place in the "real" world. As his railway carriage leaves the station, "*Il Conde's* profile, much aged already, glided away from me in stony immobility, behind the lighted pane of glass."

These six tales abound with rather disturbing insights into the nature of belief. The process of believing seems to be obscure and unpredictable in its workings; the believer is a protean creature capable of wild leaps of faith. Santierra's ardent revolutionaries are corrupted by the intense emotions aroused by their idealism, for "the heat of passionate convictions passing into hatred, removes the restraints of honor and humanity from many men." Midway in his career as an anarchist, Sevrin suffers a depletion of the necessary optimism and reverses his role to become an anti-anarchist, though his fanatic nature remains unchanged. The force of Doña Erminia's overbearing belief, her egoistic hatred, transforms the dull and motiveless Gaspar Ruiz into a man of implacable anger. A fiery radical forgets his vision of a new world order in rapt meditation upon the perfect explosive device. The protean quality in the believer and the obscure and random nature of the act of belief account for the identity crises which several of these characters suffer—both the believers (e.g., the girl in **"The Informer"**) and the objects of society's gratuitous belief (e.g., Paul the mechanic in **"An Anarchist"**). Though the metamorphosis of a character's belief is not as fully rendered here as in some of Conrad's longer works, these tales do present a more shocking and ironic revelation of it through their very brevity and detachment.

The stories afford no easy answer to the question of the moral value of man's will to believe. The self-delusion of the amateur anarchist is treated with scathing contempt, yet some of the tales show respect for human belief 's uncanny power to impose upon reality a subjective meaning often unwarranted by objective evidence and against the beliefs of the community. Neither Doña Erminia's cruel and amoral egoism nor the Count's kindly, refined egoism are supported by others' evaluations of their characters or by anything outside their own lonely beliefs; yet they do not hesitate to pay for their lofty self-esteem with their lives. This potent belief, sanctified by sacrifice, yet questionable in its extreme distortion of objective reality, is quite different from the gross gullibility which often, as in **"An Anarchist,"** is founded not upon substantial belief, but upon doubt. The task of evaluating one or another condition of belief is hopelessly complex in these stories, most of which present a "choice of nightmares," two or more alternatives of nearly equal aversion or horror—the pedantic, morally irrelevant connoisseur, the cynical Mr. X, the gesturing girl; the self-deluded idealist General Santierra and the audacious Doña Erminia; the Count and the Camorra chief—and no criterion for judging belief emerges as valid. The Count's subjective belief is honored, though with some reservation, while the amateur anarchist's neglect of reality is scorned. Doña Erminia's intensity of belief, her egoism, almost redeems her, but among the anarchists of **"The Informer"** the stronger the belief the more certain it is to be neglected for the sake of irrelevances. The stories show a full range of attitudes, from compassion to harsh irony, in their judgments of the vagaries of human belief.

The moral value of self-deluded idealism is particularly hard to judge. Harry Gee is evidently unaware of the moral skepticism which lies hidden beneath his apparent moralism—even when he admits that an anarchist victory would not only destroy outward law and order, but would also invalidate his beliefs. One is tempted to the conclusion that even the most apparently sincere delusion is never innocent.

The tales' most striking revelations of man the believer occur in just such vignettes as Harry Gee's apologia, the Count's natural, unassuming claim to affinity with the ancient Roman aristocracy, Santierra's slip into a self-deluding phrase just following a moment of anguished honesty, Sevrin's desperate affirmation, before the anarchist fanatics, that his seeming treachery, properly viewed, is integrity, for he has practiced it "from conviction." Conrad merely lets his character talk, with no analytical probing, the undisturbed belief-process is caught off guard and exposed with subtlest irony. In the midst of a casual or earnest speech comes a simple phrase, and its illumination reveals, far within, the noble egoism, the raw selfishness, the fear or doubt at the springs of belief—and the character goes on talking. (pp. 27-44)

Addison C. Bross, "A Set of Six: *Variations on a Theme,*" *in* Conradiana, *Vol. 7, No. 1, 1975, pp. 27-44.*

Christof Wegelin (essay date 1975)

[*Wegelin is a Swiss-born American educator, editor, and critic. In the following essay, he examines the importance of Captain MacWhirr's voice in "Typhoon," contending that it represents the voice of all humankind.*]

Conrad's early tale **"Typhoon"** (1902) is frequently regarded as a masterpiece, although critics disagree about its hero, Captain MacWhirr. Some, with the first mate of the ship *Nan-Shan,* regard him as a fool, some, with the chief engineer, appreciate his sturdy honesty. There is much to be said on both sides. The story opens and closes with the question of the captain's character; that question is thematically central. But it is also puzzling, for MacWhirr is both hero and fool, foolish hero and heroic fool, almost as if a man *must* be a fool to play the role of the hero, to seek the opportunity for heroism. He steers with care, but in order to save time and fuel he steers straight into a hurricane instead of around it and exposes his ship to a battering so severe that she barely survives. MacWhirr lacks imagination; but this same lack of imagination, which threatens him with loss of ship and life and in less serious moments exposes him to ridicule, is of a piece with the fortitude with which he faces disaster. The first two chapters show him largely in caricature, as the fool of his literal mind. But at the end of Chapter Two, as the *Nan-Shan* plunges into the storm-troubled waters and all the stars disappear, the dolt turns into a figure of strength. Now, in the black night of danger, Jukes, the first mate, who has been the author's instrument of ridicule and the captain's most insistent critic aboard ship, is "uncritically glad to have his captain at hand." And MacWhirr is revealed as an image of the absurd hero, in the face of indifferent nature at once foolish and admirable, powerless and resolute.

Once the storm strikes, there is little the captain can do to save his ship. Within its confines he is master: when fighting breaks out below deck he can command that order be restored. But his moral imperative, the "sense of the fitness of things" to which nature has no counterpart, impels him to demand order even when he is without control. He instructs the mate to "Keep her at it as long as we can." In the contest with the alien and chaotic elements surrounding and almost engulfing the human community of the ship, he functions as a token and promise of the continued presence of humanity. This is his significance for Jukes, the mate, and it is epitomized by the captain's voice. In the light of common day, the unimaginative and literal MacWhirr of the rounded back and big red fleshy ears has frequently looked ridiculous—to Jukes certainly, and also to the reader. But in the black night of the storm, when man has lost control and can no longer see, what remains is the voice—man's primary distinction from mute and inarticulate nature, the instrument of thought and song and hence of what we like to call immortality.

The importance Conrad has assigned this voice underlines the Captain's role as absurd hero. The Captain's voice dominates the chapter (iii) in which the ship first meets the full fury of the storm. The very first time the shaken Jukes hears it, it steadies him with its affirmative. "Is it you, sir? Is it you, sir?" Jukes keeps shouting frantically when he finds himself clasped by the stout arms of his captain. "And he heard in answer a voice, as if crying far away . . . the one word 'Yes!' " When Jukes fears for the life of the ship, the captain's voice becomes a spring of hope: "Will she live through this?" Jukes asks, and again he hears "with amazement the frail and resisting voice in his ear, the dwarf sound, unconquered in the giant tumult," which says, "She may!" and "Let's hope so!" and then, in a crescendo of force and firmness, "Keep on hammering . . . builders . . . good men. . . . " Although the captain and his mate are in a close hug, the storm lets only snatches come through, but "the voice of his commander" starts to "march athwart the prodigious rush of the hurricane" and brings to Jukes a "strange effect of quietness like the serene glow of a halo." In the next two chapters (iv and v) Jukes is on a mission below deck, but the captain speaks from the bridge through the speaking tube, and his voice, deliberate though small, continues to thwart the debilitating effect of the powers of nature on Jukes as well as to bolster the men in the engine room. Functioning as a leitmotif, the word *voice* dots the pages like the markers of a design. Constantly Conrad keeps it before us as a witness to the stubborn human presence, "a small voice [which] shoved aside the shouting hurricane quietly," which "kept the hurricane out of Jukes' ear." If on occasion the mate is tempted to capitulate before the demands made on his endurance, "the remembrance of Captain MacWhirr's voice made this impossible." Always it is "ready for him" with encouragement, direction, purposeful command; always it opposes itself to the ferocity of the elements.

The value of the captain's self-assertion does not depend on victory; success is not measured by survival. His last instructions to Jukes, given just before the second attack of the storm on the now badly mauled ship as a kind of testament in case of his own death, reinforce this impression:

> "Don't you be put out by anything," the Captain continued, mumbling rather fast. "Keep her facing it. They may say what they like, but the heaviest seas run with the wind. Facing it—always facing it—that's the way to get through. You are a young sailor. Face it. That's enough for any man. . . . "

If the heaviest seas do run with the wind, such knowledge may be useful. But in fact the survival of the *Nan-Shan* is largely accidental, for the chaos which surrounds the ship is not amenable to human reason or governance. Getting through need not be taken literally, however; the essence of the captain's wisdom lies in facing the demands of the moment without regard for the final absurdity of death. That his will is absolute, independent of the hope of success, is corroborated in retrospect in a letter which reveals that in the early morning hours of the second day of the storm "Captain MacWhirr did actually think that his ship could not possibly live another hour in such a sea, and that he would never see his wife and children again."

For Conrad the voice of his captain is symbolic. Indeed for the reader, if not for Jukes, it gradually ceases to be an individual voice and becomes the voice of the species. One passage makes its archetypal significance all but explicit, and the expansion of meaning made the passage available for use in another context. Here is the passage from **"Typhoon"**:

> And again [Jukes] heard that voice, forced and ringing feebly, but with a penetrating effect of quietness in the enormous discord of noises, as if sent out from some remote spot of peace beyond the black wastes of the gale; again he heard a man's voice—the frail and indomitable sound that can be made to carry an infinity of thought, resolution and purpose, that shall be pronouncing confident words on the last day, when heavens fall, and justice is done—again he heard it, and it was crying to him, as if from very, very far—"All right."

The parenthesis in the second half of the paragraph translates the voice of the captain in the storm into the medium of all human thought and of human speech "on the last day." But though some of the images are Biblical, the speaker is not the repentant sinner but the indomitable hero. Moreover, MacWhirr's voice appears to Jukes "as if sent out from some remote spot of peace"—almost a voice *from* heaven, not pleading to it. And allusions elsewhere in the story suggest the same inversion. In its quiet smallness, the voice in which MacWhirr directs Jukes may remind us of the "still small voice" in which the Lord directs Elijah; its setting may recall the voice in which He answers Job "out of the whirlwind." But while the allusions may tell us something about the reliance of the shaken Jukes on his captain, the captain, unlike the Biblical Lord, is not master of the elements. And the frail but indomitable voice of the final confrontation is explicitly man's.

The idea of that final day seems to have intrigued Conrad. In an essay on Henry James published three years after **"Typhoon"** [in *Notes on Life and Letters,* 1949] he elaborated the images he had used in the story:

> When the last aqueduct shall have crumbled to pieces, the last air ship fallen to the ground, the last blade of grass have died upon a dying earth, man, indomitable by his training in resistance to misery and pain, shall set this undiminished light of his eyes against the feeble glow of the sun. The artistic faculty, of which each of us has a minute grain, may find its voice in some individual of that last group, gifted with a power of expression and courageous enough to interpret the ultimate experience of mankind in terms of . . . art.

If any one will be moved to speak in that last moment of a "last flicker of light on a black sky," it will be "the imaginative man." The typhoon of the story may be said to prefigure in microcosm the final destruction of the earth, Captain MacWhirr's voice the voice of man's final interpreter, the writer. Conversely, the essay conceives the writer's role in terms befitting the captain of a ship: "Action in its essence, the creative art of a writer of fiction may be compared to rescue work carried out in darkness against cross gusts of wind swaying the action of a great multitude." The transmutation of the literal-minded MacWhirr is not so surprising as it may appear. Heroism is not only born of the occasion; it is also limited by it. Disdained by destiny, Conrad tells us, MacWhirr "had sailed over the surface of the oceans as some men go skimming over the years of existence" without ever having been made to see the ultimate violence and terror of life—until the night of his trial. Then, in the fury of the storm, the archetypal human voice is born in him—the medium of the resolution demanded by the occasion. Of the captain no more is required as no more is possible to him; but in other circumstances that voice, coming from other lips, will be capable of transcendent service.

The version of Judgment Day parenthetically suggested in **"Typhoon"** and elaborated in the paragraph from the essay on James has been made famous by Faulkner's Nobel Prize speech, and there can be little doubt that—as Eric Solomon has pointed out—the final paragraph of that speech owes something of its rhetoric to Conrad. But if comparison with the Biblical Judgment Day points up the emptiness of Conrad's sky and man's loneliness on the dying earth among the ruins of his works, comparison with Faulkner further underlines Conrad's sense of the absurdity of man's existence and of the limits set to the poet's power. There is nothing in Conrad to match Faulkner's famous "I decline to accept the end of man," nothing to match his belief that with the poet's support man will not only endure but "prevail." Whether represented by the captain of a storm-tossed ship or by the poet witnessing the last setting of the sun, Conrad's man is in the end impotent. For the cosmic and the human sphere remained for Conrad utterly distinct. A passage in one of his autobiographical essays in *A Personal Record* makes this clear:

> The ethical view of the universe involves us at last in so many cruel and absurd contradictions, where the last vestiges of faith, hope, charity, and even of reason itself, seem ready to perish, that I have come to suspect that the aim of creation cannot be ethical at all. I would fondly believe that its object is purely spectacular: a spectacle for awe, love, adoration, or hate, if you like, but in this view—and in this view alone—never for despair! Those visions, delicious or poignant, are a moral end in themselves. The rest is our affair—the laughter, the tears, the tenderness, the indignation, the high tranquility of a steeled heart, the detached curiosity of a subtle mind—that's our affair!

Here as elsewhere in Conrad, macrocosm and earthly microcosm are without converse: awe, love or hate on our side, but for answer only silent beauty, and a beauty which may well be in the eye of the beholder.

The conclusion of the passage returns us to the role of the artist—"gifted with a voice in order to bear true testimony" to the "sublime spectacle." But despite his strong moral bent, Conrad thought of the artist or writer not as man's advocate, but as a recorder in the sense of the much quoted preface to *The Nigger of the "Narcissus,"* where he says: "My task . . . is, by the power of the written word to make you hear, to make you feel—it is, before all, to make you see." The "aim of art," he says there, "is not in the clear logic of a triumphant conclusion; it is not in the unveiling of one of those heartless secrets which are called the Laws of Nature"; rather it is to "arrest, for the space of a breath, the hands busy about the work of the earth." It is to give a *full* account of the spectacle of life, or, as he put it in *A Personal Record,* to give "unwearied self-forgetful attention to every phase of the living universe." *To every phase*—this is the call of the artist's conscience as distinguished from that of the moralist. Wherever one dips into Conrad, the writer's virtue as he conceived and practiced it is in the truth of the report. **"Typhoon"** is an example, and the multiple perspective in which we see Captain MacWhirr illustrates his author's devotion to the multiplicity of truth. In the words of Robert Clifton, a recent critic of the story, the battered *Nan-Shan* "simultaneously signifies MacWhirr's heroism, the expense of his 'heroism,' the absurdity of his claim to the title, and the fortuitousness of his being alive to wear it—all of which are undeniable"; and the greatness of the story "lies in its fidelity to the independent truth of each view." At the same time, the refusal to choose between the various views is a correlative of the author's purely spectacular conception of a universe empty of ethical norms.

Some such conception and the accompanying sense of alienation in a cosmos indifferent to charity and justice was of course in the air when Conrad wrote **"Typhoon."** One thinks for instance of Hardy. But Stephen Crane, who also liked to portray men in the grip of the elements, serves better than any one else to place Conrad. And a passage about men in a storm on the Nebraska plain catches Conrad's double perspective on MacWhirr perfectly. "The conceit of man," Crane wrote in "The Blue Hotel," "was explained by this storm to be the very engine of life. One was a coxcomb not to die in it." On our "space-lost bulb" we need to be heroes to live and we need to be fools to be heroes. Only coxcombs have the energy to survive. Heroism, as Conrad's captain demonstrates, is admirable and absurd at the same time, and in a universe of gigantic and expanding dimensions it is without sanction, entirely "our affair." Both Conrad and Crane anticipate recent existentialist thought. But their lesser egotism—the irony with which Crane habitually treats man's "conceit" and Conrad's modesty in speaking of our ethical norms as illusions—distinguishes them from some more recent figures. Yet, one moment aboard the *Nan-Shan* arrests what recent existentialists along with Conrad and Crane might call the quintessential human condition, and once more the captain's voice sounds the lonely assertion of freedom beyond despair: "Will the ship pull through?" Jukes has asked. "But," says Conrad, "the wind devoured the reply, out of which Jukes heard only the one word, pronounced with great energy '. . . . Always. . . . ' " (pp. 45-50)

Christof Wegelin, "MacWhirr and the Testimony of the Human Voice," in Conradiana, *Vol. 7, No. 1, 1975, pp. 45-50.*

Chinua Achebe (essay date 1977)

[Achebe is a Nigerian novelist, short story writer, and poet. His first novel, Things Fall Apart *(1958), examines the tragic effects of colonialism on traditional African culture and is one of the most famous works written in English by an African author. In the following excerpt, he labels Conrad a "bloody racist" and* Heart of Darkness *a work of racist literature.]*

[It] is the desire—one might indeed say the need—in Western psychology to set Africa up as a foil to Europe, a place of negations at once remote and vaguely familiar in comparison with which Europe's own state of spiritual grace will be manifest. (p. 2)

Joseph Conrad's ***Heart of Darkness*** . . . better than any other work that I know displays that Western desire and need. . . . Of course, there are whole libraries of books devoted to the same purpose, but most of them are so obvious and so crude that few people worry about them today. Conrad, on the other hand, is undoubtedly one of the great stylists of modern fiction and a good storyteller in the bargain. His contribution, therefore, falls automatically into a different class—permanent literature—read and taught and constantly evaluated by serious academics. ***Heart of Darkness*** is indeed so secure today that a leading Conrad scholar has numbered it "among the half-dozen greatest short novels in the English language." (pp. 2-3)

Heart of Darkness projects the image of Africa as "the other world," the antithesis of Europe and therefore of civilization, a place where man's vaunted intelligence and refinement are finally mocked by triumphant bestiality. The book opens on the River Thames, tranquil, resting peacefully "at the decline of day after ages of good service done to the race that peopled its banks." But the actual story takes place on the River Congo, the very antithesis of the Thames. The River Congo is quite decidedly not a River Emeritus. It has rendered no service and enjoys no old-age pension. We are told that "going up that river was like travelling back to the earliest beginnings of the world."

Is Conrad saying, then, that these two rivers are very different, one good, the other bad? Yes, but that is not the real point. It is not the differentness that worries Conrad but the lurking hint of kinship, of common ancestry. For the Thames too "has been one of the dark places of the earth." It conquered its darkness, of course, and is now at peace. But if it were to visit its primordial relative, the Congo, it would run the terrible risk of hearing grotesque, suggestive echoes of its own forgotten darkness, and falling victim to an avenging recrudescence of the mindless frenzy of the first beginnings.

I am not going to waste your time with examples of Conrad's famed evocation of the African atmosphere in ***Heart of Darkness.*** In the final consideration it amounts to no more than a steady, ponderous, fake-ritualistic repetition of two sentences, one about silence and the other about frenzy. (p. 3)

The eagle-eyed English critic, F. R. Leavis, drew attention nearly thirty years ago to Conrad's "adjectival insistence upon inexpressible and incomprehensible mystery." That insistence must not be dismissed lightly, as many Conrad critics have tended to do, as a mere stylistic flaw. For it raises serious questions of artistic good faith. When a writer while pretending to record scenes, incidents, and their impact is in reality engaged in inducing hypnotic stupor in his readers through a bombardment of emotive words and other forms of trickery, much more has to be at stake than stylistic felicity. Generally, normal readers are well armed to detect and resist such underhand activity. But Conrad chose his subject well—one which was guaranteed not to put him in conflict with the psychological predisposition of his readers or raise the need for him to contend with their resistance. He chose the role of purveyor of comforting myths.

The most interesting and revealing passages in ***Heart of Darkness*** are, however, about people. . . . Herein lies the meaning of ***Heart of Darkness*** and the fascination it holds over the Western mind: "What thrilled you was just the thought of their humanity—like yours . . . Ugly."

Having shown us Africa in the mass, Conrad then zeroes in, as you would say, half a page later, on a specific example, giving us one of his rare descriptions of an African who is not just limbs or rolling eyes:

> And between whiles I had to look after the savage who was fireman. He was an improved specimen; he could fire up a vertical boiler. He was there below me, and, upon my word, to look at him was as edifying as seeing a dog in a parody of breeches and a feather hat, walking on his hind legs. A few months of training had done for that really fine chap. He squinted at the steam gauge and at the water gauge with an evident effort of intrepidity—and he had filed his teeth, too, the poor devil, and the wool of his pate shaved into queer patterns, and three ornamental scars on each of his cheeks. . . .

As everybody knows, Conrad is a romantic on the side. He might not exactly admire savages clapping their hands and stamping their feet, but they have at least the merit of being in their place, unlike this dog in a parody of breeches. For Conrad, things being in their place is of the utmost importance.

"Fine fellows—cannibals—in their place," he tell us pointedly. Tragedy begins when things leave their accustomed place, like Europe leaving its safe stronghold between the policeman and the baker to take a peep into the heart of darkness. (pp. 3-5)

Towards the end of the story, Conrad lavishes a whole page quite unexpectedly on an African woman who has obviously been some kind of mistress to Mr. Kurtz and now presides (if I may be permitted a little imitation of Conrad) like a formidable mystery over the inexorable imminence of his departure. . . .

This Amazon is drawn in considerable detail, albeit of a predictable nature, for two reasons. First, she is in her place and so can win Conrad's special brand of approval, and, second, she fulfills a structural requirement of the story: a savage counterpart to the refined, European woman with whom the story will end. . . .

The difference in the attitude of the novelist to these two women is conveyed in too many direct and subtle ways to need elaboration. But perhaps the most significant difference is the one implied in the author's bestowal of human expression to the one and the withholding of it from the other. It is clearly not part of Conrad's purpose to confer language on the "rudimentary souls" of Africa. They only "exchanged short grunting phrases" even among themselves, but mostly they were too busy with their frenzy. There are two occasions in the book, however, when Conrad departs somewhat from his practice and confers speech, even English speech, on the savages. The first occurs when cannibalism gets the better of them:

> "Catch 'im," he snapped, with a bloodshot widening of his eyes and a flash of sharp white teeth—"catch 'im. Give 'im to us." "To you, eh?" I asked; "what would you do with them?" "Eat 'im!" he said curtly.

(p. 6)

The other occasion was the famous announcement:

> Mistah Kurtz—he dead. . . .

At first sight these instances might be mistaken for unexpected acts of generosity from Conrad. In reality they constitute some of his best assaults. In the case of the cannibals the incomprehensible grunts that had thus far served them for speech suddenly proved inadequate for Conrad's purpose of letting the European glimpse the unspeakable craving in their hearts. Weighing the necessity for consistency in the portrayal of the dumb brutes against the sensational advantages of securing their conviction by clear, unambiguous evidence issuing out of their own mouth, Conrad chose the latter. As for the announcement of Mr.

Kurtz's death by the "insolent black head in the doorway," what better or more appropriate *finis* could be written to the horror story of that wayward child of civilization who wilfully had given his soul to the powers of darkness and "taken a high seat amongst the devils of the land" than the proclamation of his physical death by the forces he had joined?

It might be contended, of course, that the attitude to the African in ***Heart of Darkness*** is not Conrad's but that of his fictional narrator, Marlow, and that far from endorsing it Conrad might indeed be holding it up to irony and criticism. Certainly Conrad appears to go to considerable pains to set up layers of insulation between himself and the moral universe of his story. He has, for example, a narrator behind a narrator. . . . But if Conrad's intention is to draw a *cordon sanitaire* between himself and the moral and psychological malaise of his narrator, his care seems to me totally wasted because he neglects to hint however subtly or tentatively at an alternative frame of reference by which we may judge the actions and opinions of his characters. It would not have been beyond Conrad's power to make that provision if he had thought it necessary. Marlow seems to me to enjoy Conrad's complete confidence—a feeling reinforced by the close similarities between their two careers.

Marlow comes through to us not only as a witness of truth, but one holding those advanced and humane views appropriate to the English liberal tradition which required all Englishmen of decency to be deeply shocked by atrocities in Bulgaria or the Congo of King Leopold of the Belgians or whatever. (p. 7)

The kind of liberalism espoused here by Marlow/Conrad touched all the best minds of the age in England, Europe, and America. It took different forms in the minds of different people but almost always managed to sidestep the ultimate question of equality between white people and black people. . . .

[Conrad] would not use the word brother however qualified; the farthest he would go was kinship. (p. 8)

It is important to note that Conrad, careful as ever with his words, is not talking so much about *distant kinship* as about someone *laying a claim* on it. The black man lays a claim on the white man which is well-nigh intolerable. It is the laying of this claim which frightens and at the same time fascinates Conrad, "the thought of their humanity—like yours . . . Ugly."

The point of my observations should be quite clear by now, namely that Conrad was a bloody racist. That this simple truth is glossed over in criticisms of his work is due to the fact that white racism against Africa is such a normal way of thinking that its manifestations go completely undetected. Students of ***Heart of Darkness*** will often tell you that Conrad is concerned not so much with Africa as with the deterioration of one European mind caused by solitude and sickness. They will point out to you that Conrad is, if anything, less charitable to the Europeans in the story than he is to the natives. A Conrad student told me in Scotland last year that Africa is merely a setting for the disintegration of the mind of Mr. Kurtz.

Which is partly the point. Africa as setting and backdrop which eliminates the African as human factor. Africa as a metaphysical battlefield devoid of all recognizable humanity, into which the wandering European enters at his peril. Of course, there is a preposterous and perverse kind of arrogance in thus reducing Africa to the role of props for the breakup of one petty European mind. But that is not even the point. The real question is the dehumanization of Africa and Africans which this age-long attitude has fostered and continues to foster in the world. And the question is whether a novel which celebrates this dehumanization, which depersonalizes a portion of the human race, can be called a great work of art. My answer is: No, it cannot. I would not call that man an artist, for example, who composes an eloquent instigation to one people to fall upon another and destroy them. No matter how striking his imagery or how beautiful his cadences fall, such a man is no more a great artist than another may be called a priest who reads the mass backwards or a physician who poisons his patients. (pp. 8-9)

Naturally, Conrad is a dream for psychoanalytic critics. Perhaps the most detailed study of him in this direction is by Bernard C. Meyer, M.D. In his lengthy book, Dr. Meyer follows every conceivable lead (and sometimes inconceivable ones) to explain Conrad. As an example, he gives us long disquisitions on the significance of hair and haircutting in Conrad. And yet not even one word is spared for his attitude to black people. Not even the discussion of Conrad's anti-semitism was enough to spark off in Dr. Meyer's mind those other dark and explosive thoughts. Which only leads one to surmise that Western psychoanalysts must regard the kind of racism displayed by Conrad as absolutely normal despite the profoundly important work done by Frantz Fanon in the psychiatric hospitals in French Algeria. (pp. 10-11)

There are two probable grounds on which what I have said so far may be contested. The first is that it is no concern of fiction to please people about whom it is written. I will go along with that. But I am not talking about pleasing people. I am talking about a book which parades in the most vulgar fashion prejudices and insults from which a section of mankind has suffered untold agonies and atrocities in the past and continues to do so in many ways and many places today. I am talking about a story in which the very humanity of black people is called in question. It seems to me totally inconceivable that great art or even good art could possibly reside in such unwholesome surroundings.

Secondly, I may be challenged on the grounds of actuality. Conrad, after all, sailed down the Congo in 1890 when my own father was still a babe in arms, and recorded what he saw. How could I stand up in 1975, fifty years after his death, and purport to contradict him? My answer is that as a sensible man I will not accept just any traveller's tales solely on the grounds that I have not made the journey myself. I will not trust the evidence even of a man's very eyes when I suspect them to be as jaundiced as Conrad's. And we also happen to know that Conrad was, in the words of his biographer, Bernard C. Meyer, "notoriously inaccurate in the rendering of his own history."

But more important by far is the abundant testimony about Conrad's savages which we could gather if we were so inclined from other sources and which might lead us to think that these people must have had other occupations besides merging into the evil forest or materializing out of it simply to plague Marlow and his dispirited band. (pp. 11-12)

Conrad did not originate the image of Africa which we find in his book. It was and is the dominant image of Africa in the Western imagination, and Conrad merely brought the peculiar gifts of his own mind to bear on it. . . . Africa is to Europe as the picture is to Dorian Gray—a carrier onto whom the master unloads his physical and moral deformities so that he may go forward, erect and immaculate. Consequently, Africa is something to be avoided, just as the picture has to be hidden away to safeguard the man's jeopardous integrity. Keep away from Africa, or else! Mr. Kurtz of ***Heart of Darkness*** should have heeded that warning, and the prowling horror in his heart would have kept its place, chained to its lair. But he foolishly exposed himself to the wild irresistible allure of the jungle, and lo! the darkness found him out. (p. 13)

Ultimately, the abandonment of unwholesome thoughts must be its own and only reward. Although I have used the word *wilful* a few times in this talk to characterize the West's view of Africa, it may well be that what is happening at this stage is more akin to reflex action than calculated malice. Which does not make the situation more but less hopeful. . . .

[Although] the work which needs to be done may appear too daunting, I believe that it is not one day too soon to begin. (p. 14)

Chinua Achebe, "An Image of Africa," in Research in African Literatures, *Vol. 9, No. 1, Spring, 1978, pp. 1-15.*

Joan E. Steiner (essay date 1980)

[In the following excerpt, Steiner contends that in "The Secret Sharer" Conrad used the literary convention of the double to create both "clear-cut dualities" and "persistent ambiguities."]

Because **"The Secret Sharer"** is among those works given the most attention by Conradian critics, one is tempted to conclude that little or nothing significant remains to be said about it. Endlessly debated, for example, is Leggatt's role as *Doppelgänger*—since the captain-narrator specifically refers to him no less than eighteen times as "my double" and employs variant terms, "my other self," "my second self," "my secret self," and "my secret sharer," as many or more times, it is impossible to ignore. While the doubling here is, in some respects, less complicated than that in some of Conrad's other works, such as ***Heart of Darkness*** and *Victory,* it confirms his thorough mastery of a convention that had already undergone considerable development in the hands of his nineteenth-century predecessors. By using the double as the central image in a tale exploring a number of ostensibly clear-cut dualities and, simultaneously and paradoxically, as the focus of persistent ambiguities that blur those dualities, Conrad transforms the device into one peculiarly his own. Thus more does remain to be said about Conrad's handling of the doubling relationship in **"The Secret Sharer."**

In his study, *Doubles in Literary Psychology,* Ralph Tymms traces the evolution of the *Doppelgänger* from its origins in primitive belief, where it was frequently associated with dreams and hallucinations and with such visual phenomena as mirror images, shadows, and supernatural manifestations, through its major appearances in literature up to the end of the nineteenth century. In so doing, he points to the development of two conceptions, doubling by duplication, in which the counterpart appears as a twin or, in its essential aspects, a physical duplicate, and doubling by division, in which the counterpart appears as a twin or, in its essential aspects, a physical duplicate, and doubling by division, in which the counterpart represents one major facet of character, customarily spiritual or psychological in nature. In addition, he describes the alternation between allegorical or ethical doubles, which express dualism in human nature in terms of good and evil, and realistic or psychological doubles, which depict dualism in terms of reason and emotion or the conscious and unconscious.

Of particular importance in the development of the *Doppelgänger* was E. T. A. Hoffmann. Intrigued by the discoveries of the Mesmerist psychologists, who clinically developed theories of dual consciousness and postulated the existence of a "night side" of the mind, Hoffman incorporated their ideas in his fiction. Reviewing a number of representative tales, Tymms finds Hoffmann's greatest contribution to be his identification of the unconscious self with another individual and in some cases subjective transference of this part of the personality to that physical double, either real or imaginary. By associating inward dualism with outward physical likeness, Hoffmann thus combined the previously separate concepts of doubling by division and doubling by duplication. Moreover, influenced by the observation of the Mesmerist psychologist, G. H. Schubert, that "emotions (which act most directly on the unconscious mind) are ambiguous in character," Hoffmann placed greater emphasis on psychological than on allegorical aspects of the *Doppelgänger* relationship.

Examining the portrayal of Leggatt in light of this information, I find it significant that Conrad alludes directly to Hoffmann's tales in *Under Western Eyes,* the work he interrupted to write **"The Secret Sharer,"** for the correspondences are too great to ignore. Thus, like Hoffmann, Conrad combines doubling by duplication and doubling by division in his representation of Leggatt and also places greater emphasis on the psychological than on the allegorical aspects of Leggatt's relationship with the captain.

With respect to Leggatt's role as double by duplication, the captain, in addition to making numerous references to their identical attire and observing that the "sleeping-suit was just right for his size," initially notes other physical similarities between Leggatt and himself, including age and appearance, and concludes with an image associated with the double from the beginning: "It was, in the night, as though I had been faced by my own reflection in the depths of a sombre and immense mirror." Throughout the story, moreover, the captain frequently reminds us of this physical similarity.

By noting experiential parallels as well, Conrad extends his portrayal of the double by duplication beyond that of most of his predecessors. Thus both the captain and Leggatt, we learn, served on the Conway maritime training ship. Moreover, accounts of Leggatt's experiences on the *Sephora* indicate that he, like the narrator, was "the only stranger on board," making his first voyage as an officer among men who had been together for some time and who distrusted him. Because Leggatt appeals to him "as if our experiences had been as identical as our clothes," the captain is able to understand the circumstances of the murder "as though I were myself inside that other sleeping-suit."

Because critics have concentrated on Leggatt's role as double by division, many have taken an extreme position on his significance. Some, following the lead of Albert J. Guerard, who has variously interpreted Leggatt as "some darker, more interior, outlaw self" [*Conrad the Novelist*], and as a "more instinctive, more primitive, less rational self" revealing man's "potential criminality" [introduction to ***Heart of Darkness*** and **"The Secret Sharer"**], regard him as a predominantly negative figure. Others, by contrast, view Leggatt as the embodiment of that "ideal conception of one's own personality" that the captain has secretly set up as a standard by which to measure his behavior. While each position has some validity, both fail to consider sufficiently all aspects of Leggatt and hence the ambiguities inherent in his character, as well as in his relationship with the captain.

Heretofore ignored by critics, Conrad's remarks in *The Mirror of the Sea* concerning his own first command aboard the *Otago* provide some insight into his view of Leggatt. Specifically, he asserts that the two qualifications necessary for a trustworthy seaman are, paradoxically, a healthy sense of insecurity and "an absolute confidence in himself," both of which Leggatt reveals by the time he meets the narrator, but neither of which the narrator initially possesses. The latter's serenity at the outset, reflected in the opening descriptive paragraph, is disrupted when, just before the "tide of darkness" obliterates the scene before him, he notices the presence of another ship, which destroys for him the "solemnity of perfect solitude," as the "multitude" of stars and "disturbing sounds" from the crew destroy "the comfort of quiet communion" with his ship. Thus his preparation for Leggatt has begun.

Subsequently, the captain reveals facets of his character that further suggest his readiness for Leggatt's arrival and for their ensuing relationship. Acknowledging that he is "somewhat of a stranger" to himself and aware that he is "doing something unusual," he impulsively takes the anchor watch himself. Motivated partly by compassion for his men, he suggests this "unconventional arrangement" chiefly because he wishes to be alone in order to "get on terms" with his strange ship. Under the illusion that "the sea was not likely to keep any special surprises expressly for my discomfiture," he proceeds to commit a further breach of discipline by leaving his watch to go below for a cigar and, presumably, to put on his sleeping suit, then returns to rejoice naively "in the great security of the sea as compared with the unrest of the land, in my choice of that untempted life presenting no disquieting problems." Just as his initial description of the indistinguishable welding of land and sea reflects a naive sense of integration, so this simplistic dichotomy between land and sea reflects his growing sense of duality.

Immediately thereafter, he is confronted with a disquieting problem that results directly from his impulsive behavior and destroys his sense of security. Annoyed at finding that a rope ladder has not been hauled in, he asks himself "whether it was wise ever to interfere with the established routine of duties even from the kindest motives." After discovering Leggatt, however, he impulsively commits another breach of discipline by letting him come aboard. Upon noting the establishment of a "mysterious communication" with him and providing him with a "sleeping-suit of the same grey-stripe pattern" as his own, the captain makes the first reference to him as "my double."

That the self-confident Leggatt is presented, in part, as a positive figure of light, i.e., of life and strength, is, I think, indisputable. Three times while he is in the water he is described as "phosphorescent," and as he sits naked on deck before putting on the sleeping suit, he appears "glimmering white in the darkness." Moreover, we learn later that it is the riding light, burning "with a clear, untroubled, as if symbolic flame, confident and bright in the mysterious shades of the night," that directs him to the ship and saves him from having to swim " 'round and round like a crazed bullock.' " And at the end, of course, he leaves the hat, "white on the black water," that serves as the "saving mark" for the captain.

Through most of the story, the captain, despite his feeling of identity with Leggatt, contrasts his own deficiencies with Leggatt's strengths. After Leggatt's account of the murder and his subsequent confinement, for example, the narrator notes, "There was nothing sickly in his eyes or in his expression. He was not a bit like me, really," and imagines the manner of his thinking over the incident as "a stubborn if not a steadfast operation; something of which I should have been perfectly incapable." Later, when the captain feels that he is "appearing an irresolute commander," he envies Leggatt's looking "always perfectly self-controlled, more than calm—almost invulnerable." And after the incident of near-discovery, he marvels at "that something unyielding in his character which was carrying him through so finely. . . . Whoever was being distracted, it was not he. He was sane."

Leggatt's strength of character was also evident during the storm aboard the *Sephora.* " 'It wasn't a heavy sea,' " Leggatt says, " 'it was a sea gone mad! . . . a man may have the heart to see it coming once and be done with it—but to have to face it day after day. . . .' " When the sea produced a corresponding madness in the crew, everyone on the *Sephora* failed. Most culpable of all was the captain, Archbold, whose " 'nerve went to pieces altogether.' " After watching the main topsail blow away, he was unable to give the order for the reefed foresail, but " 'whimpered about our last hope.' " This experience, according to Leggatt, " 'was enough to drive any fellow out of his mind. It worked me up into a sort of desperation,' " yet he maintained enough presence of mind to give orders and set the foresail.

As commander of the *Sephora,* Archbold theoretically should be a strong figure, one whose "seven-and-thirty virtuous years at sea, of which over twenty of immaculate command," ought to make him an ideal example to the narrator. Instead, he serves as kind of pathetic double whose moment of failure forcefully emphasizes the ever-present dangers facing the narrator and the precariousness of his position, both personally and professionally. Unlike Leggatt, Archbold appears "completely muddled" about what has happened, unable to face the implications of his behavior or to comprehend his share in Leggatt's guilt. In addition to serving as a reminder of the possibility of failure, he both figuratively mirrors the narrator's inability to master his command, his growing sense of madness, and his fear of the crew, and literally intensifies the suspicion and distrust of that crew.

Despite Leggatt's positive aspects as a figure of light, his act of killing identifies him also with darkness. Textual evidence indicates that, in his role as double by division, Leggatt, like many of Hoffmann's *Doppelgängers,* serves as the embodiment or projection of the unconscious and that the captain's relationship with him, as Guerard observes, takes the form of the archetypal night journey or "provisional descent into the primitive and unconscious sources of being," resulting in spiritual change and rebirth. Thus, Leggatt arrives at night, appearing to the captain initially as a "naked body" flickering "in the sleeping water"—at once actual environment and metaphor of the unconscious—and then as a being "complete but for a head. A headless corpse," i.e., one without intellect. Moreover, as we have seen, the captain's discovery of him comes as the direct result of his own impulsive behavior, just as Leggatt, by his account, has impulsively jumped off the *Sephora* and, on arriving here, impulsively asked for the captain.

Once Leggatt is on board and dressed in a sleeping suit, which he wears throughout his stay, the captain, as if to check his bearings, examines his double's face under a lamp before the "warm, heavy, tropical night closed upon his head again." Thereafter, Leggatt is identified predominantly with night, for it is then that he and the narrator communicate in whispers, it not being "prudent to talk in the daytime." Finally, Leggatt plans his escape for night, noting " 'as I came at night, so I shall go.' " Here, night and darkness have traditional connotations of the mysterious and the irrational.

In addition to this identification of his "second self" with night, the narrator's frequent allusions to the sleeping suit, "the garb of the unconscious life," are in keeping with the traditional psychological representation of the *Doppelgänger* as a manifestation of the unconscious or "night side" of the mind. Traditional, too, are the narrator's metaphorical allusions to his double as a ghost, suggesting his "possession" by Leggatt. Shortly after Leggatt's arrival, for example, the captain surmises that if his chief mate were to come on deck, "he would think he was seeing double or imagine himself come upon a scene of weird witchcraft; the strange captain having a quiet confabulation by the wheel with his own grey ghost." To prevent such an occurrence, the captain takes Leggatt below to his cabin, where Leggatt must be "as noiseless as a ghost" in the attempt to keep "my second self invisible." And when that attempt is subsequently threatened by the incident of near-discovery, the captain observes, "An irresistible doubt of his bodily existence flitted through my mind. Can it be, I asked myself, that he is not visible to other eyes than mine? It was like being haunted. . . . I think I had come creeping quietly as near insanity as any man who has not actually gone over the border."

Indeed, under the stress of the emotional crisis brought on by Leggatt's sudden appearance and his own self-doubt, the captain, like many of the protagonists in Hoffmann's tales, experiences an increasingly acute dissociation or disintegration of personality, leading to incipient madness. After his double has gone to bed, for example, he tries to clear his mind of "the confused sensation of being in two places at once." The next morning, he forces himself to leave the cabin to go on deck and to breakfast with the crew, noting that "all the time the dual working of my mind distracted me almost to the point of insanity." Then, after Archbold's visit, he fears that he is making a bad impression on his first mate because "with my double *down there,* it was most trying to me to be on deck. And it was almost as trying to be *below.* . . . But on the whole I felt less torn in two when I was with him" (my emphasis).

While Conrad's portrayal of Leggatt reveals his thorough familiarity with and dependence on the traditional *Doppelgänger,* his depiction of the ambiguity of Leggatt's character and behavior also reflects his originality and independence. That such ambiguity was intentional is evident in his reworking of materials of the *Cutty Sark* incident to soften the character of the first mate and introduce extenuating circumstances. Thus, unlike Sidney Smith, Leggatt had to contend not only with the exhausting strain of the storm and serious threat to the ship, but also with a captain who had gone to pieces. Moreover, his ability to give orders and take action in such a crisis clearly enabled him to save the *Sephora* and the lives of her crew. Finally, the victim, presumably a repeated offender " 'simmering all the time with a silly sort of wickedness,' " disobeyed Leggatt not once but twice, and at the moment of their second encounter they were struck by a wave whose ferocity lasted for over ten minutes, causing Leggatt instinctively to keep hold of his assailant's throat.

The captain, knowing "the pestiferous danger of such a character where there are no means of legal repression," pronounces his double "no homicidal ruffian," yet he also recognizes Leggatt's "guilt." And Leggatt does not absolve himself of responsibility. Considering the killing " 'very wrong indeed,' " he confesses, " 'It's clear that I meant business, because I was holding him by the throat still when they picked us up.' " Moreover, while he later indicates that he wants to prevent more killing, he twice admits the possibility of his committing further acts of violence.

To interpret Leggatt as an essentially "outlaw" or "criminal" self and as a predominantly negative influence on the captain is to distort his significance, however, for he demonstrates that the irrational or instinctive elements in human nature can be a source of strength as well as weakness, good as well as evil. Recognizing this ambiguity, the captain understands how "the same strung-up force which had given twenty-four men a chance, at least, for their lives, had, in a sort of recoil, crushed an unworthy mutinous existence." Leggatt's effect on the captain is similarly ambiguous but ultimately, I think, more positive than negative.

After a few words of conversation with the "calm and resolute" Leggatt upon his arrival, for example, the captain indicates that "the self-possession of that man had somehow induced a corresponding state in myself." And the following morning, despite his fear of Leggatt's discovery, he reflects, " 'I must show myself on deck.' " Facing his suspicious officers, who have heard about his strange behavior, he deftly handles them by giving his "first particular order" and remaining to see it executed. Moreover, feeling "the need of asserting myself without loss of time," he reprimands the second mate for insolence and seizes the opportunity to have "a good look at the face of every foremast man." Though all these actions are deliberate and self-conscious rather than instinctive, they reveal a positive effort to assert control.

Simultaneously, however, the captain's constant awareness of Leggatt, "as dependent on my actions as my own personality," intensifies his sense of duality and incipient madness. Emphasizing the division between his rational and irrational selves, he notes that during the day, Leggatt sits in "the recessed part of the cabin" where he is "half-smothered" by coats. The dangers of the split are evident when enough wind arises to get the ship underway. Although pleased to feel "for the first time a ship move under his feet to his own independent word," he is disturbed by the realization that "I was not wholly alone with my command; for there was that stranger in my cabin. Or rather, I was not completely and wholly with her. Part of me was absent," i.e., his instinctive self:

> There are to a seaman certain words, gestures, that should in given conditions come as naturally, as instinctively as the winking of a menaced eye. A certain order should spring on to his lips without thinking; a certain sign should get itself made, so to speak, without reflection. But all unconscious alertness had abandoned me. I had to make an effort of will to recall myself back (from the cabin) to the conditions of the moment.

Beyond the influence directly attributable to his function as *Doppelgänger,* Leggatt affects the captain's behavior in other ways that are equally ambiguous. Newly appointed to command, he begins the voyage, as we have seen, as a stranger. At the outset, his isolation is "imposed" by circumstances and by youth. Although Leggatt's situation on the *Sephora* was similar initially, his severe physical and moral isolation began only after the killing, when he was confined to his cabin for nine weeks. Thus, on his arrival at the ship he indicates that he has had " 'a confounded lonely time' " and is grateful that the captain saw and spoke to him, for " 'I wanted to be seen, to talk with somebody.' " Through his relationship with the captain, he temporarily becomes less isolated psychologically, while the latter becomes less a stranger to himself.

Yet their relationship has moral and physical, as well as psychological, consequences for the captain. On the one hand, by harboring a fugitive from justice, he places personal or individual loyalty above the traditions of the community. In effect, then, he betrays his function as captain, for his failure to perform any but the most perfunctory duties prevents his getting to know his ship and crew, while his increasing anxiety promotes hostility and distrust that intensify his moral and physical isolation. On the other hand, his loyalty to Leggatt not only demonstrates admirable compassion, but leads to the self-knowledge and self-mastery he must have if he is to succeed both personally and professionally and avoid the weaknesses demonstrated by Archbold and Leggatt.

While he discovers the advantages and dangers of unconscious or instinctive forces in human nature, however, the captain also comes to realize that awareness of one's "second self" does not necessarily lead to desirable or predictable results, for his own nature and/or "accidents which count for so much in the book of success" may cause him to be unfaithful to his ideal conception. Temporarily immobilized by this knowledge, he must summon the courage and self-confidence to act in spite of it. Once again, it is his "calm and resolute" double who forces the issue by his "sane" insistence that he be marooned as soon as possible, making the captain realize that his hesitation is "a mere sham sentiment, a sort of cowardice."

The maneuver to facilitate Leggatt's escape initially involves little risk, for the narrator plans only to take the ship in to "half a mile" from shore, "as far as I may be able to judge in the dark," yet Leggatt's warning to " 'be careful' " makes him realize that "all my future, the only future for which I was fit, would perhaps go irretrievably to pieces in any mishap to my first command." As if to avert this possibility, the captain spends most of his time on deck giving firm and calm commands to his dubious crew and only sufficient time with his "double captain" to work out plans for the escape.

What alters the original plan is Leggatt's unexpected behavior. Going below to see him just before supper, the captain notes that "for the first time there seemed to be a faltering, something strained in his whisper." Moreover, later in the sail locker, when he impulsively rams his hat on his "other self," Leggatt at first "dodged and fended off silently." Immediately after returning to the deck, the narrator decides "it was now a matter of conscience to shave the land as close as possible—for now he must go overboard . . . Must! There could be no going back for him." As a result, he finds himself facing a test similar to that in which Leggatt succeeded/failed. There is a significant difference, however, for not only does he once again impulsively create a morally ambiguous situation out of loyalty to Leggatt, unnecessarily risking the lives of his crew and the safety of his ship, but his external challenge is provided by the land rather than the sea.

That the captain has "absorbed" the unyielding character

of his double and achieved insight into his own potential weaknesses is clear from his description of his behavior during the risky maneuver. Immediately after deciding to "shave the land," he tells us that "my heart flew into my mouth at the nearness of the land on the bow. Under any other circumstances I would not have held on a minute longer." Gaining command of his voice, he issues orders quietly in an attempt to calm his understandably nervous crew. Even when "the black southern hill of Kohring seemed to hang right over the ship like a towering fragment of the ever-lasting night," and later, when the ship is "in the very blackness of " the land, "already swallowed up as it were, gone too close to be recalled, gone from me altogether," he maintains self-control and continues to give orders confidently. Then in an incident parallel to that confronting Leggatt on the *Sephora,* the chief mate, resembling both Archbold and the mutinous sailor, goes to pieces and starts talking back to the captain. Unlike Leggatt, however, the captain maintains control of himself, subduing the mate by clinging to and shaking his arm, not his throat, while firmly issuing orders. Finally, as the ship's "very fate hung in the balance," he suddenly remembers that he is "a total stranger" to her and does not know how she is to be handled. Only the appearance of the white hat, which indicates the backward movement of the ship, enables him to give the saving command. Having demonstrated confidence and self-control, he hardly gives a thought to his "other self" and regards him now, not as a spiritual double, but as "mere flesh."

The hat not only suggests a transference and ultimate reintegration of personality, but also, as it were, a transference of destiny. The narrator must subdue his unrestful, self-conscious, and overly introspective "land" self which has proved potentially harmful to his success as captain. Yet he must retain some measure of that insecurity prompted by his newly acquired recognition of ever-present danger from within and without. His description of his confrontation with the land, juxtaposing events on board ship with frequent references to darkness and night and images of death and Hades, graphically conveys his awareness of the significance of this test. By consciously facing danger and challenging his vulnerability, the captain overcomes his crippling sense of duality and demonstrates his ability to command, thereby belatedly earning the respect of his crew.

Yet ability alone does not save the ship, for without the assistance provided by the hat, the captain might have had many more deaths to account for than Leggatt. Aided by circumstance in avoiding actual betrayal, he is free to establish a bond of fellowship with his crew and pursue his chosen profession at sea. Deprived of similarly fortunate circumstance, Leggatt commits an act of betrayal, a breach of human solidarity, that condemns him to moral and physical isolation. However, just as he helps the captain to prepare for a "new destiny," so the latter serves a similar function for him. In presenting this mutual aspect of the doubling relationship, Conrad further demonstrates his originality. Specifically, in addition to saving Leggatt's life and relieving his loneliness, the captain is able to give him what he most needs—compassionate understanding—and with it an increasing capacity to reflect, as well as a renewed determination, with which to face his exile on land.

Thus, while the narrator notes that Leggatt, on his arrival, seems "to struggle with himself," expressing "something like the low, bitter murmur of doubt. 'What's the good?' " Leggatt, subsequently confirming this impression, emphasizes that " 'you speaking to me so quietly—as if you had expected me—made me hold on a little longer.' " Thereafter, the narrator's references to necessary lengthy silence, combined with his descriptions of Leggatt's posture during the day, which as Thomas R. Dilworth observes is that of a thinker or mediator ["Conrad's Secret Sharer at the Gate of Hell," *Conradiana,* 1977], suggest that Leggatt becomes increasingly introspective. Further suggesting this process is the narrator's growing number of references to Leggatt's head and to Leggatt and himself with their heads together. Thus, having initially seen Leggatt as "complete but for a head," the narrator ultimately envisions him with his "homeless head."

The results of Leggatt's introspection and the narrator's understanding are apparent in his comments on his predicament. As we have seen, he acknowledges the murder from the outset. Considered in the context of his allusions to being " 'a Conway boy' " and the son of a parson, his question, " 'Do you see me before a judge and jury on that charge?' " seems to be prompted, not by a desire to avoid punishment, but rather by shame at having failed to live up to the traditional values of his family and his profession. A similar motive is suggested when, in describing Archbold's refusal to let him escape, he says he wanted " 'nothing more' " and then bitterly compares himself to Cain.

This scene with Archbold is symbolically re-enacted when Leggatt, asking the captain to maroon him, once again indicates that he wants " 'no more' " and refers to Cain's fate. There is a crucial difference here, however. He now wants to avoid a trial, not because of shame, but because, never having faced a crisis in which rapid, instinctive action is imperative, the men trying him would not be able to understand his behavior: " 'What can they know whether I am guilty or not—or of *what* I am guilty, either?' " he asks. He is willing to accept Cain's punishment, he tells the captain, " 'as long as I know that you understand. . . . It's a great satisfaction to have got somebody to understand. You seem to have been there on purpose.' "

Earlier, the narrator has remarked of Leggatt, "The very trust in Providence was, I suppose, denied to his guilt." Now, however, Leggatt says that he is " 'not naked like a soul on the Day of Judgment. I shall freeze on to this sleeping-suit. The Last Day is not yet.' " In short, acting somewhat in the role of Providence, as Leggatt acts for him in leaving the hat, the captain gives Leggatt compassion and protection not unlike that which God demonstrated toward Cain in allowing him to expiate his guilt by wandering the earth. Just as he has had to subdue some of his "land" self in preparing for life at sea, so Leggatt must subdue some of his "sea" self in preparing for life on land, a process symbolized by the captain's view of him looking at the navigation chart, "following with his eyes his own figure wandering on the blank land of Cochin-

China, and then passing off that piece of paper clean out of sight into uncharted regions." As noted earlier, the transference not only of personality but also of destiny is suggested when, visualizing himself "wandering barefooted, bareheaded, the sun beating on my dark poll," the captain gives Leggatt his hat. Subsequently marking the spot where he "lowered himself into the water to take his punishment" and where the captain gains control of his ship, the hat contributes to Leggatt's redemption, making him "a free man, a proud swimmer striking out for a new destiny."

Metaphorically, the lowering of Leggatt into the water and passing "out of sight into unchartered regions" suggest the resubmergence of the captain's unconscious and the reintegration of his personality. Thus, during his night journey, the narrator has moved, with the assistance of his double, from immature and naive integration through a period of severe disorientation and disintegration to a more mature reintegration resulting from self-knowledge and self-mastery. (pp. 173-84)

Joan E. Steiner, "Conrad's 'The Secret Sharer': Complexities of the Doubling Relationship," in Conradiana, *Vol. 12, No. 3, 1980, pp. 173-86.*

Hunt Hawkins (essay date 1982)

[In the following excerpt, Hawkins defends Conrad against charges that he presented a racist view of Africans in Heart of Darkness.]

Recently Conrad has come under fire from several Third World writers for his depiction of non-Europeans. The attack began in 1975 when the Nigerian novelist Chinua Achebe declared Conrad was "a bloody racist" and recommended ***Heart of Darkness*** cease to be regarded as great art. Achebe renewed his attack in 1980 in the *Times Literary Supplement,* saying that in Conrad's novella the humanity of Africans was "totally undermined by the mindlessness of its context and the pretty explicit animal imagery surrounding it." This attack has also been pressed by the Indian critic Frances B. Singh. In a 1978 article [in *Conradiana*] entitled "The Colonialistic Bias of ***Heart of Darkness***" she maintained Conrad's story "carries suggestions that the evil which the title refers to is to be associated with Africans, their customs, and their rites." Thus while Conrad may have been nominally anti-imperialist, he ultimately would have favored the subjugation of Africans: "as long as he associates the life of depravity with the life of blacks then he can hardly be called anti-colonial."

It would surely be a mistake to dismiss these attacks out of hand. Besides bringing a fresh perspective to Conrad studies, they carry a measure of truth. The limitations of ***Heart of Darkness,*** at least as a picture of African colonization, may be clearly seen by comparing it with Achebe's *Things Fall Apart,* a novel about the British takeover of an Ibo village at the end of the nineteenth century. Unlike Achebe's comprehensive presentation of Ibo life, Conrad's story barely shows the Congolese. None of the African characters has a name. With the exception of Kurtz's mistress, no African appears for more than a full paragraph. We do not go into the minds of any of the Africans to see the situation from their point of view. In fact, they barely speak, being limited to a total of four pidgin sentences. Moreover, Marlow uses some frankly derogatory language in describing Africans. At various points in the story he refers to them as "savages," "niggers," "the prehistoric man," and "rudimentary souls." He applies the following adjectives to their appearance or behavior: "grotesque," "horrid," "ugly," "fiendish," and "satanic." His explicit animal comparisons are with ants, hyenas, horses, and bees. Thus the image which Conrad projects of African life could hardly be called flattering.

On the other hand, it is overly severe simply to write Conrad off as a racist. His attitude is complex, itself critical of racism, and, I believe, ultimately sympathetic to non-European peoples. A better understanding of his complexity may be gained by studying the series of defenses which can, and have, and should be offered on his behalf.

The first defense is that Conrad's Congo story is really more concerned with Europeans than Africans. The Kenyan novelist Leonard Kibera has said [in *International Fiction Review,* 1980]: "I study ***Heart of Darkness*** as an examination of the West itself and not as a comment on Africa." We should remember Conrad had little personal experience of Africa. He spent less than six months in the Congo, mostly in the company of white men. He did not speak any African languages. Thus he did not have the background to give an intimate portrait of African life, and surely was wise not to attempt it. The main focus of his story is on European characters—Marlow, Kurtz, the Intended, the pilgrims—and the European forces which drive them such as the need for money, or the absence of European restraints, such as policemen and the opinion of neighbors. Africa as anything other than a geographical location seems to come little into play. Still, Achebe is quite right in saying this does not excuse Marlow's dehumanizing comments about Africans. And Frances Singh feels that Conrad ultimately blames Kurtz's degeneration on the evil influence of the Africans themselves.

A second possible defense of Conrad would be that the tribal life of the Congolese in 1890, the year of his visit, was in fact much less idyllic than we might wish to imagine. This subject has been inadequately studied, and objective evidence is almost impossible to obtain. The written documentation which remains was recorded entirely by Europeans and Americans. Even in their private, unpublished diaries and letters, these soldiers, officials, traders, and missionaries would have had a vested interest in seeing as degraded the Africans they were trying to subdue, rule, exploit, and convert. However, while we perhaps cannot reach the final truth, we can at least establish the norm of European perception against which to measure Conrad.

We should also recall the immediate historical background to the situation in the Congo in 1890. When Stanley first crossed Africa in 1877, he left the Arab slave trader Tippo Tib at Stanley Falls. By the time Conrad arrived there thirteen years later, pressure from Arab slaving, along with increasing Belgian exploitation, had devastated the region. Thus the tribes of the upper Congo—specifically, the Bangala, the Balolo, the Wangata, the Ngombe, the Bapoto, and the Babango—were evidently a great deal more disordered and violent than tribes in other parts of Africa, such as the Ibo. According to contemporary European reports, cannibalism and human sacrifice were rife on the upper river.

In [*In Savage Africa; or, Six Years of Adventure in Congo-Land, 1892*], E. J. Glave, the young Englishman who preceded Johannes Freiesleben (Fresleven in ***Heart of Darkness***) as captain of the steamer *Florida,* said, "Cannibalism exists amongst all the peoples on the Upper Congo east of 16° E. longitude," that is, east of Kinchassa. Most other observers agreed on the extent although there was disagreement about whether cannibalism in particular tribes was solely for religious ceremonies or for food or simply for pleasure. The English missionary John McKittrick reported in 1890 that among the Balolo, "As far as I was able to observe or ascertain, human flesh is not bought and eaten merely for food. It *is* eaten, but mainly as a superstitious rite connected with funerals." A different view, however, was presented by A. J. Wauters, editor of *Mouvement Géographique,* the company journal for the *Société Anonyme Belge pour le Commerce du Haut-Congo,* and the influential friend who got Conrad his job. Wauters maintained that throughout the Congo basin, "A notre avis, l'anthropophagie est avant tout d'origine physiologique: elle est née de la faim, du besoin de se procurer de la chair." He blamed cannibalism in regions with abundant food on "l'instinct de l'imitation, qui a amené une véritable perversion du goût." E. J. Glave made the same charge concerning the tribes along the Ubangi River, a tributary of the Congo: "Having purchased slaves they feed them on ripe bananas, fish, and oil, and when they get them into good condition they kill them." And Leopold Courouble, a state official, reported that the Bangala, who compose Marlow's cannibal view in ***Heart of Darkness,*** defined human beings as "la viande qui parle." In addition to ceremonial eating of their own dead and their enemies, they also ate purchased slaves.

Human sacrifices in the Congo appear to have occurred primarily at the funerals of chiefs. E. J. Glave wrote: "Horrible ceremonies of human sacrifice result from the belief prevailing amongst these people of an existence carried on underground after death, as on earth, a life in which the departed ones require the services of slaves and wives to attend to their several wants." Glave said that at Lukolela about one-third of a dead chief's slaves and about half of his wives were killed. Also a small child might be placed in the grave alive "as a pillow for the dead chief." John McKittrick said that at the funerals of Balolo chiefs young boys were stuffed with food, partially hung, and then "brutally beaten to death." The bodies of the victims were eaten and each head "stuck up on a pole before the dead man's house." Among the Wangata, too, after the victims were killed, "le crâne fut exposé sur un pieu au milieu du village." Human sacrifices also apparently occurred on other occasions: "Ces sacrifices ont lieu . . . aux grandes fêtes lunaires, au moment d'entreprendre une guerre, aux fêtes pour l'intronisation d'un grand chef." Glave adds that Chief Ibaka at Bolobo made human sacrifices to appease the anger of evil spirits.

The apparent practices of Africans on the upper Congo horrified the Europeans. Father Emeri Cambier called the Congo "a land given over to the devil" and Rev. W. Holman Bentley said the Africans were "children of the devil." A particularly interesting response came from a man who might be supposed relatively impartial, George Washington Williams, a black American journalist who in 1883 published a *History of the Negro Race in America* and is now well-respected as a pioneer Afro-American historian. Williams visited the Congo in 1890, the same year as Conrad. He was appalled by Belgian exploitation and became the first total opponent of King Leopold's regime. But at the same time he was shocked by the Africans. In an open letter of protest to Leopold, Williams reported that "Cruelties of the most astounding character are practiced by the natives, such as burying slaves alive in the grave of a dead chief." He also said, "Between 800 and 1,000 slaves are sold to be eaten by the natives of the Congo State annually." Thus, although Williams denounced the cruelty of Leopold's soldiers, one of his complaints against the regime was, ironically, that it was "deficient in the moral, military, and financial strength necessary to govern."

It is uncertain to what extent Conrad may have witnessed any of these practices. He made no mention of them in his Congo diaries, but he did later tell Arthur Symons, "I saw all those sacrilegious rites." Unlike other Europeans, however, Conrad did not view such rites, even conceived at their worst, as a justification for African subjugation. Contrary to what Frances Singh says, Conrad did not become a supporter of imperialism. In a protest letter sent to Roger Casement in 1903 as a contribution to the fledgling Congo reform movement, Conrad declared,

> Barbarism per se is no crime deserving of a heavy visitation; and the Belgians are worse than the seven plagues of Egypt insomuch that in that case it was a punishment sent for a definite transgression; but in this the Upoto man is not aware of any transgression, and therefore can see no end to the infliction. It must appear to him very awful and mysterious; and I confess that it appears so to me too.

As a third defense of Conrad, we should realize that ***Heart of Darkness*** is a powerful indictment of imperialism, both explicity for the case of King Leopold and implicitly (despite Marlow's comments on the patches of red) for all other European powers. Conrad graphically demonstrates that "The conquest of the earth, which mostly means the taking it away from those who have a different complexion or slightly flatter noses than ourselves, it not a pretty thing." If Conrad's image of the Africans seems negative, his presentation of the Europeans is much more so. As Ellen Mae Kitonga notes in the Kenyan journal *Busara* [1970], "However unflattering . . . this portrait of the African, that of his 'civilizers' is much less flattering and all too realistic." The Europeans are shown as possessed by "a flabby, pretending, weak-eyed devil of a rapacious and pitiless folly." They, too, are compared with animals. The uncle of the manager has a "short flipper of an arm" and the members of the Eldorado Exploring Expedition are "less valuable animals" than their donkeys.

While ***Heart of Darkness*** may suggest, as Frances Singh argues, that Kurtz has been corrupted by the evil practices of the Africans, the suggestion is slight. For the most part Conrad makes clear that the corruption comes from Europe and from Kurtz himself. Kurtz is driven to the Congo in the first place by the imperatives of the European class structure. His Intended's parents disapprove their engagement because he "wasn't rich enough." His main motive in trading for ivory, then stealing it, is to accumulate enough money to be a success in Europe. Even on the verge of death, he is thinking of Europe, dreaming of having "kings meet him at railway stations on his return." Kurtz also has other, less material, lusts, and these are brought to the surface by his isolation from external restraints. Through his possession of guns, he finds himself in a position of seemingly magical power over the Africans with nothing to hold him back. As the Russian says of Kurtz, "He came to them with thunder and lightning." Kurtz proceeds to set himself up as god of the lake tribe, presiding over "certain midnight dances ending with unspeakable rites," presumably human sacrifices. In doing this, it is important to note, he is not so much being corrupted by African practices as corrupting Africans through his abuse of his power. On his own initiative, he is aggrandizing himself in conscious hubris. Conrad very carefully distinguishes between what Kurtz does and what the Africans do, and while he finds great fault with the former, he finds little with the latter. As in his 1903 letter in which he wrote "Barbarism per se is no crime," Conrad in ***Heart of Darkness*** exonerates the Africans by having Marlow say of Kurtz, "I seemed at one bound to have been transported into some lightless region of subtle horrors, where pure, uncomplicated savagery was a positive relief, being something that had a right to exist—obviously—in the sunshine." Significantly, the harshest adjective which Marlow applies to Africans—"satanic"—is not for something they do on their own but for their participation in Kurtz's ceremonies.

Neither Achebe nor Singh fully appreciates Conrad's condemnation of Kurtz specifically and European imperialism generally. Achebe sees these condemnations as patronizing "liberalism" and "bleeding-heart sentiments" which fail to recognize African equality. But most Third World critics, even if they do not approve Conrad's depiction of non-Europeans, applaud his forceful anti-imperialism. D. C. R. A. Goonetilleke, a critic from Sri Lanka, has said, "Conrad belongs to the distinguished minority of radical contemporary critics of imperialism" [*Developing Countries in British Fiction*]. Wilson Harris, the Guyanese novelist, sees Conrad's novel as an attack on European liberalism itself. And C. Ponnuthurai Sarvan, in a detailed rebuttal to Achebe, writes, "Nor can Conrad's very forceful criticisms of colonialism be lightly passed over as weak liberalism" [*International Fiction Review,* 1980]. Conrad clearly expresses his condemnation of European exploitation and cruelty in such memorable scenes as the French ship firing into the continent, the chain-gang building the railway, and the contract-laborers languishing in the "grove of death."

A fourth defense of Conrad is that over against his seemingly negative statements about Africans, he in fact makes many quite positive comments. Achebe dismisses these comments, but to be fair, we must take them into account. As P. J. M. Robertson notes, Conrad praises Africans for their "energy, vitality, natural dignity." Kurtz's mistress is "superb . . . magnificent . . . stately." And the black paddlers off the coast have "a wild vitality, an intense energy of movement." At a deeper level, Conrad has Marlow commend the cannibals in his crew as "fine fellows . . . men one could work with." Moreover, they possess a mysterious inner restraint in not eating the whites on board even though they are starving. Thus, in a novel which is a relentless, sceptical inquiry into the basis of moral behavior, one which questions morality founded on principles or providence, the cannibals with their "inborn strength" provide one of the few signs of hope.

The other sign of hope is Marlow himself. Marlow (who may be more biased than Conrad) starts out thinking of the Africans as grotesque, horrid, ugly, and fiendish. In the course of the story, however, he develops a great deal of sympathy for them. Although he has little means of communication with Africans, he makes an effort to understand them and put himself in their place. He realizes that in Africa drums may have "as profound a meaning as the sound of bells in a Christian country," and he imagines how Englishmen would react if their country were invaded by African colonizers. Unlike Kurtz, Marlow resists the temptation to exploit Africans. Instead he does what little he can to help them by giving his biscuit to the man in the "grove of death" and by pulling his whistle so the "pilgrims" cannot slaughter Kurtz's followers. As a result of his experience, Marlow overcomes his prejudices enough to acknowledge the "claim of distant kinship" put upon him by his helmsman through their shared work and shared mortality. Thus Marlow comes to urge his audience to recognize "their humanity—like yours."

Such a recognition on the part of Marlow, and Conrad, was remarkable for his era. At the turn-of-the century many European intellectuals and politicians fully anticipated the extermination of the "inferior races." For example, the same year ***Heart of Darkness*** was written, Lord Curzon, then Undersecretary of State for Foreign Affairs, said, "From the necessities of politics . . . the living nations will gradually encroach on the dying" [*The Colonial Encounter*]. C. P. Sarvan has praised Conrad because, while he "was not entirely immune to the infection of the beliefs and attitudes of his age," he was "ahead of most in trying to break free." We must give Conrad his due by realizing that out of the hundreds of European reports emerging from the Congo in the 1890's, his was by far the most sympathetic to the Congolese.

A fifth, and final, defense of Conrad on the charge of racism is that he himself opposed it. His opposition is perhaps clearest in his Malayan novels where he shows nothing but contempt for white men who claim superiority solely on the basis of their skin color. The most striking example of such a man is Peter Willems in *An Outcast of the Islands.* When Willems falls in love with Omar's daughter, Aïssa, he feels he is "surrendering to a wild creature the unstained purity of his life, of his race, of his civilization." Later, after the love is gone, Willems cannot stand Aïssa's staring at him. He calls her eyes "the eyes of a savage; of a damned mongrel, half-Arab, half-Malay. They hurt me! I am white! I swear to you I can't stand this! Take me away. I am white! All white!"

Conrad's scorn for posturing Europeans in these novels is matched by his sympathy and respect for Malayans. With much greater experience of Asia than Africa, Conrad had the confidence to attempt detailed, rounded portraits of such characters as Mrs. Almayer, Lakamba, Babalatchi, Abdulla, Omar, Aïssa, Karain, Rajah Allang, Doramin, and Jewel. While not all of these characters are admirable, Conrad in every case shows an understanding of their suffering at the hands of Europeans and their subsequent anger. And the characters Dain Maroola, Dain Waris, Hassim, and Immada are among the most noble in Conrad's entire work. D. C. R. A. Goonetilleke has praised Conrad by saying, "His Malayan world is predominantly authentic in all its varied spheres. . . . He is able to rise above conventional Western prejudices." And Ezekiel Mphahlele, the black South African writer, says in considering *Almayer's Folly* and *An Outcast of the Islands,* "The three outstanding white novelists who portray competently characters belonging to cultural groups outside their own are Josef Conrad, E. M. Forster and William Faulkner" [*The African Image*]. Perhaps Conrad was not able to break entirely free from the racial biases and epithets of his age. But we should recognize his special status as one of the few writers of his period who struggled with the issue of race, and we should appreciate the remarkable fair-mindedness he achieved. (pp. 163-69)

Hunt Hawkins, "The Issue of Racism in Heart of Darkness," *in* Conradiana, *Vol. 14, No. 3, 1982, pp. 163-71.*

Patrick Brantlinger (essay date 1985)

[*In the following excerpt, Brantlinger examines the controversy surrounding* Heart of Darkness.]

In a 1975 lecture at the University of Massachusetts, Nigerian novelist Chinua Achebe attacked ***Heart of Darkness*** as "racist." Conrad "projects the image of Africa as 'the other world,' the antithesis of Europe and therefore of civilization, a place where man's vaunted intelligence and refinement are finally mocked by triumphant bestiality." Supposedly the great demystifier, Conrad is instead a "purveyor of comforting myths" and even "a bloody racist." Achebe adds: "That this simple truth is glossed over in criticisms of his work is due to the fact that white racism against Africa is such a normal way of thinking that its manifestations go completely undetected." Achebe would therefore like to strike Conrad's novella from the curriculum, where it has been one of the most frequently taught works of modern fiction in English classes from Chicago to Bombay to Johannesburg.

Achebe's diatribe has provoked a number of vigorous defenses of ***Heart of Darkness,*** which predictably stress Conrad's critical stance toward imperialism and also the wide acceptance of racist language and categories in the late Victorian period. Cedric Watts, for example, argues that "really Conrad and Achebe are on the same side" [*Yearbook of English Studies,* 1983]. Achebe simply gets carried away by his understandable aversion to racial stereotyping. "Far from being a 'purveyor of comforting myths,' " Watts declares, "Conrad most deliberately and incisively debunks such myths." Acknowledging that Conrad employed the stereotypic language common in his day, Watts contends that he nevertheless rose above racism:

> Achebe notes with indignation that Conrad (in the 'Author's Note' to *Victory*) speaks of an encounter with a 'buck nigger' in Haiti which gave him an impression of mindless violence. Achebe might as well have noted the reference in *The Nigger of the 'Narcissus'* . . . to a 'tormented and flattened face—a face pathetic and brutal: the tragic, the mysterious, the repulsive mask of a nigger's soul.' He might have noted, also, that Conrad's letters are sprinkled with casual anti-Semitic references. It is the same in the letters of his friend [R. B. Cunninghame] Graham. Both Conrad and Graham were influenced by the climate of prejudice of their times. . . . What is interesting is that the best work of both men seems to transcend such prejudice.

Their work "transcends prejudice," Watts believes, partly because they both attack imperialism. Watts is one of the many critics who interpret ***Heart of Darkness*** as an exposé of imperialist rapacity and violence. Kurtz's career in deviltry obviously undermines imperialist ideology, and the greed of the "faithless pilgrims"—the white sub-Kurtzes, so to speak—is perhaps worse. "The conquest of the earth," Marlow declares, "which mostly means the taking it away from those who have a different complexion or slightly flatter noses than ourselves, is not a pretty thing when you look into it too much." There is nothing equivocal about that remark; Conrad entertained no illusions about imperialist violence. But Marlow distinguishes between British imperialism and that of the other European powers: the red parts of the map are good to see, he says, "because one knows that some real work is done in there." ***Heart of Darkness*** is specifically about what Conrad saw in King Leopold's African empire in 1890; the extent to which his critique can be generalized to imperialism beyond the Congo is unclear.

The politics of Conrad's story are complicated by its ambiguous style. I will use "impressionism" as a highly inadequate term to refer to its language and narrative structure, in part because Fredric Jameson uses it in his diagnosis of the "schizophrenic" nature of *Lord Jim* [*The Political Unconscious: Narrative as a Socially Symbolic Act*]. Conrad's "impressionism" is for some critics his most praiseworthy quality, while for others it appears instead to be a means of obfuscation, allowing him to mask his "nihilism," or to maintain contradictory values, or both. Interpretations of ***Heart of Darkness*** which read it as only racist (and therefore imperialist), or conversely as only anti-imperialist (and therefore anti-racist), inevitably founder on its "impressionism." To point only to the most obvious difficulty, the narrative frame filters everything that is said not just through Marlow, but also through the anonymous primary narrator. At what point is it safe to assume that Conrad/Marlow express a single point of view? And even supposing that Marlow speaks directly for Conrad, does Conrad/Marlow agree with the values expressed by the primary narrator? Whatever the answers, ***Heart of Darkness,*** I believe, offers a powerful critique of at least certain manifestations of imperialism and racism, at the same time that it presents that critique in ways which can only be characterized as both imperialist and racist. "Impressionism" is the fragile skein of discourse which expresses—or disguises—this "schizophrenic" contradiction as an apparently harmonious whole.

In *Conrad and Imperialism,* Benita Parry argues that "by revealing the disjunctions between high-sounding rhetoric and sordid ambitions and indicating the purposes and goals of a civilisation dedicated to global . . . hegemony, Conrad's writings [are] more destructive of imperialism's ideological premises than [are] the polemics of his contemporary opponents of empire." Perhaps. It is at least certain that Conrad was appalled by the "high-sounding rhetoric" which had been used to mask the "sordid ambitions" of King Leopold II of Belgium, Conrad's ultimate employer during his six months in the Congo in 1890. ***Heart of Darkness*** expresses not only what Conrad saw and partially recorded in his "Congo Diary," but also the revelations of atrocities which began appearing in the British press as early as 1888 and which reached a climax twenty years later, when in 1908 the mounting scandal forced the Belgian government to take control of Leopold's private domain. During that period the population of the Congo was reduced by perhaps one half; as many as 6,000,000 persons may have been uprooted, tortured, and murdered through the forced labor system used to extract ivory and what reformers called "red rubber" from "the heart of darkness." Conrad was sympathetic to the Congo Reform Association, established in 1903 partly by his friend Roger Casement whom he had met in Africa, and Casement got him to write a propaganda letter in which Conrad says: "It is an extraordinary thing that the conscience of Europe which seventy years ago . . . put down the slave trade on humanitarian grounds tolerates the Congo state today." There follows some patronizing language contrasting the brutalities visited upon the Congolese with the legal protections given to horses in Europe, but Conrad's intention is clear enough.

There is little to add to Hunt Hawkins' account of Conrad's relations with the Congo Reform Association. Its leader, Edmund Morel, who quoted Conrad's letter to Casement in *King Leopold's Rule in Africa* (1904), called ***Heart of Darkness*** the "most powerful thing ever written on the subject." But as Hawkins notes, apart from writing the letter to Casement, Conrad backed away from involvement with the Association. Other prominent novelists who'd never been to the Congo contributed as much or more to its work. Mark Twain volunteered "King Leopold's Soliloquy," and Sir Arthur Conan Doyle wrote a book for the Association called *The Crime of the Congo.* Hawkins notes that Conrad "had little faith in agitation for political reform because words were meaningless, human nature unimprovable, and the universe dying"—hardly views that would encourage engagement in a cause like that of the Association [*PMLA,* 1979].

All the same, in at least one other work of fiction Conrad registered his abhorrence of King Leopold's rape of the Congo. This is the minor but highly revealing fantasy which Conrad co-authored with Ford Madox Hueffer, *The Inheritors: An Extravagant Story* (1901). Conrad's role in its writing may have been slight, but was still substantial enough to make plain that he shared the views expressed in it. Briefly, the protagonist meets a beautiful young woman who claims to come from the "fourth dimension" and to be one of those who "shall inherit the earth."

> The Dimensionists were to come in swarms, to materialise, to devour like locusts. . . . They were to come like snow in the night: in the morning one would look out and find the world white. . . . As to methods, we should be treated as we ourselves treat the inferior races.

Far from being meek, the "inheritors" are obviously modern-day imperialists, satirically depicted as invaders from a "spiritualist" alternative world. But apart from the young woman and one other character, the invasion does not occur during the course of the novel, although the satire upon imperialism is maintained through the portrayal of the Duc de Mersch and his "System for the Regeneration of the Arctic Regions." Like King Leopold, "the foreign financier—they called him the Duc de Mersch—was by way of being a philanthropist on megalomaniac lines." He proves ultimately to be no philanthropist at all, but just the sort of "gigantic and atrocious fraud" that Conrad believed Leopold to be. All one needs to do to read *The Inheritors* as an attack on Leopold's African regime is to substitute "Congo" for "Greenland." The hero, journalist Arthur Granger, helps to expose "the real horrors of the système Groënlandais—flogged, butchered, miserable natives, the famines, the vices, diseases, and the crimes." The authors are not even particular about the color of the eskimo victims: one character says that the Duc "has the blacks murdered."

Hueffer and Conrad write some scorching things in *The Inheritors* about "cruelty to the miserable, helpless, and defenceless." But the facts of exploitation in the Congo are perhaps less distressing to them than the lying idealism which disguises it:

> More revolting to see without a mask was that falsehood which had been hiding under the words which for ages had spurred men to noble deeds, to self-sacrifice, to heroism. What was appalling was . . . that all the traditional ideals of honour, glory, conscience, had been committed to the upholding of a gigantic and atrocious fraud. The falsehood had spread stealthily, had eaten into the very heart of creeds and convictions that we learn upon our passage between the past and the future. The old order of things had to live or perish with a lie.

I will come back to the possibility that the worst feature of imperialism for Conrad may not have been its violence toward the "miserable" and "helpless," but the lying propaganda used to cover its bloody tracks.

As Hawkins and others have pointed out, Conrad did not base his critique of imperialist exploitation in ***Heart of Darkness*** solely on what he had seen in the Congo. What he witnessed was miserable enough, and he was also made personally miserable and resentful by disease and the conviction that his Belgian employers were exploiting him. But, as he assured Casement, while in the Congo he had not even heard of "the alleged custom of cutting off hands among the natives." The conclusion that Casement drew from this and other evidence was that most of the cruelties practiced in the Congo were not traditional, but were the recent effects of exploitation. The cutting off of hands was a punishment for noncooperation in Leopold's forced labor system, and probably became frequent only after 1890. And just as Conrad had seen little or no evidence of torture, so, Molly Mahood conjectures [in *The Colonial Encounter*], he probably saw little or no evidence of cannibalism, despite the stress upon it in his story.

It thus seems likely that much of the "horror" either depicted or suggested in ***Heart of Darkness*** does not represent what Conrad saw, but rather his reading of the literature which exposed Leopold's bloody system between the time of his return to England and the composition of the novella in 1898-99. While Conrad's "Congo Diary" and every facet of his journey to Stanley Falls and back has been scrutinized by Norman Sherry and others, much less attention has been paid to what Conrad learned about the Congo after his sojourn there. The exposé literature undoubtedly confirmed suspicions which Conrad formed in 1890; the bloodiest period in the history of Leopold's regime began about a year later. According to Edmund Morel [in *King Leopold's Rule*]: "From 1890 onwards the records of the Congo State have been literally blood-soaked. Even at that early date, the real complexion of Congo State philanthropy was beginning to appear, but public opinion in Europe was then in its hoodwinked stage."

The two events which did most to bring Leopold's Congo under public scrutiny after Conrad's time there were the 1891-94 war between Leopold's forces and the Arab slave-traders and the murder of Charles Stokes, English citizen and renegade missionary, by Belgian officials in 1895. The conflict with the Arabs—a "war of extermination," according to Morel—was incredibly cruel and bloody. "The first serious collision with the Arabs occurred in October 27, 1891; the second on May 6, 1892. Battle then succeeded battle; Nyangwe, the Arab stronghold, was captured in January, 1893, and with the surrender of Rumaliza in January, 1894, the campaign came to an end." Conrad undoubtedly read about these events in the press and perhaps also in later accounts, notably Captain Sidney Hinde's *The Fall of the Congo Arabs* (1897). Arthur Hodister, whom Sherry claims as the original of Kurtz, was an early victim of the fighting, having led an expedition to Katanga which was crushed by the Arabs. According to Ian Watt, "*The Times* reported of Hodister and his comrades that 'their heads were stuck on poles and their bodies eaten' " [*Conrad in the Nineteenth Century*]. This and many similar episodes during the war are probable sources of Conrad's emphasis upon cannibalism in ***Heart of Darkness.***

Cannibalism was practiced by both sides in the war, not just the Arabs and their Congolese soldiers. According to Hinde, who must also be counted among the possible models for Kurtz, "The fact that both sides were cannibals, or rather that both sides had cannibals in their train, proved a great element in our success." Muslims, Hinde points out, believe that they will go to heaven only if their bodies are intact, as opposed to multilated, chopped up, eaten. So cannibalism was in part a weapon of fear and reprisal on both sides, and in part also a traditional accompaniment of war among some Congolese societies. Hinde speaks of combatants on both sides as "human wolves" and describes numerous "disgusting banquets." A typical passage in his account reads: "What struck me most in these expeditions was the number of partially cut-up bodies I found in every direction for miles around. Some were minus the hands and feet, and some with steaks cut from the thighs or elsewhere; others had the entrails or the head removed, according to the taste of the individual savage. . . . " Hinde's descriptions of such atrocities seem to be those of an impartial, external observer, but in fact he was one of six white officers in charge of some four hundred "regulars" and "about 25,000" "cannibal" troops. His expressions of horror seem only what are expected of an Englishman, but they are also those of a participant and contradict more honest expressions of sadistic fascination with every bloodthirsty detail.

While it seems likely that Conrad read Hinde's lurid account, he must have known about the war from earlier accounts such as those in *The Times.* To cite one other example, in a series of journal extracts published in the *The Century Magazine* in 1896-97, E. J. Glave documented "cruelty in the Congo Free State." According to Glave, "The state has not suppressed slavery, but established a monopoly by driving out the Arab and Wangwana competitors." Instead of a noble war to end the slave trade, which is how Leopold and his agents justified their actions against the Arabs, a new system of slavery was installed in place of the old. Glave continues: "sometimes the natives are so persecuted that they [take revenge] by killing and eating their tormentors. Recently the state post on the Lomami lost two men killed and eaten by the natives. Arabs were sent to punish the natives; many women and children were taken, and twenty-one heads were brought to [Stanley Falls], and have been used by Captain Rom as a decoration round a flower-bed in front of his house." Captain Rom, no doubt, must also be counted among the possible models for Kurtz. In any event, the practice of seizing Congolese for laborers and chopping off the hands and heads of resisters continued and probably increased after the defeat of the Arabs, as numerous eyewitnesses testify in the grisly quotations which form the bulk of Edmund Morel's exposés. According to a quite typical account by a Swiss observer: "If the chief does not bring the stipulated number of baskets [of raw rubber], soldiers are sent out, and the people are killed without mercy. As proof, parts of the body are brought to the factory. How often have I watched heads and hands being carried into the factory."

When Marlow declares that "the conquest of the earth . . . is not a pretty thing," he goes on to suggest that imperialism may be "redeemed" by the "idea" which lies behind it. But in the real world idealism is fragile, and in ***Heart of Darkness,*** except for the illusions maintained by a few womenfolk back in Brussels, it has almost died out. In "going native," Kurtz betrays the "civilizing" ideals with which he supposedly set out from Europe. Among the "faithless pilgrims," there are only false ideals and the false religion of self-seeking. "To tear treasure out of the bowels of the land was their desire," says Marlow, "with no more moral purpose at the back of it than there is in burglars breaking into a safe." The true nature of European philanthropy in the Congo is revealed to Marlow by the chain gang and the "black shadows of disease and starvation," left to die in the "greenish gloom," whom he sees at the Outer Station. These miserable "phantoms" are probably accurate depictions of what Conrad saw in 1890; they may also be taken to represent what he later learned about Leopold's forced labor system. In any case, from the moment he sets foot in the Congo, Marlow is clear about the meaning of "the merry dance of death and trade." It thus makes perfect sense to interpret ***Heart of Darkness*** as an attack on imperialism, at least as it was operative in the Congo.

But in the course of this attack, *all* "ideals" threaten to turn into "idols"—"something," in Marlow's words, which "you can set up, and bow down before, and offer a sacrifice to." Conrad universalizes "darkness" partly by universalizing fetishism. Lenin, Rosa Luxemburg, and other Marxist critics of empire described the era of "the scramble for Africa"—roughly 1880 to 1914—as one when the "commodity fetishism" of "late capitalism" was most intense, a notion which Edward Said touches upon in analyzing *The Nigger of the 'Narcissus.'* If the "natives" in their darkness set Kurtz up as an idol, the Europeans worship ivory, money, power, reputation. Kurtz joins the "natives" in their "unspeakable rites," worshipping his own unrestrained power and lust. Marlow himself assumes the pose of an idol, sitting on shipdeck with folded legs and outward palms like a Buddha. And Kurtz's Intended is perhaps the greatest fetishist of all, idolizing her image of her fiance. Marlow's lie leaves Kurtz's Intended shrouded in the protective darkness of her illusions, her idol-worship.

But the difficulty with this ingenious inversion, through which "ideals" become "idols," is that Conrad portrays the moral bankruptcy of imperialism by showing European motives and actions to be no better than African fetishism and savagery. He paints Kurtz and Africa with the same tarbrush. His version of evil—the form taken by Kurtz's Satanic behavior—is "going native." In short, evil *is* African in Conrad's story; if it is also European, that's because some number of white men in the heart of darkness behave like Africans. Conrad's stress on cannibalism, his identification of African customs with violence, lust, and madness, his metaphors of bestiality, death, and darkness, his suggestion that traveling in Africa is like traveling backward in time to primeval, infantile, but also hellish stages of existence—these features of the story are drawn from the repertoire of Victorian imperialism and racism that painted an entire continent dark.

Achebe is therefore right to call Conrad's portrayal of Africa and Africans "racist." It is possible to argue, as does Parry, that Conrad works with the white-and-black, light-and-darkness dichotomies of racist fantasy in order to subvert them, but she acknowledges that the subversion is incomplete: "Although the resonances of white are rendered discordant . . . black and dark do serve in the text as equivalences for the savage and unredeemed, the corrupt and degraded . . . the cruel and atrocious. Imperialism itself is perceived as the dark within Europe. . . . Yet despite . . . momentous departures from traditional European usage . . . the fiction gravitates back to established practice, registering the view of two incompatible orders within a manichean universe." The "imperialist imagination" itself, Parry suggests, works with the "manichean," irreconcilable polarities common to all racist ideology. Achebe states the issue more succinctly: "Conrad had a problem with niggers. . . . Sometimes his fixation on blackness is . . . overwhelming."

Identifying specific sources for Conrad's later knowledge of the horrors of Leopold's regime is less important than recognizing that there were numerous sources, swelling in number through the 1890s. Conrad reshaped his firsthand experience of the Congo in the light of these sources in several ways. As I have already suggested, the emphasis on cannibalism in ***Heart of Darkness*** probably derives in part from Conrad's reading about the war between Leopold's agents and the Arabs. At the same time, the war is not mentioned in the novella—indeed, the Arab rivals of the Belgians for control of the Congo are conspicuous only by their absence. The omission has the important effect of sharpening the light-and-dark dichotomies, the staple of European racism; "evil" and "darkness" are parceled out between only two antithetical sides, European and African, "white" and "black." But while Conrad/Marlow treats the attribution of "evil" to the European invaders as a paradox, its attribution to Africans he treats as a given. Further, the omission of the Arabs means that Conrad does not treat cannibalism as a result of war, but as an everyday custom of the Congolese, even though he probably saw no evidence of it when he was there. Exaggerating the extent and nature of cannibalism is also standard in racist accounts of Africa.

In simplifying his memories and sources, Conrad arrived at the dichotomous or "manichean" pattern of the imperialist adventure romance, a pattern radically at odds with any realist, exposé intention. Perhaps ***Heart of Darkness*** expresses two irreconcilable intentions. As Parry says, "to proffer an interpretation of ***Heart of Darkness*** as a militant denunciation and a reluctant affirmation of imperialist civilisation, as a fiction that [both] exposes and colludes in imperialism's mystifications, is to recognise its immanent contradictions." Moreover, the argument that Conrad was consciously anti-imperialist, but that he unconsciously or carelessly employed the racist terminology current in his day will not stand up, because he was acutely aware of what he was doing. Every white-black and light-dark contrast in the story, whether it corroborates racist assumptions or subverts them, is precisely calculated for its effects both as a unit in a scheme of imagery and as a focal point in a complex web of contradictory political and moral values.

Conrad knew that his story was ambiguous: he stresses that ambiguity at every opportunity, so that labeling it "anti-imperialist" is as unsatisfactory as condemning it for being "racist." The fault-line for all of the contradictions and ambiguities in the text lies between Marlow and Kurtz. Of course it also lies between Conrad and both of his ambivalent characters, not to mention the anonymous primary narrator. Is Marlow Kurtz's antagonist, critic, and potential redeemer? Or is he Kurtz's pale shadow and admirer, his double, and finally one more idolator in a story full of examples of fetishism and devil worship? Conrad poses these questions with great care, but he just as carefully refuses to answer them.

In the world of ***Heart of Darkness,*** there are no clear answers. Ambiguity, perhaps the main form of "darkness" in the story, prevails. Conrad overlays the political and moral content of his novella with symbolic and mythic patterns which divert attention from Kurtz and the Congo to "misty halos" and "moonshine." The anonymous narrator uses these metaphors to describe the difference between Marlow's stories and those of ordinary sailors:

> The yarns of seamen have a direct simplicity, the whole meaning of which lies within the shell of a cracked nut. But Marlow was typical . . . and to him the meaning of an episode was not inside like a kernel but outside, enveloping the tale which brought it out only as a glow brings out a haze, in the likeness of one of these misty halos that sometimes are made visible by the spectral illumination of moonshine.

The passage announces that locating the "meaning" of the story won't be easy, and in fact may be impossible. It seems almost to be a confession of defeat, or at least of contradiction. Conrad here establishes as one of his themes the problem of rendering any judgment whatsoever—moral, political, metaphysical—about Marlow's narrative. It is precisely this complexity—a theme that might be labeled the dislocation of meaning or the disorientation of values in the story—which many critics have treated as its finest feature.

In *The Political Unconscious,* Fredric Jameson argues that Conrad's stories—*Lord Jim* is his main example—betray a symptomatic split between a modernist "will to style," leading to an elaborate but essentially hollow "impressionism," and the reified, mass culture tendencies of romance conventions. In a fairly obvious way, ***Heart of Darkness*** betrays the same split, moving in one direction toward the "misty halos" and "moonshine" of a style which seeks to be its own meaning, apart from any "kernel" or center or embarrasingly clear content, but also grounding itself in another direction in the conventions of Gothic romance with their devalued mass culture status—conventions which were readily adapted to the heroic adventure themes of imperialist propaganda. This split almost corresponds to the contradiction of an anti-imperialist novel which is also racist. In the direction of high style, the story acquires several serious purposes, apparently including its critique of empire. In the direction of reified mass culture, it falls into the stereotypic patterns of race-thinking common to the entire tradition of the imperialist adventure story or quest romance. This double, contradictory purpose, characteristic perhaps of all of Conrad's fiction, Jameson calls "schizophrenic."

By "the manichaeanism of the imperialist imagination," Parry means dividing the world between "warring moral forces"—good versus evil, civilization versus savagery, West versus East, light versus darkness, white versus black. Such polarizations are the common property of the racism and authoritarianism which constitute imperialist political theory and also of the Gothic romance conventions which were appropriated by numerous writers of imperialist adventure tales—G. A. Henty, Rider Haggard, Robert Louis Stevenson, Conan Doyle, John Buchan, Rudyard Kipling, and Conrad among them. As Martin Green points out [in *Dreams of Adventure*], "Conrad of course offers us an ironic view of that genre. But he affirms its value." Conrad is simultaneously a critic of the imperialist adventure and its romantic fictions, and one of the greatest writers of such fictions, his greatness deriving partly from his critical irony and partly from the complexity of his style—his "impressionism." But the chief difficulty with Jameson's argument, I think, is that the "will to style" in Conrad's text is also a will to appropriate and remake Gothic romance conventions into high art. On some level, the "impressionism" of Conrad's novels and their romance features are identical—Conrad constructs a sophisticated version of the imperialist romance—and in any case both threaten to submerge or "derealize" the critique of empire within their own more strictly esthetic project. As part of that project, providing much of the substance of "impressionism," the romance conventions which Conrad reshapes carry with them the polarizations of racist thought.

In analyzing Conrad's "schizophrenic writing," Jameson notes the proliferation of often contradictory critical opinions which mark the history of his reception: "The discontinuities objectively present in Conrad's narratives have, as with few other modern writers, projected a bewildering variety of competing and incommensurable interpretive options. . . . " Jameson proceeds to list nine different critical approaches, from "the 'romance' or mass-cultural reading of Conrad as a writer of adventure tales [and] the stylistic analysis of Conrad as a practitioner of . . . [an] 'impressionistic' will to style," to the "myth-critical," the Freudian, the ethical, the "ego-psychological," the existential, the Nietzschean, and the structuralist readings. Jameson leaves off of the list his own Marxist-political reading; what he wishes to suggest is how often criticism ignores or downplays the contradictory politics of Conrad's fiction. Raymond Williams voices a similar complaint [in *The English Novel from Dickens to Lawrence*]:

> It is . . . astonishing that a whole school of criticism has succeeded in emptying ***Heart of Darkness*** of its social and historical content. . . . The Congo of Leopold follows the sea that Dom-

> bey and Son traded across, follows it into an endless substitution in which no object is itself, no social experience direct, but everything is translated into what can be called a metaphysical language—the river is Evil; the sea is Love or Death. Yet only called metaphysical, because there is not even that much guts in it. No profound and ordinary belief, only a perpetual and sophisticated evasion. . . .

There are wonderfully elaborate readings of Marlow's journey as a descent into hell, playing upon Conrad's frequent allusions to Homer, Virgil, Dante, Milton, Goethe, and devil worship. And there are just as many elaborate readings of the story as an "inward voyage" of "self-discovery," in which its geopolitical language is treated as symbolizing psychological states and parts of the mind. Conrad, Albert Guerard reminds us [in *Conrad the Novelist*], was Freud's contemporary, and in ***Heart of Darkness*** he produced the quintessential "right journey into the unconscious." Guerard adds that "it little matters what, in terms of psychological symbolism, we . . . say [Kurtz] represents: whether the Freudian id or the Jungian shadow or more vaguely the outlaw." Perhaps it matters just as little whether we say the story takes place in Leopold's Congo or in some purely imaginary landscape.

The point, however, is not to take issue with Guerard and other critics who concentrate on the "impressionism" of Conrad's story, but rather to restore what their readings neglect. In a great deal of contemporary criticism, words themselves have ceased to have external referents. Williams does not take Jameson's line in accusing Conrad's "will to style" of emptying ***Heart of Darkness*** of its "social and historical content"; instead, he accuses criticism of so emptying it. The "will to style"—or rather the will to a rarefied critical intelligence—devours us, too, leaving structuralists and deconstructionists, Althusserians and Foucauldians, and so forth. And yet Conrad has anticipated his critics by constructing a story in which the "meaning" does not lie at the center, not even at "the heart of darkness," but elsewhere, in "misty halos" and "moonshine"—forever beyond some vertiginous horizon which recedes as the would-be critic-adventurer sails toward it.

[In *Red Rubber,* E. D. Morel writes]:

> The crowds [in one village] were fired into promiscuously, and fifteen were killed, including four women and a babe on its mother's breast. The heads were cut off and brought to the officer in charge, who then sent me to cut off the hands also, and these were pierced, strung, and dried over the camp fire. The heads, with many others, I saw myself. The town, prosperous once, was burnt, and what they could not carry off was destroyed. Crowds of people were caught, mostly . . . women, and three fresh rope gangs were added. These poor 'prisoner' gangs were mere skeletons of skin and bone. . . . Chiyombo's very large town was next attacked. A lot of people were killed, and heads and hands cut off and taken back to the officers. . . . Shortly after the State caravans, with flags flying and bugles blowing, entered the mission station at Luanza . . . and I shall not soon forget the sickening sight of deep baskets of human heads.

While the primary narrator and many critics seem to believe that the meaning of ***Heart of Darkness*** lies in "the spectral illumination of moonshine," Marlow knows better. "Illumination" proves as false as most white men—as false as white "civilization"; the "truth," or at least the meaning of Conrad's story, lies in "darkness." That is why, once Marlow learns about the shadowy Kurtz, he is so impatient to get to the Central Station. And yet Kurtz seems inadequate as a central character or the goal of Marlow's quest—vacuous, a mere "shade," a "hollow man." That, however, may be part of Conrad's point. Ian Watt has identified at least nine possible models for Kurtz, including Henry Morton Stanley, Arthur Hodister, and Charles Stokes, who left the Church Missionary Society for an African wife and life as a gun-runner and slave-trader. In 1895 Stokes was executed in the Congo for selling guns to the Arabs, an event which, close on the heels of the war, provided a focus for British public indignation. To Watt's list of models for Kurtz I have already added Captain Hinde, author of *The Fall of the Congo Arabs,* and Captain Rom, who decorated the borders of his flower garden with skulls. The Belgian officer responsible for Stokes's illegal execution, Captain Lothaire, must also be counted.

But just as Conrad probably drew upon many sources in depicting the horrors of the Congo, so he probably had many models for Kurtz in mind. *All* of the white officers in charge of Leopold's empire were in essence Kurtzes, as the eyewitness testimony published by the Congo Reform Association demonstrates. And what about the eyewitnesses? Were they always so objective or so morally appalled as they claimed to be? What about Conrad himself? Although his role in the building of Leopold's "Congo Free State" was minor and also prior to the worst horrors, Conrad must have recognized his own complicity and seen himself as at least potentially a Kurtz-like figure. In the novella, the African wilderness serves as a mirror, in whose "darkness" Conrad/Marlow sees a death-pale self-image.

The massive evidence of wholesale torture and slaughter under the direction of Leopold's white agents suggests not only that there were numerous Kurtzes in the "heart of darkness," but also that, as Hannah Arendt contends in *The Origins of Totalitarianism,* nineteenth-century imperialism prepared the ground in which fascism and Nazism took root after World War I. Arendt has Kurtz and other Conrad characters in mind when she describes the appeal of "the phantom world of colonial adventure" to certain types of Europeans:

> Outside all social restraint and hypocrisy, against the backdrop of native life, the gentleman and the criminal felt not only the closeness of men who share the same color of skin, but the impact of a world of infinite possibilities for crimes committed in the spirit of play, for the combination of horror and laughter, that is for the full realization of their own phantom-like existence. Native life lent these ghostlike events a seeming guarantee against all consequences because anyhow it looked to these men like a "mere play of shadows. A play of shadows, the dominant race could walk through unaffected

> and disregarded in the pursuit of its incomprehensible aims and needs." The world of native savages was a perfect setting for men who had escaped the reality of civilization.

A great many Kurtz-like Europeans "went native" in Africa, often to the extent of practicing genocide as a hobby; some were even rumored to practice cannibalism. According to Sir Harry H. Johnston, first governor of British Central Africa, "I have been increasingly struck with the rapidity with which such members of the white race as are not of the best class, can throw over the restraints of civilization and develop into savages of unbridled lust and abominable cruelty." [*British Central Africa.*] Kurtz is not a member of the *worst* "class" of the white race, however; Conrad is talking about a quite common pattern of behavior.

One of the most remarkable perversions of the criticism of ***Heart of Darkness*** has been to see Kurtz not as an abomination—a "hollow man" with a lust for blood and domination—but as a "hero of the spirit." That phrase is Lionel Trilling's. In his well-known essay describing the establishment of the first course in modern literature at Columbia University, Trilling explains why he put Conrad's novella on the reading list:

> Whether or not . . . Conrad read either Blake or Nietzsche I do not know, but his ***Heart of Darkness*** follows in their line. This very great work has never lacked for the admiration it deserves, and it has been given a . . . canonical place in the legend of modern literature by Eliot's having it so clearly in mind when he wrote *The Waste Land* and his having taken from it the epigraph to "The Hollow Men." [*Beyond Culture: Essays on Literature and Learning*]

Despite the "hollow man" association between Eliot's poem and Conrad's novella, Trilling claims that "no one, to my knowledge, has ever confronted in an explicit way [the latter's] strange and terrible message of ambivalence toward the life of civilization." In *Sincerity and Authenticity,* Trilling adds that Conrad's story is "the paradigmatic literary expression of the modern concern with authenticity," and continues: "This troubling work has no manifest polemical content but it contains in sum the whole of the radical critique of European civilization that has been made by [modern] literature."

Although Trilling mentions the Congolese background of the story, it is less important to him than the larger question of the nature of "European civilization." Marlow's quest for Kurtz becomes a quest for the truth about that civilization. Trilling arrives at his view of Kurtz partly the way Marlow does, because Kurtz at the end of his satanic career seems to confront "the horror, the horror." "For Marlow," says Trilling, "Kurtz is a hero of the spirit whom he cherishes as Theseus at Colonus cherished Oedipus: he sinned for all mankind. By his regression to savagery Kurtz had reached as far down beneath the constructs of civilization as it was possible to go, to the irreducible truth of man, the innermost core of his nature, his heart of darkness. From that Stygian authenticity comes illumination. . . . "

Marlow does paradoxically come to admire Kurtz because he has "summed up" or "judged" in his final moments: "He was a remarkable man." Marlow's admiration for Kurtz, however, carries a terrific burden of irony which Trilling seems not to recognize. Kurtz has not merely lost faith in civilization and therefore experimented with "Stygian authenticity"—he is also a murderer, perhaps even a cannibal. He has allowed his idolators to make human sacrifices in his honor and, like Captain Rom, has decorated his corner of hell with the skulls of his victims. I suspect that Trilling arrives at his own evaluation of Kurtz as a "hero of the spirit" in part because he himself does not find "the horror" all that horrible, even though the deaths of 6,000,000 Congolese is a high price to pay for the "illumination" of "Stygian authenticity." But Trilling's interpretation of Kurtz's dying words—"the horror, the horror"—does not take account of what transpired in Leopold's Congo. "For me it is still ambiguous whether Kurtz's famous deathbed cry refers to the approach of death or to his experience of savage life."

According to Trilling's view, either Kurtz thinks death "the horror," or Kurtz thinks African "savagery" "the horror." There is another possibility, of course, which is that Kurtz's dying words are an outcry against himself—against his betrayal of civilization and his Intended, against the smash-up of his early hopes, and also against his bloody domination of the people he has been lording it over. No one would ever mistake Conrad's other traitors to civilization as "heroes of the spirit." I am thinking, for example, of Willems who goes wrong and then "goes native" in *An Outcast of the Islands,* or of the ironically sympathetic murderer Leggatt in **"The Secret Sharer."** Even Lord Jim is no "hero of the spirit," but a moral cripple who manages to regain a semblance of self-respect only after fleeing to Patusan. But how was it possible for Trilling to look past Kurtz's criminal record and identify "the horror" either with the fear of death or with African "savagery"? Achebe gives part of the answer: "white racism against Africa is such a normal way of thinking that its manifestations go completely undetected"—so normal that acts which are condemned as the vilest of crimes when committed in the supposedly civilized West can be linked to a "heroism of the spirit" and to "Stygian authenticity" when committed in Africa against Africans.

But the other part of the answer, it seems to me, is that Trilling is right. Conrad himself identifies with and ironically admires Kurtz. He, too, sees him as a "hero of the spirit," although "the spirit" for Conrad is perhaps not what Trilling thinks it is. For Conrad, Kurtz's heroism consists in staring into an abyss of nihilism so total that the issues of imperialism and racism pale into insignificance. It hardly matters if the abyss is of Kurtz's making. No more than Trilling or perhaps most Western critics, I think, did Conrad concern himself deeply about "unspeakable rites" and skulls on posts. These appear in Marlow's account like so many melodrama props—the evidence of Kurtz's decline and fall, yes—but it is still Kurtz who has center stage, with whom Marlow speaks, who is the goal and farthest point of the journey. Kurtz's black victims and idolators skulking in the bushes are also so many melodrama props.

Kurtz is not only the hero of the melodrama, he is an artist, a "universal genius," and a quite powerful, eloquent "voice" as well. As Achebe points out, the African characters are, in contrast, rendered almost without intelligible language. The headman of Marlow's cannibal crew gets in a few phrases of Pidgin-minstrelese, something about eating some fellow Africans. These are the black Kurtz worshippers, shrieking and groaning incoherently in the foggy shrubbery along the river. Kurtz's "superb and savage" mistress, though described in glowing detail, is given no voice, but in spite of this I like to imagine that she, at least, entertained no illusions about Kurtz or about imperialism, unlike the prim, palefaced knitters of black wool back in Brussels. "It's queer how out of touch with truth women are" says Marlow, but of course he means *white* women. Kurtz's black mistress knows all; it's just unfortunate that Marlow did not ask her for an interview.

The voices which come from the "heart of darkness" are almost exclusively white and male. As a nearly disembodied, pure "voice" emanating from the very center of the story, Kurtz is a figure for the novelist, as is his double Marlow. True, the "voice" which speaks out of the "heart of darkness" is a hollow one, the voice of the abyss; but Marlow still talks of Kurtz's "unextinguishable gift of noble and lofty expression." The "voice" of Kurtz has "electrified large meetings," and through it Kurtz "could get himself to believe anything—anything." Is Conrad questioning or mocking his own "voice," his own talent for fiction-making, for lying? Is he aware that the "will to style," his own tendency to "impressionism," points toward the production of novels which are hollow at the core—which can justify any injustice—which contain, perhaps, only an abyss, a Kurtz, "the horror, the horror"? Yes, I think so. It is just this hollow "voice," so devious and egotistical, so capable of self-deception and lying propaganda, which speaks from the center of "the heart of darkness" to "sum up" and to "judge."

Besides a painter, musician, orator, and "universal genius," Kurtz is also, like Conrad, a writer. What he writes can be seen as an analogue for the story and also its dead center, the kernel of meaning or non-meaning within its cracked shell. True, Kurtz has not written much, only seventeen pages, but "it was a beautiful piece of writing." This is his pamphlet for the "International Society for the Suppression of Savage Customs," which Marlow describes as "eloquent, vibrating with eloquence, but too high-strung, I think":

> The opening paragraph . . . in the light of later information, strikes me now as ominous. He began with the argument that we whites, from the point of development we had arrived at, 'must necessarily appear to [savages] in the nature of supernatural beings—we approach them with the might as of a deity,' and so on, and so on. 'By the simple exercise of our will we can exert a power for good practically unbounded,' etc., etc. From that point he soared and took me with him. The peroration was magnificent, though difficult to remember, you know. It gave me the notion of an exotic Immensity ruled by an august Benevolence. It made me tingle with enthusiasm. This was the unbounded power of eloquence. [And here I will add, "This was the unbounded will to style."] There were no practical hints to interrupt the magic current of phrases, unless a kind of note at the foot of the last page, scrawled evidently much later, in an unsteady hand, may be regarded as the exposition of a method. It was very simple, and at the end of that moving appeal to every altruistic sentiment it blazed at you, luminous and terrifying, like a flash of lightning in a serene sky: 'Exterminate all the brutes!'

Viewed one way, Conrad's anti-imperialist story condemns the murderous racism of Kurtz's imperative. Viewed another way, Conrad's racist story voices that very imperative, and Conrad knows it. At the hollow center of ***Heart of Darkness,*** far from the "misty halos" and "moonshine" where the meaning supposedly resides, Conrad inscribes a text which, like the novel itself, cancels out its own best intentions.

But now Kurtz's dying words can be seen as something more than an outcry of guilt, and certainly more than a mere expression of the fear of death or of loathing for African "savagery." They can be seen as referring to the sort of lying idealism which can rationalize any behavior, to a complete separation between words and meaning, theory and practice—perhaps to the "impressionistic" deviousness of art and language themselves. On this metaphysical level, I think, Conrad ceases to worry about the atrocities committed in the Congo and identifies with Kurtz as a fellow-artist, a "hero of the spirit" of that nihilism which Conrad himself found so attractive.

On several occasions, Conrad compared the artist with the empire builder in a way that obviously runs counter to his critique of imperialism in ***Heart of Darkness.*** In *A Personal Record,* Conrad writes of "that interior world where [the novelist's] thought and . . . emotions go seeking for . . . imagined adventures," and where "there are no policemen, no law, no pressure of circumstance or dread opinion to keep him within bounds." And in the first manuscript of **"The Rescuer,"** which as John McLure points out [in *Kipling and Conrad: The Colonial Fiction*] contains "by far" Conrad's "most sympathetic" treatment of imperialism, empire-builders are "one of those unknown guides of civilization, who on the advancing edge of progress are administrators, warriors, creators. . . . They are like great artists a mystery to the masses, appreciated only by the uninfluential few." Kurtz is empire-builder, artist, universal genius, and voice crying from the wilderness all in one. But he has lost the faith—vision or illusion—which can alone sustain an empire and produce great art. Nihilism is no basis upon which to found or administer a colony, and it is also no basis on which to write a novel, and again Conrad knows it. In suggesting his affinity to Kurtz, he suggests the moral bankruptcy of his own literary project. But once there were empire-builders and great artists who kept the faith. Conrad frequently expresses his admiration for the great explorers and adventurers, from Sir Walter Raleigh and Sir Francis Drake through James Brooke, the white rajah of Sarawak, and David Livingstone, the greatest of the many great explorers of the "Dark Continent."

Conrad's critique of empire is never strictly anti-imperialist. Instead, in terms that can be construed as conservative rather than nihilistic, he mourns the loss of the true faith in modern times, the closing down of frontiers, the narrowing of the possibilities for adventure, the commercialization of the world and of art, the death of chivalry and honor. Here the meaning of his emphasis on the lying propaganda of modern imperialism becomes evident. What was once a true, grand, noble, albeit violent enterprise is now "a gigantic and atrocious fraud"—except maybe, Marlow thinks, in the red parts of the map, where "some real work is done." Staring into the abyss of his life, or at least of Kurtz's life, Conrad sees in his disillusionment, his nihilism, the type of the whole—the path of disintegration which is modern history. It is not just Africa or even just Kurtz who possesses a "heart of darkness"; Conrad's story bears that title as well.

But I am not going to end by announcing in "a tone of scathing contempt" the death of Conrad's story as a classic, like the insolent manager's boy announcing: "Mistah Kurtz—he dead." I agree with Trilling that "authenticity," truth-telling, so far from being a negligible literary effect, is the essence of great literature. The fact that there are almost no other works of British fiction written before World War I which are critical of imperialism, and hundreds of imperialist ones which are racist through and through, is a measure of Conrad's achievement. I do not believe, moreover, that the real strength of ***Heart of Darkness*** lies in what it says about atrocities in King Leopold's Congo, though its documentary impulse is an important counter to its "will to style." As social criticism, its anti-imperialist message is undercut both by its racism and by its impressionism. But I know few novels which so insistently invoke an idealism which they don't seem to contain, and in which the modernist "will to style" is subjected to such powerful self-scrutiny—in which it is suggested that the "voice" at the heart of the novel, the voice of literature, the voice of civilization itself may in its purest, freest form yield only "the horror, the horror." (pp. 363-83)

Patrick Brantlinger, "Heart of Darkness: Anti-Imperialism, Racism, or Impressionism?" in Criticism, *Vol. XXVII, No. 4, Fall, 1985, pp. 363-85.*

FURTHER READING

Bibliography

Teets, Bruce, and Gerber, Helmut E. *Joseph Conrad: An Annotated Bibliography of Writings about Him.* Dekalb: Northern Illinois University Press, 1971, 671 p.
Exhaustive primary and secondary bibliography of Conrad's works.

Biography

Baines, Jocelyn. *Joseph Conrad: A Critical Biography.* New York: McGraw-Hill, 1960, 523 p.
Called an indispensable work by many critics. Baines includes detailed biographical material.

Conrad, John. *Joseph Conrad: Times Remembered.* New York: Cambridge University Press, 1981, 218 p.
Reminiscences by Conrad's youngest son.

Gillon, Adam. *Joseph Conrad.* Boston: Twayne Publishers, 1982, 210 p.
Biography of Conrad, portraying him as a great novelist, thinker, artist, and seaman.

Karl, Frederick R. *Joseph Conrad: The Three Lives, A Biography.* New York: Farrar, Straus and Giroux, 1979, 1008 p.
Detailed critical biography. This highly regarded, exhaustive study includes information regarding the milieu in which each of Conrad's works was written, the relationship between Conrad's inconsistent temperament and his literary output, and the influence of friends and collaborators on his works.

Meyer, Bernard C. *Joseph Conrad: A Psychoanalytic Biography.* Princeton, N.J.: Princeton University Press, 1967, 396 p.
Psychoanalytic study of Conrad's life, interspersed with discussions about his works.

Criticism

Bruss, Paul S. " 'Typhoon': The Initiation of Jukes." *Conradiana: A Journal of Joseph Conrad* 5, No. 2 (1973): 46-55.
Analyzes the character of Jukes in "Typhoon."

Crankshaw, Edward. *Joseph Conrad: Some Aspects of the Art of the Novel.* London: John Lane, 1936, 248 p.
Important early study of Conrad's literary artistry, treating all his novels as a unified artistic achievement. Crankshaw does not dwell upon isolated aspects of the works, but rather on the author as a craftsman. The book includes a discussion of *Heart of Darkness.*

Crews, Frederick. "The Power of Darkness." *Partisan Review* XXXIV, No. 4 (Fall 1967): 507-25.
Posits that *Heart of Darkness* is a form of dream narrative that conveys many of Conrad's deepest personal traumas and misgivings.

Curle, Richard. "Conrad's Diary." *The Yale Review* XV, No. 2 (January 1926): 254-66.
Contends that *Heart of Darkness* was inspired by the Congo experiences of Conrad. Curle, Conrad's longtime friend, introduces an extract from Conrad's diary illustrating the striking similarity between his real-life and fictional voyages.

Cuthbertson, Gilbert M. "Freedom, Absurdity, and Destruction: The Political Theory of Conrad's *A Set of Six.*" *Conradiana: A Journal of Joseph Conrad* 6, No. 1 (1974): 46-52.
Examines three ideas in *A Set of Six:* freedom, absurdity, and destruction, arguing that the thematic linkage was unintentional on Conrad's part.

Dean, Leonard F., ed. *Joseph Conrad's "Heart of Darkness": Backgrounds and Criticisms.* Englewood Cliffs, N.J.: Prentice-Hall, 1961, 184 p.
Includes the novella, historical information, extracts from Conrad's diary, and critical interpretations.

Emmett, V. J., Jr. " 'Youth': Its Place in Conrad's *Oeuvre.*" *Connecticut Review* 4, No. 1 (October 1970): 49-58.

Studies "Youth" as the forerunner of *Heart of Darkness* and *Lord Jim.*

Graver, Lawrence. *Conrad's Short Fiction.* Berkeley: University of California Press, 1969, 239 p.

Evaluates Conrad's achievement in short fiction, from his earliest short stories—"The Black Mate," "The Idiots," and "An Outpost of Progress"—to his major stories: "Youth," "Typhoon," "The Secret Sharer," and *Heart of Darkness.*

Kimbrough, Robert, ed. *"Heart of Darkness": An Annotated Text, Backgrounds and Sources Criticism.* Rev. ed. New York: W. W. Norton & Co., 1971, 267 p.

Includes text of *Heart of Darkness,* background information, extracts from Conrad's letters and diary that relate to the novella, a bibliography, and criticism.

Lafferty, William. "Conrad's 'A Smile of Fortune': The Moral Threat of Commerce." *Conradiana: A Journal of Joseph Conrad* 7, No. 1 (1975): 63-74.

Summarizes "A Smile of Fortune," focusing on the theme of moral identity.

Lothe, Jakob. "From Conrad to Coppola and Steiner." *The Conradian* 6, No. 3 (September 1981): 10-13.

Discusses similarities and disparities between Conrad's work and two later treatments of the same subject—Francis Ford Coppola's film *Apocalypse Now* and the novella *The Portage to San Cristobal of A. H.,* by George Steiner.

Madden, Fred. "Marlow and the Double Horror of *Heart of Darkness.*" *The Midwest Quarterly: A Journal of Contemporary Thought* 27, No. 4 (Summer 1986): 504-17.

Distinguishes two types of horror in *Heart of Darkness:* outward horror derived from nature and inward horror derived from the "seductive power of men."

Mathews, James W. "Ironic Symbolism in Conrad's 'Youth'." *Studies in Short Fiction* 11, No. 2 (Spring 1974): 117-23.

Discusses Conrad's use of the "internal narrative" in "Youth."

Moynihan, William T. "Conrad's 'The End of the Tether': A New Reading." *Modern Fiction Studies* 4, No. 2 (Summer 1958): 173-77.

Proposes that "The End of the Tether," "Youth," and *Heart of Darkness* are thematically related because all three stories portray a similar Conradian hero.

Mudrick, Marvin, ed. *Conrad: A Collection of Critical Essays.* Englewood Cliffs, N.J.: Prentice-Hall, 1966, 182 p.

Twelve critical essays on Conrad's fiction, including Stephen A. Reid's "The 'Unspeakable Rites' in *Heart of Darkness*" and Daniel Curley's "Legate of the Ideal."

Murphy, Michael. " 'The Secret Sharer': Conrad's Turn of the Winch." *Conradiana: A Journal of Joseph Conrad* 18, No. 3 (1986): 193-200.

Asserts that the Young Captain in "The Secret Sharer" is an unreliable narrator. The critic writes: "By this I do not mean, of course, that I think he is lying, but simply that he is not telling the whole story."

Ressler, Steve. "Conrad's 'The Secret Sharer': Affirmation of Action." *Conradiana: A Journal of Joseph Conrad* 14, No. 3 (1984): 195-214.

Examines "The Secret Sharer" as a romantic counterpart to the tragic *Under Western Eyes.*

Stallman, R. W. *The Art of Joseph Conrad: A Critical Symposium.* East Lansing: Michigan State University Press, 1960, 354 p.

Excellent collection of essays including works by André Gide, Vernon Young, and Albert Guerard.

Walton, James. "Mr. X's 'Little Joke': The Design of Conrad's 'The Informer'." *Studies in Short Fiction* 4, No. 1 (Fall 1966): 322-33.

Discusses "The Informer" as a neglected but masterful work.

Wiley, Paul L. *Conrad's Measure of Man.* Madison: University of Wisconsin Press, 1954, 227 p.

Discussion of Conrad's protagonists as men divided between mind and will, virtue and vice, morality and instinct.

Zuckerman, Jerome. " 'A Smile of Fortune': Conrad's Interesting Failure." *Studies in Short Fiction* 1, No. 2 (Winter 1964): 99-102.

Argues that "A Smile of Fortune" is a failure in the Conrad canon because Conrad's "sense of form" is faulty in the story.

Additional coverage of Conrad's life and career is contained in the following sources published by Gale Research: *Contemporary Authors,* Vol. 104; *Dictionary of Literary Biography,* Vols. 10, 34, 98; *Something about the Author,* Vol. 27; and *Twentieth-Century Literary Criticism,* Vols. 1, 6, 13, 25.

Herman Hesse

1877-1962

(Also wrote under pseudonyms of Herman Lauscher and Emil Sinclair) German-born Swiss novelist, poet, short story writer, editor, and critic.

INTRODUCTION

Recipient of the 1946 Nobel Prize for Literature, Hesse garnered critical esteem and popular success primarily for his novels, which he termed "biographies of the soul." Although not as well-regarded as his novels, Hesse's short stories and novellas are generally viewed by critics as competent variations on the major theme that recurs throughout his longer works: the individual's search for truth and identity through what he called the "inward journey." Strongly autobiographical, Hesse's fiction has struck a responsive chord in readers worldwide, especially among young people who readily identify with his rebellious, passionately spiritual heroes and their struggle to transcend the materialism of bourgeois society through aestheticism, mysticism, and love.

Hesse's early short fiction collections, *Eine Stunde hinter Mitternacht* and *Hinterlassene Schriften und Gedichte von Hermann Lauscher,* reflect his affinity for eighteenth- and nineteenth-century German Romanticism. These pieces typically feature misunderstood outsiders who retreat from society and engage in melodramatic fantasies about love and death. Hesse maintained a lifelong fascination with fantasy and folklore and he greatly admired *Arabian Nights* and the Brothers Grimm's *Fairy Tales.* Their influence surfaces in *Märchen* (*Strange News from Another Star and Other Tales*) and *Piktors Verwandlungen* (*Pictor's Metamorphoses and Other Fantasies*). In these volumes of fantasies, allegories, and fables, magic is accepted as a given: wish fulfillment, transformation, and the animation of objects occur as a matter of course.

In 1916 and 1917, Hesse underwent psychoanalysis with Dr. Josef Lang, a disciple of Carl Gustav Jung. He emerged from these sessions with the ambition to follow "Weg nach Innen," or an inward path, which he hoped would result in increased self-knowledge and the fulfillment of his artistic potential. Inspired also by the philosophy of Friedrich Nietzsche, Hesse vowed to reject traditional religion and morality and to lead a life of isolation and individualism. This new outlook gave rise to perhaps his most acclaimed story, "Klein und Wagner" ("Klein and Wagner"), which appears in *Klingsors letzter Sommer* (*Klingsor's Last Summer*). This tale is a fictionalized account of Hesse's break with his family in 1919, his dispiriting journey throughout Switzerland, and the grief of his first two weeks in the Ticino, the residence in southern Switzerland where he would live until 1931. The protagonist Friedrich Klein is a respectable citizen, reliable worker, and devoted husband and father who has never truly pondered his inner life. One day, unable to contain his frustration and discontent, he flees from his family and acts out his latent criminal and libidinal impulses. This new lifestyle, however, leads to further angst and after a week Klein decides to commit suicide. While drowning, he ironically experiences an epiphany of life's fundamental unity and significance.

The novella *Siddhartha: Eine indische Dichtung* (*Siddhartha*) is widely considered Hesse's finest achievement in short fiction. Hesse conceived of the story in 1911 following his extended visit to southeastern Asia in search of the peace of mind that he believed Oriental religions could offer. Instead, Hesse found only abject poverty and vulgarized Buddhism and left before reaching his final destination, India. In *Siddhartha,* the title character is a Brahmin, the highest caste in Hinduism, who seemingly has everything, yet feels spiritually hollow. He renounces his former life and embarks on a quest for wisdom and God. With his friend Govinda, he seeks Gotama the Buddha, who reputedly has achieved perfect knowledge. After speaking with Buddha, however, Siddhartha realizes that he cannot accept his doctrine of salvation from suffering.

Siddhartha then immerses himself in carnal and mercantile pursuits but comes no closer to knowledge. Disillusioned that all these paths have failed, Siddhartha becomes a ferryman and, after repeatedly crossing the river, he experiences total bliss. Bernard Landis commented: "[Siddhartha perceived the river] to be the mirror of all life, past, present, and future. All was One, and One was All. Spirit and flesh, mountain and man, blood and stone were all a part of the one continuous flow of existence. True peace was obtained in the only way possible, through a unity of the self with the universal, eternal essence."

Another emotional and spiritual crisis in the late 1920s led Hesse to write *Die Morgenlandfahrt* (*The Journey to the East*). In this novella, Hesse hoped to overcome his fear about his life and art and to establish order. The autobiographical hero H. H. earns entrance into the Order of Eastern Wayfarers, a group of elite intellectuals and artists from the past and present who are engaged in a perennial pilgrimage to the East. Each member seeks the ultimate meaning of life, which assumes a different objective for every individual. H. H.'s aim is to see Princess Fatima, who is, in Inder Nath Kher's words, "his fate and *anima,* the archetypal mother who represents the center . . . and the circumference of the psyche." When the esteemed community breaks up, H. H. loses contact with Leo, who is regarded as both servant and master of the circle and the embodiment of true friendship. After ten years of suffering and searching, they meet again and H. H. is allowed back into the Order. Leo gives H. H. his lost ring, which, Inder Nath Kher asserted, "symbolizes marriage and wholeness, self-illumination and grace." In *The Journey to the East,* Hesse reaffirms what he believed was the superiority of the timeless realm of art and thought.

Although critics generally concur that Hesse's most compelling and innovative writing appears in his novels, they acknowledge that his short fiction, particularly *Siddhartha* and *The Journey to the East,* ably conveys major concepts found in his longer works. Hesse's preoccupations—the quest for truth and self-discovery, the dualistic nature of existence, the conflict between spirit and flesh, the individual's need for freedom, the primacy of art and love—have profoundly affected readers worldwide, especially the young. Due largely to his ability to universalize his personal crises and private torments, Hesse has remained one of the most popular German-language authors of the twentieth century.

PRINCIPAL WORKS

SHORT FICTION

Eine Stunde hinter Mitternacht 1899
Hinterlassene Schriften und Gedichte von Hermann Lauscher 1901
Knulp: Drei Geschichten aus dem Leben Knulps 1915
[*Knulp: Three Tales from the Life of Knulp,* 1971]
Klingsors letzter Sommer: Erzählungen 1920
[*Klingsor's Last Summer,* 1970]
Siddhartha: Eine indische Dichtung 1922
[*Siddhartha,* 1951]
Piktors Verwandlungen: Ein Marchen 1925
[*Pictor's Metamorphoses, and Other Fantasies,* 1981]
Die Morgenlandfahrte: Eine Erzählung 1932
[*The Journey to the East,* 1957]
Stories of Five Decades 1972
Strange News from Another Star 1973

OTHER MAJOR WORKS

Peter Camenzind (novel) 1904
[*Peter Camenzind,* 1961]
Unterm Rad (novel) 1906
[*Beneath the Wheel,* 1968]
Gertrud: Roman (novel) 1910
[*Gertrud and I,* 1915]
Roßhalde (novel) 1914
[*Rosshalde,* 1970]
Demian: Die Geschchte einer Jugend von Emil Sinclair (novel) 1919
[*Demian,* 1923]
Der Steppenwolf (novel) 1927
[*Steppenwolf,* 1929; revised translation, 1963]
Krisis: Ein Stück Tagebuch (poetry) 1928
[*Crisis: Pages from a Diary,* 1975]
Narziss und Goldmund: Erzählung (novel) 1930
[*Narcissus and Goldmund,* 1968]
Das Glasperlenspiel: Versuch einer Lebensbeschreibung des Magister Ludi Josef Knecht sant Knechts hinterlassene Schriften (novel) 1943
[*Magister Ludi,* 1949; later translated as *The Glass Bead Game,* 1969]
Mein Glaube (essays) 1971
[*My Belief: Essays on Life and Art,* 1974]

Johannes Malthaner (essay date 1952)

[*In the essay excerpted below, Malthaner describes the spiritual journey of the title character in* Siddhartha *and suggests that his quest reflects Hesse's attempt to regain his harmonious relationship with the world.*]

Herman Hesse, the German-Swiss poet and novelist, is relatively little known in this country although a good deal of publicity has been given him since he was granted the Nobel prize for literature in 1946. This "unpopularity" of Hesse is only partly due to the fact that he writes in a foreign tongue—until very recently only very few of his works have been available in English translations—, even now his books are little in demand outside of university circles. That means that Hesse has not caught the fancy of the American public, that he has so far no large popular following. The main reason for this is, as I see it, that his novels do not have a strong plot around which the action revolves and therefore lack suspense or excitement. They are largely autobiographical and deal with questions of "Weltanschauung", of a philosophy of life. The plot is used by Hesse to drape his thoughts around it, to have an opportunity to present his innermost thoughts and the struggle for an understanding of the great problems of life. Hesse is, and always has been, a god-seeker; he has a message for his fellow-men, but one must "study" him, read and reread his works carefully if one wants to get the full benefit of their message. His works are not so much for entertainment but rather want to give food for thought; they have therefore a very strong appeal for the serious-minded reader but not for the masses that crave excitement and entertainment instead of beauty and depth.

Herman Hesse's novel ***Siddhartha*** is just such a work of literature, and it is of special interest to the student of literature, and of Hesse in particular, because it marks an important step in the development of Hesse and is unique in German literature in its presentation of Eastern philosophy.

The novel is largely autobiographical and has a long and interesting history. It is no doubt true of all great works of art that they do not just happen, that they are not products of chance. Great works of literature have their roots way back in the life of their writers, they have grown out of life and are part of the life of their creators; great works of literature are not factory products but grow and ripen slowly to full bloom. This is especially true of ***Siddhartha.***

Siddhartha was published in 1922 but has its roots in the earliest childhood of Hesse. His parents had been missionaries to India, his mother having been born in India of missionary parents; but on account of the poor health of Hesse's father the family had to return to Europe and came to Calw, a small Black Forest town, to help the maternal grandfather of Hesse, Dr. Gundert, the director of their mission and a famous Indian scholar and linguist. Indian songs and books, frequent discussions about India with visiting missionaries and scholars, a large library of Indian and Chinese writings, also many objects of Eastern art created great interest and left a deep impression on Hesse ever since his childhood.

The first part of ***Siddhartha,*** up to the meeting with the courtesan Kamala, was written before 1919 and was first published in the literary magazine *Neue Rundschau.* Siddhartha is the son of a rich Brahman of India. He is a good obedient son and the joy of his parents, but one day he awakens to the realization that his life is empty, that his soul has been left unsatisfied by his devotion to duty and the strict observance of all religious ordinances. He wants to find God who so far has been to him only a vague idea, distant and unreal, although he tried to serve him with sincerity of heart to the best of his understanding. Young Siddhartha realizes that he is at a dead end and that he must break away. So he leaves home leaving behind him all that he so far had loved and treasured, all the comforts, giving up his high social position, and becomes a Samana, an itinerant monk, with no earthly possessions anymore, accompanied by his boyhood friend Govinda who has decided to follow Siddhartha's lead. By fasting and exposing his body to the rigors of the weather, Siddhartha wants to empty himself completely of all physical desires so that by any chance he may hear the voice of God speaking to his soul, that he may find peace.

Hesse's books are confessions, and the story of Siddhartha is his own story describing his own doubts and struggle. He, too, had rebelled: against the pietistic orthodoxy of his parents and the strict school system in Germany that destroyed any attempt of independence in its pupils. So he ran away to shape his own life. Self-education is the main theme of most of the novels of Hesse, especially of the books of his youth. Self-education has been for centuries a very favorite theme in German literature and men like Luther, Goethe, Kant, and many other leading German writers and philosophers were the inspirers of German youth in their longing for independence.

It is significant that Hesse gave to a collection of four stories published in 1931, in which he included ***Siddhartha,*** the title of ***Weg nach Innen, Road to Within.*** Indeed, Siddhartha turns away from the outside observance of religious rituals and ordinances to a life of contemplation. So also does Hesse himself after the outbreak of World War I. Up to the war, Hesse had lived a rather quiet and self-satisfied life. After years of hard struggle to win recognition as a poet, he had found first success which brought him not only social recognition and financial security but also many friends and a home. But the war brought him a rather rude awakening out of his idylic life on the shore of Lake Constance where he had lived a rather happy and retired life. His apparently so secure and well-ordered world came crashing down over his head. The vicious attacks by the German press and by many of his former friends for his stand against the war psychosis—Hesse was living at that time in Switzerland although he was still a German citizen—forced him to reexamine the fundamental truths on which he had built his life. He had become distrustful of religion as he saw it practised, and of education which had not prevented the western world of being plunged into a murderous war. Where was the truth? On what foundation could a man build his life? All had been found wanting.

Siddhartha is Hesse's attempt to restore his faith in mankind, to regain his lost peace of mind, and to find again a harmonious relationship with his world. A new more spiritual orientation takes place. He does no longer believe in the natural goodness of man, he is thrown back unto himself and comes to a new concept of God: No longer does he seek God in nature but, in the words of the Bible, he believed that "the Kingdom of God's is within you".

Hesse confesses that he had been pious only up to his thirteenth year but then had become a skeptic. Now he becomes a believer again, to be sure it is not a return to the orthodox belief of his parents, he wants to include in his new concept of religion not only the teachings of Jesus but also those of Buddha and of the Holy Scriptures of India as well. (pp. 103-06)

Returning to our story, we find that Siddhartha also as a Samana has not come nearer his goal of happiness and peace. It seems to him that his religious fervor had been nothing but self-deception, that all the time he had been in flight from himself. The hardships which he had endured as a Samana had not brought him nearer to God.

At this period of his life, Siddhartha hears of Gotama Buddha of whom it was said that he had attained that blissful state of godliness where the chain of reincarnations had been broken, that he had entered Nirvana. Siddhartha goes to find him, hears him teach the multitude, and then has a private conversation with the Holy One; but it becomes clear to him that the way of salvation can not be taught, that words and creeds are empty sounds, that each man must find the way by himself, the secret of the experience can not be passed on. So he leaves also Gotama Buddha and all teachers and teachings. Govinda, his friend, stays with Gotama and so Siddhartha cuts the last link with his past. He is now all alone. And he comes to the sudden realization that all through the years so far he has lived a separate life, that he actually never had sought a real understanding of his fellow men, that he knew very little of the world and of life all about him. For the first time in many years he really looks about him and perceives the beauty of the world. The world about him, from which he had fled, he now finds attractive and good. He must not seek to escape life but face it, live it.

This is the startling new discovery Siddhartha makes and so he decides to leave the wilderness. He comes to the big city where he sees at the gate the beautiful Kamala, the courtesan. He finds her favor and she teaches him the ways of the world. He discards his beggar's clothes and becomes in short time a very successful merchant. But his heart is neither in his love nor in his business; all the pleasures of the world can not still the hunger of his soul. He finds the world wanting, too, and, moreover, he must realize after a few years that the worldly things, the acquiring of money, have gradually taken possession of his life, that he is being enslaved and harassed by the necessity of making money in order to satisfy his extravagant tastes, that he has become a busy and unfree man whose thoughts dwell less and less on the eternal things.

So he cuts himself loose from all that he had acquired, leaves once again everything behind him, and goes back to the river which he had crossed when he gave up his life as a Samana.

At this point there is a long interruption in the writing of ***Siddhartha.*** Hesse realized that his knowledge of Eastern philosophy was not sufficient; he devoted himself therefore to a very thorough study of Indian philosophy and religion. After a year and a half he takes up the writing of the story again. It is quite evident, however, that the emphasis has shifted. Description from now on is practically absent, and the tone is lighter, the language, too, is not so heavy, not so mystic but transparent and more elevated. The whole concentration is on the spiritual element. Instead of long discussions of philosophies and systems, we find the emphasis now on Faith. He perceives that only through faith, not by doing or by teachings, can man penetrate to the source of light, can he find God.

At the bank of the river Siddhartha sits for a long time and lets his whole life pass in review before him. He finds that even the evil things which he had done lately had been necessary as an experience in order to bring him to an understanding of what life really was. But he also becomes discouraged because all his endeavors so far had not given him the desired insight and peace of soul. There was nothing left in life that might entice him, challenge him, comfort him; he finds himself subject to an unescapable chain of cause and effect, to repeated incarnations, each of which means a new beginning of suffering. Will he ever be able to break this chain? Will he ever be able to enter Nirvana? He doubts it and is at the point of drowning himself when the mysterious word "OM" comes to his mind. "OM" means "having completed", in German "Vollendung". He realizes the folly of his attempt to try to find peace and an end to his sufferings by extinguishing his physical being. Life is indestructible. Siddhartha realizes, too, that all life is one, that all creation is an indivisible one, that trees and birds are indeed his brothers; he sees his great mistake in trying always to do something instead of just to be.

He joins Vasudeva, the ferry man, who shows him the great secret of the river, namely that for the river the concept of time does not exist: The river just is, for the river there is no past, no future, no beginning, no end; for the river is only the presence. And for man, too, Vasudeva tells him, happiness is real only when causality—that is time—has ceased to exist for him. The problem is not, as Siddhartha had always understood it, to find perfection, but to find completion, "Vollendung".

One more lesson Siddhartha had to learn. When he left Kamala she had known that she would bear him a child, but she did not tell Siddhartha because she realized that she could not and must not hold him back, that Siddhartha had to go his own way. Later, too, she felt the emptiness of her life; so one day she decides to seek Gotama Buddha of whom she had heard. Her way leads her to the river where, unknown to her, Siddhartha lived and stopping at the bank of the river to rest, she is bitten by a poisonous snake. Siddhartha finds her dying and recognizes her. After he had buried her, he takes his son, a boy of some twelve or fourteen years of age, to him. Siddhartha feels keenly the loss of Kamala, but it is not sadness that is in his heart for he knows now that all life is indestructible, that Kamala has only entered a new life, life in a wider sense, that in every blossom, in every breeze about him there is Kamala. He is not separated from her, never will be, in fact she is nearer to him now than ever before.

Siddhartha devotes himself to the education of his son but must make the painful experience that his love is not appreciated and his endeavors are repulsed. His son does not want the life Siddhartha thinks best for him, he wants to live his own life, and thus breaks away from his father as Siddhartha in his own youth had broken away from his own father. With the loss of his son, there is nothing left that binds Siddhartha to this world. He realizes that this had to come, so that he would no longer fight what he considered fate but give himself unreservedly to his destiny; thus Siddhartha has overcome suffering at last and with it has attained the last step of his completion, he has entered into Nirvana; now peace has come to Siddhartha at last. (pp. 106-09)

Johannes Malthaner, "Hermann Hesse: 'Siddhartha'," in The German Quarterly, *Vol. 25, No. 2, March, 1952, pp. 103-09.*

Bernard Landis (essay date 1953)

[*In the excerpt below, Landis asserts that* Siddhartha *encompasses all of Hesse's major themes, including the division of the universe into the masculine and the femi-*

nine, the cult of suffering, and the everlasting conflict of new against old.]

[The theme of Hesse's fiction] is the duality of man, racked with the conflict engendered by desire for sensual experience, counterbalanced by admonitions of the intellect and the striving for spiritual self-realization. The quest is the resolution of that dichotomy through a unification of sex and suffering, music and mysticism, art and death.

The duality of Hesse, clearly depicted in the mother-father worlds of ***Siddhartha,*** has a metaphysical basis that is best illustrated in his first major novel, *Demian,* where the central question is: what is man? He believes that men are all born of a common womb, yet strive to express their own individualities. This thought parallels that expressed by Carlo Levi in *Of Fear And Freedom*: in the beginning all was mass, and mass comprised all. Out of this indifferent substance, Hesse saw humanity surge forth to determine itself. With the severance of man's umbilical cord with nature, there arises an uncontrolled terror of unknowingness. Impelled to hasten back to prebirth serenity, an impossibility, man is impaled on the cross whose vertical element is dread of a doubtful liberty and whose horizontal component is dread of a deathful passiveness. In Hesse's works, this anguish is developed and transposed to the perpendicular tides of doubt concerning the values of man's animal self on the one hand, and fear of spiritual sterility on the other. (pp. 59-60)

Siddhartha continues the search for self-realization that was begun in *Demian.* The first lines of the book disclose the familiar father-mother worlds that exist to some degree in each of Hesse's novels: the dominating, intellectual spirit of the former and the pulsating, emotional heart of the latter. These concepts, especially of the earth-mother as source and protectress, govern each sphere of life. Elsewhere Hesse has written: "I cannot rid myself of the idea that instead of Death with his scythe, it will be my mother who takes me to herself once more and leads me back into non-existence and innocence."

Siddhartha, the strong and handsome son, was made of both his parents; from his father the Brahmin he learned the art of contemplation, and through his mother he understood the quiet dreams and emotions symbolized by their garden. Nevertheless, he was restless. For all his knowledge, he was unhappy. A vital element was missing in his personal ontology.

To find that elixir which would bind his disorganized parts, Siddhartha began a determined pursuit of self-discovery. No parental pleas could hold him back. Just as Sinclair learned in *Demian* that "it was entirely wrong to wish to give the world anything. A man has absolutely no other duty than this: to seek himself, to grope his own way forward, no matter whither it leads," so it was with Siddhartha.

He left his home and joined a group of ascetics whose one goal was peace, the peace that was gained through loss of consciousness of the self. To this end he fasted, blistered his flesh, cut it on thorns, sustaining every conceivable physical and mental torture. "A dead jackal lay on the sandy shore and Siddhartha's soul slipped into its corpse; he became a dead jackal, lay on the shore, swelled, stank, decayed, was dismembered by hyenas, was picked at by vultures, became a skeleton, became dust, mingled with the atmosphere." While this life did not provide the solution to Siddhartha's dilemma, it was an integral part of his development. Actually the theme, or cult, of suffering is common to Hesse's entire body of writing. This is not surprising since Hesse, a veritable genius of suffering, was profoundly influenced by Novalis, who had written: "A man should be proud of suffering. All suffering is a reminder of our high estate."

The years of punishment sharpened Siddhartha's perception but in no way brought him any closer to the final *truth* he sought. He left the ascetics and the holy men and continued his quest for personal resolution in the world of daily affairs. There he deftly learned all the tricks of trade, the games of gambling, and mastered the art of love. The greater his success in achieving material gain, the further away from his goal he traveled. He was surfeited with worldly pleasure, but his senses decayed and happiness eluded him.

At last, the sterility of this life weighed heavily upon him and he abandoned his possessions to reenter the forests with nothing but loin cloth and walking stick. Aged and worn, he assumed the life of a ferryman. He traversed the currents of the river day and night, when finally he was cognizant of contentment. For the river gave up its secrets to him. He perceived it to be the mirror of all life, past, present and future. All was One, and One was All. Spirit and flesh, mountain and man, blood and stone were all a part of the one continuous flow of existence. True peace was obtained in the only way possible, through a unity of the self with the universal, eternal essence, through a mystic identification with Sansara and Nirvana.

Siddhartha contains all of the fundamentals of Hesse's philosophy: the division of the universe into masculine and feminine worlds, the cult of suffering, anathema of dogma, antipathy to group action, the concept of the garden-forest as a source of security, and the everlasting conflict of new against old, birth against death, in the recurring life cycle. (pp. 60-1)

Each man must traverse the hell of his inner self, his subconscious and unconscious, turning the self inside out to clean the wounds inflicted in the battles between flesh and spirit, and fuse the two. This undertaking of suffering may lead to death; yet to Hesse it is the only way to truth and salvation. For out of the ashes like the phoenix, reincarnated man can return—an avatar of love. (p. 63)

Bernard Landis, "The Philosophical Fiction of Hermann Hesse," in Accent, *Vol. XIII, No. 1, Winter, 1953, pp. 59-63.*

Leroy R. Shaw (essay date 1957)

[*Shaw is a Canadian-born American educator and critic who has written extensively on German literature. In the excerpt below, he describes* Siddhartha *as the story of a man who achieves transcendency through the realization that the search for this state and its achievement are si-*

multaneous realities. Shaw also maintains that Hesse communicates this idea through a complex "welding of meaning and form" in which the former evolves from the latter.]

[Hesse's 1911 voyage to India convinced him] that oneness, whatever it was and wherever it existed, would produce a harmonious condition in which every contrast and all opposing forces had finally been resolved. Furthermore, it had become clear that the unity he desired did not reside in any particular philosophy or place, but that it belonged to "a subterranean and timeless world of values and the spirit" of which the visible marks of a civilization were only an external manifestation. Unity, in short, resided only in the timeless. With this realization the problem of finding unity became, for Hesse, the problem of transcending the limitations imposed by the domain of time. He had to learn to accept the present, but with the knowledge that it was only the embodiment of an essence which time itself had no power to destroy.

Siddhartha: Eine indische Dichtung (1922), is in part a testimony to this awareness, in part a vision of the manner in which Hesse thought his problem might be solved. India, and the way of Buddhism, are joined to his own experience in the story of a man who achieves unity and the timeless through the realization that search, and the attainment of search, are simultaneous realities of existence. In the discussion which follows I shall try to show how Hesse was able to communicate this vision through an intricate and remarkable welding of meaning and form. ***Siddhartha*** stands almost alone in modern German fiction as an example of a work in which the structure *is* the idea, the latter growing organically out of the former and not fully revealed until the last element of composition has been fitted into its proper place.

Siddhartha, young "son of the Brahmans," is propelled by the same search, and has the same foreknowledge of the goal, as Hesse himself. In the opening chapter of the *novelle* he is pictured meditating upon the magic syllable OM, "the word of words" which stands for Perfection or the Perfected. . . . OM, the alpha and omega of every Vedic text, is a symbol for that "holy power," as Heinrich Zimmer describes it, which "turns into and animates everything within the microcosm as well as in the outer world," a power without form or substance itself and yet the source of everything that was, is, or shall be. Brahman, the impersonal and universal godhead, is one aspect of this power, and Atman, the individual soul or Self, is an expression for the infinite aspects which are identical to it. To merge within this micro-macrocosmic essence, then, and by this merging find the unity which is without time and yet made manifest only in the multiplicities of time, is the goal Siddhartha envisages as the perfect fulfillment of his way upon earth.

The vocabulary of Indian philosophy suggests first of all the several dimensions concentrated in the single action of this *novelle.* Although Siddhartha's story recapitulates the search of a contemporary westerner, it also recalls the hyperconscious striving of an immemorial Eastern tradition as well. "The search for a basic unity underlying the manifold of the universe," according to Zimmer, had been "the chief motivation" of Indian philosophies since the time of the earliest Vedic hymns. ***Siddhartha*** is a legend, therefore, a story which is the amalgam of several possible actions, each of which has its origin in a discrete moment of historical time and yet is simultaneously identified with a multitude of other actions taking place on other levels of experience.

Legend as the framework of the *novelle* offers the first clue to the manner in which Hesse imagined the attainment of a timeless reality. A second is given in Siddhartha's unusual foreknowledge of the goal. Like Hesse's own yearning to "go back into the source of life," Siddhartha's undertaking bears the characteristic of a return to, or from another point of view, of a discovery, by the self, of something that is already there. In his own words, he seeks "athomeness in Atman," a goal which is at the same time the place from which he has already departed. Unlike the classic novel of development, the story of Siddhartha's way to perfection is not the logical and inevitable unfolding of one event out of the other towards an end which could not have been foreseen from the beginning; it is rather an ever-expanding awareness of a reality already known, a progression which is at the same time a regression to a condition forever in being. We must be prepared, therefore, for a type of structure in which the various moments of the protagonist's life are presented as parts of a whole that is already existent even though it has not yet been realized in his actual experience. The events of the story occur in the fleeting instant, to be sure, but an instant in which the goal as well as the search, the process of what is developing as well as the end of development, are both implied.

With these facts in mind we may turn now to the implications of Hesse's title, with its suggestive reminder that the historical Buddha, Gotama Sakyamuni, acclaimed during his own lifetime as One who had found the way to Perfection, himself bore the given name of Siddhartha. It is striking that the life of Hesse's protagonist runs almost parallel to the little that is known of the Buddha's obscure history. The latter involves three basic events: the leave-taking from his father's house, the frustrating years wasted in vacillation between the pursuit of worldly desires and a life of extreme asceticism, and finally, the determination of the Middle Path as the only road to Enlightenment. Siddhartha also follows this course, if not in strict chronological sequence, still in the same pattern of significant experiences. The sole difference here—which, as I shall try to show, amounts to only a superficial distinction—consists in the fact that the Buddha left a body of sermons and teachings which are not advanced by Hesse's hero.

The parallel just noted, which forms the structural backbone of this work, comes from Hesse's desire to superimpose upon his story of the seeker a portrait of the sage who had already found his way. Being and Becoming are both represented in the story, therefore, the former in the existence of a man who has found unity, the latter in the presence of a man who has identified himself with perfection although he is still approaching it. In this sense, time, the troubled present in which one seeks the way, is transcended in the *novelle* by the timeless fact of the goal already achieved. Siddhartha, indeed, is both seeker and sage, the

One in whom perfection hovers as a silent attendant within the actions of the One who is still unperfected. His actual encounter with the Buddha in the course of the story anticipates this absolute crossing of the timeless with time, for here the aspect of life which is Becoming meets the aspect of a life already in Being, the One who is already perfect encounters himself in the process of attaining perfection. The fact that these two aspects do not coalesce at this point, and that Siddhartha refrains from declaring himself a disciple of Gotama although acknowledging the latter as a living Buddha, is essential to Hesse's message, for it signifies the distance which experience always intrudes between the seeker and his goal. Time, the sum of moments which the Buddha has already transcended in himself, must first be lived out in Siddhartha's own life.

The course of Siddhartha's discovery of the Self, his realization, so to speak, of the Buddha who is already within him, is therefore a process of acquiring the wisdom of the historical Sakyamuni while he himself is finding the way to enlightenment. The external design of the *novelle*—its division into two major parts, of which the first contains four, the second eight separate sections—corresponds in extremely subtle fashion to the Buddha's celebrated doctrine of the Four Noble Truths and the Eightfold Path to salvation from human suffering. This is not to say that ***Siddhartha*** is intended as a biography of the Buddha, or as a literal presentation of his doctrine, but that it has drawn upon the essential language of Buddhism in order to support Hesse's identification of the One-in-Being with the One-Becoming by tracing the seeker's acquisition of those virtues which are the special wisdom of an enlightened sage.

The first part of the *novelle,* written near the end of the First World War, brings Siddhartha the knowledge of Buddha's Four Noble Truths. The experiences recounted here reflect certain events in Hesse's life up to his return from India and convey the realization, already noted, that the problem of finding unity was a problem of transcending time and that, paradoxically, the way into this timeless realm led through the multiple fields of the Here and Now. In the second part of the *novelle,* then, Siddhartha undertakes this journey through experience and arrives at the goal he is seeking.

Buddha's First Noble Truth is revealed to Siddhartha while he is still a son of the Brahmans dwelling in his father's house. The world of the father is a world of things as they have become, determined by the past and geared to the perpetual repetition of an unchanging way of life. Ritual and formula govern this world, and life in it revolves around the rendering of sacrifices and offerings at "the accustomed time," the performance of established duties from which not even the "most blameless" of men, Siddhartha's own father, is free. He must "cleanse himself every day, strive for purification every day, every day anew."

The world of the father, then, is fixed in the moment and regulated according to the set times of an inherited manner of existence. What will come is the same as what has been; the present exists only as the appointed moment for acting within a cycle of time that is forever revolving around the same course. This, Hesse indicates, is the world into which all men are born—orthodox, traditional, determined by the past—a world in which they suffer not only from the imposition of a way of life that is not of their own making, but also because time, the necessity of living according to a ritualized moment, stands between them and the reality they seek. Between Brahman and Atman, the universal godhead and the Self that is supposed to be identical to it, lies the ethic of the gods and their demands, mere formulas for life which are no less "ephemeral and subject to time" than man himself. Thus Siddhartha, as a son of the Brahmans, suffers from the impossibility of translating the consciousness of truth, his foreknowledge of the goal, into the actual experience of living free from the repeated phases of established time.

When he leaves this world of the father, Siddhartha sets out with his friend Govinda to find a place in which "the cycle of time might be eluded, the end of causes [found], and an eternity without suffering would begin." Like the historical Buddha, he joins the jackal men called Samanas, fanatic ascetics for whom enlightenment was to be found only through denial of the flesh and all worldly desires. Among the Samanas Siddhartha tries "to kill memory and his senses," to deny the sum of things as they had been, withdraw from the present, and close himself off from the possibility of further experience. He tries, in short, to escape from time. The arts of the Samanas are conscious attempts of the intellect, exercising itself through the will, to free the self from all temporal effects. Through fasting, Siddhartha tries to make himself physiologically independent of the moment; through thinking, to control what the moment might bring him and to determine his own attitude towards it; and through waiting, to suspend the moment between a part he has rejected and a future condition which he hopes to will into existence. The purpose of Siddhartha's life among the Samanas may be summed up in the rhyming words *leer* and *nicht mehr:* to be no longer subject to the experience of time, but to be "empty of thirst, empty of desire, empty of dream, empty of joy and sorrow," to become a void which only Atman-Brahman, the timeless unity of his search, would be sufficient to fill.

The way of asceticism succeeds only in revealing to Siddhartha the second of Buddha's Noble Truths—that the cause of suffering is the craving for something which can never be satisfied: "Although Siddhartha fled from himself a thousand times, lingered in nothingness, in an animal, in a stone, the return was inevitable, the hour unavoidable when he came back to find himself once more, in moonlight or in sunshine, in shadow or in rain, when he became himself again, Siddhartha once more, and again felt the torture of an imposed cycle of time." No matter what his way of escape, then, Siddhartha always returns to the self restricted by time. Thus he realizes not merely that asceticism can bring him no salvation, but also that it is impossible to solve the problem of time by trying to crush it with an act of will. His attempts to escape from suffering only lead to further suffering; the denial of the moment serves only to accelerate the temporal cycle. Siddhartha has learned that the timeless may not be found apart from the medium of that self which time is still in the process of making. Being does not reveal itself through the negation of Becoming.

In "Gotama," the next chapter of the *novelle,* Siddhartha discovers the third of Buddha's Noble Truths through an encounter with the historical sage himself. The presence of the Enlightened One proves that there is a way of release from suffering. Gotama has made "the highest wisdom his own; he has remembered his previous lives, he had reached Nirvana and returned no longer into the cycle of time, he immersed himself no longer in the murky stream of illusionary forms." In Buddha, then, the searching Siddhartha sees a living demonstration of the fact that it is not necessary to depart from time in order to know the timeless. Yet at the same time the presence of the Buddha, who has learned to preserve the memory of what was and yet not be bound to it, who has found his place in the present and yet is still at home in Atman, is a reminder that the roots of the timeless are embedded in the experiences acted out within the world of time.

Siddhartha's recognition of Gotama is unhesitating and unequivocal: "I have not doubted for a moment that you are Buddha, that you have reached the goal, the highest, which so many thousand Brahmans and sons of the Brahmans are looking for." Nevertheless, he does not become a disciple of Buddha, as his friend Govinda does, for reasons which are both pertinent and revealing. The Samanas had taught him to look upon experience only with his intellect; under this influence, he cannot overlook a logical error in the Buddha's teaching. Gotama, he claims, had clearly demonstrated "the unity of the world, and the interconnection of all that happens," but he had himself broken that unity by advising one to overcome the world and seek salvation outside of it. In contradiction to his own presence, therefore, Gotama seems to Siddhartha to preach that timelessness lies in abjuration of the world and of present time.

Buddha himself answers this argument in warning Siddhartha against a too zealous and trusting attention to words: "Be on your guard, o eager seeker for knowledge, before the thicket of opinions and the strife over words." Buddha may speak this way, indeed, because he knows that wisdom is not limited to his own doctrine and because that doctrine has been promulgated solely for the sake of those, like Govinda, who depend upon another's word in order to receive a hint as to their own way into enlightenment. Eventually, when he has reached the wisdom the Buddha now possesses, Siddhartha will admit the justness of Gotama's admonition. "Salvation and virtue, even Sansara and Nirvana," he will tell Govinda, "are only words. There is no Nirvana as such; there is only the word."

Siddhartha refuses to become a disciple of Buddha for another reason which is more fundamental, perhaps, since it leads to a revelation of the fourth Buddhistic truth. "One thing," he says to Gotama, "is not contained in your clear and most respected doctrine; it does not contain the secret of what the Buddha has experienced himself." Buddha, in other words, cannot direct Siddhartha towards his goal because the way lies through Siddhartha's knowledge of himself. This is at one and the same time a confession that a man may not learn salvation from any teacher, even if that teacher be Buddha himself, and a recognition that the path to unity and the timeless lies through one's own experience of temporality, in that very process of Becoming which seems to contradict the absolute state of Being. (pp. 204-11)

"Govinda," the final chapter of the *novelle,* is a paean of "right rapture," the Enlightened One rejoicing in his enlightenment and yet mocking the glory of his knowledge by his admission that it is impossible to communicate it fully. In Siddhartha's conversation with his friend one can hear Buddha's warning that wisdom does not reside in the doctrine, that beyond the word lies the mystery, the silence out of which the sounds have come and into which they inevitably return. Although trying to define the Being which is in and around him, Siddhartha knows that words are one-sided, robbing truth of its impartiality, emphasizing the rightness of one point of view at the expense of an opposite which is no less true. It is because this is so that Siddhartha cautions Govinda against believing in time, for "if time isn't real, then the span which seems to exist between the world and eternity, between sorrow and blessedness, between good and bad, is also a deception."

As he reviews his life for Govinda, Siddhartha reflects that *einst,* the powerful adverb by which men try to distinguish between past and future, marks no real division in the fundamental oneness of their lives. It is a mistake to think of oneself as on the way to enlightenment, in the sense of progressing by stages in which one leaves off one thing as one acquires another, for enlightenment exists within one at every moment of present time. "In every sinner there is, now and today, the future Buddha; his future is all already there, in him, in you, in everyone there is the becoming, potential, hidden Buddha." Similarly, unity, whether within or outside oneself, is not to be attained by trying to put it together as one would a puzzle out of many pieces, for it is present and entire in every object. Thus Brahman, the holy power identical with the Self, the timeless unity of all creation, is simply the reality discovered by lifting the deceptive veil of time as it is experienced in one's own life. Unity resides in the readiness, at each individual moment of time, to see the timelessness beneath, "to see all that has been, life being and life becoming, as simultaneously existent."

In the last paragraphs of the *novelle* Govinda, the everlasting disciple and uncomprehending seeker, has a vision of this truth as he looks into the face of his friend:

> He no longer saw Siddhartha's face, he saw instead other faces, many faces, a long series, a streaming river of faces, hundreds and thousands, all of which came and went and yet seemed to be there all at the same time, all of them changing continually and renewing themselves, and yet which were all Siddhartha. . . . And thus Govinda saw that this smiling mask, this smiling of unity within the streaming forms, this smiling of simultaneity within the thousand births and deaths, this smiling of Siddhartha was exactly the same, was exactly identical to the quiet, delicate, impenetrable, perhaps goodnatured, perhaps mocking, wise, thousandfold smile of Gotama, the Buddha.

Thus the goal Siddhartha has realized for himself, the destruction of multiple time, is imaged for Govinda in the face of a living Buddha. And with this we too, who have attended the search like Govinda without a full knowledge of its implications, arrive at the wisdom which Hesse has made manifest through the unique form of eternal Being discovering itself in the process of Becoming. There is after all no difference between seeker and sage, no difference between Siddhartha and Gotama, no disunity possible for the Enlightened One who has found his way to the wisdom of the other shore. (pp. 220-22)

Leroy R. Shaw, "Time and the Structure of Hermann Hesse's 'Siddhartha'," in Symposium, *Vol. XI, No. 2, Fall, 1957, pp. 204-24.*

Hans Beerman (essay date 1959)

[*In the following excerpt, Beerman relates* Siddhartha *to Hindu scripture, which is found in the* Bhagavad-Gita, *and its message of "loving devotion to the universe" as the means of spiritual liberation.*]

[Hesse] produced some twenty-five important works. While some of these belong to the realm of poetry, his most important novels are autobiographical in nature or fall into the category of *Erziehungsromane.* The *Erziehungsroman,* or novel of education, commonly shows the protagonist in his effort to cope with the demands that life throws up to him. How do I live best? How can I master the art of living the abundant life? These are most often the problems confronting Hesse's leading personalities. In nearly every one of his works there is thus some attempt at soul-searching. Most of his characters try desperately to come to terms with themselves, and most try to achieve a certain measure of self-realization. There is always the problem of man's spiritual loneliness, the effort to find one's way in a world where individualism and introspection are suspect. (pp. 27-8)

Hesse has repeatedly condemned our age as materialistic and devoid of spirit. It is an epoch that only pays lip service to the ideals of Western civilization and thereby has sunk to a low level of culture where lofty thoughts have been replaced by greed and technics. Man does not envision any more the ideal possibilities of life but has become corrupt. Hesse calls our age "the journalistic age—the era of the digest." . . .

Disappointed and disgusted with the bloodshed and the loss of individualism during the last fifty years in Europe, Hesse has felt himself increasingly attracted to Eastern idealism. (p. 28)

Among critics it is generally agreed that ***Siddhartha*** is the best written of his works. It telescopes most of the ideas and problems presented in his previous works and brings most clearly into focus the Eastern tendencies of thought which can be found as a *sous-entendu* in nearly all his mature writings.

Hinduism is characterized by its emphasis on fact. Never has it leaned as heavily on authority as other religious beliefs. . . . Hinduism is not a founded religion—it does not center around any historical events. It is experiential in character. Its distinctive characteristic has been its insistence on the inward life of the spirit. . . . The *Gita,* or the Song of the Lord, occupies a unique place in the philosophical literature of India. In conjunction with the *Upanishads* and the *Brahmasutras,* it is the most popular authority for Indian orthodox religion and philosophy. . . . In the philosophical part of [the *Gita*] we encounter the *Bhagavad-Gita,* in which the most prominent religious ideas of ancient and modern India are expressed. . . . [The] *Gita* teaches that the vital force of life is devotion or love. . . . It is the easiest road to salvation, to encounter the personal God. . . . [Action] *per se* is not condemned, provided that work is done in the right frame of mind. . . . [Human] action, to be effective, has to be free from all traces of duality (notions of good and evil) and also from the tripartite idea of man, who might think of himself as a separate doer, as an instrument, and who might worry about the results of any action he performs. (pp. 29-30)

The *Gita* is also a scripture on yoga. This Sanskrit term implies the union of the individual soul with the Universal Soul. Man is to realize: (*a*) that the relative universe has to be overcome; (*b*) that worldly life is to be transformed into spiritual consciousness. (p. 31)

Siddhartha, brilliant, handsome and a favorite son of a Brahmin, is disgusted and dissatisfied with his life at home. . . . The main cause for his disgust is the violent contradiction between the teachings and the actual life of the Brahmins, particularly the antinomies of ecclesiasticism and the philosophical spirit. As modern man, Siddhartha cannot believe in the magical power of the ritual. The tragic gulf between dogma and actuality is too barefaced for him. (p. 32)

Siddhartha does not find supreme bliss, and he leaves the Brahmins, feeling the attraction to the life of a Samana, a wandering monk. He thus follows the precepts of Brahminism. He tries to grasp the essence of the Spirit by rejecting the sensual side of life. . . . Unfortunately, even at the height of his asceticism he only experiences "a flight from the Self, a temporary palliative against the pain and folly of life." . . . With increased intensity he goes on searching for Truth. He hears about the preaching of Gautama Sakyamuni, the Buddha. He decides to meet and possibly join him, even though he is unconvinced that Buddha's teachings will do him any good. (pp. 32-3)

Siddhartha meets the Buddha, but his teachings confirm him more and more in his conviction that Buddha's methods will not bring him any closer to Self-realization. While Gautama's way of life does satisfy his logical needs, it does not answer his metaphysical longings. He is not interested in attaining Nirvana—he wants to search for a world of Becoming in which the plurality of the world of sensual perception shall give rise to Unity. Thus, Siddhartha turns away from the teachings of Buddha, unable to tolerate for himself the negativistic, life-denying character of Gautama's message. . . . Siddhartha rather wants to learn through personal experience how one goes about finding Fulfillment; Buddha's experience is not his own. . . . (p. 33)

He is possessed with the probing of the human problem of individuation. . . . Realizing that by his intensive search for the Atman (Oversoul) he has been compelled to dispel his energies from the discovery of the personal Self, he confesses: "I was seeking Brahman, Atman, I wished to destroy myself, to get away from myself, in order to find in the unknown innermost, the nucleus of all things, Atman, Life, the Divine, the Absolute. But by doing so, I lost myself on the way." . . . The turning point has been reached in the life of Siddhartha. Having previously tried to transcend the visible world, he now turns toward its sensual characteristics as a means for Realization. (p. 34)

Time passes by. Siddhartha has increasingly become involved with the world. His soul rebels against the worldly life—more and more he dimly senses that the aim of Self-realization, his deepest *raison d'etre,* is lost to him. (p. 35)

One night, after carnal excess, he is so overwhelmed with disgust for his life that his sick soul rebels, and he again renounces all his property, leaves town, and becomes a homeless wanderer again. . . . His disgust changes to desperation, and he is about to commit suicide, when suddenly out of the very depth of his subconscious there flashes the saving concept, the knowledge of his youth. "He was conscious of Brahman, of the indestructibleness of life; he remembered all that he had forgotten, all that was divine." . . . He has changed into the new Siddhartha who recognizes that both mental and sensual activities have led him to private individuation and separateness. He now understands that only loving devotion is able to save him from himself. To have one's heart and mind absorbed in love brings us to Unity with all creatures, seems to unveil the mysteries of the universe.

Siddhartha has now attained the peace of mind he has longed for all his life. (pp. 36-7)

Siddhartha, however, has not yet reached the last perfection. When the courtesan, his former mistress, succumbs to a snakebite near the ferry, he discovers that he has a son, who was conceived during the last night he spent with her. This son is now left with him. Only too painfully Siddhartha realizes that he is unable to communicate with him, even though his love toward his own flesh and blood tears his heart. Annoyed by his father's attitudes, which he can neither understand nor bear, his son runs away. After a period of deepest anguish of soul Siddhartha comes to realize that his pain was caused by his blind, one-sided love for his son. In a wonderful charismatic experience this love slowly changes to an all-absorbing devotion to the Absolute; Siddhartha is saved and absolved from his individuation. . . . It was this deepest suffering that brought about the last serenity of Knowledge and complete inner peace.

Looking retrospectively at the career of Siddhartha, we can now summarize Hesse's ideas about how life should be lived. Siddhartha's life as a Brahmin and ascetic, later as a merchant, exemplifies the wrong turns of the road that the protagonist took. Neither the life of the thinker nor that of the man of power and force of will bring him inner peace. . . . Siddhartha only finds peace and self-realization in a quiet, contemplative existence. It is not abstract thought that liberates man, but loving devotion to the universe. (pp. 37-8)

[We] are aware that Siddhartha's attitudes and his final Realization clearly follow the essence of the *Bhagavad-Gita.* . . . His experience is not unique nor private and subjective. It can be the experience of anyone. . . . Most of the works of Hesse dealing with spiritual problems implicitly, if not explicitly, point to this best solution for living. (p. 39)

Hans Beerman, "Hermann Hesse and the 'Bhagavad-Gita'," in The Midwest Quarterly, *Vol. I, No. 1, October, 1959, pp. 27-40.*

Ernst Rose (essay date 1965)

[*Rose is a German-born American critic and scholar who has written extensively on European literature. In the following excerpt from his critical study* Faith from the Abyss: Hermann Hesse's Way from Romanticism to Modernity, *he focuses his examination of the short fiction collection* Klingsor's Last Summer *on the title story and its theme of "giving up on oneself."*]

In 1920 Hesse published three . . . tales under the common title ***Klingsor's Last Summer.*** The first **"Kinderseele" ("Childhood"),** was written in 1918 and suggested the Nietzschean solution of *Demian.* It re-created one of those fateful moments of childhood when obedience to parental commandments is no longer taken on trust and the first thought of evil enters the innocent mind. It also portrayed the first painful assertion of coming independence. The story was the last one to be preoccupied with Hesse's own childhood. After **"Kinderseele,"** his attention was wholly devoted to problems of maturity.

However, **"Klein and Wagner"** (1919-1920), the second story, avoids a Nietzschean assertion. It tells the story of a man who can cope neither with the exigencies of his former bourgeois existence nor with the newly awakened sensuousness of his subconscious, and in the end simply gives up the struggle in Schopenhauerean despair. Klein starts out as a respectable bank employee and family man. But he is unable to keep up his middle-class pretensions without embezzling money and forging passports. Finally he runs away from his responsibilities and tries to start a new life. He lets himself be guided by the suppressed demon in his soul, by the evil *anima.* His secret idol becomes the murderer Wagner, a South German school teacher who ruthlessly slaughtered his whole family and then killed himself.

When Klein arrives in a small Italian lakeside resort, he pays for everything with embezzled money. He has an adventure with an innkeeper's wife, who has been deserted by her husband. Then he starts a stormy affair with the dancer Teresina. After one particularly violent scene, Klein is seized by the desire to murder Teresina and immediately sets out to execute his plan. But he is unable to find a knife and therefore runs away.

At the shore of the lake he comes across a boat, which he enters and pushes into the water. When it has drifted far

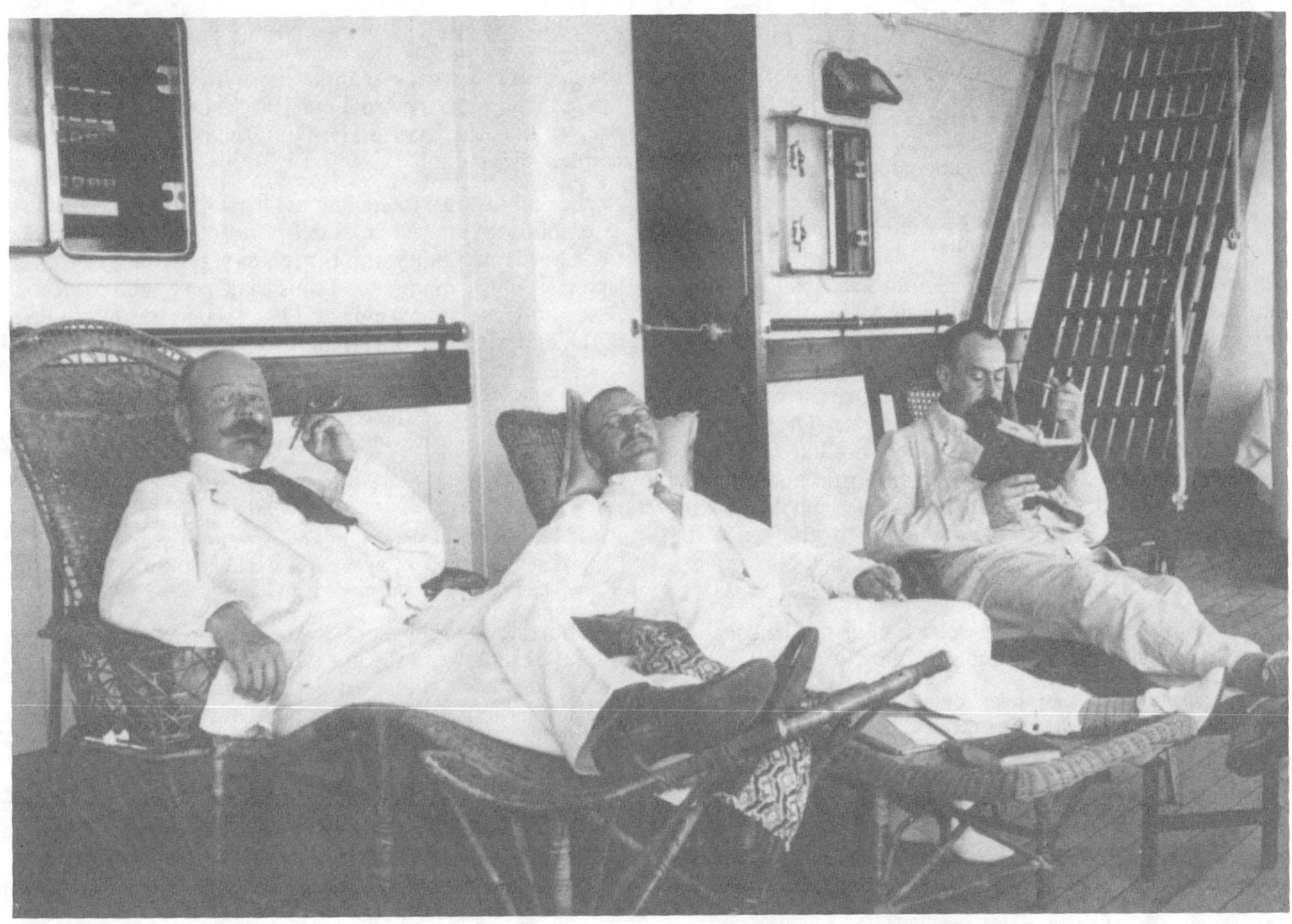

Hesse (center) and his friend the painter Hans Sturzenegger (right) en route to India, September 1911.

enough, Klein climbs overboard and lets himself fall. He cannot really face himself in the way that *Demian* espoused Nietzschean self-knowledge. Klein is too weak to lead a completely asocial life, and he is likewise unable to resume his former bourgeois existence. So he chooses the path of least resistance and gives himself up. This avoidance of a decision fills his soul with a vision of infinite bliss. He has annihilated his unsatisfactory personality and become united with the universe, of which he has been but one fleeting moment. Extinguishing himself, Klein can submerge in God, whose praise is his ultimate utterance. (pp. 59–60)

This giving up of oneself, this "letting oneself fall," is also the predominant theme of **"Klingsor's Last Summer" ("Klingsors letzter Sommer,"** 1919), the third story of the book. The title itself indicates that self-abandonment is stressed, for "last" here means "ultimate, final, suicidal." In the beginning of the story it is stated soberly that Klingsor has died, although the narrator mentions at the same time that his life has become surrounded by myths. Actually, only the intoxicated and exuberant Klingsor is symbolically rejected at the end, and a tame and conventional contemporary emerges. This solution is highly ironical. In truth, it is no solution at all. Klingsor's life is an attempt to live in both worlds—in the untamed world of the senses and the ordinary world of contemporary civilization. The result is little more than a passing escapade.

On the surface, Klingsor's story is merely trying to capture the exceptional Ticino summer of 1919. But this summer stands for the totality of sensual existence; a totality exhilarating by its vitality and continuously succumbing to death and decay at the same time. Death is always hovering before Klingsor's mind and is tinging his bursts of uninhibited self-enjoyment with melancholy. "Klingsor was looking at the black doors. Death stood outside. He saw him standing. He smelled death like one smells rain drops in the scattered leaves of the highway." Decline and downfall are also new birth and resurrection: every end is a beginning. Here, Hesse is taking leave of the setting sun of nineteenth-century Europe, from the friendly evening calm of Keller's *Seldwyla* stories, and starting out in a new, violent world of inner disturbances and searing sincerity. There is in the story all the melancholy of decay and dying, and all the explosiveness of sensuous passion and intoxication.

Klingsor is painting "free paraphrases of reality" in very few colors; but these colors are uncommonly bright. He is absorbed in the profound drinking songs of his favorite poet Li Tai Po, and often calls himself Li Tai Po. Klingsor flirts with chaos. He is

> acutely touched by every longing, sick with every vice, enthusiastically inspired by the knowledge of his own demise, prepared for every progress, ripe for every reaction, wholly glow and wholly lassitude, dedicated to fate and pain like the drug addict to poison, lonely, caved in, ancient, Faust as well as Karamasoff, animal as well as wise man, wholly bore, wholly without ambition, wholly naked, full of childish fear of death and full of tired readiness to die.

Klingsor's life pulsates between Dionysian abandon and continuous awareness of death, between searing passion and contemplative meditation. He drinks the cups of wine and of love in great gulps, yet he knows that this episode will not last forever. Some day in the future the wind will rustle over his grave. But he will not be alone. The "eternal mother" will then bend over him, she who, like Goethe's "Mothers" in *Faust,* symbolizes the immortal mainspring of ever-recurring life in the midst of the perishable world. She also symbolizes Hesse's resignation to his fate. Yet there is not only Goethe in his mind, but also Nietzsche. ("Louis the Cruel" is a Nietzschean term.)

In conformity with the abandoned mood, the landscape setting is transformed into a magic unreality.

> Beneath him descended down into dizzying depths the old terrace garden, a thicket of ample tree tops—palms, cedars, chestnuts, Judas trees, red beeches, eucalyptus—in dark shadows intertwined with climbers, lianas, glycinias. Over the black trees lay the shine of the pale, big, tinny reflecting leaves of the summer magnolias, amongst them enormous, snow-white blossoms, half opened, big like human heads, pale like the moon and like ivory, from which a peculiarly penetrating and enervating fragrance drifted over. Music came from an undetermined distance, flying on tired wings, perhaps from a guitar, perhaps from a piano, one could not make it out. In the poultry yards there suddenly shrieked a peacock two or three times and tore the forest night with the short, evil, and wooden sound of his pained voice, as if all the sufferings of the animal world sounded shrilly from primeval depths. Starlight was flowing through the valley, a white, tall, deserted chapel peaked like old magic from the infinite forest. The lake, the mountains, and the sky intermingled in the distance.

Klingsor completely forgets himself in these nightly musings, and his friend Louis the Cruel tries in vain to induce him to face reality. For Klingsor, art is not merely a substitute for sensuality; he does not pain for want of something better. In a painting by Luigi (i.e., Louis), he loves most of all a small spot taken up by a little flag. "In this small, stupid, pink flag is all the woe and all the resignation of the world, and also all the good laughter over the woe and the resignation." The spiritual and the sensual belong together and must not be separated.

Klingsor embraces life in all its aspects, be they ever so fleeting and momentary. We partake with him in a mountain climb to Monte Gennaro; in the flights of his fancy to Africa and Nagasaki, to India and to the South Seas; in his wining and dining with his friends in the beautiful July nights. And amid all these elations, Klingsor is changing. He savors the melancholy of the change from life to death and back again to new birth. He sends one of his realistic paintings to Louis the Cruel and a drinking song to his other friend Hermann the poet written in the manner of Tu Fu. . . . (pp. 61-3)

In the end he tries to encompass his whole personality by assembling all his faces in a self-portrait. He neither wants to escape from reality into the realm of pure fancy, nor resign to it in the manner of Louis the Cruel, who professes to see no sense in anything and has succumbed to the lure of the material. But the attempted integration of both attitudes is unsuccessful.

> At the end of these whipped-up days he put the finished picture into the unused, empty kitchen and locked it up. He never showed the picture to anyone. Then he took Veronal and slept for a whole day and a whole night. Afterwards he washed and shaved, put on new underwear and new clothing, went to town and bought fruit and cigarettes, as a present for Gina.

To understand **"Klingsor's Last Summer,"** one must read a great deal between the lines. Hesse does not make it easy for the reader in this most personal of his books. At the same time he is filling our minds with unforgettable images. The name of Klingsor is taken from the unfinished novel *Heinrich von Ofterdingen* by Novalis, who had found it in Wolfram von Eschenbach's *Parzival* as the name of a powerful magician. . . . Hesse frequently described his view of the world as magical, and he liked to designate his own calling as that of a magician. One might therefore be tempted to call Klingsor a self-portrait, if Klingsor did not have so many different faces. Hermann the poet, who calls himself Tu Fu, is intended as a self-portrait of Hesse. Louis the Cruel is a parody of the painter Louis Moilliet, while the Armenian magician is a mask for the architect Josef Englert. Finally, Hesse brought Ruth Wenger into this story. (Half a decade later she became his second wife.) She appears as the queen of the mountains from the parrot house in Corona. Yet all of these people are changed and transformed; their portraits emerge as expressionistic explosions. The book is in no way a simple diary. (pp. 63-4)

Ernst Rose, in his Faith from the Abyss: Hermann Hesse's Way from Romanticism to Modernity, *New York University Press, 1965, 175 p.*

Theodore Ziolkowski (essay date 1965)

[*An American educator and critic, Ziolkowski is best known as the author of* The Novels of Hermann Hesse: A Study in Theme and Structure *(1965) and as the editor of numerous English translations of Hesse's works. A professor of German language and literature, Ziolkowski contends that literature cannot be studied from a single national perspective; accordingly, throughout his career he has promoted the value of comparative literary studies. In the following excerpt from an essay originally published in the above study, he discusses Hesse's symbolic use of the river in* Siddhartha.]

The central symbol around which the plot and substance of [***Siddhartha***] are organized is the river. Unlike those in *Demian,* this symbol is not complicated or complemented by other symbols or motifs; it alone bears the full burden of communication. The river, as so often in literature from Heraclitus to Thomas Wolfe, is a symbol for timelessness, and with this symbol Hesse aligns himself with many other modern authors who are obsessed with the problem of the tyranny of time: Proust, T. S. Eliot, Hermann Broch, Thomas Mann, and Faulkner, to mention only a few. In Hesse's case this symbol of simultaneity is expanded to include the realm, already anticipated in *Demian,* in which all polarity ceases: totality. It is a realm of pure existence in which all things coexist in harmony. Fluidity is a corollary of what, in *Demian,* we called magical thinking, or what Siddhartha expresses thus: ". . . of every truth it can be said that the opposite is just as true!" For in any system that regards all polar extremes as invalid, as interchangeable, traditional values are indeed in a state of flux. Hence we find in ***Siddhartha*** many symbols of fluidity, and this extends even to the vocabulary, which returns to expressions of fluidity just as consistently as the language of *Demian* to the style of the Bible. Further: another corollary to the principle of magical thinking is metamorphosis. Just as fluidity might be regarded as the mode of totality in space, metamorphosis—in the Indian sense of transmigration of the souls—is its mode in time. Thus the concept of the "cycle of transformations" (*Kreislauf der Verwandlungen*) plays an important role in the argument of the book, for Siddhartha's ultimate goal, as exemplified in the final vision, is to escape the wheel of metempsychosis by realizing that all possible transformations or potentialities of the soul are possible not only consecutively, but simultaneously in the human soul. "In deep meditation there is the possibility of annulling time—to regard everything that has been, that is, and that will be, as simultaneous." Siddhartha explains this idea to Govinda by using the example of a stone: ". . . this stone is stone: it is also animal, it is also God, it is also Buddha. I love and venerate it not because it might someday become this or that—but because it has long been all these things and always will be . . . " Siddhartha's redemption lies in the fact that he has escaped the circle of metempsychosis: his Nirvana is no more than the recognition that all being exists simultaneously in unity and totality. As Hesse states it in his diary excerpts: "Nirvana, as I understand it, is the liberating step back behind the *principium individuationis;* that is, religiously expressed, the return of the individual soul to the All-soul."

All of this is nothing new: we met it in Demian's magical thinking and in many of Hesse's essayistic utterances. And in the story **"Pictor's Metamorphoses,"** which was written in the same year (1922), Hesse transports us to a fairytale realm where the hero actually does undergo the various transformations that Siddhartha experiences only psychologically. Through the powers of the magic carbuncle Pictor is physically transformed into a tree and other natural objects. But nowhere else has Hesse employed a more appropriate symbol for his ideas than here: for the river is in essence fluidity and simultaneity. This is made clear repeatedly:

> This is what you mean, isn't it: that the river is everywhere at the same time—at its source and at its mouth, at the waterfall, at the ferry, at the rapids, in the sea, in the mountains—everywhere, at the same time—and that for the river there is only the present, without the shadow of a future.

In the river Hesse found the perfect symbol for his views. Demian's Abraxas, Harry Haller's Magic Theater, and the Glass Bead Game itself are all symbols for precisely the same concept; but they are invented or esoteric symbols that have to be explained, whereas the aptness and significance of the river is instantly apparent to the reader. But Hesse did not stop at the symbolic function of the river. He uses it in addition as the central structural element. Substance, symbol, and structure are so closely welded that it is almost impossible to separate these functions, for the meaning is not put into words, as in the other works, but must be derived from the action of the book itself.

It is only on the river, this realm of totality and effacement of polarities, that Siddhartha could have experienced the visionary dream that he has as he departs from Govinda to experience the life of the senses in the city.

> Sad was the appearance of Govinda, sadly he asked: Why did you leave me? Thereupon he embraced Govinda, wrapping his arms about him, and as he drew him to his breast and kissed him, it was no longer Govinda, but a woman, and from the woman's garments there burst a full breast; Siddhartha rested his head upon this breast and drank, sweet and strong tasted the milk of this breast. It tasted of woman and man, of sun and forest, of animal and flower, of every fruit, of every passion. It made him drunk and unconscious.

In this dream, which comes to Siddhartha as he spends the night in the ferryman's hut beside the river, we have a transition from Siddhartha's previous ascetic life, personified by Govinda, to his new life in the arms of Kamala. But here on the river itself the two realms—spirit and senses—are united in the embrace of the strange hermaphroditic figure of his dream (a figure strongly reminiscent of the male-female dream-ideals of Sinclair in *Demian*). This dream plays a key role in the structure of the novel, for it is at once a transition between two parts as well as an anticipation of yet a third part, in which the two worlds will be reconciled in Siddhartha's vision of totality and simultaneity on the river. (pp. 81-4)

Theodore Ziolkowski, "Siddhartha: The Landscape of the Soul," in Hesse Companion, *edited by Anna Otten, Suhrkamp Verlag, 1970, pp. 71-100.*

Bhabagrahi Misra (essay date 1968)

[*In the essay excerpted below, Misra discusses the Indian elements of* Siddhartha *and proposes that Hesse combines these into "an organic cultural whole" which serves as a vehicle for his essentially existentialist themes.*]

Siddhartha is a product of a special religious awareness in its ritualistic and philosophic pattern, revaluing humanity and the primitive elements in human nature. Some critics have tried to evaluate ***Siddhartha*** in the light of the Four Noble Truths and Eightfold path of Buddha. But this approach seems to be fallacious, since, in essence, ***Siddhartha*** is a revolt against the Buddhist way. ***Siddhartha*** is a constant oscillation between life's opposite poles, reaching a conclusion, unlike Buddha:

> If they are illusions, then I am also illusion, and so they are always of the same nature as myself. It is that which makes them so lovable and venerable. That is why I can love them. And here is a doctrine at which you will laugh. It seems to me, Govinda, that love is the most important thing in the world. It may be important to great thinkers to examine the world, to explain and despise it. But I think it is only important to love the world, not to despise it, not for us to hate each other, but to be able to regard the world and ourselves and all things with love, admiration and respect.

In conflict with his age and modernism in particular, Hesse engrossed himself in exploiting Indic tradition to seek 'Unity or Oneness', in finding the meaning of life. ***Siddhartha*** is an attempt to find out this 'Oneness' and to restore faith in humanity, as a psychological release from his mental tension. This quest of Hesse is reflected in his statement before his voyage to India 'to see the sacred tree and snake (of Buddha) and to go back to that source of life where everything had begun and which signified the oneness (Einheit) of all phenomena'.

For achieving this 'timeless reality', Hesse utilised the legendary tale of Buddha as the frame-work of his novel, and has [according to Theodore Ziolkowski] 'transplanted various motifs from the life of Buddha to the life of Siddhartha—not as typological prefiguration, but in order to sustain the legendary quality of the narrative.' ***Siddhartha*** is therefore, a story with its origin in a historic time, but transcending to 'timeless reality', expounding all levels of human experiences.

The creation of Siddhartha as a separate character from the historic Buddha seems to be based on the etymological meaning of the word 'Siddhartha'. Siddhartha means, 'one who has attained his goal'. Hesse attempts to establish that Siddhartha could find all solace in life and peace, even being opposed to the Buddhist way; thus proving the etymological meaning of his name to be true.

The story starts with the traditional conflict between the Brahmanical and Buddhist way. Buddha was the most eloquent expression of protest against the traditional theology, Brahmanical priesthood and sacerdotal ritualism, establishing a more rationalistic, liberal and subjective thinking. Siddhartha, therefore, is introduced in the first chapter of the novel as a Brahmin's son, rigorously observing all the hieratic, externalistic and ritualistic pattern in daily life, but still lingering at heart to comprehend the 'Brahman'. Learning the art of practising contemplation, offering sacrifices, listening to religious discourses, and reciting hymns from *Veda* and *Upanishads* could not satisfy him. He decides to try the path of the Samanas (ascetics). This attitude in itself shows, how Hesse tries to expound the conflict in the religious tradition of India. This is reflected in his statement about Siddhartha:

> Govinda knew that he would not become an ordinary Brahmin, a lazy sacrificial official, an avaricious dealer in magic sayings, a conceited worthless orator, a wicked sly priest or just a good stupid sheep amongst a large herd.

But at the time of leaving his father's house, Siddhartha waits for the permission of his father in the traditional Indian way, and succeeds in getting his permission for the devotion to his aim in life. In the first chapter itself, Siddhartha rejects the Brahmanical way of ritualistic life. In the second chapter he joins the Samanas. But he realizes that the asceticism does not lead him on the proper path. Through self-denial, and following the ascetic rules he 'killed his senses, he killed his memory, he slipped out of his Self in a thousand different forms. He was animal, carcass, stone, wood, water, and each time he reawakened', thus reaching at a conclusion:

> Govinda, I believe that among all the Samanas, probably not even one will attain Nirvana. We find consolations, we learn tricks with which we deceive ourselves, but the essential thing—the way—we do not find.

He hypnotises the eldest Samana and gets his permission to leave. Before leaving, Govinda suggests:

> Siddhartha, you have learned more from the Samanas than I was aware. It is difficult, very difficult to hypnotise an old Samana. In truth, if you had stayed there, you would have soon learned how to walk on water.

Siddhartha rejects the suggestion of Govinda, and proceeds to listen to the teachings of Gautama the Buddha with Govinda, leaving behind the old samanas to 'satisfy themselves with such arts', as walking on waters.

In the next two chapters Hesse introduces Gautama Buddha and his followers in a legendary setting in the 'Jetavana grove, which the rich merchant Anathapindika' had presented to Buddha and his followers. Siddhartha and Govinda listened to the teachings of Buddha. Govinda joins the teacher, but Siddhartha departs from him in search of the 'unity of time', 'overwhelmed by a feeling of icy despair'. He now finds that the world from which he has so far tried to flee is attractive. As Hesse puts it:

> That was the last shudder of his awakening, the last pains of birth. Immediately he moved on again and began to walk quickly and impatiently, no longer homewards, no longer to his father, no longer looking backwards.

In the next four chapters known as Kamala episode, Siddhartha has been exposed to the pleasures and pain of the worldly man. On his way to the city he meets for the first time the longing for sex. Here Hesse is presenting a picture from the classical Indic 'Art of Love'. But the village setting and its detailed description is unsuitable for this presentation. Perhaps Hesse feels that the classical learning of the art of love had even permeated to the rural folk. As soon as Siddhartha sees a young woman on the way she greets him. She then placed her left foot on his right and made a gesture, such as a woman makes when she invites a man to that kind of enjoyment of love which the holy books call 'ascending the tree.' Next he proceeds to the city, meets Kamala, a courtesan, learns the art of love from her, discards his beggar's cloth and becomes a successful merchant. In course of his conversations with Kamala in their first meeting, Siddhartha explains that resolution is the key to success in each sphere. Siddhartha explains to her:

> That is what Siddhartha learned from the Samanas. It is what fools call magic and what they think is caused by demons. Nothing is caused by demons; there are no demons. Everyone can perform magic, everyone can reach his goal, if he can think, wait and fast.

This is how Hesse tries to explain the nature of magic as an art. Here comes a breaking point in the construction of the story. Hesse finds himself unable to move further in shaping Siddhartha. He states:

> My Indic poem got along splendidly as long as I was writing what I had experienced: the feelings of Siddhartha, the young Brahman, who seeks the truth, who scourges and torments himself, who has learned reverence, and must now acknowledge this as an impediment to the Highest Goal. When I had finished with Siddhartha the sufferer and ascetic, with the struggling and suffering Siddhartha and now wished to portray Siddhartha the victor, the affirmer, the subjugator—I could not go on.

He devotes himself in studying thoroughly Indian philosophy and religion. After a break of about one and half years he picks up new strength and vigour to lead Siddhartha to a conclusion that not by teaching or any specific action one can find peace. To equate the divine principle in the universe with the self, one has to look deep into oneself, and the world around.

The whole emphasis of the plot is swayed by a feeling to explain the supernatural element which motivates and guides all human actions. It seems that Hesse, from the study of 'the actual religious India of the Gods', perceived that only through faith and not by following any particular teaching can man find peace in life.

In the following chapters Siddhartha's self-analysis is the main theme of Hesse's description. Siddhartha meets Vasudeva, a ferryman, and spends the rest of his life with him. Here Siddhartha learns the 'timeless unity' from the river. At the bank of this river he meets Kamala, Govinda and his son. This is how Hesse reunites the plot. Thus Siddhartha in his own way achieves eternal bliss.

Comparing the legendary tale of Buddha and the plot construction of ***Siddhartha,*** it is found that there is a strong sense of parallelism. Buddha left his wife and child to become an ascetic. Similarly, Siddhartha leaves his wife Kamala and his still unborn child to seek truth. Both of them have spent some time of their lives with the Samanas and have practised yoga. Revelation came to Buddha under the sacred Bodhi tree, whereas Siddhartha takes important decision under the mango tree. River is the final place in both of their lives where they realise the ultimate truth. These parallel incidents prove to a certain degree that Hesse imitated the legendary life of Buddha in constructing the moral allegory of ***Siddhartha.*** But the incidents in the life of Siddhartha have been rearranged in an opposite direction than that of Buddha to meet his purpose, in creating Siddhartha as a protest against Buddhist way. Another important character in the novel is Vasudeva, who plays a dominant role in the life of Siddhartha. Though Vasudeva is portrayed as a simple, unconcerned, lone ferryman, many of his statements lead the reader to believe that Hesse created Vasudeva on the model of Krishna's role in the *Bhagavad-Gita.* After Siddhartha's revelation, Vasudeva leaves him for ever. Before leaving he says:

> I have waited for this hour, my friend. Now it has arrived, let me go. I have been Vasudeva, the ferryman, for a long time. Now it is over. Farewell hut, farewell river, farewell Siddhartha.

Hesse had felt in his heart that though Buddhism was a very pure form of religion, its only shortcoming is the 'destruction of the image-worlds'. As such, Siddhartha realises the truth, being in communication with a number of gods of the Hindu pantheon, on the mental plane. Vasudeva through his words and deeds commands a reverence from Siddhartha.

The function of the Indic tradition in Hesse's novel, therefore, aims at comprehending [in Ziolkowski's words] 'chaos and cosmos', which 'exist within man, not in the world outside; and the selection (or creation) of an adequate deity is based upon man's reaction to those inner impulses'. In his essay 'My Faith', he says 'that my Siddhartha puts no cognition, but love at first place: that it disdains dogma and makes the experience of unity the central point'. The struggle of the principle of existence is inevitably bound up with the rise and fall, births and deaths. In other words, life is maintained through a sort of birth and death at each and every step. Hesse tries to point out this, in the life of Siddhartha. At each step, Siddhartha reawakens to face the world outside. In the first chapter he rejects the Brahmanical way, next the Buddhist way and the worldly way. Finally, he reaches such a point in life when realisation comes of itself.

In seeking to assess and convey the reactions of his time, Hesse draws examples, incidents and characters from the legendary history of India. Through a well-knit story he presents a biographical account of Gautama Buddha, descriptions of gods, symbols, religious faiths and even the natural setting of India, from scattered sources to represent an organic cultural whole of India. Perhaps he felt that a knowledge of the past in myths and legends provides adequate evidence of man's continual struggle. This struggle alone leads to perfection. As he puts it through Siddhartha:

> The world, Govinda, is not imperfect or slowly evolving along a long path to perfection. No, it is perfect at every moment; every sin already carries grace within it, all small children are potential old men, all suckling have death within them, all dying people eternal life. It is not possi-

> ble for one person to see how far another is on the way; the Buddha exists in the robber and dice player; the robber exists in the Brahmin. During deep meditation it is possible to dispel time, to see simultaneously all the past, present and future, and then everything is good, everything is perfect, everything is Brahman.

Through the analysis of Siddhartha he tries to present his view about the eternal value of culture and religion. To him, 'as far as the eternal in man is concerned, the teachings of Jesus, Lao Tse, Veda, Goethe are the same. There is only one teaching and there is only one religion'. To establish this one religion, Hesse has tried to use a variety of psychological functions, incantations, rites, sacred formulae, mythology, theology, magic, charms, emotional reaction in Siddhartha's life. The supernatural power and its relationship to human beings is an essential point on which Hesse seems to be working. The conflict about this relationship does not lie in the external world, but in one's own self.

As [S. R.] Townsend observes, '. . . Hesse considers art, music, poetry, meditation, and humour as eternal values, i.e., phases of the absolute the awareness of which makes man's striving worthwhile.' For making 'man's striving worthwhile', Hesse chooses traditional materials and even form, for the creation of his literary art. Speaking about his literary career Hesse states:

> As a writer, I believe, I have always been a traditionalist. With few exceptions I was always satisfied with the traditional form, a standard pattern, a model. It was never important to me to offer novelty of form, or to be an avant–gardist or pioneer.

In ***Siddhartha*** too, he adapted the traditional legendary form, but reshaped the legendary tale of Buddha to create Siddhartha as an imaginative non-conformist. In his attempt to find out the meaning of life in Siddhartha, his attitude is existentialistic. In a continuum of 'Romantic tradition' at one end and 'Existentialistic attitude' at the other, ***Siddhartha*** encompasses a variety of materials from classical Indic tradition. (pp. 114-22)

Bhabagrahi Misra, "An Analysis of Indic Tradition in Hermann Hesse's 'Siddhartha'," in Indian Literature, *Vol. 11, No. 2, 1968, pp. 111-23.*

Colin Butler (essay date 1971)

[*In the following essay, Butler faults* Siddhartha *for what he regards as the title character's solipsistic philosophy which upholds escapism as the exclusive path toward truth.*]

Siddhartha is a fictitious biography. A sort of *Bildungsroman,* it records the passage of a special individual through selected key experiences until he attains to a position of competence in dealing with what little life is left to him. The nature of Siddhartha's preoccupations and development, and the stylistic devices used to relate them, suggest that the work is the repository of certain truths regarding human existence in general; and so the question naturally arises as to how acceptably Hesse presents and discusses them. In order to decide this, what is being offered must be defined as exactly as possible. In this undertaking, Hesse proves less than helpful.

Although generously endowed with intelligence, good looks, a winning personality, and all other requirements for what would normally be considered a successful life, Siddhartha is not content. He is conscious of a discrepancy between conventional assumptions and personal satisfaction which neither adulation nor material advantage nor received interpretations of life's meaning can overcome. The apparent cause of Siddhartha's discomfort is the inception of an awareness of himself as a question-begging phenomenon in a situation which provides no ready answers. . . . However, while it is undeniable that the absence of discernible metaphysical certainties may give rise to acute anxiety, it is not true that sackcloth and ashes are the only possible response. However much of a philosophical wild goose chase the search for the overall meaning of existence may be, it takes a gloomy person to jump to the conclusion that because life is meaningless in a particular sense, it is also worthless in a general sense.

But, at least at the time of ***Siddhartha,*** Hesse could be a very gloomy person indeed; and by failing to make clear from the beginning that any appraisal of life and hence of the situation of the individual (or, as in practice is more often the case, *vice versa*) is determined as much by personality as by metaphysical speculation, he admits a confusion by which his entire story will be conditioned. It is wholly in keeping with the kind of mind which naturally inclines to seek external explanations for internal distress that Siddhartha's real concern rapidly turns out to be not the onset of self-awareness as such, the fancifully-phrased *principium individuationis,* but the narrower problem of the absence of a "Ziel," an *a priori* absolute purpose. Nor is it surprising that self-awareness is consistently identified to such an extent with the absence of a "Ziel" that no real distinction is possible between them. This is a very convenient simplification for Hesse, for by becoming aware of the error of looking for a "Ziel," Siddhartha will appear to solve the "problem" of individual existence at the same time. For the moment, however, Siddhartha is allowed to pursue his mistaken course, and as a result resolves to annihilate his Self (i.e., his doleful sense of individual identity), since a Self without purpose is held to invite the drastic solution of better no Self at all.

Siddhartha's activities with the Samanas could not be other than unsuccessful. One cannot consciously rid oneself of oneself (short of actually committing suicide), since any ridding process undertaken with that intention will only further confirm the presence of a conscious self. Once Siddhartha realizes this, the exercises of the Samanas lose their point for him; if continued, they would become merely an end in themselves, which is exactly the opposite of what he wants. Siddhartha's meeting with the Buddha is of greater moment, not only because it brings him face to face with a living success, but also because it introduces three elements that will be important later on. First, the imprecise religious connotation: the Buddha is a priest and has found "the way." Second, however, the Buddha is not a priest in the orthodox Western sense, nor does his way lead to the Kingdom of Heaven or to any equivalent of it. In other words, Siddhartha becomes acquainted with a secular solution to life's problems that has the aura, but not the essence, of a religious solution in the usual sense of the word. Third, the word most frequently associated with the Buddha is "Vollkommenheit," or other words and phrases amounting to the same thing. The inference is that ultimate truth ("the way") and this undefined "Vollkommenheit" are inseparable; which allows the fallacy to be insinuated that attainment to the latter automatically entails the discovery of the former. And so terms such as "Erlösung," "Erkenntnis," "das Wesentliche," and "der Weg der Wege" are employed indiscriminately, and Siddhartha's quest is now for personal happiness, now for an answer to "die Unsinnigkeit des Lebens," now for knowledge, and now for a purpose in life. Predictably, Siddhartha's eventual solution (it is a comfort to know that life lends itself so readily to blanket solutions) will be a *potpourri* of all of these, for *the* way of understanding reality will also turn out to be the most satisfying. It could be, of course, that the attempt to gain an objective understanding of reality might well issue in the realisation that the kind of satisfaction Siddhartha is looking for is just not possible. But in ***Siddhartha*** the wish is always father to the thought, and so the illegitimate identification of objective truth and subjective contentment is allowed to run its course.

On leaving the Buddha, Siddhartha indulges in a period of stock-taking. He transfers attention back to himself, accepts the reality of the phenomenal world, which he has previously held to be illusory, and accepts for the first time the isolation of the seeker operating without the support of pre-established certainties. His objective remains the same: to find the sense of life as if there were a single sense to be found. Only the location of his enquiries and his *modus operandi* are changed. Having abandoned the possibility of forcing a solution by intellectual action, he will now try his luck with the senses. (pp. 117-19)

Siddhartha's capacity for sensual experience is, like that of all Hesse's protagonists, singularly limited. Ultimately this is due to a deficiency on Hesse's part, but in terms of ***Siddhartha*** its effect is to invalidate the contrast that is purportedly being established. Siddhartha's removal from the country to the town was obviously intended to symbolize a complete change in Siddhartha's experience of reality and so to prepare the way for the conclusion that neither intellectual effort nor unconceptualized sensual gratification is sufficient by itself to cope with the demands of a problematical existence. If this is to be done convincingly, however, Siddhartha's change of environment must be accompanied by an appropriate change in expectations on his part. Yet this is precisely what fails to occur.

Siddhartha's life in the village is a catalogue of failures—failures which the uninitiated would incline to attribute directly to his inability to develop a capacity for spontaneity. That, however, would be all too simple an explanation. As in the episode with the Samanas, Siddhartha's various occupations are expected to provide him with a reason for living. His excursion into the world of business proves unsatisfactory, not because of the inherent tedium of buying and selling, but because, from Siddhartha's point of view, business is only one of a number of pastimes which *mutatis mutandis* are all equally available to him and which are also all equally imperfect. Again, his relationship with Kamala, the courtesan, is irretrievably compromised by dint of the fact that it is basically a deliberate and artificial course of instruction. Neither trading, nor sexual expertise, nor gambling is *per se* of sufficient teleological significance to provide Siddhartha with the feeling that here at last he has found the way. And so he not unnaturally generalises his situation and succumbs to the notion that *all* human activity is "Sansara," a game.

At this point the question arises: has Siddhartha's position in any way been advanced since the end of the first part of the book? A superficial difference is immediately apparent, namely, that whereas he has hitherto been filled with confidence, he is now filled with despair. He is considerably older now, and the visible signs of physical deterioration are an undeniable reminder of the inevitability of death—which, of course, makes the discovery of a "Ziel" that much more desirable. And as far as the story's symbolical meaning is concerned, by the end of the second part Siddhartha is presumed to have exhausted if not the whole range of human experience, then at least sufficient of its two constituent areas for him to infer the impossibility of ever finding a solution to his problems. From another point of view, however, his position is not much altered. For although he has quantitatively increased the range and number of his experiences, the criterion of ultimate insufficiency by which he has found all of them wanting indicates that his sojourn in the village has amounted to no more than the continuation of old attitudes into new circumstances. If anything, Siddhartha has regressed. . . . To be sure, Hesse is careful to point out that Siddhartha has forsaken his Samana's asceticism and drifted into the ways of the world. But there is a real and important difference between his eventual seediness, and the vigorous, whole-hearted indulgence of the fleshpots which the rudimentary capacity to enjoy being alive would provide, even if intellectually the business of living did not make any more sense than before. Even a bad Samana is still a Samana.

If all this is true, what appears to be the antithetical development of the book is really nothing of the kind, despite the fact that its formal arrangement suggests that a genuine antithesis was Hesse's intention. For if both the criteria and the conclusions remain substantially the same in both parts, it can hardly be contended that Siddhartha has been exposed to the advantages and disadvantages of an alternative appreciation of reality before he contemplates suicide, let alone that *all* of life's options have been exhausted. Again the fault lies with Hesse, whose outlook on life is much more inflexible than the attempted comprehensiveness of his story indicates. But given this inflexibility on Hesse's part, it is inevitable that if Siddhartha is to find any kind of solution, it will remain the product of a mentality that *faute de mieux* thinks in terms of purposes and absolutes, even though a number of apparent modifications will have to be made if the reader is not to be left with the impression that suicide might have been the best response after all.

Reduced to their essentials, the problems that have beset Siddhartha have been transitoriness, death, and the absence of a sense of fulfillment. Having foregone the opportunity in the second part of the book to consider life from any angle other than *sub specie aeternitatis,* and having resolutely refused to recognize in any meaningful way that Siddhartha's trouble derives as much from his congenital inability to adapt to life as from his sense of metaphysical isolation, Hesse is faced with the daunting task of discovering the world to be perfect in the face of its manifest imperfections, and at the same time of accommodating Siddhartha's personal disconsolateness. He begins by having Siddhartha persuade himself that he can apprehend reality in its entirety. In addition, a cyclic principle is perceived which, unlike Siddhartha's earlier assumption of linear progression (which for him necessitated the question: to what end?), means that reality is not only physically self-contained, with all matter recurring infinitely, but that it is philosophically self-contained as well. In virtue of the totality of his vision, Siddhartha may be sure that no upsetting factors exist beyond the confines which a merely partial view of things would entail; and in virtue of this newly-discovered cyclic principle, the nature and meaning of existence may be explained without reference to any supra-terrestrial arbiter. Suddenly the world is filled with meaning. The idea of the death of God which had made Siddhartha's search for a "Ziel" at once so necessary and so tortuous is accepted and dismissed as superfluous at the same time; and everything is perfect ("vollendet") at last, particularly as the minor inconveniences of life such as pain, sorrow, and murder are apparently as amenable to assimilation in the grand view of things as are the large metaphysical issues. (pp. 119-22)

In the light of Siddhartha's revelation, what had hitherto appeared to be problems now present no difficulty. First, since reality now makes sense beyond a peradventure, one has no longer to cast about for a sense in it, or for a "Ziel": to appreciate one's inclusion in the unity of all things ("Einheit") is enough. Second, the same sense of belonging to an homogeneous reality automatically ensures the annulment of the *principium individuationis.* (Again, it might be asked why one has to regard reality as being complete before one can feel one belongs to it.) Third, once the unsubstantiated assumption is made that time is not intrinsic to reality, transitoriness can be dismissed with equal facility; for in what is maintained to be a situation of *nunc stans,* that is, the eternal circulation of what is already at hand, transitoriness is a concept without meaning. . . .

Siddhartha's attempt to mitigate the consequences of self-awareness by retailoring reality to his own specifications still in fact depends for its effectiveness on self-awareness. What has changed or rather, what has been decreased, is the *anxiety* which has hitherto been inseparable from Siddhartha's sense of individuation. . . . It is in the light of this that Hesse's treatment of death has to be interpreted. For the disquiet which has made it so hard for Siddhartha to live will certainly make it hard for him to die unless a good deal of ingenuity is employed. (p. 122)

[It is possible] that even if ***Siddhartha*** is mistaken in conception and misleading in detail it might remain a significant novel by virtue of the excellence of its style and its subtle analysis of the human soul. However, in view of Siddhartha's drab uniformity of response to situations which are already severely limited in type and variety; of his conviction, which is eventually "justified," that all of life can be reduced to a single point of view; of his latent homosexuality (a characteristic of most of Hesse's protagonists, notably Narcissus and Joseph Knecht); and of the fact that despite all this Siddhartha is still the most developed character in the novel: both the book and its eponymous hero must invite the adjective "immature"—that is, they consistently draw large conclusions from a small fund of experience without being aware that they are doing so. Much has been made by Hesse's expositors of Siddhartha's love for his son, and Hesse clearly regarded it as important. Yet it is also true that he found it necessary to remove both the son and Kamala, the only characters in the story with whom Siddhartha manages to establish anything like an intimate relationship, before proceeding to a conclusion that is solipsistic and abstract. It would be foolish to deny the presence of real feeling in those parts of the book that deal with the son. But it is to Hesse's discredit that he obscures its true nature and significance by subjecting it to pretentious rationalizations. Whatever the explicit reasons advanced for the son's departure; for Kamala's premature demise; and, for that matter, for Govinda's ultimate exclusion: the real reason for those excisions is that Hesse found himself in each case having to treat an emotion to which he could only respond with the regret and incompetence of the deprived spectator. In the last analysis, love is short-changed; and instead of "l'amor che move il sole e l'altre stelle" we are presented with the substitute rearrangement of heaven and earth that is Siddhartha's barren vision.

If the foregoing analysis of the content is true, little need be said about the style; for if the content is unacceptable, it is difficult to see how its linguistic formulation can effect any kind of meaningful improvement. It may well be that Hesse manifests a certain gift for creating atmosphere (personally, I must admit to finding ***Siddhartha*** laboured and unconvincing). But the atmosphere of ***Siddhartha*** deceives rather than enhances; it makes up in cloudy strangeness for what the book lacks in precise insight. A superficial Orientalism and what Theodore Ziolkowski calls "symbolic lyricism" may be exotic enough to make for a certain immediate appeal; but they also serve to conceal the fact that Hesse's real reason for turning to the East was not an accession of faith, but an abortive attempt to escape the problems of an obdurately Western understanding of reality. (pp. 123-24)

Colin Butler, "Hermann Hesse's 'Siddhartha': Some Critical Objections," in Monatshefte, *Vol. 63, No. 2, Summer, 1971, pp. 117-24.*

The Times Literary Supplement **(essay date 1971)**

[*In the excerpt below, the reviewer faults Hesse's use of symbolism in the stories of* Klingsor's Last Summer, *yet praises his portrait of philosophical and psychological dissolution.*]

All three stories in ***Klingsor's Last Summer*** are about dissolution. Two contrast it with duty, as a form of social indiscipline; the third treats it more subtly in relation to the artist's life.

"A Child's Heart" is a reminiscence, thirty years on, about the narrator as a child compulsively stealing figs from his father's desk, knowing it is wrong, not really wanting the figs, acting agonizingly to frustrate his own desire for affection and approval and security. One sometimes wonders if there is any other theme in German literature than the conflict of individual and authority. It is, of course, central to human existence, but art works its wonders on the periphery, shaping the casual indication. From the periphery, the imagination is tempted towards the centre, discovering implied worlds beyond thought. But when, as here in Hesse, symbols are intellectually central, there is no progress for the unconscious. This is a tender tale told from a distance, both remote and obvious, a literary exercise which even explains the child's hidden motivation (and the child's ignorance of this motivation) in case the symbols have not done their job. . . .

The second story, **"Klein and Wagner"**, is a variation on Thomas Mann's *Death in Venice.* Klein is a respectable civil servant who has suddenly broken away from his environment and his respectability. He is a criminal (i.e., the assertive individual) who has stolen a large sum of money and fled to the South (the region of indiscipline), complete with forged papers and revolver (symbol of anti-social passion, the revolver perhaps borrowed from its nail on the blood-red walls of the attic in Musil's *Törless*). Hesse seems to thumb through a thesaurus of instantly intelligible symbols, but readers are not led on by symbols they can immediately understand; they are stimulated by those they cannot understand yet know to be true. Watching Hesse in this story is like watching a competent weightlifter; one admires his muscles but not his imagination. His hero's death is inherent in the beginning, as Aschenbach's ending, his dissolution, is present always in his dissolute self. The difference between Hesse and Mann comes out clearly in the conclusion of their stories. Klein ends in the water; Hesse literally drowns his hero in the threatening ocean of forms and describes in detail his frenzy of feeling during the suicidal act. One remembers with gratitude the economy of Aschenbach's hardly noticed death on the beach. It is necessary to have a certain sense of humour to avoid making the tragic seem ridiculous.

In [**"Klingsor's Last Summer"**] Hesse develops the one satisfying feature of **"Klein and Wagner"**—that sense of kinship with all forms which comes with the melting of the individual boundary. The paradox of extreme individualism is that it leads to the elimination of the individual. The painter Klingsor moves through a succession of blazing summer days, realizing his genius through sensual seizure of experience. Colours and shapes assault him; he enjoys the pleasures of food and drink and women. Hesse's women are from a Romantic dream—the peasant with brown eyes, to be tumbled in five minutes in the heather, or the pale royal figure who proves surprisingly accessible to the hero's desires.

There is fine writing in this story. The violence of colour and temperature (human as well as meteorological) is matched by urgency of prose. Scenes connect obliquely in a satisfying because not immediately comprehensible way. The painter's growing vision of eternal metamorphosis dominates the story. This is the great flowering before decay, so the story is both a lament for transitoriness and an affirmation of continuity, even if Klingsor claims he believes only in doom. Hesse relates this sense of doom to the situation of European man, and interrupts his tale to tell us so. He is in general more successful with nature than with man, presumably because he cannot attribute thoughts to nature, or lines of dialogue like "Come to my heart, you matt dusky green trees!" At the end of this marvelous summer Klingsor paints his self-portrait, which turns out to be not only an image of all men but of all nature too, cliffs and trees and water. This is a fine thought splendidly expressed. . . .

"Long, Hot Summer," in The Times Literary Supplement, *No. 3631, October 1, 1971, p. 1166.*

Karen O. Crenshaw and Richard H. Lawson (essay date 1972)

[*In the essay excerpted below, Crenshaw and Lawson discuss Hesse's use of fairy tale elements to convey a sense of timelessness in* Die Morgenlandfahrt.]

Die Morgenlandfahrt, since it is written in the form of a fairy tale, is exempt from the necessity of continuous narration, from many of the conventions of cause and effect, and from the consequences of time. Hesse has freed himself from the restraint of having, in effect, to defend the technique of time distortion within a realistic or psychological novel. Time, forming a commentary on what is expected versus what is actual in a fairy-tale world, functions as a distancing device, and this tale, as fairy tales do, becomes abstract and cerebral. (pp. 53-4)

The fairy-tale form is especially conducive to changes and permutations of time. If by being set in a mythical or vague locale, the fairy tale achieves a kind of universality, then this universality is reinforced by a parallel vagueness of time: "einmal," "once upon a time." Such formulas do not eliminate time; rather, they allow enough temporal detail to effect a balance between alienation and understanding on the part of the listener or the reader.

The transcending of chronological time and the compromising—if not ignoring—of logic may well be a more successful technique for describing existence than is the use of logical consequence. It would, accordingly, seem well adapted to the subtle and effective expression of a philosophy. Hesse's fairy-tale stage, foreshadowed—at least so far as the important category of time-treatment goes—in *Demian* and *Der Steppenwolf,* and represented precisely by

Die Morgenlandfahrt, embraces his most successful expression of a philosophy.

As actual and fictitious places are mixed in ***Die Morgenlandfahrt,*** for example, on the one hand, Famagusta, and on the other, Morbio Inferiore, so the time element is neither unreal nor real; it draws from both categories. The actual journey to the East took place shortly after World War I. We infer the nonsequential nature of time from the simultaneity, or at any rate nonchronological juxtaposition of familiar historical data, for example, the implied simultaneity of post-World War I and the Hohenstaufen conquest of Sicily. Already one step further removed, and consonant with the narrative intermixture of history and fiction, is the juxtaposition of historical time, again, say, post-World War I, and a literary figure from a different era, thus Don Quijote. Such instances are plentiful, but we need not depend entirely on their evidence. Hesse clearly indicates his concept, first, of time as flowing, undemarcated, a stream. . . . And, second, each component of this diachronic procession, whether an individual or a group" . . . was only a wave in the eternal stream of souls, in the eternal homeward urge of the spirits. . . . "

Once the world of marked and counted time is overcome—"eine von Geld, Zahl und Zeit betörte Welt" and its appurtenances like railroads and timepieces—once all this is overcome, then the way is open for diachronic experience. Narration—telling, a function of time measurement—becomes difficult. . . . And, now with the blending of the spatial and the temporal, it is but one step from the diachronic to the synchronic: " . . . our East was not only a country and something geographical, but it was also the home and youth of the soul—it was the everywhere and nowhere, it was the unification of all eras." With the conversion of all times into one, H. H. is quite free of the tyranny of chronological time and of the latter's corollary: cause and effect. A so-called future event, or even a fictional event, may bring about a present result. . . . (pp. 54-5)

Magic, that familiar fairy-tale component, bears a primary relationship to nonsequential time, for it can bypass sequential time, and space as well. The use of magic as a description or metaphor of psychological states is limited only by the limits of the mind. Hesse uses this kind of fairy-tale description in ***Die Morgenlandfahrt*** to emphasize the weaknesses of man's normal, that is, chronological perceptions of time. The musician and fairy-tale reader, H. H., having lost his perception of timelessness, or inner time, sees life in terms of a sequence of logical events which have happened since his break with the Brotherhood. These events, comprising the latter half of the tale, are at such paradoxical variance with the timeless prospectus of the first half that they produce a remarkable structural tension and, correspondingly, a growing uneasiness, a desire for resolution, on the part of the reader. That H. H., even as he resolves "never to count . . . always to know faith to be stronger than so-called reality," nonetheless believes that these events can be set down in a history, is, of course, the crowning indication of his compartmentalization and of his separation from actual, that is, from synchronic time.

H. H. realizes that time was indeed transcended by the Brotherhood, but now that he is outside of the Brotherhood, he can no longer see how it was done, nor even the essential contradiction—the source of the reader's disquiet—in his own relationship to time. He struggles unwittingly with this contradiction but he is quite unable to formulate it: how can he express timelessness, the *Einswerden* of time, in terms of a history, a chronology of events in a cause-and-effect chain?

His renewed contact with the Brotherhood after a time-lapse is a measure of his sensed but unformulated need. The preliminary and external sign of this need is his "fixe Idee," his constant adverting to Leo, the capable, ever-present servant on the journey to the East, the Leo with whose disappearance at Morbio Inferiore H. H.'s connection with the journey dissolved. . . . H. H.'s need has become so great that he is again receptive to the Brotherhood. Its timeless world has continued to exist all around H. H. ever since he had left it for the chronological world.

H. H.'s reunion with the Brotherhood, effected by the rediscovered Leo, takes place in a faceless building, among millions of well-catalogued archives, under the scrutiny of a vague and shifting company of characters. His reunion with timelessness is a reunion with a mystical—perhaps Jungian—higher personality. The characters whom he had tried to describe and record as separate personalities became the different manifestations of the united Brotherhood when he himself could again perceive them in the state of timelessness. That a reunion with timelessness is to occur, that time will dissolve, that chronological time will cease to hold sway over H. H. is foretold even as Leo leads him by a much-detoured, zigzag route to the headquarters of the Brotherhood. Once more the familiar alignment of spatial multiplicity and temporal reduction to oneness, the latter process in the case of H. H. not yet quite complete. . . . (pp. 55-6)

The final demonstration of the fallacy of chronological sequence, and of cause and effect, is almost anti-climactic, almost trivial, as, with H. H. in the archives, the fairy-tale thread weakens, and the mystical dominates. H. H. is permitted to see three presumed histories of the journey to the East and the affair at Morbio Inferiore—his own account and those of two other would-be historians. Needless to say, the accounts do not agree, and were there ten rather than three, H. H. now realizes, "all ten would probably have contradicted one another . . . No, our historical endeavors had come to nought. . . . " As the separately described personalities became a variety of manifestations of the Brotherhood when H. H. perceived them in timelessness, so the chronology of separate events which he had tried to analyze and order is now seen as a merely momentary, temporal manifestation of timelessness.

The highly developed function of time in ***Die Morgenlandfahrt,*** as both a way and an obstacle to timelessness, the latter state achieved with the final dissolution of the personality into the greater unity, has its inchoate antecedents in *Demian.* To be sure, the earlier novel is arranged on a conventional narrative framework. Events happen one after another; previous events have logical consequences. The plot can be told, and the clear sequence of events requires a reliance on time as an absolute. (pp. 55-7)

In *Der Steppenwolf* the narrative sequence is still further weakened, as Hesse increasingly subjectifies time. Chronological time is no longer a reliable framework. (p. 57)

Clearly Hesse's development of timelessness as the alternative to chronological time, and above all as the solvent for time-bound personality in its quest toward a higher unity, has, with *Der Steppenwolf,* reached the point where it is pushing through and around the confines of the realistic or psychological novel. Further development will require a more congenial genre, one better adapted to transcending chronological time. That, as we have seen, is the fairy tale, and with ***Die Morgenlandfahrt*** Hesse's innovative time technique attains a parity with his innovative time function. (p. 58)

Karen O. Crenshaw and Richard H. Lawson, "Technique and Function of Time in Hesse's 'Morgenlandfahrt': A Culmination," in Mosaic: A Journal for the Comparative Study of Literature and Ideas, *Vol. 3, Spring, 1972, pp. 53-9.*

Theodore Ziolkowski (essay date 1972)

[*In his introduction to* Stories of Five Decades, *excerpted below, Ziolkowski assesses the development of Hesse's short fiction. (For an alternative perspective on Hesse's short fiction see Pawel's essay dated 1973.)*]

In 1921 Hermann Hesse's publisher urged him to prepare a selected edition of his works. But as Hesse read through the products of his past twenty-two years of literary activity, he came to the sobering conclusion that "there was nothing there to select." A realistic appraisal of his own abilities prevented him from invoking, even for purposes of comparison, the works of the grand masters of narrative: Cervantes, Dostoevsky, Balzac. Yet even when he considered such models as Turgenev or the nineteenth-century Swiss writer Gottfried Keller, Hesse realized that he was "by no stretch of the imagination a storyteller." For all his works, he belatedly saw, dealt not with the world but only with his own "secret dreams and wishes," his own "bitter anguish." "There was no doubt in my mind that, of all my stories, not a single one was good enough as a work of art to be worth mentioning."

Hesse's gloomy reassessment of 1921 anticipates his reflections on "the questionable art of storytelling" in the introduction to his late tale **"The Interrupted Class."** True storytelling, he argues, is possible only in societies in which the narrator can take for granted a common basis of language, values, and understanding between himself and his readers. But the fragmentation produced by the proliferation of beliefs and ideologies in the twentieth century has destroyed that common ground, isolating the author as merely one among countless alienated individuals in a pluralistic world. In his own efforts to use revered models of the past in order to come to grips with his essentially modern experience, Hesse had been, as he put it, a "deceiver deceived." As a result, he made up his mind henceforth to eschew "the good old tradition of storytelling" and to seek new modes of expression that, though less perfect and less beautiful, would provide a more honest reflection of the consciousness that he sought to render. These attempts, which produced his major novels beginning with *Demian* (1919), are the works with which most readers now identify Hesse.

Hesse's disenchantment with his early works and his determination to create a new style resulted directly from his experience with psychoanalysis in the years 1916 and 1917, during which he underwent some seventy sessions with Josef B. Lang, a disciple of Jung. The reevaluation of all his beliefs, sparked notably by the writings of Jung and Nietzsche, prompted him to turn frankly inward to the problems of his own consciousness. As a result, narratives that can be called "stories" in any conventional sense virtually disappear from his work. Instead, Hesse increasingly favored literary forms that enabled him to examine his own past and present, singling out for particular scrutiny those moments at which individual experience achieves the level of universal validity. "Fiction" begins to give way to essays that move from the private to the public, from the real to the symbolic, and to autobiographical reflections that turn out to be less an account of his life than an attempt to comprehend its meaning. And in his "fiction," from *Demian* to *The Glass Bead Game* (1943), "storytelling" in the traditional sense recedes in order to allow large mythic patterns to emerge. The forms that Hesse favored in the second half of his life—essay, autobiography, and mythic-symbolic narrative—constitute three different modes of access to the single problem that obsessed him: his own consciousness and its place in a timeless reality that transcends immediate temporal concerns.

Yet this seemingly abrupt change of direction *nel mezzo del cammin,* to cite one of Hesse's favorite poets, is no reason for us to reject the earlier works, as Hesse himself felt inclined to do in that moment of disillusionment in 1921. As we look back at them—with the benefit of hindsight, to be sure—we can see foreshadowed there not only the themes of alienation and introspection but even the style of mythic generalization that has attracted a new generation of readers to Hesse in the second half of the twentieth century. And in the 1941 introduction to a new edition of his first prose a somewhat mellower Hesse conceded that even such juvenalia as ***An Hour beyond Midnight*** (1899) and ***The Posthumous Writings and Poems of Hermann Lauscher*** (1901) are crucial documents for the history of his development.

Hesse's first published prose piece [**"The Island Dream"**] opens when a "shipwrecked dreamer" lays down his oars to greet the isle of his dreams. But his eye is suddenly caught by his reflection in the dark-green waters of the bay, and for two paragraphs, until he finally turns his attention back to the shore, he loses himself in the contemplation of his own image. The Narcissus pose was quite fashionable at the turn of the century, and it is hardly surprising to find the twenty-two-year-old Hesse adopting it in the prose sketches he published under the rather recherché title ***An Hour beyond Midnight.*** The dated tone of these misty lines and their conventional image seem quite remote from the style of Hesse's mature works. Yet, as we trace the development of Hesse's fiction, we shall be sent back repeatedly to that passage in which the young writer presented himself to the world, for it anticipates several characteristics of his subsequent oeuvre.

The style of Hesse's prose changes quite noticeably in the course of the fifty years from the early *poèmes en prose* to such late narratives as **"The Interrupted Class"** (1948). In the first decade of the century Hesse experimented with a variety of styles before he found the voice that is familiar to the readers of his major novels. The nine pieces of ***An Hour beyond Midnight,*** for instance, constitute a textbook case of *fin de siècle* aestheticism. In explicit imitation of [Maurice] Maeterlinck, Hesse created there a precious language of elegant archaisms and sonorous alliterations in order to do justice to what he called (in the 1941 introduction) "the dreamland of my poetic hours and days, which lay mysteriously somewhere between time and space." But within two years Hesse turned sharply away from the cult of *l'art pour l'art* and the other worldly spirituality of his chief model, the Romantic poet Novalis. In ***The Posthumous Writings and Poems of Hermann Lauscher*** he exploited the ironic techniques of E. T. A. Hoffmann in order to distance himself from his own immediate past and what he had come to regard as its romantic excesses. In the person of Lauscher, as he noted in an expanded edition of 1907, Hesse wanted to "bury my own dreams." Using a fictional device that anticipates the framework of *Steppenwolf* (1927), Hesse introduces himself here in the guise of an editor who is publishing the works of his friend Lauscher "as documents of the curious soul of a modern aesthete and eccentric." Although Lauscher's poetic works, we are told, display the "carefully polished, precious form" that characterized Hesse's own first prose and poetry, the five pieces—ranging from Lauscher's recollections of his childhood to his **"Diary, 1900"**—are marked for the most part by a stridently contemporary style, evident in the student slang, the vulgarisms, and the strained imagery of **"November Night."**

After the success of his novel *Peter Camenzind* (1904), however, Hesse's style underwent yet another transformation as he moved away from the preciosity of his first prose vignettes and the radically anti-bourgeois shock tactics of ***Hermann Lauscher*** and settled upon the mellow tones of melancholy realism that dominated his works for the next decade. In a series of stories typified by **"The Marble Works," "The Latin Scholar,"** and **"The Cyclone,"** he depicted the life of shopkeepers, servant girls, and artisans in small-town Germany, explicitly modeling his narrative style on the stories of Gottfried Keller. Here Hesse seemed to be celebrating the very *gutbürgerlich* culture of the Wilhelmine era that he had previously so indignantly rejected. Appropriately enough, these tales, collected in volumes with such down-to-earth titles as ***In This World*** (1907), ***Neighbors*** (1908), and ***Byways*** (1912), assured his popularity with an audience content with the *status quo* and blithely closing its eyes to all the portents of the social revolution that was soon to erupt into World War I.

During these same years Hesse was also writing fiction of a strikingly different sort—stories that appeared in various newspapers and journals but were not collected until much later, when Hesse published them in such volumes as ***Story Book*** (1935) and ***Dream Journeys*** (1945). In **"The City"** (1910) Hesse sketches a pessimistic parable on the rise and fall of culture, which anticipates by almost ten years both [Oswald] Spengler and Hesse's own postwar cultural criticism. In his lyrical account of **"The Wolf"** (1907), an animal that is hounded to death by an insensitive mob of peasants, we encounter for the first time in Hesse's works the wolf motif that became increasingly obsessive until it generated the novel *Steppenwolf.* And nothing could be further from narrative realism than the fantasy about **"A Man by the Name of Ziegler"** (1908), who is driven mad when he comes to understand the language of animals. In such works as these we have a foretaste of the magically surreal style that characterizes the major novels of the twenties and thirties, as well as such later "stories" as **"Inside and Outside," "An Evening with Dr. Faust,"** and **"Edmund."**

Yet in all these tales—from the perfumed aestheticism of the earliest prose poems through the realism and surrealism of the following decades down to the rarefied classicism of the stories collected in the volume ***Late Prose*** (1951)—we detect beneath the kaleidoscope of styles a consistent theme that is announced in the opening lines of **"The Island Dream."** For the image of narcissism betrays an introspective consciousness that has rejected the world outside for the sake of its own inner reality. The isle of beauty in that first volume, to which the young writer retreated from his humdrum existence as a book dealer in Tübingen, is nothing but a symbol for the realm of the imagination, where lovely ladies wander through fragrant groves or play Chopin in incense-laden, candle-lit chambers. Indeed, many of the early pieces are little more than aesthetic sublimations of those adolescent sex dreams in which a timid boy sees himself surrounded by choirs of adulating girls who cling to his every banal utterance with devoted attentiveness and who are perceptive enough to recognize genius in the proud youth scorned by the "real" world. But if we look behind the conventional pose and the dated exterior, we see in these vignettes the underlying theme of the alienated individual who rejects external reality for an inner realm of timelessness created by his own imagination. This is precisely the attitude that we encounter twenty-eight years later in the author of **"Dream Journeys"** (1927), who emphatically prefers the visions of his own fantasy to anything that mere "reality" has to offer. In a more radical form, the student Edmund (in the story of that title) does not flee from reality; instead, he forces the external world to conform to the reality of his vision when he strangles his skeptical teacher in accordance with the dictates of an Indic tantra.

But it is not only in the early escapist pieces and the late surreal stories that we find Hesse's characteristic tendency toward subordination of external reality to inner vision. It is also evident in many of the prewar stories, despite their ostensible "realism" after the fashion of Gottfried Keller. For all these schoolboys, students, missionaries, and apprentices turn out to be outsiders just as much as the magnificent wolf that, in the story of 1907 [**"The Wolf"**], is struck down by the peasants. The action in these stories is never narrated for its own sake, as Hesse realized in 1921. Everything happens for the benefit of the hero, who is shocked out of childhood innocence into the consciousness of maturity by the events that he witnesses. The phenomenon of **"The Cyclone,"** for all the beauty of the nature description, is important only to the extent that it reflects the violent sexuality to which the adolescent is exposed for the first time. By the same token, the characters of these stories seem to act or to be acted upon—e.g., the injury of Tina's fiancé in **"The Latin Scholar"** and Helene Lampart's death in **"The Marble Works"**—mainly so that the hero or narrator can gain insight into human nature and, ultimately, into his own consciousness. Storytelling for its own sake recedes, in other words, as external action is reduced to little more than material for the meditations of the hero on his road to self-awareness. Characteristically, in most of these stories the hero is not so much a participant in the action as, rather, a witness of it; and he often turns out to be a first-person narrator like the shipwrecked dreamer of the first prose piece—a Narcissus obsessed with the image of his own consciousness.

The tendency toward introspection is paralleled from first to last by a criticism of the world from which the author-hero is fleeing. In ***Hermann Lauscher*** this critique amounts to little more than the student's attempt to *épater le bourgeois.* In the parable in which society ladies flock to admire **"Harry, the Steppenwolf "** (1928), Hesse is lampooning an attitude that we recognize today as "radical chic." But even during the decade preceding World War I, Hesse's "wolf " frequently bit the hand that fed it—or, at least, bought its books. **"Robert Aghion"** (1913) can be read as a bitter attack on the arrogant colonializing mentality of Western man and the haughty complacency of Christianity. And **"The Homecoming"** (1909) belongs to that substantial genre of literature in which a man returning home after years abroad suddenly sees unmasked all the malice and pettiness of his own society. In many of these stories, by the way, Hesse portrays with considerable precision his own home town in southern Germany, Calw, which in its fictional form is called Gerbersau. In 1949 all of Hesse's early tales about provincial southern Germany were published in a two-volume edition entitled simply ***Gerbersau.*** It is probably safe to say that the German public, in a mood of intense self-scrutiny after two world wars, was able to perceive in those early stories much of the social criticism that was not obvious to their first readers.

If we now return to Hesse's first prose piece, **"The Island Dream,"** we note another characteristic that is anticipated there. After the narrator has beached his boat on the sand and wandered for a time, he lies down to rest in the shade of a cypress grove. Presently he is awakened from his slumbers by the cheerful cries of some young women who are tossing a golden ball in a nearby clearing. When the ball happens to land near him, he picks it up and reveals himself to the women, who, after recovering from their fright, greet the young wanderer and invite him to join them. By this point most readers will have realized that Hesse is alluding here to the story of Odysseus and Nausicaä, who meet in precisely the same way; and the remainder of Hesse's tale closely parallels Homer's account of Odysseus' sojourn among the Phaeacians. Now if we look at Hesse's other stories, we find that many of them are similarly catalyzed by a literary source. A second episode from ***An Hour beyond Midnight,*** **"Incipit vita nova,"** is sparked by Dante's work of that title. (A similar use of Dante's *Vita Nuova* occurs some twenty years later in the chapter of *Demian* entitled "Beatrice.") The episode **"November Night"** in ***Hermann Lauscher*** is prefigured by the scene in Auerbach's Cellar from Goethe's *Faust.* **"The Marble Works"** is in part an updated version of Gottfried Keller's well-known story concerning "A Rustic Romeo and Juliet." The legend of **"The Field Devil"** is based on the medieval Saints' Lives, while another story relates an episode **"From the Childhood of Saint Francis of Assisi."** In fact, almost every tale subsequently incorporated into the volume of ***Story Book*** retells a legend or an episode from history. Thus, **"Chagrin d'Amour"** uses a fictional background borrowed from Wolfram von Eschenbach's epic *Parzival* as the setting for a plot suggested by a French folk song (revived by Joan Baez). Similarly, the inscription that precipitates the "magic" in the story **"Inside and Outside"** is taken from a poem by Goethe ("Epirrhema"). The action of **"Edmund"** is inspired by an Indic tantra. And the parable of **"Harry, the Steppenwolf "** amounts to a playful extension of Kafka—whose works Hesse was one of the first to admire—since the Steppenwolf occupies a menagerie cage recently vacated by a panther resembling the one that replaced Kafka's Hunger Artist.

To point out these sources is in no way to belittle Hesse's achievement. In the first place, he demonstrated his powers of creative imagination by "inventing" actions to accommodate the allusion (e.g., the tantra, or the French folk song, or the quotation from Goethe) that inspired the story. That is, his stories amount to more than the retelling of familiar tales in new words. (As an editor and anthologist, by the way, Hesse compiled a number of volumes during these years, ranging from his own translations of medieval and Renaissance tales to volumes of Romantic poetry and modern fiction.) In the second place, and more importantly: twentieth-century literature—from Joyce's *Ulysses* and Thomas Mann's *Doctor Faustus* to Eliot's *The Waste Land* and Brecht's *St. Joan of the Stockyards*—has made us increasingly conscious of the basic "literariness" of literature, which has come to be considered not so much an imitation of life in the Aristotelian sense as a playful manipulation of elements that already exist in an autonomous world of art. Precisely this kind of manipulation of existing forms occurs in Hesse's major novels. *Demian* is indebted, as many of the chapter headings and quotations suggest, to episodes in the Bible, from Genesis to Revelation. And ***Siddhartha*** (1922) gets its title as well as its basic outline from legends surrounding the life of Buddha. So the allusion, in **"The Island Dream,"** to Odysseus among the Phaeacians anticipates the prefigurational techniques that Hesse, along with many of the other major writers of the century, was to develop with considerable sophistication.

The use of literary sources is related, moreover, to the tendency toward introspection. For the realm that Hesse opposes to everyday reality—in ***An Hour beyond Midnight*** as well as such later stories as **"Dream Journeys"**—is explicitly a realm of art. It became increasingly clear to

Hesse, in the course of his life, that "eternity" is a frame of mind: the ability to perceive what Harry Haller, in *Steppenwolf,* calls "the golden trace" that gives life its meaning. Hesse was much more at home in that timeless spiritual realm than in the "real" world. He consistently resisted attempts to make of him a public figure, preferring to spend his days and hours in the relative isolation of a farmhouse on the shores of Lake Constance (1904-12), a villa in the suburbs of Bern (1912-19), and two different dwellings in the Swiss Alps above Lugano (1919-62). In his later years, behind a sign requesting "No Visitors Please," he devoted himself to his writing, to his painting, and to his books—notably, to the German literature of the period 1750 to 1850, in which he always claimed to feel spiritually most at home, and later to the world of Oriental culture that increasingly claimed his interest. From a writer of this sort, who by choice has shut himself off from the contemporary world, we would not reasonably expect a fertile invention of exciting fictional narratives set in the everyday reality of modern European society. But we would legitimately expect to encounter evidences of that cultural realm in which he preferred to spend his time—hence Saint Francis, Faust, the wisdom of India, and the many other references of that order. The Glass Bead Game, in the novel of that title, is Hesse's most brilliant image for the timeless realm of culture: for that institution has the sole function of enabling the men of Castalia to play with the cultural values of the past and present just as easily as one plays upon the various consoles of an organ. In those early stories, with their literary allusions and their rich associations of quotation and form, we sense the inchoate outlines of that cultural realm to which Hesse's introspective tendency ultimately led him.

Apart from literature and culture, the second principal source of Hesse's fiction is his own life. We have already noted that increasingly during the twenties Hesse turned to pure autobiography in the attempt to come to grips with his past. Up to that point, however, his stories represent the best reservoir of biographical information. **"The Latin Scholar"** describes the year when Hesse, before dropping out of school for good, was attending a *gymnasium* in a town near Calw. **"The Cyclone"** depicts the period when the youth was back in Calw, working as an apprentice in the local tower-clock workshop. The episodes of ***Hermann Lauscher*** provide a lightly fictionalized account of Hesse's life in Tübingen, where he worked as a bookseller by day while, at night, he sought refuge in an aesthetic realm "an hour beyond midnight." **"Robert Aghion"** combines Hesse's own firsthand observations during his voyage to Indonesia in 1911 with stories from the history of his family, several of whom had spent years as missionaries in India during the nineteenth century. But in all these stories, as well as the novels from these early years, biographical experience serves not as a starting point for the exploration of reality and other people; rather, it leads him inevitably back into his own consciousness for the encounter with himself. It was this realization, in 1921, that caused Hesse to reject these early works as failures, at least from the standpoint of traditional storytelling, and to say that they represented nothing more than his "secret dreams," his own "bitter anguish."

If we return for a final time to Hesse's earliest story [**"The Island Dream"**], we can see a clear indication of the difference between his juvenalia and the works of his maturity. There, as the shipwrecked dreamer approaches the island of his dreams, his attention is distracted by his reflection in the waters of the bay. Almost fifty years later, a similar situation recurs in Hesse's recollection of **"The Interrupted Class."** Sent on an errand by his teacher, the twelve-year-old pauses on a bridge to watch the fish in the river below; but as he looks into the water he falls into a state of rapt contemplation in which he forgets all temporality until he is startled by the chiming of the church clock, which summons him back to reality. This parallel exemplifies the fact that to an astonishing degree Hesse's works consist of varying configurations of the same limited group of images—in this case, an epiphany produced by gazing into a body of water. But the image first occurs in a fictional setting that represents an escapist flight from reality. The shipwrecked dreamer, after all, has left the world behind for an aesthetic realm where nothing interferes with his rapturous contemplation of his own reflection. The late variation of the image has an entirely different context: for the autobiographical reminiscence forces Hesse to come to grips with an episode from his childhood that he had successfully repressed for many years. The first image stands under the sign of Narcissus, who is lost in worshipful contemplation of himself; the second leads the author into a consideration of the individual's ethical responsibilities in the world into which he has been thrust and with which he must somehow cope. The first image represents the young Hesse, still trying to express himself by means of literary forms appropriated reverently from respected masters; the second reveals the old Hesse, who has reverted frankly to autobiographical reminiscence in an effort to understand his own consciousness, since "the questionable art of storytelling" has unmasked itself as inadequate.

From all that has been said, it should be evident that more than mere caprice dictated the choice of stories in this volume. The contents pages reflect the fact that most of Hesse's stories were written before World War I; those that appeared thereafter moved ever closer to autobiography, to the essay, and to the parable, tendencies that are apparent in such late narratives as **"The Interrupted Class,"** **"Dream Journeys,"** and **"Harry the Steppenwolf,"** ***Stories of Five Decades*** (none except **"Inside and Outside,"** **"Tragic,"** and **"Dream Journeys"** has ever before been available in English) provides a representative selection that displays the full range of Hesse's storytelling and the course of its development. It includes pieces from every major period and every important collection. And if some of his stories have been omitted for reasons of space, no aspect of his work is neglected. (Most of the omitted stories fall into one of two categories: realistic tales from the "Gerbersau" period, and the retelling of medieval and Renaissance stories and legends.) Since the boundary line between fiction on the one hand and pure autobiography or essay on the other becomes increasingly tenuous in Hesse's work, only one narrative from the last years is included here. (pp. vii-xix)

[In ***Stories of Five Decades***], one can follow Hesse's development from the aestheticism of his neoromantic youth to

Hesse at work in Casa Bodmer, 1937.

the classicism of his old age. And the reader who knows Hesse mainly through his major novels of the twenties and thirties will be surprised to encounter him here in a variety of earlier incarnations. Yet the greatest surprise of all, surely, is to see how faithful Hesse remained to himself from start to finish and with what unremitting honesty he tested and discarded literary forms until he found the mode that was adequate for the expression of his own consciousness. Hesse's gloomy rejection of his early work in 1921 did not mark a radical break with his past but rather a turning point. Far from toning down the "secret dreams" that he detected in his prewar stories, Hesse transposed them from minor into major, proclaiming the realm of his imagination as his characteristic and principal theme. (pp. xix-xx)

Theodore Ziolkowski, in an introduction to Stories of Five Decades, *by Hermann Hesse, translated by Ralph Manheim and Denver Lindley, Farrar, Straus and Giroux, 1972, pp. vii-xx.*

Ernst Pawel (essay date 1973)

[*In the following review of* Stories of Five Decades, *Pawel rejects Ziolkowski's assumption in the collection's introduction (see essay dated 1972) that Hesse's short fiction documents his artistic and intellectual development. Rather, he argues that they demonstrate the static and essentially narcissistic nature of Hesse's vision.*]

[***Stories of Five Decades***] contains 23 stories, from the lush **"Island Dream,"** written in 1899, to the sparse and introspective **"Interrupted Class,"** dated 1948. Theodore Ziolkowski, a Hesse scholar at Princeton who provides a perceptive introduction, is responsible for the selections, which he arranged in chronological order so as to document the writer's artistic and intellectual development. Though sound in principle, the idea backfires in practice; for what this collection in fact demonstrates is the essentially static nature of Hesse's vision, his steadfast refusal to outgrow adolescence and his commitment to it as a permanent state of being. The stance marks him as a man ahead of his time and anticipates currently fashionable attitudes; but its implications are certainly too problematic to justify unqualified admiration for Hesse's ability to remain—in the editor's phrase—"faithful to his essential self."

In his dealings with the world Hermann Hesse was a complex but eminently sound and level-headed human being endowed with robust common sense. Thus—in stark contrast, for instance, to his friend and rival Thomas Mann—

he chose pacifism and exile in World War I and accurately foresaw the eventual triumph of barbarism in his native land; disgust with German politics and politicians made him settle in Switzerland as early as 1923. This needs to be stressed, not only because this side of him appears so rarely in his work, but also because it engendered some of the tensions between reason and its opposite that afflict so many quintessentially Western intellectuals at war with their heritage, who seek salvation in the scrutable spirituality of an idealized far-out East. In Hesse's case the impulse was slowed and very nearly aborted by a confrontation with the real-life Orient of 1913; it took him many years to get over the shock and recapture, in his vastly popular ***Siddhartha,*** the pristine idyll of an earlier vision.

But what provided the creative spur and largely determined the direction of his quest was self-absorption, a self-involvement truly heroic in its intensity. Like most of his fiction, these shorter pieces all testify to an obsession with his own consciousness so exclusive as to almost obliterate the shape and substance of external reality, which impinges, if at all, only as an ominous shadow fraught with terror. Stylistically he in time outgrew the treacly *fin-de-siècle* romanticism of his youthful efforts, four mercifully brief samples of which are included in this book; the fact that effusions such as **"November Night"** and **"The Marble Works"** were concocted by a man in his thirties seems hard to believe. But his gradual shift toward a quasi-existentialist mood, while adumbrating broad developments in European literature and deflating his prose, implies no substantial maturation. His existentialism amounts to no more than romanticism turned inside-out and stripped of the silver lining—a self-indulgent solipsism raised to a more or less fine art.

This cult of self imposes its perennial theme, explored here in metaphoric variations ranging from outcast and exile to broken-hearted lover, misunderstood artist, disappointed disciple and lone wolf caged or hunted. Hesse, of course, developed into a subtle and resourceful writer, and several of the pieces in this book are successful on their own terms; two of them—one dealing with the fate and faith of a Protestant missionary in India (possibly inspired by the author's father), the other with a crisis of conscience in the life of a 12-year-old—must rank with the best of his work. But their scope remains strictly limited to the self-same sufferings of one man's quivering soul. Despair at being strangers in a world they never made is not confined to the young; Hesse, however, exploits it with an articulately youthful self-pity that never quite ripens into compassion and goes a long way, I suspect, toward explaining his special appeal to adolescents of all ages.

Whether or not it was also a factor in his breakdown at age 44 must remain conjectural. A Jungian analysis, including personal contact with the Master himself, appears to have played a significant part in his recovery, though too much may have been made of its influence on his work. Hesse's flight into mysticism began long before he encountered Jung's cosmology and probably accounts for his choice of treatment in the first place. Moreover, self-transcendence, supreme goal and promise of all Eastern wisdom, has a special therapeutic relevance for cases of painful ego engorgement. What Jung did provide, however, was a system and a set of symbols, basic equipment for any pedantic rationalist plodding through Nirvana and hell-bent on capturing the ineffable in the language of the here-and-now.

The effects are strikingly apparent in all of Hesse's post-crisis fiction. His ornately lyrical *Weltschmerz* gave way to the even-voiced and somewhat hypnotic prose of his best and best-known novels, ***Siddhartha,*** *Narcissus and Goldmund* and *The Glass Bead Game,* perfectly attuned to the posture of wise man at peace with himself and the world beyond worlds. Yet no matter how hard he tried to convince himself, Hesse was too honest a writer ever to be wholly consistent, and even the most didactic of his later writings contain rumblings of continuing conflict. For the truth he found was not his own; traces of Western skepticism, of that rationalist despair against which he struggled all his life, persistently lurk just beneath the calm surface of his carefully crafted serenity.

It is, in fact, this very conflict which raises Hesse above the level on which his new-found popularity has come to rest. The message, as so many of these stories suggest rather in spite of themselves, is clearly not the man; but he wanted desperately to believe in its simplistic banality, and in this at least he is not alone.

Ernst Pawel, "Committed to Adolescence as a Permanent State of Being," in The New York Times Book Review, *February 11, 1973, p. 7.*

The Antioch Review (essay date 1973)

[In the excerpt below, the reviewer considers the relationship between the stories of Strange News from Another Star *and Hesse's psychological state during the years of their composition, praising the tales for their magical fusion of dream and reality.]*

[***Strange News from Another Star***] comprises seven tales published in German in *Märchen* and an eighth story, **"Flute Dream."** Written between 1913 and 1918, the stories reflect Hesse's mood in those years. His criticism of the war had caused a break with his native country; sickness in his family, uncertainty about his vocation as a writer, and rejection of conventional intellectual life caused him great stress. Above all, he was torn between the life of the mind and that of the senses—intellect and feeling, contemplation and action, ethics and aesthetics. Surrounded by difficulties from without, insecure with himself, Hesse concentrated on the "refuge within," the "point where there is only I, where the world cannot reach."

All eight tales deal with the search for liberation within a suprapersonal consciousness. The protagonist has lost the secure world of childhood and is, in terms of Jungian psychoanalysis (which Hesse underwent at this time), on "a long, hard detour home." He must endure misery until he regains paradise as an awakened man. **"Iris," "Augustus," "The Poet,"** and **"The Hard Passage"** are powerful examples of this quest. In the other stories—**"Flute Dream," "Strange News from Another Star," "Dream Se-**

quence," and **"Faldum"**—the same search is present, but is less dominant because other themes are added. All of the tales are pervaded by a magic spell—a childlike playfulness and a sense of wonder. Inner and outer world, dream and reality are presented in perfect fusion. When the King (**"Strange News from Another Star"**) says, "I do not know whether you are a child or a wise man," he may very well express the reader's appraisal of the author. (p. 498)

A review of "Strange News from Another Star," in The Antioch Review, *Vol. 32, No. 3, 1973, p. 498-99.*

Daniel P. Deneau (essay date 1973)

[*In the following review of* Stories of Five Decades, *Deneau characterizes the volume as a readable collection that reflects Hesse's artistic development throughout his career.*]

Stories of Five Decades is a readable collection of fiction, and it is designed primarily to clarify and illustrate Hesse's "development" during his long, productive career.

The first fifteen selections were written between 1899 and 1913 and thus antedate Hesse's major novels. Though hopelessly dated curiosities, the three *fin de siècle* romantic effusions (all 1899) which open the volume are important, [editor Theodore] Ziolkowski argues, because they anticipate characteristics (for instance, the use of literary sources and "an introspective consciousness") appearing throughout Hesse's fiction. The argument is tenable enough, especially in the case of the first and longest piece, **"The Island Dream."** Fortunately, Hesse reacted rapidly and violently against the languid aestheticism of his early twenties. The fourth selection, an excerpt from ***The Posthumous Writings and Poems of Hermann Lauscher*** (1901), is a crude but at least energetic account of student carousing, clearly inspired by the Auerbach's Tavern sequence in *Faust.* The remaining early narratives are of two types.

Influenced by Gottfried Keller, for at least a decade Hesse continued to produce a series of relatively long and, by early nineteenth-century standards, realistic narratives; if the six selections included in ***Stories of Five Decades*** are truly representative, then Hesse also remained preoccupied with the subject of young men and their first loves, their vocations, and their hometown environments. Naturally, there are variations, least notably in **"The Marble Works"** (1904), **"The Latin Scholar"** (1906), and **"The Cyclone"** (1913), most notably in **"Walter Kömpff"** (1908), **"The Homecoming"** (1909), and **"Robert Aghion"** (1913). Like a number of Thomas Mann characters, Walter Kömpff is a man whose "maternal and paternal traits seemed unable to blend"; his divided nature leads to vocational, social, and religious problems, and finally to suicide. The protagonist of **"The Homecoming"** is no longer young, but he, too, discovers love, as well as some mature understanding of his native town. Robert Aghion, a young missionary in India, faces the problems of love and vocation, but his story is also designed as a reflection on the proselytizing spirit of Christianity. Generally, these six related narratives are sensitive and straightforward character studies. They fill more than half (180 pp.) of ***Stories of Five Decades*** and therefore must be considered an important phase of Hesse's "storytelling."

Interspersed with the long, realistic narratives are five other quite different selections, perhaps best described as short fables and fantasies. As Ziolkowski notes, these works were "not collected until much later" and give us "a foretaste of the magically surreal style that characterizes the major novels of the twenties and thirties." Three of the stories—**"The Wolf"** (1907), **"The Field Devil"** (1908), and **"The City"** (1910)—do not have human protagonists. **"The Wolf"** is a lyrical account of "the youngest and most beautiful of the wolves, a proud beast, strong and graceful," and slain by the much less beautiful and less beauty-perceiving peasants. **"The Field Devil"** is a curious and imaginative tale of yearning and rejection: the "satyr or field devil" is forced into the desert by advancing Christianity and is not allowed inside the Christian circle. Imitating the penitential practices of Father Paul, the little devil dies; at the moment of his death God seems to accept his sacrifices, but the "pious pilgrims" who discover the corpse flee in horror at what they take "to be a mockery on the part of the Evil One." Hesse's wolf and field devil appear to me to be the most sympathetically rendered "characters" in the volume. **"The City"** is a very different matter: it describes man and nature engaging in a cycle of growth and decay and is not, as Ziolkowski claims, "a pessimistic parable on the rise and fall of culture." Based on medieval sources, the very simple and delicate **"Chagrin d'Amour"** (1908) is unlike anything else in the volume. Finally, **"A Man by the Name of Ziegler"** (1908) swallows an alchemist's pill, understands the languages of the animals, and is driven mad by his new view of his own species. The parable seems to be a semi-comic version of the same theme developed lyrically in **"The Wolf."** These brief tales definitely enrich the collection.

After his personal crisis of 1916-1917, Hesse developed into a productive and important novelist, as his well-known record extending from *Demian* (1919) to *The Glass Bead Game* (1943) clearly attests. During the same period, however, he virtually abandoned short fiction, though he did continue to publish several volumes of stories written in earlier years. Ziolkowski explains that "the boundary line between fiction on the one hand and pure autobiography or essay on the other becomes increasingly tenuous in Hesse's work"; and in a brief preface to **"The Interrupted Class,"** the last selection in ***Stories,*** Hesse reflects on "the questionable" or "mere art of storytelling," which in this context may mean particularly short fiction, and explains that "roughly" from *Demian* onward he was led further and further away from this "good old tradition." It is not surprising, then, that Hesse's last three decades of "storytelling" (1919-1948) are represented in ***Stories of Five Decades*** by only eight selections, filling only eighty-four pages. Judged as narratives, these selections are less engaging than many of their predecessors. For the sake of completeness, the following enumeration may be necessary. In **"From the Childhood of Saint Francis of Assisi"** (1919) a sensitive adolescent tries to relate his present conduct to his vocational dream of knighthood; in **"Inside and Outside"** (1920), a psychological study without a speck of human interest, a devotee of science learns to believe in "magic"; in **"Tragic"** (1923), since the age of practicing poets has passed, a poet-become-typesetter struggles to fulfill his vocation by correcting deformed sentences; in **"Dream Journeys"** (1927), the most important of the group and previously translated, a man of letters experiences the beauty of dream life but realizes his inability to capture his dream in art; in **"Harry, the Steppenwolf"** (1928), a piece of comedy, Harry in the form of a wolf occupies the cage vacated presumably by Kafka's panther (see the conclusion of "The Hunger Artist") and bites the hand of a soul sister who attempts to feed him; in the weirdly humorous **"An Evening with Dr. Faust"** (1929), Faust and an associate, through a device supplied by Mephistopheles, listen to the mysterious sounds of the future—a radio program; in **"Edmund"** (1934) a student concentrates on an Indic tantra and then joyously strangles his professor, thus making reality correspond to his vision (this one, I suggest, should be kept out of the anthologies); and in **"The Interrupted Class"** (1948), an essay-narrative, Hesse reminisces pleasantly on a school day in childhood. Such evidence makes generalizations difficult. Perhaps the humor, the stress on an inner world, and some gloomy reflections on the twentieth century are ingredients worth mentioning.

To my knowledge, Theodore Ziolkowski's introduction is to date the most useful survey of Hesse as a writer of short fiction, but this introduction is also an example of the critical intellect forcing the creative record to yield too much consistency. Ziolkowski emphasizes Hesse's consistent "introspection," "criticism of the world," "use of literary sources," and repetition "of the same limited group of images." Given the twenty-three representative selections, all of these points seem to have some validity but are expressed in an exaggerated manner. For instance, Ziolkowski is quite unconvincing when he asserts that "Hesse's characteristic tendency toward subordination of external reality to inner vision" is evident even in the early realistic narratives. True, some of these stories do have autobiographical sources and do portray young men gaining in self-awareness, but that, I think, is not precisely the same as "introspection" and "subordination of external reality to inner vision." Ziolkowski is something worse than unconvincing when he cites two characters who stare into water (the "shipwrecked dreamer" of 1899 and the child in **"The Interrupted Class"** of 1948) and then declares that "this parallel exemplifies the fact that to an astonishing degree Hesse's works consist of varying configurations of the same limited group of images—in this case, an epiphany produced by gazing into a body of water." Nonsense. The point could be a valid one, but as stated and exemplified here, it appears to be unworthy of any serious attention. (pp. 425-27)

As presented in ***Stories of Five Decades,*** the short fiction of Hesse appears to me to have the virtue of variety, and the very great virtue of clarity. This fiction certainly is not trivial, but it also does not seem to require strenuous contemplation. It is good, readable fiction, to which youthful admirers of Hesse's novels and those academic critics who particularly value complexity probably will remain indifferent. (p. 427)

Daniel P. Deneau, in a review of "Stories of Five Decades," in Studies in Short Fiction, *Vol. 10, No. 4, Fall, 1973, pp. 425-27.*

Kurt J. Fickert (essay date 1974)

[*Fickert is a German-born American educator and critic whose works on German authors include* Hermann Hesse's Quest *(1978). In the essay below, he closely analyzes the short story "Klein und Wagner," emphasizing its portrayal of the creative act.*]

"Klein und Wagner" stands apart among Hesse's stories; it occupies a unique position midway between the objectively told, "plot" stories of his early years and the relentlessly introspective, symbolic prose of the years following the First World War. Both the framework of a story and the unstructured contours of psychoanalytic probings characterize **"Klein und Wagner."**

Ostensibly the story of an embezzler who flees to Italy and meets his death in a quasi-suicidal drowning, **"Klein und Wagner"** tells, as is immediately apparent, a parallel tale about a "good citizen" who makes a violent break with his bourgeois past and attempts, unsuccessfully, to live his life in a climate of passionate abandon. The title itself indicates the multiplicity of levels on which the story functions. First it refers to Friedrich Klein, the embezzler. Without great subtlety Hesse has, of course, chosen the name "Klein" as a term of opprobrium for the middle-class mentality. In "Wagner" he has invented a device with a great deal of ambiguity. For the name Wagner, as Friedrich Klein slowly and painfully discovers, pertains not only to Richard Wagner, for whose music Klein in his youth had a passing enthusiasm, but also to a criminal Wagner, whose achievement was the notoriety of his having murdered his wife and children. There is the possibility that the combination Friedrich Klein also represents a similar juxtaposition of genius—Friedrich, i.e., Hölderlin or Schiller or Hegel—and criminal, i.e., Klein himself. There can be no doubt, however, about the significance of the name Wagner as a link between creativeness and hidden, probably lawless depths in the soul since Hesse provides a third and climactic interpretation. Wagner represents, he reveals, "The Magic Theater" of the psyche: "The theater with the sign 'Wagner,' was this not he himself; was this not the call to come into himself, into the unknown land of his true soul (*Innern*)? For he himself was Wagner—Wagner was the murderer and the pursued man in him; however, Wagner was also the composer, the artist, the genius, the seducer, the penchant for pleasure, sensuality, luxury." It becomes apparent, then, that in **"Klein and Wagner"** Hesse has written in the guise of fiction with autobiographical overtones another expose of the problematical nature of the artist.

At the time of the composition of **"Klein und Wagner"** Hesse had taken a decisive step toward realizing his lifelong ambition: to be not merely a writer but an author, a *Dichter*. . . . His freedom to pursue, almost fanatically, greatness as an author was achieved by sacrificing the security of a bourgeois existence as a sometime popular writer and by plunging precariously into the murky depths of self-analysis in order to plumb the source of creativeness. (pp. 180-81)

The story begins with the embezzler Klein's attempt to rationalize his criminal behavior. His explanation that he stole in reaction to a loveless (or at least an unhappy) marriage is patently insufficient. Hesse proceeds to analyze his protagonist further, arriving at conclusions which pertain to his own situation as much as they do to Klein's. "The Philistine and pretender in him had not wanted to let the voice of his heart persevere (*gelten*)." As Hesse penetrates deeper into the nature of his break with his past, he leaves the realms of fiction and autobiography far behind and ponders the anti-social, amoral character of the (Romantic) artist *per se.*

"He himself, however, the criminal, does only that which he has in him (to do)." With these words Hesse equates the function of the artist with that of the criminal and paints in a moment of insight and self-hatred a portrait of the artist in his egotism like that of Dorian Gray. But Hesse emphasizes instead the necessity for the artist's "criminality": self-betrayal, the betrayal of his family, his kind, his fellow-man. The artist's disavowal of any responsibility except for a narcissistic celebration of the self (the equivalent of a retreat to the exclusive self-interest of early childhood or even to the womb) turns him, so Hesse now suggests, into a "saint," a seer, a visionary. When Friedrich Klein looks at himself, he sees "the face of the select (*Gezeichneter*), stamped by fate with a sign, older and yet younger than his former face, mask-like and yet marvelously transparent and illumed (*durchglüht*)." In one of his letters Hesse identifies the philosophical source of his being able to convert criminal behavior into transcendence: "I myself have learned from Indian philosophers to distinguish between essence (*Sein*) and action (*Tun*), to see in the 'criminal' the makings of a saint (*den möglichen Heiligen*)." The combination of visionary propensities and a disposition to react to established norms by pursuing contrary (and therefore aberrant) and extremely individualistic aims constitutes the artistic temperament, as Hesse has, on several occasions, conceived it to be. (pp. 181-82)

After Hesse has probed Klein's soul for the roots of his erratic behavior and has found there the basis for his own antiestablishment feelings and a key to the amorality of the artist, he presents the second part of his story, the love affair between Klein and Teresina. She is a dancer and a coquette (if not a prostitute); like the name Wagner she represents a conjoining of art and antisocial behavior. Upon becoming acquainted with her, watching her performance, Klein comments, in terms more suitable to a philosopher contemplating aesthetics than to an embezzler, on the group of dancers and musicians to which Teresina belongs and their activity: "They danced out for the rich people, the guests of the resort, (the pattern of) the beautiful which lay in their lives and to which they themselves were incapable of giving expression and which, without such assistance, they couldn't even sense." The relationship between Klein and Teresina, which begins on a physical plane (although even here Hesse's description of the girl strikingly parallels that of Hermine in *Steppenwolf,* an obviously symbolic figure), soon develops overtones of the abstract. Teresina becomes a guide, a much more tangible Beatrice, on the way to an appreciation of the amoral aspects of the personality—lust, sex, gambling, a spendthrift existence. It is necessary for Klein—and much more for Hesse the *Dichter*—to learn to affirm these values which appear to the good citizen to be incontrovertibly negative. The element of play which underlies the distractions pursued by the demimonde has an affinity with that which engenders the creative process. Klein now perceives a creative urge in himself: "He had been overcome—something like being choked—by the overwhelming need to relate his experiences and thoughts, to give them form, to speak of them aloud, to call them out to himself. . . . (And this was progress, release (*Erlösung*), confirmation." Klein even arrives at a philosophic definition of art: "was nothing else than observation of the world (while) in a state of grace, of illumination . . . ". Of course, having reached an understanding of the concept of "Wagner," the combination of artist and murderer, Klein now experiences the dark side of his liberation through Teresina, too. His affair with her ends with an abortive attempt on his part to kill her as she lies asleep. For Klein the failure to commit the ultimate crime is convincing evidence of his inability to live outside of the sphere of bourgeois conscience and leads to his suicide, an act of atonement. For Hesse, the flight from the enactment of the murder of Teresina represents abandonment of the task of exploring the true self, in Jungian terms, a turning aside from the obligation to deal definitively with the persona. On the level of an explication of the artistic impulse, this aspect of the story of **"Klein und Wagner,"** the attempted murder of Teresina, concerns the incestuous relationship which, it is suggested, underlies the creative process. The act of creation is an act of love (Klein: "To be able to love something—what redemption!" But the awareness comes that this love is for all women and principally for the mother. Carl Helbling explains: "(The mother) is the symbol of self-sacrificing and productive love, on which the artist feeds. Contact with woman produces his creativeness." Once again in the ecstasy and self-hatred of the artist Klein feels impelled to commit a destructive act, first the murder of Teresina, for which his energies fail him, then his suicide, which succeeds.

Klein's drowning, the third part of the story of **"Klein und Wagner,"** has an ambivalent character because of the multilayered structure of the plot. In regard to the fiction of the embezzler Klein, his suicide is the logical outcome of the tensions in his life which he cannot resolve; he dies, not actually wanting to, out of necessity rather than as a result of a pathological impulse. Opposed to this death as release is the motif of Klein's death as defeat in the attempt to achieve a breakthrough to individuation, in an autobiographical reading of the story. In dealing with the nature of the artist, however, Hesse has painted a picture of Klein's last moments suffused with the light of triumph. The drowning, described at length, becomes a symbol for letting one's self fall, in Hesse's terminology the equivalent of the creative act. In a presentiment of the ecstacy of absolute (God-like) freedom to create Klein has already once before experienced, in letting himself fall, the creative moment: "In this most desirable state one had inspirations, memories, visions, phantasies, insights of a unique sort." Now, as he drowns, he transcends the conflicts which have thwarted him, the bourgeois inhibitions, the misadventures in self-analysis, the frustrations of the *Dichter,* and he smiles the smile of the prophet and seer, the murderer and creative artist. "His smile said that also Wagner's deed had been a road to redemption . . . that it, too, was a symbol and that murder and blood and atrocity are not things which actually exist, but are only values of our own, self-racking soul." At the last he perceives the harmony which encompasses and expunges all strife; he finds the secret of existence and the source of the artist's creative impulse. "Within oneself one contained everything which mattered." Openness to all aspects of life, acceptance of the amorality of the soul distinguish the *Dichter* from the writer who will not acknowledge his own self-hatred, his debauchery and his aspiration. [Heinrich Geffert] has summed up Hesse's thinking on the subject of the nature of the artist in this way: "Just this distinguishes—so Hesse feels—the artist and imaginative person from the good citizen (*Burger'*), the fact that the artist surrenders to the impulses (*Regungen*) of the unconscious while the good citizen has a security force (stationed) between the depths of the soul and the consciousness."

With Klein's immersion in the all, symbolized here as so often in Hesse's works by water, his story ends. In its many ramifications it has evolved a fictitious account of crime and punishment, written with a quality of suspense rare in Hesse even in the earlier, more objective novels and reappearing perhaps only in *Narziss und Goldmund;* it has unfolded, too, the confession of a seeker after the true self, complete with overtones of occidental psychology and oriental philosophy. However, there is a stratum in **"Klein und Wagner"** which has not always been so apparent to readers and critics, although this level of meaning constitutes a motif ubiquitous in the works of Hesse. **"Klein und Wagner"** concerns itself, beginning with its title, with the nature of the *Dichter,* or more generally, the artist. The first part of the story touches upon the quality of the outsider in the artist, his break with society and the self-revulsion engendered by the immolation of the artist, depicted as a criminal act, the destruction of human ties. In the second section Hesse deals with heterosexual love as the source of creative power, but this positive aspect of the creative process has its elements of danger and self-destructiveness, too. Only in the third segment of Hesse's portrait of the artist is there a celebration of the creative act, of letting one's self fall. This victory is achieved at a price, nevertheless; Klein must die in order that Wagner may live. (pp. 183-86)

Kurt J. Fickert, "The Portrait of the Artist in Hesse's 'Klein und Wagner'," in Hartford Studies in Literature, *Vol. VI, No. 2, 1974, pp. 180-87.*

Joseph Mileck (essay date 1978)

[*Mileck is a Romanian-born American educator and critic who is best known for his studies of Hesse's works, including* Hermann Hesse and his Critics *(1958) and* Hermann Hesse: Biography and Bibliography *(1977). In the following excerpt from* Hermann Hesse: Life and Art, *he links the events surrounding Hesse's second marriage to his vision of the self and art in "Klingsor's Last Summer."*]

Autobiography had been mythicized in *Demian* and dramatized in **"Klein und Wagner."** It was fantasized in **"Klingsors letzter Sommer."** Klein is what Hesse was late in the spring of 1919; Klingsor's story is a memorial to the summer of 1919. Klingsor, born on July 2, forty-two years old, and unattached, painter, poet, philosopher, and hypochondriac troubled by death, possessed by a passion for life and for art, and given to revelry and depression, is obviously Hesse himself; Klingsor's circle of friends was Hesse's; and the setting is clearly Ticino. Klingsor's unrestrained mode, frantic tempo, and intoxicating absorption of life in Castagnetta had become Hesse's in Montagnola. From the small, iron-railed stone balcony of his *palazzo,* Klingsor views the luxuriant steeply terraced garden below and the lake and mountains in the distance, just as Hesse was wont to gaze at that very view from the same little balcony of his Casa Camuzzi. With the exception of his concluding self-portrait, all of Klingsor's paintings were Hesse's own watercolors, his own fanciful paraphrasing and poeticizing of the visible world in brilliant transparent hues. Klingsor's poetry is just as Hessean in both its matter and manner. And Klingsor, like Hesse, had once made a necessary trip to the Orient, and he, too, had found nothing there that could not also be found in the Western world.

Large though Klingsor looms, he is actually only one of two self-projections. His intimate friend, the blond poet Hermann, a reserved writer of sad lyrics, is the second. Demian, unlike the second self-projection of Hesse's earlier tales (e.g., Richard of *Peter Camenzind,* or Heilner of *Unterm Rad*), has no reality of his own; he is Sinclair's externalized ideal self and nothing more. Klein's ideal self is not even externalized; it remains an inner voice. In **"Klingsors letzter Sommer,"** Hesse reverted to his earlier mode of double self-projection; the second projection, though shadowy, is once more as real as the first. Klingsor is what Hesse had become in the summer of 1919, and Hermann is the more withdrawn and contained person Hesse had been, the person who was to emerge again after Klingsor had spent himself. These two self-projections are appropriately equated with the Chinese poets Li Tai Pe and Thu Fu, adventurer and sufferer, respectively.

Louis the Horrible (*Louis der Grausame*), Klingsor's close friend, fellow painter, and restless inveterate traveller, was none other than Hesse's itinerant painter-friend Louis Moilliet. Like his literary counterpart, Moilliet was always an unpredictable visitor, fancied himself a gourmet, and was something of a footloose lover. He, too, was inclined in brash argument to extol man's animality and to discount his spirituality, he also painted circuses, clowns, and flagpoles, and his famous carrousel is Klingsor's favorite painting. *Der Grausame* was also Hesse's actual epithet for Moilliet: a facetious allusion to his unusual self-containment, and to his cultivated carefree manner and mocking tone. The Magician (*Der Magier*), the black-bearded ever-smiling Armenian astrologer who carouses and contends with Klingsor, trying to disabuse him of his treasured fear of death, and who was again to appear as Jup the Magician (*Jup der Magier*) in ***Die Morgenlandfahrt*** (1931), was another of Hesse's close friends: buoyant, dark-haired Josef Englert, a Jew and ardent student of astrology with whom Hesse had enjoyed similar bouts of alcohol and argument, and who was also known as *Der Magier.* Klingsor's July excursion to Kareno to meet a Queen of the Mountains (*Königin der Gebirge*) was only Hesse's fantasized recollection of his own first visit on July 22 to the Wengers in Carona. The young and exotic Queen of the Mountains was Ruth Wenger, and her enchanting yellow palace with its two small balconies and a colorful parrot painted on its gable, an accurate description of her parents' *Papageienhaus* (House of the Parrot). Two barking dogs and the persistent notes of a piano tuner at work greet Klingsor's party just as they had Hesse's. Klingsor is entranced by his red-garbed Queen of the Mountains as immediately as Hesse had been fascinated by Ruth and her red dress. He is also convinced, as Hesse at first had been, that he is too old for his new attraction, and that to worship was more in order than to woo. Dark-haired Ersilia's songs and turquoise parasol delight Klingsor as much as Margarethe Osswald's singing and green parasol had delighted Hesse. Agosto was Margarethe's husband Paolo, and the paintress and the doctor from Barengo, Klingsor's remaining companions to Kareno, were Dr. Hermann Bodmer and his wife Anny, friends of Hesse's from Sorengo. Gina the young typist with whom Klingsor is infatuated, and Edith with whom he exchanges love letters were still other of Hesse's close friends. And it is also unlikely that the various women whom Klingsor chances to encounter on his peregrinations and who attract him briefly did not also have their counterparts in actual life. (pp. 148-51)

"Klingsors letzter Sommer" mirrors Hesse's own efforts to [give himself unreservedly to the self and to life] when he settled in Montagnola, and it also indicates that to let himself fall into life proved to be much more difficult for Hesse than anticipated. He and Klingsor learned quickly that to let oneself fall into life is not quite to be equated with letting oneself fall into death, that the latter is an act of desperation involving a rejection both of the self and of life, and the former can only be an act of faith, involving an affirmation and acceptance of not only the self but also of both life and death.

Klingsor tries to begin where Klein [of **"Klein und Wagner"**] leaves off. He has also broken through the shell of traditional values and beliefs. In his case, however, there are no residual shell fragments to impede flight. Unlike Klein's, his emancipation is complete; he has managed to leave society and his socialized self behind him without any moral compunctions. He has ceased to think and to feel like a respectable member of society, lives his own morality, and nurtures his own values. He is in accord with and accepts both himself and life. He has come to terms with his immediate self and with immediate life, but not with death: neither with his own death, nor with death, the final fact of life. Haunted by the specter of death and possessed by fear, Klingsor is unable just to let himself fall into life. Klein, at odds with himself and with life, slips into death. Klingsor, at odds with death, plunges into life. Klein blots himself and life out. Klingsor tries with reckless abandon to blot out the reality of death by rushing headlong into oblivious experience. He revels in life and glories in his art, but to no avail; sex, alcohol, and painting are ineffectual weapons against death. Klingsor's life, albeit resplendent and fruitful, is as desperate an adventure as Klein's death.

Klingsor is obviously terrified by death, but as The Magician argues, he also loves death and all the agonies associated with it. And he does so for good reason. It is to death that he owes his all. Death is the positive thrust in his life and in his art. But for his fear of death, he would not live as intensively as he does and has always wanted to, and but for death he would not be the artist that he is. Thanks to death, his life is the blissful agony he actually wants it to be.

Demian explains to Sinclair that man is troubled by anxiety only when not in accord with himself, when facets of his being remain relatively unknown to and are rejected by him. In **"Klein und Wagner,"** this argument is extended to life at large; man is beset by anxiety only when he cannot or will not accept himself for what he is and life for what it is. Such a person can only resist and not flow with life. Klein is an instance in question: severely at odds with both himself and with the world, he is possessed by every conceivable fear, is unable to live, and cannot rightly die. Anxiety-ridden because he is unable to accept the fact of death, Klingsor is just as incapable of letting himself fall into life. This step into the void becomes possible for him only when he is finally able to come to terms fully with both life and death. This rare moment is depicted symbolically in Klingsor's struggle with his self-portrait.

Hesse is careful to explain that this self-portrait is a unique challenge, a necessary human ordeal involving Klingsor's very destiny and self-justification. All his preceding anxiety and his intoxicating flight into life and art had been fear of and flight from this ultimate task. At the beginning of his undertaking, Klingsor is still sorely troubled by the specter of death. However, once immersed in his struggle, all his longstanding anxiety vanishes and flight, which had characterized his life, comes to an end. He can now surrender himself to his portrait with ecstatic abandon and emerges triumphant.

Klingsor's painting is not just the culminating artistic experience of an exciting summer, but the crowning human achievement of his life. A lifetime of thinking, feeling, and acting the self, and a concomitant learning to know the self climax in a bold confrontation with the self and with life at large. Klingsor's painting of his self-portrait symbolizes this confrontation and his resultant affirmation and acceptance of the self and of life. The portrait is all Klingsor ever was, and ever will be, all he has ever felt, thought, and experienced, and will ever feel, think, and experience. It is his birth, life, and his death, also mankind of the past, the present, and of the future. It is all that was and ever will be: being in all its eternity. And it is to this that he yields himself without fear and without reservations.

In **"Klein und Wagner,"** Hesse had suggested that art was nothing but an observing of the world by a person in a state of grace. Klingsor's painting is his observation of life at just such a moment of illumination: his epiphany. He is now in accord with all, no longer suffers from anxiety, and is finally able to let himself fall into life. He manages to achieve in life what Klein had experienced fully only in death. At this critical juncture, Hesse's narration terminates in its usual abrupt manner. The next and last chapter in Klingsor's self-realization, that period when he actually lets himself fall into life, that culminating stage symbolically anticipated in his self-portrait, remains untold. As usual, Hesse took his protagonist only to the point he himself had reached, or thought he had reached. Sinclair had proceeded beyond Veraguth, Klein beyond Sinclair, and Klingsor goes beyond Klein. Siddhartha, in turn, will proceed beyond Klingsor. He alone of these protagonists is able to live fully the ideal proposed in *Rosshalde.*

After *Rosshalde,* self-living, self-knowing, and ultimate self-realization became the most persistent and the foremost of Hesse's concerns. To live oneself more fully was to know oneself more thoroughly and to realize oneself more completely. Each of the succession of major tales from *Rosshalde* to ***Siddhartha*** is centered about this personal challenge, each takes up where its predecessor leaves off, and together they reflect a continuous and progressively more extensive and more subtle probing of the problem. These tales are linked almost as intimately as their chapters, and in a similar concatenative manner. One or two major themes are broached toward the end of one chapter and developed in the next, which itself introduces yet another new theme or two, again to be treated subsequently; each tale, in turn, explores the theory or new possibility put forward in the abrupt termination of the preceding tale, and itself ends abruptly, broaching a new theory or possibility which is then tested in the subsequent tale. One might say that Hesse's protagonists from *Rosshalde* to ***Siddhartha*** live or try to live the concluding thoughts of their immediate antecedents, and think the actions of their immediate successors. Veraguth lives Kuhn's espoused life of equanimous resignation, finds it wanting, and proposes to be what he essentially is. Sinclair is intent upon realizing Veraguth's proposal, but must first emancipate himself from tradition and evolve his own ethos; having become his real self, he is prepared to be himself. Klein attempts what Sinclair is about to embark upon; self-living proves impossible with only partial emancipation, but on the threshold of death, Klein finds new hope in an envisaged will-less acceptance of the self and of life. Klingsor learns that this new approach to life, predicated upon the affirmation and acceptance of reality in its entirety, is possible only after a lifetime of intensive living. Siddhartha is accorded what Klingsor is denied; having experienced and exhausted both his spirituality and his animality, he is able in affirmation and acceptance to let himself fall into life and to enjoy the last phase of self-realization.

The major thematic linkage of these tales is reinforced by a series of subsidiary concerns that also evolve from work to work. Particularly significant among these is the theme of love and the trying polarities of the spiritual and the sensual, of time and timelessness, and of multiplicity and oneness. A young and as yet inexperienced Sinclair embraces love in all its spirituality and sexuality; for a more mature Klein, love is only sex and a flight from loneliness, a grand disillusionment, a threat, and a torture; in his interaction with women, Don Juanish Klingsor is either an old rake or a callow youth, love is one of life's flighty intoxications, a brief sexual encounter, or a passing worship; and Siddhartha knows only erotic passion or social compassion, he indulges in the former and settles for the latter. Love, that gentle, tender, benevolent, and lasting bond between man and woman, remains as foreign to these protagonists as it had been to their predecessors, and as it would be to their successors. For Harry Haller and Goldmund, love continues to be primarily a sexual experience, a necessary therapeutic diversion for the former, and a delightful steady pastime for the latter. And with ***Die Morgenlandfahrt*** and *Das Glasperlenspiel,* sexual love yields entirely to social love. Sinclair affirms both man's spirituality and his animality, Klein proves to be adequate in neither realm, Klingsor wallows in each, and Siddhartha experiences and transcends both. But Siddhartha's was only an ideal and not an actual resolution of the spirit-flesh problem (*Geist* and *Natur*). This polarity, for Hesse the most critical of life's many painful dualities, was to continue to plague his protagonists for years to come. In his illumination immediately preceding his death, Klein experiences a miraculous timelessness and the essential simultaneity and oneness of all life. He now concludes that time is merely an invention of the mind, a torture instrument devised by man, and a notion that must be discarded if man is to be free. These brief asides of **"Klein und Wagner"** become an extended argument in **"Klingsors letzter Sommer,"** and a veritable philosophy in ***Siddhartha,*** a philosophy that argues timelessness in time and oneness in multiplicity. (pp. 153-57)

In Klingsor's legend, Hesse was as usual much more intent upon inner portraiture than upon narration. Description, comment, dialogue, and reported inner monologue prevail. What little real narrative there is, is confined to the preface. Actually a double portrait is executed: that which emerges as the story proceeds along its erratic course, and the unusual self-portrait of the conclusion. Hesse's characterization of the painting pertains just as much to the splintered tale preceding it: a marvelously harmonized tapestry in brilliant hues, an exercise in surrealism, a self-analysis unsparing in its psychological insights, and a ruthless, screaming confession. And what some of Klingsor's embittered opponents maintain about his self-portrait, unsympathetic literary critics could also, and with just as little cause, say about the tale itself: a product and proof of insanity, monomaniacal self-adoration, and self-glorification.

That **"Klingsors letzter Sommer"** is self-analysis and confession in a surrealistic vein, replete with colors and sounds reflecting and accentuating the turbulence of Klingsor's emotions and the feverishness of his thoughts is obvious enough. Immediately, however, the story seems to be anything but a marvelously harmonized tapestry, comprising as it does, ten disparate segments, jarringly juxtaposed, and assigned to one summer but otherwise only vaguely related in time: an informative preface, a study of Klingsor the man and the artist, four random episodes—a brief visit by Louis, a gay outing to Kareno, an evening of dour philosophy and wild revelry with The Magician and sundry friends, and Klingsor's sexual encounter with a peasant woman—a letter to Edith, another to Louis, a poem sent to Hermann, and a description of Klingsor's self-portrait. At first glance, this fractured structure with its romantic confusion of genres (descriptive prose, dramatic dialogue, poetry, and letters) could suggest an uncontrolled effervescence, imagination on the rampage, an undisciplined spewing forth of gaudy sentiment resulting in a hapless work of art. The tale may indeed have been written in this eruptive fashion. However, genesis notwithstanding, closer examination discloses that Hesse, like Klingsor given madly to his self-portrait, had proceeded intuitively and unerringly to produce a work of art that is anything but hapless, that is indeed a marvelously harmonized tapestry: art in which all elements of form are consonant with each other, and of which the form as a whole is in accord with the substance. The tale's untraditional, splintered structure and its lack of homogeneity—intuitive craft and not just chance—mirror and highlight the unorthodox, chaotic structure of Klingsor's lifestyle, and his inner discord. The hectic flow and the frantic rhythm of Hesse's sentences reflect and accentuate Klingsor's alternately frantic and ecstatic inner state. Nature, in turn, evocatively depicted, and excitingly animated by garish color and brilliant sound, becomes an accentuating mirror for his chronic restlessness and an appropriate backdrop for his frenzied reflections. Hesse's very language assumes Klingsor's bursting vitality and vibrates sympathetically and strongly with his persistent mania. It is vitalized by its rainbow of lively colors and its symphony of insistent sounds, its lavish similes, exotic metaphors, and startling oxymora, and by its extensive recourse to restive rhetorical questions and exclamations, and to anaphora and parataxis. Language itself is made to suffer Klingsor's agonies and ecstasies; it lends his story unusual impact and gripping immediacy. In **"Klingsors letzter Sommer,"** form became its own meaning. Form does not merely reinforce the content, it retells it in its own way. This is intuitively controlled artistry at its best. (pp. 158-59)

Joseph Mileck, in his Hermann Hesse: Life and Art, *University of California Press, 1978, 397 p.*

Theodore Ziolkowski (essay date 1981)

[*In his introduction to* Pictor's Metamorphoses, and Other Fantasies *excerpted below, Ziolkowski investigates the relevance of fantasy—manifested as folktale, literary fairy tale, dream, satire, and rumination—to Hesse's short fiction.*]

In an autobiographical sketch entitled "Childhood of the Magician" (1923), Hermann Hesse confessed that it had been his overriding ambition, while he was a child, to become a magician. This ambition stemmed from a dissatisfaction with what people conventionally call reality. . . . Hesse came to realize that his whole subsequent life had been motivated by the desire for magic powers—though by magic he now meant the transformation of reality, the creation of a wholly new reality, in his writing.

Certainly the distrust of everyday "reality"—it is characteristic that he customarily bracketed the term with quotation marks to indicate what he regarded as its tentative, problematic nature—remained a conspicuous theme in Hesse's thought throughout his life. . . . [In a 1940 letter Hesse stated] that "it is becoming apparent that the so-called 'reality' of the technologists, the generals, and the bank directors is growing constantly less real, less substantial, less probable." (pp. vii-viii)

In 1940 his denial of "so-called reality" concluded with the claim that "all spiritual reality, all truth, all beauty, all longing for these things, appears today to be more essential than ever."

This perceived dichotomy between contemporary "reality" and eternal values produces the tension that is characteristic of Hesse's entire literary oeuvre. The heroes of his best-known novels—Demian, Siddhartha, Harry Haller of *Steppenwolf,* Goldmund, H. H. in ***The Journey to the East,*** and Joseph Knecht, the magister ludi of *The Glass Bead Game*—are men driven by their longing for a higher reality that they have glimpsed in their dreams, their visions, their epiphanies, but tied by history and destiny to a "reality" that they cannot escape. At times, however, Hesse sought to depict that other world outright, and not simply as the vision of a figure otherwise rooted in this world. (p. viii)

By far the most common form of fantasy practiced by Hesse was the fairy tale or, to use the somewhat broader German term, the *Märchen.* Symptomatically, his earliest extant prose composition was a fairy tale entitled **"The Two Brothers"** (included here in the piece called **"Christmas with Two Children's Stories"**). In this *Märchen* from the pen of the ten-year-old Hesse, a crippled child runs away from home because he is despised by his strong and handsome older brother. Arriving in the mountains, he is adopted by the dwarfs who mine diamonds there. Years later, the older brother, having lost the use of his right arm in the wars, wanders into the mountains. Meeting his brother, whom he fails to recognize, he begs a crust of bread. The younger brother leads him into the cave and offers him, instead, all the diamonds that he can dig out by himself. When the one-armed beggar is unable to extract a single jewel, his host says that he would gladly permit the man's brother to assist him. Thereupon the beggar, breaking into tears, admits that he once had a brother, small and crippled yet good-natured and kind, whom he had callously driven away. At this display of remorse, the younger brother discloses his identity, and the two brothers live happily together ever after.

When he analyzed this bit of juvenilia many years later, Hesse noted that it was based not upon his own experience—he had never wittingly seen a diamond, much less a mountain of jewels inhabited by dwarfs—but upon his reading, notably the Grimms' *Fairy Tales* and the *Arabian Nights.* These two collections, with which Hesse became acquainted as a child, remained his favorites throughout his lifetime. In 1929 he singled out the *Arabian Nights* for inclusion in his ideal "Library of World Literature," calling it "a source of infinite pleasure." Although all the peoples of the world have produced lovely fairy tales, he continues, "this classic magic-book suffices for our library, supplemented solely by our own German *Märchen* in the collection of the Brothers Grimm."

Hesse was not simply stating the obvious on the basis of limited knowledge; he knew what he was talking about. In an extended career of book reviewing, he appraised many collections of fantasies from countries all over the world. . . . (pp. ix-x)

Hesse was not merely a connoisseur of fairy tales; he also understood something about their history and theory. He knew that folktales employ a limited stock of familiar motifs that recur in constantly varying configurations, and he was aware of the Oriental sources of many European tales as well as the ancient sources of many medieval tales. Fairy tales, he wrote in 1915 (in an essay on "German Storytellers"), are documents that reaffirm "the eternally identical structure of the human soul in all peoples and all lands." The fairy tales of the world provide us with incomparably valuable examples of "the genetic history of the soul."

In the light of this predilection, it is hardly surprising that Hesse undertook, from time to time, to write *Märchen* of his own—works in which the techniques and motifs of the international repertoire of fairy tales are much in evidence. At first glance, this fascination seems predictable in a writer who often asserted his fondness for Oriental culture and German romanticism, two of the principal sources for the fairy tales of the world. Yet we must not take too much for granted. Why, to put it most simply, does a mature writer in the twentieth century write fairy tales?

We can start with Hesse's thoughts. When he compared his early story **"The Two Brothers"** with a similar tale written some sixty years later by his grandson, Hesse observed that in both cases a wish is magically fulfilled, and in both cases the narrator has constructed for his hero a role of moral glory, a "crown of virtue." In short, both tales are characterized by elements of the supernatural (magical wish fulfillment) and by an explicit ethical dimension.

We see precisely the same pattern underlying Hesse's most entrancing fairy tale, **"Pictor's Metamorphoses."** When Pictor first enters the garden of paradise, he is captivated by the continual transformations that all nature is undergoing: he sees a bird turn into a flower, the flower into a butterfly, and the butterfly into a colored crystal with magical powers. Before he has fully comprehended the laws of transformation, yet eager to become a part of that wonderful process, he seizes the magic stone and overhastily wishes to be transformed into a tree. After his metamorphosis, Pictor realizes that he is still not part of the cycle of transformation because, unlike all the other creatures in the garden, he has remained single, he is not a pair. Hence he is doomed to retain a specific form. Many years later a young girl comes into the garden, picks up the stone, and is transmuted into the tree along with Pictor. Now, in their new unity, they undergo transformation after blissful transformation. In other words, the device of double wish fulfillment is used to illustrate a moral situation: the first wish creates the plight which is subsequently resolved by the fulfillment of the second wish.

Hesse is also capable of using the elements of the *Märchen* for purposes of humor or irony. In **"Tale of the Wicker Chair,"** a talking chair precipitates the ethical insight: a young dilettante has been inspired by reading a biography of Van Gogh to try to paint the simple objects in his garret. When he discovers how difficult it is to paint even a wicker chair, he decides to give up painting for what he considers the easier job of writing. In a later *Märchen* it is suggested that "Bird" may be the bird from **"Pictor's Metamorphoses"**; but he is also an allegorical projection of Hesse himself, who was known to his third wife by the nickname *Vogel* ("bird"). At first regarded fondly as a queer eccentric by the inhabitants of Montagsdorf (Monday Village, a pun on Montagnola, the Swiss village where Hesse lived), "Bird" is eventually driven away when a price is put on his head by foreign governments and the villagers begin to shoot at him. Again we find the magical transformation—which psychoanalysis calls a theriomorphic projection—that gives rise to a heavily allegorical tale with pronounced ethical implications. Indeed, the whole tale is very lightly veiled autobiography. But here Hesse has added a further ironic twist. After Bird's disappearance, various legends begin to circulate about him. "Soon there will be no one left who can attest that Bird ever actually existed." Future scholars will no doubt prove, Hesse suggests, that the legend is nothing but an invention of the popular imagination, constructed according to folkloristic laws of mythmaking. Here Hesse uses the form of the *Märchen* to make an ironic comment on the academic study of fairy tales, which tends through its analysis to disenchant the very object of its study, as well as the scholarly assessments of his own works, to several of which he alludes playfully in the text.

In every case, then, from the fairy tale of the ten-year-old Hesse to the ironic fable of the sixty-year-old, the narratives that Hesse specifically labeled as *Märchen* display two characteristics that distinguish them from his other prose narratives. There is an element of magic that is taken for granted: wish fulfillment, metamorphosis, animation of natural objects, and the like. And this magic incident produces in the hero a new dimension of ethical awareness: the necessity of love in life, the inappropriateness of ambition, and so forth. To be sure, wonders and miracles occur in other forms of fantasy employed by Hesse: but elsewhere the miracle is regarded as an interruption or suspension of normal laws. In the legends, for instance, the miracle represents an intervention by some higher power (e.g., **"The Merman"** or **"Three Lindens"**) that underscores the special nature of the occurrence. The figures in the fairy tales, in contrast, accept the wonders as self-evident: they do not represent any intrusion of the supernatural into the rational world, because the entire world of the *Märchen* operates according to supernatural laws. Little Red Riding Hood takes it for granted that the wolf can talk; the wicked stepmother in "Snow White" consults her magic mirror just as routinely as a modern woman might switch on her television set; and the tailor's son is not astonished at a table that sets itself with a feast when the proper formula is uttered. Hesse's *Märchen* share this quality of self-evident magic. Pictor does not question the powers of the magic stone; the aspiring young artist is not astonished when the wicker chair talks back to him.

However, a world in which magic is taken for granted does not in itself suffice to make a fairy tale: it must also be a world with an explicit ethical dimension. Oversimplified interpretations have argued that the world of fantasy is one in which things happen in accord with the expectations of naïve notions of good and evil, right and wrong. More sophisticated theorists offer a different explanation: the fairy tale begins with a situation of ethical disorder and finally, after resolving the conflicts, reestablishes a new order. Still others regard the *Märchen* as the poetic expression of man's confidence that we live in a meaningful world. All the theorists agree that the supernatural events do not occur simply for the delectation of the reader or listener; rather, the fairy tale reminds us through its magic that despite all appearances to the contrary there is meaning and order in the world. As Bruno Bettelheim points out in *The Uses of Enchantment,* "the child can find meaning through fairy tales," which offer an experience in moral education through which he brings order into the turmoil of his feelings. This is precisely the message of Hesse's *Märchen:* the characters are brought to an awareness of some principle of meaning that they had previously misunderstood. Indeed, the ethical dimension is pronounced in all fantasies, whether or not they display the explicitly supernatural element that characterizes fairy tales.

The impulse toward fantasy remained powerful in Hesse's temperament throughout his life. The fairy tale of **"The Two Brothers"** was written in 1887, when he was ten years old; **"The Jackdaw"** was a product of his seventies. Between those two extremes, the various forms of fantasy that Hesse employed reflect accurately the stages of his development as a writer. **"The Two Brothers,"** as Hesse recognized, was patterned closely after the so-called *Volksmärchen,* or popular fairy tales, that he knew as a child from the collection of the Brothers Grimm. His later fantasies are more profoundly indebted to the so-called *Kunstmärchen,* or literary fantasy, that has constituted one of the major genres of German literature for the past two centuries. In 1900, when he was finding his way as a writer and experimenting with the various forms offered by the German romantic tradition, Hesse was inspired principally by E. T. A. Hoffmann, whom he regarded as the "Romantic storyteller of the greatest virtuosity." **"Lulu,"** an autonomous section of the early novel entitled ***The Posthumous Writings and Poems of Hermann Lauscher*** (1901), is based explicitly and in specific detail on Hoffmann's classic fantasy *The Golden Flower Pot* (1813). The tale was inspired by a holiday trip that Hesse made in August of 1899 with a group of friends from Tübingen who called themselves (as in the story) the *petit cénacle* and whose names and sobriquets are playfully modified in the text. By means of the Hoffmannesque device of an encapsulated myth, Hesse succeeds in narrating the story of their collective infatuation with the innkeeper's niece (named in reality Julie Hellmann) in such a manner that it occurs on two levels: a "realistic" one as well as a fantastic or higher one. Through his skillful and ironic imitation of the romantic conventions Hesse paid his greatest tribute to Hoffmann.

Soon Hesse rejected the neoromanticism of his youth and turned to a less fanciful type of narrative after the fashion of the great nineteenth-century realists. To be sure, the impulse toward fantasy was not simply to be denied. In **"Hannes,"** Hesse offered a realistic depiction of a contemporary who—because his consciousness has not yet undergone the characteristically modern dissociation and who therefore still enjoys a *Märchen* mentality that enables him to see God in the thunderclouds and to encounter Jesus on remote rural paths—is regarded by his neighbors as a simpleton. In general, however, having to find other outlets for his fantasy, Hesse chose a form consistent with his current realism—the legend, a genre in which the supernatural was not entirely implausible because it could be attributed to the mythic consciousness that existed in remote times and places (patristic Gaza in **"The Enamored Youth,"** Renaissance Italy in **"The Merman,"** seventeenth-century Berlin in **"Three Lindens,"** and prehistoric jungles in **"The Man of the Forests"**). As we noted, however, the supernatural occurrences in the legends are regarded as an interruption of normal "reality" and not, as in the fairy tales, as self-evident. But Hesse soon found other ways of dealing with fantasy.

Dreams always played a lively role in Hesse's psychic life, as he tells us in the late essay "Nocturnal Games." The ominous precognitive dream of war related in **"The Dream of the Gods"** (1914) is significant because it signaled the unleashing of the powers of fantasy that Hesse had sought for more than a decade to suppress. During World War I, a variety of pressures—the death of his father, the deteriorating mental health of his first wife, the responsibilities for his three young sons, the burdens of his war-relief work in Switzerland—produced in Hesse an emotional crisis so severe that, in 1916 and 1917, he sought help in psychoanalysis. It was Jungian analysis, with its emphasis on dreams and their interpretation, that enabled Hesse to recover the childlike contact with the world of fantasy that he had attempted so long to repress. Hesse recognized what he owed to the insights of depth psychology. In a review of Oskar A. Schmitz's *Fairy Tales from the Unconscious* (*Märchen aus dem Unbewußten,* 1933), Hesse observed: "Finally, with the aid of a psychoanalytical method, he overcame the inhibitions that cut him off from his own fantasy and wrote these very readable fairy tales." Hesse is speaking from personal experience because several of the fairy tales that he wrote during the war are barely disguised metaphors for the recovery of the past through psychoanalysis: notably, **"Iris"** and **"The Hard Passage."** And in many of his fictional works—e.g., *Demian* and *Steppenwolf*—dreams function as an outlet for fantasy.

Hesse was fully aware of the significance of the wartime *Märchen* and dreams in his personal development. In August of 1919 he wrote his publisher that *Demian* along with the *Märchen* that he composed from 1913 to 1918 were "tentative efforts toward a liberation, which I now regard as virtually complete." By means of the fairy tale, he had succeeded in reestablishing the link with the unconscious that had been ruptured. Yet the fairy tale as a genre was only a passing phase in his literary career. In another letter of August 1919, he wrote to a friend that "the *Märchen* were for me the transition to a new and different kind of writing; I no longer even like them." This wholesale rejection of his *Märchen* was a bit premature; some of his most charming efforts in the genre were still to come. However, the tone begins to change from the high seriousness of the wartime fables to the irony of **"The Painter"** and **"Tale of the Wicker Chair,"** which anticipate Hesse's movement toward social satire in the twenties.

It is no accident that these two fantasies deal with painters, for toward the end of the war years Hesse had discovered in painting a new avocation. For a time, indeed, he toyed with the notion of attempting an entirely new career as an artist rather than a writer. Although this shift did not come about, Hesse continued to paint until the end of his life. (pp. xi-xix)

Following the separation from his first wife in 1919, Hesse moved to southern Switzerland, where he at first lived a relatively isolated life. Coming to realize eventually that this solitude was neither natural to him nor productive, the mid-fortyish writer courted and, in 1924, was briefly married to a much younger woman, the singer Ruth Wenger. **"Pictor's Metamorphoses"** amounts to an allegorical account, in fantasy form, of that love affair. The painter, entering the paradise of Ticino (as depicted in the accompanying aquarelles), first lives alone as a tree and then, recognizing his mistake, reenters the natural cycle of transformations by attaching himself to a beautiful young woman. (p. xx)

While a fascination with the unconscious world of dreams is conspicuous in expressionism, students of the period have emphasized in particular the socio-critical purposes to which the fairy tale was often devoted. The next group of Hesse's fantasies is certainly consistent with that generational tendency (notably, **"The Tourist City in the South," "Among the Massagetae," "King Yu,"** and **"Bird"**). The techniques of the fantasy—reification of abstract concepts within the framework of a simplified moral system—lend themselves to the exposure of existing social and cultural ills. Hesse shared the expressionist sense that the old social order was collapsing and that a new humanity was going to emerge from that chaos. So Hesse's use of the *Märchen* reflected the literary trends of the times, a fact of literary history that should be kept in mind if we hope to evaluate these works properly.

Hesse's late stories, while they bring no new variations in form, nevertheless display his continuing experimentation with the forms of fantasy. Indeed, the narrative is often encapsulated within a speculative framework in which the writer reflects on the nature of fantasy. **"Nocturnal Games"** embeds the account of several dreams in a rumination on the meaning of dreams in Hesse's life. **"Report from Normalia,"** the fragment of an unfinished novel that might well have grown into a satirical counterpart to the utopian vision of *The Glass Bead Game,* depicts a Central European country "in the north of Aquitaine." "Normalia," we are told, emerged by expansion from the parklike grounds of a onetime insane asylum to become the most rational nation in Europe. But Hesse, making use of a fictional device that has recently appealed to writers of the absurd, casts doubt on all our assumptions concerning "normality." The narrator, it turns out, is ultimately unsure whether the former madhouse he inhabits has indeed become the seat of sanity in a mad world or whether it is not in fact still a madhouse. In **"Christmas with Two Children's Stories"** the two fairy tales—Hesse's own and the tale written by his grandson—generate a theoretical digression on the function and nature of fantasy. And in **"The Jackdaw"**—another example of Hesse's recurrent identification with birds—Hesse shares with us the manner in which his imagination plays with reality to generate stories about an unusually tame bird that he encounters at the spa in Baden. "And yet our imagination is not always satisfied with the most plausible explanation, it also likes to play with the remote and the sensational, and so I have conceived of two further possibilities beyond the probable one."

While fantasy in the unadulterated form that it displays in **"Pictor's Metamorphoses"** (where we are dealing literally with an "other-world" in Tolkien's sense) occurs infrequently in Hesse's mature works, it is fair to say that the tendency toward fantasy is evident in his writing from childhood to old age. Indeed, fantasy can be called the hallmark of Hesse's major novels of the twenties and thirties, the surreal quality that disturbs critics of a more realistic persuasion: for instance, the Magic Theater in *Steppenwolf* or the fanciful scenes in ***The Journey to the East,*** where reality blends into myth and fantasy. Indeed, fantasy is a state of mind into which Hesse and his literary surrogates enter with remarkable ease. . . . In sum: any complete appreciation of Hesse must take into account this central tendency in his work. The most concentrated period of *Märchen* composition occurred, as noted, from 1913 to 1918, and the eight fantasies of those years were published in 1919 in a volume with the simple generic title ***Märchen*** (translated as ***Strange News from Another Star and Other Tales***). However, the sustained obsession with fantasy in its various manifestations—folktale, literary fairy tale, dream, satire, rumination—is apparent only in a collection like [***Pictor's Metamorphoses and Other Fantasies***]. (pp. xxi-xxiv)

It would be a mistake to regard the tendency toward fantasy, in Hesse or other writers, as mere escapism. True, the classic periods of fantasy have been those ages (Napoleonic Germany, Victorian England, Weimar Germany, and America in the 1960s) when technological reality was perceived as so overwhelming that the individual began to question its values and measure them against other ideals. But fantasy, with its explicitly didactic tendency, represents not so much a flight from confrontation as, rather, a mode in which the confrontation can be enacted in a realm of esthetic detachment, where clear ethical judgments are possible. Indeed, fantasy often reveals the values of a given epoch more vividly than the so-called realisms it may bring forth. In any case, a generation that decorates its walls with the calendars of the Brothers Hildebrandt while perusing Tolkien's *Lord of the Rings,* that hastens from meetings of the C. S. Lewis Society to performances of space fantasies like *Star Wars,* has mastered the semiotics necessary to decode the hidden signs of **"Pictor's Metamorphoses"** and Hesse's other fantasies. (pp. xxiv-xxv)

Theodore Ziolkowski, in an introduction to Pictor's Metamorphoses and Other Fantasies, *by Hermann Hesse, translated by Rika Lesser, Farrar, Straus and Giroux, 1982, pp. vii-xxv.*

Inder Nath Kher (essay date 1987)

[*Kher is an Indian critic and scholar whose studies encompass nineteenth-century American literature, British Romanticism, the modern European novel, and South Asian literature. In the excerpt below, he discusses the character H. H.'s struggle to enter the "timeless realm of the spirit" in* The Journey to the East.]

Before he was fourteen, Hesse had a burning desire to become a poet and a magician, in order to be able to heighten and transform what people call "reality". This desire occupied him all his life and manifested itself in a variety of fictional forms. In this context, it should be stated at once that in Hesse's novel(s) we should not expect to find any systematic treatment or exegesis of the philosophical thought of the East; rather, we should observe how Hesse dedicated himself to a creative interpretation or an aesthetic enactment of his sources, and what they became in his imagination. Through its various myths, legends and symbols, the East epitomizes for Hesse the realm of the spirit which embodies man's ultimate oneness and unity with the cosmos, in which all the polarities of existence are reconciled, and in which man finds the springs of his wholeness. To reach this timeless realm of the spirit was Hesse's goal. His art, however, highlights the process which underlines the struggle towards the goal; it dramatizes the tension and anxiety of Hesse's fragmented heroes before they finally envision the everlasting possibility of becoming whole and serene.

The Journey to the East (1932), Hesse's prologue to his monumental novel *The Glass Bead Game* (1931-1943), represents his most intricate and poetic pattern of consciousness, woven with great care and love. It incarnates the conception of life as a game, to be played with humour and detachment. Detachment is paradoxical: it is like eating and not eating, as the two birds, inseparable companions, do in the *Mundaka Upanishad.* H. H. or Hermann Hesse, both author and persona, belongs to the League or the ideal community of artists, thinkers, and religious leaders of past and present, who are involved in a perpetual journey to the East:

> I had joined a pilgrimage to the East, seemingly a definite and single pilgrimage—but in reality, in its broadest sense, this expedition to the East was not only mine and now; this procession of believers and disciples had always and incessantly been moving towards the East, towards the Home of Light.

In this journey, the ultimate meaning of life is being pursued individually and collectively. The individual seekers name their goals differently; a great treasure called "Tao", the magical powers of the serpentine Kundalini, the greatest happiness of life in Kashmir etcetera. H. H.'s life-goal is to "see the beautiful Princess Fatima," his fate and *anima,* the archetypal mother who represents the center (Anima Pia) and the circumference of the psyche. The League and the Journey then become the interior metaphors; through the creative imagination, the external aspects of the Journey, its temporal and sequential characteristics, are interiorized, and in this vision of simultaneity, all *time* and *space* are conquered:

> We not only wandered through Space, but also through Time. We moved towards the East, but we also travelled into the Middle ages and the Golden Age; we roamed through Italy or Switzerland, but at times we also spent the night in the tenth century and dwelt with the patriarchs or the fairies. During the times I remained alone, I often found again places and people of my own past. I wandered with my former betrothed along the edges of the forest of the Upper Rhine, caroused with friends of my youth in Tübingen, in Basle or in Florence, or I was a boy and went with my school-friends to catch butterflies . . . our goal was not only East, or rather the East was not only a country and something geographical, but it was the home and youth of the soul, it was everywhere and nowhere, it was the union of all times.

The emphasis is always on *movement* and *continuity.* The protagonist is continually moving towards the goal—the homeland of the soul and childhood. This movement is sustained by magic and poetry which enable us to transcend reality. H. H. describes "one of the most beautiful experiences" of the Journey in these highly symbolic words:

> From the castle's turrets of Bremgarten, the fragrance of *lilac* entered my bedroom. I heard the *river* flowing beyond the *trees.* I climbed out of the window in the *depth of the night,* intoxicated with happiness and yearning. I stole past the knight on guard and the sleeping banqueters down to the river-bank, to the *flowing waters,* to the white, gleaming *mermaids.* They took me down with them into the cool, *moonlit crystal world of their home,* where they *played* dreamily with the crowns and golden chains from their treasure-chambers. It seemed to me that I *spent months* in *the sparkling depths,* yet when I emerged and swam ashore, thoroughly *refreshed,* Pablo's reed-pipe was still to be heard from the garden far away, and the moon was still high in the sky. I saw Leo *playing* with two white poodles, his clever, boyish face radiating happiness. [critic's italics]

But at times the magic circle breaks up, and when this happens H. H. suffers from the tensions and polarities of the Journey. His sense of harmony is threatened, or even lost, when Leo, the ideal servant suddenly disappears from the League. He faces the ultimate crisis of his life during the years when he searches for Leo. Leo exemplifies true friendship, simplicity, discipline, service, faith, grace and sacramentation. Like Vasudeva in ***Siddhartha,*** he is the image of a wise old man. Like Demian, Siddhartha, Pablo-Mozart, and Joseph Knecht (the heroes of Hesse's other novels), he is both servant and master of existence. In short, he is the symbol of the Self which H. H. has yet to *find within himself.* The loss of this symbol brings chaos and disillusionment, and the Journey becomes meaningless. When H. H. finally meets Leo after a gap of ten years, Leo does not recognize him at first. During his alleged absence, Leo has "not aged at all"; he still whistles very well which reminds H. H. of his past as a musician; H. H. has "sold his violin," the act which represents his present state of disharmony and despair. Leo tells him that life is a game: "That is just what life is when it is beautiful and happy—a game. Naturally, one can also do all kinds of other things with it, make a duty of it, or a battleground, or a prison, but that does not make it any prettier." This reminds us of Schiller's classical assertion that "man fulfils his destiny only when at play." Leo also throws light on H. H.'s own defection from the League at Morbio. In this process of revelation, Leo's own presumed disappearance from the League and his final reappearance become metaphors for the protagonist's own loss of Self and its rediscovery. The accuser becomes the self-accused and appears before the High Throne of the League to discover that his early manuscript concerning "The Story of the Journey to the East" is extremely indequate and that "it must be written again, and again right from the beginning." With this humbling experience and a somewhat new awareness of his Self, H. H. searches into the "inexhaustible archives" of the League to make a fresh start. There he finds a "tiny locket which contains a miniature portrait of a ravishingly beautiful princess, Fatima. He breathes the rare, magic fragrance from the delicate violet cloth in the medallion, the *mandala* of the Self, but eventually moves on for "other stronger charms." Like Harry Haller in *Steppenwolf* H. H. must go beyond the love of a woman, although the Anima figure or projection is one of the most significant stages in one's journey towards psychic integration. At his trial, H. H. comes to know for the first time that Leo the servant is also the President of the League. He also sees in Leo "the figure of Albertus Magnus, the ferryman Vasudeva, the artist Klingsor, and others." Leo, the President and Judge, acquits H. H., the self-accuser, and welcomes "him anew into the League." Leo, the humble servant, gives H. H. his lost ring which Leo has kept for him. The ring symbolizes marriage and wholeness, self-illumination and grace. H. H. begins to *understand* himself, Leo, and the League; he now turns to the archives of the League with renewed passion and faith, and one day, discovers a small waxlike model:

> It was a figure that really consisted of two; it had a common back. I stared at it for a while, disappointed and surprised. Then I noticed a candle in a metal candlestick fixed to the wall of the niche. A matchbox lay there. It lit the candle and the strange double figure was now brightly illuminated. . . . I discovered a second candle in the wall and lit this also. I now saw the double figure representing Leo and myself, not only becoming clearer and each image more alike, but I also saw that the surface of the figures was transparent and that one could look inside as one can look through the glass of a bottle or vase. Inside the figures I saw something moving, slowly, extremely slowly, in the same way that a snake moves which has fallen asleep. Something was taking place there, something like a very slow, smooth but continuous flowing, or melting; indeed, something melted or poured across from my image to that of Leo's. I perceived that my image was in the process of adding to and flowing into Leo's, nourishing and strengthening it. It seemed that, in time, all the substance from one image would flow into the other and only one would remain: Leo. He must grow, I must disappear.

In this epiphanous moment, Leo, representing both male and female aspects of the psyche, father and mother—beloved archetypes, fulfils H. H. in all respects, spiritual and sexual. The images of the burning candle and the double figure signify fulfilled sexuality. Only by losing his separate identity or ego, H. H. or the persona finds himself a step closer to some repose. But, as William Barrett says: "There is no resolution; life is a perpetual movement toward a resolution that never ceases. . . . There is no escape from the wheel of birth and death. Man's only salvation is to learn to live in balance with the eternal and ceaselessly shifting play of opposites." In this last act of the novel, Hesse reveals the endless possibilities of life, its varied manifestations, shapes and forms, as well as their fundamental relatedness. This sweeping vision of unity and simultaneity that underlies the apparent fragmentation of human life receives its ultimate expression in *The Glass Bead Game* (1943) which Hesse dedicates to the Journeyers to the East. (pp. 44-9)

Inder Nath Kher, "Metaphor and Reality in Hermann Hesse's 'The Journey to the East'," in The Literary Criterion, *Vol. XXII, No. 3, 1987, pp. 41-50.*

FURTHER READING

Criticism

Boubly, Mark. *Hermann Hesse: His Mind and Art.* Ithaca, N.Y.: Cornell University Press, 1967, 338 p.

Contains detailed examinations of Hesse's major works, including *Siddhartha* and the *Journey to the East,* with an emphasis on structural patterns.

Brown, Madison. "Toward a Perspective for the Indian Element in Hermann Hesse's *Siddhartha.*" *The German Quarterly* 49, No. 2 (March 1976): 191-202.

Asserts that Hesse was unconcerned with authentically portraying Indian culture and religious beliefs in *Siddhartha,* but rather used them as a means to convey his themes.

Casebeer, Edwin F. "*Siddhartha:* The Completed Hero." In

his *Hermann Hesse,* pp. 23-54. New York: Thomas Y. Crowell, 1972.

Explication of *Siddhartha* which posits that the novella is "so central to the world of the other major Hesse novels that it provides the quickest and most thorough initial experience of Hesse with the least expenditure of time."

Derrenberger, John. "Who is Leo?: Astrology in Hermann Hesse's *Die Morgenlandfahrt.*" *Monatshefte* 67, No. 2 (Summer 1975): 167-72.

Focuses on the character Leo while discussing the symbolic function of astrology in *Die Morgenlandfahrt.*

Farquharson, R. H. "The Identity and Significance of Leo in Hesse's *Morgenlandfahrt.*" *Monatshefte* 55, No. 3 (March 1963): 122-28.

Posits that Hesse based the character Leo on his pet cat Löwe, a playful act that, according to Farquharson, proves Hesse had outgrown his "deadly earnest view of life."

Fickert, K. J. "Symbolism in Hesse's 'Heumond'." *The German Quarterly* 34, No. 2 (March 1961): 118-22.

Contends that "Heumond" "foreshadows the complexities of the later Hesse in a symbolism which seems to have thrust itself upon the author, and it stands as a model for the Hessean short story of the early period."

Hughes, Kenneth. "Hesse's Use of *Gilgamesh*-Motifs in the Humanization of Siddhartha and Harry Haller." *Seminar* 5, No. 2 (Fall 1969): 129-40.

Investigates how Hesse used the Babylonian epic *Gilgamesh* to transcend Christian moral doctrine and portray the self-actualization of the main characters in *Siddhartha* and *Steppenwolf.*

Kher, Inder Nath. "Hermann Hesse's *Siddhartha:* The Landscape of the Inner Self." *The Literary Half-Yearly* XIV, No. 1 (January 1973): 17-29.

Describes Siddhartha's quest for a superconscious vision in which "awareness of the world and of multiplicity is completely obliterated."

Middleton, Christopher. "Hermann Hesse's *Morgenlandfahrt.*" In his *Bolshevism in Art and Other Expository Writings,* pp. 239-51. Manchester, England: Carcanet Press, 1978.

Uses *Morgenlandfahrt* to explore Hesse's narrative technique.

Narasimhaiah, Sanjay. "*Siddhartha:* Between the Rebellion and the Regeneration." *The Literary Criterion* 16, No. 1 (1981): 50-60.

Faults Hesse's "imperfect understanding of India" as he traces Siddhartha's movement away from narcissism to spiritual transcendence.

Paslick, Robert H. "Dialectic and Non-Attachment: The Structure of Hermann Hesse's *Siddhartha.*" *Symposium* 27, No. 1 (Spring 1973): 64-75.

Contends that in *Siddhartha* the opposing forces of the intellectual and the natural must be "dialectically united in the central spirit whose very life consists in the continual non-attached vibrations between the abstract poles of human existence: the ideal and the real, the universal and the particular."

Spector, Robert Donald. "Artist Against Himself: Hesse's *Siddhartha.*" *The History of Ideas Newsletter* IV, No. 3 (Summer 1958): 55-8.

Asserts that *Siddhartha* represents Hesse's rejection of existentialist philosophy as a doctrine for the literary artist and posits that essential truth must be experienced rather than taught.

Additional coverage of Hesse's life and career is contained in the following sources published by Gale Research: *Contemporary Authors,* Vols. 17-18; *Contemporary Authors Permanent Series,* Vol. 2; *Contemporary Literary Criticism,* Vols. 1, 2, 3, 6, 11, 17, 25, 69; *Dictionary of Literary Biography,* Vol. 66; and *Something About the Author,* Vol. 50.

Shirley Jackson

1919-1965

American short story writer, novelist, and nonfiction writer.

INTRODUCTION

The author of several critically acclaimed novels, Jackson is best known for her psychological horror story "The Lottery." Often regarded as a satire of human behavior and social institutions, this frequently anthologized story exemplifies some of the central themes of Jackson's fiction, including the victimization of the individual by society, the tendency of people to be cruel and conformist, and the presence of evil in everyday life. Written in a deft, unadorned prose style and often set in small-town communities, Jackson's short stories are characterized by blithe situations that belie their disturbing effects.

The publication of "The Lottery" in the *New Yorker* in 1948 precipitated a controversy that launched Jackson's literary career and established her reputation as a writer of strange, unsettling fiction. The story elicited hundreds of letters from readers, most of whom felt betrayed by the unexpected, gruesome ending. Frequently described as a modern parable, "The Lottery" depicts events of a June morning in a rural American town where the citizens have gathered for an annual lottery. Amid laughter and gossip, slips of paper are drawn from a box until housewife Tessie Hutchinson receives the slip with a black mark on it. Immediately, the other villagers begin stoning her. Earlier in the story, Jackson hints at the possibility of a human sacrifice in the farming community when one of the characters quotes the local adage, "Lottery in June, corn be heavy soon." Critics have interpreted the story as a satire of several social evils, including sexism, racial prejudice, and the willingness of people to engage collectively in abhorrent behavior.

Many of Jackson's other stories focus on family and societal relations, mental illness, and the supernatural. In the often-anthologized tale "After You, My Dear Alphonse," an examination of racial prejudice, a housewife is startled when her young son brings home a black friend and then becomes irritated that the child does not confirm her stereotyped conceptions of black society. In "The Renegade" a woman is stunned when her ostensibly kind neighbors brutally advise her to kill a disobedient dog. Several of Jackson's stories occur on the borderline between fantasy and reality, including "The Daemon Lover," which involves a woman whose fiancé fails to appear on the morning of their wedding; afterward she spends hours searching for him and finally begins to doubt her own sanity, wondering if he ever existed. "Louisa, Please Come Home" revolves around a young woman who runs away on her sister's wedding day, ignoring her family's broadcasted and printed pleas that she return. After four years she relents, but her family fails to recognize her and refuses to accept her identity. Jackson's stories often confront the shortcomings of human nature through irony and black humor. In "Charles" the narrator relates her child's joyful daily accounts of the exploits of the class troublemaker, Charles. However at the school's open house, she discovers that there is no Charles in the kindergarten; the troublemaker is her son. The popular story "One Ordinary Day, with Peanuts" concerns a married couple who recount to each other their experiences during a particular day. While one of them has performed such acts as sending stray dogs to the pound and shoplifting, the other has been kind, feeding birds and helping elderly women cross busy streets. Every day, they switch roles. Jackson's last published story, "The Possibility of Evil," appeared in 1965. The tale centers on Adela Strangeworth, an elderly woman whose only joy in life, besides tending her prize rosebushes, is sending anonymous notes to people in her town informing them of their "wickedness." When she inadvertently drops a note on her way to the mailbox one day, her identity is revealed, and she soon receives a note herself: "Look out at what used to be your roses."

Jackson's subtle narrative technique and her uncompromising examination of the dark side of human nature have earned her a reputation as an important short story writer. Mary Kittredge asserted that Jackson's fiction "was the result of an exquisitely sensitive double vision that would have seemed an affliction to less determined or talented writer. She saw the magic in the mundane, and the evil behind the ordinary. She saw that the line between the cruel and the comedic is sometimes vanishingly narrow."

PRINCIPAL WORKS

SHORT FICTION

The Lottery; or, The Adventures of James Harris 1949
The Magic of Shirley Jackson (short stories and novels) 1966
Come Along with Me (short stories, lectures, and novel) 1968

OTHER MAJOR WORKS

The Road through the Wall (novel) 1948; also published as *The Other Side of the Street,* 1956
Hangsaman (novel) 1951
Life among the Savages (nonfiction) 1953
The Bird's Nest (novel) 1954; also published as *Lizzie,* 1957
Witchcraft of Salem Village (juvenile nonfiction) 1956
Raising Demons (nonfiction) 1957
The Sundial (novel) 1958
The Haunting of Hill House (novel) 1959
We Have Always Lived in the Castle (novel) 1962

Donald Barr (essay date 1949)

[Barr is an American educator and critic. In the following review of The Lottery, *he associates Jackson's stories with a class of fiction that he terms "literary but popular."]*

The short story remains the most vigorous branch of American literature because it is in pretty direct contact with its audience, which is a large one.

The upper-middle-class magazine, which carries what might be called literary but popular fiction, has never been healthier and more liberal than it is today. Most of the stories in Shirley Jackson's new book, ***The Lottery; or, The Adventures of James Harris,*** appeared first in these upper-middle magazines and are fairly representative of the class. They all have the easy, economical style and unobtrusive dialogue which are now a standard requirement. Most have a certain shape and movement to them, although there are one or two of the old poignant-pointless school. Distinct incident has staged a come-back in short fiction, but still serious writers like Miss Jackson often use it more for revealing characters and situations than for any development which could be called a plot.

These twenty-five stories reveal both that Miss Jackson has a very effective talent as an ironist and that the magazines are clinging too long to certain patterns in stories. The middle-class emotion of embarrassment has been substituted for many of the human passions, and passion itself is very often treated in such a way that the reader is only embarrassed by it. The mixture of the macabre and the familiar—hell yawning beneath the commonplaces of life—and especially the combination of cruelty and the childlike is a standard theme, which Miss Jackson treats not as a source of macabre humor, as Saki treated it, but as a source of macabre embarrassment.

In this connection it is hard to see why the title story created such a sensation when it appeared in *The New Yorker* last year. It is a good story, but there are far better in the book. An unnerving, but not unfashionable, helplessness in the face of city life, of one's children, of country prejudice, and of one's fellow women in general, runs through all the stories.

It seems unfair to dwell on the shortcomings of one of the most interesting books of short stories we have had in some time, but the erudite quotations which adorn it and the recurring use of the name James Harris give a false unity to the book and confuse the meaning of the individual stories. For the better stories—like **"The Tooth," "Charles"** and **"The Flower Garden"**—are fine enough and various enough to stand by themselves and to show that writers like Miss Jackson may well do what must be done to broaden the range of their medium and market.

Donald Barr, "A Talent for Irony," in The New York Times Book Review, *April 17, 1949, p. 4.*

James Hilton (essay date 1949)

[Hilton was an English journalist and novelist who achieved his greatest success with the novels Lost Horizon *(1933) and* Goodbye, Mr. Chips *(1934). In 1935 he moved to the United States, where he became known as a book reviewer and radio announcer. In the following review of* The Lottery, *Hilton comments on what he considers the nightmarish atmospheres of Jackson's short stories.]*

It was perhaps Freud who, by interpreting dreams in relation to life, paved the way for those who see life in the irrefutable focus of a dream. Not, of course, a soft focus, still less "an exquisite embodiment of the poet's visions, gilding with refulgent light our dreamy moments, and laying open a new and magic world before the mental eye" (to quote the eminent Mr. Curdle); but rather the nightmare mood of some blackhearted fairy tale in which nobody lives happily, whether before, during or after. Yet there can be enough truth in it, of a frantic kind, to mirror aptly certain things in our own lives and times.

This is the sort of short story that Miss Shirley Jackson constructs. One of hers, **"The Lottery,"** attracted much attention when it first appeared in *The New Yorker,* and now comes a book of them, containing **"The Lottery"** and taking its title from that memorable piece. The whole collection will enhance Miss Jackson's reputation as a writer not quite like any other of her generation. Indeed, she sees life, in her own style, as devastatingly as Dali paints it, and like Dali also, she has a sound technique in her own art. There is a beguilingness in the way she leads her readers to the precise point at which the crucial shock can be administered.

The stories are of varying length and quality, but there is in nearly all of them a single note of alarm which reminds one of the elemental terrors of childhood—as when the pages of a book are unsuspectingly turned upon a frightening picture, or a shadow moves into sudden shape upon a wall. The story called **"The Lottery,"** for instance, opens with a quietly detailed description of how lots are cast one summer morning in an American village (we are not told where or when), the occasion being evidently one that takes place every year by traditional sanction. Not till the end do we discover its terrible purpose. The effect is in the calm narration culminating, almost casually, in dreadfulness—a method that has often been employed for macabre humor, as in *Arsenic and Old Lace,* or in the immortal disclosure that "Deep into the well / Which the plumber built her / Aunt Maria fell / We must buy a filter." But Miss Jackson plays it not for a laugh but for the unprofitable question of what exactly does she mean—as unprofitable as to puzzle over some night-horror that fades into incomprehensibility a moment after waking.

Other stories in this collection are less fearful but almost as cruel in their implications. Up to a point they are documented, realistic; modern New York is often the scene where Miss Jackson's thwarted characters expose themselves—the girl secretary in a half-shyster literary agency, genteel dwellers in cheap apartments, strugglers and stragglers in Greenwich Village, and the reptilian James Harris, a recurrent character who adds a slightly insane dimension wherever he appears. It is a seedy world with savage undertones, and Miss Jackson portrays it without mercy. If one might choose for special mention another of these stories, it could well be the one called **"Trial by Combat."** Beneath the surface of this seemingly straightforward anecdote of an old lady who steals trifles there is the uneasy curved space in which Miss Jackson's art flourishes; it is a very odd, specialized, unholy and, therefore, thoroughly contemporary art, and the reader who finds himself allergic to it will enjoy this book very much.

James Hilton, "The Focus of a Dream," in New York Herald Tribune Weekly Book Review, *May 1, 1949, p. 4.*

Cleanth Brooks and Robert Penn Warren (essay date 1959)

[Brooks and Warren are considered two of the most prominent figures of the school of New Criticism, an influential movement in American criticism during the mid-twentieth century. Although the various New Critics did not subscribe to a single set of principles, all stressed close textual analysis in the interpretation of a work of art rather than historical or biographical discussion. In the following excerpt from their textbook Understanding Fiction, *Brooks and Warren consider the relationship of form and meaning in "The Lottery."]*

The plot [of **"The Lottery"**] is so simple that to some readers it may seem to lack sufficient complication to be interesting. The story seems to do no more than recount the drawing of lots to determine which citizen of the village shall be stoned to death. There is no conflict—at least of the kind that occurs between tangible forces—no decision to be arrived at, no choice between two goods or two evils. There is no development of plot through human struggle and effort: the issue of life and death turns upon pure chance. The suspense secured is the simplest kind possible: which unlucky person will chance determine to be the victim?

Even this suspense is largely undercut by the fact that character interest in the story is also at a minimum. We are not brought close up to any of the characters. We learn little about their inner natures. There is nothing to distinguish them from ten thousand other people and indeed it becomes clear that they represent no more than the typical inhabitants of a New England village. The author seems deliberately to have played down any distinguishing traits. The victim herself, it is made very clear, is simply the typical small-town housewife.

Yet the story makes a very powerful impact, and the handling of plot and character must finally be judged, in terms of the story's development, to be very skillful. Obviously this story . . . has been sharply tilted toward theme. The reaction of most readers, as a matter of fact, tends to center on this problem: what does the story—granted its power—mean? It is not really a story about the victim, Mrs. Hutchinson. It is not literally about life in an American village, since the events portrayed are fantastic events. What then is the story "about"?

Before trying to answer the question specifically, one ought to say that this story is a kind of *fable*. . . . The general flatness of characterization—the fact that the characters are all simply variants of the ordinary human being, and the fantastic nature of the plot make this rather clear. The most famous early fables, Aesop's fables, for example, give us fantastic situations in which animals are actuated by human motivations, speak like human beings, and reveal themselves as rather transparent instances of certain human types. But Aesop's fables usually express a fairly explicit comment on life which can be expressed as a moral. For example, a popular translation of the fable of the fox and the grapes concludes with the moral tag: "It is easy to despise what you cannot get."

The family resemblance of **"The Lottery"** to the fable is concealed in part by the fact that **"The Lottery"** does not end with a neat moral tag and indeed avoids focusing upon a particular meaning. This latter point, however, we shall consider a little later.

The general pattern of this story may also be said to resemble that of the *parable*. . . . In a parable the idea or truth is presented by a simple narrative in which the events, persons, and the like, of the narrative are understood as being directly equivalent to terms involved in the statement of the truth. (pp. 72–3)

[In a parable, characterization is reduced to a minimum]. And the action is reduced to a minimum too. We need only so much of narrative as will make the point that the speaker wishes to make. But if **"The Lottery"** in its relative thinness of characterization and its relative simplicity of narration resembles the parable, it is obviously not a naked parable. The author has taken pains to supply a great deal of concrete detail to make us "believe" in her village, in its goings on this morning of June 27th. It is also obvious that she has preferred to give no key to her parable but to leave its meaning to our inference. One may summarize by saying that **"The Lottery"** is a normal piece of fiction, even if tilted over toward the fable and the parable form. Yet the comparison with these two forms may be useful in indicating the nature of the story.

What of its meaning? We had best not try to restrict the meaning to some simple dogmatic statement. The author herself has been rather careful to allow a good deal of flexibility in our interpretation of the meaning. Yet surely a general meaning does emerge. This story comments upon the all-too-human tendency to seize upon a scapegoat and to visit upon the scapegoat the cruelties that most of us seem to have dammed up within us. An example out of our own time might be the case in which some sensational happening occurs in a family—a child is kidnapped, or a youthful member of the family is implicated in a weird crime. The newspapers sometimes hound the family past all decency, and we good citizens, who support those newspapers, batten upon their misery with a cruelty that would shock us if we ever could realize what we were doing. Or to take another case, a man's patriotism is impugned quite falsely; or, whether the charge against him is false or true, let us say that his wife is completely guiltless. Yet she is "stoned" by her self-righteous neighbors who are acting, of course, out of pure virtue and fervent patriotism. These two instances are merely suggestive. Neither would answer fully to the terms of the story, but they may indicate that the issues with which the story is concerned are thoroughly live issues in our time.

But the author has been wise not to confine the meaning to any precise happening of the sort we have suggested. For evidently she is concerned with the more general psychological basis for such cruelty as a community tends to manifest. **"The Lottery"** makes such points as these: the cruel stoning is carried out by "decent" citizens who in many other respects show themselves kind and thoughtful. The cruel act is kept from seeming the cruel thing it is by the fact that it has been sanctioned by custom and long tradition. When Mrs. Adams remarks that "Some places have already quit lotteries," Old Man Warner says, "Nothing but trouble in *that.* Pack of young fools." A further point is this: human beings find it difficult to become exercised over ills not their own. Once a family group sees that the victim is not to be selected from among themselves, they proceed to observe matters with a certain callous disinterest. Moreover, even the individual members of the Hutchinson family are themselves relatively unconcerned once each discovers that he is not the victim chosen. Thus, "Nancy and Bill, Jr., opened theirs at the same time, and both beamed and laughed, turning round to the crowd and holding their slips of paper above their heads." The French moralist Rochefoucald ruefully observed that we obtain a certain pleasure from news of misfortune to friends. There is truth in this, and our story savagely makes a related point. Only the victim protests "It isn't fair," and she makes her protest only after she has chosen a slip of paper marked with the black spot. We remember that earlier Mrs. Hutchinson had said to Mrs. Delacroix in neighborly good humor, "Clean forgot what day it was," and both had "laughed softly" together.

"The Lottery," then, deals indeed with live issues and issues relevant to our time. If we hesitate to specify a particular "point" that the story makes, it is not because the story is vague and fuzzy, but rather because its web of observations about human nature is too subtle and too complex to be stated in one or two brief maxims.

What requires a little further attention is a problem of a quite different sort: how does this story differ from a tract or a treatise on human nature? Are we actually justified in calling it a piece of fiction?

An answer to these questions might run like this: This is obviously not a tract or merely an essay. The village is made to exist for us; the characters of Old Man Warner and Mr. Summers and Mrs. Hutchinson do come alive. They are not fully developed, to be sure, and there is a sense in which even the personality of the victim is finally subservient to the "point" to be made and is not developed in its own right and for its own sake. But, as we have said, this is not a "naked parable"—and the fact that we get an impression of a real village and real people gives the sense of grim terror.

The fictional form thus justifies itself by making vivid and forceful what would otherwise have to be given prosaically and undramatically. But it does something else that is very important: it provides a special shaping of the reader's attitude toward the climactic event and toward that from which the climactic event stems. The reader's attitude has been moulded very carefully from the very beginning. Everything in the story has been devised to let us know how we are to "take" the final events in the story. (pp. 74-6)

The very fact that an innocent woman is going to be stoned to death by her friends and neighbors and that this is to happen in an American small town during our own present day of enlightenment requires a special preparation. The apparently fantastic nature of the happening means that everything else in the story must be made plausible, down-to-earth, sensible, commonplace, everyday. We must be made to feel that what is happening on this June morning is perfectly credible. Making it seem credible will do two things: it will increase the sense of shock when we suddenly discover what is really going on, but it will ultimately help us to believe that what the story asserts does come to pass. In general, then, the horror of the ending is counter-balanced by the dry, even cheery, atmosphere of the scene. This contrast between the matter-of-factness and the cheery atmosphere, on one side, and the grim terror, on the other, gives us a dramatic shock. But it also indicates that the author's point in general has to do with the awful doubleness of the human spirit—a doubleness that expresses itself in the blended good neighborliness and cruelty of the community's action. The fictional form, therefore, does not simply "dress up" a specific comment on human nature. The fictional form actually gives point and definition to the social commentary. (p. 76)

Cleanth Brooks, in an interpretation of "The Lottery," in Understanding Fiction, *edited by Cleanth Brooks and Robert Penn Warren, second edition, Appleton-Century-Crofts, Inc., 1959, pp. 72-6.*

"[Writing's] as much fun as sending the children off to school. My husband fights writing; it is work for him, at least he calls it work. I find it relaxing. For one thing, it's the only way I can get to sit down. There is delight in seeing a story grow; it's so deeply satisfying—like having a winning streak in poker."

—Shirley Jackson, 1949.

Granville Hicks (essay date 1966)

[*Hicks was an American critic whose famous study* The Great Tradition: An Interpretation of American Literature since the Civil War *(1933) established him as the foremost advocate of Marxist critical thought in Depression-era America. During this period, Hicks believed it was the task of literature to confront sociopolitical issues. After 1939 Hicks denounced communist doctrine and adopted a less stringently ideological posture in his literary criticism. In the following excerpt from a review of* The Magic of Shirley Jackson, *Hicks notes the diversity of Jackson's literary forms and styles, while observing that her stories are dominated by the idea of evil lurking below the surface of life.*]

Shirley Jackson, who died a year ago at the age of forty-five, has never received the appreciation she deserves. I cannot boast that I was one of the few who recognized from the first the power and excellence of her work. I was impressed, as were many other people, by **"The Lottery"** when it appeared in *The New Yorker* in 1948, and there were other early things that I liked; but then I was thrown off by the many pieces she wrote about her children. These I encountered mostly in women's magazines that I found in the offices of doctors and dentists, and I realize now that I should have been careful about drawing conclusions; but I decided that Miss Jackson was no more interesting than most of the other writers for those magazines. Then, pretty much by accident, I read *We Have Always Lived in the Castle* when it was published in 1962, became aware of what I had been missing, and read everything else of hers I could find.

Now there is an omnibus volume, ***The Magic of Shirley Jackson*** which has a brief, frank, and poignant preface by her husband, Stanley Edgar Hyman. The book contains a novel, *The Bird's Nest;* both of the volumes made out of the family sketches, *Life Among the Savages* and *Raising Demons,* and eleven short stories, including of course **"The Lottery."** . . .

Hyman says that people have been surprised that "the author of her grim and disturbing fiction" should have written "two light-hearted volumes about the spirited doings of our children." "Shirley Jackson," he goes on, "wrote in a variety of forms and styles because she was, like everyone else, a complex human being, confronting the world in many different roles and moods. She tried to express as much of herself as possible in her work, and to express each aspect as fully and purely as possible." This is all very well, and I am not going to suggest that Miss Jackson's complexity at times seems schizoid; but I do think that some of the sketches are merely talented potboilers and needn't have been included in this collection.

Among the short stories are two or three funny sketches, such as **"My Life with R. H. Macy,"** but most of them are dominated by Miss Jackson's sharp sense that despair, cruelty, and madness lie just below the surface of life. **"Pillar of Salt," "The Renegade,"** and **"Elizabeth"** are all stories of that sort, and in three pages **"Colloquy"** makes a pointed comment on American life. One of the finest is **"The Flower Garden,"** in which a better than average small-town housewife abandons her good intentions to follow the racist prejudices of her neighbors. The best is the most famous, **"The Lottery."** By whom is Mrs. Hutchinson stoned to death? By the ordinary people of the town, pleasant people, often good people, who nevertheless turn joyfully to violence and cruelty when the release of the blacker elements of their natures is sanctioned by tradition. What is frightening in recent pictures of the anti-Negro riots in Chicago is not that one occasionally sees the face of a demented fanatic but that most of the participants, even some of those wearing swastikas, look like typical American kids out for a good time. (p. 31)

Miss Jackson was certainly not the first writer to assert that there is evil in everybody, but what might be merely a platitude becomes a great truth because of the depth and consistency of her own feeling about life and because she was so extraordinarily successful in making her readers feel what she felt. She plunges the reader into a world of her creating and leaves him wondering about what he has always believed to be the real world. (p. 32)

Granville Hicks, "The Nightmare in Reality," in Saturday Review, *Vol. XLIX, No. 38, September 17, 1966, pp. 31-2.*

Shirley Jackson (essay date 1968)

[*The essay below is an edited version of a lecture on "The Lottery" that was originally delivered by Jackson in 1960. The lecture was later published as "Biography of a Story" in* Come Along with Me *in 1968.*]

On the morning of June 28, 1948, I walked down to the post office in our little Vermont town to pick up the mail. I was quite casual about it, as I recall—I opened the box, took out a couple of bills and a letter or two, talked to the postmaster for a few minutes, and left, never supposing that it was the last time for months that I was to pick up the mail without an active feeling of panic. By the next week I had had to change my mailbox to the largest one in the post office, and casual conversation with the postmaster was out of the question, because he wasn't speaking to me. June 28, 1948, was the day *The New Yorker* came out with a story of mine in it. It was not my first published story, nor my last, but I have been assured over and over that if it had been the only story I ever wrote or published, there would be people who would not forget my name.

I had written the story three weeks before, on a bright June morning when summer seemed to have come at last, with blue skies and warm sun and no heavenly signs to warn me that my morning's work was anything but just another story. The idea had come to me while I was pushing my daughter up the hill in her stroller—it was, as I say, a warm morning, and the hill was steep, and beside my daughter the stroller held the day's groceries—and perhaps the effort of that last fifty yards up the hill put an edge to the story; at any rate, I had the idea fairly clearly in my mind when I put my daughter in her playpen and the frozen vegetables in the refrigerator, and, writing the story, I found that it went quickly and easily, moving from beginning to end without pause. As a matter of fact, when I read it over later I decided that except for one or two minor corrections, it needed no changes, and the story I finally typed up and sent off to my agent the next day was almost word for word the original draft. This, as any writer of stories can tell you, is not a usual thing. All I know is that when I came to read the story over I felt strongly that I didn't want to fuss with it. I didn't think it was perfect, but I didn't want to fuss with it. It was, I thought, a serious, straightforward story, and I was pleased and a little surprised at the ease with which it had been written; I was reasonably proud of it, and hoped that my agent would sell it to some magazine and I would have the gratification of seeing it in print.

My agent did not care for the story, but—as she said in her note at the time—her job was to sell it, not to like it. She sent it at once to *The New Yorker,* and about a week after the story had been written I received a telephone call from the fiction editor of *The New Yorker;* it was quite clear that he did not really care for the story, either, but *The New Yorker* was going to buy it. He asked for one change—that the date mentioned in the story be changed to coincide with the date of the issue of the magazine in which the story would appear, and I said of course. He then asked, hesitantly, if I had any particular interpretation of my own for the story; Mr. Harold Ross, then the editor of *The New Yorker,* was not altogether sure that he understood the story, and wondered if I cared to enlarge upon its meaning. I said no. Mr. Ross, he said, thought that the story might be puzzling to some people, and in case anyone telephoned the magazine, as sometimes happened, or wrote in asking about the story, was there anything in particular I wanted them to say? No, I said, nothing in particular; it was just a story I wrote.

I had no more preparation than that. I went on picking up the mail every morning, pushing my daughter up and down the hill in her stroller, anticipating pleasurably the check from *The New Yorker,* and shopping for groceries. The weather stayed nice and it looked as though it was going to be a good summer. Then, on June 28, *The New Yorker* came out with my story.

"One of the most terrifying aspects of publishing stories . . . is the realization that they are going to be read, and read by strangers. I had never fully realized this before, although I had of course in my imagination dwelt lovingly upon the thought of the millions and millions of people who were going to be uplifted and enriched and delighted by the stories I wrote. It had simply never occurred to me that these millions and millions of people might be so far from being uplifted that they would sit down and write me letters I was downright scared to open; of the three-hundred-odd letters that I received [the summer "The Lottery" was published] I can count only thirteen that spoke kindly to me, and they were mostly from friends."

—Shirley Jackson, 1960.

Things began mildly enough with a note from a friend at *The New Yorker:* "Your story has kicked up quite a fuss around the office," he wrote. I was flattered; it's nice to think that your friends notice what you write. Later that day there was a call from one of the magazine's editors; they had had a couple of people phone in about my story, he said, and was there anything I particularly wanted him to say if there were any more calls? No, I said, nothing particular; anything he chose to say was perfectly all right with me; it was just a story.

I was further puzzled by a cryptic note from another friend: "Heard a man talking about a story of yours on the bus this morning," she wrote. "Very exciting. I wanted to tell him I knew the author, but after I heard what he was saying I decided I'd better not."

One of the most terrifying aspects of publishing stories and books is the realization that they are going to be read, and read by strangers. I had never fully realized this before, although I had of course in my imagination dwelt lovingly upon the thought of the millions and millions of people who were going to be uplifted and enriched and delighted by the stories I wrote. It had simply never occurred to me that these millions and millions of people might be so far from being uplifted that they would sit down and write me letters I was downright scared to open; of the three-hundred-odd letters that I received that summer I can count only thirteen that spoke kindly to me, and they were mostly from friends. Even my mother scolded me: "Dad and I did not care at all for your story in *The New Yorker,*" she wrote sternly; "it does seem, dear, that this gloomy kind of story is what all you young people think about these days. Why don't you write something to cheer people up?"

By mid-July I had begun to perceive that I was very lucky indeed to be safely in Vermont, where no one in our small town had ever heard of *The New Yorker,* much less read my story. Millions of people, and my mother, had taken a pronounced dislike to me.

The magazine kept no track of telephone calls, but all letters addressed to me care of the magazine were forwarded directly to me for answering, and all letters addressed to the magazine—some of them addressed to Harold Ross personally; these were the most vehement—were answered at the magazine and then the letters were sent me in great batches, along with carbons of the answers written at the magazine. I have all the letters still, and if they could be considered to give any accurate cross section of the reading public, or the reading public of *The New Yorker,* or even the reading public of one issue of *The New Yorker,* I would stop writing now.

Judging from these letters, people who read stories are gullible, rude, frequently illiterate, and horribly afraid of being laughed at. Many of the writers were positive that *The New Yorker* was going to ridicule them in print, and the most cautious letters were headed, in capital letters: NOT FOR PUBLICATION or PLEASE DO NOT PRINT THIS LETTER, or, at best THIS LETTER MAY BE PUBLISHED AT YOUR USUAL RATES OF PAYMENT. Anonymous letters, of which there were a few, were destroyed. *The New Yorker* never published any comment of any kind about the story in the magazine, but did issue one publicity release saying that the story had received more mail than any piece of fiction they had ever published; this was after the newspapers had gotten into the act, in midsummer, with a front-page story in the San Francisco *Chronicle* begging to know what the story meant, and a series of columns in New York and Chicago papers pointing out that *New Yorker* subscriptions were being canceled right and left.

Curiously, there are three main themes which dominate the letters of that first summer—three themes which might be identified as bewilderment, speculation, and plain old-fashioned abuse. In the years since then, during which the story has been anthologized, dramatized, televised, and even—in one completely mystifying transformation—made into a ballet, the tenor of letters I receive has changed. I am addressed more politely, as a rule, and the letters largely confine themselves to questions like what does this story mean? The general tone of the early letters, however, was a kind of wide-eyed, shocked innocence. People at first were not so much concerned with what the story meant; what they wanted to know was where these lotteries were held, and whether they could go there and watch. (pp. 1192-95)

Shirley Jackson, "On the Morning of June 28, 1948, and 'The Lottery'," in The Story and Its Writer: An Introduction to Short Fiction, *edited by Ann Charters, St. Martin's Press, 1983, pp. 1192-95.*

Guy Davenport (essay date 1968)

[Davenport is an American scholar who has published critically acclaimed essays, translations, fiction, and poetry. In the following review of Come Along with Me, *he examines Jackson's qualities as a writer.]*

It was in plain old clapboard and potted geranium reality that Shirley Jackson recognized the strange discontinuousness of things which she elucidated with such unnerving insight. That the familiar can become alien, that the level flow of existence can warp in the batting of an eye, was the theme to which she most often returned. She liked characters whose minds seemed to be untidy and a touch hysterical, but whose fanatic grasp of reality is in some inexplicable way deeper than we can understand. The motivations she preferred to study were never those of reason nor yet of circumstances nor of passion—but of some dark quality in a psychological weather when the glass is falling and the wind beginning to wrinkle.

Like all splendidly accomplished artists, especially those highly sensitive to human suffering, she began to move her choice theme toward the comic, finding in her peculiar subjects, as with Mozart and Mann, a gaiety born of sharpness of understanding. Thus her last novel, only 25 pages of which she lived to write, is still about the nonconsecutive universe but is written with abandoned and frivolous hilarity. It is about a widow who suddenly moves to another town, changes her name while mounting a pair of steps, and proceeds to reactivate the extrasensory knack she had as a child and which marriage had shifted. Shirley Jackson's comic sense had always been a rare one; in this unfinished novel she was clearly going to let it have its day.

Stanley Edgar Hyman, the historian of ideas and Shirley Jackson's husband, has gathered sixteen stories [in ***Come Along with Me***], five of them unpublished, and three "lectures" (a word too dull for these lively talks), one of which is an appalling record of the public's response to her famous story, **"The Lottery."**

Of the unpublished stories, the surprise is in **"The Rock,"** a tale so emblematic that the setting (as settings tend to do in Shirley Jackson) carries the meaning, and the characters wander around like ghosts. Mr. Hyman wisely demonstrates the range of Shirley Jackson's imagination in his choice of stories. There are domestic comedies on the one hand and pure fantasies on the other. There are clinical penetrations into madness and senility, and allegories of fairly portentous philosophical weight. Yet everything this author wrote, no matter how innocent the surface, had in it the dignity and plausibility of myth.

Everyone has felt the anthropological echo in **"The Lottery,"** and if we look carefully at her characters and plots we can see how subtly they suggest rites and mysteries. Writing itself was a kind of ritual for her, a defining of pressures and tensions which cannot be named but which can be dispelled if approached closely enough. In this concept of the writer as a sorcerer dealing in pervasive fears she resembles two other brilliant writers, Eudora Welty and Flannery O'Connor, with whom she shared the ability to construct narratives of strictest contemporary reality that nevertheless prove to be transparent of surface, allow-

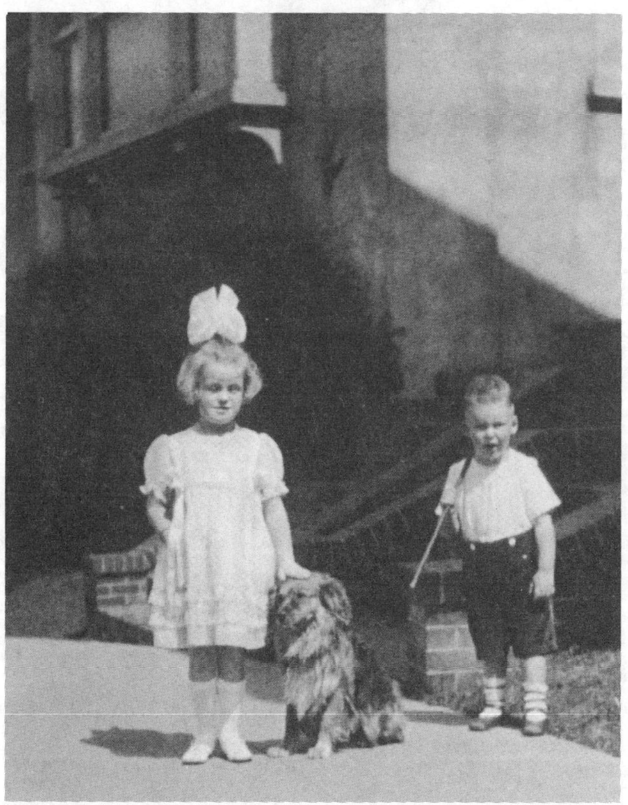

Jackson at age three, with her younger brother Barry, outside their family's San Francisco apartment.

ing motifs and fables as ancient as our civilization itself to show through.

This last novel, for instance, was clearly to have been about the escape of a captured spirit into a different life that would turn out, as so often before in Shirley Jackson's tales, to be a deeper loneliness but one more tolerable because it is at least in one's own terms and by one's own choice. Only things haunted by our own touch are worth having; our hell is to live with things haunted by another's hands. Shirley Jackson knew better than any writer since Hawthorne the value of haunted things.

Guy Davenport, "Dark Psychological Weather," in The New York Times Book Review, *September 15, 1968, p. 4.*

Robert L. Kelly (essay date 1971)

[Kelly is an American educator and critic. In the excerpt below, he offers an interpretation of "The Witch," focusing on Jackson's blending of what he considers ordinary and supernatural elements.]

Shirley Jackson's **"The Witch"** . . . is a masterful examination of the bizarre secrets man skillfully covers with an epidermis of innocence. This story is a devilish puzzle which defies rigid interpretation but openly invites complacent students to sift, sort, and contest tidbits of evidence.

In **"The Witch"** the initial calmness encircling the family on the coach is deceptive. As the lad's steady gaze devours the countryside, his mind trips lightly over pictures of bridges, rivers, and cows. The witch-sighting arouses a casual concern in Johnny and the report to his mother is basically a whimsical oration in self-reflection. However, with stage precision a man now enters the coach. By substituting *elderly* for the thrice-repeated *old* the boy had previously used, Jackson briefly suspends the horror of connection.

The man's cigar and the boy's lollipop form an immediate subtle link of evil. When Johnny says, "My father smokes cigars," here is a double dip of diabolism. A cigar is a sophisticated substitute for a lollipop. Johnny's statement here, followed by the visitor's "All men smoke cigars," raises the possibility that this man also has a paternal claim. The elderly man constantly ignores the mother and her daughter and spotlights a steady beam on Johnny. When he asks Johnny, "Do you love your sister?" the boy appears a hypnotic prisoner and can only stare. Disassociated from the scene, the mother smiles and returns "peacefully to her book."

When the man begins his macabre story, so strong is the communicative interchange between the man and the boy that the mother is "helpless" to interrupt. After the man narrates the gory massacre of his sister, he then nudges Johnny, who snaps back to reality with an indifferent "This man cut up his little sister" addressed to his mother. Yet a transference of corruption encompasses Johnny's next statement: "The conductor will eat my mommy. We'll chop her head off." The storyteller explodes the startling sequel, "And little sister's head too." The absurdity of the final touch by Johnny, "My mommy will eat you," is greeted by raucous laughs while the mother remains gripped in a tedious taciturnity.

Seconds after the intruder's exit, the mother's stress of the word *teasing* only emphasizes her fear. Now Johnny casually returns to the "dullness" of the window. The story ends with his lollipop-licking reply, "Prob'ly he was a witch."

I quickly agree with the doubters that a sure interpretation of this tale is impossible. However, an artistic blend of the commonplace, the supernatural, the symbolic, and the grotesque indubitably supports a theme of evil intent. The initial coach setting is the epitome of monotony and the final scene is the superficial equal of that same boredom. One remembers Young Goodman Brown's return from the devil's campfire. The village was unchanged; yet Brown's mind tremored with shadowy fears, he "scowled and muttered to himself," and "his dying hour was gloom." Although Jackson's Johnny has also changed, his pliant young mind cannot identify this alteration. Johnny is also similar to a miniature Manchurian candidate; he is the victim of a sinister idea transplant. While the final sentence in **"The Lottery"** ripples with repulsion, the last sentence in **"The Witch"** is the armor of innocence which now mockingly covers an evil power cell.

Jackson's use of the supernatural intrigues and baffles. Did Johnny actually see an evil face in the window, and whose face was it? First, let us assume that an awkward reflection of light skittered the glass with a grotesque image of Johnny's mother. She was sitting directly across the aisle. After sighting the witch, the lad's use of *she* proves the femininity of this vision. Also, the boy's routine greeting of "Hi" to the man is further proof that this man did not resemble the witch. Yet the boy's final statement in the story illustrates his knowledge that the man might be a witch after all.

The lollipop has monumental significance. Directly after Johnny receives the lollipop from his mother, he sees the witch. The visitor's exaggeration of the quantity of lollipops he bought his sister magnifies the role of sweet-toothed seduction. And the story ends as it begins—the mother gives Johnny a lollipop. While this solitary lollipop symbolizes a petite bribe, the million constitute a suffocating cloak of spiderwebbing control, and ultimately the complete control one scheming, selfish mind can accomplish over a victim.

The murder is bizarre but also symbolic in its demonstration of the horrid brutality that relates to mental dominance. Here is Satan's branding iron sizzling into Johnny's soul. The girl is strangled, dismembered, bludgeoned, and eaten, an unforgettable sequence for its absurdity and gore.

Despite the mother's sincere scorn of this man, unknowingly she remains his partner in evil. Her urgent plea to Johnny that the man was just teasing lacks penetration. Let us examine the last two paragraphs.

> "He was just teasing," the mother said, and added urgently, "just *teasing.*"
>
> "Prob'ly," the little boy said. With his lollipop he went back to his own seat and settled down to look out the window again. "Prob'ly he was a witch."

The first *prob'ly* does not refer to teasing, but is the fragmented thought which Johnny completes in the last sentence. While Johnny's earlier reference, "There was a big old ugly old bad old witch outside" showed emotion and imagination, this final remark shows calmness and reflection. Now Johnny *knows* that witches neither possess broomsticks nor endure suffocating solitude in fairy tale collections. Unfortunately, however, the lad doesn't recognize the evil influences which now surround him; namely, the visitor's mind tampering and his mother's weak-kneed inability to guide him around Sin's yawning door.

Like the pathetic aunt in Saki's "The Storyteller," Johnny's mother in **"The Witch"** lacks imagination. In each of these stories the male "visitor" bristles with a sinister personality and then makes an abrupt exit. The two intruders win the ultimate victory, a mental corruption; however, the degree of severity varies. Despite several interruptions of bitterness, a humorous tone still radiates through "The Storyteller"; however, humor in **"The Witch"** is nonexistent.

Ironically, the mother is the witch whose reflection Johnny sees in the window; but she is an unknowing carrier of evil. Although the visitor's story barely covers a few minutes, the action is representative of this family scene. By constantly pampering her baby daughter, the mother detaches herself from Johnny's questioning mind. Her remarks to the boy are trite and always lack substance and conviction. But most important, she has already begun to turn Johnny against his sister. The man's departure is the crucial time for the mother to comfort her son.

> She stood looking at the little boy wanting to say something, and finally she said, "You sit still and be a good boy. You may have another lollipop."

So, as the story closes, Johnny's mind begins to roam evil pathways. While the mother bounces around giving the baby feverish attention, the grotesque witch face again jumps across the window, but the lad's mind is now so aflame with imagination that he probably isn't seeing anything. (pp. 1204-06)

Robert L. Kelly, "Jackson's 'The Witch': A Satanic Gem," in English Journal, *Vol. 60, No. 9, December, 1971, pp. 1204-08.*

John G. Parks (essay date 1978)

[In the following essay, Parks asserts that "The Possibility of Evil" is characteristic of many of Jackson's short stories in terms of subject matter, theme, form, and style.]

"The Possibility of Evil," one of Shirley Jackson's superb stories, provides a key to much of her fiction. It contains many of the elements basic to her work, including a sensitive but narrow female protagonist, a gothic house, economy of language, intimations of something "other" or "more," a free-floating sense of depravity, experiences of dissociation, and a final turn about in events or a judgment.

At seventy-one, Miss Adela Strangeworth, the protagonist of **"The Possibility of Evil,"** lives alone in the house on Pleasant Street built two generations earlier by her family. She is proud of her house—"with its slimness and its washed white look"—and especially proud and protective of the beautiful roses that lined the front of the house. She knows everyone in town, and she loves her town so much that she has never spent more than a day away from it her entire life. In fact, "she sometimes found herself thinking that the town belonged to her." As she goes about her life she wonders about the behavior of her fellow townsmen, and sometimes comments, if not to them, then to herself.

For a year now Miss Strangeworth has been sending little notes to various townspeople, using common colored writing paper and writing with a dull stub pencil in a childish block print. She did not sign her name. "She was fond of doing things exactly right." The notes were cruel, gossipy, and vicious, based on half-truths or on none at all. "Miss Strangeworth never concerned herself with facts, her letters dealt with the more negotiable stuff of suspicion." She was always after the "possible evil lurking nearby," because "as long as evil existed unchecked in the world, it was Miss Strangeworth's duty to keep her town alert to it. . . . There were so many wicked people in the world and only one Strangeworth left in the town. Besides, Miss

Jackson at work in her study, which some friends believed contained over 100,000 books.

Strangeworth liked writing her letters." This is her secret contribution to keeping her town sweet and clean, her private war with the forces of evil. After her nap and dinner she takes her evening walk in order to mail the notes she had written that day. She thinks: "There was so much evil in people. Even in a charming little town like this one, there was still so much evil in people." Preoccupied, she did not notice when one of her letters fell onto the ground. But two teenagers saw it and picked it up; since Miss Strangeworth did not hear them when they called her, they decided to deliver the letter to the address; they thought: "Maybe it's good news for them." Miss Strangeworth awakes the next morning happy that three more people will receive her notes: "Harsh, perhaps, at first, but wickedness was never easily banished, and a clean heart was a scoured heart." But when she opens her own mail that morning she finds a little letter very much like the ones she sends. "She began to cry silently for the wickedness of the world when she read the words: Look Out at What Used to Be Your Roses."

Like many Jackson stories this one has a parable-like quality about it—we do not know where or when the story takes place; we are given just enough information to see the universality of the human problem involved. Even with the undercurrent of comic irony the story is reminiscent of many of Hawthorne's tales, his characters haunted by the idea of a knowledge beyond knowledge and so utterly committed to achieving it that they become perverted in the process, such as Goodman Brown and Ethan Brand. Here, Shirley Jackson summons up one more fierce Puritan who personally takes on the forces of evil, and who thus demonstrates, in William Van O'Connor's phrase, "the evil lurking in the righteous mind." Miss Strangeworth is not aware that her own humanity is corroded by making the struggle against evil her sole reason for living. She is corrupted by her own narcissism. As Lionel Rubinoff observes: ". . . by pretending to be angels we shall surely become devils. . . . [Because] the possibility of real virtue exists only for a man who has the freedom to choose evil." This freedom Miss Strangeworth cannot and will not give, because she herself holds an evil belief: "a belief that one *cannot do wrong,*" to use D. H. Lawrence's remarks about one of Hawthorne's characters. Lawrence concludes: "No men are so evil to-day as the idealists, and no women half so evil as your earnest woman, who feels herself a power for good." Paradoxically, Miss Strangeworth is doing evil in order to further good. Miss Strangeworth reveals the unscrupulosity of the devout, and the only people more unscrupulous than the devout are the frightened, and they are often the same people.

Shirley Jackson reveals a fundamental problem here, one especially crucial in American culture: the revelation of the imagination that sees evil only *out there,* and which thus must be smashed at any cost. Miss Strangeworth does not see that evil is a component within us all that can be transcended only through its recognition and acceptance. Heinrich Zimmer, writing of the meaning of an ancient tale, says:

> The function of evil is to keep in operation the dynamics of change. Cooperating with the beneficient forces, though antogonistically, those of evil thus assist in the weaving of the tapestry of life; hence the experience of evil, and to some extent this experience alone, produces maturity, real life, real command of the powers and tasks of life. The forbidden fruit—the fruit of guilt through experience, knowledge through experience—had to be swallowed in the Garden of Innocence before human history could begin. Evil had to be accepted and assimilated, not avoided.

Accordingly, Lionel Rubinoff observes: "It is the excessive rationalistic and abstract apocalyptic imagination that defines evil as an object of scorn, or as an incurable disease. The apocalyptic imagination is sober, passive, and detached. It seeks to reduce mystery to rational order. It sits in judgment, protected by certainty, and condemns." This is Miss Strangeworth before she opens her own letter of judgment which may have torn the veil of innocence from her imagination and open her to a reconsideration of "the possibility of evil."

Though she is northern and urban Shirley Jackson is here reminiscent of Flannery O'Connor, who frequently brought a "moment of truth" to her characters, though it usually arrived too late, as in her story "Greenleaf." Writing about her own work Flannery O'Connor said: "St. Cyril of Jerusalem . . . wrote: 'The dragon sits by the side of the road, watching those who pass. Beware lest he devour you. We go to the Father of Souls, but it is necessary to pass by the dragon.' No matter what form the dragon may take, it is of this mysterious passage past him, or into his jaws, that stories of any depth will always be concerned to tell." This aptly describes what Shirley Jackson is doing in her fiction. She brings many of her characters by or into the dragon, or, to change the image, she brings them to the edge of the abyss: some fall, some cling desperately to the edge, and only a few find their way to safety, but such are evil's possibilities. (pp. 320-23)

John G. Parks, "The Possibility of Evil: A Key to Shirley Jackson's Fiction," in Studies in Short Fiction, *Vol. 15, No. 3, Summer, 1978, pp. 320-23.*

Richard Pascal (essay date 1982)

[In the following excerpt, Pascal examines the theme of escape in "The Tooth," while suggesting the relevance of this theme to other concerns in Jackson's short fiction.]

To attentive readers of Shirley Jackson's work, it came as no surprise to discover that the novel she was working on at the time of her death was to be about a middle-class woman who has abandoned her lifelong home town and former identity. "I erased my old name and took my initials off everything, and I got on the train and left," says the heroine of *Come Along With Me,* articulating the desire felt by many other Jackson protagonists to liberate themselves from communal and domestic obligations and referents. For the best-selling authoress of *Life Among the Savages* and *Raising Demons,* those sprightly autobiographical chronicles which reassuringly make light of the anxieties of bourgeois domestic life, the fantasy of running away from it all was a constant fictional preoccupation. In her stories and novels she explores with remarkable skill and insight the impulse to escape from the familial universe which her non-fiction implicity celebrates. In this as in many other respects, the best of her fiction is deserving of wider critical interest than it has hitherto received. My objective in this discussion is to examine the escape theme in one of the most fascinating stories, **"The Tooth,"** and to offer by way of introduction some suggestions about Jackson's treatment of it elsewhere and its relevance to other concerns apparent throughout her work.

Prominent among the latter is the conception of the small communal group which is bound together less by love and respect than by fear, guilt, and dumb tradition. In story after story the small town or neighborhood is depicted as a nexus of sanctioned intrigue against whatever is individual, different, or alien, and in which the ties that bind may also strangle. In **"The Lottery,"** even the individualism of valuing one's own life is ritualistically and horrifyingly exorcised by the community. In **"The Summer People,"** two vacationers from the city who stay on in a small resort community past the traditional Labor Day leavetaking discover that that tradition is to the townsfolk a taboo, the breaking of which entails forfeiture of normal services and amenities and leads, ultimately, to dark hostility. Sometimes the communal group is simply the family, oppressively nuclear. Elsa Dayton in **"A Day in the Jungle"** leaves her home and husband because they represent a life of stifling quotidian regularity; marriage has been for her a succession of "hideous unprivate months." Catharine Vincent in **"I Know Who I Love,"** leaving home as a young woman, ceases immediately to think about her nagging parents, and does so only "dutifully" after they have died. The sense of duty, inspired not by love or deep moral awareness, but by anxiety and insecurity, is to the family in Jackson's fiction what custom is to the small community: a bonding mechanism whose primary function is to ensure cohesiveness.

Opposed to the regulated world of the small group is the realm of freedom and self-centeredness represented, usually, by the city. To those in recoil from the confines of the small group, the city stands as a glistening dream of freedom in which communally inculcated patters of self-abnegating behavior do not hold. Thus Elsa, during her day in the "jungle" of the downtown area to which she has fled from her suburban home, is "very much aware of the fact that for the first time she moved knowingly and of choice through a free world." Such freedom, not merely to do what one likes, but to create a life and a self of one's own, is the promise which the city seems to hold. Yet the inverse of the freedom to create a new self is the destruction of the old, which the city also seems to portend. In **"Pillar of Salt,"** the impression of things crumbling is continually with Margaret during her visit to New York, and she suspects that the disintegrating buildings, streets, and vehicles are symptomatic of the city's effect on people: it is the place where they "come apart." At the end of the story she is utterly panicked by the swarming anonymity of the crowds on the streets outside, and at not being noticed familiarly. Similarly, Elsa Dayton's fears of accidental injury during her day downtown really amount to an insecurity about her ability to hold the jungle of an unfamiliar world at bay. Without the constant external verification of identity which the small community provides, the self may seem to lose its reality and the world may crumble crazily.

These, then, are the two realms between which many of Shirley Jackson's heroines gravitate. In the family or town or neighborhood the ties may chafe, but they do hold you together; in the city there are no ties, and *you* must hold you together—assuming there is a "you" which can exist independently, out of familiar context. Some of the most interesting moments in Jackson's fiction are those in which the flight from familiarity to the realm of strangeness and freedom causes a character's sense of identity to weaken or even vanish. Such experiences of fundamental tremors in the self 's sense of who it is aren't easily explicable as schizoid disturbances or breakdowns, a line of analysis which assumes a pre-existent central self to feel disturbed or break down. What seems to fascinate Shirley Jackson most is the possibility that behind the self which we ordinarily assume to be irrevocably engrained, if not preordained, there is nothing immutably necessary which we can call our own: it is, for her, an idea which is both frightening *and* alluring.

In **"The Tooth,"** Clara Spencer, a middle-class housewife, boards an evening bus for New York from the small town which is her home. The reason for the overnight journey is that she must see a dentist about a severe flareup of a toothache which she has suffered from intermittently for years. Just prior to her departure, she complains to her husband of feeling " 'so *funny*,' " and he expresses concern that there might be something seriously wrong with her. To this she responds uneasily, " 'It's just a *toothache* . . . nothing very serious about a *toothache*,' " and the reason for her unease is hinted at a moment later when, after shivering at the suggestion that the tooth might have to be pulled, she says, " 'I just feel as if I were all tooth. Nothing else.' " On the bus she feels "closed in alone with the toothache," and later, in the dentist's office, her tooth seems to her to be "the only part of her to have any identity." When told by the dentist that she must go to an extractionist, the questions she wants to ask him (though she refrains) are "What about me? or, How far down do the roots go?" He replies to her spoken question, " 'What will they do?' " but also, in a sense, to the imagined ones, by saying " 'They'll take that tooth out . . . Should have been done years ago.' "

In retrospect, then, her husband's earlier assertion that she has been having that same toothache off and on for as long as he has known her indicates clearly that the tooth represents the deeply rooted lifetime-old self inculcated by the domestically oriented small community, and further implies that she was never happy being that self. From their parting conversation at the bus station, we are given an impression of the life-style which the community instills. The talk is all of plans and duties, not of love or personal wishes and the nearest her husband comes to a declaration of affection is this:

> 'You know, Clara,' he made his voice very weighty, as though if he spoke more seriously his words would carry more conviction and be therefore more comforting, 'you know, I'm glad you're going down to New York to have Zimmerman take care of this. I'd never forgive myself if it turned out to be something serious and I let you go to this butcher up here.'

Their relationship is a sombrely moral connection in which the important gratification is not erotic or emotional, just the satisfaction derived from knowing that one's weighty obligations have been discharged with impeccable conscientiousness. Once launched on her journey Clara never thinks of her husband or children, and what she and he are really concerned about in their farewell conversation is mutual reinforcement of faith in the mores of the family and the small community.

For Clara, the reinforcement is insufficient. Shortly after boarding the bus she is chatting with the bus driver without fully understanding why, "except that it was late at night and people isolated together in some strange bus had to be more friendly and communicative than at other times." Faced with a universe of motion and darkness and armed only with the isolated self, Clara feels the Jackson "city experience" immediately upon departure from home. The world of structured familial and communal relationships seems very fragile to her as, sitting toward the back of the bus, she senses that "only the thin thread of lights along the ceiling of the bus held them together, brought the back of the bus where she sat along with the front of the bus where the driver sat."

But sitting next to her then is "Jim," a stranger who, she is foggily aware, assists her in the roadside restaurants where the bus stops periodically, and who offers her his shoulder upon which to rest her head while she dozes. She is also dimly conscious of strange things he is telling her, about a beautiful island "farther than Samarkand." Jim is clearly fantastic, a creation of Clara's overstrained mind. This is implied throughout the story: in a restaurant, for example, she asks him " 'What do you want?' " and he points to a cup of coffee and a sandwich *she* then consumes; without having been told, he knows that she is going to see a dentist; when he leaves her in New York she does not see him go, even though she is watching very carefully; and at the end of the story, thinking she is running hand in hand with him "barefoot through hot sand," she doesn't notice the tellingly "curious glances" of pedestrians passing by on the city sidewalk. A substitute for and alternative to not just her husband, but the entire domestic society which she has left behind, he provides guidance just when she feels most disorientingly apart from other people. As a creature of her imagination he is really an aspect of herself, of course, and for her to follow his directions and hearken to his seductive verbal travelog is to tell herself what to do and what to want. But so used is she to thinking of the "Clara" identity as her very self that she cannot consciously assume proprietorship of her egocentric impulses, and so she must objectify them and render them somewhat distant in a dream figure.

In essence, it is the realm of passive, ego-centripetal wish-fulfillment, the world of pleasant dreams, that Clara seems to yearn for. The combined effects of codeine, whiskey, a sleeping pill, and lack of food have propelled her into a state of dreamlike altered consciousness, making her feel comfortable about "being carried along without effort of her own." In the course of her drugged journey of enchantment, she doesn't quite have the *ultimate* dream, but, as it were, dreams of having it. The land "farther than Samarkand" described by "Jim" represents that ultimate dream, and its appeal is that it inverts the basic values and features of the tightly strictured communal group. This is apparent from the very nature of the place, which seems to be a tropic isle with an ambiance of lazy, unfocussed eroticism, in sharp contrast to the world of sterile matrimonial devotion which Clara has just left. More deeply, though, it is its asocial quality which is most alluring about the faraway land. There, there are voices and songs but, it would seem, no other people—or, at least, none who impress themselves upon one's attention. Similarly, life there is characterized by guiltless, recumbent passivity: " 'Nothing to do all day but lie under the trees.' " When there is nothing to do, consequences are impossible, and so too are responsibility and decisiveness.

Ironically, however, when the enchantment is at its deepest and she is most passive, a new power of determination is liberated within her. Her state of dreamlike consciousness reaches its peak during the extraction as a result of the anaesthetic she has been given:

> First of all things get so far away, she thought, remember this. And remember the metallic sound and taste of all of it. And the outrage.
>
> And then the whirling music, the ringing confusedly loud music that went on and on, around and around, and she was running as fast as she could down a long horribly clear hallway with doors on both sides and at the end of the hallway was Jim, holding out his hands and laughing, and calling something she could never hear because of the loud music, and she was running and then she said, 'I'm not afraid,' and someone from the door next to her took her arm and pulled her through and the world widened alarmingly until it would never stop and then it stopped with the head of the dentist looking down at her and the window dropped into place in front of her and the nurse holding her arm.
>
> 'Why did you pull me back?' she asked, and her mouth was full of blood. 'I wanted to go on.'

Clara's commands to herself to remember her sensations during the initial phase of the operation and her subsequent cry of "I'm not afraid," reveal that she is finally making an effort to embrace her mental and emotional life at its deepest level and to accept the consequences, hazards, and indignities of that commitment. In the midst of the disorienting whirl of unstructured mental and physical sensations, the figure of Jim reappears to provide guiding direction. It is still a dream at the end of that hallway, of course, as is made clear when she feels herself being pulled back into the world of waking reality which widens beyond the scope of control of her isolated ego. But the bravery and dignity of Clara's avowal that she wanted to go on cannot be attributed dismissively to an inability to face the alarming breadth of reality unaided by the wishful imagination. Jackson's careful rendering of the experience stresses that the difference between inability and unwillingness in this regard is not altogether meaningful or clear, and that Clara is admirably aware on some level of having chosen her own fate. Thus, moments after the operation, this exchange takes place:

> 'God has given me blood to drink,' she said to the nurse, and the nurse said, 'Don't rinse your mouth or it won't clot.'

She is willing to drink the blood in her mouth as an act of expiation, though more in payment than atonement, for the sin of choosing to live for herself. But the nurse misses the deeper implication of her words and seems, sanely proferring formulaic advice, shallow and automaton-like by comparison.

Subsequently, in the crowded Ladies' Room, Clara seems more self-sufficient and can cope almost calmly with the loss of her previous identity. With only a "slight stinging shock" she realizes that she has no idea which of the several faces reflected in the mirror is hers, and that "no one was familiar in the group, no one smiled at her or looked at her with recognition." It is an extreme of the Jackson "city experience" of enswarming anonymity and loss of the identity-sustaining familiar context. Yet Clara's response is merely a "queer numbness in her throat." On discovering which of the faces is hers, her reaction is only sullenness at not having a chance to "take" one of the pretty ones, and she immediately sets about letting her hair down, applying rouge to her pallid cheeks, and drawing "an emphatic rosy mouth" on her lips. The old Clara would never have done those things, not simply because they bespeak sexual self-awareness and narcissism, but even more so because they are done with such emphatic determination to seize control of self and circumstance. She proceeds to stride "purposefully" to the elevator, as the neurotically driven old Clara would never have done, to seek a lover the old Clara would never have admitted to herself that she desired, much less sought. When "Jim" appears out of the crowd to take her hand, she remembers that she has lost her bottle of pain-killing codeine pills and left in the Ladies' Room a slip of paper containing the nurse's instructions for alleviating painful aftereffects of the extraction. But neither is needed, for the real pain she has suffered throughout her life was the result of being forced to maintain her old identity, and its absence seems an anodyne. Jim is a fantasy and she may be insane, but there is nonetheless a "happily ever after" ring to the story's ending: "her hand in Jim's and her hair down on her shoulders, she ran barefoot through hot sand."

It should be noted, in conclusion, that Shirley Jackson intended the figure of "Jim" to be associated with James Harris, the "daemon lover" of Child Ballad 243, who entices a married woman to abandon her family and run away with him on a voyage which, she realizes too late, is destined for hell. Thus some readers might be tempted to regard the story as a sort of Freudian version of the morality tale contained in the old ballad: the sin of feeling solipsistically happy and free, it might seem, is punished by the damnation of madness. Certainly the story's ending, while hardly moralistic, has the thrust of a cautionary warning about the consequences of succumbing to the seductive murmurings of that "daemon lover," one's wishful imagination. Yet even as the warning is imparted, the lure of the fantasy world is powerfully felt, and it is far from clear that the passing pedestrians who walk upon what they know to be the sidewalk are wiser or happier than Clara, running barefoot through imagined sand. Jackson's careful suspension of judgement at the end helps to explain why **"The Tooth"** is an oddly more unsettling story than a straightforward Freudian line of analysis would allow: she refuses to assume unblinkingly the value and desirability of the "reality principle," of remaining aware of things, people, and events as they objectively are (or are generally understood to be). It is, in her fictional universe, the small communal group which champions that principle, discouraging individual gratification in favor of duty and, necessarily therefore, instilling intense awareness of reality as sternly independent of the wishful self. But if self-gratification replaces communal responsibility as the supreme and guiding value for the individual, the world of private fantasy, or of reality as colored by personal desires, may come to seem a superior kind of reality. Rarely concerned with the moral implications of the quest for self-gratification and pure personal freedom, for Shirley Jackson the intriguing considerations tend to be strategic: whether and how the self can make good its escape, and what the rewards and consequences might be. She knows very well that running away with the daemon lover may mean going to hell. But she knows equally well why so many individuals thrill to his talk of a land "farther than Samarkand." (pp. 133-39)

Richard Pascal, " 'Farther than Samarkand': The Escape Theme in Shirley Jackson's 'The Tooth'," in Studies in Short Fiction, *Vol. 19, No. 2, Spring, 1982, pp. 133-39.*

Peter Kosenko (essay date 1985)

[*In the following excerpt, Kosenko analyzes "The Lottery" from a Marxist and feminist perspective.*]

In her critical biography of Shirley Jackson, Lenemaja Friedman notes that when Jackson's story **"The Lottery"** was published in the June 28, 1948 issue of the *New Yorker* it received a response that "no *New Yorker* story had ever received": hundreds of letters poured in that were characterized by "bewilderment, speculation, and old-fashioned abuse." It is not hard to account for this response: Jackson's story portrays an "average" New England village with "average" citizens engaged in a deadly rite, the annual selection of a sacrificial victim by means of a public lottery, and does so quite deviously: not until well along in the story do we suspect that the "winner" will be stoned to death by the rest of the villagers. One can imagine the average reader of Jackson's story protesting: but we engage in no such inhuman practices. Why are you accusing us of *this*?

Admittedly, this response was not exactly the one that Jackson had hoped for. In the July 22, 1948 issue of the *San Francisco Chronicle* she broke down and said the following in response to persistent queries from her readers about her intentions: "Explaining just what I had hoped the story to say is very difficult. I suppose, I hoped, by setting a particularly brutal ancient rite in the present and in my own village to shock the story's readers with a graphic dramatization of the pointless violence and general inhumanity in their own lives." Shock them she did, but probably owing to the symbolic complexity of her tale, they responded defensively and were not enlightened. (p. 27)

A survey of what little has been written about **"The Lottery"** reveals two general critical attitudes: first, that it is about man's ineradicable primitive aggressivity, or what Cleanth Brooks and Robert Penn Warren call his "all-too-human tendency to seize upon a scapegoat"; second, that it describes man's victimization by, in Helen Nebeker's words, "unexamined and unchanging traditions which he could easily change if he only realized their implications." Missing from both of these approaches, however, is a careful analysis of the abundance of social detail that links the lottery to the ordinary social practices of the village. No mere "irrational" tradition, the lottery is an *ideological mechanism.* It serves to reinforce the village's hierarchical social order by instilling the villagers with an unconscious fear that if they resist this order they might be selected in the next lottery. In the process of creating this fear, it also reproduces the ideology necessary for the smooth functioning of that social order, despite its inherent inequities. What is surprising in the work of an author who has never been identified as a Marxist is that this social order and ideology are essentially capitalist.

I think we need to take seriously Shirley Jackson's suggestion that the world of the lottery is her reader's world, however reduced in scale for the sake of economy. The village in which the lottery takes place has a bank, a post office, a grocery store, a coal business, a school system; its women are housewives rather than field workers or writers; and its men talk of "tractors and taxes." More importantly, however, the village exhibits the same socioeconomic stratification that most people take for granted in a modern, capitalist society.

Let me begin by describing the top of the social ladder and save the lower rungs for later. The village's most powerful man, Mr. Summers, owns the village's largest business (a coal concern) and is also its mayor, since he has, Jackson writes, more "time and energy [read money and leisure] to devote to civic activities" than others. (Summers' very name suggests that he has become a man of leisure through his wealth.) Next in line in the social hierarchy is Mr. Graves, the village's second most powerful government official—its postmaster. (His name may suggest the gravity of officialism.) And beneath Mr. Graves is Mr. Martin, who has the economically advantageous position of being the grocer in a village of three hundred.

These three most powerful men who control the town, economically as well as politically, also happen to administer the lottery. Mr. Summers is its official, sworn in yearly by Mr. Graves. Mr. Graves helps Mr. Summers make up the lottery slips. And Mr. Martin steadies the lottery box as the slips are stirred. In the off season, the lottery box is stored either at their places of business or their residences: "It had spent one year in Mr. Graves' barn and another year underfoot in the post-office, and sometimes it was set on a shelf in the Martin grocery and left there." Who controls the town, then, also controls the lottery. It is no coincidence that the lottery takes place in the village square "between the post-office and the bank"—two buildings which represent government and finance, the institutions from which Summers, Graves, and Martin derive their power.

However important Mr. Graves and Mr. Martin may be, Mr. Summers is still the most powerful man in town. Here we have to ask a Marxist question: what relationship is there between his interests as the town's wealthiest businessman and his officiating the lottery? That such a relationship does exist is suggested by one of the most revealing lines of the text. When Bill Hutchinson forces his wife, Tessie, to open her lottery slip to the crowd, Jackson writes, "It had a black spot on it, the black spot Mr. Summers had made the night before with [a] heavy pencil in [his] coal-company office." At the very moment when the lottery's victim is revealed, Jackson appends a subordinate clause in which we see the blackness (evil) of Mr. Summers' (coal) business being transferred to the black dot on the lottery slip. At one level at least, evil in Jackson's text is linked to a disorder, promoted by capitalism, in the material organization of modern society. But it still remains to be explained *how* the evil of the lottery is tied to this disorder of capitalist social organization.

Let me sketch the five major points of my answer to this question. First, the lottery's rules of participation reflect and *codify* a rigid social hierarchy based upon an inequitable social division of labor. Second, the fact that everyone participates in the lottery and understands *consciously* that its outcome is pure chance gives it a certain "democratic" aura that obscures its first codifying function. Third, the villagers believe *unconsciously* that their commitment to a work ethic will grant them some magical immunity from selection. Fourth, this work ethic prevents them from understanding that the lottery's actual function is not to encourage work *per se* but to reinforce an inequitable social *division* of labor. Finally, after working through these points, it will be easier to explain how Jackson's choice of Tessie Hutchinson as the lottery's victim/scapegoat reveals the lottery to be an ideological mechanism which serves to defuse the average villager's deep, inarticulate dissatisfaction with the social order in which he lives by channeling it into anger directed at the *victims* of that social order. It is reenacted year after year, then, not because it is a mere "tradition," as Helen Nebeker argues, but because it serves the repressive ideological function of purging the social body of all resistance so that business (capitalism) can go on as usual and the Summers, the Graves and the Martins can remain in power.

Implicit in the first and second points above is a distinction between universal participation in the lottery and what I have called its *rules* of participation. The first of these rules I have already explained, of course: those who control the village economically and politically also administer the lottery. The remaining rules also tell us much about who has and who doesn't have power in the village's social hierarchy. These remaining rules determine who gets to choose slips in the lottery's first, second and third rounds. Before the lottery, lists are "[made] up of heads of families [who choose in the first round], heads of households [who choose in the second round], [and] members of each household in each family [who choose in the last round]." The second round is missing from the story because the family patriarch who selects the dot in the first round—Bill Hutchinson—has no married male offspring. When her family is chosen in the first round, Tessie Hutchinson objects that her daughter and son-in-law didn't "take their chance." Mr. Summers has to remind her, "Daughters draw with their husbands' families." Power in the village, then, is exclusively consolidated into the hands of male heads of families and households. Women are disenfranchised.

Although patriarchy is not a product of capitalism *per se*, patriarchy in the village does have its capitalist dimension. (New social formations adapt old traditions to their own needs.) Women in the village seem to be disenfranchised because male heads of households, as men in the work force, provide the link between the broader economy of the village and the economy of the household. Some consideration of the other single household families in the first round of the lottery—the Dunbars and the Watsons—will help make this relationship between economics and family power clearer. Mr. Dunbar, unable to attend the lottery because he has a broken leg, has to choose by proxy. The rules of lottery participation take this situation into account: "Grown boy[s]" take precedence as proxies over wives. Mrs. Dunbar's son Horace, however, is only sixteen, still presumably in school and not working; hence Mrs. Dunbar chooses for Mr. Dunbar. Jack Watson, on the other hand, whose father is dead, is clearly older than Horace and presumably already in the work force. Admittedly, such inferences cannot be supported with hard textual evidence, but they make sense when the text is referred to the norms of the society which it addresses. Within these norms, "heads of households" are not simply the oldest males in their immediate families; they are the oldest *working* males and get their power from their insertion into a larger economy. Women, who have no direct link to the economy as defined by capitalism—the arena of activity in which labor is exchanged for wages and profits are made—choose in the lottery only in the absence of a "grown," working male.

Women, then, have a distinctly subordinate position in the socio-economic hierarchy of the village. They make their first appearance "wearing faded house dresses . . . [and walking] shortly after their menfolk." Their dresses indicate that they do in fact work, but because they work in the home and not within a larger economy in which work is regulated by finance (money), they are treated by men and treat themselves as inferior. When Tessie Hutchinson appears late to the lottery, other men address her husband Bill, "Here comes your Missus, Hutchinson." None of the men, that is to say, thinks of addressing Tessie first, since she "belongs" to Bill. Most women in the village take this patriarchal definition of their role for granted, as Mrs. Dunbar's and Mrs. Delacroix's references to their husbands as their "old [men]" suggest. Tessie, as we shall see later, is the only one who rebels against male domination, although only unconsciously.

Having sketched some of the power relations within the families of the village, I can now shift my attention to the ways in which what I have called the democratic illusion of the lottery diverts their attention from the capitalist economic relations in which these relations of power are grounded. On its surface, the idea of a lottery in which everyone, as Mrs. Graves says, "[takes] the same chance" seems eminently democratic, even if its effect, the singling out of one person for privilege or attack, is not.

One critic, noting an ambiguity at the story's beginning, has remarked that "the lottery . . . suggests 'election' rather than selection," since "the [villagers] assemble in the center of the place, in the village square." I would like to push the analogy further. In capitalist dominated elections, business supports and promotes candidates who will be more or less atuned to its interests, multiplying its vote through campaign financing, while each individual businessman can continue to claim that he has but one vote. In the lottery, analogously, the village ruling class participates in order to convince others (and perhaps even themselves) that they are not in fact *above* everyone else during

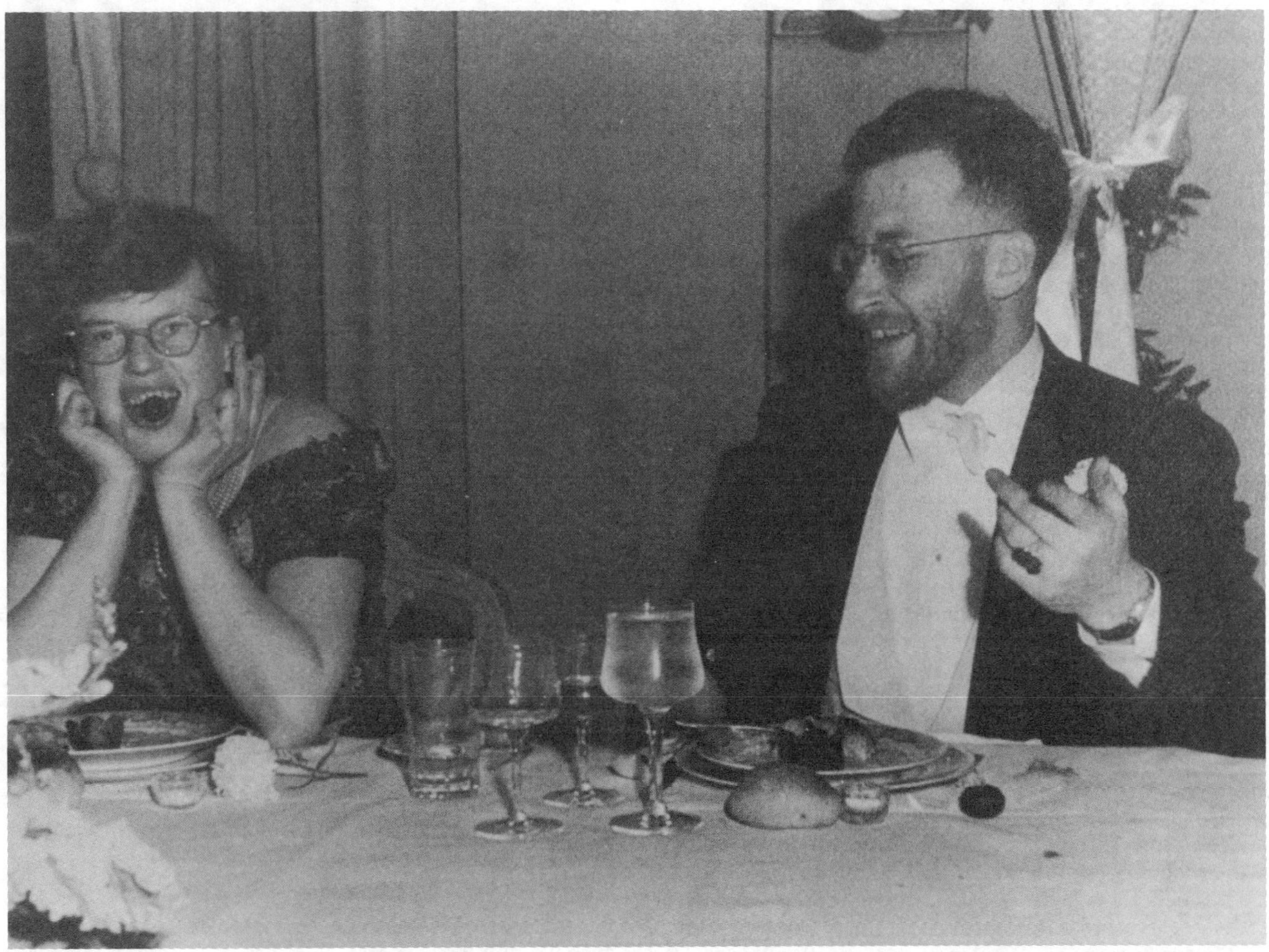

Jackson and her husband Stanley Edgar Hyman at his brother's wedding reception in 1946.

the remainder of the year, even though their exclusive control of the lottery suggests that they are. Yet just as the lottery's black (ballot?) box has grown shabby and reveals in places its "original wood color," moments in their official "democratic" conduct of the lottery—especially Mr. Summers' conduct as their representative—reveal the class interest that lies behind it. If Summers wears jeans, in order to convince the villagers that he is just another one of the common people, he also wears a "clean white shirt," a garment more appropriate to *his* class. If he leans casually on the black box before the lottery selection begins, as a President, say, might put his feet up on the White House desk, while leaning he "talk[s] interminably to Mr. Graves and the Martins," the other members of his class, and "seem[s] very proper and important." (Jackson has placed these last details in emphatic position at the end of a paragraph.) Finally, however democratic his early appeal for help in conducting the lottery might appear—"some of you fellows want to give me a hand?" Mr. Martin, who responds, is the third most powerful man in the village. Summers' question is essentially empty and formal, since the villagers seem to understand, probably unconsciously, the unspoken law of class that governs who administers the lottery; it is not just *anyone* who can help Summers.

The lottery's democratic illusion, then, is an ideological effect that prevents the villagers from criticizing the class structure of their society. But this illusion alone does not account for the full force of the lottery over the village. The lottery also reinforces a village work ethic which distracts the villagers' attention from the division of labor that keeps women powerless in their homes and Mr. Summers powerful in his coal company office.

In the story's middle, Old Man Warner emerges as an apologist for this work ethic when he recalls an old village adage, "Lottery in June, corn be heavy soon." At one level, the lottery seems to be a modern version of a planting ritual that might once have prepared the villagers for the collective work necessary to produce a harvest. (Such rituals do not necessarily involve human sacrifice.) As magical as Warner's proverb may seem, it establishes an unconscious (unspoken) connection between the lottery and work that is revealed by the entirety of his response when told that other villages are considering doing away with the lottery:

> "Pack of crazy fools . . . listening to the young

> folks, nothing's good enough for *them.* Next thing you know, they'll be wanting to go back to living in caves, nobody work any more, live *that* way for a while. Used to be a saying about 'Lottery in June, corn be heavy soon.' First thing you know, we'd all be eating stewed chickweed and acorns. There's *always* been a lottery."

But Warner does not explain *how* the lottery functions to motivate work. In order to do so, it would have to inspire the villagers with a magical fear that their lack of productivity would make them vulnerable to selection in the next lottery. The village women reveal such an unconscious fear in their ejaculatory questions after the last slip has been drawn in the first round: "Who is it?" "Who's got it?" "Is it the Dunbars?" "Is it the Watsons?" The Dunbars and the Watsons, it so happens, are the least "productive" families in the village: Mr. Dunbar has broken his leg, Mr. Watson is dead. Given this unconscious village fear that lack of productivity determines the lottery's victim, we might guess that Old Man Warner's pride that he is participating in the lottery for the "seventy-seventh time" stems from a magical belief—seventy-seven is a magical number—that his commitment to work and the village work ethic accounts for his survival. Wherever we find "magic," we are in the realm of the unconscious: the realm in which the unspoken of ideology resides.

Old Man Warner's commitment to a work ethic, however appropriate it might be in an egalitarian community trying collectively to carve an economy out of a wilderness, is not entirely innocent in the modern village, since it encourages villagers to work without pointing out to them that part of their labor goes to the support of the leisure and power of a business class. Warner, that is to say, is Summers' ideologist. At the end of his remarks about the lottery, Warner laments Summers' democratic conduct: "Bad enough to see young Joe Summers up there joking with everybody." Yet this criticism obscures the fact that Summers is not about to undermine the lottery, even if he does "modernize" it, since by running the lottery he also encourages a work ethic which serves his interest. Just before the first round drawing, Summers remarks casually, "Well, now . . . guess we better get started, get this over with, so's we can go back to work." The "we" in his remark is deceptive; what he means to say is "so that you can go back to work for me."

The final major point of my reading has to do with Jackson's selection of Tessie Hutchinson as the lottery's victim/scapegoat. She could have chosen Mr. Dunbar, of course, in order to show us the unconscious connection that the villagers draw between the lottery and their work ethic. But to do so would not have revealed that the lottery actually reinforces a *division* of labor. Tessie, after all, is a woman whose role as a housewife deprives her radically of her freedom by forcing her to submit to a husband who gains his power over her by virtue of his place in the work force. Tessie, however, rebels against her role, and such rebellion is just what the orderly functioning of her society cannot stand. Unfortunately, her rebellion is entirely unconscious.

Tessie's rebellion begins with her late arrival at the lottery, a *faux pas* that reveals her unconscious resistance to everything the lottery stands for. She explains to Mr. Summers that she was doing her dishes and forgot what day it was. The way in which she says this, however, involves her in another *faux pas:* the suggestion that she might have violated the village's work ethic and neglected her specific job within the village's social division of labor: "Wouldn't have me leave m'dishes in the sink, now, would you Joe?" The "soft laughter [that runs] through the crowd" after this remark is a nervous laughter that indicates, even more than the village women's singling out of the Dunbars and the Watsons, the extent of the village's unconscious commitment to its work ethic and power structure. When Mr. Summers calls her family's name, Tessie goads her husband, "Get up there, Bill." In doing so, she inverts the power relation that holds in the village between husbands and wives. Again, her remark evokes nervous laughter from the crowd, which senses the taboo that she has violated. Her final *faux pas* is to question the rules of the lottery which relegate women to inferior status as the property of their husbands. When Mr. Summers asks Bill Hutchinson whether his family has any other households, Tessie yells, "There's Don and Eva. . . . Make them take their chance." Tessie's daughter Eva, however, *belongs* to Don and is consequently barred from participating with her parents' family.

All of these *faux pas* set Tessie up as the lottery's likeliest victim, even if they do not explicitly challenge the lottery. That Tessie's rebellion is entirely unconscious is revealed by her cry while being stoned, "It isn't fair." Tessie does not object to the lottery *per se,* only to her own selection as its scapegoat. It would have been fine with her if someone else had been selected.

In stoning Tessie, the villagers treat her as a scapegoat onto which they can project and through which they can "purge"—actually, the term *repress* is better, since the impulse is conserved rather than eliminated—their own temptations to rebel. The only places we can see these rebellious impulses are in Tessie, in Mr. and Mrs. Adams' suggestion, squelched by Warner, that the lottery might be given up, and in the laughter of the crowd. (The crowd's nervous laughter is ambivalent: it expresses uncertainty about the validity of the taboos that Tessie breaks.) But ultimately these rebellious impulses are channeled by the lottery and its attendant ideology away from their proper objects—capitalism and capitalist patriarchs—into anger at the rebellious victims of capitalist social organization. Like Tessie, the villagers cannot articulate their rebellion because the massive force of ideology stands in the way.

The lottery functions, then, to terrorize the village into accepting, in the *name* of work and democracy, the inequitable social division of labor and power on which its social order depends. When Tessie is selected, and before she is stoned, Mr. Summers asks her husband to "show [people] her paper." By holding up the slip, Bill Hutchinson reasserts his dominance over his wayward wife and simultaneously transforms her into a symbol to others of the perils of disobedience.

Here I would like to point out a curious crux in Jackson's treatment of the theme of scapegoating in **"The Lottery"**;

the conflict between the lottery's literal arbitrariness and the utter appropriateness of its victim. Admittedly, Tessie is a curious kind of scapegoat, since the village does not literally choose her, single her out. An act of scapegoating that is *unmotivated* is difficult to conceive. This crux disappears, however, once we realize that the lottery is a metaphor for the unconscious ideological mechanisms of scapegoating. In choosing Tessie through the lottery, Jackson has attempted to show us whom the village might have chosen if the lottery had been in fact an election. But by presenting this election as an arbitrary lottery, she gives us an image of the village's blindness to its own motives.

Possibly the most depressing thing about **"The Lottery"** is how early Jackson represents this blindness as beginning. Even the village children have been socialized into the ideology that victimizes Tessie. When they are introduced in the second paragraph of the story, they are anxious that summer has let them out of school: "The feeling of liberty sat uneasily on most of them." Like their parents, they have learned that leisure and play are suspect. As if to quell this anxiety, the village boys engage in the play/labor of collecting stones for the lottery. Moreover, they follow the lead of Bobby Martin, the one boy in the story whose father is a member of the village ruling class (Mr. Summers and Mr. Graves have no boys), in hoarding and fighting over these stones as if they were money. While the boys do this, the village girls stand off to the side and watch, just as they will be expected to remain outside of the work force and dependent on their working husbands when they grow up.

As dismal as this picture seems, the one thing we ought not do is make it into proof of the innate depravity of man. The first line of the second paragraph—"The children assembled first, of course"—does not imply that children take a "natural" and primitive joy in stoning people to death. The closer we look at their behavior, the more we realize that they learned it from their parents, whom they imitate in their play. In order to facilitate her reader's grasp of this point, Jackson has included at least one genuinely innocent child in the story—Davy Hutchinson. When he has to choose his lottery ticket, the adults help him while he looks at them "wonderingly." And when Tessie is finally to be stoned, "someone" has to "[give] Davy Hutchinson a few pebbles." The village makes sure that Davy learns what he is supposed to do before he understands why he does it or the consequences. But this does not mean that he could not learn otherwise.

Even the village adults are not entirely hopeless. Before Old Man Warner cuts them off, Mr. and Mrs. Adams, whose last name suggests a humanity that has not been entirely effaced, briefly mention other villages that are either talking of giving up the lottery or have already done so. Probably out of deep-seated fear, they do not suggest that *their* village give it up; but that they hint at the possibility, however furtively, indicates a reservation—a vague, unconscious sense of guilt—about what they are about to do. The Adams's represent the village's best, humane impulses, however, which the lottery represses.

How do we take such a pessimistic vision of the possibility of social transformation? If anything can be said against **"The Lottery,"** it is probably that it exaggerates the monolithic character of capitalist ideological hegemony. No doubt, capitalism has subtle ways of redirecting the frustrations it engenders away from a critique of capitalism itself. Yet if in order to promote itself it has to make promises of freedom, prosperity and fulfillment on which it cannot deliver, pockets of resistance grow up among the disillusioned. Perhaps it is not Jackson's intention to deny this, but to shock her complacent readers with an exaggerated image of the ideological *modus operandi* of capitalism: accusing those whom it cannot or will not employ of being lazy, promoting "the family" as the essential social unit in order to discourage broader associations and identifications, offering men power over their wives as a consolation for their powerlessness in the labor market, and pitting workers against each other and against the unemployed. It is our fault as readers if our own complacent pessimism makes us *read* Jackson's story pessimistically as a parable of man's innate depravity. (pp. 27-32)

> *Peter Kosenko, "A Marxist/Feminist Reading of Shirley Jackson's 'The Lottery'," in* New Orleans Review, *Vol. 12, No. 1, Spring, 1985, pp. 27-32.*

Mary Kittredge (essay date 1985)

[*Kittredge is an editor, critic, and short story writer whose fiction has appeared in such publications as* Twilight Zone *and* Isaac Asimov's Science Fiction Magazine. *In the excerpt below, Kittredge provides a brief sketch of Jackson's life and career, focusing on her short fiction.*]

No one, I think, was better than [Shirley Jackson] at skewering an emotion, a setting, or a small event on a sharply-honed turn of phrase, then holding it up to the clearest light where it could be seen wriggling, humorously or horribly as the occasion required.

In addition to imagination, industry, and acute insight, she developed, by the "simple" method of daily practice, a pyrotechnical command of ordinary language, which she used economically but to spectacular effect. Whether in her domestic comedies or her stories and novels of psychological horror, she combined acute observation with absolute mastery of tone and clarity of expression.

She achieved her excellence in the face of numerous obstacles, by dint of singleminded application to her craft. In adolescence she kept a diary in which she recorded her writing progress, and she continued producing a consistent thousand words every day even when, after moving with her family from California to Rochester, depression forced her to leave college.

Fears and feelings of inferiority afflicted her throughout her life, sometimes to a crippling degree; among other things, she was sensitive about her appearance, apparently with some reason.

Rare photographs of her show a high, clear forehead, a wryly intelligent expression, and a pretty smile; she has been described as "a big, good-looking California girl." She was, however, always doubtful of her own attractiveness and conscious of her size, which later in life became much more than a cosmetic problem.

When one of her characters remarks that she does not like buying dresses in "a special behemoths department," we get an unhappy sense of how Jackson must have felt about being too big, not only for good looks but for good health. Whether she ever attempted to change is unclear. But towards the end of her life her weight became quite literally self-destructive; she grew so heavy, it is said, that when she walked small bones in her feet threatened to break, and her size cannot have helped but contribute to the heart failure that killed her at the age of 46, on August 8, 1965.

In addition to emotional and physical problems, there were other burdens; these, however, she seems to have borne not just willingly, but happily. Having beaten back if not tamed the depression that made her leave Rochester, she returned to college at Syracuse in 1937. There Stanley Edgar Hyman sought her out on account of his admiration for her story, **"Janice,"** a very short piece about a girl who disguises her cry for help by dramatizing her own attempted suicide.

In 1940, the year she graduated from Syracuse, she married Hyman, who was then at the beginning of a very respectable career as a literary critic. They seem to have been ideally suited to one another, and they began immediately to produce a family. Living first in Greenwich Village, then in North Bennington, Vermont, moving briefly to Westport, Connecticut, they finally settled in North Bennington where Hyman accepted a position at Bennington College and where they remained for the rest of their lives.

Her two "fictionalized" accounts of their domestic life convey a happiness that could not have been entirely invented; family love fairly shines through the pages of *Raising Demons* and *Life Among the Savages.* Even in the most cooperative family, however, the duties of a homemaker, faculty wife, and mother of four would pose an obstacle to all but the most disciplined and determined of writers—which she was.

"The Lottery," her best-known story, appeared in the *New Yorker* in 1948, and brought a measure of fame which surprised her, and with which she was not entirely comfortable. In addition to a deluge of crank letters, some of them more disturbing than the original story, **"The Lottery"** encouraged misunderstanding of her work and curiosity about herself.

Neither phenomenon could have been very enjoyable, but taken together she found them frustrating indeed. Perhaps because she had practiced her craft so diligently from childhood on, she did not care to be trivialized as "the Virginia Werewolf of seancefiction," as she was sometimes called, nor did she enjoy talking or writing about her work. Neither did she care for the misguided sensationalism to which she and her stories were subjected by articles in the Sunday supplements. (pp. 3-5)

The work she produced in her short but full existence seems to divide itself neatly into opposing categories of comedy and tragedy. *Raising Demons,* at first glance, could not have sprung from the same consciousness as the doomed-dog story, **"The Renegade."** But on closer inspection all Jackson's work shows a single theme, and that theme is magic.

Here is the small town of the 1950's, where the soda-fountain owner will hand you a blank check to pay for your childrens' lunches.

Here is that same town again, getting ready to murder your family's pet with a nail-studded choker.

The visions seem equally clear and true. There is some evidence that Shirley Jackson regarded her humorous books as "potboilers," but from this distance it is not so easy to dismiss them. They are the other side of horror; they show us what life is like when the magic works, when the good spells hold. The domestic rituals described in them are the routines that keep life from disintegration.

In *Raising Demons* and *Life Among the Savages,* the horror is not absent; it is merely held at bay, as the titles themselves forcefully hint. If we pour in energy enough, these books suggest, we can hold off entropy for a while. With casseroles and shopping trips, coin collections and Little League, we may ring ourselves with the common charms that keep madness away. One thinks of the praying maiden in the Thurber cartoon: "Lord, please let me be just an ordinary girl."

But she was not. She was a writer of skill and vision, who saw that without constant and energetic applications of magic, things come apart, we shatter and fall. In her tales of haunting, madness, and murder, she described the disorder that may result when magic is ignored, or badly used, or mistaken through carelessness, lack of imagination, laziness, or simple bad luck.

In most of the novels, disorder is characterized by mental instability, a difficulty with which Shirley Jackson was familiar, and in all of them the main character retreats or is driven from the real world, into a life of the imagination. The heroine's perceptions, however mad, are presented as reasonable and her actions as well-justified.

The continuing conflict, Real World vs. Imaginary life, surfaces in each of Jackson's horror novels, and in each it is more completely developed. In each, the grasping tentacles of madness and the anatomy of magic—white, black, and the shades between—are drawn in more delicate detail. (pp. 6-7)

Shirley Jackson's short stories differ from her novels mainly in that their thematic conflict is generally resolved when the story opens. Many of them are vignettes demonstrating the barrenness of lives devoid of magic, or in which it has been misperceived; in **"Elizabeth,"** for example, the main character fantasizes that her life will be transformed as if by magic. Under her armor of cynicism, she is as childish as the victim in *The Haunting of Hill House,* dreaming of rescue while failing to understand that she must break the spell of passivity for herself.

Some of the stories demonstrate the arbitrariness of luck; in **"The Tooth,"** a sane and sensible woman takes a painkiller, loses her mental equilibrium, and through no fault of her own is unable to find her way back to sanity.

In **"The Daemon Lover,"** a lonely woman is seduced into madness by the man of her dreams, her rescue fantasy smashed just as it seemed realized. Whether or not he ever existed outside her dreams is a question left for the reader to decide.

A few of the stories feature blithe survivors, like the unfinished heroine of *Come Along with Me.* **"My Life With R. H. Macy"** is a short romp with a girl who refuses to be reduced to a number. **"One Ordinary Day, With Peanuts,"** features a suitably nutty married couple, one of whom dispenses serendipity while the other doles out irritations to the world.

In the Edgar Allan Poe Award-winning story, **"Louisa, Please Come Home,"** a young woman deliberately transforms herself into a survivor, then discovers that she has done the job too well, changing herself so thoroughly that her family no longer recognizes her when at last she does respond to their plea.

"The Lottery," by which Shirley Jackson's work was introduced to a wide readership, has been subjected to so much interpretation and amateur psychologizing that it would be too bad to subject the poor battered object to any more comment. Suffice it to say that something about that story really got to people; in the first weeks after it appeared in the *New Yorker,* upwards of three hundred readers of the story wrote to the magazine, mostly in protest or to cancel their subscriptions.

It was, and is, a shocking story. It is also beautifully imagined, sparely and gracefully written, a one-two punch of a story which, if we are to believe the author's own account (and I do) was created entire in a single morning, early on a sunny June day in 1948. The next day, Shirley Jackson typed a clean copy, almost word for word the original first draft, and sent it off to her agent at Brandt and Brandt in Manhattan.

The rest, as they say, is history.

The story has been anthologized so thoroughly that anyone who recognizes Shirley Jackson's name at all says, **"The Lottery,"** in an almost Pavlovian response. It was dramatized for the stage, and for television, and in one particularly unlikely adaptation was transformed into a ballet. It has been read in English textbooks by generations of high-school students, and if my informal survey has any validity, it is the only thing many people remember of what they read in that period. It made her fame, and surely assisted in making what was to be her fortune. Despite the anger and suspicion with which it was originally met, it has jolted hundreds of thousands, perhaps millions, of readers.

In its history, in its subject and theme, in its manner of production, and in its effect on Shirley Jackson's life and career, **"The Lottery"** at once demonstrates and validates the major theme of the author's life and work:

If you practice the ritual, you'll get the magic.

First of all, **"The Lottery"** appeared on the page with what must have seemed like magical ease. In "Biography of a Story," Shirley Jackson describes writing it "quickly and easily, moving from beginning to end without pause." In three weeks, it had been sold to the *New Yorker.* The whole episode resembles a simple stroke of good luck, until we consider that before **"The Lottery"** appeared as if by automatic writing, Shirley Jackson had already written, by conservative estimate, five million words.

She wrote those five million words while attending college, and while she suffered the depression that forced her to drop out of college. She wrote them while founding, with Stanley Edgar Hyman, a literary magazine called *The Spectre,* and while conducting what was apparently a fairly active college social life. She wrote them before and during her marriage to Hyman; she wrote while she was pregnant, and she wrote while caring for a house, a husband, two children, and herself. She did not always feel well, she was not always at ease, and she was never without other important responsibilities.

On that sunny June morning in 1948, she did not just sit down to write; she first fed and dressed the baby, put the baby in the stroller and walked to the grocery store, did her shopping, pushed the baby and the groceries back uphill to her house, got herself, the baby, the stroller, and the groceries inside, put the groceries away, and got the baby settled.

Then she sat down and wrote a classic short story, perhaps the most important horror short of the twentieth century. She had practiced the ritual to the tune of five million words; on that June morning, she got some of the resultant magic. She finished **"The Lottery,"** one supposes, in time to give the baby lunch. (pp. 9-11)

In the handling of her own emotional difficulties she was not always so successful. Her attitude about these problems, insofar as it is now known, was apparently as determined as her attitudes about everything else. She would, for example, set tests for herself: to go into a grocery store alone, or later to cross the street *and* go into the store. To the degree that she was able to control it, her life was going to go the way she wanted it to, and that was that. In one of her essays on writing, "Experience and Fiction," she puts it this way:

> Let me just point out right here and now that my unconscious mind has *been* unconscious for a number of years now and it is my firm intention to keep it that way. When I have nightmares about a horrid building it is the horrid building I am having nightmares about, and no one is going to talk me out of it; that is final.

It wasn't final, but whatever she fought, she fought to a draw—and kept writing.

In all the aspects of her life, in fact she fought whatever obstacles she encountered at least to a draw. Her success in the horror genre, like her successful domestic comedy, was the result of an exquisitely sensitive double vision that would have seemed an affliction to a less determined or talented writer. She saw the magic in the mundane, and the evil behind the ordinary. She saw that the line between the cruel and the comedic is sometimes vanishingly narrow.

She wrote it all down, day after day, on good days and bad, creating enormous pleasure for her contemporary audience and contributing at least one story to the ranks of the best horror that has been written. Perhaps the worst that can now be said about Shirley Jackson's work is that there simply was not enough of it.

But then, there is never enough of that brand of magic. (p. 12)

Mary Kittredge, "The Other Side of Magic: A Few Remarks about Shirley Jackson," in Discovering Modern Horror Fiction, *edited by Darrell Schweitzer, Starmont House, 1985, pp. 3-12.*

Fritz Oehlschlaeger (essay date 1988)

[*In the excerpt below, Oehlschlaeger views Jackson's design of the lottery process in "The Lottery" as a key to the story's meaning: that the lottery's "primary social consequence involves women's turning over the control of their fertility to men."*]

In a 1979 article Richard H. Williams notes what he takes to be a "flaw" in the two-stage process by which the victim is selected in Shirley Jackson's **"The Lottery."** Readers of the story will recall that the first round of the drawing determines a household from which the victim is to be drawn; the second round, the single victim from within that household. Williams points out that under such a system "individuals who are members of smaller families are more likely to be chosen as the sacrificial victim," and he then proposes a new plan that would keep the two-stage process but have the same effect as simply "selecting one individual at random from the village" ["A Critique of the Sampling Plan Used in Shirley Jackson's **'The Lottery',"** *Journal of Modern Literature*]. But perhaps instead of correcting the story's "flaws," we should look at the lottery as Jackson designs it for a key to its meaning. The nature of the process by which the victim is selected gives each woman a very clear incentive to produce the largest possible family. Each child she has gives her a better chance of surviving if the marked paper falls to her household in the first round. What I am suggesting, then, is that one way the story can be seen is as the depiction of a patriarchal society's way of controlling female sexuality. Helen Nebeker has argued that the story presents a ritual that has outlived the fertility function it once had in an earlier myth-oriented time. Such an argument overlooks the real and continuing function of the lottery as it is organized. That function remains the encouraging of fertility within marriage, along with the patriarchal domination that accompanies it.

A conflict between male authority and female resistance is subtly evident throughout **"The Lottery."** Early in the story, the boys make a "great pile of stones in one corner of the square," while the girls stand aside "talking among themselves, looking over their shoulders at the boys." Later, as the Hutchinsons file up to draw their papers from the box, it is a girl who whispers, "I hope it's not Nancy." This girl's expression of a purely personal feeling is perceived by Old Man Warner as a threat to the social order, as is indicated by his bitterly exclaiming, "It's not the way it used to be," when presumably everyone subordinated personal feelings to the social demands of the ritual. It is also a woman, Mrs. Adams, who presents the story's most significant challenge to the lottery. When at one point her husband Mr. Adams remarks that "over in the North village they're talking of giving up the lottery," Old Man Warner gives vent to a tirade on the folly of departing from what has always served its purpose. Mr. Adams makes no response, but his wife does, pointing out to the Old Man that "some places have already quit lotteries," an oblique but nevertheless real gesture of resistance. That Jackson wants us to read Mrs. Adams's statement as a gesture of resistance is reinforced by what she does with the Adamses at the end of the story. Mr. Adams is at the front of the crowd of villagers as they set upon Tessie Hutchinson. No mention, however, is made of Mrs. Adams's being involved in the stoning.

There is a strong pattern of detail in the story, then, suggesting that those who are most discomfited by, or resistant to, the lottery are women. On the other hand, men control the lottery. Mr. Summers and Mr. Graves are its official priestly administrators, and when they need help, they inquire whether any of the "fellows" might want to give a hand. The lottery is arranged by families and households, women being assigned to the households of their husbands, who draw for them in the initial round. That the society is a heavily patriarchal one is suggested in many other ways as well. As the people gather at the outset of the story, the women stand "by their husbands," and Jackson sharply distinguishes female from male authority: when Mrs. Martin calls her son Bobby, he "ducked under his mother's grasping hand and ran, laughing, back to the pile of stones," but when "his father spoke up sharply," Bobby "came quickly and took his place between his father and his oldest brother." Later when Mrs. Hutchinson complains that the draw has been unfair, her husband tersely and authoritatively commands her, "Shut up, Tessie." And when it becomes clear that Tessie has drawn the marked paper, Bill "forced the slip of paper out of her hand" and "held it up" for the crowd to see. The details Jackson chooses to describe the administrator of the lottery, Mr. Summers, and his wife further clarify the nature of male power and female submission in the lottery's community. Mr. Summers is given his position because people feel "sorry for him" as one who "had no children" and whose "wife was a scold." The woman who is without children is dismissed as a "scold," a challenge to male authority. The childless man, on the other hand, is elevated to a place of special responsibility and even sanctity.

The reading of **"The Lottery"** I am developing is reinforced, too, by looking at the story within the contexts established by its most important allusions. Certainly the whole motif of a woman's being stoned to death recalls the eighth chapter of the Gospel of St. John, in which Jesus frees the woman taken in adultery by directing that man who is without sin among the scribes and Pharisees to cast the first stone. The elements of the Gospel episode strikingly parallel those of **"The Lottery."** In each, a priestly caste made up of men seeks to use its spiritual authority to control female sexuality. In both the Gospel and the short story, a woman confronts the Law, and some, like that Pharisee Old Man Warner, argue that the individual must be sacrificed to maintain community structure. But Jesus speaks a new word, insisting, as he does so often, that the Law is made for men and women, not men and women for the Law. His wisdom, his good news, is the antithesis of Old Man Warner's. Unfortunately there is no one in **"The Lottery"** to rebuke the powers so forthrightly as Jesus does in 8 *John.* The powers get their scapegoat; the woman pays. Only perhaps in 8 *John* does the woman escape paying, and that is, of course, because another scapegoat stands in her place.

The name of Jackson's victim, Tessie Hutchinson, links her to two women who do pay. Helen Nebeker relates "Tessie" to "Theresa" and "Anastasia," but this seems to me to overlook a much more obvious allusion to Tess of the D'Urbervilles. Hardy's novel is about the way "the woman pays" for crimes committed by men who hold sexual and spiritual power. Tess is victimized by the lust of Alec D'Urberville and by the spiritual pretensions of Angel Clare. Tess's final retreat to the place of ritualistic sacrifice, Stonehenge, and her execution may well have had some germinal influence on Jackson's conception of **"The Lottery."** Certainly Jackson's ending is especially reminiscent of Tess's last moments at Stonehenge as the men close in upon her from behind the encircling stones and the "whole country is reared" to prevent her escape.

The name of Jackson's victim also links her to Anne Hutchinson, whose Antinomian beliefs, found to be heretical by the Puritan hierarchy, resulted in her banishment from Massachusetts in 1638. While Tessie Hutchinson is no spiritual rebel, to be sure, Jackson's allusion to Anne Hutchinson reinforces her suggestions of rebellion lurking within the women of her imaginary village. It indicates too that what the men of Jackson's village seek to kill is a principle of rebellion that is specifically female and, I would argue, based in sexuality. We should remember that Hawthorne associates Anne Hutchinson with another woman taken in adultery and accused by Pharisees, her partner among them. As Hester is led out of prison [in *The Scarlet Letter*], she passes the wild rose bush that may have "sprung up under the footsteps of the sainted Anne Hutchinson." As Michael Colacurcio has shown, Hawthorne's association of the two women reflects an understanding that Anne Hutchinson's threat to his Puritan ancestors was partially sexual. In *Magnalia Christi Americana,* Cotton Mather treats her as a "seducer" whose ideas were "monstrous births." Edward Johnson, in *Wonder-Working Providence of Sion's Saviour,* writes of Mistress Hutchinson's ability to show him "a way, if I could attaine it, even Revelations, full of such ravishing joy that I should never have cause to be sorry for sinne, so long as I live." Here, Colacurcio notes, is "the perception, registered in anger and in fear, that antinomian doctrine is not separable from the tone and from the unsettling consequences of awakened female sexuality." (pp. 259-61)

Jackson's choice of her victim's name strongly reinforces her suggestion about how the lottery is designed primarily to control women, but it ought not to be read as an indication that Tessie is a heroine with the stature of an Anne Hutchinson or Hester Prynne. Tessie fails to be a heroine, and the way that she does so testifies to the success with which the male-dominated order has imposed itself upon her. It is crucial to note that her most grievous failure lies in betraying another woman, her married daughter, by suggesting that she be considered a member of the Hutchinson household for the second stage of the lottery. Jackson emphasizes women's turning against one another, too, through her pointed depiction of the brutality of Mrs. Delacroix and Mrs. Graves in setting upon Tessie. At the beginning of the story, the girls stand together watching the boys gather the stones, but as those girls become women, the involvement in marriage and childbearing that the lottery encourages pits them against one another, blinding them to the fact that all power in their community is male.

Jackson had a clear precedent in New England history of ritual, collective murder in which women responded to the pressures of male authority by betraying one another: the trial and execution of the Salem witches. Some years after she wrote **"The Lottery,"** Jackson wrote about the witchcraft hysteria in a book for adolescents called *The Witchcraft of Salem Village.* Some of the similarities between that book and the story are so close as to suggest that the witch trials may have been in Jackson's mind when she was writing **"The Lottery."** The description of people gathering for the first day's examination of the witches, for instance, closely parallels the opening of **"The Lottery"**: "By early morning, almost the entire population of the village was assembled, the grownups talking anxiously and quietly together, the children running off down the road and back again, with wild excited shouts." As the lottery is conducted by a pair of men, so the witch examinations are presided over by a pair of magistrates, one of whom, Hathorne, is clearly, like Mr. Summers, in control. In addition, Jackson's explanation of how the delusion began could apply equally well to the reasons behind the lottery's continuing hold on its people. Discussing the role of Mr. Paris, minister in Salem village and father of one of the children believed to be afflicted by the witches, Jackson remarks: "No one dared to leave the only protection offered the people—the protection of Mr. Paris and their church. Eventually they came to believe that if they worked together wholeheartedly and without mercy they could root out the evil already growing among them." These lines reiterate the central, terrifying import of **"The Lottery"**: that people can be brought to work together wholeheartedly and without mercy if they believe that their protection depends upon it.

A very important similarity between Massachusetts at the time of the witchcraft hysteria and the village of Jackson's story lies in the relations of power between men and women. As in Jackson's village, all power in the witchcraft trials lay with men: Mr. Paris; Magistrates Hathorne and Corwin; Deputy Governor Thomas Danforth; Judges James Russell, Isaac Addington, Major Samuel Appleton, and Captain Samuel Sewall. The "afflicted" in the trial were girls, who, like Tessie Hutchinson, responded to the pressure of male authority by betraying others of their own sex. Although Jackson does not include specific demographic information about the witches in her book on Salem, it is worth adding that Tessie Hutchinson conforms rather well to the profile of women found to be witches. Carol Karlsen has shown that the group most vulnerable to accusations of witchcraft included women between the ages of forty and sixty, or past the prime childbearing years. Accused women in this age group were also more likely to be executed than younger women suspected of witchcraft. The ages of Tessie's four children indicate that she is past the years of her peak fertility. Jackson does not give us all these ages specifically, but we do know that Tessie has a daughter old enough to be married, a son whose "overlarge" feet and order in the lottery mark him as an adolescent, a twelve-year-old daughter Nancy, and a boy so young that he must be helped to draw his piece of paper. Tessie is, then, both a woman approaching middle age and one who has had recent difficulty in conceiving children, as the age gap between Nancy and little Dave indicates. I am not arguing that there is collusion between the men who administer the lottery and Bill Hutchinson to eliminate Tessie because she has passed the peak years of childbearing. What I am suggesting, however, is this: that given the purpose of fertility within marriage that the design of the lottery unquestionably fosters, Tessie is an extremely appropriate victim.

It might be objected to my line of argument that the lottery also apparently has male victims. But such is obviously a necessary part of the process by which it retains its hold over the people who participate in it. A lottery that killed only women over forty could hardly expect to retain popular support for long, at least in part because it would lose its mystery. The lottery must appear to be fair, and it must give the villagers the sense of being narrowly spared by a mysterious power and thus justified. Still I would insist that we cannot discount Tessie's charge that the lottery is not fair. On one level, as John H. Williams has pointed out, the lottery is indeed unfair; its two-stage design means that the selection of a victim is not a purely random process. Moreover, we cannot deny Tessie's charge by saying that all the operations of the lottery appear to be fairly handled, for an obviously flawed lottery would neither mystify the villagers nor interest the reader. Neither can we argue for its fairness by saying that no one, other than Tessie, comments on any unfairness, for obviously everyone has a very strong stake in believing it was conducted fairly. In short, if the lottery is unfair, it is reasonable to assume that its lack of fairness would be evident only to the victim.

A reading of the story in the several contexts I have supplied here dramatically underscores what is evident from the design of the lottery itself: that its primary social consequence involves women's turning over the control of their fertility to men. Jackson depicts a society in which authority is male, potential resistance female. As in the history of Anne Hutchison and *The Scarlet Letter,* women in **"The Lottery"** represent the personal, the conviction that, as Michael Colacurcio has said of Hester Prynne, life is more than "the sum of its legally regulated outward works." The young girl's simple hope that the victim not be her friend Nancy is the force that would destroy the lottery, as Old Man Warner recognizes. Suppression of the personal is the function of the lottery, which it accomplishes primarily by causing women to submit control of their sexuality to men of secular and priestly authority. The design of the lottery is without flaw; it serves perfectly the patriarchal purpose of denying women consciousness by insisting that they remain part of nature, part of the fertile earth itself. (pp. 262-64)

Fritz Oehlschlaeger, "The Stoning of Mistress Hutchinson: Meaning and Context in 'The Lottery'," in Essays in Literature, *Vol. XV, No. 2, Fall, 1988, pp. 259-65.*

James Egan (essay date 1989)

[*In the following excerpt, Egan focuses on Jackson's use of domestic and fantastic elements in her short fiction.*]

Shirley Jackson is probably best known for her tales of latent evil and dark rituals, notably **"The Lottery'** (1948), and for such overtly Gothic pieces as *The Haunting of Hill House* (1959). Yet her range was considerable, including absurdist short stories, psychological thrillers, and two works of biographical domestic humor, *Life among the Savages* (1953) and *Raising Demons* (1957). Critical consensus about Jackson seems to hold that she had mastered both the familial and the macabre and could incorporate into each idiom a wit that was at times wry and self-deprecating, at times disquieting. One of her favorite but least discussed motifs is the domestic, the familial, and the rituals associated with it. I propose to argue that a substantial part of her work may be interpreted as either the expression of an idyllic domestic vision or the inversion of that vision into the fantastic and Gothic. Jackson controls the tenor of her domestic and fantastic parables primarily by her sophisticated use of wit, irony, and paradox and by juxtaposing the premises of her domestic tales to those of her fantastic ones. An awareness of Jackson's treatment of the familial and its opposite not only allows us to examine the ways in which she transforms domestic into horrific, but the evolution of her world view as well. (p. 15)

[Much of Jackson's] serious fiction revolved around the motif of the domestic—the creation, maintenance, and destruction of the familial idyll. Her characters often search for domestic sanctuary, and the places those searches lead to, the complications and illusions they set in motion, are a mainstay of her work. Versions of the sanctuary range widely, from the realistic to the fantastic and Gothic. In contrast to her later tales, **"Men with Their Big Shoes"**, **"Elizabeth"**, **"I Know Who I Love"**, and **"The Little House"** could be classified as grim and sobering, but realistic just the same. **"Men with Their Big Shoes"** involves an aging and cynical maid, Mrs. Anderson, a disruptive invader from an unhappy marriage, who poisons the well of domestic bliss for her employer, young Mrs. Hart. A sort of domestic bully, Mrs. Anderson tries to force her employer to accept her version of domesticity, dropping hints about the loose habits and moral undependability of husbands. She treats Mrs. Hart as a daughter, a daughter who should provide Mrs. Anderson with a place to live in case her husband throws her out of her own home. The

Jackson's social circle included many prominent literary figures. Here, novelist Ralph Ellison sits behind the living room bar at one of Jackson's many parties.

innocent, trusting, romantically inclined younger woman is constantly prevailed upon to suspect the notion of marital happiness she had been living by. **"Elizabeth"** recounts the story of an unmarried New York professional woman who works as an editor in a marginal literary agency. Elizabeth cannot help but reflect on her drab, dreary apartment and office and dreams of making both more comfortable and homelike. She has a nominal romantic relationship with Robbie, her employer, but the relationship makes her feel as frustrated and depressed as her living quarters do, so much so that she reacts with hostility toward Daphne, the young secretary Robbie has recently hired. Though she seems to have given up on Robbie as a potential husband, Elizabeth cannot refrain from jealousy over Daphne as a potential rival. Faced with a shrunken daily life, devoid of domestic bliss or even comfort, she frantically makes a date with Jim Harris, a writer whose work she had previously handled. The story ends inconclusively, but images of escape and romance color Elizabeth's perception of Harris; she sees the possible realization of her dreams of the conventional and domestic.

"I Know Who I Love" details the domestic misery of a woman named Catharine, daughter of a prim minster of a father who regarded her as a "trap" and "an unnecessary expense". She endures cruel treatment by her high school peers and eventually shoulders the burden of a hectoring, dying mother. Because of Catharine's wretched home life, her feelings of rejection and her parents' suspicious treatment of Aaron, the only man who showed her attention and affection, she faces a sad, empty life in New York City. Catharine has been so badly damaged by her upbringing that she simply accepts her present lot. Family failures have set the tone for her misery. Elizabeth, protagonist of **"The Little House"**, has apparently found a domestic sanctuary, a tidy home left to her by a dead aunt. When she first arrives to take possession of the house, she feels the thrill of promise and envisions rearranging the house to suit her. But Elizabeth's idyll quickly fades. Two neighbors, the elderly, maiden Dolson sisters, pay a "friendly" visit and suggest that her aunt was murdered, speculating about how the murderer might have gotten in. Elizabeth tries desperately to return to her first vision of the little house as a sanctuary but she becomes nervous and panics. Her dream has been shattered by rudimentary human evil—the gossip and meddling of the Dolson sisters.

Some searches for the domestic and familial lead Jackson's characters into the realm of the fantastic, resulting in tales which contain what Tzvetan Todorov and others consider the primary themes of fantastic discourse: metamorphosis; "Pan-determinism" (special causality); "fragmentation and multiplication of the personality; the collapse of the limits between subject and object . . . and the transformation of time and space". Given the variety of fantastic variations on the familial theme, Lenemaja Friedman's claim that Jackson will occasionally introduce a fantastic twist to dislocate the normal amounts to a substantial understatement. An early story, **"Like Mother Used to Make"**, displays a bizarre domestic metamorphosis. Fussy David and sloppy Marcia, two neighbors in a city apartment building, arrange to have dinner at David's, a dinner he prepares with care in his tidy, comfortable, "private" flat, a place he considers a retreat from a "discourteous" outside world. Marcia's apartment appears very much the opposite of his—disheveled, carelessly decorated, unharmonious. As the two sit down to dinner, they are disturbed by a knock on Marcia's door: Mr. Harris, one of Marcia's co-workers, has dropped by unexpectedly, and she invites him to dinner. Harris apparently thinks that David's apartment is Marcia's and that she has prepared the meal. Neither David nor Marcia disturbs the illusion. David proceeds to wait on the two and eventually serves dessert, but still Harris refuses to leave, settling in instead. Finally, David leaves his own apartment, walks over to Marcia's and begins to tidy it up. David's obsession with domesticity has led to a bizarre role reversal, a transformation. He becomes the "homey" Marcia the real Marcia refuses to become. Having had his own domesticity interrupted, he begins to create it again in a different location, a fantastic reversal of stereotypical male and female familial roles.

"The Beautiful Stranger" represents a more radical departure into the fantastic. As Margaret waits at the train for her husband to return from a business trip, she experiences an "intimation of strangeness" and an "odd sense of lost time." At first, the man who steps from the train seems to be her husband, but she quickly comes to realize that he is not. A fantastic transformation of time and space has occurred, for the stranger knows things about Margaret and her daily life that he could not reasonably have known. Yet she welcomes him and finds sanctuary in his mannerisms and plans for their life. The fantastic comforts her for awhile but another fantastic reversal occurs at the story's end. After going to town to buy a present for the stranger she returns to her home to face disorientation and confusion. She cannot identify her house and ends up alone and alienated, again caught up in a fantastic reversal of domesticity. Fantastic motifs likewise surface in **"The Daemon Lover"**, another early short piece, featuring an anonymous thirty-four-year-old woman who waits anxiously for her fiancé, James Harris, to arrive on their wedding day. She lives alone, without sanctuary, and Harris has offered her the prized domestic ritual of marriage. She waits but he does not arrive, so she sets out in search of him. Hostile strangers offer no help, constantly rebuffing the increasingly desperate woman. Eventually she gets a small clue and goes to an apartment where Harris was rumored to have lived. She knocks and hears voices but no one answers the door at his alleged last address. Her needs and illusions have sent her in pursuit of an illusion. Was there ever a James Harris? Have the limits between subject (her) and object (him) collapsed? The lines between real and imagined, self and Other, may have vanished. She reacts with confusion and anxiety to what she considers an impossibility, a predicament not uncommon in fantastic tales. The woman's yearning for the domestic may also have made her the victim of a metamorphosis in which her lover has become her torturer, leading her on an odyssey of humiliation. Absurdity surfaces in the plight of Louisa in **"Louisa, Please Come Home"**. Louisa feels stifled by the familial, by what she feels are the constraints of wealth, normality, and social status, so she runs away from home on her sister's wedding day. She likes her new freedom in a new city, Amityville, but ironically she quickly moves into another domestic sanctuary, a boarding house presided over by the motherly Mrs. Peacock. Paul, a friend when she lived with her family, finds Louisa and returns her to her parents, who have broadcast pleas on the radio for her to come back. Metamorphosis occurs when she confronts her parents: they don't recognize her. Louisa has been transformed into a stranger, even though she answers correctly several questions that, presumably, only she could have answered. Ironically, though she'd like to stay home now, her parents accuse her of a hoax, an experience they've suffered through several times in the past year. Jackson suspends the laws of probability here to suggest that Louisa's identity and personality have been dissolved; her parents are confounded by the illusion of a multiple personality, when, in fact, their missing daughter stands before them. In **"Beautiful Stranger", "The Daemon Lover"**, and **"Louisa, Please Come Home"**, Jackson's light domestic wit has become dark, relentless, ironic humor. She presents victims who are tricked and trapped. If comedy occurs here, the joke is on these unfortunate women. In Louisa's case a bizarre double reversal occurs—first she tricks her family by deserting them, and then they return the favor. (pp. 17-18)

[Throughout] her career Shirley Jackson examined the ways in which the ideals of the domestic and familial were created, nurtured, attacked from various quarters, escaped from, weakened, parodied, and destroyed. Particularly in *Life among the Savages* and *Raising Demons* she used the cathartic power of her humor to support her vision of a nurturing domestic world. Wit and the self-deprecating comic were a means of preserving order, of coping with life's daily disruptions, of avoiding entanglement in narcissistic illusions. Her comic domestic perspective concentrated on physical rather than psychological problems and troubling issues were largely excluded from that perspective. Even in her early short fiction, however, dissonance occurs. Characters can be found in bleak cosmetic settings, cut off from family love and support, or eager to escape from domestic lives which stifle them. Occasionally these characters simply accept the lack of the familial, and occasionally they reach out for domestic sanctuaries. As Jackson's fiction evolved over time, some of her protagonists reached desperately for the domestic tranquillity absent from or distorted in their lives, and their yearning for sanctuary led them into the fantastic or Gothic, into situations which proved to be open-ended, unpredictable, paradoxical, and illusory. These searches lack the regenerative wit of the chronicles. If they contain humor at all, it tends to be dark and ironic, with the searchers the victims of cosmic jokes in many cases. (p. 23)

James Egan, "Sanctuary: Shirley Jackson's Domestic and Fantastic Parables," in Studies in Weird Fiction, *No. 6, Fall, 1989, pp. 15-24.*

FURTHER READING

Bibliography

Herrick, Casey. "Shirley Jackson's 'The Lottery'." *Bulletin of Bibliography* 46, No. 2 (June 1989): 120-21.

Secondary bibliography compiled as a supplement to Robert S. Phillips's 1966 checklist of Jackson criticism (see below).

Phillips, Robert S. "Shirley Jackson: A Chronology and a Supplementary Checklist." *The Papers of the Bibliographical Society of America* 60, Second Quarter (1966): 203-13.

Includes a chronology of Jackson's life and writings by and about Jackson through 1966.

Biography

Oppenheimer, Judy. *Private Demons: The Life of Shirley Jackson.* New York: G. P. Putnam's Sons, 1988, 304 p.

Excellent, detailed biography containing numerous photographs and extensive interviews with Jackson's children and friends.

Criticism

Breit, Harvey. "Talk with Miss Jackson." *The New York Times Book Review* (26 June 1949): 15.

Interview that followed the publication of "The Lottery" in which Jackson discusses her writing techniques and favorite authors.

Gibson, James M. "An Old Testament Analogue for 'The Lottery'." *Journal of Modern Literature* 11, No. 1 (March 1984): 193-95.

Asserts that a close literary parallel to and possible source of "The Lottery" is an Old Testament story found in the Book of Joshua.

Halsband, Robert. "Sketch Potpourri." *Saturday Review of Literature* XXXII, No. 19 (7 May 1949): 19, 36.

Review of *The Lottery* in which Halsband divides the stories into three types: prosaic, socially conscious, and fantastic. Under this rubric, Halsband labels "The Lottery" a "failure" as a horror story, though he concedes that the tale "has at least publicized the work of a subtle and literate storyteller."

Hyman, Stanley Edgar. "Shirley Jackson: 1919-1965." *Saturday Evening Post* 238, No. 25 (18 December 1965): 63.

Tribute by Jackson's husband.

Lainoff, Seymour. "Jackson's 'The Lottery'." *The Explicator* XII (March 1954): Item 34.

Discusses the influence of Sir James G. Frazer's *The Golden Bough* on Jackson's story.

Nebeker, Helen C. " 'The Lottery': Symbolic Tour de Force." *American Literature* 46 (March 1974): 100-07.

Essay examining the various levels of symbolism in "The Lottery."

Welch, Dennis M. "Manipulation in Shirley Jackson's 'Seven Types of Ambiguity'." *Studies in Short Fiction* 18, No. 1 (Winter 1981): 27-31.

Examines the irony and "subtle and comic ambiguity" of the story and suggests that the narrative implies that one character may be the victim of a ruse practiced by two other ostensibly well-meaning people.

Additional coverage of Jackson's life and career is contained in the following sources published by Gale Research: *Concise Dictionary of American Literary Biography, 1941-1968; Contemporary Authors,* Vols. 25-28; *Contemporary Authors New Revision Series,* Vol. 4; *Contemporary Literary Criticism,* Vols. 11, 60; *Dictionary of Literary Biography,* Vol. 6; and *Something about the Author,* Vol. 2.

Katherine Mansfield

1888-1923

(Born Kathleen Mansfield Beauchamp; also wrote under the pseudonym Boris Petrovsky) New Zealand short story writer, critic, and poet.

INTRODUCTION

Mansfield is a central figure in the development of the modern short story. An early practitioner of stream-of-consciousness narration, she applied this technique to create stories based on the illumination of character rather than the contrivances of plot. Her works, which treat such universal concerns as family and love relationships and the everyday experiences of childhood, are noted for their distinctive wit, psychological acuity, and perceptive characterizations.

Mansfield was born into a prosperous family in Wellington, New Zealand, and attended school in England in her early teens. She returned home after completing her education but was thereafter dissatisfied with colonial life, and at nineteen she persuaded her parents to allow her to return to England. She became pregnant shortly after leaving home and entered into a hasty marriage with George Bowden, a young musician, and left him the next day. Her mother arranged for her removal to a German spa, where she miscarried. Mansfield returned to England after a period of recuperation, during which she wrote the short stories comprising her first collection, *In a German Pension.* Offering satiric commentary on the attitudes and behavior of the German people, these stories focus on themes relating to sexual relationships, female subjugation, and childbearing. Critics have found that these stories, although less technically accomplished than Mansfield's later fiction, evince her characteristic wit and perception—in particular her effective portrayal of female psychology—as well as her early experimentation with interior monologue. Between 1911 and 1915 Mansfield published short stories and book reviews in such magazines as the *Athenaeum,* the *Blue Review,* the *New Age,* the *Open Window,* and *Rhythm.* In 1912 she met editor and critic John Middleton Murry and was soon sharing the editorship of the *Blue Review* and *Rhythm* with him. The two began living together and married in 1918, when Bowden finally consented to a divorce.

In 1915 Mansfield was reunited in London with her brother, Leslie Heron Beauchamp, shortly before he was killed in a military training accident. Beauchamp's visit is believed to have reinforced Mansfield's resolve to incorporate material drawn from her New Zealand background into her fiction. The collections *Bliss, and Other Stories,* and *The Garden Party, and Other Stories*—the last that Mansfield edited and oversaw in production—contain many of the New Zealand stories, including "Prelude," "At the Bay," "The Garden Party," "The Voyage," and "A Doll's House," as well as other examples of her mature fiction. The success of these volumes established Mansfield as a major talent comparable to such contemporaries as Virginia Woolf and James Joyce. Never in vigorous health, Mansfield was severely weakened by tuberculosis in the early 1920s. Nonetheless, she worked almost continuously, writing until the last few months of her life. She died in 1923 at the age of thirty-four.

Early assessments of Mansfield were based largely on the romanticized image presented by Murry in extensively edited volumes of her private papers, as well as in reminiscences and critical commentary that he published after her death. His disposition of her literary estate is considered by some commentators to have been exploitative: he profited from the publication of stories that Mansfield had rejected for publication, as well as notebook jottings, intermittent diaries, and letters. The idealized representation of Mansfield promulgated by Murry, termed the "cult of Katherine," is undergoing revision by modern biographers aided by new editions of her letters and journals.

Mansfield's best and most characteristic work is generally considered to be contained in *Bliss, and Other Stories* and *The Garden Party, and Other Stories.* These volumes include many of Mansfield's highly regarded New Zealand stories as well as the widely reprinted and often discussed "Bliss," "The Daughters of the Late Colonel," "Je Ne Parle Pas Français," and "Miss Brill," which are considered among the finest short stories in the English language. These stories display some of Mansfield's most successful innovations with narrative technique, including interior monologue, stream of consciousness, and shifting narrative perspectives. They are commended for the facility with which Mansfield represented intricate balances within family relationships, her depictions of love relationships from both female and male points of view, and her portrayals of children, which are considered especially insightful. Mansfield is one of the few authors to attain prominence exclusively for short stories, and her works remain among the most widely read in world literature.

PRINCIPAL WORKS

SHORT FICTION

In a German Pension 1911
Prelude 1918
Bliss, and Other Stories 1920
The Garden Party, and Other Stories 1922
The Doves' Nest, and Other Stories 1923
The Little Girl, and Other Stories 1924; also published as *Something Childish, and Other Stories,* 1924
The Aloe 1930
The Short Stories of Katherine Mansfield 1937
Undiscovered Country: The New Zealand Stories of Katherine Mansfield 1974

OTHER MAJOR WORKS

Poems (poetry) 1923
Journal of Katherine Mansfield (journal) 1927
The Letters of Katherine Mansfield. 2 vols. (letters) 1928
Novels and Novelists (criticism) 1930
The Scrapbook of Katherine Mansfield (journal) 1939
Katherine Mansfield's Letters to John Middleton Murry: 1913-1922 (letters) 1951
The Urewera Notebook (journal) 1978
The Collected Letters of Katherine Mansfield. 2 vols. (letters) 1984-87
The Critical Writings of Katherine Mansfield (criticism) 1987
Letters between Katherine Mansfield and John Middleton Murry (letters) 1988
Poems of Katherine Mansfield (poetry) 1988

Malcolm Cowley (essay date 1922)

[*Cowley was a prominent American critic who wrote extensively on modern American literature. In the following excerpt, he assesses Mansfield's short fiction and discusses her second volume of short stories,* The Garden Party, and Other Stories.]

There is no doubt that the stories of Katherine Mansfield are literature. That is, their qualities are literary qualities. No one would think of dramatizing these stories, of condensing them into pithy paragraphs, or of making them into a scenario for Douglas Fairbanks. They do not dissolve into music, like Mallarmé, or materialize into sculpture like Heredia. The figures are not plastic; the landscapes are not painted, but described, and they are described, usually, through the eyes of a character, so that they serve both as a background and as a character study. In the same way Katherine Mansfield does not treat events, but rather the reflection of events in someone's mind. Her stories are literature because they produce effects which can be easily attained by no other art.

Nobody ever dies in one of her stories; nobody ever marries or is born. These pompous happenings occur off-stage, discreetly, a day before the curtain rises or a year after its descent; so do most other events on which her stories touch. . . . [There] is no plot; instead she tries to define a situation. That is why her stories give the effect of overflowing their frame; an event has a beginning and an end, but the consequences of a situation continue indefinitely like waves of sound or the familiar ripples of a pool. This is the effect produced by the best of her work, but actually it is nothing more than a moment out of the lives of her characters; a moment not of action but of realization, and a realization of one particular sort.

These stories, at least the fifteen contained in her second volume [***The Garden Party, and Other Stories***], have a thesis: namely, that life is a very wonderful spectacle, but disagreeable for the actors. Not that she ever states it bluntly in so many words; blunt statement is the opposite of her method. (p. 230)

[The characters] discover life to be wonderful and very disagreeable. . . . The moment from their existence which Katherine Mansfield chooses to describe is the moment of this realization.

The method is excellent, and the thesis which it enforces is vague enough and sufficiently probable to be justified aesthetically. Only, there is sometimes a suspicion—I hate to mention it in the case of an author so delicate and so apparently just, but there is sometimes a suspicion that she stacks the cards. She seems to choose characters that will support her thesis. The unsympathetic ones are too aggressively drawn, and the good and simple folk confronted with misfortunes too undeviating; she doesn't treat them fairly. (p. 231)

[This] volume, compared with the first, adheres more faithfully to the technique of Chekhov, and the adherence begins to be dangerous. He avoided monotonousness only, and not always, by the immense range of his knowledge and sympathy. Katherine Mansfield's stories have no such range; they are literature, but they are limited. She has three backgrounds only: continental hotels, New Zealand upper-class society, and a certain artistic set in London. Her characters reduce to half a dozen types; when she deserts these she flounders awkwardly, and especially when she describes the Poorer Classes. Lacking a broad scope, she could find salvation in technical variety, but in her second volume she seems to strive for that no longer.

To read her first book was to make a voyage of adventure, or maybe even to open Chapman's Homer. She had borrowed a little from her English contemporaries, but not enough so that one could identify her sources. She has borrowed a great deal from Chekhov, but her characters were other and more familiar. In general the stories were her own experiments and successful experiments; that is why it was exhilarating to read them. One did not quite know what she would write next. . . . ***The Garden Party*** has answered that question. It is almost as good as **"Bliss"** but not much different; from Katherine Mansfield it is immensely disappointing. (pp. 231-32)

Malcolm Cowley, "The Author of 'Bliss'," in The Dial, *Chicago, Vol. 73, August 22, 1922, pp. 230-32.*

David Daiches (essay date 1936)

[*Daiches is a prominent English scholar and critic. He is especially renowned for his studies of such writers as Robert Burns, Robert Louis Stevenson, and Virginia Woolf. In the following excerpt, he discusses Mansfield's fictional methods and principal aims as an author.*]

The short stories of Katherine Mansfield, though not many in number, contain some of the most sensitive writing in our literature. (p. 83)

She has imposed upon herself a much severer discipline than the majority of story-tellers dare to do; she writes only to tell the truth—not the truth for the outsider, for the observer who watches the action from the street corner, but the truth for the characters themselves and so the real meaning of the situation.

A situation can have "meaning" from many different points of view. The point of view may be ethical, or aesthetic, or dependent on any scheme of values the author wishes to apply. Katherine Mansfield consciously and deliberately avoided any such external approach. For her the meaning of the situation meant its potentialities for change in the lives of the characters, in so far as such a change had reference to aspects of experience known and appreciated by feeling and suffering beings in general. There is always this ultimate reference to life in its wider aspect, though it does not take the form of the description of the most impressive or superficially the most "significant" elements in life. It is not the course of the action itself that has this connection, but, in so many cases, this element of *change* which links up her stories with general human activity. The varying and unstable qualities of human emotions and the very essence of these qualities are illustrated by the point, the dynamic element in the story which is brought out in the presentation. It is a point the mere *observer* would miss—some subtle change of emotional atmosphere or realisation by the characters of something new, something different and cogent, though they might not themselves be aware of what it is. Thus the "truth of the idea" meant to Katherine Mansfield the meaning of the situation for those concerned in it, and this had implications far beyond the individual instance, though these implications were not stressed or commented on: this meaning she nearly always saw as involving some kind of change. (pp. 84-6)

In **"The Garden Party"** the story rests on the change from the party atmosphere to the atmosphere of sudden death in the carter's cottage, and the *meaning* of that change. All the other elements, the description, the dialogue, the character sketching, are subordinated to this. (p. 87)

[With] Katherine Mansfield much . . . depends on the actual presentation of the story. Neither she nor her characters make lengthy comment; the meaning of the situation is never *stated,* but implied. Her endeavour is to put the story in a position to illuminate itself; the parts throw light on the whole and the whole throws light on the parts so that, for example, the change at the end puts new meaning into what has gone before, putting everything into a new perspective which we had not been aware of until we arrived at the end. (pp. 91-2)

That she had a tendency in [a sentimental] direction is shown by occasional false touches throughout her work. . . .

As a rule Katherine Mansfield manages to bring out the significance of a situation with greater economy and a surer touch. (p. 93)

Objective truth was always Katherine Mansfield's aim in her stories. She wished to become the supreme recorder, free from all personal bias and even interest. . . . Yet sometimes the reader is left a little in doubt whether the story is told in terms of the thought of the observer or the observed. The meaning of the situation is the meaning for those concerned in it, but occasionally we find the writer herself entering into the situation for an instant. (pp. 94-5)

We find this occasionally throughout the stories—the spectator becoming too interested to hold aloof and allowing her own consciousness to enter. It is just because her approach is usually so objective that we notice those occasions where, only for a moment, she allows the subjective element to enter. Of course, in pure description the author must talk to some extent in her own person, but once the characters are set going and the story is told in terms of *their* minds any intrusion by the author is dangerous. There are few authors who intrude so rarely as Katherine Mansfield, who, when she does intrude, does it in this almost imperceptible way, substituting her own imagination directly just for a sentence or two. . . . (pp. 95-6)

Only in her less successful moments does Katherine Mansfield give us some notion of the difficulty of the achievement involved in her successful work. Her writing at its best has a purity rare in literature. . . . She wrote no more than she saw, but she saw so much in the least human activity that she never needed to do more than record her observations. (pp. 96-7)

Katherine Mansfield's method lies somewhere between the traditional one and that of Joyce and other modern writers. She refuses to sacrifice her powers of independent observation, but at the same time she takes note of nothing which is not in the highest sense relevant to the situation she is presenting. She frees herself by a deliberate effort from any irrelevant emotion or pre-supposition. (p. 106)

Sometimes Katherine Mansfield succumbs to the temptation of substituting her own clear vision for the blindness of those whose reactions she is portraying. But she never does this sufficiently to interfere with the reality of the story or with that creation of atmosphere which is one of her greatest achievements. (p. 108)

Katherine Mansfield's development was the result of increased consciousness of what she wanted to achieve in her writing. She was not one of those writers who improve with practice automatically. (p. 113)

The time has come when we can look back on Katherine Mansfield's work and place it in its true perspective. We can see it now as one of the greatest contributions to the development of the art of the short story ever made. Her work has shown new possibilities for the small-scale writer, and by the uniqueness of its achievement points the way to a new critical approach to that age-long problem, the relation of "art" to "life." No writer in either the creative or the critical field has yet shown himself of the calibre to profit to the full from this twofold contribution to literature. (pp. 113-14)

David Daiches, "The Art of Katherine Mansfield," in his New Literary Values: Studies in Modern Literature, *1936. Reprint by Books for Libraries Press, 1968, pp. 83-114.*

Elizabeth Bowen (essay date 1956)

[*Bowen was an Anglo-Irish fiction writer and critic whose novels and short stories are often compared to those of Mansfield for their stylistic control and subtle insight into human relationships. In the following excerpt, Bowen discusses Mansfield's narrative experimentalism, the range of her topics, and her development as a writer.*]

[Katherine Mansfield] died in January 1923. . . . One's impression, from her husband's account, is that the end when it did come took her by surprise: she had been beginning again to expect life. And from then on everything, purged of dross of falseness, was to have been different. She was thirty-four, young as a woman, as an artist at the beginning of her maturity—that is, she had entered into her full powers without being yet certain how to command them.

It is with maturity that the really searching ordeal of the writer begins. Maturity, remember, must last a long time. And it must not be confused with single perfections, such as she had accomplished without yet having solved her abiding problems. She had had throughout no guide but her own light, nothing outside to check by, no predecessor. Chekhov was her ally, but not authority. In her field, Katherine Mansfield worked by herself. (pp. vi-vii)

. . . . .

"Katherine Mansfield's death, by coming so early, left her work still at the experimental stage." This could be said—but would it be true? To me, such a verdict would be misleading. First, her writing already *had* touched perfection a recognizable number of times; second, she would have been bound to go on experimenting up to the end, however late that had come. One cannot imagine her settling down to any one fixed concept of the short story—her art was, by its very nature, tentative, responsive, exploratory. There are no signs that she was casting about to find a formula: a formula would, in fact, have been what she fled from. Her sense of the possibilities of the story was bounded by no hard-and-fast horizons: she grasped that it is imperative for the writer to expand his range, never contract his method. Perception and language could not be kept too fresh, too alert, too fluid. Each story entailed a beginning right from the start, unknown demands, new risks, unforeseeable developments. Often, she worked by trial-and-error.

So, ever on the move, she has left with us no "typical" Katherine Mansfield story to anatomize. Concentrated afresh, each time, upon expression, she did not envisage "technique" in the abstract. As it reached her, each idea for a story had inherent within it its own shape: there could be for it no other. That shape, it was for her to perceive, then outline—she thought (we learn from her letters and journal) far more of perception than of construction. The story *is* there, but she has yet to come at it. One has the impression of a water-diviner, pacing, halting, awaiting the twitch of the hazel twig. Also, to judge from her writings about her writing, there were times when Katherine Mansfield believed a story to have a volition of its own—she seems to stand back, watching it take form. Yet this could happen apart from her; the story drew her steadily into itself.

Yet all of her pieces, it seems clear, did not originate in the same order. Not in all cases was there that premonitory stirring of an idea; sometimes the external picture came to her first. She found herself seized upon by a scene, an isolated incident or a face which, something told her, must *have* meaning, though she had yet to divine what the meaning was. Appearances could in themselves touch alight her creative power. It is then that we see her moving into the story, from its visual periphery to its heart, recognizing the "why" as she penetrates. (It could seem that her great scenic New Zealand stories came into being by this process.) Her failures, as she uncompromisingly saw them, together with her host of abandoned fragments, give evidence of the state of mind she voices in anguished letters or journal entries—the sensation of having lost her way. She could finish a story by sheer craftsmanship; but only, later, to turn against the results.

Able and fine as was her intelligence, it was not upon that that she depended: intuitive knowing, vision, had to be the thing. She was a writer with whom there could be no secondary substitute for genius: genius was vision. One might speak of her as having a burning gaze. But she faced this trouble—vision at full intensity is not by nature able to be sustained; it is all but bound to be intermittent. And for Katherine Mansfield those intermittences set up an aesthetic disability, a bad, an antipathetic working condition. Under such a condition, her work abounded, and well she knew it, in perils peculiar to itself. She dreaded sagging of tension, slackening of grip, flaws in interior continuity, numbness, and, most of all, a sort of synthetic quality which could creep in. She speaks of one bad day's work as "scrappy and dreamy." Dreaminess meant for her, dilution.

Subjects, to be ideal for Katherine Mansfield, had to attract, then hold, her power called vision. There occurred a false dawn, or false start, when a subject deceived her as to its possibilities—there were those which failed her, I feel, rather than she them. . . . There was not a subject which did not tax her—raising, apart from anything else, exacting problems of treatment, focus, and angle. Her work was a succession of attempts to do what was only just not impossible. There is danger that in speaking of "attempts" one should call to mind those which have not succeeded: one forgets the no less attempt which is merged in victory. Katherine Mansfield's masterpiece stories cover their tracks; they have an air of serene inevitability, almost a touch of the miraculous. (But for the artist, remember, there are no miracles.) Her consummate achievements soar, like so many peaks, out of the foothills of her working life—spaced out, some nearer together in time than others. One asks oneself why the artist, requited thus, could not have been lastingly reassured, and how it could have happened that, after each, troughs of frustration, anxiety, dereliction should have awaited her once again?

The truth was, she implacably cut the cord between herself and any completed story. (She admits, in the journal: "It took me nearly a month to 'recover' from **'At the Bay.'** I made at least three false starts. But I could not get away from the sound of the sea, and Beryl fanning her hair at the window. These things would not *die down.*") She must not look back; she must press forward. She had not time to form a consistent attitude to any one finished story: each stood to her as a milestone, passed, not as a destination arrived at. Let us say, she reacted to success (if in Katherine Mansfield's eyes there was such a thing) as others react to failure: there seemed to be nothing left but to try again.

To be compelled to experiment is one thing, to be in love with experiment quite another. Of love for experiment for its own sake, Katherine Mansfield shows not a sign. Conscious artist, she carries none of the marks of the self-consciously "experimental" writer. Nothing in her approach to people or nature is revolutionary; her storytelling is, on its own plane, not much less straightforward than Jane Austen's. She uses no literary shock tactics. The singular beauty of her language consists, partly, in its hardly seeming to *be* language at all, so glass-transparent is it to her meaning. Words had but one appeal for her, that of speakingness. (In her journal we find noted: "The *panting* of a jaw.") She was to evolve from noun, verb, adjective, a marvelous sensory notation hitherto undreamed of outside poetry; nonetheless, she stayed subject to prose discipline. And her style, when the story-context requires, can be curt, decisive, factual. It is a style generated by subject and tuned to mood—so flexible as to be hardly *a* style at all. One would recognize a passage from Katherine Mansfield not by the manner but by the content. There are no eccentricities.

Katherine Mansfield was not a rebel, she was an innovator. Born into the English traditions of prose narrative, she neither revolted against these nor broke with them—simply, she passed beyond them. And now tradition, extending, has followed her. Had she not written, written as she did, one form of art might be still in infancy. One cannot attribute to Katherine Mansfield the entire growth, in our century, of the short story. Its developments have been speedy, inspired, various; it continues branching in a hundred directions, many of which show her influence not at all. What she did supply was an immense impetus—also, did she not first see in the story the ideal reflector of the day? We owe to her the prosperity of the "free" story: she untrammeled it from conventions and, still more, gained for it a prestige till then unthought of. How much ground Katherine Mansfield broke for her successors may not be realized. Her imagination kindled unlikely matter; she was to alter for good and all our idea of what goes to make a story. (pp. ix-xii)

. . . . .

One cannot, I think, discuss this artist's work in terms of ordinary progress. One is, rather, aware of greatened deepening and heightening. She taxed herself more rather than less as she went on—she herself remarked the loss of her first facility. The rate at which she abandoned stories shows (apart from the dislocations of sickness) how ever more demanding her art became: at the start she had asked less of it, or it less of her. That burning gaze of hers, her vision, gained in intensity: by the end almost nothing it turned on remained opaque. Her interpretations became more searching—what was spiritually happening to Katherine Mansfield gives signs of itself in the stories, one by one. Her art followed her being's, it would seem, inevitable course. (p. xv)

. . . . .

[There is evidence in Katherine Mansfield's] early stories that she could have been a writer of more than one kind. Alternations went on throughout her working life. In her letters appears a brusque, formidable, masculine streak, which we must not overlook in the stories. Her art has backbone. Her objectiveness, her quick, sharp observations, her adept presentations—are these taken into account enough? Scenically, how keen is her eye for the telling detail! The street, quayside, café, shop interior, teatime terrace, or public garden stand concretely forward into life. She is well documented. Her liking for activity, for the crowd at play, for people going about their work, her close interest in process and occupation, give an extra vitality to stories. Admire the evening Chinamen in **"Ole Underwood,"** or Alice, the servant in **"At the Bay,"** taking tea with Mrs. Stubbs of the local store.

She engraves a scene all the more deeply when it is (as few of her scenes are not) contributory to a mood or crisis. Here, at the opening of **"The Voyage,"** are the awarenesses of a little girl going away with her grandmother after her mother's death:—

> The Picton boat was due to leave at half-past eleven. It was a beautiful night, mild, starry, only when they got out of the cab and started to walk down the Old Wharf that jutted out into the harbour, a faint wind blowing off the water ruffled under Fenella's hat, and she had to put up a hand to keep it on. It was dark on the Old Wharf, very dark; the wool sheds, the cattle trucks, the cranes standing up so high, the little squat railway engine, all seemed carved out of

> solid darkness. Here and there on a rounded woodpile, that was like the stalk of a huge black mushroom, there hung a lantern, but it seemed afraid to unfurl its timid, quivering light in all that blackness; it burned softly, as if for itself.

Fancifulness, fantastic metaphor, play more part in her London (as opposed to New Zealand) scene-setting. Less seems taken for granted. **"The Wrong House"** . . . furnishes one example. Here, in a residential backwater, an unloved old woman looks out of a window:—

> It was a bitter autumn day; the wind ran in the street like a thin dog; the houses opposite looked as though they had been cut out with a pair of ugly steel scissors and pasted on to the grey paper sky. There was not a soul to be seen.

This factual firmness of Katherine Mansfield provides a ballast, or antidote, to her other side—the high-strung susceptibility, the almost hallucinatory floatingness. Nothing is more isolated, more claustrophobic than the dreamfastness of a solitary person—no one knew the dangers better than she. Yet rooted among those dangers was her genius: totally disinfected, wholly adjusted, could she have written as she did? Perhaps there is no such thing as "pure" imagination—all air must be breathed in, and some is tainting. Now and then the emotional level of her writing drops: a whimsical, petulant little-girlishness disfigures a few of the lesser stories. Some others show a transferred self-pity. She could not always keep up the guard.

Katherine Mansfield was saved, it seems to me, by two things—her inveterate watchfulness as an artist, and a certain sturdiness in her nature which the English at their least friendly might call "colonial." She had much to stand out against. She was in danger of being driven, twice over, into herself—by exile to begin with, then by illness. In London she lived, as strangers are wont to do, in a largely self-fabricated world.

She lived, indeed, exactly the sort of life she had left New Zealand in hopes of finding. Writers and intellectuals surrounded her—some merely tempestuous, some destructive. She accustomed herself to love on a razor's edge. Other factors made for deep insecurity. She and her husband were agitatingly and endlessly short of money; for reasons even other than that they seemed doomed to uproot themselves from home after home. As intelligentsia, they were apt to be preyed upon by the intelligentsia-seeking sub-*beau monde*—types she was to stigmatize in **"Bliss"** and again in **"Marriage à la Mode."** Amid the etherealities of Bloomsbury she was more than half hostile, a dark-eyed tramp. For times at a stretch, there was difficulty as to the placing of her stories; individually, their reception was uncertain: no full recognition came till the volume ***Bliss.*** In England she moved, one gets the impression, among nothing but intimates or strangers—of family, familiar *old* friends, neighbours, girlhood contemporaries there were none. Habits, associations were lacking also: here was a background without depth, thwarting to a woman's love of the normal. From this parched soil sprang the London stories.

To a degree it was better, or always began by being better, in the South of France. She felt a release among Mediterranean people and the Midi light reminded her of New Zealand's. It was at Bandol, late in 1915, that she began ***The Aloe,*** original version of **"Prelude,"** and thereby crossed a threshold. At Bandol was suffered the agony out of which the story had to be born. She had come to Bandol to be alone with loss: her brother Chummie, over with the army from New Zealand, had been killed fighting in France. His last leave had been spent with Katherine in London. (pp. xvi-xviii)

[Beginning in late 1919 she] wrote the august, peaceful New Zealand stories. They would be miracles of memory if one considered them memories at all—more, they are what she foresaw them as: a re-living. And, spiritually as in art, they were her solution. Within them fuse the two Katherine Mansfields: the sturdy soul and the visionary are one. The day-to-day receives the full charge of poetry.

> And now one and now another of the windows leaped into light. Someone was walking through the empty rooms carrying a lamp. From a window downstairs the light of a fire flickered. A strange beautiful excitement seemed to stream from the house in quivering ripples.

This is the child Kezia's first, late-night sight of the Burnells' new home. Katherine Mansfield the artist is also home-coming.

. . . . .

The writer was a woman of strong feeling. How quick were her sympathies, vehement her dislikes, total her angers, penitent her forgivingness, letters and journal show. If we had not these, how much would we know of her from her stories? Impersonality cannot but be the aim of a writer of anything like her calibre, and she fought to keep her stories clear of herself. But, human temperament and its workings being her subject, how could she wholly outlaw her own? And temperament played in her work an essential part—it was to provide as it were the climate in which ideas grew and came to flower. That throughout years of her creative life Katherine Mansfield was a sick woman, and that tuberculosis engenders a special temperament, or intensifies the one there already, must be allowed for. It has been more than allowed for—there is danger, in her case as in Keats's, that the medical history be overstressed. We are to marvel at the persistent strength with which Katherine Mansfield the artist threw off the sickroom. She was conscious only of her vocation—she *was* to write, she wrote, and wrote as she did. It may be that brutalities on the part of fate made her the more feel singled out, set apart. The battering at her health accounts for the inequalities of her accomplishment: that there was any trace of the pathological in the art itself, I imagine nobody could assert.

She was not by nature dispassionate. In the New Zealand, the "far-away people" stories, conflict seems stilled—there is an overruling harmony, the seer come to rest with the seen. Katherine Mansfield's ethics and partisanships come through far more in the English pieces (possibly because of their thinner fabric) and in some of those set in the South of France—though in **"The Young Girl"** and

"The Doves' Nest" we again have a shining impartiality. . . . She loved righteousness and hated iniquity: what, for her, constituted those two? She was on the side of innocence and honour: honesty, spontaneity, humbleness, trustfulness and forebearingness distinguish characters she is fond of. No less could she embody what she detested: cruelty or heartlessness, affectation, neurotic indulgence, cowardice, smugness. Indignation at injustice, from time to time, makes her no less inflammatory a writer than Charles Dickens. She concerns herself with bad cases rather than bad systems: political awareness or social criticism do not directly express themselves in the stories. How hard is her bearing against oppressors, how tender her leaning towards victims! Unimaginativeness, with regard to others, seemed to her one of the grosser sins. The denial of love, the stunting of sorrow, or the cheating of joy was to her not short of an enormity—she had an intense regard for the human birthright.

How good is Katherine Mansfield's character-drawing? I have heard this named as her weak point. I feel one cannot insist enough upon what she instinctively grasped—that the short story, by reason of its aesthetics, is not and is not intended to be the medium either for exploration or long-term development of character. Character cannot be more than *shown*—it is there for use, the use is dramatic. Fore-shortening is not only unavoidable, it is right. And with Katherine Mansfield there was another factor—her "stranger" outlook on so much of society. I revert to the restrictedness of her life in England, the eclecticism of her personal circle. She saw few people, saw them sometimes too often. This could account for her tendency to repeat certain types of character. This restless New Zealand woman writing of London deals with what was more than half a synthetic world: its denizens *are* types, and they remain so—to the impoverishment of the London stories. The divorce of the intelligentsia from real life tends to be with her an obsessive subject—aggravated more than she knew, perhaps, by her sense of being far from her home base. Her sophisticates are cut out sharply, with satire; they are animated, expressive but two-dimensional.

In the South of France stories, characters are subsidiary to their environment; they drift like semi-transparent fish through the brilliantly lighted colours of an aquarium. Here, Katherine Mansfield's lovely crystallization of place and hour steals attention away from men and women. Could *she* not bear to examine these winter visitors—idle, half-hearted and non-indigenous? Tense Anglo-Saxons, they contrast with physically equable busy natives—beauty cheats them, Nature withholds her secret. Patient is the husband without a temperament; true is Miss Brill to her fur necktie; the young girl is a marvel of young hauteur. Yet these three, even, no more than brush one's memory: the South of France stories are about moods.

Katherine Mansfield, we notice, seldom outlines and never dissects a character: instead, she causes the person to expose himself—and devastating may be the effect. The author's nominal impassivity is telling. I should not in the main call her a kind writer, though so often she is a pitiful one. Wholly benevolent are her comedies: high spirits, good humour no less than exquisite funniness endear to us **"The Daughters of the Late Colonel," "The Doves' Nest," "The Singing Lesson."** Nor is the laugh ever against a daydreamer.

The New Zealand characters are on a quite other, supreme level. They lack no dimension. Their living-and-breathing reality at once astonishes and calms us: they belong to life, not in any book—they existed before stories began. In their company we are no longer in Katherine Mansfield's; we forget her as she forgot herself. The Burnells of **"Prelude," "At the Bay,"** and **"The Doll's House"** are a dynasty. Related, though showing no too striking family likeness, are the conversational Sheridans of **"The Garden Party."** Of Burnell stock, graver and simplified, are elderly Mr. and Mrs. Hammond of **"The Stranger"**—Katherine Mansfield's equivalent of James Joyce's "The Dead." Alike in Burnells, Sheridans, and Hammonds we feel the almost mystic family integration. Husbands and fathers are convincing; men give off an imposing masculinity. These men, women, old women, young girls, children are in a major key. I do not claim that the New Zealand stories vindicate Katherine Mansfield's character-drawing—the *drawing* is not (to my mind) elsewhere at fault. What she fails at in the European stories is full, adult character-*realization*—or, should one say, materialization? Her Londoners are guessed at, her New Zealanders known. As to the Burnells she had information of the kind not gained by conscious experience. Writing of these people, she dwells upon them—her art grew not only from memory but from longing.

The New Zealand stories are timeless. Do the rest of the Katherine Mansfield stories "date"? I find there is some impression that they do—an impression not, I think, very closely checked on. To an extent, her work shows the intellectual imprint of her day, many of whose theories, tenets, preoccupations seem now faded. It is the more nearly *mondaine,* the "cleverer" of her stories which wear least well. Her psychology may seem naive and at times shallow—after all, she *was* young; but apart from that much water has flowed under bridges in thirty years. **"Bliss," "Psychology"** and **"Je Ne Parle Pas Français"** (technically one of her masterpieces) give out a faintly untrue ring. And one effect of her writing has told against her: it was her fate to set up a fashion in hyper-sensitivity, in vibratingness: it is her work in this vein which has been most heavily imitated, and travesties curdle one's feeling for the original. The idea of her as a literary Marie Laurencin, sponsor of a brood of gazelle-eyed heroines, tends too much to be a prevailing one. In fact in her verve, raciness, husky sensuous poetry, life-likingness, and sense of the moment's drama, she is more often sister to Berthe Morrisot.

She wrote few love stories; those she did today seem distant, dissatisfying. Staking her life on love, she was least happy (I think) with love in fiction. Her passionate faith shows elsewhere. *Finesses,* subtleties, restless analysis, cerebral wary guardedness hallmark the Katherine Mansfield lovers. Was this, perhaps, how it was in London, or is this how Londoners' *amours* struck young New Zealand? She had left at the other side of the world a girlhood not unlike young Aunt Beryl's: beaux, waltzes, muslin, moonlight, murmuring sea . . . We revert to that entry near the close of her journal:— "Take the case of K. M. She has led, ever since she can remember, a very typically false life. Yet, through it all, there have been moments, instants, gleams, when she felt the possibility of something quite other."

The stories are more than moments, instants, gleams: she has given them touches of eternity. The dauntless artist accomplished, if less than she hoped, more than she knew. Almost no writer's art has not its perishable fringes: light dust may settle on that margin. But against the core, the integrity, what can time do? Katherine Mansfield's deathless expectations set up a mark for us: no one has yet fulfilled them. Still at work, her genius rekindles faith; she is on our side in every further attempt. The effort she was involved in involves us—how can we feel her other than a contemporary? (pp. xix-xxiv)

Elizabeth Bowen, in an introduction to Stories *by Katherine Mansfield, edited by Elizabeth Bowen, Vintage Books, 1956, pp. v-xxiv.*

Ian A. Gordon (essay date 1974)

[*Gordon is a Scottish editor and critic. In the following excerpt, he discusses the stories Mansfield based on her memories of New Zealand.*]

> The longer I live the more I turn to New Zealand. I thank God I was born in New Zealand, A young country is a real heritage, though it takes one time to recognise it. But New Zealand is in my very bones.
>
> —Katherine Mansfield

(p. ix)

It has always been recognised that some of [Katherine Mansfield's] best stories are based on her Wellington memories. The full extent of her commitment has been obscured by the sheer mechanics of publishing a writer whose work is done in the short story form. The two collections she edited herself, ***Bliss*** and ***The Garden Party,*** are made up of work of various dates of composition, settings ranging over England, the Continent and New Zealand. She assembled both collections simply from what she had available that was fit and ready for publication in volume form. After her death, four more collections of her work were published. The choice and the manner of presentation in each was determined by [her husband, John Middleton] Murry. He did a series of successive garnerings from her manuscripts, resulting in ***The Doves' Nest*** in 1923, ***Something Childish*** in 1924, the ***Journal*** in 1927, and the ***Scrapbook*** in 1939. Many of the manuscripts are now in the Turnbull Library in Wellington, and a careful examination of these shows that the editorial choice for each collection was quite haphazard. Apart from the fragmentary diary entries (which find their way into the so-called ***Journal***) there was no rationale in Murry's arrangement. Later editions of all her collections have not altered the random order; they are simple reprints. The reader and critic of the final ***Collected Stories*** (which is itself no more than a gathering of simple reprints of the original single volumes) is faced with a series of brilliant single achievements, on which he must impose what unity he can.

Unity there was, and [***Undiscovered Country***], by reprinting in a re-arranged order Katherine's 'New Zealand' stories and sketches, is an attempt to underline those themes that dominated her life as a mature artist. By presenting only the New Zealand stories, some masterpieces—notably **'Life of Ma Parker'** and **'The Daughters of the Late Colonel'**—find no place. The loss is offset by a cohesion that Katherine might herself have imposed had she lived to organise the final arrangement of her work. Her mind was working in that direction. In one of her notebooks (begun in August 1920) she writes that she must 'really get down to my novel *Karori*'. The present collection is probably as close as we shall ever come to *Karori.* It is a family chronicle, seen from the point of view of a child growing up, and told with sophisticated technique. In these stories and sketches, the family name changes; the personal names change too. But we are clearly reading the chronicle of one family, lovingly remembered, memories of 'real' experience merging imperceptibly with the fiction of a creative imagination, the whole distanced by time and space, and unified by the selecting eye of a great prose artist.

. . . . .

> I want to write recollections of my own country. Yes, I want to write about my own country till I simply exhaust my store. Not only because it is a 'sacred debt' that I pay to my country because my brother and I were born there, but also because in my thoughts I range with him over the remembered places. I am never far away from them. I long to renew them in writing.
>
> Ah, the people—the people we loved there—of them, too, I want to write. Another 'debt of love'. Oh, I want for one moment to make our undiscovered country leap into the eyes of the Old World. It must be mysterious, as though floating. It must take the breath. It must be 'one of those islands' . . . I shall tell everything, even of how the laundry-basket squeaked at 75.

Katherine in the 1911 story, **'A Birthday',** had come to terms with her adolescent self. She could now recollect with pleasure—and with advantages—what she had left behind. Two stories, published in 1912, show further use of New Zealand themes. **'The Woman at the Store'** is a violent tale of the colonial backblocks conjured up by a memory of the camping journey of 1907; **'The Little Girl'** is a tender narrative of a father and a small daughter who finally come to understand each other. In **'New Dresses',** of the same date, the whole family play their part. There are, in the next year or so, further New Zealand stories, but interspersed with much else.

What determined the final direction of her writing was the arrival in early 1915 of [her brother, Leslie Beauchamp, nick-named] Chummie, on his way to join the army. He spent his leave with Katherine, and brother and sister spent hours in Katherine's little 'top room' in London, luxuriating in childhood memories. For Katherine the floodgates opened, and she began a series of sketches and reminiscences. Two, **'The Wind Blows'** and **'The Apple Tree'**, appeared towards the end of the year. By October Chummie was dead, killed in a training accident.

The death of her brother was traumatic to Katherine. She fled from Murry, who was powerless to console her. Devastated by grief, and yet utterly professional, she completed in the South of France by early 1916 a long story, **'The Aloe'**, on the Karori years of the family. It was later revised and re-named **'Prelude'**. Thereafter, at intervals in the few years that were left to her, the great, and the lesser, New Zealand stories occupy more and more of the private room of her mind. They did not emerge immediately. The 1917 stories are mainly sketches and she offered few for publication. 1918 saw **'Sun and Moon'** and **'A Married Man's Story'** and the following year some short pieces. It was not till 1920 that she was able to settle down and see clearly how to complete the task she had set herself and for the remainder of her writing life (she ceased in mid-1922) she was working with concentrated fury: **'The Stranger'**, **'Sixpence'**, **'An Ideal Family'**, **'Her First Ball'**, **'The Voyage'**, **'At the Bay'**, **'The Garden Party'**, **'The Doll's House'**, **'Weak Heart'**, **'Taking the Veil'**, **'The Fly'**, **'Six Years After'**, and many lesser—some of them not so much lesser as unfinished—stories sped from her pen; all of them segments of the family chronicle, much of it her most enduring work. When she ceased writing after **'The Fly'**, **'Six Years After'** and **'The Canary'** (all elegies for her dead brother) she had fully repaid her sacred debt. Both as a writer and as a human being she had simply exhausted her store.

. . . . .

> Father at the last was wonderfully dear to me. I mean to be held and kissed and called my precious child was almost too much—to feel someone's arms round me and someone saying, 'Get better, you little wonder. You're your Mother over again'. It's not being called a wonder. It's having love present, close, warm, to be felt and returned.

To uncover an artist's source material offers no explanation of the artistry. Reading Katherine's New Zealand stories raises an immediate question: what was she doing in these stories? She was, first, reconstituting in literary form a Victorian New Zealand middle-class family and the inter-relationship of its members. It is what the English novel had been doing for a couple of centuries. But she was a creative writer of fiction, not a documenting sociologist. She was, specifically, not painting a picture of *her* family. Both critics and biographers have been led astray by a too-ready and facile identification of her characters and the real-life figures that lay behind them. This kind of assumption belittles her achievement and falsifies some of the important people in her life. Even when she appears to be no more than 'remembering'—witness the sketch called (though the actual title was probably provided by Murry) **'A Recollection of Childhood'**—she is creating much more than she is remembering. It is a 'recollection' of a baby sister, Gwen, who died in childhood. One has only to remind oneself that, at the time of Gwen's death, Katherine had just passed her second birthday, to see that the **'Recollection'**, with its rounded and sharply-realised characterisation and its so authentic dialogue, is pure imaginative creation of a high order.

Almost all of the stories are envisaged from the point of view of a girl growing up, the child Kezia in the 'Burnell' group, the adolescent Laura in the 'Sheridan' group. This central figure (seeing eye and focus of the narrative) has, of course, much of Katherine herself. But Kezia-Laura is not quite the Katherine (whom all called Kass) of the 'real' family. Katherine organised her material as a family chronicle, seen through the eyes of one of the younger girls, the four 'real' sisters variously drawn on for the three—sometimes two—sisters of the stories, the narrative focus shifting between the youngest and the second youngest.

If one must be chary of reading too much of the detail of the stories as authentic reminiscences, one must also avoid leaning too heavily on the stories—or any isolated element in them—for biographical information. (pp. xiii-xvii)

Everything in the stories is unquestionably based on experience. Katherine wrote of nothing that she had not herself experienced. But it is always experience transmuted. The children in **'Prelude'** and **'At the Bay'** live the happy world of fantasy she had known as a child. The girls in **'Kezia and Tui'** reflect her friendship in Miss Swainson's school with her Maori class-mate Maata. The Laura-Laurie pair, with the twinned names, mirrors her close relationship with her brother Chummie. The boy hero of **'The Scholarship'**, who wins an award that will take him away from his 'darling little town' to Europe ('and God knows—if he'd ever see it again') echoes Katherine's own relief (and also her private fears) when her father gave her a kind of 'scholarship' that made possible the final departure from New Zealand. Sometimes she will even blend experience from her later life with earlier memories. **'Cassandra'** is a 'Sheridan' story. But the heroine, Cassandra, is now grown up, married, and appeals to her mother for consolation when she thinks her husband has betrayed her. A temporary distrust of Murry provided one part of the story; her New Zealand 'Garden-Party' family provided the other. And Katherine was scholar enough to indicate the assumption of adult burdens by a mere shift in name: the innocent Kass has become Cassandra, the classical forecaster of doom.

Katherine's final achievement in her New Zealand stories was to create, in sharply-realistic and contemporary prose, a romantic dream-world. New Zealand becomes an Arcadian country—'it must', she wrote in one of her notebooks, 'be mysterious, as though floating'. The material was the landscape of houses and gardens in remembered streets, rural Karori, the harbour, the trips to the Sounds, the sea and the beaches. The people ('Ah the people—the people we loved there') are idealised, happy, encapsulated in a world that never was, like the figures in one of Katherine's best-loved poems, Keats' *Ode On A Grecian Urn.*

When she stepped outside that pastoral world . . . she loses touch: she can only reproduce what she overheard or read in the more sensational pages of the local newspaper. What could a girl of her background know of Millie or Ole Underwood or the Woman in the Store, she with her fastidious distaste for the smell of cooking mutton chops, 'commercial travellers and second-class, N.Z.'? This was, arguably, a more 'real' New Zealand than Katherine Mansfield's. In the years of her growing up, New Zealand was publicly attempting to 'leap into the eyes of the Old World', by offering its particular version of a new world in the political acts of Richard John Seddon and the writings of William Pember Reeves. Katherine Mansfield's alternative offer was the 'undiscovered country', a landscape of the mind, a pastoral dream with a higher reality of its own.

. . . . .

> I have a passion for technique. I have a passion for making the thing into a *whole* if you know what I mean. Out of technique is born real style, I believe. There are no short cuts.
>
> I choose not only the length of every sentence, but even the sound of every sentence. I choose the rise and fall of every paragraph to fit her, and to fit her on that day and at that very moment. After I'd written it I read it aloud—numbers of times—just as one would *play over* a musical composition—trying to get it nearer and nearer to the expression—until it fitted her.
>
> I want to write a kind of long elegy . . . perhaps not in poetry. Nor perhaps in prose. Almost certainly in a kind of *special prose.*

Katherine's ultimate achievement was to create a new kind of fiction in a new kind of prose. In her early work there is plenty of sharply observed character, accurately rendered dialogue, neat story-line. But the author is always on the outside, observing and reporting. The beginnings of a new method first appear in **'The Little Governess'**, written in 1915. It was not, however, until she set herself down in early 1916 to write the first version of **'Prelude'** that she finally broke through to a new structure and a new technique, which are the hallmarks of all her later work. There was clearly nothing in her New Zealand memories by themselves that could have made her the finished artist she now became. It was simply that having found her theme, she found her manner.

The structure of Katherine's stories after 1915 abandons the somewhat mechanical progression of events of her earlier work. She herself called the new structure 'the Prelude method—it just unfolds and opens'. The stories are organic and not mechanical in structure, multi-cellular like living tissue. **'Prelude'** has twelve such 'cells', as has **'At the Bay'. 'The Stranger'** has two. Other stories have a single-cell structure. 'The Prelude method' was flexible. Some cells contain brisk narrative (Pat killing the duck in **'Prelude'**; the breakfast scene in **'At the Bay'**); in others action slows to passive absorption (Kezia in the old house in **'Prelude'**); or to static inactivity, the central character of the cell lost in the mind's recesses (Linda Burnell 'dreaming the morning away' in **'At the Bay'**); sometimes the central 'character' of a cell is not a person but a landscape, a seascape, a gardenscape, but all very much part of the 'story'. There is little 'plot', in the traditional sense, but as each cell 'unfolds and opens' the reader is brought in to share the life of the family.

The reader is brought in. How does she achieve this feat of a shared experience? Partly, it is brought about because Katherine herself in her New Zealand stories was able to share in every experience she recorded. 'I've *been* this man, *been* this woman', she wrote Murry after completing **'The Stranger'**, 'I've stood for hours on the Auckland wharf. I've been out in the stream waiting to be berthed—I've been a seagull hovering at the stern and a hotel porter whistling through his teeth. It isn't as if one sits and watches the spectacle. That would be thrilling enough, God knows. But one *is* the spectacle for the time'.

For Katherine, to *be* the spectacle required only her own power of sympathetic recall. To induce her reader to *be* the spectacle was a different matter. It required an originality of technique and a use of prose that is her major contribution to the craft of fiction. It is done at different levels. At one end of the scale, entire passages are interior monologues, the events seen or felt from the point of view of one or other of the characters. The reader is placed 'inside' the character, as in the recorded reverie of Linda in **'At the Bay'** or in the double and overlapping thought-processes of husband and wife in **'The Stranger'.** The technique can be extremely subtle—after three paragraphs of description, Kezia in the seventh section of **'At the Bay'** makes her first spoken entry with a question 'What are you looking at, my grandma?' Kezia has, in fact, been present throughout, the whole prior 'description' of beach landscape having been seen—and recorded—through her eyes. The reader has from the first line been placed 'inside' Kezia's mind, and he is well prepared for her spoken entry because she has been 'in' the scene from the beginning. Technical feats of this degree of virtuosity are regular in the developed Mansfield stories.

Her virtuosity extends down the scale, from the entire shape and structure of a story, through all its components, right down to the level of sentence and phrase. Everything is carefully planned, and carried off brilliantly. One of her most skilful stylistic and structural devices is to switch (within the sentence) from the 'voice' of the narrator to the overheard 'voice' of one of her characters:

> The grandmother's lap was full and Linda Burnell could not possibly have held *a lump of a child* on hers for any distance. **('Prelude')**
>
> 'Bring me some fresh blotting-paper', he said sternly, 'and look sharp about it.' And while *the old dog* padded away . . . **('The Fly')**
>
> He scarcely troubled to clasp her, and they moved away so gently, *it was more like walking than dancing.* **('Her First Ball')**
>
> Finally he flung his overcoat on to the bedside. *At last the fool was gone.* **('The Stranger')**

In each of the above passages, the words I have italicised each indicate a shift in 'voice' from that of the narrator to that of Linda, the Boss, Leila, and Hammond. Each character has been brought directly 'inside' a sentence that began as neutral and externalised narrative.

Katherine wrote many of her stories in a 'kind of special prose', which draws on the stratagems of poetry, notably an unobtrusive—but powerful—use of symbolism: the dying of the bedroom fire in the final pages of **'The Strang-**

er'; the balloonings of Ma Parker's apron (but only by an 'icy wind'); the counterpointed 'gold' and 'white' imagery of the opening of **'An Ideal Family'**, announcing its theme of youth and age; the over-riding symbol that extends even to the title in **'The Aloe'** and **'The Fly'**; the blue/gold symbolism in the early pages of **'The Garden Party'**, which gives way at the tragic end of the story to a collocation of dark/smoky/flicker/shadow/black. There is nothing in the best writing of Katherine Mansfield that is not planned and executed with consummate skill. She is one of the most professional writers in the language and her writing can stand up to the most rigorous analysis. . . . (pp. xvii-xxi)

> *Ian A. Gordon, in an introduction to* Undiscovered Country: The New Zealand Stories of Katherine Mansfield, *edited by Ian A. Gordon, Longman Group Limited, 1974, pp. ix-xxi.*

Andrew Gurr and Clare Hanson (essay date 1981)

[*In the following excerpt, the critics consider the diversity demonstrated in Mansfield's fiction and comment on some principal characteristics, including Mansfield's status as a New Zealand expatriate, her use of the modern, plotless short story form, and the influence of Symbolism on her work.*]

As a writer Katherine Mansfield produced no single magnum opus. Consequently there is no obvious focus for assessing her achievement or even for identifying her distinctive qualities. Readers who follow Leonard Woolf's preferences will take ***In a German Pension*** as her most characteristic achievement, and rank the other stories accordingly ['Her gifts were those of an intense realist, with a superb sense of ironic humour and fundamental cynicism. She got enmeshed in the sticky sentimentality of Murry and wrote against the grain of her own nature,' Leonard Woolf, in his *Beginning Again: An Autobiography of the Years 1911-18,* 1964]. The childhood stories will seem stickily sentimental, products of a maudlin escapism. Readers who find her social analysis, particularly of the oppressed position of women, to be her most conspicuously acute and illuminating feature will similarly range the stories according to a preference for which there is a good deal of supporting evidence but which still provides only a limited perspective on the whole achievement. And the view which takes the New Zealand stories, especially **'Prelude'** and the other stories written for the *Karori* collection, as most characteristic will also be limited in so far as it draws attention away from the distinctive qualities of the stories set in Bavaria or London or France. It is difficult to find a central organising principle for assessing her achievement that does not lead to neglect of some aspect of her work. She shines out through too many lantern-faces for any single perspective to give an adequate view. The best we can do is identify the different perspectives, and which face they lead up to. Of them all, probably the broadest is the one relating her exile to the powerful evocation of New Zealand in the major stories of her last years.

The last seven years of her life, the years of her mature achievements from **'Prelude'** onwards, were years of retreat into art isolation made perfect only inside the private circle of the childhood world that she constructed with such meticulous precision. She continued to use Murry and Ida Baker for physical protection, but in her stories she went where neither could hope to follow. She had written work based on her relationship with Murry—**'Je Ne Parle Pas Français'**, **'The Man without a Temperament'**, **'Psychology'**—but all of them were in some degree part of the dialogue which they maintained throughout their lives together. As such they perhaps lack the complete detachment and freedom, which writing out of more distant recollections provided.

Rather more than half the stories in her total *oeuvre* are based on or set in New Zealand. Murry's version of her outlook—that she hated the closed-off complacency of bourgeois suburban New Zealand until Leslie's death, when, as she put it, 'quite suddenly her hatred turned to love'—is a thorough oversimplification. She was trying out a narrative by 'Kass' about two little 'Beetham' girls early in 1910 (**'Mary'**, published in the *Idler,* March 1910. 'Kass' also appears in **'The Little Girl'** of 1912). **'A Birthday'**, set amongst the Bavarian stories of ***In a German Pension,*** has a New Zealand setting. The story which first drew Murry's attention, **'The Woman at the Store'**, written towards the end of 1911, was based on her memory of the camping holiday she underwent (over 240 miles on horseback) in the Ureweras shortly before she finally left New Zealand in 1908. And two stories written in 1915 before she began **'The Aloe'** have distinct affinities with the later New Zealand material. **'The Apple Tree'**, first published in the *Signature* in October 1915 under the title **'Autumn I'**, is a gently derisive anecdote about her father, told from the viewpoint of his children, girl and boy. **'The Wind Blows'**, published as **'Autumn II'** in the *Signature,* is a more oblique piece about brother and sister, poignant, discontinuous, foreshadowing the symbolist technique which evolved as **'The Aloe'** changed in the following years to **'Prelude'**. Both stories were presumably triggered by the reminiscences of their childhood that she was sharing with Leslie at the time. His death, which took place just before the two stories appeared, changed the tentative, exploratory impulse into a powerful compulsion. From then on she drove towards the ultimate goal of a complete evocation of Karori in a series of minutely detailed epiphanies.

'Prelude' showed her that her New Zealand background was the best quarry for her artistic materials. It contained so much of the experience which, up to that time, she had most deeply lived. Only such experience could be the proper food for her art. This realisation is recorded in a famous journal entry of 1916:

> I feel no longer concerned with the same appearance of things. The people who lived or whom I wished to bring into my stories don't interest me any more. The plots of my stories leave me perfectly cold. Granted that these people exist and all the differences, complexities and resolutions are true to them—why should *I* write about them? They are not near me. All the false

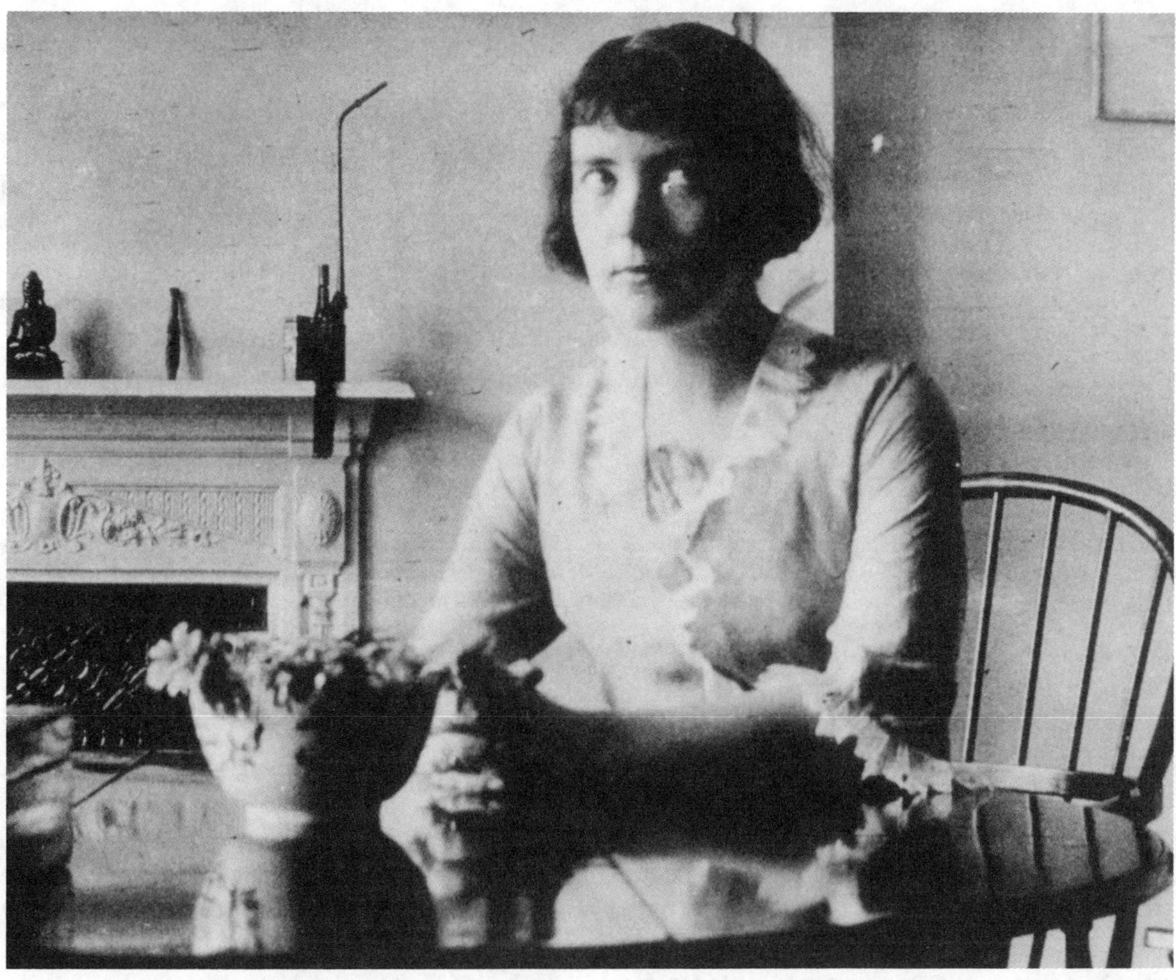

Katherine Mansfield, 1913.

threats that bound me to them are cut away quite.

> Now—now I want to write recollections of my own country. Yes, I want to write about my own country till I simply exhaust my store . . .
>
> Ah, the people—the people we loved there—of them, too, I want to write. Another 'debt of love'. Oh, I want for one moment to make our undiscovered country leap into the eyes of the Old World. It must be mysterious, as though floating. It must take the breath. It must be 'one of those islands . . .'

From this point on, when she began to see her New Zealand background as an artistic positive, something which would both nourish her as an artist and enable her to express something wholly individual, she gained enormously in confidence as a writer.

There is no doubt that she worked at her highest creative level on material that was removed from her in space and time. This is because she was a Symbolist writer, interested not in social contexts and realities, but in the imaginative discovery or recreation of the ideal hidden within the real. With the aid of distance in time and space it is the idealising imagination, or perhaps more precisely what Pater [in 'The Child in the House,' in his *Miscellaneous Studies,* 1910] would call 'the finer sort of memory', which can best discover the ideal essence of experience, which is obscured in the confusion of immediate impressions and perceptions.

Katherine Mansfield and Rudyard Kipling are among the very few writers in English to establish a reputation entirely on the basis of the short story form. It is no accident that they were writing at approximately the same time. The development of the short story in England lagged behind that in America and Russia chiefly because of differences in opportunities for magazine publication. By the 1890s, however, a huge expansion in the numbers of quarterlies and weeklies created the situation described by H. G. Wells [in his introduction to his *The Country of the Blind, and Other Stories*]:

> The 'nineties was a good and stimulating period for a short story writer . . . No short story of the slightest distinction went for long unrecognised . . . Short stories broke out everywhere.

Two entirely different types of story flourished together at the close of the nineteenth century. First, there was the story with a definite plot, which was the lineal descendant of the Gothic tale; and second, there was the new, 'plotless' story, concentrating on inner mood and impression rather than on external event. The latter was associated especially with the *Yellow Book,* the famous 'little magazine' of the nineties, and with the circle of writers gathered round its publisher John Lane—George Egerton, Ella D'Arcy, Evelyn Sharp and others. The innovatory quality of many of the stories published by these writers, and the contribution that they made to the development of the short story, is now becoming increasingly evident.

The plotless story seems to arise naturally from the intellectual climate of its time. In a world where, as the German philosopher Nietzsche declared, God was dead, and evolutionary theory had produced a sharp sense of man's insignificance in a changing universe, the only alternative seemed to be the retreat within, to the compensating powers of the imagination. With such a retreat came the stress on the significant moment, which would be called 'vision' or 'epiphany' by later writers such as James Joyce—the moment of insight which is outside space and time, vouchsafed only fleetingly to the imagination, but redeeming man's existence in time.

In fiction a shift in time-scale seems to accompany this emphasis on the moment. Throughout the nineteenth century the unit of fiction had been the year—from *Emma* to *The Ambassadors* we can say that this was so. In the late nineteenth and early twentieth century, the unit of fiction became the day. Elizabeth Bowen has written of this, saying that Katherine Mansfield was the first writer to see in the short story 'the ideal reflector of the day'. It is perhaps significant, however, that many other writers began their careers with short story writing in this period—Forster, for example, with the aptly named *The Eternal Moment,* and also D. H. Lawrence, James Joyce, and Virginia Woolf. It can even be suggested that the novels of these writers—Lawrence excepted—are in a sense simply extended short stories. Virginia Woolf 's *Mrs Dalloway* is an obvious example, but there is also Joyce's *Ulysses,* originally projected as a story for his collection of stories called *Dubliners,* to be titled 'Mr Hunter's Day'. It is as though the short story is the paradigmatic form of the early twentieth century, best able to express its fragmented and fragmentary sensibility.

Katherine Mansfield certainly saw her kind of story as a quintessentially modern form, a point she makes more than once in her reviews of fiction for the *Athenaeum.* She was also very conscious in her use of epiphany as the focal point of her stories. In one of her reviews she discusses the way in which internal crisis has replaced external crisis of plot in modern fiction, at the same time warning against the loss of all sense of crisis or significance which she detected in the work of some modern novelists:

> Without [the sense of crisis] how are we to appreciate the importance of one 'spiritual event' rather than another? What is to prevent each being unrelated—complete in itself—if the gradual unfolding in growing, gaining light is not to be followed by one blazing moment?

It is usual in discussing Katherine Mansfield as a story writer to emphasise the influence of Chekhov on her technique. The relationship between her fiction and the plotless story of the nineties, however, is probably more important. She modelled her early stories on those of the *Yellow Book* writers, and it is from them, not Chekhov, that she would have learnt the techniques of stylised interior monologue, flashback and daydream which became so important in her work. By 1909, which was when she probably first read Chekhov, his techniques must have seemed distinctly old-fashioned by comparison with much English fiction.

Chekhov was probably more interesting to her as a type of the artist, especially after she contracted the tuberculosis from which he also suffered, rather than being a specific influence on her work. The two writers differ fundamentally in that Chekhov is a far more realistic writer than Katherine Mansfield. His characters are always rooted firmly in a social context, and social forces are shown to have a decisive influence on the course of their lives and feelings. The difference is best shown by a comparison of his story 'Sleepy' with Katherine Mansfield's version of it, **'The-Child-Who-Was-Tired'** (1909). Chekhov's story is a restrained, pathological study, in which action is convincingly related to a specific social and psychological context. Katherine Mansfield's story is a symbolic fable, in which certain elements of the original plot are exaggerated and key images repeated in order to express a general, rather than a specific truth: the harshness of woman's lot in life. Although she read and admired Chekhov's stories throughout her career, a limit must be set on any comparison between the two writers. Any easy identification of the two is misleading.

Katherine Mansfield's talents were peculiarly suited to the short story form, as, in a different way, were those of Kipling. She did, however, try on at least three occasions to write a novel. There is the early attempt, *Juliet* (1906); then a novel to be based on the life and experiences of a schoolfriend she had known both in London and New Zealand, *Maata* (written intermittently between 1908 and 1915); finally the novel, *Karori,* which was to be built around the **'Prelude'** and **'At the Bay'** material, and to be based on the Burnell family. She was planning this last novel as late as 1921-22. Speculation about what she might or might not have written is futile, but clearly she continually wanted to experiment with new forms and to widen the boundaries of her talent. Another way of getting out of the critical rut of seeing her solely as a master of the concentrated short story is to recognise the clear development in her later work towards the use of the story cycle form. Two distinct cycles emerge: that centering on the Burnell family (**'Prelude'—'At the Bay'—'The Doll's House'**) and that centering on the Sheridans (**'The Garden Party'—'Her First Ball'—'By Moonlight'—'The Sheridans'**). Although they are all New Zealand stories, the two cycles are quite separate, and are clearly associated in Katherine Mansfield's mind with different themes. Broadly speaking, the Burnell sequence is concerned with the difficulties of the child or young adult coming to terms with the brutal realities of life (the egotism and cruelty of other people, the pressures of sexuality and so on), whereas in the Sheridan sequence there is a much more elegiac note: the theme is, as Katherine once wrote of Hardy's poems,

> that love and regret touched so lightly—that autumn tone, that feeling that 'Beauty passes though rare, rare it be . . . '

The fact that the two sequences were quite distinct is clear from a journal note written as Katherine Mansfield was planning **'The Sheridans':**

> I must begin writing for Clement Shorter today [this refers to a contract she had with the *Sphere*] 12 'spasms' of 2,000 words each. I thought of the Burnells, but no, I don't think so. Much better, the Sheridans, the three girls and the brother and the Father and Mother and so on . . .
>
> And in that playing chapter what I want to stress chiefly is: Which is the real life—that or this?—late afternoon—these thoughts—the garden—the beauty—how all things pass—and how the end seems to come so soon.

The stories in the Sheridan and Burnell cycles are linked together by character, setting and theme, and by repeated images and motifs. A 'dynamic pattern of recurrent development' is established, so that the reader's experience of an individual story is enriched by and enriches his experience of the others in that sequence.

Katherine Mansfield did not herself separate the short story and novel form as absolutely as genre-conscious modern critics have done, and the cycle of related stories may be seen as a kind of bridge for her between the two forms—rather as in William Faulkner's *Go Down Moses,* or, more relevantly, in Joyce's *Dubliners,* a sequence of stories linked together loosely but firmly by a common setting, related characters and related themes. Joyce similarly employs the symbolist technique of imagery repeated throughout the stories.

The relationship between Symbolism and Katherine Mansfield's short story art has been insufficiently recognised. It is accepted that her contemporary, Joyce, was influenced decisively by his early contact with Symbolist literature, but Katherine Mansfield's critics and biographers have failed to register the similar influences at work in her case. They have dismissed her early writing in the Symbolist mode as immature and, by implication, irrelevant, not seeing the intimate connection between this early work and the particular nature and scope of her achievement.

The main influence on her in the period up to 1908 when she left New Zealand for the last time was that of Arthur Symons, who also influenced so many other early twentieth-century writers, notably Yeats and Eliot. Symons's role was as a communicator and purveyor of ideas. It was through his critical books that Katherine Mansfield was introduced to French Symbolist poetry and to other diverse, broadly Symbolist writers like the Belgian Maurice Maeterlinck and the Italian Gabriele D'Annunzio. She also absorbed very thoroughly the condensed version of Symbolist aesthetic theory which Symons presented in his books. Indeed, her early attempts to piece together an aesthetic rely almost entirely on the writings of Symons, and to a lesser extent Wilde. From these two, she took ideas which continually influenced her art. One was the Symbolist belief that in literature an abstract state of mind or feeling should be conveyed not through descriptive analysis but through concrete images or symbols. Such a theme must be evoked, not described, if it is to be successfully conveyed in art. If we read her stories in the light of this ideal—one which she refers to repeatedly in letters and notebooks—it becomes apparent that in a Mansfield story almost every detail has a symbolic as well as a narrative function. The details, or images, are intended to work in concert to create a mood or evoke a theme which is never directly stated. These oblique and indirect stories must thus be read with the same close responsiveness as a Symbolist or Modernist poem, if the full effect is to be realised.

She was also influenced by the Symbolist belief in the organic unity of the perfect work of art. Even in her earliest stories she strove to achieve the 'unity of impression' advocated by Poe, and she wrote many years later that 'If a thing has really come off it seems to me there mustn't be one single word out of place, or one word that could be taken out.' This particular quotation might tend to suggest that she was concerned only with a superficial perfection of style, but her other references to the 'essential form' of the true work of art make it clear that for her such form was truly organic, uniting form and content indissolubly.

Though the work of art could be considered as analogous to natural organic life, it was also, paradoxically, outside organic life, outside reality. She certainly inherited the Symbolist belief in art as an autotelic activity, a fact which should be stressed as a corrective to the impression, frequently given by critics, that she was a writer with a 'mission' or purpose. In fact she was clear in her belief that, though art must be nourished by life, it had its own laws and nature, which were quite distinct from those of reality. The artist must be completely aware of the distinction, and must not confuse the two spheres, nor attempt to impose his vision on life:

> That is to say, reality cannot become the ideal, the dream; and it is not the business of the artist to grind an axe, to try to impose his vision of life upon the existing world. Art is not an attempt of the artist to reconcile existence with his vision; it is an attempt to create his own world *in* this world.

From Symbolist theory and practice came her interest in extending the boundaries of prose expression. Baudelaire and Mallarmé in their prose poem experiments were interested in steering prose away from its innate structural tendency towards abstraction and analysis, towards a more concrete expressiveness. They and other Symbolist writers—including Pater—attempted to convey meaning in prose not only through the use of words as conceptual counters, but also by exploiting the 'physical properties' of language, and 'sound sense'. They repeatedly used the musical analogy for prose, to signify an ideal of nondiscursive expressiveness, and this is an image which is also used by Katherine Mansfield, for the same reasons, in her frequent discussions of what she was trying to do with her prose medium. For example, she wrote of **'Miss Brill':**

> After I'd written it I read it aloud—numbers of times—just as one would *play over* a musical composition—trying to get it nearer and nearer to the expression of Miss Brill—until it fitted her.
>
> (pp. 14-23)

Katherine Mansfield's reputation is of a writer with an exquisite and delicate sensibility. Her writing is most often described as though it were a kind of verbal equivalent of an Impressionist painting, and stress is laid on the physical 'surface' of her work—its tone, colour and texture. She is commonly praised for her acuteness of ear, her visual memory, her exquisite rendering of impressions of the natural world. There is a string of verbal nouns—flash, colour, sparkle, glow—by means of which her critics have tried to convey the effect that her work has had on them. But it can more usefully and accurately be compared to Post-Impressionist rather than to Impressionist painting, for we need more emphasis on the solidity of the structure of her stories and on their weight of implication. (p. 24)

Andrew Gurr and Clare Hanson, in their Katherine Mansfield, *St. Martin's Press, 1981, 146 p.*

C. A. Hankin (essay date 1983)

[*In the following excerpt from her* Katherine Mansfield and Her Confessional Stories, *Hankin analyzes the narrative structure, imagery, and themes of "At the Bay."*]

The major work of Katherine Mansfield's last years—indeed, arguably her greatest story—is **'At the Bay'**. Frank O'Connor, one of her more severe critics, has given his verdict that **'At the Bay'** and **'Prelude'** are Katherine Mansfield's 'masterpieces and in their own way comparable with Proust's breakthrough into the subconscious world' ['An Author in Search of a Subject,' in his *The Lonely Voice*].

Apart from the length of these works, which makes them more nearly novellas than short stories, and their unusually large cast of characters, they are different thematically from her other stories. The loneliness and emotional apartness which separates one human being from another is in some way central to virtually every story she wrote; and it is central also in **'Prelude'** and **'At the Bay'.** But in these longer works there is an attempt to counteract existential loneliness by presenting characters as they live together within the companionable structure of the family and, in **'At the Bay',** of the universe. As a consequence, the narratives operate on two different levels. There is the surface level, which shows us the comings and goings of family members in the course of an ordinary day; and there is a deeper level which, probing the isolation of individual minds, constantly questions (by implication) the security offered by the family. **'At the Bay'** is both gentler and profounder than **'Prelude'** because here Katherine Mansfield achieves a philosophic resolution to the emotional contradictions of family life.

In another sense, too, these stories stand apart from her other writing. Both were written in response to the certain knowledge of death. Distraught by her brother's death in 1915, Katherine quickly linked his fate with her own death, which she felt must follow. **'Prelude'** became a conscious act of reparation, an attempt to expunge the bitterness she harboured towards her family. By the time she came to write **'At the Bay'** in 1921, the death she had wished so dramatically for herself was looming closer. One doctor had finally admitted that her case was hopeless, and she wrote in her journal, 'Why am I haunted every single day of my life by the nearness of death and its inevitability?' As a healthy young writer, Katherine Mansfield had savoured death in countless romantic, literary gestures. Dying in 1921, she wanted to celebrate life. 'What can one say of the afternoons? Of the evening? The rose, the gold on the mountains, the quick mounting shadows?' she wondered in her journal. 'But the late evening is the time—of times. . . . To write something that will be worthy of that rising moon, that pale light.' With its affirmation of the oneness of the world of nature and the world of man, **'At the Bay'** is surely that story. For what Katherine Mansfield needed to plumb now was not so much the mysterious depths of human relationships: it was the mysterious ebb and flow of life itself. The death which she faced alone had to be seen in the wider, universal perspective of the death—and renewal—of all natural forms. Thus individual suffering, individual regret, give way in this story to a greater but shared pain at the knowledge of life's shortness.

The relationship of death to life is therefore central to the thematic structure of **'At the Bay',** and critics have given it due weight. They have perceived other thematic patterns in the work as well. [In her *Katherine Mansfield*] Saralyn Daly emphasises an inherent contrast between the principles of order and disorder; [in his *The Fiction of Katherine Mansfield*] Marvin Magalaner stresses the significance of freedom versus imprisonment. But, while Magalaner finds that 'as an artistic representation of what life is about [**'At the Bay'**] is masterful', he says that it 'lacks the complexity of imagery and association of **"Prelude"** '. For him, 'the relevance of each episode to the others is not always clear . . . for the good reason that it is not there except in a nebulous, hazy fashion'.

The problem with understanding and evaluating **'At the Bay'** is that no critic has fully explored the rich thematic texture of the narrative, or the wealth of imagery which gives it both power and coherence. Indeed, to analyse the story closely is to see that everything *is* relevant and interconnected and that, if anything, **'At the Bay'** is a more complex work than **'Prelude'.** In the latter, Katherine Mansfield was primarily concerned with the emotional tensions underlying family life. In **'At the Bay'** these tensions are still present, but intertwined with them is an anxiety about death.

What has partly confused readers of these two major stories is Katherine Mansfield's continual refinement of a technique reflecting her early immersion in symbolism. In her adolescent 'Vignettes' she had struggled to find ways at once to represent and disguise 'the forbidden'; when she came to write the ***German Pension*** stories she gave both objects and actions symbolic meaning that was sometimes obtrusive; but by the time she wrote her last, great New

Zealand stories she had learned to handle symbolism so delicately that it virtually defies detection. In **'At the Bay'** there are no such concrete and identifiable symbols as the swelling bird and the thorny aloe tree. Her technique here is a logical extension of her earlier methods, but it is different. With the utmost subtlety she endows the impersonal forces of nature with some of the psychological attributes which in **'Prelude'** were invested in male and female characters, especially in Linda and Stanley Burnell. The most prominent vehicles of symbolic meaning in **'At the Bay'** are the pervasive motifs of the sun as it marks the time, and the sea. Associated with the fiery heat of the sun is forceful masculinity; the sea, which both gives and destroys life, is linked with women in her various guises.

While the cast of characters in **'At the Bay'** is almost the same as in **'Prelude'**, the emphasis has changed, then. Although Linda and Jonathan Trout dream of what might have been, and Beryl at night again conjures up a lover, Katherine Mansfield does not attempt to explore deeply the frightening fantasies of individual minds. The characters' thoughts are revealed to us, but not the workings of their subconscious. And so the symbols which in **'Prelude'** expose the subconscious are no longer prominent. Instead, Katherine Mansfield weaves into her narrative motifs whose universality suggests something very like the Jungian collective unconscious.

As if representing this, the omniscient author quietly uncovers for us the world of nature in its least observed moods, interprets the universal significance of these moods, and shows us the instinctive closeness of human beings to their natural surroundings. 'Very early morning. The sun was not yet risen', the story opens. The voice of the author describing the natural world blends into the background of the narrative. Part of the background also, and at the same time central to the meaning of almost every episode, are the motifs of the sun and the sea.

Inseparable from the sun in its movement through the sky is the idea of time. Time is a structural device which emphasises the limitation of the action to one day and unifies the separate sections of the work. But it also conveys a sense of the unity of all living beings. Time is integral to the author's thematic concern with life's shortness; and it thus bears a weight of meaning which is primarily philosophical. The sun, on the other hand, is frequently associated with psychological themes. Both the patterning of incidents and the attitudes of the characters suggest a correlation between the power and potential destructiveness of the sun, and masculinity. Significantly, Stanley Burnell's daily movements parallel the sun's: he rises with the sun and returns home when the sun sets. And, just as the presence of the sun is felt in virtually every episode of the story, so does the figure of Stanley Burnell, whether present or absent, command more attention than any other character.

The complexity of meaning and patterning in **'At the Bay'** derives partly from the portrayal of some characters' instinctive avoidance of the sun (and heat) and others' conscious association with these forces. Mrs Harry Kember's perverse unnaturalness is characterised by her deliberate and excessive exposure to the sun's heat. Unlike the wholesome and motherly Mrs Fairfield, who protects herself with 'a black hat tied under the chin', Mrs Harry Kember has allowed herself to become 'burnt out and withered. . . . When she was not playing bridge . . . she spent her time lying in the full glare of the sun. She could stand any amount of it; she never had enough. All the same, it did not seem to warm her.' Always known by her husband's forename, 'Harry', Mrs Kember appears to have identified herself with the male element: childless, lacking in femininity, insinuatingly lesbian, she seems to Beryl 'like a horrible caricature of her husband'.

Unlike Mrs Kember, the little Burnell girls go down to the beach wearing sunbonnets; and their mother, in episode VI, is depicted remaining out of the sun in the shady garden. Linda's exposure to the male element in the form of Stanley Burnell (with whom living was like being 'in a house that couldn't be cured of the habit of catching on fire') has left her broken and chilled. Linda, in her fruitfulness, should seem the opposite of Mrs Kember: the archetype of natural woman. But she is not. She is a mother who 'did not love her children. . . . No, it was as though a cold breath had chilled her through and through on each of those awful journeys; she had no warmth left to give them.'

The sun of which Linda will have no part—just as she wants no part of her husband's life-giving potency—is in the next episode depicted as oppressive. 'The sun beat down, beat down hot and fiery on the fine sand, baking the . . . pebbles. It sucked up the little drop of water . . . it bleached the pink convolvulus . . .'. At this point in the narrative, when the sun is at its hottest and most destructive and Kezia and her grandmother are taking their siesta, the theme of death is raised openly. The fate of Uncle William, who, the old woman says, 'went to the mines, and . . . got a sunstroke there and died', underlines the sun's power to kill and maim. As the afternoon wears on and the sun's heat diminishes, the intensity of emotion associated with it abates. Even so, the association between heat and masculinity lingers on in episode VIII when Alice, the servant girl, who carries 'a very dashed-looking sunshade', walks out to visit Mrs Stubbs, the local storekeeper. Mrs Stubbs, with her long bacon knife and her photographs of herself beside such suggestively phallic objects as a Grecian pillar, a giant fern tree and a towering mountain, is another woman with the attributes of a man. Her primus stove exudes heat and, as she talks cheerfully of Mr Stubbs's death, Alice uneasily wishes that she was back home.

The symbolic connotations of the sun in **'At the Bay'** have escaped critical notice, but the complementary motif of the sea has not. Saralyn Daly points out that the sea dominates the entire story, although she does not probe its symbolic meaning. Marvin Magalaner recognises such a meaning and suggests that 'the Jungian idea of water as an ever-moving feminine flow, the archetype of fecund woman . . . may be applicable here'. Water, he says, 'bears a heavy weight of historical, mythical, and psychological meaning'. But he chooses not to pursue the idea of the sea-as-woman. Instead he links the sea-as-life with the theme of freedom versus escape.

One difficulty in coming to grips with the weight of meaning carried by the sea in **'At the Bay'** is that this motif, like that of the sun, embodies meanings that are both philosophical and psychological. Philosophically, the time-sun motif is associated with the theme of death; the sea carries the contrary mythic resonance of birth. In the opening paragraph, the voice of the author describing the gradual awakening of life at the bay hints at the mysteries of creation: 'Perhaps if you had waked up in the middle of the night you might have seen a big fish flicking in at the window and gone again.' The reassuring, mythic overtones of this section give way to something different, however, when Stanley Burnell and Jonathan Trout come out for their morning swim. Possessive of the water, Stanley in his resentment of Jonathan's presence there first acts as if the sea were feminine: part wife, part mother. To be immersed in its depths is to partake of its life-giving qualities—to be reborn and revitalised. But to remain too long in its womb-like embrace (as does Jonathan) is dangerous.

There is a sense, then, in which the sea in **'At the Bay'** is symbolically invested with some of the psychological attributes of woman, especially in her role of mother. In **'Prelude'** there were two mothers: Mrs Fairfield, whose presence was reassuring and unifying, and Linda, the reluctant mother, whose rejection of her role provoked anxiety and divisiveness in the family. While both mothers are present in the later story, their functions have subtly changed. The sea, not Mrs Fairfield, is the presiding mother-deity, the unifying force around which all the characters gather; and the sea (or water) acquires also the negative attributes of Linda in her rejecting, emotionally destructive moods. It is significant that water is especially inimical to men. Both Stanley and Jonathan are left unfulfilled—'cheated'—by their early morning swim. After Stanley leaves for work, Alice underlines the dangers that water holds for the opposite sex. Exclaiming, 'Oh, these men', she holds the teapot 'under the water even after it had stopped bubbling, as if it too was a man and drowning was too good for them'. The idea of water as destructive to men is later picked up comically when Mrs Stubbs reveals to Alice the cause of her husband's death: 'it was dropsy that carried him off at the larst. Many's the time they drawn one and a half pints from 'im at the 'ospital.'

The pervasive motifs of the sun and sea (or water) provide a unifying framework for **'At the Bay'** and very subtly reinforce the emotional tensions in the work. If the sun's heat has the strength and potential destructiveness of a man, water, the opposing element, has a woman's power to deny as well as to bestow life. Revealed with deceptive casualness, an inherent hostility of female towards male imparts emotional relevance to the separate episodes. The first hint of such an antagonism is provided in the opening section by Florrie, the female cat. 'What a coarse, revolting creature!' she thinks as the male sheep-dog passes by. In episode III, after the blustering, bullying Stanley Burnell has left the house, there is a sense of conspiracy among the women: 'Oh, the relief, the difference it made to have the man out of the house. Their very voices were changed as they called to one another; they sounded warm and loving and as if they shared a secret.' As if aware of this feeling, Stanley overreacts to the loss of his walking-stick: 'The heartlessness of women! The way they took it for granted it was your job to slave away for them.' Alice's thought that drowning is too good for a man sums up the latent hostility of this early-morning scene—the only scene where all the family are shown together.

Later, at the beach in mid-morning, the battle between the sexes is portrayed openly. The Samuel Josephs boys and girls continually have to be restrained from fighting one another; and we learn that Mrs Harry Kember is so alienated from her husband that 'some of the women at the Bay privately thought he'd commit a murder one day'. Halfway through the story the theme of sexual hostility reaches an emotional climax. Linda, sitting meditatively apart from the others, makes the admission (paralleling her admission of sexual hatred for Stanley in **'Prelude'**) that the time not spent in calming her husband and listening to his story is 'spent in the dread of having children . . . that was her real grudge against life'. Nor is the theme dropped at this point. In a lighter vein, Mrs Stubbs that afternoon revels in her freedom from married life, enigmatically calling the death of her husband 'a judgmint'. And the frightened turning away of a woman from a man's sexual advances dominates the ending of the story. Beryl, in the closing episode of **'At the Bay'**, wrenches herself free from Mr Harry Kember. Frozen with horror by his 'bright, blind, terrifying smile', she runs from him calling, 'You are vile, vile.'

In **'At the Bay'**, as in **'Prelude'**, there is another side to a woman's resentment and fear of male sexuality: a mother's rejection of her children. Linda's dread of having children is conveyed quite explicitly in the central episode of **'At the Bay'**. She decides that it is 'useless pretending' to love her children and that, as for the baby boy, 'he was mother's, or Beryl's, or anybody's who wanted him.' Linda's unexpected surge of feeling for the smiling infant does not cancel out her earlier expressions of indifference towards her children, and Kezia seems instinctively to understand her mother's attitude. As in **'Prelude'**, she turns to the grandmother for maternal care and is fearful at the prospect of abandonment. 'You couldn't leave me. You couldn't not be there', she agonises, at the thought of her grandmother's death.

It is not only Kezia who exhibits a degree of emotional insecurity, however. Nearly all other members of the family demonstrate, in one way or another, that they, too, yearn for love and suffer from anxiety about separation. Lottie, for instance, is afraid that the two older sisters will hurry to the beach leaving her behind; at the end of the day the children playing in the wash-house are fearful that the grown-ups have forgotten—or abandoned them. 'No, not really forgotten. That was what their smile meant. They had decided to leave them there all by themselves.' But the grown-ups themselves are emotionally anxious. There is Jonathan Trout, who goes about with 'a look like hunger in his black eyes' and whimsically asks Linda for 'a little love, a little kindness'. Beryl, in the closing scene, wants a lover because 'it's so frightfully difficult when you've nobody'. Perhaps Stanley, more than all the adults, suffers from his dependence on being loved and a sense that his needs are constantly thwarted. Trying to punish his wife for her lack of concern over him, he calls out as he goes to work, 'No time to say good-bye!' But Linda, as if she had never noticed, replies to his request for forgiveness at the end of the day with a cutting 'what must I forgive you for?'

There is, then, a clear psychological patterning in **'At the Bay'** which is reinforced by the motifs of the sun and the sea. Less important thematically, yet helping connect the different episodes of the story, is Katherine Mansfield's use of animal imagery. In **'Prelude'**, the repeated bird motif had emphasised a common bond among the female characters: their childbearing function and its ramifications in their emotional lives. Animal imagery in **'At the Bay'** serves several purposes. It adds to the impression that human beings are hardly separable from the natural world in which they live; it introduces a note of humour into the story; and, more significantly, it links the characters and conveys some essential aspects of their personalities. Thus the likening of Mrs Harry Kember with her 'strange neighing laugh' first to a horse and later, when she swims, to a turtle and a rat, underlines her physical perverseness. In this grotesque presentation of the woman there is an implied condemnation of the mannish lesbian who would poison some such vulnerable person as Beryl. The quite different comparison of Alice and Mrs Stubbs to cats is a humorous way of suggesting the common ground they share, and it is a means of reducing the anxiety caused by the appearance of yet another masculine woman in the form of Mrs Stubbs. Animal imagery has sexually ambiguous overtones when Linda, musing in the garden during the morning, fleetingly thinks of her husband as looking like 'a trapped beast'. At the end of the day Jonathan Trout walks with Linda in the same garden and philosophically likens himself to an insect, feeble in its entrapment.

A more light-hearted use of animal imagery occurs in episode IX which is devoted to the children. Earlier, the grandmother's affectionate understanding of Kezia's personality had been expressed when she called her 'my squirrel' and 'my wild pony'. Playing animal snap in the washhouse, the children assume animal names which suggest their own characters. Pip, the dominant boy cousin, identifies himself with the strong, masculine bull; Rags, who follows his brother obediently, becomes a sheep; Lottie, whose personality is still fluid, changes from a donkey (which she behaves like) to a dog, whose part she cannot play. Isabel, a conceited boaster, appropriately becomes a crowing rooster; and Kezia, who is sensitive but able to hit back, is given the role of a bee with power to sting.

The qualities of a masterpiece resist definition. **'At the Bay'** is especially difficult to explicate because the story which appears so simple on the surface is in fact extraordinarily complex. Thematically, it encompasses a whole range of feelings about human life. Woven into the texture of the narrative is a sense of the psychological conflicts between men and women, parents and children. These are the problems of youth, and in the natural course of things give way to the pressing problem of age: anxiety about death. Katherine Mansfield's achievement in this story is to weave into one tapestry the preoccupations of youth and age, and so to balance psychological truths against philosophical truths that they seem indistinguishable. Thus life, death and sexuality are intertwined; and the same motifs which convey a mystical sense of man's continuing life in the endless round of creation are linked with a woman's fear of the hazardous process of giving birth.

But it is not just with the beginning and end of life that the author is philosophically concerned: it is with how best to use the interval between birth and death. There is a choice, Katherine Mansfield implies, between safety and danger: between existing in a kind of inertia or waking sleep (and failing to realise one's potential); and extending life's boundaries through exploration or active discovery.

The contrast between inertia and exploration, like that between death and life, is conveyed through a sequence of motifs which runs through the entire narrative. References to sleep recur in the first half of **'At the Bay'.** In the opening section we hear the soothing sounds of 'the sleepy sea'; then the reemergence of human life is signalled when 'the first sleeper turned over and lifted a drowsy head'. Taking his morning swim with Stanley, Jonathan Trout is preoccupied with the 'extraordinary dream' he had last night. Later in the morning, Mr Harry Kember with his 'slow, sleepy smile' is compared to 'a man walking in his sleep', while his wife is shown lifting 'her sleepy face . . . above the water'. In the garden, Linda Burnell 'dreamed the morning away', the baby boy 'sound asleep' at her side. Not until episode VII when Kezia and her grandmother are taking their siesta together, does the motif of sleep give way to the more sombre one of death.

Katherine Mansfield conveys her sense that exploration, with all its dangers, is preferable to inertia—indeed, necessary, if life is to be experienced to the full—through the characters themselves. In the second episode she implicitly compares the attitudes to life of Stanley and Jonathan Trout. Stanley, who exults as he enters the sea that he was 'first man in as usual! He'd beaten them all again', reacts like an explorer beaten to his goal when he discovers that Jonathan is already swimming. In contrast to Stanley's energy and competitiveness is the other man's lassitude, his preference to 'take things easy, not to fight against the ebb and flow of life, but to give way to it'. The suggestion that life is something to be explored, and that there are discoveries to be made, recurs in the fourth episode. The little Burnell girls look like 'minute puzzled explorers' as they hurry to join their boy cousins searching for 'treasure' in the sand. 'Look what I've discovered', cries Pip.

In the following episode Beryl, on another part of the beach, explores a new and potentially dangerous relationship with Mrs Harry Kember while Linda, lying inactive under the manuka tree, muses about her youthful dreams of exploring with her father 'up a river in China'. Marriage has limited her opportunities, forced on her a different role: 'It was always Stanley who was in the thick of danger. Her whole time was spent in rescuing him.' As the day wears on, the motif of exploration persists. Kezia's uncle William 'went to the mines' in Australia in search of adventure. On a smaller scale, Alice, timidly venturing along a deserted road to visit Mrs Stubbs, is testing out something new. And later the children playing in the darkening wash-house continue their exploration of life's possibilities: 'You were frightened to look in the corners . . . and yet you had to look with all your might.' Similarly frightened but courageous, Beryl, in the final episode, follows through to its conclusion her thought, 'If I go on living here . . . anything may happen to me.' Foregoing the safety of her bedroom, she responds to Harry Kember's mocking challenge, 'you're not frightened, are you? You're not frightened?' by stepping out into the darkness to meet him.

Linda's discussion with Jonathan Trout in episode X brings this theme to a climax and draws together the different threads of the story. 'I've only one night or one day, and there's this vast dangerous garden, waiting out there, undiscovered, unexplored', he laments. Jonathan acquiesces in his entrapment: 'Weak . . . weak. No stamina', he confesses. Linda shares with her brother-in-law a sense of life's shortness, a frustration at the ties of marriage and a passivity which precludes change. But his admission of inertia and defeat is for her an emotional turning-point—and a moment of discovery. The circumstances of Linda's life prevent her from extending the limits of her physical existence, from exploring space: yet she is able to make discoveries of another kind. In the morning she had discovered in spite of herself a new feeling for her baby boy; now, as Jonathan bemoans his helplessness, she inwardly compares him with her husband. The recognition that Jonathan is 'not resolute, not gallant, not careless' causes her to see Stanley in an altered light. She makes her second major affirmation that day when he returns home from work. 'Enfolded in that familiar, eager, strong embrace', Linda rediscovers her love for him as she smiles at, and accepts, his foibles.

Such an affirmation of life is essential to the resolution of the philosophical problem which is raised in **'At the Bay'.** The question, 'Why be born at all?' is implicit in Linda's meditation in the garden that morning. All through the narrative, however, the interpreting voice of the author suggests her own answer to the problem of life's dualisms—to the fact that human beings must live with the knowledge of their own inevitable end; that they are divided between a longing to explore the dimensions of life, and a fear to leave the known and familiar; that they aspire to freedom from family ties yet are emotionally dependent on each other; and that some are forced to accept sexual roles that they would rather be without.

Katherine Mansfield's answer, so subtly conveyed that it is hardly noticeable, is that there is a 'mysterious fitness' and unity in the natural order. Involving the reader with her inclusive 'you', she so merges the world of nature and the human world that they are barely distinguishable. In the mythic opening section where 'you could not see where [the hills] ended and the paddocks and bungalows began', the sea, the little streams and the vegetation not only seem timeless: they seem consciously alive. The awakening animal and human life partakes of nature's timelessness. With his 'velvet trousers tied under the knee', the old shepherd might be appearing from an earlier century, while his sheep which 'seemed to be always on the same piece of ground' are virtually interchangeable with the 'ghostly flocks and herds' which answer them from under the sea.

As we watch the mists lift on yet another morning, we sense an implied reassurance that everything is constantly reborn, that nothing really dies. Another such reassurance about the continuity of life in nature occurs midway through the story. In episode VII, when human beings have withdrawn from the sun's heat, the natural world is again seen to reassert its own life. The voice of the author compares the weed-hung rocks to 'shaggy beasts come down to the water to drink' and each pool to 'a lake with pink and blue houses clustered on the shores'. The voice asks, 'Who made that sound? What was going on down there?'

Against the backdrop of this interchangeable, perpetual life there is an intrinsic rightness to the grandmother's acceptance that death 'happens to all of us sooner or later'. The philosophical problem of death is raised for the third and last time in episode X, when Jonathan and Linda talk in the garden. Earlier in the day, Linda had reflected on the cruel paradox that the petals which 'shone as if each was the careful work of a loving hand' were destined to be wasted. Now, the voice of the author seems to merge with Linda's thoughts in one possible, negative explanation of the wastage inherent in creation: the beams in the sky 'remind you that up there sits Jehovah, the jealous God, the Almighty. . . . You remember that at His coming the whole earth will shake into one ruined graveyard.' And yet all the time counteracting this notion of a tyrannical, Old Testament God is the beauty of nature: the 'rose-coloured clouds', the blue sky overhead which faded and 'turned a pale gold', and the beams which finally seem to Linda 'infinitely joyful and loving'.

From Tolstoy, Katherine Mansfield copied into her journal in 1921, 'Life is everything. Life is God. All is changing and moving and that motion is God.' Imperceptibly, in **'At the Bay',** she resolves the paradox of life and death by fusing a Wordsworthian concept of the oneness of nature and man with her perception that nature itself shares in the attributes of a loving Christian God. And so at the end of this story which juxtaposes a woman's dread of childbearing with the necessity for birth and renewal, we are prepared to return to the beginning—and the continuance of life: 'A cloud, small, serene, floated across the moon . . . and the sound of the sea was a vague murmur, as though it waked out of a dark dream.' (pp. 222-34)

C. A. Hankin, in her Katherine Mansfield and Her Confessional Stories, *St. Martin's Press, 1983, 271 p.*

Clare Hanson (essay date 1985)

[In the following excerpt from her history of the short story form, Short Stories and Short Fictions, 1880-1980, *Hanson closely examines Mansfield's use of Symbolist technique, structure, and imagery in "The Escape."]*

If the use of indirect free form by such writers as Joyce, Virginia Woolf and Katherine Mansfield marked a major step towards the elimination of an authoritative narrator-figure distinct from the characters of fiction, the experiments of Hemingway, Katherine Mansfield, and later Samuel Beckett, with dialogue and monologue take us one stage further, removing even the sense of authorial intervention implied by the use of the third-person pronoun and anterior tense. (p. 77)

Hemingway and Katherine Mansfield shared a belief that prose was an under-exploited medium, an 'undiscovered country still'. [Katherine Mansfield] devoted herself exclusively to the short fiction form. Her fictions, like those of Joyce and Virginia Woolf, are founded on Symbolist principles. Her early notebooks show that she developed a consciously Symbolist aesthetic from her reading of Pater, Wilde and in particular Arthur Symons. She also borrowed the techniques of French Symbolist poetry for her early prose-poems and sketches. She developed the short fiction form deliberately, introducing into it Symbolist poetic techniques like those employed by T. S. Eliot and Ezra Pound. It says a good deal about Katherine Mansfield's conception of the short 'story' form that we find her writing to Virginia Woolf to explain that 'The Love Song of J. Alfred Prufrock' was 'really a short story'. The idea points to the lyrical concentration of her work.

Katherine Mansfield's fictions are built on a technique of suggestion. The themes are not stated directly but conveyed obliquely through concrete images. The idea of the concrete image can be extended in this context to mean the entire composition of a fiction and not just a single motif.

The strength of Katherine Mansfield's Symbolist technique can be fully appreciated only through close reading. **'The Escape'** (1920) is, like her other fictions, a total image, a carefully composed expressive appearance in which each naturalistic detail also functions symbolically, contributing to the expression of a mood or state of mind. The central image is that of the journey, but while this determines the story's narrative structure we know nothing of the purpose of the journey, its setting in place, or the names or appearance of the two travellers.

To demonstrate the complex unity of the story, structure and imagery must be considered as they unfold together. The first paragraph establishes with economy the characteristics of the two main actors. The woman's nervous, overwrought state is indicated by the exaggerated, repetitious speech patterns of her stylised interior monologue. The man seems by contrast lazy and easy-going, forgetful of the time and unable to organise bills and trains.

As the woman surveys in retrospect a scene at the station where the couple missed their train, the details she recalls act as objective correlatives to convey her morbid sensibility. She remembers the children at the windows of the train as 'hideous', recalls the 'glare' and 'the flies' and people who seemed to gather round oppressively. She has been almost overcome by one detail: 'the woman who'd held up that baby with that awful, awful head. . . . "Oh, to care as I care—" '. But, we realise, she cares not for the woman, nor for the baby, but for herself. Her narcissism is underlined in the next paragraph, when we return to the present and she comforts herself, 'pitifully, as though she were saying to somebody else "I know, my darling," she pressed the handkerchief to her eyes'.

On our perception of her narcissism the narrative shifts over to the husband's point of view. He looks at the bag from which his wife has taken her handkerchief and surveys its contents, all of which are thematic motifs in themselves—powder puff, rouge stick, a bundle of letters, pills 'like seeds', a broken cigarette, a mirror, 'white ivory tablets' of notepaper. 'He thought: "In Egypt she would be buried with those things".' But it is spiritual death which is evoked in the imagery of the next section of the story.

The external landscape is presented mainly through the woman's eyes, and she sees only squalid, straggling houses and the boils on the back of the driver's neck—though the narrator also intervenes briefly to point to the beauty which she does not see. The wind then starts 'in front of the carriage a whirling, twirling snatch of dust that settled on their clothes *like the finest ash*' (my italics). Dust and ash are associated with mortality and the death of the body, also with spiritual states of aridity and sterility. It is the suggestion that the springs of the life of the spirit are dried up that is important here.

The emotional distress of the couple is contrasted with the glee of a troop of ragged children who appear 'shrieking and giggling', coming downhill in the opposite direction. The children are 'sunbleached' and natural. They have gathered flowers which they offer to the couple, but they have gathered them artlessly, without any care for effect, mixing different types of flower—'any kind of flowers'—some of them already faded. This natural offering, mixed as life itself, is immediately rejected by the woman who has already been established as one who prefers the artificial to the natural. She flings the flowers back at the children who experience a 'queer' (unnatural) shock.

Before the carriage reaches the summit of the hill tension is increased by a final detail. The man makes as if to smoke but the woman stops him—' "If you could imagine," she said, "the anguish I suffer when that smoke comes floating across my face". . . . ' The smoke, like the powder, raises more dust.

The turning point comes when the woman realises that her parasol has been knocked out of the carriage. At this she is 'simply beside herself': 'My parasol. It's gone. The parasol that belonged to my mother. The parasol that I prize more than—more than . . . ' (Katherine Mansfield's ellipsis). The parasol is the literal embodiment of the fragile protective shell to which the woman clings, the artifice which she sets between herself and the world, herself and her husband, herself and her deeper self. 'Spitefully', therefore, she insists on going to look for the parasol, refusing help for 'if I don't escape from you for a minute I shall go mad'.

In this speech is embodied the central paradox of the fiction for in the next section we see how it is the husband, and not the wife, who 'escapes' from the present, or rather, transcends it.

As the woman moves away the man 'stretches himself out'; a constraint is lifted. He is motionless, and the sun beats down on him: 'The wind sighed in the valley and was quiet. He felt himself, lying there, a hollow man, a parched, withered man, as it were, of ashes. And the sea sounded, "Hish, hish".' In these lines the author invokes images suggesting spiritual death. The man feels himself to be a man of ashes, his spirit turned to dust. His spring of life is parched and withered and he lies helpless, feeling 'hollow' because he is a body without a spirit. His lying in the valley where the wind sighs also has Biblical associations—we recall the valley of dry bones of Ezekiel. But as Eliot tells us in 'Ash Wednesday', the question is 'shall these bones live?'. In the passage quoted above we realise that the man, unlike his wife, is aware of his state, a precondition of redemption or rebirth. He also notices the beauty of the sea. These intimations prepare us for what follows:

> It was then that he saw the tree, that he was conscious of its presence just inside a garden gate. It was an immense tree with a round, thick silver stem and a great arc of copper leaves that gave back the light and yet were sombre. . . . As he looked at the tree he felt his breathing die away and he became part of the silence. It seemed to grow, it seemed to expand in the quivering heat until the great carved leaves hid the sky, and yet it was motionless.

The tree is beautiful and has the quality of inalienable presence that enables the man to lose himself in contemplation of it. He feels for a moment at one with the external world. Yet there is something behind the tree—'a whiteness, a softness, an opaque mass, half-hidden—with delicate pillars'. It is from behind the tree that a voice rises in song, at first also part of the peace and silence, but gradually 'as the voice rose, soft, dreaming, gentle, he knew that it would come floating to him from the hidden leaves and his peace was shattered'. It is through the human art of song—as opposed to the artifice associated with his wife—that the man's moment of vision is deepened and his consciousness extended:

> What was happening to him? Something stirred in his breast. Something dark, something unbearable and dreadful pushed in his bosom, and like a great weed it floated, rocked . . . it was warm, stifling.

The great weed which floats and rocks suggests both more and less than the man's general spiritual malaise. It indicates his relationship with his wife as the specific situation from which he cannot 'escape'. Yet the relationship between husband and wife is symbolic of the wider net of circumstance within which the human spirit is held. From this there can be no escape as such, only the possibility of transcendence. It is in this sense that the man 'escapes', as he contemplates the tree and listens to the song during his 'timeless moment':

> He tried to struggle, to tear at it, and at the same moment—all was over. Deep, deep, he sank into the silence, staring at the tree and waiting for the voice that came floating, falling, until he felt himself enfolded.

The man comes to full consciousness of his position, of the exhaustion of his spirit and the impasse reached with his wife. But in the same moment the beauty of the tree and of the woman's voice make their way into his heart as surely as 'the weed' and are accepted not as passing distractions, but as having as much validity as his suffering. The man transcends his subjective misery because he sees and admits as equally existent the beauty of the external world and of art. Such a moment of vision is the quintessence of modernist short fiction. (pp. 77-81)

Clare Hanson, "Moments of Being: Modernist Short Fiction," in her Short Stories and Short Fictions, 1880-1980, *The Macmillan Press Ltd., 1985, pp. 55-81.*

Kate Fullbrook (essay date 1986)

[Fullbrook is an English educator and critic whose Katherine Mansfield *classifies Mansfield as an important English Modernist. In the following excerpt from that work, Fullbrook assesses some salient characteristics of Mansfield's late fiction through close examination of three stories that are considered among her best and most representative: "Je Ne Parle Pas Français," "Bliss," and "Miss Brill."]*

During the last five years of her life Katherine Mansfield was dying, and for much of that time she knew it. Her literary production during this period was extremely high in volume and in quality, and her ***Journal*** records a pressing desire to write as much as she could as a means to combat her growing isolation. The letters as well as the ***Journal*** during this time exhibit a constant attention to the origins of her fiction, and also record Katherine Mansfield's sense of her art as the last area of freedom left in her life. In these letters she makes an important analogy between her writing and the work of the impressionist and post-impressionist painters as both being concerned with a freeing of the imagination from entrenched forms. Manet, Renoir and Cezanne are all sympathetically mentioned, and in a particularly interesting letter in 1921 to Dorothy Brett (herself a painter) Katherine Mansfield reminisces about the importance to her of seeing a Van Gogh at the First Post-Impressionist Exhibition in 1910:

> Wasn't that Van Gogh shown at the Goupil ten years ago? Yellow flowers, brimming with sun, in a pot? I wonder if it is the same. That picture seemed to reveal something I hadn't realized before I saw it. It lived with me afterwards. It still does. That and another of a sea-captain in a flat cap. They taught me something about writing, which was queer, a kind of freedom—or rather, a shaking free.

The 'shaking free' she mentions here ties in with another, earlier statement, this time to Murry in 1918, in which Katherine Mansfield tried to describe the impetus behind her work. 'I've two "kick offs" in the writing game,' she wrote:

> *One* is joy . . . that sort of writing I could only do in just that state of being in some perfectly blissful way *at peace.* Then something delicate and lovely seems to open before my eyes, like a flower without thought of a frost or a cold breath—knowing that all about it is warm and

> tender and 'ready'. And *that* I try, ever so humbly, to express.
>
> The other 'kick off' is my old original one, and (had I not known love) it would have been my all. Not hate or destruction (both are beneath contempt as real motives) but an *extremely* deep sense of hopelessness, of everything doomed to disaster, almost wilfully, stupidly . . . There! as I took out a cigarette paper I got it exactly—*a cry against corruption*—that is *absolutely* the nail on the head. Not a protest—*a cry*, and I mean corruption in the widest sense of the word, of course.

Both of these stated and contrary motives are evident in the late fiction, with its characteristic moments of wonder at seeing the world in new and surprising ways, and in its underlying disgust with entrenched forms. But the second motive, Katherine Mansfield's original 'kick off', *'a cry against corruption'*, is by far the more important, and provides the impetus for positing new descriptions of 'joy', especially in the late fiction, where Katherine Mansfield's capacity to invent images of post-expressionist vividness and originality surpasses that of any earlier period in her writing.

In the late stories Katherine Mansfield's analysis of gender remains the central instance of her presentation of corruption, which becomes increasingly angry and at times despairing. The characters' masks become heavier. The women characters suffer most, in bodies and rooms and clothes and houses and, ultimately, minds, that are tantamount to prisons. They are hopeless in their seeming powerlessness, unable to assert the autonomy that would also destroy the only identities that they are certain they possess. They continue to be open to various kinds of predation by men that Katherine Mansfield habitually describes as assault. But the men suffer too, from brutalisation of character and false suppression of vulnerability that makes them animals on one hand and emotionally stunted on the other. Under such conditions, word and gesture fail. Katherine Mansfield sees the orthodox pattern of sexual dominance and submission as itself corrupt—when a women character is drawn as dominant, even momentarily, cruelty and distortion are still the operative issues. Sexually, one devours or is devoured. Katherine Mansfield's vision becomes a kind of Darwinian sexual nightmare, a naturalistic view of life that nevertheless denies its inevitability by pointing always to a different order of values signalled by the antagonism of the writing.

The play of the unconscious, too, is given an even bigger part in the late writing, with the self progressively seen as not only fragmented but unknowable. If Katherine Mansfield stresses the mystery of the self *to* the self, a concomitant point is that its inpenetrability to others becomes almost insuperable. Dialogue is seen more and more as a crude and blind gesture across an abyss from one masked and terrified individual to another. And yet the writing, working with the same linguistic tools, strains to reveal that which in the fictional world is portrayed as hidden. For all these reasons, Katherine Mansfield's late writing is profoundly interesting, and the small selection of stories treated here can only provide a suggestion of its power and range.

'Je Ne Parle Pas Français' and **'Bliss'** were written early in 1918, and both register blazing indictments against the sexual mores and opinions of the time. These stories also attempt to devise new ways to represent sexual pleasure and the vagaries of desire that brand both traditional and contemporary 'progressive' views on the subject as inadequate and inimical to understanding.

Katherine Mansfield thought that **'Je Ne Parle Pas Français'** marked an epoch in her development as a writer. As she finished it she wrote to Murry saying: 'I don't want to exaggerate the importance of this story or to harp upon it . . . But what I felt so seriously as I wrote it was—ah! I am in a way *grown up* as a writer—a sort of authority.' The next day she wrote about it with similar confidence: 'I *did* feel (I do) that this story is the real thing and that I did not once (as far as I know) shirk it.'

The excellence of the story lies in its narrative in which the central character is the only direct source of information. The conventions of fiction typically make such a character a locus of sympathy for the reader. Katherine Mansfield plays this convention against itself, denying the inevitability of the correspondence between self-revelation and identification of the reader with the self that is revealed. That she was able to do so had great implications for the status of the reader, and it is scarcely surprising that most of Katherine Mansfield's critics have had difficulties with coming to terms with this story which has probably been the most clumsily read of all her fiction.**'Je Ne Parle Pas Français'** is a brilliantly rendered monologue which reveals the central, corrupted consciousness of Raoul Duquette—gigolo, pimp, *poseur*, artist *manqué* and bisexual fraud—a veritable social monster and a master of contradictions. As he sits in a café, watching the customers, prostitutes and workmen who verify his own feelings of superiority, he recalls his adventure with an English couple and the amusement he derived from the failure of their elopement. Mixed with his pleasure is a seemingly casual attempt at self-justification for his part in the couple's drama. The hidden, but truly revealing theme of his memories is his regret at his failure to exploit sufficiently either the man, Dick Harmon, or the woman, Mouse. Regret, insists Duquette, is an indulgence he never claims: 'I have made it a rule of my life never to regret and never to look back.' But the story is about the pressure of the past on the present and it is deeply concerned with regret—Duquette's regret at losing two particularly enticing victims; the regret of Dick and Mouse at the failure of love; and the angry regret of the governing intelligence of the story on the state of the world it analyses.

Like many modernist works, the time-scheme of the story is convoluted, flickering from the present, to the childhood of Duquette, to the middle-distance of memory. Each level of personal history is tainted by the corruption that culminates in Duquette's narrative itself.

Duquette presents himself as a victim. Repeatedly molested as a child by a laundress, and bribed with cakes for his silence, he has grown into a languid egoist who fancies himself a realist, man of the world and 'first-rate' mind. He dubs his perversity the mark of an artist. Any action, he feels, is permitted to him so long as he has the power to 'feel' intensely, and this is precisely the power he fears he now lacks. In Duquette, Katherine Mansfield attacks a familiar view of the artist as an impresario of the emotions, and condemns it in her delineation of his moral bankruptcy.

Duquette is the complete charlatan. Launching himself as a serious writer he decides that his subject will be the sexual underworld: 'the submerged world. But not as others have done before me. Oh no! Very naively, with a sort of tender humour and from the inside, as though it were all quite simple, quite natural.' This is, of course, what Duquette is giving us in his monologue but with effects other than those he intends. This self-appointed chronicler of tender degradation first meets Harmon at a fashionable Parisian literary party and begins his assault on him—sending him a copy of his aptly titled book, *False Coins,* and telling him about his own 'submerged' life. Duquette at first marks the Englishman as one of his own kind and is highly surprised when Harmon produces a photo of his mother, 'Dark, handsome, wild-looking, but so full in every line of a kind of haggard pride.' Duquette revises his reading of Harmon (though Harmon actually *has* shown the Frenchman a talisman of his 'submerged' life), decides he is a highly desirable social and sexual target, and compares his disappointment when he finds Harmon has left Paris to that of a frustrated fox-terrier.

Harmon soon returns and asks Duquette to engage rooms for himself and a woman. On the day of their arrival the Parisian invents two literary successes for himself (a serial, *Wrong Doors,* and a book of poems, *Lost Umbrellas*). At the station, Harmon, distraught, looks like his mother, 'haggard and wild and proud', while the woman, left behind to tend to the luggage, looks, to Duquette's astonishment, like a baby. Carrying a grey, furry muff that she strokes constantly, Mouse's first words to him are a statement of incapacity—' "*Je ne parle pas français*" '. Duquette is puzzled and observes Mouse in the taxi that takes all three to the hotel.

> For Mouse was beautiful. She was exquisite, but so fragile and fine that each time I looked at her it was as if for the first time . . . She had dark hair and blue or black eyes . . . She wore a long dark cloak . . . Where her arms came out of it there was grey fur-fur round her neck too, and her close-fitting cap was furry.
>
> 'Carrying out the mouse idea,' I decided.

At the hotel, Mouse makes tea with quiet desperation while Harmon unaccountably leaves to post a letter. In fact, he posts himself. The letter he does write is left for Mouse:

> 'MOUSE, MY LITTLE MOUSE, It's no good. It's impossible. I can't see it through. Oh, I do love you. I do love you Mouse, but I can't hurt her. People have been hurting her all her life. I simply dare not give her this final blow. You see, though she's stronger than both of us, she's so frail and proud. It would kill her—kill her Mouse. And, oh God, I can't kill my mother! . . . '

Astounded again, Duquette is also fascinated as Mouse's tears fall: 'With her eyes shut, with her face quite calm except for the quivering eyelids. The tears pearled down her cheeks and she let them fall.' Stranded, with only a little money, at once too frightened and too dignified to pursue Harmon, unable to go back because ' "all my friends think I'm married," ' Mouse is left in Duquette's hands. He too abandons her. As he leaves the hotel he realises: 'Why they were suffering . . . these two . . . really suffering. I have seen two people suffer as I don't suppose I ever shall again . . . ' The connoisseur of 'feeling' feels nothing but surprise at its existence. In the café, safely buffered by time, Duquette fantasies about what he could have done with Mouse—pimped for her, kept her for himself, overseen the destruction of an innocence he is not likely to encounter again. Even he cannot understand why he walked away:

> Even now I don't fully understand why. Of course, I knew I couldn't have kept it up. That had a great deal to do with it. But you would have though, putting it at its lowest, curiosity couldn't have kept my fox-terrier nose away . . .
>
> *Je ne parle pas français.* That was her swan song for me.

The *'français'* that Mouse does not speak is the 'language' of corruption, egoism and of the stated valuing of emotional sensation that in fact fears it. It is a language that Duquette speaks to perfection, that Harmon, with his incestuous leanings and need to avoid adult autonomy by remaining his mother's child, also knows. Dick Harmon, like his namesake John Harmon in Dickens's *Our Mutual Friend,* which Katherine Mansfield read with admiration as she wrote **'Je ne parle pas français'**, is a man travelling in disguise, his capacity for love governed by another's 'will'. Mouse, an image of women as prey, is the ultimate victim, a vulnerable, furry morsel for any 'fox-terrier'. She is perfectly isolated, simply left behind like one of the lost umbrellas in Duquette's spurious book. Mouse is suspended in the narrative, eternally weeping, eternally betrayed in a world in which all but she are initiated into a duplicitous language of desire. She is triply open to attack: by Harmon, who promises a love he cannot deliver; by Duquette, who finds her fragility an invitation to despoilation. Finally, Mouse is self-endangered by her acquiescence to a tradition of feminine honour and feminine passivity expressed in her mouse disguise, her name and her remark about marriage.

The success of the story lies not only in the evocation of evil from the inside (Katherine Mansfield is doing in prose in this story something akin to what Robert Browning did in poetry in *The Ring and the Book*), but also in the multiple readings the tale will bear. From one point of view, the story is one in which traditional maidenly innocence inexplicably stays the hand of radical malevolence. From another, this innocence does not triumph, it is simply abandoned in a world where it is useless. Mouse's innocence is a colluding factor in her suffering. Her unexamined trust of her lover leads to a disaster that invalidates all the patterns of life she knows. From another point of view this is a story about inescapable victimisation and universal warping of desire—Duquette's by the laundress, Harmon's by his mother, Mouse's by the men and by the mask of her feminine role—that generates more victimisation and deformation in turn. In all these views love is either thwarted or irrelevant, and suffering and betrayal are the central facts of experience. Each character is painfully static. Only the reader sees enough to understand the evil of their situation and the only voice heard is that of Duquette, the voice of the world itself, insulating itself from an emotional response to its circumstances.

Finally, the story is most decidedly an attack on a view of art in which, like Duquette, the artist substitutes sexual 'sophistication' for moral judgement. There is a clear hierarchy of condemnation in the story, with the woman as the ultimate prey of the evil that congests the social patterns of which the story speaks.

In **'Bliss'**, Katherine Mansfield again challenges contemporary views regarding sexual sophistication at the same time as she tries to invent a new way to write about the awakening of female desire. Her views on the subject are extremely interesting, and accounts of her 'priggishness' in declining to write explicitly about sexual intercourse in her fiction have completely misconstrued the nature of her objections.

In this matter, Katherine Mansfield's views ran counter to her era, during which the familiar, and by now almost obligatory twentieth-century vocabulary of sexual response in fiction was being devised. In 1920, during the time she worked steadily as a reviewer of contemporary fiction for the *Athenaeum* under Murry's editorship, she announced her disgust with the growth of a particular kind of explicit eroticism in fiction by women writers:

> I don't know whether it's I that have 'fallen behind' in this procession but truly the books I read nowadays astound me. Female writers discovering a freedom, a frankness, a licence, to speak their hearts, reveal themselves as . . . sex maniacs. There's not one relationship between a man and a woman that isn't the one sexual relationship—at its lowest. Intimacy is the sexual act. I am terribly ashamed to tell the truth; it's a very horrible exposure.

It is not only women authors who prompt this response; Katherine Mansfield criticises both Joyce and Lawrence for the same reason. For example, she complains that the characters in Lawrence's *The Lost Girl* are merely 'animals on the prowl . . . they submit to physical response and for the rest go veiled-blind-*faceless-mindless.* This is the doctrine of mindlessness.'

In talking about sexual response herself, Katherine Mansfield works closely to the conventions of obliqueness that characterised nineteenth-century fiction—conventions of metaphor and symbolic suggestion that point to the inextricability of body and mind in desire, rather than adopting the twentieth-century 'empirical' conventions that represent sexual activity as a collision of bodies—mechanical and unproblematic occasions for the manufacture of 'natural', physiological pleasure. Katherine Mansfield understood very clearly that the ideas behind these new conventions were extremely suspect, that they meant, as Stephen Heath puts it in *The Sexual Fix,* 'not liberation but a myth, an ideology, the definition of a new mode of conformity' which contained as many unacceptable and unexamined implications for women as more recognisably traditional notions of women's sexual blankness or rapaciousness. This does not mean that Katherine Mansfield was not interested in the subject, she would scarcely belong to this century if she were not. But the *kind* of account she gives of desire works in a different direction to that of most other modernist writers.

'Bliss' takes account of the impact of socially dictated patterns which structure the individual's conception of what should legitimately satisfy desire, and enacts the wonder and distress that follows from an awakening to the insufficiency of those definitions. Katherine Mansfield sees desire as diffuse and unpredictable, and in the story shows her awareness of the fine mesh of social definition that is supposed to contain, express and control the desires of an advanced, western woman.

It is because of this social theme that **'Bliss'** is crowded with people, in this case members of a smart London arty set, the kind of sophisticated social group that Katherine Mansfield often pilloried. The bantering cleverness of her satire of the set—Mrs Norman Knight, with her coat patterned with monkeys, plays crudely for shock value; Eddie Warren enthuses about a line in the latest poem in the latest review: ' "Why Must it Always be Tomato Soup?" '—gives a representation in the narrative of the pretensions it mocks. The group is wrapped in conventions, though it takes itself to be frightfully liberated and knowing.

Liberation and knowledge are exactly what are in question for Bertha Young, the thirty-year-old hostess of the party that takes place in the story and whose consciousness is reflected in the writing. As far as she consciously knows, she has everything she has been told she could want:

> She was young. Harry and she were as much in love as ever, and they got on splendidly and were really good pals. She had an adorable baby. They didn't have to worry about money. They had this absolutely satisfactory house and garden. And friends—modern thrilling friends, writers and painters and poets and people keen on social questions—just the kind of friends they wanted. And then there were books, and there was music, and she had found a wonderful little dressmaker, and they were going abroad in the summer and their new cook made the most superb omelettes . . .

As she consciously rifles through her assets, Bertha tries hard to find the item that will 'prove' to herself she is happy. The barely suppressible waves of emotion that Bertha identifies as 'bliss' at the opening of the story are really signs of the hysteria that threatens to overcome her and that negates her conviction of well-being. She feels that this 'bliss', despite her modern 'freedom', is something she must hide:

> Oh, is there no way you can express it without being 'drunk and disorderly?' How idiotic civili-

> sation is! Why be given a body if you have to keep it shut up in a case like a rare, rare fiddle?

The story makes it clear that Bertha is caught between two 'civilised' conventions of female desire—the convention that outlaws women's physicality as taboo and unnatural, and, on the other hand, the alternative 'modern' convention that speaks endlessly of desire, defining it and channelling it into patterns that may not accord with individual experience. Even though Bertha's life is supposedly so free, it is, in fact, arranged so that she is restrained from physical contacts of all kinds, though the *talk* about such satisfactions is endless. The result is that the physical contacts she does make electrify her.

Katherine Mansfield deploys various emblems of female sexuality through the story and shows Bertha responding to them. Arranging bowls of fruit becomes such a sensuous activity that Bertha can hardly control herself. Being allowed to feed her baby, who is really 'mothered' by a nurse, pushes her again to the brink of hysteria. As much in control of the imagery as in **'Prelude',** Katherine Mansfield provides the analogues to the danger of sensuous response that so torments Bertha in images of the 'wild' life of the animals and plants that persist in their elemental forms in the city. Even in Bertha's bright modern world, in which consciousness is supposed to have banished secrets, there is her garden, full of its own life in the dusk of her psyche:

> At the far end, against the wall, there was a tall, slender pear tree in the fullest, richest bloom; it stood perfect, as though becalmed against the jade-green sky. Bertha couldn't help feeling, even from this distance, that it had not a single bud or faded petal. Down below, in the garden beds, the red and yellow tulips, heavy with flowers, seemed to lean upon the dusk. A grey cat, dragging its belly, crept across the lawn, and a black one, its shadow, trailed after. The sight of them, so intent and quick, gave Bertha a curious shudder.

Bertha attempts a 'modern' reaction to the scene. ' "What a creepy thing cats are!" she stammered.' The garden, with its flaming Blakean pear tree, heavy Rubensesque tulips and Lawrencian cats, is redolent with sexual suggestion for Bertha, who only unconsciously registers her response to the scene. The image is well chosen. The walled garden itself has been a classic image for unawakened female sexuality since the Middle Ages: here it works as a feature of Bertha's ordinary landscape that suddenly explodes into meaning for her. Katherine Mansfield makes all these associations work in this metaphorical garden of the unawakened woman. The paradox is that Bertha's 'fast' set bases its swagger on its freedom regarding sexual matters. Bertha's acquiescence to these mores is, then, radically fraudulent, though she does not know this. Everything she is is based on a lack of knowledge.

Bertha dresses for her party in the colours of her garden, the bridal colours of white and green of the pear tree and the sky. If Bertha is dressed as a bride, her most interesting guest, Pearl Fulton, is dressed in the silvery, pearly colours of the moon, echoing primitive connections between the moon and full female sexuality. While the dinner guests jabber on (' "Isn't she very *liée* with Michael Oat?" "The man who wrote *Love in False Teeth?*" '), Bertha feels herself in sudden, wordless intimacy with Pearl who surveys the scene indirectly through 'heavy eyelids'. Her bedroom eyes and bedroom manner work powerfully on Bertha who is pulled toward her. Again the 'bliss' returns and Bertha looks for a sign that Pearl has also felt the disturbing link between them. Bertha tries to account for her feelings: 'I believe this does happen very, very rarely between women. Never between men,' she thinks while looking again for a sign from the first adult object of her newly awakened but misunderstood desire. Pearl gives the sign. She asks to see Bertha's garden.

> 'Have you a garden?' said the cool, sleepy voice.
>
> This was so exquisite on her part that all Bertha could do was to obey. She crossed the room, pulled the curtains apart, and opened those long windows.
>
> 'There!' she breathed.
>
> And the two women stood side by side looking at the slender flowering tree. Although it was so still it seemed, like the flame of a candle, to stretch up, to point, to quiver in the bright air, to grow taller and taller as they gazed—almost to touch the rim of the round, silver moon.
>
> How long did they stand there? Both, as it were, caught in that circle of unearthly light, understanding each other perfectly, creatures of another world, and wondering what they were to do in this one with all this blissful treasure that burned in their bosoms, and dropped, in silver flowers, from their hair and hands.

Or so Bertha interprets their communion. The reader, of course, is meant to see things differently. While Bertha dramatically reveals the garden of her sexual potential in triumph to a creature who has finally become the focus for her crystallised desire in a way that Bertha herself does not understand, she does not know that she is standing with a woman who is already emblematically identified with the full moon high above the garden, and already in her own communion with the phallic implications of the pear tree which Bertha disregards, but which are also a part of its significance. Symbolically, both women are bathed in the light of the moon of female sexuality, but Pearl already *is* the moon; Bertha is merely the guardian of a garden, hidden behind windows and curtains, stunned by the moon's light.

Bertha's free-flowing sexual response moves from Pearl to her own husband. For the first time she desires him. As she takes cognisance of this amazing new sensation, she identifies the source of the 'bliss' she has been fighting back. And as she looks around to take possession of him when the guests leave, she sees him kissing Pearl. They are lovers. She understands that she has discovered her sexuality only in time to see its first two objects already in full possession of the pleasure she is only on the threshold of knowing. Bertha is left alone, on the edge of an abyss, her bliss turned to dismay, and with the pear tree, bisexual emblem of her just discovered sexual need, 'as lovely as ever and as full of flower and as still.'

Mansfield, 1917.

The ending is one of absolute and bleak exclusion; the outlets for Bertha's belated sexual flowering are suddenly blocked; a possibility is left senseless and dead in her hands. Katherine Mansfield's simultaneous control of a Jazz Age story as characteristic of the period as F. Scott Fitzgerald's, and of a deep structure drawing on a pattern of images that effortlessly shapes the story demonstrates the power of her late technique. The symbols are selected and placed with great tact and evocativeness, suggesting their multiple meanings without ever insisting on them. (For example, Pearl is associated with the moon but also with the grey cat dragging its belly through Bertha's walled garden, her sexuality seen as both utterly transcendent and utterly sordid. At the same time the moon and the cat are both functions of Bertha's unconscious, overdetermined in their meaning by her heightened emotional state.) But the most telling aspect of the story is the ending, with Bertha pushed from the chatter of her self-consciously modern, sophisticated life into the internal crisis whose source she has just discovered and whose cure was theoretically within her reach until the moment she was ready to grasp it.

The double structure of symbol and social critique provides two axes along which Katherine Mansfield can make her observations about the cultural base of women's psychology. Modern assumptions about sex are indirectly shown to be ill-suited to understanding the waywardness and unpredictability of individual response. The 'advanced' notions of the **'Bliss'** clique are as useless as the more traditional orthodoxy operative in most of the other stories. The ethical undertones of the story are still more complex. **'Bliss'** not only raises difficult questions about loyalties inside and outside of marriage and that place that sexuality holds within it, but also about the kind of freedom enacted as self-serving practice. Betrayed by both male and female, and part of a set that would not recognise Pearl and Harry's affair as betrayal at all, Bertha's distress must be masked by the hypocrisy of a social posture of openness. Superficial poses of freedom lead here to inauthenticity as surely as surfaces of repression do. The group still closes ranks against the outsider. Bertha is a victim of a psychological game she had no conscious idea she was playing.

If Katherine Mansfield's stories about women psychologically alone in the smart sets of London and New Zealand are painful, those written about women left outside the protective screens of men, money and class are often devastating in their emotional impact. Along with her contemporary, Jean Rhys, Katherine Mansfield has a reputation for her stories of the *femme seule,* and many of her late stories fit into this category. This sub-genre is in many ways a continuation of the nineteenth-century 'governess' novel—we are close to the conventions of *Jane Eyre* here—with the change that there is no hope for a happy ending, no matter how qualified, no chance that the excluded woman will be fitted back, on any terms, into the relationships that are meant to define and enclose her life.

Katherine Mansfield's **'Miss Brill'**, written in 1920, is probably her most famous sketch of a woman alone. As she explained in a letter, she worked to put the story together in terms of 'a musical composition—trying to get it nearer and nearer to the expression of Miss Brill—until it fitted her'. Once again, Katherine Mansfield's mature narrative method operates in the story as the writing strives to convey the experience of Miss Brill through the presentation of events in the vocabulary and cadences of her mind.

'Miss Brill' is the loneliest of all of Katherine Mansfield's stories about lonely women. It is sometimes compared with James Joyce's 'Clay', but is different in tone, in its ultimate significance, and in its impression of participation in the miseries of the woman's consciousness which is portrayed. Like Joyce's little laundress, so extravagantly willing to be pleased by a world that gives her little but hard knocks, Miss Brill is eager to be part of a scene that ruthlessly excludes her. But whereas in the *Dubliners* story we are asked to pity Maria, and we are not sure of the extent to which she absorbs the humiliation we so painfully see, in **'Miss Brill'** the reader is more closely implicated, both with the character and with the world, as we are made to watch the character take the full force of the transformation of her consciousness of herself from participant to exile. It is a cruel process, and Katherine Mansfield refuses to temper any detail of its typicality.

Miss Brill lives alone in France, patching together an income from scraps of English teaching and from reading the newspaper to an invalid. She keeps herself going by reining her expectations in tightly with a chirpy, inconsequentiality of mind and with her conformity to a tattered notion of gentility. Her surroundings smack of the deprivation of a lone woman—a dark little room, her meagre treat of a honey-cake which she looks forward to each week as her only self-indulgence. She most significantly identifies herself with her fur-piece, a decayed thing she keeps in a box under her bed, and which represents to her all the luxury and adventure in life that she convinces herself she shares. She values, too, the sensuality and flirtatiousness of the fur, itself an emblem of the traditional man-fascinating ways out of poverty for a woman that she still obliquely believes apply to herself. But the fur, her only friend, is not what it used to be; even Miss Brill can see that.

> Dear little thing! It was nice to feel it again. She had taken it out of its box that afternoon, shaken out the moth-powder, given it a good brush, and rubbed the life back into the dim little eyes . . . But the nose, which was of some black composition, wasn't really at all firm . . . Little rogue! Yes, she really felt like that about it. Little rogue biting its tail just by her left ear.

The lonely woman feels herself as roguish as her fur as she slips out to the public concert which is her Sunday entertainment. For her, the afternoon in the park is concert and theatre combined, for she feels herself part of a complex drama as she watches the other concert-goers from her bench. She prides herself on her understanding of life and her ability to interpret strangers' affairs from a distance. But her keenest pleasure is in eavesdropping, and at first she is disappointed, as a woman starved for words, with the silent old couple sharing her bench. When a pair of young lovers replace them she is delighted; she loves lovers, they are an unexpected treat. She sees them as the hero and heroine in a thrilling drama she directs and in which she participates. Smiling, she listens to their conversation:

> 'No, now now,' said the girl. 'Not here, I can't.'
>
> 'But why? Because of that stupid old thing at the end there?' asked the boy. 'Why does she come here at all—who wants her? Why doesn't she keep her silly old mug at home?'
>
> 'It's her fur-fur which is so funny,' giggled the girl. 'It's exactly like a fried whiting.'

Miss Brill drags herself back to 'her room like a cupboard' and, without looking, puts the fur into its box. 'But when she put the lid on she thought she heard something crying'. The extraordinary pathos of the story and of Miss Brill herself derives from the depth of the central character's courage and self-control which is nevertheless expended in acquiescence to a view of a woman's function that is bound to abase her. The story portrays a consciousness distancing itself from its own suffering isolation with a tremendous degree of pain and yet with a dignity that is in itself a kind of virtue. Miss Brill is written off as a horror by a code that condemns her on the grounds of sex, age, beauty, poverty and singleness, the same code that Miss Brill herself uses to explain her disappointment with the old couple on the beach and which now comes full circle to indict her as less than human. This is a portrait of a woman caught by the contradictions of social preconceptions that she herself has internalised. What Miss Brill stuffs into the box under the lonely bed of the *femme seule* is, according to the logic of the image, herself. (pp. 86-106)

Kate Fullbrook, in her Katherine Mansfield, *The Harvester Press, Sussex, 1986, 146 p.*

Gillian Boddy (essay date 1988)

[*Boddy is an educator and critic from New Zealand. In the following excerpt from her* Katherine Mansfield: The Woman and the Writer, *she considers Mansfield's development as a short story writer, discussing influences, styles, themes, characterization, and literary techniques.*]

A brief look at K. M.'s letters and journals shows that she was a compulsive writer. Her international reputation as one of the world's best-known short story writers, based on only eighty-eight collected stories, remains secure today. Nevertheless K. M. believed:

> You know . . . I shall not be 'fashionable' long. They will find me out . . . I like such awfully unfashionable things—and people. I like sitting on doorsteps, and talking to the old woman who brings quinces, and going for picnics in a jolting little wagon, and listening to the kind of music they play in public gardens on warm evenings, and talking to captains of shabby little steamers, and in fact, to all kinds of people in all kinds of places. But what a fatal sentence to begin. It goes on for ever. In fact, one could spend a whole life finishing it. But you see I am not a highbrow. Sunday lunches and very intricate conversations on Sex and that 'fatigue' which is so essential and that awful 'brightness' which is even more essential—these things I flee from.

This was how she saw her work and her place in literature. It was, she knew, from life's 'tremendous trifles' that she created her stories. She chose ordinary people, everyday events: a charwoman, a child's dolls house. In this, the creation of something timeless from simple things, she was an innovator. (p. 153)

Her work has been constantly debated, analysed, criticised. For some critics she was a writer's writer, to others a teller of tales. Others saw her work not as stories but as fragments or recollections. A more recent attempt to define the exact nature of her writing is Professor C. K. Stead's analysis of them as 'fictions' as opposed to narratives. At several stages in her life K. M. hoped to write a novel—these attempts included *Juliet, Young Country,* **'The Aloe'**, *Maata, Karori.* Even **'The Aloe',** since published as a separate volume, was never truly completed. It seems very possible that her particular creative gift was for the short story alone; that her unique flashes of creativity could not be sustained. Perhaps she was right in saying that she could never write, 'a whole novel about anything'.

Three of her greatest stories, **'Prelude', 'The Daughters of the Late Colonel'** and **'At the Bay'** are similar to novels in that they are divided into twelve sections or episodes, an unusual device. Each episode has a different focus. They are also longer than the average short story. Many of her New Zealand stories also fall into two cycles: one, the larger, about the Burnell family, the second about the Sheridans. K. M. seems to have felt able to sustain her interest, and the reader's, in these characters. Indeed the stories most critics regard as her finest are from these two groups. Professor Ian Gordon's *Undiscovered Country* fits these together with other stories and journal entries in such a way as to suggest what a novel based on these might have been like. Did K. M. therefore do herself an injustice in saying she would not succeed in writing a novel? If not a novel, perhaps the novella, a piece of prose the length of Ernest Hemingway's *The Old Man and the Sea,* might have been a possible form?

Some of her comments about reviewing do suggest that she regarded contemporary novels 'as simply rubbish on the whole'. For her the short story was apparently the superior genre and the one at which she would have been content to excel.

K. M.'s earliest vignettes published in the *Native Companion,* and her 1908 story **'The Education of Audrey'** show the unmistakable influence of Oscar Wilde in their subject matter, exotic mood and ornate style. From this she moved towards a more naturalistic type of story. Many of the early stories published in ***In a German Pension*** and ***Something Childish but Very Natural*** are immature, superficial, and technically often weak. She herself commented in February 1920:

> I cannot have the ***German Pension*** republished under any circumstances. It's far too *immature* . . . it's not good enough. . . . It's positively juvenile and besides that it's not what I mean: it's a lie.

Though they were often bitter, cynical and disillusioned satires, those early stories foreshadowed her later ones in style, theme and characterisation. There is wit, perception and some early, if uneven attempts at the interior monologue technique which she later developed so successfully. Often overlooked, they contain the prototypes of characters who would later fully develop 'in the round'—Frau Brechenmacher's husband was to evolve into the 'Boss' in **'The Fly'** and the Binzer family became the Burnells.

Many of the ***German Pension*** stories focus on the situation of a young woman, often alone and vulnerable to avaricious, prying strangers. Her ambivalence about her own sexuality and women's traditional child-bearing role was also explored in them. The young bride in **'Frau Brechenmacher Attends a Wedding'** had 'the appearance of an iced cake all ready to be cut and served in neat little pieces to the bridegroom.' Little Frau Brechenmacher lay waiting for her drunken chauvinistic husband, 'her arm across her face like a child expecting to be hurt'. Often the central rather ingenuous female figure was frequently forced to face reality when predatory, physically stronger men made unexpected crude advances.

Frequently the characters in these early stories are caricatured through exaggeration and oversimplification, even labelled as such—Herr Rat, the Young Man, the Coral Necklace. Others are more fully and skillfully developed. The skill with realistic dialogue is already evident, the setting and atmosphere are often clearly evoked. The sharp, sometimes cruel observation of human frailties and stupidities revealed through selected telling details is already fundamental to her stories. The later subtlety is not yet a feature but certain techniques that mark her later writings are already part of her style. These include the compounding of words for effect as in 'a "fancy-not-recognising-that-at-her-first-glance" expression'; the skilful variation of sentence length, including the 'ungrammatical' minor sentence; the quick flash of colour; and the frequent use of simile and metaphor. The central character, often the same woman narrator, is already sometimes revealed through implication and symbolism rather than external description.

These early stories contain the embryonic treatment of the themes she would continue to explore—the essential aloneness and isolation of the human predicament; the conflict between love and disillusionment, between wistful childlike idealism and life's harsh reality, between beauty and ugliness, joy and suffering. For K. M., the juxtaposition of these themes seemed to illustrate life's inevitable paradoxes.

After the destruction of the war she wrote:

> Now we know ourselves for what we are. In a way its a tragic knowledge. Its as though, even while we live again we face death. But *through Life:* thats the point. We see death in life as we see death in a flower that is fresh unfolded. Our hymn is to the flower's beauty—we would make that beauty immortal because we *know* . . .

Eventually she was to see beauty in the inevitability of life's paradoxes but in those early stories it only repelled and frightened her.

Two of her first adult stories set in New Zealand, **'The Education of Audrey'** written in 1908, and **'Old Tar'** have received little critical attention. Each is interesting for different reasons. Not only does **'The Education of Audrey'** show the strong influence of Oscar Wilde, its atmosphere redolent with candles and gardenias, it is also the only one of her stories to combine New Zealand and London in setting. Like its predecessor, the unfinished *Juliet,* it is not great writing but rather quaintly contrived and pretentious, particularly in its philosophising about 'Art' and 'Life'. The heroine's capitulation in the last line is also uncharacteristic. Nevertheless it contains some vivid moments and, more importantly, the use of a phrase that was to become almost a talisman—'Do you remember?' One passage in which Audrey reflects on her inappropriately childlike feelings of happiness is strikingly similar to the opening paragraphs of **'Bliss',** written some ten years later. A comparison of the two suggests something of her development over those years.

'Old Tar', printed in the *Westminister Gazette* and the *New Zealand Times* in 1913, also offers some intriguing comparisons. The theme of disillusionment, of reality shattering a dream, was one she would rework more successfully many times. Nevertheless this is a stronger story, the touches of colour are painted with a surer brush: 'There was no wind; just a breeze rippled over the grass and shook the manuka flowers like tiny white stars down the yellow clay banks of the new road.' This surely is the world of **'The Aloe', 'Prelude'** and **'The Doll's House'.** In her description of Tar, 'a little pale freckled boy with a flop of black hair', K. M. gives us one of her first pictures of a 'real' child. Mrs. Tar who:

> turned into a fine lady and talked of nothing but the inconvenience she'd suffered living in the

> shop for the sake of her 'usband's father and his sentimentalness.

is one of many characters who would be epitomised through the humour of their speech. This and the phonetic spelling of Tar's speech were two devices she continued to use in order to create realistic dialogue. What is more significant is the strong presence in this early New Zealand story of the sea, and of the wind 'snuffling' around the big white house as it was to do later in **'The Aloe'** and **'Prelude'.**

A study of these stories and other early stories such as **'How Pearl Button Was Kidnapped'**, **'A Birthday'**, the haunting **'The Woman at the Store'**, **'Ole Underwood'** and **'Millie'** show that the New Zealand setting and memories which K. M. was to explore so effectively had already been recognised, valued and drawn upon. Thus her 'New Zealand' short stories were not, as was so often thought, the sudden, direct result of her brother Leslie's death in 1915. She returned to this storehouse of memories yet again, early in 1915. This time the results were to be far more significant.

In February 1915 K. M. met her brother briefly and accidentally in London. In Paris in March she began 'my first novel', now identified as **'The Aloe'.** She had in fact begun several 'novels' before: the adolescent *Juliet,* and *Maata* in August 1913, for which she had written a draft outline of thirty-two chapters but had finished only two by mid-November that year. A third had been begun in December that year, *Young Country,* set in Wellington, but only two chapters were again completed. Her ambitious calculations for '24 pages per day i.e. 5000 words—for 15 days 75,000 words' were not carried out.

'The Aloe' would be different. K. M. was still working on it during May 1915. During Leslie's visit to London that summer they revisited the past together. **'The Wind Blows'** was written out of those memories and published in October, the month he died.

Ignoring the war and her own chaotic existence and deep unhappiness she turned again, in her grief, to New Zealand and tried to recreate those early days of their shared childhood:

> I want to write about my own country until I simply exhaust my store—not only because it is 'a sacred debt' that I pay to my country because my brother & I were born there—but also because in my thoughts I range with him over all the remembered places. I am never far away from them. I long to renew them in writing.
>
> Ah the people, the people we loved there—of them too I want to write—another 'debt of love'. Oh, I want for one moment to make our undiscovered country leap into the eyes of the old world. It must be mysterious, as though floating—it must take the breath. It must be 'one of those islands'. . . . I shall tell everything—even of how the laundry basket squeaked at '75'—but all must be told with a sense of mystery—a radiance—an after glow because you my little sun of it, are set. You have dropped over the dazzling brim of the world. Now I must play my part. . . .

It was not easy however to fulfil that sacred debt, to give shape to those memories until, on rediscovering **'The Aloe'** among her papers, she knew it was right and began work on it again.

In **'The Aloe'** and in later stories such as **'At The Bay'** and **'The Doll's House'** she showed her particular skill in creating the world of children, a world of light and shade, overshadowed by the problems of the adult world. She captured the very sound of their voices, their moments of loneliness, fear and happiness. She was one of the first short story writers to evoke this childhood world so clearly, and to regard it as important enough to write about. We share their games of make believe, fantasies, important projects and adventures, their delights and guilt. Few knew better than K. M. the reality and value of the past within us:

> I think the only way to live as a writer is to draw upon one's real, familiar life—to find the treasure. . . . And the curious thing is that if we describe this which seems to us so intensely personal, other people take it to themselves and understand it as if it were their own.

There have been few writers whose life and work seem so inseparable, but there seems little point in debating whether it was her experiences in New Zealand or in England which had the greater influence on her work—she could not have written as she did without the particular combination of both those very different worlds, her own peculiar form of 'geographical schizophrenia'. Rebelling in her youth against the narrow, conventional bourgeois life of colonial New Zealand she had fled to London, Europe and 'Life'. Her experiences there provided her with the basis for many of her stories, including the German ones preferred by Leonard Woolf. Satirical, increasingly sophisticated, they had a quality of toughness in their clear-sighted depiction of society and its values. Increasingly disillusioned by that world, by her contemporaries and by the frequently unsatisfactory nature of her relationship with Murry; by her illness and increasing isolation; by the growing awareness that she had no certain future, she turned back increasingly to the past. Eventually she used those last pictures of childhood in what she acknowledged to be a 'dream' New Zealand, to reconcile the discordant elements in her European stories and many earlier New Zealand ones; and to attempt to resolve the conflicts in herself and in the world as she had known it. D. H. Lawrence remarked of his *Sons and Lovers* that, 'one sheds one's sicknesses in books'. For K. M., too, writing was a kind of therapy.

In her best stories K. M. created something beyond the limitations of time and place. They were the spontaneous but carefully crafted product of her experience of life:

> Even if one does not acquire any fresh meat—one's vision of what one possesses is constantly changing into something rich and strange, isn't it? I feel mine is. 47 Fitzherbert Terrace, p.e., is colouring beautifully with the years and I polish it and examine it and only now is it ready to

> come out of the store room and into the uncommon light of day.

Frequently K. M. recognised the strong autobiographical element in her work even when she had not consciously intended it. She described it later to Murry, 'Funny thing is I think you'll always come walking into my stories. . . . "The man she was in love with".' And, she warned him, 'You will recognise some of the people.' All too often, particularly in New Zealand, people were recognised and quite naturally did not always welcome that recognition. Even the names of many of her characters show the link between fact and fiction, as in Fairfield, the anglicised version of Beauchamp. To her father she wrote in 1922:

> I meant to draw your attention, if I may, to one little sketch, **'The Voyage'**, which I wrote with dear little Grandma Beauchamp in mind. It is not in any way a likeness of her, but there are, it seems to me, traces of a resemblance.

To L. M., whose full name was Ida Constance Baker, she wrote from Cornwall about her story **'Carnation'**, 'I've even put you in as Connie Baker!' Later **'The Lady's Maid'** was perhaps a kind of recognition of L. M.'s selflessness. Certainly she was the model for the sympathetic, gently humorous portrayal of Constantia in **'The Daughters of the Late Colonel'**. At times too K. M. felt she had actually brought 'the dead to life again'.

Interestingly, the first page of the manuscript of **'The Doll's House'** begins, 'When dear old Mrs Hay went back to Wellington . . . ' K. M. then crossed the name out, replacing it with the more anonymous town. Similarly, the early story **'A Birthday'** is clearly set in Tinakori Road, despite the family's German names. At other times K. M. could not herself trace the origin of a particular story. It just evolved. After all,

> When does one *really begin* a journey—or a friendship—or a love affair? It is those beginnings which are so fascinating and so misunderstood. There comes a moment when we realise we are already well on our way—déjà.

Certainly it is difficult to disentangle fact from fiction. K. M. deliberately chose at times to write about her own experiences, her own emotions and fantasies, but often she seems not to have fully understood them herself. They reveal far more of her, her attitudes and her complex personality than she intended. This adds to their fascination—and their relevance. In her intriguing, detailed study of the 'psychological basis' of K. M.'s stories, C. A. Hankin remarks: 'Regardless of what she might say in her letters, however, Katherine Mansfield's truest expression of what she felt for the people close to her appears in her stories' [*Katherine Mansfield and Her Confessional Stories*].

One fascinating example of the way in which K. M. used her own experiences deliberately as the basis for a story seems to have been overlooked. Readers and critics have all agreed that the story **'An Indiscreet Journey'**, is based on K. M.'s own journey to visit Carco in Gray in 1915, the four-day escapade Murry dismissed as a 'fiasco'. In the story the narrator has a letter written to 'My dear niece' asking her to visit her aunt in 'X'. Written by her soldier lover it was, in fact, a ruse intended to convince the Commissaire Militaire that her journey through wartime France was legitimate.

Among Murry's letters to K. M. is one small sheet in another handwriting. Dated 26 March 1915, this letter in French from Aix-les-Gray to 'Ma Chère amie' is signed 'Marguerite Bombard'. It thanks K. M. for her last letter from Paris, speaks of their meeting there again after the war as they had promised, but suggests that in the meantime she should visit Gray as 'Maman' has put a room at her disposal. The letter continues very affectionately then instructs K. M. to obtain a pass. Marguerite Bombard's letter was, like the lover's in the story, an 'unfamiliar letter in the familiar handwriting'. It is, in fact, the only known letter still in existence from Carco to K. M. K. M. had returned to Paris to stay in Carco's flat on 18 March. It would appear she had written to him and he felt sufficiently confident to reply in this way, suggesting another visit. Perhaps they had parted on better terms than Murry had imagined? Her reply, if there was one, is unknown. She returned to England on 31 March, revisiting Paris for twelve days in May. Like the original escapade, the idea of transforming Marguerite Bombard (alias Carco) into Julie Boiffard, Aix-les-Gray into 'X' and the inclusion of the letter in the story was the kind of game that K. M. would have enjoyed.

Her own experiences provided her with the raw material, but she did not seek merely to give a photographic reproduction. Perhaps too much emphasis has been placed on analysing precise autobiographical details; on discussing whether portraits of certain people were either fair or accurate or whether a certain place was really as she described. Like an impressionist painter she worked to convey the light and shade, the overall impression or mood; details were altered, outlines blurred and places, people or occasions merged into a composite picture. Art always transcended reality and real events or people were shaped and manipulated to fit the impression she wished to create.

K. M. was a dedicated artist with 'a passion for technique', determined to find clarity, to 'write simply, fully, freely. . . . ' Truth, above all, came to be the aim of her writing:

> You see for me—life and work are two things indivisible. It's only by being true to life that I can be true to art. And to be true to life is to be *good, sincere, simple, honest.*

She hoped in this way to enable others to see clearly. She felt eventually that neither her life nor her earlier work had been 'true'.

Throughout her life K. M. was constantly evaluating her style ('horrible expression!') and her craft, looking for greater discipline and clarity, altering and perfecting her method of narration, working to find that 'special prose' that was neither poetry nor prose. A comparison of **'The Aloe'** and the final version **'Prelude'** shows how stringent she was in her criticism of her own work.

Vincent O'Sullivan's elegant edition of **'The Aloe'** with its parallel printing of **'Prelude'** on the facing pages assists such a comparison and gives an accessible insight into

K. M.'s creative process. She reworked the original story to tighten it in both structure and style in order to gain the particular effects she desired and, as a result, there is greater precision and coherence. A succession of adjectives is replaced by one precise word; extraneous details stripped away; interesting but superfluous characters, incidents and narrative passages are eliminated. Other incidents or details are added, particularly those which reveal more of the central characters.

A comparison of **'The Common Round'** and **'Pictures'** shows the same ruthless discipline. Some manuscripts show considerable alteration, revision affecting single words or whole passages. Others seem to have flowed spontaneously, requiring little change despite occasional marginal notes such as 'too much description!' Even **'The Daughters of the Late Colonel',** written as it was at such a furious pace, was not greatly altered on a later reading, although the title was changed from 'Non-Compounders'—a reference to school days at Queen's College.

There is careful craftsmanship in her varied style, at times curt, terse, brittle, at others flowing, almost poetry, depending on the mood or situation she was describing. Her sentence construction reflected this care. She was well aware of the effect of a minor or simple sentence, in contrast to longer complex ones. To achieve the specific overall effect she desired she worked consciously at her technique. Even her use of dashes and dots was deliberate—it was not simply a matter of 'a feminine dash'. Of **'Miss Brill',** her 'Insect Magnificat' she wrote:

> I choose not only the length of every sentence, but even the sound of every sentence. I choose the rise and fall of every paragraph to fit her, and to fit her on that day at that very moment. After I'd written it I read it aloud . . . until it fitted her. . . . If a thing has really come off it seems to me there mustn't be one single word out of place, or one word that could be taken out. That's how I AIM at writing. It will take some time to get anywhere near there.

K. M. developed the ability to enter the very minds and souls of her characters. The process of writing was 'a kind of *possession'*. Describing her story **'The Voyage'** she wrote:

> I might have remained the grandma for ever after if the wind had changed that moment. And that would have been a little bit embarrassing for Middleton Murry.

As a result of this remarkable empathy, some of her finest characters are revealed through their own thoughts, memories and feelings and not by external analysis or dissection so that the reader too is able to identify with them as they meet her own requirement that:

> New people have appeared in that other world of ours, which sometimes seems so much more real and satisfying than this one. That they have a life and a being of their own we do not question; even that they 'go on' long after the book is finished.

The reader slips without noticing from one character's mind to another; there is no break or narrative comment necessary. We do not need to be told at the beginning of **'The Doll's House'** that 'perhaps the smell of paint would have gone off' is said in disapproving tones by an adult. We simply know.

One word can reveal the point of view through which an incident or character is seen, and simultaneously more about the character whose vision we share. Through K. M.'s skill with dialogue the characters become living, speaking people. The choice of words, the catching of subtleties of contrasting pronunciation, intonation and inflection convey so much. The children usually speak in short sentences, simply, in 'children's language'. The adolescents and adults speak quite differently depending on their mood. From this we infer a great deal about the speakers. A skilled actress and impersonator, she had a remarkable facility with dialogue, especially children's, which allows her stories to be successfully dramatised, not only for television and radio but in the classroom and on stage. Her own dramatic pieces show how she herself experimented in the area of drama. A sense of rhythm and timing, an awareness of the nuances of speech characterise much of the dialogue, in these and other stories. These dramatic experiments also showed her how a story could progress without a narrator. She was to continue to work towards this elimination of the narrator in her writing, so having a profound influence on short story writing.

Moments of lethargy at times led to an almost physical inability to put pen to paper and consequent deep depression:

> I do still lack application. . . . There's so much to do and I do so little. Life would be almost perfect there if only when I was *pretending* to work I always was working. . . . Look at all the stories that wait and wait just at the threshold. Why don't I let them in? . . . *Next day* Yet take this morning for instance. I don't want to write anything. Its grey, its heavy and dull and these stories seem unreal & not worth doing. I don't want to write; I want to *Live.*

Nevertheless she was determined always to become 'a better writer'. Writing to Murry, she condemned Virginia Woolf for ignoring the war in her novel *Night and Day* which seemed to her 'a lie in the soul. . . . I feel in the *profoundest* sense that nothing can ever be the same—that as artists we are traitors if we feel otherwise; we have to take it into account and find new expressions new moulds for our new thoughts & feelings.' In her published review of the book she was more tactful, but Virginia Woolf was not deceived. K. M. felt the need to develop her own techniques, 'how are we going to convey these over tones, half tones, quarter tones, these hesitations, doubts, beginnings, if we go at them *directly?* . . . I do believe that there is a way . . . It's the truth we are after, no less (which, by the way, makes it so exciting)'.

Characteristically, she often felt she had failed. In the middle of the manuscript of **'Her First Ball'** she wrote:

> All that I write—all that I am—is on the border

> of the sea. It's a kind of playing. I want to put *all* my force behind it, but somehow, I *cannot!*

It was always the next story which would contain everything. In her search for 'the new word' she rejected the style and content of her early stories as well as many of the conventions of short story writing. Even at Fontainebleau, when her work was widely recognised, her idea of the short story was changing. Tired of her 'little stories like birds bred in cages', she hoped some new kind of writing would be the natural result of the spiritual rebirth she envisaged. She had always realised that carefully selected details were incredibly important, 'one can get only so *much* into a story; there is always a sacrifice.'

Inevitably it was her own attitudes which determined that selection. There was 'an infinite delight & value in detail' but it was not for detail's sake alone. Through the careful selection of detail she could *suggest,* and that should be enough. She could not tell anybody 'bang out' about the

> 'deserts of vast eternity'. . . . They are my secret. I might write about a boy eating strawberries or a woman combing her hair on a windy morning & that is the only way I can ever mention them. But they *must* be there. Nothing less will do.

Therefore, instead of telling 'directly' she frequently worked obliquely through implication, suggestion and symbolism. The little lamp in **'The Doll's House'** must surely be one of the most readily understood symbols in prose. A reader may know nothing of terms such as 'symbolism' but the little lamp will inevitably take on a deeper significance. Ordinary inanimate objects seem almost to take on a life of their own.

One of the most important techniques K. M. used in order to 'convey those over tones, half tones' was the use of contrast. At times the carefully developed contrasts provide the framework or structure for the story's events and also suggest the themes.

Frequently too the use of colour, light and shade are important in creating the atmosphere vital to the stories. In **'At the Bay',** the morning sun streamed through the open window 'on to the yellow varnished walls and bare floor. Everything on the table flashed and glittered. In the middle there was an old salad bowl filled with yellow and red nasturtiums.' The beginning of **'The Woman at the Store',** however, is very different: 'The white pumice dust swirled in our faces, settled and sifted over us . . . the sky was slate colour. . . . There was nothing to be seen but wave after wave of tussock grass.' Another contrast is the setting of **'The Wind Blows'** which is mainly an uncharacteristic monochrome.

Another of the characteristics of K. M.'s writing to which critics have paid much attention is her use of imagery. She seems to have been a writer who thought naturally in metaphor. Particularly apt images remain in the reader's mind. Our Else is 'a tiny wishbone of a child . . . a little white owl.' She and her sister are chased away from the doll's house 'like two little stray cats'. Sleek, insinuating, Mrs Harry Kember in **'At the Bay'** swims away 'like a rat'. In **'The Woman at the Store'** the narrator remarks:

> there is no twilight in our New Zealand days, but a curious half-hour when everything appears grotesque—it frightens—as though the savage spirit of the country walked abroad and sneered at what it saw.

When writing about children the imagery is peculiar to their world and strikingly apt, so the doll's house, for example, is 'spinach green', its door like 'a little slab of toffee'. Frequently she used animal imagery and symbolism as a device for hinting at hidden layers of meaning. A striking example of this occurs in **'Bliss'** when Bertha Young stands looking at the tall pear tree 'perfect . . . against the jade-green sky'. Below 'a grey cat, dragging its belly, crept across the lawn, and a black one, its shadow, trailed after. The sight of them, so intent and so quick, gave Bertha a curious shiver.'

The use of symbolism linking the concrete and the abstract, one of the most remarkable features of her work, was at times contrived, as she herself felt in **'Mr and Mrs Dove'.** In other stories a single action or detail skilfully conveys an emotion, image and mood, the external and the internal become one. Certain images recur from her earliest sketches at Queen's College. Others like the wind, flowers and insects and particularly the metaphor of the fly occur constantly, both in her notes and letters as well as in her stories. Like the sun, sea and darkness, mist and trees, they were all an integral part of her vision of life and the fabric of her stories.

Impatient with those who specialised in 'cheap psychoanalysis' she herself was a perceptive writer of unusual psychological insight, so it is not surprising that much has been written about her symbolism and her imagery. (pp. 154-68)

Generally her symbols and images are skilfully woven into the vivid texture of the story; at other times one is selected as the centre of the total pattern, such as the lamp in **'The Doll's House'**, the pear tree in **'Bliss'.** The use of natural elements in particular provides a central symbolism, a recurrent underlying motif linking many of her stories. These then were some of the methods that typified K. M.'s writing, enabling her to convey evanescent moods, to capture the essence of a fleeting moment. But what of the total pattern, the form of her stories?

Describing the form of **'Prelude'** to Dorothy Brett she remarked, 'It's more or less my own invention', and that form was to be gradually perfected and refined. Other important features of that form were the stream of consciousness technique, her use of flashbacks and her skill in conveying the multipersonal viewpoint. These are clearly illustrated in **'The Daughters of the Late Colonel'**—'a huge long story of a rather new kind. It's the outcome of the **'Prelude'** method—it just unfolds and opens . . . It's a queer tale though.' Past and present become fused as the story evolves through the characters' minds. The external narrator is almost eliminated. As so often in her work, the reader is dropped into the story and simply confronted by a particular situation. There is not preliminary establishing and identification of time and place. The reader is immediately involved; it is assumed that he or she has any necessary prerequisite knowledge and is, in a sense, part of the story too.

Some stories make use of interior monologue throughout, others combine some interior monologue or stream of consciousness with more conventional techniques. It is the multi-personal viewpoint, in particular, which has marked her writing. Often, although the story is told through a variety of viewpoints, the focus is most frequently on the central protagonist so that we share that character's experience in particular. At other times, characters or events are viewed through the eyes of different characters, being described in the language and syntax peculiar to that character. As a result of the multi-personal viewpoint we often see the characters from several angles, providing us with a constantly changing perspective.

Today K. M.'s 'episodic' or 'slice of life' technique is perhaps taken for granted but her stories were really the first of significance in English to be written without the conventional plot. The expected sequence of events: exposition, rising action, climax and conclusion have often been replaced by concentration on a moment or episode or loosely linked series of moments. The interest lies not so much in what *happens* but in *why* it happens.

The famous American short story writer, Edgar Allan Poe, had laid down clearly the principles of short story writing. English writers such as Kipling and H. G. Wells had continued to write stories with a carefully structured plot. Other writers, little known today had, however, been experimenting in a magazine, the *Yellow Book,* famous in the 1890s. There does not, however, appear any clear reference in her letters and journals to the *Yellow Book,* and she herself believed that what she was attempting was innovatory.

Sylvia Berkman, who like Marvin Magalaner and T. O. Beachcroft sees many similarities in her work to that of James Joyce, describes her stories as 'the swift, illuminated glimpse into a character or situation at a given moment' [*Katherine Mansfield: A Critical Study*]. By showing us a character at a particular moment so much more is disclosed. At times, it is as if by giving the reader that glimpse of a specific character at a specific moment, as if through an open doorway, she shows them making a gesture or speaking in a way that is typical of that character. That moment allows the reader's imagination to do the rest.

The conventions of time and tense become irrelevant. This flexible manipulation of time was something K. M. was still consciously trying to perfect in the last years of her life. 'What I feel it needs so peculiarly is a very subtle variation of "tense" from the present to the past & back again—and softness, lightness. . . . '

There is no step-by-step development of plot but this does not mean, as one critic has suggested, that we are not moved by her stories because 'nothing happens' to her characters, or that they are merely 'incidents' not short stories. For her people, as for the rest of us, there are the moments of 'the soul's desperate choice'; the moment of crisis, external or internal, the discovery of 'the big snail under the leaf—the spot in the child's lung'. Her stories may appear formless but there is, in fact, a careful pattern of parts. They were tightly constructed, around that moment of crisis or turning point which in a way determined the pattern of the story. She explained this apparent lack of ordered events:

> The diversity of life and how we try to fit in everything. Death included. That is bewildering . . . things ought to happen differently. First one and then another. But life isn't like that. We haven't the ordering of it . . .

Not surprisingly, she once showed great indignation about:

> a stupid man . . . bringing out an anthology of short stories and he said the more 'plotty' a story I could give him the better. What about that for a word! It made my hair stand up in prongs. A nice 'plotty' story, please. People *are* funny.

This view did not lessen her admiration for Jane Austen's skill with plot. 'She makes modern episodic people like me, as far as I go, look very incompetent ninnies.' She and Jane Austen were, however, alike in their rather deliberately limited range of subject matter and their ironic pictures of sophisticated society's pretensions and conventions, for K. M. had gradually abandoned her early malicious, sometimes clumsily obvious satire for a more subtle and delicate irony.

Occasionally, too, like earlier writers such as Jane Austen, she addressed the reader in an intimate tone, inviting participation in the story and collusion with the narrator. K. M.'s last story, **'The Canary'**—a monologue—involves the reader in such a way, 'there does seem to me something sad in life. . . . I don't mean the sorrow that we all know. . . . '

Often that sadness was juxtaposed with humour, an aspect that has been too often overlooked. She was a writer with an acute wit, a gift for mimicry and a true sense of the ridiculous. At times the humour was obvious and satirical, as in the German stories, with the caricature of the Norman Knights in **'Bliss'**; at others it is more subtle, a delicate irony. **'The Daughters of the Late Colonel'** illustrates a gentle compassionate humour in the portrayal of two spinster sisters who had dared to bury their bullying father 'without asking his permission'. **'At the Bay'** is not only a superb evocation of mood and feeling, it is also a story with considerable humour.

The humour in her work was often gained from a single word, sometimes deliberately misspelled, mimicking the speaker's voice, even when it is a silent voice heard only in the character's mind. It is derived from exaggeration and caricature, from a careful contrasting of characters, the placing of a character in a particular situation; from the use of cleverly selected details, unconscious self revelation, word association.

H. E. Bates, while recognising a vivid clarity and a strangely personal quality, found her writing frequently immature and monotonous; the stories told in 'a kind of mental soliloquy, fluttering, gossipy, breathless' by her characters, 'all chattering overgrown schoolgirls busy asking and answering breathless facile questions about love and life and happiness' [*The Modern Short Story*]. This surely is a very narrow view which ignores many of her characters. Certainly some are weakly drawn types—particularly in the early stories—but others are truly alive, not drawn on a grand scale, but real people in a real world.

It is true that the majority of the characters in K. M.'s stories are female. She was frequently concerned with the particular relationships in which women were involved—with their children, with each other and with men. The role of women in society is central to much of her work, and most obviously so in the German stories.

It is therefore, as H. E. Bates and others have suggested, at times a 'female' world we are shown. In **'The Luftbad'**, which is set in a women's sunbathing enclosure in Wörishofen where the women are 'in their nakeds' there are, not surprisingly, no men. The point of view from which we view incidents, characters and relationships is frequently female and it is more often the female characters who win our sympathy. Some, like Beryl in **'At the Bay'**, are disillusioned by unexpected and coarse male advances. In others, the male characters' potential for seduction or physical violence is only hinted at.

Often too the worlds of male and female seem quite separate, only tenuously linked. The men seem quite alien at times to that world in which women are comfortable. One of K. M.'s most unattractive characters, Harry Young in **'Bliss'**, epitomises this. He 'loved doing things at high pressure', was an ambitious greedy poseur who dismissed his baby daughter with the words, 'My dear Mrs Knight, don't ask me about my baby. I never see her. I shan't feel the slightest interest in her until she has a lover'. In **'At the Bay'** Stanley leaves home feeling 'The heartlessness of women! The way they took it for granted it was your job to slave away for them while they didn't even take the trouble to see that your walking stick wasn't lost.' Meanwhile, without the irritant of his presence, even the women's voices changed, 'they sounded warm and loving as if they shared a secret.'

In the same story, however, Jonathan Trout is shown as an atypical male. He is more articulate than Stanley, willing to talk about 'cranky' ideas and dreams; happier talking in the garden than sitting in his 'jail' of an office. Through him K. M. gives a picture of what men might be if only they were allowed to be, and had the courage to break free from the role society has traditionally allotted them. Linda, who finds Jonathan attractive, is aware that even beneath Stanley's everyday exterior there is a more sensitive man.

The traditional role of women in society is also closely examined. Linda spends her time calming Stanley down, 'and what was left of her time was spent in the dread of having children'. The woman 'at the store' was once a barmaid 'pretty as a waxdoll' who 'knew one hundred and twenty-five different ways of kissing'. After six years of marriage and four miscarriages she has become a pathetic figure. 'Her front teeth were knocked out, she had red pulpy hands', she is driven to murder by loneliness and despair. Elsewhere, as in **'Pictures'** and **'Miss Brill'**, K. M. explores the dilemma of older women, lonely, without family or support.

At times the male and female characters do achieve a kind of closeness and understanding, though it is rarely sexual but more akin to the kind of sympathetic bonding that often links the women in her stories. More often though the men are shown to be too inarticulate, uncommunicative and emotionally unevolved for this intimacy to take place. The boss in **'The Fly'** who 'had arranged to weep' but 'no tears came' is perhaps the most frightening example of such men, and at the same time a plea for them to change. Clearly then her characters are not 'all chattering overgrown schoolgirls' as H. E. Bates would have us believe. (pp. 168-72)

In moving away from the concept of the short story as a narrative and in suggesting through her work the immense possibilities of what could be done once the artificialities of conventional plot were eliminated, K. M. had a profound influence on the development of the modern short story—an influence freely acknowledged by Elizabeth Bowen and others. As T. O. Beachcroft states, she belongs with 'Eliot, Joyce and Virginia Woolf' as 'part of a new dawn'. Once K. M. and others had claimed the right to experiment, others followed, frequently achieving a combination of the two methods.

It is particularly interesting to look at the views of her contemporaries. Thomas Hardy, John Galsworthy and H. G. Wells all regarded her very highly, whereas D. H. Lawrence had answered Catherine Carswell's enthusiasm for **'Prelude'** with the impatient reply, 'Yes, yes, but prelude to what?' She would, he felt, reject the stories that contained her unique combination of sentiment and charm and stop writing until she could find a different kind of story. It was a strangely accurate prediction. Although he saw similarities to Dickens in her vivid use of specific details and colour and her touches of humour, Lawrence felt that Murry was wrong about her, and wrong to try to promote her work so assiduously after her death:

> She was *not* a great genius. She had a charming gift, and a finely cultivated one. But *not more.* And to try, as you do, to make it more is to do her not true service . . . she is delicate and touching—but not great! Why say great.

While dryly admitting her jealousy, Virginia Woolf felt that K. M. was one of the best women writers. **'Prelude'** was one of the first volumes published by the Hogarth Press because Virginia felt it to be, 'a good deal better than most stories'. In her diary she went further, recognising in it 'the living power, the detached existence of a work of art'.

Their relationship was a difficult one, however, and Virginia found little to admire in K. M.'s later stories. Shortly after her friend's death which, she said, had moved her greatly, she wrote to Jacques Raverat:

> My theory is that while she possessed the most amazing *senses* of her generation so that she could actually reproduce this room for instance, with its fly, clock, dog, tortoise if need be, to the life, she was as weak as water, as insipid, and a great deal more commonplace, when she had to use her mind. That is, she can't put thoughts, or feelings, or subtleties of any kind into her char-

> acters, without at once becoming, where she's serious, hard, and where she's sympathetic, sentimental.

It is also possible to criticise the very restricted circumscribed range of her work, but like Jane Austen she chose to write only of what she had known and seen. 'The artist takes a *long look* at life. He says softly, "So this is what life is, is it?" And he proceeds to express that. All the rest he leaves.' Nevertheless she was well aware of the limitations imposed upon her by her illness and her isolation: 'I'm so *stale*—oh for a "weekend" or even a ciné or a theatre or the sound of music'.

Naturally K. M. was considerably disturbed when it was suggested to her that had she not been ill, she might never have been able to write as she had.

Her illness certainly led to a feeling of urgency, 'It's always a race to get in as much as one can before it disappears'. She seemed often to write in bursts, sudden moments of crystallisation. A particularly interesting example of this occurs in the manuscript of **'The Doll's House'.** One page begins with the story's last few lines. Beneath an erratically drawn line is the preceding section about Willie Brent, 'he'd come to the front door. . . . ' Beneath that is a much earlier section, part of the scene at the school, 'Lil Kelvey's going to be a servant when she grows up. . . . ' An arrow indicates how these fragments were to be finally fitted together, like pieces in a jigsaw.

In spite of illness, unhappiness and bleak frustration K. M. retained a tremendous spontaneous enthusiasm for life. 'God! I'm *rooted* in Life. Even if I hate Life, I can't deny it. I spring from it and feed on it.' Often this enthusiasm had been for her vision of life, rather than for life's reality. Yet she knew she must learn to accept that reality: 'I don't believe a writer can ever do anything *worth* doing until he has—in the profoundest sense of the word—ACCEPTED Life.' Gradually she came to know herself; to gain the courage to accept life for what it really was:

> But do you really feel all beauty is marred by ugliness and the lovely woman has bad teeth? I don't feel quite that, . . . Beauty triumphs over ugliness in Life. That's what I feel. And that marvelous triumph is what I long to express. . . . Life is, all at one and the same time, far more mysterious and far simpler than we know. It's like religion in that. If we want to have faith, and without faith we die, we must *learn* to accept.

Some of her finest stories are about that triumph, and that acceptance, and with her ability to capture fleeting moods and vibrant warm colours they have enduring relevance.

Some stories do not work, but at her best, K. M. succeeded in writing something between 'a poem and a reflection, a novel and an anecdote'. All readers will have those stories which for him or her epitomise the particular quality of her writing and which lead them to glimpse a moment of truth; the realisation of the inevitability of life and the 'beauty in that inevitability'.

Despite John Middleton Murry's efforts, the amount of work on which her worldwide reputation rests is comparatively slight. Her technical innovations and skill alone would have had an important influence on modern writing. Her finest stories are, however, far more than technical masterpieces. In speaking to that 'secret self we all have', they establish her place in literature. Through her we see the world we have always known—but we see it more clearly. (pp. 180-82)

Gillian Boddy, in her Katherine Mansfield: The Woman and the Writer, *Penguin Books, 1988, 325 p.*

Rhoda B. Nathan (essay date 1988)

[*In the following excerpt, Nathan assesses Mansfield's contributions to the short story form.*]

Assessing an artist's contribution to his field is tricky at best. The subject must be scrutinized in his time, in the universal terms of his craft, for his original work, and in his derivative techniques. He must be measured against other practitioners of the genre, those past and contemporaneous. His good work must be separated from his mediocre efforts, his early work from his last. Periods of productivity must be weighed against arid patches in his creative landscape. Katherine Mansfield is not exempt from such treatment. Even the negative critical judgment of colleagues and critics in her day must be counterbalanced against favorable reviews. For example, her friend and fellow writer Virginia Woolf wrote this about her less than half a year after her death: "While she possessed the most amazing *senses* of her generation . . . she was as weak as water when she had to use her mind." The truth or falsity of Woolf's harsh criticism must be balanced against the indisputable fact that Mansfield's short stories continue to be anthologized frequently in our own day while those of her more distinguished rival do not.

In one area, at least, the task of critical evaluation is simplified by the author's scope. Mansfield, unlike most of her colleagues, wrote only short stories. Although she began one full-length novel, *Juliet,* she abandoned it. Notes in her *Journal* hint at another novel extending the New Zealand theme and tentatively called *Karori,* but nothing came of it. Her contribution was to the short story only. She is probably unique in this distinction. There is scarcely a writer of her time, and few since, who did not go on to write at least one novel. Whether she lacked the broader powers and vision to construct novels, as some of her detractors have hinted, is moot. The stories she left are sufficient. Berating her for failing to write at least one distinguished novel is analogous to faulting the composer Hugo Wolf, master of the German art song, or lied, for not writing at least one celebrated opera.

The conventionality of Mansfield's fiction—the term is not used in a pejorative sense—is another useful factor in limiting and directing critical evaluation. All the standard elements of the short story are present in most of her fiction in harmonious balance, much as the well-crafted stories of specialists such as J. F. Powers, J. D. Salinger, and John Updike during their *New Yorker* period. When Mansfield was experimental, it was primarily in her composition of a handful of spoken monologues, often constructed as flashbacks that reveal character, plot, theme, and tone. Her best short stories, **"Miss Brill," "The Garden Party," "Bliss,"** and **"The Dill Pickle,"** among others, are narrated conventionally from a subjective point of view. They comprise integrated elements of the short story as it has been defined by theorists such as Poe in the nineteenth century and Frank O'Connor in the twentieth.

The single most palpable quality permeating Mansfield's stories is her perfectionism. The exemplary New Zealand cycle, episode by episode, through character and conflict, develops with single-minded intensity a unified theme of complex family life recollected through a veil of nostalgia for an unrecoverable past. The action varies but the setting is remarkably unified, supporting the controlled tone of longing. In its finished state, **"Prelude"** offers the clearest evidence of its author's relentless polishing. Compared to **"The Aloe,"** the original version of the story written just a year earlier, the final story shows clear evidence of "much reshaping and rewriting," according to Murry's introductory essay. In short order the reader discovers the truth of Murry's description of the first version as "less perfect," and agrees with him that the belated publication of **"The Aloe"** many years after Mansfield's death does indeed offer the "more critically minded a unique opportunity for studying Katherine Mansfield's method of work."

It is instantly apparent that the intensity and compression of **"Prelude"** are achieved through the author's conscientious, almost excruciating, editing. Throughout the text single words have been altered, excised, and shifted from one position in a given phrase to another. The casual reader might not notice these seemingly insignificant changes,

John Middleton Murry.

but the text in its entirety shines more brightly as well as gaining in precision. For example, in **"The Aloe,"** when Lottie and Isabel are put to bed in the new house, they lie down "back to back, just touching." In **"Prelude"** Mansfield amends the phrase to "their little behinds just touching." The second description is anatomically more correct, as the children's bodies are curled into a ball, and only their backsides touch in that position. If they were "back to back," they would be envisioned in a ramrod posture, unnatural if not downright impossible. Further, there is something childlike and vulnerable about the second phrase that is well suited to the affectionate tone. In contrast, an amendment away from the infantile is made in one of the most dramatic sequences in **"Prelude."** When the handyman has decapitated the duck for that evening's dinner, Isabel, watching the headless body waddling along the path, squeals, "It's like a funny little railway engine." The original version in **"The Aloe"** was "It's like a funny little darling engine." The seemingly trivial substitution of the word "railway" for "darling" is more calculated than would appear. If indeed "these kids are real," as one impressed reader was to observe, their "realness" had to be consciously convincing. Isabel was the eldest and the most likely to frame a simile or analogy drawn from her own experience. The adjective "darling" would be more suitable to the young inexperienced Kezia.

Other judicious editing excised repetitions of descriptions such as the portrait of Mrs. Fairchild that appears twice in the original. The character of Stanley Burnell is softened into a more sympathetic figure in **"Prelude."** In **"The Aloe"** he is described as a "ginger whale," but in **"Prelude"** his ginger whiskers remain but he is drawn in more human terms. By and large, it is a small alteration but a shrewd one. It would be difficult for the reader to imagine the beautiful and fastidious Linda Fairfax agreeing to wed and bed with a "ginger whale."

There are larger slashes in **"Prelude"** that are instantly apparent. **"The Aloe"** contains an eleven-page digression that Mansfield removed, probably to incorporate it into a third part of the cycle. In the interest of preserving a unified point of view she did well, because in these pages her narrative shifts suddenly from Kezia, who has been the center of sentience, to her mother. It justifies Linda's detachment from her children through a flashback showing her devotion to her father, her longing to travel, and her resistance to marriage. But the section, which is indeed illuminating, threatens the integrity of the whole and Mansfield wisely excised it. Ultimately Linda's point of view is presented more subtly in **"At the Bay,"** where she and the other adults are the focal figures. One other lengthy episode involving Linda, Beryl, and another sister at afternoon tea, probably designed to show the differences in the three Fairfax sisters—and surely a reflection of the Beauchamp sisters—is scrapped and saved for another story. It is preserved in an unfinished state in the ***Scrapbook.***

Character in fiction is either "flat" or "round," which is to say stereotypical or multidimensional. Mansfield's characters are primarily round—that is, faceted and like "real" people. Even her minor characters—Pat the handyman in the New Zealand stories, Cyril, the wastrel grandson in **"The Daughters of the Late Colonel,"** and the "literary gentleman" in **"The Life of Ma Parker"**—have distinguishing qualities that individualize them. For example, when Hennie, the small boy in **"The Young Girl,"** buries his face in his cup of chocolate, his childish delight is captured in his emerging nose, on which hangs a blob of cream. His wholehearted immersion in the treat and his subsequent scarlet-faced humiliation frame him as an endearing child and as an effective counterpart to his sullen sister.

Mansfield can sink a character through a single word and still avoid creating a "type." The irritating genteel nurse in **"The Daughters of the Late Colonel"** has a laugh "like a spoon tinkling against a medicine glass." In **"Marriage á la Mode"** Moira Morrison's arty triviality is encapsulated in her painstaking analysis of the appearance of her legs under water, which she concludes are "the palest mushroom colour" to everyone's edification. A Russian cigarette case pulled from the pocket of the unnamed former lover in **"The Dill Pickle"** tells the story of his selfishness. It is a mute reminder of a broken promise and its owner's callousness. His onetime companion is reminded of their dreams of traveling to Russia together and of his fulfilling their shared plans without her. His guilelessness in offering her the Russian cigarettes in their native case and his hearty recounting of his adventures make his unthinking cruelty memorable.

As well plotted and carefully constructed as Mansfield's stories are, they cannot be confined to any single tradition. The two recognized historical "schools" are the psychological tradition laid down by Poe and the socially observant tradition associated with Maupassant. There are other categories as well: the plotted and the plotless story, the stories of initiation, symbolist stories, and so on. The categories are both endless and overlapping, but Mansfield, like other writers, cannot be confined to any single formula, whether it be the rules set down in Poe's "The Philosophy of Composition," Chekhov's social realism, James's psychological realism, Maurice Maeterlinck's symbolism, or Joyce's stream-of-consciousness technique. Her short stories do not fit into any single framework, any more than does the entire body of Cheever's or Updike's short fiction. As she wrote, she continued to experiment. **"Her First Ball"** and **"The Garden Party"** are stories of initiation. They are also fully plotted psychological studies. They have some traces of social realism. **"Je ne parle pas français"** is a rare attempt at plotlessness. The story **"Psychology"** is not psychological but a fragment designed to produce a "single effect" with "deliberate care" in obedience to the Poe formula.

Mansfield's youthful devotion to Wilde's brittle comedy surely is responsible for the languid witty dialogue in **"Marriage á la Mode"** and **"Bliss." "A Cup of Tea"** is the perfect magazine story. It has all the elements required for a popular journal, including a surprise ending. Its slick commercial "feel" does not negate the perfection of its construction. **"Poison"** and **"Taking the Veil"** are effective demonstrations of the symbolist credo that states of mind are most effectively conveyed through concrete images. **"The-Child-Who-Was-Tired,"** Mansfield's most feeling and conscious tribute to Chekhov's social realism, is actually far removed from Chekhov's profound but abstract social concern. Chekhov's "Sleepy" expresses his outrage against societal abuse; it is a protest against oppression and close to political socialism. Mansfield's version is more personal and limited. Her sad story focuses on the child herself as a helpless object of personal cruelty, not social injustice. Her symbolical ending of the child's dream gives the story a twist towards the allegorical. Chekhov's has none of that fanciful quality. His story is close to being a documentary of social inequity, its central character serving as an instructive example of victimization.

The following stories reveal still other debts to traditional sources even as they bear the stamp of her originality. **"The Canary,"** a first-person oral monologue to an unseen audience, is reminiscent of Poe's unidentified monologists whose narrations explain their current emotional state in terms of their past history. The speaker in **"The Canary"** begins: "You see that big nail to the right of the front door? I can scarcely look at it now and yet I could not bear to take it out." The story is secondary to the tone and symbolism. The speaker is highly agitated. Her loneliness is implicit in her attachment to the dead bird, itself a symbol of her yearning for beauty in a pinched sterile life. The nail that held the suspended cage remains on the wall as a symbol of her loss and pain. It is a nail driven through her heart.

In **"The Garden Party"** also, literal objects have a wider symbolic reverberation than their limited objective selves. When Laura Sheridan leaves the party on her mission to the bereaved family of the dead man, "the kisses, voices, tinkling spoons, laughter, the smell of crushed grass [are] somehow inside her." As the great lawn recedes in the distance behind her, a newer unfamiliar reality is symbolized by the narrow dark lane leading to the cramped hovel in her line of vision. "Women in shawls and men's tweed caps" supplant the trailing skirts and frock coats of the afternoon's festivities. Shadows replace sunlight, silence follows the murmur of tea-party chatter. Only the large garden-party hat, still propped on Laura's bowed head, remains constant, worn in the dusk as a badge of penance as it has been worn in daylight as a symbol of her corruption.

Socially observant narrative that makes its point through irony in the Maupassant tradition may be discerned in plotted stories like **"Sixpence."** Mrs. Bendall, a timid woman, is bullied by Mrs. Spears, an overbearing visitor, into goading her husband to whip their beloved small son. The child's infraction is minor, and the family is loving and forgiving. Under subtle criticism of her "superior" neighbor, Mrs. Bendall is made to feel incompetent and lax in the performance of her "moral" duty, introducing a new and ugly atmosphere into her peaceful home. Her tired husband, angry at being assaulted by his overwrought wife to do *his* duty as a man, whips the child, and is crushed by the child's forbearance in his pain and humiliation. The worm has been found in the apple. The child forgives his parents but their happiness has vanished.

The irony of the serpent's evil in this Eden is implicit in

the throwaway remark about Mrs. Spears's own "exemplary" sons. They have indeed attained perfection in deportment, but it is noted that they prefer to play outside their home, in the toolshed, behind the kennel, even in the trash bin. Her callers marvel that "you would never know there was a child in the house." Mrs. Bendall then recalls that "in the front hall of her neighbor's well-run home, under a picture of fat, cheery old monks fishing by the riverside, there was a thick dark horsewhip."

The contrast between Mrs. Spears's "soft sugary voice" and the repeated brutal whippings that have shaped her children's decorum is an irony lost on Mrs. Bendall but not on the reader. Her visitor's hypocrisy in the execution of her maternal obligation is yet another unnoted irony. Does Mrs. Spears administer the whippings? Of course not. It would be unseemly for a mother, the symbol of nurture. Who does it then? Why, their father, of course—the respected symbol of authority. Ironically, just as Mrs. Bendall, under the influence of her persuasive friend, is working herself up to persuading her husband to inflict corporal punishment on his beloved child, he "staggers up the hot concrete steps . . . hot, dusty, tired out," and spoiling for a fight. He needs no convincing. "He felt like a man in a dark net. And now he wanted to beat Dicky. Yes, damn it, he wanted to beat something." The story ends on yet another ironic note. The beaten child, holding up his face in forgiveness, wipes out the father's rage and accepts the sixpence offered him in penance by his father, who is now beating himself for his unprecedented act of brutality.

This is a story crammed with irony. Whereas little Dicky Bendall makes his small mischief in the open, Mrs. Spears's model sons do theirs secretly, away from the bullwhip. In the arena of conflict the tables are turned and turned again. The timid mother is ironically stripped of authority in her own home and is forced into violating her principles. The "superior" guest is exposed as inferior in human terms. All the plotting of the two women to force the man to act abhorrent to his nature proves to be unnecessary. He has come home in a brutalized condition and was ready to assault someone. **"Sixpence"** is withal a touching story in its understanding of frailty and the ironies of interpersonal maneuvering for power. The symbols of the omnipresent whip, the sugary voice, and the sixpence coin are effective emblems of control and subordination. It is worth noting that Mansfield must have taken Chekhov's observation about "props" in the theater seriously and adapted them to her own use of symbols. His remark that the audience may be sure that the gun hanging on the wall in the first act is bound to go off in the third is applicable to Mansfield's use of emblems, from the first mention of the tight headband on Mr. Bendall's head to the angry pucker left by his hat when he beats his child at the end.

Mansfield culled her characters from all levels of society, from the privileged station of the Sheridans to the shabby rooms of Ma Parker, from New Zealand to the Continent, from the beefy Germans of the Bavarian Alps to the fleshless spinsters of post-Victorian England. Her themes are manifold. Like all serious writers she tried to tell the truth about her own life, the life about her, and the imagined life. In short, her contribution to the genre of the short story cannot be neatly categorized. She ranged far and she roamed freely, but certain conclusions may be drawn as a guide to the basic constants in her fiction.

Her technique is invariably efflorescent—from the bud to the flower, so to speak. She begins with a single incident or clue, such as the landlady's intrusion into Miss Ada Moss's room in **"Pictures"** or the unblemished weather on the day of the Sheridans' garden party. We take it on faith that the tension in the story will derive from that single bit of information. She rarely disappoints us. She builds on the fragment layer by layer, establishing the mood—almost always an atmosphere of psychological tension—until the small incident, which Henry James used to call the "germ," unfolds into crisis, climax, and resolution.

A prevailing mood of tension is a constant in Mansfield's work. Unlike her literary model Chekhov, who did little by way of manipulation after he laid down the bare facts of his characters' troubles, she adds, alters, and controls. Miss Brill's illusory self-image is shattered when she is forced to confront herself in a glass held up by her detractors. Laura Sheridan's innocence is destroyed step by step in a calculated series of ugly events that oblige her to confront the truth about her insulated life and the tragedy of others. The unsuspecting lover in **"Poison"** is forced by an insignificant incident—his mistress's casual inquiry about the mail—to face her inconstancy. Unrelieved tension is the governing mood of the allegorical **"A Suburban Fairy Tale,"** generated by irremediably obtuse parents and their imaginative child.

In stories such as **"Prelude," "Her First Ball," "The Doll's House,"** and **"Bliss,"** tension is created through a contrived alternation between fulfillment and deprivation, satisfaction and yearning, self-indulgence and guilt. Their total sustained effect is one of delicate balance between opposing forces that prevail to the end. Witness the unanswerable question Bertha asks at the end of **"Bliss"** and Laura's unfinished question at the end of **"The Garden Party."** They keep their climate of mystery to the very end because their underlying tension is unresolved.

Finally, Mansfield's stories are usually "good reads." Their meaning is accessible even to the general reader who does not wish to trouble his head about the hidden significance in her fables. Their point of view is almost uniformly subjective, and their dialogue is witty, often sparkling. Her narration is economical and colorful, rarely discursive. Her most successful stories are those that originate in her own childhood, her love affairs and marriages, and the characters she encountered in her travels. Her least successful stories are static monologues such as **"A Married Man's Story"** and **"The Lady's Maid."** Taking Brander Matthews's definition of the true short story as "complete and self-contained" and marked by a "single effect" ["The Philosophy of the Short Story," in *Short Story Theories,* Charles E. May, editor] we may conclude that Mansfield's finest stories have the requisite "totality" of the prescription. If she failed to rise to James's mandarin detachment, or Chekhov's selfless compassion, or Joyce's psychological intensity, she left at least two dozen works of brilliance and polish and a smaller number of perfect stories. (pp. 143-53)

Rhoda B. Nathan, in her Katherine Mansfield, *Continuum, 1988, 168 p.*

Sydney Janet Kaplan (essay date 1991)

[*Kaplan is an American educator and feminist critic. In the following excerpt from her critical study* Katherine Mansfield and the Origins of Modernist Fiction, *she examines Mansfield's use of modernist technique.*]

The early modernist claims for the preeminence of subjectivity (for example in Dorothy Richardson and May Sinclair) are tempered by Mansfield's (and Woolf's) suspicions about their grounding in egoism. A recognition of interconnections, of the ways subjectivity is informed by social and cultural imperatives—especially as they are inculcated in family structure—remains a distinctive feature of Mansfield's epistemology. Mansfield's questioning of subjectivity occurs despite the seeming multiplicity and fluidity of the treatment of consciousness in her fiction. That questioning becomes apparent in two ways: through the satirical tone that emerges as the result of juxtaposition and selection, and through her efforts to achieve a *transformed* subjectivity, to *become* the object through an intuitive, Bergsonian "sympathy" with its internal structure. The latter tends to work by seeming to re-infiltrate a semblance of "objectivity" into the text.

Yet we know that for Mansfield, "objectivity" is as suspect a term as its opposite. She actually creates an *illusion* of objectivity in her fiction, an illusion whose source is the mastery of technique. The hidden author herself, insisting on her own access to truth, on the authenticity of her interpretation of reality, shows a mastery that she will not relinquish. She expresses it as a concern for "craft," for a precision in the use of details:

> It's a very queer thing how *craft* comes into writing. I mean down to details. *Par example.* In **"Miss Brill"** I choose not only the length of every sentence, but even the sound of every sentence. I choose the rise and fall of every paragraph to fit her, and to fit her on that day at that very moment. After I'd written it I read it aloud—numbers of times—just as one would *play over* a musical composition—trying to get it nearer and nearer to the expression of Miss Brill—until it fitted her. . . . If a thing has really come off it seems to me there mustn't be one single word out of place, or one word that could be taken out.

This technical "mastery," as is apparent in the encoded masculine in the word itself, might be interpreted (although I do not do so) as a kind of "masculinist" behavior, a recapture by the patriarchy, or, in orthodox Freudian terms, evidence of penis envy, masculine identification, and so forth. The problem for assertive, energetic, intelligent women is often this one: the cultural inscription of the masculine on all *active* creative endeavor. [The critic adds a footnote that "A notorious example of an attack on Mansfield generated by this type of cultural inscription is that of the short-story writer Frank O'Connor, who complains of Mansfield's 'assertiveness,' and considers her search for experience as 'a typical expedient of the woman with a homosexual streak who envies men and attributes their imaginary superiority to the greater freedom with which they are supposed to be able to satisfy their sexual appetite. It is the fallacy of Virginia Woolf's *A Room of One's Own*' " (*The Lonely Voice*).]

Mansfield does not accede to the assumed dominance of male authority and control. She takes an activist feminist position (and I am defining "activist" here not in terms of specific political actions, but as direct protest against injustice) when she insists on her authority to speak, to argue that one course of behavior is better than another. Rather than succumb to uncertainty, to never-knowingness, she takes up an ethical stance, what she calls her "cry against corruption," which is evident in the late story **"The Fly"** (1922), where she demonstrates how power corrupts, how patriarchal dominance victimizes. In this instance the small and powerless victim is a fly that struggles to escape from the inkwell of a businessman, who mindlessly lifts and submerges it with his pen. Because of the man's refusal to relinquish control, the fly ultimately is drowned. Although Mansfield allows the reader to understand that this man's sadistic behavior is a reaction to his despair over the death of his son, she does not condone it. The man is wrong, no matter how much he has suffered. Nothing justifies his mistreatment of the "other" (and certainly, "other" here brings with it a full realization of how the man has projected his own vulnerability into another creature).

In some ways Mansfield appears to be in agreement with other modernists about the alienation and decay of the postwar world, but that does not mean that she would ever have taken the same political direction as her friend D. H. Lawrence, for example, let alone that of T. S. Eliot or Ezra Pound. Mansfield's deepest suspicions were aroused by authoritarianism in any form, as her lifelong critique of male dominance gives clear evidence. In this respect she resembles some of the other female modernists, particularly Woolf and H. D., whose writings evidence strong opposition to authoritarianism. But Mansfield's growing personal isolation—although caused by her increasingly debilitating illness—reflects as well her disassociation from politics and from efforts for social change, a severance that may have resulted from her association with Murry and her exclusion from the dominant centers of cultural power. Despite her sense of alienation from political life, however, she was far more ambivalent about the notion of modern civilization as the "waste land" than some of her male contemporaries. She expressed an alternating (or perhaps simultaneous) awareness of "joy" and "hopelessness," and both of these were bound up with her self-definition as a writer. In an often quoted letter to Murry which bears repeating here, Mansfield explains:

> Ive two 'kick offs' in the writing game. *One* is joy—real joy—the thing that made me write when we lived at Pauline, and that sort of writing I could only do in just that state of being in some perfectly blissful way *at peace.* Then something delicate and lovely seems to open before

> my eyes, like a flower without thought of a frost or a cold breath—knowing that all about it is warm and tender and 'steady'. And *that* I try, ever so humbly to express.
>
> The other 'kick off' is my old original one, and (had I not known love) it would have been my all. Not hate or destruction (both are beneath contempt as real motives) but an *extremely* deep sense of hopelessness—of everything doomed to disaster—almost wilfully, stupidly—like the almond tree and 'pas de nougat pour le noël'—There! as I took out a cigarette paper I got it exactly—*a cry against corruption* that is *absolutely* the nail on the head. Not a protest—a *cry,* and I mean corruption in the widest sense of the word, of course—

This letter, written before the end of the war, reveals Mansfield gradually shifting her focus of concern as a writer. I say "gradually" because I do not think it is possible to see any sharp break between stages of her work, and as her early letters and fiction suggest, there is a consistency of style and substance throughout her career. Yet the contrast between the youthful hope and enthusiasm over the "new" in her letters of 1906-8 and the suffering and disgust expressed in letters but a decade later is startling and unsettling. A letter to Ottoline Morrell on May 24, 1918, is even bleaker than the one to Murry:

> But the ugliness—the ugliness of life—the intolerable corruption of it all—Ottoline. How is it to be borne? Today for the first time since I arrived, I went for a walk—Anne Rice has been telling me of the beauty of the spring—all the hedges one great flower, of the beauty of these little 'solid' white houses set in their blazing gardens—and the lovely hale old fishermen. But—the sea stank—great grey crabs scuttled over the rocks—all the little private paths and nooks had been fouled by human cattle—there were rags of newspaper in the hedges—the village is paved with *concrete* and as you passed the 'tiny solid white houses' a female voice yells: "you stop it or Ill lay a rope end across eë."

During the last months of the war, but especially during the first years after its conclusion, Mansfield's longstanding emphasis on women's victimization was subsumed into a larger concern with oppression and victimization on a global scale. If one considers the works of other modernists who have been considered "major" writers in the canon—Lawrence, Pound, Woolf, Eliot, Stein—only Mansfield centers her work so deeply on the victimization of individuals. Joyce certainly was sensitive to such victimization in his earlier book, *Dubliners,* which shares with Mansfield's short fiction an emphasis on the epiphanic moment; but Mansfield's late work does not move away from this primary focus on human suffering. **"The Garden Party," "The Doll's House," "Life of Ma Parker," "The Fly," "Miss Brill," "Revelations," "The Canary"** are "cries against corruption," expressions of outrage against a society in which privilege is so marked by indifference to the misery of others that it must demean or ignore any unmediated reaction to injustice, such as Laura's recognition that "we can't possibly have a garden-party with a man dead just outside the front gate" (**"The Garden Party"**).

Mansfield's artistic vision never loses its grounding in a nineteenth-century, *ethical* conception of literature's purpose. And it is here that her intense and long-standing fascination with the great Russian writers is most apparent. Mansfield was not alone in her devotion to the Russians; their influence was felt by twentieth-century writers ranging from Shaw to Joyce. Her devotion most certainly was abetted by Murry's nearly obsessive study of Dostoevsky during the period when she was writing **"Prelude."** Virginia Woolf also felt the Russians' overpowering influence. In the essay "Modern Fiction," she had insisted: "The most elementary remarks upon modern English fiction can hardly avoid some mention of the Russian influence, and if the Russians are mentioned one runs the risk of feeling that to write of any fiction save theirs is waste of time. If we want understanding of the soul and heart where else shall we find it of comparable profundity?"

For Mansfield, the connection with the Russians also signified her own personal identification with their portrayals of human suffering, and, in the case of Chekhov, a sense of like identity, a realization that she and he were condemned to death by the same disease. A preoccupation with the relentless course of that disease forms the persistent undercurrent of Mansfield's later writing. It helps to explain her seeming disgust with some of the male modernists' outspokenness about sex and other bodily processes. Such attitudes about sexuality are in great contrast with her youthful experimental posture toward the subject and hint at a kind of latent prudishness which is often the other side of promiscuity. Her biographers relate these later attitudes to a sense of guilt about her youthful sexual adventures, but I am not entirely convinced by that argument. More important, it seems to me, is the fact of her dying, the overriding reality to all her later discourse on sexuality. A remark in her journal in 1918 gives an unnerving glimpse of her recognition that Murry was withdrawing from her as a sexual partner: "Do you remember when you put your handkerchief to your lips and turned away from me—In that instant you were utterly, utterly apart from me—and I have never felt quite the same since."

One finds a certain body consciousness permeating all facets of Mansfield's writing, but its locus now shifts from sexuality to disease; its depiction is distorted by the reality of what Elaine Scarry [in her *The Body in Pain: The Making and Unmaking of the World*] calls "the inexpressibility of physical pain." There are only brief glimpses of that pain in Mansfield's letters and journals, and it is noteworthy how often its attempted expression quickly swerves to concentrate on her relation to Murry. A journal entry of August 12, 1920, is illustrative:

> I cough and cough and at each breath a dragging, boiling, bubbling sound is heard. I feel that my whole chest is boiling. I sip water, spit, sip, spit. I feel I must break my heart. And I can't expand my chest; it's as though the chest had collapsed. Life is—getting a new breath: nothing else counts. And J. is silent, hangs his head, hides his face with his fingers *as though* it were

> unendurable. 'This is what she is doing to me! Every fresh sound makes *my* nerves wince.' I know he can't help these feelings. But, oh God! how wrong they are. If he could only for a minute, serve me, help me, give *himself* up. I can so imagine an account by him of a 'calamity'. 'I could do nothing all day, *my* hands trembled, I had a sensation of *utter* cold. At times I felt the strain would be unbearable, at others a *merciful numbness* . . .' and so on. What a fate to be self-imprisoned!

Mansfield's attitude about this physical suffering is suffused with a sense of the impossibility of its being shared, of its alienating effect.

In her stories, too, the sufferer is nearly always placed in conjunction with another person who is emotionally incapable of responding to her pain. Such a juxtaposition occurs in **"The Man without a Temperament,"** which is closely based on Mansfield's relationship with Murry and her disappointment over his behavior during her illness. It also occurs in **"Life of Ma Parker"** (1920), where the horror of Ma Parker's husband's death from consumption is treated at a slant, through the irony of the "literary gentleman's" sentimentalized attitudes about the working class:

> "A baker, Mrs. Parker!" the literary gentleman would say. For occasionally he laid aside his tomes and lent an ear, at least, to this product called Life. "It must be rather nice to be married to a baker!"
>
> Mrs. Parker didn't look so sure.
>
> "Such a clean trade," said the gentleman.
>
> Mrs. Parker didn't look convinced.
>
> "And didn't you like handing the new loaves to the customers?"

Ma Parker counters the sentimentalized portrait of the "clean trade" with her memories of endless work, bearing thirteen children and losing seven of them, and then the death of her husband: "It was flour on the lungs, the doctor told her at the time." The image of flour, of "white powder," "a great fan of white dust," works to undercut the superficial hypocrisy of the literary gentleman's supposed sympathy. He does not allow himself to be aware of the pain behind her description of her losses; rather, he moves back into complacency: "shuddering, and taking up his pen again." Thus he consigns Ma Parker to the helpless silence in which she finds herself at the end of the story, alone, on the street, questioning: "wasn't there anywhere in the world where she could have her cry out—at last?"

Pain can also be filtered through the words of others, through Keats, for example. And [in her journal] Mansfield quotes from his letters: "Nothing is so bad as want of health—it makes one envy scavengers and cinder-sifters.' (*August* 23, 1820)". Chekhov, Keats, and Mansfield become, in this context of bodily suffering from tuberculosis, a triad of initiates to the secrets of pain, to a higher state of consciousness known only to those who have undergone its rituals. By identifying herself with these two others, she shares in their "genius" as well. And this was very much the point for Murry when, after Mansfield's death, he began to create his portrait of the suffering, spiritual Katherine Mansfield. Clearly, Murry encouraged her identification with Keats and Chekhov. In a letter of March 10, 1918, for instance, he urged her to change the name of a character in **"Bliss"** because he felt the name tended toward caricature: "It is a Dickens touch & you're not Dickens—you're Tchehov—more than Tchehov." Or, "You are as classic as Tchehov in your way."

Murry once called Chekhov "the only great modern artist in prose" ["Thoughts on Tchehov," in his *Aspects of Literature*], and many of the terms he used to express his admiration for the Russian author he also used elsewhere to praise the writing of Katherine Mansfield. That Murry saw her as England's answer to Chekhov is clear by implication. Murry tells us that Chekhov's attitude "is complete, not partial. His comprehension radiates from a steady centre," and that as a writer he "had slowly shifted his angle of vision until he could discern a unity in multiplicity." Murry believed that Chekhov had much to teach the modernists:

> Tchehov is . . . a good many phases in advance of all that is habitually described as modern in the art of literature. The artistic problem which he faced and solved is one that is, at most, partially present to the consciousness of the modern writer—to reconcile the greatest possible diversity of content with the greatest possible unity of aesthetic impression. Diversity of content we are beginning to find in profusion—Miss May Sinclair's latest experiment shows how this need is beginning to trouble a writer with a settled manner and a fixed reputation—but how rarely do we see even a glimmering recognition of the necessity of a unified aesthetic impression! The modern method is to assume that all that is, or has been, present to consciousness is *ipso facto* unified aesthetically. The result of such an assumption is an obvious disintegration both of language and artistic effort, a mere retrogression from the classical method.

Murry's analysis of Chekhov's importance to modernism takes up many of the same aesthetic concerns that Mansfield was also expressing—at the same time (August 1919)—in her reviews for *The Athenaeum.* Less than two months before Murry's remarks about Chekhov were published, Mansfield reviewed May Sinclair's stream-of-consciousness novel *Mary Olivier:* "For the difference between the new way of writing and the old way is not a difference of degree but of kind. Its aim, as we understand it, is to represent things and persons as separate, as distinct, as apart as possible." And Mansfield complains, in a manner similar to her criticism of Dorothy Richardson, that Sinclair's method prevents her from seeing how "one thing is to be related to another thing." In fact, Mansfield suggests that "it is too late in the day for this new form, and Miss Sinclair's skilful handling of it serves but to make its failure the more apparent." (pp. 188-96)

For many years Mansfield's reputation was bound up with a continuing critical discussion of Chekhov's influence on her work. While this focus undoubtedly was abetted by

Murry's valorization of the Mansfield-Chekhov link, Mansfield herself encouraged such discussion. Her letters and notebooks contain many references to Chekhov. For example, in a letter of 1919 to S. S. Koteliansky, with whom she worked on translating Chekhov's letters for *The Athenaeum,* she remarked:

> I wonder if you have read Joyce and Eliot and these ultra-modern men? It is so strange that they should write as they do *after* Tchekhov. For Tchekhov has said the last word that has been said, so far, and more than that he has given us a sign of the way we should go. They not only ignore it: they think Tchekhov's stories are almost as good as the 'specimen cases' in Freud.

Typical of the standard critical discussion of Mansfield's indebtedness to Chekhov is that of Gilbert Phelps [in his *The Russian Novel in English Fiction*] in 1956. He remarks:

> There were undoubtedly elements in her own temperament and sensibility that found a genuine stimulus in Chekhov. It came naturally to her to develop her stories by the gradual accumulation of impressionistic scenes, to use random details, casual incidents, unconscious gestures and remarks, making them suddenly responsible for the whole emotional content of a tale, as a small lever launches an unexpected weight, and to choose themes of melancholy, frustration, indifference.
>
> In this sense Chekhov's influence acted mainly as a confirmation of personal preferences and a stimulus to their expression. . . .
>
> And of course Katherine Mansfield does not possess Chekhov's comprehensive vision of the relation of man to his social background, and to the vaster backgrounds of Nature. She does not possess his fundamental sanity, or his objectivity, or his self-discipline. And though she learned a good deal from him it was certainly not from him that she derived the sentimentality, the parochialism, the coyness and preciosity which mar so much of her work.

Phelps repeats some of the typical complaints of critics in the '40s and '50s about the Chekhov-Mansfield connection, complaints that unconsciously register a criticism of the feminine. Phelps considers Mansfield's use of devices similar to Chekhov's as something that "came naturally to her" rather than the result of intellectual effort and craftsmanship. Phelps's contrast of the "natural" to the "objective," the "comprehensive" to the "parochial," reiterates the pattern of exclusion which phallocentric criticism has used to trivialize the achievements of women. The choice of the words "sentimentality," "coyness," and "preciosity" in the last sentence encodes the conventional negative description of the feminine as well.

Critics like Phelps frequently mark the difference between Chekhov and Mansfield in terms of scope and breadth. That Chekhov's view of the world was broader, more comprehensive, and that the range of his experience was larger, are obvious and commonplace conclusions by now. What is important is to remember that Chekhov's breadth resulted from the knowledge of the world allowed him as a man: a man with a profession that gave him the freedom to mingle with all types of people, protected by his professional role as a physician but also enabled by it to learn about those people in quite intimate ways. He had the kind of freedom belonging to men which Woolf described in *A Room of One's Own.* Although Mansfield's attempt at independence brought her more experience than many women of her generation, she was not allowed or expected to have the same range of experience as men. As we have seen, her pursuit of experience continually brought her back to the contingencies of women's vulnerability in a male-dominated society.

Mansfield has been called everything from a mere "follower" of Chekhov to a blatant plagiarizer of one of his stories. The reader who wishes to trace the connections between Mansfield's fiction and Chekhov's has ready material at hand. Yet I believe that this line of inquiry—much overworked—is fruitless unless it is accompanied by attention to gender difference. I believe that the critical fixation on Mansfield's debt to Chekhov obscures the complexity of her development as a modernist, pushing one line of influence into the foreground while other, less critically acceptable lines are hidden in the background.

In some sense, Chekhov was the foil to Wilde—at least in the Bloomian sense of "anxiety of influence." The opposition is clearest if we play with the notion of Mansfield having two literary "fathers," Wilde and Chekhov. Wilde as father, as we have seen, is connected in Mansfield's development with aestheticism, but also with her lesbianism. The emotional/intellectual complex related to Wilde is thus bound up with secrecy, posing, sexual guilt, and repression. Wilde's influence makes itself felt in her writing through experimentation and *impersonation.* Its finale is spectacular, tragic death linked with public shame. Chekhov is in some ways an escape from Wilde to a more socially acceptable model. His influence is connected with realism but also with heterosexuality, and it is bound up with a drive toward achievement and approval, maturity of vision, and *impersonality.* Its finale is private rather than spectacular: early death through tuberculosis, suffering linked with that of humanity in general. But this "mature" father also suggests the hidden, the secret, in another sense than Wilde. Although Mansfield's role as "daughter" to Chekhov signals a partial reconciliation with the patriarchy, her absorption in him also contains an element of secrecy and guilt. Rather than the pose or mask associated with the Wilde influence, Chekhov's is associated with expropriation—even with plagiarism.

In an early Burnell story, **"The Little Girl,"** published in *Rhythm* in October 1912, Kezia inadvertently uses the manuscript of a speech her father has written as the stuffing for a pincushion she is making for his birthday present. He punishes her severely with the blows of a ruler against her hands. "You must be taught once and for all not to touch what does not belong to you." But the "theft" from the father is followed by a retreat to the maternal when Kezia turns for comfort to her grandmother and sits cuddled on her lap, venting her anger at masculine authority: "What did Jesus make fathers for?" This story's encoded suggestion of daughterly revolt against the prerogatives of patriarchal authority in language may be connected with this whole issue of Mansfield's alleged plagiarism of Chekhov. For while the child endures punishment over the destruction of her father's words, by the end of the story she has gained his love. The anger against the unjust punishment (she had protested: "But it was for your b-b-birthday") is suppressed, and later, when both her grandmother and mother are away, it returns in the form of fear unleashed through the dream-state: "The butcher with a knife and a rope . . .grew nearer and nearer, smiling that dreadful smile, while she could not move, could only stand still, crying out, 'Grandma, Grandma!' She woke shivering, to see father beside her bed, a candle in his hand." The father takes her into his own bed to comfort her:

> He lay down beside her. Half asleep still, still with the butcher's smile all about her, it seemed, she crept close to him, snuggled her head under his arm, held tightly to his pyjama jacket.
>
> Then the dark did not matter; she lay still.
>
> "Here, rub your feet against my legs and get them warm," said father.
>
> Tired out, he slept before the little girl. A funny feeling came over her. Poor father! Not so big, after all—and with no one to look after him. . . . He was harder than the grandmother, but it was a nice hardness. . . . And every day he had to work. . . . She had torn up all his beautiful writing. . . .
>
> "What's the matter?" asked father. "Another dream?"
>
> "Oh," said the little girl, "my head's on your heart; I can hear it going. What a big heart you've got, father dear."

There is both recapitulation and triumph in the end of this story. The child has established rapport with the father, as Kate Fullbrook has observed, by the "imagining of commonality with her father rather than on recognition of his superiority or his power." She has defused the fear of difference by considering it "a nice hardness." But it is important to see at the same time how the last line, "What a big heart you've got, father dear," retains a level of the original fear of the male inculcated by his patriarchal authority, his will to punishment. For as C. A. Hankin notes in her excellent Freudian reading of the story, the phrase is an echo of Red Riding-Hood's refrain in the old nursery tale. "What big teeth you have, Grannie dear," she utters before the wolf leaps up to answer, "All the better to eat you with, my dear." The last line of **"The Little Girl"** thus suggests a multiple reading, including accommodation, acceptance, fear, and a masochistic sexual desire. Hankin's emphasis on the story's repeated references "to the mouth," including the father's kiss, loud speaking voice, and most significantly, his "great speech," is illuminating, especially in the contrast of these examples of the father's oral prerogative with Kezia's stuttering, her own difficulty with speech. Hankin sees this stuttering as a sign "not just of fear but also of hostility. The same repressed hostility causes her apparently accidental destruction of his speech."

Feminist theory brings additional complexity to this focus on speech. Using feminist revisions of Lacan, critics are paying attention to the various ways women writers have subverted the authority of phallocentric speech. A recent book, for example, is called [*Stealing the Language: The Emergence of Women's Poetry in America,* Alicía Suskin Ostriker], an important essay ["Still Practice, A/Wrested Alphabet: Toward a Feminist Aesthetic," *Art & Anger: Reading Like a Woman,* Jane Marcus]. The trope of expropriation has become a convention of many feminist critical texts. Mansfield's alleged plagiarism of Chekhov's "Sleepy" in her story **"The Child-Who-Was-Tired"** (1909) takes on a different meaning when interpreted within this context of feminist revolt. A number of critics have taken the similarity of plot outline in the two stories as evidence of plagiarism, but [in their *Katherine Mansfield* Clare Hanson and Andrew Gurr] maintain there is a great difference between them. They see Chekhov's as "a restrained, pathological study, in which action is convincingly related to a specific social and psychological context" and Mansfield's as "a symbolic fable, in which certain elements of the original plot are exaggerated and key images repeated in order to express a general, rather than a specific truth: the harshness of woman's lot in life." This emphasis on "woman's lot" allows us to bring the subject back within the scope of feminist analysis. Like much feminist writing, Mansfield's story is an attempt to deconstruct a phallocentric myth by retelling it. The basic plot to both stories concerns an overworked, mistreated child servant who is so driven to exhaustion by her cruel employers that she smothers their baby in order to finally get some sleep. It is revealing that Mansfield uses an image she will repeat, quite literally, years later in **"Prelude."** When the child covers the baby's face with the bolster, he struggles "like a duck with its head off, wriggling." The submerged anger at the male infant who must be nurtured at the cost of her own emotional life is released—if only momentarily—in the image of castration.

Mansfield's devotion to Chekhov is also related to the continuing preoccupation with the concept of the artist in her journal, letters, and critical writings. This preoccupation had its roots in the '90s valorization of art above experience—in Wilde's attachment to artifice—but it soon shifted to a belief in the artist's deeper understanding of experience rather than exception from it, a version of the romantic view of the artist as visionary and sufferer. By the time of her late fiction, Mansfield had enlarged this preoccupation to include the newer, postwar concern with authenticity, destruction of hypocrisy, and admiration for craft. Such concern is expressed in the following letter written to her brother-in-law, Richard Murry, on February 3, 1921, during a time of personal and aesthetic consolidation, a time of coming to terms with both her impending death from tuberculosis and her decision to continue her struggle to live as a creative artist:

> Here is painting, and here is life. We can't separate them. Both of them have suffered an upheaval extraordinary in the last few years. There is a kind of tremendous agitation going on still, but so far anything that has come to the surface seems to have been experimental, or a fluke—a lucky accident. I believe the only way to *live* as

> artists under these new conditions in art and life is to put everything to the test for ourselves. We've got, in the long run, to be our own teachers. There's no getting away from that. We've got to win through by ourselves. Well, as I see it, the only way to do that honestly, dead truthfully, shirking nothing and leaving nothing out, is to put everything to the test. (Your desire for technical knowledge is a kind of profound *symbol.*) Not only to face things, but really to find out of what they are composed. How can we know where we are, otherwise? How can we prevent ourselves being weak in certain places? To be *thorough,* to be *honest,* I think if artists were really thorough & honest they would save the world. . . . Your generation & mine too, has been 'put off' with imitations of the real thing and we're bound to react violently if we're sincere. This takes so long to write & it sounds so heavy. Have I conveyed what I mean to even? You see I too have a passion for technique. I have a passion for making the thing into a *whole* if you know what I mean. Out of technique is born real style, I believe. There are no short cuts.

The practice of "technique," that "passion for making the thing into a *whole,*" had become a mission for Katherine Mansfield by 1921, a purpose in living; but her dedication to it was not a sudden development. Her emphasis on craft relates to her long-standing appreciation for technical perfection, beginning with her adolescent immersion in the study of music, her continued practice and imitation of different literary styles in the years of her apprenticeship as a writer, and continuing in adulthood through her interest in painting encouraged by her close friendships with artists such as Dorothy Brett, Mark Gertler, and Anne Estelle Rice. Mansfield's and Murry's brief, tumultuous friendship with the sculptor Henri Gaudier-Brzeska and Murry's knowledge of and involvement with continental avant-garde artists through his editorship of *Rhythm* were equally influential. Late in the same year of the letter to Richard Murry, on December 5, 1921, Mansfield wrote to Dorothy Brett about her recollections of the first Postimpressionist exhibit in 1910:

> Wasn't that Van Gogh shown at the Goupil ten years ago? Yellow flowers—brimming with sun in a pot? I wonder if it is the same. That picture seemed to reveal something that I hadn't realised before I saw it. It lived with me afterwards. It still does—that & another of a sea captain in a flat cap. They taught me something about writing, which was queer—a kind of freedom—or rather, a shaking free. When one has been working for a long stretch one begins to narrow ones vision a bit, to fine things down too much. And its only when something else breaks through, a picture, or something seen out of doors that one realises it. It is—literally—years since I have been to a picture show. I can smell them as I write.

Mansfield's use of the expression "a shaking free" is reminiscent of her description of the revelatory moment in the journal passage "The Flowering of the Self," written more than a year earlier ("our persistent yet mysterious belief in a self which is continuous and permanent . . . [which] shakes the flower free and—we are alive—we are flowering for our moment upon the earth"). Thus it is clear that "shaking free" as an aesthetic issue is interwoven with a metaphysical shaking free as well.

Throughout her career, Mansfield recognized that one of her central strengths was her sensitivity to visual stimuli. From the "vignettes" of her youth to her most sophisticated longer works of fiction, Mansfield's descriptions convey a sense of being "composed." Often they seem like verbal equivalents of paintings. A good example is a fairly early one, from a narrative of 1915, **"An Indiscreet Journey":**

> A green room with a stove jutting out and tables on each side. On the counter, beautiful with coloured bottles, a woman leans, her breasts in her folded arms. Through an open door I can see a kitchen, and the cook in a white coat breaking eggs into a bowl, and tossing the shells into a corner. The blue and red coats of the men who are eating hang upon the walls. Their short swords and belts are piled upon chairs.

Although Mansfield was herself an experimenter and interested in experimentation in the arts in general, she kept up her guard against the temptations of innovation for its own sake—the lure of the mechanical trick, the flaunting of convention, the clever phrase. All departures from the traditional must have a foundation in the search for meaning. To merely record whatever impinges on the mind was never enough for Katherine Mansfield. As with her complaint about Dorothy Richardson, she would insist that "until these things are judged and given each its appointed place in the whole scheme, they have no meaning in the world of art."

To proceed as if all objects and values are equal in significance prevents emphasis and shadowing. But most of all it might prevent "that divine *spring* into the bounding outline of things" Mansfield spoke of in her letter to Brett. For "how are we to appreciate the importance of one 'spiritual event' rather than another? What is to prevent each being unrelated—complete in itself—if the gradual unfolding in growing, gaining light is not to be followed by one blazing moment?" And here, perhaps, we may realize the ultimate direction of Katherine Mansfield's "passion." In that "one blazing moment" she evokes epiphany, the movement of so many of her own stories to that moment of enlightenment, exposure, understanding—the instant when the walls come down. (pp. 196-205)

Sydney Janet Kaplan, in her Katherine Mansfield and the Origins of Modernist Fiction, *Cornell University Press, 1991, 233 p.*

FURTHER READING

Bibliography

Kirkpatrick, B. J. *A Bibliography of Katherine Mansfield.* Oxford: Clarendon Press, 1989, 396 p.

Includes extensive listings of books and pamphlets, contributions to books, periodicals, and newspapers, books translated by Mansfield, translations of Mansfield's works into foreign languages, large print editions, Braille, embossed, and talking books, extracts from unpublished letters, journals, and other material, stage and film scripts, radio and television productions, ballet, musical, and stage productions, films, and manuscripts.

Biography

Alpers, Antony. *The Life of Katherine Mansfield.* Rev. ed. London: Viking Penguin, 1980, 466 p.

Extensively researched biography that includes critical commentary.

Mantz, Ruth. *The Life of Katherine Mansfield.* London: Constable & Co., 1933, 349 p.

Biography sanctioned and overseen by John Middleton Murry.

Meyers, Jeffrey. *Katherine Mansfield: A Biography.* London: Hamish Hamilton, 1978, 306 p.

Revises the idealized portrait of Mansfield created by Murry.

Moore, James. *Gurdjieff and Mansfield.* London: Routledge & Kegan Paul, 1980, 261 p.

Dual biographical accounts of Mansfield and psychic healer Gurdjieff intended to correct longstanding misperceptions about their lives and their association just before Mansfield's death.

Moore, Leslie [pseudonym of Ida Baker]. *Katherine Mansfield: The Memories of L. M.* London: Joseph, 1971, 240 p.

Reminiscences by a longtime friend and companion of Mansfield.

Murry, John Middleton. *The Autobiography of John Middleton Murry: Between Two Worlds.* New York: Julian Messner, 1936, 500 p.

Includes extensive biographical information about Mansfield.

Tomalin, Claire. *Katherine Mansfield: A Secret Life.* London: Viking, 1987, 292 p.

Biography that addresses several events in Mansfield's life that have been neglected by previous biographers.

Criticism

Aiken, Conrad. "Mansfield, Katherine (1921)," "Mansfield, Katherine (1922)," and "Mansfield, Katherine (1927)." In his *Collected Criticism,* pp. 291-93, 293-97, 297-99. London: Oxford University Press, 1958.

Favorable reviews of *Bliss, and Other Stories, The Garden Party, and Other Stories,* and the *Journal of Katherine Mansfield,* assessing Mansfield as an important literary talent.

Baldeshwiler, Eileen. "Katherine Mansfield's Theory of Fiction." *Studies in Short Fiction* VII, No. 3 (Summer 1970): 421-32.

Examines statements about narrative form and technique drawn from Mansfield's published letters, journals, and book reviews.

Bateson, F. W., and Shahevitch, B. "Katherine Mansfield's 'The Fly': A Critical Exercise." *Essays in Criticism* XII, No. 1 (January 1962): 39-53.

Reprints Mansfield's "The Fly" and offers a close textual analysis. R. A. Jolly, R. A. Copland, and E. B. Greenwood responded to this essay (cited below).

Beachcroft, T. O. "Katherine Mansfield." In his *The Modest Art: A Survey of the Short Story in English,* pp. 162-75. London: Oxford University Press, 1968.

Addresses the question of Anton Chekhov's influence in a discussion of Mansfield's innovative use of the short story form.

Berkman, Sylvia. *Katherine Mansfield: A Critical Study.* New Haven: Yale University Press, 1951, 246 p.

Important biographical and critical survey.

Blanchard, Lydia. "The Savage Pilgrimage of D. H. Lawrence and Katherine Mansfield: A Study in Literary Influence, Anxiety, and Subversion." *Modern Language Quarterly* 47, No. 1 (March 1986): 48-65.

Contends that in the novels *The Lost Girl* and *Women in Love* by Lawrence and the short stories "Je Ne Parle Pas Français," "Bliss," and "Marriage á la Mode" by Mansfield, each writer was responding to messages conveyed in the work of the other.

Boyle, Ted E. "The Death of the Boss: Another Look at Katherine Mansfield's 'The Fly'." *Modern Fiction Studies* XI, No. 2 (Summer 1965): 183-85.

Disputes the interpretation by John V. Hagopian (cited below) of the boss as a largely sympathetic figure with an imperfect understanding of death, suggesting that the story deals with the spiritual death of the boss.

Brewster, Dorothy, and Burrell, Angus. "Soundings: Fiction of Anton Chekhov and Katherine Mansfield" and "Salvaging the Short-Story: Chekhov and Mansfield—Continued." In their *Dead Reckonings in Fiction,* pp. 42-70, 71-100. New York: Longmans, Green and Co., 1925.

Assesses shared characteristics of the fiction of Chekhov and Mansfield, noting in particular that both avoided the traditional short story form emphasizing plot and climax.

Brophy, Brigid. "Katherine Mansfield." In her *Don't Never Forget: Collected Views and Reviews,* pp. 255-63. New York: Holt, Rinehart and Winston, 1966.

Biographical and psychological sketch of Mansfield that has been interpreted as hostile despite Brophy's professed admiration for Mansfield.

Corin, Fernand. "Creation of Atmosphere in Katherine Mansfield's Stories." *Revue des langues vivantes* 22, No. 1 (1956): 65-78.

Examines ways in which Mansfield created atmosphere—defined as the general emotional effect, mood, and tone of a piece of fiction—and considers the function of atmosphere in her fiction.

Cox, Sidney. "The Fastidiousness of Katherine Mansfield." *The Sewanee Review* XXXIX, No. 2 (April-June 1931): 158-69.

Contends that Mansfield's life and works are characterized by her fastidious nature, which lent a quality of precision to her fiction.

Daiches, David. "Katherine Mansfield and the Search for Truth." In his *The Novel and the Modern World,* pp. 65-79. Chicago: University of Chicago Press, 1939.

Discusses Mansfield's application of a highly individual,

nontraditional set of values in her works, resulting in her illumination of an intensely personal, nonobjective truth.

Gottwald, Maria. "New Approaches and Techniques in the Short Story of James Joyce and Katherine Mansfield." In *Literary Interrelations: Ireland, England and the World,* Vol. 2—*Comparison and Impact,* edited by Wolfgang Zach and Heinz Kosok, pp. 41-7. Tübingen: Gunter Narr Verlag, 1987.

Examines affinities between the literary techniques of Joyce and Mansfield.

Gregory, Alyse. "Artist or Nun." *The Dial* LXXV (November 1923): 484-86.

Negative review of the posthumous collection *The Doves' Nest,* published by John Middleton Murry.

Gubar, Susan. "The Birth of the Artist as Heroine: (Re)production, the *Künstlerroman* Tradition, and the Fiction of Katherine Mansfield." In *The Representation of Women in Fiction: Selected Papers from the English Institute, 1981,* edited by Carolyn G. Heilbrun and Margaret R. Higonnet, pp. 19-59. Baltimore: Johns Hopkins University Press, 1983.

Includes discussion of Mansfield's fiction in an assessment of ways in which "the changing reality and image of childbearing" is reflected in women writers' views of themselves.

Hagopian, John V. "Capturing Mansfield's 'Fly'." *Modern Fiction Studies* IX, No. 4 (Winter 1963-64): 385-90.

Summarizes some critical interpretations of "The Fly" and offers a reading that rejects extra-textual, biographical interpretations in favor of the conclusion that the story "is an embodiment in language of an emotionally-charged, powerfully poignant human experience" not peculiar to Mansfield.

Hynes, Sam. "Katherine Mansfield: The Defeat of the Personal." *The South Atlantic Quarterly* LII, No. 4 (October 1953): 555-60.

Contrasts Mansfield's stylistic clarity with what Hynes terms the chaotic moral structure of her fiction. Defining moral structure as "the view of the world which emerges from [the] work," Hynes pronounces a coherent structure necessary to artistic maturity and asserts that Mansfield never successfully achieved such a structure in her fiction.

Jolly, R. A.; Copland, R. A.; Greenwood, E. B.; and Bateson, F. W. "The Critical Forum: Katherine Mansfield's 'The Fly'." *Essays in Criticism* XII, No. 3 (July 1962): 335-51.

Responses by Jolly, Copland, and Greenwood to F. W. Bateson and B. Shahevitch's "Katherine Mansfield's 'The Fly': A Critical Exercise" (cited above) addressing perceived inadequacies of that analysis. Bateson's response to the criticisms is also included.

King, Russell S. "Katherine Mansfield as an Expatriate Writer." *The Journal of Commonwealth Literature* VIII, No. 1 (June 1973): 97-109.

Examines how Mansfield's expatriate status influenced her view of art, the characters she portrayed, "and, perhaps, even the manner in which she [shaped] her stories around a moment of conscious or unconscious revelation."

Kleine, Don W. " 'The Garden Party': A Portrait of the Artist." *Criticism* V, No. 1 (Winter 1963): 360-71.

Considers the dual nature of the conclusion of "The Garden Party," in which the protagonist's acquisition of adult perceptions about life and death also illuminates for the reader "the ardent, entranced sensibility" of a young girl.

Kobler, J. F. *Katherine Mansfield: A Study of the Short Fiction.* Boston: Twayne, 1990, 172 p.

Comprehensive critical study focusing on Mansfield's development as a short story writer.

Littell, Robert. "Katherine Mansfield." *The New Republic* XXXIV, No. 430 (28 February 1923): 22.

Obituary tribute commending Mansfield's ability to portray "moods, and small joys, and small griefs."

Magalaner, Marvin. *The Fiction of Katherine Mansfield.* Carbondale and Edwardsville: Southern Illinois University Press, 1971, 148 p.

Critical survey of Mansfield's work, focusing on technique, psychology, language, and theme.

Maugham, W. Somerset. "The Short Story." In his *Points of View,* pp. 142-88. London: Heinemann, 1958.

Discusses Mansfield's life and works in a chapter devoted to study of the short story.

Maxwell-Mahon, W. D. "The Art of Katherine Mansfield." *Unisa English Studies* XVII, No. 1 (April 1979): 45-52.

Examines Mansfield's published journals and letters for explicit statements of the artistic principles underlying her fiction. Maxwell-Mahon is critical of John Middleton Murry for publishing an edited synthesis of diaries, informally kept notebooks, and other loose personal papers as Mansfield's *Journal.*

Modern Fiction Studies, Special Issue: Katherine Mansfield 24, No. 3 (Autumn 1978): 337-479.

Includes biographical and critical essays by T. O. Beachcroft, Geraldine L. Conroy, Richard F. Peterson, Mary Burgan, Marvin Magalaner, Don W. Kleine, and Adam J. Sorkin, and a secondary bibliography by Jeffrey Meyers.

Neaman, Judith S. "Allusion, Image, and Associative Pattern: The Answers in Mansfield's 'Bliss'." *Twentieth Century Literature* 32, No. 2 (Summer 1986): 242-54.

Traces allusion, imagery, and associations in the short story "Bliss" to the Bible and to William Shakespeare's *Twelfth Night.*

Nebeker, Helen E. "The Pear Tree: Sexual Implications in Katherine Mansfield's 'Bliss'." *Modern Fiction Studies* 18, No. 4 (Winter 1972-73): 545-51.

Analyzes the sexual symbolism of the pear tree in the short story "Bliss."

O'Connor, Frank. "An Author in Search of a Subject." In his *The Lonely Voice: A Study of the Short Story,* pp. 128-42. Cleveland: World Publishing Co., 1963.

Assesses Mansfield's personality and fiction.

O'Sullivan, Vincent. "The Magnetic Chain: Notes and Approaches to K. M." *Landfall 114* 29, No. 2 (June 1975): 95-131.

Discusses literary influences, imagery, and the biographical content of Mansfield's fiction.

Palmer, Vance. "Katherine Mansfield." *Meanjin* XIV, No. 2 (Winter 1955): 177-85.

Discusses the genesis of the "cult of Katherine" in the editions of Mansfield's journals and letters prepared and published by John Middleton Murry, and commends the attempt of biographer Antony Alpers to present a more balanced account of Mansfield's life.

Rohrberger, Mary. "The Modern Short Story—Analyses of Representative Works: Katherine Mansfield, 'The Fly'." In her *Hawthorne and the Modern Short Story: A Study in Genre,* pp. 68-74. The Hague: Mouton & Co., 1966.

Examines aspects of the symbolic role of the boss in Mansfield's short story "The Fly."

Satterfield, Ben. "Irony in 'The Garden-Party'." *Ball State University Forum* XXIII, No. 1 (Winter 1982): 68-70.

Contends that Mansfield's portrayal of Laura Sheridan, the protagonist of "The Garden Party," was intended ironically to underscore the character's lack of comprehension when faced with the reality of death and intimations of her own morality.

Schneider, Elisabeth. "Katherine Mansfield and Chekhov." *Modern Language Notes* L, No. 6 (June 1935): 394-97.

Considers similarities between Chekhov's short story "Spat khochetsia," which appeared in English translation in 1903, and Mansfield's "The-Child-Who-Was-Tired" from *In a German Pension* (1911), suggesting that Mansfield's story was an "unconscious imitation" rather than a work of plagiarism.

Stead, C. K. "Katherine Mansfield and the Art of Fiction." *The New Review* 4, No. 42 (September 1977): 27-36.

Examines biographical sources of Mansfield's fiction.

Sutherland, Ronald. "Katherine Mansfield: Plagiarist, Disciple, or Ardent Admirer?" *Critique: Studies in Modern Fiction* V, No. 2 (Fall 1962): 58-76.

Contends that similarities between short stories by Mansfield and Chekhov can be attributed to Mansfield's admiration for the Russian author and not to plagiarism.

Taylor, Donald S. "Crashing the Garden Party, I: A Dream—A Wakening." *Modern Fiction Studies* IV, No. 4 (Winter 1958-59): 361-62.

Response to Warren S. Walker's "The Unresolved Conflict in 'The Garden Party' " (cited below), suggesting that contrary to Walker's contention, the clash between the social attitudes of the protagonist, Laura Sheridan, and those of her mother, is not dropped, but rather, is subordinated in Laura's larger struggle to comprehend death.

Thomas, J. D. "Symbol and Parallelism in 'The Fly'." *College English* 22, No. 4 (January 1961): 256, 261-62.

Examines the symbolic value of the fly in Mansfield's story and draws parallels between the characters of the boss and Woodifield.

Walker, Warren S. "The Unresolved Conflict in 'The Garden Party'." *Modern Fiction Studies* III, No. 4 (Winter 1957-58): 354-58.

Suggests that of two chief conflicts addressed in "The Garden Party"—the struggle between the fear and acceptance of death and the clash of social attitudes between Laura and her mother—the second is left unresolved. Donald S. Taylor (cited above) and Daniel A. Weiss (cited below) responded to this essay.

Weiss, Daniel A. "Crashing the Garden Party, II: The Garden Party of Proserpina." *Modern Fiction Studies* IV, No. 4 (Winter 1958-59): 363-64.

Response to Warren S. Walker's "The Unresolved Conflict in 'The Garden Party' " (cited above), suggesting that the resolution of class conflict in the story is "a subordinate component of the primary theme—Laura's discovery of death, and its coextensiveness with life."

Wright, Celeste Turner. "Darkness as a Symbol in Katherine Mansfield." *Modern Philology* LI, No. 3 (February 1954): 204-07.

Addresses the symbolic nature of darkness in Mansfield's fiction, where it often signifies loneliness and isolation.

Additional coverage of Mansfield's life and career is contained in the following sources published by Gale Research: *Contemporary Authors,* Vol. 104; and *Twentieth-Century Literary Criticism,* Vols. 2, 8, 39.

Carson McCullers

1917-1967

(Full name Lula Carson Smith McCullers) American novelist, short story writer, dramatist, essayist, and poet.

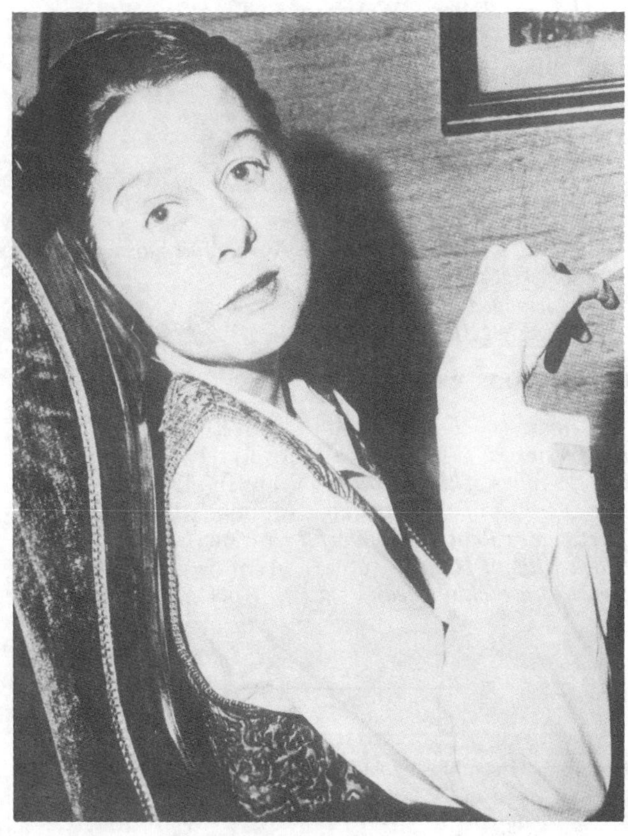

INTRODUCTION

One of the most prominent writers of the American South during the mid-twentieth century, McCullers is best known for her novels *The Heart Is a Lonely Hunter* and *The Member of the Wedding.* McCullers is also admired for the quality of her short fiction, particularly the novella *The Ballad of the Sad Café,* which is often regarded as the most fully accomplished examination of her major themes: psychological isolation and the failure of communication in love relationships. While *The Ballad of the Sad Café* contains disfigured and physically handicapped characters—a gothic element common to her longer works—most of her short stories rely on everyday situations and ordinary protagonists to examine various aspects of human love.

McCullers's first story, "Wunderkind," was published in the December 1936 *Story* magazine, and she continued to publish short fiction throughout her career. In 1943 *Harper's Bazaar* published *The Ballad of the Sad Café,* which was eventually collected in the 1951 omnibus *The Ballad of the Sad Café: The Novels and Stories of Carson McCullers.* The story revolves around a bizarre love triangle in a small Southern town: Miss Amelia, an androgynous woman, is drawn to Cousin Lymon, a hunchbacked dwarf who is a stranger in town. Lymon, in turn, is attracted to Amelia's handsome husband, Marvin Macy, who returns to town seeking revenge against his abusive wife after several years in prison. Before Macy's arrival, the dreary town enjoys a transformation attributable to Lymon's entertaining presence in a café that Miss Amelia opens in the town's general store. Eventually Macy and Lymon unite against Amelia, destroying the café and then leaving town. The novella concludes with Amelia, a physically and spiritually broken woman, closing her business and living out her remaining years as a recluse. Critics consider *The Ballad of the Sad Café* McCullers's richest treatment of the theme of isolation in love. The central characters of the novel are seen to reveal McCullers's conception of the arbitrary nature of love, and how individuals are attracted to people who possess traits they desire but lack themselves. The relationships comprising the love triangle in the novel also focus on the insurmountable separateness of the lover from the beloved and reveal McCullers's views on the enormous capacity for manipulation within love relationships. In its use of physically deformed characters, who, in the opinion of critics, suggest the human inability to fully give and receive love, *The Ballad of the Sad Café* most resembles McCullers's longer works.

The majority of McCullers's short fiction avoids the use of grotesques in exploring themes of isolation and love, relying instead on characters who are normal physically yet emotionally crippled by their incapacity to communicate effectively. While these pieces are inherently limited in scope, several are highly regarded for their slice-of-life renderings of modern love. "Wunderkind" concerns an adolescent's grappling with insecurity over her development as a musician and her awakening sexual urges toward her male piano teacher. "A Domestic Dilemma" focuses on a Southern family who are transplanted to suburban New York City. The plot relates the events of one evening, when the central character returns from work to find his children unattended and his wife inebriated. His emotions alternate between anger and compassion as he feeds and bathes the children, becoming keenly aware of their physical resemblance to their mother. The story concludes as the husband climbs into bed and reaches toward his sleeping wife, reflecting upon "the immense complexity of love." In "A Tree. A Rock. A Cloud.," which takes place in a diner, a tramp discourses on the "science of love." Addressing a young boy, he maintains that by first learning to love such inanimate objects as those listed in the story's title, one develops the ability to love everything and everyone. According to critics, youth and inexperience prevent the boy from fully comprehending the tramp's message, and the story is seen as a reflection of McCullers's concern with the inadequacy of human communication. Such poignant examinations of love and the frailty of human relationships in her novels and short fiction have placed McCullers—along with her contemporaries Flannery O'Connor, Eudora Welty, and Tenessee Williams—among the most celebrated modern authors of the American South.

PRINCIPAL WORKS

SHORT FICTION

The Ballad of the Sad Café: The Novels and Stories of Carson McCullers 1951
The Mortgaged Heart 1971
The Collected Stories 1987

OTHER MAJOR WORKS

The Heart Is a Lonely Hunter (novel) 1940
Reflections in a Golden Eye (novel) 1941
The Member of the Wedding (novel) 1946
The Member of the Wedding (drama) 1950
The Square Root of Wonderful (drama) 1958
Clock without Hands (novel) 1961
Sweet as a Pickle, Clean as a Pig (poetry) 1964

Coleman Rosenberger (essay date 1951)

[*In the following review, Rosenberger discusses the thematic unity of the works collected in* The Ballad of the Sad Café.]

Here in one omnibus volume, which includes her three novels, a half dozen short stories, and an unfamiliar longer one [**"The Ballad of the Sad Café"**] which gives the volume its name, is the whole fabulous world of Carson McCullers: the dwarfed and the deformed, the hurt and the lonely, the defeated and the despised, the violent and the homicidal—all the masks and symbols which she has employed over a decade of writing to shock the reader into a shared experience of her own intense sense of human tragedy. When *The Heart Is a Lonely Hunter* was published in 1940, it was widely recognized as an original and mature work, and the acclaim for it was mixed with mild astonishment that the book should be the work of a twenty-three-year-old writer. Something like that first astonishment is induced by the present collection, which exhibits what an impressive and unified body of work has been produced by Mrs. McCullers at an age when many another writer has hardly started upon his career. For ***The Ballad of the Sad Café*** makes abundantly clear, which was not generally seen at the time of their separate publication, that *Reflections in a Golden Eye* and *The Member of the Wedding* extend and broaden the themes of her first book, as do the shorter pieces, so that each takes its place in an expanding structure in which each part augments and strengthens the rest.

A recurring theme throughout Mrs. McCullers' work—perhaps the central theme—is the human tragedy of the failure of communication between man and man, and the sense of loss and separation and loneliness which accompanies that failure. The theme is examined and illuminated through minor characters as well as major ones. We see the drunken Blout in *The Heart Is a Lonely Hunter* pouring out his torrent of words to the deaf mute and exclaiming "You are the only one in this town who catches what I mean." Or the old man of **"A Tree. A Rock. A Cloud."** in his wild and earnest pre-dawn monologue directed at the uncomprehending paper boy. Or Frankie in *The Member of the Wedding* running beside the man on the tractor to shout words he could not hear through the noisy excitement.

In Mrs. McCullers' world of symbols, the urgent need to communicate is most often presented in the guise of the physically maimed or deformed, who are at once the favored and the damned. Frankie ticks off the freaks she had seen at the Chattahoochee Exposition—The Giant, the Fat Lady, The Midget, The Wild Nigger, The Pin Head, the Alligator Boy, the Half-Man Half-Woman—and recalls that "it seemed to her that they had looked at her in a secret way and tried to connect their eyes with hers, as though to say: we know you." And the artist, with his own compelling need to communicate, is one of the freaks of the world. (pp. 1,13)

The establishment of communication, the breaking down of the barriers of a torturing separateness, is the ultimate achievement of Mrs. McCullers' characters. The urgency which drives Frankie to become "A Member of the Wedding" is the conviction that "All other people had a we to claim, all other except her. The soldiers in the army can say we, and even the criminals on the chain-gangs." Again the theme is stated explicitly in **"The Twelve Mortal Men,"** the brief epilogue to the story of Miss Amelia. The voices of the twelve chained convicts on the road gang join in an intricately blended music: "And what kind of gang is this that can make such music? Just twelve mortal men, seven of them black and five of them white boys from this county. Just twelve mortal men who are together."

The six short stories which are here printed in book form for the first time, and the title piece, have apparently been drawn from Mrs. McCullers' whole writing career. The stories are not dated—the earliest copyright is 1936, when Mrs. McCullers was nineteen—and there is little to suggest the possible order of composition. If one were to guess, it would be that **"Wunderkind"** is the earliest. It is the story of the heartbreak of a fifteen-year-old girl who knows that she will not be a great pianist, a Wunderkind.

Such a brief gloss can give little of the quality even of the shorter pieces, such as **"The Jockey"** or **"Madam Zilensky and the King of Finland."** The jockey, dressed carefully in his tailored suit of green Chinese silk, is seen for a moment when he is on the edge of disintegration brought on by the injury of his companion and their separation. Madam Zilensky, composer and teacher, is also seen in a moment of crisis. She inhabited a private world in which she lived vicariously in the imagination, but in response to a story of hers about seeing the King of Finland, Mr. Brooks coldly observed: "But there is no King of Finland." And "never afterward could Mr. Brooks forget the face of Madam Zilensky at that moment. In her eyes there was astonishment, dismay, and a sort of cornered horror. She had the look of one who watches his whole interior world split open and disintegrate."

"The Sojourner" and **"A Domestic Dilemma"** and **"A Tree. A Rock. A Cloud."** are, in their various ways, stories of the separateness which may exist in the "we" of man and wife. It is, however, in the title story, ***The Ballad of the Sad Café,*** that Mrs. McCullers' achievement is seen at its most intense. A short novel, or long short story, or novella—it runs to some sixty pages in the present closely printed volume—it is condensed and disciplined and brilliant writing, which carries the reader along so easily on the wave of the story that he may not at first be aware how completely he has been saturated with symbolism. The story opens and closes with Miss Amelia's house as it now is, lonely, estranged, separate, boarded up. Between is an account of the coming and the departure of the hunchback and Marvin Macy. The hunchback, the deformed, the freak, the artist, was possessed of the "instinct to establish immediate and vital contact between himself and all things in the world." Before disaster came at last, Miss Amelia pushed back the barriers of separateness for a time, and the strange café was established as a place of warmth and fellowship in the desolate town. Miss Amelia and the hunchback and Marvin Macy, the instrument of the disaster, are a grotesque crew. But as Mrs. McCullers patiently explains: "The hearts of small children are delicate organs. A cruel beginning in this world can twist them into curious shapes. The heart of a child can shrink so that forever afterward it is hard and pitted as the seed of a peach. Or again, the heart of such a child may fester and swell until it is a misery to carry within the body, easily chafed and hurt by the most ordinary things." Mrs. McCullers' freaks are not to be dismissed: they are Everyman. (p. 13)

Coleman Rosenberger, in a review of "The Ballad of the Sad Café," in the New York Herald Tribune Book Review, *June 10, 1951, pp. 1, 13.*

V. S. Pritchett (essay date 1952)

[Pritchett is a highly esteemed English novelist, short story writer, and critic. Considered one of the modern masters of the short story, he is also one of the world's most respected and well-read literary critics. Pritchett writes in the conversational tone of the familiar essay, a method by which he approaches literature from the viewpoint of a lettered but not overly scholarly reader. A twentieth-century successor to such early nineteenth-century essayist-critics as William Hazlitt and Charles Lamb, Pritchett employs much the same critical method; his own experience, judgment, and sense of literary art are emphasized, rather than a codified critical doctrine derived from a school of psychological or philosophical speculation. In the following excerpt, Pritchett favorably assesses The Ballad of the Sad Café *and defines McCullers's literary genius.]*

From a brief indication of the locale and theme of a great many American novels, it has become pretty easy to fill in the rest. The spell of American loquacity comes on one like some interminable talk in a train; it is the spell of the literal mind which breaks down any human situation into the "I said" and "he said" of circumstance and which has submitted life to the mild, friendly chewing of the human jaw. There is a limp democratic charm in this manner of writing: all jaws are equal, all are moving. The liberating quality in a large number of quite ordinary American novels, indeed, seems to spring from the notion that it is enough to talk in our own sagging way through everything. But that idea has long ago lost its novelty. Large areas of very talented American writing are mere repetition work, a hurried laying-down of the macadam of a literature, an expert bustling around to see that all streets are paved, and the talking mind does this more quickly than any other. What we look for is the occasional American genius—the Faulkner, for example—who will build his own original, imaginative or intellectual structures in some small corner of the plan.

Such a genius is Miss Carson McCullers, the most remarkable novelist, I think, to come out of America for a generation. Coverage is ignored by her. She is a regional writer from the South, but behind her lies that classical and melancholy authority, that indifference to shock, which seem more European than American. She knows her own original, fearless and compassionate mind. The short novels and two or three stories now published in ***The Ballad of the Sad Café***—the sing-song Poe-like title so filled with the dominant American emotion of nostalgia—make an impact which recalls the impression made by such very different writers as Maupassant and D. H. Lawrence. What she has, before anything else, is a courageous imagination; that is to say one that is bold enough to consider the terrible in human nature without loss of nerve, calm, dignity or love. She has the fearless "golden eye" of the title of one of her stories. She is as circumspect as Defoe was in setting down the plain facts of her decaying Southern scene—a boring military camp, the dying little mill town with its closed café and empty streets, the back-kitchen life of a widower's daughter—and yet the moment she picks out her people, they are changed from the typical to the extraordinary. Like all writers of original genius, she convinces us that we have missed something which was plainly to be seen in the real world. So that if it is a matter of freaks like a gangling, mannish, hard-spitting, hard-hitting old virgin, or the hunchback dwarf she falls in love with, we are made to see that ordinary human love can transform them as it can any other creature: and, reversing the situation, when love gives its twist to a pair of dull officers and their wives at a military station, they become as strange, in their way, as the freaks. Like a chorus the mass of ordinary people crowd round these afflicted hearts. It may be objected that the very strangeness of the characters in a story like ***The Ballad of the Sad Café*** is that of regional gossip and in fact, turns these characters into minor figures from some American Powys-land. They become the bywords of a local ballad. But the compassion of the author gives them their Homeric moment in a universal tragedy. There is a point at which they become "great." A more exact definition of the range of her genius would be to say that human destiny is watched by her in the heart alone. She is—but in the highest and most sensitive degree—limited to the subject of personality.

On that subject she is a master of peculiar perception and an incomparable story-teller. The ***Ballad,*** though it concerns oddities, is a most ingenious and surprising work and, as in her other stories, its invention and surprise are found not in plot but in the contemplation of the characters themselves. She winds her way backwards and forwards into her people in a way that is sometimes too dilatory, but at every digression she cannot fail to come upon some new bearing on their fate. The almost intolerable, magnetised suspense of her stories comes from the leisure of telling and her power to catch the fatal changes in people. The little hunchback in the ***Ballad*** appears first of all as a miserable, weeping abortion at Miss Amelia's store; a meal, a bed, an act of kindness turn him into a hard, proud little fellow; the astonishing love Miss Amelia suddenly thrusts on him—it is described as a sudden hunger of "lonesomeness"—turns him further into a chattering tyrant and dandy. He civilises this terrible virgin who had once thrown a husband out of her room on her bridal night. The dwarf softens her mad quarrels, her cheating and violence; at night she sits up with him because he is afraid of the dark and has a terror of death. But if two strange beings are remade by love, the dwarf strengthened by it, the woman weakened, they are now vulnerable to betrayal. And it is at this moment that Miss McCullers's powers as a storyteller come out, for every trivial detail that has gone before now plays its part in the terrible personal tragedy; the destruction of the heart of Miss Amelia. Miss Amelia fears that when her convict husband comes out he will kill the dwarf; what she does not reckon with is that emulation and slavishness underlie the vanity of the dwarf and that he will idiotically fall for the convict and will betray her. The betrayal occurs in the phenomenal set wrestling-match which takes place between this man-woman and her husband. Here is an example of Miss McCullers's eye for circumstance:

> The fight took place on Ground Hog Day, which is the second of February. The weather was favourable, being neither rainy nor sunny, and with a neutral temperature. There were several signs that this was the appointed day, and by ten o'clock the news spread all over the county. Early in the morning Miss Amelia went out and cut down her punching bag. Marvin Macy sat on the back step with a tin can of hog fat between his knees and carefully greased his arms and his legs. A hawk with a bloody breast flew over the town and circled twice round the property of Miss Amelia. The tables in the café were moved out to the back porch, so that the whole room was cleared for the fight. There was every sign. Both Miss Amelia and Marvin Macy ate four helpings of half-raw roast for dinner, and then lay down in the afternoon to store up strength. Marvin Macy rested in the big room upstairs, while Miss Amelia stretched herself out on the bench in her office. It was plain from her white stiff face what a torment it was for her to be lying still and doing nothing, but she lay there quiet as a corpse with her eyes closed and her hands crossed on her chest.
>
> (p. 137)

Miss McCullers is a writer of the highest class because of her great literary gifts; but underlying these, and not less important, is her sense of the completeness of human experience at any moment. She is a classic, not a convert. (p. 138)

V. S. Pritchett, in a review of "The Ballad of the Sad Café," in The New Statesman & Nation, *Vol. XLIV, No. 1117, August 2, 1952, pp. 137-38.*

Ihab Hassan (essay date 1961)

[*Hassan was born in Cairo, Egypt, in 1925. He moved to the United States in 1946 and has held teaching and lecturing positions at many universities throughout the world. In the following excerpt, Hassan explores the doctrine of love presented in* The Ballad of the Sad Café *and the short stories.*]

Since the publication of *The Heart Is a Lonely Hunter* in 1940, when its author was only twenty-three years old, Carson McCullers has been recognized as one of the most likely talents in the South, one who brought strange and artful gifts of sensibility to the contemporary novel. The strangeness, however, reminded some readers of Poe's artifices, and it persuaded them to discredit her fiction as simply gothic. The judgment is aberrant and at best specious. It is true that Mrs. McCullers lacks the scope, strength, and fury of Faulkner, lacks his dark apprehension of the Southern past and his profound insight into the American wilderness, symbols both of our guilt and innocence. And it is also true that Mrs. McCullers, hypnotized as she seems to be by the burning point where love and pain secretly meet, foregoes a certain richness of surface which, let us say, Eudora Welty seldom foregoes. Still, the gothic element, the personal principle in Mrs. McCullers' work, excludes none of the larger aspects of the Southern tradition to which it belongs. In his recent introduction to *Great Tales of the Deep South,* Malcolm Cowley has summarized well these aspects of the Southern literary mind: a mind preeminently aware of custom and ceremony yet deeply responsive to the elemental nature of existence, a mind anxious to preserve the sense of place and time, of family and community, of folk life and, above all, of oral discourse. Its basic assumption seems to be, as Robert B. Heilman has noted, that "the concrete evidence of the human being is that he does not change much, that he may actually be harmed by the material phenomena usually implied by *progress,* and that in any case his liability to moral difficulty remains constant. Formal and conservative, oriented at once toward the personal and the mythic, therefore symbolic, the Southern imagination seems determined to capture man in his very essence. Hence its marked anti-pragmatic bias: "In the *ethos* of Jefferson and Yoknapatawpha, the essence of man lies in being, not in having or doing," John Maclachlan has remarked of

Faulkner's country. It is precisely the being of man that modern civilization has put on trial, and the Southern novel has sought the means, wayward sometimes and excessive, to redefine.

Within the framework of these general assumptions the gothic imagination of Carson McCullers is put to play. Yet being gothic, which is to say Protestant—for the gothic may be conceived as a latent reaction to the Catholic hierarchy under God—being both Protestant and gothic, her imagination derives its peculiar force from a transcendental idea of spiritual loneliness. Our business will be to consider the spectacle of love and pain which constitutes her fiction, and in which the idea of spiritual isolation comes repeatedly to focus. For so broad a view, some provisional clarification of terms is necessary.

To say that Mrs. McCullers has a gothic penchant is but to note, and note superficially, her interest in the grotesque, the freakish, and the incongruous. Such qualities, to be sure, exert a large influence on the contemporary imagination; and they stand in a necessary and paradoxical relation to the facts of Southern life which emphasize the power of tradition and pull of community. For alienation, like monstrousness, can become a dramatic condition only when viewed against those special norms—however vestigial—which make divergences from them meaningful. There is another sense, however, in which the gothic element may be defined more pertinently. The gothic insists on *spiritualization,* the spiritualization of matter itself, and it insists on *subjectivism.* We have it from Erwin Panofsky that "late Gothic art broke up into a variety of styles" reflecting the ideological developments of the Middle Ages; these developments were "unified by a subjectivism" which extended from the visual arts to the political sphere. The gothic impulse is also transcendental: it reaches out in a piercing line to the sky. The distinction Allen Tate has made, in *The Forlorn Demon,* between the symbolic and the angelic imagination is apposite. The first, like Dante's, is Catholic: "It never begins at the top; it carries the bottom along with it, however high it may climb." The second, like Poe's, is both gothic and Protestant: in a transcendental effort of the will, "It declares itself independent of the human situation in the quest of essential knowledge." It should not be difficult to see how the mysticism of Suso and Eckhart, the idea of prayer in Luther, the experience of spiritual horror without sensible correlative in Poe, and the gothic nightmare of alienation in the fiction of Carson McCullers fall into a somber sequence. But Protestant as the fundamentalist tradition of the South may be, and gothic as its experience of guilt and tragedy is likely to appear, it is the peculiar stamp of subjectivism, wistful and bizarre, that emerges like a watermark on every page Mrs. McCullers has written. Such introversion, we know, is a result of the disjunction between self and world which contemporary life has magnified. The disjunction is formalized into a cross to which the characters of Carson McCullers are bound, and often bound without hope of remission.

Yet it is only fair to add that her attitude is more complex than we imply. There is, of course, one sense in which Mrs. McCullers can be said to celebrate the lonely and the outcast, the frail children of the earth, those, like Singer in her first novel, who have in their face "something gentle and Jewish, the knowledge of one who belongs to a race that is oppressed." Adolescents and freaks are her rueful heroes because the first are as yet uninitiated and the latter are forever unacceptable; both do not belong, and in both physical incompleteness is the source of a qualitative, a spiritual difference. And lonely as her characters are, encased as they are in their dreams, most private of human expressions, their actions usually serve only to intensify their solitude. Their situation is, as Oliver Evans has noted, "not so much a comment on the futility of communication as it is on the undesirability of it." But there is still another sense, deeper and more significant, in which Carson McCullers can be said to underscore the inadequacy of subjectivism, of silence. Indeed, the integrity of her vision depends on her guiding insight into the tensions of our situation, caught as we are between immersion of the self in a mass society and dissipation of the world leading to madness, crime, or hermeticism.

The challenge of form is the measure of insight; the formal tension between the self and the world in the novel corresponds to the thematic juxtaposition of the power of love and the presence of pain in the vision of Carson McCullers. It is in ***The Ballad of the Sad Café*** that the doctrine of love, implicit in all her fiction, is most clearly enunciated. The passage deserves extensive quotation:

> First of all, love is a joint experience between two persons—but the fact that it is a joint experience does not mean that it is a similar experience to the two people involved. There are the lover and the beloved, but these two come from different countries. Often the beloved is only a stimulus for all the stored up love which has lain quiet within the lover for a long time hitherto. And somehow every lover knows this. He feels in his soul that his love is a solitary thing. He comes to know a new strange loneliness and it is this knowledge that makes him suffer. . . . Let it be added that this lover . . . can be man, woman, child, or indeed any human creature on this earth.
>
> Now, the beloved can also be of any description. The most outlandish people can be the stimulus of love. . . . Therefore, the value and quality of any love is determined solely by the lover himself.
>
> It is for this reason that most of us would rather love than be loved. . . . And the curt truth is that, in a deep secret way, the state of being beloved is intolerable to many. The beloved fears and hates the lover. . . .

Here are some consequences of this remarkable statement: to love is to suffer, to intensify one's loneliness. Love needs no reciprocation; its quality is determined solely by the lover; and its object can be as "outlandish" as the world may offer. Hence the grotesque nature of the objects of love in Carson McCullers' fiction: hunchbacks, deaf mutes, weddings, clouds. Hence also the desexualization of love since the love relation, often incongruous, does not admit of sexual communion. "By nature all people are both sexes," Mrs. McCullers says. "So that marriage and the bed is not all by any means." Singer, Brannon, Penderton, Amelia, and the men-women freaks who appear in her fiction are all bisexual, which is to say asexual. Then, too, without reciprocity, love becomes a crazy whirligig, the object of one love becoming the subject of another—witness Macy, Amelia, Lymon, in ***The Ballad of the Sad Café.*** Finally, love as a pure attitude of the lover toward *any* object seems to arrogate to itself the powers of God. As Tate puts it with regard to Poe, man as "angelic delegate of God" is empowered to perform His functions: "Not only is every man his own God; every man *is* God."

As a strategy of the deeper self, love is often expected both to protect man against his own inadequacies and redeem the inescapable fact of pain in the world. But the idea of love Mrs. McCullers proposes is not so palliative. By far the most startling consequence of her notion is love's avowal of pain, of *death* itself. Love, in intensifying the lover's pain, in precluding communion, and in electing outlandish recipients, seeks its own impediments. A revealing parallel is suggested by Denis de Rougemont in his book, *Love in the Western World.* De Rougemont argues that certain types of love which seek continually to defeat their end mask the fearful powers of the death wish. Boundless Eros, or transcendental Love, "despises Venus even when in the throes of sensuality," and whether it manifests itself in Courtly Love or Manichaean mysticism, it "intensifies our desires only to offer them up in sacrifice." Its real end is death. The omnipresence of pain in the work of Carson McCullers, the spectacle of a love forever seeking its own denial, leads us to a similar conclusion. Love, to be sure, redeems, but only provisionally. The critical limit imposed on the privacy of love—death, sacrifice, withdrawal—is exceeded again in the greater privacy of pain. The failure of communion ends in individual immolation, but the presence of pain makes of all men martyrs. Pain, we see, binds men in a universal brotherhood—like a chain gang—even more than love can. No longer an external threat to the self, pain, as psychoanalysts say, becomes introjected: it acts internally in the higher interests of the self. Thus the single affirmative note in Mrs. McCullers' work, sounded almost accidentally, is sounded by those who simply suffer and endure: by Portia and Brannon in her first novel, by members of the chain gang in her last story. "Radiance" and "darkness," "ecstasy" and "fright"—these are the words with which the two works end, words that predict no resolution to the human condition. They are interchangeable! (pp. 205-11)

It is interesting that the least and the most successful of Mrs. McCullers' works, *Reflections in a Golden Eye* and ***The Ballad of the Sad Café,*** 1951—the story was published in magazine form in 1943—should strike us as a variation on the same fictional genre. There is a statement by Frank O'Connor which serves to clarify the genre, and serves also to put both works in a nice relation to the tradition of the novel. "If Jane Austen were writing *Pride and Prejudice* in the modern way," O'Connor says in *The Mirror in the Roadway,* "the hero would never need to reveal his arrogance by all those subtle touches which Jane Austen analyzed. He would have been satisfied with a peacock on the lawn, and Elizabeth Bennett would have ultimately wrung its neck. . . . The main thing is that the character would be represented by an image corresponding to the author's view of his principal obsession or the author's view of his part in a poetic phantasmagoria. Either way, his character and role are determined, and his part in the story is more metaphorical than real." The characters of ***The Ballad of the Sad Café*** are both metaphors and grotesques (grotesques almost in Anderson's sense); the plot moves in the familiar pattern of a whirligig spinning out the impossible intricacies of love and pain; and the style, unconscious of its power, transforms this eccentric tale into something as universal as the old ballads about love and dread, madness and revenge.

The decayed house of Miss Amelia, its porch half-painted, its shuttered windows boarded, appears in the first scene of the story and in its last. The house, edifice to love betrayed, to loneliness irrevocable, stands in a small, dreary Southern town. The winters are short and raw, the summers white with glare and fiery hot. From behind its shutters, the strange face of Miss Amelia occasionally peers, a face "sexless and white, with two gray crossed eyes which are turned inward so sharply that they seem to be exchanging with each other one long secret gaze of grief." Firmly and with a sense of finality the narrative unfolds in retrospect before it comes to pause once again, at the end, on the same scene; the gothic touches never seem out of place, so strong is the feeling of mystery and doom. The story itself is simple. Miss Amelia, a powerful blunderbuss of a person, more than six feet tall, owns the only store in town. At the age of nineteen, she is courted by a strong, darkly handsome loom-fixer, Marvin Macy, with an "evil reputation"—he is supposed to carry around the dried, salted ear of a man he killed in a razor fight. Under the spell of love, Macy reforms temporarily, and Miss Amelia marries him in her slow, absent way. But the marriage, which is never consummated, lasts only a few days; Miss Amelia, despite all of Macy's pitiful protestations, beats him out of bed, and subsequently out of the house, after despoiling him of his possessions. Macy vanishes to lead a violent criminal life in other counties. Some years after, Lymon, the hunchback, appears at the doorstep of Miss Amelia, a tired and forlorn figure, seeking shelter, timidly claiming the rights of a dubious kinship. Lymon touches a hidden chord in Miss Amelia's character, touches in her a formless instinct, neither wholly feminine nor altogether maternal. She takes him in; he becomes Cousin Lymon; and the miraculous transformation in her life, of which the new café is evidence, induces a comparable transformation in the town. For Miss Amelia had ceased to be alone and ceased to find herself the beloved: she has suddenly become the lover, with all the pain, perplexity, and uncertain joy which attend that condition. Cousin Lymon thrives on her affections; alternately sour and saucy, mischievous and coy, he soon becomes the natural center of the café. But quick as Lymon is to respond in his egocentric fashion to any external interest, and much though he may be pampered by Amelia, he must secretly wilt, as Mrs. McCullers would have it, until *he* can find an object for *his* love.

The object is ironically provided by the sinister return of Macy, recently out of the penitentiary and bent on vengeance. The hunchback becomes immediately, outrageously, attached to Macy; he follows him around like a crippled mongrel, wiggling his ears, a figure of humble and obscene subjugation. And so the wheel has come full circle. Macy can torture Miss Amelia through the hunchback almost at will. The tension rises to an intolerable pitch, the showdown is preordained. The showdown is a marvelous and frightening scene, a grim wrestling match between the tigerish Macy and the virginal Amazon, Miss Amelia. It takes place by tacit consent on Ground Hog Day in the café, is witnessed by the whole town, and presided over by Lymon who stands watch on the counter, an unholy trophy of man's eternal struggle with Evil, with Death itself, which is the negation of Love. And just as Amelia is about to win the day, Lymon alights screaming and clawing on her back, to give the victory, after all, to Macy. The intruding *alazon* is not confuted or expelled: he triumphs. Lymon and Macy go off together after wrecking the café, wrecking the town really, and wrecking Amelia. Miss Amelia immures herself, the town resumes its sleep of death. "There is absolutely nothing to do in the town. Walk around the millpond, stand kicking at a rotten stump, figure out what you can do with the old wagon wheel by the side of the road near the church. The soul rots with boredom. You might as well go down to the Forks Falls Highway and listen to the chain gang." Yes, the chain gang. It is the envoy of the ballad, its hidden refrain: "The voices are dark in the golden glare, the music intricately blended, both somber and joyful. . . . It is music that causes the heart to broaden and the listener to grow cold with ecstasy and fright. . . ." Unlike Pascal who saw in the image of a chain gang looking at each other sorrowfully and without hope a parable of the human condition, Mrs. McCullers manages to summon for once, in the song of "twelve mortal men," the indestructible joy of endurance and transcendent pain.

The novelette sets a standard of performance for Mrs. McCullers and gives authority to a certain gothic vision, at once quaint and elemental, stark and involuted, which writers like Truman Capote and Tennessee Williams have been inclined to explore. What the novelette does not set forth is a new conception of the irrefragable conflict between the selfhood of man and the otherness of reality, between private need and communal fulfillment. Hints of man's buried life, here as elsewhere in Mrs. McCullers' work, flash darkly to the surface. There is Miss Amelia's whiskey, for instance, which has the power to reveal the secret truth in a man's heart, and which goes a long way toward creating the convivial fellowship of the café, creating the sense of pride and openness and ceremony: "There, for a few hours at least, the deep bitter knowing that you are not worth much in this world could be laid low." But good whiskey alone is not enough; the broad sense of community in the café springs from a more personal source—Miss Amelia's love for the hunchback. It is a love, of course, that remains wholly desexualized; as the town puts it, there is no "conjunction of the flesh" between Amelia and Lymon. For love, it seems, must remain beyond sexual reach, untainted by casual gratification or instinctive need.

Few readers will insist that Mrs. McCullers' image of love should be touched by the Corneillian attributes of reasonableness and high-soulfulness—the age requires another image, less rational, perhaps, and more grotesque. But many readers will regret that no one in the novelette seems to have full access to his experience, to have any ultimate or even provisional understanding of it. In a sense, the work denies the possibility of *recognition,* and avoids, therefore, the fictional equivalent of tragedy, a feature symptomatic of an age in which experience seems, more than ever, unyielding to human intelligence. Moreover, when love specifies the only contact between the hero and his world, heroism itself becomes not merely a call to isolation as in tragedy, but also an inducement to surrender all volition. Without volition no external field for our interests or our actions can ever be defined. The wages of alienation are always compounded. Irony prevails. It is the envoy, the style of anonymous celebration and immitigable sadness, that raises the work to the condition of a haunting performance. The style of pretended ballad reticence and naïveté, of folk motifs and stark tragedy, of augurs and foreshadowing, of incremental repetition and telescoped action—the enfabled style seems to incarnate the very spirit of story-telling whose medium is language in and for itself. (pp. 223-27)

The themes of Mrs. McCullers' stories are not likely to surprise the readers of her novels and their manner is far less distinguished—with the exception of **"A Tree, A Rock, A Cloud,"** which contains the germ of her doctrine of love, the stories seem by comparison both nerveless and contrived. But the deficiencies of Carson McCullers in the short form only serve to enhance her mastery of the intermediate form. And her mastery of that form in turn underscores the limitations of her sensibility.

Against "the beautiful and blest *nouvelle,*" as Henry James called it, no American need cavil. It is a genre as congenial to the pace of the American mind, the quick, nervous apprehension of our experience, as it is eminently suited to the intense lyrical gifts of so many contemporary writers. But "intense" and "lyrical" are words often used to denote a literary fruit growing out of slightly morbid soil. We are quick to sense that the subjective bias of Mrs. McCullers' imagination is but an artful response to the forces that have driven the self into recoil, and that the scope of her novelettes, unlike that of the novel, permits her characters to elude the repeated assaults of reality, permits them, that is, to leave their wishes unconverted into dramatic action.

It is upon the unconverted, and even inconvertible, wish as it seeks embodiment in love and suffering that the art of Carson McCullers has fastened. In so doing, her fiction, in good Southern style, declares itself opposed to the general aspects of our culture. The quality of that resistance, however, is passive, and it suggests a limit this side of quietism which the literary imagination may not safely transgress. For though love is the great opposing principle which Mrs. McCullers embraces in her fictional critique of our civilization, the failure of love—and love seems always to fail—leaves man encapsulated in a state not very distinguishable from anguished solipsism. The aesthetic and social consequences of this predilection are not hard to recognize. Mrs. McCullers is not only forced to do with the slighter form of the novelette but also to invoke that tone of writing whose affinities with the "buried life" are closest: the tone of romance, poetry, and dream fantasy. The fate of her lowly heroes, however—always chosen among the innocent, the grotesque, and the sacrificial—shows that her work falls somewhere between the realm of tragic experience, where defeat acquires a meaning that transcends the fact of defeat, and the province of irony, where absurdity qualifies the intelligibility of all human suffering. In this perspective, as we saw, the typical proud hero of tragedy merges into the lineaments of a self-deprecating hero of irony to appear again in the guise of a scapegoat. Since the characters of Carson McCullers are granted a more limited freedom than the hypothetical audience in our society may be thought to enjoy, it is the need for freedom, conceived in the broadest sense consonant with our humanity, that her sacrificial victims most urgently express in the very instant of their immolation. Beyond love and beyond pain, striking through the closing circle of their consciousness, the heroes of Carson McCullers evoke a secret idea, some elusive imperative or dream, which by its very absence from their lives must haunt our own. It is this idea, delimited so implicitly, so shyly, by her fiction, that Capote, Salinger, and Bellow seek to make progressively more explicit in theirs. (pp. 227-29)

Ihab Hassan, "Carson McCullers: The Aesthetics of Love and Pain," in his Radical Innocence: Studies in the Contemporary American Novel, *Princeton University Press, 1961, pp. 205-29.*

Chester E. Eisinger (essay date 1963)

[*Eisinger is an American educator. In the following excerpt from his* Fiction of the Forties, *Eisinger focuses on the significance of failed dialogue in McCullers's short fiction and examines the relationships between lovers and their beloved in* The Ballad of the Sad Café.]

In an essay on "The Understanding of Fiction," John Crowe Ransom argues that fiction brings us into a primitive world of spontaneous and natural affections. He opposes the primitive to the intellectual and sentiment to idea. Since an art work must touch the heart, the substance of fiction should be drawn from feeling and not mind. Such a theory becomes at once a justification of the poetic vision as a means of apprehending experience. It gives sanction to a writer's commerce in a fabulous rather than in a literal truth. Out of these rich implications, such a theory makes a beginning in the description of Carson McCullers' work. She is governed by the aesthetics of the primitive. This means that her overview is essentially anti-realistic. She has cut herself off from the world of ordinary experience and ordinary human beings who might entertain ordinary ideas. Her people are bizarre, freakish, lonely, hermaphroditic. This aesthetic dictates an intense concentration on man's most urgent emotional needs: a communion of dialogue and love. For her, further, the truth of the fable is the truth of the heart. It is not concerned with abstractions about the structure of society or with ideological conflicts in the contemporary world. She has banished these sociological and intellectual matters from her fiction, narrowing its range, perhaps to its detriment, in favor of memory and mood, and above all, feeling. This aesthetic demands a poetic prose and a style which, in Mrs. McCullers' case, often appears childlike. Her prose has a deliberately jerky rhythm and uneven pace, creating a movement which is designed to give the impression of simplicity. Toward that same goal of simplicity, she is occasionally monotonous in tonal qualities and repetitious, again deliberately and to good effect. Her extravagant use of color and sensuous descriptions of food are further evidences of her immersion in the world of the senses.

The purpose of her aesthetic lies in the artist's need to communicate his vision, a need that Mrs. McCullers says she feels intensely. "The function of the artist," she has written, "is to execute his own indigenous vision, and having done that, to keep faith with this vision." If to keep faith is to pursue consistently a single theme, then she has succeeded. For everywhere in her fiction she works at variations on the theme of moral isolation. It is the paradoxes of loneliness and love that impel her characters to a wretched abandonment of hope and leave them to feed on the pain of frustrated communion. She is fascinated by the loneliness of individuals in a world full of individuals. She is possessed by the unceasing failures in the consummation of love, because the lover is always rejected by the beloved, who would himself be a lover, and the lover thus goes on dying, into infinity, his spiritual death.

Capote's characters, seeking the self within the self, follow a twisted path to an abysmal zero at a dead end. Mrs. McCullers' maimed half-people hope to make themselves whole by entering into a fructifying human relationship. She understands the need of the individual to define himself by something outside himself. This is the motive force behind her play on the dialogue of love. The desolation of her characters, and her own pessimism, lie in the failure to achieve the kind of communion that Martin Buber has described, the meeting of *ich und du,* joined in a mystical reciprocity. "What do we expect when we are in despair and yet go to a man?" asks Buber. "Surely a presence by means of which we are told that nevertheless there is meaning." When there is genuine dialogue, then there is genuine community, which "is the being no longer side by side but *with* one another of a multitude of persons. And this multitude, though it also moves towards one goal, yet experiences everywhere a turning to, a dynamic facing of, the other, a flowing from *I* to *Thou.*" In genuine dialogue, men, or men and women, establish a living mutual relation. In monologue disguised as dialogue, each speaks with himself "in strangely tortuous and circuitous ways and yet imagines [he has] escaped the torment of being thrown back on [his] own resources." Lovers often engage in such monologue, enjoying their own glorious souls. Mrs. McCullers' implicit hope is that lovers, all men and women, might flow toward each other as the imperatives of Buber's mystical insight bids them do. But the visible assumptions of her theory of love doom them to inevitable failure and condemn them to eternal loneliness. Their fate is to be at the end what they were at the beginning—half-people.

But it must also be said that the failure of dialogue lies in the carefully selected characters Mrs. McCullers permits to engage in it. She has stacked the deck to guarantee ruptured communion and fruitless love by choosing people whose need, to be sure, is demonstrable but whose capacities are crippled. It is her gothic imagination that dictates this narrowly specialized range of character. It is the gothic principle that drives her to a consideration of the outsider: the adolescent who has no place and no sex, the deaf mute, the beloved hunchback, the bisexual adult, or the maternal male. These bizarre characters, alienated from society and the self, dramatize the problem of their ambiguous sex in a life that is curiously desexualized. Mrs. McCullers has said that flight in itself interests her. The remark has meaning not in images of terror from which her characters flee, for this is not the pattern of her fiction. It is flight from normative behavior; it is the frantic flight of the divided soul between the poles of male and female in the prison of the self that interests her. It is her gothic vision that denies a final resting place to this tortured soul, for no resolution of its dilemma is possible. (pp. 243-45)

In 1951 ***The Ballad of the Sad Café*** appeared, a volume containing the title story, six shorter stories, and . . . three novels. The subjects of the short stories are music (Mrs. McCullers went to New York from her home in Columbus, Georgia, to study music; Mick Kelly wishes to go away to study music), the imaginative experiences of the inner life, and the problems of love. The characters are the inevitable children or the equally omnipresent grotesques. One story, **"A Tree. A Rock. A Cloud.,"** deserves comment, because here Mrs. McCullers works out a hierarchy of love and reveals how thoroughly she has engrossed herself in this subject. An old man who has suffered the pathos of loneliness and lost love undertakes a scientific study of love, making his life a pilgrimage toward understanding it. His conclusion is that men should begin by loving a tree, a rock, a cloud, and at last, a woman. Love is the kelson of creation by which everything in the cosmos is united, the insentient thing of nature and the aspiration of the soul. Out of the life of love comes a transcendent understanding. This mystical and monistic idealism, so suggestive of Whitman, is the happiest view of love Mrs. McCullers gives us, although this conviction that love is all comes to us from a broken man.

The Ballad of the Sad Café offers, in partial contrast, the theory that lover and beloved are different. The beloved, who may be the most outlandish sort of person, is merely the stimulus for love. The lover determines the value and quality of the love. Everyone wants to be a lover and not a beloved, as everyone wants to be a subject and not an object. The beloved hates the lover, but the lover will accept any relationship with the beloved. This doctrine is explicitly stated in ***The Ballad,*** which is written to illustrate it. It is a doctrine which makes inevitable the futility of love and denies the possibility of communion. It condemns man to spiritual isolation.

The story begins on this note of isolation, speaking of the dreary town, "lonesome, sad, and like a place that is far off and estranged from all other places in the world." It is an appropriate setting for the strange tale of three lover-beloved relationships, all in the pattern described. Marvin Macy loves Miss Amelia. Miss Amelia loves Cousin Lymon. Cousin Lymon loves Marvin. None of these people is lovable. Marvin is a fearless, cruel man. He is a Satan: there is evil in him, and he never sweats, even in August. Miss Amelia is a dark, firmly muscled, cross-eyed woman who stands six feet two. Cousin Lymon is a hunchback from nowhere. Love reforms Marvin, but when he is rebuffed by Amelia, he is enraged. He leaves town, becomes a criminal, and goes to the penitentiary. The lover scorned by the beloved is ruined. Then Cousin Lymon arrives in town, claiming kinship with Miss Amelia. She takes him in. She is a hard woman who had never before offered anybody a meal or a drink. But they drink together, and it is whisky that can warm the soul and reveal the message hidden there: Miss Amelia's soul was warmed, and the message was a message of love. The new Amelia and Cousin Lymon, who had an instinct "to establish immediate and vital contact between himself and all things in the world," open a café, where it is observed that Amelia has changed for the better. Being in love, she is not so quick to cheat; she lavishes gifts and attention upon Cousin Lymon. He takes but does not give.

Then Marvin Macy returns to town. Cousin Lymon is immediately drawn to him, although he treats Lymon with cruel indifference. Amelia suffers helplessly. Then Cousin Lymon brings Marvin home to live with him and Amelia. She can do nothing. "Once you have lived with another, it is a great torture to have to live alone . . . it is better to take in your mortal enemy than face the terror of living alone." But the intolerable situation cannot last. On Ground Hog Day, when a bloody hawk is circling overhead, Amelia and Marvin fight. Just when she has the fight won, Cousin Lymon leaps upon her back. At this act, her will to win is lost, and Marvin beats her. She is broken by the perfidy of her beloved. Marvin and Cousin Lymon steal many of her things, destroy her property, try to poison her, and then leave town together. She boards up her premises and goes into seclusion. The town is as lonely as it was at the beginning. One might as well go down and listen to the chain gang sing. There, twelve men, white and black, "who are together," make music that seems to swell out of the earth and the sky. Here, where freedom is denied, men live harmoniously together in community.

Mrs. McCullers explains the ballad as she goes along. The magic potion, the desolation of the place, the portents of disaster, the criminal character have all given it the air of mystery and the aura of simplicity—not at all factitious—upon which the idea of a ballad may draw. The bitter ironies of love in the three parallel relationships reveal once again the desexualized treatment Mrs. McCullers characteristically gives to love. It is twice-fruitless in that it is always frustrated and always barren. Free men, at least, are alone and ultimately without love. This is the persistent and universal gothic horror that transcends the choice of the humpbacked dwarf as a love object or of a leaning, deserted-looking, boarded-up house as the site of the sad café.

Out of the still and twisted world in which her imagination dwells, Mrs. McCullers has drawn some truths that come home to all men. She has illuminated the possibilities for loneliness and the capacities for deviant behavior that mark the human lot. But there is a troubling sense of something wanting in what she does. The world of the adolescent child is, after all, only a promise of life to come in adulthood. The crazy, private world of her freakish and tortured adults is on the periphery of our experience, even if a significantly disturbing one. It is a narrow corner of human existence that she has chosen to exploit in her fiction. Her view of man's fate, therefore, adds little, in the largest sense, to the dimensions of our understanding. The gothic view of life has conjured up the terror of life but has not weighed the consequences of that terror. Mrs. McCullers knows something of the conditions under which life must be carried on, but she has gone beyond this to examine how men might endure under these conditions. There is no room in her work for the *consequences* of human action; there is no sense of the continuity of life. She has succeeded perhaps too well in creating an art form that is cut off from life. It is a form cut off from society, from morality, from religion, from ideas, from concern with man's burden or with man's hope. It is a special art form, and its special quality makes it symptomatic of the phenomena we have always with us—a disturbed psyche and a disturbed time. (pp. 256-58)

Chester E. Eisinger, "The New Fiction," in his Fiction of the Forties, *The University of Chicago Press, 1963, pp. 231-307.*

Louise Y. Gossett (essay date 1965)

[*In the following excerpt, Gossett discusses violence as an aspect of dispossessed love in McCuller's short fiction.*]

The motif of Carson Smith McCullers' fiction is love, its modes, demands, successes, defeats, grace, and shame. Whatever force, instinct, or need holds the human community together, this is love. The falling apart of the community is signaled by the breakdown of communications between persons, by physical and spiritual isolation, by hatred and fear, by sexual perversion, or by economic and racial injustice, and violence accompanies all negations. Within each negation, however, there is a drive toward a positive alliance. No matter how distorted the relationship may be, Mrs. McCullers has compassion for every attempt of the human being to become a *we* instead of an *I*, as the adolescent heroine of *The Member of the Wedding* puts the problem. Thus the author is charitable toward the violence and grotesqueness which develop when the impulse to love goes astray, and she treats deviations more with mercy than with horror. This mercy, however, is less rigorous than that expressed by Flannery O'Connor. Mrs. McCullers feels sympathy for the yearning of her characters for something better than the confusion into which they have fallen. Miss O'Connor feels compassion for characters because as human beings they suffer bodily and spiritual deformities. Their misery, in fact, is an inevitable consequence of their humanity. Mrs. McCullers, on the other hand, sees the derangement of human life as a passing failure to be solved by a human restoration of beneficial relationships. Violence in her fiction therefore lacks the inexorable moral toughness present in the work of Miss O'Connor.

Despite the prevalence of conflict, frustration, grief, pain, and fear in Mrs. McCullers' work, the mood is seldom morbid or bitterly melancholy. Although the characters suffer grotesque physical or psychological disfigurement, they struggle toward meaning, even though it may never come. The sense of nothingness and despair which at times overwhelms the characters of William Goyen and Truman Capote also visits her people, but they project the feeling into some form of violence. The suffering, then, instead of being brooded over is acted out in fighting, murder, or mutilation, or is spoken out in vehement arguments.

The South which Mrs. McCullers uses is made up of the lower and middle economic strata in small cities or in hamlets: petty bourgeoisie who own cafés or jewelry shops; cotton mill workers, oppressed by long hours and inadequate wages; Negroes—professional men and servants—whose wisdom and patience are only partially available to either black or white. Their environment includes long glaring summers of heat and short changeable winters, drab houses and odors of poverty, blocks of shops, offices, and factories; and streets where faces have "the desperate look of hunger and of loneliness." Occasionally there are flashes of the red cotton land and black pine woods beyond the towns. The prevailing bleak ugliness accords with the violence of the lives traced by Mrs. McCullers, a use of Southern locale similar to that of Flannery O'Connor. (pp. 159-60)

In her fiction violence and distortion are parts of the often frightening labyrinthine complexity of love. Fear, infidelity, anger, and violence frequently overcome her characters long before they have found any passage through the labyrinth. Mrs. McCullers portrays the full terror of these defeats, but she never adopts the introspective morbidity of the defeated.

Love as a relationship which permits genuine communication between persons is the goal of most of Mrs. McCullers' characters. Thus the goal in itself represents nothing violent or distorted, but thwarting its achievement inevitably destroys order in both the outer and the inner worlds. (p. 161)

Loneliness is as inescapable in Mrs. McCullers' fictional world as it is in that of Eudora Welty or William Goyen.

The anguish and fear to which loneliness subjects human beings may be contained within the words of a tortured spirit or it may erupt into violence and antisocial behavior. For the unnamed man in the café, in **"A Tree. A Rock. A Cloud"** who talks to a bewildered paper boy, words rather than acts describe the wildness of his search for an unfaithful wife and the resolution of his sorrow in learning to love by beginning with a tree, a rock, or a cloud, a design also recommended by Judge Cool in *The Grass Harp.* Madame Zilensky (**"Madame Zilensky and the King of Finland"**) lies boldly in order to have a life which she can share with others, and Mr. Brook, who once tried to force his colleague to admit her outrageous exaggerations, feels that he has attempted to murder her. Children are especially vulnerable to a breach in the confidence they have established with adults. In their defenselessness they may strike out to inflict a reciprocal injury. Hugh Harris (**"The**

Haunted Boy") is tortured by the memory of having found his mother after she had cut her wrists. After her recovery he remains anxious, and when she forgets to leave a note explaining why she will not be at home when Hugh returns from school, he reacts with hysterical anger and fear.

The sickening sweep into the oblivion of complete isolation is one of the constituents of violence which Mrs. McCullers portrays with special effectiveness. The consequences of a broken trust may be violent enough to change the personality of a character. (pp. 162-63)

Although Mrs. McCullers often portrays adults as physically and emotionally ruined people, she brings her adolescents through violence to a healthy measure of maturity. This ability to achieve wholeness distinguishes their growth from that of many young people in twentieth-century literature about the suffering adolescent. The struggle of the adolescent who appears in the fiction of William Goyen or Truman Capote injures or defeats him with a deadly finality. Mrs. McCullers prefers to educate rather than to destroy her adolescents with violence. (p. 164)

The presence of a social pattern, such as the family or the community to which the adolescent is related, checks the violence which occurs in the development of young characters in the fiction of Southern writers like Mrs. McCullers and Eudora Welty. In one short story, **"A Domestic Dilemma,"** Mrs. McCullers makes the removal of the structure of Southern life contribute to domestic violence. Transplanted to New York, Emily disintegrates without the matrix of family and friends to provide a context for her life. The weaknesses which Emily would have controlled had she been filling a place in a known social structure break out as alcoholism and neglect of her children. Her husband Martin sees nothing ahead but "degradation and slow ruin."

If the adolescents in Mrs. McCullers' novels escape psychic injuries, the adults are not so fortunate. The force of strong emotions—whether normal or abnormal, all are forms of love in Mrs. McCullers' view—has warped many of her characters. Furthermore, she often uses disfigured bodies and impaired minds to underscore all that is problematic in human relations. Such hazards become proofs of the incomprehensible perversity of love in which the mutually repellent are not only attracted to one another but also are held together in unlikely relationships. This theme is explicitly developed in ***The Ballad of the Sad Café*** when repressed, mannish, managerial Miss Amelia falls in love with Cousin Lymon, a shriveled hunchback, and the hunchback in turn bestows his affection on Marvin Macy, a handsome rake who loves and marries Miss Amelia. The circle of pursuing and fleeing lovers repeats the wheel figures indicative of human separateness in *The Heart Is a Lonely Hunter.* The violence which attends the revolution of this charged circle in ***The Ballad of the Sad Café*** develops in the direct manner of folk literature which the title promises. Like an image of her spirit of pleasure which Miss Amelia had distorted through greed and violent litigiousness, the misshapen cousin quickly restores geniality, courtesy, and graciousness to the dreary mill town by turning Miss Amelia's store into a café. And like an embodiment of Loki, he is also the principle of disorder in the midst of order; for "when he walked into the room there was always a quick feeling of tension, because with this busybody about there was never any telling what might descend on you, or what might suddenly be brought to happen in the room." The conflict of affections among the principals quickly foments a fight like a match between folk heroes as Miss Amelia and Macy hammer at one another. Cousin Lymon breaks Miss Amelia's heart by aiding Macy and going off with him after the two wreck her house. The waddling figure of the hunchback dragging his green shawl after him and nibbling a mixture of cocoa and sugar to sweeten his sour teeth intensifies the conflict by making the attachments seem strangely arbitrary and grotesque. In the tradition of the ballad there are no explanations for erratic behavior which without motive disrupts the expected quiet and provokes the unexpected violence.

Freaks serve Mrs. McCullers as illustrations of the attraction-repulsion equation. Frankie Addams [in *The Member of the Wedding*] fears the possibility of ugliness in herself, an ugliness which she believes is implied by the connection the carnival freaks seem to establish with her. Biff Brannon [in *Reflections in a Golden Eye*], on the other hand, is fascinated by all the maimed, diseased, and misshapen who come to his café. The compassion which he expresses in his generosity to them is an extension of the human community, an affirmation of the author's belief that man in all conditions merits dignified treatment. Outward deformity in Mrs. McCullers' characters is not simply a reflection of twisted inner lives to express a tragic vision of life as Dayton Kohler proposes [in "Carson McCullers: Variations on a Theme," *English Journal,* XL (1951)]. Instead, Mrs. McCullers stresses the accidental rather than the inevitable nature of this condition; it is one of the chances of life that shows up love for the paradox of violence and calm, gentleness and cruelty, beauty and ugliness which it is. The lives of the physically afflicted like Cousin Lymon or John Singer [in *The Heart Is a Lonely Hunter*] contain their private tragedies of isolation and despair, but they also generate love and restrain violence. Within themselves and in the relationship of others to them they have an effect similar to Miss Amelia's liquor: it causes joy and suffering but it reveals the truth and warms the soul. (pp. 166-69)

Because she is attracted by the countless forms of love, Mrs. McCullers necessarily portrays violence as a private rather than a public matter. She does not seek to explain warped personalities and twisted loves on the basis of environment or heritage. All that is certain, as the Macy brothers in ***The Ballad of the Sad Café*** illustrate, is the unpredictable nature of love. Abandoned by their parents but loved by their foster-mother, they develop opposite temperaments. Henry becomes patient and shy, easily touched by the misfortunes of others; Marvin turns rough and cruel, a center of violence. For the most part in Mrs. McCullers' fiction problems of the present occupy the stage to the exclusion of the past, and the author does not search for explanations in history as does Faulkner. Nor does she prepare a broad condemnation of modern society, except in relation to race. . . . Mrs. McCullers makes no attempt to prove that the experiences which she portrays are prototypes of specifically modern behavior; she is content simply to make vivid the violence of the psychological and physiological illnesses that result from thwarted or abnormal love.

Although treating a subject close to Eudora Welty's theme of love and isolation, Mrs. McCullers uses violence less as a revelation to the characters involved than as an external description of their condition. There is a minimum of exposition of the unconscious. Most of the characters, except the adolescents and the psychotics, can identify their emotions and evaluate their connection with other people. Mrs. McCullers prefers direct reporting of tension and violence to the ambivalence of fantasy which Miss Welty develops. She also treats grotesque characters objectively and matter-of-factly. In ***The Ballad of the Sad Café*** she uses a device like the folk narrator to lengthen the aesthetic distance between the freakish characters and the reader. Events of violence in her fiction, however, always bring the reader in close to the narration.

In each of the novels an act of violence forms the climax in which tensions are not so much resolved as openly expressed and rearranged. New combinations of love will follow, but there is little or no indication that they will protect the characters from continuing conflict, for the complexities of love will inevitably provoke violence. (pp. 176-77)

Louise Y. Gossett, "Dispossessed Love: Carson McCullers," in her Violence in Recent Southern Fiction, *Duke University Press, 1965, pp. 159-77.*

Dale Edmonds (essay date 1972)

[*In the following excerpt, Edmonds discusses "Correspondence," focusing on McCullers's portrayal of the adolescent protagonist.*]

Although Carson McCullers is known primarily as a novelist, she is also the author of a small but interesting body of short fiction. Of the even dozen short stories (not including portions of novels) she published over the years—from **"Wunderkind"** in 1936 to **"The March"** in 1967—at least half may be classified as good, and perhaps three or four may be considered distinguished. Her best stories (with one exception, as I will note later) were collected in the edition of her works published by Houghton Mifflin in 1951: ***The Ballad of the Sad Café; The Novels and Stories of Carson McCullers.*** The following stories appear in this edition: **"Wunderkind," "Madame Zilensky and the King of Finland," "A Domestic Dilemma," "A Tree. A Rock. A Cloud.," "The Sojourner,"** and **"The Jockey."** The last three stories were chosen for the O. Henry Memorial Award volumes for the years in which they initially appeared and each has been reprinted more than once. To date there has been little critical commentary on Mrs. McCullers' short fiction, except for that concerning **"A Tree. A Rock. A Cloud.,"** which usually is seen in relation to recurring themes in the novels.

The short fiction Mrs. McCullers published after 1951 is of distinctly inferior quality. **"The Haunted Boy,"** which appeared in both *Mademoiselle* (November) and *Botteghe Oscure* (16) in 1955, and **"Who Has Seen the Wind?"** which appeared in *Mademoiselle* (September, 1956) are cliché-ridden and ineffective. However, both stories are better than Mrs. McCullers' last published pieces of short fiction; **"Sucker,"** a bit of juvenilia unfortunately resurrected for *The Saturday Evening Post* (Sept. 28, 1963), and **"The March,"** an embarrassing, if well-intentioned, fictionalized account of a "Freedom March" that found its way into *Redbook* in March, 1967.

Other than those mentioned, the only other published works of short fiction by Carson McCullers are two stories that appeared prior to the 1951 Collected Edition but were not included in it. The exclusion of **"Art and Mr. Mahoney"** (*Mademoiselle,* February, 1949) is understandable, for it is an only mildly amusing account of the impact of culture in the provinces. But one might question the exclusion from the Collected Edition of an early story called **"Correspondence,"** which appeared in *The New Yorker* for February 7, 1942. In addition to its intrinsic merits, **"Correspondence"** reflects a side of Mrs. McCullers' talent that the collected short fiction does not reveal: her gift for light comedy. My purpose here is to summarize and comment upon this story in the hope that it may be exhumed from the state of total neglect in which it currently reposes, and to suggest that Mrs. McCullers' short fiction is more varied in tone than is generally supposed.

"Correspondence" consists of four fictional letters from Miss Henrietta "Henky" Evans of Darien, Connecticut, to Manoel García of Rio de Janeiro. Henky ("people in the neighborhood all call me Henky because Henrietta sounds sort of sissy," she says in a P.S. to her first letter) has taken Manoel's name from a list of South American students tacked on the blackboard at her school. The first letter, dated November 3, 1941, is warm, outgoing, filled with information—some of it embarrassingly frank—about the writer. Henky is "going on fourteen years of age" and in her first year at high school. She reveals that she is tall and her figure "is not very good on account of I have grown too rapidly." She imagines Manoel as having "liquid black eyes, brown skin, and black curly hair," and declares that she has always been crazy about South Americans, although she has not known any. Also in the course of this first letter Henky states her religious beliefs (she does not believe in God, but is not an atheist, because she thinks "there is some kind of a reason for everything and life is not in vain"), discloses her career aspirations ("Sometimes I think I want to be an arctic explorer and other times I plan on being a newspaper reporter and working in to being a writer"), and mentions her lack of rapport with her classmates ("It is not that I am terribly unpopular or anything like that but I am just not so crazy about the other Freshmen and they are not so crazy about me"). The letter ends with Henky's exuberant plans for a visit by Manoel to Darien during the next summer vacation, then reciprocal year-long visits between the two ("I have not yet spoken to my parents about it," Henky adds, "because I am waiting until I get your opinion on it"). She closes the letter, "Your affectionate friend, Henky Evans."

Henky is still awaiting Manoel's opinion on November 25, 1941, the date of the second letter. She says she is worried because three weeks have passed and she has not heard from him, but rationalizes that perhaps communications take longer than she had anticipated because of the war. In this second letter Henky presses upon the unresponsive Manoel more details of her personal life: she is in bed with a bad case of hives; she is studying Latin as she is about to flunk it; she has been reading about reincarnation ("That means, in case you have not happened to read about it, that you live a lot of lives and are one person in one century and another one later on"). The second letter ends with Henky's avowal that every afternoon she waits for the postman, and has a "kind of a hunch" that she will hear from Manoel that very day. She signs the letter "Affectionately yours, Henky Evans."

The third letter, dated December 29, 1941, begins, "Dear Manoel García: I cannot possibly understand why I have not heard from you. Didn't you receive my two letters? Many other people in the class have had letters from South Americans a long time ago. Nearly two months have gone by since I started the correspondence." But once again Henky rationalizes about the understandably reluctant Manoel's failure to respond: "maybe you have not been able to find anybody who knows English down there and can translate what I wrote. . . . Maybe both letters were lost. . . . But perchance there is some reason I do not know about. Maybe you have been very sick in the hospital or maybe your family moved from your last address." Despite Henky's tolerant attitude, the tone of the third letter is a bit more formal: "I still sincerely want us to be friends and carry on the correspondence because I have always been so crazy about foreign countries and South America and I felt like I knew you right at the first." She closes the letter, "I beg to remain, Sincerely yours, Henrietta Evans."

The fourth and last letter, dated Jan. 20, 1942, is quite cool in tone: "I have sent you three letters in all good faith and expected you to fulfill your part in the idea of American and South American students corresponding like it was supposed to be." Henky tells the silent Manoel that nearly every other person in class received letters, and some friendship gifts, "even though they were not especially crazy about foreign countries like I was." Henky says that she gave Manoel the benefit of the doubt concerning his failure to answer, "But now I realize what a grave mistake I made." She asks "Why would you have your name put on the list if you did not intend to fulfill your part in the agreement? All I want to say is that if I had known then what I know now I most assuredly would have picked out some other South American." The final letter closes, "Yrs. truly, Miss Henrietta Hill Evans." There is a final P. S.: "I cannot waste any more of my valuable time writing to you."

Henky Evans is another of Mrs. McCullers' gawky, adolescent girls who are on the outside yearning to become part of a "we." The author reveals both her plight and her personality vividly in the letters that comprise **"Correspondence."** In fact, the character Henky Evans marks a transition between Mick Kelly of *The Heart Is a Lonely Hunter,* Mrs. McCullers' first novel, (published in 1940), and Frankie Addams of *The Member of the Wedding* (published in 1946). Like Henky, Mick is bored, virtually friendless, and self-conscious about her size and growing evidence of femininity. Mick finds herself retreating to the unreality of what she calls an "inside room" consisting of music, fantasies about foreign lands, grandiose plans for the future, and John Singer, the deaf mute to whom she pours out her dreams. But there is a significant difference in Mrs. McCullers' treatment of the characters Mick and Henky: Mick is depicted with scarcely a trace of humor. Hers is a somber tale of traumatic sexual initiation, sudden deprivation (in the suicide of Singer), and banishment from her "inside room" to a presumed life of drudgery as a clerk in the local five-and-ten-cent store. For all the power and passion in Mrs. McCullers' portrayal of Mick Kelly, the reader's credibility is taxed by the aura of unrelieved gloom and tragic inevitability which surrounds her.

Henky Evans of **"Correspondence"** is much closer in spirit to Frankie Addams of *The Member of the Wedding,* the most fully realized character in all of Mrs. McCullers' fiction. Henky may be seen as a "way station" between Mick Kelly and Frankie Addams, revealing the development of Mrs. McCullers' ability to create convincing characters. Frankie Addams, like her predecessors Mick and Henky, is an awkward adolescent girl, discovering in herself the first signs of womanhood. Like Mick, Frankie spends much of her time building air castles about foreign countries. But unlike Mick's, Frankie's fantasies are not desperate, almost schizophrenic means of escape from the poverty and despair of her daily existence, but are predictable adolescent daydreams—as are the fantasies of Henky Evans in **"Correspondence."** Another point about Frankie Addams in *The Member of the Wedding* that often is overlooked is that she is essentially a comic figure, comically conceived and comically rendered. There is pathos in her attempt to find a "we of me," a connection with someone and something outside of the unsatisfying "we" of herself, the Negro maid Berenice Sadie Brown, and her six-year-old cousin John Henry West, that makes her seek to become a "member" of her brother's wedding. But although this attempt ends in disaster—Frankie flings herself in the dust behind the departing honeymoon car screaming "Take me!"—Frankie possesses the natural resilience of youth, and soon is wrapped up in school and her new friend Mary Littlejohn.

Of course Mick, Henky, and Frankie are three different characters, in three different works of fiction—they should not necessarily think, act, and end up alike. My point is that Henky Evans in **"Correspondence"** represents a transitional stage between the somber and, to me, not very believable character Mick Kelly, and the wholly successful Frankie Addams. It is the essential leavening of humor, as displayed in the letters of Henky Evans in **"Correspondence,"** that is responsible for the success of Frankie Addams.

My final point about **"Correspondence"** has to do with the style of Henky's letters. In this story, for the first time in her career, Mrs. McCullers revealed marked skill in capturing and conveying the idiom of adolescence, a skill that reached its zenith in her remarkably effective handling of Frankie's point of view in *The Member of the Wedding.* In none of her works published before **"Correspondence"** (early short stories and the novels *The Heart Is a Lonely Hunter* and *Reflections in a Golden Eye*) was this skill evident. In this respect Henky Evans reminds me of Salinger's Holden Caulfield, who would not appear until a decade later. As has become a truism about Holden's account, the language of Henky's letters strikes the reader as absolutely right. The examples I quoted earlier should need no further elaboration in supporting this contention, but I might call particular attention to the exuberance and concomitant pathos of adolescence that keep breaking through Henky's studied attempts to sound sophisticated. One can imagine the consternation of Manoel García as he reads that the unknown American girl is unpopular with her classmates, that she has a bad case of hives, that she believes in reincarnation—and all the rest.

I would be reluctant to say as much as I have about **"Correspondence,"** since the story succeeds so well on the immediate level, except for the fact that it has been virtually forgotten. **"Correspondence"** is no stunning achievement, but it is a unified and effective minor work of short fiction. It deserves to be redeemed from the obscurity of the pages of an early wartime *New Yorker* to amuse—perhaps delight—readers who are still capable of being touched by the universal plight of adolescence. (pp. 89-92)

Dale Edmonds, " 'Correspondence': A 'Forgotten' Carson McCullers Short Story," in Studies in Short Fiction, *Vol. IX, No. 1, Winter, 1972, pp. 89-92.*

McCullers on the "grace of labor":

It is like a flowering dream. Ideas grow, budding silently, and there are a thousand illuminations coming day by day as the work progresses. A seed grows in writing as in nature. The seed of the idea is developed by both labor and the unconscious, and the struggle that goes on between them.

I understand only particles. I understand the characters, but the novel itself is not in focus. The focus comes at random moments which no one can understand, least of all the author. For me, they usually follow great effort. To me, these illuminations are the grace of labor. All of my work has happened this way. It is at once the hazard and the beauty that a writer has to depend on such illuminations. After months of confusion and labor, when the idea has flowered, the collusion is Divine. It always comes from the subconscious and cannot be controlled.

McCullers in "The Flowering Dream: Notes on Writing," 1959.

Joseph R. Millichap (essay date 1973)

[Millichap is an American educator, poet, critic, and scriptwriter. In the following essay, Millichap discusses stylistic and technical aspects of The Ballad of the Sad Café *in relation to the ballad form in literature.]*

Carson McCullers' novels, particularly *The Heart Is a Lonely Hunter* (1940) and *Member of the Wedding* (1946), often have been misread as Gothic and grotesque fictions, categories derived by critics from her works in these modes, *Reflections in a Golden Eye* (1941) and ***Ballad of the Sad Café*** (1943). Strangely enough, the same critics, intent on demonstrating their Procrustean theories in all of her work, often misunderstand ***Ballad*** by insisting on the universality of elements which are obviously peculiar to the point of aberration. The use of the bizarre theory of love offered by the narrator of ***Ballad*** as a formula for interpreting all of McCullers' fiction has hampered analysis not only of the *novella* itself but of her other works as well. The description of her narrative as a ballad, so obviously presented in the title, provides a key to understanding which unlocks the novella's difficulties of literary mode, point-of-view, characterization, and plot structure.

The literary ballad evolved from the ballad of tradition, which in turn is rooted in folklore, because the literary artist wished to exploit the archetypal energy of the ballad world and the formal simplicity of the ballad structure. Professor Gerould, the best known authority on the ballad, has provided in *The Ballad of Tradition* a succinct definition based on a wide knowledge of the *genre.* "The ballad is a folk song that tells a story with stress on the crucial situation, tells it by letting the action unfold itself in event and speech, and tells it objectively with little comment or intrusion of personal bias." Though McCullers' ballad is neither song nor folk art, and though its narrator certainly intrudes a great deal of personal opinion, the narrative also presents many of the characteristics Professor Gerould mentions in his definition and develops in his elaboration of it. McCullers' ballad concentrates on the strange love triangle formed by a manly giantess, a selfish dwarf, and a demonic bandit. The action unfolds in a few weird events which culminate in an epic battle waged purposely on Groundhog Day to decide the death or rebirth of love. The setting is a romantic wasteland where piney woods and swamps counterpoint the stunning heat of August afternoons. The concrete symbols of the ballad world both explain and motivate the action; buildings lean in precarious decay; trees twist grotesquely in the moonlight; birds and animals provide mysterious analogues to human action.

Clearly this is the traditional world of the ballad, a world of passion and violence, of omens and portents, of the full wild impulsiveness of archetypal human behavior. The particular world of this ballad is a Georgia mill village, a place like all the Southern back country, "a place that is far off and estranged from all other places in the world." The Southern hinterlands preserved the folk qualities as well as the folk songs of the Scotch border country. Therefore, the line between the real world and the ballad world is often indistinct in the American South and in McCullers' fictions which are set there. Unlike the larger mill city which serves as the setting of most of her fiction, the mill village is not used to probe economic conditions or regional problems in a realistic manner. Even the chronological setting is unimportant; it might be 1920 or 1940; for the village in ***Ballad*** exists in the temporally imprecise world of human passion.

Of course, McCullers' ballad is a literary one, wrought by a modern, conscious artistry not by the folk mind or by an artless imagination. The literary ballad has always been a difficult form; it can be hauntingly effective, as in Keats' "La Belle Dame Sans Merci," resoundingly dull, as with many of Scott's attempts, or unintentionally humorous, as Longfellow's "The Wreck of the Hesperus." The structural and stylistic integrity of the story, especially of narrative voice marks her literary ballad as an unqualified success. McCullers presents a narrator who can spin the fine fabric of romantic fiction from the raw materials of mill-village life without violating either realm. In ***Ballad*** a ballad-maker evokes from the world of the Georgia back-country a timeless, compelling story of human passion. His voice fixes the style of the novel—a perfect blend of the literate and colloquial, the objective and personal, talky observation. The existence of this filtering personality assures the novella's achievement.

Neither McCullers nor the typical third person omniscient voice, narrates; the ballad-maker tells the tale. A part of the town himself, he knows people, places, and history, often commenting like a chorus of spectators from the village (the refrain of the ballad sometimes has this same function). At the same time he is possessed of knowledge that only an omniscient author could have. Therefore, he must be creating the narrative from the history of this particular mill-village and demonstrating the operations of human passion to his listeners.

This device also releases McCullers from responsibility for the universalization of the fantastic observations on the mutual exclusiveness of love so often ascribed to her by earlier critics (such as Oliver Evans, Ihab Hassan, and Klaus Lubbers). The narrator defines love as "joint experience between two persons," the lover and the beloved. The experience between them is not necessarily the same for each party, for the lover and the beloved "come from two different countries." The lover attaches his love to some person, often without rational purpose. He creates an imaginary world surrounding the beloved and then releases his stored creative energies on this dream vision. "Therefore, the value and quality of any love is determined solely by the lover himself." The narrator continues: "It is for this reason that most of us would rather love than be loved. Almost everyone wants to be the lover. And the curt truth is that, in a deep secret way, the state of being beloved is intolerable to many. The beloved fears and hates the lover, and with the best of reasons. For the lover is forever trying to strip bare his beloved. The lover craves any possible relation with the beloved, even if this experience can cause him only pain."

The ballad-maker's theory of love is substantiated by the character relationships in the novella, but the limited number of cases prevents immediate acceptance of it as a universal law of human nature; it clearly remains the narrator's hypothesis, not McCullers'. The theory depicts one facet of the love's dynamics, but other loves have other patterns. In her later novels and stories love does live for a few people, at least for a time. Yet the earlier novels have partially demonstrated this pattern. In *Heart,* Singer often lashes out against the lonely hearts, who have forced themselves on him as lovers, though he is most often simply puzzled by their behavior. The tangled relationships of *Reflections* are sometimes marked by hate, for example, Leonora's hatred of Capt. Penderton, but most often by indifference. In the limited context of this novella, the ballad world, this one tragic aspect of love is exaggerated to the point where it looms as its totality. The ballad creates a picture without delicate shading; therefore, the projection of one tragic aspect of love can be accepted romantically as the whole definition of this complex human phenomena. The same fascinating effect exists in many of the traditional ballads, in "Barbara Allen" for instance, where an analogous love-hate relationship exists between the courtly lover and the disdainful beloved.

The narrator's theory of love arises out of the weird triangle that forms the structural center of this novella. There are three characters of importance: Miss Amelia Evans, Cousin Lymon, and Marvin Macy. Miss Amelia is loved by Marvin Macy whom she rejects; she loves Cousin Lymon; he turns from her to an idolatrous love for Marvin Macy, who despises the dwarf. A neat triangular diagram is formed.

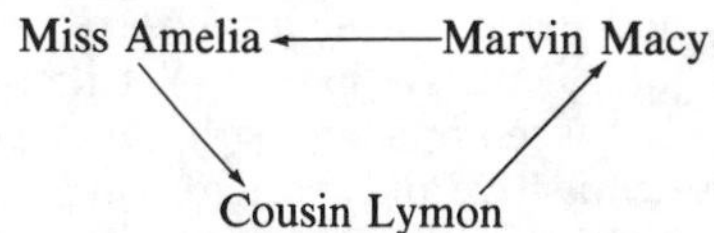

The ballad relates the story of this diagram, and the story aptly illustrates the ballad-maker's generalizations about love. As in both *Heart* and *Reflections* a geometrically patterned relationship of characters is the basis of symbolism and structure.

After the description of the town, which opens the tale, the narrator introduces Miss Amelia. On the hot, empty afternoons of August, the season when the town seems most desolate and isolated, her strange face peers down crazily from an upper window of the town's largest structure which is now boarded up and fast decaying. The building has "a curious, cracked look that is very puzzling," and Miss Amelia's haunted face with her severely crossed eyes provides the human analogue of the structure. The ballad-maker is also the Southern storyteller, the courthouse or country store loafer who will pass this dull August day retelling the story of the building and its strange inmate. The third paragraph introduces the history of the café, and of Miss Amelia, Cousin Lymon, and Marvin Macy. The narrator wanders back to the misty times before the café even existed; the ballad is being spun.

Earlier the café had been a store which Miss Amelia had inherited from her widowed father; "Big Papa" had raised the motherless girl almost like a son. The big-muscled Amazon easily assumed her masculine role and even surpassed her daddy in becoming the leading entrepreneur of the region. She supplies the mill workers and the surrounding farmers with groceries, hardware, and sundries. She also produces for sale her own chitterlings, sausage, sorghum, and whiskey. The quality of her versions of these Southern staples, especially her whiskey, is superior to any others; in fact the liquor becomes almost a magic potion which creates joy and insight.

> For the liquor of Miss Amelia has a special quality of its own. It is clean and sharp on the tongue, but once down a man it glows inside him for a long time afterward. And that is not all. It is known that if a message is written with lemon juice on a clean sheet of paper there will be no sign of it. But if the paper is held for a moment to the fire then the letters turn brown and the meaning becomes clear. Imagine that the whiskey is the fire and the message is that which is known only in the soul of a man—then the worth of Miss Amelia's liquor can be understood.

Miss Amelia is also the doctor, sawmill operator, and major property owner of the mill-village. Supernatural elements are present in her doctoring, as Miss Amelia's cures are drawn from the folk medicine of the region and her own mysterious researches into the properties of roots and herbs. Her benevolent or white witchcraft adds to the magical atmosphere of the tale. (An example is her use of "pot liquor," the juices left in the pot after cooking vegetables, as a rub for Lymon's frail body; Southern folk superstition still attaches magical healing powers to this brew.) Her whiskey and her medicine are also representative of a basically human, creative nature. Yet there is another side of her always competing with these generous instincts. She is acquisitive and avaricious in all her business dealings, quick to "go to law" or to use her big fists to defend her property rights. The store stands as her citadel; its transition into a café is essentially the story of Miss Amelia's humanization through love.

She has an earlier chance for human contact in her marriage, but it proved a dismal failure. Marvin Macy, her husband, is another larger-than-life character, as legendary in the mill town and its environs as Miss Amelia. An unhappy childhood caused by irresponsible parents made him into a figure of evil. His corruption is belied by his physical appearance. "For Marvin Macy was the handsomest man in this region—being six feet one inch tall, hardmuscled, and with slow gray eyes and curly hair." Moreover he is materially successful with a good job as a loom-fixer at the mill. Yet beneath these bright surfaces some dark force impels him to acts of outrageous evil. He carries as a talisman the salted ear of a man he killed in a razor duel, while another pocket contains "marijuana weed." As the demon lover of the region, he has degraded the sweetest young virgins, performing these depredations as coolly as he cuts the tails off squirrels in the pine woods. Yet Miss Amelia, because she is essentially unfeminine, cannot be seduced; Marvin confuses her asexuality and father fixation with personal strength, and this mistake makes him love her. He imagines that her self-sufficient strength can turn him from his dissolute ways, make him a responsible person, and restore the happiness he lost in childhood. In fact, he is asking her to be a mother to him, to replace his own lost mother.

The incestuous undertones of his love are mirrored in Miss Amelia's acceptance of him; she simply wants someone to take Big Papa's place as a companion and business partner. Both Amelia and Marvin project their unconscious desires onto the other, and both will be mightily disappointed. Marvin's love for Amelia does have an immediately reformative effect, and, until she rejects him, he is serious and well-behaved. Miss Amelia, hating him for his love, despising her own feminine role, and always driving a hard bargain, never allows their marriage to be consummated, not even when Marvin wills her all his possessions, and after ten days she drives him off her property.

Cousin Lymon is the strangest member of this outlandish trio. His past is mysteriously clouded; there can be no proof of his own version of his history, and even the village loafers regard it suspiciously. He does not elaborate in any way on his first revelation. When asked where he has come from, he replies uncertainly, "I was traveling." Even his appearance conceals the past of this mysterious stranger.

> His eyes were blue and steady as a child's but there were lavender crepy shadows beneath these blue eyes that hinted of age. It was impossible to guess his age by his hunched queer body. And even his teeth gave no clue—they were all still in his head (two were broken from cracking pecans), but he had stained them with so much sweet snuff that it was impossible to decide whether they were old teeth or young teeth. When questioned directly about his age the hunchback professed to know absolutely nothing—he had no idea how long he had been on the earth, whether for ten years or a hundred! So his age remained a puzzle.

The dwarf has much of the child about him. He possesses ". . . an instinct to establish immediate and vital contact between himself and all things in the world." His child's love of treats and spectacles—movies, fairs, cock-fights, revivals—provides insight into his personality, as does his child's curiosity and quarrelsomeness. Thus in many ways Cousin Lymon seems akin to the fairy children of folk tale and ballad—pixies, elves, leprechauns.

Miss Amelia is attracted to him by these childish qualities. Among people she likes only "the nilly-willy and the very sick," those she can see as easily molded and changed by her strong hands. In a sense the sickly, childish dwarf appears pliable. His physical deformities are also part of his attraction for Amelia and the others; touching a hunchback's hump is regarded as good luck in folk tradition. He becomes a strange combination of man, child, and pet that Amelia can love as she could not love her husband. He is a man loved without sex, a child acquired without pain, and a companion which her limited personality finds more acceptable than a husband or a child. Their relationship, like Amelia's marriage, is symbolically incestuous and immaturely formed.

The very nature of her attitude toward him ultimately causes his rejection of her for Marvin Macy. Some bond of natural kinship exists between the two adolescent men. When they first see each other they exchange a stare, ". . . like the look of two criminals who recognize each other." Cousin Lymon has a child's fascination with outlaws and an adolescent's admiration of the rebel and outcast. More importantly, the criminal is a father figure; Marvin Macy's tall, straight body and masculine swagger are qualities opposite to Lymon's, qualities which are not a part of the child's role he must play with Amelia. Therefore, he begins to reject Amelia, just as Marvin Macy hates him as representative of his failed marriage. A new dimension of hate is added to the love triangle,

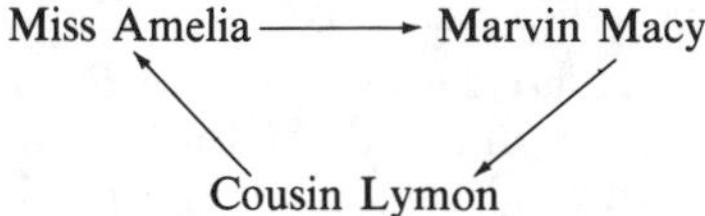

Plot is developed tightly and economically so as to dramatize the creation of these triangles and to emphasize the role of the balladeer-narrator. After beginning in the "present" with the description of the town, the narrator shifts back many years to the arrival of Cousin Lymon, the mysterious stranger who completes the triangle. The movement is natural; he switches to the beginning of the café in the relationship between Lymon and Amelia. This movement also initiates the temporal and seasonal motifs which form an important part of the novella's symbolism. Cousin Lymon arrives in April with the spring, symbolic of creation, youth, and love. When the villagers suspect that Amelia has murdered the tiny stranger the weather turns cold once again, but winter's gloom is dispelled by the warmth of the café when Lymon is discovered alive and well. Amelia's marriage took place in winter and the groundhog sees his shadow before the final battle, a portent of the triumph of hate over love and six more weeks of winter. The temporal shift at the opening is to the "once upon a time" past when things were happier, and the season is appropriate for Amelia's love creates the café and both flourish for the following six years.

The narrator quickly moves the story through these years of human growth for Miss Amelia, symbolized by the emergence of the café. Since the events of these years are ordinary and repetitive he merely summarizes them. The seasons pass in their regular order, and the passage of time is productive of joy and love. The store evolves into a real café with tables and chairs, decorations, and a mechanical piano. Like Biff Brannon's New York Café in *Heart,* Miss Amelia's place has a spiritual function as well as a material one. At the café there were at least a few hours when "the deep bitter knowing that you are not worth much in this world could be laid low." Miss Amelia even neglects to lock the door; clearly a change has taken place.

The years pass in this fruitful manner until Marvin Macy comes back to the village; bad luck follows him to his home town. Though it is autumn the weather turns hot again at his return, spoiling the barbecue and chitterlings just made. A whole family dies from eating spoiled pork. The natural rhythms of the seasons are broken for the first time in six years, when Marvin Macy arrives with the fall like some Hades of Dixie bringing death, desolation, and waste. As the fall turns to winter Marvin Macy's fearful reputation increases, and in direct proportion so does Cousin Lymon's adoration of him. On January 2 it snows, a strange occurrence in the mill village, and Marvin Macy somehow assumes credit for this meteorological miracle. Miss Amelia in her agitation comes to hate Macy even more deeply than she has in the past. They often circle each other, fists clenched, in ritualistic fashion, and the community waits tensely for the conflict to explode. Miss Amelia's degeneration is symbolized by the poison she puts in Marvin's food; her witchcraft is now destructive, her magic black with hate. After the snow Cousin Lymon brings his beloved to stay in the rooms over the café; this final displacement of Amelia precipitates the total collapse on February 2, Groundhog Day. The date proves significant because Cousin Lymon sees the groundhog observe his shadow, an indication of six more weeks of winter ahead and a prefigurement of Marvin Macy's destructive triumph. Other portents are observed on this ominous day: "A hawk with a bloody breast flew over the town and circled twice around the property of Miss Amelia."

The climactic battle begins at seven o'clock, as Miss Amelia sets great store by the mystical number seven. Significantly the fight takes place in the café; the center of companionship and symbol of love has become a place of hatred and combat. The two fighters are evenly matched, and they lunge at each other like wildcats. After a half hour of stunning punches and wild kicks, they become locked in a fearsome wrestling hold.

The ballad-maker points out that this is the style of fighting natural to country people and that the heroic struggle will be decided by this contest of raw strength and will power. After several agonizing moments Miss Amelia emerges as stronger; slowly, she bends her opponent to the floor and gets a strangle hold on him. She has won. But at this instant of victory Cousin Lymon springs onto her back, flying across the room like "a hawk," and turns the advantage to his beloved Marvin. Before the crowd can react Miss Amelia is severely beaten, and left in disgrace. She drags herself into the office, and the crowd disperses. Cousin Lymon and Marvin Macy leave that night, but, before they go, they completely wreck the café: food, whiskey, decorations, the mechanical piano. The café ends as Miss Amelia's love ends. Slowly she shrivels into an old maid; her muscles shrink and her eyes cross to look inward. After three years of lonesome waiting for Cousin Lymon to return, she has the store-café boarded up. Retreating into the upstairs rooms, she remains there alone and isolated. The town takes on a new loneliness also; a perpetual August drought envelops it in a claustrophobic malaise. Time hangs heavy and dull.

> Yes, the town is dreary. On August afternoons the road is empty, white with dust, and the sky above is bright as glass. Nothing moves—there are no children's voices, only the hum of the mill. The peach trees seem to grow more crooked every summer, and the leaves are dull gray and of a sickly delicacy. The house of Miss Amelia leans so much to the right that it is now only a question of time when it will collapse completely and people are careful not to walk around the yard. There is no good liquor to be bought in the town; the nearest still is eight miles away, and the liquor is such that those who drink it grow warts on their livers the size of goobers, and dream themselves into a dangerous inward world. There is absolutely nothing to do in the town. Walk around the millpond, stand kicking at a rotten stump, figure out what you can do with the old wagon wheel by the side of

> the road near the church. The soul rots with boredom. You might as well go down to the Forks Falls highway and listen to the chain gang.

The chain gang illustrates the prison house aspect of the human condition. The coda, entitled **"Twelve Mortal Men,"** emphasizes how man can achieve creativity, in this case the beautiful work songs and ballads of the gang, even in the most difficult situations if there is harmony and co-operation. The last sentence of the novella points out that they are only " . . . twelve mortal men who are together." The picture of the chain gang contrasts with the reader's final vision of Miss Amelia. She could release her creative efforts when she was "together" with Cousin Lymon; alone she can accomplish nothing. Where love and harmony exist much can be created; sadly enough, they exist in few places and for short times—human failings quickly frustrate them, and they are often replaced by hate and isolation. McCullers' other novels demonstrate this condition in the modern social world; the strange ballad of the café that becomes sad traces the roots of these difficulties in the timeless province of the lonely human heart. (pp. 329-39)

Joseph R. Millichap, "Carson McCullers' Literary Ballad," in The Georgia Review, *Vol. XXVII, No. 3, Fall, 1973, pp. 329-39.*

Panthea Reid Broughton (essay date 1974)

[Broughton is an American educator, author of William Faulkner: The Abstract and the Actual, *and editor and contributor to* Stratagems for Being: Essays on the Writings of Walker Percy. *In the following excerpt, Broughton discusses themes of spiritual isolation and rejection of the feminine in* The Ballad of the Sad Café.*]*

Mrs. McCullers once said of her work "my central theme is the theme of spiritual isolation. Certainly I have always felt alone." In her ***The Ballad of the Sad Café,*** the setting itself serves as metaphor for such spiritual isolation. She begins this novella by establishing the dreariness, lonesomeness, and sadness of a setting which seems "estranged from all other places in the world." The largest building in the town, we are told, is old, boarded up, and leans far to one side. The house has "about it a curious, cracked look" which results, we discover, from its having once been haphazardly half-painted. The house is not, however, uninhabited. On hot afternoons a face may linger at the window for an hour or so before the shutters are closed once more: "It is a face like the terrible dim faces known in dreams—sexless and white, with two gray crossed eyes which are turned inward so sharply that they seem to be exchanging with each other one long and secret gaze of grief."

All of this sounds curiously gothic. We have the impression that the town itself is a grotesque, warped by its isolation, and that the building, with its cracked appearance, its dilapidated one-sided construction, and its boarded-up façade, might serve as symbol for whatever life remains in it and in the town. For life here is hopelessly inward, separated, and estranged. Selfhood means only confinement in the solitude of one's own heart.

With D. H. Lawrence, Carson McCullers believed that "we need one another" and that we attain our very individuality itself in living contact, the give-and-take of human relations. Lawrence felt that without such relationships, we are nonentities. In ***The Ballad*** McCullers presents us with an unnamed Southern town and with a woman, Miss Amelia Evans, who together almost manage to escape aloneness and nonentity. The effort, however, is as abortive as the abandoned paint job on the front porch of her house.

When the building Miss Amelia owns becomes a café rather than a dry goods store, Miss Amelia and the townspeople as well almost succeed in breaking out of their separateness. On the occasion when Miss Amelia first breaks her rule and allows liquor to be drunk on the premises, an atmosphere of "company and genial warmth" suddenly emerges. "For," McCullers writes, "the atmosphere of a proper café implies these qualities: fellowship, the satisfactions of the belly, and a certain gaiety and grace of behavior."

In other words, through the café people do manage to overcome their aloneness. They begin to share their liquor, and when the café closes, Miss Amelia for the first time forgets to bolt her door. Trust in one another, founded on a new sense of human dignity, pervades. The change may best be seen in Miss Amelia who, along with Cousin Lymon, becomes actually sociable and is "not so quick to cheat her fellow man and to exact cruel payments."

Most studies of ***The Ballad*** emphasize only McCullers' theme of spiritual alienation and irreparable loneliness; they seem to disregard the fact that aloneness was, for a time at least, actually overcome. But Carson McCullers is very explicit about the achievement of "an air of intimacy . . . and a vague festivity" in the café. Her theorizing about the café is crucial enough to deserve quoting at some length:

> But it was not only the warmth, the decorations, and the brightness, that made the café what it was. There is a deeper reason why the café was so precious to this town. And this deeper reason has to do with a certain pride that had not hitherto been known in these parts. To understand this new pride the cheapness of human life must be kept in mind. There were always plenty of people clustered around a mill—but it was seldom that every family had enough meal, garments, and fat back to go the rounds. Life could become one long dim scramble just to get the things needed to keep alive. And the confusing point is this: All useful things have a price, and are bought only with money, as that is the way the world is run. You know without having to reason about it the price of a bale of cotton, or a quart of molasses. But no value has been put on human life; it is given to us free and taken without being paid for. What is its worth? If you look around, at times the value may seem to be a little or nothing at all. Often after you have sweated and tried and things are not better for

> you, there comes a feeling deep down in the soul that you are not worth much.
>
> But the new pride that the café brought to this town had an effect on almost everyone, even the children. . . . Children love to sleep in houses other than their own, and to eat at a neighbor's table; on such occasions they behave themselves decently and are proud. The people in the town were likewise proud when sitting at the tables in the café. They washed before coming to Miss Amelia's, and scraped their feet very politely on the threshold as they entered the café. There, for a few hours at least, the deep bitter knowing that you are not worth much in this world could be laid low.

Although, then, the "people in this town were unused to gathering together for the sake of pleasure," they do manage for a time to do so and consequently to escape the humdrum everydayness of their lives and the sense of their own worthlessness. But the effort cannot be maintained; the café is closed and the people retreat once again into their own separateness and aloneness. The convivial nights in the café end ostensibly because Marvin Macy and Cousin Lymon have ransacked the place, carving obscene words on the tables and bringing shame and sadness to Miss Amelia. But I should like to suggest that the café's violent end was already inherent in the consciousness of Amelia and her patrons.

McCullers makes a comparison between useful commodities which have a clearly established value and human lives which do not. The comparison is seminal here because it is a lack of confidence in their own human worth which renders the townspeople incapable of sustaining the transcendent affirmation which was the café. For the dreary desperation of the town with its one-industry economy has conditioned the people to hoard themselves as well as their money. As Tocqueville long ago surmised, spiritual isolation is closely aligned with competitive capitalism. Here the normative pattern for dealing with the world and its people is the transaction. Now the transaction may be efficient, abstract, uninvolved, and profitable, but it is also dehumanized. In the business transaction people are used, not respected. Their worth is calculated in terms of dollars and cents. Of course, as McCullers writes, there is "no feeling of joy in the transaction," only the determination not to risk too much. And so, among a people "unused to gathering together for the sake of pleasure" the experience of joy cannot be sustained. To expend the soul in an open give-and-take relationship with another is too much of a risk; it seems safer, and more expedient, to approach another only to take rather than to risk being taken.

The three central characters exemplify this habit of defining human relationships pragmatically. Ravishing the young girls in the town, Marvin Macy has exploited human relationships to assert his will. Miss Amelia has exploited them to make a profit. (We learn that until the arrival of Cousin Lymon, she has never invited anyone to eat with her, "unless she were planning to trick them in some way, or make money out of them.") And even Cousin Lymon, who has "an instinct to establish immediate and vital contact between himself and all things in the world," exploits these contacts for excitement; for Lymon, who loves a spectacle, tries to create tension in the café by badgering and setting hostilities on edge. Furthermore, each of these characters, when he is the beloved, only exploits the other's affection. Amelia appraises Marvin's gifts and then shrewdly puts them up for sale; Lymon uses his sickliness, like his trick of wiggling his ears, whenever he wants "to get something special out of Miss Amelia." And Marvin, of course, uses Lymon's devotion to get his own back from Amelia.

Now, John B. Vickery may suggest that there is comedy in the characters' inability to synchronize their successive roles as lover and beloved; I would insist, on the other hand, that the situation is tragic. For these characters simply do not know how to love. As the lover, each is a slave; as the beloved, each is a tyrant. None can achieve a satisfactorily balanced human relationship. He cannot love without sacrificing his own individual integrity, nor can he be beloved without exerting his power and superiority. His problem directly results from the deeply ingrained assumption that one approaches a human relationship only to exploit, not to enjoy. These characters cannot overcome a value system in which it is better to subjugate than to share, better to use than to love. They live in the world that McCullers describes in her poem "Saraband:"

> The world that jibes your tenderness
> Jails your lusts.

In this world, the virtues of openness, receptivity, tenderness, and compassion are held in such contempt that no one can comfortably express them.

In this town if a man shows his feelings he is labeled contemptuously a "Morris Finestein;" Finestein, we are told, was a little Jew sensitive enough to cry whenever people called him a Christ-killer and foolish enough to live in this town (before, that is, an unnamed but easily imagined calamity overcame Finestein and he was compelled to move away to Society City). The reference to Finestein is important because it reveals the town's concept of sexual roles. McCullers writes "if a man were prissy in any way, or if a man ever wept, he was known as a Morris Finestein." In other words to be sensitive, to weep, is to be effeminate. The human virtues of tenderness and sensitivity are considered to be exclusively feminine and decidedly superfluous and downright contemptible by a pragmatic and rationalistic society. The human psyche has then been split, "cracked," if you will, into qualities which are feminine and contemptible on the one hand and masculine and admirable on the other.

Sexual characteristics, then, are so rigidly dichotomized that they cannot be held in balance. One is either servile and feminine, or, preferably, dominant and masculine. Ideally, as the psychoanalyst Karl Stern writes in his study entitled *The Flight from Woman,* "Man in his fullness is bisexual," or, as Carson McCullers herself puts it, "By nature all people are both sexes." But here, in this novella, people cannot be both sexes at once. Marvin Macy, for instance, who is described as the "cause" of all the trouble, is ruthlessly masculine. With his razor and knife and the sharpened stick he uses to pick his teeth, he is viciously phallic. McCullers describes him as an "evil character" with a "secret meanness" about him. She explains:

> For years, when he was a boy, he had carried about with him the dried and salted ear of a man he had killed in a razor fight. He had chopped off the tails of squirrels in the pinewoods just to please his fancy, and in his left hip pocket he carried forbidden marijuana weed to tempt those who were discouraged and drawn toward death. Yet in spite of his well-known reputation he was the beloved of many females in this region—and there were at the time several young girls who were clear-haired and soft-eyed, with tender sweet little buttocks and charming ways. These gentle young girls he degraded and shamed.

Macy, then, dominates and destroys others in order to enhance his own ego. To admit his need of another is equivalent, in this frame of mind, to abolishing his own ego. That is why Marvin Macy's attachment to Miss Amelia is such a pathetic thing. Her indifference only provokes further, more desperate, acts of self-abasement from him, but to no avail. Miss Amelia continues to ignore the man Macy and to turn his gifts to profit. It is only normative though, as McCullers remarks in one of her short stories, that "you hate people you have to need so badly." Thus Macy cannot but resent Amelia, not only for spurning him, but for making him so despicably servile. And so Marvin Macy vows to get even, and he does.

Macy's behavior represents the extremes of sadism and masochism which Erich Fromm tells us are not emotionally dissimilar. And I should like further to suggest that his unhealthy behavior, whether aggressively masculine or servilely feminine, results from a social ethos which has destroyed a human sense of balance. Karl Stern describes this contemporary psychic phenomenon as a "Flight from Woman" and explains that, with modern men and women "The very possibility of being in the least dependent or protected, or even being loved, amounts to nothing less than a phantasy of mutilation or destruction."

Certainly, with Miss Amelia, the experience of having an operation for kidney stones was an experience of mutilation. She seems to have been unable to survive the experience of being totally helpless and dependent, unless she could justify it in pragmatic, business-like terms. Thus she kept the kidney stones and later has them set as ornaments in a watch chain for Cousin Lymon. McCullers writes, "It had been a terrible experience, from the first minute to the last, and all she had got out of it were those two little stones; she was bound to set great store by them, or else admit to a mighty sorry bargain." Miss Amelia, then, has real difficulty in justifying any experience unless, that is, she can extract from it something practical and tangible, preferably in the shape of a profit. And so that is why the café and love seem doomed from the start. The pattern of pragmatism is too deeply entrenched for these people to sustain, for long, the experience of delight for its own sake.

Here each person has such a deep-seated fear of tenderness that he cannot admit his need of another without self-effacement, followed by hatred of the self and resentment of the needed one as well. Karl Stern describes this psychic phenomenon as "an undue emphasis on the technical and the rational, and a rejection of what for want of a better term we call 'feeling,' [which] go with a neurotic dread of receiving, a fear of tenderness and of protection, and are invariably associated with an original maternal conflict." Now both Marvin Macy and Amelia Evans, and apparently Lymon too, have been deprived of the security of motherly love, and each of them has a real dread of receiving and an inability to show tenderness or love except at the price of self-abandonment.

With her father, himself described as a "solitary man," Amelia may have been, despite her six-foot-two-inch stature, known as "Little" but with everyone else she is the big one, the dominant force. Amelia is "like a man," then, not because she wears overalls and swamp boots, nor because she is six feet two inches tall (though McCullers does remark that Amelia's height is indeed "not natural for a woman"), nor even because Amelia settles her disputes with men by a wrestling match; Amelia is "like a man," instead, simply because of her insatiable need to dominate. The assumption here is that it is masculine to dominate, to force one's shape upon matter, whereas it is feminine to be receptive and malleable. In these terms, Miss Amelia is as masculine as Marvin Macy; for we learn that "with all things which could be made by the hands, Miss Amelia prospered." But also, that "It was only with people that Miss Amelia was not at ease. People, unless they are willy-nilly or very sick, cannot be taken into the hands and changed overnight to something more worthwhile and profitable. So that the only use that Miss Amelia had for other people was to make money out of them. And in this she succeeded." Unless they are sick, she deals with people only to make a profit (until, that is, the café opens). And she deals with sick people because they are malleable. With them she can achieve a symbiotic union which confirms her sense of power even more than litigations and profit-making do. Thus this fiercely materialistic woman need charge no fees for doctoring, for power is its own reward. Miss Amelia, however, is incapable of dealing with female complaints. At the mention of a female problem she reacts "like a great, shamed, dumb-tongued child;" she is then, as much as the cruelly phallic Marvin Macy, in flight from the feminine.

With the coming of Lymon and the opening of the café, of course, Miss Amelia tries to change, to become female. She still wears overalls and swamp boots, but on Sundays she now wears a dress. She is "not so quick to cheat her fellow man." She becomes more sociable and even takes Lymon into her confidence about "the most delicate and vital matters." But these matters are mostly details about her property—where she keeps bankbook, keys, and whisky barrels. Certainly she never confides in Lymon about her ten-day marriage to Marvin Macy.

Miss Amelia tries very hard to be open and tender, for she does love Lymon, but she simply does not know how to show that love. She gives him presents when he is cross, and she spoils him as a foolish mother does a child, but she is unable to maintain a reciprocal relationship with him. Instead she smothers him in a symbiotic relationship which must itself be the cause of his deep fear of death, for, as McCullers explains, "the lover is forever trying to strip bare his beloved."

Miss Amelia is then no more capable of manifesting a healthy femininity than Marvin Macy is. She is alternately hard and soft, but cannot manage to balance the qualities or to be both at once. She is, as McCullers explains, "divided between two emotions." Thus when Marvin Macy returns, she puts aside her overalls and wears always the dark red dress as symbol of her accessibility. She tries giving Marvin free drinks and smiling at him in a "wild, crooked way." But she also sets a terrible trap for him and tries to poison him. And she is no more successful at destroying him than she is at attracting him. She remains then the figure in the boarded-up house, white and sexless, the eyes turning increasingly inward upon themselves.

Amelia is left in the prison of her aloneness because the stereotyped patterns by which she encountered others were exclusively those of dominance or subjugation. She has known no way to love without self-abasement. Nor has Marvin Macy. Nor has Cousin Lymon. And self-abasement can only result in resentment and eventual retaliation, so Marvin Macy has his turn taking from Amelia and then, with Lymon's help, destroys the café in order to get his own back from her.

All these relationships are organically incomplete because no one knows how to give without vitiating his own integrity and no one knows how to take without enhancing his sense of personal power. These characters need to dismiss the sexual stereotypes of extremity and to learn to be strong without cruelty, tender without servility. The problem, then, is to reclaim the virtues of tenderness and receptivity from their exclusive association with whatever is female and weak, and to reinstate them as virtues which are essential to all humanity; for, without accepting these virtues as a dignified aspect of mankind, the human community cannot survive. (pp. 34-42)

Once toward the end of McCullers' story, Marvin Macy laughs at Miss Amelia and says, " 'Everything you holler at me bounces back on yourself.' " His denunciation provides an apt image for the entire novella. For ***The Ballad of the Sad Café*** may be interpreted as a fable which shows us that rejecting those characteristics labeled as exclusively feminine bounces back on the rejector and renders men and women alike incapable of loving and thereby escaping the prisons of their own spiritual isolation.

Now, we may have learned from contemporary cinema that we have "a failure to communicate" and from the popular song that "what the world needs now is luv, luv, luv," but only modern fiction has, to date, been subtle and serious enough to bring us to some understanding of why we have a communication gap and of how love can bridge that gap. In this tradition, McCullers' ***Ballad*** is especially significant; for to read it is to experience the solitude of the heart and to understand how misconceptions of love only reinforce that solitude. (p. 42)

Panthea Reid Broughton, "Rejection of the Feminine in Carson McCullers' 'The Ballad of the Sad Café'," in Twentieth Century Literature, *Vol. 20, No. 1, January, 1974, pp. 34-43.*

Melvin J. Friedman (essay date 1976)

[Friedman is an American educator, author, and editor of many books of literary criticism, including (as writer) Stream of Consciousness: A Study of Literary Method *and (editor)* The Added Dimension: The Art and Mind of Flannery O'Connor. *In the following excerpt, Friedman considers how the stories collected in* The Mortgaged Heart *foreshadow and reflect McCullers's novels.]*

Many of the stories (or "exercises," as Margarita Smith prefers to call some of them) in ***The Mortgaged Heart*** appear to have been prematurely removed from the drawing board. . . . The tentative and miscellaneous nature of ***The Mortgaged Heart*** depends crucially on the introductory directives and frequent apologies of Margarita Smith. It is a patchwork quilt of short pieces, fiction and nonfiction, stitched together with some editorial finesse by Carson McCullers' sister. (p. 144)

The best of McCullers—and that is very good indeed—is to be found in her two novels and three novellas. There is very little left to sustain ***The Mortgaged Heart*** which illumines mostly the darker corners of the writer's workshop.

With this said, one should consider the collection in some detail. The three main divisions of the book, "short stories," "essays and articles," and "poetry," are preceded by editorial notes which offer useful biographical props and explain the principles of selection: "to show in part the growth of a writer." The growing-up process involves change and that is rarely in evidence. The numbing sameness of the language, authorial voice, techniques, and literary strategies—despite the fact that ***The Mortgaged Heart*** covers most of the years of Carson McCullers' life as a writer—alerts us rather cruelly to the vast distances separating her remarkable longer fiction (*The Heart Is a Lonely Hunter* through *The Member of the Wedding*) from her intermittent efforts in the shorter form. Even then, unexplainably, her best short stories, like **"A Tree, a Rock, a Cloud"** and **"The Sojourner,"** are left out of Margarita Smith's gathering.

This worst-foot-forward approach seems to offer a kind of negative principle of selection for ***The Mortgaged Heart.*** Things are included, we are told, largely for their unavailability: "So this book is to give some idea of the early work of a writer and to illustrate, within the range of material chosen from her least-known work, the development of that talent." (Actually some of her later work is included; in fact, four of the stories are referred to as "later stories" and several of the essays were written quite late in her career.) One wonders about the purpose served by such a collection. Margarita Smith herself is beset by uncertainty: "I am plagued with doubt because I wonder why Carson did not collect some of this material while she was living since money was always a problem."

The early stories and "exercises" do supply a measure of "foreshadowing." The first story in ***The Mortgaged Heart,*** **"Sucker"**—as Oliver Evans already remarked in his excellent *The Ballad of Carson McCullers*—anticipates elements in the later work. One occurrence is almost exactly duplicated in *The Heart Is a Lonely Hunter.* Just as the nickname Bubber gave way to George in the novel so we are told in next-to-the-last paragraph of the story: "I don't even want to call him Sucker any more and unless I forget I call him by his real name, Richard." The circumstances of the name-change are more than passingly similar.

"Court in the West Eighties," the next story in the collection, shifts scene to New York City and reveals a somewhat different narrative focus although it is written, like **"Sucker,"** in the first-person. The storyteller here is more an observer than a participant. She settles her attention on a red-haired man, with a "calm drowsy face," who lives across the court from her. Margarita Smith suggests in her editor's note that the redhead may have anticipated Singer in *The Heart Is a Lonely Hunter;* indeed he stands toward the narrator in much the way Singer existed in the imaginations of Mick Kelly, Jake Blount, and Dr. Copeland. Here is the storyteller trying to account for her fascination: "It is not easy to explain about this faith I had in him. I don't know what I could have expected him to do, but the feeling was there just the same." She says again in the final paragraph of the story: "But no matter how peculiar it sounds I still have this feeling that there is something in him that could change a lot of situations and straighten them out."

There is a sense of anonymity about virtually everything in **"Court in the West Eighties"**; the characters are identified as the man with the red hair, the cellist, the young couple, a friend of mine. Everything seems quite conjectural, including the final words: " . . . in a sense it is true." This unwillingness to name, to identify with precision carries over into the novels and novellas. The opening sentence of *The Heart Is a Lonely Hunter* could scarcely be less revealing: "In the town there were two mutes, and they were always together." The last two sentences of the opening paragraph of *Reflections in a Golden Eye* proceed in the same intentionally vague manner: "There is a fort in the South where a few years ago a murder was committed. The participants of this tragedy were: two officers, a soldier, two women, a Filipino, and a horse." "The town itself is dreary" are the opening words of ***The Ballad of the Sad Café.*** Cities and towns are usually not named in the novels and novellas . . . and . . . their settings seem more parabolic than real. **"Court in the West Eighties,"** despite the mention of New York City, seems to gain its sense of place more from the imagination of its narrator than from any series of believable urban circumstances.

The unnamed, rather haunting figure of the cellist reappears in the next story, **"Poldi."** This piece is much closer to what Robbe-Grillet was later to speak of as an "instantané." (Sylvia Chatfield Bates, in her comment following it, accurately describes it as a " 'picture' story.") The temperament of the musician is on display here as it is in other selections in ***The Mortgaged Heart.*** We know from Oliver Evans how Carson McCullers came north to study at Juilliard and how a curious twist of fate thwarted her efforts in that direction. We get a sense of mockery in **"Poldi"** which we don't get in the longer works—like *The Heart Is a Lonely Hunter*—in which musical concerns are introduced. Poldi can appear quite ridiculous when she says: " 'I believe my playing has deepened much in the last month . . . Life does that to me—it happens every time something like this comes up. Not that it's ever been like this before. It's only after you've suffered that you can play.' "

The fragility-of-childhood theme figures prominently in the next two stories, **"Breath from the Sky"** and **"The Orphanage."** The second is little more than a sketch and does not seem very different from several of the pieces grouped under "essays and articles" later in the collection. There is indeed some fine expository prose here, including a brief series of near-poetic turns on a subject central to all of Carson McCullers' work: "The memories of childhood have a strange shuttling quality, and areas of darkness ring the spaces of light. The memories of childhood are like clear candles in an acre of night, illuminating fixed scenes from the surrounding darkness." This deserves a place next to the famous passage about the lover and the beloved in ***The Ballad of the Sad Café*** and the *we of me* passage in *The Member of the Wedding.*

One can only agree with Sylvia Chatfield Bates's estimation of the next story, **"Instant of the Hour After"**: "I like this the least of anything you have done . . . " The kind of in-joke, sophisticated conversation, with the occasional literary allusions, is not what Carson McCullers does best. She manages somewhat better with it in the later story, **"Who Has Seen the Wind?"**, probably because she fleshes out her material and gives it some narrative thrust. Yet the best of her early work is concerned with children and adolescents (or with ingenuous older men like the redhead in **"Court in the West Eighties"**). These types, in fact, predominate in most of the remaining stories in ***The Mortgaged Heart.***

"Like That" returns to the matter and method of **"Sucker."** The colloquially-tuned voice of the adolescent manages the narration. The disappointments which come from growing up are as central to this story as they were to the earlier one. The final sentence of the story establishes the fear and uncertainty so essential to McCullers characters like Mick Kelly and Frankie Addams: "I don't want to grow up—if it's like that."

"Wunderkind" is clearly not among Carson McCullers' "least-known work" as it has long been available in a collection called ***The Ballad of the Sad Café and Other Stories;*** it is apparently reprinted here for sentimental reasons: " . . . it marks the beginning of her [Carson McCullers'] professional career." It continues some of the musical preoccupations of **"Poldi."** Adolescence and its torments are again of central importance. The former prodigy fails on her crucial day—the day the story is mainly concerned with although much of its substance is gained through flashback—to play even the most elementary piece of music. Failed talent and frustration are revealed through the staccato syntax and movement of next-to-the-final paragraph: "Her coat. The mittens and galoshes. The school books and the satchel he had given her on her birthday. All from the silent room that was hers. Quickly—before he would have to speak."

The principal character in **"The Aliens"** is also a musician.

(There are all kinds of musical references which reinforce the poetic base of the story and give it a kind of melodic texture.) But his being a Jew, with a strong sense of the Diaspora, is more important. His bus ride south, accompanied part of the way by a young southerner, carries with it strong symbolic properties. The allegorist in Carson McCullers is very much in evidence, especially in a sentence like this: "The journey of this fugitive—for the Jew had fled from his home in Munich two years before—more nearly resembled a state of mind than a period of travelling computable by maps and timetables." One of the music teachers in **"Wunderkind"** was identified, in a passing reference, as a Jew, but this fact held no special consequences for the story.

"The Aliens" seems to uncover a tendency to make the Jew a metaphor for suffering and alienation in Carson McCullers' work. It should be recalled that Singer was taken for a Jew by Dr. Copeland in *The Heart Is a Lonely Hunter.* Singer's original name, we know from *"The Flowering Dream,"* was Harry Minowitz (with its distinctly Jewish ring); when Singer finally emerged in the finished novel, the name Harry Minowitz was given to the Jewish boy who had the fleeting adolescent sexual relationship with Mick Kelly. Finally, it should be noted that Jake Blount accused Biff Brannon of looking "like a Jew in Germany." The response by Biff was that he was "an eighth part Jew." The Jew's special kind of poetry and his enviable remoteness give him a favored position in most of Carson McCullers' fiction. . . . (pp. 146-49)

"Untitled Piece," the next selection in ***The Mortgaged Heart,*** indicates how close Carson McCullers was to writing *The Heart Is a Lonely Hunter.* Margarita Smith may be right in suggesting that it could have been the beginning of a novel *manqué* or abandoned. In any case, it offers a view of a family very like Mick Kelly's, although the vantage point is very different from *The Heart Is a Lonely Hunter.* The story gains its frame from the son Andrew's returning to his home town in Georgia after a three-year absence. Much of it proceeds through flashback. One of the central symbols is the glider he and his sister Sara had been working on many years before: " . . . and perhaps he kept remembering it because the things he had felt at that time were so much like the expectancy this journey now brought." Music is also a vital concern of this story; it shapes the situation as well as the imagery. At one point we are told: "Music to them [Andrew and Sara] was something like the glider should have been." Two Jews figure prominently: Aunt Esther who takes Sara off with her to Detroit; and Harry Minowitz who is an older and less attractive version of the character in *The Heart Is a Lonely Hunter.*

There is no mistaking the proximity of this "exercise" to Carson McCullers' first novel, especially to the Mick Kelly sections. The next step on the way to the novel is the **"Author's Outline of 'The Mute'"** which appeared for the first time as the appendix to Oliver Evans' book on Carson McCullers. These blueprints for the novel offer an intriguing view of her workshop. It is the same kind of glimpse of the creative process as we get from something like Gide's *Journal of "The Counterfeiters."* The comparison is especially apt when we see how preoccupied both novelists were with the possibilities of musical analogies and references in fiction. Here is Gide in the opening paragraph of his *Journal:* "I am like a musician striving, in the manner of César Franck, to juxtapose and overlap an andante theme and an allegro theme." Here is Carson McCullers in the final section of her outline: "This book is planned according to a definite and balanced design. The form is contrapuntal throughout. Like a voice in a fugue each one of the main characters is an entirety in himself . . . "

This "outline" is one of the more valuable items in ***The Mortgaged Heart.*** It is placed at the end of the section which Margarita Smith calls the "Early Stories." In a sense it ends Carson McCullers' apprenticeship with all its self-consciousness and youthful indulgences. It exposes the rawness of her nerves and the innocence of her compositional habits. We rarely get such an unedited view of the sensibility of the writer. We certainly do not get this close to Gide in his *Journal of "The Counterfeiters."*

The four "later stories" still do not seem to be vintage McCullers. Most critics of her work seem to prefer the novellas to the novels and both in turn to the short stories. Ihab Hassan, in *Radical Innocence,* speaks of "the deficiencies of Carson McCullers in the short form." Dale Edmonds, in his pamphlet on her in the "Southern Writers Series," is more charitable: "Of the dozen stories (not including portions of novels) Carson McCullers published over a span of nearly thirty years, at least half may be classified as good, and perhaps three of these may be considered distinguished." He singles out for special mention **"Correspondence,"** which is the first of these "later stories" included in ***The Mortgaged Heart.*** This piece is made up of four letters sent by an American teenage girl, Henky Evans, to a prospective pen-pal in Brazil. The letters are never answered. Mr. Edmonds places it in the mainstream of the *œuvre:* "Another of Mrs. McCullers' gawky adolescent girls on the outside yearning to become part of a 'we,' Henky is characterized extremely well by her letters."

"Art and Mr. Mahoney" is little more than a blown-up anecdote. **"The Haunted Boy,"** however, deserves serious attention. It has something in common with another McCullers story, not included in ***The Mortgaged Heart,* "A Domestic Dilemma."** In each case a psychologically disturbed mother and wife is the center of attention. We see **"A Domestic Dilemma"** through the eyes of the husband who despairs of his wife's excessive drinking. **"The Haunted Boy"** offers the vantage point of the teenage son who fears that his mother has had another nervous breakdown. The "terror of the afternoon"—while the son imagines that all kinds of horrible things have happened to his mother—is relieved by her unexpected appearance following a harmless shopping expedition. The sense of relief pervades the last sentence of the story: "Although he felt he would never cry again—or at least not until he was sixteen—in the brightness of his tears glistened the safe, lighted kitchen, now that he was no longer a haunted boy, now that he was glad somehow, and not afraid."

"Who Has Seen the Wind?" is less characteristic of Carson McCullers' manner than almost any other story included in ***The Mortgaged Heart.*** It seems, however, well placed in the collection, coming as it does at the end of the short story section. Indeed it offers a natural bridge from the stories to the essays. It contains some interesting literary theorizing and some judgments of other writers, especially Proust; it perhaps belongs side by side essays like "The Vision Shared" and "The Flowering Dream: Notes on Writing."

"Who Has Seen the Wind?" concerns the author of a successful first novel and a failed second novel who seems unable to manage a third. His marriage has fallen to pieces; even his cocktail-party behavior has taken on certain unpleasant eccentricities. At the end of the story he searches irrationally and distractedly for his wife who has left him.

We are told several times in the long opening paragraph about the blank page which faces the author, Ken Harris. Carson McCullers seems to be speaking here about the problems the writer encounters when confronted with "le vide papier que la blancheur défend" (Mallarmé's famous image). Ken Harris is spared temporarily by a six P.M. cocktail party at which he manages to introduce Proust in the opening conversation. (He incorrectly speaks of "that last party of the Duc de Guermantes"; the final party he refers to occurred at the home of the Prince and Princesse de Guermantes—the kind of mistake allowable when discussing almost any other writer but Proust who was so careful in the distinctions he made among the nobility. One suspects that this lapse may have been intentional on Carson McCullers' part as a way of indicating Ken Harris' carelessness in his literary judgments.) Other writers like Joyce, Thomas Wolfe, and Thoreau are also mentioned in the text. One noticed the same kind of literary name-dropping in **"Instant of the Hour After."** But it is not, certainly, a characteristic of her work. (pp. 149-52)

There is the uncomfortable feeling of late that Carson McCullers' position in Southern literature is suffering some sort of decline. An example of what I have in mind was recently expressed in an essay by Robert Drake, "Cultivating My Antique Garden," *Modern Age,* Spring 1972. . . . He says, in the course of overviewing the Southern literary scene: " . . . despite Mrs. McCullers' genuine triumphs, she ultimately betrayed her own gift and began willing herself to venture away from her true country into foreign lands, even to write up the news of the day, which is always fatal for the truth-telling novelist." ***The Mortgaged Heart,*** alas, is not likely to change Drake's mind. (p. 154)

Melvin J. Friedman, "'The Mortgaged Heart': The Workshop of Carson McCullers," in Revue des langues vivantes, *Vol. 42, 1976, pp. 143-55.*

Robert Phillips (essay date 1978)

[Phillips is an American educator, poet, editor, critic, short story writer, and advertising executive. In the following excerpt, he focuses on the spiritual isolation of the central characters in McCullers's short fiction.]

The work of Carson McCullers is whole cloth. Few writers have maintained such a consistent vision. Moreover, few writers have such a clear conception of their preoccupations and themes. In "The Flowering Dream: Notes on Writing" (included in ***The Mortgaged Heart,*** edited by Margarita G. Smith) McCullers wrote:

> Spiritual isolation is the basis of most of my themes. My first book was concerned with this, almost entirely, and all of my books since, in one way or another. Love, and especially love of a person who is incapable of receiving it, is at the heart of my selection of grotesque figures to write about—people whose physical incapacity is a symbol of their spiritual incapacity to love or receive love—their spiritual isolation.

There, in one paragraph, McCullers answered satisfactorily all the queries raised concerning *why* in her novels she wrote almost exclusively of grotesques. Elsewhere, in "A Personal Preface" to her second play, *The Square Root of Wonderful,* she again stated, "I suppose my central theme is the theme of spiritual isolation. Certainly I have always felt alone."

Now if we take the lady at her word, and I believe we should, this theme of spiritual isolation is the cornerstone to her house of fiction. One of the smallest rooms of that house is the region of her short stories. While there already is a considerable body of criticism concerning her four novels and the fifth novella, very little has been said about her shorter fiction—particularly the fourteen stories published in the posthumous collection, ***The Mortgaged Heart.*** Which is a pity, because of the total of nineteen stories to be found there and in the earlier omnibus collection, ***The Ballad of the Sad Cafe,*** several are quite superb fiction. Certainly all are typical McCullers, with this exception: they are all less likely to be labeled "Gothic" or "grotesque" when compared to her novels. For whatever reason, there is less physical abnormality in the stories. Instead of mutes and dwarfs, what we generally encounter here are people isolated by circumstance rather than physical appearance or malady. Instead of freaks we find an inner freaking-out.

What does Carson McCullers mean by "spiritual isolation"? I have taken the phrase to mean, simply, personal dissociation—the feeling of being severed from society, disunited from others, lonely, separate, different, apart. Certainly that state characterizes Frankie Addams of *The Member of the Wedding,* one of McCullers's more "normal" characters, just as it does Cousin Lymon of the ***Ballad,*** a more "abnormal" one. Obviously the term "spiritual isolation" applies to the freaked-out as well as to the freaks.

One of the amazing things in considering McCullers is not only how many variations she played upon this theme in book after book, story after story, and two plays, but also how early that vision was formulated. It is to be found in her very first story, **"Sucker,"** written when she was a seventeen-year-old school girl. There the title character, Sucker, is an orphan, and therefore unrelated to the family with whom he lives. The young author described him beautifully: "his face had the look of a kid who is watching a game and waiting to be asked to play." Sucker desperately wants to be loved, to become a member of the family. In this respect he is a young Frankie Addams, who wanted so very much a "we of me."

At first **"Sucker"** seems to be the story of the narrator, Pete, and the pull between *agape* (Pete and Sucker) and *eros* (Pete and Maybelle). But by the time of the story's climax, the awful scene in which Pete tells Sucker he doesn't care for him one bit, we realize the story bears the correct title after all. It *is* Sucker's story, the story of an outsider who tries to fit in. In one epiphany he is made to realize he never will, and thus he freaks out and becomes a hardened rebel.

Though it was her first story, **"Sucker"** contains the seeds of the later McCullers's philosophy of love, which she expounded upon in a famous passage in the ***Ballad of the Sad Cafe.*** In **"Sucker"** she tells us, "There is one thing I have learned, but it makes me feel guilty and is hard to figure out. If a person admires you a lot you despise him and don't care—and it is the person who doesn't notice you that you are apt to admire. This is not easy to realize." (pp. 65-7)

Being an orphan, then, was McCullers's first projection of a spiritually isolated being. She used the same projection in **"The Orphanage."** Yet another early story, **"Breath from the Sky,"** depicts a young woman orphaned from her family not by parental death, but by her own invalidism. Both her shorn hair and the cut flowers are symbolic of the sapping of her strength, the nipping of the bloom of her youth. The story centers on her realization of the helplessness of her situation. She is overcome by the lustiness of her brother and sister, and even the bounding, healthy dog. While a move three hundred miles north to Mountain Heights is supposed to help her, the simple move from the inside of the house to the yard has in itself made her feel enervated and stricken. The trip surely will estrange her both in body and in spirit.

Some of Carson McCullers's most successful characterizations of the isolated individual are, of course, her adolescents—characters like Mick Kelly and Frankie Addams, who belong neither to the adult world nor to the world of childhood. One such in-betweener is the thirteen-year-old younger sister in the early story **"Like That."** Perceiving the pain of growing into womanhood experienced by her older sister, she resists rather than embraces maturation. Like Sucker, she rebels, only her rebellion is against such overwhelming forces as menstruation, sexuality, premature death.

Another adolescent is the heroine of **"Correspondence,"** a slight epistolary story of a one-way correspondence undertaken by a Frankie Addams type, here named Henrietta Evans. Henrietta, estranged from her fellow freshmen, seeks release through a South American pen pal. He never answers, and the psychic changes inflicted upon the girl are reflected in changes in her signature—she transforms herself from "Henky Evans" to "Henrietta Evans" to "Miss Henrietta Hill Evans"—a ploy also practiced by F. Jasmine Addams, formerly known as Frankie. This little story clearly illustrates McCullers's theme of man's revolt against his own inner isolation and his urge to express himself as fully as possible. That there is no response from the other country is indicative of McCullers's negative world view.

Not all of McCullers's suffering adolescents are female. In the long **"Untitled Piece"** a boy called Andrew Leander seems a male Frankie, and his father is also a jeweler. The action takes place during one crazy summer, and Bernice Sadie Brown has somehow been transmogrified into a younger black named Vitalis. In his attempt to become joined to something, Andrew commits an act of unpremeditated miscegenation with Vitalis, then flees the town in guilt. His one act of union and love has forced his separation and fear. A later story, **"The Haunted Boy,"** depicts a teenager named Hugh who is also isolated, in his case in the knowledge that his mother is mad and that he may once again discover her in a suicide attempt. The story is marred by a pat ending, but Hugh's fear is made extraordinarily real. One does not soon forget his terror at the simple act of opening the upstairs bathroom door.

Another category of McCullers's characterizations of young people is that of the adolescent as musician. As if being adolescent were not sufficiently special and disjoining, McCullers knew that for an adolescent who studied music the situation would certainly be exacerbated. **"Wunderkind"** is one of the most famous of all her stories, even though there are several that are better. It concerns the realization of a fifteen-year-old music student that she simply does not possess the emotional capacity to match her facile pianistic technique. Outside she is all glitter; inside, she knows she is empty. There is no sensationalism here, yet the epiphany is as traumatic as Alison's severing her own nipples with garden shears (in *Reflections in a Golden Eye*). In the novels McCullers strove for grand moments; in the stories, for quiet occasions which nevertheless are vital occasions. When the washed-up *wunderkind* flees her piano teacher's studio and hurries "down the street that had become confused with noise and bicycles and the games of other children," the reader comprehends the loss of the girl's childhood, sacrificed to the music she cannot really play well. She is an emotional freak who is outwardly normal.

Another youthful musician appears in **"Poldi,"** an early tale of hopeless love. The young protagonist admires and perhaps even loves an older cellist, who in turn, naturally thinks of him merely as "a little brother." The cellist, in turn, loves a pianist named Kurt, whom she has seen only three times in her life. It is the McCullers love formula at work again. As in **"Sucker," "The Haunted Boy,"** and the **"Untitled Piece,"** McCullers successfully transforms herself into a young male. That her ability to do this may have roots deeper than mere considerations of technique and point of view is suggested by the revelations of Virginia Spencer Carr's exhaustive biography of the author, *The Lonely Hunter.*

Bridging the generation gap between the author's younger and older short story protagonists is the eighteen-year-old university student in the early tale **"Court in the West Eighties."** This is a character who neither acts nor is acted upon, but merely records the scenes about her in an apartment house which serves as a microcosm of the macrocosm. She seems to make a God figure of one inhabitant, a serene, red-headed man: "The sun made a haze of light around his bright hair that was almost like a sort of halo." He is perhaps an early precursor of John Singer of *The Heart Is a Lonely Hunter.* He is also a demiurge, looking on unfeelingly while a young jobless couple living across the court slowly starve. McCullers injects a potent symbol into the story in the form of a balloon man—that is, a man made of balloons, bearing a silly grin and hanging perpetually from one apartment window. He is an effigy mocking mankind and man's helplessness. In the world of McCullers's imagination we are all dangling, hanged men.

In McCullers's stories portraying adults confronting adult problems—or rather, not confronting them, since most either freak out or flee the situation rather than face it—the characters are occasionally absolutely normal in appearance. Later, however, they are rendered symbolically grotesque, as in **"Instant of the Hour After,"** a mood piece in which a young married couple's love for one another is inexplicably destroying them. In the story's chief symbol they are seen as two figures in a bottle—small, perfect, yet white and exhausted, like "fleshly specimens in a laboratory." This image is quite akin to that of the pickled fetus in **"The Orphanage."** The story also predates the conflict of the later and vastly superior **"A Domestic Dilemma."**

In **"A Domestic Dilemma,"** the isolated character is a housewife, physically transplanted from Alabama to New York. Unable to adjust to the changes involved in the move or to make friends, she seeks escape through drinking. Without the artifice of alcohol her interior life is insufficient. Just as the son in **"The Haunted Boy"** lives in fear that his crazy mother may again harm herself, so too this suburban housewife's husband is haunted by her earlier drunken accident with one of the children and by the possibility that it could happen again. A threat of undefined disaster underlies his days. Far worse is his fear that her daily drunken behavior is causing invisible psychic damage to the two children—damage which can only increase as the immunity of incomprehension passes. In this, my personal favorite of her shorter fiction, McCullers explores love/hate relationships in marriage and what she calls "the immense complexity of love."

This inability to adjust to physical change signals a state of spiritual isolation in several of the best stories by McCullers, including **"The Sojourner"** and **"A Tree. A Rock. A Cloud,"** as well as the more superficial **"Art and Mr. Mahoney."**

"The Sojourner" is a meditation on what McCullers terms "the improvisation of human existence." Some people adjust to life's variations, some do not. John Ferris, this story's protagonist, has not adjusted to the anxieties of transience and solitude brought about by his divorce. On the other hand, his former wife has adjusted, and he makes the discovery of his own emotional poverty during a visit to her and her new family. It is as traumatic for him as the *wunderkind*'s discovery of her own shortcomings. He perceives immediately that his ex-wife has created a rich new life for herself, with two children and a second husband. He, by contrast, has put down no roots. Recently even his father has died, reminding him of wasted years and death, cancelling out the past in a life which has no present or future. Physically he is an expatriate from America; emotionally he is an expatriate from the human heart. At the end he is vowing to reach out, to create a meaningful relationship with his mistress's son, an act he may or may not be able to accomplish.

The disintegration of a marriage also creates another disintegrated soul in **"A Tree. A Rock. A Cloud."** The story relates the encounter in a café of a twelve-year-old boy and an old cuckold. It is not so much a plotted story as the plodded meditations of the old man on the nature of love—surely one of Mrs. McCullers's favorite topics. Love here is expounded as a condition which must be achieved through small steps. Rather than presuming to begin one's love life with a woman—what the old man (and McCullers) calls "the most dangerous and sacred experience in God's earth"—we should instead begin in very small ways, loving tiny inanimate objects first: a tree, a rock, a cloud. Only when we can relate to the minimal can we hope to possess the maximal.

That the old man's experience of losing his wife has stunted him emotionally is undeniable. His science of love can be taken as mere justification of his remaining womanless. Like Coleridge's ancient mariner, he is forever having to unburden himself upon strangers. But there is something more to be said for his love-science. That McCullers sides with him is made clear by the actions she attributes to Leo, the café owner. Leo not only treats his regular customers stingily, but also does not love himself enough to nourish his body adequately. He grudges himself a bun. But then, in McCullers's love affairs, everyone seems to be grudging their buns.

The twelve-year-old paperboy listener, drinking his coffee in a café of adults drinking their beer, is another McCullers alien. He is as out of his element in the café as Ferris is in Paris. The paperboy is further endowed with a physical difference. One shoulder is lower than the other, from the weight of the paper sack. This qualifies him as a freak in a café which prefigures Miss Amelia's place, in the ***Ballad,*** as a place of fellowship and understanding.

Mr. Mahoney's inability to adjust, in **"Art and Mr. Mahoney,"** is less dramatic. He is a man of great cultural pretensions and little education to back them up. Inadvertently he reveals his ignorance by clapping at the wrong time in a piano concert. "I should think that anybody with a grain of sense knows enough not to clap until everybody else is clapping," his wife hisses, forgetting, of course, that if this were so, there would never be any applause. Ultimately Mr. Mahoney must face the realization that he belongs more to the town's coarser elements than to the refined. The sound of his applause in the silent auditorium symbolizes his interior isolation. His little embarrassment, however, can in no way be compared to the illuminations experienced by the *wunderkind* and Ferris and the haunted boy, and **"Art and Mr. Mahoney"** remains a trivial story.

A more traumatic dissociation takes the form of writer's

block in **"Who Has Seen the Wind?"** and pathological lying in **"Madame Zilensky and the King of Finland."** **"Who Has Seen the Wind?"** is the rather melodramatic tale of Ken, a writer who is blocked after two books. His inability to communicate is driving him mad. His is a much more severe case of the blues experienced by Henrietta Evans in **"Correspondence."** In the story's best moment Ken experiences, in the act of trying to talk out the plot of his third unwritten novel to a friend at a party, an extreme case of *déjà vu:* seven or eight years before, he had told the same friend the same plot at the same kind of party. Just as no one has "seen" the wind, creative inspiration goes and comes, is ungraspable. Ken's unreturned correspondence with the muse is another example of McCullers's use of the writer's art as the means by which an individual rebels against isolation and silence.

The tale of **"Madame Zilensky"** is a superb one of a woman so dedicated to music that she is alien to the rest of the world, consequently compensating through lies—living vicariously the experiences she never had time to experience. The action of the story revolves about her forced confrontation with the truth, an encounter in which she manages to gain the upper hand and preserve her precious illusions. Madame Zilensky's need for illusions in order to exist is greater than her unmasker's need for truth. Indeed, he feels he will have killed her if he continues to confront her.

In a curious final paragraph, McCullers makes a comment on the nature of what passes for "reality." When the Madame's accuser thinks he sees a dog running backward in the street, we perceive that reality is events refracted through the human brain, and each person's reality is relative to his own mental state at the time.

In **"The Aliens,"** which is a sketch rather than a story, we are given speculations on the nature of grief from the mouth of a wandering Jew. There once was a time, I hear, when many provincial people thought a Jew was a freak, with horns and a tail. McCullers's Jew has neither horns nor tail, and can in no way qualify as a freak. She uses his Jewishness to emphasize his displacement. He is an alien on the bus of life, as it were—rootless and totally other.

This brings us through eighteen of McCullers's nineteen short stories, and if one discounts a paperboy with a lowered shoulder, we have yet to encounter a freak, in the physical sense. That would disappoint many of McCullers's critics, who seem to think she wrote of nothing else. But with the nineteenth story (nineteenth only in my survey, not in the order of their writing), we do find a freakish fellow. He is the title character in **"The Jockey."** With his diminutive physical stature and his life of mandatory dietary deprivation, he is a man-child in the world of men. A freak.

But more than size and diet separates this jockey from his peers. He is morally outraged by the behavior of the trainer, the bookie, and the rich man who populate the story. Their insensitivity is typified by the grossness of their appetites. When the jockey takes a mouthful of their french fries and spits it out, he symbolically rejects their values.

In contrast to the physical and material values of these men, McCullers posits a symbol of the soul—green-white August moths which flutter about the clear candle flames. The soulful jockey and the moths are one. The image is a good one, because in this gallery of wanderers and aliens, failures and outcasts in a world in which all traditional values are, if not reversed, unrecognizable, all are seeking but one thing—the freedom of the moth, the unification of the spirit with the environment, the soul with the body of this earth. In these nineteen short stories, with only one certified freak among them, Carson McCullers depicts this quest with less sensationalism than in the novels, and often with true distinction. (pp. 67-73)

Robert Phillips, " 'Freaking Out': The Short Stories of Carson McCullers," in Southwest Review, *Vol. 63, No. 1, Winter, 1978, pp. 65-73.*

Alice Hall Petry (essay date 1988)

[Petry is an American educator and author of many books and articles on American Southern writers. In the following essay, she examines "Wunderkind."]

It is one of the more peculiar phenomena of literary history that once an author becomes critically and/or popularly acclaimed, his or her earliest efforts often acquire a new status. Instead of being approached as discrete works of art, worthy of evaluation on their own terms, too often they tend to be utilized primarily as source material. They are mined for whatever embryonic elements—characters, events, motifs—were destined to reemerge, fully fleshed, in the later, greater works. Or, what is even more intriguing, those early efforts that draw upon autobiographical elements (as do so many) cease to be regarded as works of fiction, and hence they do not attract the kinds of serious scholarly attention which they deserve. Such has been the fate of one of Carson McCullers's earliest efforts, **"Wunderkind,"** written in a creative writing class taught by Sylvia Chatfield Bates, and published when she was only nineteen years old. **"Wunderkind"** is much anthologized and widely acknowledged as the thinly-veiled autobiographical record of McCullers's "burnout" as a student of the piano while in her mid-teens. It surely is that; but it also is vastly more. If one goes beyond the facile equation of "Frances is Carson," and in particular if one recognizes that the protagonist's difficulties are considerably more profound than a high schooler's disenchantment with practicing the piano, then it becomes clear that **"Wunderkind"** is essentially a remarkable rendering of an adolescent's turmoil over her growing awareness of her sexual passion for her music teacher, Mr. Bilderbach; and her turmoil is rendered no less acute by her tendency to regard him as a father figure. As shall be seen, **"Wunderkind"** features what are considerably more than what Oliver Evans terms "sexual overtones": Frances's sexual feelings for her teacher, far from "confusing" and "complicating" their relationship, are its very basis. They do not mar the story; they *make* it.

Surely **"Wunderkind"** is one of the most emotionally-intense stories McCullers ever wrote; and part of that intensity is due to the fact that the sources of the young protagonist's turmoil, although they are beginning to dawn on her, cannot quite be articulated by her. Hence the absolute importance of the story's limited point of view: fifteen-year-old Frances is undergoing a crisis; her distress is palpable throughout the story; but it is only through her confused actions, statements and memories (much of **"Wunderkind"** consists of a series of flashbacks) that the reader—far more than Frances—comes to realize that her difficulties are sexual in nature.

The limited point of view is enhanced by the strictures of the story's spatial and temporal setting. In what is apparently less than half an hour, Frances enters the confining arena of the crisis (the living room and studio of her piano teacher), reaches the breaking point and flees from what is virtually an emotional torture chamber. But the impulse to bolt is not really a sudden one: the circumstances leading up to it had been building for at least the three years during which she had studied under Bilderbach, and they had been intensifying during the previous four months; and they owe infinitely more to Frances's relationship with Bilderbach than they do to her relationship with music per se.

As so often happens in teacher/student situations (especially long-term, one-on-one tutorial arrangements), Bilderbach is more like a parent than an instructor, or what Margaret B. McDowell aptly terms "a second father." Frances had received her cherished label of "wunderkind" from him three years before, as well as her pet name "Bienchen" (literally, "little bee"). These are both Germanic names, and it comes as no surprise that Frances "wished she had not been born and brought up in just Cincinnati." Longing to deny the American name and identity derived from her biological father (who is given the American generic name of "dad"), Frances would much prefer a background like that of her surrogate father, the Dutch-Czech, German-bred Bilderbach. Frances clearly wishes desperately to please Bilderbach, who paternally gives her lessons in his cozy home, buys her a satchel for her birthday and kindly offers her milk and apple cake. Her distress over being unable to play the piano well—and, concomitantly, the *source* of her being unable to play well—is her overwhelming desire to satisfy the expectations of her father figure. The actual piano playing, then, is less an end than a means.

Even so, it is vital that music be the means by which Frances seeks to please Bilderbach. McCullers is not simply drawing upon her own background as a student of piano; rather, she is drawing heavily upon the capacity of music to evoke intense emotional responses, including sexual ones: **"Wunderkind"** would never materialize as a story if Bilderbach were teaching Frances to pitch horseshoes. Indeed, the very description of Bilderbach and Lafkowitz's duet underscores the sexuality of the music: "The music in the studio seemed to be urging violently . . ."; the two men were "lustfully drawing out all that was there." Come to that, Lafkowitz's only criticism of Frances's performance of Bach's Fantasia and Fugue is that it lacked sexual passion:

> "Frances—" Mister Lafkowitz had said then, suddenly, looking at her with his thin mouth curved and his eyes almost covered by their delicate lids. "Do you know how many children Bach had?"
>
> She turned to him, puzzled. "A good many. Twenty some odd."
>
> "Well, then—" The corners of his smile etched themselves gently in his pale face. "He could not have been so cold—then."

And Bilderbach himself responds physically to Frances's playing: she could "see his hands rise climactically from the chair arms and then sink down loose and satisfied when the high points of the phrases had been passed successfully." The powerful sexual dimension of the piano music leads to the complex central motif of the story: Bilderbach and Frances respond to each other not just as teacher and student, and not just as father and daughter, but virtually as lover and beloved. And although Frances may not have been aware of this at age twelve, it is becoming frighteningly apparent at fifteen.

The blurring of the pedagogical, paternal and amorous dimensions of Bilderbach is subtle but quite insistent. Frances has watched Bilderbach carefully, as might a student or a daughter: he has a "chunky, guttural" voice and "stolid footsteps;" and she has observed "the quick eyes behind the horn-rimmed glasses." But she also has studied features which, although benign out of context, assume a carnal aura the more they are repeated in the story: "the lips full and loose shut and the lower one pink and shining from the bites of his teeth; the forked veins in his temples throbbing." She also has studied his "muscular back" and has noted that, compared to Bilderbach's, Lakfowitz's voice was "almost like a woman's." Even her recollection of her first lesson with Bilderbach, when she was twelve years old, has an insistently sexual undercurrent of which, in retrospect, she seems to have been vaguely aware: "His deep voice sounded as though it had been straying inside her for a long time. She wanted to reach out and touch his muscle-flexed finger that pointed out the phrases, wanted to feel the gleaming gold band ring and the strong hairy back of his hand." Indeed, even the lessons themselves are couched in sexual terms . . . , and, not surprisingly, Frances repeatedly has dreams of vortexes with the face of Bilderbach—his "lips urging softly, the veins in his temples insisting"—at the center. In sum, Bilderbach may seem "crotchety" to an outsider, but to Frances he is singularly attractive.

Unlike a good father or teacher, Bilderbach has (albeit apparently unconsciously) been nurturing Frances's sexual response to him and to the music with which he is intimately associated. Hence his surname: although superficially it is a variation of "bilderbuch" (literally, "picture book"), it also echoes "bildner-Bach"—a "shaper" or "molder" ["bildner"] of a Bachesque (i.e., sexual) response to music. Indeed, at times he treats Frances like a mistress. After Saturday's lessons, for example, he has her spend the night in his house and return home by streetcar the following morning. Even though her overnight stays are evidently platonic, their resemblance to love trysts could not have been lost totally on either Bilderbach or the adolescent girl who has been wondering for two years why he has no children. Similarly, when Frances graduates from junior high school, Bilderbach personally takes her downtown and selects the cloth for her dress: "His thick fingers smoothed over the filmy nets and crackling taffetas. . . . He held colors to her face, cocking his head to one side, and selected pink"; he also supervised the sewing of the dress, insisting upon such "grown-up" features as "ruffles around the hips and neck and a fancy rosette on the shoulder." This demonstrates considerably more personal interest than the buying of a book-satchel, and is the sort of behavior few fathers would exhibit, let alone piano teachers. Even Bilderbach's most casual remarks often sound like a man speaking to his mistress: " 'You see, Bienchen, I know you so well—as if you were *my own girl.* I know what you have . . .' " (emphasis added).

Is it any wonder, then, that Frances—looking back at the events, feelings and remarks of the past three years from the vantage point of a budding sexual awareness—is nervous and confused, even distraught, as the story opens? Destined momentarily to be behind closed doors once again with a man to whom she responds physically, and who himself has a confused, quasi-sexual interest in her, Frances irrationally behaves like a woman who is trying to revive a cooling relationship with her lover. She talks to the departing Lafkowitz "to put off going into the studio a moment longer"; she vows to have a good lesson " 'like it used to be' "; and she refuses Bilderbach's proffered cake " 'till afterward' ". Although in fact this is a girl wishing to recreate the happy, asexual world of her childhood, the very *language* is that of a woman wanting to regain the bliss of earlier coitus, but fearing that it will be unsatisfactory. This astonishing use of language is particularly apparent in the story's climactic scene, the abortive final lesson with Bilderbach.

It opens with Bilderbach, a teacher trying to soothe his student, sounding more like a lover trying to console his mistress for a lack of sexual responsiveness: " 'This afternoon we are going to begin all over. Start from scratch. Forget the last few months.' " Rather provocatively straddling his chair ("The heavy volume before him seemed to balance dangerously on the chair back"), Bilderbach intensely watches her perform; and the acutely self-conscious Frances, who never used to mind his closeness, now finds that her unresponsive fingers are like "limp macaroni"—an image often associated with impotent males. Bilderbach then suggests that she play "The Harmonious Blacksmith":

> [I]mpulsively he squatted down to the floor. "*Vigorous,*" he said.
>
> She could not stop looking at him, sitting on one heel with the other foot resting squarely before him for balance, the muscles of his strong thighs straining under the cloth of his trousers. . . .
>
> She could not look down at the piano. The light brightened the hairs on the backs of his outspread hands, made the lenses of his glasses glitter.
>
> *"All of it," he urged. "Now!"*
>
> She felt that the marrows of her bones were hollow and there was no blood left in her. Her heart that had been springing against her chest all afternoon felt suddenly dead. She saw it gray and limp and shriveled at the edges like an oyster.
>
> His face seemed to throb out in space before her, come closer with the lurching motion in the veins of his temples. . . . Her lips shook like jelly and a surge of noiseless tears made the white keys blur in a watery line. "I can't," she whispered. "I don't know why, but I just can't—can't any more."
>
> His tense body slackened and, holding his hand to his side, he pulled himself up. (emphasis added).

Were this scene read out of context, one would assume that it was a failed sexual encounter, not a piano lesson. The sexual tension is not lost on Frances: like Rabbit Angstrom, unable to handle the demands and implications of sexual maturity, she runs: ". . . she stumbled down the stone steps, turned in the wrong direction, and hurried down the street that had become confused with noise and bicycles and the games of other children."

It is a child's response to stress; and this regressive behavior is to be expected from someone whose happiest moments came when Bilderbach was just her teacher/father and she was his "wunderkind"—an asexual, prelapsarian world to which she can never return, no matter how hard she runs. After all, a "wunderkind," by literal definition, is a "kind"—a *child.* It was an appropriate label for a twelve-year-old, but at fifteen Frances is occupying the tenuous world of the adolescent. As she has been outgrowing her status as a child, she is simultaneously being pressured into adulthood—and with that transformation comes the awareness (even if it cannot yet be articulated) that she has been responding to Bilderbach on a physical level.

The situation had apparently been coming to a head for at least four months, and both Bilderbach and Frances had been noticing the change. Whether it was due to the onset of menarche (hence the repeated references to "months") or perhaps from masturbation (hence the unexplained sore finger: "The sight sharpened the fear that had begun to torment her for the past few months") or simply her increased awareness of Bilderbach's maleness, the fact remains that the intimacy of a one-on-one situation is something she can no longer handle.

Thus their rather pathetic attempts to deny her budding womanhood. When she cannot play the Beethoven sonata (a mature piece), he assumes the voice "he used for children" and urges her to play a simple, early piece, "The Harmonious Blacksmith." Frances, meanwhile, who feels "clumsy and overgrown" even compared to Mr. Lafkowitz, irrationally insists that she is like Heime, a prepubescent boy ("She was like Heime. She had to be."). No wonder she is so dismayed at seeing his photograph: it is not that he is more successful than she musically, but rather that "*he* hadn't changed much in six months" (emphasis added). She measures herself against a fellow "wunderkind," Heime—a pun on "hymen"?—and is found wanting.

McCullers brilliantly conveys the confused feelings of this girl entering womanhood while longing for childhood by focusing upon the fried egg given to her at breakfast that morning. Although Frances is still enough of a child to prefer eating four chocolate bars instead of breakfast, she is sufficiently trapped in the adult world that she is being forced to eat decent meals: ". . . this morning her dad had put a fried egg on her plate and she had known that if it burst—so that the slimy yellow oozed over the white—she would cry. And that had happened. The same feeling was upon her now [while waiting for her final encounter with Bilderbach]. The egg is a perfect symbol of female sexuality, as well as of embryonic potential that will never be realized. The bursting of the egg is an apt emblem of both a sexual encounter (in particular, loss of virginity) and a difficult situation coming to a head—a quality often evoked in McCullers's fiction. At the same time, the very oozing of the egg suggests a situation out of control, while her seemingly irrational crying over the broken egg is a classic symptom of adolescent anxiety. No wonder the distress she felt at breakfast (with "dad") is identical to that she feels while anticipating the final piano lesson (with her other "father").

The presentation of Bilderbach as Frances's father enriches the complex sexual dimension of the story. At fifteen, Frances is at the age when the adolescent girl reportedly begins to experience what Freud termed the "Electra complex"—a passionate interest in the father, which must be rejected if the girl is to enter into meaningful adult heterosexual relationships. The act of running "in the *wrong* direction" towards "*other* children" suggests, however, that instead of passing into the next psycho-social stage, Frances is trying pathetically to regain her status as a child. This is regression, not an "act of courage." One can see why McCullers herself vigorously discounted those interpretations which posit **"Wunderkind"** as simply an embellished autobiographical account of how she abandoned music for writing. Once one becomes aware of the story's pervasive sexual dimension, one sees that it is virtually a case study of a rite de passage (albeit an abortive one). **"Wunderkind"** does, to quote Miss Bates, evoke "a mood and a crisis"; but where critics have done the story a disservice is to fail to determine the precise nature of the crisis. In the words of Erik Erikson, "each successive step [in an individual's psychosocial development] is a potential crisis because of a radical change in perspective." And Frances, looking back at the three previous years from the perspective of her newly-dawning sexual consciousness and anticipating an indefinite number of years in close proximity with Bilderbach, cannot face the reality of her situation. Frances's incapacity to play the piano—perhaps, indeed, her *deliberate* (even if unconscious) decision to play poorly so as to disappoint, and hence distance herself from, her teacher—is a symptom of Frances's crisis, rather than the crisis itself.

Purely as a text, **"Wunderkind"** is thus a remarkable fictional achievement, and especially so considering the youth of the author. But McCullers's precocious skill and sensitivity as a writer seem even more remarkable in light of the possibility that **"Wunderkind"** is the fictionalized transmutation of her personal feelings for her own teacher. McCullers's piano instructor in Columbus, Georgia, was not a man but Mary Tucker; there is, thus, the possibility that **"Wunderkind"** offers an embellished, fictionalized account of McCullers's sexual attraction to Mrs. Tucker—but presented, of course, within the "safe" paradigm of a girl's heterosexual feelings for her male teacher. McCullers's uncertainty over how to deal with these lesbian impulses may explain her abrupt and final decision to abandon a musical career when the object of her affections suddenly revealed she was moving to Maryland—a decision so firm and sweeping that McCullers literally would not allow anyone even to mention Mrs. Tucker's name in her presence for many weeks. Hurt by what she apparently perceived as her beloved's abandonment of her, young McCullers struck back at Mrs. Tucker in the only possible ways: in real life, by rejecting her teacher's dream of a musical career for her talented protegée; in fiction, by having the female student, rather than the teacher, do the running away.

The sexual crisis underlying **"Wunderkind"** was obviously painful for McCullers; but as so often happens in literary history, her personal trauma led to great art. By turning from a career in music to one in literature, Carson McCullers was able to create not only **"Wunderkind"** but a series of works in an unusually wide variety of literary genres. Her pain was, ultimately, our gain. (pp. 31-8)

Alice Hall Petry, "Carson McCullers's Precocious 'Wunderkind'," in The Southern Quarterly, *Vol. XXVI, No. 3, Spring, 1988, pp. 31-9.*

Margaret Walsh (essay date 1988)

[*In the following excerpt, Walsh explicates* The Ballad of the Sad Café *as an anti-fairy tale.*]

For ***The Ballad of the Sade Cafe,*** a tale of unrequited, misdirected, and unredeeming love, Carson McCullers has plucked some choice specimens from fairyland's magic tree. Although ***Ballad*** has not been discussed as a fairy tale, in it McCullers revisits the land of enchantment, redraws its map, and rewrites the expected happy ending. She thereby confirms what we have suspected but have not wanted to hear: that love does not always redeem and that personal transformations are not always lasting.

What McCullers actually writes is an anti-fairy tale. A fanciful text filled with country humor, outlandish characters, and bizarre happenings carries McCullers' disturbing message, and it is the author's choice of ballad context that permits fantastic exaggeration, a feature common to ballad and fairy tales. Other shared properties found in McCullers' story are the stock characters of dwarfs and giants; enchantments and marvelous transformations; magic numbers, spells, and elixirs; and the telling of a story dramatically, with emphasis on action and climax and without deep characterization or analysis.

Many ballads, like McCullers' story, end unhappily; and contrary to popular notions, some fairy tales do also. In tales of enchantment, according to Iona and Peter Opie in their collection of classic fairy tales, dreams and wishes seldom come true; when they do, the recipient often looks foolish. These stories invariably contain an unnatural state, from which the hero or heroine must be released or disenchanted. "Cinderella," "Sleeping Beauty," and various animal tales, such as "Beauty and the Beast," are but a few examples. A trusting, generous love, rather than magic, usually effects these fairy tale transformations: such happy endings are earned the old-fashioned way and not merely granted. Her deliberate subversion of love makes McCullers' story an anti-fairy tale.

Two kinds of enchantment's most familiar and ambiguous personages, dwarfs and giants, are central to McCullers' ballad, and they can be helpful, stupid, or frightful. Whether kind or wicked, dwarfs are exclusively male, are full-grown at three years and have a beard at seven (magical numbers in myth and folklore). They often have big heads and bumps on their backs, and they favor gray or green apparel. Many are loquacious, and most love festivities, especially moonlit feasts with music and dancing. The helpful dwarfs in "Snow White" are probably most familiar, but many manikins are mischievous, such as Rumpelstiltskin, or nasty and ungrateful, as in "Snow White and Rose Red," or simply thoroughly bad, e.g., "The Yellow Dwarf." Lymon Willis is McCullers' faithfully-sketched fairy-tale dwarf in all except the beard. Like the dwarfs in these tales, he represents an unexpected, unstabilizing, and sometimes threatening character who confronts others with danger or uncertainty and the need to make decisions. (p. 43)

Dwarfs are often paired with bloodthirsty, vicious, and solitary giants. The most famous giants are those encountered by two Jacks, one a fearless giant killer, the other a shiftless and spoiled boy who strikes a bargain for some magic beans. McCullers' giants, though at times isolated and belligerent, are derivative of those in myth and legend, especially in their epic fight scenes and in the heroine's Amazonian dimensions.

McCuller's balladeer, beginning at the end of his tale, tells of the terrible transformation of the rich young heroine into a crone; she lives entombed in a leaning, boarded-up house with "a curious, cracked look," from which a horrible, witchlike face, "sexless and white with two gray crossed eyes" stares. The face is that of Amelia Evans, legendary in reputation, "born dark, somewhat queer of face, raised motherless by her father." She weighs one hundred and sixty pounds, has "bones and muscles like a man," and is "six feet two inches tall, in itself not natural for a woman." Amelia arranges her hair in a mannish, brushed-back style, smokes pipes, wears overalls and swamp boots, and is a "fine fighter—a little heavy on her feet, but knowing all manner of mean holds and squeezes"; like her mythical counterparts, the Amazons, those warlike women who kept men at bay, Amelia "cared nothing for the love of men."

Amelia's sad transformation, actually her second, is one of many in McCullers' ballad. Her former husband, Marvin Macy, also undergoes two transformations, one by love and one by rejection, both at the hand of Amelia; though she spurns the attention of men, she herself is the object of Macy's mysterious and adoring attachment. Why Macy falls in love, we never know; nor is the narrator privy to the reasons. He paints Macy as a lengendary lover, the area's best-looking man, tall and muscular, the charming ravisher of numerous young maidens, "an evil character" known for carrying animal tails, marijuana, and the salted ear of a vanquished enemy in his pockets. Macy has all the makings of a handsome prince waiting to be released from imprisonment in a terrible form; when overcome by his unlikely love for Amelia, he is transformed into a thrifty, mannerly, pious suitor. He adores Amelia in humble silence for two years before declaring his love. Inexplicably, she marries him, but being loved does not transform Amelia; there is no tender initiation into connubial bliss for this sleeping sexual partner who is not awakened to her female role by her prince. In desperation, Macy strips himself of his possessions as he has already stripped himself of his pride and self-respect, and he offers them to his bride. Amelia responds to this unselfish supplication with avaricious brutality, and she finally casts Macy out, leaving him impoverished, humiliated, and vengeful. Once a prisoner of love under a spell, the freed Macy takes up a life of crime, only to become a prisoner again, this time of the state. For Macy, a generous love has not led to a rewarding relationship; for him, bewitched by Amelia, love itself was an enchantment.

Though Amelia's husband could not change her, Lymon Willis does, and he is the center of McCullers' tale. A pitiful wayfarer from parts unknown, a four-foot hunchback of indeterminate age, with spindly "crooked little legs," "a great warped chest," an oversized head, and a "sharp little mouth," he presents a pre-adolescent image. Bettelheim ascribes such a pre-pubertal state to fairy-tale dwarfs, who, he adds, "are certainly not men in any sexual sense." Asexuality, with its freedom from sexual demands, may be one of Lymon's attractions for Amelia.

Lymon not only inspires change, but also undergoes a remarkable alteration himself. When he fails to reappear after accepting Amelia's hospitality, the town is sure that she has murdered him. When the townsmen ominously gather at the store, they gape as the resurrected dwarf descends majestically from Amelia's apartment, shining and sparkling clean, and robed in a floor-length, lime-green, fringed, wool shawl. His "large, pale ears" adding to his elfin appearance, he is dressed in a "pair of tightfitting little knee-length breeches, black stockings, and shoes of a special kind, being queerly shaped" with ankle laces—in all, a description worthy of the most authentic fairy-tale dwarf.

At his debut, Amelia lets the regenerated dwarf, now Cousin Lymon, be the center of attention. When she emerges from her office, her face is soft and glowing. From that moment, the town itself and Amelia's store begin metamorphoses as well. The local denizens had been unaccustomed to socializing, but after the dwarf 's arrival, a new sense of geniality fills the store; in its rebirth as a cafe, it becomes the town's new home, and its roaring, glowing stove becomes a community hearth reminiscent of the ancient archetype, a womb-like sanctuary, a place of warmth and security.

The simultaneous metamorphoses of Amelia, Lymon, and

the town are accomplished within the traditional mythological period for symbolic deaths and regenerations: "And so ended three days and nights in which had come an arrival of a stranger, an unholy holiday, and the start of the cafe." Eventually the town's transformation, like all others in the story, will be reversed: after Amelia's defeat and Lymon's departure, the cafe will die, its demise taking three years as its birth had taken three days and nights.

In Lymon's presence, however, the cafe blossoms, with bright paper flowers, red curtains, and a player piano. Too, Amelia flowers: on Sundays she wears "a dark red dress that hung on her in a most peculiar fashion," and she takes Lymon visiting, to movies, fairs, and distant spectacles. Over the ensuing six year, the changes in Amelia are obvious in her "deep ringing laugh," and "the sassy, tuneful trickery" of her whistling. Watching Lymon, her face has "a bright, soft look," and her voice carries "the undertone of love" when she mentions his name.

In true fairy tale fashion, McCullers' manikin is a liar and braggart, a "mischief maker," a cause of acrimony and bickering, and the most popular attraction at the cafe. He struts about with a puerile inquisitiveness and cannot "bear to be left out of anything." According to the narrator, he has "an instinct to establish immediate and vital contact between himself and all things in the world. Such images reinforce Lymon's pre-adolescent and asexual aura.

When Macy returns, Lymon is mesmerized by his glamour. To attract Macy's attention, Lymon uses every trick in his repertoire, from wiggling "his large pale ears with marvelous quickness and ease" to fluttering his eyelids, waving, and dancing, but to no avail. Here again, McCullers stresses the bewitching power of love: the town concludes that Macy has put Lymon under a "charm," or that "an unnatural spirit" has taken possession of the dwarf. The result of love's spell on Lymon is a complete reversal of his roles, from Amelia's pampered *enfant terrible,* to groveling pet and and obstreperous child, taunting and mocking Amelia, tagging along after Macy like a stray dog.

In retaliation for his own previous degradation, Macy mistreats Amelia's beloved Lymon, thereby precipitating the call to combat. In the final clash, it is the dwarf who flies clutching and clawing like an evil bird onto Amelia's back and causes her defeat. Just before sunrise, Macy and his new companion smash Amelia's still, steal into her rooms, lay waste to all the valuables, and go off together. In the end, then, Lymon is a destructive, ungrateful dwarf, but Amelia is not rescued by a prince in bear's clothing; her prince has reverted to his beastly ways as a result of her beastly treatment of him. Amelia is left unloving and unloved, bereft of both roles, the unfulfilled role of wife to Marvin Macy and adopted role of parent to Cousin Lymon.

Lymon and Amelia's physical relationship is like that of child indulged by a fond, doting parent. Amelia's special feelings for the sufferings of children cannot be called maternal. *Parental* is a better term to describe such moments as the one when Amelia draws a boundary line (as one would for a child) around the barbeque pit so that Lymon will not injure himself while she is away, or when, after sitting up with the sleepless dwarf, "she arranged the mosquito netting over his bed and waited until he had finished with his prayers." She spoils him outrageously, doctors him with chest plasters and liniments, and misses him terribly when he does not go with her on trips. For his part, Lymon shadows her like a child, marches in her footsteps on hunting trips, and scrambles on her back to wade across the streams during excursions in the swamp.

The narrator introduces the question of whether there is a sexual element in this relationship and then leaves the answer to conjecture; this is allowed by the story's ballad form, but it causes confusion. After pointing to the incongruities of the situation, Amelia being "a powerful blunderbuss of a person . . . and Cousin Lymon a weakly little hunchback reaching only to her waist," the storyteller adds, "The good people thought that if those two had found some satisfaction of the flesh between themselves, it was a matter of concerning them and God alone." What the balladeer considers is the experience of asexual love, for the "lover" discussed is "man, woman, child, or indeed any human creature on earth." Lymon's sexless demeanor makes this feasible; however, vaguely sexual language is used several times to describe the relationship between Amelia and Lymon.

As noted, the ballad form allows sexual ambiguity because it leaves us ignorant of the emotions and sexual desires of the characters and dependent on the narrator's description of their behavior. Of the three, Macy is the only character whose sexuality is described in a traditional, though negative, manner. Amelia's characterization is more problematic, even paradoxical. We never know if Amelia has sexual yearnings, unless we count as evidence hints from the ballad singer about her wearing a "peculiar red dress" and the "lonesome look of a lover." The text does not support such a surmise; in fact, it leaves gender designation as technical, anatomical. Amelia's appearance and behavior are radically unconventional, and the mental and physical traits she exhibits are decidedly masculine. Her ambivalence to things female is seen in Amelia's doctoring. When confronted with female complaints, "She would stand there, for all the world like a great, shamed dumbtongued child." The question is not whether Amelia rejects or denies femininity, which is entirely foreign to her nature; it is rather a matter of the author's declining to provide her with any feminine traits to be denied. Lymon is asexual in all but name and dress: when he is with Amelia, his words and actions never have sexual over- or undertones. Neither is Lymon's behavior toward Macy sexual, innuendos from the balladeer notwithstanding: "The hunchback was smiling at Marvin Macy with an entreaty that was near to desperation." Lymon's conduct is like that of a child who worships someone more experienced (He is enthralled because Macy has been to Atlanta and the penitentiary.), wealthier, or more powerful than he is.

Lymon is an unsettling chimera, the unstable element at love's center. We might consider him as other than an actual or concrete character: if, in the land of enchantment a lowly toad can represent inchoate sexuality, then surely this dwarf can manifest psychological reality, specifically the psyches of Evans and Macy; read in this way, ***Ballad*** becomes for each of them a terrible story of self-revelation. Clues to a richer metaphorical interpretation of Lymon's monstrosity lie in the similar reactions he elicits from both Marvin and Amelia. When he first appears, Amelia listens thoughtfully, her gaze averted. Arrested by Lymon's deformity, she reaches out, fascinated: "Gingerly, the one long brown forefinger, she touches the hump on his back." Because Amelia has previously acknowledged few relatives and has rarely invited anyone to eat, drink or visit with her, her uncharacteristic acceptance of Lymon's claim to kinship leads onlookers to conclude that she has been overindulging in her famous homemade whiskey—a truly magic elixir and a possible cause for all that later occurred, according to the balladeer. In words that bring to mind a witch overseeing her brew, the singer relates how Amelia often "spent whole nights in her shed in the swamp silently guarding the low fire of the still." The most magical effect of the "clean," "sharp," liquor is revelatory; the ballad singer compares it to invisible writing on a paper held before a fire: "Imagine that the whiskey is the fire and that the message is hidden there." The secrets waiting to be unveiled within Amelia's breast (depending on whether we see her as a disturbed female, a troubled human being, or a combination of both) are her grotesquely developed human responses and her unrealized, abortive female emotions. The possible metaphorical unity of Amelia and her adopted cousin is revealed as they retire for the night. Amelia welcomes her new companion—whether hideously deformed relation or horribly distorted alter ego, and as they ascend to her rooms, the stairway light makes "one great, twisted shadow of the two of them."

Lymon is the first to see the returned Marvin. Whether the dwarf represents the grotesque inner psychological life of Amelia or the ludicrous outward form love can take when finally expressed, Marvin's look is of one who sees and understands. He knows that if he had personally sent Lymon to engage his former wife's affections, the moment could not have been more propitious for her devastation. The use of Lymon as a vehicle for revenge reveals another of his metaphorical roles. At this first encounter, the mutual gaze of Macy and Lymon is "like the look of two criminals who recognize each other." What Macy also recognizes is a visible expression of the hatred and desire for revenge that have filled his breast since Amelia's rejection of his love.

No matter how McCullers' story is read, sexuality is given a slanted presentation within its pages. The author's scales have gone askew, falling heavily on the male side, with but a scant portion, and a negative one at that, to the female. As a consequence, we find that while those traditionally female components of the binary male/female equation (e.g., emotion, intuition, gentleness, sensitivity, candor) are not absent from McCullers' story, they are punished, not rewarded. For example, when a beastly male like Macy is tamed by love, it is unrequited, and he is defeated, leaving his unreformed, violent mate richer and more powerful; when the previously unfeeling Amelia shares everything in her life with Lymon, he forsakes her; when Lymon receives love, he abandons the person who gives him a new life of affection and self-respect.

This brings us to the question of why this is an anti-fairy tale: unlike the redeeming love of fairy tales, love in McCullers' tale is the spell that weakens the will, the enchantment that can dwarf giants. To lay oneself bare to love is to be open to disloyalty, to be meek, powerless, and defenseless, to be at the mercy of love's unpredictability. Though the tale is recounted with good humor, ultimately these characters seem the victims of a grim cosmic joke. Such a bleak picture of an irrational universe of feeling cannot be declared invalid, but it can be seen as unsatisfying and unconsoling, which, of course, it has every right to be. But even in a random universe, the odds on a coin toss are that heads will come up at least half the time; here in McCuller's world, every flip comes up tails, and the moral seems to be that a visitor to the Sad Cafe should not plan to live happily ever after. (pp. 44-8)

Margaret Walsh, "Carson McCullers' Anti-Fairy Tale: 'The Ballad of the Sad Cafe'," in Pembroke Magazine, *No. 20, 1988, pp. 43-8.*

Virginia Spencer Carr (essay date 1990)

[Carr is an American educator, journalist, and author of a biography on McCullers (see Further Reading*). In the following excerpt, Carr surveys McCullers's short fiction, relating characters and situations in the stories to people and events in McCullers's life.]*

In tale after tale, regardless of its date of composition, the conflicts depicted by McCullers are intensified by the "immense complexity of love," a phrase that the author coined for one of her most successful short stories, **"A Domestic Dilemma."** Such love may be between a husband and his wife, an adolescent piano pupil and her teacher, a simple boy and a male cousin he idolizes, a "haunted" youth and his suicidal mother, a seemingly indifferent mother and her tubercular daughter, a jockey and his injured friend, a young girl "in love with a wedding" (or enamored of a Brazilian pen pal who never writes back), an Amazonian woman and a hunchback dwarf, and countless other fictional potential conjoinings that never quite materialize. Most of the latent love relationships in McCullers's short fiction never reach maturity, and for good reason. As her narrator expressed it in ***The Ballad of the Sad Café*** (and evident, as well, throughout her writings), "The value and quality of any love is determined solely by the lover himself," and such myopic vision by its very nature destines one's love to go unnoticed or bitterly unrequited.

To McCullers, a lover was always vulnerable unless he loved someone—or some thing—from whom he expected nothing in return. In **"A Tree. A Rock. A Cloud,"** a beery tramp confides to a pink-eared newspaper boy, a stranger to him, his "science of love," which he conceived after being abandoned by his wife. The tramp's sterile formula has led him to love things that cannot love back—first, a goldfish, then a tree, a rock, a cloud. But he invites the catcalls of mill workers in the all-night café in which he accosts the child and tells him: "Son! Hey Son! . . . I love you". Despite his declaration, the tramp knows that he can walk out alone into the predawn silence and never see his so-called "beloved" again. Loving a woman is the "last step" to his science, he tells the boy. "I go cautious. And I am not quite ready yet". The reader feels intuitively that the dissolute tramp will never be ready for the final step. He will not risk again his vulnerability to *eros.*

Whereas all of McCullers's novels are set in the South, only six of her short stories—**"A Tree. A Rock. A Cloud," "Art and Mr. Mahoney," "The Haunted Boy," "The March,"** and two apprentice pieces, **"Breath from the Sky"** and **"The Aliens"**—make such a setting explicit. At least ten of her stories have obvious settings in the North, and three of her earliest stories (**"Sucker," "Like That,"** and **"The Orphanage"**) have settings that could be anywhere (although the characters, dialogue, and events offer a kind of southern authenticity to the setting, which could well be McCullers's hometown in Georgia or the fictional towns in which *The Heart Is a Lonely Hunter* and *The Member of the Wedding* are set). Her characters who do, in fact, live in the North are often transplanted southerners whose home region remains a memory of pain and anguish. (pp. 128-30)

[A] significant characteristic unique to the short stories is the way in which McCullers transformed her personal reality into fiction. Whereas readers who know something of McCullers's girlhood in Georgia (or who knew the author personally) can recognize readily the autobiographical elements in the novels—especially in her depiction of Mick Kelly, Frankie Addams, and Jester Clane—the self-portraits in her short fiction are more cleverly disguised. On the other hand, McCullers's husband appears almost full cloth in three of the short stories: **"Instant of the Hour After," "Who Has Seen the Wind?"** and **"A Domestic Dilemma."** In the novels, Reeves McCullers can be recognized only in the characterization of Jake Blount.

The most prevalent theme in the novels—rejection or unrequited love—repeats itself, as one might expect, in her short fiction. McCullers's characters must learn again and again the lesson of *eros,* just as their creator herself had to learn it many times—and to live with it—over the years. The theme is firmly established in her apprentice story, **"Sucker."** *Sucker* is the nickname of a gullible twelve-year-old boy who idolizes his older cousin, Pete, in whose home he has lived for many years, his parents having been killed in a car accident. Pete, who narrates the tale in an effort to come to grips with Sucker's evolvement into a hardened preadolescent, presents a truism that becomes a refrain, as it were, throughout McCullers's fiction: "If a person admires you a lot you despise him and don't care . . . it is the person who doesn't notice you that you are apt to admire". Pete was in love with Maybelle, a popular older girl who took a casual interest in him until her head was turned by a boy with a yellow roadster. She admits to the crestfallen Pete early in the story that she has "never cared a rap" about him, and he, in turn, attacks Sucker: "Nobody cares anything about you! And just because I felt sorry for you sometimes and tried to act decent don't think I give a damn about a dumb-bunny like you . . . a dumb Sucker."

To cope emotionally with his cousin's betrayal, the boy assumes a façade of hardness (much as Bubber Kelly does in *The Heart Is a Lonely Hunter* when his sister Mick tries to frighten him with thoughts of Sing Sing and an electric chair "just his size"), and it is Pete who yearns to undo the damage. But it is too late. Sucker looks at him in a "new hard way" and insists upon being called by his real name *Richard.* Sucker's physical growth burgeons during the three months immediately following his fall from innocence, and the physiological changes are matched by psychological ones. Richard acts tough and hard with his friends, and when they come to the room he still shares with Pete, the older youth laments that even the room is no longer his: "He [Sucker] sprawls across the bed in those long corduroy pants with the suspenders and just stares at me with that hard, half sneering look. I don't care a flip for Maybelle or any particular girl any more and it's only this thing between Sucker and me that is the trouble now."

McCullers wrote **"Sucker"** when she was seventeen and trying to deal with her own trauma of what she saw as abandonment upon learning that her piano teacher's husband was being transferred to a distant infantry fort—a move that meant that she would have to continue her lessons with someone else. In her eyes, the entire Tucker family was *her* family, and she was devastated. Not since the acute jealousy that her infant sister had aroused by her "intrusion" (as McCullers saw it) into the Smith household at birth had she felt so personally undermined. The characters whose shrill cries of being "cheated" resound repeatedly throughout McCullers's fiction certainly owe much of their genesis to McCullers's response to the Tucker family's move.

Frances, the main character in **"Wunderkind"**—and Sucker, her counterpart—are the earliest versions of McCullers's countless adolescents who are torn in time, dislodged from the safety of childhood, yet not ready, either, for the world of adults. **"Wunderkind,"** written a few months after **"Sucker,"** was another early attempt by McCullers to objectify her wretched perception of having been renounced. Frances, more boldly autobiographical than Sucker, is a young piano pupil who perceives that she is no longer a *wunderkind* and wrestles with what she should do about it. In this tale it is the piano teacher who, ultimately, is abandoned. Important to the initiation theme in **"Wunderkind"** is the reader's recognition of the paradoxical nature of love and human charity. Frances teeters between adolescence and maturity in an unsuccessful struggle to play for her teacher (whom she loves), with the passion, sensitivity, and technique she had shown when they first began working together. Equally responsible for the dilemma is Mr. Bilderbach, Frances's teacher, who resists admitting, because he loves her, that her talent is unpromising. His pupil seems like a daughter to him, and he welcomes special opportunities to give her presents, which she views with resentment as "charity." She has no interest in anything but music, and all she can think about is "playing the music as it must be played, bringing out the thing that must be in her, practicing, practicing, playing so that Mister Bilderbach's face lost some of its urging look." Through her teacher, Frances becomes aware not only of her own musical ineptitude, but also of her evolving sexuality. As she strives to please him she is aware that his "deep voice sounded as though it had been straying inside her for a long time. She wanted to reach out and touch his muscle-flexed finger that pointed out the phrases, wanted to feel the gleaming gold band ring and the strong hairy back of his hand."

In an attempt to play another Beethoven *variation,* Frances longs to start the dirge "with subdued viciousness and progress to a feeling of deep, swollen sorrow," but her "hands seemed to gum in the keys like limp macaroni," and she could not even imagine the music. "I can't. I don't know why, but I just can't—can't anymore," she whispers, then clutches her belongings—her music, her coat, her mittens and galoshes, the book satchel he had given her for her birthday, everything "from the silent room that was hers"—and flees the house. Frances's painfully acquired self-knowledge leads to her stumbling flight from the master's studio, to which she knows she will never return. The girl's profound sense of loss is shared by her teacher as well, but in their confusion and hurt, neither can admit it. (pp. 130-35)

Some twenty-five years after its publication, McCullers reflected that just as Tennessee Williams had written *The Glass Menagerie* as a memory play, so, too, had she written **"Wunderkind"** as a memory, but not the "reality of the memory"; rather, it was a "foreshortening of that memory. It was about a young music student. I didn't write about my real music teacher—I wrote about the music we studied together because I thought it was truer. The imagination is truer than the reality." (p. 135)

"Like That," another apprentice tale, was purchased by Whit Burnett for *Story* magazine in 1936, along with **"Wunderkind,"** but it remained unpublished until it surfaced years later in the *Story* archives at Princeton University. Burnett felt that a story whose central incident revolved around a young woman's first menstruation should be suppressed until "more liberal times."

Similar in theme and narrative mode to **"Sucker," "Like That"** is an interior monologue by a pubescent girl about her older sister's coming of age ("Sis" is eighteen and "grown-up now"), but the real initiation is the narrator's. If being grown-up means acting "like that," she wants nothing to do with it. "I know there's no way I can make myself stay thirteen all my life," she says, "but I know I'd never let anything really change me at all—no matter what it is." She recalls the satisfying years of growing up—of making fudge, playing three-handed bridge with their brother (who at eighteen is also experiencing growing pains), and sharing holidays, books, and secrets with her brother and sister before her sudden awareness that "growing up" alters everything. She speaks painfully of her discovery that "Sis" had just "started with what every big girl has each month," and frightened and angry, she tells "Sis": "Anybody can tell. Right off the bat. . . . It looks terrible. I wouldn't ever be like that."

Later in the tale (marked by a five-year interval), the narrator makes a new discovery. She has just surmised that her sister has undergone a new initiation—a sexual one—that further confirms her coming of age. The younger girl does not know exactly what has happened, but she hears the "sharpness" in her sister's voice, is troubled by her sister's sad looks and silent, terrible weeping following a date with Tuck, a college student, and recognizes that her relationship with her sister has changed permanently. The name *Tuck* (another echo of *Mary Tucker,* McCullers's former piano teacher) and the narrator's anguish as a result of the incident reveal a more blatant use of persona and events from the author's own life than usual. Unwilling to forsake childhood, the narrator rides her bicycle, skates, goes to football games, wears bobby socks, withdraws from the group in the basement of the school gym when they begin "telling certain things—about being married and all," vows never to wear lipstick—not "for a hundred dollars"—and declares that she is "hard boiled" and will not "waste her time trying to make Sis like she used to be." The child's hostility toward change foreshadows Mick's in *The Heart Is a Lonely Hunter,* and in her pain of conversion, she is a combination of Sucker and Pete.

Still another early memory piece and a more somber initiation tale than the other apprentice pieces is **"The Orphanage."** McCullers can be taken here, too, for the unidentified narrator of this prosaic slice-of-life that has no plot or character development (and very little movement). Yet there is drama in the tale as the narrator looks back upon an incident that occurred when she was six or seven and had an older friend Hattie, whom she identifies as her "initiator." When the narrator and her cousin Tit (a male cousin her age) promise not to reveal to anyone else what she is going to show them, Hattie retrieves from a closet shelf a "dead pickled baby" in a jar that her brother had brought home "when he was learning to be a drug store man." It was an orphan, she told them. The narrator had always been intrigued by the town's orphanage and often passed it with her grandmother (for it was on the main thoroughfare to downtown), but Hattie's revelation of the "pickled orphan" haunts the narrator and provokes wild, fearful dreams.

McCullers interrupts her tale midway to observe that the "memories of childhood have a strange shuttling quality, and areas of darkness ring the spaces of light . . . [like] clear candles in an acre of night, illuminating fixed scenes from the surrounding darkness." Even though the children whom the narrator saw playing on their swings and exercise bars were orphans, they had each other as an "assorted whole." McCullers's coda of the chain gang in ***The Ballad of the Sad Café*** became her telescoped treatise on the same subject. Another version of being an envious outsider watching children at play was rendered more directly in McCullers's essay "The Flowering Dream: Notes on Writing." The frustration felt by a character who has been excluded from things in which he/she desperately wants to share is treated again and again in McCullers's fiction, just as the author herself experienced it repeatedly in life.

Yet another early tale of rejection set in the South, but developed quite differently, is **"Breath from the Sky,"** published posthumously—as were these other early pieces—for the first time in ***The Mortgaged Heart.*** In **"Breath from the Sky,"** Constance, a fragile girl of fourteen or fifteen, is about to be sent away to a sanitarium in Mountain

Heights (Georgia) for treatment for what appears to be advanced tuberculosis. Constance fears that she will never return home and that her younger brother and sister will live out their carefree lives as though she had never existed. Made implicit by the point of view through which the story unfolds is the fact that, regardless of appearances, Constance's mother is not indifferent to her daughter's plight. Rather, the older woman's apparent insensitivity is simply her means of dealing with the tragedy. Ultimately, the story is as much the mother's as it is the ailing daughter's. Not surprisingly, readers of this early tale who lived in Columbus, Georgia, and knew both McCullers and her mother (Marguerite Waters Smith), readily perceived Constance's mother to be a thinly disguised portrait of the author's own.

Throughout McCullers's canon, it is noteworthy that the children she depicts have no strong emotional ties with their mothers. Lamar Smith believed that his sister "did not want to strip herself 'that bare' and reveal her utter dependency" on their mother. "Sister was too vulnerable," he continued. "She was our mother's favorite child, and somehow my sister Rita and I understood this. We were convinced that Sister was a genius, and that our mother was, also, for letting that genius flower." McCullers's fictional mothers—if they are mentioned at all—either die in childbirth, as does Frankie's in *The Member of the Wedding;* are too preoccupied with helping to support the family when the father cannot, as does Mick's in *The Heart Is a Lonely Hunter;* drink too much, as does Emily Meadows in **"A Domestic Dilemma"**; or attempt suicide, as does Hugh's in **"The Haunted Boy."** On the other hand, the fathers in her fiction are treated rather compassionately. Like Mick's and Frankie's fathers, they suffer because they fail to communicate with their daughters, who are only vaguely aware of their sense of loss and appear reticent to deal with them directly.

In **"Court in the West Eighties,"** a long and less well-developed apprentice piece than most of the others in the posthumous collection edited by McCullers's sister, the narrator is an eighteen-year-old university student in New York City who comments upon the people living in the court whom she views from her window. The neighbor who intrigues her most is a red-headed man who keeps milk and crocks of food on his window sill, and who looks out upon the court just as she does. "We were near enough to throw our food into each others' windows, near enough so that a single machine gun could have killed us all together in a flash," observes the narrator, her flair for the dramatic similar to her creator's. When trouble brews among several of the residents of the court, the young woman is certain that the man with the red hair "was the one person able to straighten it out. . . . I had a feeling that nothing would surprise him and that he understood more than most people." Despite her ratiocination, the narrator knows that neither she nor the strange man with the red hair could possibly straighten out things for any of them, that one simply lives his own life and endures it. Although the tale is slight and clearly an apprentice piece, it is important to readers of McCullers's first novel in that the narrator and the man she watches are sensitively drawn prototypes of Mick Kelly and John Singer, who were germinating as early as 1935 when McCullers first went north.

Two other stories, **"The Aliens"** and a fragment identified as **"Untitled Piece,"** are also important early versions of materials that appeared eventually in McCullers's novels (and published for the first time in ***The Mortgaged Heart***). One of the earliest prototypes of John Singer is Felix Kerr in **"The Aliens."** A displaced Jew, Kerr is journeying south by bus to make a home for the family he has left in Europe. The story, which takes place in August of 1935, is actually a dialogue between the Jew and the passenger who sits beside him, a naïve farm boy. The tale remains static until a black woman, who appears "deformed—although not in any one specific limb," gets on the bus; her body as a whole is "stunted, warped and undeveloped." To the Jew, everything about her seems repugnant, and he asks the youth: "What is the matter with her?"

"Who? You mean the nigger?" the youth replies. "Why there's nothing the matter with her. . . . Not that I can see." Bound by the parameters of his farm, the boy is as maimed in his own social perception as the woman is in her physical grotesqueness. Ironically, both the woman and the youth get off the bus at the same stop, inextricably linked by their environment. The youth has unwittingly revealed that he is as isolated in his own region as the wandering Jew is in this foreign land (and as the black woman herself must be)—all three, social pariahs. Alone once more, Kerr, thinking of his wife and their younger daughter who will join him soon, is suddenly stricken with an inconsolable grief for another daughter whose whereabouts and welfare remain a mystery to him.

The fragmented family appears throughout McCullers's canon, a theme she experimented with again and again in her early work. Her longest story, published as **"Untitled Piece"** in ***The Mortgaged Heart,*** is important, too, for its seeds that flower later in *The Heart Is a Lonely Hunter.* The tale is told from the point of view of Andrew Leander, who leaves his Georgia home at seventeen for New York City and returns at twenty-one, the full initiate. Like most of McCullers's short fiction, the story is a memory piece concerning Andrew's awakening and his ambivalent feelings toward his family as he gains self-awareness. Andrew has two sisters (Sara and Mick) and no mother, only the young black houseservant Vitalis, who—like Portia in *The Heart Is a Lonely Hunter* and Berenice Sadie Brown in *The Member of the Wedding*—functions as a surrogate. Andrew recalls the sounds, scents, and events in his life when he was on the edge of puberty—a maturation that he and his sister Sara had yearned for, yet tried to forestall. Andrew—whose father is a jeweler—is not only a Mick Kelly figure, but a prototype, as well, of Jake Blount and Dr. Copeland in *The Heart Is a Lonely Hunter.* He is also similar to Harry Minowitz, with whom Mick has her first sexual experience (both Harry and Andrew flee to distant cities after their encounters). But in McCullers's **"Untitled Piece,"** Harry Minowitz is an actual character, a Jew who borrows a workbench from Andrew's father on which to set up his business as a watch repairman. It is the Minowitz of this tale who eventually evolves into John Singer, the deaf-mute.

McCullers's **"Untitled Piece"** is the best single prototype of any of her longer fiction and affords an intriguing study of the creative process. The reader who is well acquainted with *The Heart Is a Lonely Hunter* can see how McCullers developed her characterizations, used and discarded incidents, reassigned various character traits, and created the tightly controlled structure that was missing from her untitled apprentice work.

Although Andrew is never a fully rounded character—largely because he tells his own rambling story—McCullers succeeded in recreating his distorted vision and slow search for selfhood, punctuated by a series of Joycean epiphanies. Andrew's restless search for identity resembles that of Stephen Daedalus (by this time McCullers had read *Portrait of an Artist as a Young Man,* as well as Joyce's Dubliner tales, and was admittedly influenced by them). Andrew's father is much like the father of Frankie Addams, who works deftly and lovingly at his jeweler's bench, his eyes seeing only the immediate task before him. The "eye that wore the jeweler's glass" is distorted, and the other eye is "squinted almost shut." Although he sometimes stares out at people passing his window on the street, he does not speak to them, nor does he communicate successfully with either Sara or his son (Andrew's father closely resembles the fathers of Mick and Frankie, both of whom owe their genesis to McCullers's father).

After his sexual initiation, Andrew abandons his plans to go to Georgia Tech to study engineering and goes instead to New York City, that spot "on an aerial map . . . far away . . . frozen and delicate." When he returns to the South three years later, his odyssey having come full circle, he is drunk and sick for home.

These apprentice pieces and McCullers's "Outline to 'The Mute' " comprise more than half of ***The Mortgaged Heart*** and make a significant contribution to the reader's appreciation of her work as a whole. (pp. 136-45)

"Poldi" is an engaging tale of unrequited love, but it is less successful than most of the other early pieces. Although the physically unattractive Poldi Klein, a cellist, appears to be the main character, it is the hapless lover Hans (who resembles Sucker in many ways) with whom the reader ultimately sympathizes. Hans—from whose viewpoint the story unfolds—is a grieving, pimply-faced pianist who has loved inordinately the overweight, unattractive cellist for two years without her having the slightest awareness that his devotion is anything more than concern for her well-being. Poldi, on the other hand, has been in love with a succession of men who have little awareness that she even exists. At the story's opening, Hans visits the cellist's studio again, this time determined to confess his feelings and to rescue her from her destitute state (Poldi cannot even afford to repair her damaged instrument); however, before he can convey his feelings, she informs him that she has declared in a note her unbridled love for someone else (then offers countless reasons for the man's silence). When Hans gently reminds her that her new beloved is engaged to marry someone else, Poldi replies: "Yes. But it's a mistake. What would he want with a cow like her?" The neglected Hans realizes that the woman's illusions are essential if she is to survive, and he does what he can to confirm them.

Hans's decision to support the woman's fantasy reinforces the similarities between **"Poldi"** and McCullers's tale of another musician, **"Madame Zilensky and the King of Finland."** Madame Zilensky, a composer and piano teacher, becomes a pathological liar in an attempt to escape through fantasy an awareness of her fragmentation in a disordered world. Just as the metronome provides a mechanical tempo for her performance and teaching of music, so, too, do her lies and fantasies impose an illusory order upon her personal life. Madame Zilensky's downfall comes when her supervisor, known only as Mr. Brook, challenges one of her harmless deceptions after she tells him of having seen the King of Finland go by on a sled as she stood in front of a *pâtisserie* in Helsingfors (Helsinki). Later, it occurs to Brook that Finland has never had a king, that the country is a democracy, and he can hardly wait to expose her.

Yet, by stripping the woman of her illusions—unwilling, as it were, to *brook* the lie—Brook strips Madame Zilensky of her soul as well. In this early tale McCullers establishes with no uncertainty her conviction that illusions are essential if one is to endure life's painful realities. When one's dream is ravished by grim ratiocination, the dreamer, too, is destroyed. McCullers, however, does not allow the destroyer to go unpunished. Almost at once Brook experiences a "great commotion of feelings—understanding, remorse, and unreasonable love," and he covers his face with his hands. "Yes. Of course. The King of Finland. And was he nice?" Brook asks the stricken woman, but the situation is irreparable.

Whereas the tale appears to focus on the unfortunate woman (as does **"Poldi"**), the important reversal in the action concerns Brook himself, who is described early in the story as a solitary man who loathes "academic fiddle-faddle" and takes a trip alone to Peru instead of joining his music colleagues in Salzburg. A silent observer, Brook reminds the reader of Biff Brannon, the café owner in *The Heart Is a Lonely Hunter.* He is tolerant of the peculiarities of others and claims even to relish them. In the course of the story, he learns something about himself as well, just as Brannon has his moment of revelation at the novel's close. An hour after Brook had handily dispatched Madame Zilensky, he sits alone in his room, vaguely disquieted, as he grades papers for his counterpoint class. Suddenly he views from the window the neighbor's old Airedale waddling down the street. At first the dog behaves as usual, then inexplicably appears to be "running along backward." That the dog is actually running backward—in a kind of crab or mirror counterpoint—is illusory, and Brook dismisses the phenomenon as impossible. Yet, in destroying the illusions of Madame Zilensky, Brook also fragments himself. The solitary professor may be able to teach and grade counterpoint, but, ironically, he cannot allow counterpoint to exist in his own life. These two dissimilar human beings might have come together contrapuntally in a rare spiritual communion and thus ease their self-estrangement—just as two dissimilar themes or melodies may run counter, yet concurrently, to combine into a harmonious single entity—but the two fragmented halves that they finally represent are too dissonant to make a whole.

"The Sojourner," a more subtle and mature story of unrequited love, is a "remembrance of things past" juxtaposed with the painful present. This lyrical tale has its origins, like so many of McCullers's other stories, in her troubled life with her husband. It, too, employs music in its resolution and deals with displacement and a character's need for order in a disordered society.

John Ferris, from whose point of view the story is told, is a displaced southerner who has come home from Paris to attend the funeral of his father in Georgia. Back in New York City for scarcely twenty-four hours before boarding a plane to return to Paris, he sees his former wife, Elizabeth, quite by chance and follows her briefly without her knowing it. Suddenly, Ferris literally "wheels" from her to distance himself once more from the bittersweet memories interwoven with the "jealousy, alcohol and money quarrels" that had destroyed "fiber by fiber" the "fabric of married love." He had thought himself invulnerable to old emotions, yet seeing her again (when he calls her, she invites him to dinner), meeting her husband and their two beautiful children, hearing her perform at the piano a Bach prelude and fugue (then an elusive melody that he could not place), he was "lost in the riot of past longings, conflicts, ambivalent desires." Elizabeth's playing is interrupted by the maid announcing dinner, and, later, on the plane en route to Paris, Ferris tries to recapture her "singing melody," but it is too late. His self-perception at this moment is that he is suspended between two worlds—an idealized world suggestive of what might have been (symbolized by Elizabeth's music and her face, "a madonna loveliness, dependent of the family ambiance") and his own disordered world, a "succession of cities, of transitory loves; and time, the sinister glissando of the years, time always." Having a lover who was already married to someone else was safe, just as the old tramp's declaration to a strange child—"Son, I love you"—was safe. So long as neither risks his vulnerability, his "science of love" is secure. (pp. 146-50)

In **"The Haunted Boy,"** another story of wounded adolescence and rejection set in Georgia, Hugh is haunted by the fear that he will return from school one day and discover his mother lying in a pool of blood on the bathroom floor, just as he had discovered her a few months earlier after a failed suicide attempt that resulted in her being sent to the state mental hospital in Milledgeville. Although the boy's mother has recovered and is back home when the story opens, Hugh cannot forgive his mother for what he sees as her attempt to abandon him. The boy's hostility and sense of guilt drive him to his friend John for succor, but John is insensitive to Hugh's unspoken needs, and, thus, cannot share his burden. Hugh recognizes in his distress, finally, that he hates John, reasoning that "you hate people you have to need so badly!"

Young Hugh's admission reflects the ambivalence of McCullers's own feelings toward her mother, with whom she felt increasingly uncomfortable (in direct proportion to her dependency upon her) after her husband's suicide. Yet in making her protagonist an adolescent boy (a gender disguise that the author employed in much of her fiction), McCullers successfully objectified her ambivalent love-hate-guilt feelings, feelings that she tried repeatedly to suppress in her life and to conceal from her mother. Friends of McCullers who knew her mother may have viewed the tale as a thinly disguised fiction of a "haunted girl." McCullers probably began work on the story in 1954, but the exact date of composition is unknown. Her mother died of a bleeding ulcer in 1955, five months before **"The Haunted Boy"**—ultimately yet another version of the author's thesis on love presented in ***The Ballad of the Sad Café***—was published.

McCullers ends this tale, too, in strange fashion compared to her usual final resolutions. It is Hugh's father who now partially redeems him. Whereas he had distanced himself from his son during his wife's crisis, he now praises Hugh for his courage in accepting the experience and treats him like a grown-up for the first time. **"The Haunted Boy"** provides one of the few father figures in McCullers's fiction who make any positive impression upon a son or daughter. Although the ending is mawkish and lacks conviction, the reader appreciates the boy's emergence from moral isolation into self-knowledge.

"Correspondence"—McCullers's only story in the epistolary form—is one of McCullers's best and most tightly controlled conversions of life into art. The tale consists solely of four letters from Henky Evans, another Frankie Addams character (though she lives in Darien, Connecticut), who pours out her adolescent heart to a Brazilian pen pal who never writes back. Henky's salutations and closings reveal her growing awareness of failure and rejection as she moves from "Dear Manuel" and "Your affectionate friend, Henky Evens" to "Dear Mr. Garcia" and "Yrs. truly, Miss Henrietta Hill Evans." In her final letter Henky demands to know why the youth had "put his name on the pen pal list" if he did not intend to fulfill his part of the agreement. In a postscript she adds: "I cannot waste any more of my valuable time writing to you." It is unlikely that Henky Evans—who lacks Frankie Addams's resilience—will put her name on a pen pal list again or otherwise risk her vulnerability.

In actuality, McCullers interrupted her work on ***The Ballad of the Sad Café*** to write this story, one prompted by her husband's failure to answer her letters while she was spending her first summer at Yaddo Artists Colony. As she saw it, Reeves McCullers—like Henky's South American pen pal—had defaulted on his contract. McCullers resolved to waste no more "valuable time" on her marriage and immediately initiated divorce proceedings, having learned that her husband had gone away secretly with their best friend.

"The Jockey," another poignant story of loss that McCullers wrote at Yaddo the same summer that she wrote **"Madame Zilensky and the King of Finland"** and **"Correspondence,"** was set in Saratoga Springs, a spa town famous for its August races. . . . The external conflict in this tale is between the jockey Bitsey Barlow—whose description brings to mind that of the hunchback dwarf in ***The Ballad of the Sad Café***—and a trio whom he accosts in the restaurant: the owner of the horse that Barlow rode the day of the incident, the horse's trainer, and a bookie. Whether the jockey had ridden to victory that day or lost the race was not the issue, nor does the omniscient narrator comment upon it. What *does* cause concern, and provides the catalyst to the action, is the realization that the jockey's best friend (who rode for the same owner and trainer) will never ride again because of the injuries he sustained in an earlier race. "Libertines," Barlow hisses when he finds the trio at dinner over a sumptuous meal, his impotent rage reminiscent of Jake Blount's in *The Heart Is a Lonely Hunter.* The jockey sees his adversaries as animals incapable of concern for the maimed rider. The trio wants only to *replace* the wounded jockey as quickly as possible. A horse with a broken leg is shot, but the unfortunate jockey in a callous environment is trapped forever, implies McCullers.

The frustrated jockey and his disabled companion have been caught, cheated—like Mick in *The Heart Is a Lonely Hunter* and others in her fictional landscape—because the cards are stacked against them. McCullers continued to rail against the "ironies of fate" as she turned repeatedly during the summer of 1941 from her book-length tale of the hapless Frankie Addams who is hopelessly in love with a wedding, to the writing of short stories concerning unrequited love—artistic achievements from which she could gain more immediate release from her disappointments and frustrations.

A story that McCullers wrote several years later that depicts philistines of a different sort is **"Art and Mr. Mahoney,"** published in *Mademoiselle* and selected by McCullers's sister for inclusion in ***The Mortgaged Heart*** for its deft detail and sharp satire of provincial manners and the prostitution of art. It is not the title character Mahoney, but his wife, who is the true philistine. Mahoney, once a country boy, now owns a brick yard and mill and is a pillar of society in his small southern town in which the pretentious patrons of little theater plays and concerts wear "chiffon and corsages and decorous dinner jackets" to the high school auditorium and attend what they think of as "gala" receptions. Mahoney can talk handily about abstract art and "repertory" and assume the "proper expression of meek sorrow" at a concert or lecture, having been "well drilled" by his culturally groomed wife. The couple's position in their smalltown world of art and culture seems secure until Mahoney makes his "fatal" mistake: he claps too soon during a Chopin sonata played by Jose Iturbi at the season's opening concert. Mahoney was "so dead sure it was the end that he clapped heartily half a dozen times before he realized, to his horror, that he clapped alone." The man's shame is exceeded only by his wife's humiliation. At a party afterward, an acquaintance of Mahoney's who does not "know a sonata from the *Slit Belly Blues,*" yet who has done nothing to provoke ostracism, safely approaches the humiliated offender and declares with "a slow wink of covert brotherhood" that the subscription tickets Mahoney had sold ought to entitle him "to an extra clap" if he wanted one.

The tale—told from Mahoney's point of view, yet rendered through an omniscient voice that one takes for McCullers's own—affords the reader scant sympathy for the offender; yet more to the point, the author offers no hope of redemption for Mrs. Mahoney either, who can neither forgive her husband nor recognize her own duplicity in the charade. The woman is ignorantly and permanently entrapped in smug conventionalism, a fate more damning than death itself, suggests McCullers.

The concept of the "immense complexity of love"—a phrase from her short story **"A Domestic Dilemma"**—surfaces often in McCullers's writings, especially in her domestic tales that reflect aspects of her life with Reeves McCullers. The earliest story of domestic discord, **"Instant of the Hour After,"** was written when the author was nineteen. It depicts a wretched evening in the life of a young husband and wife whose marriage is disintegrating because of his inability to control his drinking. Although the wife (unnamed) loves her husband, she is put off by his torrent of meaningless words and sarcasms when he is drunk. She wonders vaguely what life might have been like had she married their friend Phillip, who often came to their apartment to play chess. (pp. 151-57)

"Instant of the Hour After" is McCullers's only story in which both the husband and wife drink heavily. The young wife in the tale sees herself entrapped with her husband in a bottle, "skeetering angrily up and down the cold blank glass like minute monkeys" until they collapse, exhausted, "looking like fleshy specimens in a laboratory. With nothing said between them." Despite her teacher's urging that she revise the tale, McCullers chose not to do so, apparently having found the material too painful and personal to attempt to rework it.

The second tale in which marital harmony is disrupted by alcohol is **"A Domestic Dilemma."** Its tone is reminiscent of **"Instant of the Hour After."** This time it is the sherry-tippling housewife Emily Meadows who precipitates the conflict. Emily drinks furtively and cannot be trusted with the safe rearing of their two young children. Her husband Martin—from whose point of view the story unfolds—assumes much of the responsibility for the dilemma, for he has uprooted his wife from the south and moved her to an unnamed suburban town on the Hudson River. Homesick and unable to adjust to the "stricter, lonelier mores of the North," Emily stays to herself, reads magazines and murder mysteries, and finds her interior life "insufficient without the artifice of alcohol." Martin has been uneasy about their children ever since Emily, in a state of intoxication, had allowed their infant daughter to slip from her arms while carrying her naked from her bath. Having hired a housekeeper as a result of the accident, the young husband now worries only on Thursday afternoons, the servant's afternoon off. The tale opens on such a Thursday as a domestic crisis is in progress.

Martin has just discovered that Emily had sprinkled red pepper (rather than cinnamon) on the children's buttered toast, then left them alone to eat while she sipped sherry in the bedroom upstairs. After a confrontation with Emily and a drunken scene in the kitchen in front of the children, Martin fixes soup and insists that she eat; then he puts her to bed—his dull hard anger "like a weight upon his chest"—before bathing the children and settling them for the night. His anger rises as he thinks of their vulnerability, and he reflects, too, upon his own youth, which he sees being "frittered by a drunkard's waste." Later, as he undresses for bed and observes his wife in the darkened room in "tranquil slumber," he becomes suddenly overwhelmed by tenderness. He perceives his daughter in the arch of Emily's handsome brow and his son in her chin and high cheekbones. Then, inexplicably and at once, the "ghost of the old anger" and all thoughts of "blame or blemish" vanish, and he slides into bed trying not to awaken his wife. Ultimately, sorrow parallels desire "in the immense complexity of love," and his hand seeks the "adjacent flesh."

"A Domestic Dilemma" aptly demonstrates McCullers's narrative gift for understatement and her ability to handle a story told from a man's point of view that is equally as sensitive and sympathetic as one told from the woman's perspective.

Still another complex tale of love and domestic crisis brought on by alcohol is **"Who Has Seen the Wind?"** This long tale dealt McCullers considerable pain, too, in the writing. Whereas the alcoholic husband in **"Instant of the Hour After"** was a young man of twenty, his later counterpart is almost forty. Written exactly twenty years after **"Instant of the Hour After," "Who Has Seen the Wind?"** is the story of Ken Harris, an author of one successful novel and a bitterly unsuccessful second novel. At this point in his life, Harris cannot write at all, but sits staring at a blank sheet in the typewriter and sporadically alternating *X* and *R* on the keys. At a recent cocktail party he had warned a young writer that a "small, one-story talent" is the "most treacherous thing that God can give." Harris feels betrayed, too, by his wife (who supports him by her editing job in the city) because she refuses to take seriously his repeated urgings that they move to an apple farm, an idyllic dream they had once shared. When she refuses her husband in bed as well, telling him "No. Never again," and pleads with him to seek help for his sickness, he threatens to stab her with her sewing scissors. Harris is desolate when he discovers a few moments later that she has left him alone with his psychotic fears, and he lurches with "luminous lost eyes" into a blinding snowstorm and "the unmarked way ahead." Yet as he stumbles toward his own certain death at the story's end, he stops a policeman to report that his wife is crazy and has just tried to kill him. "She ought to be helped before something awful happens," he instructs. (pp. 157-60)

One final short story, **"The March,"** was published in *Redbook* a few weeks before McCullers's death. A thin civil rights story set in the South, it was not included in either of the posthumous collections of her work. Most readers (if they know it at all) agree that **"The March"** does not approach the quality of excellence in her other short fiction. She had intended the tale to be the first of a trilogy of short stories, but she was unable to complete the other two before her death. McCullers's best short stories remain those that she wrote during her young womanhood in the 1930s and 1940s. (p. 161)

Virginia Spencer Carr, in her Understanding Carson McCullers, *University of South Carolina Press, 1990, 181 p.*

FURTHER READING

Biography

Carr, Virginia Spencer. *The Lonely Hunter: A Biography of Carson McCullers.* New York: Doubleday & Co., 1975, 600 p.

Extensive biography of McCullers includes photographs, genealogy, concise chronology, bibliography, and index.

Evans, Oliver. *The Ballad of Carson McCullers.* New York: Coward-McCann, 1965, 220 p.

Biographical and critical study of McCullers's life and works includes photographs and extensive discussions of "Wunderkind" and "A Tree. A Rock. A Cloud." Evans also reprints McCullers's notes on "The Mute," which became the basis for her first novel *The Heart Is a Lonely Hunter.*

Criticism

Baldanza, Frank. "Plato in Dixie." *The Georgia Review* XII, No. 1 (Summer 1958): 151-67.

Examines the presentation of Platonic philosophy, specifically, theories of Platonic love, in McCullers's short story "A Tree. A Rock. A Cloud."

Bloom, Harold, ed. *Modern Critical Views: Carson McCullers.* New York: Chelsea House Publishers, 1986, 159 p.

Anthology of critical articles and excerpts on different aspects of McCullers's fiction, includes essays by Marguerite Young, Tennessee Williams, Gore Vidal, Oliver Evans, Klaus Lubbers, and Louise Westling.

Cook, Richard M. *Carson McCullers.* New York: Frederick Ungar, 1975, 150 p.

Dedicates a chapter to each of McCullers's longer works, including *The Ballad of the Sad Café* with many references and comparisons to such short stories as "Wunderkind," "Sucker," and "A Tree. A Rock. A Cloud."

Dazey, Mary Ann. "Two Voices of the Single Narrator in *The Ballad of the Sad Café.*" *The Southern Literary Review* 17, No. 2 (Spring 1985): 33-40.

Observes that McCullers's narrator in *The Ballad of the Sad Café* employs two voices: one simple and straightforward; the other complex and philosophical.

Gaillard, Dawson F. "The Presence of the Narrator in Carson McCullers's *The Ballad of the Sad Café.*" *Mississippi Quarterly* 25, No. 4 (Fall 1972): 419-27.

Discusses McCullers's adherence to the ballad form in *The Ballad of the Sad Café* and uses extensive quotes from the story to identify the narrator as an intelligent and perceptive individual.

Gervin, Mary. "McCullers's Frames of Reference in *The Ballad of the Sad Café.*" *Pembroke Magazine* 20 (1988): 37-42.

Attempts to locate sources of the story in mythology, folk epics, Greek philosophy and drama, as well as French, German, and Russian literature.

Graver, Lawrence. *Carson McCullers.* St. Paul: University of Minnesota Press, 1969, 44 p.

Provides a brief overview of McCullers's body of work, focusing mainly on the novels. Graver admires McCullers's fiction with reservations about her thematic repetition and lack of philosophic depth.

McDowell, Margaret B. *Carson McCullers.* Boston: Twayne, 1980, 158 p.

Dedicates chapter to discussion of short stories, poems, and McCullers's second play. Other chapters individually examine the longer works and McCullers's approach to writing in general.

McNally, John. "The Introspective Narrator in "The Ballad of the Sad Café." *South Atlantic Bulletin* XXXVIII, No. 4 (November 1973): 40-44.

Examines the story's shifting narrative points of view and presents the narrator as a fully realized character whose observations introspectively shape the tale.

Perrine, Laurence. "Restoring 'A Domestic Dilemma'." *Studies in Short Fiction* 11, No. 1 (Winter 1974): 101-104.

Refutes article by James W. Grinnell (*Studies in Short Fiction* 9 [Summer 1972]: 270-271). Argues that Martin's situation, not Martin himself, is the source of dilemma.

Perry, Constance M. "Carson McCullers and the Female *Wunderkind.*" *The Southern Literary Journal* 19, No. 1 (Fall 1986): 36-45.

Seeks to explicate McCullers's first published short story through biographical details.

Vickery, John B. "Carson McCullers: A Map of Love." *Wisconsin Studies in Contemporary Literature* 1, No. 1 (Winter 1960): 13-24.

Finds McCullers's representation of the relationship between lover and beloved in *The Ballad of the Sad Café* to be the "clearest and simplest" presentation of "the archetypal pattern of love."

Additional coverage of McCullers's life and career is contained in the following sources published by Gale Research: *Concise Dictionary of American Literary Biography, 1941-1968; Contemporary Authors,* Vols. 5-8, rev. ed., 25-28, rev. ed. [obituary]; *Contemporary Authors Bibliographical Series,* Vols. 1, 3; *Contemporary Authors New Revision Series,* Vol. 18; *Contemporary Literary Criticism,* Vols. 1, 4, 10, 12, 48; *Dictionary of Literary Biography,* Vols. 2, 7; *Major 20th-Century Authors;* and *Something about the Author,* Vol. 27.

Leo Tolstoy

1828-1910

(Also transliterated as Tolstoi, Tolstoj, Tolstoi) Russian novelist, short story and novella writer, essayist, dramatist, and critic.

INTRODUCTION

Tolstoy is regarded as one of the greatest writers in the history of world literature. Primarily admired as a novelist, he is also esteemed for his folk tales, short stories, and novellas. The short fiction he wrote throughout the course of his sixty-year literary career depicts a broad spectrum of life in nineteenth-century Russia and reflects the development of his aesthetic, political, and religious convictions. These works are generally divided into an early period, before he wrote his major novels *War and Peace* and *Anna Karenina,* and a later period, the works of which were influenced by his moral and spiritual crisis of the late 1870s.

Tolstoy began writing fiction during his service in the army in the 1850s. During this time he completed his first novel, *Detstvo* (*Childhood*), which is often discussed as a work of short fiction. *Childhood* presents the observations of a young man over the course of two days. The simple occurrences in Nikolenka's domestic life suggest larger issues that would later become prominent in Tolstoy's fiction. For example, a conversation the narrator overhears between his father and a family servant attests to the injustices inherent in the relationship between masters and servants as well as the often hypocritical behavior of the wealthy. Tolstoy's next work, three sketches collectively entitled *Sevastopolskiye rasskazy* (*Sebastopol*), chronicles his experiences in the Crimean war. The first sketch reflects his initially patriotic and enthusiastic participation in the war, while the other two indicate his disillusionment with war after witnessing the hardships it causes. Tolstoy next began work on *Kazaki* (*The Cossacks*), which Ivan Turgenev described as the "finest and most perfect production of Russian literature." In this novella, Olenin, a young nobleman, leaves his home in the city to live among the Cossacks, a group of frontierspeople in a village in the Caucasus Mountains. Enchanted by their simple life-style, their vigorous nature, and their ability to live off the land, Olenin attempts to abandon his former values and mode of living for those of the Cossacks. Many critics describe *The Cossacks* as Tolstoy's finest work of his early period, praising it as a vivid depiction of Tolstoy's belief that a simple life, as represented by the Cossacks, is morally superior to that of the self-indulgent urban aristocracy, and citing its extraordinarily realistic characterizations.

Tolstoy's later works of short fiction reflect the spiritual and moral crisis outlined in his essay *Ispoved* (*A Confession*), wherein he questioned the meaning of his existence in light of the inevitability of death. His attempt to resolve this crisis took the form of a radical Christianity, the doctrines of which ultimately included nonresistance to evil and abstinence from sexual relations even within marriage. This conversion prompted Tolstoy to repudiate much of his previous work, and it profoundly influenced everything he wrote thereafter. At this point in his career, he focused on producing two types of fiction: simple tales written in a folk tradition for uneducated readers and short fiction presenting his moral preoccupations of this period. The folk tales, such as "Brazhe iepko, a bozhe krepko" ("Evil Allures, but Good Endures"), were designed as examples of "universal art," which successfully instills in its audience the highest sentiment Tolstoy believed an artist can express—that of religious feeling. These tales have been praised for delivering their didactic point in an artful manner. Much the same estimation has been accorded Tolstoy's short fiction of this time, including the novella *Smert Ivana Ilyicha* (*The Death of Iván Ilych*). In this work, the protagonist is an egotistical, superficial man who discovers meaning in his life only when on the verge of death. The mysterious illness from which Ilych suffers provides inactive and introspective periods during which he observes the selfless behavior of Gerasim, his servant. Faced with the prospect of his own mortality, Ilych realizes that his unhappiness and pain results from the self-serving life he has led. Ranking *The Death of Iván Ilych* among Tolstoy's greatest works, critics praise the powerful effects Tolstoy achieved through a simple, unadorned style. In *Khozyain i rabotnik* (*Master and Man*), Tolstoy similarly explores the effects of impending death on a man's perceptions of his life. Brekhunov, like Ivan Ilych, is egocentric and materialistic, character traits that contrast dramatically with the artless and instinctual behavior of his servant Nikita. The two men travel together to a nearby town, encountering a bizarre, apocalyptic snowstorm along the way. After hours of frustrated attempts to reach shelter, Nikita accepts his fate and lies down to die; Brekhunov experiences a revelatory moment in which he is faced with and rejects the values of his past, and he consequently saves Nikita's life by sacrificing his own. While many critics acknowledge the emotional power of the story's conclusion, others assert that Brekhunov's transformation is too sudden to be credible.

In *Kreitserova sonata* (*The Kreutzer Sonata*), a novella emphasizing Tolstoy's controversial views on sexuality, Tolstoy asserts that physical desire is an obstacle to relations between men and women and may result in tragedy. The protagonist murders his wife in a jealous rage, claiming that the deterioration of their marriage began on their honeymoon, when they first began a sexual relationship. While many commentators have criticized the story for its unrealistic plot, others have expressed sentiments similar to those of Anton Chekhov: "You will hardly find anything as powerful in seriousness of conception and beauty of execution." Commenting on the contradictions that inevitably arise in discussing a body of work created over sixty years by a man of Tolstoy's complexity, Raymond Rosenthal has remarked that "Tolstoy was a rationalist and a desperate God-seeker, a hater of all orthodoxy and a stifled dogmatist, a steadfast believer in the essential goodness and creativity of man and one of the keenest intellects ever to expose man's vices and duplicities."

PRINCIPAL WORKS

SHORT FICTION

Detstvo 1852
[*Childhood* published in *Childhood and Youth,* 1862]
Otrochestvo 1854
[*Boyhood* published in *Childhood, Boyhood, Youth,* 1886]
Sevastopolskiye rasskazy. 2 vols. 1855-56
[*Sebastopol,* 1887; also published as *Sevastopol,* 1904-05]
Yunost 1857
[*Youth* published in *Childhood and Youth,* 1862]
Semeinoe schaste 1859
[*Family Happiness,* 1888]
Kazaki 1863
[*The Cossacks,* 1878]
Polikushka 1863
[*Polikouchka,* 1888]
Smert Ivana Ilyicha 1886
[*Iván Ilyitch* published in *Iván Ilyitch, and Other Stories,* 1887; also published as *The Death of Iván Ilych,* 1946]
Kreitserova sonata 1890
[*The Kreutzer Sonata,* 1890]
Khozyain i rabotnik 1895
[*Master and Man,* 1895]
Otetz sergii 1898
[*Father Sergius* published in *Father Sergius, and Other Stories and Plays,* 1911]
The Novels and Other Works of Lyof N. Tolstoi. 22 vols. (novels, novellas, short stories, dramas, essays, and sketches) 1899-1902
Khadzhi Murat 1911
[*Hadji Murád* published in *Hadji Murád, and Other Stories,* 1912]
L. N. Tolstoi: polnoe sobranie proizvedenie. 90 vols. (novels, novellas, short stories, dramas, essays, and sketches) 1928-58

OTHER MAJOR WORKS

Voina i mir (novel) 1869
[*War and Peace,* 1886]
Anna Karenina (novel) 1877
[*Anna Karenina,* 1886]
Ispoved (essay) 1882
[*A Confession,* 1885]
V chiom moya vera (essay) 1884
[*What I Believe,* 1885]
Vlast tmy (drama) 1888
[*The Dominion of Darkness,* 1888; also published as *The Power of Darkness* in *Plays,* 1910]
Plody prosvesh cheniya (drama) 1889
[*The Fruits of Enlightenment,* 1890]
Chto takoe iskusstvo (essay) 1898
[*What Is Art?,* 1898]
Voskresenie (novel) 1899
[*Resurrection,* 1899]
I svet vo tme svetit [first publication] (unfinished drama) 1911
[*The Light That Shines in Darkness,* 1912]
Zhivoy trup (drama) 1911
[*The Living Corpse,* 1912]
Tolstoy's Letters. 2 vols. (letters) 1978

A. P. Chekhov (letter date 1890)

[*A Russian dramatist and short story writer, Chekhov is considered one of the greatest authors of the late nineteenth and early twentieth centuries. In the following excerpt from a letter written to A. N. Pleshcheev in 1890, he asserts that* The Kreutzer Sonata, *while imperfect, is a provocative and potent work.*]

I won't say [***The Kreutzer Sonata***] is a work of genius, or one that will last for ever, I am no judge of these matters, but in my opinion, among everything being written here and abroad, you will hardly find anything as powerful in seriousness of conception and beauty of execution. Without mentioning its artistic merits, which in places are outstanding, one must thank the story if only for the one thing that it is extremely thought-provoking. As I read it I could hardly stop myself crying out: 'That's true!' or 'That's wrong!' Of course it does have some very annoying defects. . . . [There is one] point which one will not readily forgive its author, namely the brashness with which Tolstoy pontificates on things he does not know and out of stubbornness does not want to understand. Thus his pronouncements on syphillis, foundling hospitals, women's repugnance for copulation and so on are not only debatable but also show him to be a complete ignoramus who has never taken the trouble during the course of his long life to read a couple of books written by specialists. Still these defects fly off like feathers in the wind; considering the merits of the story you simply do not notice them, or, if you do, it is only annoying that the story did not avoid the fate of all works of man, all of which are imperfect and possess faults. . . . (pp. 395-96)

A. P. Chekhov, in a letter to A. N. Pleshcheev on February 15, 1890, in Tolstoy: The Critical Heritage, *edited by A. V. Knowles, Routledge & Kegan Paul, 1978, pp. 395-96.*

D. N. Ovsyaniko-Kulikovsky (essay date 1905)

[*In the following excerpt from* Tolstoy the Artist *(1905), Ovsyaniko-Kulikovsky examines what he considers the inflexible moral code underlying* The Death of Iván Ilych.]

Of what particularly is Ivan Ilich guilty before Tolstoy's moral code? His sins are as numerous as they are 'terrible'. Even in his youth,

> when he was a lawyer he was just as he was later, throughout his whole life: a capable man, cheerfully good-natured and sociable, but carrying out strictly what he considered his duty; *he considered his duty everything that people from the highest social strata considered to be his duty.* He was not ingratiating either as a boy or as a grown man, *but from his earliest years he was drawn to people from the highest social standing, like a fly is drawn to a light, he adopted their habits, their outlook on life and entered into friendly relations with them.*

Later when he was a civil servant charged with special duties in the provinces, this 'defect' took the form of fawning upon his superior and even his superior's wife. Furthermore his careerism did not cross the line of generally accepted respectability, like the misdemeanours of his youth, inasmuch as Ivan Ilich had a relationship with one of the ladies who thrust themselves on dandified lawyers; there was also a milliner; he had gone drinking with newly-arrived aides-de-camp and had 'gone to a street some way away after supper'. But 'none of this could be called by anything bad' for 'everything was done with clean hands, wearing clean shirts, speaking French and, most importantly, in the highest society and consequently with the approval of high-born people'.

Ivan Ilich is also guilty of not being a stoic but an epicurean; his ideal is an easy life, decent and pleasant. From this viewpoint he looked upon family life too. His marriage to Praskovya Fyodorovna seemed to him completely compatible with his 'programme'.

> To say that Ivan Ilich married because he loved his fiancée and found in her sympathy for his outlook on life, would be as unjust as to say that he married her because people in his social milieu approved the union. He married because of both these considerations: he made life pleasant for himself by taking such a wife and also did what high-society people considered correct. And so Ivan Ilich got married.

He is also guilty of treating everything in life, including both his work and even his family life, somewhat formally, one could say 'bureaucratically'. So, while serving as a civil servant charged with special duties and later as a coroner, he

> very quickly adopted the habit of keeping at a distance all circumstances which were not connected with his work and of clothing any highly complicated matter in such a way that it appeared on paper only in its external details, excluding completely his personal opinions, and, most importantly, observing all required formality.

It is exactly the same in his family life where Ivan Ilich finds it most convenient and pleasant to keep to the same system—to observe all the generally accepted 'formalities' of family life without participating in the intimate life of his family. In his family he is 'a civil servant'. Furthermore, he did not become like this at once, but after a year of marriage when spiritual discord developed between the couple and Praskovya Fyodorovna adopted the tactics of ceaselessly complaining, moaning and generally behaving badly. Then Ivan Ilich

> understood that married life, while offering a certain convenience to one's life, was a very complicated and serious affair, to which, in order to fulfil his duty, i.e. to lead a respectable life of which others would approve, it was necessary to work out a definite attitude, just as to his work. And this is just what he did. He demanded from family life only those comforts of dinner at home, of looking after the house, of bed, which she could give him and, most importantly, the proprieties of external forms which are set by social opinion.

Family life gave him annoyance and unpleasantness and contradicted his 'ideal of an easy, pleasant and respectable life'. And so he spiritually deserts his family and recognizes this desertion as something normal and even 'the object of his life'. 'His object consisted in freeing himself as much as possible from these unpleasantnesses and giving them the character of harmlessness and respectability.' He achieved this by spending as little time as possible in the family and also 'ensured it by having other people present'. It is unpleasant, cold and empty at home and he seeks some 'spiritual home' in his work, in his civic obligations. He becomes more and more ambitious. . . . But he shows himself as bankrupt in this as he does in family life—and again he is 'guilty'.

He is guilty in that he is incapable of introducing any, as it were, 'breath of life' into his civic obligations, that he has no calling for his work, but merely training, skill and official thoroughness; he only observes the rites of his work so as to receive his salary on the twentieth of the month and works only for promotion up the salary scale. In a word he is guilty of being a man of office routine and making a career. When he is unsuccessful in his work and looks for another post, he goes to St Petersburg

> for one thing: to obtain a post at 5,000-a-year. He was not choosy about any Ministry or any particular type of work. He only wanted a post, a post with 5,000, in the administration, banking, with the railways, in Empress Maria's household, even in the Customs—but certainly with 5,000, and certainly out of the Ministry where no one knew how to value him.

If we gather together all these factors of his guilt and then add them to all those little characteristics which Tolstoy so skilfully groups together in order to expose as clearly as possible the spiritual emptiness and vulgarity of Ivan Ilich, then we will have a conclusion as follows: Ivan Ilich is brought before the moral court because he is an average, ordinary man who has no 'divine spark'. The moral consequence, so artistically shown by Tolstoy, is that the defendant has no real love for his work, has no real feelings for his family; as a citizen, as a pillar of society he is a blank; he has no convictions that he has worked out in his own head or from his own experience; as a moral individual he is nothing. From this spiritual poverty he is sentenced to death, and the heavy process of dying will be for him a kind of moral penalty and at the same time—expiation. In dying he will gradually come to a realization of the emptiness, vulgarity and disorder of the life he has led, will see its nothingness and will feel all the horror of his spiritual loneliness. And he will die, transfigured and enlightened by the consciousness of the fact 'that his life had not been as it should' that his life had indeed been 'the most empty and commonplace' and also 'the most terrible'.

To discover and show this 'most terrible' in 'the most empty and commonplace life' was the object of the artistic experiment, carried out with such rare mastery. This is perhaps Tolstoy's most successful experiment.

But this 'most terrible' which Tolstoy found in the life of Ivan Ilich can possibly appear in various different lights, dependent upon the reader's particular point of view. One could profit from the results of Tolstoy's artistic experience without sharing the artist's dogma and without making such severe demands upon Ivan Ilich as Tolstoy makes. For him Ivan Ilich is a real moral freak who can 'be straightened out' only by death. For us this exclusive point of view is not obligatory. We meet people like Ivan Ilich on almost every corner but we do not at all consider them freaks. And actually Ivan Ilich is not a bad man, not an evil man; he is honourable, and incorruptible, etc. Although most of these characteristics are negative in that they show not so much the presence of good as the absence of bad, they none the less give us a picture of a very respectable person. Knowing that Ivan Ilich even before the Great Reforms when he served as a civil servant showed himself a man who could not be bought, that later in his position of coroner or procurator he did not misuse his power and even tried to soften its influence, etc., we have every right to include Ivan Ilich among so-called 'good people'. And the name of these good people is legion. And it seems to us that to investigate and judge these people from the standpoint of high religious and moral demands, as does Tolstoy, there are insufficient grounds. I dispute in the given circumstances the 'jurisdiction' and the 'choice of instances'. Tolstoy wants every such Ivan Ilich to be a fully developed moral and religious personality, rising above the given level of commonplace conceptions; he wants this average, morally insignificant man to be a participant in life, to react critically (and in this respect from a high moral standpoint) to established forms, morals and the accepted proprieties in order, in the end, to avoid being a petty egotist and not to look on life as a pleasant and orderly passing of the time, but see its meaning and value in serving some higher ideal. Tolstoy demands too much. . . . From the Ivan Iliches one can demand but one thing: that they do not descend below the average level, in a moral and civic sense, and do not prevent from living and acting those who rise above it. If they satisfy this modest, minimal requirement, we shall say to them: May health go with you! Labour and multiply! . . .

In describing the domestic disorder, the eternal arguments and disagreements between Ivan Ilich and his wife, in showing that 'arguments were always on the point of flaring up', Tolstoy gives us a type of abnormal family life, when there is no real love between the couple, only a sensual attraction in the satisfaction of which their mutual enmity flares up even more and takes on the explicit character of an organized loathing for each other. There were (in between the rows) a few periods of that mutual affection which comes over couples, but they did not last long. These were little islands at which they anchored for a time, but then again put out to their sea of suppressed hatred, expressed in their alienation one from the other. This serves as the starting-point for another artistic experiment in which the complicated question of the ethics of sexual relations in general and those of marriage in particular could be put point-blank. An adept at ascetic morals, Tolstoy will come to the dubious conclusion that sexual relations, no matter whether within or outside marriage, contradict man's ethical nature and that man, as a moral being, should abstain from them. The fact that the consequences of the carrying out of this principle would lead to the demise of the human race is of no concern to the moralist. For him the 'moral law' is superior to humanity and must triumph even at the price of the destruction of humanity—a point of view that humanity itself will never accept and which science and critical philosophy will refute and disprove. (pp. 420-24)

D. N. Ovsyaniko-Kulikovsky, in an extract from Tolstoy: The Critical Heritage, *edited by A. V. Knowles, Routledge & Kegan Paul, 1978, pp. 419-24.*

Leo Shestov (essay date 1932)

[*Shestov was a Russian literary critic and the author of* Tolstoi and Nietzsche: Philosophy and Preaching *(1900). In the essay below, which originally appeared in a more extensive version in 1932, he discusses Tolstoy's perspective on death in his later works of short fiction, particularly "The Diary of a Madman" and* Master and Man.]

Aristotle says somewhere that every one has his own particular world in his dreams, while in his waking state he lives in a world common to all. This statement is the basis, not only of Aristotle's philosophy, but also of all positive scientific philosophy, before and after him. Common sense also looks upon this as an indisputable truth. Can man give up self-evident truth? Certainly not. Nobody, not even God Himself, can ask this of him. *Deus impossibile non jubet.* God does not ask the impossible. That is a self-evident truth which is admitted equally by common sense, by science, and even by the Catholic Church, impregnated with mysticism though it may be.

But death takes no heed of this. It has its own truths, its own self-evidence, its possibilities and its impossibilities, which do not agree with our ordinary ideas, and which we, therefore, cannot understand. Only a few exceptional men have succeeded, in rare moments of extreme tension and excitement, in hearing and understanding the mysterious language of death. This understanding was given to Tolstoy. What did death reveal to him? What were the impossibilities which were changed into possibilities for him? Death does, as a matter of fact, unlike common sense, demand the impossible of man. In spite of Aristotle, it drags him out of the world common to all. How does this happen? How can the impossible become possible?

Among Tolstoy's posthumous works there is a short, unfinished story called **"The Diary of a Madman."** The subject is very simple. A rich landowner, having learned that an estate was for sale in the province of Penza, makes up his mind to go down, have a look at it and buy it. He is very pleased about it; according to his calculations, he will be able to buy it at a very low figure, almost for nothing. Then, *suddenly,* one night at an hotel on the way, without any apparent reason, he is seized by a horrible, insufferable anguish. Nothing in his surroundings has changed, nothing new has happened, but until now everything had always inspired him with confidence, everything had seemed to him to be normal, necessary, well-regulated, soothing; he had felt the solid earth beneath his feet and reality on all sides of him. No doubt, no questions! Nothing but answers! Then suddenly, in an instant, in the twinkling of an eye, everything is transformed as though by a magic wand. Peace, answers, the solid earth, consciousness of right, and the easy feeling of lightness, simplicity and certainty which springs from this—all suddenly disappear. Around him are nothing but looming questions with their inevitable train of importunate anxiety, of doubt, and senseless, gnawing, invincible terrors. The ordinary means by which these painful thoughts are usually routed are completely ineffectual.

> I tried to think of things which interested me; of the acquisition of the estate, of my wife. Not only did I find nothing pleasant in these thoughts, but they were all as nothing to me. The horror of my wasted life overshadowed everything. I tried to go to sleep. I lay down, but no sooner was I on my bed than terror roused me again. And anxiety! An anxiety like one feels before one is going to be sick, but it was moral. Fear, anguish—we think of death as terrible, but when we look back upon life, it is the *agony of life which overwhelms us!* Death and life seemed in some way to be confounded with one another. Something tore my existence to rags, and yet could not succeed in tearing it completely. I went once more to look at my fellow-sleepers; I tried again to get to sleep; but terror was ever before me, red, white, and square. Something was tearing, but it still held.

Thus Tolstoy pitilessly strips himself before our eyes. There are few writers who show us truths like these. And if one wants, if one is able to see this truth—for even naked truth is not easy to see—then a whole series of problems arise which are out of all relation with our ordinary thoughts. How are we to apprehend these groundless terrors which so suddenly appeared, red, white, and square? In the world which is common to us all, there is not and cannot be a "suddenly"; there can be no action without a cause. And its terrors are not red, nor white, nor square. What happened to Tolstoy is a challenge to all normal, human consciousness. Now it is Tolstoy who has been suddenly and causelessly seized by terror; to-morrow it may be another, then a third, and one fine day it will be the whole of society, the whole of mankind who will be attacked. If we take seriously what we are told in **"The Diary of a Madman"** there is no third alternative; either we must repudiate Tolstoy and cut him off from our midst as lepers and others suffering from contagious diseases were cut off in the Middle Ages; or else, if we consider his experiences justifiable, we must be prepared for others to undergo the same, for the "world common to us all" to fall to pieces and men to begin to live in their own separate worlds, not in dreams but in their waking moments.

Common sense, and science which derives from it, cannot hesitate for a moment before this dilemma. Tolstoy is in the wrong with his senseless anxieties, his unreasonable terrors, and his mad uncertainty. It is "the world common to us all" which is right, with its solid beliefs, its eternal, satisfying truths, clear, defined, and accessible to all. If the person concerned had not been a world-famous writer, his fate would have been quickly decided; he would have been exiled from society as a dangerous and unhealthy member. But Tolstoy is the pride and glory of Russia; it is impossible to treat him like this. Although what he says appears utterly meaningless and unacceptable, one goes on listening to him, one goes on reckoning with him.

"To-day," he continues,

> they took me before the provincial council for a mental examination. Opinions were divided. They argued, and finally decided that I was not mad. But that was because I constrained myself not to speak frankly during the medical inspection. I was not frank because I am afraid of the lunatic asylum. I am afraid that there they

> would not allow me to accomplish my madman's work. They declared that I was subject to fits and other things of the sort, but that I was of sane mind. *They certified this, but I know that I am mad.*

It is beyond question that *he* is right, not *they.* All his life Tolstoy was aware that there was something in his soul driving him out of the world common to all. He tells us that it had happened to him before, although not often, to experience crises like that which occurred on the road to Penza. From childhood upwards, he would suddenly find himself overwhelmed on quite trivial occasions by intolerable terrors which would brutally deprive him of all joy in life and of all sense of the normality and natural balance of existence. . . .

The pleasures, preoccupations, and all the innumerable business affairs of life naturally distracted Tolstoy's attention from his extraordinary visions for many years. And then, as he tells us, he had an instinctive dread of the madhouse, and an even greater dread of madness, of having to live in his own individual world instead of in the common world. Therefore he made desperate efforts to live like every one else, and to see only what is contained within everyday limits.

"The Diary of a Madman" is in a sense the key to Tolstoy's work. . . . Only death and the madness of death are able to awaken man from the nightmare of existence. This is what Tolstoy's **"Diary of a Madman"** also tells us—not the short unfinished story which bears this title, but the whole of what he wrote after *Anna Karenina.* His "madness" lay in the fact that everything which had formerly seemed to him to be real and to have a solid existence, now appeared illusory, whereas all that had seemed illusory and unreal now seemed to him the only reality.

The review the *Russian Archive* published in 1868 an article by Tolstoy which, for no reason that I know, has never been republished since; it is called "A Few Words about *War and Peace.*" It contains some extremely significant passages showing Tolstoy's attitude towards serfdom. He had been reproached with not having sufficiently depicted the character of the times in *War and Peace.* "To these reproaches," Tolstoy declares,

> I should reply as follows: I know quite well what are the characteristics of the times, which are supposed to be wanting in my novel: the horrors of serfdom, the burial of women alive, the flogging by men of their grown sons, Saltychike, etc., but I do not consider that this character, as we imagine it to-day, conforms to reality, and therefore I did not want to describe it. I have studied letters, memoirs, and hearsay, but have not found that these horrors were more frequent then than now or at any other period. People loved in those days, were jealous, sought truth, virtue, or were the slaves of their passions just as now; the intellectual and moral life was the same—often, indeed, more refined than to-day, especially in the upper classes. If we represent these times to ourselves as particularly cruel and brutal, it is only because the novels, stories, and legends of that period have only preserved what was exceptionally brutal or strikingly savage.

Tolstoy was forty years old when he wrote these lines. It is the age when the intellectual powers reach their zenith. In Tolstoy, at that age, the days of Arakcheev awaken no horror, no disgust; yet we remember that as a child he gave way to mad despair on seeing a little boy beaten or hearing his nurse and the steward quarrelling. He certainly knew what to think of Arakcheev and his men, he also knew what serfdom was and the condition of the peasants under the despotic rule of the landed proprietors; but he did not want to "see" it; reason, which should know all things, forbade. Why? Because such a vision would have been useless. It would have destroyed that *ordo et connexio rerum* which had established itself historically in the face of so many difficulties, and upset the common world outside whose boundaries there exists nothing but madness and death. Unvarnished truth, that truth which runs contrary to the vital needs of human nature, is worse than any lie. This is what Tolstoy thought when he wrote *War and Peace,* when he was still entirely possessed by Aristotle's ideas, when he was afraid of madness and the asylum and hoped that he would never have to live in an individual world of his own. But when he was obliged to say to himself, "They certified that I was sane, but I know that I am mad"; when he felt himself expelled from the world common to all, then he was obliged, willy-nilly, to look at things with his own eyes and not with every one else's. Then the character of Arakcheev's day appeared to him quite otherwise. Formerly he had spoken of "the refined existence of the upper classes." Later he spoke of the cruel, coarse, and debased "uppermost classes."

The outward seeming is spick and span and elegant, but beneath this beautiful appearance there are folly, emptiness, vile cruelty, narrow, inhuman selfishness. The Rostovs, Bezukhovs, and Bolkonskis change before our eyes into Sobakevich, Nozdrev, and Chichikov. There is no longer even Gogol's laughter, only his tears.

In another short story, also unfinished, **"The Morning after the Ball,"** written in 1903, when the author was seventy-five years old, Tolstoy, with obvious intention, confronts his old and new visions. The story is in two parts; the first describes, with an art unequalled in Russian literature before or since, a gay, elegant, and amusing ball. It is a really marvellous ball: there are music and dancing, there is champagne, the young people are of the highest class, charming and aristocratic; naturally there is also a charming young lady there and a young man who is in love with her; it is he who tells the story. An hour after the ball, the narrator, still gay, excited, and possessed by his "refined" emotions, is witness of quite another scene in the street; a Tartar deserter is being made to run the gauntlet. And this is being done at the orders of the colonel, the father of the charming young girl, the very man who, to the universal delight, himself had danced the mazurka with his daughter at the end of the ball, displaying such charm and old-world gallantry. I have said that the scene at the ball is described by Tolstoy with inimitable art; the torture of the Tartar is described with no less strength and feeling. I will not quote extracts, for the story is well known. The important point is to compare and contrast the two ways of looking at reality. And considering the whole of Tolstoy's work, one might say, metaphorically of course and with certain reservations, that in his youth Tolstoy described life as a fascinating ball; and later, when he was old, it was like a running of the gauntlet. When he was old, it was not only the time of Arakcheev and Nicholas I which seemed to him like a mad and oppressive nightmare; he could not even endure our own comparatively mild ways. His own family became unendurable to him, that family which he had described in such idyllic colours in *Anna Karenina.* And he saw himself under an aspect as hideous as that of the people with whom he lived. As it is said in Scripture, one must hate one's father and mother, wife and children, and even oneself; there is evidently no other way for the man who is shut out from the world common to us all. . . .

He who wants to learn the truth must first learn the art of reading works of literature. It is a difficult art. To know how to read is not enough. It is for this reason that rough drafts, and notes thrown hastily on paper, are so valuable. A sketch, a few words, a half-formed thought, can often tell us more than a finished work; the man has not yet had time to adapt his visions to the demands of society. The introduction which was to prepare the way, and the conclusion which rounds it off, are alike missing. The brutal, naked truth rises to its full height, like a rock above the waters, and no one has yet attempted to "justify" its stark savagery, neither the author himself nor his sedulous biographer.

This is why I have lingered so long over **"The Diary of a Madman,"** an unfinished and incomplete story. Tolstoy in his finished works obstinately insists that he is working for the cause of common sense; that his one object is to strengthen men's faith in common sense. Only once, in this short sketch, did he allow himself to call what happened in his soul by its true name. "They certified that I was sane; but I know that I am mad." This confession gives us the key to what is most important and significant in Tolstoy's hidden life.

We must not, however, forget that Tolstoy was not always in this state of "madness," even during his last years. There were only passing attacks; sometimes he lived in his own particular world, sometimes in the world common to all. Wild unreasoning terrors suddenly welled up, God knows whence; they disappeared, overthrowing and breaking the treasures which reason had amassed; they dissipated themselves and vanished, God knows how or whither, as abruptly as they had arisen. And then Tolstoy became a normal man once more, he was like every one else, except for certain strange ways, pale reflections of the storms which had passed or which were brewing. Hence the inequalities of his character and actions, the flagrant contradictions on which his many enemies have maliciously insisted. Tolstoy was even more afraid of madness than of death, yet at the same time he hated and despised his normal state with his whole soul. And his restless, impetuous inconsequence reveals more to us than the even and reasonable consistency of his accusers.

Many people, in the effort to calm themselves and dissipate the uneasiness which seizes them on reading Tolstoy's works, have thought to explain his struggles and his wild outbursts as the result of his fear of death. They think that such an explanation would free them once and for all from every difficulty and would also re-establish in their old strength the solutions which he had rendered null and void. This proceeding is not new, but it is effective. Aristotle had already suggested it when, with firm hand, he traced a definite line to mark the limit beyond which human endeavour and inquiry must not go. The ultimate mystery must not be approached, the idea of death must not be allowed to take possession of the human soul.

But Plato taught otherwise. . . .

Eight years after ***The Death of Ivan Ilych,*** Tolstoy wrote ***Master and Man.*** These two stories are, in spite of their surface dissimilarity, so intimately connected with one another that they seem to be only variations on a single theme. Since Tolstoy had been forced out of the common way by the terrors which he had described to us in **"The Diary of a Madman,"** one single thought, one single problem pursued and obsessed him. If Plato is right in saying philosophers "concern themselves with nothing but dying and death," . . . then we must admit that few of our contemporaries have so wholly devoted themselves to philosophy as Tolstoy. Tolstoy begins by describing to us, in these two stories, a man in the ordinary circumstances of existence, circumstances which are well known and universally admitted. Then suddenly, in ***Master and Man*** (the ca-

Tolstoy and his brother Nikolay in 1851, before serving in the army in the Caucasus.

tastrophe is even less prepared than in ***The Death of Ivan Ilych***), he transports his characters to that solitude which could not have been more complete in the bowels of the earth or in the depths of the sea. Vassili Andreivich Brekhunov is a "self-made man," a rich villager, of the corporation of merchants, proud of his intelligence and of the fortune which he has won. He owes nothing to any one but himself, to his own talents, his own energy, for everything that he possesses; and he is, moreover, convinced that he possesses a great many excellent things. He genuinely despises those who have not succeeded in carving out their own path through life; misfortune and incapacity are synonyms in his eyes. He would probably repeat with others: "Trust in God, but look out for yourself," but in his mouth these words would mean: "God's duty is to help those who do not sit with folded arms." If he had had a theological education he would have said: *Facienti quod in se est Deus infallibiliter dat gratiam,* and he would protest against those who affirm that *Deum necessitare non posse.* But he does not know Latin and expresses the same ideas in Russian with no less emphasis. The man worthy of the name is the one who has the means to make himself beloved of God by his own efforts. Masses, fat wax candles, and all the rest are not for a miserable moujik like the workman Nikita, who earns with difficulty a few kopeks to supply his immediate needs. But he, Vassili Andreivich, can do anything. By his own energy and intelligence he has assured his welfare here below and his eternal salvation above.

The consciousness of his righteousness, indeed of his election, never leaves him. He even cheats with conviction. Two days before the festival which marks the opening of the story, Marfa, the servant Nikita's wife, has come to Vassili Andreivich and has obtained from him white flour, tea, sugar, the eighth of a measure of brandy, three roubles' worth altogether, besides five roubles in money. She has thanked him for all this as though he had done her a special favour, although at the lowest computation he owed Nikita twenty roubles for his work.

> "Are we agreed on our bargain?" Vassili Andreivich had said to Nikita: "if you want anything you shall have it from me, and you shall pay me in labour. I am not like others where you must wait, make out bills and then pay fines into the bargain. No, I am a man of honour. You serve me and I will not desert you." As he spoke thus Vassili Andreivich was quite sincerely convinced that he was Nikita's benefactor, so persuasive were his arguments and so wholeheartedly did all those who depended on him, beginning with Nikita himself, support him in the opinion that, far from exploiting other people, he was loading them with benefits.

Tolstoy insistently underlines this gift which Vassili Andreivich possessed of being able to convince himself and others of his rectitude. It was a precious gift. To it Vassili Andreivich owed the comfort of his position. A few pages later on Tolstoy quotes another example of his talents. He is trying to sell Nikita a worthless horse.

> "Well, take the bony horse; I won't charge you much for him," cried Brekhunov, feeling agreeably excited and joyfully seizing the opportunity to drive a bargain, which he loved of all things. "Give me fifteen roubles or so instead, it will buy one at the horse fair," said Nikita, who knew quite well that the bony beast which Vassili Andreivich was trying to pass off on him was worth seven roubles at the outside, and that it would be reckoned against him at twenty-five. He would not see the colour of his money again for many a long day.
>
> "It is a good horse. I want your good as well as my own. Word of honour! Brekhunov deceives no one. I would rather lose on the bargain myself. I am not like others. I give you my word that the horse is a good one," he cried in the special tone which he used in order to talk over and deceive buyers or sellers.

Brekhunov, as we have seen from these extracts, was no ordinary man. Being a merchant, he could only make use of his great powers over himself and others for a modest end, bargaining. But if fate had seen fit to put him in a more exalted position, if he had had the necessary education, his voice, which was now only used to confuse his fellow merchants in their ideas, to deceive buyers and sellers, would certainly have been used for other purposes. Who knows to what he might not have persuaded the masses which he could then have addressed? The secret of talent lies in the ability to work upon men. Conversely, success, general approbation, is the atmosphere which talent needs for its development. Crowds need leaders, but leaders also need crowds.

Tolstoy knew this; the hero of his story was no ordinary character; he had a powerful will and a clear intelligence, in his own way he was a genius. Such is the personality which Tolstoy will now tear out of his natural setting and put abruptly into the midst of new conditions, facing him with the absolute solitude which we have already met in ***Ivan Ilych.***

Nikita goes out with Brekhunov and together they are caught in a snowstorm. But Nikita's agony in the snow is of no interest either to Tolstoy or to us. Perhaps Brekhunov is right when he prepares to abandon his faithful servant and says: "It doesn't matter to him whether he dies or not. What was his life like? He won't regret his life. But I, thanks be to God, I still have something to live for!" Nikita prepares to die as he has lived, peacefully, with that calm submission which, losing itself in the grey uniformity of the surrounding world and obeying eternal laws, makes no particular individual impression which can be seized and retained in the mind of the observer. Tolstoy himself cannot guess at what happens in Nikita's mind when life ceases and death begins in it under the snow which covers him. Perhaps this is why Nikita lives and Brekhunov dies. Tolstoy wanted to confront life with death; but a rich life, full to the brim, confident in itself and its sacred rights and without even a suspicion that an implacable enemy infinitely stronger than itself is watching it at every turn. Even when it turns out that master and man have lost their way and that they will have to pass the night buried under the snow, Brekhunov will not admit that his reason and his talents, which have already got him out of so many difficult situations, will betray him now; that in a few hours his stiffened hands will let fall the *potestas clavium,* which gave him the proud right to look upon the future with the same confidence as the present.

This is what he is thinking of while Nikita, in his thin clothes, drowses under the falling snow and tries to protect his shivering body against the raging of the bitter wind. Brekhunov is warmly clad, as yet he does not feel the cold, and from past experience is confident he never will.

> ". . . What did we possess in my father's time? Nothing much; he was no more than a rich peasant. An inn, a farm; that was all. And I, what have I collected in fifteen years? A shop, two inns, a mill, barns for grain, two farm properties, a house and its outbuildings all under iron roofs." He thought of all that with pride. "It is quite different from my father's time. Who is now famous throughout the whole district? Brekhunov! And why? Because I never lose sight of business. I work. I am not like others who are always sleeping or else running their heads into some foolishness or other."

Brekhunov continues for a long time to sing the praises of these reasonable, active principles, the source of all "good" on earth. And I repeat: if Brekhunov had received a superior education, he would have been capable of writing an excellent philosophical or theological treatise, which would have made him famous, not only in his own district but throughout all Russia and Europe.

But here we come to the second part of the story, where an unexpected reality suddenly supervenes and affords the critique of this treatise which Brekhunov might have written.

In the middle of this reasoning Brekhunov began to doze.

> But he suddenly felt a shock and awoke. Whether it was that the horse had tugged at a few straws from behind his head, or whether it was the effect of some internal uneasiness, he suddenly awoke and his heart began to beat so violently and quickly that it seemed as though the whole sledge were trembling beneath him.

This was the beginning of a whole series of events of which Brekhunov had no suspicion in spite of his long life, his powerful intelligence, and his rich experience. Around him was the boundless plain, boundless, at least, to him, and snow, cold, and wind, Nikita, already numbed by the cold, and the shivering horse. He felt unreasonable but insistent and overmastering terror. "What to do? What to do?" This is the regular question which every man asks when he finds himself in a difficult situation. It presents itself to Brekhunov, but this time it seems completely absurd. Hitherto, the question had always held the elements of its own answer, it had at least always shown him the possibility of an answer. But this time it held nothing of the sort. The question excluded all possibility of an answer; there was *nothing to be done.*

Brekhunov was no coward. He had been in many difficult places in his lifetime, and had always been ready to fight any adversary, even one stronger than himself. But his present situation was such that it would have been impossible to imagine anything more terrible. The enemy was formidable and—this was the worst part of it—completely invisible. Against what could he direct his blows? Against whom could he defend himself? Brekhunov's reason could not admit that such a thing was possible.

When they had stopped at Grichkino, an hour earlier, everything had seemed so comfortable, so natural, so easy to understand. One was able to talk, to listen to other people, drink tea, give orders to Nikita, drive the bay. And now there was nothing to be done but to look on and feel oneself freeze. Where is truth, where is reality? Over there at Grichkino, or here on this plain? Grichkino had ceased to exist for ever; must one then doubt the reality of its existence? And with it the reality of the existence of all the old world? Doubt everything? *De omnibus dubitandum?* But did great Descartes really doubt everything? No, Hume was right: the man who has once doubted all things will never overcome his doubts, he will leave for ever the world common to us all and take refuge in his own particular world. *De omnibus dubitandum* is useless; it is worse than storm and snow, worse than the fact that Nikita is freezing and that the bay is shivering in the icy wind.

Always so strong, so clear-minded, Brekhunov tries, for the first time in his life, to take refuge in dreams.

> He began once more to reckon up his profits, the sums which were due to him. He began to boast to himself again, and to take pleasure in his excellent situation; but at every moment fear slipped into his thoughts and interrupted their pleasant flow. Try as he might to think of nothing but his accounts, his transactions, his revenues, his glory and his wealth, fear little by little took possession of his whole soul.

It will seem strange that Brekhunov, like King Solomon in Ecclesiastes, told over the tale of his riches and his glory. But this was just what Tolstoy wanted, and he knew what he wanted. If the great king himself had been in Brekhunov's place, the situation would not have been changed in any way. Riches and glory added nothing to Brekhunov's strength, nor diminished in any way that of his invisible adversary. For the lowly and humble Nikita it was much easier. "He did not know whether he was dying or whether he was falling asleep, but he was equally ready to do either."

All his existence, utterly devoid alike of glory and wealth, had accustomed Nikita to the thought that he was not his own master, that he must not ask any one to render him an account, or to explain what was happening. He had never understood anything, and he continued not to understand; there was not much difference. But for Brekhunov it was quite another matter. He was accustomed to being his own master, and to having clear and distinct explanations given him; everything indefinite and indeterminate was intolerable to him. To live in the unknown is to live under a strange power which slays or spares us as it will. Can one have confidence in it? Why should it have mercy on us? It will certainly condemn us. One cannot believe any one or anything, except oneself. And in any case, before believing one must ask *cui est credendum*—whom shall we believe? You must not be surprised that Brekhunov takes to talking Latin and quoting St. Augustine, for it was certainly no more surprising than everything else which was happening to him.

And Brekhunov, gathering together all his strength for the last time, firmly declared: "I will never believe in this silence, in this forsaken solitude, in the snowstorm, the shivering horse, freezing Nikita, this cold and dreary desert, and this infinite waste." Reason was still alive within him, and reason which had always taught him what to do would guide him again. There was still some possible answer, although a lying terror was whispering to him that he must yield.

Brekhunov decides to abandon Nikita and take his chance, mounts the horse and goes off in search of the road.

This was undoubtedly a reasonable decision; the only reasonable decision. Was he to die, caught by the cold, like a dog, he, Brekhunov, who for so many years had filled Russia and Europe with the fame of his inns, his house, his barns with their iron roofs?

Brekhunov makes a last, supreme effort to defeat his invisible foe. But what he does, what he is forced to do, in no way resembles what one would call "action". He urges on his horse, which obeys him docilely, but his strength of mind, in which he had always had so much confidence, now betrays him. Without noticing it, he continually changes the direction of his march. Everything overwhelms him, he is trembling more from fear than from cold now—a quite absurd and unreasonable fear of every tussock which appeared through the snow. To his distracted eyes every outlined object was as a phantom. He suddenly found himself placed in circumstances so contrary to his usual reasonable, positive nature, that everything appeared to him stupid and absurd as in a fairy tale. But where is truth? In that old world, with that old reason where everything is clear and comprehensible, or here? Until now there had been nothing hostile or terrible or mysterious in that tussock or in those dried grasses. They had been subject to man and useful to him. What then, is the force that suddenly takes possession of them? Why do they inspire him with such terror? And not they alone; this immense, mournful desert appears peopled with phantoms who until now, as he had positively known, did not exist and could not exist.

> Suddenly a terrible cry rang in his ears and everything trembled and moved beneath him. Vassili Andreivich clung to the neck of his horse, but the neck trembled and the cry rang out again, more terribly still. For a few minutes Vassili Andreivich could not take heart again, could not understand what had happened. But all that had happened was simply that the horse had neighed with all its powerful voice, either to give itself courage or else, perhaps, to call for help. "Oh, curse you," said Brekhunov, "how you frightened me!" But even when he understood the real cause of his terrors, he did not succeed in overcoming them.

The last chance of safety disappeared, terror invaded his soul and took possession of it. Explanations which had formerly driven away all his doubts and fears were now powerless and brought him no comfort. "One must think, one must be calm," said Brekhunov to himself; but in vain. He had already crossed the fatal border line, he was cast off for ever from solid earth, where order reigns and laws and methods which have been securely established for the ascertaining of truth. The phantoms with which the desert is peopled will disappear no more, whether or no he succeeds in explaining that the dried grasses are nothing but a vegetable growth and the cry of terror no more than the neighing of his horse. And, moreover, are these descriptions accurate? Has that black bush not got some occult force which had escaped Brekhunov's sagacity until now? . . .

Brekhunov falls from his horse into a snowdrift, the horse goes on and leaves him alone, utterly alone in the snow. "The forest, the farmsteads, the inns, the house under its iron roof and the barns . . . will his heir—what," he thinks, "will become of these? But what is happening? This cannot be." Suddenly he remembers the tuft of grass which the wind had shaken and which he had passed twice already. "Such a terror invaded him then that he could not believe in the reality of all that was happening to him. He thought, "Is not this a dream?" And tried to awake. But it was not a dream."

He tried to remember the theories of knowledge which even a few hours earlier had given him the power to distinguish between the real and the visionary, dreams from waking; but these principles, hitherto so clear and definite, had effaced themselves and could no longer guide him. They defined nothing, taught nothing, and could not deliver him. Then he gave up all scientific theories and remembered that he had one last resource left to which he had not resorted until now, having felt no need of it, and having kept it in reserve for a last emergency.

"Queen of Heaven, Holy Father Nicholas, Lord of Renunciation. . . ." He thought of the Mass, of the ikon with its dark face in the gilded frame, of the candles which he sold for this ikon, the candles which were immediately brought back to him, hardly burnt at all, and which he hid in a drawer of his writing table. Then he began to pray to this same St. Nicholas that he would save him, and promised him a Mass and candles.

> But he immediately and very clearly understood that this face, those ornaments, the candles, the priest, the Mass might all be very important, very necessary even, over there in church, but that they could not help him in any way, that there had not been and was not any connection between the candles and the religious ceremonies, and his present situation.

But what does this new reality call to mind? Nothing that Brekhunov knows, except dreams. Brekhunov's powerful and well-balanced understanding can imagine nothing, it feels itself lost in the midst of the dreams which press in on reality, he struggles like a madman and does just the opposite of what could help him. "Only, no confusion! No haste!" He repeats to himself these well-learned and tried rules of reasonable action and methodical search. But his terror grows, and instead of looking for the road, calmly and carefully, according to rule, he begins to run, falls, picks himself up again, falls once more and loses the last remnants of his strength. Thus he arrives, quite by accident, at the sledge where Nikita is lying. There, at first, from old habit, he makes proof of great activity. Then suddenly a complete change comes over him, such as could not have been deduced by any ordinary rules, from his empirical character.

Before Nikita, who, as it seems to him, is about to die, in the face of inevitable death, Brekhunov suddenly resolves to break completely with his past. Whence this decision comes, and what it means, Tolstoy does not explain; and presumably he does well, for the fact admits of no explanation; in other words, we can establish no connection between the force which drives a man towards the unknown, and the facts that we have previously known about him. This break means, in the words of Plato and Plotinus, "a flight from the known," and any explanation, in so far as it tries to re-establish broken ties, is only the expression of our wish to maintain the man in his former place, to prevent him from accomplishing his destiny.

"Vassili Andreivich," Tolstoy tells us, "stood for some moments in silence, and then, *suddenly,* with the same decision with which he used to clinch a successful bargain by a hand-shake, he took a step backwards, rolled up the sleeves of his coat and set about rubbing life back into Nikita's half frozen body." Can you explain this "sudden" and "suddenly" from which spring the decisions of those who are forsaking the common world? Brekhunov suddenly descends from the height of his glories to warm that worthless peasant Nikita. Is it not an obvious absurdity? But it is still to a certain extent the old Brekhunov; one feels his need to do something, in order not to have to look IT in the face. In the words which he addresses to Nikita we still catch a ring of the old boasting tones, the old self-glorification. Brekhunov still tries instinctively in his old way to escape the inevitable. He is still afraid to let drop from his trembling hands the *potestas clavium* which obviously no longer belongs to him.

"Ah, there you are! You are all right! . . . And you talk of dying. Don't get up, keep warm. That's what we do, we cunning ones. . . ." Vassili Andreivich begins to hold forth. But he could not go on in the same strain. And he was obliged to throw this act, too, overboard. "That's what we do . . ."—this phrase might have been of some use to him formerly, but now, after the decision of this autocratic "suddenly," it is of no use at all, even though crowned by supreme self-abnegation. Something else is wanted, something quite different.

> To his great astonishment he was unable to go on, for his eyes filled with tears and his lower jaw began to tremble. He stopped talking and could only swallow the lump in his throat. "I have been frightened," he thought to himself, "and now I am very weak." But this weakness was not unpleasant; it caused him a peculiar feeling of joy such as he had never previously known.

Brekhunov rejoiced in his weakness; the same Brekhunov who all his life had gloried in his strength, according to the laws of common humanity, persuaded that he was not and could not be happy except in his full strength; and in this conviction he had disputed the *potestas clavium,* the power to bind and loose, with Heaven itself. This joy which was born of weakness, was the beginning of the miraculous, inconceivable, enigmatic change which we call death. Brekhunov, Tolstoy tells us, tries once more to get back for a moment into the old world; he boasts to someone that he has saved Nikita, that he has sacrificed his life to him; but these abrupt stirrings of the old consciousness, the consciousness of strength, become shorter and shorter and eventually cease altogether. Then there remains in him only the joy of his weakness and his liberty. He no longer fears death; strength fears death, weakness does not know this fear. Weakness hears the appeal coming from the place where, long pursued and despised, she has found her eventual refuge. Brekhunov renounces, eagerly and with feverish haste, his inns, his barns, and all the great ideas, including the *potestas clavium,* which had gathered in his soul and been the boasts of the other, the learned, Brekhunov. And now an admirable mystery is revealed to him. " 'I come, I come,' he cried joyfully with his whole being. And he felt that he was free and that nothing held him back any more." And he went, or rather he flew on the wings of his weakness, without knowing whither they would carry him; he rose into the eternal night, terrible and incomprehensible to mankind.

The end of ***Master and Man*** turned out to be a prophecy. Leo Nicolaievich Tolstoy also ended his days on the steppe, in the midst of storms and tempests. Thus destiny will end. The glory of Tolstoy was spread abroad throughout the whole world while he still lived. And yet, in spite of that, soon after his eightieth birthday, which was celebrated in the four quarters of the globe, in every language—an honour which no one before his day had enjoyed—he yet left all and fled from his home one dark night, not knowing whither or wherefore. His works, his glory, all these were a misery to him, a burden too heavy for him to bear. He seems, with trembling, impatient hand, to be tearing off the marks of the sage, the master, the honoured teacher. That he might present himself before the Supreme Judge with unweighted soul, he had to forget and renounce all his magnificent past. (pp. 157-72)

Leo Shestov, "The Last Judgment: Tolstoy's Last Works," in Tolstoy: A Collection of Critical Essays, *edited by Ralph E. Matlaw, Prentice-Hall, Inc., 1967, pp. 157-72.*

E. M. Forster (essay date 1942)

[Forster was a prominent English novelist, critic, and essayist whose works reflect his liberal humanism. His most celebrated novel, A Passage to India *(1924), is a complex examination of personal relationships amid the conflicts of the modern world. Although some of Forster's critical essays are considered unsophisticated in their literary assessments, his* Aspects of the Novel *(1927), a discussion of the techniques of novel writing, is regarded as a minor classic in literary criticism. In the following excerpt from an essay written in 1942, he discusses* The Cossacks, The Death of Iván Ilych, *and*

"The Three Hermits" as illustrations of the high value Tolstoy placed on leading a simple life.]

Three short stories by Tolstoy—namely ***The Cossacks, The Death of Ivan Ilyitch,*** and **"The Three Hermits"**—may help us towards an understanding of him.

They are very different, these stories. ***The Cossacks*** is an early work, full of adventure, it swings ahead, it's about war and love and mountains and ambushes, and it takes place at the foot of the Caucasus. ***The Death of Ivan Ilyitch,*** written later, is a story of illness and suffering indoors, where we never breathe the fresh air. **"The Three Hermits"** (also a late work) is a folk-tale about some Holy Men who were so stupid that they could not even learn the Lord's Prayer.

The three stories, although so different, have one thing in common. They all teach that simple people are best. That was Tolstoy's faith. It took various forms at various times of his life and led him into all sorts of contradictions—sometimes he believed in fighting, sometimes in non-violence and passive resistance, sometimes he was a Christian, sometimes he wasn't, was sometimes an ascetic, sometimes a voluptuary, but the idea that simple people are best underlies all his opinions from start to finish. He was himself far from simple—one of the most complex and difficult characters with whom the historian of literature has to deal, he was an aristocrat, an intellectual, a landowner who thought property wrong, he was ravaged with introspection and remorse. But that's his faith, simplicity.

In one of his earlier revolts against society he had retired to the Caucasus and joined the Russian Army there. At that time conditions were primitive, and savage tribes would descend from the mountains to raid the lowlands to the north. To check them the Russian Government subsidised the Cossacks, who were almost equally wild. The Cossacks lived in their own villages, but were a military organisation who manned outposts and co-operated with the regular army. They were independent and charming, they loved violence and pleasure, and the women as well as the men went free. The life warmed Tolstoy's imagination, and is responsible for his first masterpiece. ***The Cossacks*** is loosely written and the plot is simple. A young Russian officer is stationed in a village and falls in love with a Cossack girl, Marianka. She is betrothed to a wild local youngster, who has made good by killing a tribesman. There are complications, and just as the Russian thinks he has won the girl over, the young Cossack is desperately wounded by the tribesman's brother; Marianka turns away from the officer in fury and returns to her own people, whom she had been tempted to desert. Thus epitomised, the plot sounds thin and stagey, but it is alive by the character-drawing, by the wealth of incident, and by the splendid descriptions of scenery. It's a story of youth, written by a young man.

> Yes, this is the kind of man I am [says one of the Cossacks]. I am a hunter and there isn't another hunter in the regiment like me. I can find and show you every kind of animal and bird—what they are and where they are, I know all about them. And I have got dogs and two guns and nets and a mare and a falcon; got everything I want, thank God! You perhaps may become a real hunter but don't boast of it. I will show you everything. That's the kind of man I am! I will find the scent for you. I know the beast. I know where his lair is and where he goes to drink or lie down. I will make a shooting hut and I will sit there all night and keep watch for you. What is the use of sitting at home? One only gets warm and gets drunk. And then the women come and make a row, and one's angry. Whereas there—you go out and you smooth down the reeds and you sit and watch as a brave young fellow should. You look up at the sky and see the stars: you look at them and guess the time. The wood stirs and you hear a little noise, and a boar comes out to roll in the mud. You hear how the young eagles cry and how the cocks or the geese in the village answer them—geese only till midnight of course. All this I know.

The Cossacks was published in 1863. It made a great sensation in Russia. He followed it with *War and Peace* and *Anna Karenina,* and by the time he wrote ***The Death of Ivan Ilyitch*** he was famous.

Ivan Ilyitch is a successful public servant who rises to become a judge. He is a decent fellow—he has had to pull strings to get on, of course, but everyone has to do that—if you're in the civil service yourself you realise that, don't you? He married, and for love. Romance doesn't last, of course, and by the time he and his wife are middle-aged they quarrel a good deal. That's not unusual—if you yourself are middle-aged you've experienced it perhaps. When he becomes a judge he takes a charming house at St. Petersburg. He is interested in the house, and supervises its decorating, climbs on a ladder to show a workman how to hang a curtain; he slips and in saving himself knocks his side against the corner of a picture frame. The bruised place aches a little, but the discomfort soon passes off, and that's nothing, is it? He went on with his worldly and respectable life, attended the courts, got in with the best people, gave parties. He had a terrible row with his wife over some cakes. She called him a fool because he had ordered too many and he threatened her with divorce. You know the sort of thing. Still it passed. The only trouble was—he didn't feel quite well. There was a nasty taste in his mouth at times, his temper got worse, and there was an uncomfortable feeling—not exactly a pain—in his side, where he had banged it against the picture frame. He is persuaded to consult the doctor who diagnoses—either a loose kidney or appendix trouble. He resumes his daily life—but the pain gets worse.

I won't inflict on you further details of this gruesome story—the most powerful Tolstoy ever wrote. The end is—agonising death, death embittered by Ivan Ilyitch's knowledge that he is in everyone's way, and that they will be thankful when he is gone, and by the polite pretence around him that he is going to recover. In this bitterness there is one compensation. Among his servants is a young peasant called Gerasim, whose job it is to do the rough work in the house. Gerasim is strong, good-tempered and unsophisticated, and spends his time in doing things for other people without making any fuss. "Death will come to all of us, so what's a little trouble, your honour?" says Gerasim. And Ivan Ilyitch discovers before the end that something is wrong with his life; unlike Gerasim he has lived only for himself—even when he was in love with his wife it was for the sake of his own pleasure, and that's what has been wrong. The illumination comes, and at the supreme moment he understands. "In the place of death there was light."

In ***The Death of Ivan Ilyitch*** Tolstoy criticises modern civilisation. In **"The Three Hermits"** he shows what civilisation needs. A bishop, an excellent man, is on a voyage, and hears of an island where three hermits live, saving their souls. He determines to visit them, and finds them indeed holy and sincere, but so ignorant that they do not even know the Lord's Prayer. He teaches them, but they are so stupid that they have the greatest difficulty in learning it; they try again and again, one gets it right, another gets it wrong; however, the Bishop is patient, and does not re-embark until the lesson is learnt. He has the satisfaction of leaving the hermits in a row on the shore, saying the Lord's Prayer fairly accurately. By now it is night and the full moon has risen. The ship continues her course, and in the middle of the night something is seen following her rapidly over the sea. It is the three hermits. They have forgotten the Lord's Prayer, and they are running over the surface of the waves to ask the Bishop to teach them again.

You will see now what I mean by saying Tolstoy believes in simple people. And he believed in a different sort of simplicity at various times in his life. When he was young, and himself a bit of a rip, he believed in the Cossacks, because they were spontaneous and loved animal violence and pleasure. In ***The Death of Ivan Ilyitch*** he has shifted his affection to the Russian peasant, Gerasim, who is placid and imperturbable and unselfish. And in **"The Three Hermits"** he recommends a third type—the saint who is an imbecile in the world's judgment, but walks on the water through the powers of the spirit. Tolstoy was inconsistent. Here are some of his inconsistencies, and they laid him open to attack. But he never wavered in his central faith: simplicity. (pp. 208-12)

E. M. Forster, "Three Stories by Tolstoy," in his Two Cheers for Democracy, *Harcourt Brace Jovanovich, Inc., 1951, pp. 208-12.*

Theodore Redpath (essay date 1960)

[Redpath is an English educator and critic. In the excerpt below, he examines the evolution of Tolstoy's short fiction, which he divides into two periods: the first including those works written in the decade before War and Peace *and* Anna Karenina, *and the second comprising the literature written after his moral and spiritual conversion.]*

Tolstoy always thought that a work of art must be deeply personal and original, and scrupulously faithful to life. But he was also, from the first, concerned with literary texture and form.

When Tolstoy's literary career seriously began he drew at once on personal experiences. The curious fragment, **"A Story of Yesterday,"** his most ambitious attempt before ***Childhood,*** offers a minute record of his experiences of twenty-four hours. It was, however, no mere transcription of life, but a highly self-conscious re-arrangement and amplification of a number of Tolstoy's diary entries, stretching over many days. The work is lively, and vividly displays two features typical of Tolstoy's work—the extended internal monologue and the portrayal of mental events and characteristics through their physical manifestations. Tolstoy abandoned it, however, to create a work of art out of a remoter period of his life.

Childhood, Tolstoy's first published work, is an attempt to recapture the distilled essence of childhood through a series of distinct episodes recounted so as to bring to life not only the scenes and situations, but the feelings experienced, and especially those of the child-'hero', Nikolenka. The work is not only vital but elegant. The primary literary influence was Sterne's *Sentimental Journey,* and we find, indeed, the *Journey's* spare selectiveness, momentary intensity and limpid style, but ***Childhood*** has more genuine warmth, greater moral seriousness, more depth and variety of feeling, and rather less whimsicality. Tolstoy himself, in his Preface, asks his reader to read the tale 'looking for the parts that grip your heart, and not for such as make you laugh'. Yet without the comic passages the grip on our hearts would be perceptibly loosened. Tolstoy's attempt to deflect the reader's attention from the gratuitous humour of which he had a strong vein is noteworthy, especially as we find him also during this early phase naming humour as one of his criteria of literary value. Even in ***Childhood,*** however, serious intentions and the urge to fun are sometimes reconciled by yoking humour for satiric purposes—a procedure more fully exploited in **"Sevastopol in May,"** fairly frequent in *War and Peace* and *Anna Karenina,* and very common in work of the last period. Yet, at first, satire itself was not wholly acceptable to Tolstoy, and we find diary entries expressing his reluctance to use the powerful satiric gift which he could not suppress.

A salient feature of ***Childhood*** is the thoroughgoing watchfulness of the analysis of Nikolenka's emotional reactions. This is particularly striking in episodes where these reactions were unusually powerful, as in the vivid scene of the holy fool Grisha praying to God in the attic allotted to him on one of his visits to the great house, while the children huddle together in the dark, listening, and watching him as he stands out clearly in the moonlight. Tolstoy emphasizes the unforgettably moving impression Grisha's confession of sins made on Nikolenka, and amplifies its religious significance; but having done so he inexorably records the fading of the child's emotion, because his curiosity was satisfied, his legs were stiff, and he wanted to join in the whispering and romping of the other children. This is an early instance of the union of immense feeling with unsentimental honesty so frequent in Tolstoy's writing. Whether he *was* rigorously honest in such passages is irrelevant. In literature it is the impression of honesty that counts, not honesty itself.

Childhood is a harbinger of Tolstoy's mature fiction in other ways also. The theme of death, which was to haunt him later, is already present, and, indeed, has the last word. And an attitude which was perhaps lifelong in Tolstoy is expressed in the brief sentence about the death of the housekeeper, Natalya Savishna:

> She achieved the best and greatest thing in life—
> she died without regrets and without fear.

The animal excitement of the hunting scene is a foretaste of the great chapters of *War and Peace.* The anxieties and absurdities of Nikolenka make the child the father of Pierre. ***Childhood*** also has many of the formal features which were to become typical. There is the abrupt beginning. There are the short chapters. There are the digressions, in which Tolstoy expresses, through his protagonist, his opinions on life, people, and art. These features again partly derive from Sterne. There are also, however, some of the very opinions (for instance, the intense dislike of hypocrisy, and the mistrust and contempt for artificial writing), which will run through Tolstoy's whole career.

But ***Childhood*** is not merely a precursor of Tolstoy's mature work, it is fine in its own right—chiefly perhaps in virtue of its controlled lyrical nostalgia, its moral power, the brilliant choice of scenes, the economy of the writing, the vivid impact of the characters, and the sure touch shown in the psychology of childhood.

Tolstoy soon began to think of ***Childhood*** as the first part of a large novel on the 'Four Epochs' of his life to date, childhood, boyhood, youth, and early manhood. He seems to have wanted to trace his own growth and work it into art, to comment on his changing environment, and to show the weakness of an intelligent and sensitive person in face of his growing egoism and vanity, and of the influences of artificial education and worldly society.

Tolstoy never wrote the fourth part of this novel. ***Boyhood*** and ***Youth,*** the second and third parts, are less remarkable than ***Childhood,*** though they maintain its general structure—a series of set scenes with little attempt to mould them into a continuous narrative. The scenes are generally less striking, though in ***Boyhood*** the storm scene is wonderfully perceptive, and the history lesson a sheer delight, while in ***Youth*** the hero's awkward behaviour in society, and his confused sensations about young women, as well as the episodes of the University examinations and their aftermath, offer splendid instances of the self-critically ironical humour which so often forms an element in Tolstoy's 'dialectic of the soul'.

While he was writing of these earlier experiences, Tolstoy was living a life of a very different kind—the Army life of the Caucasus and later of the Crimean War. Besides giving perspective and sometimes irony to Tolstoy's view of his past, this formed the stuff of some new works of fiction.

Several of these—for instance, **"The Raid," "Recollections of a Billiard Marker,"** the Sevastopol Sketches, and **"The Wood-felling"**—were thrown into the press, but the best of them, ***The Cossacks,*** was nursed and rounded into one of Tolstoy's very finest works. Much of the other work, however, has three signal features, its fresh, powerful, and often stern impressions of the details of campaigning life, its scathing satire on the glory of war as such, and its depreciation of the vain showy soldier in comparison with the quiet man who accepts emergencies and does his duty without any eye to reward.

The Sevastopol Sketches have a place apart, not only because they were written from first-hand experience of an event of major importance, but because of the strong and somewhat conflicting feelings expressed in them. **"Sevastopol in December 1854"** is a glorification of the defenders, but in **"Sevastopol in May 1855"** we find bitter condemnations of war and exposure of the meanness and egoism of many of the participants. This is continued in **"Sevastopol in August 1855,"** yet here patriotism fires Tolstoy again, and he is stung with shame and indignation at the Russian defeat. A similar conflict of feelings appears in *Anna Karenina,* about the Serbo-Turkish war.

The Cossacks is somewhat complex in conception. The story of Olenin, disillusioned at twenty-four with the empty card-playing existence of a young man about Moscow, travelling to the Caucasus in search of a new life, settling for a time on a Cossack *stanitsa* [a Cossack village settlement], falling in love with a beautiful Cossack girl, who turns him down for a young Cossack brave, is used by Tolstoy for some large-scale polemic purposes. First, though subordinately, he deflates romanticized conceptions of life in the Caucasus, such as those retailed by Lermontov and Bestuzhev-Marlinsky. Though he portrays the warlike side of Cossack life, he also emphasizes the peaceful occupations of the Cossacks, their cultivation of vines and fruit trees, maize, millet, melons, and pumpkins, and their fishing and hunting. Secondly, and dominantly, Tolstoy is concerned to contrast the productiveness and moral worth of Cossack life with the aimless wastefulness of the *jeunesse dorée* of Moscow. Even the operations of war seem to him justified, as defence of the Russian frontiers against Moslem marauding or invasion. The main Cossack characters, old Yeroshka, young Lukashka, and the splendid and strong girl Maryana, are all shown as full of health, vitality, and moral dignity. Again, while refusing to indulge in false lyricism, Tolstoy finds poetic inspiration in these characters and the Cossack way of life, and in the beauty of the Caucasian mountains. Many of the impressions come to us through the mind of Olenin, who also represents the passionate searches for a morally satisfying attitude to life which we find in Tolstoy's diaries of 1851-4. Much as Olenin loves the Cossack life, however, he is unable to assimilate himself to it, and his rupture with Maryana and subsequent departure are told of with insight and bleak frankness. The elements could not mix; and this is yet another criticism of Olenin's background. Olenin is more struck by the Cossacks than they are by him. Especially fascinating for him is Daddy Yeroshka, the enormous old hunter, with the deep bass voice, and tremendous zest for life, action, story-telling, and joking, and the belief that at the end 'the grass grows over you, and that's all'. Yeroshka's courage is companioned by the sense that all this killing of Chechens and Cossacks, who ought to live at peace, is a very foolish business. In his talks with Olenin he gives his solutions to some of Olenin's (and Tolstoy's) deepest questions about existence; and the solutions spring from an unfailing vitality which neither Olenin nor Tolstoy had in that measure. Yeroshka is the symbol for the early Tolstoy of that same life-force whose claims we shall see strangely reasserted nearly half-a-century later in ***Hadji Murad.***

The Cossacks (with ***Childhood***) stand supreme among the work of Tolstoy's first period. Its vivid presentation of external and internal life, its combined use of objective description, spoken language, and psychological presentation, and the clarity and forceful expression of the ultimate guiding ideas, are probably unrivalled in Tolstoy.

One short work on which Tolstoy was also engaged during those Army years stands apart both from the stories of recollection and from those of campaigning life. This is ***A Landowner's Morning,*** in which Tolstoy gives expression to the heart-searchings and problems of a young landowner who wishes to do the best by his peasants. This is a fragment of a large novel, *The Novel of a Russian Landowner,* which Tolstoy had planned in 1852, and which was intended to be dogmatic and instructive. The story presents the main problem well, but makes it seem like an impasse, and it may well be that Tolstoy abandoned the large work because he could not find any solution which satisfied him.

Two Hussars, **"Lucerne,"** and ***Family Happiness*** belong to the period after Tolstoy's return from Sevastopol in November 1856 and before his decision late in 1859 to found a school at Yasnaya Polyana. ***Two Hussars,*** originally called *Father and Son,* is the story of two brief amatory episodes in a provincial town. The first involves the father, the second, some decades later, the son. The guiding idea is to contrast the bold openness and full-bodied romanticism of an earlier and better epoch, with the cynical egoism, meanness, and timidity of life in the mid-century. In this respect we have a foretaste of *War and Peace.* **"Lucerne"** is one of the products of Tolstoy's first journey abroad. It is a short, indignant protest at the inhumanity of the elegant tourists, staying at the Schweizerhof Hotel, who listened enthralled to an itinerant guitarist, but did not throw a single copper when the music was over. This burning and moving work is the expression of Tolstoy's disgust at the moral weakness of Western European 'civilization'. (It should perhaps be added, however, that Tolstoy was equally disgusted, on his return to Russia, with the barbaric beatings, thieving and lawlessness he encountered there.) After the failure of his story of a dipsomaniac musician, **"Albert"** (publ. 1858), Tolstoy came out both against professional writing and against art which concerned itself with contemporary social and political questions, instead of matters of universal import. It was during this phase that he wrote ***Family Happiness,*** based on his relations with Valerya Arseneva, a girl he had nearly married about two years before. In the story the hero and heroine actually marry, and there is much friction owing to their difference of age and outlook, though eventually both friction and passion cease, and they settle down to a peaceful and contented existence. The story also brings out the threat to family happiness and genuine human values, from worldly life in high society. ***Family Happiness*** is a fine work, generally underrated even now, but cold-shouldered with gross injustice at the time by those critics who were concerned to maintain the socio-political elements in fiction. There is throughout the work a delicate touch for concrete detail both physical and psychological, and a firm grasp of the main theme, which is made extremely convincing. As a result of the ill-success of ***Family Happiness*** with critics and public, Tolstoy was discouraged, and decided to give up writing fiction. He started his school at Yasnaya Polyana. His renewed contact with the peasants, however, soon made him think of writing peasant stories. This idea bore real fruit during his second journey to Western Europe to study educational methods. Tolstoy started ***Polikushka*** in Brussels in March 1861, and it was published two years later. ***Polikushka*** is a heart-rending tale of a rather incompetent serf who fervently wishes to please his owner, and is entrusted with an errand. He fails through a series of accidents, with the help of some drink, and, as a result, hangs himself. The blend of powerful feeling with robust and somewhat malicious humour in this story is a frequent one in Tolstoy. Here the humour is partly that of the peasants themselves, but it is so fully realized by Tolstoy, and his own humour is so similar, that one can understand the suggestion that, despite his aristocracy, he was basically himself a *muzhik.*

So far Tolstoy had written almost entirely from personal experience. All his themes, moreover, were contemporary. Some had a social or political bearing. All had serious moral content. And Tolstoy had been persistently concerned to depict reality vividly and naturally, to give no quarter in self-analysis, and not to blink harsh realities, such as the horrors of war.

In much of this Tolstoy was simply following the general practice of the 'Realistic School' *(Naturalnaya Shkola)* which included writers as various as Herzen, Grigorovich, Turgenev, Dostoyevski, and Goncharov. Many diary entries between 1847 and 1857 show Tolstoy's admiration for writers of this 'School'.

Tolstoy's originality lay largely in his character and in his special experiences as child of the nobility, landowner, and soldier. By and large he simply worked superlatively well on this material within the bounds of an established tradition.

In some of the later work of this phase, however, he does try to push beyond the bounds of personal experience. In ***Family Happiness,*** for instance, he imaginatively extends suggestions from an episode in his own life into description of a married life he had not yet known; and he even tells the story from the woman's point of view. In ***Polikushka*** he brilliantly projects himself into the mind of the peasant. (pp. 46-55)

. . . . .

Soon after he completed *Anna Karenina* Tolstoy was overwhelmed with that sense of despair which brought about his moral crisis and 'conversion'. Thereafter his religious attitudes almost wholly dominate the fiction, and though sometimes he writes as a hierophant, and sometimes as a sinner, the moral religion behind the work is one and the same.

Many of the aspects of this religion are expressed with great intensity in many of the short stories he wrote, in simple style, for the people. These almost all teach explic-

Tolstoy with Maxim Gorky.

itly that the only life worth living is a life dedicated to God's will. Some teach what Tolstoy thought specifically followed from this. In **"Two Old Men"** the pilgrim who never reaches Jerusalem because he attends on the way to the misfortunes of a peasant family is shown to have acted better than the pilgrim who visits all the Holy Places. In **"Ivan the Fool,"** where Tolstoy makes great use of irony and shock-exposure ofcurrent military violence and capitalistic exploitation, the teaching is that the peaceful performance by every individual of his fair share of manual labour is a primary human duty, that money and soldiers are only instruments of egoistic ambition, and that military attack can be conquered by non-resistance. **"The Imp and the Crust"** is a fanciful temperance parable. **"How Much Land Does a Man Need?"** is a powerful indictment of greed for land. One of the subtlest tales is **"The Empty Drum,"** an attack on state violence.

Some of these stories Tolstoy invented. Others are re-written folk-tales. Most of them have an urgency which springs from Tolstoy's poignant realization of the continual threat of death which hangs over everyone, and his fervent belief in the vital importance of Christian love and mutual help between all human beings. The texture and form of the best of the stories are supreme. The moral naturally grows out of the narrative, which is generally conducted with great skill: in some cases hurrying on with a grotesque rapidity reminiscent of Voltaire, in others moving with quiet care and earnestness; occasionally, too, dwelling for a moment, to gather power, on the physically horrifying or the nightmarish. Telling effect is often achieved by the familiar ballad and folk-tale technique of recounting episodes in series. The moral tendency of these stories, on the other hand, is open to criticism. Even the view that love and kindness are valuable whatever their consequences is not really so attractive as it might seem; but the exaggerated optimism as to the likelihood of the unkind being converted by the kind, hatred overcome by love, and violence by verbal reproach or passive resistance, is positively dangerous. Ivan was lucky to keep his kingdom. Such optimism was perhaps necessary for propagandic effect. It would not encourage love and kindness to show how often they fall on stony ground. But they do so far more often than Tolstoy's stories suggest.

Some of these popular tales actually sketch cases of conversion, but this theme is more elaborately treated in other works of the last period: ***The Death of Ivan Ilych, Master and Man,*** and the posthumous fragment, **"Memoirs of a Madman."** The powerful **"Memoirs"** have considerable biographical interest, but are not a work of art. The other two works are artistic wholes. In both the protagonist is converted, from egoism to love for others, under the stress of acute mental and physical agony in the face of impending death. It is well-nigh unbearable to read of the mounting torture of Ivan Ilych, the official who dies through a simple fall which occurred while he was re-decorating his new St. Petersburg home. Slightly less cruel because less monotonous is the suffering the reader has to endure as the egoism of the master Brekhunov is broken down during a bewildering nocturnal blizzard, and he comes to sacrifice himself by lying on the body of his servant to protect him from the cold, so freezing to death. The uncanny power of these narratives is undeniable. Indeed, especially in ***Ivan Ilych,*** it seems rooted in the pathological. Such experiences scarcely bear thinking of, and *in themselves* belong to those parts of life that are best not dwelt on, and, indeed, if possible, best forgotten. Tolstoy, however, does not dwell on them *for themselves,* but for the sake of his conception of Christian love. In this respect ***Master and Man*** seems the more convincing. Ivan Ilych could only too easily have died in despair. Brekhunov is faced with a definite choice, and his decision grows naturally from the situation. In both tales, however, the anguish springs from an unhealthy intensity, close to madness.

Another main theme of the longer fiction of the last period is the danger, and even hatefulness, of sexuality. This theme is the exclusive concern of ***The Kreutzer Sonata*** and of the two posthumous tales, **"The Devil"** and ***Father Sergius;*** and it is fused with the theme of spiritual regeneration in *Resurrection.* In ***The Kreutzer Sonata*** the highly-pitched outpourings of the hero, Pozdnyshev, who has murdered his wife, have a shrillness which approaches insanity. Tolstoy skilfully disowns this insanity, continually referring to Pozdnyshev's irritable excitability, and at one point even making him admit himself 'a sort of lunatic'. His opinions, however, Tolstoy does not disclaim, and, indeed, they are obviously the *raison d'être* of the book. Like Iago, Pozdnyshev dismisses as non-existent any love between the sexes, distinct from sensuality. Like Byron, another libertine, he is acutely sensitive to the sordid character of the marriage-market. Women are trained from childhood to capture men; and so they dominate society—through sensuality. The social consequences are far-reaching. 'All the luxuries of life are demanded and maintained by women. Women, like queens, keep nine-tenths of mankind in bondage to heavy labour.' Husbands like this sensuality and cultivate the sexuality of their wives. Sexual intercourse, however, in Pozdnyshev's view, is quite unnatural ('Ask a child, ask an unperverted girl'). To the question how the human race would continue without it, his retort is: Why should it continue? If life is for life's sake, there is no reason for living, and then Schopenhauer, Hartmann, and the Buddhists would be right in thinking we ought not to live, and should renounce the will to do so. If, however, life's aim is goodness, that would be more easily attained by stamping out the passions, and especially the strongest passion, sexual love. These positions of Pozdnyshev's are crucial, and, I think, basically unsound. If life were for life's sake, life would provide its *own* reason for living; or else it would *require no reason.* If, however, life's aim were goodness, it is unlikely that the extinction of the passions would achieve life's aim. It might be a greater achievement to attain goodness with the passions than without them; and for many it might be *impossible* without them to achieve goodness at all. But Pozdnyshev fails at other points too. Besides denying any love between the sexes distinct from sensuality, he dubs the sensuality 'something abominable, swinish, which it is horrid and shameful to remember'. Such a view as Pozdnyshev's is not surprising in one who started sexual life as he or Tolstoy did. But those sexual careers were misfortunes, and the doctrines engendered by them have no claims to the title of universally valid moral teaching. Even *were* sexual love nothing but sex, it would not follow that the sexual act is an act of shame. Much more could be said of the wild errors of Pozdnyshev's diatribes. But one would still have to admire the force of the writing, and the seriousness of the moral ideals behind it.

Similar horror at sex underlies **"The Devil"** and ***Father Sergius,*** but these are tightly-controlled narratives of specific cases. They do not make exaggerated generalizations; and they are compact. Yet they do not canvas such a range of aspects of sex as ***The Kreutzer Sonata*** does. **"The Devil"** is the powerful story of a landowner, Irtenev, who, at first 'for health's sake', and later under the spell of personal fascination, has clandestine sexual relations with the wife of a local peasant. After a time Irtenev marries a woman who makes an exemplary wife. The peasant woman's curiosity, however, and chance meetings, work on Irtenev till he becomes obsessed with her attractions. Even an absence of several months does not cure him, and, in a fit of despair, he kills himself, or, in an alternative version, the peasant woman. The suspense of the narrative and the close description of the stream of the landowner's tortured consciousness are masterly. One of the less obvious but highly Tolstoyan morals of the story is that a man who has sexual relations with a woman is responsible for her subsequent sexual life, so that if she grows loose he bears the guilt. The work is directly an attack on the irresponsible morality of some members of the landowning classes of that time; but its moral implications obviously do not rest there. As to the obsession, Tolstoy carefully points out that, though judicially Irtenev was pronounced insane, he was really on the same level of sanity as the general run of humanity. The implication is clearly that such sexual passion could attack and destroy *anyone,* and is not to be trifled with by such practices as indulging in sex 'for health's sake'. Yet the attitude to sex in this story is not so negative as in ***The Kreutzer Sonata.*** The possibility of an entirely satisfying marriage is not excluded, even though not actualized.

In ***Father Sergius*** Tolstoy tells the tale of an aristocratic Guards officer, who, when he learns that his fiancée has become the Emperor's mistress, renounces the world, and enters a monastery. The story deals with the subsequent spiritual development of Sergius, in particular relation to his resistance to sexual temptations. It is, in my view, a finer achievement than either ***The Kreutzer Sonata*** or **"The Devil."** The sense of the nature of true spiritual progress is impressive. The positive values behind Tolstoy's repudiation of lust and sexual love are here recorded more clearly than in any of the fiction save *Resurrection.* The sequence of episodes, showing the subtle interrelation of pride and lust, is managed with the greatest skill, and the whole tale is outstandingly economical. Tolstoy was indeed justified when, after reading part of it to some friends, he exclaimed with closed eyes: 'The old man wrote it well!' (pp. 74-9)

One work of fiction completed by Tolstoy [after his conversion] is of special value and interest: ***Hadji Murad,*** the tale of the Chechen chieftain who fought under Shamil, but, in revenge for his leader's hostility, the murder of his father and brother, and seizure of his wife and children, goes over to the Russians in hope of receiving command of an army with which to destroy his enemy. Owing to intrigue and delay, Hadji Murad does not get his army; and so flees from the Russians with the intention of recapturing his family by a bold coup, with the help of a few henchmen. The Russians pursue him and surround him in a swamp, where he goes down, fighting to the last. The verve of the narrative and the Homeric vividness of the detail are remarkable; and so is the fact that the converted Tolstoy should have written such a story. The full weight of Tolstoy's sympathy seems to be with the resistant mountaineer. Not a trace of the long-cherished philosophy of non-resistance or Christian forbearance, or even of self-perfection, is present. Certain other work written by Tolstoy in the late 'nineties and first decade of the new century has a similar character; but ***Hadji Murad*** is the best example of the tendency. Though Tolstoy recognizes Hadji Murad's love of power and thirst for gain, he lays stress on his deep family love, his daring, resolution, initiative, and longing for a free and full life. It is tempting to see here a re-assertion of Tolstoy's sub-conscious egoistic life-force against the oppressive claims of his stern conscience. There is an interesting diary entry for 5 August 1902: 'I have been writing on Hadji Murad, partly with pleasure, partly against the grain and with shame.' Whatever the biographical significance of the story, however, there is, in any case, something peculiarly satisfying in the spirit behind the work: the passionate love and care for life and its details, and for genuine strong natural impulses, untamed either by the hypnotic force of an effete civilization, by the ruthless despotism of a barbarian overlord, or by the inner workings of over-careful conscience. The story does indeed also contain . . . a vitriolic exposure of the irresponsibility of Nicholas I and his ministers; but powerful as these episodes are in themselves one cannot but suspect them of exaggeration and unfairness, and this weakens their force. Some Soviet critics try to see also in the story propaganda for the union of all Caucasia with Russia, and a scorn of the reactionary Murid fanaticism which constituted some of Shamil's power over his followers. I fail to find the first in the story at all, and the second seems at most present in a very mild degree. The story impresses one rather with the great threat to life and happiness which lies in the two contrasting despotisms of Shamil and Nicholas; with the poetic power of this wild and dangerous Caucasian life, rising at moments to a tragic intensity, which several times finds expression in the poignant spellbinding old Caucasian songs; and by its compelling sympathy with the fine wild chieftain, tenacious of life to the last, hanging on like the red wild thistle, the only living thing in the field to survive the passage of the plough—the symbol with which Tolstoy begins his tale, and with which he ends it.

Generally, however, the fictional work of Tolstoy's last years embodies his religious convictions, sometimes with particularly striking artistry, as in the posthumous stories, **"The Forged Coupon," "After the Ball,"** and **"Alyosha the Pot." "The Forged Coupon"** is the remarkable story of the horrifying ramifications of an original misdeed by some schoolboys, followed by a corresponding narrative of the chain-reactions set up by an act of repentance, which ultimately lead to the spread of happiness. Tolstoy thought, with some justification, that he had here opened up a new form. It certainly admirably expresses the central conviction that the moral tendency of everything one does is vitally important. **"After the Ball"** tells first of a ball at which a young man dances for most of the evening with a girl of eighteen, intoxicated with love; and then of the shattering of that love the very next day when he sees the girl's father, a colonel, order the cruel 'gauntletting' of a deserter. The purposely brutal intensity of the contrast and the restrained force of the explicit moral indignation are superb. **"Alyosha the Pot"** is quite different. It is the miniature life-history of a good, simple boy, put upon by everyone, who dies young of an accident, but who, throughout his brief life, and right up to his death, has been actuated by nothing but serene resignation and goodwill. It is a touching epitome of the human values Tolstoy had come most to admire. (pp. 83-5)

Theodore Redpath, in his Tolstoy, *Bowes & Bowes Publishers Limited, 1960, 126 p.*

Raymond Rosenthal (essay date 1962)

[In the following excerpt, Rosenthal offers an appreciation of Tolstoy's skill as a writer of fables and fairy tales.]

Leo Tolstoy wrote fables and fairy tales throughout his adult life. It is incorrect therefore to associate them solely with the later period of his writing career, when his religious conversion led him to regard what he called the "religious" and "universal" arts as the only arts worth the trouble of creation. . . . [These tales] bear dates that stretch from Tolstoy's early manhood, soon after he had finished *War and Peace* and just before he began *Anna Karenina,* right down to the last years of his long and arduous life. True, many diverse impulses and necessities went into the making of these fables. Yet the form itself was for him a cherished one—cherished for its purity, simplicity, and directness, the qualities in both men and art he valued most—and he always returned to it, as one returns to a restful, green, beloved spot.

Like most perduring aesthetic predilections, Tolstoy's love of the fable can be traced back to his childhood. It was Nicholas, Tolstoy's eldest brother, who instilled it in him. Tolstoy has told the story of this childhood revelation so movingly that it must be quoted at length.

> He [Nicholas] was a wonderful boy, and later a wonderful man. Turgenev used to say of him, very truly, that he lacked only certain faults to be a great writer. He lacked the chief fault needed for authorship—vanity—and was not at all interested in what people thought of him. The qualities of a writer that he possessed were, first of all, a fine artistic sense, an extremely developed sense of proportion, a good-natured, gay sense of humor, an extraordinary, inexhaustible imagination, and a truthful and highly moral view of life; and all this without the slightest conceit. His imagination was such that for hours together he could tell fairy tales or ghost stories or amusing tales in the style of Mrs. Radcliffe, without a pause and with such vivid realization of what he was narrating that one forgot that it was all invention. . . . It was he who, when I was five and my brothers Dmitry six and Sergey seven, announced to us that he possessed a secret by means of which, when disclosed, all men would become happy: there would be no more disease, no trouble, no one would be angry with anybody, all would love one another and all would become 'Ant-Brothers.' . . . We even organized a game of Ant-Brothers, which consisted in sitting under chairs, sheltering ourselves with boxes, screening ourselves with handkerchiefs, and cuddling against one another while thus crouching in the dark. . . . The Ant-Brotherhood was revealed to us but not its chief secret—the way for all men to cease suffering any misfortune, to leave off quarreling and being angry, and become continuously happy—this secret he said he had written on a green stick buried by the road at the edge of a certain ravine . . . there was also a certain Fanfaronov Hill, up which he said he could lead us if only we would fulfill all the appointed conditions. These were: first, to stand in a corner and *not* think of a white bear. I remember how I used to get into a corner and try (but could not possibly manage) not to think of a white bear. . . .

It is clear that in describing the game his brother Nicholas invented, Tolstoy has also described that magical entertainment, the fairy tale. The analogy is complete. The fairy tale's rules are like those of a game arbitrary and capricious—without imagination you can't possibly play!—but, once accepted, absolutely binding; its obstacles are delightfully mysterious and excruciating—oh, that bulky, inescapable white bear!—but, in recompense, its final rewards are vast and splendidly miraculous. To continue playing this game is, unfortunately for mankind, past the powers of most adults, yet Tolstoy did play it and perhaps more than anything else this is the proof of his genius. When he was over seventy he remembered the "green stick" in these words: "The ideal of Ant-Brothers lovingly clinging to one another, though not under two armchairs, but of all mankind under the wide dome of heaven, has remained unaltered in me. As I then believed that there existed a little green stick whereon was written the message which would destroy all evil in men and give them universal welfare, so I now believe that such truth exists and will be revealed to men and will give them all it promises." Indeed, Tolstoy felt so strongly about this that he asked to be buried at the spot where the green stick was supposed to be hidden; and after his death his wish was carried out by his wife and children.

Now Tolstoy's life is usually divided into three distinct periods: his youth, when he wrote the stories of his literary apprenticeship, such as ***Childhood, Tales of Sevastopol,*** and ***The Cossacks;*** his maturity, when the fresh, keen-sighted realism that characterized his first work took on a deeper, intellectual dimension in his masterpieces *War and Peace* and *Anna Karenina;* and his old age, when his religious conversion seemed to transform a spontaneous artist into a single-minded and almost compulsive moral teacher. But if one remembers the story of the green stick and appreciates its continuing significance in Tolstoy's life, these neat divisions break down. Indeed, after his religious conversion Tolstoy decided that his main task as a writer was to express "the religious perception of his time," and this religious perception illuminated precisely the need for human brotherhood. Thus it is evident that the childhood experience with his brother Nicholas had a mythic value for Tolstoy—that is, it was for him both deeply meaningful and strangely unfathomable, as all myths are—and in his last period, when he devoted himself almost entirely to writing fables and folktales, he was in fact trying to give universal form to a mythic experience which was exquisitely intimate and personal.

This accounts for the way in which his last tales, such as **"Ivan the Fool," "Esarhaddon, King of Assyria,"** and **"Emelyan and the Empty Drum,"** are at once similar to the run of fables and fairy tales yet very much unlike them. The manner of their difference lies in Tolstoy's effort to allegorize and explain the mythic content of his original childhood experience. In most fairy tales, the hero's humility and kindness are the human traits which permit him to overcome the dangers and obstacles in his path and win his just reward; and he is rewarded with wealth or happiness or the princess's hand because he is humble and kind. In Tolstoy's tales, however, the hero's humility and kindness are simply the preconditions for the achievement of greater wisdom and self-awareness, and his reward is never wealth or personal success but rather his ability to conquer, both for himself and others, a new and deeper area of human value and responsibility. Thus, if one believes that a folktale or fable is merely an entertainment, providing the same sort of formal pleasure that one gets from Mallarmé's poetry or abstract painting, then Tolstoy's tales, which above all intend to "prove" the reality and urgency of a whole moral world, can only be criticized as a misuse of the form.

I must admit that I am not at all disturbed by Tolstoy's manhandling of the fabulistic proprieties. One could expect just that when a genius of his particular gifts encounters an ancient form and bends it to his special purposes. The wonder of it is that these stories, despite all the ideological and moral preachments they carry, are yet so successful as sheer stories. Much has been made in recent years of the lacerating conflicts that plagued Tolstoy in his old age. But none of these critics have turned their analytical attention to the fables and folktales. If they had considered them, they would quickly have seen that Tolstoy's realism, the acute and absolute perception which operates so directly and beautifully in his great novels and, at the same time, made it so difficult for him to find an all-embracing intellectual system that would satisfy his heart as well as his head, has here achieved an ideal, well-nigh perfect transfiguration. It is a starkly simple transfiguration, but with all of Tolstoy's essential personal qualities still intact—his straightforwardness, his shrewdness, his incisive intellectual power, his mordant humor. (pp. ix-xii)

Artists can triumph only in their art; in life they undergo the defeats and miseries of the common human lot. It is true that Tolstoy's emotional and intellectual conflicts remained with him to the day of his death, unresolved and perhaps unresolvable. But it is also true that in his last fables and folktales he gave triumphant expression to the bare essentials of his spirit. And I would contend that, viewed in this light, Tolstoy in his old age no longer seems disheartened and death-haunted, a master of words weary of his art, but rather a serene and accomplished sage who knew the value of words and used them with inspired frugality.

I am not trying to unravel Tolstoy's enormous complexity by offering a quaint, fairy-tale view of him. The colossal creator who composed the great novelistic symphonies will not yield up his secret so easily. But the fact remains that side by side with this titan stands the humble, unassuming man who wrote the simple tales. And the simplicity that speaks in these tales is quite palpably not a contrived or affected simplicity, for, as every writer knows, of all literary genres the simple tale is the hardest to fake and the easiest in which to detect the insincere and false. What's more, Tolstoy's simplicity was not a facile achievement. It arose out of a vastly complicated intellectual ferment. Consider: Tolstoy was a rationalist and a desperate God-seeker, a hater of all orthodoxy and a stifled dogmatist, a steadfast believer in the essential goodness and creativity of man and one of the keenest intellects ever to expose man's vices and duplicities. And yet, though pulled in so many divergent directions, Tolstoy somehow managed "to become as a child" and to write the slight, pellucid, sardonic tales that one reads in [his fables and fairy tales].

There are many explanations, and good ones, of the titanic Tolstoy. There is Maxim Gorky's deeply perceptive memoir, in which he sees Tolstoy as a demonic enchanter, a part of nature itself, an old, sick man sitting by the coast, "the wind blowing the silvery hairs of his beard: he was looking into the distance out to sea, and the little greenish waves rolled up obediently to his feet and fondled them as if they were telling something about themselves to the old magician." There is Thomas Mann's organ-rolling eloquence: "The Homeric, the timeless epic was strong in Tolstoy, as perhaps in no other artist in the world. His work has the epic's long oceanic swell, its majestic monotone; its powerful, astringent freshness and tang, its immortal healthiness and realism." But, strangely enough, few writers have bothered to deal with the simple Tolstoy, the Tolstoy of the fables and folk tales.

They have dealt, it is true, with the Tolstoy whose ideas for the redemption of mankind were so dogmatically and passionately expressed, and for some reason they imagined that by doing so they were also dealing with the Tolstoy I am talking about. They were wrong. In general their oversight was due, I believe, to embarrassment, the sort of embarrassment that often seizes writers and critics when confronted with an elemental fact that cries out for an elemental epithet. For the truth of the matter is that Tolstoy was able to write these tales with such purity and grace because he possessed that Biblical virtue—loving-kindness. It was his supreme virtue, both as a man and as an artist. His biographer Aylmer Maude has given us the best insight into this by his vivid description of Tolstoy as a child. "He was," Maude reports one of Tolstoy's relatives as saying, "like a ray of light. He would come into the room with a happy smile as if he had made a discovery about which he wished to tell everyone." The miracle is that the grown-up Tolstoy somehow retained that virtue. In his great novels it is this quality of openheartedness that makes his characters so alive and astonishingly real. And in preparing to write his fables he gave this emotion unreservedly not to a sensual society matron or a morose, stubborn general but to the young peasant boys whom he had brought together to teach in the school on his estate.

For Tolstoy was perhaps the first proponent of the theory and practice of progressive education. He fervently believed that "to teach and educate a child is impossible and senseless on the simple ground that the child stands nearer than I do, nearer than any adult does, to that ideal of harmony, truth, beauty and goodness to which, in my pride, I wish to lead him." Of course, believing as he did, Tolstoy ran his school in such a manner that he was as much the pupil as the teacher. Eventually this educational experiment was abandoned and later on he revised and modified some of his more extreme views on the subject. But there was one lasting acquisition from all his educational fervor and enthusiasm—a reading primer which Tolstoy labored over long and finally published in 1872, a few years after he had written *War and Peace.* Among such books this primer is perhaps unique, for it is the outcome of the collaboration of a refined genius of language with the raw genius of the folk, as represented by the young peasant boys in Tolstoy's school.

In fact, when writing all his folktales, Tolstoy not only accepted but eagerly sought the corrections and elaborations of the peasants among whom he lived. Although we have it straight from him that vanity is a driving force in any writer, it seems that he was capable of holding his own in check, even of obliterating it, for the sake of a sharp phrase, an apt example, or a happier turn of speech. One of the many disciples that Tolstoy's doctrines gathered about him in his last years tells us how the old man, after reading his just completed story **"Ivan the Fool"** to a group of peasants, asked one of them to repeat it in his own words. The peasant, who had a remarkable gift for words, altered the story considerably. But Tolstoy was delighted by his changes, copied them down rapidly, and published the story in the new form the peasant had given it. He explained to his disciple that he always did that; it was, he said, "the only way to write stories for the people."

It is this last point that has aroused the wrath of so many critics. They object to the whole notion of "stories written for the people." They protest against the didactic, preaching note. They attack the moralistic tone that distorts the variety and fullness of life in order to promulgate a message, however good or reasonable. They contrast the early Tolstoy who wrote the masterpieces with the late, dogmatic Tolstoy who, they say, had withered into a doctrinaire of his own feelings and views. I do not intend to argue with them. [Tolstoy's fables and fairy tales] will either be enjoyed for [their] own sake and prove me right in holding that the Tolstoy of the fables is as precious to us as the Tolstoy of the masterpieces, or [they] will fail to delight readers and therefore prove me wrong.

I can only hope that what happened to G. K. Chesterton happens to all the people who read [Tolstoy's tales]. Chesterton, a volatile man and a vehement preacher, set out to refute the "preaching" Tolstoy but ended with:

> The real distinction between the ethics of high art and the ethics of manufactured and didactic art lies in the simple fact that the bad fable has a moral, while the good fable is a moral. And the real moral of Tolstoy comes out constantly . . . , the great moral which lies at the heart of all his work, of which he is probably unconscious. . . . It is the curious cold white light of morning that shines over all the tales, the folklore simplicity with which 'a man and a woman' are spoken of without further clarification, the love—one might almost say the lust—for the qualities of brute materials, the hardness of wood, and the softness of mud, the ingrained belief in a certain kind of ancient kindliness sitting beside the very cradle of the race of man.

(pp. xii-xvi)

Raymond Rosenthal, in a foreword to Fables and Fairy Tales *by Leo Tolstoy, translated by Ann Dunnigan, New American Library, 1962, pp. ix-xvi.*

Elizabeth Trahan (essay date 1963)

[*In the excerpt below, Trahan considers Tolstoy's* Master and Man *as an essentially symbolic narrative in an examination of the story's religious themes and nature imagery.*]

In his essay *What is Art?* (1897), Tolstoj rejects contemporary art as involved, affected and obscure. He attacks the French Symbolists for their incomprehensibility and heaps ridicule on Richard Wagner for his use of myths and leitmotifs. Good art, Tolstoj suggests, must express universally valid religious or at least humanitarian feelings, experienced by the author and transmitted through direct emotional infection, as is accomplished in the great religious writings, in folk legends, fairy tales and folk songs. When reviewing his own writings from this critical position, Tolstoj is forced to reject all his literary masterpieces. He can only find two instances of "good" art, two of his ***Tales for Children*** (1872)—**"The Prisoner of the Caucasus"** and **"God Sees the Truth but Waits."**

Today, however interesting we may find the essay on art, we will hardly use it as a basis for evaluating Tolstoj's works. Not **"The Prisoner of the Caucasus"** or **"God Sees the Truth but Waits"** but *War and Peace, Anna Karenina,* ***The Death of Ivan Il'ič,*** and ***Master and Man*** are generally considered Tolstoj's best works. Yet, paradoxically, in one respect the bias of Tolstoj's theoretical position seems to have affected most critics. Tolstoj is usually discussed in terms of his "realism" or as a moralist, and is rarely given credit for any formal experimentation. Yet already *War and Peace* (1865-69) and *Anna Karenina* (1873-77) make use of certain formal devices, such as interior monologue, free association, structural patterns based on parallels and contrasts, significant detail, even some symbolic, i.e., open metaphors. ***The Death of Ivan Il'ič*** (1886), in addition, uses "leitmotifs" very much in Richard Wagner's manner, and contains sensory associations of a directness or subtlety very close to that emphasis on nuances and depth which characterizes Baudelaire and the French Symbolists. Finally, ***Master and Man*** (1894), one of Tolstoj's last stories, is, as I will try to show, a truly modern symbolic narrative.

The plot of ***Master and Man*** is simple. Vasilij Andreič Brexunov, the master, and Nikita, his man, set out on a business trip to a village some seven miles away. They are confronted by a blizzard, repeatedly lose their way and are finally forced to spend the night in their sledge. Brexunov freezes to death but saves Nikita by shielding him with his body. Initially a selfish, stubborn bully, he now dies willingly and gladly, with a vision of Christ and a belief in the unity of all life. Nikita's life is saved, and he quietly lives out his lifespan.

The juxtaposition of two contrasting characters and their ways and views of life had been a favorite device of Tolstoj's ever since ***Three Deaths,*** written in 1858. But only on the most immediate level is ***Master and Man*** the story of Brexunov and his servant Nikita. While Nikita does not change throughout the story, Brexunov undergoes a complete transformation. The indifferent churchwarden becomes a true believer; the greedy and self-confident egotist, a humble and self-effacing human being. ***Master and Man*** is actually Brexunov's story, for he emerges as both master and man.

As a tale of moral regeneration and religious consolation, the story is thematically close to many of Tolstoj's popular tales, and to his conception of "good" art. Moreover, the detached, simple folk idiom used—much of its charm is, unfortunately, lost in translation—gives the story the naïveté and wisdom of a folk legend. At the same time, even a superficial reading reveals a certain mysterious, magic quality which suggests additional dimensions. Certain words are repeated like incantations. The howling of the wind and the circling of the snow provide an ominous refrain. The sledge and its occupants move in circles which they seem unable to break through. The number "three" occurs some fifteen times in the story, suggesting a bewitched, alien world. And close attention to the text reveals the presence of metaphors and symbols which not only deepen and transform the surface reality of the plot but which form connected patterns and provide additional levels of meaning. Through these symbols, Brexunov's religious awakening becomes a pilgrimage from the village of *Kresty* (The Crosses) to the Cross, almost a reiteration of Christ's Road to Calvary. The personal crisis of Brexunov, the Liar—*brexat'* is "to tell lies"—becomes the experience of an existential moment, the culmination of man's struggle with nature both without and within. Brexunov's final insight not only bestows meaning upon his existence but, through the correspondence of the symbols used, reveals Brexunov's essence to be a reflection of the essence of that external force which he had challenged.

The setting for the story may have been suggested to Tolstoj by a personal experience. During the winters of 1891-92 and 1892-93, he was engaged in famine relief work in the district of Rjazan'. Mme. Raevskaja, at whose estate he was staying, describes how on February 15, 1892, worried about Tolstoj's long absence during a blizzard, they set out after him and found him crossing a snowy field on foot, left behind by his horse. Once before, Tolstoj had written a story based on his own experience of a blizzard during a twenty-two hour trip in January of 1854. ***The Snowstorm*** (1856) describes realistically an all-night ride, in which the horses instinctively find their way to safety. If contrasted to the early story, the formal emphasis and achievement of ***Master and Man*** becomes immediately apparent.

The immediate incentive for the story must have been provided by Flaubert's *Légende de Saint Julien l'Hospitalier.* Tolstoj wrote ***Master and Man*** only a few months before two introductions, one to the works of Guy de Maupassant, the other to S. T. Semenov's *Peasant Stories.* Both introductions reveal Tolstoj's preoccupation with literary criticism. The criteria stated later in *What is Art?* are here anticipated by Tolstoj's emphasis on the significance and universality of the theme, on the proper relation of form to content, and on the author's "sincerity." In the introduction to Semenov's stories, Tolstoj points to Flaubert's tale as an example of an author's lack of sincerity: "The last episode of the story which ought to be the most touching represents Julien lying on a bed together with a leper and warming him with his body. . . . The whole thing is described with great skill, but in reading this story I am always left perfectly cold and indifferent. I feel that the author would not have done and would not have cared to do what his hero did, and I therefore have no desire to do it, and experience no emotion on reading of this marvellous exploit."

Tolstoj's criticism of Flaubert's story shows not merely the inadequacy of his criterion of "sincerity" but his lack of insight into Flaubert's approach. A comparison with ***Master and Man*** again becomes illuminating: *La Légende* *de Saint Julien l'Hospitalier* was written as a deliberate—and probably eminently sincere—attempt to re-create the mood and spirit of the Middle Ages. It is filled with allegorical objects and animals, miracles and coincidences, set against the backdrop of a medieval, stable universe. The story provides an excellent example of what Erich Kahler calls "descending symbolism"—a symbolism dependent on and determined by a pre-established reality. Tolstoj's story, on the other hand, becomes modern both by its emphasis on psychological character treatment and by its "ascending" symbolism. Here a set of freely created unique forms achieves a consummate representation of the author's vision. In contrast to Flaubert's story, the intensity of the vision now absorbs the communicative purpose, and the story's message can no longer be separated from the work itself.

The comparison of Brexunov and his man, Nikita, is achieved largely by direct description, as well as Tolstoj's long favored devices of parallelism and contrast, often used to reflect ironic ambivalences. But since this comparison forms the story's basis, it must be traced at least briefly before we can turn to Brexunov's psychological development and its symbolic significance.

Initially, Brexunov, Church Elder and Merchant of the Second Guild, views the world entirely in terms of his personal power and economic success. Though his estate thrives, both wife and child are "thin and pale." Brexunov's tone toward his wife is rude and condescending, and his son exists for him merely as a personal heir. Nor is Brexunov's attitude toward Nikita positive, though he considers himself Nikita's benefactor. As shown by his taunting remarks about the cooper and by his attempt to sell Nikita a bad horse, Brexunov is as indifferent to Nikita's feelings and to his financial plight as to his physical well-being.

Nikita's relations with his environment, on the other hand, are harmonious. The master's little boy loves him, the mistress worries whether he will be warm enough, and he pleases everyone by his cheerful and obliging manner. He has the peasant's straightforward simplicity and fatalism, his closeness to nature and animals. Nonetheless, Nikita is no saint. When drunk—and he is called a habitual drunkard early in the story—he can become a veritable fiend. But while his master freely imbibes both before his departure and in Griškino, Nikita resists all temptation, remains sober and thus more aware of the hazards and necessities of their situation.

Ironically, just as Brexunov's two fur-lined coats do not save him while Nikita survives in his thin coat, so Brexunov's personal energy and business acumen turn out far less effective than the simple reasoning of those around him. Nikita would have chosen the safer road, trusted the horse's instinct and, undoubtedly, spent the night safely at Taras' house. Only upon his wife's nagging does Brexunov take Nikita along. This step might have saved his life, had he paid attention to Nikita from the start. It saves his soul when he finally does. It is similarly ironic that, while Nikita derives real comfort from placing his sins and fate into God's hands, Brexunov, the Church Elder, can find no consolation in religion. Instead, he vainly seeks reassurance in the memory of his own achievements and the excitement of future goals.

We do not know whether Nikita would have survived the night without Brexunov's self-sacrifice; but we know that he was ready for death, without any reproach toward his master or God. It almost seems a reward for his unswerving loyalty that Nikita is permitted to die his own death—*nastojaščaja smert'*—the traditional solemn death of the believer, at home in his bed, surrounded by his family and with a lighted taper in his hand.

Even though the last paragraph is devoted to Nikita, ***Master and Man*** is not his story. The ending merely completes the comparison between him and his master, beyond their actions and attitudes to their actual death experience. In many ways, Nikita is more positive. His actions and decisions, in contrast to Brexunov's, seem appropriate and "right." By his fatalistic acceptance of life in all its manifestations, he reminds us of Natal'ja Savišna in ***Childhood,*** the coachman Fedor in ***Three Deaths,*** Platon Karataev in *War and Peace,* Gerasim in ***The Death of Ivan Il'ič.*** All of them are contrasted positively to men of greater individuality who are assailed by doubts, fears, and temptations. In Platon, the type finds its culmination. He is less a person than a symbol, a "personification of the spirit of simplicity and truth" *(War and Peace,* Part Twelve, Ch. XIII). He does not take the center of the stage, but the secret of his happiness is coveted by Pierre Bezuxov as much as that of the peasant—whose name, incidentally, is again Platon—by Konstantin Levin. In ***The Death of Ivan Il'ič,*** the balance begins to shift. Ivan Il'ič incorporates to some extent Gerasim's humble and joyful submissiveness into his own world view. In ***Master and Man,*** the change is completed. However "right" Nikita's attitude and however peaceful his death, not he, the just man, is exalted but Brexunov, the repentant sinner, who, after a desperate struggle with nature, submits to it and finds God.

The contrast between Nikita and Brexunov is extended into their attitude toward nature. While Nikita accepts it even in its extreme manifestation—the cold and pitiless fury of the blizzard—Brexunov challenges it as he had challenged everything around him before. But while he had been able to impose his will on men and animals, he suffers defeat when he confronts nature with the same ruthless disregard.

When Brexunov's path is blocked by the ravine, he suffers the first decisive defeat, the defeat of his actions. When he vainly seeks reassurance in memories of the past and dreams of the future, he suffers the defeat of his achievements. Finally, when he, no longer master of himself but driven by fear and the instinct of self-preservation, makes one more attempt at physical escape, he suffers the defeat of his values. But like Dostoevskij's Ridiculous Man who, on his dream flight, is stripped of layer upon layer of the armor with which he had fortified himself against life, so Vasilij Brexunov, facing non-existence in a nightmarish and awesome no-man's land, moves step by step toward the core of his existence. He faces his existential crisis alone, weak, unable to muster the support of any ethical, moral, or religious consolations. But now, untrammeled by shackles of conventions and prejudices, a deep inner strength surges up in him. Brexunov begins to find a new self and new values.

Brexunov's attempt to revive Nikita may initially have been due to his fear of being left alone again, of having to submit to death and acknowledge defeat. But the "peculiar joy such as he had never felt before," the "strange and solemn tenderness," and the "joyous condition" which he experiences, bear witness to the fact that a change is taking place within him. Now his thoughts circle around Nikita and the peasant's image fuses with that of the past. Finally, Brexunov sees himself back in the past, when he is immobile, unable to react to his old environment. That this fact does not fill him with fear or indignation, again shows how profoundly he has changed. Formerly an impatient and irascible master, he is now waiting patiently and joyfully for his own Master. His submission is complete: he acknowledges the merit for the good deed as not his but Christ's and follows Him with humility.

The religious theme which asserts itself so powerfully at the end, is latently present from the very beginning. Brexunov lives in a village called The Crosses and, as it turns out, indeed in the shadow of the Cross. His challenge takes place on the second day of the feast of St. Nicholas, who is not only the saint of all Russia and specifically of peasants, merchants and wayfarers, but also of temperance—and a wonderworker. Nikita, who has taken a vow of abstinence and who successfully resists all temptation on the crucial day, is obviously under the protection of St. Nicholas. But on Brexunov the Saint works his miracle.

Initially Brexunov is a sinner. Though a church elder, he ignores the holy day and desecrates church funds by borrowing them for private gain. In Griškino, he sits down at the head of the table for what becomes his last supper. To be sure, with his "protruding, hawk-like eyes," his three thousand rubles and his greed for gain he is still closer to Judas than to Christ. His answer to the anguished complaints of the old man about his son's greed is unconcerned. Brexunov does not realize that his own test has begun.

It is interesting that a counting of heads reveals the presence of thirteen adults in Taras' house: the old couple, two of their sons and one grandson—Petruša—with his wife, Taras' four daughters-in-law, the neighbor, Brexunov, and Nikita. But though such detailed account is given of all twenty-two members of Taras' household as to suggest a purpose, the allusion is again blurred by the fact that only the men sit around the table.

Several other, similarly marginal references occur. The sledge which Brexunov overtakes is driven by one Simon who, however casually encountered, might have shared Brexunov's burden, had he chosen to accept his help. The man who opens the gate to Taras' house for them and again guides them onto their way is called Peter and, for all his willingness, he turns back at the crucial moment and abandons them, if unknowingly, to their fate. These allusions gain weight, as Brexunov recalls one Sebastian who froze to death. The uncommon name clearly evokes the Saint and the possibility of martyrdom and glory. Even more direct is the allusion to treason when Brexunov thinks he hears a cock crow. Not much later, he abandons Nikita with the sacrilegious words: "He won't grudge his life but I, thank God, have something to live for. . . . "

When Brexunov sets out alone for the wilderness—the wormwood becomes its appropriate symbol—his punishment seems imminent. Though there is little resemblance between Brexunov's flight into the snowy waste and Christ's withdrawal into the Garden of Gethsemane, Brexunov, not unlike Christ, experiences supreme anguish. He, too, turns to prayer asking that the cup be taken away from him, only to realize the vanity of such prayer. When Brexunov returns to Nikita, he is ready for his burden. As he lies down on his servant with his arms spread out, he, in a sense, mounts the Cross.

During the moment of extreme anguish Brexunov recalled the recent church service and the tapers which he would sell and resell. Lying on Nikita he again recalls service and tapers, but now their images merge with that of Nikita. In sacrificing himself for this man, Brexunov reiterates Christ's sacrifice, and in his last vision Christ comes for him in person and thereby accepts the sacrifice.

Even though Brexunov's symbolic death is somewhat similar to Billy Budd's he is no Christ figure like Billy Budd or like Prince Myškin. Nor does his wrong-doing approach the scope of that of St. Julien. Brexunov is merely a sinner who through suffering returns to love and through love to Christ. Franz Kafka, in *A Country Doctor,* likewise describes a ride through a blizzard, and the doctor, too, lies down to warm a dying human being. There, however, the symbols are used with savage irony. The country doctor lies down willingly, and attempts to escape as soon as he can—only to find his escape turn into a trap, an eternal pilgrimage through "the frost of this most unhappy of ages." Brexunov's religious development, on the other hand, remains thematically entirely within the framework of traditional Christianity, a fitting illustration of Luke 15:7: "I say unto you, that likewise joy shall be in heaven over one sinner that repenteth, more than over ninety and nine just persons, which need no repentance." The symbolic presentation, however, gives Brexunov's final gesture a scope and significance which by far transcends his actual transformation into a humble and dedicated servant of Christ.

The religious symbolism of ***Master and Man*** represents only one strand in the symbolic pattern of the story. With its use of allegorical names and its actual depiction of a religious vision, it remains to some extent superimposed upon the story. The nature imagery, on the other hand, becomes so intrinsic a part of the narrative, permeates it so completely and intensively that the story becomes an excellent example of what, earlier, I called "ascending" symbolism.

The circle becomes the key symbol of the story. It is menace and trap, futility and despair, but it also represents the unity of life and death, the Chain of Being. The snow whirls around master and man, the wind circles around them, their road turns into circles. Brexunov, by defying the circle as long as he can, rejects every road leading out of it, until there remains only the one leading into its very center—the heart of nature and the self. Darkness and the abyss provide its signposts. Though Brexunov fails to recognize their deeper significance, they effectively stop his outer journey, and the inner journey to the core of the self can begin. Again Brexunov's quest moves in circles, those of his thoughts, then those of his last trip. Finally Brexunov reaches the innermost circle, in which the I and the Thou merge.

The circular symbol is enhanced by the continual recurrence of the number "three," which also adds a supernatural dimension to the reality of the plot. Brexunov starts out during the third hour, with three thousand rubles in his pocket. Three times they set out. Three times Nikita takes over. Three times they see the same cluster of moaning willows, three times they pass the frozen wash, three times wormwood is mentioned. They have three encounters—with Isaj, the horse thief, the three peasants whom they overtake, and Taras and his household in Griškino. Petruša speaks of three domestic councellors. Three times Nikita climbs out to search for the path, the third time reappearing three sazhens further. Three times Brexunov tries to light a cigarette and, after successfully lighting three matches, he is unable to light the last three.

Other secondary images likewise support and extend the symbolic structure. The frozen wash which "is struggling," "fluttering desperately in the wind," and the white shirt which "in particular struggled desperately, waving its sleeves around"—not only reflect the fury of the storm but become portents of doom, of man in distress, of a shroud, a frozen body, perhaps even a crucifixion. The willows are moaning "dismally" and "desperately," "swaying" and "whistling"; the wormwood which is "desperately tossed about by a pitiless wind" fills Brexunov with utmost terror and seems to him his own reflection, as he "awaits an inevitable, swift and meaningless death." These images call to mind Pascal's *pensée* on man as a reed, "le plus faible de la nature"; they also suggest Job 21: 18: "They are as stubble before the wind, and as chaff that the storm carrieth away."

A series of frightening sounds provides the aural backdrop for the visual imagery and fills the air with the clamor appropriate for Judgment Day: the wild whistling of the wind, the threatening howl of a wolf, the eerie and pitiful cry of the frightened horse.

Tolstoy with Anton Chekhov.

The poem which Petruša quotes with such joy at its aptness—it is a colloquialized version of the first stanza of Puškin's *Winter Evening*—indeed expresses the Protean power of the storm:

> Storms with mist the sky conceal,
> Snowy circles wheeling wild.
> Now like savage beast 'twill howl,
> And now 'tis wailing like a child.

Brexunov dies only thirty sazhens (70 feet) off the road and half a verst (about one-third mile) from the village, trapped by the blizzard in a magic circle which he cannot break through. Nor can man break through nature's circle of life and death; he can only transcend it by leaving the realm of nature, of life. And while Brexunov follows *His* call, around his dead body the snowstorm once more asserts its symbol of the circle: "All around the snow was whirling as before. The same snow squalls were circling about, covering the dead Vasilij Andreič's fur coat. . . . "

The blizzard has lifted Brexunov out of time and space—the time and space of his everyday life—into the vastness of nature, pure, bare, and invincible, stripped of sham values and comforts, and encompassing both life and death in close proximity. The business trip, begun with a disregard for nature's power, continued as one man's challenge, becomes a desperate struggle against the element until nature asserts itself. It forces Brexunov to acquiesce, to accept death at its hands; but it also enables him to understand its secret and to find his own existence and essence in love. An almost mystical union with nature through a supreme act of love becomes his ultimate fulfillment. "Nikita is alive so I too am alive," is Brexunov's final unreserved and unselfish affirmation of life. This is not merely a creed based on the Christian virtues of humility and brotherly love, but a belief in the eternal flow and transfer of life, a Buddhist rather than Christian concept. Käte Hamburger, in her excellent study on Tolstoj [*Tolstoi. Gestalt und Problem*], sees the unique accomplishment of ***Master and Man*** in this visually accomplished act of love, which by far transcends the token gesture of love made by Ivan Il'ič. Yet even ***Master and Man,*** if more faintly than Tolstoj's other works, echoes its author's own inner split. Despite his self-sacrifice, Brexunov does not come to terms with death nor does he, in Rilke's words, "die his own death."

Of all of Tolstoj's heroes, only Prince Andrej comes close to dying his own death, aside from such "children of God," as Natal'ja Savišna, Platon Krataev, or Nikita. Prince Andrej turns away from life with the same aloofness with which he had turned away from each successive phase of his life. Neither Ivan Il'ič nor Brexunov dies his own death. Ivan Il'ič's dying is awful far beyond the sins of his lifetime, while Brexunov, petty sinner that he was, dies an undeservedly beautiful and glorious death. Nor does either of them—in fact, none of Tolstoj's fictional challengers of death—ever come to terms with it. Even Prince Andrej cannot face death squarely. He turns it from an end into a beginning, "an awakening from life"—

an escape. Brexunov's story in many ways parallels that of Ivan Il'ič. Confronted by death, both men face the crisis of their existence, and both are forced to reject the values of their past. Yet neither is able to accept death—they merely dismiss or ignore it. For Ivan Il'ič it "ceases to exist," as the immense relief after an almost unbearable suffering floods his entire being till nothing else has room. Brexunov finds a dual escape from facing death: the Christian consolation of a personal immortality and a—basically contradictory—emphasis on the abandonment of individuality in an identification with all life. In neither case is death accepted as part of life, as its end.

Brexunov is much simpler than Ivan Il'ič. He lives by feelings and urges rather than thoughts, and even his act of love and submission takes place on the same instinctive level, brought about by a moment of overwhelming fear rather than a crisis of consciousness. He rejects his past after he has found new values, whereas Ivan Il'ič dismissed his entire life before he had found anything to take its place. Ivan Il'ič was battered and tossed about by his pain until the last shreds of his strength and dignity were gone. Therefore, his final gesture of love may be weak, and his dismissal of death an escape, yet his courage and his suffering give him a heroic scope which Brexunov lacks.

Ironically, though ***Master and Man*** was prompted by Tolstoj's effort to demonstrate "sincerity," to achieve a direct emotional infection, the impact of the story cannot compare to the impact of Ivan Il'ič's terrible struggle with death. Tolstoj's own fear of death proved stronger than his love of man or God. However, esthetically, ***Master and Man*** evokes a serenity and pleasure as none of Tolstoj's other works do. The story not only occupies a unique place in Tolstoj's creative output and points to an unsuspected range of his talent, but, both complex and superbly simple, it becomes the most nearly perfect of his works of art. (pp. 258-67)

Elizabeth Trahan, "L. N. Tolstoj's 'Master and Man'—A Symbolic Narrative," in Slavic and East-European Journal, *Vol. VII, No. 3, 1963, pp. 258-68.*

Ernest J. Simmons (essay date 1968)

[*Simmons was an American critic and educator. In the excerpt below, he surveys Tolstoy's later short stories, written between 1870 and 1905.*]

After his first two major full-length novels, *War and Peace* and *Anna Karenina,* Tolstoy did not neglect the short story form which had played so prominent a part in his youthful literary endeavors. In any comparison of his accomplishments in this genre during the early and later periods, one is struck by the somewhat limited output in the second in terms of the forty years involved. Several reasons for the disparity come to mind, but perhaps the important one is that Tolstoy's enormous success in the novel served to lessen his interest in the short story.

Still more striking is the marked thematic difference between the short stories in the two periods. With a few exceptions those in the later period do not appear to have been written to enhance a literary reputation. Most of them seem to be inspired by an uneasy conscience or a deliberate subjective purpose, yet among them are several short stories that have often been acclaimed as Tolstoy's greatest. Of course, the difference in his approach and subject matter was connected with the spiritual crisis he underwent at the beginning of the 1880's, an experience which . . . altered the course of his life as well as his attitude toward art.

The earliest group of these short stories, written in 1872 between *War and Peace* and *Anna Karenina,* Tolstoy regarded as "Tales for Children." He was dubious about the practice of writing stories specifically for youngsters and would probably have agreed with Chekhov's advice that one should select for children something truly artistic that has been written for adults. The tales in this group appear to be closely connected with Tolstoy's return to pedagogical pursuits in 1870, one result of which, as we have seen, was his ***ABC Book*** containing a complete educational curriculum for beginning pupils. In preparing its reading selections, he pored over collections of Russian mediaeval legends and the folk tales of a dozen countries, paying particular attention to the style of those he translated. The simplicity and clarity of these folk narratives plainly influenced the original tales he wrote for his ***ABC Book.*** In fact, more than ten years before he began to think seriously about the ideas that guided his notable treatise, *What Is Art?,* he had hit upon one of its salient contentions—that the language of sophisticated literature was less effective, artistically, than the language of the so-called popular literature of uneducated folk.

There is much of the fetching artlessness of folk tales in **"God Sees the Truth, but Waits,"** for the emotional power of its message of forgiveness gains in impressiveness by virtue of the uncontrived simplicity of motivation and characterization. In the end, Aksyonov's triumphant faith in God transforms an unjust punishment into an act of beatification. The theme of a merchant who was condemned for a crime he did not commit and who accepted his tribulations in a spirit of Christian forgiveness was a favorite of Tolstoy's, and he used it earlier, in memorable circumstances, in the story told in *War and Peace* by the peasant, Platon Karataev.

Though a youngster might not easily perceive the moral significance of **"God Sees the Truth, but Waits,"** he would have no difficulty appreciating the simple feelings of fear, courage, pity, and endurance which Tolstoy illustrated without didacticism in **"A Prisoner in the Caucasus."** Moreover, the youngster would understand and approve the efforts of Dina, the charmingly portrayed little Tartar girl, to free the Russian officer Zhilin, captured by her people, even though she risked severe punishment. She was won over not so much by the clever toys he made for her as by his courage, fearlessness, and strength of character, which aroused in her feminine feelings strange in one so young. The adult reader, however, will take pleasure in the work as a well-told story of adventure in the tradition of Tolstoy's early Caucasian tales, but at the same time differing from them in its special individuality and in its clarity and sincerity of expression. And again, like the early Caucasian short stories, it is based on a personal experience—once, in an exposed position as a cadet in the Russian forces, Tolstoy barely escaped capture by the Tartars.

The third and last story in this group for children, **"The Bear-Hunt,"** likewise grew out of an actual incident—in 1858 Tolstoy, while hunting with a friend, was attacked by a huge bear that had been wounded, and he almost lost his life. Though the details of the real and fictional accounts are quite similar, in the latter one may observe the transmuting power of Tolstoy's art manifesting itself in the wonderfully realistic descriptions of winter scenes on the first day of the hunt, the sleeping and awakening in the woods, and much else, all of which appears to be entirely imaginary.

It is worth pointing out that Tolstoy regarded **"God Sees the Truth, but Waits"** and **"A Prisoner in the Caucasus"** as the best of all his many short stories. In consigning the whole corpus of his works to the category of "bad art" in *What Is Art?* he made exceptions of these two tales, placing the first in the highest category of "religious art" and the second in the category of "universal art."

It has been pointed out that after his spiritual conversion Tolstoy devoted himself to the theory and practice of a new faith that amounted to a form of Christian anarchism incompatible with the kind of emphasis he had been placing on fiction. There is even a suggestion that he would like to have broken cleanly with art just as he flatly rejected the kind of life he had previously led. If now, however, he was unable to abandon imaginative writing, he was determined that it would be consistent with the new morality and ethics to which he subscribed. And it must be said that nearly everything he did write after his conversion was conceived and executed, in varying degrees, in the spirit of his new faith. That is, he sought to create in terms of the categories he established in *What Is Art?*—religious art that transmits feelings of love of God and one's neighbor, and universal art that transmits the very simplest feelings common to all men. The remarkable fact is that not a few of these works must be included among his most memorable artistic achievements.

The qualities Tolstoy now sought in art he detected in the old religious legends and folk tales he had combed in connection with the complication of his ***ABC Book.*** The fact that the Russian masses lacked easy accessibility to inexpensive editions of such literature prompted him to explore the matter. One consequence was the establishment, in 1884, of a publishing firm called *Intermediary,* the main purpose of which was to make available to the people cheap booklets containing fiction and illustrations reflecting the essence of Tolstoy's Christian teaching. Initially the business was headed by his disciple V. G. Chertkov.

In 1882 Tolstoy had published **"What Men Live By,"** a beautiful retelling of the old legend of the angel sent to earth by God to teach men to live by love. Chertkov, impressed by the widespread popularity of this short story, urged Tolstoy to contribute similar tales to *Intermediary.* He did, and no doubt the initial popularity of the firm's booklets may be attributed to the fact that three of the early ones contained stories from his pen. His conviction that the masses would read good literature if they could afford to buy it was proved to the hilt, for these *Intermediary* booklets, Russian's "paperbacks," priced at the equivalent of a cent, sold twelve million copies in the first four years of the existence of the firm.

The second grouping among these later short stories could be described as "Folk Tales and Legends." It is made up of a series of narratives written mostly for *Intermediary* and hence aimed primarily at peasants and workers, but their simplicity and charm delight young and old of all social classes. Sources of most if not all of these stories may be found in oral and written literature of the folk, but in retelling the tales Tolstoy has made them entirely his own. He declared in an article, "Truth in Art" (1887), that "there are fairy tales, parables, legends, in which marvellous things are described that never happened or ever could happen, and these legends, fairy tales, and fables are true, because they show wherein the will of God has always been, and is, and will be: they show the truth of the kingdom of God."

In these pieces for *Intermediary* he strove to retain the artlessness of folk literature, its customary trappings of devils, imps, supernatural happenings, repetition of motifs, and otherworldly plots, but at the same time he used them to impart his own moral and religious convictions. And the narrative style he employs has nothing of the saturated realism of his previous fiction. It has the biblical simplicity of one of his favorite tales, that of Joseph and his coat of many colors. The unknown author of this story, Tolstoy writes in *What Is Art?* "did not need to describe in detail, as would be done nowadays, the blood-stained coat of Joseph, the dwelling and dress of Jacob, the pose and attire of Potiphar's wife, and how adjusting the bracelet on her left arm she said, 'Come to me,' and so on, because the content of feeling in this tale is so strong that all details except the most essential—such as that Joseph went out into another room to weep—are superfluous and would only hinder the transmission of emotion. And therefore this tale is accessible to all men, touches people of all nations and classes young and old, and has lasted to our times and will last for thousands of years to come."

"Two Old Men" (1885), **"Where Love Is, God Is"** (1885), and **"The Repentant Sinner"** (1886) fall into Tolstoy's category of "religious art" which transmits feelings of love of God and one's neighbor. The moral of the first story—that the best way to keep one's vow to God and to do His will is for each man to show love and do good to others—does not seem contrived in this appealing narrative of the two old friends who set out on a pilgrimage to Jerusalem. One fails to get there because of his compulsion to help a starving family on the road, whereas his comrade, who reaches the goal and performs all the conventional acts of worship, comes away religiously unmoved. The bland flavor of biblical narrative suffuses **"Where Love Is, God Is,"** and the same may be said of **"The Repentant Sinner,"** but the "instructional" purpose of both stories is allowed to remain too close to the surface.

Characteristic folk-tale content and narrative method predominate in the remaining stories of the group, except for the very brief pieces, **"Evil Allures, but God Endures"** (1885), **"Little Girls Wiser than Men"** (1885), and **"Elias"** (1885), which Tolstoy wrote as illustrative texts to accompany pictures reproduced in *Intermediary.* His intention is to portray the simplest feelings common to all men which, as indicated, he later associated with the category, "universal art." In this respect he succeeds, sometimes quite brilliantly. However, in pure folk literature a moral lesson, if any, is never made explicit, and whenever present it is subordinated to narrative interest in incident and character. This is not always the case with Tolstoy. Though the story of the enmity of peasant neighbors in **"A Spark Neglected Burns the House"** (1885) is absorbing, the old father's moral preaching conveys the impression that the incidents were deliberately devised to prove that one must forgive one's enemies and, if necessary, turn the other cheek.

On the other hand, **"Ivan the Fool"** (1885) is an unblemished folk tale, in which Ivan emerges as a convincing popular hero. There is some humor in Ivan's repeated frustration of the devil's designs on him, and in his dedication to hard work there is an exemplification of a solid folk virtue which is contrasted with the vain hopes of easy success on the part of his two brothers. It has been said that the story contains an indictment of militarism and commercialism, but if this is so the indictment is never allowed to obtrude upon the artistic unity of the narrative. The same may be said of the so-called anti-war element in **"The Empty Drum"** (1891), another effective retelling of a folk tale which, according to Tolstoy, was still current in the Volga region. There is also humor in **"The Three Hermits"** (1886). The rather pompous bishop, after teaching the Lord's Prayer to the ignorant hermits on an island, decides they need no further lessons in the faith when he discovers them running on the surface of the water in pursuit of his ship to seek further instruction from him.

The moral lesson in **"The Imp and the Crust"** (1886) is a natural part of the story, in which the devil finally tricks the kind peasant into drunkenness. If Tolstoy's handling of this gem of a folk tale is regarded as a plea for temperance, it is a conclusion that must be drawn by the reader, for it is never explicitly stated in the text. Tolstoy's dramatization of the story, a comedy entitled *The First Distiller* (1886), . . . does turn out to be an amusing piece of forthright temperance propaganda.

Though interesting characteristics of the Russian peasantry are reflected in **"A Grain As Big As a Hen's Egg"** (1886) and **"The Godson"** (1886), the first appears to have been written specifically to demonstrate that people then, unlike their forebears, have ceased to live by their own labor and depend on that of others. The second is oddly complicated for a story in the folk-tale tradition, perhaps because Tolstoy imposed upon it the dual purpose of showing that one must care more about others than about oneself, and that one must not fear death if one wishes to make one's heart fast to God. It is unnecessary to append a moral to the well-known and consummately narrated **"How Much Land Does a Man Need?"** (1886), for the whole story is about the traditional greed of the peasants for land. The failing betrays one of them, who in the end discovers too late that all the land he requires is the six feet in which he is buried. This uncompromising object lesson in the vanity of human wishes was later repudiated by Chekhov in his tale "Gooseberries," where the narrator pointedly declares: "Man needs not six feet of earth, not a farm, but the whole globe, all nature, where he will have room for the full play of all the capacities and peculiarities of his free spirit."

Before the end of the 1880's Tolstoy appears to have lost interest in turning popular legends and tales into short stories that would illuminate his religious and moral convictions. In 1903, however, a special circumstance led him to attempt more stories of this kind. He was invited to contribute to a volume on behalf of persecuted Jews of Russia, especially those attacked that year in the terrible pogroms at Kishinev. Other distinguished authors, including Chekhov, gladly offered manuscripts for the proposed book. Tolstoy's three brief stories for this purpose were translated into Yiddish by the eminent Jewish writer Sholom Aleichem and appeared in a volume published in Warsaw.

The economy of means in the first of these stories **"Esarhaddon, King of Assyria,"** with its simple moral preachment that when you harm others you harm yourself because all life is one, is matched by **"Work, Death, and Sickness,"** a retelling, says Tolstoy, of a religious legend current among South American Indians. Here, in four short pages, he drives home the lesson that work ought to unite all men so that they might live in unity and love. The last of these tales written to aid the Jewish sufferers, **"Three Questions,"** is equally succinct in detailing the manner in which a baffled king discovers answers to his problems.

The final group, his last short stories, consists of four which Tolstoy never published in his lifetime. In them he reverts to his early manner of fiction-writing before his spiritual conversion, with the difference that he still remains influenced by the special concerns of his new faith. At times he draws upon personal experiences as he did in so many of his previous creative works. This is especially true of **"Memoirs of a Madman,"** which he began to write as early as 1884 and apparently never finished to his own satisfaction. It is a rather thinly disguised fictionized treatment of the oppressive fear of death, which he experienced before his religious change, and its relation to his growing belief that the kind of life he led then was irrational, fit only for a madman, and must be abandoned. Scenes of the visitation of death are as intensely and brilliantly realized as Prince Andrew's striking encounter with death in *War and Peace.*

In **"After the Ball"** (1903), the seventy-five-year-old Tolstoy goes back for inspiration to a love affair as a youthful student at Kazan University. But how vividly and freshly he evokes the atmosphere of the past by employing the saturated realism and psychological probing of his earlier art! At the end of the story, however, there lurks the aged Tolstoy's implied condemnation of the state as a kind of conspiracy not only to exploit citizens, but to demoralize them as well. For after the ball, when the young Ivan Vasilyevich, his mind still filled with the ecstasy of love, accidentally witnesses the horrifying spectacle of a deserter being fatally clubbed through the gauntlet of his fellow-soldiers at the command of a colonel, who is his beloved's father, the hero's passion for the daughter not only grows cold, but he mentally vows never to enter any form of government service.

There can be no doubt that **"Fedor Kuzmich"** (1905) was intended to be a long narrative, but even in its present unfinished state it may stand as a rather well-rounded short story. Again Tolstoy returns to artistic memories and methods of an earlier period, specifically to the historical novel, *War and Peace,* and one of its principal characters—Alexander I. Though there seems to be no diminution in his skill in handling the material of historical fiction, it is also clear that Alexander's attraction for him now is based more on ideological than artistic considerations. Accepting the allegation, believed by many at the time, that Alexander falsified his death in 1825 and secretly disappeared and became a repentant and holy hermit in Siberia, Tolstoy undertook to portray him in this light. Obviously he was intrigued by the analogy between his own hopes and aspirations in his last years and those of this emperor, who supposedly turned his back on a worldly existence in order, in poverty and humility, to live a religious life of thought and good deeds.

In the few highly concentrated pages devoted to **"Alyosha"** (1905), one of the last short stories Tolstoy wrote, he is again the pure artist, untroubled and uninfluenced by moral or religious preachments. Or perhaps it would be better to say that all he believed and hoped for is artistically sublimated in the radiant image of "Alyosha the pot," the simple peasant drudge who in his cheerful, self-sacrificing service to others discovers that perfect peace which Tolstoy sought for in vain at the end of his life. The story is a perfect masterpiece in miniature. (pp. 135-45)

Ernest J. Simmons, in his Introduction to Tolstoy's Writings, *The University of Chicago Press, 1968, 219 p.*

R. F. Christian (essay date 1969)

[*In the following excerpt, Christian discusses Tolstoy's short fiction from the years 1856-63.*]

During [the years 1856-63], Tolstoy's literary output was not especially high. ***The Cossacks*** apart, his main published works, in chronological order of publication, were ***The Snowstorm*** (1856), ***Two Hussars*** (1856), **"Meeting a Moscow Acquaintance in the Detachment"** (1856), **"Lucerne"** (1857), **"Albert"** (1858), ***Three Deaths*** (1859), ***Family Happiness*** (1859) and ***Polikushka*** (1863). In their different ways they are a very clear reflection of Tolstoy's beliefs, interests and prejudices, but from a literary point of view their compass is too small to accommodate the overt didacticism and moral pamphleteering which in diluted form in a larger work could be taken painlessly, and perhaps even enjoyed. In a word, they do not give sufficient rein to the reader's imagination. ***The Snowstorm*** grew out of an incident on a journey from the Caucasus. It is an unhappy amalgam of narrative description and recollections of childhood which come and go as the narrator dozes off on his journey through the night. (***The Cossacks,*** it will be remembered, employs a similar device.) In the manner of Turgenev's *A Sportsman's Sketches* it paints largely sympathetic portraits of ordinary working people—the various peasant drivers who brave the storm. There is no suspense or excitement about the story, nor does the snowstorm lead to complications and adventures of the kind which Pushkin crowded with far greater economy into a much smaller space in his tale of the same title. Perhaps the only point of literary interest is the device, familiar enough in Tolstoy's later writing, of connecting the details of dreams with phenomena happening simultaneously in the outside world (a bell ringing outside appearing in the dream as a dog barking or an organ playing), and the moment of waking from a dream with the last sensation carrying over from the dream (the sensation of something pressing on one's foot being so strong that the dreamer rubs his foot immediately on awakening).

For his next published story Tolstoy took as his theme the contrast between the past and the present in the persons of a father and son of markedly different character, the younger generation suffering by comparison with the older. The basis of the story is a simple juxtaposition, neat and regular, and executed with an almost geometrical precision. The first eight chapters are devoted to the father, the second eight to the son. An amusing and ironical, if cumbersome and sententious, preface rings the praises of the good old days in a lengthy period, in fact one sentence, of a type which Tolstoy was particularly fond of using (for example in *The Decembrists*): 'In the 1800s, at a time when there were no railways, no highroads, no gaslight [etc., etc.]—in those naïve days when . . . when . . . when . . . [etc., etc.]—in the naïve days of Masonic Lodges, Martinists, the Tugenbund [etc., etc.]—there was a meeting of landowners in the provincial town of K.' Tolstoy had been reading *The Newcomes* shortly before, and the similarity with a passage from the 'Overture' to Thackeray's novel ('There was once a time when the sun used to shine brighter than it appears to do in this latter half of the nineteenth century . . . ') is particularly striking. The second half of the story (Chapter 9) starts by picking up the preface to the first part in a style and idiom which immediately recall the construction of **"Sevastopol in May,"** and within this framework Turbin father and son, after an interval of twenty years, visit the same place, meet the same people and enact the same sequence of card-playing and philandering—but in a totally different spirit and with a totally different effect. The father is a handsome roué, gambler and seducer, but he is gallant, generous and charming. The son inherits the same weaknesses, but behaves in a mean, cold and calculating way. Tolstoy's English biographer, Aylmer Maude [in *The Life of Tolstoy*], draws attention to the English flavour of ***The Two Hussars*** when he calls it 'a rollicking tale with flashes of humour resembling Charles Lever's' and it has been well observed that Turbin *pére* is portrayed in a somewhat Dickensian manner, while Turbin *fils* is in the Thackeray vein. Translated into Russian terms, the father is a Pushkin hero, the son a Gogolian. 'One might say', observes Eykhenbaum, exaggerating his valid point for the sake of emphasis, 'that in ***The Two Hussars*** a comparison is drawn between Dubrovsky and Khlestakov [*Lev Tolstoi,* Vol. 1]. In its jocular, light-hearted tone, its wealth of plot interest, its absence of any serious thought, its surface level of description and its lack of psychological profundity, the story is hardly typical of its author—perhaps indeed one should call it an 'entertainment', and within its unpretentious limits a very successful one.

Less successful are Tolstoy's next two stories, which have the common theme of the artist and society. [The critic explains in a footnote that " **'Meeting a Moscow Acquaintance in the Detachment,'** which appeared in 1856, failed to make any impression at all," and therefore is not addressed in this essay.] **"Albert"** owes its origin to an encounter between Tolstoy and a gifted but drink-besotted violinist, which is elaborated into a conflict between the brilliant, unstable and childishly helpless artist-alcoholic and a Tolstoyan philanthropist, determined to save the artist for society and at the same time to reap the satisfaction of his own good deed. The trouble with the story, which came with difficulty and had five different titles at different stages of its composition, is that there is nothing to suggest the brilliance of the musician—merely the author's verbal assurance. In *Doctor Zhivago* Pasternak succeeded in creating a poet by allowing him to write great poems. In *Anna Karenina* Tolstoy managed to create a convincing portrait of a painter by showing how the ordinary trivial incidents of everyday life, his quarrels with his wife, his shopping at the tobacconist's, were intimately bound up with his own creative life. With music the problem is more difficult, as Thomas Mann found in trying to convince readers of *Doctor Faustus* that Leverkühn is a great composer, although the method Tolstoy was later to use with Mikhailov would appear to be equally applicable to the art of music—one can feel the temper and mood of the artist and something of his spiritual elation and depression. But in the last resort one has to take it on trust that a fictional painter or composer or violinist is a great artist. Tolstoy's Albert is a man of 'intuition', not of theories or ideas; whatever he says or does or whatever he plays is done instinctively. So far so good. But what does he do when he is not playing? He drinks. There is no other dimension to his life. In an early draft Tolstoy had envisaged broadening the scope of the story by introducing an artist and a connoisseur of music to discuss Albert's case and debate his usefulness to society in words reminiscent of the questions put to the poet by the crowd in Pushkin's poem [*The Poet and the Crowd*]. But the final version is less ambitious. Tolstoy himself was very dissatisfied with it, but sent it nevertheless to *The Contemporary.* Nekrasov decided he could not publish it for the following reasons: 'The thing mostly to blame for your failure is the unsuccessful choice of subject which, quite apart from the fact that it is very hackneyed, is almost impossibly difficult and thankless. While the seamy side of your hero is plain for all to see, how can you express in a tangible and convincing manner his brilliant side? And if that is not there, there is no story . . . ' Tolstoy duly revised the story and Nekrasov published it with grave misgivings, which were justified by its cold reception. Equally coldly received by critics and readers alike was **"Lucerne,"** which focuses on the attitude of society to the artist rather than on the personality of the artist himself. Its overt tendentiousness and irascibility really puts it beyond the range of *belles lettres* into the category of polemical journalism. Its origin can be found in a diary entry for 7 July 1857 when Tolstoy was staying at a Swiss tourist centre, and in a long letter to his friend Botkin. The diary reads:

> Walked to *privathaus.* On the way back at night—cloudy, with the moon breaking through—heard several marvellous voices. Two bell towers on a wide street. Little man with guitar singing Tyrolean songs—superb. Gave him something and invited him to sing opposite the Schweizerhof. He got nothing and walked away ashamed, the crowd laughing as he went . . . Caught him up and invited him to the Schweizerhof for a drink. They put us in a separate room. Singer vulgar but pathetic. We drank. The waiter laughed and the doorkeeper sat down. This infuriated me—swore at them and got terribly worked up . . .

The incident is inflated into a story and then deflated again into a paragraph at the end of it, as though implying that the content of the story could really be expressed in a few lines and emphasising for the reader's benefit that 'this is fact, not fiction':

> On the 7th of July 1857 a poverty-stricken strolling player sang and played the guitar for half an hour in front of the Schweizerhof Hotel in Lucerne where the very rich people stay. About a hundred people listened to him. The singer asked them all three times to give him something. Not one of them gave him anything, and many people laughed at him.

The very rich people being mainly English, Tolstoy prefaces **"Lucerne"** with a withering denunciation of their arrogance, complacency, insensitivity, and cold, silent awareness of their own superiority. 'And yet not all these frozen people are stupid and unfeeling,' he adds in a moment of generosity; 'then why do they deprive themselves of one of life's greatest pleasures—the enjoyment that comes from the intercourse of man with man?' The trouble with these national generalisations, and in the same context the pointed contrast between the irregularity of the beauty of nature and the artificially straight, man-made quay built to please the English, is not whether they are true or false, but that they are gratuitously disbursed by the author and do not emerge as deductions which the discriminating reader can make from the characters themselves and their mutual relationships. Tolstoy's peculiar gifts of vital characterisation and searching mental and spiritual analysis are hardly put to use at all. It is true that the narrator allows himself a certain vindictive delight in describing the pleasure of deliberately not making way for a complacent Englishman but jostling him with his elbow—a psychological moment which brings to mind a similar scene in *Notes from the Underground* where the hero asserts his individuality by crowding off the pavement a man who has offended him—Tolstoy's healthy anger contrasting typically with the poisonous spleen of Dostoevsky's 'underground man'. But psychologically the story does not register, and one's reactions are purely mental ones to the logic or otherwise of the statements put out. It is true that this incident would have been impossible in any French, German or Italian village? Could a hundred people, even though they were English, remain almost completely silent throughout a meal? What basis of comparison is there between a luxury hotel in Switzerland and a cheap Paris *pension* as a criterion for judging the respective habits and manners of the English and the French? These *ex cathedra* statements are the prerogative of the journalist, not the artist. There is no characterisation. The singer is given no identity. He has virtually nothing to say. The incident over, there is some tedious moralising and rhetoric to the effect that the ways of God are inscrutable, and that the poor downtrodden singer may perhaps be happier than the rich well-fed tourist, and that the author has no right to pity the singer or be angry with the aristocracy. Needless to say, the story was not well received by Tolstoy's friends, the Botkins and the Annenkovs, who could hardly be expected to sympathise with his contemptuous attitude to educated Westerners. Turgenev very shrewdly summed up **"Lucerne"** as a mixture of Rousseau, Thackeray and the short Orthodox Catechism—'Go your own way and go on writing,' he said, 'only not moral-political sermons like **"Lucerne,"** of course!' If the story is still remembered today, it is as the first piece of Tolstoy's fiction which is unambiguously, consistently and irascibly hostile to the West European *bourgeoisie.*

Three Deaths reads like a parable illustrating a simple idea, expressed by the familiar Tolstoyan device of contrast. In his own words:

> My idea was: three creatures died—a lady, a peasant and a tree. The lady is pathetic and repulsive because she lied all her life and lied on the point of death. Christianity as she understands it has not solved the problem of life and death for her. Why die when you want to live? With her mind and her imagination she believes in the future promises of Christianity, but all her being kicks against it and she has no other consolation (except a pseudo-Christian one). She is repulsive and pathetic. The peasant dies peacefully just because he is not a Christian. His religion is different, although from habit he observed the Christian ritual. His religion is nature, which he lived with. With his own hands he felled trees, sowed rye and cut it, and slaughtered sheep. Sheep were born, children were born, old men died—and he fully understood this law and never transgressed it like the lady, but looked it fairly and squarely in the face. *Une brute,* you say, and what's wrong with being *une brute? Une brute* is happiness and beauty, harmony with the whole world, not discord, as with the lady. The tree dies peacefully, nobly and beautifully. Beautifully because it does not lie, does not break down, is not afraid, has no regrets. This is my idea . . .

Three Deaths is a fairly faithful illustration of this idea. The overt class message is not likely to convince those who do not believe that because a person is a 'lady' she is for that reason more likely to be mendacious and repulsive, or that because a man is a peasant he is *ipso facto* likely to have a more beautiful and harmonious soul. The story is too short for the characters to be developed, and one has to accept the author's word that the one has more inner peace of mind than the other for the reasons implied. The religious message that the letter of Christianity is mortifying but the pagan spirit of 'natural' religion is quickening evokes a more sympathetic response than the thesis that 'ladies' are nasty because they are 'ladies'. But Leskov handles it more artistically, because more discreetly, in his powerful story *At the End of the World.* The death of the tree is an embarrassment. How can a tree die nobly and fearlessly? Or ignobly and with trepidation? In fact Tolstoy, in recapitulating his idea in the letter quoted above, appears to have forgotten that he had described the tree as 'tottering on its roots in fear'. The background to the story, as befits its sympathy for the natural life, is the seasons of the year. It is autumn, cold, grey, damp and nasty when the peasant dies and when nature is dying with him. It is spring when the lady dies, and all that is natural bursts into life. Although the story is so short, there is no mistaking Tolstoy's stamp on every page. The husband of the dying woman thinks of the consequences for himself of her death. The dying peasant who gives his new boots away, instinctively acts for the good of others. The unavailing presence of the doctor and the priest at the woman's bedside emphasises Tolstoy's prejudice against the ritual practices of sacred and secular healers—the negative side of his positive belief that in the important crises of life and death, help comes not from without but from within. The opportunity is not missed to draw attention to the fact that the husband addresses his wife in French, not Russian. It is a measure of the artistic limitations of this story that Tolstoy, who rightly believed that a work of literature should not be able to be summarised but is capable of being expressed only in the way in which it has been expressed, should have been able to condense the full essence of ***Three Deaths*** into a dozen lines of summary without much sacrifice or distortion.

Tolstoy's next published work of fiction, ***Family Happiness,*** was written against the background of a topical social problem which was very close to his heart—the place of women in society and in the home. The novels of George Sand, the writings of Proudhon and Michelet, and Tolstoy's own courtship of Arseneva all served to remind him that he was not married but would like to be, and that he must first clarify his ideas about the nature of love, the purpose of marriage and the rôle of the ideal husband and wife. 'Il faut que tu crées ta femme,' wrote Michelet. Tolstoy agreed. His letters to Arseneva (1856), with whom he seriously contemplated marriage, are the best source material for ***Family Happiness,*** although a good case has been made out to support Tolstoy's liking for the climate of ideas generated by Proudhon's *De la Justice dans la Révolution et dans L'Église,* parts of which are devoted to marriage, and Michelet's *L'Amour,* both of which appeared in the year (1858) when Tolstoy was making his first start on ***Family Happiness,*** and both of which defend marriage against the recently fashionable advocacy of 'free love'. The letters to Arseneva, which advise her among other things to go for a walk every day and to put on her corsets and stockings by herself, and which reproach her for her bad taste in hats, also plan the details of the ideal married life with scrupulous and pedantic care. They recommend where to live in summer and winter, how many rooms an apartment should have and on what floor, what the husband should do to make his peasants happy, what he should teach his wife, and how she should divide her time between music, reading, and helping her husband . . . With these plans in mind, Tolstoy embarks on his first attempt at treating the theme of love in fiction, and not surprisingly does so in a calculating, static and predictable manner, making his characters play to the rules of the game as *he* understands them. The story is told in the first person, and takes the form of the reminiscences of a married woman—her courtship, marriage, brief idyllic happiness, estrangement, and eventual reconciliation based on the subordination of selfish love to the wider ideal of duty to the family ('love of my children and the father of my children'). The woman emerges a little more fully than the man—she may have owed something to Esther in *Bleak House,* as well as to Arseneva—and it is a remarkable achievement on Tolstoy's part to have conveyed the innocent awakening of a young girl's love in a manner which many women readers have found truthful and convincing. But it is poetry of atmosphere rather than subtlety of characterisation which one remembers in the early chapters of the story, which have a greater charm than the later schematised version of married life; for after all, Tolstoy had courted Arseneva, not married her. The following passage is the prelude to a moonlight walk which Masha, the narrator, takes with her future husband and her chaperone:

> 'Just look what a night it is!' Sergei Mikhailych called out from the drawing-room, as he stood by the open French window looking into the garden.
>
> We joined him, and it really was such a night as I have never seen since. A full moon shone above the house behind us so that it was not visible, and half the shadow cast by the roof, the pillars and the verandah awning lay slanting and foreshortened on the gravel path and the round lawn. Everything else was bright and bedecked with the silver of the dew and the moonlight. The broad path through the flower beds—on one side of which the shadows of the dahlias and their supports lay aslant—ran on, all bright and cold and with its rough gravel glittering, until it vanished in the mist. The roof of the conservatory shone bright through the trees and a gathering mist rose from the glen. Bright too were the branches of the lilac bushes, already partly leafless. One could make out every single dew-drenched flower. Light and shade so mingled together that the avenues seemed to be not paths and trees, but transparent houses, swaying and vibrating. To our right, in the shadow of the house, everything was black, indistinguishable and uncanny. But all the brighter and more conspicuous in the darkness was the fantastic, leafy crown of a poplar tree which for some reason was oddly poised there aloft in the bright light close to the house, and had not vanished far away into the retreating dark blue sky.
>
> 'Let's go for a walk,' I said.
>
> Katya agreed, but told me to put on my galoshes.
>
> 'There's no need to,' I said. 'Sergei Mikhailych will give me his arm.'
>
> As if that could stop me getting my feet wet . . .

Typical of Tolstoy is the juxtaposition of light and darkness, the repeated emphasis on a single word—in this case 'bright'—the careful description of shadows and of what they obscure or leave revealed, the simple, spontaneous remarks punctuating a lyrical narrative which never soars too high but keeps close to the earth which is the source of Tolstoy's power—and the occasional, quiet flash of humour. There are many such passages in the first half of ***Family Happiness,*** but they are less frequent in the later stages where interest in mood and its associations with nature gives place to a predetermined transition from one state to another. The dialogue becomes at times inept, and there are some embarrassing passages which might have been culled from an old-fashioned schoolgirl's magazine: when, for example, the wife is momentarily tempted by the prospect of a society liaison:

> I was so longing to throw myself headlong into the abyss of forbidden pleasures which was suddenly opening up and drawing me in . . .
>
> 'I am so unhappy,' I thought, 'let more and more misfortunes fall upon my head.'
>
> He embraced me with one arm and bent over my face. 'Let shame and sin be heaped still higher on my head.'
>
> 'Je vous aime,' he whispered in a voice which was so like my husband's. I thought of my husband and child as erstwhile dear creatures with whom all was now over. But suddenly round the corner I heard the voice of L. M. calling me. I pulled myself together, snatched my arm away and without a glance at him, almost ran after L. M.

This is hardly sounding the depths of a woman's heart. Nor is the motivation for the heroine's renunciation of society a convincing one. Why does she return to her husband? Is it a change of heart, or simply a sense of pique at being out of her depth? Or just a desire for peace and quiet? The husband, too, seems tired. There is a flavour of Turgenev at his most wistful—the past is gone, youth is over, there is no excitement in store but only the desire for a quiet life in which passion is replaced by habit. Will the woman be satisfied? She ought to be, according to the plan. But the story breaks off where it should really start. Towards the end it shows all the signs of hasty composition. Some of its episodic characters are denoted merely by initials. It has no complexity or natural growth; and while its beautiful evocation of the raptures of youthful, romantic love more than compensates for its sketchiness and didacticism, the story as a whole left Tolstoy so dissatisfied that he did not wish to publish it. Was fiction, he wondered, his real calling? Were there not more urgent jobs to be done? In 1860 he wrote to Fet:

> There is nothing to prevent lovers of the classics, of whom I am one, seriously reading poems and stories and seriously discussing them. But now we need something else. We don't need to learn,

but we do need to teach Martha and Taras at least a little of what we know.

There was an interval of nearly four years before Tolstoy, by this time a married man, ventured into print again with ***The Cossacks*** (begun ten years previously) and ***Polikushka,*** which he started in Brussels in 1861, the year of the emancipation of the serfs. In between, his literary efforts had been devoted more or less exclusively to his educational journal *Yasnaya Polyana.* And because of his school activities and his close daily contact with peasant children it was only fitting that his next work of fiction should be devoted very largely to the peasantry. ***Polikushka*** in fact is Tolstoy's first story to have a peasant as its central figure. He is a serf with a tarnished reputation, entrusted by his mistress, who has tried to reform him, with the responsible task of collecting a sum of money from a neighbouring town. He loses the money on the journey home and commits suicide. His baby child is accidentally drowned in its bath. His wife goes out of her mind. Threaded into the plot is the story of another peasant, whose nephew is the victim of the recruiting system and whom he is too mean to buy off. He finds the money, returns it to the mistress and is presented with it, not as a reward but in the belief that it is 'unlucky money'. The peasant is so troubled by his dreams and so persuaded that 'money causes sin' that he uses it to ransom his nephew and reunite him with his family. The story may be read in different ways, for it is neither moralistic nor overtly didactic like the stories of the later 1850s. Those who regard it as a salutary illustration of the theme that money is the root of all evil are rebuked by Tolstoy's former secretary, Gusev, who declares categorically that the basic theme is 'the moral oppression of serfdom'. But this contention ignores the universal applicability of the mental anguish of a man who feels he has let down a person who has helped and trusted him. A Soviet Polikushka might have done the same thing if his 'benefactor' had been his factory manager. The ownership of one person by another, disgraceful as it is, is not the real cause of human misery—not but what a reading of ***Polikushka*** strengthens one's antipathy to the evils of serfdom, the squalid lives of its victims and the iniquities of the recruiting system. But here the emphasis is surely on the moral dilemma of trust seemingly betrayed, and this is enhanced by the detachment with which Tolstoy writes without betraying his own sympathies and without apportioning vices and virtues, praise and blame, in a schematic and preordained manner. The tragedy is not the inevitable outcome of serfdom (Rebecca West once somewhat flippantly observed that it could have been avoided if there had been a reliable postal service) but it is enacted against an unlovely background where the peasant Dutlov is, if anything, a more unattractive character than the mistress of the village. Virtually unnoticed by the critics, it won the qualified praise of Turgenev in a letter to Fet and the unqualified disapproval of Fet himself. Turgenev wrote:

> After you had gone I read Tolstoy's ***Polikushka*** and marvelled at the power of his great talent. Only an awful lot of material is wasted and there was no need for him to have drowned the son. It's terrible enough without that. But there are some truly wonderful pages.

Fet, on the other hand, complained:

> Everything about ***Polikushka*** is crumbling, putrid, poverty-stricken, painful . . . it is all accurate and truthful, but so much the worse for that. It is the deep, broad foot-mark of a giant, but a foot-mark which has turned off into a bog. I am not against the subject, but against the absence of any ideal purity. Venus, arousing desire, is evil. She should only sing of beauty in marble. The stench itself should acquire fragrance in the creative process, after passing through *Das Labyrinth der Brust* of the artist. But ***Polikushka*** smells of its corrupted environment . . .

Tolstoy replied:

> You are right of course. But there are not many readers like you. ***Polikushka*** is drivel on the first subject that comes into the head of a man who 'wields a good pen'.

Fet's strictures hardly deserve attention, but it is surprising that none of these writers saw fit to comment on Tolstoy's unusual experiment of describing Polikushka and his background not in standard literary Russian but in a language more appropriate to the manner in which one peasant might talk about another. In his earlier tales Tolstoy had frequently couched the dialogue of his soldiers in non-literary form, but this is the first important example of his adapting his own narrative style to the character and milieu he is describing. Patchy and uneven, ***Polikushka*** is nevertheless a powerful and moving story, the very objectivity of which immediately places it on a higher artistic plane than **"Albert"** or **"Lucerne."**

It is very probable that in the same year as ***Polikushka*** was published, Tolstoy also wrote ***Strider,*** which did not, however, appear until 1885. This unorthodox and imaginative story of the life and death of a horse, the central part of which is related by the horse itself, is poignant and affective. The consequences of being different (a piebald and a gelding), the themes of alienation, injustice and the inconstancy of love inevitably arouse pity; while the vision of human beings and their system of private property, incomprehensible from a horse's point of view, provides the sort of opportunity for trenchant and well-aimed satire which some earlier writers found in the juxtaposition of European and oriental civilisations based on widely different conventions. (pp. 82-96)

R. F. Christian, in his Tolstoy: A Critical Introduction, *Cambridge at the University Press, 1969, 291 p.*

Nancy Dworsky (essay date 1975)

[*In the excerpt below, Dworsky examines* Hadji Murád *as an expression of several themes central to Tolstoy's writings.*]

When, between 1865 and 1869, Tolstoy was writing *War and Peace,* he perfected a narrative technique that presented his world view more convincingly than any of the arguments he advanced to support it. The essence of this narrative technique, which he himself labeled "peep-show," consists in its use of relatively short scenes that jump between places, times, people, activities, social strata, and even narrative perspectives, without evident order or direction, but with the result that stories develop and grow with beginnings, middles, and endings, and relate to one another to form an epic panorama. What emerges from reading this is a conviction that somehow, however random the process of living and acting may seem, life holds together and makes sense. In this Tolstoyan world individual people act freely in accordance with their will and character, but the sum of all such actions when seen from a distant perspective shows a pattern that could not be changed by any person living within the framework of the whole.

Indeed, Tolstoy does not deal at all with the possibility of people trying to evade fate or change it, except to satirize those in positions of power who believe that their will is the causative factor in events. Rather than a struggle between man's will and mysterious forces of fate, Tolstoy presents a vision of rightness, appropriateness—the classical *ta prepa*—in that which happens. It is at the same time a reflection of the Homeric concept of fate where one knows what was fated simply because it has happened, and an affirmation of organic continuity and wholeness. *War and Peace* exemplifies both, not as alternatives but as complementary perspectives on the same phenomena.

Polikushka, a short story written in 1863, employs the same narrative technique and shares the same world view. It is not concerned with history and does not deal with family formations and dissolutions as *War and Peace* does, but it affirms an organic view by crossing between families at a single moment in time. The tragedy and death of Polikushka provides the salvation of Dutlov. By the sympathetic presentation of both tales, the reader is invited to grieve and to rejoice at the same time and about the same event: he is invited to accept the wholeness and interdependence of life and death in the narrative, rather than to judge, make distinctions and criticize the action.

How remarkable, then, that Tolstoy returned to this narrative technique late in his life when he was embroiled in desperate judgment, criticism, and rejection of all that he saw around him. Yet he did so in ***Hadji Murad,*** begun in 1896, completed in 1904, and only published in 1911 after his death. This short novel presents Tolstoy's last clear-eyed vision of the world. Critics have called it "a masterpiece of the highest order" but have not found it to reflect Tolstoy's most serious concerns. Indeed, Henri Troyat says that "it is a strange thing that Tolstoy should have written this tale, devoid of all religious considerations, whose extraordinary beauty alone is enough to content the reader." But in this late work Tolstoy addresses themes central to his whole intellectual life. Not only does the novel speak again to the corruption inherent in power, and to the beauty of the noble savage. It also explicates an understanding of art and culture that moves beyond his theoretical essays, and it exposes a vision of himself that is more convincingly humble than all his religious exhortations.

In ***Hadji Murad*** Tolstoy made the narrative technique of *War and Peace* serve a dreadful vision of random destructiveness, where effects of action are not only independent of will or intent, but are separable from both, and unpredictable from any perspective—truly inevitable, because truly irrational. This is the vision derived from the death of the peasant Avdeev early in the novel. It was caused simply by the high spirits of Poltaratsky who orders firing for no reason. Avdeev's death might recall ***Polikushka*** in its benefit to his wife, pregnant by a salesclerk with whom she was living, for "now no one could reproach her any more, and the clerk could marry her." But here her relief does not reassure us, since it is qualified by her guilt and by the deep hopelessness of "her whole ruined life."

The vision of irrationality is reinforced by the raid on the Tatar *aoul* that was caused by a flattering remark of a courtier to the tsar, a remark that had an effect only because the tsar was suffering from bad temper at the time. No sensible relation can be seen between the tsar's order and the burning of the *aoul* and polluting of the well; the causes and effects have nothing to do with one another. And this is a very different matter from the ineffectuality of orders given at battles in *War and Peace.* While Tolstoy satirizes Napoleon at Borodino for thinking his orders affect the battle, his satire is directed only at misplaced self-importance. Effective or not, all the generals in a battle are fitting parts of the large drama of history that Tolstoy so confidently knows is being played.

When Tolstoy was writing ***Hadji Murad*** his attention had shifted from the great panorama of history to a ploughed field and a broken thistle. The intent behind destroying every living thing in that field was to bring forth sustenance for man—just as the intent behind the conquest of the Tatars was to spread Christianity—but Tolstoy gives no ground for confidence that either intent will be fulfilled. All his evidence suggests that intentions bear no relation to effect.

In ***Hadji Murad*** this area of intention and fulfillment has both political and religious dimensions. On the one hand, the action concerns the extension of Russian power over the Tatar regions, with the loss of Tatar political autonomy; on the other, it concerns the extension of Christianity and the concomitant destruction of the pagan ethos. Tolstoy is, of course, not interested in military history for its own sake; he is interested in the morality of power.

In *War and Peace* where the moral dimension is most muted, Tolstoy condemned those in power not because they were ineffectual, but because they were unserious and unbeautiful. They occupy their positions on a basis of egregious self-deception which others support for their own practical purposes. Beautiful and serious feelings belong to those outside of power. Tolstoy had later examined the inhumanity inherent in positions of power in ***The Death of Ivan Ilych*** (1886). Ivan discovers during his illness that he is not an abstraction but a human being. Through his career as a lawyer he treated people as though they were abstractions, denying their individual, personal humanity. And his doctor, now in power over him, treats him as an abstraction. This is still more of a social commentary than a moral one, attached as it is to a bureaucratic milieu. It becomes, however, the basic insight that makes the Christian mystic Tolstoy also the political anarchist Tolstoy.

Tolstoy's personal moral condemnation of power came still later in, for example, the short story **"After the Ball"** (1903), written in the same period as ***Hadji Murad.*** While the emotional power of the story rests on the narrator's discovery of the reality behind social elegance, its horror derives from its moral statement. The colonel, in his capacity of colonel, is having a man beaten to death. The victim calls upon his "brothers" for mercy, but the colonel, through the exercise of his power, has turned those brothers into executioners. This is a clear and unambiguous moral judgment, standing uncomplicated by social or aesthetic considerations.

A similar situation exists in ***Hadji Murad*** when Tsar Nicholas orders punishment for the student who has struck a professor. As in **"After the Ball"** there is no ambiguity in Tolstoy's position. The tsar is a terrible and disgusting figure as, with a flourish of the pen, he condemns the young man to run the gauntlet of a thousand men twelve times because "Thank God, we have no capital punishment. And it is not for me to introduce it." Tolstoy uses abstraction here to explain, in a way, what the tsar is doing: he is playing a role, dealing with concepts and poses of justice and mercy, because there is no real person there to be beaten to death, only a written report submitted by a flunky. Nevertheless, unlike the case of Ivan Ilych, the moral judgment is clear. By having the tsar invoke God Tolstoy emphasizes to the reader that Nicholas is doing evil.

But the tsar is only one man in a position of power in ***Hadji Murad.*** This clear, unambiguously evil figure stands parallel to Shamil, his Tatar counterpart, who plays a similar scene when he tells Hadji Murad's son to write his father and tell him that unless he surrenders Shamil will put out his son's eyes. There are elements in this scene that could make Shamil appear more evil than Nicholas, or at the least—as some critics insist—equally repellent. First, there is no excuse of distance: the boy is standing in front of him. Second, Shamil is using him to further his own ambition, while the tsar has no personal stake in punishing the student. Third, the boy has committed no crime; he is condemned simply for being Hadji Murad's son. But what Tolstoy does is make each of these facts mitigate the reader's judgment of Shamil so that finally, however terrible the scene may be, the Imam is simply not as evil as the tsar.

First of all, Tolstoy prepares the reader to admire Shamil. He makes him beautiful and noble by dressing him starkly in black while his followers provide him with a gaudy bejeweled background. And the language applied to him, *e.g.* "His pale face . . . like stone, completely immobile," comes from the romantic conventions of the noble savage, perfectly familiar in Russian literature and in Tolstoy's own early works. So a certain background has been prepared before the reader faces the crucial scene.

In that scene the boy is looking at Shamil with "tremulous veneration," and while this makes the threat more terrible, it does nothing to undermine the reader's admiration of Shamil. Tolstoy turns the fact of face to face confrontation to Shamil's advantage simply by his honesty, especially in contrast to the tsar's posing and strutting with such real consequences. The same can be said of the self-serving aspects of the case: at least Shamil has a real situation to deal with—a real enemy who is fighting against him and whom he is trying to subdue. In contrast, the tsar has only his vanity to protect. He exercises destructive power purely for the satisfaction of his own ego. The guilt or innocence of the victims becomes irrelevant, for Tolstoy clearly cannot consider striking a professor to be a crime worthy of serious consequences.

These are all minor points, but they become part of a major difference between Shamil and Nicholas. Shamil is acting within a recognizable cultural context, the values of which conform to his behavior. The fact that the guiltless victim admires his persecutor and does not question the propriety of his acts underscores this. And it is further put into relief by the Russian student's crime which is one of insubordination, of rejecting the constituted authority. If the reader is horrified by Shamil it is because the reader is suffering from moral inhibitions that are foreign to the Tatar culture. Shamil is an embodiment and norm of that culture, not an individual evil person.

By contrast, Tsar Nicholas supposedly embodies a Christian culture so superior to the Tatar that it is worth destroying the beauty to realize the morality—this is the implicit parallel to ploughing the field to produce food. But the actual culture of Russia conflicts with Christian values. The customs by which people live include flattery, power, self-aggrandizement—the demands made by a hierarchical ruling structure that does not and cannot provide a framework for Christian love between people. What happens in this dislocation between cultural structure and its avowed values, is that the values become rationalizations. Christian morality becomes nothing but empty procedures that can be used for completely non-Christian ends. This is the real nature of the tsar's argument about capital punishment. Tolstoy's irony and anger is not simply directed against the tsar's abuse of power—it is a reaction to a cultural structure not fit to embody Christian values, that therefore makes coherent action impossible.

Shamil's action is not good by Christian standards, but it does not have to be in order to be valid and right within a non-Christian culture. Indeed, this is how a noble savage can be both noble and savage without being sentimentalized, as Tolstoy had shown forty years earlier in ***The Cossacks*** (1863). In that story, which avoids moral distinctions between the cultures, Olenin cannot be a Cossack simply because he is not one; he can, however, be a good Russian. In ***Hadji Murad*** the Tatars can be good Tatars, but the Christians cannot be good Christians. The difference lies in the relation between the structures of the cultures and their values. The Tatar structure, patriarchal and hierarchal, served for values of honor and courage and sexual decorum. The Russian structure of bureaucracy did not serve for values of mercy, love, and sexual purity.

This particular theme of bureaucratic social structures undermining Christian morals is the familiar base of Tolstoy's anarchism, and it goes back to *Anna Karenina* (1877), the novel that questioned the essentially amoral view of *War and Peace* and thereby precipitated a personal crisis for Tolstoy, at first moral and religious, then also political. Tolstoy presented the problem most clearly in the person of Karenin. He belongs to the sphere of Petersburg society that Tolstoy virtually dismissed in *War and Peace* as people with inferior souls, not worthy of serious consideration. In *Anna Karenina* he did consider some of them seriously and found that the possibility of spiritual growth and moral feeling that Karenin experienced at the mystery of birth was subverted by social pressures and turned into a vicious opposite in the respectable Christian mysticism practiced by Countess Lydia Ivanovna.

In the ***Death of Ivan Ilych*** Tolstoy went a step further, examining how bureaucratic life destroyed spiritual life, and still later in, for example, **"A Talk Among Leisured People"** (1890) he spelled out the point even more directly. Finally in ***Hadji Murad*** this view of a bureaucratic Christian society stood opposite a coherent, amoral pagan society, with dramatic and tragic effect. Not only is the tsar both helpless and evil, capable only of destruction both personally and politically. Even the peasants, whom Tolstoy had always held free from the corruptions of society, are in ***Hadji Murad*** victims of the discrepancy between the culture and its values. The story of Avdeev and his family exemplifies this. Not only is Avdeev's wife caught up, but also his mother, who cannot find an outlet for love except by giving needed money to the church for unnecessary works, and his father, who cannot find fulfillment in work because the draft took his son, and his brother, who takes to drink because he bears the brunt of his father's anger. All in the family do their best, but their lives go on without joy and without hope. Dissatisfied, bereaved, angry and guilty, only the pressure of necessary work saves them from despair. In ***Hadji Murad*** Tolstoy's peasants for the first time have nothing to teach us.

The life that does have something to teach us is clearly that of Hadji Murad himself. He is a compelling and disquieting figure, somehow enormously larger than anyone else in the story, boldly and clearly drawn, and yet complex and difficult to decipher. This difficulty has led critics to suggest that Tolstoy was ambivalent about his own religious values and that deep within he admired the pagan warrior more than any Christian saint. But such analysis begs the question of what, exactly, constitutes the greatness of Hadji Murad, and what are we to understand from his life?

Actually, the hero embodies two themes: his life epitomizes the destruction of paganism by Christianity, which is central to the whole narrative; and it exemplifies the role of art as mediator between a culture and individual self-realization, a theme that is extraneous to the novel except in the life of the protagonist.

The theme of destruction to allow the growth of Christianity is openly symbolized at the beginning and end by the crimson thistle destroyed by the plough. Behind this symbol is not only a tale of political history, but of moral history. To see the dynamics of that moral history, we must understand a distinction Tolstoy made—and said Western Europeans failed to make—between the good and the beautiful. The tragedy enacted in this novel is the destruction of beauty to cultivate goodness that did not, in fact, root and grow in the ploughed field.

Tolstoy, at age eighty, riding in the fields of his estate Yasnaya Polyana.

Hadji Murad is explicable and acceptable when we see him as beautiful but not good—which, for Tolstoy, necessitates a Christian standard. His life is beautiful because it displays coherence and integrity in values, actions and personality. This view of him is validated in the story by the respect and trust that Marya, the most nearly moral character, has for him. At the same time, we are prohibited from judging him good by the action of the tale. When Tolstoy shows us the Russians gratuitously and obscenely despoiling the *aoul* that had received Hadji Murad so graciously and helpfully, we non-pagan readers cannot but judge morally: Hadji Murad had no business fighting on the side of the barbarous Russians. Just as Shamil can be awesome and dreadful without being evil, so Hadji Murad can be admirable and grand without being good.

If beauty and integrity were the only components of Hadji Murad's greatness, there would be little to distinguish him from Shamil, save that he plays the protagonist's role, and is free from the corrupting pressures of power. (His dream is of gaining power, however, and once more we are reminded of his amorality.) Yet there is in Hadji Murad a greatness far beyond Shamil. It seems to arise from a dimension in his life that is lacking in that of the others—the dimension of art affecting his existence.

The role that art might play in people's lives had troubled Tolstoy for many years. In *Anna Karenina,* where art and dilettantism are discussed at some length, Tolstoy avoids what soon became for him the crucial issue: what vital function, if any, does or can art play in people's lives? Soon after *Anna Karenina* he spelled out this problem in his *Confession* (1879) where he speaks of having wanted to be a teacher without knowing what it might be that he had to teach. By 1896 in *What is Art?* he was thinking about art as a human means of communication where "One man consciously, by means of certain external signs, hands on to others feelings he has experienced, and other people, having been infected by these feelings, also experience them." Moral art would infect with moral feelings; immoral art would infect with immoral feelings. In many of his later writings Tolstoy was trying to use his own art for this purpose, both in his moral tales rewritten in a simple style, and his sophisticated narratives. For example, he would expect that ***The Kreutzer Sonata*** would infect people with his own feeling of sexual nausea. In ***Hadji Murad,*** whatever its infectious capacity, Tolstoy seems to be saying something further on the role of art in human society. And this statement is made through the life of the hero.

Two songs are crucial for Hadji Murad. One is the ballad of Hamzad that his cohorts have been singing throughout much of the story. The other is a ballad that his mother composed when he was an infant, that he tells about in his life story. The song of his mother spells out in detail the function of art in a healthy culture—that is, a culture where the values and the institutions support rather than conflict with one another. Hadji Murad's mother has been stabbed in the breast by his father for refusing to go as wet-nurse to the *khansha* because she fears her own baby will suffer. She then sings to her son that, just as she was not afraid, so he must never be afraid. By writing the song she has taken an act of defiance—one that conflicts with her cultural role of obedience—and fitted it into another cultural value: courage. Through art, her act transcends itself. And as art, it serves to perpetuate cultural values: Hadji Murad finds a demand for courage made on him by the song. Despite his mother's hopes, he cannot become brave simply by the magic of art: personal experience with fear is also necessary. But after he has felt fear, and has fled through want of courage, the song serves him as an embodiment outside himself of a quality he has developed within himself. The courage is both his personal characteristic and a cultural value, validated in a song—a song that itself arose from and transcended personal experience.

Tolstoy does not expose the "Ballad of Hamzad" in such detail: it appears more as background foreshadowing the end. Yet when that time comes, Hadji Murad can put aside all personal fears and thwarted hopes in order to die fighting like Hamzad. Here the personal demand made by immediate circumstance attains a social dimension, becomes a shared experience, through art. And it is most impressive that art works well here to tell a man exactly what Tolstoy himself so often despaired of knowing: how to die. His recurring fascination and anxiety about death appears in many characters and many situations; his attempts to dissolve the problem by scenes in which peasants die simply, or with a flash of revelation, is also attested to in many tales. But only in this case does an individual death take on a social dimension, thereby freeing the man who is about to die from the exacerbating awareness that it is his death he is dying. Ivan Ilych complained that "He was not Caius and not man in general, but had always been totally, totally different from all other creatures." But for Hadji Murad, Hamzad was not an abstract idea different from himself, but an experienced cultural reality that even made it possible for a man to die with the confidence that it was a right and proper thing to be doing.

Art works in the Tatar culture for Hadji Murad to validate his personal characteristics and give them a social context. But this does not really account for the personal greatness of the hero that the reader knows and feels. Hadji Murad surpasses his type to become a person. In this he contrasts curiously with Ivan Ilych, who rises out of his individuality to become a type. Ivan Ilych suffered all the Russian sense of anxiety and alienation coming from sophisticated self-consciousness. But in the story of his life, which was "the most simple and ordinary, and the most terrible," he became exactly like everyone else. This story is cast in the Christian frame of losing one's life in order to find it, and in ***The Death of Ivan Ilych*** there is certainly a religious overtone to Ivan's rebirth into death at the end: he finds himself by learning to think of others. And it works for the reader too: we come to know him, through his suffering and rebirth, not as an abstraction but as a person like ourselves.

The case is altogether different for Hadji Murad, where the frame is not religious but artistic. He dies an epic death, escaping from his personal life into the wider area of art, and growing to his greatest stature as an individual through this merging of himself with his tradition. Nowhere does art work this way for any of Tolstoy's Christian heroes.

The story ***Father Sergius*** (1898), written at the same time as Tolstoy was working on ***Hadji Murad,*** comes to mind as one where, if ever art were to be effective for a Christian, it should have been. Father Sergius, tempted by a young woman who is trying to seduce him, remembers the story of a saint who thrust his hand in the brazier to save himself from temptation. Using him as a model (but lacking a brazier) Father Sergius chops off his finger with an axe. It's a powerful event. It effects the salvation of the woman, in fact. But the saint's life is not effective for Father Sergius the way Hadji Murad's mother's song was for him. On the contrary, the symbolic castration he enacts is only a staying action. Finally, in raping the half-wit peasant girl who has been brought to him to cure, he acts criminally instead of simply immorally. Father Sergius, given over to pride, necessarily uses the saint's life for his own prideful end—the story has had little or no power in his life.

Throughout the whole last half of Tolstoy's life, ever since his conversion in 1878, Tolstoy was trying to teach Christianity through his writing. Yet over and over again his tales point up the ineffectiveness of art in teaching Christian morality; over and over, morals are learned by living without benefit of art. Even an angel has to experience human life in order to learn about God (in **"What Men Live By"**). The moral tales, while hoping to be infectious, seem in themselves always to be pointing out the ineffectiveness or superfluousness of any art.

It seems, then, that when he wrote ***Hadji Murad*** Tolstoy had discovered that his earlier hopes for what Christian art could accomplish were misplaced. His implicit statement about art in ***Hadji Murad*** is, more than anything else, an unusually humble explanation of failure. In a coherent culture, the Tatar's, art can teach and can inform a man's life as it does for Hadji Murad. In an incoherent culture art is ineffective. This insight, though only implicitly articulated, may explain at least in part why Tolstoy became more politically concerned in his late years, advocating and insisting on people's rejection of the institutions of society, and less involved in the making of literature: literature becomes a meaningless pastime in a society where the values and the institutions are at odds with one another. At best under these circumstances, it could be beautiful; it could not be effectively good.

Somehow, this judgment is embodied in the second thistle in ***Hadji Murad***—not that broken but unbowed "tatar" with which the tale begins and ends, but the other one that Tolstoy mentions first and not again. This one, he tears up in order to decorate his bouquet of spring flowers, only to find that it does not fit with their delicacy, and he is sad to have destroyed something beautiful for no purpose. Certainly this symbol resists facile one-to-one correlation with acts or thoughts in Tolstoy's life. But it clearly concerns his ambitions in art, and it is an admission of failure, in which he attains for once the humility that he sought so hard and which was so alien to his nature. It is as though he were saying: an artist can only be great, affecting the lives of men, in a society that is healthy. Otherwise, however inspired or gifted he may be, like Mikhailov in *Anna Karenina* or Tolstoy at Yasnaya Polyana, he can never be more than a gatherer of flowers. (pp. 138-46)

Nancy Dworsky, " 'Hadji Murad': A Summary and a Vision," in Novel: A Forum on Fiction, *Vol. 8, No. 2, Winter, 1975, pp. 138-46.*

Edward Wasiolek (essay date 1978)

[*Wasiolek is an American educator and critic who has written extensively on Russian literature. In the excerpt below, he asserts that Tolstoy intentionally presented, though imperfectly executed, two different points of view in* The Cossacks: *one objective and the other subjective.*]

The Cossacks is regularly referred to by Western and Soviet critics alike as the best of Tolstoy's early works and often as one of his most beautiful works. The tradition of praise is extraordinary since the novel has some clear deficiencies. The work does not read as something all of one piece, and one can sense something of the construction that took place in fits and starts and over a period of a decade. The novel has, for example, a curiously indecisive movement: Olenin is the central consciousness, indeed the center of interest, and it is his attempt to purify and remake himself that provides the motive force for our interest and, generally speaking, for the movement of the novel. But this line of interest is constantly being diverted by what one might call a general ethnographic description of Cossack life, where for considerable stretches one almost forgets Olenin. Nor are these details "symbolic" or "functional" in any way; they are not there as reflections of Olenin's spiritual state or as an indirect comment on him. Nor do they advance the action in any way. At best they would seem to delineate a situation or atmosphere in which Olenin attempts to find a more authentic self. It is quite possible that these descriptions are a kind of ethnographic residue from earlier versions of the tale and from its long and uneven history of writing. But it is unlikely that Tolstoy, careful writer that he was, would have left such long descriptive passages in the novel without some connection to Olenin's attempt to pass from the corruptions of Moscow to a better and purer life in the Caucasus.

John Bayley and R. F. Christian have taken the ethnographic material as evidence of Tolstoy's serious purpose to give us an objective picture of Cossack life, an end that is at odds with the subjective distortions that Olenin introduces. Bayley's key statement—picked up and approved by Christian—is: "Are we to have 'The Cossacks' or 'The Cossacks as seen by Olenin'?—that is the question which Tolstoy cannot be said to have resolved" [*Tolstoy and the Novel*]. The point is, according to Bayley, that even in those scenes where Olenin is absent, Tolstoy has so identified his own point of view with Olenin's that he is unable to give us an objective description of the Cossacks and Cossack life. It is true that the reader is at times unsure whose point of view he is getting. This situation is, however, much less frequent than Bayley would like us to believe. Bayley insists, for example, that we see the village through Olenin's eyes even though he has not yet arrived, but it is inconceivable that the following topographical and historical description could possibly be confused with Olenin's sense of things:

> To the north of it begin the sand-drifts of the Nogay or Mozdok steppes, which fetch far to the north and run, Heaven knows where, into the Trukhmen, Astrakhan, and Kirghis-Kaisatsk steppes. To the south, beyond the Terek, are the Great Chechnaya river, the Kochkalov range, the Black Mountains, yet another range, and at last the snowy mountains, which can just be seen but have never yet been scaled.

Bayley's implication that Tolstoy was unable to choose between Olenin's sense of things and some objective sense of things is a Jamesian prejudice that has been imported into Tolstoy's intentions. It is a prejudice that Lubbock had already expressed in *The Craft of Fiction* and one that English Tolstoy critics seem condemned to keep repeating. Tolstoy was not trying, and failing, to achieve a single point of view. He wanted and needed two articulated points of view. If there is some weakness in the way the points of view are handled, it does not lie in Tolstoy's inability to give us consistently either Olenin's sense of things or some general, and presumably authorial, sense of ***The Cossacks,*** but in Tolstoy's inability to achieve a sharper and more distinct separation of these two and a more emphatic affirmation of both. Tolstoy needs both the objective description and Olenin's sense of things. An objective sense of things permits us to measure and judge Olenin's misunderstandings and misperceptions. When Tolstoy tells of the somewhat casual and even slovenly way the Cossacks keep guard, even while an attack by the Abreks is in the offing, he is preparing us for the romantic and ennobling distortions of Olenin's perception of Cossack life. So, too, when he shows us Maryanka milking a cow, slopping through the mud, responding good-naturedly to a certain amount of ribaldry, he is giving us an "objective ground" against which we can measure Olenin's misperception of her as an ideal and unapproachable creature.

One cannot emphasize too strongly the importance of recognizing Tolstoy's efforts to articulate such an "objective ground," not only in this tale but in all his early works. Tolstoy assumes that there is an objective reality undistorted by the partial views of individuals. Tolstoy's view of reality is very different from that of most twentieth-century writers. By and large, writers like James, Conrad, Woolf, and Joyce assume that reality is fragmentary, subjectivized, partial, relative, and in any complete sense beyond formulation; that is, that reality is how it is seen by the individual. James's special excellence lies in his ability to catch and convey with such fine complexity the impressions of his characters, but there is no reality outside these impressions. Faulkner, for example, is at pains to tell us that there is no objective history but only the history that men carry in their minds. Even that is imperiled by memory and the passions and prejudices of those who carry the past into the present. But Tolstoy believes firmly that there is a "real" world apart from our understandings of it, and he is at pains to objectivize that real world, even though his conception of it changes with his development.

It is, of course, a matter of considerable technical interest how Tolstoy manages to communicate the presence of such a world. The communication depends very much on a strong and unambiguous authorial presence, even though the authorial presence is presented in a variety of ways. Sometimes it is direct and intrusive, but it can also be fully dramatized and presented with great subtlety. We can assume that the ethnographic matter in ***The Cossacks*** functions as an impersonal and objective ground against which we can measure the partial and changing views of Olenin. Nature in ***Childhood*** is firm, clear, and specific, and is used as a backdrop for the child's perception of various subjective distortions. In ***The Landowner's Morning, Polikushka,*** and later in *Anna Karenina,* the peasants themselves are presented as a kind of recalcitrant reality against which the efforts of the well-intentioned landowners come to naught. Whatever its embodiment, the objective reality is always presented as something impervious to the manipulations of wish and desire.

Much of the drama of Tolstoy's works—early and late—has to do with the distance between subjective understanding of such objective reality and the various efforts of characters to impose partial and personal views on the reality about them or on the reality of their own beings. Nicholas's temptation to flee before the horror of his mother's death is such a struggle, as is Masha's attempt to hold on to the charm and poetry of courtship after the "reality" of her being and the conditions of her life have changed. The beginning of "wisdom" is the recognition that one cannot remake such objective reality according to one's wishes; the completion of such wisdom lies in bringing one's own subjective world into relationship with that "independent" reality. The "right relationship" which I have posited as the central quest of Tolstoy in the early works is the identification of one's subjective being with this objective ground. To be sure, the situation is complicated by the fact that Tolstoy is not sure at this point what that objective ground is, and he can seize it partially only in discrete experiences and for the most part only in what it is not. But there is never any doubt that it exists, that it is good, and that harmony, well-being, and plenitude of life follow upon bringing oneself into alignment with it. ***The Cossacks*** represents another attempt to seize the "truth" of this objective ground and to formulate what it means to make the inner self and the outer world one.

The paradoxical character of this "right relationship" can be seen in the fact that it is experienced and embodied in a weird and mystifying scene: Olenin touches truth when he is lying in the lair of an old stag. This is the scene in which it is most difficult to separate Tolstoy's sense of things from Olenin's. For a short time the distance between them is closed, and Tolstoy's sense of right relationship and Olenin's are one; but this endures only for a short time. The renewed separation begins when Olenin begins to think on the significance of what has happened to him.

Olenin, having been shown the old stag's lair by Daddy Eroshka, sets off alone in the woods and settles unaccountably in the lair. The day is hot and the insects swarm, and Olenin's body quickly becomes covered with mosquitoes. He is about to go home because of the pain, but he decides to bear it, and gradually the sensation of pain turns into a peculiar pleasure and into a causeless happiness. He calls upon the mosquitoes to devour him, and feels himself in some way in blissful harmony with the nature about him. Olenin knows that something important has been revealed to him, that he has touched some source of life, and in gratitude he crosses himself. There seems to be no irony here. Tolstoy does not conceal his ironies, but his mockery is quiet when Olenin feels joy, crosses himself, and calls on the mosquitoes to devour him. The experience is right and Olenin is right. But it is not right for long. Shortly after the sacramental scene, Olenin begins to reason on the event, and on the meaning of life and happiness, and he comes to the conclusion that what has been revealed to him is the necessity of sacrificing himself for others. As soon as the idea of self-sacrifice forms in his mind, the joy he has felt leaves him, the wilderness grows dark, the trees look strange, and he is filled with fear of the Abreks. He has been led to the truth, but the grooves of habits lead him away from it. Nothing in the experience in the stag's lair leads him to the necessity of self-sacrifice. The mosquitoes do not sacrifice themselves but attack and eat him. Reflection distorts what he experiences. The bleeding pheasant head, severed from its body, which remains in his belt after a day of hunting, is a fitting, if not subtle, symbol of intellection and abstraction that Olenin takes away from the truth he has experienced.

The decision to sacrifice himself is wrong, and Tolstoy shows that it is wrong by what follows upon the decision. The self-sacrifice furthers Olenin's alienation from Cossack life and from Maryanka. It leads him to further idealization of his motives, to further romantic fantasies and further self-deceptions. Lukashka looks upon the horse that Olenin gives him as a bribe of some sort and is persuaded that Olenin has evil intentions against him. Because he believes he is doing something wrong in accepting the horse, Lukashka lies about the horse to his fellow Cossacks. When the villagers learn that the horse was a gift, they become suspicious of Olenin and put themselves on guard against him. The Cossacks act as if Olenin's self-sacrifice were a selfish act intended to hurt them, and they are right in their feelings. In this respect the stag's lair scene is quintessential of the novel: it summarizes Olenin's perception and misperception of himself and of the world about him, a process that takes place throughout the novel.

The misperception has begun with the opening scene in Moscow. On the eve of Olenin's departure for the Caucasus, several friends give him a farewell party. Olenin's coachman waits outside for four hours in freezing weather while Olenin indulges himself with food, drink, and sentiment. Olenin is intoxicated with self-analysis and does not notice the yawns and drooping eyes of one friend and the indifference of the other. He is interested only in himself, and his friends are interested only in themselves, but the conventional gestures and sentiments of good will and affection screen the self-interest and express what is not felt. At the moment of separation the friends bring themselves to tears and Olenin to blubbering. But once he has left, the friends talk of Olenin only for a moment before turning to the perfunctory matter of the following night's dinner. Tolstoy does not conceal the contrast between the sentiments poured out and the actual feelings experienced, nor the ironic contrast between Olenin's understanding of the situation and the understanding the reader is intended to have. Tolstoy says of Olenin, for example, after he has set off on his journey: "He remembered all the words of friendship heartily, bashfully, spontaneously (as he believed) addressed to him on his departure." The authorial presence is direct and unqualified. That Olenin is deceiving himself, Tolstoy does not hesitate to point out by commenting parenthetically on what Olenin has just thought or expressed. Immediately after the opening scene Tolstoy gives us a summary analysis of Olenin's past and character—not the kind of analysis that Olenin would have made of himself. It is dry, objective, detached, and laconic. For the most part Olenin is painted as a young man whose heart and beliefs are at variance with his actions. We are told for example: "He had come to the conclusion that there is no such thing as love, yet his heart always overflowed in the presence of any young and attractive woman. He had long been aware that honours and position were nonsense, yet involuntarily he felt pleased when at a ball Prince Sergius came up and spoke to him affably."

Olenin is a superfluous man: he believes in nothing; he has no relatives, fatherland, religion; he has accomplished nothing even though he has experimented with social life, the civil service, farming, and music. He shares too the typical preconceptions and clichés about the Caucasus. The Caucasus for him is a region of beautiful and mysterious women, precipices, perils, and rushing torrents. It is a place of pristine purity where one may become as pure as the snow-capped mountains. Olenin's sweetest vision is a tritely romantic one of a Circassian woman utterly devoted to him, living in a lonely mountain hut, waiting on the threshold for his return, her eyes deeply submissive. He would return covered with dust, blood, and fame from vanquishing innumerable enemies. His Circassian beauty would be enchanting, wild, uneducated, but in the long winter months he would patiently teach her French and introduce her to the masterpieces of French literature. The vision is banal and fantastic enough to jolt even Olenin into exclaiming "Oh, what nonsense!" but it is attractive and real enough for him to slip back into a contemplation of the vision.

Olenin's journey from Moscow to the Caucasus to find a new life and to make himself into a new man has its mythic resonances in the body of Russian literature. Olenin, as a superfluous man in search of a more authentic self, reenacts a rite that is essential to much nineteenth-century Russian literature. The "holy temple" is never far from the minds and visions of fictive and real life heroes of Russian literature and life. Tolstoy actualizes the form by changing it from the traditional political utopianism and topographical primitivism to a psychological and spiritual quest. He also deals with the quest ironically. There is nothing very pristine and elemental about Caucasian life; it is shown to be dirty, humdrum, tedious, artificial in parts (witness the Cornet's speech and actions) and very unromantic, all obvious qualities that Olenin fails to see. But all is not irony. There is something new, wild, and elemental in man, and it is something that Olenin touches briefly in the stag lair scene. Olenin looks for a new and authentic self in his imitation of Cossack life, but he does not find it, although he never realizes this.

When we meet him three months after the opening scene, he is in some respects a changed man. His sallow complexion has become red with a healthy sunburn, and he breathes of health, joy and contentment. Yet Tolstoy is careful to point out that his Cossack dress and mannerisms are awkward and imitative and that any Cossack would easily recognize him as a Russian and not as a Tartar brave. He has become a Cossack in dress but not in feeling. The form and the gesture have changed more than have the substance and the spirit. The Cossacks, sensing the unnaturalness, instinctively dislike him. He inspires constraint, distrust, and suspicion. He is very much the outsider looking in. Beletsky, in contrast, the typical nobleman, has no trouble becoming part of Cossack life in a few weeks. He is liked and accepted, as Olenin is not. The difference is that Beletsky accepts unthinkingly what he is and how he is regarded by the Cossacks: a Russian nobleman in the Caucasus who does not attempt to play a different role. Olenin sees a Caucasus that exists in his mind; Beletsky sees the Circassian town as a provincial hole, where a Russian nobleman accustomed to pleasure must find what amusement he can in any way he can. It may seem perverse that Tolstoy should put forth the superficial, pleasure-loving rake Beletsky as in some way more admirable than the ideal-seeking, self-denying Olenin. Yet there is no doubt that he is doing so. Good intentions and even good deeds are no defense against unnaturalness and falsity. If reality lies beyond the manipulations by individuals and moves in its own course regardless of the wishes, hopes, and fears of the individual, so too does inner reality. One cannot make oneself what one wants; no matter how beautiful the self one imagines, the wages are always some form of falsity and separation from one's inner reality.

Olenin's misunderstanding and misperception of himself and of the reality about him is played out repeatedly and even with some obviousness, yet the tradition of critical commentary on the novel has by and large taken Olenin's sense of things as the real sense of things. Olenin maintains—and most critics concur—that he changes in the course of the novel: that he begins as a spoiled, self-deceived, and generally useless person, but that he is somehow stronger in self-knowledge and action by the end of the novel. Except for moments of perception and consciousness, this is not true. At the end of the tale we meet an Olenin who is essentially the same: he is still romanticizing himself and his desires; he is essentially useless to the village life about him as he was useless in the capital. At the beginning of the tale he is pleased with his garrulous self-analysis; and at the end of the tale he is loquaciously absorbed in detailing his life in self-flattering terms in diary and letters. He is the superfluous man in Moscow, and he is the superfluous man in the Cossack village. When the life and death trial of the battle occurs in the struggle between the Cossacks and the Abreks, Olenin is not only useless at the scene but a positive obstacle. As always he is an observer of life and not a participant. Before the novel begins, he has played at being a farmer, civil servant, musician, and lover. And at the end of the novel, he is playing at being a Cossack, and, though he doesn't know it, he plays at being in love with Maryanka and in sacrificing himself for others. At the core of his idealizations, romanticizations, self-sacrifice is a certain self-indulgence, which Tolstoy expresses again and again. He goes to the battle between the Cossacks and the Abreks because he feels it would not look right if he did not go. After the battle he returns to Maryanka to take up where he left off, as if nothing had happened and nothing mattered but his feelings. When he returns and sees Maryanka's back turned to him, he concludes unaccountably and egotistically that she is shy, that is, that she is reacting to him. She is, of course, not thinking of Olenin but is consumed by grief. When she tells him to leave her alone, he asks obtusely why she is crying. Maryanka answers, "Cossacks have been killed, that's why." He can think only of grief in personal terms, and asks, "Lukashka?"

Olenin seldom sees a thing for what it is. He never sees the Cossack village for what it is: the environment of real people living in real conditions; and he never sees Maryanka for what she is: a practical, average, village girl, who is capable of grieving for the death of fellow Cossacks and who loves Lukashka with simplicity and dignity. Near the very end of the novel he is still writing of Maryanka in the following terms: "Every day I have before me the distant snowy mountains and this majestic happy woman." He seldom sees others for what they are because he seldom sees himself for what he is. He sees only what his mind wants and he and others are functions of this seeing. But there is the scene in the stag's lair: weird, mysterious and puzzling; yet with the unmistakable stamp of truth and reality on it. The causeless happiness that Olenin feels is a sign of that right, unreflective confrontation with truth, as much so as the leap of joy that Nikolay will feel at the sign of the old wolf in *War and Peace.* In trying to seize the truth that lies at the core of this scene, we are led inevitably to Daddy Eroshka, because it is he who has led Olenin to the stag's lair and it is he who propounds a view of life that is increasingly attractive to Olenin. Eroshka represents an elemental sensuousness as opposed to Olenin's intellectualizings, unrestraint against restraint, indulgence against self-denial. The purpose of life as it is exposited and exemplified by Daddy Eroshka is not morality nor the manifold disciplines that man has invented for himself, but the pursuit of immediate sensuous pleasure. Eroshka drinks, hunts, and lives with his senses; when he was younger, he had killed, stolen, and enjoyed the favors of women. Moral and religious prohibitions, for him, are the fantasies of the Mullah. The real law is the fire in one's blood and the appetites one feels, which one rightly asks to be satisfied. About the enjoyment of women, he says, "Is it a sin to love her? No, my dear fellow, it's not a sin, it's salvation. God made you and God made the girl too." Tolstoy summarizes his view of experience with the generalization that justifies the life Eroshka has apparently come to accept: "When you die, the grass will grow on your grave and that's all." It would seem, given the contrast that Tolstoy pursues between the two men, that Olenin has for a time in the stag's lair accepted Eroshka's view of life. The happiness he feels there seems to be the sign that Tolstoy and Olenin are siding with Eroshka.

Olenin's decision to devote his life to self-sacrifice represents a reversion to that view of life he had held prior to Eroshka's influence. Since Olenin's program of self-sacrifice is represented by Tolstoy as self-deception, then it would seem that Tolstoy is recommending Eroshka's program of simple, natural, and elemental enjoyment of life. This is essentially the way that Merezhkovsky understands the conflict in Tolstoy's attitude, using Eroshka's world view as decisive evidence that the Tolstoy of the early period resolved the conflict between satisfaction of instinct and the denial of instinct by subordinating one to the other. Eroshka is the model, for Merezhkovsky, of Tolstoy's early views and the clearest embodiment of what Tolstoy believed in and lived by.

But neither the biographical data nor the evidence of the novel itself will permit us to identify Tolstoy's views with Eroshka without serious qualification, or to accept Eroshka as the philosophical hero of the novel. If Olenin is mocked and satirized because of his romanticizations, idealizations, self-deceptions, and unconscious hypocrisies, Eroshka is similarly mocked, though more subtly. In other words the characterization and representation of Eroshka and Olenin are so made that the reader is asked to distance himself from both and to reject the beliefs of each. What happens in the stag's lair to Olenin is neither an affirmation of Eroshka's philosophy nor an affirmation of self-sacrifice as the goal of life. Neither Christian nor pagan impulses, neither love of the flesh nor hatred of the flesh, neither indulgence nor denial are affirmed in the scene. What Olenin misunderstands is something different and new, something Tolstoy has pursued since he wrote ***Childhood*** and something that is clear enough for him at this point to dramatize, if not to explain.

Both Eroshka's indulgence of self and Olenin's self-denial are wrong, and the common "untruth" is revealed by the similarity that hides beneath the contrast between the two men. On the surface they could not be more different; Olenin is the sophisticated nobleman from Moscow, reflective, dreamy and sensitive; and Eroshka is the down-to-earth woodsman and the man of action. Yet they get along well. Indeed, Olenin feels at home only with Eroshka; he makes the other Cossacks uncomfortable, but he is at ease with Eroshka and Eroshka with him. What binds the men is a common distance from the real business of life. Tolstoy makes it abundantly clear that Daddy Eroshka is not representative of Cossack life, and that he is not fully part of Cossack life any longer. In the village he is a useless old man, an object of indifference and occasional mockery, someone given to drunkenness, slovenliness, and long stories. Eroshka romanticizes his past and Olenin romanticizes his present and future. But there are two Eroshkas; the Eroshka of the village, where he is something of a pathetic figure, and the Eroshka of the woods. Tolstoy mocks Eroshka in the village, but he does not mock Eroshka of the woods, suggesting that the elemental sensuousness, which has taken perverted forms in his drunkenness, carousing, and sensuality, has its pure and true form in the woods and away from its civilized forms. This conclusion would seem to be strengthened by the manner in which Tolstoy narrates Eroshka's introduction of Olenin to the woods and to the stag's lair.

The Eroshka who takes Olenin hunting in the woods and initiates him into the elemental life of the forest is not the Eroshka who brags about his exploits, reminisces about the past, drinks, and recommends an unrestrained sensual love. In the forest he is the wise old man leading the sophisticate to the elemental conditions of life. The scene reminds us of the initiating scenes that are so common in the works of Hemingway and Faulkner. In the woods Eroshka and Olenin leave behind the sounds and forms of the village, as well as the garrulity of Eroshka and the introspection of Olenin. Eroshka is serious and ritualistic as he leads Olenin to the lair of the old stag. The next day, like Faulkner's Ike McCaslin who must brave the woods on his own, Olenin goes off by himself. There he has his sacramental moment. He finds the lair and settles himself into it, feeling by some process of decivilization that "he was not a Russian nobleman, member of Moscow society, the friend and relation to so-and-so, and so-and-so, but just such a mosquito, or pheasant, or deer." The layers fall away, and the superficies are erased, and for a moment the essential Olenin is revealed. We seem to be confronted for a moment with that core of the onion that Tolstoy seems intent on finding. The experience seems to embody some form of depersonalization, for everything that had constituted Olenin's personality and identity drop away: his social position, name, family, and friends. Such depersonalization would support Merezhkovsky's view that Olenin experiences an immersion in the general life of sense and instinct, as would Olenin's explicit identification with the stag, the mosquitoes, and the creatures of the forest. He says of the mosquitoes: "Each one of them is separate from all else and is just a separate Dmitry Olenin as I am myself." Yet this consciousness of the separate identity of the individual mosquitoes expresses not an immersion in some general life, but intense consciousness of different centers of existence and of his own center. Tolstoy believed intensely in the uniqueness of the individual. An immersion in some general impersonal life was always abhorrent to him. The scene would seem then to present us with a dilemma: it makes clear that Olenin's identity drops away and at the same time that Olenin has an intense consciousness of identity. We can extricate ourselves from the dilemma by noticing that what drops away is Olenin's general and abstract personality, something as general as the sensuous life he is presumably experiencing.

What falls away is a personality composed of such general qualities as position, name, social status, and interpersonal relationships. What falls away, too, is Olenin's conception of himself and his conception of the world about him: what he thinks he is and what society thinks he is; what society has imposed on him and what he has imposed on himself. What remains is an Olenin purified for an instant of the encrustations of the past and the future, of social and personal expectations, of thought and desire. At the height of the experience he does not think of anything or desire anything. What remains is an intense present moment, and an intense consciousness of himself and of the world about him. The "normal" Olenin has kept life at a remove by the abstractions that constitute his specious and willed perception of the world. His own conceptions, thoughts, desires keep him out of touch with reality as much as do social expectations. He touches some immediate source of life when he is emptied of past and future Olenins, and when thought (though not consciousness) and desire are quiet. The purified Olenin is not some undifferentiated and impersonal part of nature; rather, he is intensely conscious of a new identity, the condition of which is the consciousness of the unique identities of other creatures of the world. In this respect the experience is not so much different from those moments of consciousness in ***Childhood,*** when Nicholas perceives something about himself and the world about him that is different from his own expectations and the expectations of others. Nicholas is in touch with reality and some mysterious source of being when he can separate himself from the expectations of the group.

What Tolstoy is groping for is some definition that escapes the dichotomous oppositions of sense and consciousness, of civilization and primitiveness, and even that of pleasure and pain. Olenin recognizes that the experience would not have had its special happiness if he had not come to experience and accept the pain of the mosquitoes. He even admits that the pain, which almost drove him back to the village, turns into a peculiar pleasure. There is no doubt that Tolstoy has a deep-seated sense of the artificiality and sterility of social forms, but his opposition to such forms does not place him automatically on the side of what is ordinarily opposed to such forms: primitiveness, sensation, and lack of form. Just as his rejection of an abstract intellectual view of the world does not place him automatically on what we ordinarily oppose to intellection: sense. Merezhkovsky's failure to see that there was something other than a choice between sensuous self-fulfillment and self-denial is characteristic of critical opinion on Tolstoy, and explains why we have critics calling Tolstoy the champion of the rational and critics who see him as the champion of the irrational. The thrust of Tolstoy's thinking is to show that some common element underlies such oppositions.

There is a general consciousness and there is a general sensuousness. What Tolstoy is trying to express here and what he is groping for is the conditions under which the world is neither sense nor consciousness but both: something new, thoroughly individualized in sense and consciousness, and something full and good. He seems to have come upon the paradox that the intense, full, and joyful consciousness of oneself is necessarily tied to the recognition that the world about one is just as distinct and unique as one is. One becomes oneself when one permits the world to become itself. In the experience of the stag's lair, life, for Olenin, is no longer at the remove of intellection and dream. Olenin accepts himself and he accepts what is around him. What exists does not exist as a condition of what his idea of existence should be. He permits himself to be and he permits the mosquitoes to be, and no idea, desire, or wish is a condition of what should be. Olenin experiences all this, but he does not understand it.

While he is conscious of what is happening to him, he sees the world about him in sharp and individualized contours; he sees the old and the new trees, one of which is entwined with wild vines; he feels the flutter of pheasants about him and senses that they may be conscious of their slain brothers; and he perceives that the mosquitoes have as much right to exist as he has. But as soon as he begins to reason, the experience becomes confused, and when he reaches the conclusion—to sacrifice himself for others—the joy turns to foreboding, fear, and darkness in his soul. He asks himself presumably the right question: "How then must I live to be happy, and why was I not happy before?" But the very fact that he asks the question puts his present life at the remove of reflection. The experience has shown that Olenin touches deep sources of a new and vital personality when he gives up his special knowledge about what the world is and what he ought to be. Sacrifice is the very opposite of what the experience has shown him. It is a form of imposition on others as aspects of thought and desire are an imposition on one's own life. Tolstoy had already shown the egotistical and self-serving character underlying sacrifice and its baleful consequences in a number of early works, notably in the actions of Masha in regard to the poor peasant Simon in ***Family Happiness*** and the noblewoman in regard to ***Polikushka.***

What is insistent in [several of Tolstoy's works] is the conviction that something good, true, and real exists before it is spoiled by human manipulation, the forms of which, however, seem endless in complexity and subtlety. What the good, true, and real is eludes Tolstoy, at least in clear and full explanation. Whatever he examines turns out to be false. If sophistication is false, so too is simplicity and elementalness. Self-indulgence is as deceptive as is self-sacrifice. If the mind cannot be trusted, neither can the senses. Nothing, except for a few intimations, seems to resist the corrosive and destructive power of Tolstoy's analysis. Yet Tolstoy holds fast to a conviction that there is beneath all the cheating forms some core of reality and truth. The child narrator in ***Childhood*** knows what is false because he feels what is right; Masha learns what is wrong because she glimpses what is true; and Olenin experiences for a moment what is right even though he misunderstands it. (pp. 51-64)

Edward Wasiolek, in his Tolstoy's Major Fiction, *The University of Chicago Press, 1978, 255 p.*

Peter Ulf Møller (essay date 1983)

[In the excerpt below, originally published in Danish in 1983, Møller discusses Tolstoy's intention for The Kreutzer Sonata *to be an artistic and ethical reflection of Christian precepts.]*

In the years 1887-1890, while Tolstoj was working on ***The Kreutzer Sonata*** and the *Epilogue,* he was also engaged in a persistent struggle with the theoretical problems of art. A number of drafts for articles on aesthetics have been preserved from that time. They show that many of the ideas that were collected and systematized in the tract from 1897-98 had already been thought a decade earlier. The problem of art that is contained in the tale and which gave it its title is in itself evidence that it is not just a matter of contemporaneity but of an interaction between the genesis of ***The Kreutzer Sonata*** and the reflections on aesthetics. Correspondingly, the interaction is manifested in the tract in an insistent stress on the infamous way in which contemporary art both excites and embellishes sensuality.

In December 1890, when the debate on ***The Kreutzer Sonata*** was at its height in Russia, Tolstoj was visited by Aleksandr Žirkevič, a writer now mainly remembered for his reminiscences of Tolstoj. Žirkevič had made the journey to Tolstoj's estate Jasnaja Poljana in order, among other things, to receive an authoritative assessment of his talent, and his conversation with Tolstoj turned, naturally enough, on the question of what is required of good literature and of good writers. Immediately after his visit Žirkevič noted Tolstoj's words down in his diary, striving to reproduce them as exactly as possible.

In these reminiscences we find a variant of the three requirements for genuine, contagious art that Tolstoj later formulated in his tract. He explained to Žirkevič that to be of any value a work of art must have a new content (novizna soderžanija) and a talented form, and that the writer must have a "serious, warm attitude" to the subject of his work. Compared with the tract, it is only the second requirement that is different. However, this divergence disappears when Žirkevič goes on to write that Tolstoj considered the question of form to be the least important of the three and placed clarity as the goal for his own work with form. "If I sometimes work closely on the form, it is so that the content of my views can be more easily understood. People talk and shout so much about the artistry of my ***Kreutzer Sonata.*** But I have only given this artistry just enough room for the terrible truth to become visible".

With regard to the supreme ethical yardstick for art, the religious consciousness of the tract, Žirkevič's notes also contain interesting formulations, which relate this consciousness to Tolstoj's own artistic intention. Thus, Tolstoj commented on the change in his own writings after *Anna Karenina* as follows: "Only about ten years ago were my eyes opened to God's wide world, and I began to understand life. From that moment—that is at an advanced age, and almost with one foot in the grave—I became a serious artist. In every person's spiritual life there is a neutral point, and when he places himself there he can suddenly see all truth and falsehood in life. It is the same as the centre of a ball. If you wish to take in a room, you should stand in the middle of it and not place yourself under a divan by the wall. Now I have found that point".

Together with the tract on art and its drafts, Žirkevič's reminiscences give us an impression of some of the conscious reflections that governed the writing of ***The Kreutzer Sonata.*** Despite their general character they provide a key to the way in which Tolstoj planned the effect the tale was to have on its readers. They help us to understand a number of features—both in the final version and in earlier versions—and the reasons for certain changes from version to version. I have, therefore, chosen to take these reflections as my frame of reference in the following analysis of the tale.

In ***The Kreutzer Sonata*** Tolstoj quite deliberately sought to realize the requirements, both aesthetic and ethical, for Christian art that are formulated in the tract. The ethical qualities aimed at in the tale are to be found in its appeal for Christian love in the relationship between the sexes. Its straightforward message, which Tolstoj considered to be in harmony with the most advanced scientific and religious consciousness of the time, was that sexuality inhibited this love between man and woman, but that the problem would be less troublesome if people made continence their ideal. He had a simple and well-meant piece of brotherly advice to give to his fellow human beings, advice that would be of great significance for their daily lives. Through a tragic example of modern marriage, told by a repentant husband, he wished so to affect his readers' minds that they themselves would repent, become converted and strive for chastity.

Tolstoj regarded this ethical message as the most important aspect of ***The Kreutzer Sonata.*** But this does not mean that the message was there from the very beginning, and that the creative process was merely a search for a suitable form. As we shall see, it was more that the story about marriage, which he was planning and eventually got started on, gradually intensified the demand that its author should find one clear and simple truth about the relations between the sexes. It was only in the condemnation of sexuality based on the New Testament that Tolstoj finally hit upon that "neutral point", mentioned by Žirkevič, from which the complexity of life divides itself into truth and falsehood. From this point and in the name of Christian love, he was able to implement a drastic unmasking of modern marriage and the miserable sensuality of the upper classes. From this point, he was able to achieve that trinity of novelty, clarity and originality that his aesthetic theory held to be necessary if the artist's good will was to infect the reader.

The Kreutzer Sonata is about "how a man killed his wife"—so ran its title in the period before Tolstoj struck on the idea of introducing Beethoven's sonata into the tale. The story is told by the murderer himself during a train journey after he has served a relatively mild sentence, and his audience is a chance fellow-passenger, who initially only listens out of politeness. In the course of the story of the marital drama which culminates in a murder caused by jealousy, the murderer—Pozdnyšev—spells out a devastating criticism of modern marriage, and in this criticism the story of his own marriage functions paradoxically as an example of a completely normal marriage.

The explanation of this paradox is to be found in the circumstance that the murder is not Pozdnyšev's real crime. The writer Mark Aldanov has drawn attention to the rather strange sigh that escapes from Pozdnyšev's lips at the end of the penultimate draft version of the tale: "Had I only known what I now know, it would never have happened. I would never have married her, not for anything in the world". As Aldanov points out, it is not for the murder that Pozdnyšev reproaches himself. The real crime is in his sexual relationship to his wife. The murder is a kind of radicalization of this basic and widespread crime, but at the same time a moral turning-point. With the murder the original, corrupted Pozdnyšev ceases to exist and is replaced by another Pozdnyšev, the repentant and clearsighted narrator of the train journey. During and immediately after the murder Pozdnyšev undergoes a conversion, which at last makes it possible for him to regard his wife as a fellow human being instead of as a source of physical pleasure.

Woodcut from a 1920s version of The Kreutzer Sonata, depicting Pozdnyshev's first visit to a brothel.

There is, therefore, both sexual and moral symbolism in the description of the murder. Tolstoj had already compared sexual intercourse with murder in *Anna Karenina,* and in ***The Kreutzer Sonata*** this equivalence is realized in the action. The last time Pozdnyšev sticks something into his wife in a state of animal excitement, it is a dagger (in certain of the earlier drafts the murder weapon was "only" a pistol). The dagger pierces a garment, which has, in the literal sense of the word, formed his wife as a sexual object: "I noticed and remember the brief resistance of the corset and of something else and then the knife's entry into softness". After the murder he falls into a deep sleep and dreams that he is quarrelling with his wife, but that they more or less make up, which is to say that the dream re-establishes the normal pattern of their relationship. When he wakes up, however, he is confronted by the irrevocable change that has taken place—once again in the form of the same detail: "I remembered the resistance of the corset and the entry of the knife". At the very moment of the murder he has symbolically broken through a shell of sensuality that has excluded him from the true love of his fellow human beings. Shortly after, by his wife's deathbed, a veil falls from his eyes: "for the first time I saw the human being in her". He has awoken at the point from which the tale's entire stream of passionate value judgments takes its spring.

But this conversion is undeniably somewhat belated. (Pozdnyšev's name derives from "pozdno", which means late). Afterwards Pozdnyšev knows that the murder of his wife began in his youth, when he learnt to enjoy women. All at once he recognizes that men cannot have a both sexual and moral relationship with a woman, and it is this recognition that gives him his unmasking power as a narrator, makes him see "everything in a different light", "everything reversed". At the same time it is this recognition that gives his narrative its unique tone of flagellantist fervour. Pozdnyšev has discovered a corruption in himself, which he calls "debauchery" (razvrat), and which he carefully explains at the beginning of his account: "Dissoluteness does not lie in anything physical—no kind of physical misconduct is debauchery; real debauchery lies precisely in freeing oneself from moral relations with a woman with whom one has physical intimacy". "A libertine may restrain himself, may struggle, but he will never have those pure, simple, clear, brotherly relations with a woman. By the way he looks at a young woman and examines her, a libertine can always be recognized". The moral criticism of ***The Kreutzer Sonata*** is based on the unreserved assumption that there is a "wolf " in every man. It admits and regrets the way in which men automatically size up any woman with regard to her potential in bed. In its emotional source, the tale is an example of male confessional literature.

The parallel between murder and intercourse is the most concentrated expression of the view on sexual love put forward in ***The Kreutzer Sonata,*** and it is interesting to observe the process by which Tolstoj sought to express this parallel. In the seventh draft it is the wife who first discovers the fellow creature in her husband and begs for forgiveness on her deathbed, thus bringing about a corresponding transformation in him: "She beckoned me towards her and began to speak very, very softly: I went to her side. With her eyes fixed on me, she pronounced very softly: 'Forgive me, Vasja'. And these words, this look from an obviously dying woman, who no longer had any earthly needs, at once killed the animal in me. The very same animal that had felt what we so blasphemically call love for her, and which had killed her. For the first time I saw the human being in her, the sister in her, and I have no words for all the goodness and love I felt for her". This very direct emphasis that the animal that had killed the wife was also the animal that had entertained carnal feelings for her may have been necessary because in this draft the wife had not been stabbed to death but "only" shot.—From the fourth up to and including the penultimate draft, however, the most explicit formulation of this parallel came much earlier at the time when Pozdnyšev described his first visit to a brothel: "Yes, I want to tell you how I killed my wife, and in order to do so I must first tell you how I became debauched (razvratilsja). I killed her before I knew her, I killed the woman the first time I was with her without love, I killed my wife already at that time". But Tolstoj seems not to have been satisfied with his formulation, which makes the murder a once-only action, even though it is carried out at a far earlier point in time than the night when he stabbed her with a dagger. Tolstoj wished to represent the murder as something that was and is continually taking place, and he therefore moved these observations to Chapter 13, where they act as an introduction to Pozdnyšev's condemnation of contraception: "You think I am straying from my subject? Not at all! I am telling you how I killed my wife. They asked me at the trial with what and how I killed her. Fools! They thought I killed her with a knife, on the 5th of October. It was not then I killed her, but much earlier. Just as they are all now killing, all, all . . . ".

As there is only a difference of degree, but not of essence, between Pozdnyšev's stabs and what is taking place everywhere in respectable homes, the Pozdnyševs' marriage can stand as a typical marriage. There is, however, a difference of degree, which places their relationship in the sphere of the criminal and irreparable. Thus, while Tolstoj, on the one hand, had universalized the meaning of the murder, he was, on the other hand, obliged to give a realistic explanation as to why things went worse for the Pozdnyševs, than, on the whole, they do for other couples. It is here that the function of music in the tale comes in.

"Fury, too, has it laws", says Pozdnyšev just before the place in his account where the thrusts the dagger into his wife. The last part of the tale, from Chapter 19 onwards, contains a kind of demonstration of these laws, of the dialectics in the emotional crescendo that ends in murder. And as so often when Tolstoj sets out to describe what human reality is *really* like, he contrasts it with a less complete truth, the court's view of the crime. "At the trial it was decided that I was a wronged husband and that I had killed her while defending my outraged honour (that is the phrase they employ, you know). That is why I was acquitted. I tried to explain matters at the trial but they took it that I was trying to rehabilitate my wife's honour". Pozdnyšev's explanation, which the court would not listen to, but which his travelling companion does have time to hear, exposes the method in the madness. Modern married life is typically an alternation between hate and physical attraction (as Pozdnyšev experienced for the first time during his honeymoon). These fluctuations lead almost inevitably to a crisis, which can break out in different ways and with more or less force. "I maintain that all husbands who live as I did must either live dissolutely, separate, or kill themselves or their wives as I have done". In Pozdnyšev's case it is the last possibility—the murder of his wife that is enacted.

Among the accidents of fate in the final phase of Pozdnyšev's marriage music is the worst. "And it all began from that" is his comment on the apparently innocuous information that in connection with her general rejuvenation his wife has resumed her piano playing, and later he repeatedly emphasizes the role played by music in the tragedy. It is clear that in Pozdnyšev's attitude to music Tolstoj is thematizing some ideas on the emotionally contagious effect of art that were to be developed in his tract on art. While the main character is listening to his wife and the insidious Truchačevskij performing the Kreutzer Sonata, it seems to him that he is discovering "quite new feelings, new possibilities that I had not known hitherto". At that time this new condition was experienced as an agreeable elation, but the later Pozdnyšev, who is, of course, the speaker, knows better and persistently describes the effect of the music in negative terms. The presto movement is terrifying, the Kreutzer Sonata is terrifying, music as a whole is terrifying. This Pozdnyšev is speaking from a theory about music that is brief enough to be contained in a prosaic comparison: "music acts like yawning, like laughter: I am not sleepy, but I yawn when I see someone yawning; there is nothing for me to laugh at, but I laugh when I hear other people laughing. The meaning is that music transmits an alien, emotional charge, an urge to act that, for want of a real object, must find its fulfilment within the sphere of life in which the listener is placed. Thus, in Pozdnyšev's case, music becomes an artificial induction of energy from outside into the anguished basic rhythm of marriage. At the same time as Pozdnyšev feels his exclusive right to his wife's body threatened by Truchačevskij's presence, his sensibility is extended, and this releases the catastrophe.

What Tolstoj is criticizing here is the titillating, exciting effect of ethically unengaged art on the upper class of his time. Functionally, however, this criticism is subordinate to the moral message of the tale. Tolstoj wants everybody to be warned of how short a way there is between the daily hell of sensual marriage and disaster. A little music-making, and the whole thing can come crashing down in ruins. ***The Kreutzer Sonata*** is as Bjørnson so appositely put it, a "warning to our sensual life".

Over the years the clear moral intention of ***The Kreutzer Sonata,*** its unambigious advice on sexual continence, has discomfited many literary critics. They have been particularly disturbed by the fact that at the same time they have been deeply moved by the tale and have felt unable to deny its high artistic quality. As this kind of ambivalence has been a common reaction to several of Tolstoj's later works, a strong tradition has been created for drawing a distinction between Tolstoj as a *thinker* and Tolstoj as an *artist.* Instead of registering that even works that put forward the oddest ideas in all seriousness can succeed as art and then studying this paradox as an instructive question of reception aesthetics, many critics insist on tracing the paradox to contrasts in Tolstoj's mind and in the genesis of the works. It is argued that during the creative process Tolstoj was split into two conflicting personalities, each attempting to dupe the other, and satisfaction is expressed when the artist, as the more sympathetic of the two, comes out the winner.

An impressive attempt within this tradition is N. K. Gej's article on ***The Kreutzer Sonata.*** Gej's point of departure is familiar: "As an artist Tolstoj came into conflict with himself; his artistic achievement (osuščestvlenija) diverged from his intentions as a preacher". ***The Kreutzer Sonata*** gives a fairly comprehensive picture of the writer's views on love, marriage, jealousy, the relationship between the sexes, all the "damned questions" that no period and no literature have been able to avoid. But the artistic logic of the work does not coincide with the statements that Tolstoj made on these questions in the period when it was being written, and which are presented within the tale as the character's thoughts or directly as the author's viewpoint, his moral credo. In addition to these two layers and because of their presence in the work, it also contains what might be called a "credo of life". Gej develops this concept: "When Tolstoj's idea entered the riverbed of artistic representation, it came under the influence of a stronger necessity than the logical necessity of the original postulates". In brief, the course of events that is *shown* in ***The Kreutzer Sonata*** subverts the authority of Pozdnyšev's theories, even though it was the author's intention that the events should illustrate the theories and be explained by them.

The validity of this thesis is, of course, entirely dependent on the textual evidence that can be adduced to support it. Here Gej's strongest card is that Tolstoj has not described the exact nature of the relationship between Truchačevskij and Pozdnyšev's wife. In Gej's view this opens up the possibility of a genuine and profound feeling having arisen between them, perhaps with the help of the music; it may, indeed, be a love of the kind that Pozdnyšev does not believe to exist, in which case his jealousy could be inspired by the sight of the more elevated relationship that he himself was unable to realize. By virtue of, among other things, this ambivalence the tale acquires a certain unclarity of intention, which Gej calls "artistic infinity" and regards as an essential artistic quality. It is difficult to agree with him. In the first place, the lack of definite information concerning the relationship between the violinist and Pozdnyšev's wife is obviously necessary to the author's intention: whether infidelity has taken place or not is completely irrelevant to the question of where the real (as opposed to the legal) guilt lies. Secondly, it is not easy to see what benefit Tolstoj as an artist could derive from incorporating evidence that runs counter to what he wants to convince the reader of. Despite the article's metalinguistic eloquence it gives a misleading picture of Tolstoj as an incompetent who ends up pulling out nails when he is in fact trying to knock them in.

One might, instead, make the tentative assumption that Tolstoj knew what he was doing when he wrote ***The Kreutzer Sonata.*** If one takes his concurrent reflections on the nature of art into consideration, it is not unreasonable to believe that ***The Kreutzer Sonata*** is a product of a very conscious and consistent calculation of artistic effects, integrated into an ethical intention. (pp. 9-19)

Peter Ulf Møller, "The Unmasking of Love," in his Postlude to the Kreutzer Sonata: Tolstoj and the Debate on Sexual Morality in Russian Literature in the 1890s, *translated by John Kendal, E. J. Brill, 1988, pp. 1-38.*

FURTHER READING

Biography

Noyes, George Rapall. *Tolstoy.* 1918. Reprint. New York: Dover Publications, 1968, 395 p.

Examines Tolstoy's multifaceted body of literature, offering biographical information pertaining to his short fiction.

Wilson, A. N. *Tolstoy.* London: Hamish Hamilton, 1988, 572 p.

A comprehensive biographical study, including a detailed chronology of Tolstoy's life.

Criticism

Baehr, Stephen. "Art and *The Kreutzer Sonata:* A Tolstoian Approach." *Canadian American Slavic Studies* 10, No. 1 (Spring 1976): 39-46.

Explores human relationships in Tolstoy's *The Kreutzer Sonata* in terms of his aesthetic theories developed in his essay *What Is Art?* suggesting that "the basic equation underlying the many parallels between the two works, providing a key to *The Kreutzer Sonata,* is that 'life is art'."

Citati, Pietro. *Tolstoy.* Translated by Raymond Rosenthal. New York: Schocken Books, 1986, 265 p.

Examines Tolstoy's life and works, with two chapters, "Youth" and "Old Age," specifically addressing his short fiction.

Edmonds, Rosemary. Introduction to *The Cossacks; The Death of Iván Ilyich; Happy Ever After,* by Leo Tolstoy, pp. 7-10. Baltimore: Penguin Books, 1960.

Discusses Tolstoy's *The Cossacks, The Death of Ivân Ilyich,* and *Happy Ever After,* which is usually translated as *Family Happiness.* Edmonds praises the author's conveyance of realism and truth, concluding that "Tolstoy was a prophet."

Gosse, Edmund. Introduction to *Work While Ye Have the Light,* by Leo Tolstoy, unpaged. London: William Heinemann, 1890.

Biographical and critical overview of Tolstoy's literary production, including his short fiction.

Green, Dorothy. "*The Kreutzer Sonata:* Tolstoy and Beethoven." *Melbourne Slavonic Studies,* No. 1 (1967): 11-23.

Examines structural and thematic similarities between Tolstoy's *The Kreutzer Sonata* and Beethoven's work of the same name.

Hagan, John. "Ambivalence in Tolstoy's *The Cossacks.*" *Novel* 3, No. 1 (Fall 1969): 28-47.

Argues that in *The Cossacks,* major spiritual themes "are combined and developed for the first time so impressively that the work not only has intrinsic literary merit but occupies a crucial position in Tolstoy's canon, both crystallizing the achievements of his first eleven years of authorship and decisively preparing for the major works which immediately followed."

———. "Detail and Meaning in Tolstoy's *Master and Man.*" *Criticism* 11 (Winter 1969): 31-58.

Explores religious symbolism in *Master and Man,* asserting that "though transparently didactic, the story is by no means crudely so; the surface clarity and simplicity of the structure, characters, and theme belie a considerable richness and complexity of suggestive detail and symbolism which . . . link it more closely to twentieth-century modes of short fiction than we might first suspect."

Jahn, Gary R. "Tolstoj's Vision of the Power of Death and 'How Much Land Does a Man Need?' " *Slavic and East European Journal* 22, No. 4 (Winter 1978): 442-53.

Examines Tolstoy's story "How Much Land Does a Man Need?" as a reflection of Tolstoy's despair over the "power of death."

Karpman, Ben. "*The Kreutzer Sonata:* A Problem in Latent Homosexuality and Castration." *The Psychoanalytic Review* 25 (1938): 20-48.

Freudian interpretation of *The Kreutzer Sonata.* Karpman submits that *The Kreutzer Sonata* "is a thinly disguised self-portraiture of Tolstoy himself, and that the trends therein expressed may be used as clues in search for the understanding of Tolstoy's own life."

Kopper, John M. "Tolstoy and the Narrative of Sex: A Reading of *Father Sergius,* 'The Devil,' and *The Kreutzer Sonata.*" In *In the Shade of the Giant: Essays on Tolstoy,* edited by Hugh McLean, pp.158-86. Berkeley and Los Angeles: University of California Press, 1989.

Analyzes sexual conflict and narrative technique in three of Tolstoy's later works of short fiction.

Magarshack, David. Afterword to *The Death of Ivan Ilych, and Other Stories,* by Leo Tolstoy, pp. 295-304. New York: New American Library, 1960.

Discusses *Family Happiness, The Death of Iván Ilych, The Kreutzer Sonata,* and *Master and Man,* focusing on the circumstances under which they were written and the extensive revision process Tolstoy employed.

Maude, Aylmer. Preface to *"Iván Ilých" and "Hadji Murád," and Other Stories,* by Leo Tolstoy, pp. vii-xiv. London: Oxford University Press, 1935.

Introduces several of Tolstoy's short stories, describing the actual events from which they originated.

Rowe, William W. *Leo Tolstoy.* Boston: Twayne, 1986, 143 p.

Biographical and critical study containing two chapters—*"Childhood, Boyhood, and Youth"* and "How Should We Live?"—devoted to short fiction written in the early, formative stages of Tolstoy's literary career.

Schefski, Harold K. "Leo Tolstoy's Short Sketch 'Three Deaths': A Reassessment of Its Place within His Literary Work." *Studies in Short Fiction* 16, No. 4 (Fall 1979): 349-50.

Contends that the story "Three Deaths" is significant as a structural and thematic precursor to *War and Peace* and *Anna Karenina.*

Schultze, Sydney. "Meaning in 'The Snowstorm'." *Modern Language Studies* XVII, No. 1 (Winter 1987): 67-74.

Argues that in "The Snowstorm," Tolstoy's concerns with "the major problems of life, death, and how to live" culminate in the work's central vision: "a metamorphosis in the snow."

Simmons, Ernest J. Introduction to *Leo Tolstoy: Short Novels,* by Leo Tolstoy, pp. v-xv. New York: Modern Library, 1965.

Examines short novels written between 1851 and 1863, citing them as examples of Tolstoy's realism and as precursive exercises to his full-length novels.

Turner, C. J. G. "Tolstoy's *The Cossacks:* The Question of Genre." *The Modern Language Review* 73, No. 3 (July 1978): 563-72.

Addresses the changes in the genre of *The Cossacks* throughout its ten years of composition, concluding that it "is indeed a hybrid. One after another, various generic forms that Tolstoy envisaged for his work during its long gestation make their contribution to the final product."

Woodward, James B. "Tolstoy's *Hadji Murad:* The Evolution of Its Theme and Structure." *The Modern Language Review* 68, No. 4 (October 1973): 870-82.

Considers the textual history of *Hadji Murád,* noting "the sharp divergencies" between early versions and the final product.

Additional coverage of Tolstoy's life and career is contained in the following sources published by Gale Research: *Contemporary Authors,* Vols. 104, 123; *Something about the Author,* Vol. 26; and *Twentieth-Century Literary Criticism,* Vols. 4, 11, 17, 28, 44.

Appendix:

Select Bibliography of General Sources on Short Fiction

BOOKS OF CRITICISM

Allen, Walter. *The Short Story in English.* New York: Oxford University Press, 1981, 413 p.

Aycock, Wendell M., ed. *The Teller and the Tale: Aspects of the Short Story* (Proceedings of the Comparative Literature Symposium, Texas Tech University, Volume XIII). Lubbock: Texas Tech Press, 1982, 156 p.

Averill, Deborah. *The Irish Short Story from George Moore to Frank O'Connor.* Washington, D.C.: University Press of America, 1982, 329 p.

Bates, H. E. *The Modern Short Story: A Critical Survey.* Boston: Writer, 1941, 231 p.

Bayley, John. *The Short Story: Henry James to Elizabeth Bowen.* Great Britain: The Harvester Press Limited, 1988, 197 p.

Bennett, E. K. *A History of the German Novelle: From Goethe to Thomas Mann.* Cambridge: At the University Press, 1934, 296 p.

Bone, Robert. *Down Home: A History of Afro-American Short Fiction from Its Beginning to the End of the Harlem Renaissance.* Rev. ed. New York: Columbia University Press, 1988, 350 p.

Bruck, Peter. *The Black American Short Story in the Twentieth Century: A Collection of Critical Essays.* Amsterdam: B. R. Grüner Publishing Co., 1977, 209 p.

Burnett, Whit, and Burnett, Hallie. *The Modern Short Story in the Making.* New York: Hawthorn Books, 1964, 405 p.

Canby, Henry Seidel. *The Short Story in English.* New York: Henry Holt and Co., 1909, 386 p.

Current-García, Eugene. *The American Short Story before 1850: A Critical History.* Twayne's Critical History of the Short Story, edited by William Peden. Boston: Twayne Publishers, 1985, 168 p.

Flora, Joseph M., ed. *The English Short Story, 1880-1945: A Critical History.* Twayne's Critical History of the Short Story, edited by William Peden. Boston: Twayne Publishers, 1985, 215 p.

Foster, David William. *Studies in the Contemporary Spanish-American Short Story.* Columbia, Mo.: University of Missouri Press, 1979, 126 p.

George, Albert J. *Short Fiction in France, 1800-1850.* Syracuse, N.Y.: Syracuse University Press, 1964, 245 p.

Gerlach, John. *Toward an End: Closure and Structure in the American Short Story.* University, Ala.: The University of Alabama Press, 1985, 193 p.

Hankin, Cherry, ed. *Critical Essays on the New Zealand Short Story.* Auckland: Heinemann Publishers, 1982, 186 p.

Hanson, Clare, ed. *Re-Reading the Short Story.* London: MacMillan Press, 1989, 137 p.

Harris, Wendell V. *British Short Fiction in the Nineteenth Century.* Detroit: Wayne State University Press, 1979, 209 p.

Huntington, John. *Rationalizing Genius: Idealogical Strategies in the Classic American Science Fiction Short Story.* New Brunswick: Rutgers University Press, 1989, 216 p.

Kilroy, James F., ed. *The Irish Short Story: A Critical History.* Twayne's Critical History of the Short Story, edited by William Peden. Boston: Twayne Publishers, 1984, 251 p.

Lee, A. Robert. *The Nineteenth-Century American Short Story.* Totowa, N. J.: Vision / Barnes & Noble, 1986, 196 p.

Leibowitz, Judith. *Narrative Purpose in the Novella.* The Hague: Mouton, 1974, 137 p.

Lohafer, Susan. *Coming to Terms with the Short Story.* Baton Rouge: Louisiana State University Press, 1983, 171 p.

Lohafer, Susan, and Clarey, Jo Ellyn. *Short Story Theory at a Crossroads.* Baton Rouge: Louisiana State University Press, 1989, 352 p.

Mann, Susan Garland. *The Short Story Cycle: A Genre Companion and Reference Guide.* New York: Greenwood Press, 1989, 228 p.

Matthews, Brander. *The Philosophy of the Short Story.* New York: Longmans, Green and Co., 1901, 83 p.

May, Charles E., ed. *Short Story Theories.* Athens, Oh.: Ohio University Press, 1976, 251 p.

McClave, Heather, ed. *Women Writers of the Short Story: A Collection of Critical Essays.* Englewood Cliffs, N. J.: Prentice-Hall, 1980, 171 p.

Moser, Charles, ed. *The Russian Short Story: A Critical History.* Twayne's Critical History of the Short Story, edited by William Peden. Boston: Twayne Publishers, 1986, 232 p.

New, W. H. *Dreams of Speech and Violence: The Art of the Short Story in Canada and New Zealand.* Toronto: The University of Toronto Press, 1987, 302 p.

Newman, Frances. *The Short Story's Mutations: From Petronius to Paul Morand.* New York: B. W. Huebsch, 1925, 332 p.

O'Connor, Frank. *The Lonely Voice: A Study of the Short Story.* Cleveland: World Publishing Co., 1963, 220 p.

O'Faolain, Sean. *The Short Story.* New York: Devin-Adair Co., 1951, 370 p.

Orel, Harold. *The Victorian Short Story: Development and Triumph of a Literary Genre.* Cambridge: Cambridge University Press, 1986, 213 p.

O'Toole, L. Michael. *Structure, Style and Interpretation in the Russian Short Story.* New Haven: Yale University Press, 1982, 272 p.

Pattee, Fred Lewis. *The Development of the American Short Story: An Historical Survey.* New York: Harper and Brothers Publishers, 1923, 388 p.

Peden, Margaret Sayers, ed. *The Latin American Short Story: A Critical History.* Twayne's Critical History of the Short Story, edited by William Peden. Boston: Twayne Publishers, 1983, 160 p.

Peden, William. *The American Short Story: Continuity and Change, 1940-1975.* Rev. ed. Boston: Houghton Mifflin Co., 1975, 215 p.

Reid, Ian. *The Short Story.* The Critical Idiom, edited by John D. Jump. London: Methuen and Co., 1977, 76 p.

Rhode, Robert D. *Setting in the American Short Story of Local Color, 1865-1900.* The Hague: Mouton, 1975, 189 p.

Rohrberger, Mary. *Hawthorne and the Modern Short Story: A Study in Genre.* The Hague: Mouton and Co., 1966, 148 p.

Shaw, Valerie, *The Short Story: A Critical Introduction.* London: Longman, 1983, 294 p.

Stephens, Michael. *The Dramaturgy of Style: Voice in Short Fiction.* Carbondale, Ill.: Southern Illinois University Press, 1986, 281 p.

Stevick, Philip, ed. *The American Short Story, 1900-1945: A Critical History.* Twayne's Critical History of the Short Story, edited by William Peden, Boston: Twayne Publishers, 1984, 209 p.

Summers, Hollis, ed. *Discussion of the Short Story.* Boston: D. C. Heath and Co., 1963, 118 p.

Vannatta, Dennis, ed. *The English Short Story, 1945-1980: A Critical History.* Twayne's Critical History of the Short Story, edited by William Peden. Boston: Twayne Publishers, 1985, 206 p.

Voss, Arthur. *The American Short Story: A Critical Survey.* Norman, Okla.: University of Oklahoma Press, 1973, 399 p.

Ward, Alfred C. *Aspects of the Modern Short Story: English and American.* London: University of London Press, 1924, 307 p.

Weaver, Gordon, ed. *The American Short Story, 1945-1980: A Critical History.* Twayne's Critical History of the Short Story, edited by William Peden. Boston: Twayne Publishers, 1983, 150 p.

West, Ray B., Jr. *The Short Story in America, 1900-1950.* Chicago: Henry Regnery Co., 1952, 147 p.

Williams, Blanche Colton. *Our Short Story Writers.* New York: Moffat, Yard and Co., 1920, 357 p.

Wright, Austin McGiffert. *The American Short Story in the Twenties.* Chicago: University of Chicago Press, 1961, 425 p.

CRITICAL ANTHOLOGIES

Atkinson, W. Patterson, ed. *The Short-Story.* Boston: Allyn and Bacon, 1923, 317 p.

Baldwin, Charles Sears, ed. *American Short Stories.* New York: Longmans, Green and Co., 1904, 333 p.

Charters, Ann, ed. *The Story and Its Writer: An Introduction to Short Fiction.* New York: St. Martin's Press, 1983, 1239 p.

Current-García, Eugene, and Patrick, Walton R., eds. *American Short Stories: 1820 to the Present.* Key Editions, edited by John C. Gerber. Chicago: Scott, Foresman and Co., 1952, 633 p.

Fagin, N. Bryllion, ed. *America through the Short Story.* Boston: Little, Brown, and Co., 1936, 508 p.

Frakes, James R., and Traschen, Isadore, eds. *Short Fiction: A Critical Collection.* Prentice-Hall English Literature Series, edited by Maynard Mack. Englewood Cliffs, N.J.: Prentice-Hall, 1959, 459 p.

Gifford, Douglas, ed. *Scottish Short Stories, 1800-1900.* The Scottish Library, edited by Alexander Scott. London: Calder and Boyars, 1971, 350 p.

Gordon, Caroline, and Tate, Allen, eds. *The House of Fiction: An Anthology of the Short Story with Commentary.* Rev. ed. New York: Charles Scribner's Sons, 1960, 469 p.

Greet, T. Y., et. al. *The Worlds of Fiction: Stories in Context.* Boston: Houghton Mifflin Co., 1964, 429 p.

Gullason, Thomas A., and Caspar, Leonard, eds. *The World of Short Fiction: An International Collection.* New York: Harper and Row, 1962, 548 p.

Havighurst, Walter, ed. *Masters of the Modern Short Story.* New York: Harcourt, Brace and Co., 1945, 538 p.

Litz, A. Walton, ed. *Major American Short Stories.* New York: Oxford University Press, 1975, 823 p.

Matthews, Brander, ed. *The Short-Story: Specimens Illustrating Its Development.* New York: American Book Co., 1907, 399 p.

Menton, Seymour, ed. *The Spanish American Short Story: A Critical Anthology.* Berkeley and Los Angeles: University of California Press, 1980, 496 p.

Mzamane, Mbulelo Vizikhungo, ed. *Hungry Flames, and Other Black South African Short Stories.* Longman African Classics. Essex: Longman, 1986, 162 p.

Schorer, Mark, ed. *The Short Story: A Critical Anthology.* Rev. ed. Prentice-Hall English Literature Series, edited by Maynard Mack. Englewood Cliffs, N. J.: Prentice-Hall, 1967, 459 p.

Simpson, Claude M., ed. *The Local Colorists: American Short Stories, 1857-1900.* New York: Harper and Brothers Publishers, 1960, 340 p.

Stanton, Robert, ed. *The Short Story and the Reader.* New York: Henry Holt and Co., 1960, 557 p.

West, Ray B., Jr., ed. *American Short Stories.* New York: Thomas Y. Crowell Co., 1959, 267 p.

Short Story Criticism Indexes

Literary Criticism Series
Cumulative Author Index

SSC Cumulative Nationality Index
SSC Cumulative Title Index

This Index Includes References to Entries in These Gale Series

Concise Dictionary of American Literary Biography contains illustrated entries on major American authors selected and updated from the *Dictionary of Literary Biography.*

Contemporary Literary Criticism presents excerpts of criticism on the works of novelists, poets, dramatists, short story writers, scriptwriters, and other creative writers who are now living or who have died since 1960.

Twentieth-Century Literary Criticism contains critical excerpts by the most significant commentators on poets, novelists, short story writers, dramatists, and philosophers who died between 1900 and 1960.

Nineteenth-Century Literature Criticism offers significant passages from criticism on authors who died between 1800 and 1899.

Literature Criticism from 1400 to 1800 compiles significant passages from the most noteworthy criticism on authors of the fifteenth through eighteenth centuries.

Classical and Medieval Literature Criticism offers excerpts of criticism on the works of world authors from classical antiquity through the fourteenth century.

Short Story Criticism compiles excerpts of criticism on short fiction by writers of all eras and nationalities.

Poetry Criticism presents excerpts of criticism on the works of poets from all eras, movements, and nationalities.

Drama Criticism contains excerpts of criticism on dramatists of all nationalities and periods of literary history.

Children's Literature Review includes excerpts from reviews, criticism, and commentary on works of authors and illustrators who create books for children.

***Contemporary Authors* Series** encompasses five related series. *Contemporary Authors* provides biographical and bibliographical information on more than 97,000 writers of fiction and nonfiction. *Contemporary Authors New Revision Series* provides completely updated information on authors covered in *CA. Contemporary Authors Permanent Series* consists of listings for deceased and inactive authors. *Contemporary Authors Autobiography Series* presents specially commissioned autobiographies by leading contemporary writers. *Contemporary Authors Bibliographical Series* contains primary and secondary bibliographies as well as analytical bibliographical essays by authorities on major modern authors.

Dictionary of Literary Biography encompasses four related series. *Dictionary of Literary Biography* furnishes illustrated overviews of authors' lives and works. *Dictionary of Literary Biography Documentary Series* illuminates the careers of major figures through a selection of literary documents, including letters, interviews, and photographs. *Dictionary of Literary Biography Yearbook* summarizes the past year's literary activity and includes updated entries on individual authors. *Concise Dictionary of American Literary Biography* comprises six volumes of revised and updated sketches on major American authors that were originally presented in *Dictionary of Literary Biography.*

Major 20th-Century Writers contains in four volumes both newly written and completely updated *CA* sketches on over one thousand of the most influential authors of our time.

***Something about the Author* Series** encompasses three related series. *Something about the Author* contains well-illustrated biographical sketches on juvenile and young adult authors and illustrators from all eras. *Something about the Author Autobiography Series* presents specially commissioned autobiographies by prominent authors and illustrators of books for children and young adults. *Authors & Artists for Young Adults* provides high school and junior high school students with profiles of their favorite creative artists.

Yesterday's Authors of Books for Children contains heavily illustrated entries on children's writers who died before 1961. Complete in two volumes.

Literary Criticism Series Cumulative Author Index

This index lists all author entries in the Gale Literary Criticism Series and includes cross-references to other Gale sources. References in the index are identified as follows:

AAYA: *Authors & Artists for Young Adults,* Volumes 1-7
CA: *Contemporary Authors* (original series), Volumes 1-135
CAAS: *Contemporary Authors Autobiography Series,* Volumes 1-14
CABS: *Contemporary Authors Bibliographical Series,* Volumes 1-3
CANR: *Contemporary Authors New Revision Series,* Volumes 1-35
CAP: *Contemporary Authors Permanent Series,* Volumes 1-2
CA-R: *Contemporary Authors* (first revision), Volumes 1-44
CDALB: *Concise Dictionary of American Literary Biography,* Volumes 1-6
CLC: *Contemporary Literary Criticism,* Volumes 1-69
CLR: *Children's Literature Review,* Volumes 1-25
CMLC: *Classical and Medieval Literature Criticism,* Volumes 1-8
DC: *Drama Criticism,* Volume 1
DLB: *Dictionary of Literary Biography,* Volumes 1-112
DLB-DS: *Dictionary of Literary Biography Documentary Series,* Volumes 1-9
DLB-Y: *Dictionary of Literary Biography Yearbook,* Volumes 1980-1990
LC: *Literature Criticism from 1400 to 1800,* Volumes 1-18
NCLC: *Nineteenth-Century Literature Criticism,* Volumes 1-34
PC: *Poetry Criticism,* Volumes 1-3
SAAS: *Something about the Author Autobiography Series,* Volumes 1-13
SATA: *Something about the Author,* Volumes 1-66
SSC: *Short Story Criticism,* Volumes 1-9
TCLC: *Twentieth-Century Literary Criticism,* Volumes 1-43
YABC: *Yesterday's Authors of Books for Children,* Volumes 1-2

A. E. 1867-1935 .... **TCLC 3, 10**
See also Russell, George William
See also DLB 19

Abbey, Edward 1927-1989...... **CLC 36, 59**
See also CANR 2; CA 45-48; obituary CA 128

Abbott, Lee K., Jr. 19??- .... **CLC 48**

Abe, Kobo 1924-............ **CLC 8, 22, 53**
See also CANR 24; CA 65-68

Abell, Kjeld 1901-1961............ **CLC 15**
See also obituary CA 111

Abish, Walter 1931- .... **CLC 22**
See also CA 101

Abrahams, Peter (Henry) 1919- ..... **CLC 4**
See also CA 57-60

Abrams, M(eyer) H(oward) 1912-... **CLC 24**
See also CANR 13; CA 57-60; DLB 67

Abse, Dannie 1923-............. **CLC 7, 29**
See also CAAS 1; CANR 4; CA 53-56; DLB 27

Achebe, (Albert) Chinua(lumogu) 1930- .... **CLC 1, 3, 5, 7, 11, 26, 51**
See also BLC 1; CLR 20; CANR 6, 26; CA 1-4R; SATA 38, 40

Acker, Kathy 1948- .... **CLC 45**
See also CA 117, 122

Ackroyd, Peter 1949-.......... **CLC 34, 52**
See also CA 123, 127

Acorn, Milton 1923-.............. **CLC 15**
See also CA 103; DLB 53

Adamov, Arthur 1908-1970 ...... **CLC 4, 25**
See also CAP 2; CA 17-18; obituary CA 25-28R

Adams, Alice (Boyd) 1926- ... **CLC 6, 13, 46**
See also CANR 26; CA 81-84; DLB-Y 86

Adams, Douglas (Noel) 1952- ... **CLC 27, 60**
See also CA 106; DLB-Y 83

Adams, Francis 1862-1893....... **NCLC 33**

Adams, Henry (Brooks) 1838-1918 .... **TCLC 4**
See also CA 104; DLB 12, 47

Adams, Richard (George) 1920- .... **CLC 4, 5, 18**
See also CLR 20; CANR 3; CA 49-52; SATA 7

Adamson, Joy(-Friederike Victoria) 1910-1980 .... **CLC 17**
See also CANR 22; CA 69-72; obituary CA 93-96; SATA 11; obituary SATA 22

Adcock, (Kareen) Fleur 1934-...... **CLC 41**
See also CANR 11; CA 25-28R; DLB 40

Addams, Charles (Samuel) 1912-1988 .... **CLC 30**
See also CANR 12; CA 61-64; obituary CA 126

Addison, Joseph 1672-1719 .... **LC 18**
See also DLB 101

Adler, C(arole) S(chwerdtfeger) 1932- .... **CLC 35**
See also CANR 19; CA 89-92; SATA 26

Adler, Renata 1938-............ **CLC 8, 31**
See also CANR 5, 22; CA 49-52

Ady, Endre 1877-1919 .... **TCLC 11**
See also CA 107

Afton, Effie 1825-1911
See Harper, Francis Ellen Watkins

Agee, James 1909-1955 .... **TCLC 1, 19**
See also CA 108; DLB 2, 26; CDALB 1941-1968

Agnon, S(hmuel) Y(osef Halevi) 1888-1970 .... **CLC 4, 8, 14**
See also CAP 2; CA 17-18; obituary CA 25-28R

Ai 1947-................. **CLC 4, 14, 69**
See also CAAS 13; CA 85-88

Betjeman, (Sir) John 1906-1984 . . . . **CLC 2, 6, 10, 34, 43**
See also CA 9-12R; obituary CA 112; DLB 20; DLB-Y 84

Betti, Ugo 1892-1953 . . . . **TCLC 5**
See also CA 104

Betts, Doris (Waugh) 1932- . . . . **CLC 3, 6, 28**
See also CANR 9; CA 13-16R; DLB-Y 82

Bialik, Chaim Nachman 1873-1934 . . . . **TCLC 25**

Bidart, Frank 19??- . . . . **CLC 33**

Bienek, Horst 1930- . . . . **CLC 7, 11**
See also CA 73-76; DLB 75

Bierce, Ambrose (Gwinett) 1842-1914? . . . . **TCLC 1, 7; SSC 9**
See also CA 104; DLB 11, 12, 23, 71, 74; CDALB 1865-1917

Billington, Rachel 1942- . . . . **CLC 43**
See also CA 33-36R

Binyon, T(imothy) J(ohn) 1936- . . . . **CLC 34**
See also CA 111

Bioy Casares, Adolfo 1914- . . . . **CLC 4, 8, 13**
See also CANR 19; CA 29-32R

Birch, Allison 1974?- . . . . **CLC 65**

Bird, Robert Montgomery 1806-1854 . . . . **NCLC 1**

Birdwell, Cleo 1936-
See DeLillo, Don

Birney (Alfred) Earle 1904- . . . . **CLC 1, 4, 6, 11**
See also CANR 5, 20; CA 1-4R

Bishop, Elizabeth 1911-1979 . . . . . **CLC 1, 4, 9, 13, 15, 32; PC 3**
See also CANR 26; CA 7-8R; obituary CA 89-92; CABS 2; obituary SATA 24; DLB 5

Bishop, John 1935- . . . . **CLC 10**
See also CA 105

Bissett, Bill 1939- . . . . **CLC 18**
See also CANR 15; CA 69-72; DLB 53

Bitov, Andrei (Georgievich) 1937- . . . **CLC 57**

Biyidi, Alexandre 1932-
See Beti, Mongo
See also CA 114, 124

Bjornson, Bjornstjerne (Martinius) 1832-1910 . . . . **TCLC 7, 37**
See also CA 104

Blackburn, Paul 1926-1971 . . . . . . **CLC 9, 43**
See also CA 81-84; obituary CA 33-36R; DLB 16; DLB-Y 81

Black Elk 1863-1950 . . . . **TCLC 33**

Blackmore, R(ichard) D(oddridge) 1825-1900 . . . . **TCLC 27**
See also CA 120; DLB 18

Blackmur, R(ichard) P(almer) 1904-1965 . . . . **CLC 2, 24**
See also CAP 1; CA 11-12; obituary CA 25-28R; DLB 63

Blackwood, Algernon (Henry) 1869-1951 . . . . **TCLC 5**
See also CA 105

Blackwood, Caroline 1931- . . . . **CLC 6, 9**
See also CA 85-88; DLB 14

Blair, Eric Arthur 1903-1950
See Orwell, George
See also CA 104; SATA 29

Blais, Marie-Claire 1939- . . . . **CLC 2, 4, 6, 13, 22**
See also CAAS 4; CA 21-24R; DLB 53

Blaise, Clark 1940- . . . . **CLC 29**
See also CAAS 3; CANR 5; CA 53-56R; DLB 53

Blake, Nicholas 1904-1972
See Day Lewis, C(ecil)

Blake, William 1757-1827 . . . . **NCLC 13**
See also SATA 30

Blasco Ibanez, Vicente 1867-1928 . . . . **TCLC 12**
See also CA 110

Blatty, William Peter 1928- . . . . **CLC 2**
See also CANR 9; CA 5-8R

Blessing, Lee 1949- . . . . **CLC 54**

Blish, James (Benjamin) 1921-1975 . . . . **CLC 14**
See also CANR 3; CA 1-4R; obituary CA 57-60; DLB 8

Blixen, Karen (Christentze Dinesen) 1885-1962
See Dinesen, Isak
See also CAP 2; CA 25-28; SATA 44

Bloch, Robert (Albert) 1917- . . . . **CLC 33**
See also CANR 5; CA 5-8R; SATA 12; DLB 44

Blok, Aleksandr (Aleksandrovich) 1880-1921 . . . . **TCLC 5**
See also CA 104

Bloom, Harold 1930- . . . . **CLC 24, 65**
See also CA 13-16R; DLB 67

Blount, Roy (Alton), Jr. 1941- . . . . . **CLC 38**
See also CANR 10; CA 53-56

Bloy, Leon 1846-1917 . . . . **TCLC 22**
See also CA 121

Blume, Judy (Sussman Kitchens) 1938- . . . . **CLC 12, 30**
See also CLR 2, 15; CANR 13; CA 29-32R; SATA 2, 31; DLB 52

Blunden, Edmund (Charles) 1896-1974 . . . . **CLC 2, 56**
See also CAP 2; CA 17-18; obituary CA 45-48; DLB 20

Bly, Robert (Elwood) 1926- . . . . **CLC 1, 2, 5, 10, 15, 38**
See also CA 5-8R; DLB 5

Bochco, Steven 1944?- . . . . **CLC 35**

Bodker, Cecil 1927- . . . . **CLC 21**
See also CLR 23; CANR 13; CA 73-76; SATA 14

Boell, Heinrich (Theodor) 1917-1985
See Boll, Heinrich
See also CANR 24; CA 21-24R; obituary CA 116

Bogan, Louise 1897-1970 . . . . . **CLC 4, 39, 46**
See also CA 73-76; obituary CA 25-28R; DLB 45

Bogarde, Dirk 1921- . . . . **CLC 19**
See also Van Den Bogarde, Derek (Jules Gaspard Ulric) Niven
See also DLB 14

Bogosian, Eric 1953- . . . . **CLC 45**

Bograd, Larry 1953- . . . . **CLC 35**
See also CA 93-96; SATA 33

Bohl de Faber, Cecilia 1796-1877
See Caballero, Fernan

Boiardo, Matteo Maria 1441-1494 . . . . **LC 6**

Boileau-Despreaux, Nicolas 1636-1711 . . . . **LC 3**

Boland, Eavan (Aisling) 1944- . . . **CLC 40, 67**
See also DLB 40

Boll, Heinrich (Theodor) 1917-1985 . . . **CLC 2, 3, 6, 9, 11, 15, 27, 39**
See also Boell, Heinrich (Theodor)
See also DLB 69; DLB-Y 85

Bolt, Robert (Oxton) 1924- . . . . **CLC 14**
See also CA 17-20R; DLB 13

Bond, Edward 1934- . . . . **CLC 4, 6, 13, 23**
See also CA 25-28R; DLB 13

Bonham, Frank 1914- . . . . **CLC 12**
See also CANR 4; CA 9-12R; SAAS 3; SATA 1, 49

Bonnefoy, Yves 1923- . . . . **CLC 9, 15, 58**
See also CA 85-88

Bontemps, Arna (Wendell) 1902-1973 . . . . **CLC 1, 18**
See also BLC 1; CLR 6; CANR 4; CA 1-4R; obituary CA 41-44R; SATA 2, 44; obituary SATA 24; DLB 48, 51

Booth, Martin 1944- . . . . **CLC 13**
See also CAAS 2; CA 93-96

Booth, Philip 1925- . . . . **CLC 23**
See also CANR 5; CA 5-8R; DLB-Y 82

Booth, Wayne C(layson) 1921- . . . . . **CLC 24**
See also CAAS 5; CANR 3; CA 1-4R; DLB 67

Borchert, Wolfgang 1921-1947 . . . . . **TCLC 5**
See also CA 104; DLB 69

Borges, Jorge Luis 1899-1986 . . . **CLC 1, 2, 3, 4, 6, 8, 9, 10, 13, 19, 44, 48; SSC 4**
See also CANR 19; CA 21-24R; DLB-Y 86

Borowski, Tadeusz 1922-1951 . . . . . . **TCLC 9**
See also CA 106

Borrow, George (Henry) 1803-1881 . . . . **NCLC 9**
See also DLB 21, 55

Bosschere, Jean de 1878-1953 . . . . . **TCLC 19**
See also CA 115

Boswell, James 1740-1795 . . . . **LC 4**

Boto, Eza 1932-
See Beti, Mongo

Bottoms, David 1949- . . . . **CLC 53**
See also CANR 22; CA 105; DLB-Y 83

Boucolon, Maryse 1937-
See Conde, Maryse
See also CA 110

Bourget, Paul (Charles Joseph) 1852-1935 . . . . **TCLC 12**
See also CA 107

Bourjaily, Vance (Nye) 1922- . . . . **CLC 8, 62**
See also CAAS 1; CANR 2; CA 1-4R; DLB 2

Brooks, Mel 1926- .... **CLC 12**
See also Kaminsky, Melvin
See also CA 65-68; DLB 26

Brooks, Peter 1938- .... **CLC 34**
See also CANR 1; CA 45-48

Brooks, Van Wyck 1886-1963 ...... **CLC 29**
See also CANR 6; CA 1-4R; DLB 45, 63

Brophy, Brigid (Antonia)
1929- .... **CLC 6, 11, 29**
See also CAAS 4; CANR 25; CA 5-8R; DLB 14

Brosman, Catharine Savage 1934- .... **CLC 9**
See also CANR 21; CA 61-64

Broughton, T(homas) Alan 1936- ... **CLC 19**
See also CANR 2, 23; CA 45-48

Broumas, Olga 1949- .... **CLC 10**
See also CANR 20; CA 85-88

Brown, Charles Brockden
1771-1810 .... **NCLC 22**
See also DLB 37, 59, 73; CDALB 1640-1865

Brown, Christy 1932-1981 .... **CLC 63**
See also CA 105; obituary CA 104

Brown, Claude 1937- .... **CLC 30**
See also BLC 1; CA 73-76

Brown, Dee (Alexander) 1908- .. **CLC 18, 47**
See also CAAS 6; CANR 11; CA 13-16R; SATA 5; DLB-Y 80

Brown, George Douglas 1869-1902
See Douglas, George

Brown, George Mackay 1921- .... **CLC 5, 28**
See also CAAS 6; CANR 12; CA 21-24R; SATA 35; DLB 14, 27

Brown, H. Rap 1943-
See Al-Amin, Jamil Abdullah

Brown, Hubert Gerold 1943-
See Al-Amin, Jamil Abdullah

Brown, Rita Mae 1944- .... **CLC 18, 43**
See also CANR 2, 11; CA 45-48

Brown, Rosellen 1939- .... **CLC 32**
See also CANR 14; CA 77-80

Brown, Sterling A(llen)
1901-1989 .... **CLC 1, 23, 59**
See also BLC 1; CANR 26; CA 85-88; obituary CA 127; DLB 48, 51, 63

Brown, William Wells
1816?-1884 .... **NCLC 2; DC 1**
See also BLC 1; DLB 3, 50

Browne, Jackson 1950- .... **CLC 21**
See also CA 120

Browning, Elizabeth Barrett
1806-1861 .... **NCLC 1, 16**
See also DLB 32

Browning, Robert
1812-1889 .... **NCLC 19; PC 2**
See also YABC 1; DLB 32

Browning, Tod 1882-1962 .... **CLC 16**
See also obituary CA 117

Bruccoli, Matthew J(oseph) 1931- .. **CLC 34**
See also CANR 7; CA 9-12R

Bruce, Lenny 1925-1966 .... **CLC 21**
See also Schneider, Leonard Alfred

Bruin, John 1924-
See Brutus, Dennis

Brunner, John (Kilian Houston)
1934- .... **CLC 8, 10**
See also CAAS 8; CANR 2; CA 1-4R

Brutus, Dennis 1924- .... **CLC 43**
See also BLC 1; CANR 2, 27; CA 49-52

Bryan, C(ourtlandt) D(ixon) B(arnes)
1936- .... **CLC 29**
See also CANR 13; CA 73-76

Bryant, William Cullen
1794-1878 .... **NCLC 6**
See also DLB 3, 43, 59; CDALB 1640-1865

Bryusov, Valery (Yakovlevich)
1873-1924 .... **TCLC 10**
See also CA 107

Buchan, John 1875-1940 .... **TCLC 41**
See also YABC 2; brief entry CA 108; DLB 34, 70

Buchanan, George 1506-1582 .... **LC 4**

Buchheim, Lothar-Gunther 1918- .... **CLC 6**
See also CA 85-88

Buchner, (Karl) Georg
1813-1837 .... **NCLC 26**

Buchwald, Art(hur) 1925- .... **CLC 33**
See also CANR 21; CA 5-8R; SATA 10

Buck, Pearl S(ydenstricker)
1892-1973 .... **CLC 7, 11, 18**
See also CANR 1; CA 1-4R; obituary CA 41-44R; SATA 1, 25; DLB 9

Buckler, Ernest 1908-1984 .... **CLC 13**
See also CAP 1; CA 11-12; obituary CA 114; SATA 47

Buckley, Vincent (Thomas)
1925-1988 .... **CLC 57**
See also CA 101

Buckley, William F(rank), Jr.
1925- .... **CLC 7, 18, 37**
See also CANR 1, 24; CA 1-4R; DLB-Y 80

Buechner, (Carl) Frederick
1926- .... **CLC 2, 4, 6, 9**
See also CANR 11; CA 13-16R; DLB-Y 80

Buell, John (Edward) 1927- .... **CLC 10**
See also CA 1-4R; DLB 53

Buero Vallejo, Antonio 1916- ... **CLC 15, 46**
See also CANR 24; CA 106

Bukowski, Charles 1920- .... **CLC 2, 5, 9, 41**
See also CA 17-20R; DLB 5

Bulgakov, Mikhail (Afanas'evich)
1891-1940 .... **TCLC 2, 16**
See also CA 105

Bullins, Ed 1935- .... **CLC 1, 5, 7**
See also BLC 1; CANR 24; CA 49-52; DLB 7, 38

Bulwer-Lytton, (Lord) Edward (George Earle Lytton) 1803-1873 .... **NCLC 1**
See also Lytton, Edward Bulwer
See also DLB 21

Bunin, Ivan (Alexeyevich)
1870-1953 .... **TCLC 6; SSC 5**
See also CA 104

Bunting, Basil 1900-1985 .... **CLC 10, 39, 47**
See also CANR 7; CA 53-56; obituary CA 115; DLB 20

Bunuel, Luis 1900-1983 .... **CLC 16**
See also CA 101; obituary CA 110

Bunyan, John 1628-1688 .... **LC 4**
See also DLB 39

Burgess (Wilson, John) Anthony
1917- ..... **CLC 1, 2, 4, 5, 8, 10, 13, 15, 22, 40, 62**
See also Wilson, John (Anthony) Burgess
See also DLB 14

Burke, Edmund 1729-1797 .... **LC 7**

Burke, Kenneth (Duva) 1897- .... **CLC 2, 24**
See also CA 5-8R; DLB 45, 63

Burney, Fanny 1752-1840 .... **NCLC 12**
See also DLB 39

Burns, Robert 1759-1796 .... **LC 3**

Burns, Tex 1908?-
See L'Amour, Louis (Dearborn)

Burnshaw, Stanley 1906- ..... **CLC 3, 13, 44**
See also CA 9-12R; DLB 48

Burr, Anne 1937- .... **CLC 6**
See also CA 25-28R

Burroughs, Edgar Rice
1875-1950 .... **TCLC 2, 32**
See also CA 104; SATA 41; DLB 8

Burroughs, William S(eward)
1914- .... **CLC 1, 2, 5, 15, 22, 42**
See also CANR 20; CA 9-12R; DLB 2, 8, 16; DLB-Y 81

Busch, Frederick 1941- ... **CLC 7, 10, 18, 47**
See also CAAS 1; CA 33-36R; DLB 6

Bush, Ronald 19??- .... **CLC 34**

Butler, Octavia E(stelle) 1947- ..... **CLC 38**
See also CANR 12, 24; CA 73-76; DLB 33

Butler, Samuel 1612-1680 .... **LC 16**
See also DLB 101

Butler, Samuel 1835-1902 ...... **TCLC 1, 33**
See also CA 104; DLB 18, 57

Butor, Michel (Marie Francois)
1926- .... **CLC 1, 3, 8, 11, 15**
See also CA 9-12R

Buzo, Alexander 1944- .... **CLC 61**
See also CANR 17; CA 97-100

Buzzati, Dino 1906-1972 .... **CLC 36**
See also obituary CA 33-36R

Byars, Betsy 1928- .... **CLC 35**
See also CLR 1, 16; CANR 18; CA 33-36R; SAAS 1; SATA 4, 46; DLB 52

Byatt, A(ntonia) S(usan Drabble)
1936- .... **CLC 19, 65**
See also CANR 13, 33; CA 13-16R; DLB 14

Byrne, David 1953?- .... **CLC 26**

Byrne, John Keyes 1926-
See Leonard, Hugh
See also CA 102

Byron, George Gordon (Noel), Lord Byron
1788-1824 .... **NCLC 2, 12**

Caballero, Fernan 1796-1877 ..... **NCLC 10**

Cabell, James Branch 1879-1958 ... **TCLC 6**
See also CA 105; DLB 9, 78

Cable, George Washington
1844-1925 .... **TCLC 4; SSC 4**
See also CA 104; DLB 12, 74

Caute, (John) David 1936- . . . . **CLC 29**
See also CAAS 4; CANR 1; CA 1-4R; DLB 14

Cavafy, C(onstantine) P(eter) 1863-1933 . . . . **TCLC 2, 7**
See also CA 104

Cavanna, Betty 1909- . . . . **CLC 12**
See also CANR 6; CA 9-12R; SATA 1, 30

Caxton, William 1421?-1491? . . . . **LC 17**

Cayrol, Jean 1911- . . . . **CLC 11**
See also CA 89-92; DLB 83

Cela, Camilo Jose 1916- . . . . . . **CLC 4, 13, 59**
See also CAAS 10; CANR 21; CA 21-24R

Celan, Paul 1920-1970 . . . . . . **CLC 10, 19, 53**
See also Antschel, Paul
See also DLB 69

Celine, Louis-Ferdinand 1894-1961 . . . . . **CLC 1, 3, 4, 7, 9, 15, 47**
See also Destouches, Louis-Ferdinand-Auguste
See also DLB 72

Cellini, Benvenuto 1500-1571 . . . . **LC 7**

Cendrars, Blaise 1887-1961 . . . . **CLC 18**
See also Sauser-Hall, Frederic

Cernuda, Luis (y Bidon) 1902-1963 . . . . **CLC 54**
See also CA 89-92

Cervantes (Saavedra), Miguel de 1547-1616 . . . . **LC 6**

Cesaire, Aime (Fernand) 1913- . . **CLC 19, 32**
See also BLC 1; CANR 24; CA 65-68

Chabon, Michael 1965?- . . . . **CLC 55**

Chabrol, Claude 1930- . . . . **CLC 16**
See also CA 110

Challans, Mary 1905-1983
See Renault, Mary
See also CA 81-84; obituary CA 111; SATA 23; obituary SATA 36

Chambers, Aidan 1934- . . . . **CLC 35**
See also CANR 12; CA 25-28R; SATA 1

Chambers, James 1948-
See Cliff, Jimmy

Chambers, Robert W. 1865-1933. . . **TCLC 41**

Chandler, Raymond 1888-1959 . . . **TCLC 1, 7**
See also CA 104

Channing, William Ellery 1780-1842 . . . . **NCLC 17**
See also DLB 1, 59

Chaplin, Charles (Spencer) 1889-1977 . . . . **CLC 16**
See also CA 81-84; obituary CA 73-76; DLB 44

Chapman, Graham 1941?- . . . . **CLC 21**
See also Monty Python
See also CA 116; obituary CA 169

Chapman, John Jay 1862-1933 . . . . . **TCLC 7**
See also CA 104

Chappell, Fred 1936- . . . . **CLC 40**
See also CAAS 4; CANR 8; CA 5-8R; DLB 6

Char, Rene (Emile) 1907-1988 . . . . **CLC 9, 11, 14, 55**
See also CA 13-16R; obituary CA 124

Charles I 1600-1649 . . . . **LC 13**

Chartier, Emile-Auguste 1868-1951
See Alain

Charyn, Jerome 1937- . . . . **CLC 5, 8, 18**
See also CAAS 1; CANR 7; CA 5-8R; DLB-Y 83

Chase, Mary (Coyle) 1907-1981 . . . . . . **DC 1**
See also CA 77-80, 105; SATA 17, 29

Chase, Mary Ellen 1887-1973 . . . . **CLC 2**
See also CAP 1; CA 15-16; obituary CA 41-44R; SATA 10

Chateaubriand, Francois Rene de 1768-1848 . . . . **NCLC 3**

Chatier, Emile-Auguste 1868-1951
See Alain

Chatterji, Bankim Chandra 1838-1894 . . . . **NCLC 19**

Chatterji, Saratchandra 1876-1938 . . . . **TCLC 13**
See also CA 109

Chatterton, Thomas 1752-1770 . . . . **LC 3**

Chatwin, (Charles) Bruce 1940-1989 . . . . **CLC 28, 57, 59**
See also CA 85-88,; obituary CA 127

Chaucer, Geoffrey c. 1340-1400 . . . . . **LC 17**

Chayefsky, Paddy 1923-1981. . . . . . . **CLC 23**
See also CA 9-12R; obituary CA 104; DLB 7, 44; DLB-Y 81

Chayefsky, Sidney 1923-1981
See Chayefsky, Paddy
See also CANR 18

Chedid, Andree 1920- . . . . **CLC 47**

Cheever, John 1912-1982 . . . . . **CLC 3, 7, 8, 11, 15, 25, 64; SSC 1**
See also CANR 5, 27; CA 5-8R; obituary CA 106; CABS 1; DLB 2; DLB-Y 80, 82; CDALB 1941-1968

Cheever, Susan 1943- . . . . **CLC 18, 48**
See also CA 103; DLB-Y 82

Chekhov, Anton (Pavlovich) 1860-1904 . . . . . . **TCLC 3, 10, 31; SSC 2**
See also CA 104, 124

Chernyshevsky, Nikolay Gavrilovich 1828-1889 . . . . **NCLC 1**

Cherry, Caroline Janice 1942-
See Cherryh, C. J.

Cherryh, C. J. 1942- . . . . **CLC 35**
See also CANR 10; CA 65-68; DLB-Y 80

Chesnutt, Charles Waddell 1858-1932 . . . . **TCLC 5, 39; SSC 7**
See also BLC 1; CA 106, 125; DLB 12, 50, 78

Chester, Alfred 1929?-1971 . . . . **CLC 49**
See also obituary CA 33-36R

Chesterton, G(ilbert) K(eith) 1874-1936 . . . . **TCLC 1, 6; SSC 1**
See also CA 104; SATA 27; DLB 10, 19, 34, 70

Chiang Pin-Chin 1904-1986
See Ding Ling
See also obituary CA 118

Ch'ien Chung-shu 1910- . . . . **CLC 22**

Child, Lydia Maria 1802-1880 . . . . **NCLC 6**
See also DLB 1, 74

Child, Philip 1898-1978 . . . . **CLC 19**
See also CAP 1; CA 13-14; SATA 47

Childress, Alice 1920- . . . . **CLC 12, 15**
See also BLC 1; CLR 14; CANR 3, 27; CA 45-48; SATA 7, 48; DLB 7, 38

Chislett, (Margaret) Anne 1943?- . . . **CLC 34**

Chitty, (Sir) Thomas Willes 1926- . . **CLC 11**
See also Hinde, Thomas
See also CA 5-8R

Chomette, Rene 1898-1981
See Clair, Rene
See also obituary CA 103

Chopin, Kate (O'Flaherty) 1851-1904 . . . . **TCLC 5, 14; SSC 8**
See also CA 122; brief entry CA 104; DLB 12, 78; CDALB 1865-1917

Christie, (Dame) Agatha (Mary Clarissa) 1890-1976 . . . . . . **CLC 1, 6, 8, 12, 39, 48**
See also CANR 10; CA 17-20R; obituary CA 61-64; SATA 36; DLB 13

Christie, (Ann) Philippa 1920-
See Pearce, (Ann) Philippa
See also CANR 4; CA 7-8

Christine de Pizan 1365?-1431?. . . . . . . **LC 9**

Chulkov, Mikhail Dmitrievich 1743-1792 . . . . **LC 2**

Churchill, Caryl 1938- . . . . **CLC 31, 55**
See also CANR 22; CA 102; DLB 13

Churchill, Charles 1731?-1764. . . . . **LC 3**

Chute, Carolyn 1947- . . . . **CLC 39**
See also CA 123

Ciardi, John (Anthony) 1916-1986 . . . . **CLC 10, 40, 44**
See also CAAS 2; CANR 5; CA 5-8R; obituary CA 118; SATA 1, 46; DLB 5; DLB-Y 86

Cicero, Marcus Tullius 106 B.C.-43 B.C. . . . . **CMLC 3**

Cimino, Michael 1943?- . . . . **CLC 16**
See also CA 105

Cioran, E. M. 1911- . . . . **CLC 64**
See also CA 25-28R

Cisneros, Sandra 1954- . . . . **CLC 69**
See also CA 131

Clair, Rene 1898-1981 . . . . **CLC 20**
See also Chomette, Rene

Clampitt, Amy 19??- . . . . **CLC 32**
See also CA 110

Clancy, Tom 1947- . . . . **CLC 45**
See also CA 125

Clare, John 1793-1864 . . . . **NCLC 9**
See also DLB 55

Clark, Al C. 1937?-1974
See Goines, Donald

Clark, (Robert) Brian 1932- . . . . **CLC 29**
See also CA 41-44R

Clark, Eleanor 1913- . . . . **CLC 5, 19**
See also CA 9-12R; DLB 6

Clark, John Pepper 1935- . . . . **CLC 38**
See also BLC 1; CANR 16; CA 65-68

Clark, Mavis Thorpe 1912?- . . . . **CLC 12**
See also CANR 8; CA 57-60; SAAS 5; SATA 8

Clark, Walter Van Tilburg 1909-1971 .... **CLC 28**
See also CA 9-12R; obituary CA 33-36R; SATA 8; DLB 9

Clarke, Arthur C(harles) 1917- ...... **CLC 1, 4, 13, 18, 35; SSC 3**
See also CANR 2; CA 1-4R; SATA 13

Clarke, Austin 1896-1974 .... **CLC 6, 9**
See also BLC 1; CANR 14; CAP 2; CA 29-32; obituary CA 49-52; DLB 10, 20, 53

Clarke, Austin (Ardinel) C(hesterfield) 1934- .... **CLC 8, 53**
See also CANR 14; CA 25-28R; DLB 53

Clarke, Gillian 1937- .... **CLC 61**
See also CA 106; DLB 40

Clarke, Marcus (Andrew Hislop) 1846-1881 .... **NCLC 19**

Clarke, Shirley 1925- .... **CLC 16**

Clash, The .... **CLC 30**

Claudel, Paul (Louis Charles Marie) 1868-1955 .... **TCLC 2, 10**
See also CA 104

Clavell, James (duMaresq) 1924- .... **CLC 6, 25**
See also CANR 26; CA 25-28R

Clayman. Gregory 1974?- .... **CLC 65**

Cleaver, (Leroy) Eldridge 1935- .... **CLC 30**
See also BLC 1; CANR 16; CA 21-24R

Cleese, John 1939- .... **CLC 21**
See also Monty Python
See also CA 112, 116

Cleland, John 1709-1789 .... **LC 2**
See also DLB 39

Clemens, Samuel Langhorne 1835-1910 ...... **TCLC 6, 12, 19; SSC 6**
See also Twain, Mark
See also YABC 2; CA 104; DLB 11, 12, 23, 64, 74; CDALB 1865-1917

Cliff, Jimmy 1948- .... **CLC 21**

Clifton, Lucille (Thelma) 1936- .... **CLC 19, 66**
See also BLC 1; CLR 5; CANR 2, 24; CA 49-52; SATA 20; DLB 5, 41

Clough, Arthur Hugh 1819-1861 .. **NCLC 27**
See also DLB 32

Clutha, Janet Paterson Frame 1924-
See Frame (Clutha), Janet (Paterson)
See also CANR 2; CA 1-4R

Coburn, D(onald) L(ee) 1938- ...... **CLC 10**
See also CA 89-92

Cocteau, Jean (Maurice Eugene Clement) 1889-1963 .... **CLC 1, 8, 15, 16, 43**
See also CAP 2; CA 25-28; DLB 65

Codrescu, Andrei 1946- .... **CLC 46**
See also CANR 13; CA 33-36R

Coetzee, J(ohn) M. 1940- .... **CLC 23, 33, 66**
See also CA 77-80

Cohen, Arthur A(llen) 1928-1986 .... **CLC 7, 31**
See also CANR 1, 17; CA 1-4R; obituary CA 120; DLB 28

Cohen, Leonard (Norman) 1934- .... **CLC 3, 38**
See also CANR 14; CA 21-24R; DLB 53

Cohen, Matt 1942- .... **CLC 19**
See also CA 61-64; DLB 53

Cohen-Solal, Annie 19??- .... **CLC 50**

Colegate, Isabel 1931- .... **CLC 36**
See also CANR 8, 22; CA 17-20R; DLB 14

Coleman, Emmett 1938-
See Reed, Ishmael

Coleridge, Samuel Taylor 1772-1834 .... **NCLC 9**

Coleridge, Sara 1802-1852 .... **NCLC 31**

Coles, Don 1928- .... **CLC 46**
See also CA 115

Colette (Sidonie-Gabrielle) 1873-1954 .... **TCLC 1, 5, 16**
See also CA 104; DLB 65

Collett, (Jacobine) Camilla (Wergeland) 1813-1895 .... **NCLC 22**

Collier, Christopher 1930- .... **CLC 30**
See also CANR 13; CA 33-36R; SATA 16

Collier, James L(incoln) 1928- ..... **CLC 30**
See also CLR 3; CANR 4; CA 9-12R; SATA 8

Collier, Jeremy 1650-1726 .... **LC 6**

Collins, Hunt 1926-
See Hunter, Evan

Collins, Linda 19??- .... **CLC 44**
See also CA 125

Collins, Tom 1843-1912
See Furphy, Joseph

Collins, (William) Wilkie 1824-1889 .... **NCLC 1, 18**
See also DLB 18, 70

Collins, William 1721-1759 .... **LC 4**

Colman, George 1909-1981
See Glassco, John

Colter, Cyrus 1910- .... **CLC 58**
See also CANR 10; CA 65-68; DLB 33

Colton, James 1923-
See Hansen, Joseph

Colum, Padraic 1881-1972 .... **CLC 28**
See also CA 73-76; obituary CA 33-36R; SATA 15; DLB 19

Colvin, James 1939-
See Moorcock, Michael

Colwin, Laurie 1945- .... **CLC 5, 13, 23**
See also CANR 20; CA 89-92; DLB-Y 80

Comfort, Alex(ander) 1920- .... **CLC 7**
See also CANR 1; CA 1-4R

Compton-Burnett, Ivy 1892-1969 .... **CLC 1, 3, 10, 15, 34**
See also CANR 4; CA 1-4R; obituary CA 25-28R; DLB 36

Comstock, Anthony 1844-1915 .... **TCLC 13**
See also CA 110

Conde, Maryse 1937- .... **CLC 52**
See also Boucolon, Maryse

Condon, Richard (Thomas) 1915- .... **CLC 4, 6, 8, 10, 45**
See also CAAS 1; CANR 2, 23; CA 1-4R

Congreve, William 1670-1729 .... **LC 5**
See also DLB 39

Connell, Evan S(helby), Jr. 1924- .... **CLC 4, 6, 45**
See also CAAS 2; CANR 2; CA 1-4R; DLB 2; DLB-Y 81

Connelly, Marc(us Cook) 1890-1980 .... **CLC 7**
See also CA 85-88; obituary CA 102; obituary SATA 25; DLB 7; DLB-Y 80

Conner, Ralph 1860-1937 .... **TCLC 31**

Conrad, Joseph 1857-1924 ...... **TCLC 1, 6, 13, 25, 43; SSC 9**
See also CA 104, 131; SATA 27; DLB 10, 34, 98

Conrad, Robert Arnold 1904-1961
See Hart, Moss

Conroy, Pat 1945- .... **CLC 30**
See also CANR 24; CA 85-88; DLB 6

Constant (de Rebecque), (Henri) Benjamin 1767-1830 .... **NCLC 6**

Cook, Michael 1933- .... **CLC 58**
See also CA 93-96; DLB 53

Cook, Robin 1940- .... **CLC 14**
See also CA 108, 111

Cooke, Elizabeth 1948- .... **CLC 55**

Cooke, John Esten 1830-1886 ..... **NCLC 5**
See also DLB 3

Cooney, Ray 19??- .... **CLC 62**

Cooper, Edith Emma 1862-1913
See Field, Michael

Cooper, J. California 19??- .... **CLC 56**
See also CA 125

Cooper, James Fenimore 1789-1851 .... **NCLC 1, 27**
See also SATA 19; DLB 3; CDALB 1640-1865

Coover, Robert (Lowell) 1932- .... **CLC 3, 7, 15, 32, 46**
See also CANR 3; CA 45-48; DLB 2; DLB-Y 81

Copeland, Stewart (Armstrong) 1952- .... **CLC 26**
See also The Police

Coppard, A(lfred) E(dgar) 1878-1957 .... **TCLC 5**
See also YABC 1; CA 114

Coppee, Francois 1842-1908 ...... **TCLC 25**

Coppola, Francis Ford 1939- .... **CLC 16**
See also CA 77-80; DLB 44

Corcoran, Barbara 1911- .... **CLC 17**
See also CAAS 2; CANR 11; CA 21-24R; SATA 3; DLB 52

Corman, Cid 1924- .... **CLC 9**
See also Corman, Sidney
See also CAAS 2; DLB 5

Corman, Sidney 1924-
See Corman, Cid
See also CA 85-88

Cormier, Robert (Edmund) 1925- .... **CLC 12, 30**
See also CLR 12; CANR 5, 23; CA 1-4R; SATA 10, 45; DLB 52

Fink, Janis 1951-
See Ian, Janis

Firbank, Louis 1944-
See Reed, Lou
See also CA 117

Firbank, (Arthur Annesley) Ronald 1886-1926 .... **TCLC 1**
See also CA 104; DLB 36

Fisher, Roy 1930- .... **CLC 25**
See also CANR 16; CA 81-84; DLB 40

Fisher, Rudolph 1897-1934 .... **TCLC 11**
See also BLC 2; CA 107, 124; DLB 51

Fisher, Vardis (Alvero) 1895-1968.... **CLC 7**
See also CA 5-8R; obituary CA 25-28R; DLB 9

FitzGerald, Edward 1809-1883 .... **NCLC 9**
See also DLB 32

Fitzgerald, F(rancis) Scott (Key) 1896-1940 .... **TCLC 1, 6, 14, 28; SSC 6**
See also CA 110, 123; DLB 4, 9, 86; DLB-Y 81; DLB-DS 1; CDALB 1917-1929

Fitzgerald, Penelope 1916-... **CLC 19, 51, 61**
See also CAAS 10; CA 85-88,; DLB 14

Fitzgerald, Robert (Stuart) 1910-1985 .... **CLC 39**
See also CANR 1; CA 2R; obituary CA 114; DLB-Y 80

FitzGerald, Robert D(avid) 1902-... **CLC 19**
See also CA 17-20R

Flanagan, Thomas (James Bonner) 1923- .... **CLC 25, 52**
See also CA 108; DLB-Y 80

Flaubert, Gustave 1821-1880 .... **NCLC 2, 10, 19**

Flecker, (Herman) James Elroy 1884-1913 .... **TCLC 43**
See also CA 109; DLB 10, 19

Fleming, Ian (Lancaster) 1908-1964 .... **CLC 3, 30**
See also CA 5-8R; SATA 9; DLB 87

Fleming, Thomas J(ames) 1927- .... **CLC 37**
See also CANR 10; CA 5-8R; SATA 8

Fletcher, John Gould 1886-1950... **TCLC 35**
See also CA 107; DLB 4, 45

Flieg, Hellmuth
See Heym, Stefan

Flying Officer X 1905-1974
See Bates, H(erbert) E(rnest)

Fo, Dario 1929-.................. **CLC 32**
See also CA 116

Follett, Ken(neth Martin) 1949- .... **CLC 18**
See also CANR 13; CA 81-84; DLB-Y 81

Fontane, Theodor 1819-1898 ..... **NCLC 26**

Foote, Horton 1916-............. **CLC 51**
See also CA 73-76; DLB 26

Forbes, Esther 1891-1967.......... **CLC 12**
See also CAP 1; CA 13-14; obituary CA 25-28R; SATA 2; DLB 22

Forche, Carolyn 1950- .... **CLC 25**
See also CA 109, 117; DLB 5

Ford, Ford Madox 1873-1939 .... **TCLC 1, 15, 39**
See also CA 104; DLB 34

Ford, John 1895-1973............. **CLC 16**
See also obituary CA 45-48

Ford, Richard 1944-.............. **CLC 46**
See also CANR 11; CA 69-72

Foreman, Richard 1937-........... **CLC 50**
See also CA 65-68

Forester, C(ecil) S(cott) 1899-1966 .... **CLC 35**
See also CA 73-76; obituary CA 25-28R; SATA 13

Forman, James D(ouglas) 1932- .... **CLC 21**
See also CANR 4, 19; CA 9-12R; SATA 8, 21

Fornes, Maria Irene 1930-...... **CLC 39, 61**
See also CANR 28; CA 25-28R; DLB 7

Forrest, Leon 1937- .... **CLC 4**
See also CAAS 7; CA 89-92; DLB 33

Forster, E(dward) M(organ) 1879-1970 .... **CLC 1, 2, 3, 4, 9, 10, 13, 15, 22, 45**
See also CAP 1; CA 13-14; obituary CA 25-28R; SATA 57; DLB 34

Forster, John 1812-1876 .... **NCLC 11**

Forsyth, Frederick 1938-...... **CLC 2, 5, 36**
See also CA 85-88; DLB 87

Forten (Grimke), Charlotte L(ottie) 1837?-1914.................. **TCLC 16**
See also Grimke, Charlotte L(ottie) Forten
See also BLC 2; DLB 50

Foscolo, Ugo 1778-1827.......... **NCLC 8**

Fosse, Bob 1925-1987............. **CLC 20**
See also Fosse, Robert Louis

Fosse, Robert Louis 1925-1987
See Bob Fosse
See also CA 110, 123

Foster, Stephen Collins 1826-1864 .... **NCLC 26**

Foucault, Michel 1926-1984 .... **CLC 31, 34, 69**
See also CANR 23, 34; CA 105; obituary CA 113

Fouque, Friedrich (Heinrich Karl) de La Motte 1777-1843 .... **NCLC 2**

Fournier, Henri Alban 1886-1914
See Alain-Fournier
See also CA 104

Fournier, Pierre 1916-............ **CLC 11**
See also Gascar, Pierre
See also CANR 16; CA 89-92

Fowles, John (Robert) 1926- .... **CLC 1, 2, 3, 4, 6, 9, 10, 15, 33**
See also CANR 25; CA 5-8R; SATA 22; DLB 14

Fox, Paula 1923-............... **CLC 2, 8**
See also CLR 1; CANR 20; CA 73-76; SATA 17; DLB 52

Fox, William Price (Jr.) 1926- ..... **CLC 22**
See also CANR 11; CA 17-20R; DLB 2; DLB-Y 81

Foxe, John 1516?-1587............ **LC 14**

Frame (Clutha), Janet (Paterson) 1924- .... **CLC 2, 3, 6, 22, 66**
See also Clutha, Janet Paterson Frame

France, Anatole 1844-1924 .... **TCLC 9**
See also Thibault, Jacques Anatole Francois

Francis, Claude 19??- .... **CLC 50**

Francis, Dick 1920- .... **CLC 2, 22, 42**
See also CANR 9; CA 5-8R; DLB 87

Francis, Robert (Churchill) 1901-1987 .... **CLC 15**
See also CANR 1; CA 1-4R; obituary CA 123

Frank, Anne 1929-1945 .... **TCLC 17**
See also CA 113; SATA 42

Frank, Elizabeth 1945-............ **CLC 39**
See also CA 121, 126

Franklin, (Stella Maria Sarah) Miles 1879-1954 .... **TCLC 7**
See also CA 104

Fraser, Antonia (Pakenham) 1932- .... **CLC 32**
See also CA 85-88; SATA 32

Fraser, George MacDonald 1925-.... **CLC 7**
See also CANR 2; CA 45-48

Fraser, Sylvia 1935-.............. **CLC 64**
See also CANR 1, 16; CA 45-48

Frayn, Michael 1933-...... **CLC 3, 7, 31, 47**
See also CA 5-8R; DLB 13, 14

Fraze, Candida 19??- .... **CLC 50**
See also CA 125

Frazer, Sir James George 1854-1941 .... **TCLC 32**
See also CA 118

Frazier, Ian 1951-................ **CLC 46**
See also CA 130

Frederic, Harold 1856-1898...... **NCLC 10**
See also DLB 12, 23

Frederick the Great 1712-1786 ...... **LC 14**

Fredman, Russell (Bruce) 1929-
See also CLR 20

Fredro, Aleksander 1793-1876..... **NCLC 8**

Freeling, Nicolas 1927- .... **CLC 38**
See also CANR 1, 17; CA 49-52; DLB 87

Freeman, Douglas Southall 1886-1953 .... **TCLC 11**
See also CA 109; DLB 17

Freeman, Judith 1946-............ **CLC 55**

Freeman, Mary (Eleanor) Wilkins 1852-1930 .... **TCLC 9; SSC 1**
See also CA 106; DLB 12, 78

Freeman, R(ichard) Austin 1862-1943 .... **TCLC 21**
See also CA 113; DLB 70

French, Marilyn 1929-...... **CLC 10, 18, 60**
See also CANR 3; CA 69-72

Freneau, Philip Morin 1752-1832.. **NCLC 1**
See also DLB 37, 43

Friedman, B(ernard) H(arper) 1926- .... **CLC 7**
See also CANR 3; CA 1-4R

Friedman, Bruce Jay 1930-.... **CLC 3, 5, 56**
See also CANR 25; CA 9-12R; DLB 2, 28

Friel, Brian 1929-........... **CLC 5, 42, 59**
See also CA 21-24R; DLB 13

Gozzi, (Conte) Carlo 1720-1806 .. **NCLC 23**

Grabbe, Christian Dietrich 1801-1836 .... **NCLC 2**

Grace, Patricia 1937- .... **CLC 56**

Gracian y Morales, Baltasar 1601-1658 .... **LC 15**

Gracq, Julien 1910- .... **CLC 11, 48**
See also Poirier, Louis
See also DLB 83

Grade, Chaim 1910-1982 .... **CLC 10**
See also CA 93-96; obituary CA 107

Graham, Jorie 1951- .... **CLC 48**
See also CA 111

Graham, R(obert) B(ontine) Cunninghame 1852-1936 .... **TCLC 19**

Graham, W(illiam) S(ydney) 1918-1986 .... **CLC 29**
See also CA 73-76; obituary CA 118; DLB 20

Graham, Winston (Mawdsley) 1910- .... **CLC 23**
See also CANR 2, 22; CA 49-52; obituary CA 118

Granville-Barker, Harley 1877-1946 .... **TCLC 2**
See also CA 104

Grass, Gunter (Wilhelm) 1927- .. **CLC 1, 2, 4, 6, 11, 15, 22, 32, 49**
See also CANR 20; CA 13-16R; DLB 75

Grau, Shirley Ann 1929- .... **CLC 4, 9**
See also CANR 22; CA 89-92; DLB 2

Graves, Richard Perceval 1945- .... **CLC 44**
See also CANR 9, 26; CA 65-68

Graves, Robert (von Ranke) 1895-1985 ... **CLC 1, 2, 6, 11, 39, 44, 45**
See also CANR 5; CA 5-8R; obituary CA 117; SATA 45; DLB 20; DLB-Y 85

Gray, Alasdair 1934- .... **CLC 41**
See also CA 123

Gray, Amlin 1946- .... **CLC 29**

Gray, Francine du Plessix 1930- .... **CLC 22**
See also CAAS 2; CANR 11; CA 61-64

Gray, John (Henry) 1866-1934 .... **TCLC 19**
See also CA 119

Gray, Simon (James Holliday) 1936- .... **CLC 9, 14, 36**
See also CAAS 3; CA 21-24R; DLB 13

Gray, Spalding 1941- .... **CLC 49**

Gray, Thomas 1716-1771 .... **LC 4; PC 2**

Grayson, Richard (A.) 1951- .... **CLC 38**
See also CANR 14; CA 85-88

Greeley, Andrew M(oran) 1928- .... **CLC 28**
See also CAAS 7; CANR 7; CA 5-8R

Green, Hannah 1932- .... **CLC 3, 7, 30**
See also Greenberg, Joanne
See also CA 73-76

Green, Henry 1905-1974 .... **CLC 2, 13**
See also Yorke, Henry Vincent
See also DLB 15

Green, Julien (Hartridge) 1900- .. **CLC 3, 11**
See also CA 21-24R; DLB 4, 72

Green, Paul (Eliot) 1894-1981 ...... **CLC 25**
See also CANR 3; CA 5-8R; obituary CA 103; DLB 7, 9; DLB-Y 81

Greenberg, Ivan 1908-1973
See Rahv, Philip
See also CA 85-88

Greenberg, Joanne (Goldenberg) 1932- .... **CLC 3, 7, 30**
See also Green, Hannah
See also CANR 14; CA 5-8R; SATA 25

Greenberg, Richard 1959?- .... **CLC 57**

Greene, Bette 1934- .... **CLC 30**
See also CLR 2; CANR 4; CA 53-56; SATA 8

Greene, Gael 19??- .... **CLC 8**
See also CANR 10; CA 13-16R

Greene, Graham (Henry) 1904- ..... **CLC 1, 3, 6, 9, 14, 18, 27, 37**
See also CA 13-16R; SATA 20; DLB 13, 15; DLB-Y 85

Gregor, Arthur 1923- .... **CLC 9**
See also CANR 11; CA 25-28R; SATA 36

Gregory, J. Dennis 1925-
See Williams, John A.

Gregory, Lady (Isabella Augusta Persse) 1852-1932 .... **TCLC 1**
See also CA 104; DLB 10

Grendon, Stephen 1909-1971
See Derleth, August (William)

Grenville, Kate 1950- .... **CLC 61**
See also CA 118

Greve, Felix Paul Berthold Friedrich 1879-1948
See Grove, Frederick Philip
See also CA 104

Grey, (Pearl) Zane 1872?-1939 ..... **TCLC 6**
See also CA 104; DLB 9

Grieg, (Johan) Nordahl (Brun) 1902-1943 .... **TCLC 10**
See also CA 107

Grieve, C(hristopher) M(urray) 1892-1978
See MacDiarmid, Hugh
See also CA 5-8R; obituary CA 85-88

Griffin, Gerald 1803-1840 .... **NCLC 7**

Griffin, John Howard 1920-1980.... **CLC 68**
See also CANR 2; CA 2R; obituary CA 101

Griffin, Peter 1942- .... **CLC 39**

Griffiths, Trevor 1935- .... **CLC 13, 52**
See also CA 97-100; DLB 13

Grigson, Geoffrey (Edward Harvey) 1905-1985 .... **CLC 7, 39**
See also CANR 20; CA 25-28R; obituary CA 118; DLB 27

Grillparzer, Franz 1791-1872...... **NCLC 1**

Grimke, Charlotte L(ottie) Forten 1837?-1914
See Forten (Grimke), Charlotte L(ottie)
See also CA 117, 124

Grimm, Jakob Ludwig Karl 1785-1863 .... **NCLC 3**
See also SATA 22; DLB 90

Grimm, Wilhelm Karl 1786-1859 .. **NCLC 3**
See also SATA 22; DLB 90

Grimmelshausen, Johann Jakob Christoffel von 1621-1676 .... **LC 6**

Grindel, Eugene 1895-1952
See also brief entry CA 104

Grossman, David 1954- .... **CLC 67**

Grossman, Vasily (Semenovich) 1905-1964 .... **CLC 41**
See also CA 124, 130

Grove, Frederick Philip 1879-1948 .... **TCLC 4**
See also Greve, Felix Paul Berthold Friedrich

Grumbach, Doris (Isaac) 1918- .... **CLC 13, 22, 64**
See also CAAS 2; CANR 9; CA 5-8R

Grundtvig, Nicolai Frederik Severin 1783-1872 .... **NCLC 1**

Grunwald, Lisa 1959- .... **CLC 44**
See also CA 120

Guare, John 1938- .... **CLC 8, 14, 29, 67**
See also CANR 21; CA 73-76; DLB 7

Gudjonsson, Halldor Kiljan 1902-
See Laxness, Halldor (Kiljan)
See also CA 103

Guest, Barbara 1920- .... **CLC 34**
See also CANR 11; CA 25-28R; DLB 5

Guest, Judith (Ann) 1936- .... **CLC 8, 30**
See also CANR 15; CA 77-80

Guild, Nicholas M. 1944- .... **CLC 33**
See also CA 93-96

Guillen, Jorge 1893-1984 .... **CLC 11**
See also CA 89-92; obituary CA 112

Guillen, Nicolas 1902-1989 .... **CLC 48**
See also BLC 2; CA 116, 125; obituary CA 129

Guillen y Batista, Nicolas Cristobal 1902-1989
See Guillen, Nicolas

Guillevic, (Eugene) 1907- .... **CLC 33**
See also CA 93-96

Guiney, Louise Imogen 1861-1920 .... **TCLC 41**
See also DLB 54

Guiraldes, Ricardo 1886-1927 ..... **TCLC 39**

Gunn, Bill 1934-1989 .... **CLC 5**
See also Gunn, William Harrison
See also DLB 38

Gunn, Thom(son William) 1929- .... **CLC 3, 6, 18, 32**
See also CANR 9; CA 17-20R; DLB 27

Gunn, William Harrison 1934-1989
See Gunn, Bill
See also CANR 12, 25; CA 13-16R; obituary CA 128

Gunnars, Kristjana 1948- .... **CLC 69**
See also CA 113; DLB 60

Gurney, A(lbert) R(amsdell), Jr. 1930- .... **CLC 32, 50, 54**
See also CA 77-80

Gurney, Ivor (Bertie) 1890-1937 ... **TCLC 33**

Gustafson, Ralph (Barker) 1909- .... **CLC 36**
See also CANR 8; CA 21-24R; DLB 88

Guthrie, A(lfred) B(ertram), Jr. 1901- .... **CLC 23**
See also CA 57-60; DLB 6

Guthrie, Woodrow Wilson 1912-1967
See Guthrie, Woody
See also CA 113; obituary CA 93-96

Guthrie, Woody 1912-1967 .... **CLC 35**
See also Guthrie, Woodrow Wilson

Guy, Rosa (Cuthbert) 1928-........ **CLC 26**
See also CLR 13; CANR 14; CA 17-20R; SATA 14; DLB 33

Haavikko, Paavo (Juhani) 1931- .... **CLC 18, 34**
See also CA 106

Hacker, Marilyn 1942- .... **CLC 5, 9, 23**
See also CA 77-80

Haggard, (Sir) H(enry) Rider 1856-1925 .... **TCLC 11**
See also CA 108; SATA 16; DLB 70

Haig-Brown, Roderick L(angmere) 1908-1976 .... **CLC 21**
See also CANR 4; CA 5-8R; obituary CA 69-72; SATA 12; DLB 88

Hailey, Arthur 1920- .... **CLC 5**
See also CANR 2; CA 1-4R; DLB-Y 82

Hailey, Elizabeth Forsythe 1938-... **CLC 40**
See also CAAS 1; CANR 15; CA 93-96

Haines, John 1924-............... **CLC 58**
See also CANR 13; CA 19-20R; DLB 5

Haldeman, Joe 1943- .... **CLC 61**
See also CA 53-56; DLB 8

Haley, Alex (Palmer) 1921-...... **CLC 8, 12**
See also BLC 2; CA 77-80; DLB 38

Haliburton, Thomas Chandler 1796-1865 .... **NCLC 15**
See also DLB 11

Hall, Donald (Andrew, Jr.) 1928- .... **CLC 1, 13, 37, 59**
See also CAAS 7; CANR 2; CA 5-8R; SATA 23; DLB 5

Hall, James Norman 1887-1951 ... **TCLC 23**
See also CA 123; SATA 21

Hall, (Marguerite) Radclyffe 1886-1943 .... **TCLC 12**
See also CA 110

Hall, Rodney 1935- .... **CLC 51**
See also CA 109

Halpern, Daniel 1945- .... **CLC 14**
See also CA 33-36R

Hamburger, Michael (Peter Leopold) 1924- .... **CLC 5, 14**
See also CAAS 4; CANR 2; CA 5-8R; DLB 27

Hamill, Pete 1935-............... **CLC 10**
See also CANR 18; CA 25-28R

Hamilton, Edmond 1904-1977....... **CLC 1**
See also CANR 3; CA 1-4R; DLB 8

Hamilton, Gail 1911-
See Corcoran, Barbara

Hamilton, Ian 1938-.............. **CLC 55**
See also CA 106; DLB 40

Hamilton, Mollie 1909?-
See Kaye, M(ary) M(argaret)

Hamilton, (Anthony Walter) Patrick 1904-1962 .... **CLC 51**
See also obituary CA 113; DLB 10

Hamilton, Virginia (Esther) 1936-... **CLC 26**
See also CLR 1, 11; CANR 20; CA 25-28R; SATA 4; DLB 33, 52

Hammett, (Samuel) Dashiell 1894-1961 .... **CLC 3, 5, 10, 19, 47**
See also CA 81-84; DLB-DS 6

Hammon, Jupiter 1711?-1800? .... **NCLC 5**
See also BLC 2; DLB 31, 50, 31, 50

Hamner, Earl (Henry), Jr. 1923- ... **CLC 12**
See also CA 73-76; DLB 6

Hampton, Christopher (James) 1946- .... **CLC 4**
See also CA 25-28R; DLB 13

Hamsun, Knut 1859-1952....... **TCLC 2, 14**
See also Pedersen, Knut

Handke, Peter 1942- .. **CLC 5, 8, 10, 15, 38**
See also CA 77-80; DLB 85

Hanley, James 1901-1985 ... **CLC 3, 5, 8, 13**
See also CA 73-76; obituary CA 117

Hannah, Barry 1942-.......... **CLC 23, 38**
See also CA 108, 110; DLB 6

Hansberry, Lorraine (Vivian) 1930-1965 .... **CLC 17, 62**
See also BLC 2; CA 109; obituary CA 25-28R; CABS 3; DLB 7, 38; CDALB 1941-1968

Hansen, Joseph 1923-............ **CLC 38**
See also CANR 16; CA 29-32R

Hansen, Martin 1909-1955 .... **TCLC 32**

Hanson, Kenneth O(stlin) 1922- .... **CLC 13**
See also CANR 7; CA 53-56

Hardenberg, Friedrich (Leopold Freiherr) von 1772-1801
See Novalis

Hardwick, Elizabeth 1916- .... **CLC 13**
See also CANR 3; CA 5-8R; DLB 6

Hardy, Thomas 1840-1928 ... **TCLC 4, 10, 18, 32; SSC 2**
See also CA 104, 123; SATA 25; DLB 18, 19

Hare, David 1947- .... **CLC 29, 58**
See also CA 97-100; DLB 13

Harlan, Louis R(udolph) 1922-..... **CLC 34**
See also CANR 25; CA 21-24R

Harling, Robert 1951?-........... **CLC 53**

Harmon, William (Ruth) 1938-..... **CLC 38**
See also CANR 14; CA 33-36R

Harper, Frances Ellen Watkins 1825-1911 .... **TCLC 14**
See also BLC 2; CA 125; brief entry CA 111; DLB 50

Harper, Michael S(teven) 1938- .. **CLC 7, 22**
See also CANR 24; CA 33-36R; DLB 41

Harris, Christie (Lucy Irwin) 1907- .... **CLC 12**
See also CANR 6; CA 5-8R; SATA 6; DLB 88

Harris, Frank 1856-1931 .... **TCLC 24**
See also CAAS 1; CA 109

Harris, George Washington 1814-1869 .... **NCLC 23**
See also DLB 3, 11

Harris, Joel Chandler 1848-1908 ... **TCLC 2**
See also YABC 1; CA 104; DLB 11, 23, 42, 78, 91

Harris, John (Wyndham Parkes Lucas) Beynon 1903-1969 .... **CLC 19**
See also Wyndham, John
See also CA 102; obituary CA 89-92

Harris, MacDonald 1921- .... **CLC 9**
See also Heiney, Donald (William)

Harris, Mark 1922- .... **CLC 19**
See also CAAS 3; CANR 2; CA 5-8R; DLB 2; DLB-Y 80

Harris, (Theodore) Wilson 1921-.... **CLC 25**
See also CANR 11, 27; CA 65-68

Harrison, Harry (Max) 1925-...... **CLC 42**
See also CANR 5, 21; CA 1-4R; SATA 4; DLB 8

Harrison, James (Thomas) 1937- ... **CLC 66**
See also Harrison, Jim
See also CANR 8; CA 13-16R

Harrison, Jim 1937-......... **CLC 6, 14, 33**
See also Harrison, James (Thomas)
See also DLB-Y 82

Harrison, Tony 1937-............. **CLC 43**
See also CA 65-68; DLB 40

Harriss, Will(ard Irvin) 1922-...... **CLC 34**
See also CA 111

Hart, Moss 1904-1961 .... **CLC 66**
See also Conrad, Robert Arnold
See also obituary CA 89-92; DLB 7

Harte, (Francis) Bret(t) 1836?-1902......... **TCLC 1, 25; SSC 8**
See also brief entry CA 104; SATA 26; DLB 12, 64, 74, 79; CDALB 1865-1917

Hartley, L(eslie) P(oles) 1895-1972 .... **CLC 2, 22**
See also CA 45-48; obituary CA 37-40R; DLB 15

Hartman, Geoffrey H. 1929-....... **CLC 27**
See also CA 117, 125; DLB 67

Haruf, Kent 19??-............... **CLC 34**

Harwood, Ronald 1934-........... **CLC 32**
See also CANR 4; CA 1-4R; DLB 13

Hasek, Jaroslav (Matej Frantisek) 1883-1923 .... **TCLC 4**
See also CA 104, 129

Hass, Robert 1941-............ **CLC 18, 39**
See also CANR 30; CA 111

Hastings, Selina 19??- .... **CLC 44**

Hauptmann, Gerhart (Johann Robert) 1862-1946 .... **TCLC 4**
See also CA 104; DLB 66

Havel, Vaclav 1936-........ **CLC 25, 58, 65**
See also CA 104

Haviaras, Stratis 1935- .... **CLC 33**
See also CA 105

Hawes, Stephen 1475?-1523?........ **LC 17**

Hawkes, John (Clendennin Burne, Jr.) 1925- ...... **CLC 1, 2, 3, 4, 7, 9, 14, 15, 27, 49**
See also CANR 2; CA 1-4R; DLB 2, 7; DLB-Y 80

Hubbard, L(afayette) Ron(ald) 1911-1986 .... **CLC 43**
See also CANR 22; CA 77-80; obituary CA 118

Huch, Ricarda (Octavia) 1864-1947 .... **TCLC 13**
See also CA 111; DLB 66

Huddle, David 1942- .... **CLC 49**
See also CA 57-60

Hudson, W(illiam) H(enry) 1841-1922 .... **TCLC 29**
See also CA 115; SATA 35

Hueffer, Ford Madox 1873-1939
See Ford, Ford Madox

Hughart, Barry 1934-............. **CLC 39**

Hughes, David (John) 1930- .... **CLC 48**
See also CA 116, 129; DLB 14

Hughes, Edward James 1930-
See Hughes, Ted

Hughes, (James) Langston 1902-1967 .... **CLC 1, 5, 10, 15, 35, 44; PC 1; SSC 6**
See also BLC 2; CLR 17; CANR 1; CA 1-4R; obituary CA 25-28R; SATA 4, 33; DLB 4, 7, 48, 51, 86; CDALB 1929-1941

Hughes, Richard (Arthur Warren) 1900-1976 .... **CLC 1, 11**
See also CANR 4; CA 5-8R; obituary CA 65-68; SATA 8; obituary SATA 25; DLB 15

Hughes, Ted 1930-..... **CLC 2, 4, 9, 14, 37**
See also CLR 3; CANR 1; CA 1-4R; SATA 27, 49; DLB 40

Hugo, Richard F(ranklin) 1923-1982 .... **CLC 6, 18, 32**
See also CANR 3; CA 49-52; obituary CA 108; DLB 5

Hugo, Victor Marie 1802-1885 .... **NCLC 3, 10, 21**
See also SATA 47

Huidobro, Vicente 1893-1948 ..... **TCLC 31**

Hulme, Keri 1947- .... **CLC 39**
See also CA 125

Hulme, T(homas) E(rnest) 1883-1917 .... **TCLC 21**
See also CA 117; DLB 19

Hume, David 1711-1776............. **LC 7**

Humphrey, William 1924-......... **CLC 45**
See also CA 77-80; DLB 6

Humphreys, Emyr (Owen) 1919-.... **CLC 47**
See also CANR 3, 24; CA 5-8R; DLB 15

Humphreys, Josephine 1945-.... **CLC 34, 57**
See also CA 121, 127

Hunt, E(verette) Howard (Jr.) 1918- .... **CLC 3**
See also CANR 2; CA 45-48

Hunt, (James Henry) Leigh 1784-1859 .... **NCLC 1**

Hunter, Evan 1926- .... **CLC 11, 31**
See also CANR 5; CA 5-8R; SATA 25; DLB-Y 82

Hunter, Kristin (Eggleston) 1931-... **CLC 35**
See also CLR 3; CANR 13; CA 13-16R; SATA 12; DLB 33

Hunter, Mollie (Maureen McIlwraith) 1922- .... **CLC 21**
See also McIlwraith, Maureen Mollie Hunter

Hunter, Robert ?-1734 .... **LC 7**

Hurston, Zora Neale 1901?-1960....... **CLC 7, 30, 61; SSC 4**
See also BLC 2; CA 85-88; DLB 51, 86

Huston, John (Marcellus) 1906-1987 .... **CLC 20**
See also CA 73-76; obituary CA 123; DLB 26

Hutten, Ulrich von 1488-1523....... **LC 16**

Huxley, Aldous (Leonard) 1894-1963 .. **CLC 1, 3, 4, 5, 8, 11, 18, 35**
See also CA 85-88; DLB 36

Huysmans, Charles Marie Georges 1848-1907
See Huysmans, Joris-Karl
See also CA 104

Huysmans, Joris-Karl 1848-1907 ... **TCLC 7**
See also Huysmans, Charles Marie Georges

Hwang, David Henry 1957-........ **CLC 55**
See also CA 127

Hyde, Anthony 1946?-............ **CLC 42**

Hyde, Margaret O(ldroyd) 1917- ... **CLC 21**
See also CLR 23; CANR 1; CA 1-4R; SAAS 8; SATA 1, 42

Hynes, James 1956?-............. **CLC 65**

Ian, Janis 1951- .... **CLC 21**
See also CA 105

Ibarguengoitia, Jorge 1928-1983.... **CLC 37**
See also obituary CA 113, 124

Ibsen, Henrik (Johan) 1828-1906 .... **TCLC 2, 8, 16, 37**
See also CA 104

Ibuse, Masuji 1898-............... **CLC 22**
See also CA 127

Ichikawa, Kon 1915-.............. **CLC 20**
See also CA 121

Idle, Eric 1943-.................. **CLC 21**
See also Monty Python
See also CA 116

Ignatow, David 1914-...... **CLC 4, 7, 14, 40**
See also CAAS 3; CA 9-12R; DLB 5

Ihimaera, Witi (Tame) 1944-....... **CLC 46**
See also CA 77-80

Ilf, Ilya 1897-1937 .... **TCLC 21**

Immermann, Karl (Lebrecht) 1796-1840 .... **NCLC 4**

Ingalls, Rachel 19??-.............. **CLC 42**
See also CA 123, 127

Ingamells, Rex 1913-1955 .... **TCLC 35**

Inge, William (Motter) 1913-1973 .... **CLC 1, 8, 19**
See also CA 9-12R; DLB 7; CDALB 1941-1968

Innaurato, Albert 1948-........ **CLC 21, 60**
See also CA 115, 122

Innes, Michael 1906-
See Stewart, J(ohn) I(nnes) M(ackintosh)

Ionesco, Eugene 1912-........ **CLC 1, 4, 6, 9, 11, 15, 41**
See also CA 9-12R; SATA 7

Iqbal, Muhammad 1877-1938 ..... **TCLC 28**

Irving, John (Winslow) 1942- .... **CLC 13, 23, 38**
See also CANR 28; CA 25-28R; DLB 6; DLB-Y 82

Irving, Washington 1783-1859 .... **NCLC 2, 19; SSC 2**
See also YABC 2; DLB 3, 11, 30, 59, 73, 74; CDALB 1640-1865

Isaacs, Susan 1943- .... **CLC 32**
See also CANR 20; CA 89-92

Isherwood, Christopher (William Bradshaw) 1904-1986 .... **CLC 1, 9, 11, 14, 44**
See also CA 13-16R; obituary CA 117; DLB 15; DLB-Y 86

Ishiguro, Kazuo 1954- ...... **CLC 27, 56, 59**
See also CA 120

Ishikawa Takuboku 1885-1912 .... **TCLC 15**
See also CA 113

Iskander, Fazil (Abdulovich) 1929- .... **CLC 47**
See also CA 102

Ivan IV 1530-1584 .... **LC 17**

Ivanov, Vyacheslav (Ivanovich) 1866-1949 .... **TCLC 33**
See also CA 122

Ivask, Ivar (Vidrik) 1927- .... **CLC 14**
See also CANR 24; CA 37-40R

Jackson, Jesse 1908-1983 .... **CLC 12**
See also CANR 27; CA 25-28R; obituary CA 109; SATA 2, 29, 48

Jackson, Laura (Riding) 1901- ...... **CLC 7**
See also Riding, Laura
See also CANR 28; CA 65-68; DLB 48

Jackson, Shirley 1919-1965 .... **CLC 11, 60; SSC 9**
See also CANR 4; CA 1-4R; obituary CA 25-28R; SATA 2; DLB 6; CDALB 1941-1968

Jacob, (Cyprien) Max 1876-1944 ... **TCLC 6**
See also CA 104

Jacob, Piers A(nthony) D(illingham) 1934-
See Anthony (Jacob), Piers
See also CA 21-24R

Jacobs, Jim 1942- and **Casey, Warren** 1942- .... **CLC 12**
See also CA 97-100

Jacobs, Jim 1942-
See Jacobs, Jim and Casey, Warren
See also CA 97-100

Jacobs, W(illiam) W(ymark) 1863-1943 .... **TCLC 22**
See also CA 121

Jacobsen, Jens Peter 1847-1885 .. **NCLC 34**

Jacobsen, Josephine 1908-......... **CLC 48**
See also CANR 23; CA 33-36R

Jacobson, Dan 1929- .... **CLC 4, 14**
See also CANR 2, 25; CA 1-4R; DLB 14

Jagger, Mick 1944-............... **CLC 17**

Jakes, John (William) 1932- .... **CLC 29**
See also CANR 10; CA 57-60; DLB-Y 83

James, C(yril) L(ionel) R(obert) 1901-1989 .... **CLC 33**
See also CA 117, 125; obituary CA 128

James, Daniel 1911-1988
See Santiago, Danny
See also obituary CA 125

James, Henry (Jr.) 1843-1916 ... **TCLC 2, 11, 24, 40; SSC 8**
See also CA 132; brief entry CA 104; DLB 12, 71, 74; CDALB 1865-1917

James, M(ontague) R(hodes) 1862-1936 .... **TCLC 6**
See also CA 104

James, P(hyllis) D(orothy) 1920- .... **CLC 18, 46**
See also CANR 17; CA 21-24R

James, William 1842-1910..... **TCLC 15, 32**
See also CA 109

Jami, Nur al-Din 'Abd al-Rahman 1414-1492 .... **LC 9**

Jandl, Ernst 1925- .... **CLC 34**

Janowitz, Tama 1957- .... **CLC 43**
See also CA 106

Jarrell, Randall 1914-1965 .... **CLC 1, 2, 6, 9, 13, 49**
See also CLR 6; CANR 6; CA 5-8R; obituary CA 25-28R; CABS 2; SATA 7; DLB 48, 52; CDALB 1941-1968

Jarry, Alfred 1873-1907........ **TCLC 2, 14**
See also CA 104

Jeake, Samuel, Jr. 1889-1973
See Aiken, Conrad

Jean Paul 1763-1825 .... **NCLC 7**

Jeffers, (John) Robinson 1887-1962 .... **CLC 2, 3, 11, 15, 54**
See also CA 85-88; DLB 45; CDALB 1917-1929

Jefferson, Thomas 1743-1826 .... **NCLC 11**
See also DLB 31; CDALB 1640-1865

Jeffrey, Francis 1773-1850....... **NCLC 33**

Jellicoe, (Patricia) Ann 1927- ...... **CLC 27**
See also CA 85-88; DLB 13

Jenkins, (John) Robin 1912- .... **CLC 52**
See also CANR 1; CA 4R; DLB 14

Jennings, Elizabeth (Joan) 1926- .... **CLC 5, 14**
See also CAAS 5; CANR 8; CA 61-64; DLB 27

Jennings, Waylon 1937-........... **CLC 21**

Jensen, Johannes V. 1873-1950.... **TCLC 41**

Jensen, Laura (Linnea) 1948- ...... **CLC 37**
See also CA 103

Jerome, Jerome K. 1859-1927..... **TCLC 23**
See also CA 119; DLB 10, 34

Jerrold, Douglas William 1803-1857 .... **NCLC 2**

Jewett, (Theodora) Sarah Orne 1849-1909 .... **TCLC 1, 22; SSC 6**
See also CA 108, 127; SATA 15; DLB 12, 74

Jewsbury, Geraldine (Endsor) 1812-1880 .... **NCLC 22**
See also DLB 21

Jhabvala, Ruth Prawer 1927- .... **CLC 4, 8, 29**
See also CANR 2, 29; CA 1-4R

Jiles, Paulette 1943-........... **CLC 13, 58**
See also CA 101

Jimenez (Mantecon), Juan Ramon 1881-1958 .... **TCLC 4**
See also CA 104

Joel, Billy 1949-................. **CLC 26**
See also Joel, William Martin

Joel, William Martin 1949-
See Joel, Billy
See also CA 108

John of the Cross, St. 1542-1591 .... **LC 18**

Johnson, B(ryan) S(tanley William) 1933-1973 .... **CLC 6, 9**
See also CANR 9; CA 9-12R; obituary CA 53-56; DLB 14, 40

Johnson, Charles (Richard) 1948- .... **CLC 7, 51, 65**
See also BLC 2; CA 116; DLB 33

Johnson, Denis 1949-............. **CLC 52**
See also CA 117, 121

Johnson, Diane 1934-........ **CLC 5, 13, 48**
See also CANR 17; CA 41-44R; DLB-Y 80

Johnson, Eyvind (Olof Verner) 1900-1976 .... **CLC 14**
See also CA 73-76; obituary CA 69-72

Johnson, Fenton 1888-1958
See also BLC 2; CA 124; brief entry CA 118; DLB 45, 50

Johnson, James Weldon 1871-1938 .... **TCLC 3, 19**
See also Johnson, James William
See also BLC 2; CA 125; brief entry CA 104; SATA 31; DLB 51; CDALB 1917-1929

Johnson, James William 1871-1938
See Johnson, James Weldon
See also SATA 31

Johnson, Joyce 1935-............. **CLC 58**
See also CA 125, 129

Johnson, Lionel (Pigot) 1867-1902 .... **TCLC 19**
See also CA 117; DLB 19

Johnson, Marguerita 1928-
See Angelou, Maya

Johnson, Pamela Hansford 1912-1981 .... **CLC 1, 7, 27**
See also CANR 2, 28; CA 1-4R; obituary CA 104; DLB 15

Johnson, Samuel 1709-1784......... **LC 15**
See also DLB 39, 95

Johnson, Uwe 1934-1984 .... **CLC 5, 10, 15, 40**
See also CANR 1; CA 1-4R; obituary CA 112; DLB 75

Johnston, George (Benson) 1913- ... **CLC 51**
See also CANR 5, 20; CA 1-4R; DLB 88

Johnston, Jennifer 1930- .... **CLC 7**
See also CA 85-88; DLB 14

Jolley, Elizabeth 1923-............ **CLC 46**
See also CA 127

Jones, D(ouglas) G(ordon) 1929-.... **CLC 10**
See also CANR 13; CA 29-32R, 113; DLB 53

Jones, David 1895-1974 .... **CLC 2, 4, 7, 13, 42**
See also CANR 28; CA 9-12R; obituary CA 53-56; DLB 20

Jones, David Robert 1947-
See Bowie, David
See also CA 103

Jones, Diana Wynne 1934- .... **CLC 26**
See also CLR 23; CANR 4, 26; CA 49-52; SAAS 7; SATA 9

Jones, Gayl 1949-............... **CLC 6, 9**
See also BLC 2; CANR 27; CA 77-80; DLB 33

Jones, James 1921-1977.... **CLC 1, 3, 10, 39**
See also CANR 6; CA 1-4R; obituary CA 69-72; DLB 2

Jones, (Everett) LeRoi 1934- .... **CLC 1, 2, 3, 5, 10, 14, 33**
See also Baraka, Amiri; Baraka, Imamu Amiri
See also CA 21-24R

Jones, Louis B. 19??-............. **CLC 65**

Jones, Madison (Percy, Jr.) 1925- ... **CLC 4**
See also CAAS 11; CANR 7; CA 13-16R

Jones, Mervyn 1922- .... **CLC 10, 52**
See also CAAS 5; CANR 1; CA 45-48

Jones, Mick 1956?-............... **CLC 30**
See also The Clash

Jones, Nettie 19??-............... **CLC 34**

Jones, Preston 1936-1979 .... **CLC 10**
See also CA 73-76; obituary CA 89-92; DLB 7

Jones, Robert F(rancis) 1934-....... **CLC 7**
See also CANR 2; CA 49-52

Jones, Rod 1953- .... **CLC 50**
See also CA 128

Jones, Terry 1942?- .... **CLC 21**
See also Monty Python
See also CA 112, 116; SATA 51

Jong, Erica 1942-.......... **CLC 4, 6, 8, 18**
See also CANR 26; CA 73-76; DLB 2, 5, 28

Jonson, Ben(jamin) 1572(?)-1637...... **LC 6**
See also DLB 62

Jordan, June 1936-.......... **CLC 5, 11, 23**
See also CLR 10; CANR 25; CA 33-36R; SATA 4; DLB 38; AAYA 2

Jordan, Pat(rick M.) 1941- .... **CLC 37**
See also CANR 25; CA 33-36R

Josipovici, Gabriel (David) 1940- .... **CLC 6, 43**
See also CAAS 8; CA 37-40R; DLB 14

Joubert, Joseph 1754-1824 .... **NCLC 9**

Jouve, Pierre Jean 1887-1976...... **CLC 47**
See also obituary CA 65-68

Joyce, James (Augustine Aloysius) 1882-1941 ...... **TCLC 3, 8, 16, 26, 35; SSC 3**
See also CA 104, 126; DLB 10, 19, 36

Jozsef, Attila 1905-1937.......... **TCLC 22**
See also CA 116

Juana Ines de la Cruz 1651?-1695 .... **LC 5**

Julian of Norwich 1342?-1416? .... **LC 6**

Just, Ward S(wift) 1935- .... **CLC 4, 27**
See also CA 25-28R

Justice, Donald (Rodney) 1925- .. **CLC 6, 19**
See also CANR 26; CA 5-8R; DLB-Y 83

Juvenal c. 55-c. 127 .... **CMLC 8**

Kacew, Romain 1914-1980
See Gary, Romain
See also CA 108; obituary CA 102

Kacewgary, Romain 1914-1980
See Gary, Romain

Kadare, Ismail 1936- .... **CLC 52**

Kadohata, Cynthia 19??- .... **CLC 59**

Kafka, Franz
1883-1924 .... **TCLC 2, 6, 13, 29; SSC 5**
See also CA 105, 126; DLB 81

Kahn, Roger 1927- .... **CLC 30**
See also CA 25-28R; SATA 37

Kaiser, (Friedrich Karl) Georg
1878-1945 .... **TCLC 9**
See also CA 106

Kaletski, Alexander 1946- .... **CLC 39**
See also CA 118

Kallman, Chester (Simon)
1921-1975 .... **CLC 2**
See also CANR 3; CA 45-48;
obituary CA 53-56

Kaminsky, Melvin 1926-
See Brooks, Mel
See also CANR 16; CA 65-68

Kaminsky, Stuart 1934- .... **CLC 59**
See also CANR 29; CA 73-76

Kane, Paul 1941-
See Simon, Paul

Kanin, Garson 1912- .... **CLC 22**
See also CANR 7; CA 5-8R; DLB 7

Kaniuk, Yoram 1930- .... **CLC 19**

Kant, Immanuel 1724-1804 ...... **NCLC 27**

Kantor, MacKinlay 1904-1977 ...... **CLC 7**
See also CA 61-64; obituary CA 73-76;
DLB 9

Kaplan, David Michael 1946- ...... **CLC 50**

Kaplan, James 19??- .... **CLC 59**

Karamzin, Nikolai Mikhailovich
1766-1826 .... **NCLC 3**

Karapanou, Margarita 1946- .... **CLC 13**
See also CA 101

Karl, Frederick R(obert) 1927- ..... **CLC 34**
See also CANR 3; CA 5-8R

Kassef, Romain 1914-1980
See Gary, Romain

Katz, Steve 1935- .... **CLC 47**
See also CANR 12; CA 25-28R; DLB-Y 83

Kauffman, Janet 1945- .... **CLC 42**
See also CA 117; DLB-Y 86

Kaufman, Bob (Garnell)
1925-1986 .... **CLC 49**
See also CANR 22; CA 41-44R;
obituary CA 118; DLB 16, 41

Kaufman, George S(imon)
1889-1961 .... **CLC 38**
See also CA 108; obituary CA 93-96; DLB 7

Kaufman, Sue 1926-1977 .... **CLC 3, 8**
See also Barondess, Sue K(aufman)

Kavan, Anna 1904-1968 .... **CLC 5, 13**
See also Edmonds, Helen (Woods)
See also CANR 6; CA 5-8R

Kavanagh, Patrick (Joseph Gregory)
1905-1967 .... **CLC 22**
See also CA 123; obituary CA 25-28R;
DLB 15, 20

Kawabata, Yasunari
1899-1972 .... **CLC 2, 5, 9, 18**
See also CA 93-96; obituary CA 33-36R

Kaye, M(ary) M(argaret) 1909?- .... **CLC 28**
See also CANR 24; CA 89-92

Kaye, Mollie 1909?-
See Kaye, M(ary) M(argaret)

Kaye-Smith, Sheila 1887-1956 ..... **TCLC 20**
See also CA 118; DLB 36

Kaymor, Patrice Maguilene 1906-
See Senghor, Leopold Sedar

Kazan, Elia 1909- .... **CLC 6, 16, 63**
See also CA 21-24R

Kazantzakis, Nikos
1885?-1957 .... **TCLC 2, 5, 33**
See also CA 105

Kazin, Alfred 1915- .... **CLC 34, 38**
See also CAAS 7; CANR 1; CA 1-4R;
DLB 67

Keane, Mary Nesta (Skrine) 1904-
See Keane, Molly
See also CA 108, 114

Keane, Molly 1904- .... **CLC 31**
See also Keane, Mary Nesta (Skrine)

Keates, Jonathan 19??- .... **CLC 34**

Keaton, Buster 1895-1966 .... **CLC 20**

Keaton, Joseph Francis 1895-1966
See Keaton, Buster

Keats, John 1795-1821 ...... **NCLC 8; PC 1**

Keene, Donald 1922- .... **CLC 34**
See also CANR 5; CA 1-4R

Keillor, Garrison 1942- .... **CLC 40**
See also Keillor, Gary (Edward)
See also CA 111; SATA 58; DLB-Y 87;
AAYA 2

Keillor, Gary (Edward)
See Keillor, Garrison
See also CA 111, 117

Kell, Joseph 1917-
See Burgess (Wilson, John) Anthony

Keller, Gottfried 1819-1890 .... **NCLC 2**

Kellerman, Jonathan (S.) 1949- ..... **CLC 44**
See also CANR 29; CA 106

Kelley, William Melvin 1937- ...... **CLC 22**
See also CANR 27; CA 77-80; DLB 33

Kellogg, Marjorie 1922- .... **CLC 2**
See also CA 81-84

Kelly, M. T. 1947- .... **CLC 55**
See also CANR 19; CA 97-100

Kelman, James 1946- .... **CLC 58**

Kemal, Yashar 1922- .... **CLC 14, 29**
See also CA 89-92

Kemble, Fanny 1809-1893 .... **NCLC 18**
See also DLB 32

Kemelman, Harry 1908- .... **CLC 2**
See also CANR 6; CA 9-12R; DLB 28

Kempe, Margery 1373?-1440? .... **LC 6**

Kempis, Thomas á 1380-1471 .... **LC 11**

Kendall, Henry 1839-1882 .... **NCLC 12**

Keneally, Thomas (Michael)
1935- ...... **CLC 5, 8, 10, 14, 19, 27, 43**
See also CANR 10; CA 85-88

Kennedy, Adrienne 1931-
See also BLC 2; CANR 26; CA 103;
CABS 3; DLB 38

Kennedy, Adrienne (Lita) 1931- .... **CLC 66**
See also CANR 26; CA 103; CABS 3;
DLB 38

Kennedy, John Pendleton
1795-1870 .... **NCLC 2**
See also DLB 3

Kennedy, Joseph Charles 1929- ...... **CLC 8**
See also Kennedy, X. J.
See also CANR 4, 30; CA 1-4R; SATA 14

Kennedy, William (Joseph)
1928- .... **CLC 6, 28, 34, 53**
See also CANR 14; CA 85-88; SATA 57;
DLB-Y 85; AAYA 1

Kennedy, X. J. 1929- .... **CLC 8, 42**
See also Kennedy, Joseph Charles
See also CAAS 9; DLB 5

Kerouac, Jack
1922-1969 .... **CLC 1, 2, 3, 5, 14, 29, 61**
See also Kerouac, Jean-Louis Lebris de
See also DLB 2, 16; DLB-DS 3;
CDALB 1941-1968

Kerouac, Jean-Louis Lebris de 1922-1969
See Kerouac, Jack
See also CANR 26; CA 5-8R;
obituary CA 25-28R; CDALB 1941-1968

Kerr, Jean 1923- .... **CLC 22**
See also CANR 7; CA 5-8R

Kerr, M. E. 1927- .... **CLC 12, 35**
See also Meaker, Marijane
See also SAAS 1; AAYA 2

Kerr, Robert 1970?- .... **CLC 55, 59**

Kerrigan, (Thomas) Anthony
1918- .... **CLC 4, 6**
See also CAAS 11; CANR 4; CA 49-52

Kesey, Ken (Elton)
1935- .... **CLC 1, 3, 6, 11, 46, 64**
See also CANR 22; CA 1-4R; DLB 2, 16;
CDALB 1968-1987

Kesselring, Joseph (Otto)
1902-1967 .... **CLC 45**

Kessler, Jascha (Frederick) 1929- .... **CLC 4**
See also CANR 8; CA 17-20R

Kettelkamp, Larry 1933- .... **CLC 12**
See also CANR 16; CA 29-32R; SAAS 3;
SATA 2

Kherdian, David 1931- .... **CLC 6, 9**
See also CLR 24; CAAS 2; CA 21-24R;
SATA 16

Khlebnikov, Velimir (Vladimirovich)
1885-1922 .... **TCLC 20**
See also CA 117

Khodasevich, Vladislav (Felitsianovich)
1886-1939 .... **TCLC 15**
See also CA 115

Mishima, Yukio 1925-1970 .... **CLC 2, 4, 6, 9, 27; DC 1; SSC 4**
See also Hiraoka, Kimitake

Mistral, Gabriela 1889-1957 .... **TCLC 2**
See also CA 104

Mitchell, James Leslie 1901-1935
See Gibbon, Lewis Grassic
See also CA 104; DLB 15

Mitchell, Joni 1943-.............. **CLC 12**
See also CA 112

Mitchell (Marsh), Margaret (Munnerlyn) 1900-1949 .... **TCLC 11**
See also CA 109, 125; DLB 9

Mitchell, S. Weir 1829-1914 ...... **TCLC 36**

Mitchell, W(illiam) O(rmond) 1914- .... **CLC 25**
See also CANR 15; CA 77-80; DLB 88

Mitford, Mary Russell 1787-1855.. **NCLC 4**

Mitford, Nancy 1904-1973......... **CLC 44**
See also CA 9-12R

Miyamoto Yuriko 1899-1951...... **TCLC 37**

Mo, Timothy 1950-............... **CLC 46**
See also CA 117

Modarressi, Taghi 1931- .... **CLC 44**
See also CA 121

Modiano, Patrick (Jean) 1945- ..... **CLC 18**
See also CANR 17; CA 85-88; DLB 83

Mofolo, Thomas (Mokopu) 1876-1948 .... **TCLC 22**
See also BLC 3; brief entry CA 121

Mohr, Nicholasa 1935-............ **CLC 12**
See also CLR 22; CANR 1; CA 49-52; SAAS 8; SATA 8

Mojtabai, A(nn) G(race) 1938- .... **CLC 5, 9, 15, 29**
See also CA 85-88

Moliere 1622-1673 .... **LC 10**

Molnar, Ferenc 1878-1952........ **TCLC 20**
See also CA 109

Momaday, N(avarre) Scott 1934- .... **CLC 2, 19**
See also CANR 14; CA 25-28R; SATA 30, 48

Monroe, Harriet 1860-1936....... **TCLC 12**
See also CA 109; DLB 54, 91

Montagu, Elizabeth 1720-1800 .... **NCLC 7**

Montagu, Lady Mary (Pierrepont) Wortley 1689-1762 .... **LC 9**

Montague, John (Patrick) 1929- .... **CLC 13, 46**
See also CANR 9; CA 9-12R; DLB 40

Montaigne, Michel (Eyquem) de 1533-1592 .... **LC 8**

Montale, Eugenio 1896-1981... **CLC 7, 9, 18**
See also CANR 30; CA 17-20R; obituary CA 104

Montesquieu, Charles-Louis de Secondat 1689-1755 .... **LC 7**

Montgomery, Marion (H., Jr.) 1925- .... **CLC 7**
See also CANR 3; CA 1-4R; DLB 6

Montgomery, Robert Bruce 1921-1978
See Crispin, Edmund
See also CA 104

Montherlant, Henri (Milon) de 1896-1972 .... **CLC 8, 19**
See also CA 85-88; obituary CA 37-40R; DLB 72

Monty Python .... **CLC 21**

Moodie, Susanna (Strickland) 1803-1885 .... **NCLC 14**

Mooney, Ted 1951-............... **CLC 25**

Moorcock, Michael (John) 1939- .... **CLC 5, 27, 58**
See also CAAS 5; CANR 2, 17; CA 45-48; DLB 14

Moore, Brian 1921- .... **CLC 1, 3, 5, 7, 8, 19, 32**
See also CANR 1, 25; CA 1-4R

Moore, George (Augustus) 1852-1933 .... **TCLC 7**
See also CA 104; DLB 10, 18, 57

Moore, Lorrie 1957-........ **CLC 39, 45, 68**
See also Moore, Marie Lorena

Moore, Marianne (Craig) 1887-1972 ... **CLC 1, 2, 4, 8, 10, 13, 19, 47**
See also CANR 3; CA 1-4R; obituary CA 33-36R; SATA 20; DLB 45; CDALB 1929-1941

Moore, Marie Lorena 1957-
See Moore, Lorrie
See also CA 116

Moore, Thomas 1779-1852........ **NCLC 6**

Morand, Paul 1888-1976 .... **CLC 41**
See also obituary CA 69-72; DLB 65

Morante, Elsa 1918-1985........ **CLC 8, 47**
See also CA 85-88; obituary CA 117

Moravia, Alberto 1907- .... **CLC 2, 7, 11, 18, 27, 46**
See also Pincherle, Alberto

More, Hannah 1745-1833 .... **NCLC 27**

More, Henry 1614-1687............. **LC 9**

More, Sir Thomas 1478-1535 .... **LC 10**

Moreas, Jean 1856-1910 .... **TCLC 18**

Morgan, Berry 1919-.............. **CLC 6**
See also CA 49-52; DLB 6

Morgan, Edwin (George) 1920-..... **CLC 31**
See also CANR 3; CA 7-8R; DLB 27

Morgan, (George) Frederick 1922- .... **CLC 23**
See also CANR 21; CA 17-20R

Morgan, Janet 1945- .... **CLC 39**
See also CA 65-68

Morgan, Lady 1776?-1859....... **NCLC 29**

Morgan, Robin 1941-.............. **CLC 2**
See also CA 69-72

Morgan, Seth 1949-1990 .... **CLC 65**
See also CA 132

Morgenstern, Christian (Otto Josef Wolfgang) 1871-1914 .... **TCLC 8**
See also CA 105

Moricz, Zsigmond 1879-1942 ..... **TCLC 33**

Morike, Eduard (Friedrich) 1804-1875 .... **NCLC 10**

Mori Ogai 1862-1922............ **TCLC 14**
See also Mori Rintaro

Mori Rintaro 1862-1922
See Mori Ogai
See also CA 110

Moritz, Karl Philipp 1756-1793 ...... **LC 2**

Morris, Julian 1916-
See West, Morris L.

Morris, Steveland Judkins 1950-
See Wonder, Stevie
See also CA 111

Morris, William 1834-1896 .... **NCLC 4**
See also DLB 18, 35, 57

Morris, Wright (Marion) 1910- .... **CLC 1, 3, 7, 18, 37**
See also CANR 21; CA 9-12R; DLB 2; DLB-Y 81

Morrison, James Douglas 1943-1971
See Morrison, Jim
See also CA 73-76

Morrison, Jim 1943-1971.......... **CLC 17**
See also Morrison, James Douglas

Morrison, Toni 1931-..... **CLC 4, 10, 22, 55**
See also BLC 3; CANR 27; CA 29-32R; SATA 57; DLB 6, 33; DLB-Y 81; CDALB 1968-1987; AAYA 1

Morrison, Van 1945- .... **CLC 21**
See also CA 116

Mortimer, John (Clifford) 1923- .... **CLC 28, 43**
See also CANR 21; CA 13-16R; DLB 13

Mortimer, Penelope (Ruth) 1918-.... **CLC 5**
See also CA 57-60

Mosher, Howard Frank 19??-...... **CLC 62**

Mosley, Nicholas 1923-........... **CLC 43**
See also CA 69-72; DLB 14

Moss, Howard 1922-1987 .... **CLC 7, 14, 45, 50**
See also CANR 1; CA 1-4R; obituary CA 123; DLB 5

Motion, Andrew (Peter) 1952-...... **CLC 47**
See also DLB 40

Motley, Willard (Francis) 1912-1965 .... **CLC 18**
See also CA 117; obituary CA 106; DLB 76

Mott, Michael (Charles Alston) 1930- .... **CLC 15, 34**
See also CAAS 7; CANR 7, 29; CA 5-8R

Mowat, Farley (McGill) 1921- ..... **CLC 26**
See also CLR 20; CANR 4, 24; CA 1-4R; SATA 3, 55; DLB 68; AAYA 1

Mphahlele, Es'kia 1919-
See Mphahlele, Ezekiel

Mphahlele, Ezekiel 1919-.......... **CLC 25**
See also BLC 3; CANR 26; CA 81-84

Mqhayi, S(amuel) E(dward) K(rune Loliwe) 1875-1945 .... **TCLC 25**
See also BLC 3

Mrozek, Slawomir 1930-........ **CLC 3, 13**
See also CAAS 10; CANR 29; CA 13-16R

Mtwa, Percy 19??-............... **CLC 47**

Nordhoff, Charles 1887-1947...... **TCLC 23**
See also CA 108; SATA 23; DLB 9

Norman, Marsha 1947- .... **CLC 28**
See also CA 105; CABS 3; DLB-Y 84

Norris, (Benjamin) Frank(lin)
1870-1902 .... **TCLC 24**
See also CA 110; DLB 12, 71; CDALB 1865-1917

Norris, Leslie 1921-.............. **CLC 14**
See also CANR 14; CAP 1; CA 11-12; DLB 27

North, Andrew 1912-
See Norton, Andre

North, Christopher 1785-1854
See Wilson, John

Norton, Alice Mary 1912-
See Norton, Andre
See also CANR 2; CA 1-4R; SATA 1, 43

Norton, Andre 1912- .... **CLC 12**
See also Norton, Mary Alice
See also DLB 8, 52

Norway, Nevil Shute 1899-1960
See Shute (Norway), Nevil
See also CA 102; obituary CA 93-96

Norwid, Cyprian Kamil
1821-1883 .... **NCLC 17**

Nossack, Hans Erich 1901-1978..... **CLC 6**
See also CA 93-96; obituary CA 85-88; DLB 69

Nova, Craig 1945-.............. **CLC 7, 31**
See also CANR 2; CA 45-48

Novak, Joseph 1933-
See Kosinski, Jerzy (Nikodem)

Novalis 1772-1801 .... **NCLC 13**

Nowlan, Alden (Albert) 1933-...... **CLC 15**
See also CANR 5; CA 9-12R; DLB 53

Noyes, Alfred 1880-1958.......... **TCLC 7**
See also CA 104; DLB 20

Nunn, Kem 19??-................. **CLC 34**

Nye, Robert 1939- .... **CLC 13, 42**
See also CANR 29; CA 33-36R; SATA 6; DLB 14

Nyro, Laura 1947- .... **CLC 17**

Oates, Joyce Carol
1938- ..... **CLC 1, 2, 3, 6, 9, 11, 15, 19, 33, 52; SSC 6**
See also CANR 25; CA 5-8R; DLB 2, 5; DLB-Y 81; CDALB 1968-1987

O'Brien, Darcy 1939-............. **CLC 11**
See also CANR 8; CA 21-24R

O'Brien, Edna
1936- .... **CLC 3, 5, 8, 13, 36, 65**
See also CANR 6; CA 1-4R; DLB 14

O'Brien, Fitz-James 1828?-1862.. **NCLC 21**
See also DLB 74

O'Brien, Flann
1911-1966 .... **CLC 1, 4, 5, 7, 10, 47**
See also O Nuallain, Brian

O'Brien, Richard 19??-........... **CLC 17**
See also CA 124

O'Brien, (William) Tim(othy)
1946- .... **CLC 7, 19, 40**
See also CA 85-88; DLB-Y 80

Obstfelder, Sigbjorn 1866-1900.... **TCLC 23**
See also CA 123

O'Casey, Sean
1880-1964 .... **CLC 1, 5, 9, 11, 15**
See also CA 89-92; DLB 10

Ochs, Phil 1940-1976............. **CLC 17**
See also obituary CA 65-68

O'Connor, Edwin (Greene)
1918-1968 .... **CLC 14**
See also CA 93-96; obituary CA 25-28R

O'Connor, (Mary) Flannery
1925-1964 ... **CLC 1, 2, 3, 6, 10, 13, 15, 21, 66; SSC 1**
See also CANR 3; CA 1-4R; DLB 2; DLB-Y 80; CDALB 1941-1968

O'Connor, Frank
1903-1966 .... **CLC 14, 23; SSC 5**
See also O'Donovan, Michael (John)
See also CA 93-96

O'Dell, Scott 1903-............... **CLC 30**
See also CLR 1, 16; CANR 12; CA 61-64; SATA 12; DLB 52

Odets, Clifford 1906-1963 .... **CLC 2, 28**
See also CA 85-88; DLB 7, 26

O'Donovan, Michael (John)
1903-1966 .... **CLC 14**
See also O'Connor, Frank
See also CA 93-96

Oe, Kenzaburo 1935- .... **CLC 10, 36**
See also CA 97-100

O'Faolain, Julia 1932-....... **CLC 6, 19, 47**
See also CAAS 2; CANR 12; CA 81-84; DLB 14

O'Faolain, Sean 1900-..... **CLC 1, 7, 14, 32**
See also CANR 12; CA 61-64; DLB 15

O'Flaherty, Liam
1896-1984 .... **CLC 5, 34; SSC 6**
See also CA 101; obituary CA 113; DLB 36; DLB-Y 84

O'Grady, Standish (James)
1846-1928 .... **TCLC 5**
See also CA 104

O'Grady, Timothy 1951- .... **CLC 59**

O'Hara, Frank 1926-1966 ..... **CLC 2, 5, 13**
See also CA 9-12R; obituary CA 25-28R; DLB 5, 16; CDALB 1929-1941

O'Hara, John (Henry)
1905-1970 .... **CLC 1, 2, 3, 6, 11, 42**
See also CA 5-8R; obituary CA 25-28R; DLB 9; DLB-DS 2; CDALB 1929-1941

O'Hara Family
See Banim, John and Banim, Michael

O'Hehir, Diana 1922-............ **CLC 41**
See also CA 93-96

Okigbo, Christopher (Ifenayichukwu)
1932-1967 .... **CLC 25**
See also BLC 3; CA 77-80

Olds, Sharon 1942-........... **CLC 32, 39**
See also CANR 18; CA 101

Olesha, Yuri (Karlovich)
1899-1960 .... **CLC 8**
See also CA 85-88

Oliphant, Margaret (Oliphant Wilson)
1828-1897 .... **NCLC 11**
See also DLB 18

Oliver, Mary 1935-............ **CLC 19, 34**
See also CANR 9; CA 21-24R; DLB 5

Olivier, (Baron) Laurence (Kerr)
1907- .... **CLC 20**
See also CA 111, 129

Olsen, Tillie 1913- .... **CLC 4, 13**
See also CANR 1; CA 1-4R; DLB 28; DLB-Y 80

Olson, Charles (John)
1910-1970 ..... **CLC 1, 2, 5, 6, 9, 11, 29**
See also CAP 1; CA 15-16; obituary CA 25-28R; CABS 2; DLB 5, 16

Olson, Theodore 1937-
See Olson, Toby

Olson, Toby 1937- .... **CLC 28**
See also CANR 9; CA 65-68

Ondaatje, (Philip) Michael
1943- .... **CLC 14, 29, 51**
See also CA 77-80; DLB 60

Oneal, Elizabeth 1934-............ **CLC 30**
See also Oneal, Zibby
See also CLR 13; CA 106; SATA 30

Oneal, Zibby 1934-............... **CLC 30**
See also Oneal, Elizabeth

O'Neill, Eugene (Gladstone)
1888-1953 .... **TCLC 1, 6, 27**
See also CA 110; DLB 7; CDALB 1929-1941

Onetti, Juan Carlos 1909-....... **CLC 7, 10**
See also CA 85-88

O'Nolan, Brian 1911-1966
See O'Brien, Flann

O Nuallain, Brian 1911-1966
See O'Brien, Flann
See also CAP 2; CA 21-22; obituary CA 25-28R

Oppen, George 1908-1984 .... **CLC 7, 13, 34**
See also CANR 8; CA 13-16R; obituary CA 113; DLB 5

Orlovitz, Gil 1918-1973........... **CLC 22**
See also CA 77-80; obituary CA 45-48; DLB 2, 5

Ortega y Gasset, Jose 1883-1955 ... **TCLC 9**
See also CA 106, 130

Ortiz, Simon J. 1941-............. **CLC 45**

Orton, Joe 1933?-1967....... **CLC 4, 13, 43**
See also Orton, John Kingsley
See also DLB 13

Orton, John Kingsley 1933?-1967
See Orton, Joe
See also CA 85-88

Orwell, George
1903-1950 .... **TCLC 2, 6, 15, 31**
See also Blair, Eric Arthur
See also DLB 15

Osborne, John (James)
1929- .... **CLC 1, 2, 5, 11, 45**
See also CANR 21; CA 13-16R; DLB 13

Osborne, Lawrence 1958- .... **CLC 50**

Osceola 1885-1962
See Dinesen, Isak; Blixen, Karen (Christentze Dinesen)

Oshima, Nagisa 1932- .... **CLC 20**
See also CA 116

Powys, T(heodore) F(rancis) 1875-1953 .... **TCLC 9**
See also CA 106; DLB 36

Prager, Emily 1952- .... **CLC 56**

Pratt, E(dwin) J(ohn) 1883-1964.... **CLC 19**
See also obituary CA 93-96; DLB 92

Premchand 1880-1936 .... **TCLC 21**

Preussler, Otfried 1923-........... **CLC 17**
See also CA 77-80; SATA 24

Prevert, Jacques (Henri Marie) 1900-1977 .... **CLC 15**
See also CANR 29; CA 77-80; obituary CA 69-72; obituary SATA 30

Prevost, Abbe (Antoine Francois) 1697-1763 .... **LC 1**

Price, (Edward) Reynolds 1933- .... **CLC 3, 6, 13, 43, 50, 63**
See also CANR 1; CA 1-4R; DLB 2

Price, Richard 1949- .... **CLC 6, 12**
See also CANR 3; CA 49-52; DLB-Y 81

Prichard, Katharine Susannah 1883-1969 .... **CLC 46**
See also CAP 1; CA 11-12

Priestley, J(ohn) B(oynton) 1894-1984 .... **CLC 2, 5, 9, 34**
See also CA 9-12R; obituary CA 113; DLB 10, 34, 77; DLB-Y 84

Prince (Rogers Nelson) 1958?- ..... **CLC 35**

Prince, F(rank) T(empleton) 1912- .. **CLC 22**
See also CA 101; DLB 20

Prior, Matthew 1664-1721........... **LC 4**

Pritchard, William H(arrison) 1932- .... **CLC 34**
See also CANR 23; CA 65-68

Pritchett, V(ictor) S(awdon) 1900- .... **CLC 5, 13, 15, 41**
See also CA 61-64; DLB 15

Probst, Mark 1925- .... **CLC 59**
See also CA 130

Procaccino, Michael 1946-
See Cristofer, Michael

Prokosch, Frederic 1908-1989.... **CLC 4, 48**
See also CA 73-76; obituary CA 128; DLB 48

Prose, Francine 1947-............. **CLC 45**
See also CA 109, 112

Proust, Marcel 1871-1922 .. **TCLC 7, 13, 33**
See also CA 104, 120; DLB 65

Pryor, Richard 1940- .... **CLC 26**
See also CA 122

Przybyszewski, Stanislaw 1868-1927 .... **TCLC 36**
See also DLB 66

Puig, Manuel 1932-1990 .... **CLC 3, 5, 10, 28, 65**
See also CANR 2, 32; CA 45-48

Purdy, A(lfred) W(ellington) 1918- .... **CLC 3, 6, 14, 50**
See also CA 81-84

Purdy, James (Amos) 1923- .... **CLC 2, 4, 10, 28, 52**
See also CAAS 1; CANR 19; CA 33-36R; DLB 2

Pushkin, Alexander (Sergeyevich) 1799-1837 .... **NCLC 3, 27**

P'u Sung-ling 1640-1715 .... **LC 3**

Puzo, Mario 1920- .... **CLC 1, 2, 6, 36**
See also CANR 4; CA 65-68; DLB 6

Pym, Barbara (Mary Crampton) 1913-1980 .... **CLC 13, 19, 37**
See also CANR 13; CAP 1; CA 13-14; obituary CA 97-100; DLB 14; DLB-Y 87

Pynchon, Thomas (Ruggles, Jr.) 1937- ..... **CLC 2, 3, 6, 9, 11, 18, 33, 62**
See also CANR 22; CA 17-20R; DLB 2

Quarrington, Paul 1954?- .... **CLC 65**
See also CA 129

Quasimodo, Salvatore 1901-1968 ... **CLC 10**
See also CAP 1; CA 15-16; obituary CA 25-28R

Queen, Ellery 1905-1982 .... **CLC 3, 11**
See also Dannay, Frederic; Lee, Manfred B(ennington)

Queneau, Raymond 1903-1976 .... **CLC 2, 5, 10, 42**
See also CA 77-80; obituary CA 69-72; DLB 72

Quin, Ann (Marie) 1936-1973 .... **CLC 6**
See also CA 9-12R; obituary CA 45-48; DLB 14

Quinn, Simon 1942-
See Smith, Martin Cruz
See also CANR 6, 23; CA 85-88

Quiroga, Horacio (Sylvestre) 1878-1937 .... **TCLC 20**
See also CA 117

Quoirez, Francoise 1935-
See Sagan, Francoise
See also CANR 6; CA 49-52

Rabe, David (William) 1940- ... **CLC 4, 8, 33**
See also CA 85-88; CABS 3; DLB 7

Rabelais, Francois 1494?-1553........ **LC 5**

Rabinovitch, Sholem 1859-1916
See Aleichem, Sholom
See also CA 104

Rachen, Kurt von 1911-1986
See Hubbard, L(afayette) Ron(ald)

Radcliffe, Ann (Ward) 1764-1823 .. **NCLC 6**
See also DLB 39

Radiguet, Raymond 1903-1923 .... **TCLC 29**
See also DLB 65

Radnoti, Miklos 1909-1944 .... **TCLC 16**
See also CA 118

Rado, James 1939- .... **CLC 17**
See also CA 105

Radomski, James 1932-
See Rado, James

Radvanyi, Netty Reiling 1900-1983
See Seghers, Anna
See also CA 85-88; obituary CA 110

Rae, Ben 1935-
See Griffiths, Trevor

Raeburn, John 1941- .... **CLC 34**
See also CA 57-60

Ragni, Gerome 1942- .... **CLC 17**
See also CA 105

Rahv, Philip 1908-1973 .... **CLC 24**
See also Greenberg, Ivan

Raine, Craig 1944- .... **CLC 32**
See also CANR 29; CA 108; DLB 40

Raine, Kathleen (Jessie) 1908- ... **CLC 7, 45**
See also CA 85-88; DLB 20

Rainis, Janis 1865-1929.......... **TCLC 29**

Rakosi, Carl 1903- .... **CLC 47**
See also Rawley, Callman
See also CAAS 5

Ramos, Graciliano 1892-1953 ..... **TCLC 32**

Rampersad, Arnold 19??- .... **CLC 44**

Ramuz, Charles-Ferdinand 1878-1947 .... **TCLC 33**

Rand, Ayn 1905-1982........ **CLC 3, 30, 44**
See also CANR 27; CA 13-16R; obituary CA 105

Randall, Dudley (Felker) 1914-...... **CLC 1**
See also BLC 3; CANR 23; CA 25-28R; DLB 41

Ransom, John Crowe 1888-1974 .... **CLC 2, 4, 5, 11, 24**
See also CANR 6; CA 5-8R; obituary CA 49-52; DLB 45, 63

Rao, Raja 1909- .... **CLC 25, 56**
See also CA 73-76

Raphael, Frederic (Michael) 1931- .... **CLC 2, 14**
See also CANR 1; CA 1-4R; DLB 14

Rathbone, Julian 1935- .... **CLC 41**
See also CA 101

Rattigan, Terence (Mervyn) 1911-1977 .... **CLC 7**
See also CA 85-88; obituary CA 73-76; DLB 13

Ratushinskaya, Irina 1954- .... **CLC 54**
See also CA 129

Raven, Simon (Arthur Noel) 1927- .... **CLC 14**
See also CA 81-84

Rawley, Callman 1903-
See Rakosi, Carl
See also CANR 12; CA 21-24R

Rawlings, Marjorie Kinnan 1896-1953 .... **TCLC 4**
See also YABC 1; CA 104; DLB 9, 22

Ray, Satyajit 1921-............... **CLC 16**
See also CA 114

Read, Herbert (Edward) 1893-1968 .. **CLC 4**
See also CA 85-88; obituary CA 25-28R; DLB 20

Read, Piers Paul 1941- ...... **CLC 4, 10, 25**
See also CA 21-24R; SATA 21; DLB 14

Reade, Charles 1814-1884 .... **NCLC 2**
See also DLB 21

Reade, Hamish 1936-
See Gray, Simon (James Holliday)

Reading, Peter 1946- .... **CLC 47**
See also CA 103; DLB 40

Reaney, James 1926- .... **CLC 13**
See also CA 41-44R; SATA 43; DLB 68

Rebreanu, Liviu 1885-1944 .... **TCLC 28**

Robinson, Jill 1936- . . . . **CLC 10**
See also CA 102

Robinson, Kim Stanley 19??- . . . . **CLC 34**
See also CA 126

Robinson, Marilynne 1944- . . . . **CLC 25**
See also CA 116

Robinson, Smokey 1940- . . . . **CLC 21**

Robinson, William 1940-
See Robinson, Smokey
See also CA 116

Robison, Mary 1949- . . . . **CLC 42**
See also CA 113, 116

Roddenberry, Gene 1921- . . . . **CLC 17**
See also CANR 110; SATA 45

Rodgers, Mary 1931- . . . . **CLC 12**
See also CLR 20; CANR 8; CA 49-52; SATA 8

Rodgers, W(illiam) R(obert)
1909-1969 . . . . **CLC 7**
See also CA 85-88; DLB 20

Rodman, Howard 19??- . . . . **CLC 65**

Rodriguez, Claudio 1934- . . . . **CLC 10**

Roethke, Theodore (Huebner)
1908-1963 . . . . . . **CLC 1, 3, 8, 11, 19, 46**
See also CA 81-84; CABS 2; SAAS 1; DLB 5; CDALB 1941-1968

Rogers, Sam 1943-
See Shepard, Sam

Rogers, Thomas (Hunton) 1931- . . . . **CLC 57**
See also CA 89-92

Rogers, Will(iam Penn Adair)
1879-1935 . . . . **TCLC 8**
See also CA 105; DLB 11

Rogin, Gilbert 1929- . . . . **CLC 18**
See also CANR 15; CA 65-68

Rohan, Koda 1867-1947 . . . . **TCLC 22**
See also CA 121

Rohmer, Eric 1920- . . . . **CLC 16**
See also Scherer, Jean-Marie Maurice

Rohmer, Sax 1883-1959 . . . . **TCLC 28**
See also Ward, Arthur Henry Sarsfield
See also CA 108; DLB 70

Roiphe, Anne (Richardson)
1935- . . . . **CLC 3, 9**
See also CA 89-92; DLB-Y 80

Rolfe, Frederick (William Serafino Austin Lewis Mary) 1860-1913 . . . . . . **TCLC 12**
See also CA 107; DLB 34

Rolland, Romain 1866-1944 . . . . **TCLC 23**
See also CA 118; DLB 65

Rolvaag, O(le) E(dvart)
1876-1931 . . . . **TCLC 17**
See also CA 117; DLB 9

Romains, Jules 1885-1972 . . . . **CLC 7**
See also CA 85-88

Romero, Jose Ruben 1890-1952 . . . **TCLC 14**
See also CA 114

Ronsard, Pierre de 1524-1585 . . . . **LC 6**

Rooke, Leon 1934- . . . . **CLC 25, 34**
See also CANR 23; CA 25-28R

Roper, William 1498-1578 . . . . **LC 10**

Rosa, Joao Guimaraes 1908-1967 . . . **CLC 23**
See also obituary CA 89-92

Rosen, Richard (Dean) 1949- . . . . **CLC 39**
See also CA 77-80

Rosenberg, Isaac 1890-1918 . . . . **TCLC 12**
See also CA 107; DLB 20

Rosenblatt, Joe 1933- . . . . **CLC 15**
See also Rosenblatt, Joseph

Rosenblatt, Joseph 1933-
See Rosenblatt, Joe
See also CA 89-92

Rosenfeld, Samuel 1896-1963
See Tzara, Tristan
See also obituary CA 89-92

Rosenthal, M(acha) L(ouis) 1917- . . . **CLC 28**
See also CAAS 6; CANR 4; CA 1-4R; SATA 59; DLB 5

Ross, (James) Sinclair 1908- . . . . **CLC 13**
See also CA 73-76; DLB 88

Rossetti, Christina Georgina
1830-1894 . . . . **NCLC 2**
See also SATA 20; DLB 35

Rossetti, Dante Gabriel
1828-1882 . . . . **NCLC 4**
See also DLB 35

Rossetti, Gabriel Charles Dante 1828-1882
See Rossetti, Dante Gabriel

Rossner, Judith (Perelman)
1935- . . . . **CLC 6, 9, 29**
See also CANR 18; CA 17-20R; DLB 6

Rostand, Edmond (Eugene Alexis)
1868-1918 . . . . **TCLC 6, 37**
See also CA 104, 126

Roth, Henry 1906- . . . . **CLC 2, 6, 11**
See also CAP 1; CA 11-12; DLB 28

Roth, Joseph 1894-1939 . . . . **TCLC 33**
See also DLB 85

Roth, Philip (Milton)
1933- . . . . . . **CLC 1, 2, 3, 4, 6, 9, 15, 22, 31, 47, 66**
See also CANR 1, 22; CA 1-4R; DLB 2, 28; DLB-Y 82; CDALB 1968-1988

Rothenberg, James 1931- . . . . **CLC 57**

Rothenberg, Jerome 1931- . . . . **CLC 6, 57**
See also CANR 1; CA 45-48; DLB 5

Roumain, Jacques 1907-1944 . . . . . . **TCLC 19**
See also BLC 3; CA 117, 125

Rourke, Constance (Mayfield)
1885-1941 . . . . **TCLC 12**
See also YABC 1; CA 107

Rousseau, Jean-Baptiste 1671-1741 . . . **LC 9**

Rousseau, Jean-Jacques 1712-1778 . . . **LC 14**

Roussel, Raymond 1877-1933 . . . . . **TCLC 20**
See also CA 117

Rovit, Earl (Herbert) 1927- . . . . **CLC 7**
See also CANR 12; CA 5-8R

Rowe, Nicholas 1674-1718 . . . . **LC 8**

Rowson, Susanna Haswell
1762-1824 . . . . **NCLC 5**
See also DLB 37

Roy, Gabrielle 1909-1983 . . . . **CLC 10, 14**
See also CANR 5; CA 53-56; obituary CA 110; DLB 68

Rozewicz, Tadeusz 1921- . . . . **CLC 9, 23**
See also CA 108

Ruark, Gibbons 1941- . . . . **CLC 3**
See also CANR 14; CA 33-36R

Rubens, Bernice 192?- . . . . **CLC 19, 31**
See also CA 25-28R; DLB 14

Rubenstein, Gladys 1934-
See Swan, Gladys

Rudkin, (James) David 1936- . . . . . . **CLC 14**
See also CA 89-92; DLB 13

Rudnik, Raphael 1933- . . . . **CLC 7**
See also CA 29-32R

Ruiz, Jose Martinez 1874-1967
See Azorin

Rukeyser, Muriel
1913-1980 . . . . **CLC 6, 10, 15, 27**
See also CANR 26; CA 5-8R; obituary CA 93-96; obituary SATA 22; DLB 48

Rule, Jane (Vance) 1931- . . . . **CLC 27**
See also CANR 12; CA 25-28R; DLB 60

Rulfo, Juan 1918-1986 . . . . **CLC 8**
See also CANR 26; CA 85-88; obituary CA 118

Runyon, (Alfred) Damon
1880-1946 . . . . **TCLC 10**
See also CA 107; DLB 11

Rush, Norman 1933- . . . . **CLC 44**
See also CA 121, 126

Rushdie, (Ahmed) Salman
1947- . . . . **CLC 23, 31, 55, 59**
See also CA 108, 111

Rushforth, Peter (Scott) 1945- . . . . . **CLC 19**
See also CA 101

Ruskin, John 1819-1900 . . . . **TCLC 20**
See also CA 114; SATA 24; DLB 55

Russ, Joanna 1937- . . . . **CLC 15**
See also CANR 11; CA 25-28R; DLB 8

Russell, George William 1867-1935
See A. E.
See also CA 104

Russell, (Henry) Ken(neth Alfred)
1927- . . . . **CLC 16**
See also CA 105

Russell, Mary Annette Beauchamp 1866-1941
See Elizabeth

Russell, Willy 1947- . . . . **CLC 60**

Rutherford, Mark 1831-1913 . . . . . . **TCLC 25**
See also CA 121; DLB 18

Ruyslinck, Ward 1929- . . . . **CLC 14**

Ryan, Cornelius (John) 1920-1974 . . . **CLC 7**
See also CA 69-72; obituary CA 53-56

Ryan, Michael 1946- . . . . **CLC 65**
See also CA 49-52; DLB-Y 82

Rybakov, Anatoli 1911?- . . . . **CLC 23, 53**
See also CA 126

Ryder, Jonathan 1927-
See Ludlum, Robert

Ryga, George 1932- . . . . **CLC 14**
See also CA 101; obituary CA 124; DLB 60

Séviné, Marquise de Marie de Rabutin-Chantal 1626-1696 . . . . . **LC 11**

Saba, Umberto 1883-1957 . . . . **TCLC 33**

Sabato, Ernesto 1911- . . . . **CLC 10, 23**
See also CA 97-100

Sacher-Masoch, Leopold von 1836?-1895 . . . . **NCLC 31**

Sachs, Marilyn (Stickle) 1927- . . . . . **CLC 35**
See also CLR 2; CANR 13; CA 17-20R; SAAS 2; SATA 3, 52

Sachs, Nelly 1891-1970 . . . . **CLC 14**
See also CAP 2; CA 17-18; obituary CA 25-28R

Sackler, Howard (Oliver) 1929-1982 . . . . **CLC 14**
See also CA 61-64; obituary CA 108; DLB 7

Sacks, Oliver 1933- . . . . **CLC 67**
See also CANR 28; CA 53-56

Sade, Donatien Alphonse Francois, Comte de 1740-1814 . . . . **NCLC 3**

Sadoff, Ira 1945- . . . . **CLC 9**
See also CANR 5, 21; CA 53-56

Safire, William 1929- . . . . **CLC 10**
See also CA 17-20R

Sagan, Carl (Edward) 1934- . . . . **CLC 30**
See also CANR 11; CA 25-28R; SATA 58

Sagan, Francoise 1935- . . . . **CLC 3, 6, 9, 17, 36**
See also Quoirez, Francoise
See also CANR 6; DLB 83

Sahgal, Nayantara (Pandit) 1927- . . . **CLC 41**
See also CANR 11; CA 9-12R

Saint, H(arry) F. 1941- . . . . **CLC 50**

Sainte-Beuve, Charles Augustin 1804-1869 . . . . **NCLC 5**

Sainte-Marie, Beverly 1941-1972?
See Sainte-Marie, Buffy
See also CA 107

Sainte-Marie, Buffy 1941- . . . . **CLC 17**
See also Sainte-Marie, Beverly

Saint-Exupery, Antoine (Jean Baptiste Marie Roger) de 1900-1944 . . . . **TCLC 2**
See also CLR 10; CA 108; SATA 20; DLB 72

Saintsbury, George 1845-1933 . . . . . **TCLC 31**
See also DLB 57

Sait Faik (Abasiyanik) 1906-1954 . . . . **TCLC 23**

Saki 1870-1916 . . . . **TCLC 3**
See also Munro, H(ector) H(ugh)
See also CA 104

Salama, Hannu 1936- . . . . **CLC 18**

Salamanca, J(ack) R(ichard) 1922- . . . . **CLC 4, 15**
See also CA 25-28R

Sale, Kirkpatrick 1937- . . . . **CLC 68**
See also CANR 10; CA 13-14R

Salinas, Pedro 1891-1951 . . . . **TCLC 17**
See also CA 117

Salinger, J(erome) D(avid) 1919- . . . . **CLC 1, 3, 8, 12, 56; SSC 2**
See also CA 5-8R; DLB 2; CDALB 1941-1968

Salter, James 1925- . . . . **CLC 7, 52, 59**
See also CA 73-76

Saltus, Edgar (Evertson) 1855-1921 . . . . **TCLC 8**
See also CA 105

Saltykov, Mikhail Evgrafovich 1826-1889 . . . . **NCLC 16**

Samarakis, Antonis 1919- . . . . **CLC 5**
See also CA 25-28R

Sanchez, Florencio 1875-1910 . . . . . **TCLC 37**

Sanchez, Luis Rafael 1936- . . . . **CLC 23**

Sanchez, Sonia 1934- . . . . **CLC 5**
See also BLC 3; CLR 18; CANR 24; CA 33-36R; SATA 22; DLB 41; DLB-DS 8

Sand, George 1804-1876 . . . . **NCLC 2**

Sandburg, Carl (August) 1878-1967 . . . **CLC 1, 4, 10, 15, 35; PC 2**
See also CA 5-8R; obituary CA 25-28R; SATA 8; DLB 17, 54; CDALB 1865-1917

Sandburg, Charles August 1878-1967
See Sandburg, Carl (August)

Sanders, (James) Ed(ward) 1939- . . . **CLC 53**
See also CANR 13; CA 15-16R, 103; DLB 16

Sanders, Lawrence 1920- . . . . **CLC 41**
See also CA 81-84

Sandoz, Mari (Susette) 1896-1966 . . **CLC 28**
See also CANR 17; CA 1-4R; obituary CA 25-28R; SATA 5; DLB 9

Saner, Reg(inald Anthony) 1931- . . . . **CLC 9**
See also CA 65-68

Sannazaro, Jacopo 1456?-1530 . . . . **LC 8**

Sansom, William 1912-1976 . . . . **CLC 2, 6**
See also CA 5-8R; obituary CA 65-68

Santayana, George 1863-1952 . . . . . **TCLC 40**
See also CA 115; DLB 54, 71

Santiago, Danny 1911- . . . . **CLC 33**
See also CA 125

Santmyer, Helen Hooven 1895-1986 . . . . **CLC 33**
See also CANR 15; CA 1-4R; obituary CA 118; DLB-Y 84

Santos, Bienvenido N(uqui) 1911- . . . **CLC 22**
See also CANR 19; CA 101

Sappho c. 6th-century B.C.- . . . . **CMLC 3**

Sarduy, Severo 1937- . . . . **CLC 6**
See also CA 89-92

Sargeson, Frank 1903-1982 . . . . **CLC 31**
See also CA 106, 25-28R; obituary CA 106

Sarmiento, Felix Ruben Garcia 1867-1916
See Dario, Ruben
See also CA 104

Saroyan, William 1908-1981 . . . . . **CLC 1, 8, 10, 29, 34, 56**
See also CA 5-8R; obituary CA 103; SATA 23; obituary SATA 24; DLB 7, 9; DLB-Y 81

Sarraute, Nathalie 1902- . . . . **CLC 1, 2, 4, 8, 10, 31**
See also CANR 23; CA 9-12R; DLB 83

Sarton, Eleanore Marie 1912-
See Sarton, (Eleanor) May

Sarton, (Eleanor) May 1912- . . . . **CLC 4, 14, 49**
See also CANR 1; CA 1-4R; SATA 36; DLB 48; DLB-Y 81

Sartre, Jean-Paul (Charles Aymard) 1905-1980 . . . **CLC 1, 4, 7, 9, 13, 18, 24, 44, 50, 52**
See also CANR 21; CA 9-12R; obituary CA 97-100; DLB 72

Sassoon, Siegfried (Lorraine) 1886-1967 . . . . **CLC 36**
See also CA 104; obituary CA 25-28R; DLB 20

Saul, John (W. III) 1942- . . . . **CLC 46**
See also CANR 16; CA 81-84

Saura, Carlos 1932- . . . . **CLC 20**
See also CA 114

Sauser-Hall, Frederic-Louis 1887-1961 . . . . **CLC 18**
See also Cendrars, Blaise
See also CA 102; obituary CA 93-96

Savage, Thomas 1915- . . . . **CLC 40**
See also CA 126

Savan, Glenn 19??- . . . . **CLC 50**

Sayers, Dorothy L(eigh) 1893-1957 . . . . **TCLC 2, 15**
See also CA 104, 119; DLB 10, 36, 77

Sayers, Valerie 19??- . . . . **CLC 50**

Sayles, John (Thomas) 1950- . . . . **CLC 7, 10, 14**
See also CA 57-60; DLB 44

Scammell, Michael 19??- . . . . **CLC 34**

Scannell, Vernon 1922- . . . . **CLC 49**
See also CANR 8; CA 5-8R; DLB 27

Schaeffer, Susan Fromberg 1941- . . . . **CLC 6, 11, 22**
See also CANR 18; CA 49-52; SATA 22; DLB 28

Schell, Jonathan 1943- . . . . **CLC 35**
See also CANR 12; CA 73-76

Schelling, Friedrich Wilhelm Joseph von 1775-1854 . . . . **NCLC 30**
See also DLB 90

Scherer, Jean-Marie Maurice 1920-
See Rohmer, Eric
See also CA 110

Schevill, James (Erwin) 1920- . . . . **CLC 7**
See also CA 5-8R

Schisgal, Murray (Joseph) 1926- . . . . . **CLC 6**
See also CA 21-24R

Schlee, Ann 1934- . . . . **CLC 35**
See also CA 101; SATA 36, 44

Schlegel, August Wilhelm von 1767-1845 . . . . **NCLC 15**

Schlegel, Johann Elias (von) 1719?-1749 . . . . **LC 5**

Schmidt, Arno 1914-1979 . . . . **CLC 56**
See also obituary CA 109; DLB 69

Schmitz, Ettore 1861-1928
See Svevo, Italo
See also CA 104, 122

Schnackenberg, Gjertrud 1953- . . . . . **CLC 40**
See also CA 116

Schneider, Leonard Alfred 1925-1966
See Bruce, Lenny
See also CA 89-92

Schnitzler, Arthur 1862-1931 . . . . . . **TCLC 4**
See also CA 104; DLB 81

Skvorecky, Josef (Vaclav) 1924- .... **CLC 15, 39, 69**
See also CAAS 1; CANR 10, 34; CA 61-64

Slade, Bernard 1930- .... **CLC 11, 46**
See also Newbound, Bernard Slade
See also DLB 53

Slaughter, Carolyn 1946- .... **CLC 56**
See also CA 85-88

Slaughter, Frank G(ill) 1908- ...... **CLC 29**
See also CANR 5; CA 5-8R

Slavitt, David (R.) 1935- .... **CLC 5, 14**
See also CAAS 3; CA 21-24R; DLB 5, 6

Slesinger, Tess 1905-1945 .... **TCLC 10**
See also CA 107

Slessor, Kenneth 1901-1971 .... **CLC 14**
See also CA 102; obituary CA 89-92

Slowacki, Juliusz 1809-1849 ..... **NCLC 15**

Smart, Christopher 1722-1771 .... **LC 3**

Smart, Elizabeth 1913-1986 .... **CLC 54**
See also CA 81-84; obituary CA 118; DLB 88

Smiley, Jane (Graves) 1949- .... **CLC 53**
See also CA 104

Smith, A(rthur) J(ames) M(arshall) 1902-1980 .... **CLC 15**
See also CANR 4; CA 1-4R; obituary CA 102; DLB 88

Smith, Betty (Wehner) 1896-1972 ... **CLC 19**
See also CA 5-8R; obituary CA 33-36R; SATA 6; DLB-Y 82

Smith, Cecil Lewis Troughton 1899-1966
See Forester, C(ecil) S(cott)

Smith, Charlotte (Turner) 1749-1806 .... **NCLC 23**
See also DLB 39

Smith, Clark Ashton 1893-1961 .... **CLC 43**

Smith, Dave 1942- .... **CLC 22, 42**
See also Smith, David (Jeddie)
See also CAAS 7; CANR 1; DLB 5

Smith, David (Jeddie) 1942-
See Smith, Dave
See also CANR 1; CA 49-52

Smith, Florence Margaret 1902-1971
See Smith, Stevie
See also CAP 2; CA 17-18; obituary CA 29-32R

Smith, Iain Crichton 1928- .... **CLC 64**
See also DLB 40

Smith, John 1580?-1631 .... **LC 9**
See also DLB 24, 30

Smith, Lee 1944- .... **CLC 25**
See also CA 114, 119; DLB-Y 83

Smith, Martin Cruz 1942- .... **CLC 25**
See also CANR 6; CA 85-88

Smith, Martin William 1942-
See Smith, Martin Cruz

Smith, Mary-Ann Tirone 1944- ..... **CLC 39**
See also CA 118

Smith, Patti 1946- .... **CLC 12**
See also CA 93-96

Smith, Pauline (Urmson) 1882-1959 .... **TCLC 25**
See also CA 29-32R; SATA 27

Smith, Rosamond 1938-
See Oates, Joyce Carol

Smith, Sara Mahala Redway 1900-1972
See Benson, Sally

Smith, Stevie 1902-1971 .... **CLC 3, 8, 25, 44**
See also Smith, Florence Margaret
See also DLB 20

Smith, Wilbur (Addison) 1933- ..... **CLC 33**
See also CANR 7; CA 13-16R

Smith, William Jay 1918- .... **CLC 6**
See also CA 5-8R; SATA 2; DLB 5

Smolenskin, Peretz 1842-1885 .... **NCLC 30**

Smollett, Tobias (George) 1721-1771 .. **LC 2**
See also DLB 39

Snodgrass, W(illiam) D(e Witt) 1926- .... **CLC 2, 6, 10, 18, 68**
See also CANR 6; CA 1-4R; DLB 5

Snow, C(harles) P(ercy) 1905-1980 .... **CLC 1, 4, 6, 9, 13, 19**
See also CA 5-8R; obituary CA 101; DLB 15, 77

Snyder, Gary (Sherman) 1930- .... **CLC 1, 2, 5, 9, 32**
See also CANR 30; CA 17-20R; DLB 5, 16

Snyder, Zilpha Keatley 1927- ...... **CLC 17**
See also CA 9-12R; SAAS 2; SATA 1, 28

Sobol, Joshua 19??- .... **CLC 60**

Soderberg. Hjalmar 1869-1941 .... **TCLC 39**

Sodergran, Edith 1892-1923 .... **TCLC 31**

Sokolov, Raymond 1941- .... **CLC 7**
See also CA 85-88

Sologub, Fyodor 1863-1927 .... **TCLC 9**
See also Teternikov, Fyodor Kuzmich
See also CA 104

Solomos, Dionysios 1798-1857 ... **NCLC 15**

Solwoska, Mara 1929-
See French, Marilyn
See also CANR 3; CA 69-72

Solzhenitsyn, Aleksandr I(sayevich) 1918- ... **CLC 1, 2, 4, 7, 9, 10, 18, 26, 34**
See also CA 69-72

Somers, Jane 1919-
See Lessing, Doris (May)

Sommer, Scott 1951- .... **CLC 25**
See also CA 106

Sondheim, Stephen (Joshua) 1930- .... **CLC 30, 39**
See also CA 103

Sontag, Susan 1933- ... **CLC 1, 2, 10, 13, 31**
See also CA 17-20R; DLB 2, 67

Sophocles c. 496? B.C.-c. 406? B.C. ...... **CMLC 2; DC 1**

Sorrentino, Gilbert 1929- .... **CLC 3, 7, 14, 22, 40**
See also CANR 14; CA 77-80; DLB 5; DLB-Y 80

Soto, Gary 1952- .... **CLC 32**
See also CA 119, 125; DLB 82

Soupault, Philippe 1897-1990 ...... **CLC 68**
See also CA 116; obituary CA 131

Souster, (Holmes) Raymond 1921- .... **CLC 5, 14**
See also CANR 13; CA 13-16R; DLB 88

Southern, Terry 1926- .... **CLC 7**
See also CANR 1; CA 1-4R; DLB 2

Southey, Robert 1774-1843 .... **NCLC 8**
See also SATA 54

Southworth, Emma Dorothy Eliza Nevitte 1819-1899 .... **NCLC 26**

Soyinka, Wole 1934- .. **CLC 3, 5, 14, 36, 44**
See also BLC 3; CANR 27; CA 13-16R; DLB-Y 86

Spackman, W(illiam) M(ode) 1905- .... **CLC 46**
See also CA 81-84

Spacks, Barry 1931- .... **CLC 14**
See also CA 29-32R

Spanidou, Irini 1946- .... **CLC 44**

Spark, Muriel (Sarah) 1918- .... **CLC 2, 3, 5, 8, 13, 18, 40**
See also CANR 12; CA 5-8R; DLB 15

Spencer, Elizabeth 1921- .... **CLC 22**
See also CA 13-16R; SATA 14; DLB 6

Spencer, Scott 1945- .... **CLC 30**
See also CA 113; DLB-Y 86

Spender, Stephen (Harold) 1909- .... **CLC 1, 2, 5, 10, 41**
See also CA 9-12R; DLB 20

Spengler, Oswald 1880-1936 ...... **TCLC 25**
See also CA 118

Spenser, Edmund 1552?-1599 .... **LC 5**

Spicer, Jack 1925-1965 .... **CLC 8, 18**
See also CA 85-88; DLB 5, 16

Spielberg, Peter 1929- .... **CLC 6**
See also CANR 4; CA 5-8R; DLB-Y 81

Spielberg, Steven 1947- .... **CLC 20**
See also CA 77-80; SATA 32

Spillane, Frank Morrison 1918-
See Spillane, Mickey
See also CA 25-28R

Spillane, Mickey 1918- .... **CLC 3, 13**
See also Spillane, Frank Morrison

Spinoza, Benedictus de 1632-1677 .... **LC 9**

Spinrad, Norman (Richard) 1940- ... **CLC 46**
See also CANR 20; CA 37-40R; DLB 8

Spitteler, Carl (Friedrich Georg) 1845-1924 .... **TCLC 12**
See also CA 109

Spivack, Kathleen (Romola Drucker) 1938- .... **CLC 6**
See also CA 49-52

Spoto, Donald 1941- .... **CLC 39**
See also CANR 11; CA 65-68

Springsteen, Bruce 1949- .... **CLC 17**
See also CA 111

Spurling, Hilary 1940- .... **CLC 34**
See also CANR 25; CA 104

Squires, (James) Radcliffe 1917- .... **CLC 51**
See also CANR 6, 21; CA 1-4R

Stael-Holstein, Anne Louise Germaine Necker, Baronne de 1766-1817 ..... **NCLC 3**

Williams, Hugo 1942-............. **CLC 42**
See also CA 17-20R; DLB 40

Williams, John A(lfred) 1925-.... **CLC 5, 13**
See also BLC 3; CAAS 3; CANR 6, 26; CA 53-56; DLB 2, 33

Williams, Jonathan (Chamberlain) 1929-....................... **CLC 13**
See also CANR 8; CA 9-12R; DLB 5

Williams, Joy 1944-.............. **CLC 31**
See also CANR 22; CA 41-44R

Williams, Norman 1952-.......... **CLC 39**
See also CA 118

Williams, Paulette 1948-
See Shange, Ntozake

Williams, Sherley Anne 1944-
See also BLC 3; CANR 25; CA 73-76; DLB 41

Williams, Shirley 1944-
See Williams, Sherley Anne

Williams, Tennessee 1911-1983 .... **CLC 1, 2, 5, 7, 8, 11, 15, 19, 30, 39, 45**
See also CA 5-8R; obituary CA 108; DLB 7; DLB-Y 83; DLB-DS 4; CDALB 1941-1968

Williams, Thomas (Alonzo) 1926-... **CLC 14**
See also CANR 2; CA 1-4R

Williams, Thomas Lanier 1911-1983
See Williams, Tennessee

Williams, William Carlos 1883-1963 ... **CLC 1, 2, 5, 9, 13, 22, 42, 67**
See also CA 89-92; DLB 4, 16, 54, 86; CDALB 1917-1929

Williamson, David 1932-.......... **CLC 56**

Williamson, Jack 1908-........... **CLC 29**
See also Williamson, John Stewart
See also DLB 8

Williamson, John Stewart 1908-
See Williamson, Jack
See also CANR 123; CA 17-20R

Willingham, Calder (Baynard, Jr.) 1922-..................... **CLC 5, 51**
See also CANR 3; CA 5-8R; DLB 2, 44

Wilson, A(ndrew) N(orman) 1950-.. **CLC 33**
See also CA 112, 122; DLB 14

Wilson, Andrew 1948-
See Wilson, Snoo

Wilson, Angus (Frank Johnstone) 1913-............. **CLC 2, 3, 5, 25, 34**
See also CANR 21; CA 5-8R; DLB 15

Wilson, August 1945-....... **CLC 39, 50, 63**
See also BLC 3; CA 115, 122

Wilson, Brian 1942-.............. **CLC 12**

Wilson, Colin 1931-............ **CLC 3, 14**
See also CAAS 5; CANR 1, 122; CA 1-4R; DLB 14

Wilson, Edmund 1895-1972 .... **CLC 1, 2, 3, 8, 24**
See also CANR 1; CA 1-4R; obituary CA 37-40R; DLB 63

Wilson, Ethel Davis (Bryant) 1888-1980 .... **CLC 13**
See also CA 102; DLB 68

Wilson, Harriet 1827?-?
See also BLC 3; DLB 50

Wilson, John 1785-1854.......... **NCLC 5**

Wilson, John (Anthony) Burgess 1917-
See Burgess, Anthony
See also CANR 2; CA 1-4R

Wilson, Lanford 1937-....... **CLC 7, 14, 36**
See also CA 17-20R; DLB 7

Wilson, Robert (M.) 1944-........ **CLC 7, 9**
See also CANR 2; CA 49-52

Wilson, Sloan 1920-.............. **CLC 32**
See also CANR 1; CA 1-4R

Wilson, Snoo 1948-................ **CLC 33**
See also CA 69-72

Wilson, William S(mith) 1932-..... **CLC 49**
See also CA 81-84

Winchilsea, Anne (Kingsmill) Finch, Countess of 1661-1720.................. **LC 3**

Wingrove, David 1954-............ **CLC 68**
See also CA 133

Winters, Janet Lewis 1899-
See Lewis (Winters), Janet
See also CAP 1; CA 9-10

Winters, (Arthur) Yvor 1900-1968 .... **CLC 4, 8, 32**
See also CAP 1; CA 11-12; obituary CA 25-28R; DLB 48

Winterson, Jeannette 1959-........ **CLC 64**

Wiseman, Frederick 1930-......... **CLC 20**

Wister, Owen 1860-1938 .... **TCLC 21**
See also CA 108; DLB 9, 78

Witkiewicz, Stanislaw Ignacy 1885-1939 .... **TCLC 8**
See also CA 105; DLB 83

Wittig, Monique 1935?-........... **CLC 22**
See also CA 116; DLB 83

Wittlin, Joseph 1896-1976......... **CLC 25**
See also Wittlin, Jozef

Wittlin, Jozef 1896-1976
See Wittlin, Joseph
See also CANR 3; CA 49-52; obituary CA 65-68

Wodehouse, (Sir) P(elham) G(renville) 1881-1975 ... **CLC 1, 2, 5, 10, 22; SSC 2**
See also CANR 3; CA 45-48; obituary CA 57-60; SATA 22; DLB 34

Woiwode, Larry (Alfred) 1941-... **CLC 6, 10**
See also CANR 16; CA 73-76; DLB 6

Wojciechowska, Maia (Teresa) 1927-...................... **CLC 26**
See also CLR 1; CANR 4; CA 9-12R; SAAS 1; SATA 1, 28

Wolf, Christa 1929-........ **CLC 14, 29, 58**
See also CA 85-88; DLB 75

Wolfe, Gene (Rodman) 1931-....... **CLC 25**
See also CAAS 9; CANR 6; CA 57-60; DLB 8

Wolfe, George C. 1954-........... **CLC 49**

Wolfe, Thomas (Clayton) 1900-1938 .... **TCLC 4, 13, 29**
See also CA 104; DLB 9; DLB-Y 85; DLB-DS 2

Wolfe, Thomas Kennerly, Jr. 1931-
See Wolfe, Tom
See also CANR 9; CA 13-16R

Wolfe, Tom 1931-... **CLC 1, 2, 9, 15, 35, 51**
See also Wolfe, Thomas Kennerly, Jr.

Wolff, Geoffrey (Ansell) 1937-..... **CLC 41**
See also CA 29-32R

Wolff, Tobias (Jonathan Ansell) 1945-.................... **CLC 39, 64**
See also CA 114, 117

Wolfram von Eschenbach c. 1170-c. 1220 .... **CMLC 5**

Wolitzer, Hilma 1930-............ **CLC 17**
See also CANR 18; CA 65-68; SATA 31

Wollstonecraft Godwin, Mary 1759-1797 .... **LC 5**
See also DLB 39

Wonder, Stevie 1950-............. **CLC 12**
See also Morris, Steveland Judkins

Wong, Jade Snow 1922-........... **CLC 17**
See also CA 109

Woodcott, Keith 1934-
See Brunner, John (Kilian Houston)

Woolf, (Adeline) Virginia 1882-1941 .... **TCLC 1, 5, 20, 43; SSC 7**
See also CA 130; brief entry CA 104; DLB 36, 100

Woollcott, Alexander (Humphreys) 1887-1943 .... **TCLC 5**
See also CA 105; DLB 29

Wordsworth, Dorothy 1771-1855 .... **NCLC 25**

Wordsworth, William 1770-1850.. **NCLC 12**

Wouk, Herman 1915-......... **CLC 1, 9, 38**
See also CANR 6; CA 5-8R; DLB-Y 82

Wright, Charles 1935-....... **CLC 6, 13, 28**
See also BLC 3; CAAS 7; CANR 26; CA 29-32R; DLB-Y 82

Wright, Charles (Stevenson) 1932-.. **CLC 49**
See also CA 9-12R; DLB 33

Wright, James (Arlington) 1927-1980 .... **CLC 3, 5, 10, 28**
See also CANR 4; CA 49-52; obituary CA 97-100; DLB 5

Wright, Judith 1915-.......... **CLC 11, 53**
See also CA 13-16R; SATA 14

Wright, L(aurali) R. 1939-......... **CLC 44**

Wright, Richard (Nathaniel) 1908-1960 ... **CLC 1, 3, 4, 9, 14, 21, 48; SSC 2**
See also BLC 3; CA 108; DLB 76; DLB-DS 2; CDALB 1929-1941; AAYA 5

Wright, Richard B(ruce) 1937-...... **CLC 6**
See also CA 85-88; DLB 53

Wright, Rick 1945-
See Pink Floyd

Wright, Stephen 1946-............ **CLC 33**

Wright, Willard Huntington 1888-1939
See Van Dine, S. S.
See also CA 115

Wright, William 1930-............ **CLC 44**
See also CANR 7, 23; CA 53-56

Wu Ch'eng-en 1500?-1582? .... **LC 7**

Wu Ching-tzu 1701-1754 .... **LC 2**

Wurlitzer, Rudolph 1938?-..... **CLC 2, 4, 15**
See also CA 85-88

Wycherley, William 1640?-1716 ...... **LC 8**
See also DLB 80

Wylie (Benet), Elinor (Morton Hoyt)
1885-1928 .... **TCLC 8**
See also CA 105; DLB 9, 45

Wylie, Philip (Gordon) 1902-1971... **CLC 43**
See also CAP 2; CA 21-22; obituary CA 33-36R; DLB 9

Wyndham, John 1903-1969 .... **CLC 19**
See also Harris, John (Wyndham Parkes Lucas) Beynon

Wyss, Johann David 1743-1818 .. **NCLC 10**
See also SATA 27, 29

X, Malcolm 1925-1965
See Little, Malcolm

Yanovsky, Vassily S(emenovich)
1906-1989 .... **CLC 2, 18**
See also CA 97-100; obituary CA 129

Yates, Richard 1926- .... **CLC 7, 8, 23**
See also CANR 10; CA 5-8R; DLB 2; DLB-Y 81

Yeats, William Butler
1865-1939 .... **TCLC 1, 11, 18, 31**
See also CANR 10; CA 104; DLB 10, 19

Yehoshua, A(braham) B.
1936- .... **CLC 13, 31**
See also CA 33-36R

Yep, Laurence (Michael) 1948-..... **CLC 35**
See also CLR 3, 17; CANR 1; CA 49-52; SATA 7; DLB 52

Yerby, Frank G(arvin) 1916-... **CLC 1, 7, 22**
See also BLC 3; CANR 16; CA 9-12R; DLB 76

Yevtushenko, Yevgeny (Alexandrovich)
1933- .... **CLC 1, 3, 13, 26, 51**
See also CA 81-84

Yezierska, Anzia 1885?-1970....... **CLC 46**
See also CA 126; obituary CA 89-92; DLB 28

Yglesias, Helen 1915-........... **CLC 7, 22**
See also CANR 15; CA 37-40R

Yorke, Henry Vincent 1905-1974
See Green, Henry
See also CA 85-88; obituary CA 49-52

Young, Al 1939-................. **CLC 19**
See also BLC 3; CANR 26; CA 29-32R; DLB 33

Young, Andrew 1885-1971.......... **CLC 5**
See also CANR 7; CA 5-8R

Young, Edward 1683-1765........... **LC 3**

Young, Neil 1945-................ **CLC 17**
See also CA 110

Yourcenar, Marguerite
1903-1987 .... **CLC 19, 38, 50**
See also CANR 23; CA 69-72; DLB 72; DLB-Y 88

Yurick, Sol 1925-................. **CLC 6**
See also CANR 25; CA 13-16R

Zamyatin, Yevgeny Ivanovich
1884-1937 .... **TCLC 8, 37**
See also CA 105

Zangwill, Israel 1864-1926........ **TCLC 16**
See also CA 109; DLB 10

Zappa, Francis Vincent, Jr. 1940-
See Zappa, Frank
See also CA 108

Zappa, Frank 1940- .... **CLC 17**
See also Zappa, Francis Vincent, Jr.

Zaturenska, Marya 1902-1982.... **CLC 6, 11**
See also CANR 22; CA 13-16R; obituary CA 105

Zelazny, Roger 1937-............. **CLC 21**
See also CANR 26; CA 21-24R; SATA 39, 59; DLB 8

Zhdanov, Andrei A(lexandrovich)
1896-1948 .... **TCLC 18**
See also CA 117

Ziegenhagen, Eric 1970-........... **CLC 55**

Zimmerman, Robert 1941-
See Dylan, Bob

Zindel, Paul 1936- .... **CLC 6, 26**
See also CLR 3; CA 73-76; SATA 16, 58; DLB 7, 52

Zinoviev, Alexander 1922-......... **CLC 19**
See also CAAS 10; CA 116

Zola, Emile 1840-1902... **TCLC 1, 6, 21, 41**
See also brief entry CA 104

Zoline, Pamela 1941-............. **CLC 62**

Zorrilla y Moral, Jose 1817-1893.. **NCLC 6**

Zoshchenko, Mikhail (Mikhailovich)
1895-1958 .... **TCLC 15**
See also CA 115

Zuckmayer, Carl 1896-1977........ **CLC 18**
See also CA 69-72; DLB 56

Zukofsky, Louis
1904-1978 .... **CLC 1, 2, 4, 7, 11, 18**
See also CA 9-12R; obituary CA 77-80; DLB 5

Zweig, Paul 1935-1984......... **CLC 34, 42**
See also CA 85-88; obituary CA 113

Zweig, Stefan 1881-1942 .... **TCLC 17**
See also CA 112; DLB 81

SSC Cumulative Nationality Index

SSC Cumulative Title Index

Title Index

Title Index

Title Index

Title Index

Title Index

Title Index

Title Index

Title Index

Title Index

ISBN 0-8103-2558-6
90000
9 780810 325586

8832